The Cambridge Handbook of Generative Syntax

Syntax – the study of sentence structure – has been at the center of generative linguistics from its inception, and has developed rapidly and in various directions. *The Cambridge Handbook of Generative Syntax* provides a historical context for what is happening in the field of generative syntax today, a survey of the various generative approaches to syntactic structure available in the literature, and an overview of the state of the art in the principal modules of the theory and the interfaces with semantics, phonology, information structure, and sentence processing, as well as linguistic variation and language acquisition. This indispensable resource for advanced students, professional linguists (generative and non-generative alike), and scholars in related fields of inquiry presents a comprehensive survey of the field of generative syntactic research in all its variety, written by leading experts and providing a proper sense of the range of syntactic theories calling themselves generative.

MARCEL DEN DIKKEN is a professor of linguistics at the Graduate Center of the City University of New York.

CAMBRIDGE HANDBOOKS IN LANGUAGE AND LINGUISTICS

Genuinely broad in scope, each handbook in this series provides a complete state-of-the-field overview of a major sub-discipline within language study and research. Grouped into broad thematic areas, the chapters in each volume encompass the most important issues and topics within each subject, offering a coherent picture of the latest theories and findings. Together, the volumes will build into an integrated overview of the discipline in its entirety.

Published titles

The Cambridge Handbook of Phonology, edited by Paul de Lacy
The Cambridge Handbook of Linguistic Code-switching, edited by Barbara E. Bullock and Almeida Jacqueline Toribio
The Cambridge Handbook of Child Language, edited by Edith L. Bavin
The Cambridge Handbook of Endangered Languages, edited by Peter K. Austin and Julia Sallabank
The Cambridge Handbook of Sociolinguistics, edited by Rajend Mesthrie
The Cambridge Handbook of Pragmatics, edited by Keith Allan and Kasia M. Jaszczolt
The Cambridge Handbook of Language Policy, edited by Bernard Spolsky
The Cambridge Handbook of Second Language Acquisition, edited by Julia Herschensohn and Martha Young-Scholten
The Cambridge Handbook of Biolinguistics, edited by Cedric Boeckx and Kleanthes K. Grohmann
The Cambridge Handbook of Generative Syntax, edited by Marcel den Dikken

Further titles planned for the series

The Cambridge Handbook of Communication Disorders, edited by Louise Cummings
The Cambridge Handbook of Stylistics, edited by Stockwell and Whiteley
The Cambridge Handbook of Linguistic Anthropology, edited by Enfield, Kockelman and Sidnell
The Cambridge Handbook of Morphology, edited by Hippisley and Stump
The Cambridge Handbook of Historical Syntax, edited by Ledgeway and Roberts
The Cambridge Handbook of Formal Semantics, edited by Maria Aloni and Paul Dekker
The Cambridge Handbook of English Corpus Linguistics, edited by Douglas Biber and Randi Reppen
The Cambridge Handbook of English Historical Linguistics, edited by Merja Kytö and Päivi Pahta

The Cambridge Handbook of Generative Syntax

Edited by
Marcel den Dikken

CAMBRIDGE UNIVERSITY PRESS

CAMBRIDGE
UNIVERSITY PRESS

University Printing House, Cambridge CB2 8BS, United Kingdom

One Liberty Plaza, 20th Floor, New York, NY 10006, USA

477 Williamstown Road, Port Melbourne, VIC 3207, Australia

314-321, 3rd Floor, Plot 3, Splendor Forum, Jasola District Centre, New Delhi - 110025, India

79 Anson Road, #06-04/06, Singapore 079906

Cambridge University Press is part of the University of Cambridge.

It furthers the University's mission by disseminating knowledge in the pursuit of education, learning and research at the highest international levels of excellence.

www.cambridge.org
Information on this title: www.cambridge.org/9781108744362

© Cambridge University Press 2013

This publication is in copyright. Subject to statutory exception and to the provisions of relevant collective licensing agreements, no reproduction of any part may take place without the written permission of Cambridge University Press.

First published 2013
First paperback edition 2020

A catalogue record for this publication is available from the British Library

Library of Congress Cataloging in Publication data
The Cambridge Handbook of Generative Syntax / Edited by Marcel den Dikken.
  pages cm
Handbook of Generative Syntax
Includes bibliographical references and index.
ISBN 978-0-521-76986-0
1. Grammar, Comparative and general – Syntax. 2. Generative grammar. I. Dikken,
Marcel den, 1965– editor of compilation. II. Title: Handbook of Generative Syntax.
P291.C326 2013
415–dc23
                                                                    2013017092

ISBN 978-0-521-76986-0 Hardback
ISBN 978-1-108-74436-2 Paperback

Additional resources for this publication at www.cambridge.org/den dikken

Cambridge University Press has no responsibility for the persistence or accuracy of URLs for external or third-party internet websites referred to in this publication, and does not guarantee that any content on such websites is, or will remain, accurate or appropriate.

Contents

List of contributors	page vii
Preface	ix

Part I Background   1
1. Introduction   *Marcel den Dikken*   3
2. Brief overview of the history of generative syntax
   Howard Lasnik and Terje Lohndal   26
3. Goals and methods of generative syntax   *Frederick J. Newmeyer*   61

Part II Modern generative approaches to the study of sentence structure   93
4. Principles and Parameters theory and Minimalism
   Željko Bošković   95
5. Minimalism and Optimality Theory   *Hans Broekhuis and Ellen Woolford*   122
6. Lexical-Functional Grammar   *Peter Sells*   162
7. Phrase structure grammar   *James P. Blevins and Ivan A. Sag*   202
8. Tree Adjoining Grammar   *Robert Frank*   226

Part III Syntactic structures   263
9. Argument structure and argument structure alternations   *Gillian Ramchand*   265
10. The syntax of predication   *Caroline Heycock*   322
11. Lexical categories and (extended) projection   *Norbert Corver*   353
12. The functional structure of the sentence, and cartography   *Luigi Rizzi*   425
13. Adverbial and adjectival modification   *Artemis Alexiadou*   458

Part IV Syntactic processes: their nature, locality, and motivation   485

14 Economy of derivation and representation *Samuel D. Epstein, Hisatsugu Kitahara, Miki Obata, and T. Daniel Seely*   487
15 Syntax, binding, and patterns of anaphora *Ken Safir*   515
16 Raising and control *Maria Polinsky*   577
17 Agreement and Case *Mark C. Baker*   607
18 The locality of syntactic dependencies *Marcel den Dikken and Antje Lahne*   655

Part V Syntax and the internal interfaces   699

19 Ellipsis phenomena *Jeroen van Craenenbroeck and Jason Merchant*   701
20 Tense, aspect, and modality *Karen Zagona*   746
21 Negation and negative polarity *Hedde Zeijlstra*   793
22 The syntax of scope and quantification *Veneeta Dayal*   827
23 Syntax, information structure, and prosody *Daniel Büring*   860

Part VI Syntax and the external interfaces   897

24 Microsyntactic variation *Sjef Barbiers*   899
25 Parameters: the pluses and the minuses *Rosalind Thornton and Stephen Crain*   927
26 Syntax and the brain *Jon Sprouse and Ellen F. Lau*   971

References   1006
Index of language names   1140
Index   1143

Contributors

Artemis Alexiadou, Professor, Department of Linguistics, University of Stuttgart
Mark C. Baker, Professor, Department of Linguistics, Rutgers University
Sjef Barbiers, Professor, Meertens Institute (Royal Netherlands Academy of Arts and Sciences), and Utrecht University
James P. Blevins, Assistant Director of Research, University of Cambridge
Željko Bošković, Professor, Department of Linguistics, University of Connecticut
Hans Broekhuis, Senior researcher, Meertens Institute (Royal Netherlands Academy of Arts and Sciences)
Daniel Büring, Professor, Department of Linguistics, University of Vienna
Norbert Corver, Professor, Utrecht Institute of Linguistics (Onderzoeksinstituut voor Taal en Spraak), Utrecht University
Jeroen van Craenenbroeck, Assistant Professor, Center for Research in Syntax, Semantics, and Phonology (CRISSP), Hogeschool-Universiteit Brussel
Stephen Crain, Distinguished Professor, Department of Linguistics and ARC Centre of Excellence in Cognition and its Disorders, Macquarie University
Veneeta Dayal, Professor, Department of Linguistics, Rutgers University
Marcel den Dikken, Professor, Linguistics Program, CUNY Graduate Center
Samuel D. Epstein, Professor, Department of Linguistics, University of Michigan
Robert Frank, Professor, Department of Linguistics, Yale University
Caroline Heycock, Professor, Department of Linguistics and English Language, University of Edinburgh

Hisatsugu Kitahara, Professor, Institute of Cultural and Linguistic Studies, Keio University

Antje Lahne, Assistant Professor, Department of Linguistics, Universitity of Konstanz

Howard Lasnik, Distinguished University Professor, Department of Linguistics, University of Maryland

Ellen F. Lau, Assistant Professor, Department of Linguistics, University of Maryland

Terje Lohndal, Associate Professor, Department of Modern Foreign Languages, Norwegian University of Science and Technology, Trondheim

Jason Merchant, Professor, Department of Linguistics, University of Chicago

Frederick J. Newmeyer, Professor Emeritus, Department of Linguistics, University of Washington; Adjunct Professor, University of British Columbia and Simon Fraser University

Miki Obata, Assistant Professor, Faculty of Humanities, Law, and Economics, Mie University

Maria Polinsky, Professor, Department of Linguistics, Harvard University

Gillian Ramchand, Professor, Institute for Linguistics/CASTL-Center for Advanced Study in Theoretical Linguistics, University of Tromsø

Luigi Rizzi, Professor, Interdepartmental Center of Cognitive Studies on Language (Centro Interdipartimentale di Studi Cognitivi sul Linguaggio), University of Siena

Ken Safir, Professor, Department of Linguistics, Rutgers University

Ivan A. Sag, Professor, Department of Linguistics, Stanford University

T. Daniel Seely, Professor, Linguistics Program, Eastern Michigan University

Peter Sells, Professor, Department of Language and Linguistic Science, University of York

Jon Sprouse, Assistant Professor, Department of Cognitive Sciences, University of California, Irvine

Rosalind Thornton, Associate Professor, Department of Linguistics and ARC Centre of Excellence in Cognition and its Disorders, Macquarie University

Ellen Woolford, Professor, Department of Linguistics, University of Massachusetts, Amherst

Karen Zagona, Professor, Department of Linguistics, University of Washington

Hedde Zeijlstra, Assistant Professor, Department of Dutch Linguistics, University of Amsterdam

Preface

This handbook was an ambitious project – and as Sir Humphrey Appleby would never fail to remind his (Prime) Minister, Jim Hacker, in the episodes of the legendary BBC series *Yes Minister* and *Yes Prime Minister*, the epithet 'ambitious' usually means 'beyond an individual's capacity' or even 'dangerous'. If I have managed to avoid the many potential pitfalls of an undertaking of this magnitude and complexity, and have steered clear of the dangers inherent in it, I certainly have many people to thank for it.

Before I thank the people who have helped bring this project to fruition, I should mention the essential role played, at the very outset, by Maria Polinsky. If Masha had not suggested my name to the people at Cambridge University Press as a potential editor of the syntax handbook that they were seeking to publish, and had not instilled in me the necessary confidence to take this project on, I would never have been in the happy position to write this preface and to present this book to you, the reader. I will be eternally grateful to Masha for giving me this opportunity and for convincing me that I could pull this off.

Two of my compatriot colleagues, Hans Broekhuis and Norbert Corver, and my CUNY colleague Christina Tortora, also made immensely valuable contributions to this project at its inception. They served as sounding boards for the ideas that I had put together on the content and organization of the handbook. Whatever its shortcomings, the finished project is infinitely better than it would have been if I had not listened to and acted upon their input.

Masha, Hans, and Norbert all ended up contributing chapters to the handbook, and Christina served as the reviewer of one of the chapters. This leads me to some heartfelt words of gratitude toward the authors and reviewers for the handbook. It was very gratifying to see so many colleagues respond immediately and enthusiastically to my invitation to contribute a chapter to the book. Almost all the linguists I approached signed on to the project. There were a few personnel changes along the way (I am especially grateful to Jon Sprouse and Ellen Lau for stepping in so late in the game, and for going about the writing of their difficult chapter so expeditiously and efficiently), and three of the chapters originally planned and solicited did not materialize; but overall, the response to this project has been overwhelmingly positive. I thank the authors for their excellent work on their chapters.

Each chapter, besides being commented on by the editor, was sent to one external reader. The reviewers were asked to evaluate their chapter for content and presentation as well as adherence to the detailed guidelines provided by the editor to the authors. I am very grateful for the highly valuable input provided by the reviewers, which led to many substantive and presentational improvements.

At the Press, I thank Helen Barton and Joanna Breeze for their excellent support throughout the project, and Adrian Stenton for his copy-editing work. Helen deserves special thanks for always backing me on my suggestions, responding promptly to my queries, and keeping my spirits up with her positive attitude.

At the CUNY Graduate Center, I am very grateful to Michelle Johnson for helping me to keep track of progress (there was a time at which some chapters had not been written at all, others were being reviewed, a third set was being revised, and a few chapters were already finished in their revised form; Michelle's spreadsheets helped me to stay on top of things), and for her wizardry with Word's index function in linking the index entries to their occurrences in the chapters.

Finally, my special thanks go to my most precious one, my friends and my family for their support throughout this period.

Part I

Background

1

Introduction

Marcel den Dikken

1.1 The handbook of generative syntax: aims, structure, and scope

1.1.1 Aims

The Cambridge Handbook of Generative Syntax is designed to be a handbook in the truest sense of the term. To optimally meet this standard, the handbook provides (i) a historical context for what is happening in the field of generative syntax today, (ii) a survey of the variety of generative approaches to syntactic structure available in the literature, (iii) an overview of the major lexical and functional categories and their syntactic projections, (iv) a detailed presentation of the principal modules of generative syntactic theory, (v) an investigation of the interfaces between syntax and other domains of linguistic and psychological inquiry, and (vi) a discussion of linguistic variation. The handbook aims to provide the reader with a comprehensive survey of the field of generative syntactic research in all its variety, written from the perspective of the synchronic state of the art but also reviewing the historical roots of current generative syntax and providing a proper sense of the range of syntactic theories calling themselves generative.

The book is not intended as a *tabula rasa* introduction to generative syntax. Basic knowledge of generative linguistics is presupposed. The typical audience will include advanced undergraduate students and professional practitioners of linguistics as well as researchers in neighboring fields of academic inquiry. Though the book is centered exclusively on generative approaches, it does not concentrate uniquely on the Chomskyan mainstream but also includes discussion of other generative perspectives. Non-generative linguists should find at least some parts of the book of interest and accessible as well, although, inevitably, the discussion in the more specialized chapters is sometimes rather technical in nature. Though the individual chapters of the handbook have been written separately, by specialists on the topics addressed, the often quite intimate connections between the various chapters have been brought out by the many cross-references to related sections of other chapters throughout the book. In conjunction with the detailed subject index, these cross-references should make it easy for readers to find more information on specific topics within the handbook itself.

While the handbook is rich in empirical detail covering a broad range of different phenomena from a wide variety of the world's languages, the book's primary focus is the *theory* of generative syntax. For readers interested in more in-depth discussion of some of the empirical phemonena addressed in the handbook (say, clitic placement, the dative alternation, extraposition, secondary predication, or specificational copular sentences), the five-volume *Blackwell Companion to Syntax* (Everaert and van Riemsdijk 2006) should serve as a helpful companion to this book. In addition, the many references (collected at the end of the handbook in the general bibliography) should enable readers who would like to gain a deeper understanding of the issues addressed to find their way to the relevant primary literature.

1.1.2 Structure

The book is divided into six major parts. In Part I, the necessary background to the generative enterprise is provided. Section 1.2 of this Introduction gets down to this right away, by highlighting many of the foci of generative syntactic research and their interconnections. Chapter 2 subsequently offers a historical overview of generative syntax, and Chapter 3 looks critically at the central goals and the research methods of the field.

Part II presents five different generative approaches to syntactic structure, starting in Chapter 4 with the mainstream Chomskyan approach (Principles and Parameters theory and its most recent development, the Minimalist Program). Chapter 5 looks at the contributions that Optimality Theory can make to our understanding of syntax, with particular emphasis on the prospects of a combination of derivational (minimalist) and representational (OT-theoretic) approaches. Chapters 6, 7, and 8 present three outlooks on syntactic analysis that share the general objectives of the generative enterprise but make rather different assumptions on many central issues, including the question of whether there are movement operations in syntax or not, and if so, whether these operations do or do not proceed via a succession of intermediate steps. The frameworks included here are Lexical-Functional Grammar, Phrase Structure Grammar (GPSG and HPSG), and Tree Adjoining Grammar. (On the rationale for not including certain other generative frameworks, see Section 1.1.3.)

The focus of Part III is on syntactic structures. It reviews the generative approaches to argument structure and argument-structure alternations (Chapter 9), predication (Chapter 10), the structure of lexical categories

(Chapter 11) and of the sentence (Chapter 12), and the way in which modification relations are structurally established (Chapter 13). The role of functional projections is a central theme throughout this portion of the handbook.

With the basic syntactic structures in place, Part IV proceeds to a discussion of syntactic processes. It begins, in Chapter 14, by looking at the role played by economy considerations in the construction of syntactic analyses, investigating in tandem the roles played by economy of derivation and economy of representation, and the areas of tension between the two. Chapter 15 then examines the way in which referential dependencies are established in syntax. Though the syntactic issues presented by anaphora are intimately related to those arising in connection with raising, control, and the typology of nominal empty categories, a separate chapter (Chapter 16) is devoted to the latter set of topics, because of the complexity of the empirical and theoretical questions raised in the two contexts. Chapter 17 subsequently proceeds to study the ways phi-feature agreement and case marking can be dealt with in generative syntax. And Chapter 18 concludes this part of the handbook by presenting a detailed overview of the generative accounts of locality restrictions on syntactic dependencies, one of the most densely studied topics in the field.

The topic of Part V is the relationship between syntax and the internal interfaces: Phonological Form (articulation and perception) and Logical Form (meaning). The discussion is opened and closed by chapters addressing the sound side, with Chapter 19 concentrating on silence (in particular, the conditions under which parts of a syntactic structure get no phonological matrix assigned to them) and Chapter 23 addressing the relationship between syntax and prosody. Chapter 23 also looks at the links between syntactic structure and discourse or information structure. Other aspects of the interface between syntax and meaning are addressed in the chapters on tense, aspect, and modality (Chapter 20), negation and polarity (Chapter 21), and scope and related matters (Chapter 22).

The last part of the handbook (Part VI) brings together three chapters that look at linguistic variation, language development, and language production and processing, respectively. These chapters are placed in a separate part at the end of the book because their scope transcends the individual areas of syntactic investigation addressed in Parts III–V, and because they raise general questions about generative linguistic theory. A central topic in this part of the book is formed by questions relating to parameters, including their nature and the basis on which they are set. Chapter 24 sheds light on the important contributions that generative syntax makes to dialectology, and the last two chapters of the handbook concentrate on generative approaches to issues in psycholinguistics, with Chapter 25 addressing language acquisition and development, and Chapter 26 providing an introduction to experimental studies of sentence processing and production.

1.1.3 Scope: what is and is not included in this handbook

Though this handbook aims to provide a comprehensive survey of research in the field of generative syntax, there are, of course, limitations to what a project of this magnitude can successfully achieve. Some readers may not find their favorite generative framework covered in the book; others may be surprised to find no separate chapters dedicated, for instance, to computational linguistics, or the relationship between hierarchical syntactic structure and linear order, or the syntax–morphology interface, or diachronic syntax (i.e., studies of the syntactic development of adult languages over time, as distinct from syntactic development in children). But most readers will find discussion relevant to their favorite framework or research topic somewhere in the handbook, even if that framework or topic is not featured prominently in a designated chapter or section of the book.

The handbook is squarely and unapologetically focused on the Principles and Parameters approach to generative syntax – a focus that is entirely justified in view of the fact that the Principles and Parameters approach is the dominant paradigm in the field, and has generated the most in-depth discussion of virtually all of the issues covered in Parts III–VI. Part II reviews some of the major alternatives to the Chomskyan mainstream, but cannot aspire to exhaustiveness in this regard. Thus, although Relational Grammar (see Perlmutter 1980) played a significant role in the development of a clear perspective on argument structure and argument-structure alternations and helped unearth a wealth of data from a wide variety of languages, this handbook contains no chapter dedicated to it, nor to its offshoot Arc Pair Grammar (see Johnson and Postal 1980). Readers will find occasional references to Relational Grammar in the book, particularly in Chapter 9. Some attention is paid to Construction Grammar (see Goldberg 1995) in Chapters 3 and 7. The latter chapter and also Chapter 8 (and, in passing, Section 1.2.4 of this Introduction) mention Categorial Grammar (see Wood 1993). Chapter-length exposés of these frameworks were not pursued, not just because of space restrictions but also in light of the fact that these theories are not being practiced by a critical mass of linguists in the field today, and have not established themselves (yet) as 'mainstream.' The same rationale has led the handbook to remain silent on Dependency Grammar (an approach emanating from work done in the first half of the twentieth century by the French linguist Lucien Tesnière; various versions of this approach are around today; see Fraser 1994 for a brief overview) and the related theory of Word Grammar (see Hudson 1984, and Sugayama and Hudson 2005 for a recent collection of papers), which both represent sentence structure entirely in terms of dependencies between words and forgo phrase structure representations. These kinds of frameworks are chiefly popular among computational linguists – a constituency not served by a dedicated chapter in this book, for reasons of space; but readers interested in computational issues should find the discussion in Section 8.7 of significant interest. This book also contains no discussion of Dynamic Syntax (see Kempson et al. 2001, Cann et al. 2005), a theory primarily concerned with time-linear processing, and Mirror Theory (developed in Brody 2001), an approach to the syntax–morphology interface which Adger et al. (2009) show provides an interesting perspective on ordering restrictions in so-called 'free-word-order languages.'

This leads me naturally to a brief discussion of one of the central issues in current generative syntax that this handbook has not singled out as the topic for a chapter of its own: linearization. The primary reason for not including a separate chapter on this topic is the fact that it has connections with so many of the ingredients of the other chapters, hence pops up in different places throughout the book. The placement of a complement relative to its selecting head ('VO' vs.'OV,' or more generally, 'head–complement' vs. 'complement–head') used to be encoded directly in the form of a linearization instruction inherent in the phrase-structure rules (PS-rules) of the earliest generative syntax (Chapters 2, 11) or, later, in the subcategorization frames of heads (Chapters 9, 11). With the introduction of the X-bar Theory of phrase structure (Chapters 2, 11), linear order was no longer automatically built into the phrase-structure component. The question of variation among languages (and, within languages, among constituents of different categories) with respect to linear order came to be addressed at that time with reference to word-order parameters ('head parameters') of various sorts (Chapters 3, 11, 25), some couched in terms of the directionality of thematic role assignment, others in terms of the directionality of case assignment, and yet others in terms of the directionality of government. The so-called 'Borer–Chomsky conjecture' (Chapter 25), which restricted parametric variation to the properties of functional categories, made it impossible to postulate a parameter regulating the direction in which thematic roles are assigned: theta-roles are assigned by lexical categories, not by functional ones. The Hale and Keyser (1993) program aimed at providing universal configurational definitions for thematic roles (see Section 9.6.2) further dampened the prospects of a parameterization of theta-role assignment. The introduction, in early Minimalism, of the checking theory of features rendered it impossible, furthermore, to parameterize the directionality of case assignment: case was no longer considered to be a 'mark' that was 'assigned' by some head to a nominal constituent in its c-command domain (with the directionality of case assignment potentially parameterizable), but was instead conceived of as a feature that needed to be checked against a matching feature of a nominal constituent in a particular structural configuration, either a Specifier–Head relation or Agree (see Chapter 17 for details); neither of these structural relations lends itself to parametric variation. And government, which played such a pivotal role in generative syntactic theory for some time that it even lent its name to the title by which the theory was widely known in the 1980s ('Government and Binding Theory,' after Chomsky 1981), became entirely defunct at the dawn of the Minimalist Program (Chomsky 1995c; see also Section 17.3.2.1), closing the door on the possibility of a government-based directionality parameter.

An influential hypothesis that has informed the discussion about the relationship between hierarchical structure and linear order in recent times is Kayne's (1994) Linear Correspondence Axiom (LCA), which requires that hierarchical structures be translatable *in toto* and unambiguously into linear strings of terminals on the basis of the asymmetric c-command relationships holding between the non-terminals in the structure. Sections 2.4.2 and 11.4.2 present a brief introduction to this hypothesis, and Section 4.2.1 looks at the level at which it applies; see also Moro (2000) for an approach (dubbed 'Dynamic Antisymmetry') that exploits movement to convert underlying symmetry into surface asymmetry (recently recast in terms of the need to get unambiguously labeled structures; Moro 2009). No matter whether one accepts the particular way in which Kayne's LCA codifies the translation from hierarchical structure into linear order (this approach depends heavily on specific assumptions about X-bar structure which are rejected, for instance, in Chomsky's [1995c: Chapter 4] Bare Phrase Structure; see Sections 2.4.3 and 4.2.4.2), it is clear that current assumptions in generative syntax leave no basis on which to formulate a directionality parameter with reference to the base component, as was shown in the previous paragraph. All cross-linguistic and intra-linguistic variation in linear order must therefore be taken care of in a different way. Movement plays a central role in this. One approach would be to say that a particular movement operation that takes place in overt syntax in one language or construction fails to take place (overtly) in some other language or construction; an alternative that exploits the so-called copy theory of movement (see Section 4.2.4.1) would have it that the movement operation in question takes place systematically but in some languages or constructions it is the highest copy in the movement chain that is phonologically spelled out whereas in other languages or constructions a lower copy is realized, giving the surface impression of lack of movement or partial movement (on partial *wh*-movement, see Chapter 22). The fine-tuning of an approach to linearization in terms of the locus of copy spell-out depends in non-trivial ways on the timing of the linearization instructions given to the phonological component: Are such instructions given once only, at the end of the complete syntactic derivation, or in a piecemeal fashion, upon the completion of discrete subportions of the structure (the 'cyclic nodes' of early generative syntax, now called 'phases')? Some beneficial consequences of the cyclic approach to linearization are presented in Fox and Pesetsky (2005) and Ko (2005b), but work along these lines is still in its early stages, so no clear stand in this matter can be taken at this time.

It is difficult, in present-day generative syntax, to talk in terms of the syntax–morphology interface. The primary reason why no separate chapter of this handbook is dedicated to this interface is that, on most generative syntacticians' assumptions today, there really is no such interface: by and large, morphology *is* syntax. The Minimalist Program attributed a central role to morphological features as the driving force (or 'trigger') of syntactic operations. And the framework of Distributed Morphology (Halle and Marantz 1993) assembles morphologically complex structures in the course of the syntactic derivation (see Baker 1988 and related work for important ancestors of this approach). There currently remain some morphological puzzles that the syntax seems ill-equipped to take full responsibility for, which is why Distributed Morphology recognizes a number of morphological operations in the Phonological Form (PF) wing of the grammar (in its Morphological Structure component), including morphological merger, fission, and impoverishment of the feature structures delivered by the syntactic derivation. Readers interested in these morphological operations should consult the literature on Distributed Morphology (Harley and Noyer 2003 and Embick and Noyer 2006 are very accessible introductions to the framework). But for the most part, issues relating to the syntax–morphology interface are subsumed under the individual chapters in Parts III–V of this book, including discussions of the Mirror Principle (Chapter 12) and the morphosyntax of case and agreement (Chapter 17). For pointers to discussion of individual morphology-related matters, the index at the back of the book should prove useful.

Finally, let me say a few words about the absence of a chapter on diachronic variation alongside the chapter on dialectal variation. In the earliest days of linguistics as an academic discipline (see especially the work of the *Junggrammatiker* in late nineteenth-century Germany), the historical approach was very much at center-stage. The diachronic development of languages still plays an important role in generative syntax today, but the questions arising in the context of diachronic variation, from a generative point of view, are very much the same kinds of questions about variation that also arise in a synchronic context. A central issue in both domains is how best to deal with inter- and intra-speaker variation, and the optionality that it often comes in tandem with. Chapter 24 addresses these and other questions primarily from a synchronic point of view. But the answers it presents to them should prove relevant to those interested in diachronic variation as well.

I now proceed to presenting a continuous narrative that introduces the central themes and research foci of the generative-syntactic enterprise, establishes connections (or seams) between them, and highlights some of the issues for future research (the dreams). I hope this will frame the discussions in the individual chapters to follow, will give the reader a sense of how things hang together in this multifarious field.

1.2 The theory of generative syntax: themes, seams, and dreams

1.2.1 The beginnings of generative syntax, and its central goal

Though the European structuralist movement known as the Prague School had studied the pragmatic functions of sentence constituents in discourse in its Functional Sentence Perspective, in its early days the newly born academic discipline of linguistics generally paid little detailed attention to syntax. American Structuralism introduced rigorous scientific standards to the young field, but concentrated almost exclusively on morphophonemics; and Saussure had famously placed the sentence in his *parole*, hence altogether outside the formal linguistic system, the *langue*. But Harris (1951, 1957) recognized the need, in a structuralist theory of syntax, for three ingredients that would come to figure, in some form, in early generative syntax as well: *(i)* "statements which enable anyone to synthesize or predict utterances in the language," statements which "form a deductive system with axiomatically defined initial elements and with theorems concerning the relations among them"; *(ii)* "statements" which "transform certain sentences of the text into grammaticality equivalent sentences" (such as nominalization, particle placement, VP-ellipsis, question formation, addressed in some detail in Harris 1957); and *(iii)* the idea that sentences "consist of a sequence of one or more *underlying* sentences" (Harris 1951:372–73). In early generative grammar, statements of type *(i)* resurfaced as the phrase-structure rules ('PS rules') that codified the well-formed underlying syntactic representations, and those of type *(ii)* transparently foreshadowed its transformations (though in Harris's profoundly non-derivational approach, the word 'transform' in the quotation under *(ii)* should not be read in the way that transformational generative grammar later applied it). And generalized transformations could combine two sentence-level phrase markers ('kernel sentences') into one complex sentence, as in Chomsky's (1955/1975) analysis of clausal subordination – very much along the lines of *(iii)* (which itself closely reflects the Port Royal grammarians' approach to the complex sentence *Dieu invisible a créé le monde visible* 'invisible God created the visible world,' assembled out of the three simple sentences *Dieu est invisible* 'God is invisible,' *Dieu a créé le monde* 'God created the world,' and *le monde est visible* 'the world is visible').

In these formal respects, therefore, early generative grammar (with 'generative' meaning 'explicit') is a continuation of its predecessors. But it breaks radically with its structuralist antecedents in identifying the central explanandum as what Chomsky has called 'Plato's problem,' the fact that children all over the world acquire their native languages effortlessly within a short period of time, notwithstanding the poverty of the stimulus (see Chapters 2, 3, 25). What children hear in their environment is both quantitatively and qualitatively a very poor reflection of what their language is capable of: during the critical period of language acquisition, they will likely hear not a single instance of many constructions that they will end up being able to produce and process without difficulty (an oft-cited case in point is the parasitic gap construction (see Section 4.2.4.1), represented by sentences such as *Which article did you file ___ without reading ___?*, containing two gaps, the second parasitizing on the first); and conversely, they will hear lots of utterances that are not grammatically well-formed (anacolutha, false starts, utterances that end in mid-sentence, speech errors of various sorts) but they somehow manage to exclude them from the primary linguistic data on the basis of which they develop the grammar of their native language. The language learner (or, more appropriately but less elegantly, the language acquirer) is placed at center-stage in the generative enterprise – and in this respect, it is a world apart from structuralism. Here one need only recall Joos's brief commentary on Bloch's (1941) highly influential article on phonemic overlapping, in which Joos leaves little doubt about the priorities of American Structuralists (or 'descriptivists,' as they themselves preferred to be called): "Children want explanations, and there is a child in each of us; descriptivism makes a virtue of not pampering that child" (Joos 1957:96). American Structuralism is above all a practical approach to the description of language data, providing a maximally rigorous tool for setting up the phoneme inventories of (previously unanalyzed) individual languages. Structuralist methodology was very much developed from the *linguist*'s perspective, not the *language learner*'s. Chomsky changed this perspective dramatically, making the language learner the focal point, and in so doing revolutionized the field of linguistics. It is by no means the case that the logical problem of language acquisition had never figured on the research agenda before: as Chomsky (1966) himself has emphasized, the mentalist perspective owes much to the prominent seventeenth-century French philosopher René Descartes; Wilhelm von Humboldt and Otto Jespersen can be mentioned in this context as well. But Chomsky made the logical problem of language acquisition the central explanandum of the generative enterprise: it defined the highest criterion to which a generative theory of language should answer, that of explanatory adequacy (see Sections 2.1 and 3.2.5). This emphasis on acquisition led over time to the theory of principles (universal, innate) and parameters – the latter possibly confined to the functional lexicon (see Chapter 25).

1.2.2 Abstractness
From the outset, Chomsky argued for a degree of abstractness in syntactic analysis not previously adumbrated. A key argument to this effect comes from the miminal pair in (1) and (2) (on the *tough*-movement or *easy-to-please* construction, see Section 10.4.2.1).

(1) John is easy to please
(2) John is eager to please

The Harris-style "statements which enable anyone to synthesize or predict utterances in the language" are the same for (1) and (2), including the ones in (3) (stated in the format of PS-rules):

(3) a. AP → A + S_{inf}
    b. S_{inf} → *to* + VP

Yet (1) and (2) are clearly different. Interpretively, *John* is the object of *please* in (1) but its subject in (2). And syntactically, there are important differences between the two as well:

(4) a. *John's easiness to please
    b. John's eagerness to please

(5) a. John is easy for us to please
    b. *John is eager for us to please
       [*with *John* as the object of *please*]

(6) a. to please John is easy
    b. *to please John is eager

(7) a. it is easy to please John
    b. *it is eager to please John
       [*unless *it* is referential]

Structuralist syntax, with its surface orientation, fails to make the desired distinctions and fails to capture the interpretive difference between (1) and (2). By contrast, the (simplified) derivations in (8a,b) (for (1) and (2), respectively) make the interpretations of these sentences directly transparent, and at the same time they afford us a perspective on the contrasts in (4)–(7): raising operations are generally highly restricted in noun phrases (thus, there is no NP-raising in the English noun phrase: *John's appearance to like Mary* contrasts sharply with *John appears to like Mary*); *John* is represented in (8b) as the subject of *please*, blocking *us* in (5b) from occupying this position, whereas nothing prevents *us* from being the subject of *please* in (5a); *John* in (8b) is also the deep subject of *eager*, which resists a propositional subject (6b) or a placeholder for it (7b), unlike in the case of *easy*, which in (8a) does not have a deep subject.

(8) a. John is easy [(for someone) to please J̶o̶h̶n̶]   ['*tough*-movement']
    b. John is eager [J̶o̶h̶n̶ to please (someone)]   ['Equi NP deletion']

1.2.3 Phrase-structure rules and X-bar Theory

Syntactic Structures (Chomsky 1957) is Chomsky's first publication on transformational generative grammar (his *Logical Structure of Linguistic Theory* was completed in 1955 but not published until 1975). In *Syntactic Structures*, Chomsky presents a theory of phrase structure comprising phrase-structure rules, which are part of the so-called base component, and transformations, which form the transformational component. There is no separate lexicon – terminals of phrase markers (the actual words and morphemes) are assumed to be introduced by PS-rules in the same way that non-terminal nodes of syntactic representations are. The PS-rule system persists until well into the 1970s, though their purview is reduced in Chomsky (1965) by the introduction of the lexicon, so that lexical items no longer need to be introduced by PS-rules. PS-rules eventually gave way, however, to the desire to capture the fundamental endocentricity of syntactic structures in a formally explicit way. The advent of X-bar Theory (Chomsky 1970a, Jackendoff 1977; see esp. Chapter 11, this volume) and subcategorization catalyzed the analysis of syntactic structures, culminating in a uniform approach to the syntactic projections of all categories, lexical (open-class) and functional (closed-class) alike.

Generalized X-bar theoretic representations have enjoyed broad though not universal acceptance throughout the generative enterprise. Thus, one finds nodes labeled 'IP' and 'CP' in Lexical-Functional Grammar (LFG) analyses as well, although, as Chapter 6 points out, the c-structures that LFG postulates are not necessarily X-bar Theory compliant: individual structures of individual languages may employ 'S' and 'S" nodes instead, and LFG structures are not necessarily binary branching (Kayne 1984, 1994) either. Head-driven Phrase Structure Grammar (HPSG, outlined in Chapter 7) does not use categorially labeled structural nodes in its representations; it registers category in the feature structures associated with nodes, but category is just one of the many pieces of information contained in these feature structures: category membership is not given privileged status in node labeling, nor does HPSG recognize bar levels. In these respects, there are parallels between HPSG and Bare Phrase Structure, a recent development in Chomsky's (1995c) Minimalist Program that abandons the familiar X-bar theoretic representations and considers the abolition of category labels as well (see especially Collins 2002; Sections 2.4.3 and 4.2.4.2 discuss Bare Phrase Structure). In everyday practice, however, X-bar structures continue to be in general use in minimalist syntax.

1.2.4 Transformations, and non-transformational generative approaches

With the ouster of PS-rules, Harris-style 'statements which enable anyone to synthesize or predict utterances in the language' – *(i)* in Section 1.2.1, above – disappeared from the generative mainstream. Singulary and generalized transformations, corresponding to Harris's *(ii)* and *(iii)*, have never enjoyed general approval in generative syntax. They had their heyday in the 1960s and 1970s during the Generative Semantics era, but were reined in drastically by Chomsky's (1970a) rebuttal of the practice of deriving words via the application of syntactic transformations to (sometimes highly abstract) sentence-level underlying representations. While Harris (1957) mentioned nominalization as one example where we might "transform certain sentences of the text into grammaticality equivalent sentences," Chomsky centered his argument against deriving words via syntactic transformations precisely on nominalizations such as *the city's destruction by the enemy*, for which Lees (1963) had developed an analysis that derived them from passive sentences. Chomsky's argument was simple: *the city's destruction by the enemy* "is only apparently the nominalization of a passive" (Chomsky 1970a:43); the object preposing rule and the subject postposing rule that jointly characterize the passive transformation (*The enemy destroyed the city* → *The city was destroyed by the enemy*) are entirely independent of one another in the noun phrase (thus, one can have *the destruction of the city by the enemy*, where there is subject postposing without object preposing, unlike in sentential passives), and their application does not even require there to be a nominalized verb (in *John's photo*, on a reading in which John is the person shown in the photograph, and *a book by Chomsky* we are not dealing with nominalizations). Moreover, Chomsky points out that if we actually allowed nominalization to be a syntactic transformation that can take a passive sentence as its input, we ought to be able to derive nominalizations such as *the tomatoes' growth* from *The tomatoes were grown* – but in point of fact, *the tomatoes' growth* does not support a passive interpretation; it only has an intransitive one (corresponding to *The tomatoes are growing*). A transformational approach to nominalizations would thus fail to be descriptively adequate.

Chomsky's rebuttal of Generative Semantics marked a shift away from unbridled transformationalism. Around the same time, offshoots that started to branch out from the Chomskyan stem made a point of either not exploiting the transformational mechanism or using it much more sparingly. Lexical-Functional Grammar (Chapter 6) and Phrase Structure Grammar (Chapter 7) are non-transformational generative models: there is no movement in the syntax in these theories; non-local dependencies are dealt with in different ways, for instance with the aid of the 'slash category' – a mechanism that allows the syntax to keep track of the fact that, say, a verb's desire to take an object has not been met yet: in *What did you eat?*, the verb *eat* wants an object but does not get one locally; the slash mechanism registers the fact that there is an object missing, and carries this information up the tree until a suitable filler is encountered (see Chapter 7 for illustration). Categorial Grammar deals with filler–gap dependencies in a very similar way (see Chapters 7 and 8 for brief discussion). Tree Adjoining Grammar (TAG), discussed in Chapter 8, presents an interesting mix of the Chomskyan transformational approach and the non-transformational approach to filler–gap dependencies advocated by Phrase Structure Grammar and Categorial Grammar. It represents what one might call a 'locally transformational' generative grammar: there are movement transformations, but they are always local, in the sense that they never span clause boundaries. In the cyclic approach to the long-distance filler–gap dependencies of Chomsky (1973) (see Chapter 18), these are broken up into a succession of local steps: you cycle your way up the tree going from clause to clause (or from cyclic node to cyclic node). Tree Adjoining Grammar does away with this by making all *wh*-movement (and, more generally, all movement) local: movement applies within a simple elementary tree, which can never be larger than a clause; apparent long-distance dependencies result from the adjunction of a partial structure (an auxiliary tree, with the same node at its top and foot) into the simple elementary tree – a process that can in principle be repeated infinitely many times, capturing the recursiveness of the grammar in a straightforward way. Thus, in the formation of a sentence such as *Who do you think that Bill kissed?*, the *wh*-dependency between *who* and the gap following *kissed* is itself local, confined within a single clause: *who that Bill kissed* is the elementary tree representing the *wh*-dependency. We create the extra distance between *who* and the gap by adjoining the auxiliary tree *do you think*, recursive on C', into the elementary tree; and in principle we can repeat this process of adjoining auxiliary trees as many times as we want, creating more and more linear distance between *who* and the gap while keeping the structural distance between the two perfectly constant: throughout: *who* moves only within the elementary tree containing *kiss*; there is no successive-cyclic movement.

The exigencies of the Minimalist Program (Chomsky 1995c and subsequent work; see Chapter 4) have led Chomsky's followers to question the need for certain transformations (or applications of the general rule Move α) as well. Thus, some have questioned the desirability of representing NP-movement (at work in passive and raising constructions; see Chapter 16) in terms of actual movement: if one could allow thematic roles to be carried up the tree, one could potentially base-generate the subject of a passive sentence such as *Mary was kissed* directly in its surface position, voiding the need to move *Mary* from the object position of *kiss* into the subject position (see Lasnik 1999d on the absence of reconstruction effects under A-movement). Similar thoughts have been brought to bear on scrambling, which is responsible for the freedom of word order in languages such as Dutch, German, Japanese, and many others: while scrambling is traditionally believed to instantiate a movement operation, the fact that it has always been very difficult to pinpoint its status as an instance of A- or A'-movement because it tends to respond in contradictory ways to familiar diagnostics for these two processes has led some to represent scrambling in terms of base-generation instead (see e.g. Bayer and Kornfilt 1994,

Neeleman 1994b, Neeleman and Reinhart 1998; see also Section 11.11). Such a rethinking of NP-raising and scrambling phenomena without an appeal to movement impinges on the way in which argument structure and predication are represented in syntax (see Chapters 9 and 10): for instance, a restrictive requirement to the effect that all the thematic roles associated with a particular predicate head be assigned within the maximal projection of that head (usually called the VP-internal subject hypothesis) would stand in the way of an analysis of raising constructions such as *John seems to like Mary* eschewing NP-movement. But there may be reason, quite independently of the constructions at hand, to reconsider the relationship between argument structure and syntax. Some have argued that the requirements imposed by the Theta Criterion and the Projection Principle, the major arbiters of this relationship in early Principles and Parameters theory, should either be relaxed or abolished completely – with the analysis of control constructions (such as *John tried to kiss Mary*) playing a central role in this discussion (Chapter 16 addresses this matter at some length). Interestingly, the control-as-movement program (initiated by Hornstein 1999) extends movement to a domain which it had previously been thought not to apply to, and in this respect, the control-as-movement approach to some extent counterbalances developments elsewhere in the field to use movement less than before.

That not all filler–gap dependencies need to be represented in terms of movement is perhaps particularly clear in the case of topicalization, which places a topic in sentence-initial position. Topicalization often gives rise to the emergence of a so-called resumptive pronoun in the position of the expected gap (as in *John, I can't stand him*). This, in conjunction with the fact that null pronouns clearly exist in many languages (see the discussion of pro-drop in Chapter 25, for instance), may suggest an analysis that postulates a null pronoun in the position of the gap, rather than a trace or copy of the topicalized constituent. And although *wh*-dependencies are still generally treated in terms of movement, the idea that certain *wh*-constituents could be base-generated in their surface position and bind a null resumptive instead of being moved up the tree has gained significant traction since Cinque's (1990b) demonstration of the benefits of such an approach (see Section 18.4). Even if *wh*-movement as such continues to be necessary, it may be possible to simplify the derivation of long-distance *wh*-dependencies considerably, for instance by dispensing with the need for intermediate touch-downs on the edges of all subordinate clauses. Recent work by Rackowski and Richards (2005) suggests that landing on the edge of a cyclic node (called 'phase' in current terminology) may not be the only way to make extraction from that node possible – and if their argument is successful, it should lead to the conclusion that whenever the alternative mechanism for opening cyclic nodes up to extraction from them is available, the successive-cyclic movement derivation is redundant, hence unavailable (see Section 18.10). A *rapprochement* between mainstream minimalist syntax and the TAG approach to long *wh*-dependencies thus looms on the horizon – and with it, a further reduction of the theory's dependence on movement.

1.2.5 Economy of derivation, representation, and theory design

The successive-cyclic movement derivations that Chomsky (1973) gave rise to reveal perhaps particularly vividly the tension between two apparently conflicting desirata: to make the shortest movements and to make the fewest movements. This tension (addressed in detail in Chapter 14) lies at the heart of the role played in much current syntactic theorizing by considerations of economy – the joint injunctions (a) to keep one's derivational steps as short as possible (the Minimal Link Condition; economy of derivation), and (b) to keep one's representations free from superfluous symbols (the Principle of Full Interpretation; economy of representation).

The intermediate traces or copies introduced into the structure by successive-cyclic movement on the one hand have the benefit of cutting the derivation up into a series of very local steps, yet on the other hand threaten to provide the interface between syntax and semantic interpretation with a lot of uninterpretable matter (the intermediate traces/copies). For Lasnik and Saito (1984), maximal deletion of intermediate members of successive-cyclic *wh*-movement chains was their creed: since Affect α (the more general version of Move α: "do anything you want to α") was not at the time thought to come at a cost, it was best to apply it wherever possible to get rid of meaningless material. But less than a decade later, Chomsky and Lasnik (1993) approached the very same question rather differently: in the 1990s all applications of Affect α had become costly, so deletion of intermediate traces had to be eschewed unless it was forced by the need to procure a well-formed LF object. The chain formed by successive-cyclic *wh*-movement of an argument is not, as it stands, such an object: it is neither uniform (it contains a member in A-position as well as several members in A'-positions) nor a simple operator–variable structure (which should contain exactly one operator and one variable). The problem that such a chain poses for the Principle of Full Interpretation can be resolved by deleting, by way of last resort, all the intermediate traces in the chain – economy of derivation here yields to economy of representation. But a chain formed by successive-cyclic movement of an adjunct is a well-formed LF object by virtue of being uniform (all the members of the chain are in A'-positions). Chomsky and Lasnik argue that deletion of intermediate traces does not take place in such a chain – economy of derivation trumps economy of representation here: though the chain contains one or more meaningless members (the intermediate trace or traces), this is deemed acceptable for Full Interpretation as long as the multi-member chain is uniform. The adjunct chain case illustrates nicely that sometimes there seems to be no way to *fully* satisfy economy of derivation and representation at the same time: you can abstain from applying Affect α and deliver a uniform object to the LF component, but you are left with meaningless material at LF as part of this uniform object. (See Section 14.2.2, for further discussion.)

Economy considerations were initially introduced into Principles and Parameters theory as general guidelines, but in the Minimalist Program, economy started to dominate the research agenda. Like all branches of science, generative linguistics is beholden to Occam's razor, hence should not postulate mechanisms or operations that it could do without. And it has turned out over the years that many of the mechanisms and operations that earlier generative syntax considered indispensable not only could be disposed of without significant loss but would actually do the theory a disservice if they were kept. I have already mentioned X-bar Theory in this connection (recall Section 1.2.3, above). But perhaps the most striking demonstration of this comes from the levels of syntactic representation.

1.2.6 Levels of syntactic representation, and the interfaces with the interpretive systems

From its inception, transformational generative grammar made a distinction between Deep Structure (abbreviated to D-structure) and Shallow or Surface Structure (S-structure), with transformations mediating between the two levels of representation. Logical Form was later added (in the so-called T- or Y-model of grammar first presented in Chomsky and Lasnik 1977; see Section 2.3) as a third level of syntactic representation. Each of these syntactic levels was legitimated by the fact principles of syntactic theory were thought to apply to them. Thus, the Projection Principle ensures that the Theta Criterion applies to D-structure as well as to the other two levels of representation; the Case Filter (see Chapter 17) was standardly considered to hold at S-structure; and the principles of the Binding Theory (chapter 15) were variously believed to hold at D-structure, S-structure, LF, or all of the above.

It was specifically with reference to the Binding Theory that Chomsky (1995c: Chapter 3) constructed his argument that the postulation of D-structure and S-structure as levels to which principles of the theory could apply was a mistake. Perhaps even more dramatically than in 1970, when Chomsky drew the curtain on the Generative Semantics movement with the aid of one case study (nominalizations), the case against multiple levels of syntactic representation hinged on just a single datum: while *John wonders how many pictures of himself Bill took* is ambiguous in principle with respect to the choice of antecedent for *himself* (i.e., either *Bill* or *John* could be chosen to antecede the reflexive), this ambiguity disappears when *took pictures* is interpreted as an idiom ('photographed'), in which case only the *Bill*-reading is available. On the assumption that idiomatic interpretation requires constituency at LF, the non-ambiguity of this sentence on the idiom reading for *took pictures* follows directly from the Binding Theory (see Chomsky 1995c: Chapter 3 for the details) – but only if the principles of the Binding Theory are taken to apply exclusively at LF: if one allowed the Binding Theory to be satisfied at S-structure, one could derive the *John*-reading at that level entirely regardless of the interpretation assigned at LF to *took pictures*, which would make it impossible to explain the correlation between idiomaticity and antecedent choice observed in the data.

With D-structure and S-structure gone, LF is left as the only syntactic level of representation. LF interfaces directly with the Conceptual–Intentional interface. An increasing amount of discussion in the syntax literature has consequently come to be devoted to the question of how syntax answers to the legibility conditions imposed by this interface. Among the issues arising in this connection is the question of how to deal with morphosyntactic properties of syntactic structures that do not seem to be interpretable at the Conceptual–Intentional interface. Foremost among these properties are agreement (phi-feature inflection: person, number, gender) and case, discussed at length in Chapter 17. For a noun phrase, it is obviously semantically meaningful whether it is singular or plural; but its gender specification is often entirely arbitrary (think of the fact that the Spanish noun *mesa*, meaning 'table,' is feminine and *asiento* 'seat, chair' is masculine, while in German both *Tisch* 'table' and *Stuhl* 'chair' are masculine), and the case that it bears typically does not help in determining its grammatical function (an accusative-marked noun phrase can be a direct object, an indirect object, or even a subject, as in '*accusativus-cum-infinitivo*' or 'Exceptional Case-Marking' (ECM) constructions: *I consider him to be the best candidate*). These case- and phi-features are obviously important to the workings of the morphosyntax: in English, a nominative case-marked pronoun must be paired up with a finite verb as its subject, and that finite verb must normally have the same phi-features as its subject. The case- and phi-features often get a phonological realization as well (*he~him, he~she, (s)he~they*). But they do not seem to make a semantic contribution in many instances. One might say the same thing, at least in some instances, for the tense features of verbs (see Chapter 20 for detailed discussion of tense, along with aspect and modality) – though tense is clearly interpretable, the particular morphological tense feature on a finite verb often has no direct connection to the semantics of time, as in Sequence of Tenses contexts: on a reading of *John said yesterday that he was sick* where the time of his being sick is cotemporaneous with the time of his saying so, it seems that the past-tense morphology of *was* makes no semantic contribution. If indeed there are truly uninterpretable morphosyntactic features (a claim that typically distinguishes the generative approach from more functionalist perspectives), it would seem to make good sense to try and rid the syntactic representation of these features before it interfaces with the Conceptual–Intentional system, so that a full interpretation can be assigned to the output of syntax at that point.

1.2.7 Feature checking, and the trigger for movement

This led to the introduction of feature-checking theory, and it also centered attention on the driving force for syntactic operations – movement, in particular. In a restrictive theory, nothing happens for no reason. So movement must have a driving force, or 'trigger,' as Chomsky has called it. Since Chomskyan syntax has always cherished its autonomy *vis-à-vis* the interpretive components (especially semantics; but see Chapter 3 and also Section 1.2.9 for ways in which the autonomy of syntax has been weakened in some recent work), delivery of a particular semantic interpretation generally has not been considered to be a legitimate trigger for movement. Instead, the need to eliminate ('check') otherwise uninterpretable morphosyntactic features was postulated, in early Minimalism, as the trigger. Thus, a *wh*-constituent does not move to the left edge of the sentence because it wants to be there for semantic reasons (scope, for instance; see Chapter 22); rather, it was said that the *wh*-constituent shares a certain feature (let us call it a [WH] feature) with a functional head in the left periphery of the clause ('C' for 'Complementizer'), and raises to the edge of the projection of that functional head in order to ensure that the uninterpretable [WH] feature of this head is checked before the output of the syntactic derivation is handed over to the Conceptual–Intentional interface. Such checking would not necessarily require displacement of the *wh*-constituent in overt syntax: uninterpretable features that the Conceptual–Intentional interface cannot deal with should be eliminated by the end of the derivation toward LF, but that does not mean that they need to be checked before the derivation is handed over to the other interpretive component, the Articulatory–Perceptual interface (or sensori-motor system). The feature-checking theory of movement may thus provide a rationale for movement, but the answer to the question of when movement is overt and when it is not still eludes it. To account for the timing of movement, some additional diacritic needs to be introduced – feature strength (as in Chomsky 1995c: Chapters 3, 4, 14) or the 'EPP property' of more recent minimalist work (with 'EPP' standing for 'Extended Projection Principle,' originally the combination of the 'core' Projection Principle, which requires that all lexical information be syntactically projected, and the ancillary condition that all clauses must have a subject; in its more recent incarnation, 'EPP' is a generalized version of this latter condition, now requiring that displacement take place to the edge of any functional category that is specified for this property – see also Section 3.5 and Chapter 10).

The checking approach to movement is not straightforward beyond the core cases involving case and agreement. The example of *wh*-movement that I already alluded to in the previous paragraph will serve as a good illustration of the questions raised by this approach. It is easy to see that there is no requirement that each and every bearer of the morphological feature [WH] must be displaced to the edge of CP: in English, this requirement does generally hold in the case of single *wh*-questions (though quiz questions such as *The French Revolution was started by which event?* are a well-known example of genuine information questions that exhibit *wh-in-situ* even in English; see Wachowicz 1974), but it is not in effect in multiple *wh*-questions (such as *Who ate what?*, where *what* must stay *in situ*). More strikingly, there are languages whose *wh*-constituents must generally *all* be fronted in multiple *wh*-questions, but where there are individual cases in which this general requirement is obligatorily lifted (see Section 4.2.4.1 for illustration from Romanian). These cases combined raise the question of where to place the responsibility for feature checking: on the C-head, or on the individual *wh*-constituent(s)? The question of the nature of the feature that is being checked is equally non-trivial. The morphological property [WH] does not isolate the right class of elements, as is particularly clear in languages (such as German) that can use *wh*-pronouns as bare indefinites: *Ich habe was gegessen* 'I have WH eaten, i.e., I ate something' has the *wh*-pronoun *was* in VP-internal position, not at the edge of CP. The feature [Q], for 'question,' is not adequate either: *wh*-fronting is not exclusive to questions; it happens in relative clauses (*the man who Mary kissed*) and exclamative constructions (*How tall you are!*) as well. In light of these problems, it may be advantageous to think of *wh*-fronting in a rather different kind of way, not treating it as a feature-driven movement but instead as an operation that creates a particular structural configuration that is paired up with a particular semantic interpretation.

Such an approach is particularly attractive for operations that are especially hard to couch in terms of feature checking. Here we should think, in particular, of operations that are typically confined to or commonly postulated primarily for the 'covert syntax,' i.e., the portion of the syntactic derivation that transpires after the syntactic construct has already been handed over (via 'Spell-out') to Phonological Form. For negation, the literature has occasionally suggested (see especially Haegeman's work; see Chapter 21) that negative quantifiers must move into a designated specifier position (SpecNegP), either overtly (as in West Flemish) or else covertly. But Hungarian (a language that famously "wears its LF on its sleeve" and places its quantifiers in their appropriate scopal positions already in overt syntax) aside, Quantifier Raising (QR; May 1977, 1985; see Chapter 22) has standardly been treated as LF-movement to an adjunction position, with the landing-site not being preordained: QR could in principle target either VP or IP. A popular approach to QR is one that says that it must have an effect on the interpretation of the output (Fox 2000). Such an outlook is still compatible with the idea that movement takes place by way of last resort, hence in line with the general economy guidelines; but it is very different from the feature-checking approach to movement. I should add that there are accounts available in the literature that treat the raising of quantifiers in terms of movement to specifiers of designated functional categories, and could thus couch Quantifier Raising in terms of feature checking (see Section 22.2.4). Beghelli and Stowell's (1997) proposal is an important case in point. It recognizes a variety of quantification-related functional projections (including DistP for distributive quantifiers and RefP for group-denoting QPs) in the left periphery of the clause.

1.2.8 Mapping functional structure

The left periphery of the clause harbors not just quantificational expressions and *wh*-constituents of various sorts (interrogative, exclamative, relative). A rapidly growing number of studies has also exploited it as the locus of information-structural functions such as topic and focus. The case for a designated position for foci was first made forcefully in the generative literature on the basis of data from Hungarian (Horvath 1986, Brody 1990) – though more recent work on focus in this language has made it clear that it is not actually the focality of a constituent *per se* that causes it to surface in this designated position: foci are perfectly happy in their base positions lower in the structure; but when they are fronted, they are obligatorily associated with an interpretation of exhaustivity of the type also seen in English *it*-clefts (*It was Mary that John kissed* signals that, in the universe of discourse, Mary was the *only* person John kissed). Work done in the so-called 'cartographic' program (so called because of the fact that the program seeks to draw the map of the functional structures made available by Universal Grammar) has concentrated, for more than a decade now, on questions relating to the structure of the left periphery of the clause. The central issues arising in connection with this portion of syntactic structure are addressed in Chapter 12. Questions regarding the interface between syntax and information structure are taken up in Chapter 24 as well.

The original impetus to the cartographic program was Cinque's (1994) study of adjectival modification in the noun phrase and his (1999) more extensive investigation of adverbial modification in the clause. Cinque presented a wealth of empirical material taken to underpin the postulation of a large number of designated functional categories for particular modification relations (see Chapter 13 for discussion). This is one of the possible approaches to the many difficult questions posed by modification relations – relations that one finds not just in the extended projections of verbs and nouns, but also in those of adjectives and adpositions: the parallels between the four lexical domains are often quite striking, as the discussion in Chapter 11 emphasizes in some detail.

Setting up designated functional categories that serve as 'probes' and check features against 'goals' with matching features is not the only way to deal with the various phenomena that I briefly touched upon in the preceding paragraphs, however. Both the 'designated' part of this approach and the 'probing/checking' part are subject to debate. Scope and modification relations are above all relative in nature: a quantifier α has a scope that is relatively wider or narrower than that of β; a modifier γ establishes a modification relationship with some constituent relative to other modifiers present in the structure. Relative command appears to be significant in this context, not relative linear order: thus, *John knocked intentionally twice on the door* supports a reading in which *intentionally* modifies the constituent modified by *twice* (he intentionally gave two knocks), whereas *John knocked on the door intentionally twice*, which has the adverbs strung along in the same relative order, yields the opposite relative modification relation (he gave two intentional knocks), one that corresponds to the reading also obtained when the two adverbs are both to the left of the PP but with *twice* preceding *intentionally*, as in *John knocked twice intentionally on the door* (see Andrews 1983; also see Cinque 1999 and den Dikken 2006b). The relative nature of scope and modification relationships is readily encoded in terms of c-command relationships at LF; it is not immediately obvious that a theory that postulates a series of designated functional categories for specific quantification or modification types would be equally well equipped to express the relativity of the phenomena. (See Chapter 13 for relevant discussion.)

1.2.9 The autonomy of syntax

Moreover, as Section 3.3.3 stresses as well, cartographic approaches to semantic relations have a tendency to weaken the autonomy thesis (in particular, the idea that syntax is autonomous *vis-à-vis* semantics), especially if they take the fact that certain movement operations target the specifier positions of these designated functional projections to be triggered by a quintessentially semantic feature of the heads of these projections.

Such an objection can also be leveled at approaches to the interfaces between syntax and information structure and prosody (see Chapter 23 for discussion of both interfaces) that take the trigger for a syntactic movement to be the requirement on the part of a particular syntactic constituent to be focused or be outside the domain of focus, or to get stress or be outside the domain that attracts stress (see Reinhart 1995, Szendrői 2003, and also Richards 2010 for extensive discussion of the idea that syntax and prosody are entangled, and Kandybowicz and Torrence 2011 for evidence against Richards's conclusion and in favor of the traditional approach wherein syntax feeds prosody). And it applies as well to Optimality Theoretic approaches to the syntax–semantics interface and the syntax–prosody interface that postulate syntactic constraints making reference to some semantic or prosodic property. But in the case of OT, this criticism is only valid insofar as the constraints in question are assumed to be part of syntax proper. In Chapter 5, an outlook on the division of labor between derivational syntax and representational OT constraints is unfolded according to which the OT constraints are part of the Evaluator whereas minimalist-syntactic derivations are performed in the Generator portion of the system. The Evaluator is not syntax-specific, hence can harbor constraints of all kinds of flavors. A constraint that says, for instance, "the prosodically unmarked focus is the rightmost constituent in its clause" (ALIGNFOCUS; Costa 1998) is a perfectly sensible ingredient of the Evaluator, which filters the outputs of the (narrow-)syntactic derivation. It would be much harder to uphold such a statement if it were conceived of as a *trigger* for syntactic movement.

1.2.10   The locus of variation, and the nature of parameters
As the previous paragraphs have shown, it is not obvious that all instances of movement need a designated trigger in the syntax proper. Sometimes, movements apparently triggered just by morphological properties (such as phi-features or case) can have a particular semantic or phonological reflex – including the possibility that the remnant of the movement in question fails to get a phonological realization (as in ellipsis phenomena, discussed in Chapter 19). But such a reflex, whatever its nature, is read off the syntactic configuration established by the movement; it is not what sets things in motion.

Triggers for syntactic movement, to the extent that they need to be postulated (and it seems likely that there will remain an unreducible residue of purely formally driven movements), are presumably localizable in the functional lexicon: variation in the parameterizable properties of syntactic categories is likely confined to the set of functional categories (the 'Borer–Chomsky conjecture', discussed in Chapters 2, 4, 24, and 25). But whether this is the sole locus of variation among languages (i.e., whether language variation is just a matter of the parameterized lexical properties of functional categories) is a matter of considerable debate in the literature. What some have called 'microparameters' must arguably be formulated precisely in these terms; but there remain serious candidates for so-called 'macroparameters', such as Baker's polysynthesis parameter (see Chapter 25). The status of such parameters, their precise anchoring (by which I refer to the question of whether they are or are not linkable to a particular functional category), and the way they are set in the course of the language acquisition process are important questions that will continue to be discussed in the literature.

1.2.11   Testing syntactic theory experimentally
Whether we will be able to experimentally ascertain where parameters are anchored by looking at the brain's activity during the on-line production and processing of syntactic structures is one of the questions that investigations of language and the brain could provide important new insight into. Experimental techniques have evolved rapidly in recent years, having led to a veritable boom in the amount of resources made available for

various brain-scanning techniques. Alongside these recent strategies, off-line studies of the processing of linguistic input, which require far less sophisticated equipment, as well as low-tech on-line processing studies also contribute significantly to our understanding of syntax. So does the venerable tradition of studying the developmental patterns exhibited during the language-acquisition processes. Chapters 25 and 26 give an overview of the impressive results yielded by these investigations.

Whenever convergent with their own findings, theoretical syntacticians have generally welcomed these results as support for conclusions they had arrived at independently. It is still very rare to see the results of experimental studies shape and steer the debate in the theory. This is due to a significant extent to the fact that there remains a considerable gap between developments in the theory and the experimental studies: especially over the last fifteen years, mainstream Chomskyan syntax has gone through what may, to relative outsiders, appear to be a whirlwind of changes that often have not had the time to sink in properly. For instance, before the field had managed to understand Chomsky's (1995c: Chapter 3) original approach to feature strength, it was replaced with a new one in Chapter 4 of that same book, and subsequently abandoned altogether and replaced with an 'EPP feature,' alternately referred to as 'edge feature' and 'OCC(urrence) feature.' At a more general level, the consequences of the idea that movement should be postponed until LF whenever possible were still being explored when word came that Procrastinate was actually unformulable in Chomsky's (2000b) more recent single-cycle syntax and had to be replaced with its exact opposite, the Earliness Principle. When theoretical syntacticians themselves are sometimes struggling to keep up with what is being proposed and discussed, it is hardly surprising that the experimentalists are not always at the vanguard of theory development.

This will change once the dust starts to settle on Minimalist theorizing, and once the intensity of collaboration between theoretical and experimental linguists increases. To test their theories, linguists will likely continue to rely primarily on elicited native-speaker judgments from adults with normally functioning brains – a methodology that, though justifiably criticized in certain respects and therefore subject to improvement, continues to deliver generally reliable and replicable results (see Section 3.3.1). But one would expect that theoretical linguists will have their work be informed more and more by important results from experimental work on language acquisition, sentence processing, and language pathologies.

2

Brief overview of the history of generative syntax

Howard Lasnik and Terje Lohndal

2.1 Background and outline

Scientific grammar goes back to the Middle Ages, and specifically the study, by Modistic philosophers, of language as a phenomenon independent of thought. In a sense, the tradition is even older, dating back to Classical Antiquity, and spanning several cultures – after all, every traditional writing system presupposes some serious linguistic theorizing. In the humanistic Renaissance, philosophers started worrying, also, about the relation between language and mind, and as the Ages of Exploration and Reason came to be, about the problem of creativity and what it reveals about the natural world – where according to Descartes it effectively constituted a "second substance." By the time Darwin began to revolutionize our thinking about human nature, philology was a profession in its own right, so much so that the discovery of the Indo-European ancestry and how it gave rise to hundreds of different languages served as a central inspiration in Darwin's evolutionary theory. Many of the theoretical insights of linguistics in the twentieth century date back to this modern tradition, particularly as coupled together with late nineteenth- and early twentieth-century developments in mathematical logic and philosophy more generally.

Saussure (1916) initiated contemporary structural linguistics, by emphasizing how language should be conceived as separate from what it is used for, and by concentrating on how language is, not how it changes. Bloomfield (1933), Wells (1947), and Harris (1951) developed structuralism further and Noam Chomsky's work developed in particular in immediate reaction to Harris's program. A fundamental difference between structuralism and generative grammar stems from the fact that Chomsky focused on those aspects of structure that make the system recursive, whereas structuralism left those for the realm of what we nowadays call 'performance.' Structuralism in fact focused on finite levels of language, such as morphophonemics, where notions like 'linguistic feature' or the paradigmatic inventory underlying phonemics came to be understood (see again especially Harris 1951). But it was the syntax put to the side at the time that especially interested Chomsky, particularly since it was taken to address a key element in the problem of linguistic creativity. For this purpose, Chomsky borrowed from the axiomatic-deductive method in mathematical logic, developed a generation earlier in its computational formulation – more concretely via Davis (1958) (which had circulated as a draft much prior to its publication date). Chomsky systematized and generalized Emil Post's version of 'recursive function theory' (see Post 1944), and eventually came to propose formal devices of his own ('transformations,' see below).

Aside from these theoretical considerations pertaining to the precise structure of language and its implications, generative grammar from Chomsky's perspective always had a conceptual angle that informs the enterprise to this day: Syntax is seen as a natural system, somehow rooted in human psychology and biology. This point of view constituted the bulk of Chomsky's reaction to behaviorism, his later exploration of complex forms of biology, and more generally his insistence over six decades on approaching linguistic structure with the same sorts of tools and attitudes that one should assume for an intricate biological phenomenon, like adaptive immunity.

All of Chomsky's work has centered on two fundamental questions:

(1) What is the correct characterization of someone who speaks a language? What kind of capacity is 'knowledge of language'?
(2) How does this capacity arise in the individual? What aspects of it are acquired by exposure to relevant information ('learned'), and what aspects are present in advance of any experience ('wired in')?

Chomsky's earliest work, in the 1950s, raised and focused on question (1), since explicit and comprehensive answers to that question had never been provided before. Chomsky's answer posited a computational system in the human mind that provides statements of the basic phrase structure patterns of languages (phrase-structure rules) and more complex operations for manipulating these basic phrase structures (transformations). This framework, and its direct descendants, fall under the general title Transformational Generative Grammar ('generative' meaning explicit, in the sense of mathematics).

In the 1960s, the research began to shift more toward question (2), and Chomsky called the theory that was developed the Standard Theory. Chomsky coined the term 'explanatory adequacy' for putative answers to that question. A theory of language, regarded as one component of a theory of the human mind, must make available grammars for all possible human languages. To attain explanatory adequacy, the theory must in addition show how the learner selects the correct grammar from among all the available ones, based on restricted data. The theories of the 1950s and early 1960s made an infinite number of grammars available, so the explanatory problem was severe.

Through the late 1960s and 1970s, to enhance explanatory adequacy, theorists proposed more and more constraints on the notion 'possible human grammar.' Ross (1967a) was a particularly influential and pioneering study looking at locality restrictions (see Chapter 18). These moves were explicitly motivated by considerations of explanatory adequacy, though general considerations of simplicity also played a role. This culminated in the Principles and Parameters framework (Chapter 4), and more specifically in the Government and Binding approach that Chomsky (1981) proposes. The latter led to a wide range of cross-linguistic research since a core part of the program involved comparative syntax and used comparative data to help refine theoretical definitions of terms like 'government' and 'binding.'

At the same time as these developments took place, a number of researchers departed from Chomsky's specific approach. Generative Semantics, in particular, was a very prominent theory in the late 1960s; today some Generative Semantics ideas have returned, as we will discuss below. In the early 1980s, non-transformational theories such as Lexical-Functional Grammar (Kaplan and Bresnan 1982; see Chapter 6), Generalized Phrase Structure Grammar (Gazdar et al. 1985; see Chapter 7) and Tree Adjoining Grammar (Joshi et al. 1975, Joshi 1985; see Chapter 8) were also developed. We will say a bit more about these below and contextualize them to make it clear why they emerged and what the main differences are between these theories and the more mainstream Chomskyan theories.

In the late 1980s, Chomsky started to explore what has become known as the Minimalist Program, with its emphasis on simplicity in theorizing and on moving beyond explanatory adequacy in the sense of asking why the language faculty has the properties it does. This approach is most explicitly outlined in Chomsky (1995c). Recent and ongoing work by Chomsky (2000b, 2001, 2004, 2007, 2008) and many others continues to develop this framework.

This chapter is organized as follows. Section 2.2 discusses the earliest generative approaches, namely those explicated in *Syntactic Structures* (1957) and *Aspects of the Theory of Syntax* (1965). We examine some relevant differences between these two theories and we discuss some general properties of transformations. Section 2.3 discusses the syntax/semantics interface in early generative grammar and beyond, whereas Section 2.4 is an overview of how phrase structure has developed from the early days of generative grammar until today. In Section 2.5, we discuss the role in the evolving theories of rules and filters versus principles. Section 2.6 is concerned with derivations and the derivation versus representation issue. In Principles and Parameters theory, Chomsky explicitly introduced economy principles for the first time, and we give a summary of some of these in Section 2.7. A few concluding remarks are provided in Section 2.8.

2.2 The earliest generative approaches: *Syntactic Structures* and *Aspects*

Chomsky's earliest work developed in reaction to the structuralist work mentioned in Section 2.1. As a student of Zellig Harris, Chomsky was very familiar with Harris's program and he developed his own work in reaction to Harris (1951). Harris had one sentence transform into another. This approach was therefore not able to give any systematic explanation for the more abstract kind of phenomena Chomsky started to deal with in *The Logical Structure of Linguistic Theory* (1955/1975) and *Syntactic Structures*. In order to deal with these phenomena, it is necessary to relate abstract structures to abstract structures. Let us now look at some of the characteristics of Chomsky's earliest work.

Infinity and structure are the fundamental characteristics of human language, and they can both be captured, in part, by way of a context-free phrase-structure (PS) grammar. One such device (a Σ, F grammar in Chomsky's terminology) consists of:

(3) a. A designated initial symbol (or a set thereof) (Σ);
 b. Rewrite rules (F), which consist of a single symbol on the left, followed by an arrow, followed by at least one symbol.

A derivation consists of a series of lines such that the first line is one of the designated initial symbols, and to proceed from one line to the next we replace one symbol by the sequence of symbols it can be rewritten as, until there are no more symbols that can be rewritten. For instance given:

(4) a. Designated initial symbol (Σ): S
 b. Rewrite rules (F):
 S → NP VP
 NP → N
 VP → V
 N → John
 V → laughs

we can obtain a derivation as in (5):

(5) Line 1: S
 Line 2: NP VP
 Line 3: N VP
 Line 4: N V
 Line 5: John V
 Line 6: John laughs

Chomsky (1965) called rules like the last two in (4), which rewrite a particular non-terminal symbol as a single terminal symbol, lexical insertion rules – a distinction not made in the theories of Chomsky (1955/1975, 1957).

PS grammars capture constituent structure by introducing non-terminal (unpronounced) symbols. Given (5), we can connect each symbol with the symbol(s) it rewrites as. In this way we can trace back units of structure. After joining the symbols we can represent the derivation in the standard form of a tree, as in (6a). Getting rid of symbols that are mere repetitions, we end up with the collapsed tree in (6b):

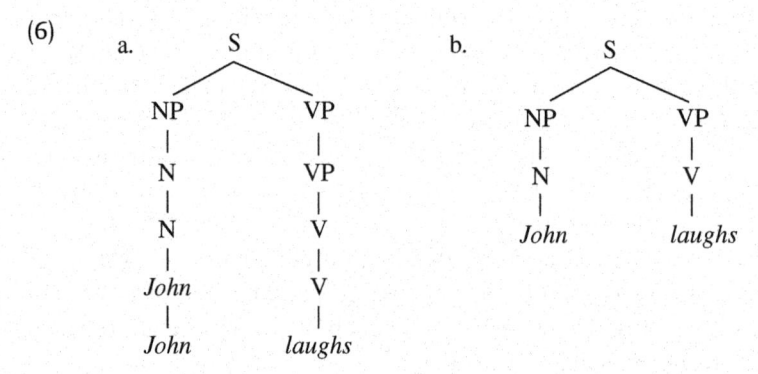

(6) a.
```
         S
        / \
       NP  VP
       |   |
       N   VP
       |   |
       N   V
       |   |
     John  V
       |   |
     John laughs
```
b.
```
         S
        / \
       NP  VP
       |   |
       N   V
       |   |
     John laughs
```

More technically, a phrase marker for a terminal string is the set of all strings occurring in any of the equivalent derivations of that string, where two PS derivations are equivalent if and only if they involve the same rules the same number of times (not necessarily in the same order). This is a result that Chomsky (1955/1975) proved by showing that for two PS derivations to be equivalent, they have to collapse down to the same PS tree. See Section 2.4.1 for further discussion.

2.2.1 Transformations and generalized transformations

Finite-state machines can easily capture infinity, one of the two fundamental characteristics of human language (see Lasnik 2000 for much discussion), and if we move one level up on the Chomsky Hierarchy (Chomsky 1956), we can avail ourselves of PS grammars. These grammars are more powerful devices that capture both infinity and structure.

Interestingly, the theory in both *Syntactic Structures* and *The Logical Structure of Linguistic Theory* (Chomsky 1955/1975, henceforth *LSLT*) did not have recursion in the base, that is, PS rules, or sequences of them, that allow self-embedding. Instead, complicated structures, hence infinity, were created by special operations, called generalized transformations, which put together the simple structures generated by the PS rules. For example, to derive *John knew that Mary understood the theory*, first the separate structures underlying *John knew it* and *Mary understood the theory* were generated by the method described above; then a generalized transformation inserted the second of these structures into the first. Metaphorically, a generalized transformation grafts one tree onto another. Put differently, in this theory recursion was in the 'transformational component.'[1] In more recent times, Tree Adjoining Grammar (TAG) developed this approach further (Joshi et al. 1975, Joshi 1985; see Chapter 8) by arguing for a system of tree rewriting. In this theory, a derivation works on a set of predefined pieces of tree structure. These pieces are called elementary trees and they are expanded and combined with one another so that structures are built through generalized transformations. Still more recently, Frank (2002) suggested a way to integrate the Minimalist approach to grammar suggested by Chomsky with TAG.

The structures created by phrase structure rules and generalized transformations could be altered by singulary transformations.[2] Singulary transformations apply to single P-markers and derived P-markers, which is to say that they apply to one tree. Chomsky showed how singulary transformations can explain the relatedness between, for example, statements and corresponding questions:

(7) a. Susan will solve the problem. → Will Susan solve the problem?
    b. John is visiting Rome. → Is John visiting Rome?

The members of each pair come from the same initial P-marker, with singulary transformations producing the divergent surface shapes. One of the great triumphs of the analysis of such pairs in *LSLT* is that it was able to use the same singulary transformation for the interrogative sentences in (7) and the superficially very different one in (8).

(8) Susan solved the problem. → Did Susan solve the problem?

This was a significant achievement since the relations are felt by native speakers to be parallel, an otherwise mysterious fact. Chomsky also showed how, in numerous situations, even properties of individual sentences cannot be adequately characterized without recourse to the descriptive power of singulary transformations. One major example involved the sequences of English auxiliary verbs, and the inflectional suffixes associated with them. The revolutionary insight here (and also in the analysis of (7)–(8)) was that these bound morphemes, especially the one carrying tense and agreement, are autonomous items as far as the syntax is concerned, capable of undergoing syntactic operations independently until eventually uniting with a verbal element (a process that came to be called 'Affix Hopping'). The Affix Hopping transformation rises above the limitations of phrase structure (which at best can simply list the possible sequences) and simultaneously captures the generalizations about linear ordering of the elements, their morphological dependencies, the location of finite tense, the form of inversion and sentence negation, and the distribution of auxiliary *do*.[3] There was, thus, considerable motivation for this new device relating more abstract underlying structures to more superficial surface representations. In fact, one of the major conceptual innovations in the entire theory is the proposal that a sentence has not just one structure, closely related to the way it is pronounced, but an additional abstract structure (potentially very different from the superficial one), and intermediate structures between these two. This is fundamental to all the analyses in the Chomskyan system.

The organization of the syntactic portion of the grammar is as follows: Application of the phrase structure rules creates a P-marker, or, in the case of a complex sentence, a set of P-markers. Then successive application of transformations (singulary and generalized) creates successive phrase structure representations (derived P-markers), culminating in a final surface representation. The syntactic levels in this theory are that of phrase structure and that of transformations, the latter giving a history of the transformational derivation (the successive transformational steps creating and affecting the structure). The representations at these levels are the P-marker and the T-marker respectively. The final derived P-marker is the input to phonological interpretation, and the T-marker is the input to semantic interpretation.[4]

Let us consider some of the formal properties of transformations as they are stated in *Syntactic Structures*. Each transformation has a structural analysis (SA) and a structural change (SC). The SA characterizes the class of structures to which the transformation applies. The SC specifies the alterations that the process carries out.

A SA is a sequence of *terms* or a set of sequences of terms. Elements that can constitute a term are listed in a general fashion in (9).

(9) a. any sequence of symbols (terminals, non-terminals, and variables) or
 b. a set of sequences of symbols *or*
 c. a Boolean combination of these

SCs are able to carry out the following elementary operations:

(10) a. adjunction of one term to another (to the right or the left)
 b. deletion of a term or sequence of terms
 c. adjunction of new material that was not in the structure before to a term
 d. permutation

A SC for Chomsky was a set of elementary operations.

Other properties of transformations are that they are ordered, and that they are specified as being optional or obligatory. For some transformations it is crucial that we be allowed but not required to apply them; for others it is necessary that we be required to apply them. Lastly, the transformations in *Syntactic Structures* also occasionally had a global dependency: They can refer back to any other stage of a derivation.

We will not go through an example of an early generative syntactic analysis here but instead refer to Lasnik (2000:53ff.) for a thorough illustration of several early transformations.

2.2.2 Chomsky (1965)

Chomsky (1965), henceforth *Aspects*, presented a revised conception of the grammar, based on an alternative way of constructing complex sentences, one that Chomsky argued was an advance in terms of simplicity and explanatory adequacy over the one in *LSLT*. In the *LSLT* framework, as discussed above, the phrase-structure rules produce simple monoclausal structures, which can then be merged together by generalized transformations. Generalized transformations were thus the recursive component of the grammar, the one responsible for the infinitude of language. In the alternative view, the phrase-structure rule component itself has a recursive character. Consider the complex sentences in (11).

(11) a. Mary reads books
     b. John thinks that Mary reads books
     c. Susan said John thinks Mary reads books

By adding a recursive 'loop' to a standard set of phrase-structure rules, we can directly create the possibility of ever longer sentences. Such a rule is given in (12).

(12) VP → V S

Under this approach to sentence embedding, unlike that in *LSLT*, there is one unified structure underlying a sentence prior to the operation of any syntactic transformations. This structure is the result of application of the phrase-structure rules and lexical insertion transformations which insert items from the lexicon into the skeletal structure.[5] Chomsky argued in *Aspects* that this underlying structure, which he there named 'Deep Structure,' is the locus of important generalizations and constitutes a coherent level of representation. Let us say a bit more about the latter concept before we move on.

Levels of representation were introduced into the theory in the following way in *LSLT*:

> We define, in general linguistic theory, a system of levels of representation. A level of representation consists of elementary units (primes), an operation of concatenation by which strings of primes can be constructed, and various relations defined on primes, strings of primes, and sets and sequences of these strings. Among the abstract objects constructed on the level **L** are **L**-markers that are associated with sentences. The **L**-marker of a sentence *S* is the representation of *S* on the level **L**. A grammar of a

> language, then, will characterize the set of **L**-markers for each level **L** and will determine the assignment of **L**-markers to sentences.
>
> (Chomsky 1975a: 6)

The child learning a language is assumed to bring knowledge of the levels to bear on the task of learning. That is, the child must learn properties of the language at each level, but knows the levels in advance, hence, knows what to look for. The levels are part of Universal Grammar. Of course, the *linguist* does not know in advance of research what the levels are. Determining them is a scientific question, one of biological psychology. Throughout the years, Chomsky and others have devoted considerable attention to determining just what the levels of representation are in the human language faculty. In *LSLT*, the levels were considered to be phonetics, phonemics, word, syntactic category, morphemics, morphophonemics, phrase structure, and transformations. Throughout the years, the levels have changed in important and interesting ways.

Chomsky's major arguments for the new level, Deep Structure, in *Aspects* were that it resulted in a simpler overall theory, and at the same time it explained the absence of certain kinds of derivations that seemed not to occur (or at least seemed not to be needed in the description of sentences of human languages). Taking the second of these points first, Chomsky argued that while there is extensive ordering among singulary transformations (situations where a derivation produces an unacceptable sentence if two transformations are applied in reverse order), "there are no known cases of ordering among generalized embedding transformations although such ordering is permitted by the theory of Transformation-markers" (Chomsky 1965:133) (see also Fillmore 1963, Lees 1963). Further, while there are many cases of singulary transformations that must apply to a constituent sentence before it is embedded, or that must apply to a matrix sentence after another sentence is embedded in it, "there are no really convincing cases of singulary transformations that must apply to a matrix sentence before a sentence transform is embedded in it" (Chomsky 1965:133).

As for the first argument, Chomsky claimed that the theory of transformational grammar is simplified by this change, since the notions 'generalized transformation' and 'Transformation-marker' are eliminated entirely. The P-markers in the revised theory contain all of the information of those in the *LSLT* version, but they also indicate explicitly how the clauses are embedded in one another, that is, information that had been provided by the embedding transformations and T-markers.

This change in the theory of phrase structure, which has the effect of eliminating generalized transformations, also has consequences for the theory of singulary transformations. As indicated above, in the *Aspects* theory, as in *LSLT*, there is extensive ordering among singulary transformations. In both frameworks, the set of singulary transformations was seen as a linear sequence: an ordered list. Given the *Aspects* modification, this list of rules applies cyclically, first operating on the most deeply embedded clause, then the next most deeply embedded, and so on, working up the tree until they apply on the highest clause, the entire generalized P-marker. Thus, singulary transformations apply to constituent sentences 'before' they are embedded, and to matrix sentences 'after' embedding has taken place. "The ordering possibilities that are permitted by the theory of Transformation-markers but apparently never put to use are now excluded in principle" (Chomsky 1965:135).

2.3 The syntax/semantics interface in early generative grammar and beyond

An important question for any syntactic theory is how syntax relates to semantics: what the precise connection is between form and meaning. In *LSLT*, the T-marker contains all of the structural information relevant to semantic interpretation. Katz and Postal (1964) proposed a severe restriction on just how this structural information could be accessed. In particular, they postulated that the only contribution of transformations to semantic interpretation is that they interrelate P-markers. The slogan at the time was that "transformations do not change meaning." As Chomsky put it, (generalized) transformations combine semantic interpretation of already interpreted P-markers in a fixed way. In the revised theory, which Chomsky called the Standard Theory, the initial P-marker, now a Deep Structure, then contains just the information relevant to semantic interpretation. To summarize the model:

> ... the syntactic component consists of a base that generates deep structures and a transformational part that maps them into surface structures. The deep structure of a sentence is submitted to the semantic component for semantic interpretation, and its surface structure enters the phonological component and undergoes phonetic interpretation. The final effect of a grammar, then, is to relate a semantic interpretation to a phonetic representation – that is, to state how a sentence is interpreted.
> (Chomsky 1965:135–36)

To carry out this program, Chomsky (1965) adopted the proposal of Katz and Postal (1964) that many seemingly 'meaning-changing' optional transformations of *LSLT* be replaced by obligatory transformations triggered by a marker in the Deep Structure. To take one example, earlier we noted that in *LSLT*, simple questions and the corresponding statements are derived from the same initial P-marker. In the revision, those initial P-markers would be very similar but not identical. The former would contain a marker of interrogation that would both signal the difference in meaning and trigger the inversion that results in the auxiliary verb appearing at the front of the sentence. Katz and Postal also noted that there are languages such as Japanese in which this Q-marker is spelled out as a separate morpheme.

At this point in the development of the theory, the model can be graphically represented as follows, with Deep Structure doing the semantic work formerly done by the T-marker:

(13) Deep Structure ⇒ Semantic Interpretation
⇓
Transformations
(operating cyclically)
⇓
Surface Structure ⇒ Phonetic Interpretation (via the 'sound-related' levels of morphophonemics, phonemics, and phonetics)

Some researchers soon challenged this framework. Generative Semantics built on the work by Katz and Postal (1964), and especially the claim that Deep Structure determines meaning (Lakoff 1971). For Generative Semantics, syntax is not the primary generative component. Rather, each meaning is represented by a different deepest representation (much more abstract that Chomsky's Deep Structure). On this view, transformations can, and often must, be far more complex and powerful than those in the *Aspects* model. There was intense debate about these issues in the late 1960s and into the 1970s before Generative Semantics largely disappeared from the scene, partly because the main practitioners came to develop different interests. However, central aspects of Generative Semantics have survived in different contemporary frameworks such as Cognitive Linguistics, Construction Grammar, and generative grammar including Chomskyan approaches. For example, Generative Semantics assumed that causative structures have a cause morpheme in the syntax, which is an approach that is found in recent work (see, e.g., Harley 1995). Baker's (1988) Uniformity of Theta Assignment Hypothesis (UTAH), which states that identical thematic relationships are represented by identical structural relationships, is, in essence, another example of a proposal from Generative Semantics that has returned. Yet another, which we will discuss below, is the elimination of Deep Structure as a level of representation.

Let us now return to the chronological history. By the time *Aspects* was published, there were already questions about initial structure as the sole locus of semantic interpretation. To take just one example, Chomsky (1957) observed that in sentences with quantifiers (see Chapter 22), the derived structure has truth conditional consequences. (14a) may be true while (14b) is false, for instance if one person in the room knows only French and German, and another only Spanish and Italian (see also Chapter 3, example (13)).

(14) a. everyone in the room knows at least two languages
 b. at least two languages are known by everyone in the room

In the theory of Chomsky (1957), this is not problematic, since semantic interpretation is based on the T-marker. However, in the *Aspects* framework, there is a problem, as Chomsky acknowledges. He speculates that the interpretive difference between (14a) and (14b) might follow from discourse properties, rather than grammatical ones. The general problem, though, came to loom larger and larger, leading to a theory in which both Deep Structure and Surface Structure contribute to semantic interpretation. The core idea was introduced by Jackendoff (1969) and then elaborated by Chomsky (1970a) (see also, e.g., Bach 1964, McCawley 1968b), and it is clearly different from the view held by Generative Semantics. In this so-called Extended Standard Theory the contribution of Deep Structure concerns 'grammatical relations' such as understood subject and object of (cf. fn. 5). The contribution of Surface Structure concerns virtually all other aspects of meaning, including scope, as in the examples mentioned just above, anaphora, focus, and presupposition.

Alongside these questions about Deep Structure as the sole locus of semantic interpretation, there were also challenges to its very existence. Postal (1972) argued that the best theory is the simplest, which, by his reasoning, included a uniform set of rules from semantic structure all the way to surface form, with no significant level (i.e., Deep Structure) in between. And McCawley (1968b) explicitly formulated an argument against Deep Structure on the model of Morris Halle's (1959) famous argument against a level of taxonomic phonemics. McCawley's argument is based on the interpretation of sentences with *respectively*, such as (15).

(15) those men love Mary and Alice respectively

McCawley argues that a *respectively*-transformation relates (16) to (15).

(16) that man (x) loves Mary and that man (y) loves Alice

For McCawley, this is a syntactic operation since it involves conjunction reduction. McCawley then notes that there is a corresponding semantic relation between (17) and (18).

(17) $\forall x : x \in M$ [x loves x's wife]

(18) these men love their respective wives

For generative semanticists, such as McCawley, since there is no syntactic level of Deep Structure, there is no a priori need to separate the two operations involved in (15)–(16) and (17)–(18). The deepest level of representation is a semantic representation. But in a theory with Deep Structure, the syntactic operation involved in (15)–(16) would necessarily be post-Deep Structure, while the operation implicated in (17)–(18) would necessarily be in a different module, one linking a syntactic representation with a semantic representation. Purportedly, then, a generalization is missed, as in Halle's classic argument.

Chomsky (1970b) considers this argument, but rejects it, claiming that it rests on an equivocation about exactly what the relevant rule(s) would be in the theories in question. Chomsky points out that it is possible to give a more abstract characterization of the transformations such that one is not syntactic and the other is not semantic. Therefore there is no argument against Deep Structure here. Chomsky does, however, accept McCawley's contention that it is necessary to provide justification for the postulation of Deep Structure. But he observes that the same is true of Surface Structure or phonetic representation, or, in fact, any theoretical construct. How can such justification be provided?

> There is only one way to provide some justification for a concept that is defined in terms of some general theory, namely, to show that the theory provides revealing explanations for an interesting range of phenomena and that the concept in question plays a role in these explanations.
> (Chomsky 1970b:64)

As far as Chomsky was concerned, this burden had been met, especially by the *Aspects* analysis of the transformational ordering constraints discussed above.[6]

One small simplification in the Extended Standard Theory model was the result of a technical revision concerning how movement transformations operate (Wasow 1972, Chomsky 1973, Fiengo 1974, 1977). Trace theory proposed that when an item moves, it leaves behind a 'trace,' a silent placeholder marking the position from which movement took place. The motivation for this was that in important respects, movement gaps behave like positions that are lexically filled, an argument first made in Wasow (1972) and Chomsky (1973). Under trace theory, the importance of Deep Structure (D-structure) for semantic interpretation is reduced, and ultimately eliminated. Once Surface Structure (S-structure) is enriched with traces, even grammatical relations can be determined at that derived level of representation. Using the term LF ('Logical Form') for the syntactic representation that relates most directly to the interpretation of meaning and PF ('Phonetic Form') for the one relating most directly to how sentences sound, we have the so-called T-model in (19) (also called the (inverted) Y-model), which was at the core of Government and Binding Theory.

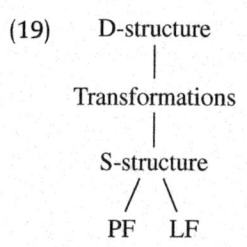

(19)   D-structure
         |
        Transformations
         |
        S-structure
         / \
        PF   LF

The precise nature of the connection between the syntactic derivation and semantic and phonological interfaces has been a central research question throughout the history of generative grammar. In the earliest generative model, the interface is the T-marker, which includes all of the syntactic structures created in the course of the derivation. Subsequent models had the following interfaces with semantics: The Standard Theory had D-structure, the Extended Standard Theory had D-structure and S-structure, whereas Government and Binding and early Minimalism had LF. Chomsky's most recent model even dispenses with LF as a level in the technical sense (Chomsky 2004). The Minimalist approach to structure building, where Merge is the basic operation, is much more similar to that of the 1950s than to any of the intervening models, which is to say that interpretation in the Minimalist model also could be more like that in the early model, distributed over many structures. In the late 1960s and early 1970s, there were already occasional arguments for such a model from phonological interpretation as well as semantic interpretation. For example, Bresnan (1971b) argued that the phonological rule responsible for assigning English sentences their intonation contour (see Chapter 23) applies cyclically, following each cycle of transformations, rather than applying at the end of the entire syntactic derivation. There were similar proposals for semantic phenomena involving scope and anaphora put forward by Jackendoff (1972). Chomsky (2000b, 2001, 2004) argued for a general instantiation of this distributed approach to phonological and semantic interpretation, based on ideas of Epstein (1999) and Uriagereka (1999), who called the approach 'multiple spell-out.' Simplifying somewhat, at the end of each cycle (or 'phase' as it has been called for the past ten years) the syntactic structure created thus far is encapsulated and sent off to the interface components for phonological and semantic interpretation. Thus, although there are still what might be called PF and LF components, there are no syntactic levels of PF and LF. Epstein argued that such a move represents a conceptual simplification, and both Uriagereka and Chomsky provided some empirical justification. We can view this conceptual simplification similarly to the elimination of D-structure and S-structure. Chomsky (1993) argued that both D-structure and S-structure should be dispensed with. Both levels are theory-internal, highly abstract and they are not motivated by conceptual necessity, as the semantic and phonological interfaces to a much greater extent are. Another way to put this is to say that the motivation for D-structure and S-structure is empirical. Chomsky argued that, contrary to appearances, it is possible to cover the same or even more empirical ground without postulating either S-structure or D-structure.[7]

The role of syntactic derivation becomes even more central on this view because there are no levels of representation at all. The syntax interfaces directly with sound and meaning.

2.4 The development of phrase structure

In this section, we will provide a history of the development of phrase structure (see also Fukui 2001 and Chapters 4, 6, 7, and 8). We will start with a brief recap of PS grammars and then move on to different versions of X-bar Theory. Lastly we will discuss the approach to phrase structure within the Minimalist Program: Bare Phrase Structure. Our focus throughout will mainly be on the Chomskyan versions of phrase structure; but we will also mention where other theories developed and why they developed.

2.4.1 Phrase structure grammars

Chomsky (1955/1975, 1957) developed a theory of phrase structure which made use of context-free PS grammars ([Σ, F] grammars). In addition, the theory was based on derivations and equivalence classes of such derivations.

Chomsky (1957:27-29, 87) defines phrase structure set-theoretically, as in (20).

(20) Given a particular [Σ, F] grammar and a particular terminal string (i.e., string of terminal symbols):
  a. Construct all of the equivalent PS derivations of the terminal string.
  b. Collect all of the lines occurring in any of those equivalent derivations into a set. This set is the *phrase marker* (PM), a representation of the phrase structure of the terminal string.

The purpose of a PM is to tell us for each portion of the terminal string whether that portion comprises a constituent or not, and, when it comprises a constituent, what the 'name' of that constituent is. Chomsky makes the following empirical claim: All and only what we need a PM to do is to tell us the 'is a' relations between portions of the terminal strings and non-terminal symbols. Anything that tells us those and only those is a perfectly adequate PM; anything that does not is inadequate as a PM.

The PS rules can generate a graph-theoretic representation like the one in (21) (see Lasnik 2000:29ff. for an illustration of how this works).

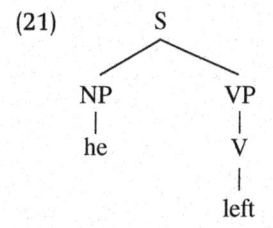

(21)
```
            S
           / \
          NP  VP
          |   |
          he  V
              |
              left
```

The tree tells us everything we have established concerning the 'is a' relations. Note, however, that the tree encodes information that goes beyond the 'is a' relations. The tree tells us that a VP is rewritten as V, and that the V is rewritten as *left*. It is an empirical question whether we need this additional information or not, say, for phonological, semantic, or further syntactic operations. If we do, then this particular set-theoretic model has to be rejected. If we do not, then the model is accepted, since we would like the minimal theory that does what has to be done. We will see later that the field has typically assumed that the set-theoretic model needs to be enriched in various ways.

Lasnik and Kupin (1977) showed that the algorithm for computing 'is a' relations needs recourse only to the terminal string and the other members of the PM that consist of exactly one non-terminal symbol surrounded by any number of terminal symbols (what Lasnik and Kupin called 'monostrings'). Hence Lasnik and Kupin proposed a construct called a *reduced phrase marker*, which includes only the terminal strings and the monostrings. See Lasnik (2000: section 1.2.6.1) for more discussion.

2.4.2 X-bar Theory

One problem in *LSLT* and *Syntactic Structures* is that the theory developed there allows PS rules like (23) alongside ones like (22) (Lyons 1968).

(22) NP → ... N ...

(23) VP → ... N ...

But there do not seem to be rules like (23). Why is this? The formalism allows both rules, and the evaluation metric (Chomsky 1965) judges them equally costly. Chomsky (1970a) was an attempt to come to grips with this problem. There it is proposed that there are no individual PS rules of the sort that did so much work in *Syntactic Structures* and even in *Aspects*. Rather, there is what is now known as the X-bar schema (see also Chapter 11). X is a variable, ranging over category names such as V, N, and so on.

Here is the version of X-bar Theory that Chomsky (1970a) presented (see also Emonds 1976 and Jackendoff 1977 for much relevant discussion).

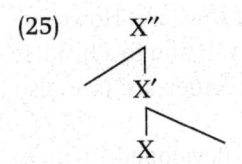

(24) X' → ... X ...
      X" → ... X' ...

(25) $\quad$ X"
       $\quad\quad$ |
       $\quad\quad$ X'
       $\quad\quad$ |
       $\quad\quad$ X

X' and X" are true complex symbols. Keep in mind that in *Syntactic Structures* NP looked like it had something to do with N, but in that system it really did not. NP was just one symbol that was written for mnemonic purposes with two letters. In X-bar Theory, a category label is a letter plus a number of bars (originally written as overbars - e.g., X̄ - but later written as primes - e.g., X' - for typographical convenience). It can be thought of as an ordered pair. X is <X, 0>, X' is <X, 1>, and X" is <X, 2>. X-bar Theory immediately explains why there are no rules like (23). This is because phrases have heads, i.e., they are endocentric, which is to say that phrases are projections of heads.

Chomsky also introduced the relational notions complement and specifier. A complement is a sister to a head. He argued that the notion complement does not play any role in transformations (Chomsky 1970a:210), that is, complements cannot be the target qua complements of any transformational operations. At this point, there were general rules like (29) that subsumed rules like the ones in (26)–(28).

(26)   NP → N Comp

(27)   VP → V Comp

(28)   AP → A Comp

(29)   Comp → NP, S, NP S, NP Prep-P, Prep-P Prep-P, etc.

The rules in (29) should instead be replaced with the rule in (30).

(30)   X' → ... X ...

The dots in (30) indicate that there are no restrictions on what can be a complement and where the complement is placed *vis-à-vis* the head.

Chomsky then proposes that in order to "introduce further terminological uniformity, let us refer to the phrase associated with N', A', V' in the base structure as the 'specifier' of these elements" (Chomsky 1970a:210).

(31)   X" → [Spec, X'] X'

On this view, a specifier encompasses a heterogeneous set as it contains a variety of pre-head elements like auxiliaries in SpecV', determiners in SpecN', adverbials in SpecV', and degree modifiers in SpecA'. As Jackendoff (1977:14) points out, it is not clear whether Chomsky considers the specifier to be a constituent or an abbreviation for a sequence of constituents, like Comp. The diagrams in Chomsky (1970a) show specifiers as constituents. Jackendoff (1977) argues against specifiers being constituents whereas Hornstein (1977) defends the claim that they are. However, beyond being a constituent and bearing a geometrical relation to a head, it is not clear what the defining characteristics of a specifier are (see also George 1980:17).

Later a biconditional version of X-bar Theory was developed, namely that phrases have heads, and heads project. Whenever a structure has an XP, it has an X (this is what Chomsky 1970a proposed), and whenever a structure has an X, it has an XP.

In Chomsky (1970a), the initial rule of the base grammar is as in (32).

(32) S → N" V"

This means that X-bar Theory is not fully general: S and S' (the latter the larger clause including a sentence-introducing complementizer like *that*) do not fit into the theory in any neat way.[8] These labels are not projections of heads, unlike the other labels in the system. However, it is worth bearing in mind that Bresnan (1970) suggests that complementizers are essentially specifiers of sentences through the rule in (33).

(33) S' → Comp S

This is in line with the general approach to specifiers during the 1970s, as complementizers here are analyzed on a par with auxiliaries, which were also specifiers.

It may be worth pausing to reflect on what pushed Chomsky to create X-bar Theory.

> The development of X' theory in the late 1960s was an early stage in the effort to resolve the tension between explanatory and descriptive adequacy. A first step was to separate the lexicon from the computations, thus eliminating a serious redundancy between lexical properties and phrase structure rules and allowing the latter to be reduced to the simplest (context-)free form. X' theory sought to eliminate such rules altogether, leaving only the general X' theoretic format of UG. The problem addressed in subsequent work was to determine that format, but it was assumed that phrase structure rules themselves should be eliminable.   (Chomsky 1995a:61)

The attempt was to do away with redundancies in favor of larger generalizations. Another way to say this is that when we impose strict constraints, the PS rules themselves vanish. It is possible to view the change from phrase structure rules to X-bar Theory in the same way as Chomsky's (1973) generalization of some of Ross's (1967a) locality 'island' constraints on movement (see Chapter 18). In both cases, instead of more or less idiosyncratic properties, we get general properties that hold across categories. Baltin (1982:2) puts the general development this way:

> The history of transformational generative grammar can be divided into two periods, which can be called expansion and retrenchment. During the early "expansion" period, a primary concern was the description of grammatical phenomena. ... The theory was correspondingly loose, and consequently failed to provide an adequate solution to the projection problem.[9] ... During the retrenchment period ... the focus of attention shifted from the construction of relatively complex ... statements to the construction of a general theory of grammar, restricted as to the devices it employed, which could be ascribed to universal grammar.

Chomsky (1970a) only discusses NPs, VPs, and APs, not PPs. One goal of Jackendoff (1977) is to bring PPs under the X-bar theoretic fold. So at the end of the 1970s, a quite general picture of phrase structure had started to emerge.

Before we move on to the early Principles and Parameters view of phrase structure, it is worth considering a general problem that both Chomsky (1970a) and Jackendoff (1977) face. The problem has been brought up most clearly by Stuurman (1985). Stuurman's goal is to defend what he calls "the single-projection-type hypothesis." Multiple projection types (X, X', X'', X^n), as assumed in Chomsky's and Jackendoff's works, are banned. Stuurman's thesis is that only one distinction is made internal to projections: the distinction between X^0 and X^1, or put differently, between a head and everything else. Stuurman argues that this provides a more restrictive phrase structure theory and a theory that is more easily learnable. Here is an example that he uses to make his claim.

In English, only the first hierarchical level projected from X^0 can dominate an NP.

(34) a. he [[met his wife] in Italy]
　　 b. *he [[met in Italy] his wife]

Stuurman (1985:8) points out that if we assume multiple projection-types, the facts in (34) can easily be captured directly at the level of PS as follows:

(35) a. $V^i \rightarrow \ldots V^j \ldots$, where $\ldots \neq NP, i > j \geq 1$
　　 b. $V^1 \rightarrow \ldots V^0 \ldots$, where $\ldots = NP, \ldots$

These restrictions are descriptively adequate, but as Stuurman stresses, they do not explain how a child can learn the distribution of NPs. Put differently, Universal Grammar (UG) does not provide a rationale for why the constraints are the way they are: Why should UG not allow NP under V^i and exclude NP under V^1? Unless the rules in (35) are universal, children need access to negative data (i.e., that (34b) is bad), which they by assumption do not have access to.[10]

Stuurman presents a different analysis where there is only one projection type. His theory, which we will not flesh out here, allows for both the structures in (36a) and (36b).

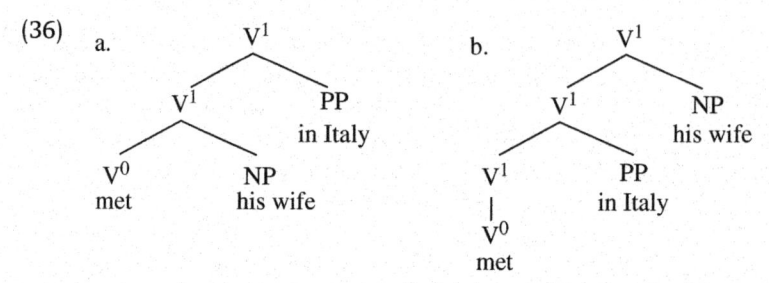

(36) a.
```
        V¹
       /  \
      V¹   PP
     /  \  in Italy
    V⁰   NP
   met   his wife
```
b.
```
        V¹
       /  \
      V¹   NP
     /  \  his wife
    V¹   PP
    |    in Italy
    V⁰
   met
```

Here one needs an independent principle that filters out the structure in (36b). This structure has an NP that is not dominated by the first X^1 up from X^0.

Stuurman argues that this filtering condition can be associated with an adjacency condition on Case Theory, following Stowell (1981) (see Chapter 16 for more discussion). That is, being a Case assigner is a lexical property, thus a property of X^0, not of X^1. (36b) is therefore ruled out independently of PS rules, as in Stowell's work.[11] Stuurman presents additional arguments for the single projection hypothesis. The point is that the view emerging in the late 1970s had important flaws, as it was too flexible and not principled enough. In the early 1980s, these flaws were addressed.

As research developed during the 1970s and 1980s, more and more of the elements that Chomsky and Jackendoff had analyzed as specifiers came to be analyzed as heads of particular functional projections (see also Abney 1987). As Chametzky (2000) points out, a notion of specifier emerged with the following characteristics: (i) typically an NP, (ii) it bears a certain relationship with the head. Stowell (1981:70) summarizes the general characteristics of X-bar Theory as follows:

(37) a. Every phrase is endocentric.
    b. Specifiers appear at the XP-level; subcategorized complements appear within X'.
    c. The head always appears adjacent to one boundary of X'.
    d. The head term is one bar level lower than the immediately dominating phrasal node.
    e. Only maximal projections may appear as non-head terms within a phrase.

These were further developed during the Government and Binding era in the 1980s. Here we will focus on Chomsky (1986a), since that work presents X-bar Theory as it is best known.

Chomsky (1986a, henceforth *Barriers*) provides a generalization of X-bar structure, though attempts had already been made in Chomsky (1981), Stowell (1981), and den Besten (1983), to mention the most important works. As we have seen, prior to *Barriers*, the maximal projections were VP, NP, AP, and PP. In addition, there was S, which gets rewritten as NP Infl VP, and S', which gets rewritten as Comp S. Comp includes at least C and *wh*-expressions. The problem is that S does not conform to X-bar Theory. It is not endocentric since it has no head, which means that there is no projection line from a head to a maximal projection. S' is also not uniformly endocentric, since when Comp is filled by phrasal material, it is not the head of S'. Because of these problems, Stowell (1981: Chapter 6) suggests that the head of S is Infl, as illustrated in (38). This is very similar to Williams (1981a:251), who suggests that S is headed by Tense.

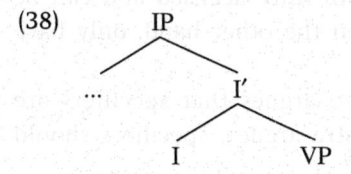

(38)   IP
        / \
    ...   I'
          / \
        I   VP

Once IP replaces S, a natural step is to reconsider S'. Stowell (1981: Chapter 6) proposes that C is the head of S'. The optional specifier then becomes the target of *wh*-movement. We then have the structure in (39) (see also Chomsky 1986a; and Section 11.5).

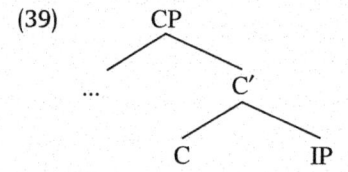

(39)
```
         CP
        /  \
      ...   C'
           /  \
          C    IP
```

With this in place, it is possible to formulate restrictions on movement based on what can appear in a head position and what can appear in a specifier position, cf. Travis (1984) and Rizzi (1990a).

The reanalysis of S and S' paves the way for a generalization of X-bar Theory. Chomsky (1986a:3) proposes that X-bar Theory has the general structure in (40), where X^* stands for zero or more occurrences of some maximal projection and $X = X^0$.[12]

(40) a. $X' = X\ X'''^*$
 b. $X'' = X'''^*\ X'$

Koizumi (1995:137) argues that the traditional X-bar schema can be seen as expressing three claims, as given in (41).

(41) a. Asymmetry: A node is projected from only one of its daughters.
 b. Binarity: A node may have at most two daughters.
 c. Maximality: A head may project (at most) two non-minimal projections.

It should be mentioned that (40) does not force binarity, since a node may have more than two daughters. One can either restrict X-bar Theory so that it does observe binarity by hard-wiring it into the X-bar Theory, or, for example, follow the proposal of Kayne (1984, 1994) that independent grammatical constraints require all branches in a tree to be binary (see below).

Chomsky (1986a:4) points out that specifiers are optional whereas the choice of complements is determined by the Projection Principle. The latter is a principle that says that representations at each syntactic level are projected from the lexicon.

Following up on the theory in *Barriers*, many researchers developed somewhat different versions of X-bar Theory. Fukui and Speas (1986) claim that there are significant differences between lexical and functional projections, e.g., VP and IP. They argue that lexical categories may iterate specifiers as long as all these positions are fully licensed and can be interpreted at LF. Functional categories, on the other hand, only have one unique specifier position.[13]

Hoekstra (1991; see also Hoekstra 1994) argues that specifiers are stipulated in X-bar Theory. Rather, Hoekstra argues, specifiers should be defined through agreement: A specifier always agrees with its head (see also Chapter 17). Hoekstra also eliminates the phrase-structural distinction between adjuncts and specifiers and argues that an adjunct can be defined as an element that does not agree with the head of the projection it is adjoined to. Recently, several researchers have argued that specifiers are problematic and should not be part of phrase structure (Hoekstra 1991, Kayne 1994, Cormack 1999, Starke 2004, Jayaseelan 2008).

Kayne (1994) puts forward a novel theory of phrase structure. He suggests there is one universal order and that this order is as in (42).

(42) specifier > head > complement

Throughout the history of generative grammar, it had generally been an assumption that languages vary in their base structure. PS rules encode this directly as in (43) for an English VP and (44) for a Japanese VP.

(43) VP → V NP

(44) VP → NP V

In the Government and Binding era, a common analysis of this variation was given in terms of the head parameter. Contrary to these analyses, Kayne claims that linear and hierarchical order are much more tightly connected. He argues that the property of antisymmetry that the linear precedence ordering has is inherited by the hierarchical structure.[14] The Linear Correspondence Axiom is the basic property of phrase structure, and familiar X-bar theoretic properties follow from it.

(45) *Linear Correspondence Axiom*
    d(A) is a linear ordering of T.   (Kayne 1994:6)

The non-terminal-to-terminal dominance relation is represented by d. This relation d is a many-to-many mapping from non-terminals to terminals. For a given non-terminal X, d(X) is the set of terminals that X dominates. A is a set of ordered pairs <X_j, Y_j> such that for each j, X_j asymmetrically c-commands Y_j. A contains all pairs of non-terminals such that the first asymmetrically c-commands the second, thus it is a maximal set. T stands for the set of terminals.

At this point, we will turn to a brief description of Bare Phrase Structure, which partly incorporates Kayne's ideas, since this is the current approach to phrase structure in Chomskyan generative grammar.

2.4.3 Bare Phrase Structure and cartography

Kayne's theory forces the elimination of the distinction between X' and XP since his linearization algorithm does not make this distinction. Chomsky (1995a, 1995c) went further and argued that X-bar levels should be eliminated altogether. This is the theory of Bare Phrase Structure (BPS; see also Section 4.2.4.2).

The gist of BPS is summarized in the following quote: "Minimal and maximal projections must be determined from the structure in which they appear without any specific marking; as proposed by Muysken (1983) they are relational properties of categories, not inherent to them" (Chomsky 1995a:61): "What I will propose is that bar level is not a primitive of the grammar at all, rather 'maximal projection' and 'minimal projection' are defined terms, and intermediate projections are simply the elsewhere case" (Muysken 1983).[15] Chomsky (1995c:242) tied this to the Inclusiveness Condition, which bans any marking of maximal and minimal projections.[16]

(46) *Inclusiveness Condition*
Any structure formed by the computation is constituted of elements already present in the lexical items. No new objects are added in the course of computation apart from rearrangements of lexical properties.
(Chomsky 1995c:228)

Another way to look at BPS is to say that phrase structure consists solely of lexical items. No extrinsic marking is necessary. This means that instead of a phrase like (47), phrases look like (48). Here we are setting aside how verbs get their inflection and where the arguments really belong in the structure – the important point at hand is the difference between the two structures.

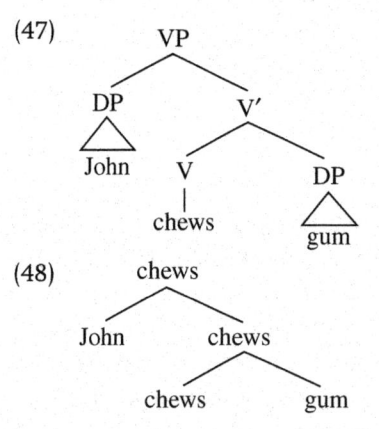

(47)
```
        VP
       /  \
      DP   V'
      /\  /  \
    John V   DP
         |   /\
       chews gum
```

(48)
```
       chews
       /    \
     John  chews
           /    \
        chews   gum
```

These lexical items are accessed at the LF interface. No units apart from the lexical items can be part of the computation. Thus bar levels have no existence within BPS. For a critical discussion of some problems with BPS, see Starke (2004) and Jayaseelan (2008).

Shortly after BPS had been developed in Chomsky (1995a, 1995c), Rizzi (1997) initiated what has become known as the cartographic approach. This approach assumes an expansion of functional structure, an expansion that is claimed to be necessary on empirical grounds. See Chapter 12 for discussion.

This concludes our rather brief overview of the history of phrase structure. A common thread has been the reduction and generalization that started with Chomsky (1955/1975). X-bar Theory was a generalization of PS grammars but at the same time a reduction in that the core primitives of the theory were fewer. Chomsky (1986a) also made significant generalizations of the X-bar Theory in Chomsky (1970a). Lastly, BPS has provided the last reduction that we have seen so far, where even the existence of bar levels is denied.

2.5 Rules and filters versus principles

Most of the early work in generative syntax was done on English. A few important exceptions were Kuroda (1965), Matthews (1965), Ross (1967a), Perlmutter (1968), and Kayne (1969). However, especially with the publication of Kayne (1975), it became more and more common to investigate different languages.[17] Kayne gave a range of different language-particular rules for French and in many cases compared them to the syntax of English. Slightly later, Jaeggli (1980) and Rizzi (1982a) conducted in-depth studies of other Romance languages. Crucially, though, this enterprise centered on formulating language-specific and construction-specific rules, and what may be universal across languages was not given as much attention.

Chomsky and Lasnik (1977) pointed out that early work in pursuit of descriptive adequacy led to an extremely rich theory of transformational grammar. For a formalization that encompasses much descriptive practice, see Peters and Ritchie (1973). Even this extremely rich theory does not encompass such devices as structure-building rules, global rules, transderivational constraints, and others that had often been proposed. Let us take a quick look at global rules and transderivational constraints.

A global rule is a rule that states conditions on "configurations of corresponding nodes in non-adjacent trees in a derivation" (Lakoff 1970:628). Thus, global rules go far beyond the usual Markovian property of transformational derivations. An example of a global rule is provided by Ross (1969). Ross observed that the island constraints on movement he proposed in Ross (1967a) only hold if the island-forming node is present in Surface Structure. The constraints do not hold, however, if a transformation ('Sluicing' in this case; see Chapter 19) subsequently deletes that node. An example illustrating this is given in (49)–(50).

(49) *Irv and someone were dancing, but I don't know who Irv and were dancing

(50) Irv and someone were dancing, but I don't know who

The conclusion drawn from this is that island constraints cannot just mention the point in the derivation at which the movement rule applies, nor just the surface structure. The constraints must mention both.

As for transderivational constraints, these are constraints that depend on properties of derivations other than the one currently being constructed. Hankamer (1973) argues for transderivational constraints based on a detailed analysis of gapping (see Chapter 19). Among others, he considers the data in (51)–(54) (pp. 26–27).

(51) Max wanted Ted to persuade Alex to get lost, and Walt, Ira

(52) ... and Walt *[wanted] Ira [to persuade Alex to get lost]

(53) ... and Walt *[wanted Ted to persuade] Ira [to get lost]

(54) ... and [Max wanted] Walt [to persuade] Ira [to get lost]

In order to block gapping in (52)–(53), Hankamer argues that a constraint is needed that makes reference to other structures that might have been created, even from different Deep Structures. In particular, the reason (51) cannot be derived from (52) or (53) is that it *can* be derived from (54). Space considerations prevent us from elaborating further, though we should acknowledge that Hankamer suggests that the constraint at issue here is universal, thus raising no learnability concerns.

Returning to our main discussion, any enrichment of linguistic theory that extends the class of possible grammars requires strong empirical motivation. This, Chomsky and Lasnik (1977) argued, is generally missing in the case of devices that exceed the framework of Chomsky (1955/1975), Peters and Ritchie (1973), and comparable work; cf. Dougherty (1973), Chomsky (1973), Brame (1976).

Note that the work of Chomsky and many others has consistently tried to reduce the descriptive power of the transformational component. The framework in *Aspects* is more restricted than the one in *LSLT*, and Chomsky (1973) is much more restricted than *Aspects*. In the 1980s, many researchers argued that we should make transformations as general as Move α, or even Affect α, as in Lasnik and Saito (1984, 1992).

Chomsky and Lasnik (1977) contributed to these developments by proposing a framework that attempted to restrict the options that are available in this narrower, but still overly permissive framework, so that it is possible to approach one of the basic goals of linguistic theory: to provide, in the sense of *Aspects*, explanations rather than descriptions and thus to account for the attainment of grammatical competence. They assumed that Universal Grammar is not an 'undifferentiated' system, but rather a system that incorporates something analogous to a theory of markedness. Specifically, there is a theory of core grammar with highly restricted options, limited expressive power, and a few parameters. Systems that fall within core grammar constitute the unmarked case; one can think of them as optimal in terms of the evaluation metric. An actual language is determined by fixing the parameters of core grammar and then adding rules or rule conditions, using much richer resources, perhaps resources as rich as those contemplated in the earlier theories of transformational grammar noted above.

Filters were supposed to bear the burden of accounting for constraints, which, in the earlier and far richer theory, were expressed in statements of ordering and obligatoriness, as well as contextual dependencies that cannot be formulated in the narrower framework of core grammar. The hypothesis in Chomsky and Lasnik (1977) was that the consequences of ordering, obligatoriness, and contextual dependency could be captured in terms of surface filters. Furthermore, they argued that the above-mentioned properties could be expressed in a natural way as surface filters that are universal, or else the unmarked case.

We see that the idea of a distinction between parameters and principles is already present in Chomsky and Lasnik (1977). However, in this framework, there are only a few parameters that affect the core grammar. Besides these parameters, there are a number of language-specific rules. An example is the filter in (55) that blocks *for-to* constructions in Standard English.

(55)   *[for-to]

(56)   *we want for to win

As Chomsky and Lasnik (1977:442) point out, this filter is a 'dialect' filter, meaning that it is not a principle of Universal Grammar. They discuss a range of filters, and some of them are like (55) in being outside of core grammar, whereas others, like the Stranded Affix filter of Lasnik (1981b), are argued to be part of Universal Grammar.

With Chomsky (1981), the conception of rules and filters changed somewhat. The part related to rules stayed intact, since there is no distinction between rules and principles. Both are assumed to be universal and part of Universal Grammar. But instead of filters that can be both language- and construction-specific, Chomsky suggested that we should conceive of variation in terms of parameters (hence the name Principles and Parameters Theory; see Chapter 4). The following quote brings out the main difference.

> If these parameters are embedded in a theory of UG that is sufficiently rich in structure, then the languages that are determined by fixing their values one way or another will appear to be quite diverse.   (Chomsky 1981:4)

The parameters are assumed to be part of UG and together they should yield both the variation we observe and an answer to Plato's problem: How do we know so much given the limited evidence available to us? In the realm of language, the question is how the child can arrive so rapidly at its target grammar given the input it gets. An important part of the theory was that parameters were supposed to represent clusters of properties: "[I]deally we hope to find that complexes of properties... are reducible to a single parameter, fixed in one or another way" (Chomsky 1981:6). Rizzi (1982a) gave a nice example of this when he argued that there are correlations between thematic null subjects, null expletives, free inversion, and *that*-trace effects (*Who do you think that __ won the race).

This model was therefore a sharp break from earlier approaches, under which Universal Grammar specified an infinite array of possible grammars, and explanatory adequacy required a presumably unfeasible search procedure to find the highest-valued one, given primary linguistic data. The Principles and Parameters approach eliminated all this. There is no enumeration of the array of possible grammars. There are only finitely many targets for acquisition, and no search procedure apart from valuing parameters. This cut through an impasse: Descriptive adequacy requires rich and varied grammars, hence unfeasible search; explanatory adequacy requires feasible search.

See Chapters 4, 24, and 25 for further discussion of parameters.

2.6 Derivations

The general issue of derivational versus representational approaches to syntax has received considerable attention throughout the history of generative grammar. A derivational approach argues that there are constraints on the processes by which well-formed expressions are generated, whereas a representational approach argues that there is a system of well-formedness constraints that apply to structured expressions (see Frank 2002 for more discussion of this general issue). Internally to the major derivational approach, transformational grammar, a related issue arises: Are well-formedness conditions imposed specifically at the particular levels of representations made available in the theory, or are they imposed 'internal' to the derivation leading to those levels?[18] Like the first question concerning whether derivations exist, it is a subtle one, perhaps even subtler than the first, but since Chomsky (1973), there has been increasing investigation of it, and important arguments and evidence have been brought to bear (see Freidin 1978 and Koster 1978a for illuminating early discussion).

However, generative theories disagree on whether derivations actually exist or not. Typically this disagreement emerges when the question of whether there are transformations is considered, since this is the main case where one can impose derivational constraints. Any phrase structure representation has to be generated somehow, and one can arguably claim that the generation of such a tree is derivational. This is not where the disagreement lies; rather, it concerns whether one can impose constraints on derivations or not. Chomskyan generative grammar, especially since the very important work of Ross (1967a), has always assumed that this is possible and that it is a virtue of the theory. However, let us consider some non-transformational theories (see also Frank 2002 for useful discussion, and Harman 1963 for a very early formulation of a non-transformational generative theory). Most of these developed in the wake of Chomsky's (1973, 1977) theorizing based on the important discoveries in Ross (1967a).

Lexical-Functional Grammar (LFG) (Kaplan and Bresnan 1982, Bresnan 2001) eliminates transformations and increases the role of structural composition. This is a theory where the lexical expressions are of crucial importance. LFG argues that lexical representations have a richer hierarchical structure than in the Chomskyan theory. The theory also assumes parallel levels of representation: constituent structure, functional structure, and argument structure all constitute independent levels of representation. Since the theory does not have transformations, dependencies are established by interaction between the different levels and by lexical entries that have been transformed by lexical rules. For example, an analysis of the passive assumes that there are two lexical entries of the verb in the lexicon and that there are linkages that determine the appropriate thematic dependencies. See Chapter 6 for more discussion of LFG.

Generalized Phrase Structure Grammar (GPSG) (Gazdar et al. 1985) eliminates transformations in a different way. In this theory, a derivation consists of context-free phrase-structure rules. Metarules that modify the phrase structure rules are used to established dependencies in a way reminiscent of Harman (1963). This is to say that *wh*-movement, for example, is captured through additional phrase-structure rules. Chapter 7 discusses GPSG in detail.

As Frank (2002:8) points out, all these non-transformational theories share with transformational theories the property that there are no privileged intermediate levels of syntactic structure. This has been the case since Chomsky (1965), but it was not true of Chomsky (1955/1975, 1957), where kernel structures constituted such intermediate structures. Put differently, something needs to prevent non-local dependencies from being created. However, a non-transformational theory that returns to a theory that is closer to that of Chomsky (1955/1975) is Tree Adjoining Grammar (Joshi et al. 1975, Joshi 1985). We briefly described this theory in Section 2.2.1 above; see also Chapter 8.

In theories of the Chomskyan sort, based on transformational movement operations, a question arises: What determines whether movement occurs? In the Move α framework, all such processes were completely free (see, e.g., Lasnik and Saito 1992 for a detailed version of this theory). There were no triggers; rather, there were representational constraints that had to be satisfied for a structure to be convergent. Even though representationalist approaches have been developed in recent years (see in particular

Brody 1995, 2002, 2003), Chomsky and most researchers within Chomskyan generative grammar have defended a derivationalist approach where movement is triggered.[19] Chomsky (1995c) argues on conceptual and, to some extent, empirical grounds that movement is always morphologically driven. That is, there is some formal feature that needs to be checked, and movement provides the configuration in which the checking can take place. Chomsky also provides reasons that, all else being equal, covert movement (movement in the LF component) is preferred to overt movement, a preference that Chomsky calls 'Procrastinate.' When movement is overt, rather than covert, then it must have been forced to operate early by some special requirement. The major phenomenon that Chomsky considers in these terms is verb raising, following the influential work of Pollock (1989). He also hints at a contrast in object shift, overt in some languages and covert in others. Chomsky (1993, 1995a, 1995c) codes the driving force for overt movement into strong features, and presents three successive distinct theories of precisely how strong features drive overt movement. These three theories, which we will summarize immediately, are of interest to our question, since the first two of them are explicitly representational in the relevant sense, while the third is derivational.

(57) a. A strong feature that is not checked in overt syntax causes a derivation to crash at PF. (Chomsky 1993)
b. A strong feature that is not checked (and eliminated) in overt syntax causes a derivation to crash at LF. (Chomsky 1995a)
c. A strong feature must be eliminated (almost) immediately upon its introduction into the phrase marker. (Chomsky 1995c)

All three of these proposals are designed to force overt movement in the relevant instances (e.g., verb raising in French, where a strong V feature of Infl will cause a violation in one of the three ways listed in (57) if overt movement does not take place) and all are framed within a Minimalist conception of grammar. The work of building structure is done by generalized transformations, as it was before recursion in the base was introduced in Chomsky (1965). This return to an earlier approach replaces a partly representational view with a strongly derivational one.

Chomsky (1993) argues that the treatment in (57a) follows from the fact that parametric differences in movement, like other parametric differences, must be based on morphological properties reflected at PF. (57a) makes this explicit. Chomsky suggests two possible implementations of the approach:

> ... 'strong' features are visible at PF and 'weak' features invisible at PF. These features are not legitimate objects at PF; they are not proper components of phonetic matrixes. Therefore, if a strong feature remains after

Spell-Out, the derivation crashes ... Alternatively, weak features are deleted in the PF component so that PF rules can apply to the phonological matrix that remains; strong features are not deleted so that PF rules do not apply, causing the derivation to crash at PF. (Chomsky 1993:198)

There is presumably only one other possible type of representational approach, given Minimalist assumptions: one that involves LF, rather than PF. Chomsky (1995a) proposes such an analysis, (57b), based on an empirical shortcoming of (57a). What is at issue is the unacceptability of sentences like (58).

(58) *John read what?

Assuming that the strong feature forcing overt *wh*-movement in English resides in interrogative C,[20] the potential concern is that C, since it has no phonetic features, might be introduced in the LF component, where, checked or not, it could not possibly cause a PF crash, since it has no phonetic features, and therefore as far as PF knows, the item does not exist at all. Yet (58) is bad as a non-echo question, so such a derivation must be blocked. This problem arises in the general context of fitting lexical insertion into the grammar. In most circumstances, there is no need for a specific prohibition against accessing the lexicon in the PF or LF component. (58) represents a rare problem for the assumption that lexical insertion is free to apply anywhere. Chomsky (1995a:60–61) suggests that the root C head has a feature that requires overt *wh*-movement. Unless this feature is checked prior to Spell-out, the derivation will crash at LF. Chomsky proposes to implement this basic idea in the following way: "Slightly adjusting the account in Chomsky (1993), we now say that a checked strong feature will be stripped away by Spell-Out, but is otherwise ineliminable" (Chomsky 1995a:61).

Chomsky (1995c) rejects the representational approach in (57a), and the conceptual argument he gives evidently applies equally to the alternative representational approach in (57b). He discounts such an account as an evasion, and proposes what he claims is a more straightforward statement of the phenomenon:

> ... formulation of strength in terms of PF convergence is a restatement of the basic property, not a true explanation. In fact, there seems to be no way to improve upon the bare statement of the properties of strength. Suppose, then, that we put an end to evasion and simply define a strong feature as one that a derivation 'cannot tolerate': a derivation $D \to \Sigma$ is canceled if Σ contains a strong feature.   (Chomsky 1995c:233)

In summary, strong features trigger a rule that eliminates them. This approach is strongly derivational. There are problems with this account (see Lasnik 2001b for detailed discussion), but the goal here has merely been to outline the ways one can think of the trigger question in either derivational or representational terms.

Since Chomsky (1995c), the assumption is that movement is triggered by feature checking. But while feature checking was originally thought to be possible only in specific derived configurations (the Spec–Head relation and head-adjunction configurations, in particular), in more recent work it is contingent merely on the establishment of an Agree relationship between a c-commanding Probe and a Goal. The introduction of the Agree mechanism divorces the movement trigger from agreement, contrary to the framework in Chomsky (1993), where elements moved to specifiers to undergo agreement with a head (see Chapter 17 for discussion). However, even if features have to be checked, it is not clear that the approach is fully derivational. The typical assumption is that a derivation crashes unless all features are checked prior to the interfaces, which in effect is a representational condition based on features. However, the operations defined on features are derivational as they unfold as the structure is being built and they are limited by grammatical principles (e.g., intervention effects or the Phase Impenetrability Condition; see Chomsky 2001, and Chapters 4 and 18 for discussion). Therefore it seems valid to say that there are both derivational and representational aspects and that both play important roles in grammar in this model.

2.7 The advent of economy principles in Principles and Parameters theory

As we have seen, a major Minimalist concern involves the driving force for syntactic movement. From its inception in the early 1990s, Minimalism has insisted on the last-resort nature of movement: in line with the leading idea of economy, movement must happen for a reason and, in particular, a formal reason. The Case Filter, which was a central component of the Government and Binding Theory, was thought to provide one such driving force. Chapter 17 illustrates this at length, so we will not discuss it here. Instead we will offer two other examples of economy principles: Relativized Minimality and the Extension Condition.

An important instance of economy is what Luigi Rizzi (1990a) called Relativized Minimality (see Chapter 18 for more discussion). Chomsky and Lasnik (1993) reinterpreted Rizzi's groundbreaking work in terms of least effort. Let us illustrate that here by way of a phenomenon called Superiority, which has often been analyzed as a Relativized Minimality effect. Consider the following examples:

(59)   Guess who bought what?

(60)   *Guess what who bought?

In this situation, there might seem to be an option. One could either front *who* or *what*. As (59) and (60) show, only the former is licit. In such a situation, you always have to pick the closest to the position where the element ends up after moving, as first observed in something like these terms by Chomsky (1973). Put differently, one should minimize the distance traveled by the moving element, an instance of 'economy' of derivation.

Another potential example of an economy condition relates to the Extension Condition. This condition requires that a transformational operation extends the tree upwards. In Chomsky (1965), the requirement that derivations work their way up the tree monotonically was introduced, alongside D-structure. Generally this is known as the requirement of cyclicity. Chomsky used this to explain the absence of certain kinds of derivations, but also as an argument against generalized transformations and for D-structure. But it was cyclicity, rather than D-structure, that was crucial in the account. As we have discussed above, Minimalism rejects D-structure and reinstates generalized transformations, but it still preserves cyclicity, thus ruling out the anticyclic derivations that were the original concern. The Minimalist Extension Condition demands that both the movement of material already in the structure (internal merge = singulary transformation) and the merger of a lexical item not yet in the structure (external merge = generalized transformation) target the top of the existing tree. Consider in this context the structures in (90)–(92).

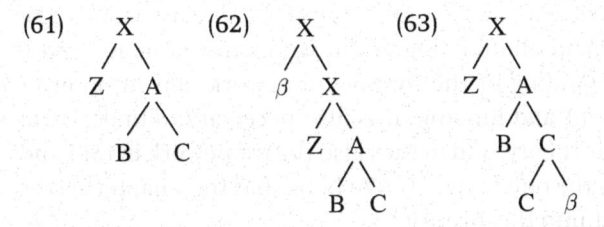

(61)
```
      X
     / \
    Z   A
       / \
      B   C
```

(62)
```
      X
     / \
    β   X
       / \
      Z   A
         / \
        B   C
```

(63)
```
      X
     / \
    Z   A
       / \
      B   C
         / \
        C   β
```

(61) is the original tree. (62) shows a derivation that obeys the Extension Condition. Here the new element β is merged at the top of the tree. The last derivation, (63), does not obey the Extension Condition because β is merged at the bottom of the tree. Importantly, there is a deep idea behind cyclicity, which again was present in Chomsky's earliest work in the late 1950s. The idea, called the No Tampering Condition in current parlance, seems like a rather natural economy condition. (62) involves no tampering since the old tree in (61) still exists as a subtree of (62), whereas (63) involves tampering with the original structure. That is, it is more economical to expand a structure than to go back and change a structure that has already been built. This becomes particularly clear if parts of the structure are shipped off to the interfaces (e.g., phase by phase as in much recent Minimalist work), where the earlier structure effectively is not available. Were one to tamper with that structure, it would require bringing the structure back into the main structure again, which seems hugely uneconomical.

2.8 Concluding remarks

The history of generative grammar is not very long. Despite this, considerable progress has been made in our understanding of the human language faculty. Numerous problems and questions remain, but it is interesting to observe that there are certain questions that have remained at the center of the theoretical development since the early beginning. For example, whereas generalized transformations were eliminated in the mid 1960s, they returned again in the Minimalist Program where D-structure was eliminated (though see Uriagereka 2008 for critical discussion). Questions of how structure is generated are still at the forefront of current research. Another major issue, since Ross (1967a), is locality (see Chapter 18). Since Chomsky (1973), locality issues have occupied a central role in linguistic theorizing. We are still lacking a complete theory of islands, so this is certainly another issue that will be on the front burner for quite some time. Phrase structure has been central since *LSLT*, though the theory of phrase structure has undergone substantial changes over the years.

These are just a few examples of recurrent themes during the brief sixty-year history of our field. In this chapter we have in particular emphasized the early period since that is often the period that is not as well known. We believe it is important to know the history of the field in order to fully understand current developments. For example, understanding the change from Government and Binding to the Minimalist Program necessitates a good understanding of the former framework. But in order to understand Government and Binding, it is also necessary to understand the Extended Standard Theory, and in turn also the framework in *LSLT* and *Syntactic Structures* and the one in *Aspects*. We hope that this chapter serves as a useful entry point into this history.

Notes

We are grateful to Juan Uriagereka for extensive help on an earlier draft and to Marcel den Dikken for his patience and encouragement, and to Marcel and an anonymous reviewer for very helpful comments that led to substantial improvements in the presentation.
1. In languages like Hungarian, sentential complementation is typically 'mediated' by a pronoun, as shown in (i).

    (i) János azt   tudja, hogy S
        János it.ACC knows that S

    This property may provide retroactive support for the *LSLT* way of generating sentential complementation. Thanks to Marcel den Dikken (p.c.) for pointing out this fact to us.

2. It should be noted that singular transformations and generalized transformations could be interspersed. There were no constraints on when either could apply.
3. For extensive discussion of this analysis, see Lasnik (2000; Chapter 2).
4. We need the T-marker as interface with semantics because the final derived P-marker typically lacks information relevant to meaning, for example grammatical relations if Passive has applied.
5. In the theory in *Aspects*, grammatical relations like *subject* and *object* are read off the syntactic structure. However, the relations themselves are semantic, so *subject* means *understood subject of*. A decade later, the theory of Relational Grammar (Perlmutter 1980) turned this view on its head, maintaining that grammatical relations are the primitives of the grammar. In Relational Grammar, grammatical relations are purely structural relations. This means that grammatical relations can be altered by transformations, and the major Relational Grammar syntactic processes had just this purpose.
6. It is worth noting that in *Aspects*, cyclicity and deep structure were intertwined. Later on, they were distinguished, which means that one has to reconsider the previous evidence for deep structure.
7. See Section 2.2.7 below for discussion of an approach to cyclicity that, unlike that in *Aspects*, does not require recursion in the base (hence D-structure). In effect, this addresses one of the major *Aspects* arguments for D-structure.
8. Though see Jackendoff (1977) for a way to in part solve this problem by identifying S with V''' in his system. See also Hornstein (1977), who argues that S should be excluded from the X-bar convention.
9. That is, the problem of 'projecting' the correct grammar from limited input data.
10. See also Stowell (1981:71–75) for criticism based on arguments from acquisition.
11. In fact, Stowell (1981) argued for the general elimination of phrase-structure rules, thus providing empirical motivation for the formalization of Lasnik and Kupin (1977).
12. This is what Chomsky said, but it is obviously not exactly what he meant. (40a) should read $X' = X\ Y'''^*$ because otherwise a verb, for example, can only take a VP complement, and similarly for (40b) and specifiers.
13. See also Stuurman (1985:182) for a similar claim, though Stuurman claims that this also holds for lexical categories.
14. We speculate that Kayne intended 'asymmetry' rather than 'antisymmetry.' An antisymmetric relation R is one where if $(a, b) \in R$ and $(b, a) \in R$, then $a = b$. Asymmetry is a stronger property: $(a, b) \in R \rightarrow (b, a) \notin R$. Since items evidently do not precede themselves, the weakening loophole of antisymmetry is not needed.

15. This way of looking at phrase structure is closely related to Speas (1990:35).
16. This condition is an obvious extension of an idea in Katz and Postal (1964:44–45), further developed in Chomsky (1965:132) when he suggests that transformations cannot introduce meaning-bearing elements.
17. This also happened as textbooks on the *Syntactic Structures* and *Aspects* frameworks were written.
18. There are of course hybrid theories as well. Chomsky (1981), for example, proposes well-formedness conditions on Deep Structure, on Surface Structure, and on the application of transformations between grammatical levels.
19. Almost from the earliest days of generative grammar, there were qualms about optional transformations: "An obvious decision is to consider minimization of the optional part of the grammar to be the major factor in reducing complexity" (Chomsky 1958/1962:154).
20. Notice that in English, the relevant strong feature could not reside in the *wh*-phrase, since in multiple interrogation, all but one of the *wh*s remain in situ, hence unchecked in overt syntax:

    (i) Who gave what to who?

3
Goals and methods of generative syntax

Frederick J. Newmeyer

3.1 Introduction

This chapter focuses on the goals and methodology of generative syntax, with special emphasis on the Principles and Parameters (P-and-P) framework.[1] Section 3.2 discusses the three principal goals of the theory, which I call the 'universalist,' the 'particularist,' and the 'typological.' The main topic of Section 3.3 is generative methodology, focusing on the relative merits of introspective versus conversational data. It also discusses and evaluates the recent trend to admit more and more types of semantic data as evidence in syntactic theorizing. Sections 3.4 and 3.5 discuss the goals and methods of non-P-and-P generative models and of Cognitive–Functional Linguistics respectively. Section 3.6 is a brief conclusion.

3.2 Goals

Generative syntax embodies three complementary goals, two of which are adopted by all practitioners of the approach and a third which is not universally accepted. The first two are to characterize what a 'possible human language' might be and to provide formal grammars of individual languages. I call these the 'universalist' and the 'particularist' goals and they are discussed in Sections 3.2.1 and 3.2.2 respectively. For most generative syntacticians, the mechanism linking the first two goals is the theory of parameters (see Section 3.2.3). The third, more controversial, goal is to explain why some grammar types appear to be cross-linguistically more common than others. This, the 'typological' goal, is the subject of Section 3.2.4. Section 3.2.5 discusses a set of goals orthogonal to the first three, namely the attainment of a set of 'levels of adequacy' that might be imposed on syntactic theory.

3.2.1 The universalist goal

Generative syntax sets as its primary goal the provision of a rigorous characterization of the notion 'possible human language.' The essence of this 'universalist' goal is to distinguish as precisely as possible the class of grammatical processes that can occur in language from that which cannot. The product of this characterization, namely 'Universal Grammar' (UG), specifies the limits within which all languages function. In an early formulation of this goal, Chomsky wrote:

> The theory thus constructed is a theory of linguistic universals ... Specification of the form of grammars *excludes certain infinite sets of sentences from consideration as possible natural languages*. ... Procedures for evaluating grammars and determining structural descriptions impose strict conditions on the kinds of units that can be attributed to a natural language and the manner of their arrangement and interconnection. This general theory can therefore be regarded as a definition of the notion 'natural language' ... (Chomsky 1962:536-37; emphasis added)

In Chomsky's view, natural scientists set parallel tasks for themselves: The goal of physicists, as Chomsky sees things, is to characterize the class of possible physical processes, that of biologists to characterize the class of possible biological processes, and so on.

This central goal has remained consistent in the past half century of generative studies. In early work, the 'central fact' to be explained was that "a mature speaker can produce a new sentence of his language on the appropriate occasion, and other speakers can understand it immediately, though it is equally new to them ... On the basis of a limited experience with the data of speech, each normal human has developed for himself a thorough competence in his native language" (Chomsky 1964b:914-15). This fact has now been recast as 'Plato's problem,' the fact that "we can know so much about language given that we have such limited evidence" (Chomsky 1986b:xxv; see also Chomsky 2000a:61).

Chomsky and other generative syntacticians have repeatedly identified UG as part of the innate endowment of the human mind, and have gone so far as to categorize (generativist) linguistic theory as a branch of the field of cognitive psychology. Thus Chomsky sees 'explanation' in linguistics as being tied ultimately to an account of the process of language acquisition by the child; one can be said to have explained a universal grammatical principle by showing that it is brought forth by the child in the acquisition process, just as one might say that the normal human propensity to have two arms and two legs is explained by providing an account of the biological preprogramming that causes this propensity to be realized. In other words, generative grammarians take a 'biolinguistic perspective,' which "regards the language faculty as an 'organ of the body' along with other cognitive systems" (Chomsky 2005:1).[2]

The innateness of linguistic constructs is motivated in part by what are called 'arguments from the poverty of the stimulus' (APS). APS emphasize that the abstractness and/or complexity of the proposed universal is so great that no conceivable mechanism of inductive learning could have resulted in its acquisition. Let us look at two cases. The first is Chomsky's well-known and often repeated argument for the innateness of the formal universal that grammatical rules are structure-dependent (see, for example, Chomsky 1975b:32–33, 1980b:40). Chomsky reasons as follows: Suppose that a child learning English unerringly forms questions such as (1b) from declaratives such as (1a):

(1) a. the man is tall
    b. Is the man tall?

In principle, the child could be working with one of two strategies for forming questions. The first is simply that they are formed by inverting the first occurrence of *is* (or an auxiliary). In the second, more complex, scenario, the child analyzes the sentence into abstract phrases and preposes the occurrence of *is* (or an auxiliary) that occurs after the first noun phrase. Questions formed from sentences such as (2a), in which the subject contains a relative clause with a copula, decide the matter – the child assumes the second hypothesis. Given the first hypothesis, the child would incorrectly produce (2b). However, following the second, the child correctly produces (2c):

(2) a. the man who is tall is in the room
    b. *Is the man who tall is in the room?
    c. Is the man who is tall in the room?

How did the child come to possess the second hypothesis? Chomsky writes:[3]

> It is certainly absurd to argue that children are trained to use the structure-dependent rule, in this case. ... A person may go through a considerable portion of his life without ever facing relevant evidence, but he will have no hesitation in using the structure-dependent rule, even if his experience is consistent with hypothesis 1. ... The principle of structure-dependence is not learned, but forms part of the conditions for language learning.
> (Chomsky 1975b:32–33)

Hoekstra and Kooij (1988) have constructed a similar argument in support of the principle of Subjacency being an innate formal universal (for more on this principle, see Chapter 18). Since this constraint prohibits the formation of *wh*-questions if a *wh*-phrase intervenes between the filler and the gap, it predicts correctly that (3a) is ambiguous as to the scope of *where*, while (3b) is not. Note that in (3a), *where* can refer both to the place of John's saying and the place of getting off the bus, while in (3b), *where* can refer only to the place of John's asking:

(3) a. Where$_i$ did John say ___$_i$ that we had to get off the bus ___$_i$?
    b. Where$_i$ did John ask ___$_i$ whether we had to get off the bus *___$_i$?

They argue that positive evidence alone could hardly suffice to enable the child language learner to come to the conclusion that (3b) does not manifest the same ambiguity as (3a) – the abstractness and complexity of the principle and the paucity of direct evidence bearing directly on it guarantee that the child could never figure Subjacency out 'for itself.' Thus knowledge of the permissible intervening structure between a *wh*-phrase and its co-indexed gap must be pre-wired into the language learner.

3.2.2 The particularist goal

The second goal is to provide formal statements characterizing the grammars of individual languages or, more accurately, the grammars of individual speakers.[4] This latter task is seen as equivalent to characterizing the tacit knowledge that native speakers have about syntactic, phonological, morphological, and semantic patterning in their language. This knowledge, once called '(linguistic) competence,' is now generally referred to as 'I-language' (where 'I' is short for 'internalized'). 'I-language' contrasts with 'E-' or 'externalized' language, or what was once called '(linguistic) performance.' 'Competence' and 'performance' themselves are modern reinterpretations of the dichotomy between *langue* and *parole*, which was bequeathed to the field about a century ago by the Swiss linguist Ferdinand de Saussure (Saussure 1916/1966). While many pre-1950s European structural linguists had no difficulty in viewing language in terms of internalized mental representations (see, for example, Jakobson 1941/1968), their American counterparts tended to think of language as essentially a species of behavior. For example, Leonard Bloomfield, probably the most influential American linguist of the first half of the twentieth century, defined 'language' as "the totality of utterances that can be made in a speech-community" (Bloomfield 1926/1957:26).

It goes without saying that the universalist and particularist goals work in tandem. On the basis of facts encountered in a particular language one might propose a principle designed to account for such facts. This principle might well seem to be no more than a language-particular one, shedding no necessary light on UG. But should it appear to be at a level of complexity or abstractness that suggests that it could implausibly be learned inductively, then it is put forward as a candidate UG principle, thereby necessitating its testing in a wide variety of languages. Should the evidence bear out its universality, then a scholar investigating a different language might well incorporate it into the set of assumptions guiding his or her analysis of that language. Hence it is perfectly reasonable methodologically ...

> ... to propose a general [i.e., universal – FJN] principle of linguistic structure on the basis of observation of a single language.
> (Chomsky 1980b:48)

If a survey of the critical literature is any indication, no other remark of Chomsky's with respect to grammatical analysis has so outraged the linguistic community. Esa Itkonen's reaction was typical:

> Those working outside the Chomskyan paradigm have found this type of statement rather preposterous ... It looks self-evident that Chomsky is merely repeating the mistakes of his predecessors who tried to construct a theory of universal grammar based on Latin or French.
> (Itkonen 1992:69)

One might conclude, then, along with Itkonen, that "Chomsky's assumption of linguistic universals is not based on data, but rather on conceptual arguments." But a look at the continuation of Chomsky's passage perhaps puts the matter in a different light:

> The inference is legitimate, on the assumption that humans are not specifically adapted to learn one rather than another human language ... Assuming that the genetically determined language faculty is a common human possession, we may conclude that a principle of language is universal if we are led to postulate it as a 'precondition' for the acquisition of a single language. ... To test such a conclusion, we will naturally want to investigate other languages in comparable detail. We may find that our inference is refuted by such investigation.
> (Chomsky 1980b:48)

In other words, any claim about universals based on a single language makes a testable falsifiable hypothesis. The more languages that are studied, the better the hypothesis is tested. And tested and falsified they are, with great regularity. There hardly exists an issue of a generative-oriented journal that does not propose the modification or abandonment of a hypothesized principle of UG on the basis of data from a previously uninvestigated language.

3.2.3 Parametric theory

Any theory of UG ipso facto separates the class of possible grammars from the class of impossible grammars. Children are literally 'born knowing' that they can exclude from possibility an infinite set of grammars that might be compatible with the environmental input that they receive. It has generally been assumed, however, that children need more than that in order to arrive at the correct grammar. To be specific, the general assumption has been that the constructs of UG are parameterized in such a way that acquiring a language involves little more than setting values for each parameter based on the appropriate environmental trigger. In earlier versions of parametric theory, it was assumed that UG principles themselves were parameterized (Chomsky 1981, Rizzi 1978b). For example, Rizzi observed that the principle of Subjacency (see Chapter 18), first proposed in Chomsky (1973), seemed to work somewhat differently in Italian than in English. For the former language, S' (now CP) appeared to be the relevant bounding node, rather than S (now TP), as in English. Rizzi suggested that Subjacency is indeed a universal principle, but with parameterized bounding nodes. Part of learning a language involves, given this approach, setting the appropriate bounding nodes on the basis of positive evidence.

Since Borer (1984a), the general assumption (sometimes referred to as the 'Borer–Chomsky conjecture'; see also Chapter 25) is that parametric variation is situated in the properties of functional categories, that is, categories that play specifically grammatical roles.[5] Auxiliaries, complementizers, and determiners are examples of functional categories. By way of illustration, McCloskey (2002) argues that whether or not a language makes productive (fully grammaticalized) use of resumptive pronouns depends on the inventory of complementizer-type elements that the language contains. And in Pesetsky and Torrego (2001), whether or not a language has Subject–Auxiliary Inversion depends on the featural properties of the node Complementizer.

The parametric approach to variation sparked an intensive cross-linguistic study of syntactic features that had been to a great extent missing in earlier versions of generative syntax. In order to arrive at the correct set of parameters and their possible settings, a wide variety of typologically different languages needs to be investigated and compared.

A major appeal of parametric theory has been that, by narrowing down the hypothesis space for the language learner, it brings us one step closer to understanding how, in the absence of direct evidence in many or most circumstances, the child can arrive at the appropriate grammar. Equally appealing was the apparent fact that parameters manifest all of the following properties:

(4) Parameters (it has been claimed):
    a. are descriptively simple.
    b. have binary settings.[6]
    c. are small in number.
    d. are hierarchically/implicationally organized, thereby accounting for both order of first language acquisition and typological generalizations.
    e. are abstract entities with a rich deductive structure, making possible the prediction of (unexpected) clusterings of morphosyntactic properties.
    f. along with their set of possible settings are innate (and therefore universal).
    g. have settings that are easily learned.
    h. can undergo rapid change (unlike morphological and grammaticalization-related changes).

For the decade following its introduction, parametric theory appeared to be so successful that the umbrella term for mainstream syntactic theory was the 'Principles and Parameters' approach. In recent years, however, the tendency has been to focus on 'microparametric' variation among languages. Instead of proposing wide-scope (macro) parameters capable of dividing the world's languages into broad typological classes (as in Baker 2001), most linguists focus on minute variation between related dialects and languages, such as might be characterizable by minor differences in their categorial inventory or organization.[7]

3.2.4 The typological goal and difficulties with parametric theory

Many, but not all, advocates of parametric theory go one step farther and attribute to UG the task of traditional linguistic typology, namely to account for why some grammar types are more common or less common than other types and why certain typological traits tend to cluster with each other, while others do not. One might call the commitment to explain such phenomena the 'typological' goal. For example, in approximately 96 percent of all languages the subject precedes the object (Tomlin 1986) and at a frequency far greater than chance, VO languages are more likely to manifest *wh*-fronting than OV languages (Dryer 1991). Facts such as these are often argued to follow from markedness relations among parameters (Travis 1989) or a hierarchy ranking some parameters over others (Baker 2001).

Parametric theory has been subject to intense scrutiny in recent years and an increasing number of linguists have expressed reservations as to its general correctness. To give one example, Cedric Boeckx was at one time the most ardent defender of parametric theory (see Boeckx 2006:55–58, 73). However, he has recently re-evaluated his position, writing:

> But although such clusters of variation did much to dispel the common impression (endorsed by structuralists) that languages can vary from one another indefinitely, it is fair to say that few of the implicational statements at the heart of traditional Principles-and-Parameters approach have stood the test of time. ... Critics are correct in stressing that the rarity of massive clustering effects takes much of the gloss away from the traditional Principles-and-Parameters model. ... I think they are correct in taking parametric clusters to be tendencies, not to be accounted for in terms of UG principles ... (Boeckx 2008:12–13)

Despite the early apparent success of parametric theory, there is reason to doubt the correctness of all of (4a–h) (see Newmeyer 2004, 2005). Given space limitations, I will briefly call attention to problems with (4c) and (4e). As far as the former is concerned, there is little reason to believe that only a small number of parameters need to be posited. Consider five out of the dozens of morphosyntactic differences that exist within and/or among English dialects:

(5) VP ellipsis (see Chapter 19):
   a. Mary gave me an expensive present for my birthday, but she shouldn't have   (North American usage)
   b. Mary gave me an expensive present for my birthday, but she shouldn't have done   (British usage)

(6) Negative concord (see Chapter 21):
   a. I don't know anything about any ballot stuffing
   b. I don't know nothing about no ballot stuffing

(7) Conjoined subject pronouns:
   a. he and I have signed up for the tour
   b. him and me have signed up for the tour

(8) Preposition stranding / pied-piping:
   a. Who did you speak to?
   b. To whom did you speak?

(9) Stylistic inversion after initial adverbials:
   a. Mary ran away
   b. Away ran Mary

If each of these analytically independent distinctions were to be handled by a difference in parameter setting, then, extrapolating to all of the syntactic distinctions in the world's languages, there would have to be thousands, if not millions, of parameters.[8] Such a conclusion is clearly unacceptable. On the other hand, if not all syntactic differences between dialects are handled by differences in parameter settings, but some by means of differences in more traditional-looking rules, then positing parameters results in little gain either in terms of ease for the language acquirer or in terms of theory-internal elegance.

As far as (4e) is concerned, let us examine briefly what is probably the most famous parameter in the history of generative grammar, the Null Subject Parameter. This parameter was proposed in (Chomsky 1981) and soon modified in Chomsky (1982), Rizzi (1982a), and Safir (1985). It predicts that the following properties should cluster cross-linguistically: null thematic subjects (NULL TS); null non-thematic subjects (NULL NTS); the possibility of subject inversion (SI); and the possibility of *that*-trace filter violations (THAT-T). The predictions of the parameter were put to the test by Gilligan (1987), who worked with a 100-language sample, which he attempted to correct for areal and genealogical bias. According to Gilligan, the data reveal that the only robust correlations among the four features are the following:

(10) a. NULL TS → NULL NTS
 b. SI → NULL NTS
 c. SI → THAT-T
 d. THAT-T → NULL NTS

These results are not very heartening for any theory that sees in null subject phenomena a rich clustering of properties. In three of the four correlations, null non-thematic subjects are entailed, but that is obviously a simple consequence of the rarity of languages that manifest *overt* non-thematic subjects. Even worse, five language types are attested whose existence neither theory predicts. As Mark Baker, one of the leading spokespersons for parametric theory, has acknowledged: "History has not been kind to the Pro-drop [i.e., Null Subject – FJN] Parameter as originally stated. It is now well-known that the cluster of properties that this parameter claimed to be related fragments in various ways when one looks at a wider range of languages" (Baker 2008a:352).

I feel that we can sum up the success of parametric syntax in one sentence: Parameters work the best where they are needed the least. By that, I mean that where we *do* find clustering, there is usually a pretty good functional explanation at hand. And where we do not find the predicted clustering, the functional explanation is much less obvious or entirely non-existent. So take the Greenbergian correlations, that is, those deriving from Greenberg (1963). These are *real* clustering effects, the most robust of which are listed in (11):

(11) Correlation pairs reported in Dryer (1992) (the 'Greenbergian correlations')

VO correlate	OV correlate
adposition – NP	NP – adposition
copula verb – predicate	predicate – copula verb
'want' – VP	VP – 'want'
tense/aspect auxiliary verb – VP	VP – tense/aspect auxiliary verb
negative auxiliary – VP	VP – negative auxiliary
complementizer – S	S – complementizer
question particle – S	S – question particle
adverbial subordinator – S	S – adverbial subordinator
article – N'	N' – article
plural word – N'	N' – plural word
noun – genitive	genitive – noun
noun – relative clause	relative clause – noun
adjective – standard of comparison	standard of comparison – adjective
verb – PP	PP – verb
verb – manner adverb	manner adverb – verb

These correlations have generally been handled within generative syntax by means of an (innate) Head Parameter, which requires complements to consistently precede or consistently follow their heads (Stowell 1981, Travis 1984, 1989, Koopman 1984). However, two points need to be made about the generalization governing head–complement order. First, it is very close to the surface and, second, there is a neat processing explanation for why it exists, first proposed in Hawkins (1994).[9] Why do VO languages tend to have prepositions and OV languages tend to have postpositions? There are four logical possibilities, illustrated in (12a–d): VO and prepositional (12a); OV and postpositional (12b); VO and postpositional (12c); and OV and prepositional (12d):

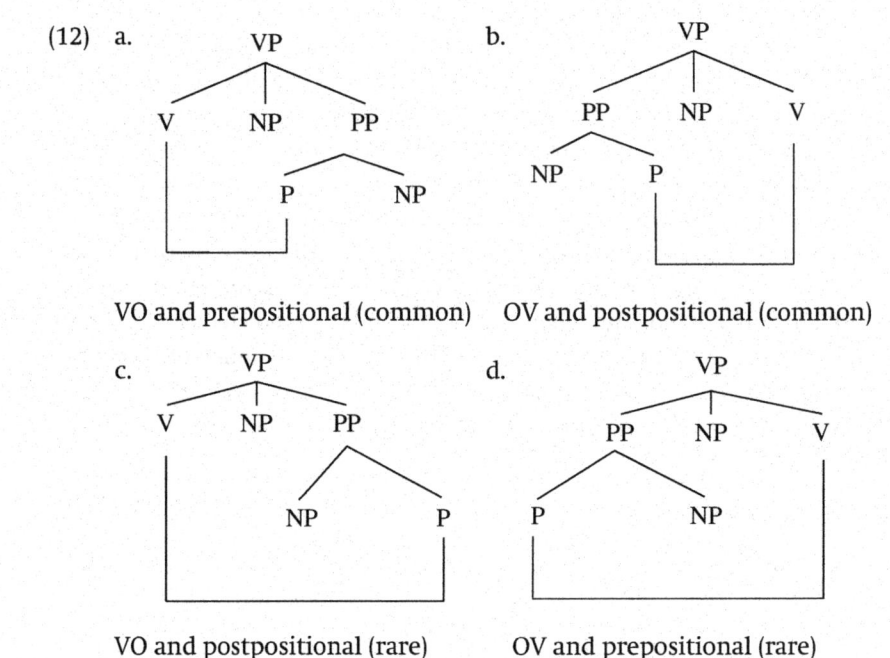

(12) a.

```
        VP
      / | \
     V  NP  PP
              \
              P  NP
```

b.

```
        VP
      / | \
     PP  NP  V
     / \
    NP  P
```

VO and prepositional (common)   OV and postpositional (common)

c.

```
        VP
      / | \
     V  NP  PP
              \
              NP  P
```

d.

```
        VP
      / | \
     PP  NP  V
     / \
    P  NP
```

VO and postpositional (rare)   OV and prepositional (rare)

In (12a) and (12b), the two common structures, the distance required for the hearer to identify all of the constituents of VP is just that distance between V and P, crossing over the object NP. But in (12c) and (12d), the uncommon structures, the identification space is longer, since it encompasses the object of the adposition as well. In other words, there is no need for a head parameter.[10]

The abandonment of parameters does not take us back to the days when linguists believed that languages could vary without limit, since a rich theory of innate knowledge limits the hypothesis space that the language learner needs to search in order to posit (on the basis of positive evidence) the particular structures of his or her grammar. To take a simple example, if UG tells the language learner that he or she needs to determine the head for each phrase, nothing is gained by the additional innate (parametric) specification that heads are on the left or on the right of their complements. The learner needs to figure that out on the basis of positive evidence anyway (for more discussion of this point, see Newmeyer 2005: Chapter 3).

3.2.5 Levels of adequacy and the 'third factor in language design'

Early work in generative grammar outlined three goals to which grammatical theory might aspire – goals that are orthogonal to the universalist, particularist, and typological goals. These goals were phrased in terms of the notion 'levels of adequacy,' that is, attainable levels of theoretical and empirical success. The lowest two levels, those of observational adequacy and descriptive adequacy, are predicated of proposed grammars. Observational adequacy is attained "if the grammar presents the primary data correctly" (Chomsky 1964b:924), by separating the grammatical sentences from the ungrammatical sentences. A descriptively adequate grammar "gives a correct account of the linguistic intuition of the native speaker, and specifies the observed data (in particular) in terms of significant generalizations that express underlying regularities in the language" (p. 924). Explanatory adequacy, unlike the lower two levels, is predicated of *theories*. A theory is explanatorily adequate if for any set of competing descriptively adequate grammars, it picks out the correct (i.e., mentally represented) one. It has always been taken for granted that explanatory adequacy can be achieved only by bringing into play evidence from outside of grammatical patterning *per se*, that is, evidence from acquisition, change, impaired speech, and so on.

Given that even descriptive adequacy has never been achieved, except perhaps for the smallest grammar fragments, many linguists were startled to read Chomsky in the early years of the first decade of the twenty-first century remarking that our level of knowledge had now allowed us to set goals that go beyond (mere) explanatory adequacy. To be specific, Chomsky has written that "we can seek a level of explanation deeper than explanatory adequacy, asking not only *what* the properties of language are but also *why* they are that way" (Chomsky 2004:105; emphasis in original). Understanding how such might be possible involves a look at what is certainly the biggest rhetorical – and perhaps substantive – shift in Chomsky's thinking in recent years. Until recently, Chomsky had always gone out of his way to stress the *uniqueness* of human language, that is, the degree to which its properties differ from those of other biological systems. And it is certainly indisputable that the principles proposed by generative syntacticians in the first forty years of the history of the discipline seemed to lack even remote homologues elsewhere in the natural world. One thinks of the Coordinate Structure Constraint of the 1960s (Ross 1967a; see Chapter 18), the Specified Subject Condition of the 1970s (Chomsky 1973; see Chapters 15 and 18), the Theta Criterion of the 1980s (Chomsky 1981; see Chapter 9), and the Linear Correspondence Axiom of the 1990s (Kayne 1994; see Section 2.4.2) as typical examples. Furthermore, there appeared to be considerable overlap in the explanatory domain of the principles that had been proposed. In the course of a discussion of attempts to diminish the high degree of redundant overlap among the principles of the Government and Binding Theory, Chomsky noted that "it has often proven to be a useful guiding intuition in research that if some property of language is 'overdetermined' by proposed principles, then probably the principles are wrong, and some way should be found to reconstruct them so as to avoid this redundancy" (Chomsky 1991a:49). He went on to write:

> Typically, biological systems are not like this at all. They are highly redundant, for reasons that have a plausible functional account. Redundancy offers protection against damage, and might facilitate overcoming problems that are computational in nature. Why language should be so different from other biological systems is a problem, possibly even a mystery. (Chomsky 1991a: 49–50)

The mystery has been solved, at least to Chomsky's satisfaction, by means of a steady diminution in the scope and complexity of syntactic principles proposed that are specific to UG and a corresponding increase in the explanatory burden of systems not unique to language. In a number of recent publications, Chomsky has called attention to "three factors that enter into the growth of language in the individual: 1., Genetic endowment, apparently nearly uniform for the species ...; 2., Experience, which leads to variation, within a fairly narrow range ...; and 3., Principles not specific to the faculty of language" (Chomsky 2005:6). As far as the first factor is concerned, Hauser et al. (2002) define the "Faculty of language – narrow sense" (FLN) as "the abstract linguistic computational system alone, independent of the other systems with which it interacts and interfaces" (p. 1571) and "hypothesize that FLN only includes recursion and is the only uniquely human component of the faculty of language" (p. 1569). Recursion (i.e., the operations of Merge and Move) is complemented exclusively by principles that can be attributed to the third factor: "properties of interface systems [sensory-motor and conceptual-intentional – FJN] and general considerations of computational efficiency, and the like" (Chomsky 2005:10).

Desirable as it may be to attribute properties of the linguistic system to independently motivated external factors, we are a long way from achieving the goal of reducing FLN/UG to recursion. For example, economy principles such as Last Resort (Chomsky 1993), Relativized Minimality (Rizzi 1990a) (as well as its cousin, Chomsky and Lasnik's 1993 Minimize Chain Links), and anti-locality (Grohmann 2003) do not fall out from recursion *per se*, but rather represent conditions (however well motivated) that need to be imposed on it (for discussion of these principles, see Chapter 18). Nor do they seem to follow directly from the 'third factor.' The entire set of mechanisms pertaining to phases (Chomsky 2001; see also Chapter 18), including what nodes count for phasehood and the various conditions that need to be imposed on their functioning, like the Phase Impenetrability Condition, seem to be inherent aspects of FLN/UG as well. To complicate things still further, some Minimalist theorists have transferred from the narrow syntax to the phonology the burden of accounting for phenomena such as extraposition and scrambling (Chomsky 1995c), object shift (Holmberg 1999), head movements (Boeckx and Stjepanović 2001), the movement deriving V2 (Verb Second) order (Boeckx and Stjepanović 2001), and much more, in part on the basis of the desire to keep the narrow syntax as 'minimalist' as possible. Yet whatever component these processes are assigned to, they are still 'syntactic.' What formal universals govern syntactic processes in PF? Nobody knows, but the default assumption has to be that they are not the same ones that govern more 'narrowly syntactic' processes. And returning to parameters, they are said by many to be as central to the Minimalist Program as they were to the antecedent Government and Binding model (see Biberauer et al. 2010). Given that there could be anywhere between hundreds and millions of parameters (see above, Section 3.2.4), all (by definition) innate, any 'recursion only' hypothesis for FLN/UG is a long way from realization, as is therefore the possibility of having transcended explanatory adequacy.

3.3 Methods

Generative syntacticians have not, in general, been very concerned with methodology.[11] Chomsky set the tone for this lack of interest in *Syntactic Structures*, writing that "One may arrive at a grammar by intuition, guess-work, all sorts of partial methodological hints, reliance on past experience, etc." (Chomsky 1957:56). Put simply, it is only the final product that counts. How one arrives at that product might be of interest to a specialist in the psychology of scientific discovery, but of little relevance to the correctness of the theory. That said, the data used in theory construction have overwhelmingly been the introspective judgments provided by native speakers. In another early publication of Chomsky's, and the only one devoted primarily to methodology, he observed that he had:

> been concerned with such data as (a) phonetic transcriptions; (b) judgments of conformity of utterance tokens; (c) judgments of well-formedness; (d) ambiguity that can be traced to structural origins; (e) judgments of sameness or difference of sentence type; (f) judgments concerning the propriety of particular classifications or segmentations; and so on. (Chomsky 1961:223)

Chomsky had no objection to exploring "objective experimental techniques for characterizing these intuitive operations" (1961:226), which he considered to be "complementary" to introspective judgments. In fact, when we look at the methodology of generative syntacticians over the years, "complementary" appears to be the appropriate word. Scores of publications have pointed to results based on experiments in the psycholinguistic lab, aspects of first and second language acquisition (see Chapter 25), language loss in aphasia, and so on in order help confirm or refute some theoretical proposal already on the table. But I am not aware of a single new hypothesis governing the nature of UG that was *proposed* on the basis of non-introspective data.

The major reason for the pre-eminence of introspective data is quite evident: They are far and away the *easiest* type of data to collect. There are no complex experiments to design and carry out, no sophisticated apparatus to buy and maintain, no subjects to recruit and instruct, and no time-consuming statistical analyses to perform. The question, of course, is whether this reliance on introspection has had negative effects. Section 3.3.1 discusses in some detail the pros and cons of the use of introspective data. Section 3.3.2 addresses the assertion of many non-generativists that only conversational data is appropriate to scholars probing the nature of grammar. And Section 3.3.3 turns to a rather different issue, namely whether judgments about meaning are relevant to the construction of a syntactic theory.

3.3.1 Introspective data: advantages and limitations

Schütze (1996), the major methodological study of the use of data in generative theorizing, provides six key reasons for the use of judgments of grammaticality. The first three are theory-independent: They provide data not obtainable from spontaneous speech or recorded corpora; they provide negative information, that is, information about what is not possible for the speaker; and they allow for the easy removal of irrelevant data, such as slips of the tongue, false starts, etc. The more controversial reasons for their use are that they allow the researcher to abstract away from the communicative function of language and thereby to focus on the mental grammar as a structural system; the factors affecting judgments tend to be less mysterious than those affecting use; and by providing an alternative path to the grammar from language use, "we have a basis on which to search for the common core that underlies both kinds of behavior" (Schütze 1996:180). These latter three reasons presuppose some degree of autonomy of the representational aspect of language from the communicative – a presupposition not shared by all of the world's linguists (see below, Section 3.5).

One frequently heard critique of introspective judgments is their putative inherent instability. But such is apparently not the case. Cowart (1997) took some constructions that have loomed large in theoretical discussions (examples involving Subjacency and *that*-trace violations, binding relations, and so on) and showed that there was a stable pattern of response to them among his subjects. That is, their relative acceptability remained the same with different groups of subjects.

It goes without saying that the greatest danger inherent in introspection is that the researcher might be unconsciously led to judge the acceptability of a sentence based on the desired theoretical outcome, rather than completely 'objectively.' As pointed out in Derwing (1973) and by many critics who followed him, an introspective judgment is no more and no less than an uncontrolled experiment. William Labov drew what for him was the "painfully obvious conclusion ... that linguists cannot continue to produce theory and data at the same time" (Labov 1972:199).

How common is it for linguists to (unconsciously) bias their judgments in favor of the theoretical proposal they are in the process of establishing? It is not clear. As argued at length in Newmeyer (1983: Chapter 2), many debates in the history of the field that appear to be data disputes are in reality anything but that. For example, in early generative syntax, the interpretive differences between actives and passives containing quantified subjects and objects was a matter of hot theoretical dispute. Consider, by way of illustration, the following pair (see also Chapter 2, ex. (14)):

(13) a. every person reads some books
      b. some books are read by every person

Chomsky (1957), in arguing for a model in which transformational rules did not necessarily preserve meaning, maintained that the meanings of (13a) and (13b) differ: In the former, *every* has wide scope over *some* and in the latter *some* has wide scope over *every*. A few years later, Katz and Postal (1964) pointed to the *ambiguity* of each of the two sentences as support for their view that such rules are indeed meaning preserving. In the following decade Lakoff's (1971) key Quantifier Lowering transformation demanded a single reading for each sentence and subsequent work in the Extended Standard Theory sometimes assigned each sentence a single representation at Logical Form and sometimes a double representation. But I really do not think that we have an example here of linguists cooking the data to fit their theoretical prejudices. As I recall the debates, all parties were agreed on the data: Both interpretations could be imposed on both sentences, but the reading where the first quantifier has higher scope is preferred without a special context that would attribute higher scope to the second. In the absence of a fleshed out discourse-pragmatic theory interacting with a purely grammatical one, linguists were "prepared to let the grammar itself decide" (Chomsky 1957:14) whether the syntax generated or did not generate structures corresponding to each possible meaning.

There are certainly cases, however, in which theories are built with appeal to the most unclear and most controversial data. Schütze (1996) provides one example. Lasnik and Saito (1984) consider it a major selling point of their theory of proper government that it accounts for the ambiguity of sentence (14):

(14)   Why do you think that he left?

In their view, *why* can be understood as questioning the reason for thinking or questioning the reason for leaving. Its putative ambiguity was a crucial piece of data in their analysis. But for Aoun et al. (1987), a major advantage of their account of proper government is that it accounts for the lack of ambiguity of the very same sentence. In this case, I see no obvious appeal to pragmatic factors to explain the difference in judgments, though of course they cannot be ruled out of the realm of possibility.

Schütze emphasizes that introspective judgments are indispensable to the linguist, but far from sufficient, and remarks that "it should be obvious that considerable care and effort must be put into the elicitation of grammaticality judgments if we are to stand a chance of getting consistent, meaningful, and accurate results" (1996:171). He concludes his study with some useful concrete suggestions involving elicitation procedures for judgments and their statistical analysis and interpretation and points to three publications that are 'exemplary' in their use of judgment data within the framework of theoretical argumentation: Grimshaw and Rosen (1990); Carden and Dietrich (1981); and Gerken and Bever (1986).

3.3.2 The richness of conversational data

Introspective data is criticized not only for its supposed unreliability, but also for its supposed irrelevance. A sizeable percentage of linguists feel that since most sentences made up by linguists are (putatively) never likely to be uttered in a real conversation, they have no bearing on the nature of grammar. For example:

> The data in generative grammar analyses are almost always disembodied sentences that analysts have made up ad hoc, ... rather than utterances produced by real people in real discourse situations ... Only the focus on naturally occurring discourse has the potential to lead to descriptions and explanations of linguistic phenomena that are psychologically plausible. (Tomasello 1998:xiii)

What these critics advocate is a near-exclusive focus on natural conversation.

Since, at least in their view, language is used more in conversation than for any other purpose, it stands to reason, they would say, that the properties of grammars should reflect the properties of conversation. As Sandra Thompson concluded an article:

> I hope to have demonstrated the heavy reliance of grammar on the goals of the communicative event. That is, understanding grammar is inseparable from understanding the principles by which language users decide how to package an entire discourse.   (Thompson 1983:64)

In other words, the complex abstract structures of generative grammar are an artifact of using example sentences that, they say, nobody would ever actually use. The conclusion that some critics draw is that if one focuses on naturally occurring conversation, grammar will turn out to be a collection of stock memorized phrases – 'formulas' or 'fragments,' as they are often called – and very simple constructions.

An examination of the Fisher English Training Transcripts reveals that nothing like that is the case (for details, see Newmeyer 2010a). These transcripts form a 170MB corpus of over 11,000 complete telephone conversations, each lasting up to 10 minutes and containing over 6,700,000 words. Conversational speech reveals a depth of syntactic knowledge that is absolutely stunning. Consider naturally occurring examples of long-distance *wh*-movement (15a) and embedded gaps in relative clauses (15b):

(15) a. B: so **what do you think that um we should do** um as far as w- we're standing right now with our position
b. B: you know **when i move away and get the things that i want to have** and retire early and enjoy you know what i mean

To produce and comprehend utterances like these, one must hold in mental storage a place for an unexpressed direct object in a different clause, and link a fronted *wh*-element or lexical antecedent to that place. We are not talking about 'fragments' or 'formulas' here, but a sophisticated engine for representing grammatical knowledge.

Anaphoric relations (see Chapter 15) are among the most recalcitrant construction types to find in corpora, given the difficulty in formulating the right search criteria. But persistence provides some interesting (and perhaps surprising) results. For example, one sometimes hears it said that cataphors (i.e., backwards anaphors) occur only in educated speech or writing. But in fact they are found in ordinary conversation, and both in pronominal and elliptical form:

(16) a. A: **when their sons die with with money he rewards the parents** and and the parents are quite happy about it
b. A: um overseas we **i don't know why we don't but everybody has flags here** we have huge flags on the street

There are also examples of both forward and backward sluicing (see Chapter 19) in conversation:

(17) a. A: i know i know i'm going to get married some time **but i don't know when**
b. A: **i just i don't know why but** i don't usually get sick in the winter time

The question is why so many linguists denigrate the linguistic resources of ordinary speakers. The answer is in part the small size of many of the corpora that are used. For example, one of the major book-length studies of conversation, Miller and Weinert (1998), limits itself to an English corpus of only 50,000 words. Perhaps not surprisingly, all of the following were missing:

(18) a. adverbial clauses of concession introduced by *although*
b. adverbial clauses of reason introduced by *since*
c. gapping
d. conditional clauses signaled by subject–auxiliary inversion
e. accusative–infinitive sequences ('Exceptional Case Marking')
f. gerunds with possessive subjects
g. gerunds with an auxiliary
h. initial participial clauses preceding a main clause
i. infinitives in subject position
j. infinitives with auxiliaries

Yet all of these occur in the Fisher corpora:

(19) a. adverbial clauses of concession introduced by *although*
B: **although they may not agree with war** then they are going to support the u._s. government and they're going to support the u._s. soldiers
b. adverbial clauses of reason introduced by *since*
A: **since i've never been much of a power grabber myself** i don't really understand people that that are
c. gapping
A: but at the same time you might not have not being in that situation might have had gave you a different outlook on the world on the world and life and such and **and me the same** so you know while we might feel like um you know we wish we had done things differently if we had things we might not feel the same way that we do now
d. conditional clauses signaled by subject–auxiliary inversion
A: **had i known then what i know now**
e. accusative–infinitive sequences ('Exceptional Case Marking')
A: um **i consider myself to be a pretty open minded person** and you know i'm friends with all kinds of different people
f. gerunds with possessive subjects
A: you know **going back to his firing of his economic advisors** you know he knows this isn't going to be

g. gerunds with an auxiliary
B: i was kinda surprised they'd i could i could fit in **because of my having been born in england** i i i thought it would just be americans

h. initial participial clauses preceding a main clause
A: **hoping i never get that far** i just wanna make sure that i don't end up on every committee and directing the choir and [laughter] you know organizing the bake sales and whatever

i. infinitives in subject position
A: to yeah to **to get to where they need to do so sunday** would kinda be like the first day of the festivities or saturday night sunday and then monday maybe a goodbye breakfast and all the family members are going back to

j. infinitives with auxiliaries
A: yeah you know **i wouldn't have wanted to to have brought - em up in a in a Christian controlled**

On the basis of the absence of these construction types from their database, Miller and Weinert conclude:

> The properties and constraints established over the past thirty years by Chomskyans are based on sentences that occur neither in speech nor in writing or only occur in writing. (Miller and Weinert 1998:379)

and then go on to question whether such "properties and constraints" could form part of the internalized competence of the average native speaker of English. But given that the average speaker utters about 16,000 words *per day* (Mehl *et al.* 2007), it is clear that nothing should be concluded from a corpus of 50,000 words.

The differences between the grammatical structures found in spontaneous conversation and those in more literary genres are almost entirely quantitative, rather than qualitative. Biber (1988) looks at sixty-seven grammatical features of English, and calculates their frequency of occurrence in twenty-three different genres. Only three of these features failed to occur in face-to-face conversations at a frequency of less than 0.1 times per thousand words:

(20) Rare features in the Biber (1988) corpus:
   a. present participial clauses (e.g. *stuffing his mouth with cookies, Joe ran out the door*)
   b. past participial clauses (e.g. *built in a single week, the house would stand for fifty years*)
   c. split infinitives (e.g. *he wants to convincingly prove that*)

All three features were rare in academic prose as well: 1.3, 0.4, and 0.0 times per thousand words respectively in that genre. And all three occur in the Fisher corpora:

Table 3.1. The most frequent grammatical features in two English genres (Biber 1988)

Rank	Face-to-face conversations	Academic prose
1	nouns	nouns
2	present tense	prepositions
3	adverbs	attributive adjectives
4	prepositions	present tense
5	first person pronouns	adverbs
6	contractions	type-token ratio[a]
7	type-token ratio	nominalizations
8	attributive adjectives	BE as main verb
9	BE as main verb	past tense
10	past tense	agentless passive

[a] That is, the number of different lexical items in a text, as a percentage.

(21) a. B: **having angst** i don't have any like firsthand experience with separations or anything cause i mean
b. A: but **compared to the comedies** now it it's tame
c. B: right and they tried **they tried to really make it so people wouldn't get a long**

Table 3.1 gives the ten most frequent grammatical features in the two genres.

The only features that made the top ten in face-to-face conversations, but not in academic prose were (unsurprisingly) first person pronouns and contractions.

In short, there is little reason to believe that a focus on naturally occurring conversation would lead to a grammatical theory that is substantially different from ones that are constructed primarily using introspective data. One might object that usage-based data *in principle* would lead to a very different looking theory than one based on introspective data, given that generative grammars capture a cognitive capacity, rather than the ability to communicate. Such an objection cannot be dismissed out of hand, but it needs to be supported by hard evidence. As I see things, however, no one form of data is theoretically privileged with respect to any other, as far as grammar construction is concerned. Introspective data, conversational data, experimental data, data from ancient manuscripts, and so on all have their place – and their pitfalls. It is interesting to note that Chomsky, despite his views cited above, made fairly critical remarks about the use of introspective data in some of his earlier work:

> It is also quite clear that the major goal of grammatical theory is to replace this obscure reliance on intuition by some rigorous and objective approach. (Chomsky 1957:94)

Perhaps the day will come when the kinds of data that we now can obtain in abundance will be insufficient to resolve deeper questions concerning the structure of language. (Chomsky 1965:21)

Has that day come? Perhaps it has. Only time will tell.

While all imaginable sources of data are welcome in the construction of a comprehensive grammatical theory, in my view it is risky to adduce data from one grammatical domain in an analysis of the properties of a different domain. To that end, the next section argues that semantic data have no relevance to considerations of syntactic theory.

3.3.3 Semantic data and syntactic autonomy

Throughout most of its history, what has distinguished generative syntax from virtually all other approaches to grammar is the hypothesis of the autonomy of syntax (AS):

(22) Autonomy of syntax: The rules (principles, constraints, etc.) that determine the combinatorial possibilities of the formal elements of a language make no reference to constructs from meaning, discourse, or language use.

Chomsky put forward three distinct arguments for AS in his earliest writings. The first is pure methodological caution: Since the nature of the form–meaning interface is one of the most difficult problems in linguistics, the worst thing would be to presuppose a semantic basis for syntax. The second is that the empirical evidence points to AS, that is to a purely formal system. In language after language, we find formal generalizations that do not map smoothly onto generalizations from meaning or use. The auxiliary rules in *Syntactic Structures* were Chomsky's first and most famous example (Chomsky 1957: Chapter 5). And third, we can use form to get at meaning: "In general, as syntactic description becomes deeper, what appear to be semantic questions fall increasingly within its scope ..." (Chomsky 1964b:936). Take the passive in *Syntactic Structures*. Chomsky motivated the transformation purely on its formal properties (the occurrence of the morpheme *be+en*, its limitation to transitive verbs, and so on). Contrary to what many believe, the rough paraphrase relation between actives and passives was *not* one of Chomsky's motivations. In fact, he went on to argue that the fact that transformations are to a large degree meaning-preserving was an empirical discovery. He could hardly have claimed to have explained the meaning-preserving properties of transformations if he had used paraphrase to motivate transformations in the first place.

Consider a later example of deeper syntactic description encompassing what has traditionally been called 'semantics.' A highly constrained theory of movement rules led to the Specified Subject Condition and Tensed-S Condition, which led to the trace theory of movement rules, which led to the possibility of surface interpretation of meaning (all of this was in

Chomsky 1973), which led to capturing certain aspects of quantifier scope structurally, as in May (1977). Notice the methodology here. There was no starting assumption that it was within the domain of syntax to explain facts about quantifier scope (as was the case in Generative Semantics) or even that quantifier scope data was necessarily food for syntactic theory. Rather, each step of syntactic analysis seemed to lead closer and closer to a syntactic treatment of aspects of quantifier scope.

In other words, in early work in generative syntax, one generally assumed a methodological counterpart to AS:

(23) Autonomy of syntax (methodological counterpart): Semantic judgments (i.e., judgments of paraphrase, ambiguity, scope, nuances of aspect and the nature of events, etc.) should not in general be used as data in the construction of a syntactic theory.

There is a nice quote from *Aspects of the Theory of Syntax* affirming AS, both in its theoretical and methodological variants:

> For the moment, I see no reason to modify the view, expressed in Chomsky (1957) and elsewhere, that although, obviously, semantic considerations are relevant to the construction of general linguistic theory ... there is, at present, no way to show that semantic considerations play a role in the choice of the syntactic or phonological component of a grammar or that semantic features (in any significant sense of this term) play a role in the functioning of the syntactic or phonological rules.
> (Chomsky 1965:226)

Since the 1980s, AS has become progressively weakened, both theoretically and methodologically, as indicated in (24a–f):

(24) Examples of the theoretical and/or methodological weakening of AS in mainstream generative syntax:
   a. The Theta Criterion (Chomsky 1981), which demands that the syntax 'know' which syntactic elements bear Θ-roles and which do not.
   b. The idea that 'c-selection' (essentially, subcategorization) is derivable from 's-selection' (essentially, the thematic properties of the items involved) (Chomsky 1986b).
   c. Uniformity of Theta Assignment Hypothesis (UTAH) (Baker 1988). Identical thematic relationships between items are represented by identical structural relationships between those items at the level of D-structure.
   d. Lexical decomposition, which derives semantically complex predicates via syntactic movement operations (Baker 1988, 1993, Hale and Keyser 1993, 1997, Borer 2003)
   e. The cartography program (Rizzi 1997, Cinque 1999), which appeals in part to semantic motivation for syntactic projections:

In fact, a restrictive theory should force a one-to-one relation between position and interpretation (p. 20) ... each projection has a specific semantic interpretation. (p. 132)   (Cinque 1999)

f. The triggering of movement (and/or the licensing of configurations) by semantic properties of heads (Rizzi 1991/1996, 1997, Haegeman 1995, 1997):

Syntactic movement ... must be triggered by the satisfaction of certain quasi-morphological requirements of heads. ... *Such features have an interpretive import (Wh, Neg, Top, Foc, ...)*: they determine the interpretation of the category bearing them and of its immediate constituents ..., function as scope markers for phrases with the relevant quantificational force in a local configuration, etc. ...   (Rizzi 1997:282; emphasis added)

The Negative Criterion appeals to the semantic-syntactic feature NEG.   (Haegeman 1997a:116)

One might wonder whether all of (24a–f) are not just good examples of syntax becoming deeper and incorporating semantics. In fact, they are not. What we have in all of (24a–f) are the workings of a dramatically changed theoretical outlook, which in some ways is the antithesis of the methodological counterpart to AS in (23). (24a–f) do not illustrate pushing back the frontiers of syntax and thereby encompassing aspects of meaning. What they illustrate is the assumption that it is the task of syntax to account for semantic judgments. The negative consequence is that it becomes more and more difficult to capture purely formal generalizations.

Let me start with an example involving English modal auxiliaries (see also Chapter 20) to illustrate my point. There are profound structural generalizations governing the modals (for details, see Huddleston and Pullum 2002):

(25) a. They occur before all other auxiliaries (*must have gone*; **have must gone*)
b. They do not occur in sequence (in Standard English) (**might could*)
c. They take neither the infinitive marker nor inflection (**to would; *she woulded*)
d. They must be followed by non-finite form of the verb or auxiliary (**I must had gone*)
e. They invert in questions and are followed by the negative morpheme (*could she run?; she could not run*)
f. All of (25a–e) apply to modals both in their root and epistemic senses: i. Root *must* = obligation, epistemic *must* = consequence; ii. Root *may* = permission, epistemic *may* = possibility; iii. Root *can* = ability, epistemic *can* = possibility.

Now, consider some of the current work on English modals. We could take the work of Tim Stowell and Karen Zagona as exemplars (Stowell 2004, Zagona 2007, 2008 since it is the most insightful as well as the most cited. In this work, surprisingly, capturing (25a-f) plays the most minor role. Rather, the goal is to find ways to represent the subtle scopal differences between root and epistemic modals structurally. So for Stowell the goal is to explain the fact that epistemically construed modals and root modals do not pattern alike in how they are interpreted relative to tense. Roughly speaking, the generalization is that tense can take scope over root modals but not over epistemic modals. Zagona argues that modals can be merged above or below Tense, and their position relative to tense determines whether they will have an epistemic or root reading. These semantic differences between roots and epistemics are real, so any comprehensive theory needs to take them seriously. But capturing them in terms of Merge order or difference in projection renders it all the more difficult to account for the fact that in terms of their formal properties, roots and epistemics are just about the same. What I mean is that the more syntactic complexity that one attributes to structures containing modals, the more difficult it becomes to provide an elegant account of (25a-f).

One might raise the objection that the above arguments are a priori. What principle, one might ask, makes it evident that the computational system should handle, say, the syntagmatic position of modals as a higher priority than accounting for their scopal properties? My reply is based on the fact that there are phenomena that are clearly syntactic, those that are ambiguously syntactic or semantic (or part of a system interfacing the two), and phenomena that are clearly semantic. The diagram in (26) illustrates:

(26)

(A) PHENOMENA THAT ARE CLEARLY SYNTACTIC	(B) PHENOMENA THAT ARE AMBIGUOUSLY SYNTACTIC OR SEMANTIC (OR PART OF A SYSTEM INTERFACING THE TWO)	(C) PHENOMENA THAT ARE CLEARLY SEMANTIC
*John has must go(ne) is an ungrammatical sentence of English	Tense can take scope over root modals but not over epistemic modals	*John will go* entails *John can go*

A reasonable methodological principle is that any adequate model of the computational system of a language has the obligation to account for phenomena of type (A) before those of type (B). Otherwise put, a model of the computational system that accounts for (B), while rendering an account of (A) more difficult, is inadequate.

We find the same problem cross-linguistically. That is, we find the positing of semantically based projections that render the purely formal generalizations all but impossible to capture. Consider the Neg Phrase projection. The default assumption now is that where we have semantic negation we have a Neg Phrase projection (see Ouhalla 1991b). But such an analysis risks to obscure the formal similarities between negatives in a particular language and other categories with the same formal properties (different for different languages). For example, negation can be a complement-taking verb, as in Tongan (Churchward 1953:56, Payne 1985:208); an auxiliary, as in Estonian (Blevins 2007); a derivational affix, as in Turkish (Payne 1985:227); a noun, as in Evenki (Payne 1985:228); and an adverb, as in English (Jackendoff 1972, Baker 1991, Ernst 1992, Kim 2000, Newmeyer 2006). The fact that the semantic properties of negatives are quite different from those of the other categories mentioned – in particular the fact that the negative particle functions as an operator – gives strong credence to the autonomy of syntax and illustrates that a Neg Phrase node, motivated almost exclusively on the basis of semantic data, might not be the optimal hypothesis.

It is an interesting question why syntax has come to be as semanticized as it has in recent years. This trend is partly due to conceptions and their implementations that were novel to the Minimalist Program, (27a–c) in particular:

(27) a. There is no optionality in grammar; hence elements move only when they are 'required to.' (Chomsky 1995c)
b. Movement must be triggered by a feature on a functional head. (Chomsky 1995c)
c. "In a perfectly designed language, each feature would be semantic or phonetic, not merely a device to create a position or to facilitate computation." (Chomsky 2000a:109)

(27a), in effect, requires that seemingly optional variants have different underlying structures. Since few if any structural variants have the same semantic properties (broadly defined), it seemed reasonable to locate their structural differences in projections with direct semantic relevance. But if projections are semantically defined and, as in (27b), movement is triggered by features of projections, then we are a step closer to the idea that movement is semantically motivated. The quote in (27c) is the icing on the cake. Linguists might disagree with each other profoundly about what a 'perfectly designed language' might look like. But if we do happen to agree with (27c), then the inevitable dynamic is one of searching for a semantic motivation for any and all syntactic operations.

But in fact I do not think that conceptions unique to the Minimalist Program have been the driving force in leading syntax to an anti-autonomist methodology. The trend was well under-way before the first Minimalist publication. I think that the basic problem is that throughout most of its history there has been no formal semantic theory that has meshed comfortably with mainstream generative syntax. So the tendency has been to 'go with what we know,' that is, to expand syntax to encompass what might seem naturally to be the domain of semantic theory.

3.4 Non-P-and-P generative approaches

All formal generative approaches to syntax outside of P-and-P have their roots in the lexicalist hypothesis, first proposed in Chomsky (1970a). In that paper, Chomsky took on the first trend to 'semanticize' syntactic structures, namely that undertaken by the framework of Generative Semantics (Lakoff 1971). For generative semanticists, semantic structure and underlying syntactic structure were identical. The lexicalist hypothesis challenged Generative Semantics by prohibiting the syntactic component from performing word-creating operations, for example, from relating transformationally items like the verb *refuse* and the noun *refusal*. The resultant deep structures hence ended up being much closer to the surface than those that Generative Semantics posited at the time. Current formal alternatives to Chomskyan theory represent the lexicalist hypothesis taken to it logical conclusion. That is, they abandon the transformational component altogether, positing no syntactic structures more abstract than those found on the surface. Most such models have what is called a 'constraint-based architecture.' In this view, grammars are based on the notion of 'constraint-satisfaction.' Instead of surface structures resulting from transformations of one structural representation into another, they are a product of constraints (or rules) that interact with each other to derive surface representations directly. So rather than employing a rule deriving passives from actives, say, they propose relations among structures occurring on the surface. Also, most non-Chomskyan formal models have adopted some form of 'model-theoretic semantics,' an approach within truth-conditional semantics in which, by means of a model, an arbitrary sentence of a language is assigned a truth value with respect to a possible state of affairs. This approach to semantics, whose impetus for linguistics was pioneered by Richard Montague (1970, 1974), provided ways of characterizing meanings directly in terms of surface structure. That result was also instrumental in leading many linguists to abandon transformational rules.

In terms of their goals and methodology, however, the alternative formal models do not appear to differ significantly from more mainstream P-and-P models. For example, an introduction to Lexical-Functional Grammar prioritizes "the search for a universal design of grammar" (Bresnan 2001:3), which is considered to be "Chomsky's great achievement." And the data utilized by this model appear to be mostly introspective or consultant-derived. Head-driven Phrase Structure Grammar (HPSG) is slightly more agnostic on the universalist goal. A recent introduction to that framework notes that its goal is to propose "constructs that *may* have universal application to human language" (Sag et al. 2003:21; emphasis added) and states that its "position is that the grammatical structures we have been developing in this text are well suited to a theory of universal grammar, whether or not this theory turns out to be highly task-specific, and that the explicitness of our proposals can be helpful in resolving the task-specificity question" (pp. 306–307). This model as well advocates the use of introspective data, though it cautions about the risks thereby entailed.

Several related approaches share the name 'Construction Grammar' (see also Sections 25.6.2 and 26.2.2.1). What they have in common is the idea that a language is a set of constructions, namely pairings of form and meaning that are not wholly predictable from their component parts. By that definition, simple words are constructions, given that they embody the notion of the 'arbitrariness of the sign' (Saussure 1916/1966). Idioms are hence constructions as well, since (by definition) their meanings are not compositionally determined from their structures. But constructions can also be broader in scope, and hence more abstract. For example, the 'Ditransitive Construction' encompasses all sentences that contain a verb followed by two NP objects, such as *John gave Mary a book, I envy you your success,* and *We elected her president* (for details, see Goldberg 1995). Models of Construction Grammar run the gamut from those with a strong affinity to HPSG (Fillmore et al. 1988) to those that resemble versions of cognitive linguistics (see below) in their basic assumptions (Goldberg 2006). Hence no sweeping statement is possible regarding the goals and methods of Construction Grammar.

3.5 Cognitive–Functional Linguistics

Most of the non-generative syntacticians of the world work in some version of Cognitive Linguistics or Functional Linguistics. Both constitute a broad family of approaches that overlap to such a degree that it is common to refer to the ensemble as 'Cognitive–Functional Linguistics.' Advocates of these approaches claim that they take "a basically psychological approach to grammar – as opposed to the formal mathematical approach of generative grammar" (Tomasello 1998:xiii). Linguistic structures are said to derive from "communicative function," since "language evolved for purposes of communication phylogenetically, and it is learned for purposes of communication ontogenetically" (p. xiv). In this view, cognitive–functional linguists, as opposed to generative grammarians, explain "linguistic skills ... in fundamentally the same terms as other complex cognitive skills" since in their approach "the structures of language are taken directly from human cognition" (p. xx).

Many cognitive-functional linguists, at least rhetorically, concern themselves with what is possible in human language. In the words of a leading practitioner:

> Linguistic theory of any approach, 'formalist' or 'functional-typological,' has as its central question, what is a possible human language? This question can in turn be paraphrased as: of the logically possible types of languages, how do we account for what types actually exist?
>
> (Croft 1990:44)

And Shibatani and Bynon (1995:19) write that "in a truly functional approach...the range of the observed variation and its internal structures defined by crosslinguistic generalizations delimit the range of possible (segments of) human languages." In other words, such cognitive-functional linguists are united with generative grammarians in the ultimate goal of linguistic theory. That which separates the different orientations is to be found at the level of specifics, in particular whether UG provides an innate module containing purely grammatical constructs. Cognitive-functional linguists in general envisage grammar "as a sub-component of a ... system in which the human linguistic capacity is linked to epistemic, logical, perceptual, and social capacities" (Siewierska 1991:1), rather than being the semi-autonomous formal entity of most generative approaches. For that reason, one rarely finds reference to the construct 'Universal Grammar' *per se* in cognitive-functional writings. Nevertheless, many adherents of this school see it as a major goal of linguistic theory to distinguish the possible from the probable.

On the other hand, there is a growing tendency within Cognitive-Functional Linguistics to reject outright the universalist goal. For example Dryer 1996, 1997) argues that structural categories cannot be equated across languages and that grammatical relations and word classes in a cross-linguistic sense are "at most a convenient fiction" (Dryer 1997:117).[12] In the latter paper Dryer points to the difficulty in identifying unambiguously the construct 'Subject' in languages such as Dyirbal, Acehnese, Cree, and Cebuano. He concludes that this difficulty arises in large part from the (in his view, mistaken) idea that there is a universal basis to the notion 'grammatical relation' that allows a Subject in one language to be identified as representing the 'same' theoretical construct as in another. Along the same lines, Croft has now concluded that "Universal Grammar does not consist of an inventory of universal categories and relations available to all speakers" (Croft 2001:34) and Martin Haspelmath has written a major piece on the non-existence of what he calls "pre-established categories" (Haspelmath 2007). Dryer and others argue that exceptionless universals are so rare that linguists' time would be better spent formulating statistical universals than searching for the absolute (or even parameterized) universals of UG.

It is interesting to note that the typological goal has in general played a much more important role in Cognitive-Functional Linguistics than in generative grammar. Indeed, most functional linguists do not make a distinction between the universalist and the typological goals, regarding the typological patterns found in language as providing the best insight into the nature of the language faculty:

> In our view, language typology lies at the very center of linguistics in that it serves directly the goals of the discipline itself: to explain, as well as describe, the facts of natural language structure. Language typology not only provides a description of the range of variation among natural languages, but also addresses itself to the *explanatory* task.
> (Hammond et al. 1988:1; emphasis in original)

Joseph Greenberg was at one and the same time the founder of modern typological studies and one of the pioneers of functional linguistics. For example, his classic paper, Greenberg (1963), which was as important for typology as was Chomsky's *Syntactic Structures* for generative syntax, went further than merely to point out the typological correlations among linguistic elements. Its last section, 'Conclusion: Some general principles,' attempts to explain why certain typological patterns exist. For example, the predominance of noun-adjective and subject-verb order is attributed to "a general tendency for comment to follow topic" (p. 100). And three universals that exemplify a "general tendency to mark the ends of units rather than the beginning" is "probably related to the fact that we always know when someone has just begun speaking, but it is our sad experience that without some marker we don't know when the speaker will finish" (p. 103).

As far as cognitive-functional methodology is concerned, I think that it is fair to say that there is a significant disparity between theory and practice. Most cognitive-functional linguists scorn the use of introspective judgments (as is indicated by the Tomasello and Thompson quotes in Section 3.3.2 above). However, in the actual practice of a great majority of such linguists, introspective data plays as important a role as it does for the majority of generativists.[13]

3.6 Conclusion

All generative syntacticians advocate the universalist goal, namely to characterize what a 'possible human language' might be, and the particularist goal, namely, to provide formal grammars of individual languages. Not all, however, share the typological goal, namely, to provide a grammar-internal explanation of why some types of grammars are more common than other types. For cognitive–functional linguists, the particularist and typological goals are paramount. Some, but not all, share the universalist goal. As far as methodology is concerned, generative syntacticians have generally relied on introspective data. While such data are not totally unproblematic, there is little reason to believe that a reliance on purely conversational data would lead to theories with significantly different properties. Cognitive–functional linguists tend to prioritize conversational and experimental data over introspective, though their day-to-day practice generally relies on the latter.

Notes

1. I am greatly indebted to Marcel den Dikken and Ricardo Otheguy for their detailed comments on an earlier draft of this chapter. Errors are my own.
2. The term 'biolinguistics' has been enshrined as the name of a journal devoted to "exploring theoretical linguistics that takes the biological foundations of language seriously" (Boeckx and Grohmann 2010). However, linguists outside the Chomskyan tradition (narrow defined) are almost universally skeptical that Chomsky's current approach has any right to describe its orientation as 'biological' (see especially Evans and Levinson 2009). Certainly no one would question the fact that generative linguists have a long way to go to achieve the success enjoyed by biologists, say by specifying the regions of DNA associated with putative grammatical universals.
3. For recent rebuttals to Chomsky's argument, see Pullum and Scholz (2002) and Reali and Christiansen (2005); for defenses, see Boeckx (2006) and Kam *et al*. (2008).
4. As Chomsky notes, "... the commonsense notion of language has a crucial sociopolitical dimension. ... That any coherent account can be given of 'language' in this sense is doubtful; surely none has been offered or even seriously attempted. Rather, all scientific approaches have simply abandoned these elements of what is called 'language' in common usage" (Chomsky 1986b:15). Grammatical theorists hence do not study 'languages,' but rather 'grammars,' that is, the internalized systems of speakers. Confusingly, however, it is commonplace in technical writing to refer to 'nominalizations in English,' 'the voiceless vowels of Japanese,' etc., rather than to 'nominalizations in the grammar of Mary Smith, a member of the sociopolitical community of (self-described) "English speakers",' 'voiceless vowels in the grammar of Tatsuya Tanaka, a member of the community of (self-described) "Japanese speakers",' etc. That is, one generally assumes that the grammar of one individual in a speech community shares relevant properties with other individuals in that speech community. The question of the

degree to which such an assumption can be maintained is an important one, albeit one that is typically ignored by generative theoreticians.

5. The word 'functional' in the technical term 'functional category' should not be confused with 'functional' in the sense of 'useful,' 'externally motivated,' etc. See the following section for discussion of the latter sense of 'functional,' as applied to grammatical elements.

6. 'The values of each parameter form no continuum and in the ideal case just amount to two (Longobardi 2003:108). However, non-binary parameters have been proposed, as in Manzini and Wexler's (1987) treatment of binding domains.

7. For discussion of the distinction between macroparameters and microparameters, see Chapters 4 and 25.

8. Richard Kayne, one of the primary advocates of parametric theory, has written that "every functional element made available by UG is associated with some syntactic parameter" (Kayne 2005:11). That alone would require the postulation of well over one hundred parameters, given the number of functional categories that have been proposed.

9. The idea that independently motivated processing principles relieve grammatical theory *per se* from the burden of accounting for many complex distributional facts about grammars has its origins in Chomsky and Miller (1963) and its early development in work in the 1970s by Thomas Bever (Bever 1970, Bever and Langendoen 1972) and Susumu Kuno (Kuno 1972, 1973a).

10. Ricardo Otheguy (personal communication) points out a that a functional explanation for a particular phenomenon does not preclude an innatist one. The Baldwin Effect (Hinton and Nowlan 1987), for example, allows for the evolution of neural mechanisms that encode (functionally) beneficial attributes/behavior in a population that has a fair amount of plasticity at birth in brain wiring. Hence, there exists a mechanism by which UG principles might have become biologized without increasing the survival and reproductive possibilities for any particular individual who, by chance, happened to have acquired one or more of them. The Baldwin Effect has been identified as a means by which functionally motivated grammatical constraints might have become innate (see Newmeyer 1991, Kirby and Hurford 1997, Kirby 1998, Bresnan and Aissen 2002). The Head Parameter would thus be a hard-wired grammatical principle grounded ultimately in processing. Other processing-based generalizations, however, are much less plausibly incorporable into UG (for discussion, see Newmeyer 2010b: Section 3.2).

11. Though pressure from linguists outside the generative tradition and from more experimentally oriented generativists has led to an increased concern with methodological issues. A case in point is the special issue of the journal *Theoretical Linguistics* (33:3, 2007) devoted to

data in generative grammar, with a number of generative contributors. Other noteworthy contributions to methodology from generative linguists are Schütze (1996), Cowart (1997), and Gibson and Fedorenko (2010a/2010b).

12. The rejection of universals of grammar was a hallmark of American Post-Bloomfieldian structuralism, where such a position followed directly from the empiricist assumptions of that approach. For example, Fries (1952) chose to call the English categories Noun, Verb, Adjective, and Adverb 'Class 1,' 'Class 2,' 'Class 3,' and 'Class 4' respectively, in order to emphasize their language-particularity.

13. As noted above, Tomasello (1998:xiii) deplores the "disembodied sentences" that are used in generative grammar. Nevertheless, only two contributors to this edited volume present segments of natural discourse, neither filling even a page of text.

Part II

Modern generative approaches to the study of sentence structure

4

Principles and Parameters theory and Minimalism

Željko Bošković

The central problem for linguistic theory, often referred to as Plato's problem, is how children are able to acquire language despite the impoverished nature of the linguistic data they are exposed to. The Principles and Parameters approach provides a viable solution to Plato's problem. The basic idea is that children are biologically endowed with a set of principles, which are invariant across languages, and a set of parameters, which provide limited options for language variation and which can be easily set on the basis of the linguistic data children are exposed to. These principles and parameters comprise what is referred to as Universal Grammar (UG), a genetic endowment which helps children acquire language and as such represents an answer to Plato's problem in the domain of language.

Principles are not subject to language variation, they hold across all languages with equal force. As an illustration, the Theta Criterion (which may be at least partially subsumable under a broader Principle of Full Interpretation, see below) is responsible for the ungrammaticality of *John is likely that Mary is sleeping*. The example contains an argument, namely *John*, which does not bear a theta-role, in violation of the Theta Criterion, which requires that all arguments bear theta-roles (as well as that all theta-roles be assigned). By providing options, parameters account for a good amount of language variation. The Head Parameter is one such parameter, posited early on in the Government and Binding Theory. According to this parameter, languages differ regarding whether their heads precede or follow complements. Thus, in English both verbs and prepositions precede their complements, while in Japanese they follow them (but see the discussion of Kayne 1994 below). Borer (1984a), however, restricts the notion of parameters by assuming that all parameters are lexical, which reduces parametric variation to differences among lexical items, a further restriction being that the variation is tied only to differences among functional elements (i.e. grammatical elements like inflection).

4.1 Government and Binding Theory

Government and Binding theory (GB) is the version of the Principles and Parameters approach that was dominant in the 1980s. GB is a modular theory which divides grammar into a number of distinct subcomponents with a powerful transformational component based on the rule Move α, which in principle allows any element to move anywhere at any point. Overgeneration is handled by having various modules filter out the undesired structures. Four levels of representation are posited where conditions of UG apply, filtering out the illicit structures: D-structure (DS), S-structure (SS), Logical Form (LF), and Phonological Form (PF). DS, SS, and LF together constitute the syntactic levels of representation. The central grammatical relation is government, a powerful grammar-internal (in a sense that it is not determined by anything outside of the grammar) relation that crucially holds in a number of otherwise distinct modules.

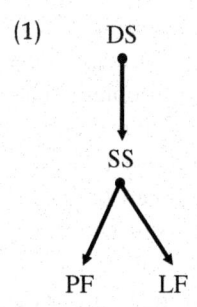

(1) DS
     ↓
     SS
    ╱ ╲
   ↙   ↘
  PF   LF

As an illustration, consider the working of the Case module (see Chapter 17), which determines the distribution of NPs. There are characteristic structural positions that are tied to particular cases; thus, the subject position of a finite clause licenses nominative and the object position accusative case, as in *He likes her*. (The relevant distinctions are overtly manifested in English only with pronouns, but in other languages, e.g., Russian, all nominals show them.) A central tenet of GB is that NPs (even those that do not overtly show case distinctions) can occur only in positions where case is assigned due to the Case Filter, which filters out all constructions that contain caseless NPs at SS. In a passive like *was arrested Mary*, *Mary* is base-generated in the object position of the verb to satisfy its thematic properties. However, since, in contrast to active verbs, passive verbs do not assign case, if *Mary* remains in this position the structure will violate the Case Filter. Another relevant condition here is the Extended Projection Principle (EPP), which requires all clauses to have a subject (see Chapter 11). One way to satisfy both the EPP and the Case Filter in the construction under consideration is to move *Mary* to the subject position, as in *Mary was arrested*. Alternatively, the EPP can be satisfied by inserting an expletive, as in **It was arrested Mary*. But then *Mary* needs to move to another position to avoid violating the Case Filter. In **Mary seems that it was arrested*, *Mary* is placed in the right position as far as the Case

Filter is concerned. However, the movement violates other modules, in particular the locality module. One relevant constraint is Rizzi's (1990a) Relativized Minimality, which prohibits movement to SpecIP (i.e. subject position) across another SpecIP. (More generally, Relativized Minimality prohibits movement to a position of type X across an element in X; see Chapter 18.) The above discussion illustrates how Move α and various conditions and modules that constrain its application work.

GB posits a distinction between overt movement, which takes place before SS (the point when the structure is sent to PF, which determines pronunciation) and hence has an effect on pronunciation, and covert movement, which takes place during the mapping from SS to LF, hence does not affect pronunciation. One argument for covert movement involves locality constraints on movement. Thus, (2) is ruled out on the reading on which *how* modifies the embedded clause (which means *how* should be generated within the embedded clause on the reading in question, in the position indicated by t(race)) because movement of *how* from the embedded clause to the matrix SpecCP (the position for fronted *wh*-phrases in questions) yields a locality violation (Rizzi's Relativized Minimality is also relevant here, since the example involves movement to SpecCP across a filled SpecCP). Significantly, Chinese (3), where all *wh*-phrases stay *in situ* (Chinese being a *wh-in-situ* language), also lacks the reading on which *how* is interpreted in the matrix clause and *why* in the embedded clause.

(2) *How do you wonder [why Mary left t]?

(3) *Ni xiangzhidao [Mali weisheme zenmeyang likai]?
    you wonder   Mary why   how   left

The unacceptability of the Chinese example on this reading can be accounted for in the same way as the unacceptability of its English counterpart if the Chinese example involves the same movements as the English example, the only difference being that in the Chinese example the movements take place in LF, hence are not reflected in the pronunciation. Under this view English and Chinese differ only in the timing of *wh*-movement.

4.2 The Minimalist Program

The most recent outgrowth of the Principles and Parameters approach is the Minimalist Program (MP). MP explores the possibility that the content attributed to UG is an optimal way of satisfying requirements imposed on the language faculty by the external systems that the language faculty interfaces with and is characterized by optimal, computationally efficient design. Language is assumed to consist of a lexicon and a computational system.

The computational system is embedded in two performance systems: articulatory–perceptual and conceptual–intentional. Two linguistic levels, namely, Phonological Form and Logical Form, are postulated as interfaces with the performance systems. Each linguistic expression, generated by the computational system, is a pair of representations at PF and LF. A computation converges at the interface levels if its structural description contains only legitimate PF and LF objects, with all of their morphological features satisfied, otherwise it crashes. However, defining linguistic expressions simply as pairs (P, L) formed by a convergent derivation and satisfying interface conditions does not suffice; the operations of the computational system that produce linguistic expressions must be optimal, in the sense that they must satisfy some general considerations of simplicity and efficient design. These considerations ban superfluous steps in derivations and superfluous symbols in representations, prefer short movements over long movements, etc. It is then no surprise that the drive for simple and non-redundant explanations (Occam's razor), a natural aspect of any scientific inquiry which has characterized the development of linguistic theory even before Minimalism (though probably not as much as the core sciences), has come to the forefront of linguistic theorizing with MP, prompting re-evaluations of the standard tenets of GB from this point of view.

MP can in fact be best understood in relation to its immediate predecessor, GB, a task to which I turn now with respect to some of the most important concepts of MP.

4.2.1 Syntactic interfaces and levels of representations

Under the traditional view that human language is a way of relating sound and meaning, the interface levels of PF and LF seem to be uneliminable. Minimalism begins with the position that these levels of representation, which are the only conceptually necessary linguistic levels, are in fact the only levels of representation. Elimination of DS and SS has led to a number of fruitful lines of research, including the exploration of the possibility of movement into theta-positions and reanalyses of DS/SS conditions as either PF/LF or derivational conditions. Consider the former (see Section 4.2.4.1 for the latter). DS is an internal interface level with the lexicon which comes with several assumptions regarding lexical insertion that are not conceptually necessary. DS is built by an all-at-once application of an operation that selects an array of lexical items and presents them in a way that satisfies X-bar Theory. Since DS is the starting point of the derivation, all lexical insertion then takes place before movement applies. But why would all lexical items have to be introduced all at once, before any movement takes place? MP abandons the 'all at once' and 'before any movement' assumptions. Instead, elements taken from the lexicon project separate subtrees which are combined to form a phrase marker by generalized transformations. Thus, in *These smart women like Mary*, *these smart women* is assembled separately and then combined with *like Mary*, which is also assembled separately. Under this approach lexical insertion can take place after movement. In fact, given the Cycle (or Extension Condition; see also Chapter 2), which requires syntactic operations to apply at the top of the tree, in *They think that Mary was arrested*, *Mary* is generated in the object position of *arrest* and then moves to SpecIP of its clause before the lexical items *they* and *think* are introduced into the structure. But if Move can take place before lexical insertion, why couldn't movement then take place into a theta-position? Such movement is impossible in a system assuming DS. DS represents the thematic structure of the sentence as a consequence of the Projection Principle, which requires that lexical properties be satisfied, and the Theta Criterion, which requires that every theta-role be assigned to an argument and that every argument bear a theta-role, applying at DS. Since no theta-positions can be left empty at DS, movement into a theta-position is not possible. In a system where DS and SS are eliminated, with the Projection Principle and the Theta Criterion holding trivially at LF (if they are not satisfied the expression in question receives a deviant interpretation), and where movement can in principle take place prior to lexical insertion, it appears that nothing would in principle go wrong with movement into a theta-position. Such movement can certainly still be banned by adopting additional assumptions (see in fact Chomsky 1995c:312–16, who basically assumes that theta-relatedness is a base property), but the point is that additional assumptions are needed to ban it, not to allow it. There is also some empirical motivation that such movement should not be banned. Consider the following example from Chilean Spanish, noted by Gonzalez (1988) and discussed in this context by Bošković (1994).

(4) a Juan le quiere gustar   Marta
    to Juan cl. wants to-like Marta
    'Juan wants to like Marta'

Juan bears an inherent case assigned by *gustar* and realized morphologically as *a*. Since inherent case is assigned together with a theta-role (Chomsky 1986b), *Juan* must then have started in the embedded clause, where it got case and a theta-role from *gustar* (*quiere* cannot assign the inherent case in question, cf. (*A) *Juan le quiere la fama* 'Juan wants fame,' which rules out a control analysis for (4)). *Juan* is in fact interpreted as the experiencer of *gustar*. However, it is also interpreted as bearing the subject theta-role of *quiere* (and subjecthood tests show that it is located in the matrix SpecIP). Given this, Bošković (1994) argues that (4) should be analyzed in terms of movement into a theta-position, where *Juan* moves from an embedded clause theta-position (where it gets *a*) to a matrix theta-position. While the possibility of movement into a theta-position is still a controversial issue, it has been argued for by a number of authors and argued to have an impact on a number of important phenomena, including control, Binding Theory, and parasitic gaps. Thus, Hornstein (1999) analyzes all traditional control structures in terms of movement into a theta-position, with the traditional controller starting in the place of PRO and moving into a higher theta-position (see Chapter 16).

The most recent theorizing has raised another issue regarding the basic design of language. Both GB and early Minimalism assume that there is a single point of Spell-out, where the derivation separates into the phonology branch and the semantics branch. But why should that be the case? While under Chomsky's (1993) single spell-out approach PF and LF considerations determine when Spell-out applies,[1] the assumption that Spell-out applies only once still hides a trace of SS. A number of authors (see especially Uriagereka 1999, Epstein 1999, Epstein et al. 1998, and Chomsky 2000b, 2001) explore the possibility that Spell-out may apply multiple times. This leads to a radically derivational nature of the computation (see Chapter 14), where the interfaces access syntactic computation as the derivation proceeds without the mediation of PF and LF levels of representation. Syntactic derivation itself plays the central role in this approach, as there are no real levels of representation. The approach has a number of conceptual advantages. Instead of cyclic syntactic construction of a complete phrase marker which is followed by a cyclic semantic composition that retraces syntactic steps, semantic composition can now proceed concurrently with syntactic structure building. Furthermore, MP assumes that syntactic computation is driven by the need to eliminate from the computation objects that are illegitimate at the interfaces, which interfaces cannot deal with. Given this, Epstein et al. (1998) raise a question: How can a syntactic operation at some intermediate point of the derivation be driven by the notion of legitimacy at the interfaces, if these interfaces can access only the final PF and LF representations? On the other hand, in the derivational multiple spell-out model where the interfaces interface with the syntax throughout the syntactic derivation, the problem does not arise. In addition to the conceptual advantages, the dynamic multiple spell-out model also has a good amount of empirical justification, see e.g. Uriagereka (1999), Chomsky (2000b), Franks and Bošković (2001), Simpson (2002), and Fox and Pesetsky (2005). As an illustration, consider the well-known problem regarding the blocking effect of *wh*-traces on *to*-contraction.[2]

(5) a. *you wanna John go there
 b. cf. you want John to go there
 c. you wanna go there
 d. cf. you want PRO to go there
 e. *Who do you wanna go there?
 f. cf. Who$_i$ do you want t$_i$ to go there?

(5a–d) show that while a phonologically null subject of an infinitive does not block *to*-contraction, a lexically realized subject blocks it. A *wh*-trace apparently patterns with the latter in that it blocks *to*-contraction, as shown by (5e–f). If *to*-contraction is a PF phenomenon, (5e) is problematic: since *wh*-trace is phonologically null, we would expect it not to interfere with *to*-contraction, just like PRO does not interfere with it in (5c–d).[3] Under the multiple spell-out hypothesis, (5e) can be accounted for in a principled way. Suppose that instead of waiting for the end of the syntactic derivation the phonology indeed interfaces with the syntax throughout the derivation. If what is sent to the phonology in (5e) is the matrix VP, *who* rather than a trace of *who* intervenes between *want* and *to* at the point when the phonology access the structure.

(6) [$_{VP}$ you want who to go there]

It is then not surprising that (5e) patterns with (5a) rather than (5c) regarding *to*-contraction. An important question arises in this respect: Which pieces of syntactic structure are sent to the interfaces? Chomsky (2000b) argues that, in contrast to active VPs, passive VPs are not sent to the interfaces. This assumption enables us to account for the well-known fact that NP-traces do not block contraction, as shown by the possibility of contraction across the NP-trace in (7).

(7) a. John is sposta leave
     b. John$_i$ is supposed t$_i$ to leave

If, in contrast to the matrix VP in (5), the matrix VP in (7) is not sent to the phonology, the phonology will only access (7) once the infinitival subject has moved from the embedded SpecIP, where it would intervene between *to* and the higher verb. As a result, the contraction is not blocked in (7) (the issue of which pieces of syntactic structure are sent to the interfaces under the multiple spell-out hypothesis is currently under debate; see Section 4.2.3 for relevant discussion).

Another very influential proposal which has to do with the way syntax interacts with the interfaces concerns Kayne's (1994) proposal (dubbed the Linear Correspondence Axiom) that linear order should be deduced from the hierarchical structure, where (roughly) if X asymmetrically c-commands Y, X precedes Y. While Kayne applies the algorithm in question in the syntax, Chomsky (1995c) proposes that the algorithm should apply in PF, i.e., on the mapping from syntax to the PF interface. An interesting consequence of this proposal is that linear order is purged from the syntax (overt syntax and LF, as well as semantics). Syntax is then simply characterized by hierarchical structure, linear order being imposed on it only in PF, presumably as a requirement of the PF interface. This approach to linearization is an example of the Minimalist agenda to reduce linguistic constraints to bare output conditions, which are determined by the external systems that the language faculty interfaces with.

Kayne's hypothesis that ties word order to structural relations has many consequences. One of them is that, since the basic spec–head–complement structure can only be mapped to the order spec–head–complement, SOV languages like Japanese must be analyzed as involving movement of the object (without the movement, the verb would have to precede the object, the two being in a head–complement relation).

4.2.2 Last resort

Minimalism has insisted on the last resort nature of movement from its inception: In line with the leading idea of economy, movement must happen for a reason, in particular, a formal reason. Case may provide one such driving force. Consider (8).

(8) Mary is certain *t* to leave

Mary cannot be case-licensed in the position of *t*. Raising to matrix SpecIP rectifies its case inadequacy, since the position into which raising has taken place licenses nominative. Once *Mary* has been case-licensed, it is no longer available for A-movement, to a case or a non-case position. This follows from Last Resort, if A-movement is driven by case considerations. Since *Mary* is case-licensed in the position of *t* in (9), Last Resort blocks further movement of *Mary*.

(9) a. *Mary is certain *t* will leave
 b. *the belief Mary to be likely *t* will leave

One fruitful line of research regarding Last Resort concerns the issue of where the formal inadequacy driving movement lies, in the target (Attract) or the moving element (Greed). Greed was the earliest approach (Chomsky 1993), revived recently in Bošković (2007b) based on considerations of successive-cyclic movement (see Sections 18.2.3 and 18.10). Under this approach X can move only if X has a formal inadequacy, and if the movement will help rectify the inadequacy. Under pure Attract, the target head always triggers movement (Chomsky 1995c), which means the target must always have a formal inadequacy to be rectified by the movement (see also Lasnik 1995 for a combination of the two approaches to Last Resort). Under this approach, movement of *Mary* in (8) is driven by T/I: the head has a property, namely the EPP, that must be satisfied by an NP which triggers movement of *Mary* (*Mary*'s case-checking is merely a beneficial side effect of the satisfaction of the attractor's requirement.) While the Greed approach easily handles (9), such constructions require additional assumptions in a target-driven system. Chomsky (2000b) posits the Activation Condition, which says X can move only if X has an uninterpretable feature, i.e., a formal inadequacy (the need to license its case-feature in the case of A-movement). The approach is still sneaking in Greed into a system where movement is supposed to be target-driven. A target-driven approach, however, has a conceptual advantage in that under this approach the driving force for movement can be satisfied immediately (as soon as the relevant element enters the structure), rather than indefinitely later in the derivation, as in the moving-element driven approach. As discussed in Bošković (2011a), there are, however, cases of movement that seem to be quite clearly driven by the properties of moving elements, like Quantifier Raising (which does not take place because the targets of Quantifier Raising would require an adjoined quantifier) or multiple movements to the same position such as multiple *wh*-fronting in languages like Romanian (see (19) below), where the very fact that all *wh*-phrases must front indicates that there is something wrong with *wh*-phrases that do not undergo movement.

4.2.3 Government

One early Minimalist objective was to re-examine all posited relations from GB, with the goal of eliminating those that were arbitrary. Attention immediately focused on government, a structural relation that was central in almost every module of GB. While this provided substantial unification it came at a significant cost, government being an arbitrary notion that did not follow from anything. There are many definitions of government in the literature. This in itself reveals its arbitrary nature, which can be illustrated by the following definition of government, a modified version of Chomsky's (1986a).

(10) A governs B if there is no XP intervening between A and B, where XP is not a complement argument other than IP, and XP does not immediately dominate YP, where YP is not a complement argument.

Government was assumed to be crucially involved in Case Theory, providing a unification of the three configurations under which case was assumed to be assigned (spec–head for nominative case, head–complement for accusative case, and head–spec of the complement for Exceptional Case-Marking (ECM)-accusative, as in *Mary believes him to be smart*), Binding Theory (the domain in which anaphors must be bound and pronouns must be free crucially had to contain a governor for the anaphor/pronoun; since PRO was assumed to be subject to binding conditions, government was also crucially involved in the distribution of PRO: see the PRO Theorem), the distribution of null complementizers (which were assumed to be subject to a government requirement), and locality of movement (which is taken rather broadly here to include the licensing of traces). A great deal of effort went into providing accounts of these phenomena that do not appeal to government, in an attempt to eliminate the notion from the grammar. The research program has proved rather successful. Since movement has been argued to determine the distribution of anaphors and pronouns (see, e.g., Chomsky 1993, Hornstein 2001, and Kayne 2002a), and the distribution of PRO has been argued to be determined either by locality of movement (under Hornstein's 1999 approach, where the controller of the traditional PRO undergoes movement) or Case Theory (under the null Case approach, where PRO bears a special case; see Chomsky and Lasnik 1993, Martin 1996, Bošković 1997; and Section 16.2.2), the locality of case-licensing and the locality of movement have become the crucial cases (see also Bošković and Lasnik 2003, Pesetsky and Torrego 2001, and Landau 2007a for elimination of government from the domain of the distribution of null complementizers). In early Minimalism, all case-licensing was reduced to the Spec–Head relation. What made that possible was adoption of object shift, an operation which moves accusative NPs to a higher position in which they enter a Spec–Head agreement relation with the verb. The operation was also assumed to apply to accusative subjects of infinitival complement clauses, which would then undergo A-movement motivated by case-licensing outside of their infinitival clauses. Some evidence for this is provided by examples like (11), where the subject of the infinitive binds an anaphor within a matrix adverbial, which indicates that it has moved into the matrix clause at the relevant point (see Postal 1974, Lasnik and Saito 1991, and Sections 15.3.2 and 16.2.3); there is some controversy regarding whether the movement is covert or overt, the latter possibility requiring overt short V-movement in English to derive the correct word order.

(11) John proved [Mary and Jane to be innocent] during each other's trials

Regarding locality of movement, early proposals attempted to deduce locality-of-movement effects from Chomsky and Lasnik's (1993) Minimize Chain Links Principle (MCLP), which requires each step of movement to be as short as possible.[4] Rizzi's (1990a) Relativized Minimality effects then follow because such effects always involve skipping of a potential landing-site, for example in *Mary seemed it was told t he left, Mary has to skip embedded SpecIP when moving to the matrix SpecIP.[5]

More recently, Chomsky (2000b, 2001, 2004) has proposed another approach to locality which plays a crucial role in a number of phenomena, including locality of movement and case licensing (for relevant discussion, see also Chapter 18). The approach is based on the notion of phase, the leading idea being that only the edge of a phase (i.e., spec and head of the relevant phrase) is available for operations outside of the phase (the Phase Impenetrability Condition (PIC)). Assuming that CP and DP are phases, a *wh*-phrase moving out of a CP and DP then can only move outside of these phrases if it first moves to SpecCP and SpecDP.[6] If these positions are filled, making such movement impossible, as in (12), the PIC is violated.

(12) a. ??What do you wonder [$_{CP}$ why John bought t]?
 b. ?*What do you like [$_{DP}$ Mary's picture of t]?

The PIC is also assumed to constrain the locality of case-licensing. Thus, *John believed that him left is ruled out because case-marking of the embedded clause subject by the matrix verb violates the PIC. In a multiple spell-out system, phases are also assumed to determine which pieces of structure are sent to the interfaces. They are also taken to determine the contents of a numeration. Chomsky (1995c) argues that the computational system does not have direct access to the lexicon throughout the derivation but only to a collection of lexical items, i.e., numeration, which serves as the starting point for the derivation. Not all lexical items in a sentence come from a single numeration. Rather, Chomsky argues that numerations correspond to phases, with each phase built from a separate numeration. The concept of numeration is itself important since economy conditions are taken to compare only derivations with the same starting point, i.e., numeration. If this were not the case, silence would always be most economical since it does not require any syntactic operations. One non-trivial question concerns the proper definition of phases; the reader is referred to Sections 18.8 and 18.9 for this issue.

4.2.4 The Inclusiveness Condition

Chomsky (1993) proposes the Inclusiveness Condition, which confines the power of syntax to (re)arrangements of lexical items, banning syntax from creating new objects. The condition is very appealing conceptually due to its restrictive nature. It has also led to re-examinations of several phenomena that have yielded very important results. I will discuss here its effects for phrase structure and the trace theory of movement, starting with the latter.

4.2.4.1 The copy theory of movement

It is a fundamental property of human language that syntactic elements can be interpreted in positions different from the ones where they are pronounced. In GB such dependencies were implemented by using movement and traces. Thus, *Mary*, which is interpreted as object of *kiss* in (13), is generated in this position and then it moves, leaving behind a co-indexed trace, a phonetically null element that has the interpretational properties of the moved element.

(13) Mary$_i$ was kissed t$_i$

Traces are prime examples of creationism in syntax and, as such, violate the Inclusiveness Condition. Chomsky (1993) therefore abandons trace theory and resurrects the copy theory of movement, according to which the trace of an overtly moved element is a copy of the moved element that is deleted in PF but available for interpretation in LF. (Copies are annotated here with superscripts.)

(14) Mary^k was arrested ~~Mary^k~~

Chomsky (1993) shows that in addition to conforming to the Inclusiveness Condition, the copy theory considerably simplifies the analysis of reconstruction phenomena (see below; see also Chapter 15). Furthermore, by making it possible to treat reconstruction as an LF phenomenon, the copy theory contributes to the research endeavor to eliminate non-interface levels of representation. Another attractive feature of the copy theory is that, by eliminating traces, it reduces the number of theoretical primitives.

However, the copy theory has brought in a new set of questions: it now has to be determined which copies reach the interfaces and why this is so. The positions in which elements undergoing movement are pronounced and interpreted are generally unique, and not necessarily identical. To ensure this under the copy theory, it is standardly assumed that only one copy of X remains at the interface levels. The question is then which copy should survive deletion.

On the LF side, there is at least some choice in deciding where deletion should take place in non-trivial chains, with a preference for deletion of the restriction of the *wh*-operator in the head of operator–variable chains. Consider (15). Chomsky (1993) argues that the upstairs reading of *himself* is obtained after the tail of the *wh*-chain is deleted (see (16a), where *himself* is locally bound by *Joe*; note that if theta-roles are features that can be checked derivationally the deletion may not need to leave anything behind). Under the downstairs reading, *himself* is deleted in the head of the *wh*-chain and remains in its tail (see (16b), where *himself* is locally bound by *Jim*).

(15)   Joe$_i$ wondered which picture of himself$_{i/j}$ Jim$_j$ bought

(16)   a. Joe wondered [$_{CP}$ [which picture of himself]^k [$_{IP}$ Jim bought [which picture of himself]^k]]
       b. Joe wondered [$_{CP}$ [which picture of himself]^k [$_{IP}$ Jim bought [which picture of himself]^k]]

Chomsky argues that there is a preference for minimizing the operator restriction in LF, which normally leads to deletion in the head of Ā-chains. This is motivated by the impossibility of coreference between *he* and *Tom* in (17). To exclude (17) while allowing the upstairs reading of *himself* in (15), Chomsky suggests that in (16a), *himself* undergoes LF anaphor movement into the matrix clause from the head of the *wh*-chain (see Chapter 15 regarding anaphor movement); deletion in the head of the *wh*-chain is then blocked because it would break the anaphor movement chain. By contrast, in (16b) the lower copy of *himself* undergoes LF anaphor movement within the lower clause so that the deletion within the head of the *wh*-chain is permitted.

(17)   a. *Mary wondered which picture of Tom$_i$ he$_i$ liked
       b. *Mary wondered [$_{CP}$ [which picture of Tom]^k he liked [which picture of Tom]^k]

While on the LF side there is clearly some choice in deciding where deletion should take place in non-trivial chains, early on it was assumed that no such choice is available in PF, the head of a non-trivial chain always being the sole survivor, based on paradigms like (18).

(18) a. [[the student]^k was arrested [~~the student~~]^k]
b. *[[~~the student~~]^k was arrested [the student]^k]
c. *[[the student]^k was arrested [the student]^k]
d. *[[the ~~student~~]^k was arrested [~~the~~ student]^k]
e. *[[~~the~~ student]^k was arrested [the ~~student~~]^k]

Such paradigms led to adopting the stipulation that lower copies cannot be phonetically realized, which was rather unfortunate since it tacitly resuscitated traces. More recent work has, however, amassed considerable evidence that 'traces', i.e., lower copies, can be phonetically realized. It turns out that just as in LF there is a preference for deletion in the head position of non-trivial chains (at least with operator–variable chains), deletion of lower copies in PF is just a preference, not the only option (see also Sections 5.2.2.3, 16.2.1, and 16.2.4). In particular, Franks (1998) argues that a chain is pronounced in the head position, with lower copies deleted in PF, unless pronunciation in the head position would lead to a PF violation. If and only if the violation can be avoided by pronouncing a lower copy of the chain, the lower copy is pronounced and the head of the chain is deleted. There is a good amount of empirical evidence for this state of affairs, which has also been shown to be deducible from independent assumptions by Nunes (2004). One such argument is given in Bošković (2002a) based on multiple wh-fronting in Romanian (for an overview of other arguments and additional references, see Bošković and Nunes 2007; as shown there, there are in fact cases where different pieces of different chain links are realized, just as in the LF procedure discussed regarding (16b)).

Romanian requires all wh-phrases to front in questions (19). However, the second wh-phrase does not appear to move if it is homophonous with the first fronted wh-phrase (20).

(19) a. Cine ce precede?
who what precedes
b. *Cine precede ce?
who precedes what
'Who precedes what?'

(20) a. Ce precede ce?
what precedes what
b. *Ce ce precede?
what what precedes
'What precedes what?'

Many languages have low-level PF constraints against consecutive homophonous phrases, which is what rules out (20b). (20a) then represents an intricate interplay between phonology and syntax, with phonology apparently overriding syntax, more precisely, the need to satisfy a PF requirement appears to override the need to satisfy a syntactic requirement. The mechanism of pronunciation of lower copies provides a straightforward way of resolving this phonology–syntax conflict. Given that Romanian has a syntactic requirement that forces all *wh*-phrases to move overtly (Bošković 2002a argues this involves focalization), the second *wh*-phrase must move in the syntax, as in (21) (irrelevant copies are ignored).

(21) [ce ce^i precede ce^i]

If the highest copy of the second *wh*-chain is pronounced, a PF violation obtains due to a sequence of homophonous *wh*-elements. This is precisely the situation where a lower copy can be pronounced under Franks's (1998) approach to the pronunciation of non-trivial chains.

(22) [ce ce^i precede ce^i]

By deriving (20a) from (21), the pronunciation of a lower copy analysis accounts for the contrast between (19b) and (20a) without violating the syntactic requirement that forces all *wh*-phrases to move overtly in Romanian and without look-ahead from the syntax to the phonology. It also resolves the problem of the phonology–syntax interaction raised by (20a), without having phonology override syntax.

There is also independent evidence that the second *ce* in (20a) indeed moves overtly. *In-situ wh*-phrases in multiple questions in languages like English differ from their moved counterparts in being unable to license parasitic gaps.

(23) a. What did John read without filing?
b. *Who read what without filing?

Significantly, the *in-situ wh*-phrase in (20a) does license parasitic gaps. The fact that the '*in-situ*' wh-phrase in (24) patterns with the moved wh-phrase in (23a) rather than the *in-situ* wh-phrase in (23b) is exactly what is expected if (20a) involves overt *wh*-movement and lower copy pronunciation.

(24) Ce precede ce fără să influenţeze?
what precedes what without subj.particle influence.3p.sg
'What precedes what without influencing?'

In addition to the issue of copy interpretation at the interfaces, the copy theory also has more general consequences for the operation Move. The basic structure building operation is Merge, which combines two things making one of them the head of the resulting structure (see Section 4.2.4.2). What Move does is take an element that is already merged into the structure, and copy it by merging it into another position. From this perspective, Move is not a primitive operation, but the combination of the operations Merge and Copy. While remerger of an element that is already merged into the structure is referred to as Internal Merge and initial merger of an element into the syntactic tree is referred to as External Merge there is then still only one basic structure-building operation, namely Merge. The mechanics of the operation will be discussed in detail in the next section.

4.2.4.2 Bare Phrase Structure and late insertion

Above, we have seen that the Inclusiveness Condition has led to the introduction of the copy theory of movement. The condition also has important consequences for phrase structure. Bar levels, vacuous projections, even the terminal/non-terminal distinction, standard tools of the GB framework present in the GB tree in (25), all violate the ban on creationism in syntax (none of them are present in the lexicon).

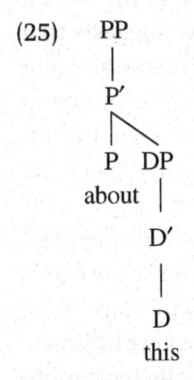

(25)
```
        PP
        |
        P'
       / \
      P   DP
    about  |
           D'
           |
           D
          this
```

This has led to a re-examination of phrase structure (and X'-theory), the result of the re-examination being known as Bare Phrase Structure (Chomsky 1995c: Chapter 4; see also Section 2.4.3 of this handbook). Consider (25) from this perspective. In (25), two lexical items, *about* and *this*, are combined by the operation Merge, which takes two syntactic objects and forms a new syntactic object out of them. The resulting object is labeled by *about*, which means that the object is a projection of *about* (i.e., it is of the same type as *about*). This gives us the following representation for (25).

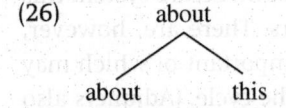

(26)
```
         about
         /  \
      about  this
```

While (26) conforms with the Inclusiveness Condition, it raises a number of interesting questions regarding how the traditional distinctions between maximal and minimal projections, complements and specifiers can be implemented in this system, given that they cannot be identified by any special marking. Consider the issue with respect to a slightly more complicated case of a double object construction, where *v* introduces the external argument, with *give* raising to *v* (the movement is ignored here; on '*v*,' see Chapter 9).

(27)
```
           v
          / \
        we   v
            / \
           v   give
          / \
        her  give
            /  \
          give everything
```

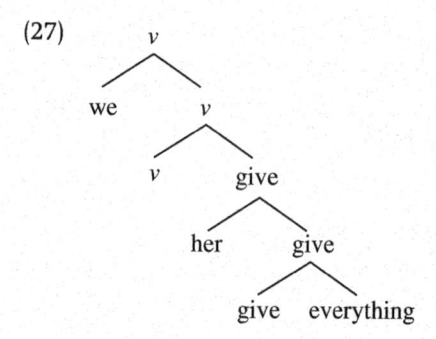

Following Muysken (1983), Chomsky argues for a relational definition of the relevant notions: a category that does not project any further is a maximal projection (e.g., the highest *give*), and one that is not a projection at all is a minimal projection (the traditional head, which is the lowest *give*). As for the complement/specifier distinction, Chomsky suggests that the most local relation with a head Y corresponds to the head–complement relation, all other relations (putting aside adjunction for the moment) being head–specifier. This means that the first merger with a head yields a complement (*everything* in (27)), all additional mergers involve specifiers (*her* in (27)).

Bare Phrase Structure has a number of very interesting consequences. First, it allows for the existence of elements that are at the same time heads and phrases. Chomsky suggests that clitics, which do seem to share some properties of both heads and phrases, are such elements (see here Bošković 2002b); note that some of the lexical items in (27) may actually have more internal structure than indicated in (27). The system also naturally allows for the existence of multiple specifiers.[7] One of the instances where this possibility has been argued to be instantiated is multiple *wh*-fronting, as in Romanian (19a)), where under Koizumi's (1994) analysis each *wh*-phrase occupies a separate SpecCP.

This system leaves adjuncts in a somewhat uncomfortable position. One of the reasons behind the postulation of adjunction was to allow for the possibility of merging multiple phrases (more precisely, more than two phrases) within the same phrase. In the Bare Phrase Structure system this can be achieved by employing multiple specifiers. There are, however, other reasons to postulate adjunction, the most important of which may be the special status of adjuncts with respect to the cycle. (Adjuncts also typically fail to enter into agreement relations and have different case requirements from arguments.)[8] As discussed above, in MP the derivation proceeds cyclically bottom-up starting with what ends up being the most deeply embedded structural unit. The requirement of strict cyclicity ensures, for instance, that it is not possible to get around the *wh*-island effect in (28a) by doing long distance *wh*-movement first (28b) and then filling the embedded clause SpecCP ((28c); for various approaches to cyclicity, see Lasnik 2006).

(28) a. ??What do you wonder why John bought?
b. What do you wonder John bought why?
c. What do you wonder why John bought?

Lebeaux (1988) argues that certain elements, in fact precisely those that have been assumed to enter the structure by adjunction, should be exempt from the cyclicity requirement. His argument is based on the following contrast:

(29) a. *Which argument that John$_i$ is a genius did he$_i$ believe?
b. Which argument that John$_i$ made did he$_i$ believe?

(29a), which involves a nominal complement, can be captured if the restriction of the operator must be reconstructed to the base position, i.e., the position it occupied prior to *wh*-movement (see in this respect the discussion of the preference for minimizing operator restriction regarding (17), above). What about (29b) then? The relevant element in (29b) is a relative clause, which is traditionally treated as an adjunct. Lebeaux observes that the grammaticality of (29b) can be accounted for if adjuncts can be inserted non-cyclically. The issue of reconstruction does not arise on the derivation on which the relative clause is introduced into the structure acyclically after *wh*-movement, since this derivation has only one copy of the adjunct, the one that is pronounced in the matrix SpecCP. Furthermore, Stepanov (2001) argues based on (30) that adjuncts not only can be, but in fact must be inserted into the structure acyclically. In particular, the fact that, in contrast to (30b), condition A is apparently violated in (30a) provides evidence that the adjunct clause must in fact be adjoined after *wh*-movement (given late adjunction, *the lawyers* cannot bind *each other* at any point of the derivation).⁹

(30) a. *What evidence that each other$_i$'s friends brought up in court did the lawyers$_i$ refuse to talk about?
b. the lawyers$_i$ refused to talk about the evidence that each other$_i$'s friends brought up in court

Obligatory late insertion of adjuncts suggests an interesting way of capturing the ban on extraction out of adjuncts. Thus, if the adjunct in (31) must be introduced into the structure late, after *wh*-movement takes place, it follows that no *wh*-movement can take place out of the adjunct (the account raises a number of questions, see in this respect the discussion in Stepanov (2001); for alternative accounts of the Adjunct Condition, see Chomsky 1986b, Takahashi 1994, Nunes and Uriagereka 2000, Starke 2001, Boeckx 2003, and Müller 2010, among others; extraction from adjuncts is also discussed in Chapter 18).

(31) ?*What did John fall asleep [after Mary had bought]?

There is another interesting question concerning late insertion: Can lexical insertion take place in PF and LF? In the GB framework it was tacitly assumed that all lexical insertion has to take place prior to S-Structure (i.e., prior to Spell-out); otherwise, the sound-meaning relation would completely collapse. Thus, if free insertion in LF were allowed (32a) could mean (32b), with *John does not think* inserted in LF (hence it would be present in the semantic representation but would not be pronounced). On the other hand, if free insertion in PF were allowed (32b) could mean (32a), with *John does not think* inserted in PF (hence it would be pronounced but it would not have semantic representation).

(32) a. Mary left
b. John does not think that Mary left

Chomsky (1995c) suggests a way of deducing the ban on PF/LF insertion. Consider the lexical item *John*. Like any lexical item, *John* is a set of features, with at least three kinds of features: formal (e.g., case-feature), phonological (the instruction how to pronounce *John*), and semantic (the instruction how to interpret *John*). Given this, the ban on late (i.e., PF/LF) insertion follows from the Principle of Full Interpretation, which requires that whatever is present at the interface levels be interpretable by the interfaces. Thus, if *John* is inserted in LF the derivation crashes because LF cannot interpret the phonological features of *John*. If, on the other hand, *John* is inserted in PF, PF will not know how to interpret the semantic features of *John*. The only way to derive a legitimate PF and a legitimate LF is for *John* to be inserted before the 'SS' is reached. PF will then strip off the phonological features of *John*, and the semantic features of *John* will proceed into LF. This line of reasoning allows lexical insertion to take place in PF and LF under certain conditions. To be more precise, it allows PF insertion of semantically null elements and LF insertion of phonologically null elements (as long as such insertion obeys the cycle, assuming the cycle holds in LF). The former may be instantiated in the case of semantically dummy elements like *do* of *do*-support. Bošković (1998) argues that the latter option is the best way to handle French *wh-in-situ*, the element that is inserted in LF being the interrogative C. As illustrated in (33)-(35), *wh-in-situ* is in fact possible in French only in the contexts where LF insertion is in principle possible, namely, when the C is phonologically null (compare (33a) and (35b)) and when it is located at the top of the tree (compare (33a) and (34b)). (Note that not all dialects of French allow overt C examples like (35a).)

(33) a. Tu as vu qui?
you have seen whom
'Who did you see?'
b. Qui as-tu vu?

(34) a. Pierre a demandé qui tu as vu.
Pierre has asked whom you have seen
b. *Pierre a demandé tu as vu qui.

(35) a. Qui   que tu   as   vu?
         whom C   you have seen
         'Who did you see?'
     b. *Que tu as vu qui?

4.2.5 Economy and optionality

The above paradigm can also be used to illustrate some issues regarding the Minimalist guideline that language is economical. The French data in (33) bring up the question of optionality. Truly optional movement does not fit well with a framework like Minimalism where all movement takes place for a reason: in such a framework either there is a reason for a movement to take place, in which case it must take place, or there is not, in which case it in fact cannot take place, given Last Resort. Everything else being equal we then would not expect to find truly optional movements. In cases like (33), it then must be the case that everything else is not equal. Under the above analysis this is indeed the case. Notice first that we cannot assume that French interrogative C optionally triggers movement. If that were the case, we would not be able to ever enforce the movement option, which would leave the ungrammaticality of (34b) and (35b) unaccounted for. Bošković (1998) then argues that French interrogative C in fact requires *wh*-movement. The difference between (33a) and (33b) is in the timing of C-insertion. In both cases, the C triggers *wh*-movement immediately upon its insertion (note in this respect that French *wh-in-situ* shows locality-of-movement effects): however, the C is inserted overtly in (33b), hence it triggers overt *wh*-movement, and it is inserted covertly in (33b), hence it triggers covert *wh*-movement (in other words, there is no overt *wh*-movement in (33a) because its trigger is not present in the structure at the relevant point of the derivation). In (34) and (35), where the LF C-insertion derivation is blocked (it is blocked in (35b) because the C is phonologically overt and in (34b) because the insertion would not take place at the top of the tree, violating the cycle), overt C insertion and overt *wh*-movement are the only options. The above discussion illustrates what one would expect to find in the cases involving seemingly optional movements: not everything is equal in the movement and non-movement options.

The French data in question also show that economy should be evaluated locally, without look-ahead. Chomsky (1993) argues that covert movement is more economical than overt movement, hence should be preferred to overt movement when both are in principle possible. From this perspective, the LF C-insertion derivation should be more economical than the overt C insertion derivation, since it triggers covert *wh*-movement, which is more economical than overt *wh*-movement. It then appears that (33a), the LF C-insertion derivation, should block (33b), the overt C-insertion derivation. Notice, however, that this is the case only if look-ahead is allowed. C-insertion itself works in exactly the same way whether it is covert or overt; there is no reason to prefer one of these options. It just happens that later down the road one of these operations will lead to a more economical movement operation. If economy considerations must be evaluated locally, without look-ahead, rather than globally, with look-ahead, we then get exactly the right outcome, with both (33a) and (33b) allowed. The data in question thus favor local economy over global economy, as one would expect from a system with efficient design (see Collins 1997 for much relevant discussion).

The system then does not always choose one option. As noted by Chomsky (1991b), more than one option is allowed if they are equally economical. In this respect, Superiority effects provide a rather nice confirmation of the idea of economy in language. Consider (36), whose structure prior to *wh*-movement is given in (37).

(36) a. Who did you tell that she should buy what?
     b. ?*What did you tell who that she should buy?

(37) You tell who that she should buy what?

The GB account of the contrast in (36) was based on Chomsky's (1973) Superiority Condition (see (38)), which basically says that if X and Y are candidates for a particular movement operation, and X asymmetrically c-commands Y, then X rather than Y undergoes the movement in question (see also Section 18.7 and its note 11; there are actually other pre-Minimalist accounts of (37); however, they all make the same prediction as (38) with respect to the Bulgarian data discussed below).

(38) No rule can involve X, Y in the structure ...X...[...Z...WYV...] where the rule applies ambiguously to Z and Y, and Z is superior to Y. The category A is superior to the category B if every major category dominating A dominates B as well but not conversely.

Turning to Minimalism, the Superiority effect in (36) is perhaps the most straightforward illustration of economy of derivation, which requires that every requirement be satisfied through the shortest movement possible. English interrogative C requires its Spec position to be filled by a *wh*-phrase, however this requirement is to be implemented. In (37) the requirement can be satisfied by moving either *who* or *what*. Since the former results in shorter movement, (36a) is preferred to (36b).[10]

While the economy account is simpler, hence conceptually preferable to the account based on (38), there is also an empirical reason to prefer the economy account. Consider the Bulgarian multiple *wh*-fronting (MWF) data in (39).

(39) a. *Koj e vidjal kogo?
           who is seen whom
     b. Koj kogo e vidjal?
        'Who saw whom?'

(40) a. Kogo kakvo e pital Ivan?
   whom what is asked Ivan
   'Whom did Ivan ask what?'
   b. ?*Kakvo kogo e pital Ivan?

In Bulgarian MWF all *wh*-phrases move to SpecCP. The *wh*-phrase that is highest prior to *wh*-movement (the subject in (39) and the indirect object in (40)) must come first in the linear order. This has been analyzed as a Superiority effect, which means that the highest *wh*-phrase moves first, the second *wh*-phrase either right-adjoins to the first *wh*-phrase, as in Rudin (1988), or moves to a lower SpecCP, as in Richards (2001). As discussed in Bošković (1999), like English C, Bulgarian C requires movement to its Spec. In addition, there is a focusing requirement on *wh*-phrases, which is also satisfied by moving *wh*-phrases to SpecCP. Consider now what should happen in constructions involving three *wh*-phrases. Let us assume that whichever *wh*-phrase moves first to SpecCP satisfies the requirement of the interrogative C to have a filled SpecCP. As a result, the *wh*-phrase that is highest prior to *wh*-movement must move first to SpecCP; this way the formal inadequacy in question is satisfied in the most economical way. The lower two *wh*-phrases then move to SpecCP to satisfy their focusing requirement. Whichever order these two *wh*-phrases move in, the requirements are satisfied through movements of the same length, i.e., the movements always cross the same maximal projections. Under the economy account we would then expect that the highest *wh*-phrase will move first, and then the other two *wh*-phrases can move in any order. On the other hand, the account based on (38) will always force the higher *wh*-phrase to move first, which means that the order of all three fronted *wh*-phrases should be fixed, reflecting their order prior to *wh*-movement. As discussed in Bošković (1999), the prediction of the economy account is borne out: the highest *wh*-phrase must move first, the order of the second and the third *wh*-phrase is free. Thus, while the dative must move before the accusative in (40), this is not the case in (41), where their order of movement is free. (Any order where the subject is not first is unacceptable.)

(41) a. Koj kogo kakvo e pital?
   who whom what is asked
   'Who asked whom what?'
   b. Koj kakvo kogo e pital?

The above data provide an argument for the economy account of Superiority and for the general notion of economy in language. It also shows that economy does not always rule out all but one option. In cases where several options are equally economical they are all allowed.

4.2.6 Covert movement/dependencies

A lively area of research in current Minimalist theorizing involves the nature of covert movement, or more generally, covert dependencies. In

GB there was a standard treatment of covert movement. Covert movement was pretty much the same as overt movement (putting aside the timing difference, the former taking place after S-structure and the latter before S-structure), except that it was assumed not to be subject to some constraints, like Subjacency (see Huang 1982a; see also Chapter 22 for alternative views). Thus, Japanese (42) was assumed to involve movement of the *wh*-phrase to SpecCP, just like its English counterpart, the only difference being that the movement was assumed to take place in LF in (42).

(42) anata-ga dare-o mita ka
      you-nom who-acc saw Q
      'Who did you see?'

Minimalism initially kept this treatment of covert movement. However, Chomsky (1995b) suggested that covert movement involves movement only of formal features. The reason behind this suggestion was the general economy principle that movement should carry as little material as possible; since movement is assumed to be motivated by the need to license/check formal features only formal features should then be affected by movement. Chomsky (1995b) suggested that this is indeed what happens in cases like Japanese (42). However, he argued that pure formal feature movement is not a possibility prior to SS. The reason for this is that such movement feeds pronunciation, and lexical items whose features are scattered in different positions (with formal features separated from other features due to feature movement) are unpronounceable.[11] Chomsky (2000b), however, reanalyzes covert dependencies in terms of Agree, which is a feature-checking operation that takes place at a distance without actual movement. Under this approach the interrogative C and the *wh*-phrase in (42) simply undergo feature checking via Agree without actual movement.[12] There are two additional treatments of covert dependencies, both of which arose as a result of elimination of the traditional LF component and the LF cycle. As noted in Section 4.1, the most recent approach to the basic design of grammar eliminates LF. Covert and overt movement then cannot be distinguished by sequential ordering in the derivation: since there is only one cycle, they both have to take place on the same cycle.[13] One way to distinguish covert and overt movement is then in terms of which copy is pronounced (see Section 4.2.4.1): the highest would be pronounced in the latter and the lowest in the former (see Bobaljik 1995 and Groat and O'Neil 1996). Another way is to assume that covert and overt movement differ with respect to the timing of the transfer to the PF interface (see Nissenbaum 2000): they both take place on the same cycle, but the phrase hosting the movement can be transferred to the PF interface either after (in the case of overt movement) or before (in the case of covert movement) the relevant movement takes place. Notice finally that the Agree approach is also consistent with the one-cycle syntax model.

Determining the proper treatment of covert dependencies is currently a lively area of research. Empirical facts, however, suggest that there may not be a single way of treating such dependencies. Thus, *wh-in-situ* does not exhibit uniform behavior cross-linguistically (compare, e.g., the behavior of the *wh-in-situ* in (23b) and (24) with respect to parasitic gap licensing), which may be difficult (though not necessarily impossible) to account for if all covert dependencies are treated in the same way.

4.2.7 Features and feature checking

Let us now look more closely at feature checking / licensing, which drives much of the syntactic computation in Minimalism. As discussed above, lexical items enter the computation as sets of features. Some of these features require feature checking, i.e. establishing relations with other features, during the syntactic computation.

There are two properties of features that are important in this respect. Chomsky (1995c) introduces the interpretable/uninterpretable feature distinction, the criterion here being semantic interpretability, or more precisely, interpretability at the LF interface. Case, for example, is taken to be an uninterpretable feature. Other features are more complicated in that they are uninterpretable only on some lexical items. For example, the number feature is uninterpretable on the verb, but interpretable on the noun. (Thus, the subject in *A student likes Mary / Students like Mary* is interpreted differently depending on whether it is singular or plural, which is not the case with the verb.[14]) Given the Principle of Full Interpretation, which requires that everything that is present at the interface levels has to be interpretable by the interfaces, uninterpretable features then have to be eliminated from the structure before the LF interface. This is accomplished through feature checking, an operation which will be discussed below.

Chomsky (2000b) introduces another important distinction: valued vs. unvalued features. Consider (43)–(45), from Serbo-Croatian (*kola* is a plurale tantum).

(43) zelena   kola   su kupljena   (Serbo-Croatian)
     green.fem car.fem are bought.fem
     'the green car was bought'

(44) zeleno   auto   je kupljeno
     green.neut car.neut is bought.neut

(45) zeleni   automobil je kupljen
     green.masc car.masc is bought.masc

The gender of the adjective and the participle depends on the gender of the noun. *Green* can be feminine, neuter, or masculine; which gender it has depends on the noun it modifies. On the other hand, nouns have a fixed gender specification: *kola* is always feminine, *auto* neuter, and *automobil* masculine. As noted by Pesetsky and Torrego (2007), this can be captured if adjectives and participles are lexically unvalued for gender: they receive their gender value after undergoing agreement with a noun that already has a valued gender. Since the gender of the noun is lexically valued it does not depend on the noun's syntactic context. Under the plausible assumption that unvalued features are illegitimate at the interfaces (the interface has to know the value of a feature to be able to interpret it), only valued interpretable features are legitimate at the LF interface. Other features need to be eliminated before reaching the interface. In principle, that could be accomplished through deletion of relevant features. However, Chomsky (2001) posits that only valued features can be deleted. Unvalued uninterpretable features then need to be valued before they can be eliminated. From this perspective, what drives the feature checking operation is valuation, i.e., the need to value unvalued features.

An element X with an unvalued feature K then probes its c-command domain to find Y with a valued K. Once X finds Y, Y values K of X. The process in question is the Agree operation. If X's K is uninterpretable, which means the LF interface cannot deal with it, it will then be deleted; if it is interpretable, it will remain in the structure. A sentence like (46) then has the following derivation:

(46) John left
    T   John
    uninterpretable unvalued   valued interpretable phi-features
      phi features   unvalued uninterpretable case feature

T in (46) triggers the Agree operation. The valued phi-features of *John* value the phi-features of T, after which the phi-features of T are deleted. Only phi-features of *John*, which are interpretable at the LF interface, then reach the LF interface level. Notice also that *John* has an unvalued case-feature. Chomsky (2001) assumes that T does not have a case-feature, the case feature of *John* being valued as nominative as a reflex of the phi-feature checking relation with finite T. It is also possible to implement case-licensing in (46) without the stipulatory notion of reflex checking. Thus, as noted by Bošković (2011b), it can be assumed that T has a valued case feature (nominative; after all finite T always licenses nominative, while the case-feature of a noun depends on its syntactic context[15]), with the case-feature of T valuing the case feature of *John*. Since deletion of valued uninterpretable features is allowed, both the case feature of *John* and the case feature of T can be deleted following the Agree relation so that they do not reach the LF interface. Finally, the Agree relation in (46) is followed by movement of *John* to SpecTP, which is triggered by a property of the target in the target-driven system (the EPP property), or by a property of the moving element in the moving-element driven system (for example the requirement that unvalued uninterpretable features function as probes, which means that they must c-command their valuators, see Epstein and Seely 2006 and Bošković 2007b).

Recall also that valued interpretable features of *John* are not deleted after undergoing a feature-checking Agree relation. This implies that they should be able to undergo such a relation more than once, an option which is realized in multiple verb constructions where each verb agrees with the subject, as in Italian (47).

(47) I   ragazzi sono   stati   invitati   (Italian)
      the boys   are.pl been.pl invited.pl
      'the boys were invited'

4.3 Conclusion

The leading idea of the Principles and Parameters approach is the existence of Universal Grammar, a genetic endowment which helps children acquire language that comprises a set of principles, which are invariant across languages, and a set of parameters, which provide limited options for language variation. Government and Binding Theory and the Minimalist Program are two implementations of the Principles and Parameters approach, with the Minimalist Program building upon Government and Binding Theory. Minimalism attempts not only to explain the properties of the language faculty but also to answer the question why these properties are the way they are (see also Chapter 3).

Notes

1. In particular, movements that take place prior to Spell-out are assumed to be driven by the need to eliminate strong features, which are illegitimate PF objects, before syntactic information is sent to PF. The principle Procrastinate, which favors LF movement, delays all movements that are not motivated by PF considerations until LF.
2. The argument for multiple spell-out based on *to*-contraction can be traced back to Bresnan (1971c).
3. See Boeckx (2000) for discussion of the *to*-contraction paradigm under the movement approach to control.
4. There is a fine line to walk on here, given Bošković's (1994) proposal that movement cannot be too short, a line of research that Grohmann (2003), Abels (2003), and Boeckx (2007a), among others, have expanded on (Grohmann calls the relevant constraint anti-locality; see Section 18.11).
5. Takahashi (1994) deduces even the ban on extraction out of subjects and adjuncts from MCLP, the idea being that the MCLP forces the element moving out of a subject/adjunct to adjoin to the subject/adjunct, which leads to a violation of independent requirements.

6. Rackowski and Richards (2005) and den Dikken (to appear), however, question successive-cyclic movement via SpecCP.
7. More precisely, multiplicity of specifiers cannot be blocked in the Bare Phrase Structure system. In this respect, the system contrasts with Kayne (1994), which disallows multiple specifiers.
8. Regarding formal implementation of adjunction, adjuncts are assumed not to change the label and bar level of their targets (see Chomsky 1995c: Chapter 4). The constituent represented by the tree in (i) is a non-minimal, maximal projection.

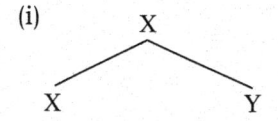

(i)
```
       X
      / \
     X   Y
```

The addition of a specifier turns the constituent into a non-minimal, non-maximal projection. The addition of an adjunct, on the other hand, does not change the bar level of the target, which remains a non-minimal, maximal projection.

9. There is also a line of research that accounts for special properties of adjuncts by assuming that adjuncts are not fully integrated into the structure (or they are on a separate plane) at the point when the processes in which adjuncts do not participate occur (see in this respect Chomsky 2001b).
10. The account can actually be extended to all relativized minimality effects. Thus, the problem with (28a) is that *what* undergoes wh-movement to the matrix SpecCP although there is a wh-phrase that is closer to the matrix SpecCP than *what*, namely *why*.
11. It is actually not clear that movement of formal features prior to SS would cause a pronunciation problem since phonological features (and this is what PF cares about) would still be present together.
12. Another non-movement approach is to assume that the Q unselectively binds the wh-phrase. This treatment, however, is not an option for all covert dependencies, which other options mentioned in this section at least in principle can be.
13. What was discussed in Section 4.1 in this respect was the multiple spell-out model. Adoption of the single cycle model actually does not require adoption of multiple spell-out; see, for example, Bobaljik (1995), Groat and O'Neil (1996).
14. The exception here is the number of pluralia tantum nouns like *kola* in (43), which does not have semantic interpretation.
15. Chomsky disallows the possibility of valued uninterpretable features essentially by stipulation. The possibility, however, needs to be allowed on empirical grounds (see Pesetsky and Torrego 2007 and

Bošković 2011b). Thus the gender feature of the nouns in (43)–(45) is valued, as discussed above, but it is also semantically uninterpretable, gender in Serbo-Croatian being an arbitrary, grammatical feature. As discussed in the text, allowing valued uninterpretable features also makes possible elimination of reflex feature checking.

5

Minimalism and Optimality Theory

Hans Broekhuis and Ellen Woolford

5.1 Introduction

This chapter discusses the relation between the Minimalist Program (MP) and Optimality Theory (OT) and will show that, contrary to popular belief, MP and OT are not inherently incompatible or competing frameworks/theories. Instead, we will show (i) that the two can well be seen as complementary parts of a more general model of grammar and (ii) that the resulting hybrid system may be superior to the two constituting parts in isolation. Before we discuss the hybrid system, we provide background on some characteristic features of MP and OT in Section 5.2. Section 5.3 shows that the hybrid system makes it possible to eliminate the EPP-features from MP by replacing them by an OT-evaluation of the output of the computational system. Although this need not necessarily be seen as a step forwards, we will show that it provides us with a theory of Scandinavian Object Shift that is far superior to the proposal in Chomsky (2001) and which raises a number of new and interesting questions concerning Holmberg's Generalization; cf. Holmberg (1986, 1999). Section 5.4 goes a step further by showing that the replacement of certain inviolable conditions on the operation Agree from MP by an OT-evaluation of the output of the computational system solves a set of intricate questions concerning Burzio's Generalization and cross-linguistic variation in the case-licensing of nominative objects.[1]

5.2 Some characteristic features of the Minimalist Program and Optimality Theory

Before we discuss the hybrid system it is necessary to briefly lay out the properties of MP and OT. The focus here will be on OT, given that MP is more extensively discussed in Chapters 2–4. An important conclusion will be

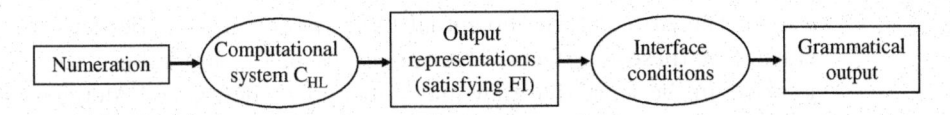

```
Numeration → Computational → Output          → Interface   → Grammatical
              system C_HL    representations    conditions    output
                             (satisfying FI)
```

Figure 5.1

that, contrary to what the name suggests, OT-syntax resembles MP in that it is not a theory but a program in the sense that it implies neither a specific theory of the generative component nor of the evaluative module that evaluates the output of the system; it is a theory of constraint interaction that computes the predictions for any generator and set of postulated constraints. We will furthermore argue that the overall modeling of the syntactic module presupposed by MP is very similar to that proposed by OT-syntax. This will make it possible to develop a new program that incorporates certain basic assumptions and guiding intuitions from both MP and OT. Sections 5.3 and 5.4 will illustrate two implementations of the hybrid program.

5.2.1 The Minimalist Program

Given that Minimalism is not a theory but a program, which refers to a family of approaches that aim at reducing syntax/grammar to its absolute minimum, we will simply pick out one of the more familiar approaches for illustration, viz., the one developed by Chomsky (1995c) and, especially, subsequent work. The overall structure of the model that has arisen since Chomsky (2000b) is given in Figure 5.1. Below, we will briefly summarize some of the properties of this model that will be central to our concern. Various other aspects of Chomsky's recent work (like phase theory) will not be discussed here; see Chapters 4 and 18 for a more complete discussion.

The derivation takes a numeration as its input, the elements of which are processed by the operations of the computational system for human language C_{HL}. The first operation is EXTERNAL MERGE (henceforth: Merge), which combines elements from the numeration and/or larger syntactic objects already formed into larger structures. The merged elements may contain unvalued formal features that must be valued by entering into the syntactic relation Agree with some other element in their syntactic (c-command) domain with corresponding valued formal features: the unvalued features thus function as probes that search within a certain domain for a goal with corresponding valued features.[2] It is further assumed that this probe can be assigned a so-called EPP-FEATURE, which requires that the goal be placed in its minimal domain (in the sense of Chomsky 1995c: Chapter 3) by means of INTERNAL MERGE (henceforth: Move). When the numeration is exhausted, the subsequent applications of Merge and Move must have resulted in an output representation that satisfies Full Interpretation, that is, which only consists of elements that can be given an interpretation by either the Conceptual–Intentional

(C-I) or the Articulatory–Perceptual (A-P) system; if not, the derivation crashes at these interfaces. The operations of C_{HL} are subject to LAST RESORT in the sense that they may only apply when forced: Merge must apply given that the derivation must result in a single syntactic object, which implies that the numeration must be exhausted at the end of the derivation; Agree is forced by Full Interpretation given that unvalued formal features cannot be interpreted by the C-I or A-P system. Move, finally, is forced by the need to eliminate the EPP-features: it is often assumed that these features must be eliminated immediately after they are introduced in the structure in order for the derivation to be able to proceed (see Chapter 4).

The computational system C_{HL} is seen as invariant among languages and defines a set of possible output representations for each numeration. The fact that languages vary in word order (that is, give rise to different output representations on the basis of similar numerations) is accounted for by assuming that languages may be parameterized with respect to the question whether a certain probe, like the unvalued formal feature(s) on the functional heads of the clause (including the light verb v^*), is associated with an EPP-feature.[3] In earlier Minimalist work, it was assumed that the option of having or not having an EPP-feature was fixed once and for all in the lexicon of the language in question, but Chomsky (2001) suggested that the EPP-features can (at least sometimes) be optionally assigned to a certain probe, which may account for certain 'optional' movements like Object Shift in Icelandic. However, given that object shift is sensitive to the information structure of the clause, Chomsky claims that (at least in this case) the assignment of an EPP-feature is subject to an effect-on-output condition: an EPP-feature can only be assigned when this has repercussions for the meaning of the clause. We will return to this in Section 5.3.

The effect-on-output condition, which in effect functions as a filter on the set of possible output representations, is an example of a larger set of so-called interface conditions (as were the global economy, bare output, interface, etc. conditions postulated in earlier and other versions of MP). Although these conditions are assumed to play an important role in selecting the grammatical output representations for a certain language L, it seems that the Minimalist community has failed so far to develop a general format that such conditions must meet. The aim of this chapter is to show that OT may fill that gap.

5.2.2 Optimality Theory

This section will briefly discuss what we will refer to as traditional OT-syntax.[4] Section 5.2.2.1 will start with presenting the basic ideas shared by researchers working within OT, which will subsequently be illustrated for syntax in Section 5.2.2.2. Section 5.2.2.3 will conclude this brief discussion of OT-syntax by showing that OT-syntax is not a theory, but instead resembles MP in that it functions as a research program.

```
Input → Generator → Candidate Set → OT-Evaluator → Optimal output
```

Figure 5.2

5.2.2.1 Shared basic ideas

'OT-syntax' refers to a family of approaches that adopt the model of grammar in Figure 5.2. The guiding intuition of OT is that the language system consists of two components, viz., a generative device called GENERATOR that produces candidate sets and a language-specific filtering device called EVALUATOR that selects candidates from these candidate sets as optimal (= well-formed) in a given language L.

Furthermore, OT adopts the basic assumption that the evaluator consists of a universal set of VIOLABLE CONSTRAINTS (usually referred to as CON) and that it is the LANGUAGE-SPECIFIC RANKING of these constraints that determines which candidates from the candidate sets are optimal in L. The determination of the optimal candidate thus proceeds as in (1), which we have adapted from Archangeli (1997).

(1) The evaluator finds the candidate that *best satisfies* the ranked constraints, such that:
    a. violation of a lower ranked constraint is tolerated if this enables the candidate to satisfy a higher ranked constraint, and
    b. ties by violation or by satisfaction of a higher ranked constraint are resolved by a lower ranked constraint.

5.2.2.2 An illustration

The way the OT-evaluator works can readily be demonstrated by means of Pesetsky's (1997, 1998) analysis of the pronunciation patterns of relative clauses. Pesetsky adopts the standard assumption that relative clauses are derived by means of *wh*-movement of (the phrase containing) the relative pronoun, followed by optional deletion of the phonological content of the relative pronoun and/or the complementizer. His aim is to provide an OT-alternative for Chomsky and Lasnik's (1977) proposal that the pronunciation patterns in (2) arise as the result of the Doubly-Filled COMP Filter and the recoverability condition on deletion.

(2)
a. the man [who$_i$ that I know t_i] a'. the book [[$_{PP}$ about which]$_i$ that he spoke t_i]
b. the man [who$_i$ that I know t_i] b'. *the book [[$_{PP}$ about which]$_i$ that he spoke t_i]
c. the man [who$_i$ that I know t_i] c'. *the book [[$_{PP}$ about which]$_i$ that he spoke t_i]
d. *the man [who$_i$ that I know t_i] d'. *the book [[$_{PP}$ about which]$_i$ that he spoke t_i]

Pesetsky's proposal also aims at accounting for the fact that the pronunciation pattern is language-specific. The contrast between the primeless examples in (2) and (3) shows that English allows a wider range of pronunciation patterns with a bare relative pronoun than French. However, when the relative pronoun is embedded in a larger constituent, like the PPs in the primed examples, the two languages behave the same.

(3)
a. *l'homme [qui$_i$ que je connais t$_i$]   a'. l'homme [[$_{PP}$ avec qui]$_i$ que j'ai dansé t$_i$]
b. l'homme [qui$_i$ que je connais t$_i$]   b'. *l'homme [[$_{PP}$ avec qui]$_i$ que j'ai dansé t$_i$]
c. *l'homme [qui$_i$ que je connais t$_i$]   c'. *l'homme [[$_{PP}$ avec qui]$_i$ que j'ai dansé t$_i$]
d. *l'homme [qui$_i$ que je connais t$_i$]   d'. *l'homme [[$_{PP}$ avec qui]$_i$ que j'ai dansé t$_i$]

Pesetsky accounts for the data in (2) and (3) by means of the universal constraints in (4), which we have slightly simplified here for reasons of exposition: (4a) is simply Chomsky and Lasnik's (1977) recoverability condition on deletion, (4b) is a constraint that favors embedded clauses introduced by a complementizer, and (4c) is a constraint that favors the deletion of function words (like complementizers).

(4) a. RECOVERABILITY (REC): a syntactic unit with semantic content must be pronounced unless it has a sufficiently local antecedent.
    b. LEFT EDGE (CP): the first leftmost pronounced word in an embedded CP must be the complementizer.
    c. TELEGRAPH (TEL): do not pronounce function words.

The analysis crucially relies on the fact that LE(CP) in (4b) and TEL in (4c) are in conflict: the former favors complementizers to be pronounced, whereas the latter favors them to be deleted. This makes it possible to account for variation between languages by varying the ranking of these constraints: when LE(CP) outranks TEL, as in (5a), we get a language in which embedded declarative clauses must be introduced by a complementizer; when TEL outranks LE(CP), as in (5b), we get a language in which embedded declarative clauses are not introduced by a complementizer; and when we assume that the two constraints are in a tie, as in (5c), we get a language in which embedded declarative clauses are optionally introduced by a complementizer.

(5) a. LE(CP) >> TEL: embedded declarative clauses are introduced by a complementizer.
    b. TEL >> LE(CP): embedded declarative clauses are not introduced by a complementizer.
    c. TEL < > LE(CP): embedded declarative clauses are optionally introduced by a complementizer.

It is important to realize that a tie like (5c) expresses that the rankings in (5a) and (5b) are *simultaneously* active in the language in question; the set of optimal candidates selected by (5c) is the union of the sets of optimal candidates selected by (5a) and (5b); see Müller (1999) for a discussion of various uses of the notion of a tie. The evaluations can be made visible by means of tableaux. Tableau 5.1 gives the evaluation of embedded declarative clauses with and without a pronounced complementizer in a language with the ranking in (5a). The two asterisks indicate that the constraint in the header of their column is violated by the candidate in question. The (a)-candidate, with a pronounced complementizer, violates TEL but this is tolerated because it enables us to satisfy the higher ranked constraint LE(CP); cf. (1a). The (b)-candidate, with a deleted complementizer, violates LE(CP), and this is fatal (which is indicated by an exclamation mark) because the (a)-candidate does not violate this constraint. The (a)-candidate is therefore optimal, which is indicated by means of the pointed finger: ☞. The shading of cells following the fatal constraint violation indicates that these cells do not play a role in the evaluation; this convention is mainly for convenience, because it makes larger tableaux easier to read.

Tableau 5.1. No C-deletion in embedded declarative clauses

		LE(CP)	TEL
a. ☞	.... [complementizer ....]		*
b.	.... [~~complementizer~~ ....]	*!	

Now consider the evaluation of the same candidates in a language with the ranking in (5b), given in Tableau 5.2. Since TEL is now ranked higher than LE(CP), violation of the former is fatal, so that deletion of the complementizer becomes obligatory.

Tableau 5.2. Obligatory C-deletion in embedded declarative clauses

		TEL	LE(CP)
a.	.... [complementizer ....]	*!	
b. ☞	.... [~~complementizer~~ ....]		*

Tableau 5.3 gives the evaluation according to the ranking in (5c), where the two constraints are in a tie, which is indicated in the tableau by means of a dashed line. Under this ranking the two rankings in (5a&b) are simultaneously active. Therefore we have to read the tie in both directions: when we read the tie from left to right, the violation of LE(CP) is fatal (which is indicated by *>), and the (a)-candidate is optimal; when we read the tableau from right to left, the violation of TEL is fatal (which is indicated by *<), and the (b)-candidate is optimal. This predicts that deletion of the complementizer is optional in this case, since a candidate is only excluded by tied constraints when there is a fatal violation in both directions; cf. the discussion of Tableau 5.5.

Tableau 5.3. Optional C-deletion in embedded declarative clauses

	LE(CP)	TEL
a. ☞ ....[complementizer ....]		*<
b. ☞ ....[~~complementizer~~ ....]	*>	

Note in passing that the ranking in (5c) accounts for the fact that the two constructions are both possible but has nothing to say about their relative frequency. This is not surprising given that we are dealing here with core syntax/competence; the relative frequency of the two constructions should rather be accounted for by some performance theory (which may be given shape as some version of Stochastic OT, mentioned in footnote 4).

Let us now return to the difference between English and French with respect to the pronunciation patterns of relative clauses. It is clear that English is a language of type (5c), given that the complementizer is normally optional in embedded declarative clauses. French, on the other hand, is a language of type (5a): the complementizer is obligatory in embedded declarative clauses. Pesetsky has shown that this also accounts for the differences between the primeless English and French examples of (2) and (3), in which a bare relative pronoun is preposed, provided that we assume that in both languages the constraint recoverability outranks the constraints TEL and LE(CP).

(6) a. French: REC >> LE(CP) >> TEL
    b. English: REC >> TEL <> LE(CP)

Tableau 5.4 provides the evaluation of the primeless French examples in (3). Since the relative pronoun has a local antecedent it is recoverable after deletion, so that all candidates satisfy REC. The (b)-candidate is the optimal candidate because it is the only one that does not violate LE(CP); the fact that this candidate violates the lower-ranked constraint TEL is tolerated since this enables the satisfaction of the higher-ranked constraint LE(CP); cf. (1a).

Tableau 5.4. Relative clauses with preposed relative pronoun

French		REC	LE(CP)	TEL
a.	l'homme [qui$_i$ ~~que~~ je connais t$_i$]		*!	
b. ☞	l'homme [~~qui$_i$~~ que je connais t$_i$]			*
c.	l'homme [~~qui$_i$~~ ~~que~~ je connais t$_i$]		*!	
d.	l'homme [qui$_i$ que je connais t$_i$]		*!	*

The evaluation of the corresponding English examples is given in Tableau 5.5, which is slightly more complex due to the fact that LE(CP) and TEL are in a tie. We are therefore dealing with two rankings at the same time: REC >> LE(CP) >> TEL and REC >> TEL >> LE(CP). The first ranking is the one we also find in French, and we have seen that this results in selection of the (b)-candidate as optimal. Under the second ranking, violation of TEL is fatal, so that the (a)- and the (c)-candidate are selected as optimal. As a result, three out of the four candidates are acceptable in English.

Tableau 5.5. Relative clauses with preposed relative pronoun

English	REC	LE(CP)	TEL
a. ☞ the man [who₁ ~~that~~ I know t₁]		*>	
b. ☞ the man [~~who₁~~ that I know t₁]			*<
c. ☞ the man [~~who₁~~ ~~that~~ I know t₁]		*>	
d. the man [who₁ that I know t₁]		*>	*<

Next consider the evaluation of the French examples in Tableau 5.6, in which a PP containing a relative pronoun is preposed. Since the preposition is not locally recoverable, deletion of it leads to a violation of the highest-ranked constraint REC: this excludes the (b)- and the (c)-candidate. Since the two remaining candidates both violate LE(CP), the lowest ranked constraint TEL gets the final say by excluding the (d)-candidate; cf. (1b). Note that this shows that the subranking LE(CP) >> TEL does not mean that the complementizer is always realized, but that this depends on the question whether it is preceded by some other element that must be realized; if so, TEL forces the complementizer to delete.

Tableau 5.6. Relative clauses with preposed PP

French	REC	LE(CP)	TEL
a. ☞ l'homme [[avec qui]₁ ~~que~~ j'ai dansé t₁]		*	
b. l'homme [[~~avec qui~~]₁ que j'ai dansé t₁]	*!		*
c. l'homme [[~~avec qui~~]₁ ~~que~~ j'ai dansé t₁]	*!	*	
d. l'homme [[avec qui]₁ que j'ai dansé t₁]		*	*!

Tableau 5.7 shows that we get the same result for the corresponding English examples: both the (b)- and the (c)-candidate are excluded by REC, and the (d)-candidate is excluded because it is harmonically bound by the (a)-candidate, that is, it has a fatal violation of TEL irrespective of whether we read the tie from left to right or from right to left. We will simply indicate violations of tied constraints that are fatal on all rankings available in the language by means of an exclamation mark.

Tableau 5.7. Relative clauses with preposed PP

English	REC	LE(CP)	TEL
a. ☞ the book [[about which]₁ ~~that~~ he spoke t₁]		*	
b. the book [[~~about which~~]₁ that he spoke t₁]	*!		*
c. the book [[~~about which~~]₁ ~~that~~ he spoke t₁]	*!	*	
d. the book [[about which]₁ that he spoke t₁]		*	*!

5.2.2.3 OT-syntax is a meta-theory or program, not a theory

Although OT-syntacticians agree that the language system consists of a generator that produces candidate sets and an evaluator that selects candidates from these sets as optimal in a given language L by means of the procedure in (1), they may have widely varying ideas on the nature of the generator and, as a result, the constraints that constitute the evaluator. The generator can take the form of virtually any imaginable generative device, as is clear from the fact that the current OT-approaches to syntax are based on very different and often incompatible linguistic theories. Some more or less random examples are given in (7).

(7) a. Lexical-Functional Grammar: Bresnan (2000), Sells (2001b; Chapter 6)
 b. Early Principles and Parameters theory: Grimshaw (1997), Pesetsky (1998); Chapter 4
 c. Minimalism: Dekkers (1999), Broekhuis and Dekkers (2000), Heck and Müller (2000), Woolford (2007), Broekhuis (2008); Chapter 4
 d. Others: Müller (2000/2001), Vogel (2006a)

Since the generators postulated by the proposals in (7) differ considerably and the generated candidate sets will therefore be constituted by candidates with entirely different properties, the postulated constraints will be quite different as well. This can be illustrated by comparing the OT-approaches proposed in Grimshaw (1997), Broekhuis (2008), and Dekkers (1999), which are all based on some version of the Principles and Parameters theory. Grimshaw's (1997) proposal was originally written in the early 1990s and is based on the pre-Minimalist Principles and Parameters framework. Among other things, this is clear from the fact that she tries to capture the directionality parameter, which was still generally adopted at that time, by means of two conflicting constraints HEAD LEFT and HEAD RIGHT (the head is leftmost/rightmost in its projection). In addition, she assumes the alignment constraints SPECIFIER LEFT and SPECIFIER RIGHT (the specifier is leftmost/rightmost in its projection). Given that Grimshaw also assumes that the structures created by the generator conform to the general X-bar-schema, the linearization of these structures follows from the language-specific ranking of these four constraints. Broekhuis (2008), which is based on the Minimalist machinery proposed in Chomsky (2000b) and later work, need not make use of Grimshaw's alignment constraints given that he adopts some form of the Universal Base Hypothesis, according to which linear order is derived from the hierarchical relations between the constituents in the output representation (as expressed by Kayne's, 1994, Linear Correspondence Axiom). In his approach, linear order therefore follows from the language-specific ranking of a set of so-called EPP-constraints, which favor movement of a goal into its probe's minimal domain, and the economy constraint *MOVE, which disfavors movement. For example, the 'strong' ranking EPP(case) >> *MOVE requires movement of the probed noun phrase into the minimal domain of the unvalued case features of the verb or the inflectional node I, whereas the 'weak' ranking *MOVE >> EPP(case) requires that the probe remain in its original position; see Section 5.3 for details. This proposal, which expresses the same intuition as Chomsky's Agree-based approach that Agree is normally sufficient for convergence, will find no place in OT-approaches that follow Groat and O'Neil (1996) in assuming that feature checking invariably triggers movement and that the linear order depends on the question whether it is the tail or the head of the resulting chain that is spelled out (see also Sections 4.2.4.1, 15.4.3, 16.2.1, and 16.2.4); such approaches will replace the EPP-constraints by, e.g., Dekkers's (1999) PARSE-F constraints, which favor pronunciation of moved constituents in the position of their formal feature (the head of the chain), and reinterpret *MOVE as a constraint that favors pronunciation of moved elements in their base position (the tail of the chain). This brief discussion demonstrates that properties of the proposed generator are immediately reflected in the nature of the postulated violable constraints of the OT-evaluator. The differences between the three OT-approaches discussed here are relatively small due to the fact that the proposed generators all find their origin in the Chomskyan generative tradition, but it will be clear that the differences between these OT-approaches and OT-approaches that are based on other traditions may be much larger. Note that the choice of the correct generator and the selection of the correct set universal constraints are, of course, both empirical issues.

5.2.3 Combining the Minimalist Program and Optimality Theory

When we compare Figure 5.1 and Figure 5.2, we see immediately that the overall structure of Chomsky's version of MP has much in common with the model assumed in standard OT. Both have a generative device that defines a set of possible structures, from which languages select a subset of acceptable sentences by means of some filtering device. From the discussion in the preceding sections, it will have become clear that the two devices are not equally well developed in the two programs. Minimalist research has focused mainly on the generative device, despite the fact that the following quote from Chomsky (1995c:220) shows that a filtering device was postulated right from the start:

The language L thus generates three relevant sets of derivations: the set D of derivations, a subset D_C of convergent derivations of D, and a subset D_A of admissible derivations of D. [Full Interpretation] determines D_C, and the economy conditions select D_A. ... D_A is a subset of D_C.

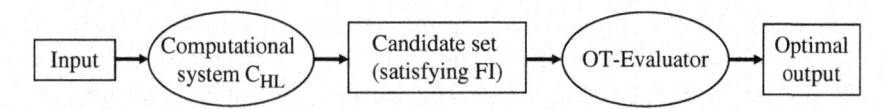

```
Input → Computational system C_HL → Candidate set (satisfying FI) → OT-Evaluator → Optimal output
```

Figure 5.3

Although the filtering device has been endowed with various names in the respective stages of the Minimalist framework (they have been referred to as global economy, bare output, interface, and effect-on-output conditions), relatively little work has been devoted to developing a coherent theory of it. The situation in OT is rather the reverse: much work has been devoted to the substantive content of the filtering device (that is, the constraints and their ranking), but virtually no attention has been paid to the generator. Given this situation it might be useful to combine the two approaches by assuming that the generative device is some version of the computational system C_{HL}, and that the filtering device is some version of the OT-evaluator, as in Figure 5.3.

A potential advantage of this hybrid MP + OT model is that it provides OT-syntax with an explicitly formulated generator and MP with at least a general format for expressing the interface conditions. Furthermore, now that both devices have been assigned an explicit format, we can seriously investigate the division of labor between the two components. For example, Broekhuis and Dekkers (2000) have noted that Pesetsky's RECOVERABILITY is rather suspect as an OT-constraint given that it is never violated: it is always the *highest* ranked constraint. This suggests that we are actually dealing with an inviolable condition on the operation Delete, which must therefore be added to the inventory of syntactic operations in C_{HL}. Given that the derivation is cyclic, the postulation of Delete makes it impossible to account for the recoverability restriction by appealing to the availability of some local antecedent. Therefore, the restriction must rather be formulated in terms of semantic features, which will have various ramifications for the analysis of the pronunciation patterns of relative clauses. We will not digress here on this specific issue any further, but refer the reader to Dekkers (1999) for further discussion.

An important point is that the hybrid model may substantially change our views on the properties ascribed to the generative and filtering devices by traditional MP/OT. Our hope is that we can simplify current MP by expressing all language-specific statements (including the more recent effect-on-output conditions discussed above) by means of language-specific rankings of otherwise universal violable constraints. For example, MP stipulates that languages differ with respect to the question of whether functional heads force movement of the phrases with which they are in an Agree-relation. A formal way of expressing this is by assuming that such heads may or may not have an EPP-feature. The following section will show that it is not only readily possible to replace the notion of EPP-feature by a small set of violable constraints, but that doing this also results in a descriptively more adequate theory.

5.3 Eliminating the EPP-features

This section, which is based on Broekhuis (2000, 2008), will discuss certain aspects of Scandinavian Object Shift (henceforth: OS). Section 5.3.1 will start with discussing Chomsky's (2001) syntactic account of OS in order to further underpin our claim that current MP employs language-specific output filters. Section 5.3.2 will propose an OT-version of Chomsky's filter and show that the postulated constraints can also be readily used to express the macroparameterizations concerning OS. Section 5.3.3 will argue that the OS data unambiguously show that, contrary to what has been claimed in some Minimalist approaches, verb movement must be considered an instantiation of syntactic movement, and provide an OT-account of some differences between the Germanic languages in this respect; it will also show that the proposed OT-accounts of OS and verb movement interact in interesting ways.

5.3.1 Chomsky's (2001) account of Icelandic Object Shift

Earlier versions of MP assumed that the option of having or not having an EPP-feature was fixed in the lexicon of the language in question, but it soon became clear that this could not be maintained. Chomsky (2001) adopts the configuration in (8), where $Object_\theta$ is the thematic position of the object and $Object_s$ is an outer specifier position of v^* created by OS triggered by the case feature on the light verb v^* (cf. Vikner 1994, 2006), provided at least that v^* is also associated with an EPP-feature.

(8) ... [$_\alpha$ Object$_s$ [Subject v^* [V ... Object$_\theta$]]]

If we assume that the lexicon determines once and for all whether v^* is assigned an EPP-feature or not, we expect languages to behave rigidly with respect to OS by categorically forcing or blocking it. This runs afoul, however, with the examples in (9), which show that Icelandic OS depends on the information structure of the clause (see also Chapter 23): OS is only possible when the object is part of the presupposition of the clause; cf. Holmberg (1999). From this, we may conclude that OS is at least partly externally motivated, and that we have to introduce additional means to account for the data in (9).[5]

(9) a. Jón keypti ekki bókina   bókina ⊄ focus
       Jón bought not the book
    b. Jón keypti bókina$_i$ ekki $t_{bókina}$ bókina ⊂ presupposition

More evidence against assuming that the lexicon fully determines whether v^* is assigned an EPP-feature or not is provided by the examples in (10), which show that OS is also sensitive to its syntactic environment: in complex verb constructions like (10), OS is excluded irrespective of the information structure of the clause, and (10a) is therefore ambiguous.

(10)
a. Jón hefur ekki keypt bókina.   *bókina* ⊂ focus or presupposition
   Jón has not bought the book
b. *Jón hefur bókina ekki keypt t_bokina

One way to rescue the earlier proposal that the lexicon determines once and for all whether *v** is assigned an EPP-feature is to follow Holmberg (1999), who claims that OS is actually not part of core grammar but a *phonological* operation that is driven by the interpretation of the object. This is formulated more precisely in (11a), which paraphrases Chomsky's (2001:31) summary of Holmberg's proposal. Holmberg (1999:15) accounts for the ungrammaticality of (10b) by postulating the additional restriction on the application of OS in (11b): OS is blocked in (10b) because it would move the object across the main verb.

(11) a. Object Shift is a phonological movement that satisfies condition (11b) and is driven by the semantic interpretation INT of the shifted object:
       (i) INT: object is part of the presupposition of the clause.
       (ii) INT': object is part of the focus of the clause.
      b. Holmberg's Generalization (1999 version): Object Shift cannot apply across a phonologically visible category asymmetrically c-commanding the object position except adjuncts.

Chomsky (2001:32) correctly argues that Holmberg's proposal is problematic because "displacement rules interspersed in the phonological component should have little semantic effect" (p. 15), and he therefore maintains that OS takes place in core syntax.[6]

Chomsky's (2001: example (61)) own solution to the problem concerning the 'optionality' of OS is given in (12), where INT and INT' are different interpretations defined as in (11a), and we will see below that this boils down to filtering out the unwanted form–meaning pairs by means of a language-specific output filter.

(12) a. *v** is assigned an EPP-feature only if that has an effect on outcome.
      b. The EPP position of *v** is assigned INT.
      c. At the phonological border of *v**P, XP is assigned INT'.

Chomsky suggests that (12a) is an invariant principle of grammar; it intends to express that *v** is only assigned an EPP-feature when the resulting movement affects the semantic interpretation of the output representation, or when it makes A'-movement possible by placing the object at the phonological edge of the *v**P-phase. Clause (12b) is likewise claimed to be an invariant principle: an object occupying the position *Object_s* in (8) in the output representation must be construed as being part of the presupposition of the clause. It is important to note that (12b) is silent on non-shifted objects, which correctly predicts that non-shifted objects in Icelandic examples like (10a) or in non-OS languages like English can be interpreted as part of either the focus or the presupposition of the clause.

Given that (12b) does not restrict the interpretation of non-shifted objects, we need something in addition to account for the fact that OS is obligatory in examples like (9b). This is where (12c) comes in, which intends to express that the object will be interpreted as being part of the focus of the clause when it is v^*P-internal *and* not c-commanded by v^*P-internal phonological material.

(13) XP is at the phonological border of v^*P, iff:
 a. XP is a v^*P-internal position; and
 b. XP is not c-commanded by v^*P-internal phonological material.

The main difference between the examples in (9) and (10) is that in the former the main verb has moved out of v^*P into T, whereas in the latter it has not and thus occupies a v^*P-internal position. Example (10a) is therefore correctly predicted to be ambiguous: since the v^*+V complex is v^*P-internal and c-commands the object, clause (12c) does not apply and the object can therefore be interpreted either as part of the focus of the clause (INT′) or as part of the presupposition of the clause (INT). Example (10b) is consequently blocked by (12a) because OS has no effect on the outcome as the object can also be assigned the interpretation INT in its base position in (10a). Therefore, in constructions like (10), the EPP-feature can only be assigned to v^* if it is needed to enable A′-movement. In (9), on the other hand, there is no v^*P-internal phonological material that c-commands the θ-position of the object. Consequently, if the object occupies this position, (12c) states that it must be assigned INT′. OS therefore has an effect on the outcome because it enables the assignment of INT, so that (12a) allows assignment of an EPP-feature to v^*.[7]

It is important to note that statement (12c) clearly functions as a filter in the sense of Chomsky and Lasnik (1977). First, it is clear that it cannot be considered an intrinsic condition on the operation Move; when we apply (12c) to the intermediate stage in (8), the desired distinction between (9) and (10) cannot be made yet, because the verb and the subject are moved out of the v^*P only at a later stage in the derivation. Chomsky (2001) therefore assumes that (12c) applies to the resulting representation at the higher phase level (CP). Secondly, (12c) is a language-specific statement: Icelandic is subject to it, and therefore OS is forced in examples like (9b); Danish, on the other hand, is not subject to it, so that (12a) blocks OS in Danish examples like (14).

(14) a. Hvorfor læste studenterne   ikke   artiklen?
     why   read the students   not   the article
  b. *Hvorfor læste studenterne artiklen$_i$ ikke t_i?

Chomsky (2001:36) presents clause (12c) as a parameter that distinguishes OS from non-OS languages, which correctly distinguishes between languages like Icelandic, which do, and Finnish–Swedish, which do not, have OS. It seems, however, that (12c) is unlike the parameters of the earlier Principles and Parameters framework in that it is not binary. This is clear from the fact that a language like Danish has limited OS: it is like Finnish–Swedish in not allowing OS of non-pronominal DPs, but like Icelandic in that OS of weak pronouns is possible; see the contrast between (14) and (15).

(15) a. Hvorfor læste studenterne den$_i$ ikke t_i?
    why read the students it not
 b. *Hvorfor læste studenterne ikke den?

This can be accounted for by refining clause (12c) as in (12c′). This clause makes the following correct predictions: (i) non-pronominal DPs that are part of the presupposition of the clause (= INT) must undergo OS in Icelandic, but not in Finnish–Swedish or Danish; (ii) definite pronouns (which are assigned INT by definition) must undergo OS in Icelandic and Danish; (iii) Finnish–Swedish does not have any kind of OS because the set of elements that is assigned INT′ in the relevant context is empty, which is indicated by '∅.'

(12) c′. At the phonological border of v^*P, XP is assigned INT′
    (i) XP = DP   (Icelandic)
    (ii) XP = weak definite pronoun   (Danish)
    (iii) XP = ∅   (Finnish–Swedish)

The discussion above has shown that Chomsky's proposal regulates OS by means of language-specific filters on the output representation. In fact, this proposal raises the question whether we still need the EPP-features. Given that the output filters decide whether a certain movement is licit or not, we may just as well assume that movements that satisfy the Last Resort Condition apply optionally; the unwanted structures can then be filtered out by appealing to the effect-on-output condition in tandem with the language-specific filter in (12c′). This would enable us to attribute cross-linguistic language variation *entirely* to the evaluator, just as in OT. In (16), we rephrase Chomsky's proposal such that reference to the notion of EPP-feature indeed becomes superfluous.

(16) a. Move is possible only if it has an effect on outcome.
 b. The derived object position is assigned INT.
 c. At the phonological border of v^*P, XP is assigned INT′
    (i) XP = DP   (Icelandic)
    (ii) XP = weak definite pronoun   (Danish)
    (iii) XP = ∅   (Finnish–Swedish)

5.3.2 An OT-account of Object Shift

Eliminating the EPP-features is of course highly desirable from a Minimalist perspective as it furthers the goal of reducing the computational system to its absolute minimum by eliminating the parameterization introduced by these features: it makes C_{HL} into a truly universal system that mechanically applies to a given input. However, given that elimination of the EPP-features shifts the explanatory burden entirely to the interface conditions, it will be clear that it is unsatisfying to appeal to more or less randomly formulated and language-specific output filters of the sort in (16); a more general theory of these filters is called for, and OT can provide the format for such a theory. Elimination of the EPP-features is also advantageous from an OT-perspective given that the resulting version of C_{HL} fully satisfies McCarthy and Prince's (1993) description of the OT-generator as consisting of linguistic operations subject to "very general considerations of structural well-formedness"; C_{HL} simply consists of general operations like Agree and Merge without any built-in language-specific properties.

We will assume that the resulting hybrid MP + OT system must meet certain Minimalist demands of design, which implies among other things that the set of constraints be small and that the formulation of the individual constraints be simple (see Broekhuis 2008 for detailed discussion). The constraints proposed here build on previous work in that they all have some correlate in the Principles and Parameters tradition (and, more specifically, in current MP). We start with formulating an OT-counterpart of the EPP-features from traditional MP by postulating a family of violable EPP-constraints, which generalizes the GB-style EPP (SpecIP must be filled) by requiring that all probes (unvalued formal features) trigger movement of their goal into their specifier.

(17) EPP(F): probe F attracts its goal.
    a. EPP(case): an unvalued case feature attracts its goal.
    b. EPP(φ): unvalued φ-features attract their goal.
    c. etc.

The EPP-constraints in (17) interact in an OT-fashion with the economy constraint *MOVE, which prohibits movement. As a result, claiming that *MOVE outranks EPP(case) is more or less equivalent to saying that no EPP-feature is assigned to probes with an unvalued case feature, whereas claiming that EPP(case) outranks *MOVE is more or less equivalent to saying that these probes are assigned an EPP-feature. The two rankings in (18a&b) thus express a macroparameterization between OS and non-OS languages. In order to facilitate discussion, we will adapt the weak/strong terminology from Chomsky (1995c) and henceforth refer to these rankings as, respectively, the WEAK and STRONG RANKING of EPP(case).

(18) a. Weak ranking: *MOVE >> EPP(case) ⇒ case features normally do not trigger OS
b. Strong ranking: EPP(case) >> *MOVE ⇒ case features normally trigger OS

An important advantage of this OT-formalization of the 'strength' property is that it follows without further ado that we can override the weak and strong rankings: languages with a weak ranking of EPP(case) will sometimes allow OS when *MOVE is outranked by some constraint A that favors it (cf. (19a)), and languages with a strong ranking of EPP(case) will sometimes disallow OS when EPP(case) is outranked by some constraint B that disfavors it (cf. (19b)).

(19) a. A >> *MOVE >> EPP(case): if A favors OS, the weak ranking of EPP (case) is overruled
b. B >> EPP(case) >> *MOVE: if B disfavors OS, the strong ranking of EPP(case) is overruled

We will assume that the constraints that override the weak/strong rankings are related to restrictions imposed by the C-I and A-P systems, for which reason we will refer to them as interface constraints. The three interface constraints relevant for our present discussion are given in (20). These constraints all correspond more or less with notions found in (16) above: the constraint D-PRONOUN essentially adopts earlier claims that phonologically reduced pronouns cannot occur vP-internally and replaces clause (16c,ii); the constraint ALIGNFOCUS, which is taken from Costa (1998), formalizes the well-known observation that new information tends to occur in the right periphery of the clause, and replaces (16c,i) above; finally, H-COMPL expresses part of Holmberg's Generalization in (11b), which Chomsky tries to capture by appealing to the notion of phonological border in (16c).[8]

(20) a. D-PRONOUN: a reduced definite pronoun must be vP-external:
*$[_{vP} \ldots \text{pron}_{[+def]} \ldots]$.
b. ALIGNFOCUS (AF): the prosodically unmarked focus is the rightmost constituent in its clause.
c. H-COMPL: a head precedes all terminals dominated by its complement

Now we have everything in place to show how the weak and strong rankings in (18) can be overridden. First, consider the case in (19a), which can be illustrated by means of the Danish examples in (14) and (15), repeated here in a slightly different form as (21), in which the angled brackets indicate alternative placements of the object. Broekhuis (2000) has argued that Danish OS in (21a) is blocked by the weak ranking *MOVE >> EPP(case). The fact that OS is nevertheless possible when the object is a definite pronoun is due to the fact that *MOVE is outranked by D-PRONOUN, which requires that the pronominal object be vP-external.

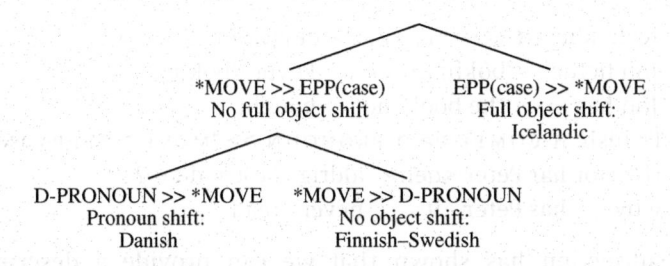

```
                              ┌──────────────┴──────────────┐
                    *MOVE >> EPP(case)              EPP(case) >> *MOVE
                    No full object shift             Full object shift:
                                                          Icelandic
              ┌──────────┴──────────┐
     D-PRONOUN >> *MOVE    *MOVE >> D-PRONOUN
       Pronoun shift:         No object shift:
          Danish              Finnish–Swedish
```

Figure 5.4

(21) Danish: D-PRONOUN >> *MOVE >> EPP(case)
    a. Hvorfor læste Peter <*artiklen> aldrig <artiklen>?
        why   read   Peter   the.article   never
    b. Hvorfor læste Peter <den> aldrig <*den>?
        why   read   Peter   it   never

This shows that we can readily account for the fact that languages differ in the extent to which they exhibit OS: languages like Icelandic allow OS both with pronominal and lexical DPs due to the fact that they have a strong ranking of EPP(case), languages like Danish have the ranking D-PRONOUN >> *MOVE >> EPP(case) and therefore allow OS of pronouns only, and languages like Finnish–Swedish do not have any form of regular OS because *MOVE outranks both EPP(case) and D-PRONOUN. This gives rise to the macroparameterization in Figure 5.4.

Now, consider the case in (19b), which can be illustrated by means of the Icelandic examples in (9), repeated here in a slightly different form as (22), in which the angled brackets again indicate alternative placements of the object. By assuming that ALIGNFOCUS in (20b) outranks EPP(case), we account for the fact that OS is excluded when the object is part of the focus of the clause given that the high ranking of ALIGNFOCUS requires it to be the rightmost constituent in its clause.

(22) Icelandic: AF >> EPP(case) >> *MOVE
    a. Jón keypti <*bókina> ekki <bókina>   bókina ⊂ focus
        Jón bought   the book   not
    b. Jón keypti <bókina> ekki <*bókina>   bókina ⊂ presupposition

Holmberg's Generalization in (11b) instantiates another case of (19b); the Icelandic examples in (10), repeated here as (23a), can be accounted for by assuming that H-COMPL also outranks EPP(case). Given that H-COMPL and ALIGNFOCUS both disfavor OS, the ranking of these two constraints cannot be established on the basis of the data discussed so far, which we have expressed by placing them within curly brackets. Example (23b) shows that Holmberg's Generalization also applies to Danish pronominal object shift, which can be accounted for by assuming that H-COMPL outranks D-PRONOUN.

(23) a. Icelandic: {H-COMPL, AF} >> EPP(case) >> *MOVE
   Jón hefur <*bókina> ekki keypt <bókina>
   Jón has   the book   not bought
b. Danish: H-COMPL >> D-PRONOUN >> *MOVE >> EPP(case)
   Hvorfor har Peter <den> aldrig læst <*den>?
   why   has Peter it   never read

This subsection has shown that we can provide a descriptively adequate account of the Scandinavian OS data discussed so far by postulating the constraints in (17) and (20), which are in fact no more than alternative versions of assumptions that are already present in the current MP framework. Interestingly, the empirical scope of the present OT-account goes far beyond the data that motivated it. For example, the proposal leads us to expect that there are also OS-languages with the ranking EPP(case) >> *MOVE >> H-COMPL; these languages resemble Icelandic in allowing non-pronominal OS, but differ from it by not being sensitive to Chomsky's (2001) version of Holmberg's Generalization in (16c), that is, by allowing the object to cross a c-commanding v*P-internal verb. Broekhuis (2008) has argued that this expectation is indeed borne out, and that Dutch and German are languages of this type.

5.3.3 The interaction of Object Shift and verb movement

The high ranking of H-COMPL in the constraint rankings of (23) does not only account for the fact that OS is excluded in complex verb constructions, but also accounts for the examples in (24), which show that whereas Icelandic also allows OS in embedded clauses, Danish does not. This contrast is related to a difference in verb movement between Icelandic and Danish. The fact that the finite verb precedes adverbial phrases like *aldrei* 'never' in (24a) shows that the finite verb undergoes V-to-I in embedded clauses in Icelandic; as a result, OS will satisfy H-COMPL and is thus correctly predicted to result in an acceptable result. The fact that the finite verb follows adverbials like *aldrig* 'never' in (24b) shows that the finite verb does not undergo V-to-I in embedded clauses in Danish; as a result, OS will violate H-COMPL and is thus correctly predicted to be impossible.

(24) a. éf spurði af hverju Pétur læsi <þessa bók> aldrei t_V <þessa bók>
       I asked   why   Pétur read this book never   (Icelandic)
   b. jeg spurgte hvorfor Peter <*den> aldrig læste <den> (Danish)
       I asked   why   Peter it   never read

The fact that Danish pronominal OS can only occur in main clauses, as shown by the contrast between the Danish examples in (23b) and (24b), can therefore be related to the fact that Danish is an asymmetric V2-language.

It is important to note that this conclusion is only sound when V-movement applies in core syntax (contra Chomsky 2004 and especially Boeckx and Stjepanović 2001, who have claimed that head-movement in general is a PF phenomenon). A simple and in our view conclusive argument in favor of syntactic verb movement can be based on the fact discussed earlier that Icelandic OS is sensitive to the information structure of the clause. We have seen in Section 5.3.1 that Chomsky (2001) concluded from this that OS must be construed as part of core syntax given that "displacement rules interspersed in the phonological component should have little semantic effect." (p. 15) Since Scandinavian OS cannot apply when the main verb remains in v^*P-internal position, it follows immediately that V-to-I must also be a rule of core syntax; see also den Dikken (2006b/2007). Since we have already seen that Holmberg's Generalization in (11b) cannot be accounted for by means of some condition on movement given that the intermediate stage given in (8) does involve movement of the object across the main verb, it must be rephrased as a filter on the output representation. This, in fact, is the only option in our current proposal.

In earlier accounts of Holmberg's Generalization, the observation that V-to-I must apply in order to license OS was normally considered the end of the story, whereas in the present approach it can be no more than half of the story given that there are in principle two ways in which H-COMPL could be satisfied: the first way is the one illustrated in (24b), where pronominal OS is *blocked* by the v^*P-internal verb; the second way would be a case in which the verb is actually *pushed up* into the I-position by pronominal OS. A full account of Holmberg's Generalization thus requires an explanation of the fact that Danish does not employ the push-up option in embedded clauses. In order to account for this, we first have to provide an analysis of V-to-I. The constraints that we will use for this are given in (25).

(25)   a. *STRAY FEATURE: amalgamate formal features of the functional heads with the root they are associated with.
       b. LEXICALLY FILL TOP F (LFTF): the highest head position in an extended projection must be lexically filled.
       c. NOLEXM: a θ-role assigning head remains in its θ-domain (a main verb does not move).

The constraint *STRAY FEATURE is a generalized version of the EPP-constraints involved in head movement: instead of postulating separate constraints like EPP(tense) or EPP(aspect), we simply require that the formal features in the extended projection of the verb (or other lexical categories) amalgamate with their lexical associate. The relative ranking of *STRAY FEATURE and *MOVE will therefore determines whether the verbal root V will move into the higher functional heads (like v or I) in its extended projection.

Table 5.1. V-to-I in the Germanic languages

RANKING	#24	MAIN CLAUSES	EMBEDDED CLAUSES	EXAMPLE
1 *MOVE >> {*STRAY FEATURE, LFTF}; ranking NOLEXM not relevant	8	–	–	Japanese
2 LFTF >> *MOVE >> *STRAY FEATURE; LFTF >> NOLEXM	3	+	–	Dutch/German Danish/Swedish
3 NOLEXM >> LFTF >> *MOVE >> *STRAY FEATURE	1	aux only	–	Proto-Germanic
4 *STRAY FEATURE >> {*MOVE, NOLEXM}; ranking LFTF not relevant	8	+	+	Icelandic
5 NOLEXM >> *STRAY FEATURE >> *MOVE; NOLEXM >> LFTF	3	aux only	aux only	English
6 LFTF >> NOLEXM >> *STRAY FEATURE >> *MOVE	1	+	aux only	Proto-Indo-European

The constraint LEXICALLY FILL TOP F can be held responsible for the asymmetric V2-property of languages like Danish: LFTF >> *MOVE >> *STRAY FEATURE predicts that in the absence of a complementizer the verb must be moved into the highest functional projection in the extended projection of the verb, whereas it will remain *in situ* otherwise.[9] When we further assume that complementizers must be selected, and can therefore only appear in embedded clauses, it will follow that V2 must apply in main clauses (and in embedded clauses that are complementizer-less for some reason).

The third constraint, NOLEXM, is adapted from Grimshaw (1997) and goes back at least to Pollock (1989): its role is to block movement of main verbs, while still allowing movement of auxiliary and modal verbs, and it is used to account for the fact that in English V-to-I is restricted to modal and auxiliary verbs, that is, cannot apply to main verbs. The three constraints in (25) in tandem with the general economy constraint *MOVE suffice to provide a basic typology of V-to-I by defining twenty-four different rankings which produce six different typological patterns. This is illustrated in Table 5.1, which was calculated by hand (a new tool that may help in performing this kind of calculations is OTWorkplace; Prince and Tesar 2010).

The first type arises when *MOVE outranks the two constraints that favor V-to-I, *STRAY FEATURE and LEXICALLY FILL TOP F, and is characterized by having no V-to-I at all. To our knowledge there are no languages of this type within the Germanic language family, but OV-languages like Japanese will be good candidates.

The second and the third types are languages with V2 in main clauses only. The weak ranking of *STRAY FEATURE blocks V-to-I in embedded clauses, whereas the ranking of LFTF above *MOVE forces V-to-I in main clauses. The second and the third type differ in the relative ranking of NOLEXM and LFTF. The third type has the subranking NOLEXM >> LFTF and therefore allows V2 with auxiliary and modal verbs only; to our knowledge there are no languages of this type within present-day Germanic, but Tonya Kim Dewey (p.c.) informs us that reconstructed Proto-Germanic is of this type; cf. Fortson (2004) and Dewey (2006). The second type has the subranking LFTF >> NOLEXM, and allows V2 in main clauses with all verbs. Swedish and Danish as well as the Germanic OV-languages are examples of this type.

The fourth type arises when *STRAY FEATURE outranks the constraints that disfavor movement, NOLEXM and *MOVE, and is defined by allowing V-to-I with all finite verbs in all contexts. This type is instantiated by Icelandic.

The fifth and the sixth type arise when we have a strong ranking of *STRAY FEATURE, but NOLEXM outranks *STRAY FEATURE. This results in languages that normally have V-to-I with auxiliary and modal verbs only. The two types differ in the relative ranking of NOLEXM and LEXICALLY FILL TOP F. When the former outranks the latter, V-to-I is restricted to auxiliary and modal verbs in all contexts: English is an example of this type. On the subranking LEXICALLY FILL TOP F >> NOLEXM, V-to-I of main verbs is restricted to main clauses, whereas aux-to-I may apply in all contexts. To our knowledge there are currently no Germanic languages of this type, but Tonya Kim Dewey (p.c.) again informs us that reconstructed Proto-Indo-European exhibits this behavior; cf. Fortson (2004) and Dewey (2006).

Let us now return to the question why Danish has the pattern in (26a) without pronominal OS and embedded V-to-I, rather than that in (26b) with pronominal OS and embedded V-to-I.

(26) a. jeg spurgte hvorfor Peter aldrig læste den
      I   asked why   Peter never read it
   b. jeg spurgte hvorfor Peter læste den aldrig t_V t_{den}
      I   asked why   Peter read it   never

This question can now be answered by having a better look at the subrankings independently established so far. We have seen that the subranking in (23b), repeated here as (27a), correctly accounts for the following two facts: Danish only has pronominal OS and pronominal OS is blocked in complex verb construction by the non-finite main verb. Our discussion of Table 5.1 has further shown that the subrankings in (27b&c) account for the fact that V-to-I is restricted to main clauses.

(27) a. H-COMPL >> D-PRONOUN >> *MOVE >> EPP(case)
   b. LFTF >> *MOVE >> *STRAY FEATURE
   c. LFTF >> NOLEXM

The question why Danish opts for the blocking of OS in (26a) instead of push-up of the finite main verbs in (26b) must be answered by appealing to the interaction of the independently motivated constraints in (27). The two obvious candidates that could handle this are D-PRONOUN and NOLEXM, given that the former favors pronominal object shift and the latter disfavors movement of main verbs: the subranking D-PRONOUN >> NOLEXM predicts that pronominal OS would push up the finite main verb into I, whereas the subranking NOLEXM >> D-PRONOUN predicts that the main verb would block pronominal OS. From this we may conclude that that Danish has the subranking NOLEXM >> D-PRONOUN. When we assume that Danish has the ranking in Tableau 5.8, where the dashed lines indicate that the constraints cannot be ordered yet on the basis of the data discussed so far, we will get the desired result.

Tableau 5.8. V-to-I and pronominal object shift in Danish embedded clauses

	H-COMPL	LFTF	NOLEXM	D-PRONOUN	*MOVE	*STRAYF	EPP(case)
☞ no pronominal OS no V-to-I				*		*	*
pronominal OS no V-to-I	*!				*	*	
no pronominal OS V-to-I			*!	*	*		*
pronominal OS V-to-I			*!		**		

For completeness' sake note that the suggestion in Tableau 5.8 that H-COMPL outranks NOLEXM has not been established yet. In Broekhuis (2008) it is argued that next to the type of OS discussed here, which he refers to as regular OS, there is second type of OS, which he refers to as short object shift, which is triggered by the φ-features on the verbal root V, which does have the property of forcing V-to-v in Danish. This can be accounted for by assuming that the constraint EPP(φ), which is responsible for short OS, is ranked between H-COMPL and NOLEXM. We do not have the space here to discuss short OS (which can be identified with the type of object movement identified for English by Johnson 1991, and Lasnik 1999a: Chapters 2 and 8), but refer the reader to Broekhuis (2008) for detailed discussion.

5.3.4 Conclusion

This section has shown that the minimalist EPP-features can readily be eliminated by postulating a set of EPP-constraints. As such, this is of course not a real gain as we simply replace one postulate by another, but Section 5.3.2 has shown that this results in a grammatical system with entirely different properties that is better equipped to capture language variation than the standard Minimalist approach, and is also readily able to account for apparently optional movements like Scandinavian OS. Furthermore, Section 5.3.3 has shown by means of a discussion of the interaction between Object Shift and verb movement that the postulation of EPP-constraints may have wide ramifications throughout the grammatical system due to the fact that they may interact. Given space limitations we have not been able to make all evaluations explicit by means of tableaux, but these can been found in Broekhuis (2008), where a much more detailed discussion of

Object Shift (including what has become known as scrambling in Dutch/ German) can be found.

This section has given a first illustration of our claim at the end of Section 5.2.3 that the hybrid MP + OT model may substantially change our views on the properties ascribed to the generative and filtering devices by traditional MP/OT. The proposed change in the MP system was of course rather limited: we simply replaced the postulate of EPP-features by that of EPP-constraints, while leaving the inviolable conditions on the operations of C_{HL} intact. However, the hybrid system requires that we investigate whether the use of such conditions is the optimal way of restricting the operations of C_{HL} or whether we can further simplify the operations of the computational system by accounting for the restrictions on these operations by means of an Optimality-Theoretic evaluation. In the next section, we will therefore investigate whether it would be profitable to reformulate the locality restrictions on case assignment in an OT-fashion as violable constraints on output representations.

5.4 Local domains and Case Theory

This section, which builds on earlier work by Woolford, shows how the hybrid MP + OT model allows us to capture an interesting typological difference with respect to the possibility of licensing nominative objects, namely that some languages allow T to value nominative on an object when the subject has inherent case, but other languages do not. (For more discussion of case, see Chapter 17.) We preserve from MP the notion that all structural cases must be licensed by a head in an Agree relation under c-command.[10] We preserve the Minimal Link Condition (MLC) on case-licensing, but split it into two. We build into the basic Agree relation a weak but inviolable version of the Minimal Link Condition which allows T to probe past a closer DP with inherent case. A strong version of the Minimal Link Condition which blocks probing past any closer DP, even one with inherent case, is formulated here as a violable constraint. This approach allows us to capture the fact (which cannot be captured by a parameter) that a closer dative blocks nominative licensing/valuation on objects in some constructions in Icelandic, but not in others.

5.4.1 The typological problem
It is well-known that languages such as Icelandic and Hindi allow nominative objects in dative subject constructions:

(28) a. barninu   batnaði   veikin   [Icelandic]
        child-DAT   recovered-from disease-NOM
        'the child recovered from the disease'   (Yip et al. 1987:223)

(28) b. Siitaa-ko laRke   pasand the   [Hindi]
     Sita-DAT boys-NOM.masc like be.past.masc.pl
     'Sita liked the boys'   (Mahajan 1991: (7))

What is not so well-known is that in other languages, such as Faroese, dative subject constructions take structural accusative objects. We will argue that nominative licensing is blocked by the closer dative in these constructions.

(29) a. mær   tørvar   góða   hjálp   [Faroese]
     me.DAT needs.3sg good.ACC help.ACC
     'I need good help'   (Thráinsson et al. 2004:256)
     b. mær   líkar   hana   væl   [Faroese]
     me.DAT likes.3sg her.ACC well
     'I like her a lot'   (Thráinsson et al. 2004:255)

Ergative subject constructions divide into the same two types; cf. Legate (2006) and Woolford (2003b, 2007) (see also Section 17.3.4). Languages such as Inuit and Hindi allow nominative objects in all constructions where the subject has inherent case, dative or ergative.[11] Note that Hindi manifests the same agreement pattern as Icelandic, where the verb agrees with all and only nominatives, regardless of whether the nominative is a subject or an object.

(30) a. Juuna-p   puisit   aallaa-v-a-i   [Inuit]
     Junna-ERG seals.NOM shoot-ind-tr-3sg.3pl
     'Juuna shot the seals'   (Bittner and Hale 1996a:(44))
     b. Raam-ne roTii   khaayii   thii   [Hindi]
     Ram-ERG bread.fem.NOM eat.perf.fem be.past.fem
     'Ram had eaten bread'   (Mahajan 1990:73)

In contrast, ergative languages such as Warlpiri do not allow nominative objects (Legate 2006), and this is true of many other Australian languages as well according to Godard (1992). Objects in Warlpiri are cross-referenced with an accusative pronominal clitic, and not with the agreement that cross-references nominative subjects (in contrast to the pattern in Hindi above):

(31) a. ngaju   ka-rna   wangka-mi   [Warlpiri]
     I.NOM pres-1sgAgr speak-nonpast
     'I am speaking'   (Hale 1982:(9a))
     b. kurdu-ngku ka-ju   nya-nyi   ngaju   [Warlpiri]
     child-ERG   pres-1sg.ACC see-nonpast me.ACC
     ' the child sees me'   (Simpson 1991:99)

Our goal here is to provide a simple account of this typological difference: that some languages allow nominative objects in constructions where the subject has inherent case, and other languages do not. We will show that this difference follows from a difference in the ranking of a violable version of the Minimal Link Constraint.

The strategy is as follows. First, the Agree relation in MP from Chomsky (2000b) is updated and formulated with only a weak version of the Minimal Link Condition, so that T is allowed to probe past a closer dative in order to value nominative on a further DP (Section 5.4.2). Where a closer dative blocks T from valuing nominative on an object, the claim here is that this is due to the application of a stronger, but violable version of the MLC, the Strong Minimal Link Constraint (Section 5.4.3). This violable constraint does not get a chance to apply in many constructions in languages such as Icelandic and Hindi, because it is outranked by another violable constraint, the Least Marked Case Constraint.[12] This constraint requires the selection of the least marked case that can be licensed on any DP, and thus favors nominative over accusative (Section 5.4.4). We will show that this constraint produces all of the effects normally attributed to Burzio's Generalization (Section 5.4.5; see also Section 17.3.2.3). The details of the analysis are presented in Section 5.4.6, where we show how a difference in the relative ranking of these two violable constraints produces the typological difference between languages which do and do not allow nominative objects in clauses with a dative or ergative subject (a subject with inherent case). We show in Sections 5.4.7 and 5.4.8 that, regardless of their ranking, both constraints are active in both types of languages. That is, the lower ranked constraint must be obeyed as long as it does not conflict with the requirements of the higher ranked constraint. Section 5.4.9 discusses whether the constraints proposed in this section apply to derivations or representations, and we dispel the myth that MP necessarily evaluates derivations, bottom up and step by step, while OT necessarily evaluates representations. We conclude in Section 5.4.10 by summarizing the benefits of the present approach.

5.4.2 The Agree (probe–goal) relation and case

This section discusses a number of assumptions concerning case valuation that will be crucial for the analysis to be developed. We assume, as in MP, that the case feature of a DP is initially unvalued, and must be valued in an Agree (probe–goal) relation with a c-commanding head, subject to locality. However, it will be crucial in this section to retain the older view that the case features of T and the verb are initially valued, as nominative and accusative respectively (rather than adopting the assumption in Chomsky 2008 that the case features of heads are also initially unvalued and that case is an automatic reflex of agreement). One desirable effect of this, as we will see below, is that it removes any need for case-assigning heads to enter into an Agree relation, since valued uninterpretable features can simply delete at the interface (Chomsky 2008). As for the definition of the Agree relation itself, rather than adopting the most recent formulation in Chomsky (2008), which is designed to accommodate multiple Agree,[13] we update the formulation of Agree from Chomsky (2000b:122), which restricts a head from establishing an Agree relation with anything except the closest DP that has a matching case feature. This updated formulation of Agree in (32) is technically new, but it closely follows the original notion of 'closest match' in claiming that a head can only probe until it finds a case feature that it can value, and after that, it must stop. In (32), this is informally formulated for case valuation. (On the role of Agree in case valuation, see also Chapter 17.)

(32) Agree relation for case valuation:
A case-assigning head can enter into a probe–goal relation under c-command only with the closest DP that has an unvalued case feature

When there is no closer DP, which is the situation in a simple unaccusative construction, nothing blocks T from licensing nominative case under c-command, even to a DP inside the VP. This occurs in unaccusative constructions in Italian and in general across languages (Burzio 1986). Note that this even holds in unaccusative constructions in Faroese, as in example (33), despite the fact that in Faroese, nominative objects are blocked in dative subject constructions like (29a) above:

(33) tað eru   komnir   nakrir gestir   í gjár   [Faroese]
     there are-pl come-pl some   guests-NOM.pl   yesterday
     'some guests came yesterday'   (Diane Jonas, p.c.)

When a closer DP is present, it will block T from probing further if it has an unvalued case feature, as in (34a), but not if its case feature is already valued, as is the situation with a DP with inherent case, as in (34b). Inherent case is valued in connection with theta marking (Chomsky 1995c:114), and we assume this occurs at the moment the DP is merged.

(34) a. T[nom] DP-[u case] DP-[u case]
     b. T[nom] DP-[dative] DP-[u case]

The formulation of Agree in (32) therefore captures the fact that T can value nominative on an object in Icelandic when there is a closer dative DP, regardless of whether or not that dative intervenes between T and the nominative in the surface word order (a point that will be important below):

(35) a. sumum   gömlum   mönnum   líkar/líka   pípuhattar
        some.DAT.pl old.DAT.pl   men.DAT.pl like.3sg/3pl   top hats.NOM.pl
        'some old men like top hats'   (Ussery 2009)

b. það líkar/líka sumum gömlum mönnum pípuhattar
expl like.3sg/3pl some.DAT.pl old.DAT.pl men.DAT.pl top hats.NOM.pl
'there like some old men top hats' (Ussery 2009)

In Section 5.4.7, we discuss a more complex type of Icelandic example that has led some (including Chomsky 2000b:130) to incorrectly conclude that a surface intervening dative always blocks T from establishing an Agree relation with a further DP. We will show that such examples violate *not* the universal Agree requirements, but rather a separate, violable constraint, which we will refer to as the Strong Minimal Link Constraint and which will be developed in the next section. The approach developed here correctly predicts when such a violation is and is not tolerated in Icelandic.

5.4.3 The Strong Minimal Link Constraint

Given that the Agree relation defined in (32) allows T to probe across a subject with inherent case, the question now is what blocks nominative objects in dative subject constructions in Faroese? The answer, we propose, is the existence of a strong version of the Minimal Link Condition, formulated as a violable constraint, the Strong Minimal Link Constraint in (36). This violable constraint prohibits T from probing past *any* closer DP, regardless of whether or not its case feature is valued.

(36) Strong Minimal Link Constraint (violable constraint):
A probe (case-assigning head) is blocked from establishing an Agree relation with a goal (DP) if there is a closer potential goal (DP), regardless of whether or not the head can enter into an Agree relation with that closer goal.

In Faroese, the Strong MLC is ranked high, and blocks T from probing past a dative. Thus, in experiencer constructions with a dative subject, the verb is the only head that can value case on the object, producing a dative–accusative pattern. The valued case feature on T in (37) simply deletes at the interface.

(37) T[nom] DP-dative V[acc] DP-accusative [Faroese]

In Section 5.4.8, we will see that, although lower ranked in Icelandic, the Strong MLC does apply when it does not conflict with another higher ranked constraint, the Least Marked Case Constraint, to which we now turn.

5.4.4 The Least Marked Case Constraint

One of the two primary types of constraints in OT is markedness constraints, which select a less marked element over a more marked element. Since nominative is a less marked case than accusative, it should be preferred over accusative in a situation where either case could be licensed.[14] We encode this generalization in our hybrid approach as a violable constraint, the Least Marked Case Constraint:

(38) Least Marked Case Constraint (violable constraint):[15]
When there is a choice of cases that could be valued on a DP, select the least marked of these cases.

In a clause with a dative subject, the Least Marked Case Constraint favors the derivation/representation in which the object gets nominative.

(39) T[nom]   DP-dative   V[acc]   DP-[nom]

The requirements of the Least Marked Case Constraint conflict with those of the Strong MLC; Section 5.4.5 gives the details of how ranking this constraint above the Strong MLC makes the right predictions for Icelandic in a variety of constructions. Since MP already has violable constraints (called economy constraints in MP) which apply 'if possible,' what we add to MP by adopting an OT-evaluation is the ability to rank such constraints, so as to govern the relative priority of their application when their requirements conflict. This will be crucial in the analysis in Section 5.4.6 of the difference between Icelandic and Faroese. Before we turn to this analysis, however, we provide additional motivation for adding the Least Marked Case Constraint in (38) to the grammar.

5.4.5 Deriving Burzio's Generalization

Woolford (2001, 2003a, 2003b) argues that the Least Marked Case Constraint produces all of the effects attributed to Burzio's (1986) Generalization, without its over- and undergeneration problems. To see this, let us begin by reviewing the data that motivated Burzio's Generalization. The primary fact is that unaccusative subjects get nominative case, even if they remain *in situ* inside the VP as in Italian.

(40) all'improvviso è entrato   un uomo   dalla finestra   [Italian]
     suddenly   entered   a   man.NOM from the window
     'suddenly a man entered from the window'   (Belletti 1988:(17))

In (40), there are two heads (T and the verb) that are known to license structural case in other constructions, and under the original formulation of Relativized Minimality (Rizzi 1990a), the closer head (the verb) is expected to block the further head (T), but it does not here. To deal with this problem, Burzio (1986) postulated that the normal accusative licensing ability of the verb is not available in this construction (and that this somehow nullifies the blocking effect expected under Relativized Minimality). As to why the verb lacks its normal accusative case feature in unaccusatives and passives, Burzio noted that both constructions lack an external argument, and he thus proposed that the verb can license structural accusative case if and only if an external argument is present. This idea was then built into MP by postulating that the light verb *v* (the head that introduces external arguments), rather than the verbal root V, introduces the accusative case feature into the structure.

Since 1986, many exceptions to the original formulation of Burzio's Generalization have been pointed out. Accusative case can be licensed without the presence of an external argument (e.g., in experiencer subject constructions in English and Faroese).[16] Moreover, accusative case is not always licensed in the presence of an external argument; an example of this is the ergative–nominative construction shown above in (30), with the pre-movement structure in (41).[17]

(41)   [T$_{[nom]}$ DP-ERGATIVE v$_{[acc]}$ … V$_{[acc]}$ DP-NOMINATIVE]

There has been a great deal of work on Burzio's Generalization effects since 1986 and most of this work has reached the same conclusion, namely that there is actually no relation between the ability of the verb to assign accusative case and the presence of an external argument; see the papers collected in Reuland (2000) and summaries of many of the proposals in the literature in Woolford (2003a). Instead, there is currently fairly widespread agreement (including Burzio 2000) that the actual descriptive generalization is something like (42):

(42)   T must license nominative case (if possible).

Most proposals that incorporate the generalization in (42) into the grammar attribute it to T, by requiring that T establish an Agree relation with some DP; see the discussion in Woolford (2003a). But why should T be special in this way? An alternative perspective would be to say that it is not T that is special, but nominative, because it is the least marked case. The explanation for the effects that motivated Burzio's Generalization are actually the result of the fact that it is more 'economical' to use the less marked nominative than a more marked case; cf. Woolford (2001, 2003a, 2003b).

Adding the Least Marked Case Constraint to the list of violable constraints thus removes any need to require T to discharge its nominative feature, or to stipulate that certain verbs (in certain languages) carry an accusative case feature while others do not. Instead, the theory will make the right predictions if all heads optionally make use of the case-feature they carry. Under the assumption noted above, that heads are merged with a valued case feature, the case feature of T will simply delete at the interface, as any valued uninterpretable feature does in Chomsky (2008).

Let us now turn to the details of how these two violable constraints Least Marked Case Constraint and Strong MLC introduced in Sections 5.4.3 and 5.4.4 produce the typological difference between languages with nominative versus accusative objects in constructions with inherently case-marked subjects described in Section 5.4.2.

5.4.6 The analysis

The typological difference between dative–nominative languages like Icelandic and dative–accusative languages like Faroese (and the parallel difference between ergative–nominative and ergative–accusative languages) reduces to a difference in the relative ranking of the Least Marked Case Constraint and the Strong MLC. In a clause where the subject has inherent case, these constraints determine which head, T or V, gets to value structural case on the object. In Icelandic, the Least Marked Case Constraint takes priority, so that nominative is used whenever it can be legally licensed. In Faroese, the Strong MCL takes priority, so that any closer DP blocks T from reaching an object DP.

(43) a. Constraint ranking in Icelandic: Least Marked Case Constraint >> Strong MLC
      b. Constraint ranking in Faroese: Strong MLC >> Least Marked Case Constraint

In Icelandic, the higher ranked Least Marked Case Constraint (which favors nominatives) eliminates the (b)-candidate in Tableau 5.9, because it uses a more marked case, accusative. This leaves the (a)-candidate with a dative–nominative pattern, as the winner. Its violation of the lower ranked constraint is irrelevant (and thus shaded in the tableau).[18]

Tableau 5.9. Icelandic experiencer subject constructions

T DP-dat V DP-	LEAST MARKED CASE	STRONG MLC
a.☞ T DP-dat V DP-nom		*
b. T DP-dat V DP-acc	*!	

The result is the reverse in Faroese, because the ranking of these two violable constraints is reversed. Here the higher ranked Strong MLC eliminates the (a)-candidate in Tableau 5.10 because it prohibits probing past the closer dative. This leaves the (b)-candidate with a dative–accusative pattern as the winner, and its violation of the lower ranked constraint is irrelevant.

Tableau 5.10. Faroese experiencer subject constructions

T DP-dat V DP-	STRONG MLC	LEAST MARKED CASE
a. T DP-dat V DP-nom	*!	
b.☞ T DP-dat V DP-acc		*

To show that this OT approach is superior to a parametric approach where these constraints would be set at 'off' or 'on' for each language, we need to see evidence that the lower ranked constraint in each language is still active. That is, it applies whenever the higher ranked constraint does not make the decision. We turn to this evidence in Sections 5.4.7 and 5.4.8.

5.4.7 The lower ranked Least Marked Case Constraint remains active in Faroese

In Faroese, although the Strong MLC outranks the Least Marked Case Constraint, there is evidence that the lower ranked constraint is still active, and not set at 'off' as a parameter. This evidence takes the form of examples where the Least Marked Case Constraint gets to make the decision. One kind of example is simple unaccusative constructions. Since there is no closer DP, neither derivation violates the Strong MLC and the decision of whether T or the verb gets to value the case of the DP therefore passes down to the lower ranked Least Marked Case Constraint.

Tableau 5.11. Faroese unaccusative constructions

T V DP-	STRONG MLC	LEAST MARKED CASE
a.☞ T V DP-nom		
b. T V DP-acc		*!

The Least Marked Case constraint selects the (a)-candidate with nominative over the (b)-candidate with accusative, because nominative is the less marked case. This is why unaccusative subjects do not get accusative case even in Faroese-type languages; cf. example (33).

An important consequence of this approach is that it removes the need to claim that unaccusative verbs cannot license accusative case. All verbs potentially license accusative case. Moreover, there is no need to allow parametric variation in the case licensing/valuing capacity of any type of head across languages under this approach: differences in the case patterns that surface follow from differences in the relative ranking of the relevant violable constraints (see Woolford 2001, 2003a, 2003b, 2007).

5.4.8 The lower ranked Strong MLC remains active in Icelandic

This section provides evidence that the Strong MLC, which is lower ranked in Icelandic, remains active, applying in constructions where the higher ranked Least Marked Case Constraint does not narrow the possible derivations down to one. This occurs when there are two candidates that use nominative case for a particular DP, but different Ts that may value that nominative. The Strong MLC then selects which derivation is more 'economical.'

Before we begin, we need to establish that the standard assumption in GB (e.g., Chomsky 1986a) that non-finite T lacks a nominative case feature was incorrect. We now know that a non-finite T can value nominative case on its object in a dative subject construction (Jónsson 1996). We see this in example (44), where only the embedded non-finite T can license/value nominative case on the embedded object, because the matrix T uses its nominative feature to value the case of the matrix subject.[19]

(44) hann   hafði   talið   [Jón-i   líka   þessir sokkar]
     he-NOM   had.sg believed John-DAT   to-like these socks-NOM
                                                        Jónsson (1996:170)

Given that non-finite T can license nominative on an object, situations arise in which the grammar must make a decision as to whether a finite matrix T or an embedded non-finite T values nominative case on an embedded object, as in the structure in (45), exemplified by the examples in (46).

(45) [T$_{[nom]}$ DP-DAT V [T$_{[nom]}$ DP-DAT V DP-NOM]]

(46) a. *?mér   virðast   [stráknum   líka   þessir bílar]
        me-DAT   seem.3pl   the boy-DAT like   these cars-NOM
        'it seems to me that the boy likes these cars'
                                                   (Watanabe 1993:418)
     b. *mér   fundust   [henn-i   leiðast   þeir]
        me-DAT   seemed.3pl she-DAT   be-bored   they-NOM
        'I thought she was bored with them'   (Taraldsen 1995:(40))

The examples in (46) show that the matrix T cannot agree with the embedded nominative DP in the construction in (45). This is predicted by the analysis developed here, as we see in Tableau 5.12 below, where the lower T wins the competition to value case on that DP (and thus agreement is not possible with the upper T). The (a)-candidate in Tableau 5.12, where the matrix T values nominative on the embedded object (indicated here by co-indexing), incurs two violations of the Strong MLC because there are two closer dative DPs. In contrast, the (b)-candidate, where the embedded T values nominative on that object, incurs only one violation because there is only one closer dative DP, and thus wins the competition. The (c)-candidate, in which the object gets accusative, is eliminated by the higher ranked Least Marked Case Constraint. Thus we see that the Strong MLC is active in Icelandic, making the decision when the higher ranked Least Marked Case Constraint cannot.

Tableau 5.12. Icelandic

	[T$_{[nom]}$ DP-dat [T$_{[nom]}$ DP-dat V$_{[acc]}$ DP-]]	LEAST MARKED CASE	STRONG MLC
a.	[T$_i$ DP-dat [T DP-dat V$_{[acc]}$ DP-nom$_i$]]		**!
b. ☞	[T DP-dat [T$_i$ DP-dat V$_{[acc]}$ DP-nom$_i$]]		*
c.	[T DP-dat [T DP-dat V$_{[acc]}$ DP-acc]]	*!	

In the winning candidate in (b), where the non-finite T values the nominative object, the matrix T shows only 3sg default agreement (since it does not establish an Agree relation with any argument) and non-finite T never shows morphological agreement:

(47) mér   fannst   [henn-i   leiðast   þeir]
     me-DAT   seemed.3sg   she-DAT   be-bored   they.NOM
     'I thought she was bored with them'   (Taraldsen 1995:(39))

Although the matrix T loses the above competition in Tableau 5.12, there are other constructions in which it is possible for a matrix T to value nominative inside an embedded non-finite clause in Icelandic. Chomsky (2008:143) notes that T can probe under c-command into a lower phase or even into a lower clause in principle, if not blocked by a closer DP. This occurs successfully in raising examples like (48), where the matrix verb optionally agrees with the embedded nominative object:

(48) Jón-i   virðast [t vera taldir [t líka hestarnir]]
     John-DAT seemed.3pl be   believed like horses.NOM
     'John seems to be believed to like horses'   (Schütze 1997:108–109)

This example differs from those in (46) above in that there is only one dative DP present. Before movement, that dative is located below T in the embedded clause. As a result, that dative intervenes in candidate (a), where the matrix T enters into an Agree relation with the embedded object, and in candidate (b), where the embedded T enters into an Agree relation with the embedded object, and thus both candidates incur one violation of the Strong MLC. Thus there is a tie. This is consistent with the fact that agreement is optional in examples like (48); cf. Ussery (2009).[20]

Tableau 5.13. Icelandic raising example

$[T_{[nom]}]$ [$T_{[nom]}$] DP-dat DP-]]	LEAST MARKED CASE	STRONG MLC
a. [T_i [T DP-dat DP-nom$_i$]]		*
b. [T [T_i DP-dat DP-nom$_i$]]		*

We can eliminate an alternate hypothesis assumed in Chomsky (2000b, 2008) that the ungrammaticality of the examples in (46) is due to fact that the closer dative intervenes in the surface string (in contrast to the raising example in (48)). There is independent evidence from examples such as (49), where an expletive subject is present, that the mere presence of an intervening dative in the surface string is not sufficient to block nominative licensing in Icelandic.[21] Here the verb can agree with the nominative object across the intervening dative:

(49) það   líkuðu   einhverjum   þessir   sokkar
      there liked.pl somebody-DAT   these   socks-NOM
      'somebody liked these socks'   (Jónsson 1996:153)

This example is predicted to grammatical under the hybrid MP + OT analysis presented here for the same reason that we saw above for the same kind of example without an expletive (e.g. (35a)). With only one T present, the higher ranked Least Marked Case Constraint must select the derivation where that T values nominative on the object, because the only alternative is the derivation in (b) where the verb values accusative:

Tableau 5.14. Icelandic experiencer subject constructions

there T DP-dat V DP-	LEAST MARKED CASE	STRONG MLC
a. ☞ there T DP-dat V DP-nom		*
b. there T DP-dat V DP-acc	*!	

5.4.9 Derivations or representations

Let us now turn to the question of whether the Strong MLC and the Least Marked Case Constraint proposed above apply to derivations or representations. Before we do so, however, let us dispel the common myth that MP intrinsically evaluates derivations, bottom up and step by step, while OT necessarily evaluates completed derivations (representations). Chomsky makes this clear for his version of MP: "Generation of an expression is not strictly 'bottom-up,' because of the parallelism of operations" (Chomsky 2007:6); "All operations within the phase are in effect simultaneous"; "their applicability is evaluated at the phase level" (Chomsky 2001:24). Prince and Smolensky (1993, 2004) designed OT to evaluate completed derivations; however, that work mentions that it would also be compatible with the overarching principles of OT to implement the theory in a different way, with step by step derivation and evaluation (Prince and Smolensky, 1993: 94–95; see also Heck and Müller 2000 for an early implementation of this idea). A version of this alternative, known as Harmonic Serialism, has been developed recently in McCarthy (2007, 2008), who argues that it is more restrictive than classic OT in desirable ways. Under Harmonic Serialism, only one change at a time can occur (e.g., deletion or insertion of a feature) and any change must lead to an improvement, the best possible one-step improvement. Thus the decision as to whether to evaluate completed representations or to evaluate each step of a derivation is independent of whether one works in MP or OT, and, consequently, one might also take either approach in a hybrid theory.

With respect to the hybrid approach to case valuation developed in this section, the Strong Minimal Link Constraint would apply correctly to completed representations under the version of MP in Chomsky (2000b) because a DP in Spec TP was defined as closer to T than an object (Chomsky 2000b). However, under the version of MP in Chomsky (2007) where an Agree relation can only be established under strict c-command, the Strong Minimal Link Constraint cannot apply to completed representations because a dative subject that has moved above T will not intervene between T and a nominative object, and thus cannot block T from probing past it. The Strong MLC would thus have to apply derivationally, at some point before the dative is moved above T. Nevertheless, there is a way to make the Strong MLC apply correctly even to completed derivations in this more recent version of MP if we take advantage of copy theory and add the idea that even an copy of a moved dative potentially blocks T from establishing an Agree relation with a lower object: [DP-dative T ~~DP-dative~~ DP-nominative].

5.4.10 Summary of benefits

In this section, we have seen that adding to MP the ability to rank violable constraints (which already exist in MP under the name economy constraints) produces desirable results of several types. By splitting up the Minimal Link Condition into two separate conditions, one weak but inviolable and the other strong but violable, and by ranking the latter with respect to a new violable constraint which requires the selection of the least marked case that can be licensed, we not only derive Burzio's Generalization (and predict its exceptions), but we can also capture differences between languages (and between constructions within a language) in whether nominative case can be licensed on an object in dative and ergative subject constructions. This hybrid approach allows us to simplify the theory and make it more restrictive by eliminating all cross-linguistic differences in the structural cases that heads can license.

5.5 Conclusion

This chapter has shown that adding an OT-evaluation to MP can be done in a very 'minimal' way, simply by introducing the idea that the output of the computational system is filtered in an Optimality-Theoretic fashion by means of a language-specific ranking of otherwise universal constraints. The introduction of such an Optimality-Theoretic evaluator eliminates the need for many other devices that are currently used in MP to capture cross-linguistic differences such as language-specific filters of the type in (16) and parameter settings. Ranked violable constraints are superior to parameters set at 'on' or 'off' for a language as a whole, because parameters do not allow a requirement to hold in some situations, but not in others within the same language. Ranked violable constraints are always active and may affect the optimal output whenever they do not conflict with higher ranked constraints. This allows us to account for intricate patterns of data involving Object Shift and case that are beyond the reach of the traditional filters and parameters. We have also shown that ranked constraints allow us to further the goal of the Minimalist Program by enabling us to eliminate other devices such as EPP-features and language-specific case features on particular heads.

Notes

1. The two authors of this chapter are no exception to the general rule that no two researchers agree on every assumption. The main goal of the discussions in Sections 5.3 and 5.4 is to illustrate the logical properties of the hybrid system: the specific proposals described here are based on earlier work of the two authors of this chapter. Taken together they do not constitute a single, consistent theory in all respects, but we did not attempt to resolve the tensions between the two proposals here, leaving this as a matter for future research.
2. With respect to case features, the views of the two authors diverge: Broekhuis adopts the view that the case feature on T and the verb are initially unvalued, while Woolford assumes that they are valued; see the discussion in Section 5.4.2.
3. Section 5.3 will show that the unvalued formal feature(s) on v^* (= the light verb that creates a transitive verb from the verbal root V) are the ones that trigger object shift (when an EPP-feature is present). The nature of these feature(s) depends on the version of MP one adopts: until recently, it was assumed that the light verb v^* has accusative case features, but Chomsky (2008) has proposed that the relevant features are φ-features and that case is simply a reflex of agreement. Section 5.3 and 5.4 will adopt the more traditional view; we refer the reader to Broekhuis (2005) for a critical assessment of the empirical motivation underlying Chomsky's more recent claim.
4. There are alternative versions of OT like Harmonic Grammar (Legendre et al. 1990), Stochastic OT (Boersma 1998), and Bidirectional OT (Blutner 2000), which diverge in various ways from the form OT discussed here, but we will not discuss these approaches here.
5. Chomsky (2001) does not address the question of why OS must cross the sentential adverbs: if these adverbs are v^*P-external and the object moves into the outer specifier of v^*P, this would not be expected. Broekhuis (2008) solves this problem by assuming that OS involves the creation of an extended projection (in the sense of Grimshaw 1997) of v^*: if Merge of the adverb applies before OS, the desired crossing will be obtained, as is shown by (ia). Note that it is not necessary to stipulate rule ordering given that the alternative order (OS before Merge of the adverb) will result in a surface string in which OS has applied string vacuously, as is shown by (ib). This derivation can be excluded by means of a surface constraint (which originates from Chomsky 1986a)

that disfavors string vacuous movement. Since we do not have the space to digress on this, we refer the reader to Broekhuis (2008) for detailed discussion.

(i)   a. [Subj I+V+v [Obj v [Adv [t_{Subj} t_v [t_V t_{Obj}]]]]]
      b. [Subj I+V+v [Adv [Obj v [t_{Subj} t_v [t_V t_{Obj}]]]]]

6. There are a number of additional problems with Holmberg's (1999) proposal, which are extensively discussed in Broekhuis (2008: Section 4.3.3). For example, (11b) is assumed to constrain both syntactic and phonological movement, and phonological movement thus simply seems to introduce an additional syntactic cycle, which is only needed to circumvent certain problems for strict cyclicity.

7. Chomsky's proposal crucially presupposes that reordering of phonological material does not satisfy (12a); if it did, object shift would be allowed in (10b) given that it inverts the order of the main verb and the object. Restricting the effect-on-output condition to semantics is surprising, however, given that in Chomsky's (1995c:294) earlier work this notion explicitly referred to properties of PF; see in this connection also Chomsky's (1986a: Section 9) Vacuous Movement Hypothesis and Williams's (2003:162) suggestion that linearization and interpretation play a similar role in making movement "visible."

8. It is not entirely clear at present whether D-PRONOUN is imposed by the A-P or the C-I system. Diesing (1997) claims that definite pronouns are variables that cannot occur in the domain of existential closure, whereas, e.g., Vogel (2006b) claims that the need of leftward movement of definite pronouns is related to the phonological weight of the pronouns. Given that emphatically stressed definite pronouns do occur vP-internally, we provisionally assume that we are dealing with a restriction imposed by the A-P system. Note further that the formulations of ALIGNFOCUS and H-COMPL are sloppy in the sense that they refer to the notion of linearity: since the constraints apply to the output of C_{HL} and linearization is part of the phonological component, we should phrase the restriction in hierarchical terms. However, given that we assume a version of the universal base hypothesis, according to which asymmetric c-command corresponds to the linear notion of precedence, this is an acceptable simplification: (20b) states that the prosodically unmarked focus may not asymmetrically c-command any other constituent within its clause, and (20c) states that the head of a head-chain must c-command the head of the A-chain of its complement.

9. Of course, the notion *lexically filled* in (25b) must be distinguished from the notion 'phonetically realized.' More specifically, it may be the case that a complementizer that is lexically present is phonetically empty as a result of the constraint TELEGRAPH; see Section 5.2.2 for discussion.

The constraint LEXICALLY FILL TOP F is similar to the nameless principle independently proposed in Zwart (2001:38).
10. Retaining the MP requirement that all cases on arguments must be licensed by a head in a legal Agree configuration eliminates the possibility of the generator generating candidates with random cases on arguments, arguments with no case at all, inserted (but unlicensed) cases, and unlicensed default case in syntax. At Spell-out (PF) an independent decision is made as to whether to spell-out the case feature from syntax.
11. For a summary of the extensive evidence that ergative is an inherent case like the dative, see Woolford (2006). For discussion, see also Section 17.3.4.1.
12. A reviewer points out that in a technical sense, every constraint applies in OT in the sense that every constraint assesses every candidate, as indicated in the tableaux. When we say that a constraint does not get a chance to apply, we mean that it has no effect on the outcome because constraints ranked above it select the optimal candidate.
13. Likewise we do not adopt the associated assumption in Chomsky (2008) designed for multiple Agree that inherently case-marked DPs have an additional structural case feature that needs to be valued.
14. Nominative is the least marked case. It appears to be present in every language, assuming that subjects labeled with absolutive case are actually nominative (Bittner 1991). This is not true for any other case; for example, Basque does not use accusative case (Bok-Bennema 1991). Moreover, nominative (absolutive) is more likely to be morphologically unmarked in languages than any other case (e.g., Blake 2001).
15. The Least Marked Case Constraint is formulated here in the style of economy constraints in MP. In pure OT, the formulation would be simplified because there is no need to include a direction to compare forms, since that is built into the architecture of OT. In addition, constraints also do not require one to consult a hierarchy; instead, constraints may be formulated based on a hierarchy, and then simply apply. Based on the markedness hierarchy of structural cases, accusative > nominative, this constraint is formulated in Woolford (2001) as simply *accusative. There is no constraint against the least marked element in a hierarchy, following Gouskova (2003).
16. Chomsky (2008) deals with this by locating the accusative case feature on the highest v of any transitive construction, including transitive experiencer subject constructions. He refers to this highest v as v^*.
17. Thus the prediction of the original formulation of Relativized Minimality (Rizzi 1990a), that a closer head should block a further head from licensing case, is not borne out. Fortunately, this prediction does not follow from the revised version of Relativized Minimality (Rizzi 2001c), which, like the Minimal Link Condition,

proposes that it is a closer goal (not a closer probe) that will block an Agree relation.
18. We have ignored a possible (c) candidate in this tableau where the inherent dative case is replaced by a nominative and the object is accusative. That candidate would be eliminated by a higher ranked faithfulness constraint Max (dative) in Icelandic. See Woolford (2001). Note that, following MP, the generator will not produce any candidate with a case that is not licensed by a head in a legal Agree relation.
19. It remains true, however, even in Icelandic, that the subject of a non-finite clause cannot be overt except in ECM constructions. The explanation for this fact remains unclear, but it appears to have nothing to do with the ability of a non-finite T to license nominative case, contra the assumption in GB (Chomsky 1986a).
20. Agreement is actually always optional with nominative objects in Icelandic according to Ussery's (2009) survey at the University of Iceland. However the percentage of speakers who prefer agreement in the raising constructions in (48), 36%, is lower than the 47% who prefer agreement in simple monoclausal dative subject construction such as (35a). Note that the situation in Tableau 5.13 is similar to that in Tableau 5.3 in that the evaluation predicts that both constructions may occur but is silent on the relative frequency of the two. We will therefore not attempt to account for the rates of morphological spell-out of agreement here; we merely use the possibility of agreement as evidence that an Agree relation can be established with the relevant T.
21. There is, nevertheless, a small reduction in the percentage of speakers who prefer morphological agreement in expletive constructions where the dative remains in situ and intervenes on the surface, as in (35b), according to Ussery (2009).

(i) a. DP-dative T V DP-nominative   46% agreement
    b. Expletive T V DP-dative DP-nominative   35.8% agreement

6

Lexical-Functional Grammar

Peter Sells

6.1 Motivation and historical development

This chapter provides an introduction to Lexical-Functional Grammar (LFG). Other article-length overviews can be found in Dalrymple (2006) and Asudeh and Toivonen (2010). The major publications concerning LFG, its motivations, and formal basis are Bresnan (1982a, 2001). Falk (2001) is an introductory textbook; Dalrymple (2001) is a more comprehensive overview, including semantics.

LFG starts from the idea that grammatical knowledge is factored into different levels of representation, which encode different kinds of information, and are in not in a one–one mapping relation. As a matter of presentation, the different levels have a different look, to indicate their different properties. LFG is a declarative syntactic theory, meaning that there are no movement or other transformational operations, and it is monotonic, meaning that no information is changed or deleted in the syntax (see Bresnan 2001: Chapter 5). A sentence is well-formed under an LFG analysis if that sentence satisfies the various relevant constraints on each level of representation.

What is most distinctive about LFG is its direct representation of grammatical relations or grammatical functions (GFs), which are also organized into a hierarchy. This GF hierarchy follows the relational hierarchy of the Relational Grammar of Perlmutter (1980), which also underlies the Accessibility Hierarchy of Keenan and Comrie (1977). The level of functional structure (f-structure) carries this information. LFG makes a sharp distinction between some grammatical information (at f-structure) and the overt structure which expresses that information (the c-structure). It is argued that many, perhaps most, significant aspects of syntactic analysis are captured at f-structure, and therefore not tied to language-specific properties of c-structure (e.g., Bresnan 2001: Chapters 1–2). F-structure expresses grammatical information which is largely invariant across languages; functional and semantic information for example. However, the surface expression of these kinds of information may vary from language to language. So while the lexicon and c-structure are the loci of cross-linguistic variation, the level of f-structure is quite stable, in the sense that synonymous constructions in different languages might have radically different c-structure representations though very similar f-structures. In general there is no one-to-one correspondence between constituents of a c-structure and elements of the corresponding f-structure, though of course there is a consistent relation between the two structures.

As f-structure is largely invariant across languages, it therefore plays a role somewhat similar to that of Logical Form (LF) in the Minimalist syntax framework, although f-structure itself is not intended to be close to a semantic representation.

The 'lexical' basis of LFG lies in its adherence to the Principle of Lexical Integrity (Section 6.4.1). Simply put, this is motivated by the key idea that structural principles upon which words are organized are substantially different from the structural principles of syntax. Due to the fundamental difference in LFG between structures and the information that those structures express (f-structure information), it is perfectly consistent in LFG to claim that the structures of words and the structures of syntax are possibly quite different, while both express the same kinds of grammatical information.

In the earliest versions of LFG, only c-structure and f-structure were represented. As noted above, f-structure expresses many of the language-invariant properties of grammar, yet the c-structures of different languages may diverge widely, and what one language expresses periphrastically (e.g., a syntactic causative) another language may express lexically (e.g., a lexical causative). Much early work in LFG focused on c-structure variation, and/or how morphologically complex single words can contribute the same information to f-structure as syntactic structures composed of simpler lexical items.

In the later 1980s, a-structure was incorporated into the theory as an integral part of the overall analysis (e.g., Bresnan and Kanerva 1989, Bresnan and Zaenen 1990). Like f-structure, a-structure also expresses some largely language-invariant properties, through the thematic hierarchy (see also Section 9.2.1).

The different levels of representation in LFG are in correspondence, but are crucially not in any simple isomorphic relationship, and hence provide dimensions of analysis within syntax which are necessarily different in character. The general conception of LFG allows in principle for many different kinds and levels of representation, in what is known as a Correspondence Architecture (Asudeh and Toivonen 2010). The parts of the architecture discussed here are shown in (1):

(1) LFG architecture

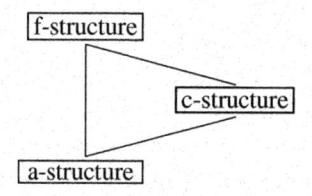

```
[f-structure]
       \
        \____[c-structure]
        /
[a-structure]
```

The rest of this chapter is organized as follows: I first present a basic outline of the interaction of the levels shown in (1) in Section 6.2, followed by more in-depth presentations of key aspects of f-structure (Section 6.3) and c-structure (Section 6.4).

6.2 The architecture of LFG and the basic style of analysis

In this section I elaborate on the architecture of grammar in (1) as it is embodied in LFG.

6.2.1 C-structure and f-structure

The syntactic analysis of any clause in LFG has two principal parts: the constituent structure (c-structure) and the functional structure (f-structure). The c-structure encodes phrasal dominance and precedence relations, represented as a phrase structure tree. In contrast, the f-structure encodes information about the functional relations between the parts, such as what is the subject and what is the predicate, what agreement features are present, and so on. A simple example is given in (2). The annotations involving up and down arrows in (2a) indicate how the information on each node in that structure takes its place in the f-structure in (2b) (see Section 6.4.2). (2) involves a clausal analysis based on the standard IP-VP structure, with argument grammatical functions of SUBJ, OBJ, and so on:

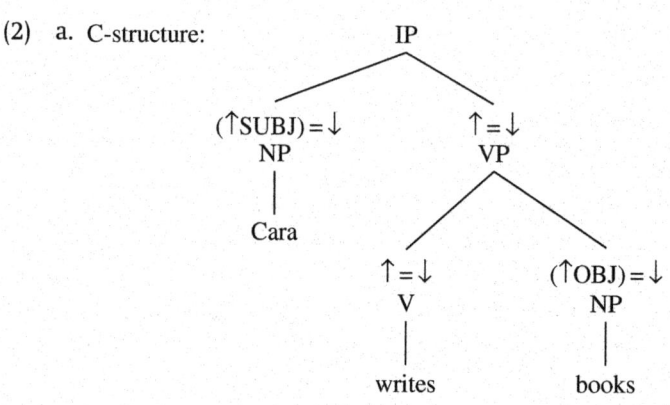

(2) a. C-structure:

```
                    IP
                  /    \
        (↑SUBJ)=↓      ↑=↓
            NP          VP
            |          /  \
           Cara       ↑=↓   (↑OBJ)=↓
                      V        NP
                      |        |
                    writes   books
```

b. F-structure:

$$\begin{bmatrix} \text{SUBJ} & \begin{bmatrix} \text{PRED} & \text{'Cara'} \\ \text{PERS} & 3 \\ \text{NUM} & \text{SG} \\ \text{GEN} & \text{F} \end{bmatrix} \\ \text{OBJ} & \begin{bmatrix} \text{PRED} & \text{'book'} \\ \text{PERS} & 3 \\ \text{NUM} & \text{F} \end{bmatrix} \\ \text{TENSE} & \text{PRES} \\ \text{PRED} & \text{'write} < (\uparrow \text{SUBJ})(\uparrow \text{OBJ}) >\text{'} \end{bmatrix}$$

In (2b), the f-structure represents the collective sum of the grammatical information that each node carries, as attribute–value pairs in a matrix. The up arrows inside PRED indicate that that PRED must have a SUBJ and OBJ in its structure – formally expressing the intuition that the verb determines what its (syntactic) arguments are.

Functional information originates in lexical items. For example, the following shows partial lexical entries for the words used in example (2a).

(3) a. *Cara* N ($\uparrow$PRED) = 'Cara'
                ($\uparrow$PERS) = 3
                ($\uparrow$NUM) = SG
                ($\uparrow$GEN) = F

   b. *books* N ($\uparrow$PRED) = 'book'
                ($\uparrow$PERS) = 3
                ($\uparrow$NUM) = PL

   c. *writes* V ($\uparrow$PRED) = 'write <($\uparrow$SUBJ)($\uparrow$OBJ)>'
                 ($\uparrow$SUBJ NUM) = SG
                 ($\uparrow$SUBJ PERS) = 3
                 ($\uparrow$TENSE) = PRES

The value of each PRED ('predicate') within the quotes indicates the semantic content of the item. The notation ($\uparrow$PRED) then can be read as "my mother's f-structure has a PRED value which is ..." The mother node will be the preterminal dominating the lexical item in question, and so in this way functional information passes from lexical items onto (f-structures associated with) constituents of the c-structure.

The verb carries the information that it has a subject and an object, that the tense is present, and that the subject has 3sg agreement features. In fact, this corresponds to an f-structure, shown in (4). Due to the '$\uparrow$=$\downarrow$' annotations on the V node and on VP, which mark the notion of head in the functional sense, this f-structure is also associated with the VP and IP nodes; hence (4) is associated with the lexical entry of the V and the whole clause at the same time.

(4) $\begin{bmatrix} \text{SUBJ} & \begin{bmatrix} \text{PERS} & 3 \\ \text{NUM} & \text{SG} \end{bmatrix} \\ \text{OBJ} & [\quad] \\ \text{TENSE} & \text{PRES} \\ \text{PRED} & \text{'write} < (\uparrow \text{SUBJ})(\uparrow \text{OBJ}) >\text{'} \end{bmatrix}$

Within the object NP, *books* carries the information that its mother's f-structure PRED is 'book'; hence this is the PRED of the N and of the NP. However, the f-structure of the NP is not directly inherited into the f-structure of the VP, but rather becomes part of the OBJ specification within that f-structure. That is to say, "PRED 'book'" etc. is not information at the same level as "TENSE PRES" and "PRED write...", but is information about the OBJ within the outermost f-structure. Hence from the object NP part we get the f-structure shown in (5).

(5) $\begin{bmatrix} \text{OBJ} & \begin{bmatrix} \text{PRED} & \text{'book'} \\ \text{PERS} & 3 \\ \text{NUM} & \text{PL} \end{bmatrix} \end{bmatrix}$

This unifies with the f-structure information coming from the V, yielding the f-structure in (6), associated with VP. The mechanism of unification entails that the different pieces of information are added up, as long as there are no conflicting requirements (see Section 6.3.1). Formally, the V part of VP describes an object of which the information in (4) must be true; the NP part of VP describes an object of which the information in (5) must be true; and hence what the VP itself describes is (6):

(6) $\begin{bmatrix} \text{SUBJ} & \begin{bmatrix} \text{PERS} & 3 \\ \text{NUM} & \text{SG} \end{bmatrix} \\ \text{OBJ} & \begin{bmatrix} \text{PRED} & \text{'book'} \\ \text{PERS} & 3 \\ \text{NUM} & \text{PL} \end{bmatrix} \\ \text{TENSE} & \text{PRES} \\ \text{PRED} & \text{'write} < (\uparrow \text{SUBJ})(\uparrow \text{OBJ}) >\text{'} \end{bmatrix}$

A similar unification to that described above happens at the IP level with the subject NP, and the result is the f-structure in (2b).

The 'lexical' and 'functional' bases of LFG are that grammatical information is introduced by lexical items, and that information is functional in nature (about f-structure). Informally, the c-structure shows how the different pieces of lexical information are aggregated in the f-structure of the whole.

6.2.2 A-structure and f-structure

In the clausal syntax of a language such as English, the structurally highest phrase structure position, SpecIP, c-commands all other argument positions. This position expresses the SUBJ (Subject) grammatical function, which outranks all the other GFs in the basic hierarchy SUBJ > OBJ > OBL (subject outranks object, which outranks oblique). And in an active clause, the SUBJ will also be the thematically highest argument, such as Agent, outranking all other arguments on the thematic hierarchy (see (10)).

The term 'Subject' has been used in the development of generative syntax as a label for a syntactic element that has any of the properties of the most prominent argument in the senses just mentioned. For example, Keenan's (1976) list of 'subject' properties, categorized as 'coding' properties and 'behavioral' properties, can also be classified according to what kinds of syntactic information they refer to. With the integration of a-structure into LFG, the subjecthood properties fall into those properties which accrue to the thematically highest argument (in a-structure) and those which accrue to the highest grammatical function (in f-structure). For example, Manning (1996:12ff.) groups different properties in the unrelated languages Tagalog and Inuit as follows, using 'Actor' as the label for the thematically highest argument:[1]

(7) Differentiated properties (Manning 1996):

Actor properties	SUBJect properties
Imperative addressee	obligatory element of clause
Equi target	relativization
antecedent of reflexive	specific/wide scope
	associates with floating quantifiers

For example, in English, an imperative form of the verb is a morphologically bare form which is interpreted with its grammatical subject as the imperative addressee. However, in other languages, the imperative addressee is always the thematically highest argument, Actor, but not necessarily the highest GF. Austronesian languages have this construction robustly, as in the Tagalog examples in (8). The voice system of Tagalog allows any argument of the verb to be SUBJ – respectively in the examples below, Actor, Goal, and Theme – and if the Actor is not the SUBJ, it is the OBJ (as seen by the NOM vs. ACC forms of the immediately postverbal clitic pronoun in the examples):

(8) a. mag-bigay ka sa kaniya ng kape
ActorV-give 2sg.NOM DAT him ACC coffee
'give him coffee'
b. bigy-an mo siya ng kape
give-DativeV 2sg.ACC 3sg.NOM ACC coffee
'give him coffee'

c. i-bigay mo sa kaniya ang kape
InstrumentV-give 2sg.ACC DAT him NOM coffee
'give him the coffee'

The imperative addressee is the Actor, regardless of surface grammatical functions.[2]

Some of the principal motivations for the correspondence architecture approach of LFG come from non-configurational languages (see Section 6.4.3), and from syntactically ergative languages. Dyirbal is one such syntactically ergative language, which means that the mapping between a-structure and f-structure is inverted compared to a syntactically accusative language – it is the lower argument of a transitive verb which maps to subject (Dixon 1994, Manning 1996). I use the terms 'Actor' and 'Undergoer' from Role and Reference Grammar (Foley and van Valin 1984) to designate the higher and lower arguments of a transitive verb, abstracting over their precise thematic content in a thematic hierarchy such as that in (10) (from Bresnan 2001:10ff.):

(9) a. Accusative linking

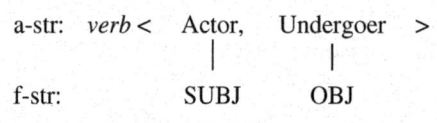

a-str: verb <   Actor,   Undergoer   >
                    | |
f-str: SUBJ   OBJ

b. Ergative linking

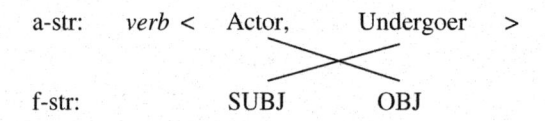

a-str: verb <   Actor,   Undergoer   >
                     \   /
                      \   /
                       \   /
                        \   /
                         \ /
                          X
                         / \
f-str: SUBJ   OBJ

(10) Thematic hierarchy
Agent > Beneficiary > Recipient > ... > Patient/Theme > Location

Bresnan (2001) cites idiom formation in Dyirbal as evidence for the hierarchy in a-structure (see also Section 9.6.2 on idiom formation). There is a stable cross-linguistic property that idioms are predominantly formed by a verb combining with its thematically lowest argument (Marantz 1984, O'Grady 1998). Idiom formation in Dyirbal as illustrated in (11) shares these properties with a language like English, showing that the hierarchy in a-structure is consistent across the two languages, even though the linking to GFs and many other aspects of clausal syntax are quite different, due to the Accusative vs. Ergative characters of the languages (on case and agreement, see Chapter 17).

(11) a. bana-l   <   Ag   Pt   >
        'break' |
                             |
                          buŋgu   "break+knee" = 'bend over, fold'
                          'knee'

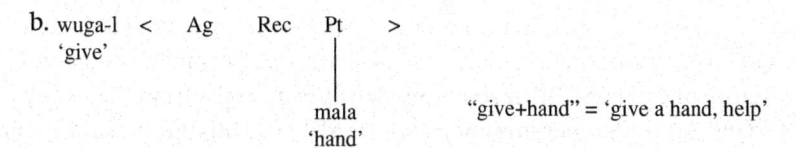

b. wuga-l   <   Ag   Rec   Pt   >
   'give' |
                        mala   "give+hand" = 'give a hand, help'
                        'hand'

As noted above, a-structure expresses some of the language-invariant properties of syntax, such as idiom formation. As a-structure is related to the lexical semantics of a predicate, we would expect a-structure properties to be cross-linguistically stable to the extent that lexical semantics is. Exactly how much semantic information is represented in a-structure is a matter of ongoing research. Butt (1995) in particular argues for a conception of a-structure which is much richer than simpler thematic role labels.

However, a-structure is not a 'pure' semantic representation, but rather, it is an abstraction from the semantic representation. It is 'syntacticized' (Alsina 1993, Manning 1996, Bresnan 2001, Arka 2003:127). While its core is to represent valence, it also expresses which arguments are direct (i.e., which map to the functions SUBJ, OBJ, OBJ2) and which are obliques, and also the relative hierarchy within the direct arguments. A-structure is also syntacticized in the sense that it represents non-thematic arguments – dependents of the PRED in f-structure which have no semantic relation to the PRED, as in the classic instance of the SUBJ of a raising predicate (see (25) below).

With this brief background on the substance of a-structure, we can now consider the mapping from a-structure to f-structure. It is largely one–one, but not invariant, due to voice alternations: in an Accusative language, in active voice, the Actor of a transitive verb is SUBJ and the Undergoer is OBJ. In passive voice, it is the Undergoer which is SUBJ, with the Actor being an oblique (OBL) or being unexpressed.

Lexical Mapping Theory (LMT) was developed in the 1980s as a way of relating a-structure and f-structure (Bresnan and Kanerva 1989, Bresnan and Zaenen 1990). It classifies GFs in terms of the semantic content that they can express: whether a given GF can express any semantic role or not (the feature 'restricted'), and whether or not a given semantic role may be expressed as a grammatical object (the feature 'objective'):

(12)

	−restricted	+restricted
−objective	SUBJ	OBL_θ
+objective	OBJ	OBJ_θ

From (12), we see that SUBJ is a GF which is unrestricted as to semantic role – any role could be expressed as SUBJ – and is not an object. OBJ is also unrestricted, but of course is an object. The other two functions are semantically restricted. For example, the OBJ, which is the function of the second NP in the [V NP NP] ditransitive frame, can only express Theme, in English.

In canonical LMT, Actor arguments in a-structure are classified as −o, while Undergoer arguments are classified as −r. This means that an Actor argument can be SUBJ (in active) or an OBL$_\theta$ (in passive), but never any kind of OBJ. An Undergoer argument can be SUBJ or OBJ, but never a thematically restricted argument.

This conception of LMT does not extend to syntactically ergative languages, in which the Actor argument of a transitive verb maps to OBJ (see (9b)). Rather, the mapping principles within LMT must be parameterized for different language types, or rather, for different mapping types; see Arka (2003: Chapter 5).

6.2.3 Mapping syntax to semantics

Given that LFG gives emphasis to f-structure as the locus of the representation of grammatical information, it is natural that semantic interpretation is determined from f-structure. An early and influential model-theoretic treatment of semantics in LFG can be found in Halvorsen (1983).

In the last decade or so, a linear logic approach to semantics has become standard in LFG research, known as 'Glue Semantics,' "because of the role of linear logic in stating how the meanings of the parts of an utterance can be 'glued together' to form the meaning" (Dalrymple 2001:230). From the syntactic perspective, the key idea in Glue Semantics is that the information in f-structure provides resources which the semantics interprets, and roughly speaking, each such resource is used in the semantic interpretation exactly once. For short introductions, see Asudeh (2006) and Dalrymple (2006).

6.3 F-structure

6.3.1 Basic properties

F-structure presents all of the grammatically relevant information about a sentence or other unit of analysis. The information must be formally precise, and is presented systematically in attribute–value matrices. Every attribute must have a value. To illustrate the format, a typically informal characterization of a verb as [+Past, 3sg] would necessarily be represented as the following f-structure in LFG. 'Past' is actually a value of the attribute TENSE, and '3sg' is actually information about the subject's agreement features:

$$(13) \begin{bmatrix} \text{TENSE} & \text{PAST} \\ \text{PRED} & \text{'verb} < \ldots > \text{'} \\ \text{SUBJ} & \begin{bmatrix} \text{PERS} & 3 \\ \text{NUM} & \text{SG} \end{bmatrix} \end{bmatrix}$$

That is, the relevant part of the structure has PAST for the value of the TENSE attribute, the semantic predicator (PRED) is whatever the verb denotes; the part shown only as '...' is where the selectional properties of the PRED are indicated. There is also some information about the grammatical features of the SUBJ: its PERS attribute has value 3 and NUM has value SG. Any f-structure which has a PRED is known as a **nucleus** – essentially the domain in which a head combines with its arguments.

The f-structure in (13) would be characterized by this set of equations on a V node in c-structure:

(14) ($\uparrow$SUBJ NUM) = SG
      ($\uparrow$SUBJ PERS) = 3
      ($\uparrow$PRED) = 'verb< ... >'
      ($\uparrow$TENSE) = PRES

The order in which the lines of information are written in (14) or displayed in (13) is irrelevant. (14) describes a set of properties (on a c-structure node) which must be true of the f-structure of that c-structure node. If we ask whether each line in (14) is true of (13), regardless of which 'order' we take the lines in (14), the answer is always affirmative.

In a full grammatical description, we would need to enumerate all of the typical attributes and values of f-structure (e.g., TENSE and its possible values, ASPECT and its possible values, etc.). Typical lists of these can be found in Dalrymple (2001:28, 2006: (17)). In any given analysis, usually only those attributes and values relevant to the argument or discussion are shown – just as only certain aspects of syntactic tree representations or derivations are shown in transformational analyses.

Some f-structure attributes take atomic values, such as PAST or PRES. Other f-structure attributes name grammatical functions (GFs), and take as their values other f-structures. Hence these embedded f-structures will themselves have PRED values, and if the PRED itself selects for any GFs, there will be further f-structure embedding. This is illustrated below, for example in (22).

The core GFs are SUBJ, OBJ, OBJ$_\theta$, OBL$_\theta$, COMP, and XCOMP. SUBJ is a core GF, but also is one of the Grammaticized Discourse Functions (GDFs; see Section 6.3.3), along with the other Discourse Functions of TOPIC and FOCUS. Bresnan (2001:98) motivates the class of GDFs as those "functions [which] are the most salient in discourse and often have c-structure properties that iconically express this prominence." The functions OBJ$_\theta$ and OBL$_\theta$ are thematically restricted: they may only express certain semantic roles. This is most simply illustrated with prepositional markers of OBL in English: OBLs marked with *from* only express Source-like meanings, OBLs marked with *to* only Goal-like meanings (possibly metaphorically extended), and so on. COMP is the function of selected complement clauses, and XCOMP is the function of clause-like complements with a controlled subject (see Section 6.3.2). The GFs ADJ and XADJ cover adjunct functions. For further detail see Asudeh and Toivonen (2010, Table 1). Functions are grouped as follows:

(15) a. Grammaticized Discourse Functions: TOPIC, FOCUS, SUBJ
b. Complement Functions: SUBJ, OBJ, OBJ$_\theta$, OBL$_\theta$, COMP, and XCOMP.

These groupings will be referred to in the discussion below, as significant structural generalizations refer to them.

In addition to values that are atomic or are f-structures, there is one more type of value in LFG: the semantic form. This is the value of the attribute PRED, and it designates the semantic form of a PRED and its selection, in terms of GFs. For example, the verb 'give' might have part of its lexical entry as follows:

(16) (↑PRED) = 'give<(↑SUBJ)(↑OBJ)(↑OBL)>'

which requires that the f-structure includes the predicate 'give' and three GFs: SUBJ, OBJ, and OBL, expressing the three arguments of the predicator (see (58b) for a corresponding f-structure).

The major constraints on syntax in LFG are in fact constraints on f-structure. Within the nucleus, the notion of 'governable GF' determines whether an f-structure is well-formed or not. The governable GFs are: SUBJ, OBJ, OBJ$_\theta$, OBL$_\theta$, XCOMP, COMP.

(17) Constraints on F-structure:
  a. Completeness: Every thematic governable GF has a PRED value.
     An f-structure is complete if and only if it contains all the governable GFs that its PRED governs.
  b. Coherence: Every governable GF is governed.
     An f-structure is coherent if and only if all of the governable GFs that it contains are governed by PRED.
  c. Uniqueness: Every attribute has a unique value. (F-structure is a function.)

For example, all the examples in (18) could be generated as possible c-structures in English. However, some of them are ungrammatical with respect to f-structure. (18a) is ungrammatical due to the Completeness Condition: there is no information about the of the verb, which is a governable GF (see (3c)); hence (18b) is well-formed. (18c) is ungrammatical due to the Uniqueness Condition: the subject NP is specifying its NUM as PL, but the verb is specifying its subject's NUM as SG. In this way, all agreement facts are captured: two different parts of the c-structure provide information about the same piece of f-structure, and this information must not be inconsistent.

(18) a. *writes books
   b. the boy writes books
   c. *the boys writes books

For a given c-structure, what is its f-structure? Consider again the English c-structure in (2a), repeated below. Its f-structure is (19a), but why is it this one, as opposed to any of the other f-structures shown in (19), each of which is well-formed as an f-structure?

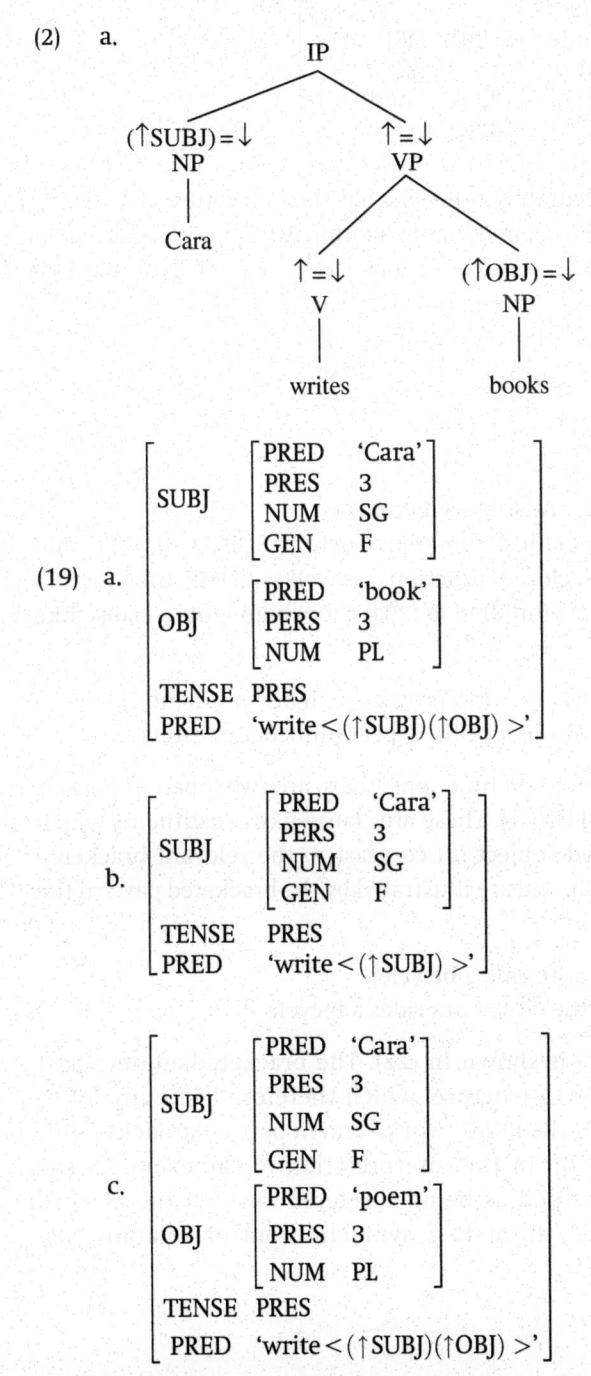

(2) a.

```
                IP
              /    \
      (↑SUBJ)=↓    ↑=↓
         NP        VP
         |        /   \
        Cara    ↑=↓   (↑OBJ)=↓
                 V      NP
                 |      |
               writes  books
```

(19) a.
$$\begin{bmatrix} \text{SUBJ} & \begin{bmatrix} \text{PRED} & \text{`Cara'} \\ \text{PRES} & 3 \\ \text{NUM} & \text{SG} \\ \text{GEN} & \text{F} \end{bmatrix} \\ \text{OBJ} & \begin{bmatrix} \text{PRED} & \text{`book'} \\ \text{PERS} & 3 \\ \text{NUM} & \text{PL} \end{bmatrix} \\ \text{TENSE} & \text{PRES} \\ \text{PRED} & \text{`write} < (\uparrow\text{SUBJ})(\uparrow\text{OBJ}) >\text{'} \end{bmatrix}$$

b.
$$\begin{bmatrix} \text{SUBJ} & \begin{bmatrix} \text{PRED} & \text{`Cara'} \\ \text{PERS} & 3 \\ \text{NUM} & \text{SG} \\ \text{GEN} & \text{F} \end{bmatrix} \\ \text{TENSE} & \text{PRES} \\ \text{PRED} & \text{`write} < (\uparrow\text{SUBJ}) >\text{'} \end{bmatrix}$$

c.
$$\begin{bmatrix} \text{SUBJ} & \begin{bmatrix} \text{PRED} & \text{`Cara'} \\ \text{PRES} & 3 \\ \text{NUM} & \text{SG} \\ \text{GEN} & \text{F} \end{bmatrix} \\ \text{OBJ} & \begin{bmatrix} \text{PRED} & \text{`poem'} \\ \text{PRES} & 3 \\ \text{NUM} & \text{PL} \end{bmatrix} \\ \text{TENSE} & \text{PRES} \\ \text{PRED} & \text{`write} < (\uparrow\text{SUBJ})(\uparrow\text{OBJ}) >\text{'} \end{bmatrix}$$

d. $\begin{bmatrix} \text{SUBJ} & \begin{bmatrix} \text{PRED} & \text{'Cara'} \\ \text{PERS} & 3 \\ \text{NUM} & \text{SG} \\ \text{GEN} & \text{F} \end{bmatrix} \\ \text{OBJ} & \begin{bmatrix} \text{PRED} & \text{'book'} \\ \text{PERS} & 3 \\ \text{NUM} & \text{PL} \end{bmatrix} \\ \text{TENSE} & \text{PRES} \\ \text{PRED} & \text{'write} < (\uparrow\text{SUBJ})(\uparrow\text{OBJ}) >\text{'} \\ \text{ADJ}_{\text{LOC}} & \begin{bmatrix} \text{PRED} & \text{'in} < (\uparrow\text{OBJ}) >\text{'} \\ \text{OBJ} & \begin{bmatrix} \text{PRED} & \text{'study'} \\ \text{SPEC} & + \end{bmatrix} \end{bmatrix} \end{bmatrix}$

Only f-structure (19a) accurately reflects what the c-structure conveys. In contrast, (19b) does not have enough information (the object is ignored); it would correspond to 'Cara writes'. (19c) has the right amount of information, but it has the wrong information about the PRED of the OBJ. And (19d) has too much information (there is a locative adjunct not expressed in any way in the c-structure), and would correspond to 'Cara writes books in the study.'

6.3.2 Structure sharing: raising and control

All of the nuclear grammatical functions such as SUBJ, OBJ, OBL, and ADJ(UNCT) are known as 'closed' functions, as well as COMP, the function of complement clauses, exemplified in (20a). (20b) highlights a clause-like adjunct:

(20) a. we expect $_{\text{COMP}}$[that further progress will be imminent]
b. $_{\text{ADJ}}$[with Cara as designer], we expect immediate results

Now in addition to these closed functions, there are two 'open' functions in LFG: XCOMP and XADJ(UNCT). These are clause-like constituents which do not have an expressed subject (in contrast to the relevant bracketed parts of the examples (20)), and are illustrated by the bracketed parts of the examples in (21):

(21) a. Cara started $_{\text{XCOMP}}$[to ride a bicycle]
b. $_{\text{XADJ}}$[working in the city], Cara rides a bicycle

The f-structure for (21b) is shown in (22). The bracketed adjunct part of (21b) is simply a VP in c-structure, which therefore lacks any information about the SUBJ of the PRED 'work,' and in particular lacks PRED information for that SUBJ. In the interpretation of the example, the SUBJ of 'work' is understood as being coreferential with the SUBJ of the main PRED 'write,' through a syntactic control relation (see Chapter 16):

(22)
$$\begin{bmatrix} \text{XADJ} & \begin{bmatrix} \text{SUBJ} & [\quad] \\ \text{PRED} & \text{'work<(↑SUBJ)>'} \\ \text{ADJ}_{\text{LOC}} & \begin{bmatrix} \text{PRED} & \text{'in<(↑OBJ)>'} \\ \text{OBJ} & \begin{bmatrix} \text{PRED} & \text{'city'} \\ \text{SPEC} & + \end{bmatrix} \end{bmatrix} \end{bmatrix} \\ \text{SUBJ} & \begin{bmatrix} \text{PRED} & \text{'Cara'} \end{bmatrix} \\ \text{PRED} & \text{'ride <(↑SUBJ)(↑OBJ)>'} \\ \text{OBJ} & \begin{bmatrix} \text{PRED} & \text{'bicycle'} \\ \text{SPEC} & - \end{bmatrix} \end{bmatrix}$$

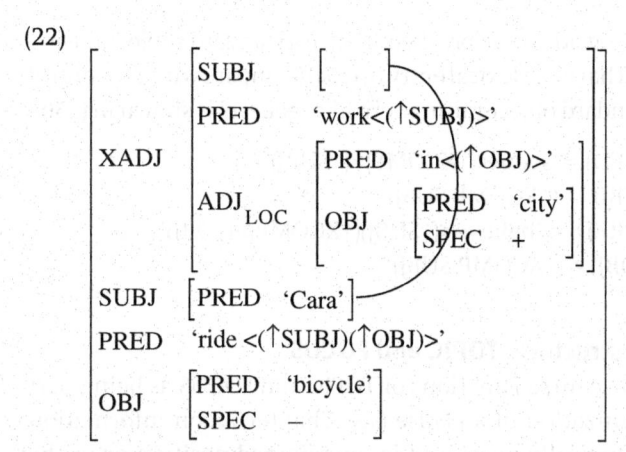

The curved line represents 'structure-sharing,' indicating that two attributes in f-structure have the same object as their value. Hence (22) shows that the SUBJ of 'work' and the SUBJ of 'ride' are the same grammatical object, the f-structure corresponding to the NP 'Cara.' Without this structure sharing, which is constructionally specified (see Bresnan 1982c), the inner nucleus of the XADJ would violate the Completeness Condition (as there would no information about its SUBJ).

The same structure sharing is used to represent lexically specified control relations, as are found with obligatory control verbs such as 'start' in (21a), or 'try' or 'persuade.' Part of the lexical entry of such verbs will specify the control relation, such as:

(23)   start V (↑PRED) = 'start<(↑SUBJ)(↑XCOMP)>'
        (↑SUBJ) = (↑XCOMP SUBJ)

Due to the fact that a verb like 'start' specifies that its XCOMP SUBJ is identified with its SUBJ, the c-structure position which would intuitively correspond to the XCOMP SUBJ must be empty, or else the Uniqueness Condition is violated. Again, the c-structure rules for English would permit an example like (23) to be generated structurally, but there is no well-formed f-structure that can be associated with this c-structure:

(24)   *Cara$_i$ started [her(self)$_i$ to ride a bicycle]$_{\text{XCOMP}}$

The overt subject of the XCOMP would require the PRED of the SUBJ of that XCOMP has value 'PRO,' coming from *her(self)*, but the upper part of the example dictates that the PRED value of XCOMP SUBJ is 'Cara.'

The syntactic relations of control and raising are indicated in the same way, in LFG, through structure sharing. The notional difference between control and raising is whether the SUBJ of the PRED which determines the structure sharing is thematic or not, and it is this property which LFG uses to indicate the difference between control and raising. By definition, GFs which are selected by a PRED and which bear a thematic (semantic) relation to that PRED are placed between the angle brackets in the semantic form of the PRED, while non-thematic GFs are outside these brackets. Hence a standard subject-raising verb like 'seem' would have the lexical entry in (25a) (compare with the control verb in (24)), and a standard object-raising verb like 'believe' is shown in (25b):

(25) a. *seem* V (↑PRED) = 'seem<(↑XCOMP)>(↑SUBJ)'
   (↑SUBJ) = (↑XCOMP SUBJ)
b. *believe* V (↑PRED) = 'believe<(↑SUBJ)(↑XCOMP)>(↑OBJ)'
   (↑OBJ) = (↑XCOMP SUBJ)

6.3.3 Information structure: TOPIC and FOCUS

LFG recognizes the Discourse Functions of TOPIC and FOCUS as being part of the syntactic organization of a clause (see Chapter 23 on information structure); TOPIC is typically expressed in an adjoined position or in the specifier of a functional category, while FOCUS may have a wider variety of expression. For example, TOPIC in English is typically expressed by a category adjoined to IP, while there is a variety of strategies for FOCUS expression. Formally, DFs must be associated with an argument or adjunct GF. This is covered by the Extended Coherence Condition (Bresnan 2001):

(26) Extended Coherence Condition
FOCUS and TOPIC must be linked to the semantic predicate argument structure of the sentence in which they occur through proper integration with the sentence's f-structure. Proper integration is either functional equality with or anaphoric binding of a grammatical function.

A simple example of how DFs are separate from nuclear GFs is provided by the Japanese marker *wa*, which marks TOPIC (Kuno 1973b). As is well known, *wa* supplants the regular nominative and accusative case markers, and a *wa*-marked TOPIC should be initial in the clause:

(27) a. Cara-ga   syoosetu-o kak-u
       Cara-NOM novel-ACC write-PRES
       'Cara writes novels'

   b. Cara-wa   syoosetu-o kak-u
       Cara-TOP novel-ACC write-PRES
       '(as for) Cara (, she) writes novels'

   c. syoosetu-wa Cara-ga   kak-u
       novel-TOP   Cara-NOM write-PRES
       'novels, Cara writes'

In Section 6.4.3 I discuss the contributions of the markers here – roughly speaking, *ga* shows that the constituent which hosts it corresponds to a SUBJ in f-structure, *o* indicates an OBJ, and *wa* indicates a TOPIC. If this is so, compared to (27a), nothing in (27b) indicates that the SUBJ phrase *Cara-wa* is also a SUBJ; but if TOPIC and SUBJ are identified in f-structure, this will give a Complete and Coherent f-structure.

Due to the fact that DFs may be expressed in the functional categories of CP and IP, even non-configurational languages may be configurational with regard to DFs, being 'discourse configurational' (É. Kiss 1995). King (1995) presents an extended account of Russian in LFG. A simple illustration of the idea of discourse configurationality is provided by the Bulgarian example (28), from Dalrymple (2001:73).

(28) Ivan kakvo pravi?
      Ivan what   do-PRES
      'What does Ivan do?'

In Bulgarian, SpecCP is a TOPIC position, SpecIP is a FOCUS position, and the finite verb sits in the I position.[3] The details of c-structure are provided below in Section 6.4, but as there are only three overt positions in (28), these are all that are represented in the phrase structure. Hence, there is no overt structure following the finite verb in I; higher up, CP is present as its Specifier is filled, but there is no head of CP:

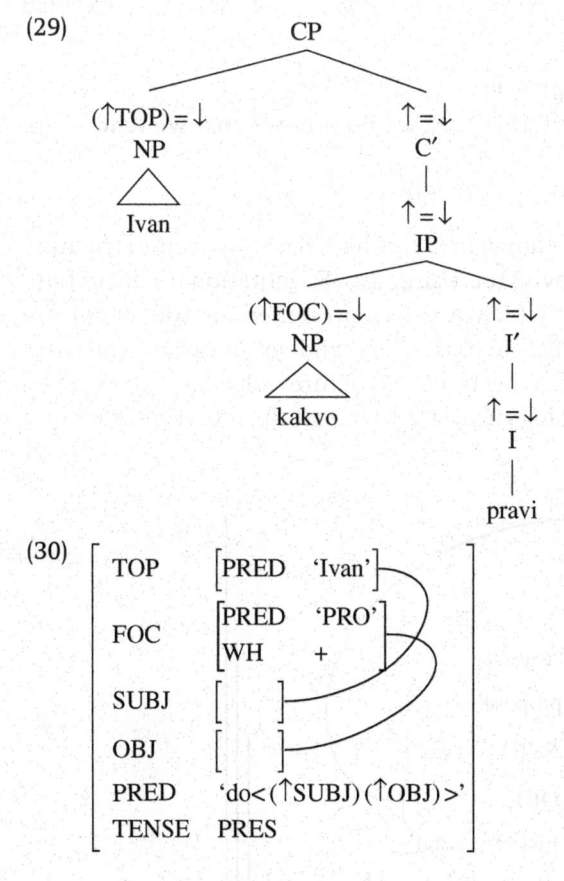

(29)
```
                    CP
         _____|_____
    (↑TOP)=↓                  ↑=↓
       NP                      C'
       △                       |
      Ivan                    ↑=↓
                               IP
                      _____|_____
                 (↑FOC)=↓              ↑=↓
                    NP                  I'
                    △                   |
                  kakvo                ↑=↓
                                        I
                                        |
                                      pravi
```

(30) ⎡ TOP   [PRED 'Ivan']   ⎤
      ⎢   ⎥
      ⎢   ⎡PRED 'PRO'⎤   ⎥
      ⎢ FOC   ⎣WH   +   ⎦   ⎥
      ⎢   ⎥
      ⎢ SUBJ   [   ]   ⎥
      ⎢   ⎥
      ⎢ OBJ   [   ]   ⎥
      ⎢   ⎥
      ⎢ PRED   'do<(↑SUBJ)(↑OBJ)>'   ⎥
      ⎣ TENSE PRES   ⎦

Each DF must be identified with some nuclear GF, as shown in (30). In this particular Bulgarian example, either NP could be SUBJ or OBJ, and the structure-sharing shown indicates the pragmatically plausible reading.

6.3.4 Long-distance dependencies

Long-distance dependencies in LFG (corresponding to A'-movement in transformational approaches)[4] are represented in f-structure, as an instance of structure sharing. If we consider such a dependency to have a top, a middle, and a bottom, the f-structure only represents the top and the bottom.

To take a canonical example of a clause-initial *wh*-phrase, in its *in-situ* position it will realize the function FOCUS, which as a DF must be integrated into the rest of the clause, at f-structure. In the first instance, this will involve structure-sharing with a nuclear GF. This happens in the syntax through an equation of 'functional uncertainty' on the clause-initial node. The functional uncertainty expression describes one of many paths into an f-structure. For instance, a general equation like (31a) associates a FOCUS on a given node with any GF within the same nucleus, or in an embedded nucleus through one or more COMP functions. For a specific example such as (31b), the specific instantiation of the equation would be as in (31c). In (31b), the notation '___' is for presentational purposes only.

(31) a. (↑FOCUS) = (↑COMP* GF)
 b. Who did you think that Cara would propose that we send ___ to France?
 c. (↑FOCUS) = (↑COMP COMP OBJ)

The f-structure of (31b) is shown in (32), which has the specific structure-sharing link described by (31c). Using an LFG notational convention, parts of the f-structure which are not presented in full detail are enclosed in double quotes, such as "who" and so on, where the extra detail is not relevant to aspects of f-structure relevant to the given discussion. (It is the analog of using a triangle to represent part of a phrase structure.)

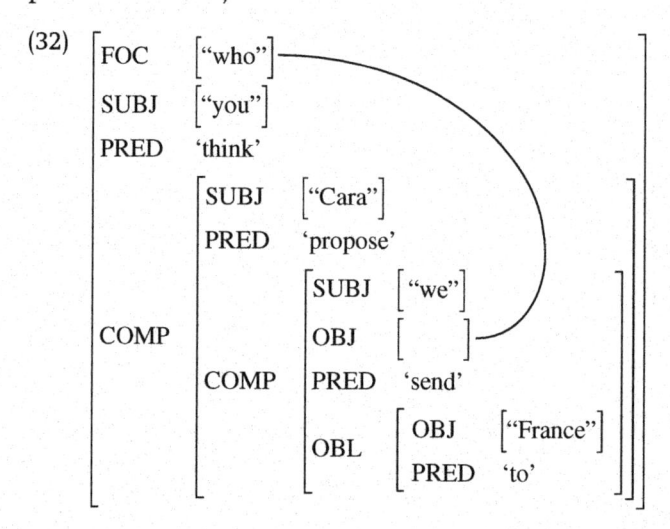

(32)
$$\begin{bmatrix} \text{FOC} & [\text{``who''}] \\ \text{SUBJ} & [\text{``you''}] \\ \text{PRED} & \text{`think'} \\ \text{COMP} & \begin{bmatrix} \text{SUBJ} & [\text{``Cara''}] \\ \text{PRED} & \text{`propose'} \\ \text{COMP} & \begin{bmatrix} \text{SUBJ} & [\text{``we''}] \\ \text{OBJ} & [\ ] \\ \text{PRED} & \text{`send'} \\ \text{OBL} & \begin{bmatrix} \text{OBJ} & [\text{``France''}] \\ \text{PRED} & \text{`to'} \end{bmatrix} \end{bmatrix} \end{bmatrix} \end{bmatrix}$$

As with the functional control examples above, no principle of c-structure requires there to be clause-internal 'empty' position, but if all internal positions are filled, and therefore if all the GFs of each PRED are overtly expressed, there is no way to have the required structure-sharing as well, fulfilling the Extended Coherence Condition as instantiated in (31a). The acceptable example corresponding to (32) does not provide any information about the OBJ of 'send' internal to the clause containing 'send', and hence that function is open in f-structure to be informationally specified in some other way. So while (33a) is a c-structure which has a well-formed f-structure (namely (32)), there is no well-formed f-structure for (33b), even though it is possible by the c-structure rules of English.

(33) a. Who did you think that Cara would propose that we send to France?
b. *Who did you think that Cara would propose that we send Ana to France?

Specifically, there is no GF with which to integrate the DF "who," and the Extended Coherence Condition is violated as a result. Once again, what appears to be a dependency in c-structure between one position and an empty or missing position is determined entirely by f-structure properties, and the way the c-structure information is integrated into f-structure.[5]

6.4 C-structure

6.4.1 Basic properties

C-structure is a representation of constituency, categorial labeling, and linear precedence relations. C-structure essentially, but not exclusively, represents the overt structure of a given string – the structure may include nodes dominating the empty string, if such nodes are motivated by some of the same principles which motivate overt structure. While in many approaches to syntax, non-overt structure is motivated by any kind of grammatical dependency (for example, one element displaced from an *in-situ* argument position, or one position controlling another position), such motivation is lacking in LFG, for all such dependencies are represented at f-structure. However, null elements in c-structure can be motivated by the participation in linear precedence relations (Section 6.4.4). An underappreciated feature of LFG is that there are very strict conditions on what counts as evidence for constituency and labeling in the overt structure, and in fact LFG places a much higher burden of proof on the motivation of its phrase structures than most other syntactic frameworks.

An overarching constraint on c-structure is the Principle of Lexical Integrity, which does not allow more than one c-structure node to correspond to a terminal element.

(34) Lexical Integrity
The terminal nodes of c-structures are morphologically complete words.

For example, if an inflected verb expresses tense and agreement, this is not evidence in LFG for c-structure nodes V, Tns, and Agr, which are somehow syntactically related. Rather, it is just a situation where a morphologically complex single word expresses more grammatical information than just the verb lexeme itself. The syntactic label of this word is determined by the c-structure properties of the language in question. Thus, in Japanese clause structure, the predicate may inflect for various kinds of grammatical information, including tense and speech level (whether the overall utterance is plain vs. polite/formal). The morphological class of verbs in Japanese are lexical items which can host both of these kinds of information in the same word. Adjectives may host tense, but not speech level; to express both kinds of information in a clause, a periphrastic construction must be used.

C-structure is pure structure; hence the only syntactic 'features' in it relate to categorial information, such as [±N, ±V] and bar level. All of the other syntactic information is projected from c-structure to f-structure. LFG does not assume that all structures, or even all languages, are structured according to X'-theory. The overall theory of c-structures does admit standard X'-type Specifier–Head–Complement structures, as well as a variety of phrase structures which fall outside this format. Within the clause, X'-structures such as IP and CP essentially provide the 'extended projection' (Grimshaw 2000) of the verb (see (37b) below). However, in some languages the analysis of the clause involves the category S – see the discussions of Welsh and Warlpiri below – to which X'-theory does not apply.

In one sense, formal constraints on c-structure are very weak: they may or may not respect X'-theory; they may be endocentric or exocentric; they may be binary or many-ways branching.[6] This is as it should be, in LFG, as all of the major constraints on c-structure follow from f-structure. For example in every mother–daughter(s) subtree, at least one daugher must be the functional head (f-head), annotated ↑=↓, or else information will not flow within the structure.

If there is a head in the c-structure, in the traditional phrase structure sense, this is the default f-head. So, for example, within VP, V is the f-head because it is the c-head; similarly I' is the f-head of IP. Other categories have an f-head but no c-head – for example, VP is the f-head of S even though the two categories S and VP have no X'-theoretic relation. Similarly, LFG has notions of 'Specifier functions' and 'Complement functions,' which contrain which GFs can be expressed in the X' syntactic positions of Specifier and Complement; but the GFs are not **defined** in terms of such c-structure positions.

Due to the information available in f-structure, c-structure as such is not needed to represent the difference between subjects and non-subjects, or between arguments and adjuncts. For example, a node V which is intermediate between V and VP would not be motivated on the basis of the fact that both arguments and adjuncts can appear within VP. From the LFG perspective, there may be little evidence in English for a V′ constituent. It is not even true that all arguments appear closer to V than all adjuncts: the fact of English is that a direct object NP must immediately follow V, but for all other arguments and adjuncts, order is somewhat free, as suggested by the examples in (35):[7]

(35) a. discuss (*frankly/*openly) one's child / the problem (frankly/openly)
      b. talk (frankly/openly) to one's child / about the problem (frankly/openly)

Lexical categories provide the core endocentric structures such as NP, VP, and possibly AP and PP, if the language has such categories as adjective and adposition.

LFG recognizes that languages may have functional categories in c-structure, such as DP, IP, and CP. These functional categories are motivated only through two kinds of evidence: either a closed subclass of lexical items which have a special distribution, or a specialized syntactic position for a grammatically defined set of categories; sometimes both kinds of evidence converge. Hence I might be motivated by a language which has a special position for finite auxiliary verbs (e.g., English), or for all finite verbs (e.g., French), but I is not motivated simply by the fact that a language has finite verbs (e.g., Japanese). The head C of CP is similarly motivated in some languages by a special closed class of complementizers, and by a high position for auxiliary or all finite verbs in certain constructions. Specifier positions are typically motivated by the positional expression of a GDF (cf. the structure for Bulgarian in (29) above).

The c-structures of a given language are chararacterized by a set of annotated phrase-structure rules which provide all of the possible structures in the language. By convention, unless otherwise specified, every member in the right-hand side of a rule is optional. For example, the simple rule in (36) could determine six different VP subtrees, with any combination of one or more of the daughter constituents present (in the relative order indicated):

(36) VP → V   NP   PP
                       (↑OBJ)=↓   (↑OBL)=↓

Ordering constraints are themselves largely stated on functional information. There are natural domains for ordering constraints (Sells 2001b) – sisters in a local c-structure subtree, and the exponents of GFs in the same nucleus.

6.4.2 Correspondences and f-structure constraints on c-structure

With different levels of representation, LFG must provide mechanisms for relating them. Any part of one level of representation may carry information about some part of another, which is determined by 'projecting' the information. The overall projection sets up correspondences between a structure at one level and a structure at another. The canonical correspondence is between c-structure and f-structure, expressed through defining equations. For example, if a c-structure node has the annotation (↑PERS) = 3, this means that the attribute PERS has the value 3 in the f-structure corresponding to that c-structure node.

Every node in a c-structure, with the exception of the root node, is annotated either with (↑GF)=↓, for some grammatical function, or else it is an f-structure head, and is annotated ↑=↓. The relationship between c-structure and f-structure is given by a projection function from c-structure nodes to f-structure attribute-value matrices. The up- and down-arrows ('↑' and '↓') refer to the f-structure that corresponds to the c-structure node where the arrow points: the 'up' refers to the f-structure of the mother node and the 'down' refers to the f-structure of the node itself. So the annotation ↑=↓ indicates the functional information associated with a given node is the same as the functional information as the mother node, and an annotation like (↑SUBJ)=↓ indicates that the functional information associated with a given node is in the SUBJ value of the mother's f-structure.

The main principles of structure–function association are given in (37), based on Bresnan (2001:102ff.), with brief paraphrases:

(37) Principles of structure–function association:
  a. C-structure heads are f-structure heads. (Every head in the usual X'-theory sense is annotated ↑=↓.)
  b. Complements of functional categories are f-structure co-heads. (The IP complement within CP is annotated ↑=↓, and the VP or S complement within IP is annotated ↑=↓.)
  c. Specifiers of the functional categories CP and IP are the grammaticalized discourse functions. (SpecCP and SpecIP are annotated with one of (↑SUBJ)=↓, (↑TOPIC)=↓, or (↑FOCUS)=↓.)
  d. Complements of lexical categories are the non-discourse argument functions. (Each sister of the head V of VP is annotated with (↑OBJ)=↓, or (↑OBL)=↓, and so on.)

It is important to have a clear understanding of these four principles. In LFG, the syntactic notion of 'head' has different manifestations, and it is useful to keep them separate. We can say that (37a) states that every c-head is an f-head. For example, within VP, the primary infomation about the functional information about VP flows up from the c-head V, and not from the complement NP. While every local subtree must have at least one f-head, there are circumstances where (i) there is an f-head but no c-head, in truly exocentric structures, or (ii) there is more than one f-head, even though there is only one c-head.

An example of an exocentric structure is provided by the rule S → NP VP within which VP is the f-head, even though VP is not the c-structure head of S (as by definition, S does not participate in X'-theory). This rule provides a standard subject–predicate organization for a clause in two situations. The first is in languages in which there is no evidence in a clause for any INFL-like element to motivate an IP structure (see Falk 2001). For example, mainland Scandinavian languages show no verb raising out of VP in non-V2 clauses (see Holmberg and Platzack 1995), though the finite verb is in C in V2 clauses. A possible structural analysis of such languages would involve CP over S – the finite verb would be in C in V2 clauses, but in V within VP in non-V2 clauses. There would be no evidence (within LFG) for an intermediate I position.

The second situation where a subject–predicate S category is motivated in LFG is one involving a configurational subject position, but lower than a finite verb in I. In this case, S is rather like the 'small clause' of the Government and Binding Theory era of transformational syntax, hosting only non-finite predicates. The resulting structures correspond to analyses involving a VP-internal subject position. This has been proposed for LFG analyses of Russian (King 1995) and Welsh (Sadler 1997), among others. The structure can be illustrated with a Welsh example, from Sadler:

(38)   a. gwnaeth hi weld y draig
          do-PAST she see the dragon
          'she saw the dragon'
       b.   IP
                        ┌───────┴───────┐
                       ↑=↓   ↑=↓
                        I   S
                        | ┌──────┴──────┐
                    gwnaeth (↑SUBJ)=↓   ↑=↓
                                NP   VP
                                △   ┌──────┴──────┐
                                hi   ↑=↓   (↑OBJ)=↓
                                         V   NP
                                         | △
                                        weld   y draig

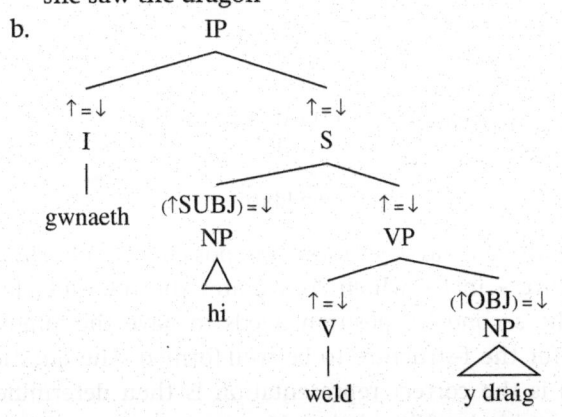

Returning to (37), (37b) provides the principle by which information flows in more complex syntactic structures, throughout the 'extended projection' connecting CP, IP, S, and VP. (37c) straightforwardly refers to specifier positions and the specifier functions. (37d) refers to c-structure complements of a lexical category such as V. Hence, in the unmarked case, complements in c-structure categories are the non-discourse GFs, and specifiers of functional categories are the discourse GFs.

The principles in (37) refer to categories in c-structure. The category labels in c-structure are subject to two different kinds of motivation: their 'pure' categorial content, and how their categorial content is evaluated within the system of structure–function mapping. Exactly how the structure–function correspondences are set up is a key part of the approach, and significant generalizations about linguistic structure follow from the statement of these correspondences. For example, in a language such as Spanish in which finite verbs appear in the c-structure in I, rather than heading V in VP, a simple transitive clause (meaning 'Cara bought a book') could plausibly have the c-structure in (a) or in (b):

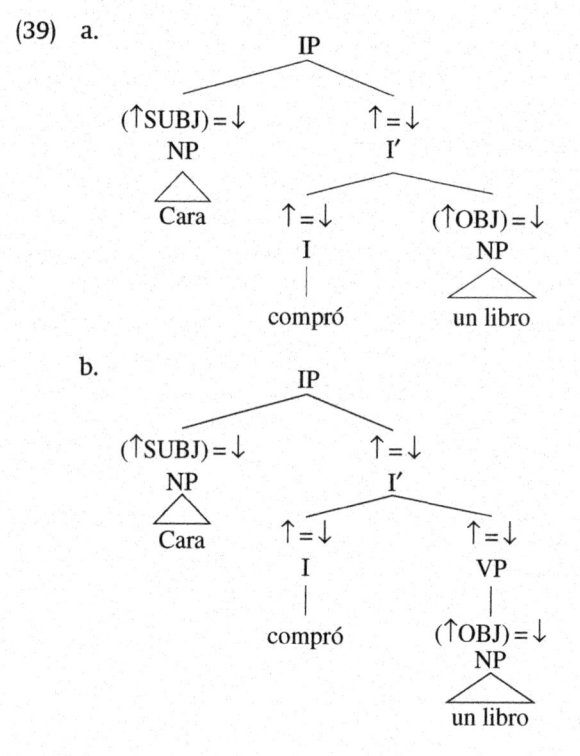

(39) a.

```
                    IP
          ┌─────────┴─────────┐
      (↑SUBJ)=↓             ↑=↓
         NP                  I'
          │          ┌───────┴───────┐
        Cara        ↑=↓          (↑OBJ)=↓
                     I               NP
                     │                │
                   compró          un libro
```

b.

```
                    IP
          ┌─────────┴─────────┐
      (↑SUBJ)=↓             ↑=↓
         NP                  I'
          │          ┌───────┴───────┐
        Cara        ↑=↓             ↑=↓
                     I               VP
                     │                │
                   compró         (↑OBJ)=↓
                                      NP
                                       │
                                   un libro
```

In these structures there is no V position, and possibly no VP. There is a verb in the structure – in I – which contributes the relevant PRED to f-structure. And the second NP position needs to have the annotation (↑OBJ)=↓ in order for the f-structure to be well-formed. The question of whether (a) or (b) is the correct representation is then determined by considering different kinds of linguistic evidence.

One kind of evidence comes from pure c-structure considerations. Clearly there is a VP node in (b) which is absent from (a). Hence (b) implies that there should be positive evidence for VP; if no such evidence could be found, this might suggest that (a) is the correct structure.

A different kind of evidence comes from the substance of the theory of structure–function annotations, such as in (37) – what kinds of annotations are natural on which nodes? Looking at (39b) first, I and VP are annotated ↑=↓, as co-heads; the specifier of IP is annotated (↑SUBJ)=↓ and the NP immediately dominated by VP is annotated (↑OBJ)=↓. In other words, what it is to be a structural object is to be an NP within VP (note that VP dominating only NP is a legitimate structure licensed by the rule in (36)). Now in contrast to this, in structure (39a) the complement of the functional category head I is directly annotated (↑OBJ)=↓. If this is the correct structure, there should be no evidence for an intervening VP node, and (a) implies a language with a lower degree of configurationality than (b). Additionally, if structure (a) is correct, (37b) could not be universal or might need to be revised. Hence, as with any theory, the overall account will emerge from a balanced consideration of empirical coverage, coherent linguistic analysis, and theoretical generality or elegance.

In addition to defining equations, the LFG formalism also makes available 'constraining equations,' which ensure that a given piece of information is provided from somewhere else in the structure. For example, the complementizer *for* in English only introduces an infinitive clause headed by *to*. If we assume that *to* has the annotation (↑TNS) = INF, then *for* would have the constraining equation (↑TNS) =$_c$ INF, which checks for the presence of this information (coming from elsewhere in the structure). Hence we might say that the appearance of *for* is licensed by the appearance of *to*.

Another dependency of this type can be illustrated by the Spanish examples in (40), in which a preverbal clitic doubles the information of an oblique PP within the VP. The clitic may appear in the structure without the PP, as in (40b), but the reverse situation is not possible, as in (40c):

(40) a. le   di   un regalo a mi madre
        3sg.DAT give.PAST.1sg a present to my mother
        'I gave a present to my mother'
     b. le   di   un regalo
        3sg.DAT give.PAST.1sg a present
        'I gave him/her a present'
     c. *di   un regalo a mi madre
        give.PAST.1sg a present to my mother
        'I gave a present to my mother'

The lexical entry for the clitic can be given as (41). The parentheses around the last line mean that the specification of the value of PRED as 'PRO' is optional – that the form may correspond to a pronoun (if the option is taken) or simply to case and agreement information (if the option is not taken). This becomes relevant below in Section 6.4.4.

(41) *le* Cl (↑CASE) = DAT
                (↑PERS) = 3
                (↑NUM) = SG
                ((↑PRED) = 'PRO')

The generalization is that if the verb appears, its OBL argument must be expressed by at least the clitic. This could be accounted for in LFG by a constraining equation on the verb, as follows:

(42)   *dar* V (↑PRED) = 'give<(↑SUBJ)(↑OBJ)(↑OBL)>'
                 (↑OBL CASE) =$_c$ DAT

The verb's entry requires that its OBL's CASE value is specified as DAT, by something else in the structure; and this comes precisely from the clitic in (41). This account works on the assumption that the full PP *a mi madre* is not specified at all for (dative) case; therefore only the clitic can satisfy the constraining equation on the verb. Once again, (40c) is a possible c-structure, but it is ruled out at f-structure due to the missing information from the clitic.

LFG also has positive and negative existential specifications, which introduce some attribute but do not provide a value. In the case of a positive existential specification, this means that some other element in the c-structure must provide the value; for a negative specification, no other element must introduce the attribute, with any value.

For example, the complementizer *that* in English must appear in a clause specified for some value of TENSE, but it does not matter which one (PAST or PRESENT):

(43) a. ... that he {was on time / is on time / be on time / *to be on time}

This can be accomplished by specifying *that* for (↑TENSE). An f-structure is only well-formed if every attribute has a value, so once the TENSE attribute is determined in the f-structure by *that*, the following clause must contain enough morphosyntactic substance to provide some value for TENSE.

Finally, to account for a distribution such as the complement of *try* in (44a), we would have a negative specification on *try* as shown in (44b), to the effect that the XCOMP of *try* cannot have any expression of tense within it:

(44) a. he tried {to leave / leaving / *is leaving / *will leave}
     b. ¬(↑XCOMP TENSE)

Assuming that infinitives and gerunds are non-finite constituents of some kind, lacking the attribute TENSE and any value for it, the distribution in the examples above would be accounted for.

6.4.3 Information flow in lexico-centric structures

Bresnan (2001) makes a distinction between syntactico-centric languages and lexico-centric languages, according to how they indicate grammatical information in their c-structures. In lexico-centric languages, the forms of words themselves indicate the grammatical role in the clause that the words play. For example, a language with robust case marking will typically allow for free(r) constituent order as the GFs of the major constituents will be recoverable from the case marking. In LFG, this is known as 'constructive case marking,' developed by Nordlinger (1998). Consider a language with ergative–absolutive case marking, in which ergative case signals that the argument that bears it is the subject in a transitive clause. Rather than ergative case being a morphological spell-out of the syntactic properties just described, in the constructive case approach, the morphological form 'constructs' these properties, shown formally in (45) with informal paraphrases.

(45) Ergative case marker:
    (SUBJ↑) OBJ   (= 'the clause in which I am subject has an object')
    (↑ CASE) = ERG   (= 'my case is ergative')

Let us see how this works out in terms of an f-structure. The up arrow ↑ in (45) picks out an f-structure, the one labeled 2 in (46):

(46) $\left[\begin{array}{ll} \text{SUBJ} & {}_2[\text{CASE} \quad \text{ERG}] \\ \text{OBJ} & [\quad] \end{array} \right]_1$

(45) says for this f-structure 2 that it is the value of a SUBJ attribute, and that in the f-structure where the SUBJ attribute is, namely f-structure 1, there is an OBJ attribute. This is the 'constructive' contribution of the case marking. (45) also says that within 2, the attribute CASE has the value ERG.

An interesting application of constructive case is found in Korean. Standard nominative case is marked by the case suffix *i/ka* (phonologically conditioned by the host); it marks subjects of canonical transitive verbs and objects of some stative predicates. As a constructive case marker, it constructs the GF SUBJ or OBJ for the constituent which hosts it. There is also an honorific marker *kkeyse* which marks subjects whose referents are honorific; unlike the plain nominative marker, it does not appear on nominative objects. Hence *kkeyse* constrains its noun host to be part of a constituent which must be a SUBJ in f-structure (Sells 1995). *kkeyse* cannot be considered the 'spell-out' of nominative case on an honorific-referring NP, but must also directly involve the SUBJ grammatical function.

As noted below example (27), Japanese also has constructive case: it is essentially like Korean, with nominative *ga* constructing the SUBJ of any predicate and the OBJ of certain stative predicates; accusative *o* only constructs OBJ. The TOPIC marker *wa* can also be given a constructive analysis, as in (47):

(47) Japanese *wa*
    (TOPIC ↑)   (= 'I am the topic of my clause')

To further illustrate constructive case marking, let us look at the LFG analyses of two examples from Warlpiri, slightly adapted from Kroeger (2004:115):

(48) a. Jakamarra-rlu   ju   jinjinyi-manu warlu   yarrpi-minja-ku
       Jakamarra-ERG 1sg.ABS order-PAST   firewood kindle-INF-PURP
       'Jakamarra ordered me to build a fire'
    b. walya kiji-rninja-ku   ka-ma   kapakapa-jarri-mi   ngaju
       earth throw-INF-PURP PRES-1sg fail-INCH-NONPAST I
       'I am failing to throw the dirt out'

Warlpiri is famously a non-configurational language (see Hale 1979), and so the rules for Warlpiri c-structure are different from what we have seen above, though they are variations on quite familiar themes. In these rules below, 'C' stands for any constituent. There is some limited configurationality in Warlpiri, and the functional category IP provides an initial position which followed by a fixed second position for auxiliary-like elements. The structures are largely non-configurational in these various senses: there is no necessary constituency, and there are no privileged positions where given GFs must be expressed. The exocentric constituent S is the complement to the functional category I, and it may consist of any number of constituents, in any order. Non-finite verbal structures may form VPs (in sharp distinction to finite verbs, which never form VPs; see Simpson 1991:106 on Warlpiri and Nordlinger 1998:28ff. on Wambaya).

There is a variety of analytical options for restricting these VPs to being non-finite (see rule (49d)). In the specific case of Warlpiri, it is possible that the non-finite constituents are in fact nominal, rather than verbal (Simpson 1991:133). However, assuming that the constituents are truly verbal, a c-structure-based approach could be provided by taking categories to be more articulated than has been suggested so far. If c-structure nodes are complex categories of features and values, as in Generalized Phrase Structure Grammar (GPSG) (Gazdar et al. 1985), the relevant c-structure rules would refer to categories such as V[–Fin], which would formally be {V +, N –, Fin –}. Finally, an f-structure solution to this restriction would annotate the V in the VP rule with $\neg(\uparrow\text{TENSE})$, which would ensure that no tensed verb could be introduced by that rule.

The c-structure rules for Warlpiri are given in (49):

(49) a. IP → C I', where C = VP, NP, V, or N
     b. I' → I S
     c. S → C$^+$, where C = VP, NP, V, or N
     d. VP → NP V
     e. NP → N$^+$

Unless otherwise noted, the annotations on the c-structure nodes are essentially freely instantiated, allowing any consituent to play any functional role in any position. Any node may be freely annotated $\uparrow=\downarrow$ or

(↑GF)=↓. However, the functional role of a given constituent is constrained by its case marking or other morphological properties, and this is constructive. (50) shows the lexical information associated with the absolutive case marker, marking the subject of an intransitive clause or an object (in the second part of (50)), is not directly mentioned as the presence of a in the f-structure would follow from other principles).

(50) Absolutive case marker:
    (SUBJ↑)   (= 'I am subject in my clause')
    ¬ (SUBJ↑) OBJ   (= 'and that clause does not have an object')
    (↑ CASE) = ABS (= 'my case is absolutive')
    OR
    (OBJ↑)   (= 'I am object in my clause')
    (↑ CASE) = ABS (= 'my case is absolutive')

For example (48a), we assign the c-structure shown in (51). The initial element is an ergative-marked noun, and we can assume that the ergative marking constructively specifies that this is the subject in a transitive clause. In the c-structure of a non-configurational languages, there is no reason to assume an NP node dominating a single N, even the initial N in (51). Hence phrasal categories such as NP and VP are reserved in Warlpiri for true multi-word constituents.

The second word in (51) is the 'auxiliary,' which appears in I, in second position, and which is an absolutive first person pronoun. This pronoun cannot be the SUBJ of the PRED of the nucleus (as the ergative-marked N has that function), so it must be the OBJ. The PRED information comes from the next word, which is the V. There is no way to integrate this into the c-structure other than to introduce it as a daughter of S (which can be a sequence of any categories). The PRED also selects for an XCOMP, and therefore the c-structure must provide some information about that XCOMP. This information comes from a non-finite VP, also under S in the c-structure. The PRED 'order' specifies that its OBJ is the same as its XCOMP SUBJ, as it is an object control verb.

The VP under S must be annotated (↑XCOMP)=↓. This can be accomplished formally by allowing free annotation on any node – if this node is annotated anything other than XCOMP, no well-formed f-structure will result; or we might take it that the final complementizer on the non-finite V is a purpose marker, which constructively creates the function, by being morphemically specified as (XCOMP↑). The f-structure, shown in (51), is effectively 'Jakamarra ordered me to kindle firewood.' For purposes of presentation, I use the glosses of the Warlpiri examples in the c-structures below, rather than the Warlpiri lexical items themselves.

(51)

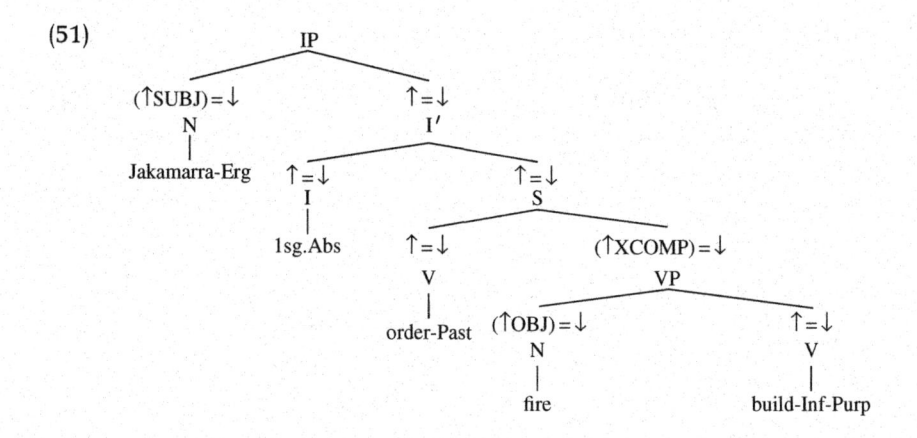

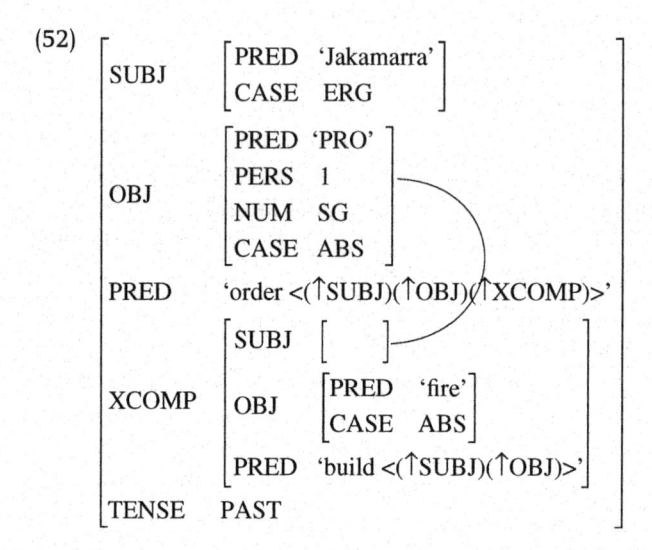

```
                        IP
         ┌──────────────┴──────────────┐
    (↑SUBJ)=↓                        ↑=↓
       N                              I'
       │              ┌───────────────┴───────────────┐
  Jakamarra-Erg     ↑=↓                              ↑=↓
                     I                                S
                     │         ┌──────────────────────┴──────────────────────┐
                  1sg.Abs    ↑=↓                                       (↑XCOMP)=↓
                              V                                              VP
                              │        ┌──────────┐                 ┌─────────┴─────────┐
                          order-Past (↑OBJ)=↓                                         ↑=↓
                                       N                                               V
                                       │                                               │
                                      fire                                      build-Inf-Purp
```

(52)
$$\begin{bmatrix} \text{SUBJ} & \begin{bmatrix} \text{PRED} & \text{'Jakamarra'} \\ \text{CASE} & \text{ERG} \end{bmatrix} \\ \text{OBJ} & \begin{bmatrix} \text{PRED} & \text{'PRO'} \\ \text{PERS} & 1 \\ \text{NUM} & \text{SG} \\ \text{CASE} & \text{ABS} \end{bmatrix} \\ \text{PRED} & \text{'order <(↑SUBJ)(↑OBJ)(↑XCOMP)>'} \\ \text{XCOMP} & \begin{bmatrix} \text{SUBJ} & [\quad] \\ \text{OBJ} & \begin{bmatrix} \text{PRED} & \text{'fire'} \\ \text{CASE} & \text{ABS} \end{bmatrix} \\ \text{PRED} & \text{'build <(↑SUBJ)(↑OBJ)>'} \end{bmatrix} \\ \text{TENSE} & \text{PAST} \end{bmatrix}$$

A comment is in order on the annotation on the auxiliary in I in (51) and in (53) below. The auxiliary itself may provide TENSE information to the main f-structure nucleus, as well as agreement information about some GF within that nucleus. The different paths of information flow on lexical items such as these actually come from different annotations with the sub-lexical structure of the word. This property is even more salient in languages with complex head-marking morphology. For details of word-internal annotations, see Bresnan (2001: Chapter 8).

Next, for example (48b), we assign the c-structure shown in (53). Here the initial constituent is a phrase, a non-finite VP, which is the XCOMP selected by the main PRED. In this example, the PRED is not transitive (it does not have an OBJ), and therefore the absolutive-marked constituents contribute to information about its SUBJ. This information comes from two nodes in the c-structure, from the auxiliary in I, and from the final word, under S.

(53)

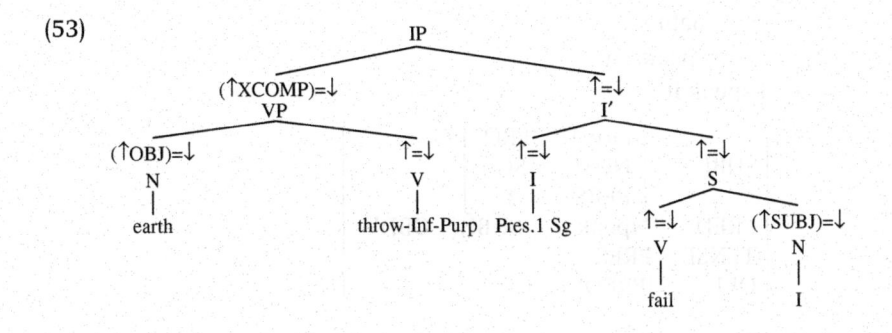

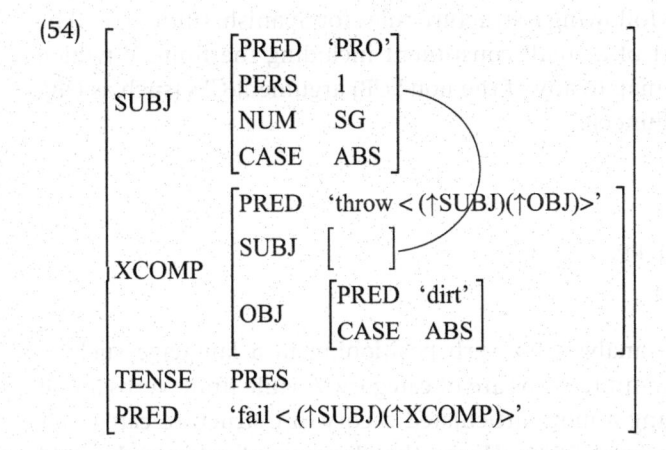

```
                              IP
                    ┌─────────┴─────────┐
              (↑XCOMP)=↓              ↑=↓
                   VP                  I'
            ┌──────┴──────┬────┐   ┌───┴───┐
       (↑OBJ)=↓   ↑=↓    ↑=↓   ↑=↓
           N       V      I     S
           │       │      │   ┌─┴──┐
         earth  throw-Inf-Purp Pres.1 Sg
                              ↑=↓  (↑SUBJ)=↓
                               V       N
                               │       │
                              fail     I
```

(54)

$$\begin{bmatrix} \text{SUBJ} & \begin{bmatrix} \text{PRED} & \text{'PRO'} \\ \text{PERS} & 1 \\ \text{NUM} & \text{SG} \\ \text{CASE} & \text{ABS} \end{bmatrix} \\ \text{XCOMP} & \begin{bmatrix} \text{PRED} & \text{'throw} < (\uparrow\text{SUBJ})(\uparrow\text{OBJ})>\text{'} \\ \text{SUBJ} & [\quad] \\ \text{OBJ} & \begin{bmatrix} \text{PRED} & \text{'dirt'} \\ \text{CASE} & \text{ABS} \end{bmatrix} \end{bmatrix} \\ \text{TENSE} & \text{PRES} \\ \text{PRED} & \text{'fail} < (\uparrow\text{SUBJ})(\uparrow\text{XCOMP})>\text{'} \end{bmatrix}$$

6.4.4 Null arguments

Above I have discussed various GFs in f-structure which have no overt correspondent in c-structure. Another instance of this circumstance involves canonical null subjects, as in classic 'pro-drop' languages. If there is the information of a pronoun present in f-structure (PRED 'PRO' and some agreement information), but no correspondent in c-structure, this is a null pronoun. (It is also possible to have an element which is present in c-structure but which contributes no information to f-structure – this would be a truly expletive element.) I will illustrate the account of null subjects as part of a slightly larger discussion of pronominal syntax in Spanish, which will allow me to show a few other aspects of a typical LFG analysis.

The Romance languages have a position for clitic pronouns which precedes a finite verb, while the canonical 'object position' follows the verb. A language like Spanish also has verbs which are inflected for the subject's agreement features, which allows clauses to be well-formed without having overt subjects, as in familiar examples like those in (55a–b), which determine the same f-structure, shown in (55c), except for different information about the PRED of the OBJ:

(55) a. hablo   español
        speak.1sg Spanish
        'I speak Spanish'

b. lo   hablo
   3sgm speak.1sg
   'I speak it'

c. $\begin{bmatrix} \text{SUBJ} & \begin{bmatrix} \text{PRED} & \text{'PRO'} \\ \text{NUM} & \text{SG} \\ \text{PERS} & 1 \end{bmatrix} \\ \text{PRED} & \text{'speak} < (\uparrow \text{SUBJ})(\uparrow \text{OBJ})\text{'}> \\ \text{TENSE} & \text{PRES} \\ \text{OBJ} & [\text{PRED'} \ldots \text{'}] \end{bmatrix}$

Let us assume the following c-structure rules for Spanish. Clitics could be introduced as part of a small constituent including the finite V (which appears in I), and map to any of the non-SUBJ argument GFs (such as OBJ, OBL, or certain adjuncts).

(56) a. IP → NP I'
     b. I' → I VP
     c. VP → V NP PP
     d. I → Cl$^+$ V

The standard LFG analysis for verb positioning in a language such as Spanish is that non-finite verbs are of category V while finite verbs are of category I, assuming a more articulated theory of c-structure categories (see King 1995, Bresnan 2001). Hence the elements of category I would appear in the I position licensed by rule (56b), and (non-finite) Vs would appear in the V position licensed by rule (56c). Rule (56d) for the clitics slightly obscures this basic approach to verb positioning, and it is necessary to restrict the V on the right-hand side of the rule to finite verbs, possibly by the use of complex categories in c-structure (see the discussion of a similar issue in Warlpiri on page 188).[8]

Any position introduced by the rules above is optional.[9] For example, it is possible to have a VP dominating the NP and PP, but no V. This would be a familiar case, a structure in which a finite verb appears external to VP, in I, but the internal arguments of that V are within VP. Consider (40a), repeated here as (57):

(57) le   di   un regalo a mi madre
     3sg.DAT give.PAST.1sg a present   to my mother
     'I gave a present to my mother'

This example receives the analysis in (58), given the rules above. The subscript numbers on some of the nodes figure in the discussion below.

(58) a.

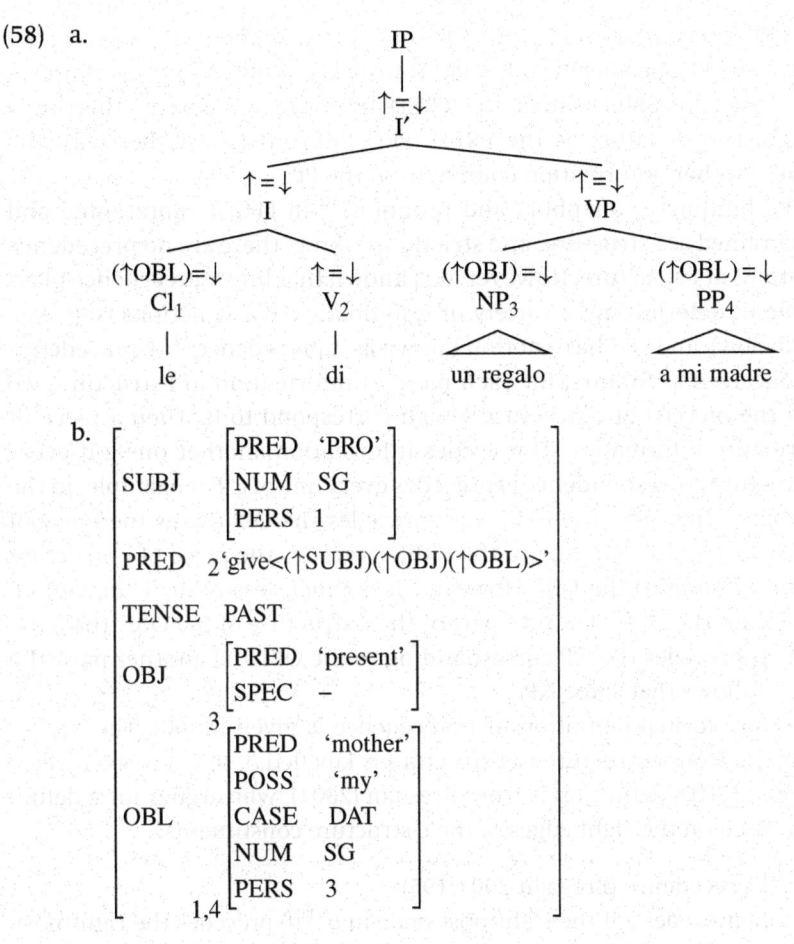

```
                        IP
                        |
                       ↑=↓
                        I'
              _____
             ↑=↓                ↑=↓
              I                  VP
       _____          _____
   (↑OBL)=↓   ↑=↓       (↑OBJ)=↓   (↑OBL)=↓
    Cl₁       V₂          NP₃         PP₄
     |         |           △           △
     le        di       un regalo   a mi madre
```

b.
$$\begin{bmatrix} \text{SUBJ} & \begin{bmatrix} \text{PRED} & \text{'PRO'} \\ \text{NUM} & \text{SG} \\ \text{PERS} & 1 \end{bmatrix} \\ \text{PRED} & {}_2\text{'give<(↑SUBJ)(↑OBJ)(↑OBL)>'} \\ \text{TENSE} & \text{PAST} \\ \text{OBJ} & {}_3\begin{bmatrix} \text{PRED} & \text{'present'} \\ \text{SPEC} & - \end{bmatrix} \\ \text{OBL} & \begin{bmatrix} \text{PRED} & \text{'mother'} \\ \text{POSS} & \text{'my'} \\ \text{CASE} & \text{DAT} \\ \text{NUM} & \text{SG} \\ \text{PERS} & 3 \end{bmatrix} \end{bmatrix}_{1,4}$$

While the clitic pronoun in (57) is 'doubling' the postverbal PP, in other examples the clitic pronoun stands as the OBL itself:

(59) le   di   un regalo
     3sg.DAT   give.PAST.1sg   a   present
     'I gave him/her a present'

The examples (57) and (59) are accounted for by the lexical entry for the clitic pronoun given above in (41), repeated below, in which the PRED information is optional:

(41)   le Cl   (↑CASE) = DAT
                (↑PERS) = 3
                (↑NUM) = SG
                ((↑PRED) = 'PRO')

Completeness and Uniqueness at f-structure determine the grammatical outcomes of the c-structures. In (59), if the PRED information in (41) is absent, the f-structure of the OBL is incomplete; if the PRED information is present, the f-structure is complete. In (57), the postverbal PP is providing the PRED information about the OBL, and therefore the clitic in (41) cannot do so as well. Specifically, if the PRED from (41) is absent, (57) is complete (as shown in (58b)), and if the PRED from (41) is present, there is a Uniqueness violation as the PRED 'PRO' information clashes with the PRED 'mother' information coming from the PP.

The binding of anaphors and pronouns[10] in LFG is represented and constrained at f-structure, and strictly speaking, there are no precedence relations at f-structure. However, it is known that linear precedence plays a role in determining a variety of grammatical constructions (see, e.g., (61) below), and LFG has a notion known as 'f-precedence.'[11] F-precedence is conceived as follows: for each piece of information in f-structure, we find the piece(s) of c-structure which correspond to it. Then a piece of f-structure information f f-precedes information another one g if every c-structure correspondent of f precedes every one of g. For example, in the f-structure in (58b), the PRED (2) f-precedes the OBJ (3), as the piece of c-structure corresponding to the PRED precedes the piece of c-structure corresponding to the OBJ. However, it is much less clear if the OBJ (3) f-precedes the OBL – because part of the c-structure of the OBL (the clitic part, 1) precedes the NP corresponding to the OBJ and another part (the PP, 4) follows that same NP.

A more formal definition of f-precedence is given in (60). The overall mapping from c-structure to f-structure is labelled φ, so φ^{-1} is the reverse mapping. This definition is from Bresnan (2001), who argues for a definition based on the right edges of the c-structure constituents.

(60) F-precedence (Bresnan 2001:195):
f f-precedes g if the rightmost node in $\varphi^{-1}(f)$ precedes the rightmost node in $\varphi^{-1}(g)$.
Under this definition, OBJ does precede OBL in (58b).

Generalizations involving linear precedence have been used in argumentation about whether null pronouns are present in c-structure or not. The following data from Mohanan (1983:665), on binding in Malayalam, are representative; see also Kameyama (1985) on Japanese for a similar argument (summarized in Dalrymple 2001:171ff., 288ff.). Mohanan observes that an overt pronoun may not precede its antecedent, while a null pronoun (indicated for presentational purposes by *pro* in (61b)) may:

(61) a. [awan   aanaye   nulliyatinə seesam] kutti$_i$ uraɲɲi
       he.NOM elephant.ACC pinched.it after   child.NOM slept
       'the child$_i$ slept [after he$_{*i/j}$ pinched the elephant]'
    b. [*pro* aanaye   nulliyatinə seesam] kutti$_i$ uraɲɲi
          elephant.ACC pinched.it after   child.NOM slept
       'the child$_i$ slept [after he$_{i,j}$ pinched the elephant]'

Why would overt and null pronouns have different precedence conditions on them? Mohanan proposes the following condition on pronoun binding:

(62) Malayalam
A pronoun must not f-precede its antecedent.

Now, if null pronouns are not represented in c-structure, but only in f-structure, they are not in any precedence relationships. Hence the null pronoun in (61b) satisfies (62), even under the *i*-indexing. Consider the c-structure relationships of the relevant parts of the examples, shown in (63a), with the f-structure of the example shown in (63b). The subscript numbers show the c-to-f-structure correspondences:

(63) a. C-structure:
   (pro_1) pinched$_2$ child$_3$

b. F-structure:
$$\begin{bmatrix} \text{SUBJ} & {}_3[\text{PRED} \quad \text{'child'}] \\ \text{PRED} & \text{'sleep} < (\uparrow \text{SUBJ}) >\text{'} \\ \text{TENSE} & \text{PAST} \\ \text{ADJ} & \begin{bmatrix} \text{PRED} & \text{'pinch'} \\ \text{SUBJ} & {}_1[\text{PRED} \quad \text{'PRO'}] \\ & \ldots \end{bmatrix} \\ & {}_2 \quad \ldots \end{bmatrix}$$

In (63b), 2 f-precedes 3, because the c-structure correspondent(s) of 2 precede the correspondent(s) of 3 in (63a). Now with regard to 1 and 3, 1 f-precedes 3 only if 1 is present in c-structure. Hence the apparently different binding properties of pronouns reduce to their different properties in different parts of the syntactic analysis.

Such a truly null argument can be considered to be introduced directly into f-structure in order to satisfy Completeness – if a verb is generated in c-structure without enough arguments, a null pronoun can be assumed in f-structure. This is a property sometimes known as 'radical' pro-drop, where any argument can be null, in languages which have no grammatical agreement. The prototypical exemplars of this type of language are the East Asian languages. This approach to introducing radically null arguments is importantly different from one in which null arguments are introduced as parts of the lexical entries of their governing verbs (see, e.g., Bresnan and Mchombo 1987 on Chichewa).

The implications of this analysis are far-reaching: if certain syntactic elements can have a range of grammatical properties without being represented in phrase structure – and there is positive evidence that they are not represented in phrase structure – then every aspect of grammatical analysis which can or must refer to those properties must also be independent of any phrase structure representation, including phenomena such as subjecthood, agreement, binding, and so on.

Now this is not so say that LFG does not recognize empty elements in c-structure as a matter of principle. Some well-known facts of Hindi (Mahajan 1990) can be used to illustrate exactly when empty elements are or are not present (Bresnan 2001:197ff.). The examples involve weak crossover effects. These effects arise when an empty category is present in an *in-situ* argument position (in the c-structure), to the right of a pronoun which is bound by an operator associated with that empty category.

The relevant facts of Hindi are very simple. Mahajan (1990:26) observed that clause-internal scrambling does not lead to a weak crossover effect, which long-distance scrambling across clauses does. Due to this difference, the *wh*-operator 'who' in (64a) can bind the following pronoun 'him,' while the same binding is not grammatical in (64b):

(64) a. kis-ko$_i$ uskii$_i$ bahin   pyaar kartii   thii?
       who-ACC his   sister(NOM) love do.IMPF.F be.PAST.F
       'Who$_i$ was loved by his$_i$ sister?'
       Lit.: '"Who$_i$ did his$_i$ sister love?'
    b. *kis-ko$_i$ uskii$_i$ bahin-ne   socaa   [ki raam-ne e_i dekhaa
       who-ACC his   sister-ERG think.PAST that Ram-ERG see
       thaa]?
       be.PAST.M
       'Who$_i$ was it that his$_i$ sister thought that Ram has seen e_i?'

In (64a), 'who' is locally determined as an OBJ due to its case marking. However, in (65b), 'who' is not the OBJ of the clause where it appears in c-structure: with respect to the main clause nucleus, it is the COMP OBJ. Bresnan (2001) argues that such non-local determination of GFs is accomplished through an empty category, which effectively sets up a dependency from its *in-situ* position to the displaced element. To repeat, while the GF OBJ for 'who' in (64a) is determined by its case marking and is determined local to its nucleus – it is the OBJ in the nucleus of its clause, this is not so in (64b). In (64b) 'who' bears only the FOCUS DF in the nucleus of the clause where it is overtly present; to be also identified as an OBJ, this must require some c-structure element determining the OBJ GF local to its own clause – the empty category *e* in (64b).

The relevant c-structure precedences in (64b) are shown in (65a). Due to the structure-sharing, 1 and 3 are identified (they are the same informational object). Hence the right edge of the FOC/COMP OBJ 'who' is actually 3. If 'his' and 'who' were co-indexed, the POSS pronoun 'his' would f-precede its antecedent, because the right edge of the POSS, 2, precedes 3, the right edge of the FOC/COMP OBJ:

(65) a. who₁   his₂   e₃

b. $\begin{bmatrix} \text{FOC} & {}_1[\quad] \\ \text{SUBJ} & \begin{bmatrix} \text{PRED} & \text{'sister'} \\ \text{POSS} & {}_2\ \text{his} \end{bmatrix} \\ \text{PRED} & \text{'think} < (\uparrow\text{SUBJ})(\uparrow\text{COMP})>\text{'} \\ \text{TENSE} & \text{PAST} \\ \text{COMP} & \begin{bmatrix} \text{SUBJ} & [\text{PRED}\quad\text{'Ram'}] \\ \text{OBJ} & {}_3[\quad] \\ \text{PRED} & \text{'see} < (\uparrow\text{SUBJ})(\uparrow\text{OBJ})>\text{'} \end{bmatrix} \end{bmatrix}$

The condition on weak crossover is once again that a pronoun may not precede its binder, and hence 'his' cannot have 'who' as a binder in (65b). If the empty category *e* were not present in c-structure, the only relevant precedence relations would be between 2 and 1, and this structural analysis would predict binding to be possible.

Now it is not the case that binding and long-distance scrambling are simply incompatible. (66) (Mahajan 1990:42) differs from (65b) in that the bound pronoun is in the lower clause, rather than the higher one, and the binding is acceptable. This is because (66) has a c-structure analysis as shown, in which the empty category corresponding to the lower verb's object locally precedes the subject within its clause. The right edge of the binder is *e*, which precedes the right edge of the bindee 'his.' Within that lower clause, the relationships for binding are effectively the same as those in (64a), and hence the pattern of grammaticality is the same:

(66) [Kis-ko$_i$ raam-ne socaa   [ki e_i uskii$_i$ bahin-ne dekhaa thaa]?]
who-ACC Ram-ERG think.PAST [that his   sister-ERG see   be.PAST.M]
'Who$_i$ did Ram think was seen by his$_i$ sister?'
Lit.: 'Who$_i$ did Ram think that his$_i$ sister had seen?'

6.5 Conclusion

One central idea of the LFG approach is that the truly universal aspects of syntax are determined with regard to f-structure information, necessarily abstracted away from the overt c-structures of a given language. Bresnan (2001:8) justifies the move away from configurational c-structure as follows: "Now it might be true that all languages do have an abstract level of grammatical structure which closely matches the surface organization of the grammars of English and other European languages. Perhaps it just happens that the biologically based universal design of grammar really does have the form of the language of the colonizers. But there is no evidence for this." Bresnan argues that a wide range of syntactic facts motivate the 'relational' or correspondence architecture in (1). In this relational architecture, correct syntactic analysis is concerned with the ways that a given phenomenon is factored among the different levels, in a way that provides insight into its language-specific properties within the context of universal grammar.

Languages such as Warlpiri (Simpson 1991), Tagalog (Kroeger 1993), and Jiwarli (Austin and Bresnan 1996) show positive evidence for non-configurationality – they have no structural asymmetries involving argument expression at c-structure – yet show evidence for asymmetries at f-structure and a-structure with familiar binding and control facts. It is at these levels that the truly universal aspects of syntax emerge.

In addition, the 'lexical' aspect of LFG, which has only been mentioned in passing here, is also central to the approach. With the exception of null elements as described above in Section 6.4.4, terminal nodes in c-structures are fully inflected words, words which are also specified for all their relevant grammatical properties. Bresnan (1982b) argues that passive is fully defined over lexical items, as passive participles can undergo further word-formation processes. This means in turn that all of the stable cross-linguistic properties of passive must necessarily be independent of any given c-structure configuration: for those properties are encoded in a single word, regardless of what phrasal syntax, if any, the word enters into.

The contrast between lexical selection for an argument and the structural expression of that argument is demonstrated strikingly by the so-called 'Verb Copy Construction' in Mandarin Chinese (Huang 1982a, Li 1990). A verb cannot combine with both a selected argument (an object in these examples) and an adjunct within the same VP, but rather the verb of the VP must be 'copied,' such that the first occurrence combines with the argument, and the second with the adjunct, as seen in (67):

(67) a. Zhangsan xue zhongwen *(xue) le san nian
       Zhangsan study Chinese *(study) ASP three year
       'Zhangsan has studied Chinese for three years'
    b. wo deng xin   *(deng) le bantian
       I   wait letter *(wait) ASP long.time
       'I have waited for mail for a long time'

Such examples have been analyzed in transformational frameworks in terms of a restriction to binary branching at the V' level (Huang 1982a) or the proposal that adjuncts need case, but that each V only assigns one case (Li 1990). An LFG analysis of the copy construction is given in Fang and Sells (2007), which adopts a version of Huang's proposal: in Mandarin Chinese, each VP is simple, and branches binarily, consisting of a head and a sister XP (argument or adjunct).

Now the difference between the (f-structure) information that a clause conveys and the phrase structure expression of that information appears in the examples in (68). It is possible to topicalize an object in Mandarin Chinese, in the presence of an adjunct within the clause. Yet from the copy construction example in (68a), the grammatical object topicalization is (68c), without the duplicated verb, rather than (68b). The notation '___' shows the intuitive position of the gap but has no formal status in the LFG analysis, which directly generates only overt structure.

(68) a. Zhangsan tan <u>gangqin</u> tan de hen hao
    Zhangsan play piano   play DE very well
    'Zhangsan played piano very well'
  b. *<u>gangqin</u> Zhangsan tan ___ tan de hen hao
    piano   Zhangsan play ___ play DE very well
  c. <u>gangqin</u> Zhangsan tan ___ de hen hao
    piano   Zhangsan play ___ DE very well

In the LFG analysis, (68a) respects the phrase structure constraints, for each VP is simple yet branching. On the other hand, (68b) violates these constraints, as the first VP does not branch overtly. (68c) once again respects the phrase structure constraints, yet has only one VP. Note that if 'object' is represented structurally, and hence if there is formally a trace in an extraction construction, the first and second VPs in (68b) ought to be well-formed, and the VP of (68c) ought to be ill-formed, for it would be ternary-branching.

As described above in Section 6.3.4, displacement in LFG involves a dependency at f-structure, but not in c-structure. A TOPIC is generated in its *in-situ* peripheral position, and is identified with some core grammatical function only in f-structure: the core function is OBJ this case. This identification has no manifestation in the c-structure of (68c). (69a) shows the way that functions are assigned to this example in c-structure, yet the f-structure is (69b):

(69) a. gangqin Zhangsan tan   de hen hao
    piano   Zhangsan play DE very well
    TOP   SUBJ   PRED ADJ
    'Chinese, Zhangsan studied very well'

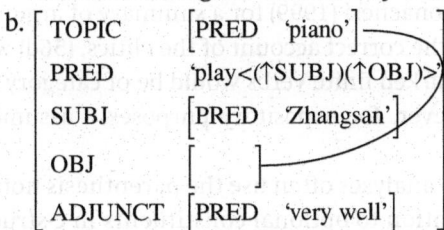

  b. $\begin{bmatrix} \text{TOPIC} & [\text{PRED} \quad \text{'piano'}] \\ \text{PRED} & \text{'play<(↑SUBJ)(↑OBJ)>'} \\ \text{SUBJ} & [\text{PRED} \quad \text{'Zhangsan'}] \\ \text{OBJ} & [\quad] \\ \text{ADJUNCT} & [\text{PRED} \quad \text{'very well'}] \end{bmatrix}$

Example (68c) shows that what a verb combines with structurally (an adjunct) need not correspond to what it combines with functionally (an adjunct and an object), and the fact that (68c) is grammatical where (68b) is not shows that there is no direct structural derivation to (68c) from (68a). As the LFG analysis does not identify the functions of a given phrase one-to-one with phrase structure positions, such apparent mismatches are not paradoxical at all, but rather illustrate the underlying intuition that only some aspects of syntactic analysis are structural, and some are functional.

Notes

I am grateful for the careful comments and thoughtful suggestions of one anonymous reviewer and the editor, Marcel den Dikken, which have significantly improved the flow and clarity of this chapter.

1. 'Equi' constructions are also known as 'Control' constructions, as described in Chapter 16.
2. I follow Kroeger (1993) and Gerassimova (2005) in the analysis of cases in Tagalog and the idea that NOM case marks the SUBJ. Similar facts about the form of imperatives are reported by Arka (2003:58) for Balinese.
3. SpecIP in LFG is usually associated with one of the GDFs, but not necessarily SUBJ. The idea that SpecIP is not universally a subject position derives from the analysis of Yiddish in Diesing (1990), who argues that all Yiddish V2 clauses are rooted in IP.
4. See Chapter 18 on A′ dependencies.
5. See Dalrymple (2001: Chapter 14) for a full discussion of long-distance dependencies, island constraints, and the analysis of specific morphological or syntactic forms determined along the binding path.
6. The typological space of phrase-structure variation is addressed by Nordlinger (1998: Chapter 2). She sets up two dimensions along which languages can be classified: (more or less) configurationality, and a head-marking/dependent-marking dimension.
7. As an analog of the idea in Government and Binding Theory that accusative case is assigned under adjacency to the assigning head, it could be in LFG that the function OBJ has only one c-structure expression in English, adjacent to its selecting head. In other words, this adjacency would be part of the configurationality of English.
8. It is possible that the clitics are actually affixes on verbs (prefixes in the case of finite verbs); see Monachesi (1999) for a summary of arguments for this position. If this is the correct account of the clitics, (56d) would be unnecessary as clitic-marked finite verbs would be of category I and positioned by (56b). However, for expository purposes, I assume the rules as given for Spanish.
9. In practice, published LFG analyses often use the parenthesis notation to indicate and draw attention to optional constituents in c-structure rules. However, the intent of the theory is that all c-structure nodes are optional, with the actual expression of categories following from well-formedness conditions at f-structure. For instance, a clause with no verb in it anywhere will have no top-level PRED, which will likely lead to an incoherent (17b) f-structure. However, a verb which is present

could be in C, or I, or V, leading to equivalent well-formedness at f-structure.
10. See Chapter 15 on referential dependencies.
11. Syntactic phenomena which might be analyzed in derivational frameworks by reference only to c-command might involve a combination of linear precedence and GF hierarchy (see page 167) constraints in LFG (see, e.g., Bresnan 2001: Chapters 9–10).

7
Phrase structure grammar

James P. Blevins and Ivan A. Sag

7.1 Origins of phrase structure analysis

To understand the properties of modern phrase structure grammars, it is useful to place their development in a wider formal and historical context. Phrase structure grammars and associated notions of phrase structure analysis have their proximate origins in models of Immediate Constituent (IC) analysis. Although inspired by the programmatic syntactic remarks in Bloomfield (1933), these models were principally developed by Bloomfield's successors, most actively in the decade between the publication of Wells (1947) and the advent of transformational analyses in Harris (1957) and Chomsky (1957). The central intuition underlying models of IC analysis was that the structure of an expression could be exhibited by dividing the expression into parts (its immediate constituents), further subdividing these parts, and continuing until syntactically indivisible units were obtained. This style of analysis was motivated in part by a belief in the LOCALITY of syntactic relations, in particular the view that the most important relations held between immediate constituents.

> The process of analyzing syntax is largely one of finding successive layers of ICs and of immediate constructions, the description of relationships which exist between ICs, and the description of those relationships which are not efficiently described in terms of ICs. The last is generally of subsidiary importance; most of the relationships of any great significance are between ICs. (Gleason 1955:133)

Within the Bloomfieldian tradition, there was a fair degree of consensus regarding the application of syntactic methods as well as about the analyses associated with different classes of constructions. Some of the general features of IC analyses find an obvious reflex in subsequent models of analysis. Foremost among these is the idea that structure involves a part–whole relation between elements and a larger superordinate unit, rather than an asymmetrical dependency relation between elements at the same level. The Bloomfieldians' preference for binary branching analyses likewise reemerges in later models of phrase structure, and their practice of extending syntactic analysis below the word level, to include stems and inflectional formatives, survives largely intact in the transformational tradition. Some other features of IC analyses are less faithfully preserved. These include general properties such as the recognition of discontinuous and overlapping constituents or the representation of intonation.[1] More specific proposals, such as the classification of elements (notably coordinating conjunctions) as 'markers' (Hockett 1958:153) were not rehabilitated until nearly thirty years later (Gazdar et al. 1985, Sag et al. 1985, Pollard and Sag 1994: Chapter 1). The encoding of dependency relations within a part-whole analysis (Nida 1966) was also suppressed until the development of feature-based models such as Lexical-Functional Grammar (LFG) (Kaplan and Bresnan 1982 and Chapter 6 of this volume) and Head-driven Phrase Structure Grammar (HPSG) (Pollard and Sag 1987 and Section 7.3.1 below) that could explicitly express valence dependencies within syntactic representations.

7.1.1 Procedures of IC analysis

The development of constituent structure analysis within the Bloomfieldian tradition was held back by, among other things, the lack of a perspicuous format for representing syntactic analyses. The formats explored by the Bloomfieldians were cumbersome, ranging from annotated circuit diagrams in Nida (1966) through the chart representation in Table 7.1 or the 'Chinese box' arrangements in Table 7.2.[2]

The shortcomings of these representational formats were particularly evident in the analysis of the discontinuous and overlapping constituents recognized by the Bloomfieldians. While generally preferring continuous (and binary) analyses, they also admitted a range of constructions that violated these preferences.

Table 7.1. Chart-based IC Analysis (Hockett 1958: Chapter 17)

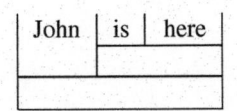

John	is	here

Table 7.2. Chinese box-based IC Analysis (Gleason 1965:157)

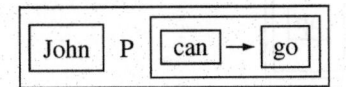

| John | P | can → go |

> Most linguists operate on the principle that cuts will be made binary whenever possible, but that cuts giving three or more ICs will not be excluded a priori. In the same way, they will make cuts giving continuous ICs wherever possible, but discontinuous ICs are not excluded on principle. (Gleason 1961:142)

The descriptive challenges that arose in extending these formats to the description of discontinuous dependencies are illustrated by the representation of phrasal verb constructions, which were taken to be discontinuous from at least Wells (1947).

> Verb phrases of the type verb+prepositional adverb *(up, away, through,* etc.) may seem to deserve being treated as constituents even when they are discontinuous: *wake up your friend* and *wake your friend up* are almost synonymous. (Wells 1947:105–106)

Expressions such as *wake up your friend* presented no new difficulties. However, the 'shifted' order in which the object intervened between the verb and particle required a means of indicating that ICs formed units at non-adjacent levels. One of the representational extensions explored by Hockett (1958) is shown in the chart in Table 7.3. Box diagrams provided a somewhat more flexible format, as illustrated in Table 7.4.

7.1.2 Phrase structure analysis

As suggested by the contrast between the analyses in Table 7.4 and Table 7.3, graph theory provided the natural formalization of the intuitions underlying models of IC analysis, though this idea was not developed until McCawley (1982). Instead, IC analyses were interpreted as representing the

Table 7.3. Chart-based analysis of 'shifted' phrasal verb

wake	your	friend	up

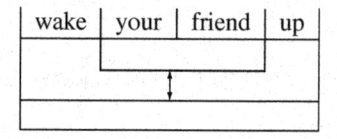

Table 7.4. Box-based analysis of 'shifted' phrasal verb

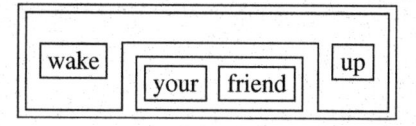

successive segmentation of an expression into sub-expressions, each of which was annotated with a word class label and, usually, other types of information. It was not until the early transformational accounts that IC analyses were incorporated into explicit grammar formalisms rather than treated as procedures of classification, and the fact that these procedures were first formalized by the Bloomfieldians' successors had the effect of simplifying them, much as the Bloomfieldians had themselves simplified Bloomfield's more intricate constructional perspective (Manaster-Ramer and Kac 1990). In Chomsky (1956), phrase structure grammars are proposed as "the form of grammar [that] corresponds to [the] conception of linguistic structure" expressed by IC analysis (p. 111). Chomsky's insight consisted in recognizing how informal procedures for segmenting and classifying expressions could be expressed by means of rules of the form $A \to \omega$ that would 'rewrite' a single word class label A by a string ω (which could consist of labels along with words and formatives). Thus a rule such as $S \to NP\ VP$ would rewrite a sentence S by a subject NP and a VP predicate, and the rule $V \to \textit{took}$ would classify *took* as a verb.

By starting with the sentence label 'S' and applying a sequence of phrase-structure rules, one could define a 'derivation' that terminated in the expression that would be the starting point for procedures of IC analysis. The syntactic analysis assigned to an expression by a phrase structure grammar was conventionally represented by a phrase structure tree, though in Chomsky's initial formulations, analyses are represented by stringsets that he termed PHRASE MARKERS.[3] These sets contain strings from equivalence classes of derivations differing from one another solely in that they apply the same rules in a different order (e.g., a derivation where the subject NP is rewritten before rewriting the VP and a second derivation where the VP is rewritten first).

7.2 Extended phrase structure systems

As clarified particularly in Scholz and Pullum (2007) and Pullum (2011), phrase structure (and transformational) grammars represent linguistic applications of the general string rewriting systems developed in Post (1943, 1947). Despite the evident success attained by grammatical models based on rewriting systems, it was soon apparent that standard systems were not always ideally suited to the description of natural languages.

7.2.1 'The difficult question of discontinuity'
In particular, initial formulations of phrase structure grammars were incapable of representing the classes of discontinuous constituents

recognized by the Bloomfieldians, a point that Chomsky (1975a) was initially freely prepared to concede.

> This [the treatment of 'long components' in the sense of Harris 1951] is an important question, deserving a much fuller treatment, but it will quickly lead into areas where the present formal apparatus may be inadequate. The difficult question of discontinuity is one such problem. Discontinuities are handled in the present treatment by construction of permutational mappings from **P** [the level of phrase structure, JPB/IAS] to **W** [the level of word structure, JPB/IAS], but it may turn out that they must ultimately be incorporated somehow into **P** itself. (Chomsky 1975a:190)

The transformational tradition never did reconsider whether discontinuities could be handled better within a phrase structure analysis and no general approach to this issue was explored within constituency-based grammars until the development of Head Grammars (Pollard 1984) and linearization-based models of HPSG (Reape 1996, Stefan Müller 1999, 2004, Kathol 2000). These models rehabilitated many of the same intuitions about syntactic and semantic units that had been explored in 'wrapping' analyses in the Montague grammar tradition, particularly in the accounts of Bach (1979) and Dowty (1982). However, Chomsky sought to reinforce the case for 'permutational mappings' (i.e., transformations) by disputing the feasibility of applying procedures of IC analysis to 'derived' constructions such as polar and information questions.

> The case for indirect representation, not based on the relation of membership, becomes even stronger when we consider such sentences as "did they see John" or "whom did they see". THESE ARE SENTENCES THAT NO LINGUIST WOULD EVER CONSIDER AS THE STARTING POINT FOR APPLICATION OF TECHNIQUES OF IC ANALYSIS – i.e., no one would ask how they can be subdivided into two or three parts, each of which has several constituents, going on to use this subdivision as the basis for analysis of other sentences, and so on. Yet there is nothing in the formulation of principles of procedure for IC analysis that justifies excluding these sentences, or treating them somehow in terms of sentences already analyzed.
> (Chomsky 1958/1962:131f.; emphasis added JPB/IAS)

In the emphasized passage, as elsewhere in Chomsky's writings about the Bloomfieldians, a position possibly consistent with the practice of Zellig Harris is incorrectly attributed to the Bloomfieldians as a group. Virtually all leading American linguists of the time, including Hockett, Gleason, Nida, Pike, and Wells, among others, not only considered applying – but in fact DID apply – procedures of IC analysis to questions in English. In particular, the analysis of polar questions was regarded as a solved problem and presented as such in the introductory textbooks of the day. In the passage below, Gleason gives what he takes to be an uncontroversial IC analysis of polar questions to exemplify the notion of discontinuous constituents.

> In English, discontinuous constituents occur. One common instance occurs in many questions: *Did the man come?* This is clearly to be cut *did ... come | the man.* (Gleason 1961:142)

This discrepancy between procedures of IC analysis and phrase structure grammars is of more than purely historical interest. One of the criticisms levelled by Chomsky against phrase structure grammars turned on their inability to represent discontinuous dependencies, particularly within auxiliary verb phrases.

> To put the same thing differently, in the auxiliary verb phrase we really have discontinuous elements ... But discontinuities cannot be handled within [Σ, F] grammars [i.e., phrase structure grammars, JPB/IAS].
> (Chomsky 1957:41)

7.2.2 Generalized Phrase Structure Grammar (GPSG)

For the most part, modern phrase structure systems preserve Chomsky's preference for describing discontinuous dependencies indirectly, usually in terms of relations between different parts of a single structure or correspondences between different types of structures. However other restrictions on phrase structure systems have been more comprehensively revised. The most severe of these was the assumption that the 'nonterminal' vocabulary of a phrase structure grammar should consist solely of atomic labels such as 'S,' 'NP,' 'V,' etc. The case for relaxing this restriction is made initially by Harman (1963), who objects that "it is irrational to restrict the amount of information expressed by the grammar to statements about grammatical category" (p. 604). The response in Chomsky (1965:210f.) dismisses Harman's proposal out of hand as a "terminological equivocation" and appears to construe any refinement of phrase structure grammars as a case of a patent infringement rather than as a genuine attempt to understand the scope and limits of constituent structure grammars. Partly as a consequence, Harman's 'defense of phrase structure' had little direct influence on the field at the time. Hence, the descriptive potential of feature 'decompositions' of atomic symbols was not fully realized until the later work on unbounded dependencies and coordination (Gazdar 1981).

By this time, a limited amount of feature decomposition had been incorporated into transformational models that adopted some version of the X-bar conventions. However, features were assigned a tightly circumscribed role in Chomsky (1970a), and these restrictions were preserved in subsequent accounts. Two constraints were particularly decisive. The first of these restricted propagation through an endocentric X-bar projection to the word class features ±N and ±V (Chomsky 1970a:52f.), excluding other types of lexical and inflectional properties. The second constraint limited feature 'percolation,' as it came to be known, more generally by "tak[ing] feature complexes to be associated only with lexical categories, and permitting] complex symbols to dominate a sequence of elements only within the word" (Chomsky 1970a:48).[4] These restrictions precluded the use of constituent structure links as a conduit for the propagation of complex feature bundles. Likewise, although the 'non-distinctness' condition on complex symbols in Chomsky (1965:84) anticipated the unification operations of later constraint-based formalisms, this condition could play no role in regulating the distribution of features within a projection.

7.2.2.1 Non-local dependencies

As with the representational constraints that barred discontinuities, restrictions on the 'flow' of feature information prevented feature-based mechanisms from encroaching on the role reserved for structure-changing rules and derivational operations in transformational models. By relaxing these restrictions, extended phrase structure models could exploit the descriptive value of feature information for describing local and non-local grammatical dependencies. Unbounded dependencies had long been taken to require the power of a transformational grammar, or at any rate to defy analysis in terms of phrase structure grammars, as suggested in the quotation from Chomsky (1958/1962) above. Hence the rehabilitation of phrase structure analysis began, somewhat counterintuitively perhaps, with an analysis of unbounded dependencies that was developed in the late 1970s but first published in Gazdar (1981). The simple intuition developed in this work was that the constituent structure links of a phrase structure tree provided a suitable conduit for the flow of information about displaced elements. The components of the analysis were equally straightforward: feature attributes that could take categories as values, the insight that information about 'missing' elements could be treated in terms of a feature (Bear 1982), and feature 'passing' conditions that could match features between the 'mother' and 'daughter' nodes in a phrase structure tree. By passing the value of a category-valued attribute along a chain of local mother–daughter nodes, a phrase structure analysis could match the properties of a 'missing' element at an 'extraction site' with those of the 'dislocated' element that typically occurred at the periphery of a construction.

The components of what came to be known as the 'slash category' analysis of unbounded dependencies are exhibited in the analysis of the English indirect question in Figure 7.1 below. The lowest occurrence of the category-valued SLASH feature encodes the properties of the missing object NP that is governed by the transitive verb *saw*. These properties

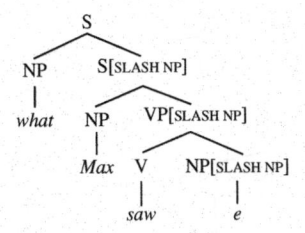

```
                        S
                     ╱     ╲
                   NP    S[SLASH NP]
                   │      ╱    ╲
                 what    NP   VP[SLASH NP]
                         │     ╱    ╲
                        Max   V   NP[SLASH NP]
                              │         │
                             saw        e
```

Figure 7.1. 'Slash category' analysis of indirect question

```
      what              Max                saw
   ─────────   ──────────────────────   ─────────
   S/(S\NP)     (S\NP)/((S\NP)/NP)      (S\NP)/NP
               ────────────────────────────────
                              S\NP
   ────────────────────────────────────────────
                         S
```

Figure 7.2. Gap-free categorial analysis (cf. Steedman 2000b)

are passed up successively to the superordinate VP and S nodes until they can be matched against the properties of the 'filler' *what*.

To a large degree, the early phrase structure analyses carried over prevailing assumptions about the structure of unbounded dependency constructions from transformational accounts. In contrast to the IC analyses adumbrated in the descriptivist tradition, the structure in Figure 7.1 assumes that the dislocated element *what* is higher in the tree as well as to the left of the extraction site. This assumption is retained in most subsequent analyses of unbounded dependencies. In addition, the structure in Figure 7.1 preserves the assumption that the extraction site is occupied by an empty placeholder 'gap.' Since this assumption had no internal motivation within phrase structure models, the analysis developed in Sag and Fodor (1994) and Bouma *et al.* (2001) dispensed with null terminals. These analyses nevertheless retain the strategy of using dedicated attributes to represent information about extracted elements. In this respect, they are unlike categorial analyses, such as Steedman (2000b), which use the slash notation both to indicate the argument of a functor and to encode information about extracted elements. In the categorial analysis in Figure 7.2, the category '(S\NP)/NP' marks the transitive verb *saw* as a functor that looks rightward for an NP to form a functor that in turn looks leftward for an NP to form an S. The overloading of this notation is reflected in the fact that the category 'S\NP' encodes the 'missing' object NP in the expression *Max saw*.[5]

As recognized by those working to extend the empirical coverage of phrase structure models, category-valued features offered a novel perspective on a range of phenomena that interacted with unbounded dependencies. In particular, the assumption that information about missing constituents formed part of the syntactic information associated with a node interacted with the independent assumption that coordination was restricted to syntactically like elements. One immediate consequence was

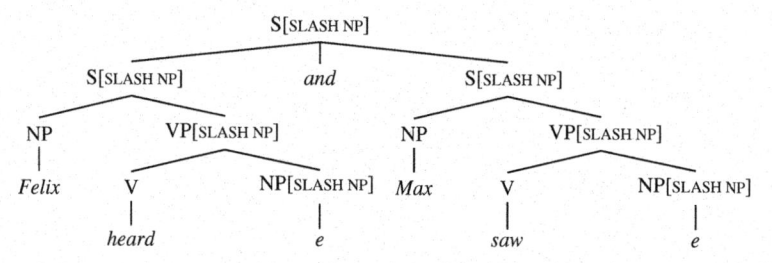

```
                         S[SLASH NP]
              ┌──────────────┼──────────────┐
         S[SLASH NP]         and        S[SLASH NP]
         ┌────┴────┐                    ┌────┴────┐
        NP     VP[SLASH NP]            NP     VP[SLASH NP]
         │     ┌────┴────┐              │     ┌────┴────┐
       Felix   V     NP[SLASH NP]      Max    V     NP[SLASH NP]
               │         │                    │         │
             heard       e                   saw        e
```

Figure 7.3. 'Across-the-board' extraction from coordinate indirect question

an account of the parallelism that Ross (1967a) had termed 'across-the-board' extraction. The central observation was that in a coordinate structure, if one conjunct contained an extraction site, then all of the conjuncts must.[6] In transformational models, this condition had been attributed to dedicated devices, such as the Coordinate Structure Constraint (Ross 1967a) or the Across-the-Board convention of Williams (1978), which, as Gazdar et al. (1982b) noted, incorporated a construction-specific and somewhat imprecise extension to the notion of phrase marker. In contrast, the parallelism requirement on extraction from coordinate structures followed on a phrase structure analysis. Two conjuncts of category X[SLASH YP] were syntactically alike, whereas a conjunct of category X[SLASH YP] and one of category X were not. In the analysis in Figure 7.3, the two conjuncts of category S[SLASH NP] are syntactically alike and can be conjoined, but neither could be conjoined with a full S to yield unacceptable examples such as *what Felix heard and Max saw the intruder* or *what Felix heard the intruder and Max saw.*[7]

Gazdar (1981) also clarified how constraints on extraction, which had typically been described in terms of conditions on rule application, could be recast in terms of restrictions on the 'paths' of category-valued features that connected extraction sites to dislocated fillers. In classical transformational accounts, there had been no reason why information about missing constituents should trace a path along the constituent structure links of a tree.[8] But once extraction was characterized in terms of the sharing of category-valued features along a sequence of mother–daughter links, it became clear that any restrictions on the extraction of elements out of specified 'island' domains (Ross 1967a) would correspond to paths in which those domains occurred somewhere along the path between extraction sites and fillers.

7.2.2.2 Local dependencies

The demonstration that complex-valued features could provide an analysis of unbounded dependencies inspired surface-based analyses of more local syntactic phenomena within the nascent community that had begun to explore the potential of monostratal models.[9] The English auxiliary system had long been an obvious candidate for reanalysis. The system consisted of a finite inventory of modal and auxiliary elements, which were subject to ordering constraints that determined a (short) maximum expansion. The expansions were indeed almost as restricted as pronominal clitic sequences in Romance languages, and, like these sequences, exhibited some of the ordering rigidity characteristic of morphological formations. Even the selectional dependencies tended to relate pairs of adjacent elements. So there was nothing that presented any intrinsic difficulties for a phrase structure analysis.

The 'affix hopping' analysis of Chomsky (1957) had long been held to be one of the crowning achievements of transformational approaches. However, Gazdar et al. (1982a) showed that the strategy of 'hopping' affixes from one point in a terminal string to another was a solution to a self-inflicted problem and hence dispensable in a model with complex-valued features. If one auxiliary element could select the verb form of the head of a phrasal complement, there was no need to assemble inflected forms in the course of a syntactic derivation. Instead, the admissible expansions could be determined by the subcategorization demands of individual elements. The first component of this analysis is a feature classification of verbal elements that distinguishes tense, aspect, and voice properties, along with form variants, such as participles, infinitives, etc. The second is a generalization of the X-bar feature conventions that allows these 'head' features to be shared between a mother and head daughter node. The final ingredient is, again, category-valued features that permit a verbal element to select a complement headed by a particular form variant.

These components are set out in detail in Gazdar et al. (1982a) and in much subsequent work within Generalized Phrase Structure models. One type of analysis that they define is illustrated in Figure 7.4. The advantages of this analysis are summarized in Gazdar et al. (1982a:613ff.), though one immediate benefit was the avoidance of the formal problems that had plagued the 'affix-hopping' analysis since its initial formulation (see, e.g., Akmajian and Wasow 1975, Sampson 1979).

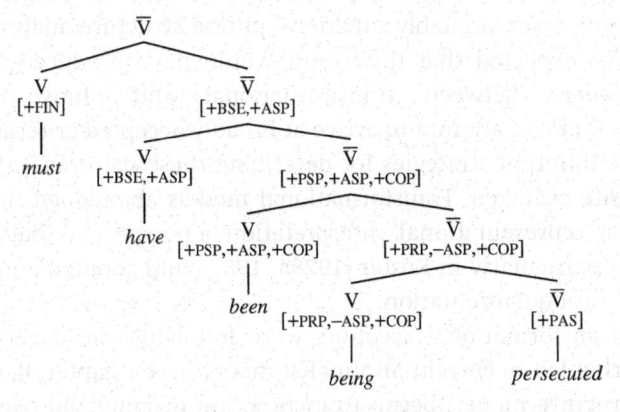

Figure 7.4. Passive auxiliary expansion (cf. Gazdar et al. 1982a:601)

```
              V̿
            [+INV]
           /      \
          V        V̄
        [+INV]   [+BSE]
          |      /    \
         did   NP      V̄
                     [+BSE]
                       |
              the man  V
                     [+BSE]
                       |
                      come
```

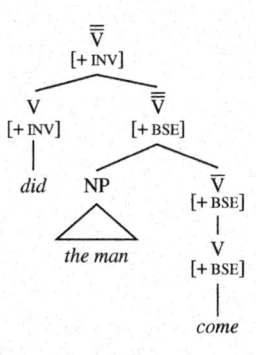

Figure 7.5. Subject–auxiliary 'inversion'

The analyses in Gazdar *et al.* (1982a) thus established that the same basic feature-passing strategy used in the treatment of unbounded dependencies could provide an account of local dependencies. Patterns of subject–auxiliary inversion were amenable to a similar analysis using grammar rules systematically related to the basic rules via metarules, a device whose utility in the grammar of programming languages had previously been established. Figure 7.5 exhibits the analysis of the polar question cited by Gleason (1955) above. The invertibility of modals and auxiliaries is encoded here via compatability with the [+INV] specification that is required of the verbal head in a phrase structure rule licensing the 'inverted' structure. Independent motivation for this feature comes from lexical restrictions on the distribution and interpretation of auxiliary elements. Some elements, such as 1sg *aren't*, are obligatorily inverted, while others, such as *better*, are obligatorily uninverted, and yet others, such as *may*, have a different range of meanings depending on whether or not they are inverted.

7.2.3 Node admissibility and constraint satisfaction

More generally, it turned out that all of the alternations and dependencies that had been described by transformational models had simple – and, in at least some cases, arguably superior – phrase structure analyses.[10] One might have expected that this result would have produced a general rapprochement between transformational and phrase structure approaches and an attempt to arrive at broadly accepted criteria for evaluating the different strategies for describing these patterns. In fact, just the opposite occurred. Transformational models abandoned their flirtation with a 'representational' interpretation, a perspective that had been developed particularly in Koster (1978a, 1987), and adopted a more resolutely derivational orientation.

While transformational accounts were following the developmental pathway that led to current Minimalist models (see Chapter 4), extended phrase structure models began to incorporate insights and perspectives from other monostratal approaches. Following McCawley (1968a), models of Generalized Phrase Structure Grammar (Gazdar *et al.* 1985) had already adopted – and, indeed, refined – a 'node admissibility' interpretation of phrase structure rules. On this interpretation, a rule such as S → NP VP is interpreted as directly 'licensing' a local subtree in which S immediately and exhaustively dominates NP and VP daughters, and the NP daughter immediately precedes the VP daughter. A node admissibility interpretation immediately eliminated the need for string-rewrite derivations and string-based representations of phrase structure ('phrase markers'). Instead, rules could be regarded as partial DESCRIPTIONS of the subtrees that they sanctioned and the admissibility of a tree could be defined in terms of the admissibility of the subtrees that it contained.

In large part, this reinterpretation of phrase structure productions supplied graph-theoretic modeling assumptions that were a better fit for the classes of IC analyses initially proposed by the Bloomfieldians. The schematization adopted within models of X-bar Theory similarly deprecated phrase structure rules within transformational models, though without substantially revising the string-based model of phrase structure represented by phrase markers (as discussed in note 3).

Furthermore, a node admissibility interpretation clarified the fact that conventional phrase structure rules bundle information about structure (mother–daughter links) together with information about order (linear arrangement of daughters). GPSG accounts showed how these two types of information could be expressed separately, by means of a set of Immediate Dominance (ID) rules that just constrained mother–daughter relations and a set of Linear Precedence (LP) statements that applied to sisters in a local tree. For example, the information represented by the phrase structure rule S → NP VP would be expressed by an ID rule S → NP, VP and the general LP statement NP ≺ VP. The absence of an applicable LP rule would not sanction unordered trees, but rather trees in which the NP and VP occurred in either order.

An overriding consideration in the development of GPSG was the goal of keeping analyses as explicit as possible and the underlying grammatical formalism as formally restrictive as possible. The central role of context-free phrase structure grammars largely reflected the fact that their properties were well understood and provided a formal basis for transparent analyses. In some cases, analyses were constrained so that they did not take GPSG models outside the class of phrase structure grammars. For example, requiring that sets of ID rules and LP statements must operate over the same local domains, ensured that they could in principle be 'reconstituted' as phrase structure grammars. LP statements were thus restricted to apply to sister nodes. As a consequence, LP statements could allow free or partial ordering of VP-internal elements, but they could not impose any ordering of subjects and VP-internal elements other than those that followed from the ordering of a subject and full VP expansion. Yet there was no direct empirical support for this restriction.

Hence the tight association between the domains of ID rules and LP statements undermined the fundamental separation of structure and order in the ID/LP format since certain types of ordering variation dictated a flat structure. This was perhaps acceptable as long as there was some independent motivation for remaining within the class of context-free phrase structure grammars. But by 1985, the demonstration of non-context-free patterns in Swiss German subordinate clauses (Shieber 1985) and Bambara compounds (Culy 1985) had weakened the empirical grounds for this restriction and the non-transformational community shifted their focus to identifying restricted classes of weakly context-sensitive grammars that were descriptively adequate. This was a natural development within the family of phrase structure approaches, given that the interest in context-free grammars had been driven by an interest in explicit formalisms with clearly defined and well-understood properties. Hence the move from the limited word order freedom defined by the ID/LP format in GPSG to 'domain union' in HPSG (Reape 1996) extended the dissociation of structure and order in ways that allowed for the interleaving of non-sisters in an explicit but non-context-free formalism.[11]

7.3 Model-theoretic grammar

In the subsequent development of phrase structure grammars, the interpretation of rules as partial descriptions of trees provided the model for a more comprehensive constraint-based or model-theoretic perspective. As in models of Lexical-Functional Grammar (Kaplan and Bresnan 1982; Chapter 6 of this volume), rules and grammatical principles came to be construed as CONSTRAINTS that described or were satisfied by corresponding types of STRUCTURES. This move to a uniform model-theoretic orientation permitted much of the complexity that had been associated with representations to be confined to the constraint language that described structures. In addition, a general model of constraint satisfaction provided a conception under which the diverse feature distribution principles of GPSG could be subsumed. The gradual accretion of constraints and conditions in GPSG had led over time to a theory in which the components that regulated feature information included feature co-occurrence restrictions and feature specification defaults, in addition to the immediate dominance rules, linear precedence statements, and other devices, such as metarules. As detailed in Gazdar *et al.* (1985: Chapter 5), the constraints in these components exhibited fairly intricate interactions. On a description-theoretic interpretation, these constraints and interactions could be modeled in a more uniform and transparent way.

The emergence of a constraint-based perspective was accompanied by the adoption of richer sets of structures and more expressive constraint languages. These developments provided clearer conceptions of the lexicon, valence, and valence alternations than had been possible in GPSG.

The phrase structure systems proposed in Chomsky (1956) had offered only very rudimentary treatments of the lexicon and valence demands, and incorporated no notion of a lexical valence-changing process. The closest counterparts of 'lexical entries' in these simple systems were rules of the form V → *sleep*, which rewrote a non-terminal symbol as a terminal element. The valence of a predicate was likewise represented implicitly by the other elements that were introduced in the same rule expansions. GPSG enriched this spartan conception by locating terminal elements within lexical entries that specified distinctive grammatical features of an element other than word class. Corresponding to the pre-terminal rules of a simple phrase structure grammar was a class of 'lexical ID rules' which introduced lexical heads indexed by a subcategorization index. This index (technically the value of a SUBCAT feature) was then cross-referenced with a class of lexical entries. For example, the rule VP → H[1] would license a local VP subtree that dominated a unary tree whose mother was V[1] and whose daughter was an intransitive verb, such as *sleep*, whose entry contained the index 1.[12]

In effect, the use of subcategorization indices achieved a limited type of context sensitivity within a context-free formalism. Yet, as Jacobson (1987:394ff.) pointed out, the fact that lexical items did not directly represent valence information created numerous complications in GPSG. The most acute arose in connection with the treatment of valence alternations. There was no way to formulate a passive rule that mapped the transitive entry for *devour* onto a (syntactically) detransitivized entry *devoured*, because entries themselves contained no direct representation of transitivity. This led to an analysis of passivization in terms of metarules that mapped a 'transitive expansion' such as VP → W, NP to a 'detransitivized expansion' such as VP[PAS] → W (where W is any string). However, it then became necessary to constrain metarules so that they only applied to lexical ID rules. But lexical ID rules were serving as proxies for under-informative entries, so the obvious solution lay in associating valence information directly with lexical items and introducing a class of lexical rules to map between entries, as suggested by Pollard (1984).

7.3.1 Head-Driven Phrase Structure Grammar (HPSG)

The models of Head-driven Phrase Structure Grammar outlined in Pollard and Sag (1987, 1994) develop a number of these revisions in the context of a broad constraint-based conception of grammar. A central component of these models is the set of assumptions that have come to be known as the 'formal foundations' of HPSG. As in LFG, grammatical constraints and lexical entries are interpreted as partial descriptions of structures, though the representational conventions and model theories of the two theories differ significantly. One representational difference concerns the interpretation of attribute–value matrices (AVMs). Whereas in LFG, AVMs of the

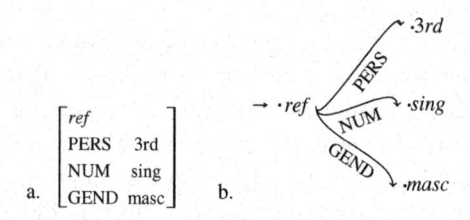

a. $\begin{bmatrix} ref \\ \text{PERS} & 3rd \\ \text{NUM} & sing \\ \text{GEND} & masc \end{bmatrix}$ b. →·ref (PERS ·3rd, NUM ·sing, GEND ·masc)

Figure 7.6. Descriptions and structures in HPSG

sort illustrated in Figure 7.6a are used to represent f(unctional)-structures, in HPSG they represent descriptions, i.e., sets of constraints. The structures DESCRIBED BY (or which SATISFY) a set of constraints are represented as graphs like the one in Figure 7.6b.

A distinctive aspect of the HPSG model theory is the role assigned to the TYPE system. The core idea is that each kind of structure is associated with certain sorts of attributes, and that each attribute is associated with a type of value. For example, a referential index (object of type *ref* in Figure 7.6) is associated with the attributes PERS(ON), NUM(BER), and GEND(ER). Each attribute takes values from a partitioned value space, which in the present case just represents traditional person, number, and gender contrasts. The empirical effects of this type system derive from two additional assumptions. The first is that structures must be TOTALLY WELL-TYPED (Carpenter 1992: Chapter 6) in the sense that they must be assigned a value for each appropriate attribute. This constraint precludes, for example, the assignment of a number-neutral structure as the analysis of English *sheep*, given that number is distinctive for English nouns (each occurence of *sheep* is unambuously singular or plural). A separate requirement that structures must be SORT-RESOLVED (Pollard and Sag 1994:18) permits only 'fully specific' feature values and thus bars disjunctive case values from occurring in a well-formed structure. Hence *sheep* could not be treated as neutral by assigning the attribute NUM a maximally general value such as *number*, which subsumes the resolved values *sing* and *plur*. Given that entries are interpreted as descriptions of lexical structures, the English lexicon can still contain a single underspecified ENTRY for *sheep*, one that specifies either no NUM attribute or a NUM attribute with a non-sort-resolved value. But the lexical structures described by the entry must be totally well-typed and sort-resolved.

These general assumptions have the effect of ensuring that structures are maximally specific and that all underspecification is confined to descriptions. A neutral description is not satisfied by a correspondingly underspecified structure but by a set of structures, each of which supplies different, fully resolved values for underspecified attributes. This technical point has a number of consequences. On the positive side, the assumption that structures must be totally well-typed and sort-resolved does some of the work of the completeness and coherence conditions in LFG, and facilitates type-based inferencing within HPSG. However, these assumptions also lead to apparent difficulties in accounting for the types of patterns described in Ingria (1990), in which the neutrality of an item seems to permit it to satisfy incompatible demands simultaneously, most prominently in coordinate structures.[13]

Note further that in a model theory that only contains fully specified structures, it is somewhat anachronistic to describe the processes that determine feature compatibility in terms of feature structure UNIFICATION, as had been the practice in GPSG and PATR-based formalisms (Shieber 1986). A more accurate characterization of a model-theoretic linguistic framework would be as CONSTRAINT-based, a term that has garnered a certain acceptance in the non-transformational community. Within HPSG, configurations in which a single object occurs as the value of multiple attributes are described in terms of STRUCTURE-SHARING, a term that refers to reentrance in the graph-theoretic models typically assumed in HPSG.

7.3.1.1 Valence, raising, and control

Raising constructions illustrate how structure sharing interacts with complex-valued attributes to provide an insightful analysis of grammatical dependencies. The term 'raising' derives from transformational analyses in which the subject of a complement is taken to be 'raised' to become an argument of the raising verb. However, complex-valued features permit an analysis in which raising involves the identification of arguments within the argument structure of a raising predicate. Patterns involving the sharing of purely morphological properties offer the clearest support for this analysis. As discussed by Andrews (1982), among others, modern Icelandic contains verbs that may govern 'quirky' non-nominative subjects. One such verb is *vanta* 'to want,' which occurs with the accusative subject *hana* 'her' in (1a). These quirky case demands are preserved by raising verbs such as *virðist* 'seems.' As example (1b) shows, *virðist* is, in effect, 'transparent' to the accusative case demands of *vanta*, which are imposed on its own syntactic subject.

(1) Quirky case in Icelandic raising constructions (Andrews 1982)
    a.   hana   vantar   peninga
         her.ACC lack.3SG money.ACC
         'she lacks money'
    b.   hana   virðist   vanta peninga
         her.ACC seem.3SG lack   money.ACC
         'she seems to lack money'

The constraints in Figure 7.7 first identify *hana* as a 3sg feminine accusative NP, and indicate that the verb *vanta* selects an accusative subject and complement (though category is suppressed here). In place of the integer-valued SUBCAT feature of GPSG, HPSG represents the core valence demands of a verb by means of list-valued SUBJ and COMPS features.

$$\text{hana:} \begin{bmatrix} \text{IND} & \begin{bmatrix} \text{PER} & \text{3rd} \\ \text{NUM} & \text{sg} \\ \text{GEND} & \text{fem} \end{bmatrix} \\ \text{CASE} & \text{acc} \end{bmatrix} \quad \text{vanta:} \begin{bmatrix} \text{SUBJ} & \langle \boxed{1}[\text{CASE acc}] \rangle \\ \text{COMPS} & \langle \boxed{2}[\text{CASE acc}] \rangle \\ \text{ARG-ST} & \langle \boxed{1},\boxed{2} \rangle \end{bmatrix}$$

Figure 7.7. Constraints on accusative NP and 'quirky' accusative-governing verb

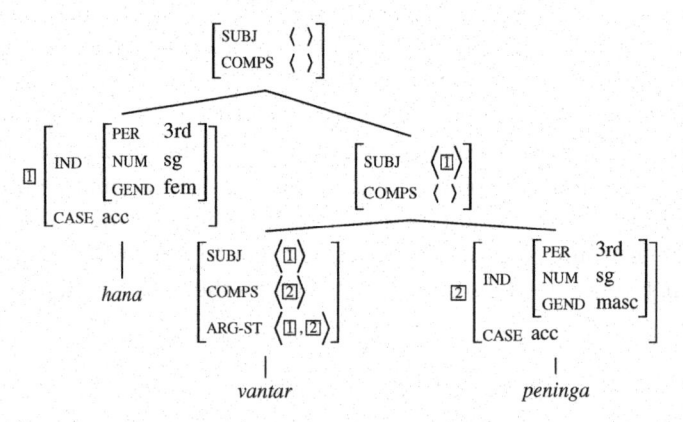

Figure 7.8. Regulation of valence demands in HPSG

The value of the SUBJ attribute can either be an empty list or a singleton list, whereas the COMPS value may contain as many dependents as a verb can select. The boxed integers in the indicated constraints for *vanta* represent the fact that the subject term corresponds to the first element of the lexical argument structure (ARG-ST) of *vanta* and the complement term corresponds to the second term. This correspondence is not established by individual entries, but instead reflects a general relationship between ARG-ST and SUBJ and COMPS lists. By treating the correspondence as canonical rather than as invariant, HPSG accommodates divergences between argument structure and grammatical relations (Manning and Sag 1999).

The analysis in Figure 7.8 then illustrates how these valence features regulate basic valence requirements. Adapting the idea of 'argument cancellation' from categorial approaches, elements are 'popped off' valence lists as arguments are encountered. Hence the term in the COMPS list of the verb *vantar* is structure shared with the syntactic object *peninga* in Figure 7.8, producing a VP with an empty COMPS list. The subject term is in turn identified with the syntactic subject *hana*, yielding a 'saturated' clause, with empty SUBJ and COMPS lists. The terms in the ARG-ST list of the verb *vanta* are also structure-shared with the syntactic arguments. However, in accordance with the locality constraints of HPSG, ARG-ST values are only associated at the lexical level, so that elements that combine syntactically with the clause in Figure 7.8 cannot access information about the dependents it contains.

Given this general treatment of valence, the transparency of *virðist* can be represented by the entry in Figure 7.9. The cross-referencing of the

$$virðist: \begin{bmatrix} \text{SUBJ} & \langle \boxed{1} \rangle \\ \text{COMPS} & \langle \boxed{2}[\text{SUBJ } \langle \boxed{1} \rangle] \rangle \\ \text{ARG-ST} & \langle \boxed{1}\boxed{2} \rangle \end{bmatrix}$$

Figure 7.9. Lexical entry of subject raising verb

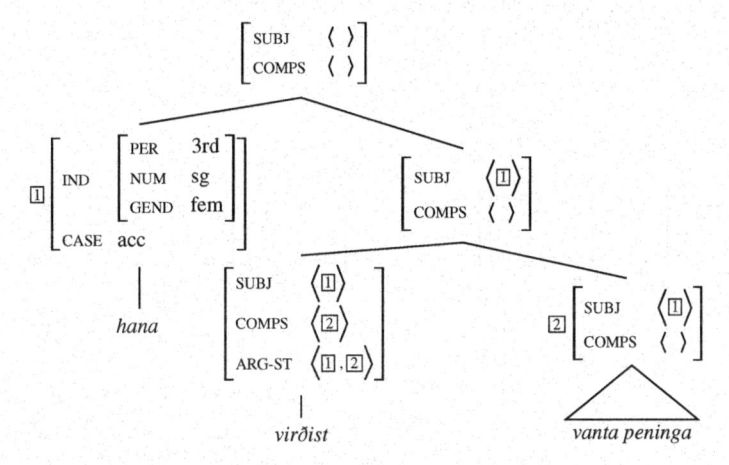

Figure 7.10. Subject 'raising' as structure sharing

two SUBJ values (via the boxed integer $\boxed{1}$) indicates that the SUBJ attribute of *virðist* literally shares its value with the SUBJ value of its complement. Identifying the values of the two SUBJ attributes ensures that any constraints that apply to the SUBJ of the complement of *virðist* will apply to its own syntactic SUBJ. Hence when *vanta* occurs as the head of the complement, as in Figure 7.10, its accusative SUBJ demands will be identified with the SUBJ demands of *virðist*. Only an accusative subject such as *hana* can satisfy these demands. So this analysis forges a direct association between *hana* and the complement *vanta peninga*, but the association is established by means of structure sharing, rather than through constituent structure displacements.

This analysis shows how the complex-valued features that provide an account of basic valence demands in Figure 7.8 interact with structure-sharing to allow the subject demands of a raising verb to be identified with those of its complement.[14] Furthermore, precisely the same elements offer an analysis of 'control' constructions, in which the higher controller merely identifies the reference of the subject of the complement. The properties of control constructions are discussed in detail in Sag and Pollard (1991), but they can be broadly subsumed under the generalization that control verbs are not transparent to the syntactic demands of the head of their complement. The contrast with raising verbs is reflected in the fact that the subject of the control verb VONA 'hope' in (2b) follows the default nominative pattern and does not inherit

$$\textit{vanast:} \begin{bmatrix} \text{SUBJ} & \langle \boxed{1}[\text{IND } \boxed{3}]\rangle \\ \text{COMPS} & \langle \boxed{2}[\text{SUBJ } \langle [\text{IND } \boxed{3}]\rangle]\rangle \\ \text{ARG-ST} & \langle \boxed{1}, \boxed{2}\rangle \end{bmatrix}$$

Figure 7.11. Lexical constraints on subject control verb

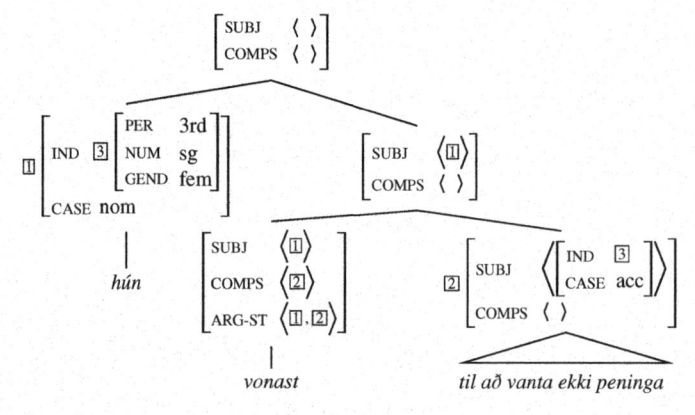

Figure 7.12. Subject 'control' as index feature sharing

the accusative case governed by its complement VANTA in (2a) (repeated from (1a)).

(2) Icelandic subject control constructions (cf. Andrews 1990:198)
  a. hana   vantar   peninga
     her.ACC   lack.3SG   money.ACC
     'she lacks money'
  b. hun/*hana   vonast   til að   vanta ekki peninga
     she.NOM/*her.ACC   hope.3SG   toward   lack not money.ACC
     'she hopes not to lack money'

The intuition that the subject of a control verb merely identifies the reference of its complement's subject is expressed by the entry in Figure 7.11, in which the index values of the two SUBJ values are identified (i.e., structure-shared). The fact that index but not case values are shared in this entry allows the subject of *vonast* to select a nominative subject and control a complement that selects an accusative subject in Figure 7.12. Exactly the same formal components determine the analyses in Figures 7.10 and 7.12; there is no analogue of distinct 'raising' and 'equi' transformations or of distinct PRO and 'trace' elements in the subordinate subject positions. Instead it is solely the locus of structure sharing that distinguishes these subconstructions.[15]

7.3.1.2 Lexical rules

The treatment of argument structure in terms of a list-valued ARG-ST feature also provides the formal basis for a lexical analysis of valence alternations in HPSG. Lexical rules can apply to an entry and modify the ARG-ST list in various ways, by adding, deleting, permuting, or reassociating elements. The new entries that are defined by these types of rules will then have different combinatory and interpretive properties, due to the cross-referencing of ARG-ST elements with valence features and with semantic representations. For example, different versions of passive lexical rules are proposed in Pollard and Sag (1987:215) and Manning and Sag (1999), and a number of other valence-changing lexical rules are proposed in the HPSG literature (see, e.g., Wechsler and Noh (2001) and Müller (2002)). However, the study of valence alternations has been less a primary focus of research within HPSG than in, say, LFG (see the discussion of Lexical Mapping Theory in Chapter 6).

7.3.1.3 The architecture of signs

Figures 7.10 and 7.12 illustrate the tree-based diagrams that are often used to exhibit HPSG analyses. These representations show the usefulness of tree-based diagrams for isolating particular aspects of an analysis, in the present case the role of valence features and structure sharing. However, the familiarity of this representational format comes at a cost, as it slightly misrepresents the SIGN-BASED nature of HPSG.[16] In GPSG, feature structures are labels that annotate the nodes of a phrase structure tree. But HPSG inverts this conception and incorporates constituent structure links within general data structures termed SIGNS. Within the version of HPSG expounded in Pollard and Sag (1994), a head–complement sign has the general structure in Figure 7.13. There are two innovative aspects of this analysis. The first is that syntactic and semantic features are consolidated into a single type of data structure, termed a *synsem*. The second is that constituent structure is represented by DTRS ('daughters') attributes that take signs or lists of signs as values. Hence the VP from Figure 7.8 above is represented, albeit somewhat less perspicuously, by the sign in Figure 7.14.

Even the fairly rich analysis in Figure 7.14 suppresses syntactic detail (not to mention all of the semantic properties incorporated within *synsem* objects). Although the highly explicit nature of the HPSG formalism may seem somewhat imposing, the formal character of the formalism is designed with the dual goals of broad-coverage theoretical description and large-scale practical implementation in mind.[17] For students (and

$$\begin{bmatrix} \text{PHON} & \text{phonological representation} \\ \text{SYNSEM} & \text{syntactic and semantic features} \\ \text{DTRS} & \begin{bmatrix} \text{HEAD-DTR} & \text{single sign} \\ \text{COMPS-DTRS} & \text{<list of signs>} \end{bmatrix} \end{bmatrix}$$

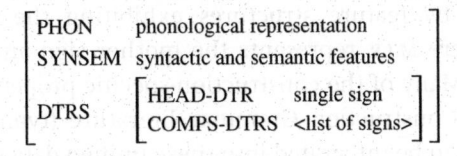

Figure 7.13. Structure of head-complement signs

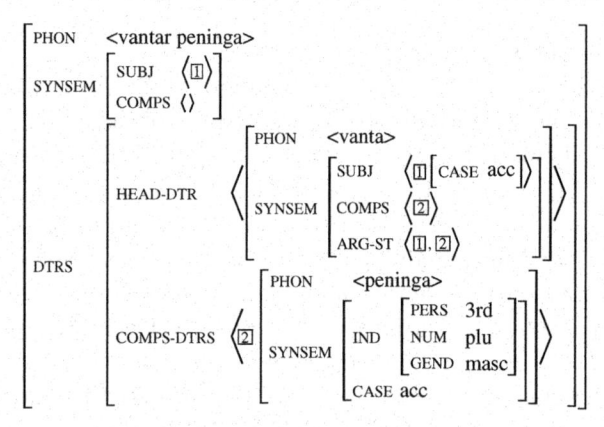

$$\begin{bmatrix} \text{PHON} & \text{<vantar peninga>} \\ \text{SYNSEM} & \begin{bmatrix} \text{SUBJ} & \langle\boxed{1}\rangle \\ \text{COMPS} & \langle\rangle \end{bmatrix} \\ \text{DTRS} & \left\langle \begin{bmatrix} \text{HEAD-DTR} & \left\langle \begin{bmatrix} \text{PHON} & \text{<vanta>} \\ \text{SYNSEM} & \begin{bmatrix} \text{SUBJ} & \langle\boxed{1}[\text{CASE acc}]\rangle \\ \text{COMPS} & \langle\boxed{2}\rangle \\ \text{ARG-ST} & \langle\boxed{1},\boxed{2}\rangle \end{bmatrix} \end{bmatrix} \right\rangle \\ \text{COMPS-DTRS} & \left\langle\boxed{2} \begin{bmatrix} \text{PHON} & \text{<peninga>} \\ \text{SYNSEM} & \begin{bmatrix} \text{IND} & \begin{bmatrix} \text{PERS} & \text{3rd} \\ \text{NUM} & \text{plu} \\ \text{GEND} & \text{masc} \end{bmatrix} \\ \text{CASE} & \text{acc} \end{bmatrix} \end{bmatrix}\right\rangle \end{bmatrix} \right\rangle \end{bmatrix}$$

Figure 7.14. Partial analysis of *vantar peninga*

$$\begin{bmatrix} \textit{construct} \\ \text{MTR} & \text{sign}_0 \\ \text{DTRS} & \text{<sign}_1,\ldots,\text{sign}_n\text{>} \end{bmatrix}$$

Figure 7.15. General structure of a *construct* (Sag 2010a: 497)

general linguists) who mainly want to understand the basic intuitions and desiderata that underlie HPSG models, a more streamlined version of the formalism is presented in Sag et al. (2003).

7.3.2 Sign-Based Construction Grammar (SBCG)

In much the same way that initial models of HPSG drew on ideas from categorial grammar and adapted techniques from AI and theoretical computer science, current models of Sign-Based Construction Grammar integrate key empirical insights from the Berkeley Construction Grammar tradition (Goldberg 1995, Kay and Filmore 1999). The conceptual unification of these traditions rests on the insight that the rich construction inventories investigated in Construction Grammar can be modeled by organizing individual constructions into inheritance networks. The formal architecture required by this analysis is already fully present in standard models of HPSG, in the form of the type hierarchies that cross-classify individual signs representing words, phrases, and clauses. The main prerequisite for a construction-based extension of HPSG is then a type of feature structure that represents constructions.

As noted in Sag (2010b, 2012), feature structure counterparts of the local trees from GPSG provide suitable candidates. Individual constructions can be represented by feature structures exhibiting the organization in Figure 7.15, where MTR represents the mother sign and DTRS a list of daughter signs. Many of the construction-specific properties investigated in the modern Construction Grammar literature (typified by Kay and Filmore (1999)) can be integrated into these unified data structures.

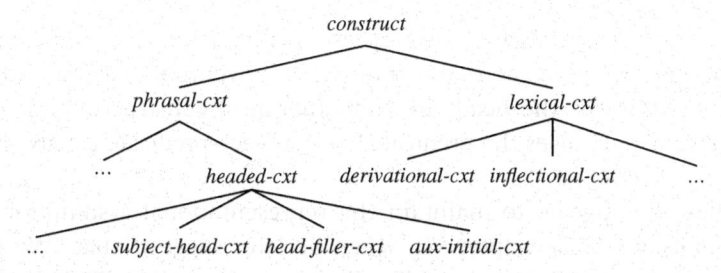

```
                          construct
                  ┌──────────┴──────────┐
            phrasal-cxt              lexical-cxt
           ┌────┴────┐              ┌─────┼─────┐
         ...      headed-cxt   derivational-cxt  inflectional-cxt   ...
              ┌──────┼──────┐
            ...  subject-head-cxt  head-filler-cxt  aux-initial-cxt
```

Figure 7.16. Partial construction type hierarchy (Sag 2010a: 499)

As in HPSG, the inheritance of properties within a construction inventory can be modeled by type hierarchies. The partial hierarchy in Figure 7.16 represents natural classes of constructions relevant to the analysis of extraction in English.

The detailed treatment of English relative and filler–gap clauses in Sag (1997, 2010a) presents a sustained argument for extending HPSG models to include a notion of construction. At the same time, these studies make a case for reconceptualizing grammatical constructions in the context of a constraint-based architecture, rather than in the exemplar-based terms assumed in traditional grammars.

These studies also illustrate the ways that phrase structure models continue to evolve, driven in part by the logic of their basic organizing principles, and in part by their ability to incorporate and extend insights from other traditions. From their origins in the string rewriting systems in Chomsky (1956), extended phrase structure models have assumed their modern form by successively integrating traditional perspectives on grammatical features and units with more formal notions such as inheritance hierarchies and constraint satisfaction. In addition to providing analyses of a wide range of syntactic constructions, these models have clarified how explicit mechanisms for regulating the distribution of grammatical information within a single syntactic representation can achieve any of the benefits that had, beginning with the work of Harris (1957), been claimed to accrue to derivational analyses.

Notes

We thank Stefan Müller and an anonymous reviewer for comments on an earlier version of this chapter.

1. A partial list of constructions that were analyzed as discontinuous by the Bloomfieldians would include parentheticals (Bloomfield 1933:186, Nida 1966:21), coordination (Bloch 1946:229), ditransitives (Pike 1943:77), complex predicates (Nida 1966:46), phrasal verbs (Wells 1947:105–106), polar questions (Pike 1943:77, Hockett 1958:158, Gleason 1955:142, Nida 1966:28), non-subject relatives (Nida 1966:27), non-subject constituent questions (Nida 1966:46, Gleason 1955:155).

2. The analysis in Table 7.2 also represents functional and even dependency information, as it illustrates the convention that "the arrow points towards the head" in a modifier-head construction and that "the **P** always faces the predicate" in a subject–predicate construction (Gleason 1965:157).
3. Chomsky appears to maintain the representational assumptions in Chomsky (1975a:chapter VII) when he later suggests that "We take these objects [i.e., levels of linguistic representation, JPB/IAS] to be phrase markers in the familiar sense represented conventionally by trees or labelled bracketings)" (Chomsky 1995c:34).
4. In the continuation of this passage, Chomsky notes that the second constraint has merely been carried over from Chomsky (1965:188) and appears willing to countenance the idea "that certain features should also be associated with nonlexical phrase categories." Yet the accompanying footnote immediately characterizes the arguments supporting previous proposals as "very weak," and Chomsky does not in fact propose a general relaxation of the constraints on complex feature bundles that would allow the inflectional features associated with a lexical category to be propagated to or shared with a phrasal projection.
5. See Steedman and Baldridge (2011) for recent synopsis of combinatory categorial approaches.
6. Though subsequent work has called into question whether this parallelism is restricted to coordinate structures (Postal 1998) and whether the constraint ultimately reflects more general semantic or discourse factors (Goldsmith 1985, Lakoff 1986, Kehler 2002).
7. The analysis in Figure 7.3 introduces the coordinating conjunction as a sister of the conjuncts, rather than associating it with the second conjunct, though nothing here hinges on this difference.
8. Indeed, there was a considerable delay before the tradition even addressed the challenge of assigning a derived constituent structure to transforms, an issue that had been raised as early as Stockwell (1962).
9. See Ladusaw (1988) for discussion of the contrast between linguistic 'levels' and 'strata.'
10. The analyses of unbounded dependencies and auxiliary selection/inversion outlined above were followed by phrase structure treatments of, among others, an expanded range of extraction constructions (Pollard and Sag 1994: Chapters 4–5, Levine and Hukari 2006), passives (Pollard and Sag 1987:215, Manning and Sag 1999), control constructions (Sag and Pollard 1991), anaphoric binding (Pollard and Sag 1992). Contemporary work in Lexical–Functional Grammar (Dalrymple et al. 1995) and Tree Adjoining Grammar (Joshi and Schabes 1997) explored a similar range of

empirical extensions. See also Johnson and Lappin (1999) for a comprehensive comparison of constraint-based and derivation perspectives.
11. Reape (1996) was widely circulated in draft form, as of 1990.
12. By virtue of the Head Feature Principle (aka the Head Feature Convention), the metavariable 'H[1]' would license a preterminal V[1] that shared the word class features of the VP mother.
13. See Blevins (2011) for a recent review and discussion of these types of cases.
14. A similar analysis is proposed within LFG in terms of 'functional control' (Bresnan 1982c).
15. There is more to say about Icelandic raising constructions and the mechanisms that allow quirky 'lexical' case to take priority over default 'structural' case. See Andrews (1982, 1990) for some discussion.
16. See also Orgun (1996) for a sign-based model of morphology compatible with HPSG assumptions.
17. Repositories of information, publications, and materials related to current HPSG implementations can be found at http://lingo.Stanford.edu/, http://hpsg.fu-berlin.de/Projects/core.html, and http://hpsg.fu-berlin.de/~stefan/Babel/. See also Müller (2010:187f.)

8

Tree Adjoining Grammar

Robert Frank

8.1 The derivation of syntactic structure

A fundamental question for syntactic theory concerns the nature of the basic computations that are used to construct grammatical representations. Within variants of transformational grammar from Chomsky (1957) to the present, answers to this question have been motivated by two fundamental properties of syntax:

- *Hierarchy*: the explanation of syntactic patterns requires reference to a hierarchically organized representation (constituency, asymmetry).
- *Displacement*: even when a language shows a canonical word order, there is systematic variation where words and phrases are displaced from their usual positions.

To account for each of these properties, variants of transformational grammar have posited a distinct operation. For hierarchy, a basic structure building operation has been posited, called Merge (or more specifically External Merge) in current Minimalist work and phrase-structure rules in previous work, which combines lexical units into hierarchical structures that can further be combined with additional lexical material or previously built structures. A separate operation, dubbed Move (or Internal Merge) in current work, is responsible for the displacement property. This operation perturbs the syntactic representation so that a previously merged constituent is attached in a different position in the structure.[1]

While the properties of hierarchy and displacement (H&D) are no doubt important ones, recall that the motivation for positing a grammar was the desire to have a finite specification of an infinite class of grammatical representations, that is, a mental grammar. What is the relationship between H&D and infinite capacity? Certainly, the H&D properties are not a sufficient condition for infinite capacity. Consider, for instance, the syntactic representations that are associated with single clauses with no coordination or modification. These are hierachical and exhibit displacement. Yet, this class is not infinite. And neither are the H&D properties necessary in an infinite class of representation. To see this, consider an infinite class of sequential (non-hierarchical) representations, i.e., strings, or an infinite class of hierarchical representations that does not exhibit displacement, with the elements occurring in a canonical order.

There is, however, a property that is necessary for an infinite class of representations to have a finite specification, namely *recursion*. By recursion, I mean the property of structures in which a consituent of one type, determined by the node label of the constituent's root, occurs inside another of the same type. Without the possibility of generating recursive representations, a grammar which begins with a finite lexicon will produce only finitely many syntactic representations, yielding a system that lacks the productivity that is characteristic of human language.

Hauser et al. (2002) recognize the importance of recursion and indeed take recursion to be at the core of the human capacity for language. However, for them recursion is not the property of representations as just discussed. Instead, Hauser, Chomsky and Fitch appear to take recursion to be a property of the computational mechanisms of grammar: a recursive process is one which can apply to its own output. Specifically, they take Merge, the operation that generates hierarchical representations, to embody this property. This notion of recursion is not sufficient to ensure productivity, though. The computational procedure underlying context-free derivations is certainly recursive, with the result of each rule application feeding the next. However, such a procedure applied to the grammar in (1) will only produce a single representations.

(1) S → NP VP
     NP → Det N
     VP → V NP

Because of the way this grammar has been written, a sequence of rewriting steps will never rewrite the same symbol twice, and consequently, the structure that is derived is not recursive in the representational sense. The case of the Merge operation is similar: depending on how the features driving merge are assigned to lexical items, it could well happen that recursive structures are not generable. And even when context-free rewriting or Merge do produce recursive structures, it is not a single application of the rewrite or Merge operation that produces recursive structure. Instead, it is a combination of operations that are implicated, requiring the presence of a set of rules or features that allow such a combination to take place.

Given the importance of recursive representations, we might consider what happens if we formulate our derivational operations so that they are directly tied to their generation. In fact, the earliest model put forward in generative syntax, that of Chomsky (1955/1975, 1957), did precisely this. Derivations began with the restricted use of context-free rewriting, using rule sets like that in (1) to produce non-recursive *kernel sentences*. Kernel sentences were then combined using operations called *generalized transformations* (cf. Chapter 2). The resulting complex structures were then given as input to *singulary transformations*, which accomplished the kind of displacement that has traditionally been taken to result from transformational operations such as Move. In this model, it is the application of generalized transformations that is directly implicated in the creation of structural recursion. However, a decade after it was proposed, in Chomsky (1965), this model was abandoned. Chomsky argued that the limitation to non-recursive phrase structure rewriting was unmotivated, and by allowing for recursive phrase-structure rules, recursive syntactic structure could be generated without any appeal to generalized transformations. Perhaps most significantly, this abandonment of generalized transformations allowed a simplification in the form of the grammar, eliminating the need to postulate a complex set of constraints (or 'traffic rules') that regulate the interaction of generalized and singulary transformations (Fillmore 1963). From current perspectives, this model was also suspect given its dependence on parochial construction-specific generalized and singulary transformations.

Recent attempts to reintegrate generalized transformations into the grammar, in the form of an abstract Merge operation, avoid the argument against parochial constraints, and have largely put aside the question of the necessity for traffic rules (though see Chomsky 2000b and Nunes 2004 for discussion of different aspects of relative ordering of Merge and Move). Yet, as already noted, these attempts have not brought with them operations that create structural recursion. It is, however, possible to do so in a way that has significant empirical and theoretical advantages, and the rest of this chapter will be devoted to a framework, Tree Adjoining Grammar (TAG), that does precisely this. In the next section, I outline the assumptions and operations of TAG. Subsequent sections explore the implications of TAG for the nature of the grammar, specifically in the domain of long-distance dependencies. Finally, I explore the role that TAG can play in discussions of the computational constraints on grammar.

8.2 The basics of Tree Adjoining Grammar

Tree Adjoining Grammar (TAG) is a formalism that builds grammatical representations through the composition of smaller pieces of syntactic structure. Joshi et al. (1975) first proposed TAG as a formalization of the idea, present in Chomsky (1955/1975, 1957) and Harris (1968), that complex sentences are constructed through the combination of simple ones, called *kernel sentences*. The significance of TAG for syntactic theory was first recognized and explored in a series of papers by Aravind Joshi and Anthony Kroch (Joshi 1985, Kroch and Joshi 1985, 1987, Kroch 1987, 1989b).[2]

Like all derivational systems, TAG derivations begin with a finite set of atomic elements. What is different in TAG is that these atoms are larger that usual: the basic objects are the kernel sentences that combine to yield complex sentences. These hierarchically structured objects, called *elementary trees*, provide what has been called an *extended domain of locality* over which grammatical regularities can be expressed. As with the phrase structure trees that are familiar from other frameworks, the nodes of an elementary tree will be decorated by labels of two sorts, *terminals* and *non-terminals*. Elementary trees adhere to the usual assumption that terminal labels, which we can tentatively identify with word forms, will only be associated with nodes along the frontier of an elementary tree.[3] Non-terminal (phrasal category) labels, in contrast, will decorate all of the internal (phrasal) nodes. Unusually, TAG also allows some frontier nodes in an elementary trees to be labeled by non-terminal symbols.

In order to produce recursive syntax from a set of elementary trees, TAG makes use of two derivational operations. The first of these is *substitution*. In this operation, an elementary tree β rooted in non-terminal X targets a frontier non-terminal in another elementary tree α that is also labeled X. The result is the insertion of the β at the node labeled X in α.

(2) Substitution:

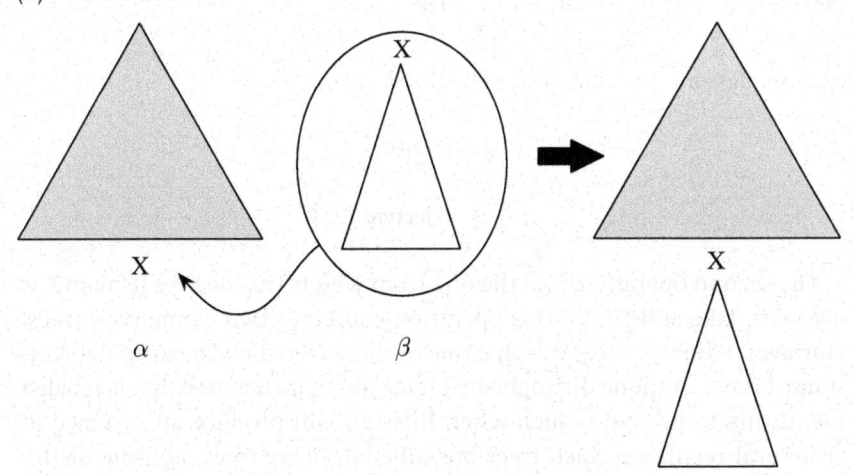

Another way to conceptualize TAG derivations is in terms of tree rewriting: at each step in the derivation a node of an already constructed tree is rewritten as a piece of structure. From this perspective, substitution can be seen as the rewriting of a frontier non-terminal as the substituted elementary tree.

In linguistic applications, the substitution operation is often used to insert the structures corresponding to arguments into a verbally headed elementary tree. Thus in the following derivation, the DP frontier nonterminals corresponding to the subject and object of *finishes* are filled via the substitution of DP-rooted elementary trees.[4]

(3) a.

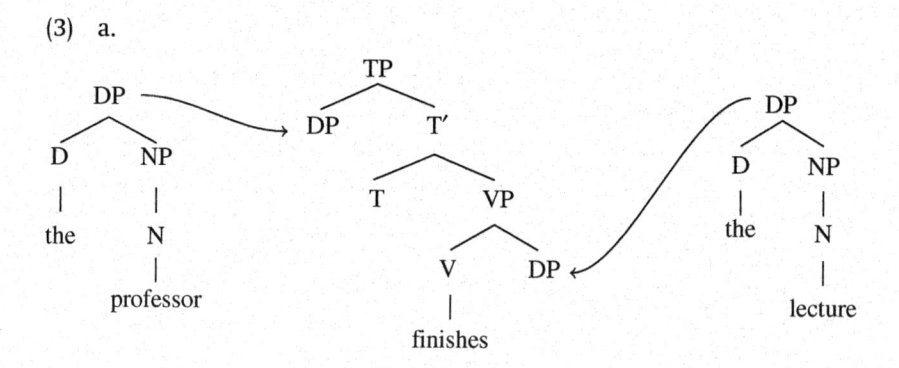

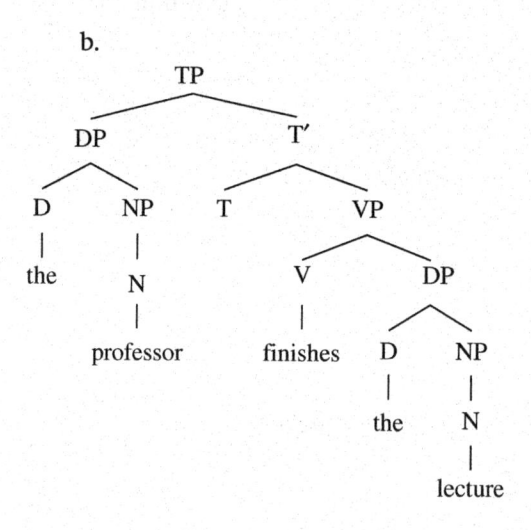

```
        DP                    TP                         DP
       /  \                  /  \                       /  \
      D    NP         →  DP     T'              ←      D    NP
      |    |               ┌────┴────┐                 |    |
     the   N                T        VP               the   N
           |                      ┌──┴──┐                   |
        professor                 V     DP              lecture
                                  |
                              finishes
```

b.

```
                    TP
                  /    \
                DP      T'
               /  \    /  \
              D   NP  T   VP
              |   |       /  \
             the  N      V    DP
                  |      |   /  \
              professor finishes D  NP
                                 |  |
                                the N
                                    |
                                 lecture
```

The second operation, and the one from which TAG derives its name, is *adjoining*. Like substition, this operation combines two elementary trees. However, adjoining requires that one of these trees be of a particular sort: it must have a unique distinguished node along its frontier that is labeled identically to its root, which when filled in will produce an instance of structural recursion. Such trees are called *auxiliary* trees, and the distinguished (recursive) frontier node is called the *foot* node. Throughout the chapter, we will identify the foot node by placing an superscripted asterisk on its label. Given an auxiliary tree α recursive on label X, adjoining targets a node labeled X in another elementary tree β by removing the subtree in β rooted at X, attaching α in its place, and reattaching the subtree of β at α's foot node. This is depicted in (4).

(4) Adjoining:

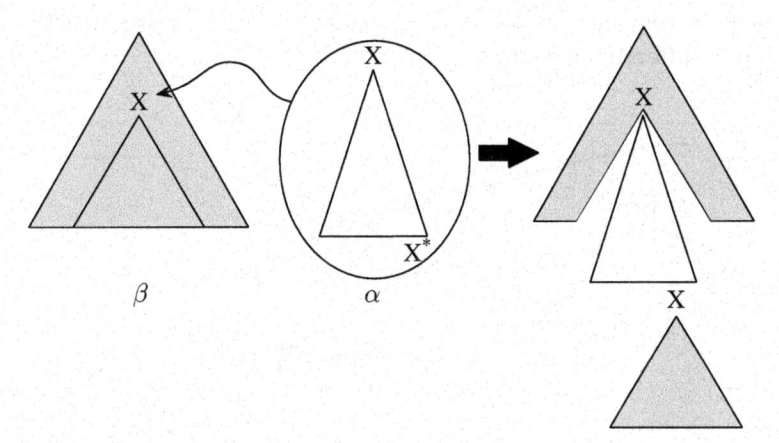

If we adopt the tree rewriting perspective on TAG, we can see that adjoining provides a way to rewrite not only nodes that are at the periphery of an elementary tree, but rather any node at all. The context surrounding the target of adjoining is expanded to accommodate the auxiliary tree, and the identity in label between the site of adjoining and the foot node of the auxiliary tree ensures that previously existing parent–child relations in the tree are preserved.

Since the structure of auxiliary trees explicitly introduces recursion, adjoining has been exploited to derive a range of recursive structures. In deriving the example in (5), for example, we derive the configuration for modification, by adjoining the VP-recursive auxiliary tree containing the adverb at the VP node in (5) to the *the professor finishes the lecture*, yielding the structure on the right.

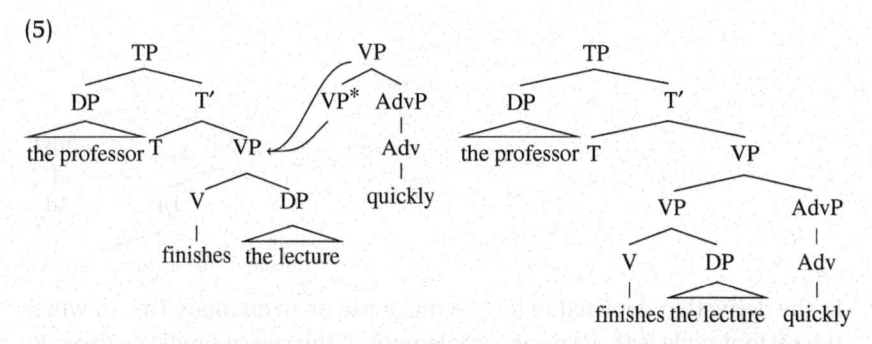

(5)

The result of this derivation is the kind of configuration typically taken to arise from the operation of (Chomsky) adjunction. In spite of the similarity in name, the TAG adjoining operation is capable of deriving a considerably wider range of structures, as we shall see directly.

The VP-recursive auxiliary tree used in (5) has a foot node that is the daughter of the root. When this property holds of an auxiliary tree, an 'adjunction structure' will result from adjoining. Yet nothing in the TAG formalism requires that to be the case. By making use of auxiliary trees in which the root and foot are more distant, we derive recursive structures of a rather different character.

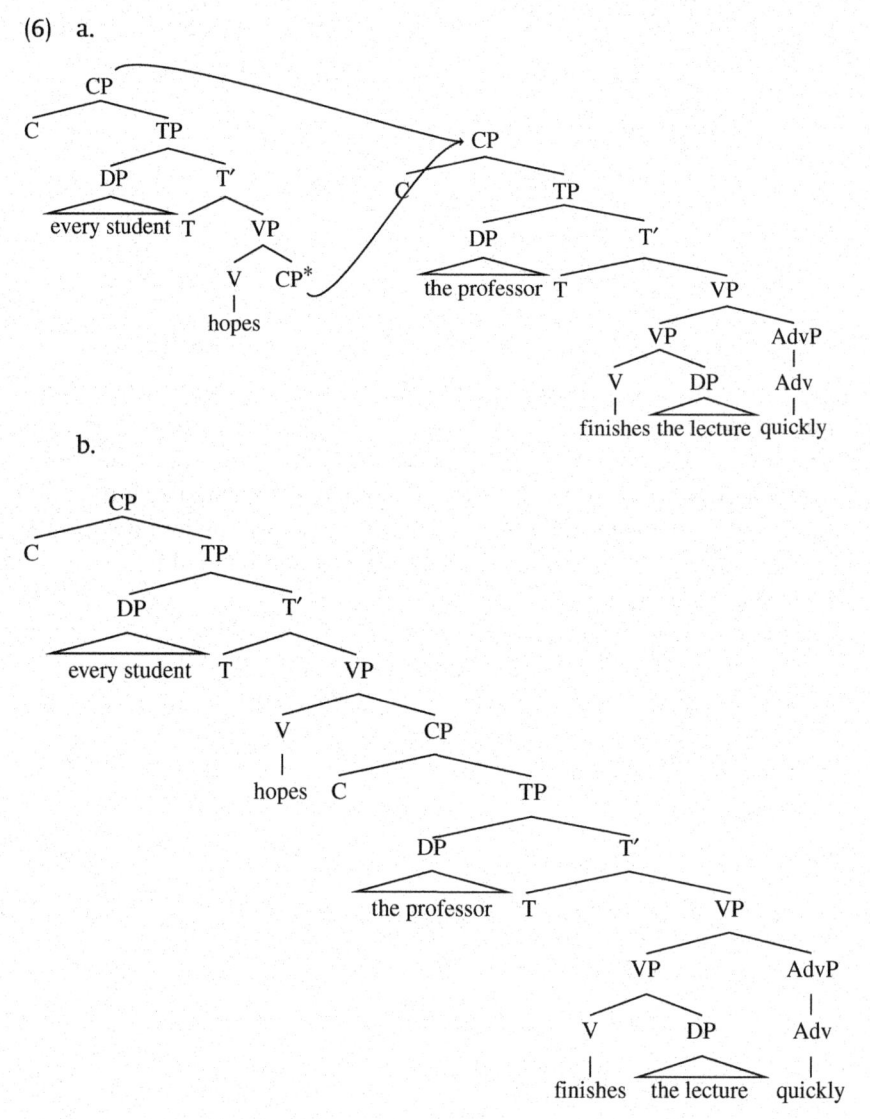

(6) a.

[tree diagram: CP auxiliary tree with "every student T hopes CP*" adjoined to a tree "the professor T finishes the lecture quickly"]

b.

[tree diagram: resulting structure "every student T hopes C the professor T finishes the lecture quickly"]

In the derivation depicted in (6), we make use of an auxiliary tree in which the CP foot node is the clausal complement of the verbal predicate *hopes*. By adjoining this CP-recursive auxiliary tree at the root of the structure derived above, we derive an instance of recursive clausal complementation.

The substitution and adjoining operations, as presented thus far, are constrained by the syntactic category of the node at which the operation takes place: substitution or adjoining of a elementary tree rooted in a node labeled X can only proceed at another node labeled X. There is, however, reason to additionally constrain the application of these operations. Take for instance the case of substitution of DP nodes, as in the derivation in (3). Because of the form of the inflected verb, the DP that is inserted into the subject, specifier of TP position must bear 3rd person singular features. To express such a constraint, without expanding the set of syntactic categories, TAG allows for the imposition of node constraints that further restrict the application of the substitution and adjoining operations. A node marked for selective substitution (SS) or selective adjoining (SA) will specify a subset of elementary trees which can substitute or adjoin. In its most basic form, an SS or SA specification can take the form of a list of elementary trees that can adjoin or substitute. In the case at hand, this would mean that the DP node in the TP specifier position would be marked with a list of all of the DP elementary trees in the grammar (a finite set) that were headed by a nominal of the appropriate form. Linguistically more satisfying approaches couch such constraints in terms of a description of the feature content of the elementary trees that can substitute or adjoin at a particular node (XTAG Research Group 2001, Frank 2002). We will also allow ourselves two further types of constraint on the adjoining operation, to render adjoining at a particular node either necessary or impossible. Such regulation takes the form of obligatory adjoining (OA) and null adjoining (NA) constraints. We will see linguistic motivations for such constraints in the next section.[5]

8.3 TAG and syntactic dependencies

The interest of TAG for linguistic theory comes not only from the prominence it assigns to structural recursion, but also from the perspective it offers on the nature of syntactic dependencies. In transformational theories, once a hierarchical structure is built using Merge, operations such as Move or Agree apply, establishing potentially non-local dependencies among the elements in the tree. In order to account for the locality properties of such dependencies, additional stipulations must be added that regulate the application of these operations. See Chapter 18 for further discussion of such locality properties. In TAG derivations, in contrast, there are no operations that apply after recursive structures are built with substitution and adjoining, and consequently no place for such stipulations. Instead, in a TAG-based theory of grammar, syntactic dependencies must be local, a view which I dub the 'Fundamental TAG Hypothesis' (Frank 2002).

(7) *Fundamental TAG Hypothesis*
Every syntactic dependency is expressed locally within a single elementary tree.

Of course there do exist many syntactic dependencies that appear to be non-local, spanning over unbounded distances. Two such cases are raising and *wh*-movement constructions, depicted in (8), and these have indeed constituted the primary motivation for a Move operation in grammatical derivations.

(8) a. {the professor}$_i$ appears t_i to have finished the lecture
    b. What$_i$ do you think the professor said t_i?

How can we reconcile the existence of these kinds of examples with the Fundamental TAG Hypothesis? Suppose we allow ourselves a T′-recursive auxiliary tree. By adjoining such a tree between the subject and the T head in an infinitival clausal elementary tree, as shown in (9), we accomplish the displacement of the subject to the left edge of the higher clause without resort to a inter-clausal movement operation. Instead, the structural relation between the embedded subject is simply 'stretched' away from its clause as a result of adjoining.

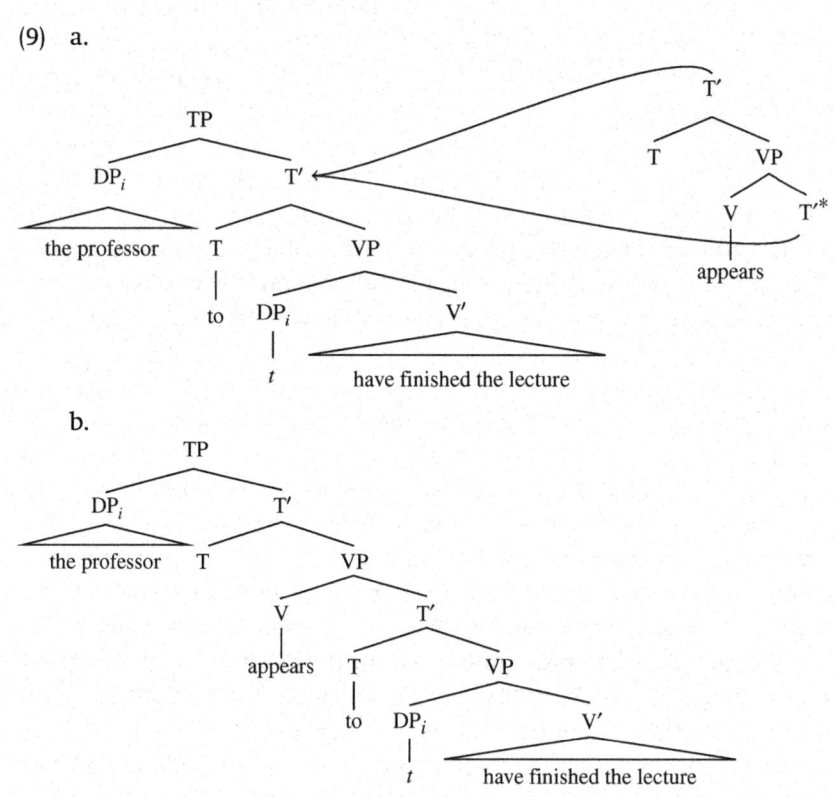

(9) a.

b.

Note that the TP tree into which adjoining takes place does contain an instance of an intra-clausal filler–gap dependency, between the DP and its VP-internal trace.[6] This is necessary because there is no way to accomplish such displacement using the mechanisms of the TAG formalism. As a result, any grammatical theory that makes use of TAG will need to avail itself of some mechanism for accomplishing displacement within elementary trees. However, following the Fundamental TAG Hypothesis, we will limit the role of this mechanism to cases of local displacement.

Observe that the infinitival TP elementary tree *the professor to have finished the lecture* does not by itself constitute a well-formed sentence: infinitival clauses must occur in embedded contexts. To ensure that this tree does not surface in this form, we make use of an Obligatory Adjoining (OA) constraint on the T′ node, which will require that an auxiliary tree with a finite verb, like the one used in this derivation, adjoin at this node. Conversely, in the case of finite clauses, we will want to prevent the adjoining of a raising-verb-headed auxiliary at the T′ node. To do so, we can impose a Null Adjoining (NA) constraint at the T′ node of such trees, blocking the adjoining of any such tree.

We can extend the distance between the displaced element and its base position without bound through additional applications of the adjoining operation. For example, to derive an instance of raising across two clauses, we first adjoin one T′ auxiliary tree to the root of another, and then adjoin the resulting complex auxiliary tree to the T′ node below the subject, as before.

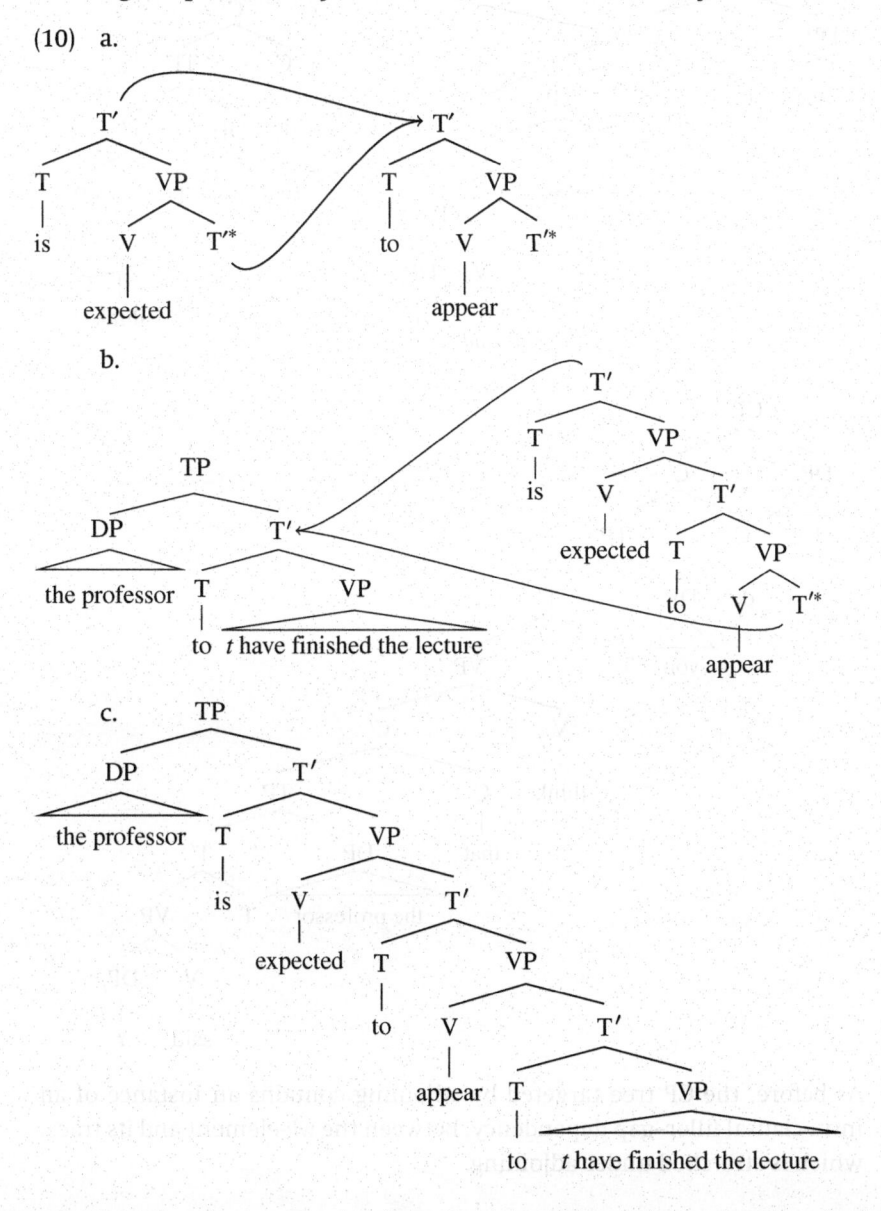

(10) a.

b.

c.

To add yet another level of embedding we would add to our derivation one more instance of adjoining into an infinitival T' auxiliary tree, and the more complex derived auxiliary tree would finally adjoin into the finite TP elementary tree. Since this pattern of adjoining can be iterated without bound, we derive the possibility of unbounded displacement.

In (11) a similar application of adjoining, this time involving a C'-recursive auxiliary tree, accomplishes the effects of cross-clausal *wh*-movement.

(11) a.

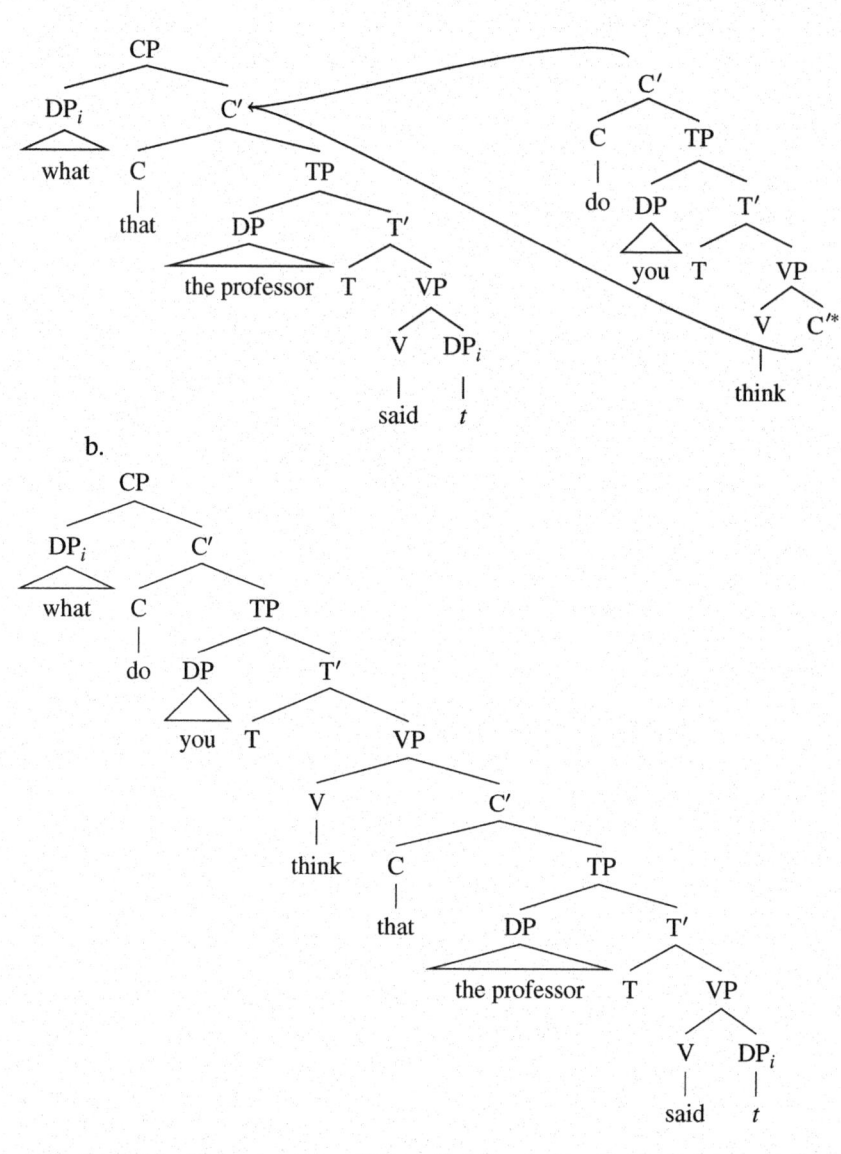

b.

As before, the CP tree targeted by adjoining contains an instance of an intra-clausal filler–gap dependency, between the *wh*-element and its trace, which is stretched under adjoining.

This view of displacement has a number of interesting consequences. First of all, it offers an explanation for why long-distance displacement must proceed via the edge of the syntactic domain out of which it takes place. Only by moving to the edge of a domain (an elementary tree) can a syntactic object be displaced to a higher domain using the adjoining operation; otherwise even after adjoining, it would be stuck below any structure that dominates it. This leads us to predict the widespread occurrence of 'successive-cyclic' movement, for instance from specifier of TP to specifier of TP, or from specifier of CP to specifier of CP. Note however that the TAG analog of successive cyclic derivation differs crucially from that which is standardly assumed, in that it eliminates all but two stages of displacement: elementary-tree-internal movement followed by adjoining. This simplified style of derivation avoids the need to posit unboundedly many intermediate traces of movement, whether between the raised subject DP and the embedded verb in (9) and (10) or between the wh-phrase in higher and the lower CP specifier positions. As I shall argue below, this simplification does not adversely affect our ability to explain the locality of displacement.[7] Finally, instances of inter-clausal A- and A'-movement are not distinguished by the kind of position to which movement takes place, since neither involves inter-clausal movement of any sort. Instead, different movement types are distinguished by the locus of adjoining.

The claim embodied in the Fundamental TAG Hypothesis in (7) is that all cases of non-locality are of the sort just discussed, being the result of a locally established dependency that is stretched as a result of the adjoining operation. Because of the connection between adjoining and the generation of recursive structure, this means that non-local dependencies have a tight connection to recusive structure, as the following corollary of (7) makes clear:

(12) *Non-local Dependency Corollary*
Non-local dependencies always reduce to local ones once recursive structure is factored out.

If this is correct, it points to a sharp link between one of the most surprising, and widely investigated properties of grammar, namely locality, and the property of syntactic recursion.[8]

In order to have empirical bite, the Fundamental TAG hypothesis and Non-local Dependency Corollary require a characterization of the structural domain that comprises an elementary tree. Just as the context-free formalism tells us nothing about the kind of phrase-structure rules that should be present in a grammar, the TAG formalism says little about the nature of elementary trees. Consequently, from the perspective of the formalism, the grammar of a language could simply consist of a list of an arbitrary finite set of (finite) trees. Such an approach would, however, fail to account for the generalizations that hold across the structures for a particular language, or across languages in generally. Just as the theory of Generalized Phrase Structure Grammar (GPSG) (Gazdar *et al.* 1985) aimed to characterize the set of phrase-structure rules in the grammar of a language, a TAG-based theory of syntax must provide an independent characterization of the set of elementary trees. Since the adoption of the TAG formalism commits us to the invariant adjoining and substitution operations, the set of elementary trees in the grammar of a language is the only locus of cross-linguistic differences, imposing substantial restrictions on the kind of variation that we will find cross-linguistically.

Unlike many frameworks in which the formal system has been inextricably tied to a particular set of substantive linguistic assumptions, TAG has been approached from a range of perspectives and ontological commitments, including Government and Binding Theory (Kroch and Joshi 1987, Kroch 1989b), Minimalism (Frank 2002, 2006), Head-driven Phrase Structure Grammar (HPSG) (Kasper *et al.* 1995), Lexicon Grammar (Abeillé 1991), and Categorial Grammar (Joshi and Kulick 1997). However, any characterization of possible elementary trees must impose some sort of upper bound on their size. Otherwise, there would be no guarantee that the set of elementary trees would be finite. Virtually all of the TAG-based work has been driven by a common intuition concerning the source of this bound: an elementary tree should be built around a single semantic predicate. Under the assumption that lexical, as opposed to functional, categories are responsible for theta-role assignment, this intuition can be translated into the assumption that each elementary tree contains a single lexical category. This does not suffice to determine the character of elementary trees, however. Specifically, it leaves open the question of how functional categories ought to be incorporated into elementary trees. This question has received a range of responses in the TAG literature. Functional heads might be generated in independent elementary trees that are adjoined to a lexical head, as proposed by Hegarty (1993) and Rambow (1993). Under such an approach, T and C heads would be introduced in auxiliary trees that are adjoined at appropriate locations in a verbally headed VP projection.

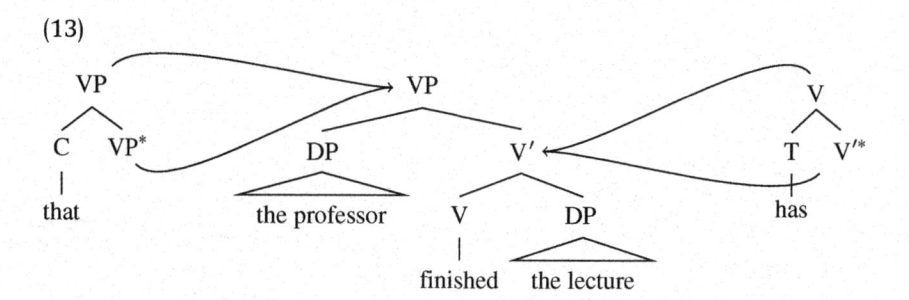

(13)

```
    VP                      VP                          V
   /  \                    /  \                        / \
  C   VP*                DP    V'                     T   V'*
  |                      /\    /\                     |
 that              the professor V   DP              has
                                 |   /\
                              finished the lecture
```

Alternatively, the functional heads might be included in the elementary tree of a lexical head, as in the trees used in the derivations given thus far.

In Frank (2002), I argued in favor of the latter possibility, constraining the form of elementary trees as follows:

(14) *Condition of Elementary Tree Minimality (CETM)*
    The syntactic heads in an elementary tree and their projections must form an extended projection of a single lexical head.

The CETM makes use of the notion of extended projection from Grimshaw (2005). Briefly, the extended projection of a lexical head H includes H's immediate projection and the projections of the 'functional shell' that surrounds H. This notion can be defined as follows:

(15) *Extended Projection*
    For lexical head L, X is an extended projection of L if
    a. X is the projection of L
    b. X is the projection of a functional head H that is sister to an exended projection of L.

Grimshaw argues that extended projections delimit the domain in which selection, agreement, feature percolation, and head movement take place. By taking elementary trees to consist of extended projections, the CETM thereby allows us to sustain the Fundamental TAG Hypothesis with respect to these phenomena. As we have seen above, the possibility of stretching the local domain defined by an extended projection through the adjoining operation allows the dependencies resulting from phrasal movement to be localized within an extended projection.

One immediate consequence of the CETM and the definition of extended projection is that a lexical head must be generated in a distinct elementary tree from its arguments. The extended projection of a V may include the functional projections of T and C (or any further functional decompositions of the clause), but not the projections of V's arguments, or of a lexical head that takes V's extended projection as its complement. As a result, the derivation of simple transitive clauses will necessarily involve the combination of multiple elementary trees, as seen in (3). In the nominal domain, the N extended projection may include functional heads D (and P, if one assumes that this is functional), but nothing higher.

As formulated in (14), the CETM restricts only the projections of heads that are themselves present in an elementary tree. This leaves open the possibility for phrasal nodes that are not part of the lexical head's extended projection to appear in an elementary tree, so long as they are not projected from any head present in the tree. In the elementary trees used in the sample derivations above, we have already seen instances of such material. One type of case involves the non-projected non-terminals that serve as the foot nodes of auxiliary trees or sites for substitution. Thus, the non-projected frontier non-terminal DP, CP, C', T', and VP nodes in the trees in (3), (5), (6), (9), (10), and (11) do not run afoul of the CETM. Another kind of non-projected node that the CETM licenses is the VP root node of the auxiliary tree in (5). This VP is not projected from a V, but is a reflection of the syntactic configuration in which VP modification takes place.

The first class of non-projected nodes correspond to the arguments of the lexical head of an elementary tree. We must regulate their appearance, so that we do not end up with substitution nodes that do not correspond to a thematic argument. One way to do this is by imposing a version of the Theta Criterion as a condition on elementary trees:

(16) θ-Criterion (TAG version)
      a. If H is the lexical head of elementary tree T, H assigns all of its theta roles in T.
      b. If A is a frontier non-terminal node of elementary tree T, A must be assigned a role in T.

The first clause of this constraint puts a lower bound on the number of frontier non-terminals of an elementary tree with lexical head H: there must be at least as many as the number of theta roles assigned by H. The second clause imposes an upper bound on the set of frontier non-terminals: the number of frontier non-terminals is at most the number of roles assigned. If the only roles that can be assigned are theta-roles, then this determines the number of frontier non-terminals exactly.[9]

8.4 Derivations in TAG-based syntax

Thus far, our approach to the task of specifying elementary tree well-formedness has been representational: elementary trees are well-formed if they satisfy a set of constraints, such as the CETM and θ-criterion. An alternative approach, laid out in Frank (2002), takes the properties of the elementary trees to result from a derivational process. Under this view, the derivation of a sentence is divided into two distinct stages: the first involves the construction of individual elementary trees, through the operations of Merge and Move familiar from Minimalist proposals, while the second combines these elementary trees using the operations of substitution and adjoining. The overall architecture is depicted in Figure 8.1. Let us consider each of these stages in turn.

The first stage of the derivation is responsible for the formation of the elementary trees that are subsequently manipulated by the TAG operations. For each elementary tree, an array of lexical items is chosen, which are combined and manipulated using the feature-driven operations of Merge and Move. Under this conception, the CETM qua representational constraint on elementary trees can be replaced with a limit on the content of the lexical array that provides the 'raw materials' for the derivation of any elementary tree: it may contain only the lexical and functional heads that together constitute a single extended projection. Such a constraint is similar in certain respects to Minimalist constraints on the content of

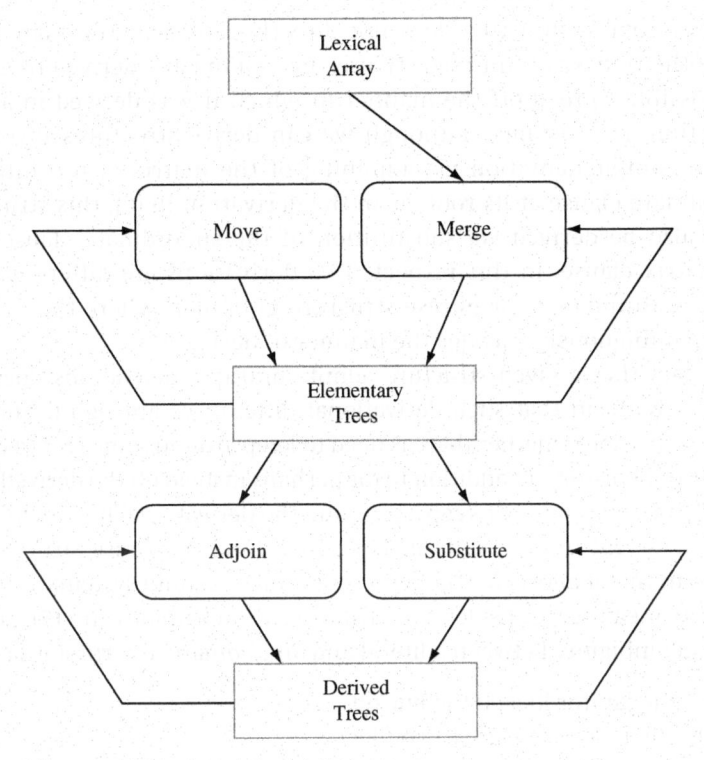

Figure 8.1. TAG-based derivational model

the subarray responsible for the derivation of a single phase: it may contain only a single phase head. In order to allow for the inclusion of foot nodes and substitution sites in elementary trees, we will depart from Minimalist views of the lexical array, allowing non-projected non-terminals to occur in the lexical array along with lexical items. The appearance of such non-terminals will be regulated by the derivational analog of the θ-criterion, in the form of a constraint on Merge: a non-projected non-terminal cannot Merge as part of an elementary tree unless it is driven by thematic features borne on a lexical head. Because of the limit we are imposing on the size of the lexical array, the Merge–Move portion of the derivation is incapable of producing structural recursion. Even if the non-projected non-terminal is identical to the root of the elementary tree, structural recursion, as I have defined it, will arise only once this non-projected non-terminal is structurally instantiated during the TAG portion of the derivation.

Let us turn next to the lower part of the derivational model in Figure 8.1, the part of the derivation involving the TAG operations of substitution and adjoining. As we have already seen, an elementary tree can be the target of multiple instances of substitution and adjoining, and the resulting tree can itself undergo substitution or adjoining into another tree. This process gives rise to what we call a *derived tree*. Note however that such a tree does not directly represent the manner in which the tree was composed. That is, by looking at a derived tree, it is not possible to read off the manner in which it was derived in a TAG derivation. For instance, although we can derive structures involving clausal complementation via adjoining of the matrix clause into the subordinate clause at its root, as in the derivation in (6), this structure could also be derived via substitution of the subordinate clause into the matrix clause. In this respect, TAG derivations are different from those in Minimalism or phrase structure grammar, where the derived tree unambiguously encodes the manner of derivation.

The fact that a given structure admits multiple derivations does not necessarily mean that such derivational differences are significant. We should ask, then, whether there is need to keep around some record of the derivational history, in addition to (or perhaps instead of) the derived tree. One argument in favor of keeping around the derivational history mirrors Chomsky's (1957) arguments in favor of a level of phrase structure in syntax, in that it allows for the representation of certain systematic differences in meaning. Consider, for instance, the examples in (17), which show an ambiguity between a literal and an idiomatic interpretation.

(17) a. the janitor kicked the bucket
      b. she is ready to bite the bullet
      c. that drink really hit the spot
      d. they spent the afternoon shooting the bull

Regardless of their interpretations, these examples are usually assumed to involve a single phrase structure representation: the potentially idiomatic material, whether interpreted idiomatically or literally, is assigned an ordinary transitive verb structure. As Abeillé and Schabes (1989) note, TAG provides an alternative in which this meaning alternation is a case of structural ambiguity, in the derivational history. Example (17a), for instance, permits two distinct TAG derivations. In one, an elementary tree headed by the verb *kicked* is targeted by substitution of two DP elementary trees, associated with the lexical material *the janitor* and *the bucket*, a derivation essentially identical to the one seen in (3). Alternatively, the derivation involves only a single substitution operation: the DP *the janitor* substitutes into a complex elementary tree headed by the non-compositionally interpreted material *kicked the bucket*.[10] In both cases, the derived tree is the same, namely that of a simple transitive clause, though the derivational history is distinct. The fact that the semantic ambiguity is represented at the level of the derivation tree suggests that it is this level that should be the object of semantic interpretation. The assumption I will make, then, is that semantic composition is mirrored by the TAG operations, though not by the operations Merge and Move implicated in the construction of the elementary trees. See Kallmeyer and Romero (2008) and Han (2007) for discussion.

To represent these derivational histories, TAG defines an object called a *derivation tree*, similar in function to the T-markers in the theory of Chomsky (1955/1975) (cf. Chapter 2). In a derivation tree, each node N corresponds to an elementary tree T, and the children of N are the elementary trees that substitute or adjoin into T during the derivation. Because there may be multiple loci for substitution and adjoining in a single elementary tree, as seen in the derivation in (3), where each of the DPs could substitute into one of two possible sites, the derivation tree also encodes the node at which the operation takes place. This allows us to represent the two derivations of (17a) as the following pair of derivation trees:

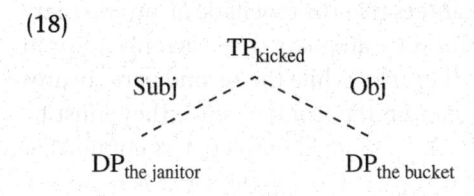

(18)

```
                TP_kicked
         Subj  ╱        ╲  Obj
              ╱          ╲
       DP_the janitor   DP_the bucket
```

(19)

```
     TP_kicked the bucket
         │
        Subj
         │
     DP_the janitor
```

In these derivation trees, elementary trees are represented via the label of their category root subscripted by the lexical material present in the tree. The dotted edges indicate that the operation involved was substitution. The 'Subj' and 'Obj' labels along the edges represent the loci of substitution.

To further illustrate the concept of derivation tree, consider the derivation of the long-distance raising example from (10).

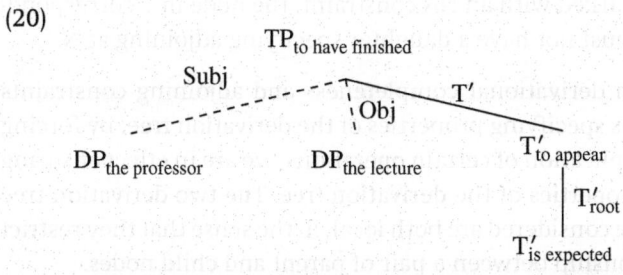

(20)

```
                    TP_to have finished
          Subj   ╱       │        ╲   T'
               ╱        Obj        ╲
        DP_the professor   DP_the lecture   T'_to appear
                                                │
                                              T'_root
                                                │
                                           T'_is expected
```

The solid edges in this derivation tree indicates that the combination was accomplished via adjoining. Such derivation trees are most straightforwardly read in a bottom-up fashion. In this derivation, then, one T'-recursive auxiliary tree *is expected* is adjoined into another one *to appear* at the T' root of the latter, with the resulting complex auxiliary tree adjoining into the infinitival transitive clause headed by the lexical verb *finished* at T'. This latter tree is also targeted by two instances of substitution, of the DP subject and object, as before.

Well-formed TAG derivations must abide by a number of formal conditions, in order to guarantee that all frontier non-terminals in the derived tree are filled by lexical material. These can be represented as follows:

(21) *Derivational Completeness*
   a. The root of a derivation tree cannot be an auxiliary tree.
   b. Any node of a derivation tree must have as many substitution daughter nodes as its corresponding elementary tree has substitution sites.

The first part of this definition guarantees that the foot node of any auxiliary tree cannot remain along the frontier since auxiliary trees can only occur in a derivation if they adjoin into another tree, while the second part ensures that substitution nodes do not remain on the frontier, since they must be targeted by substitution. As a result, Derivational Completeness entails that an elementary tree's frontier non-terminals whose appearance is regulated by the θ-criterion are filled by lexical material.

Derivations must also be structured so as to ensure the satisfaction of node constraints. For the case of selective substitution and adjoining, it is sufficient to add appropriate preconditions to the application of the TAG operations, so that these operations cannot target nodes not included in the selective specification. However, for obligatory and null adjoining constraints, we must constrain the derivation itself as follows:

(22) *Adjoining Constraints*
   a. If a derivation tree T includes an elementary tree E containing a node N marked with an OA constraint, the node in T corresponding to E must have a daughter specifying adjoining at N.
   b. If a derivation tree T includes an elementary tree E containing a node N marked with an NA constraint, the node in T corresponding to E must not have a daughter specifying adjoining at N.

The conditions on derivational completeness and adjoining constraints can both be seen as specifying properties of the derivation tree: by forcing or blocking the application of certain operations, we are in effect ensuring configurational properties of the derivation tree. The two derivation tree properties we have considered are both local, in the sense that they restrict at most the relationship between a pair of parent and child nodes.

The final property of TAG derivations imposes a similar kind of local requirement on TAG derivations, this time determining when the TAG derivational operations are possible. In the case of substitution, the derivation tree will involve two nodes A and B, with B corresponding to an elementary tree, say β, that is substituted into the elementary tree corresponding to A, say α. In this case, there is nothing more to be said beyond what was stated above in the definition of the operation: substitution simply requires that the root of β have the same label as the locus of substitution in α. In the case of adjoining, things are potentially somewhat more complex. Adjoining at a node labeled X requires a structure that is recursive on X. While such recursion can be present in an elementary auxiliary tree, one could also imagine such recursion arising from the combination of elementary trees, say via the substitution of one elementary tree into another, as follows:

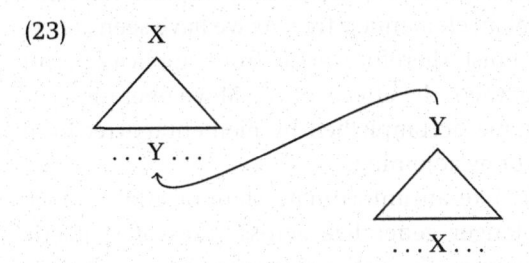

(23)

Note, however, that if such a derived structure could be used for adjoining, the determination of the well-formedness of an adjoining link in a derivation tree would necessitate a non-local process: we would need to compare the unboundedly distant root and foot node in the derived tree to determine whether the adjoining structure is appropriately recursive. To avoid this consequence, TAG derivations are constrained by the following property:

(24) Markovian Property of TAG Derivations
The well-formedness of a TAG operation is determined by the pair of elementary trees in a parent–child relationship in the derivation tree.

A Markovian process is one in which the possible next steps are determined only by the current state and not on the past. In the context of TAG derivations, this means all TAG operations should be thought of as operations that combine one elementary tree into another. By the Markovian assumption, any prior modification of an elementary tree via substitution or adjoining will not affect its ability to enter into subsequent derivational operations. Hence, even if a recursive structure can be created during the derivation, as it was in (23), it cannot serve as an input to the adjoining operation, unless the recursion was already present in one of the elementary trees (as it is in (20)). Said in a pithier way, in a TAG derivation auxiliary trees must be born and not made. Formally speaking, the Markovian property guarantees that the set of derivation trees of a particular TAG are particularly simple: they are what is called a *local set*, that is, they constitute a set of trees generable by a context-free grammar. Interestingly, as we shall see in Section 8.7, the derived trees need not have this property, and can encode dependencies beyond those expressible in a context-free grammar.

8.5 Redundancy in displacement?

Under the derivational architecture depicted in Figure 8.1, the Merge and Move operations apply only during the first stage of the derivation; once an elementary tree is used as input to one of the TAG operations, it may no longer be the target of Merge or Move operations. This has the effect of limiting the power of the Move operation, as it can only displace elements within the bounded domain of an elementary tree. As we have seen above, long-distance displacement must therefore arise from applications of adjoining. Under this picture, then, the effects of the Move operation are now divided in two, with some accomplished by elementary-tree-local Move, and others taken care of by adjoining.

On first glance, this seems like an unfortunate state of affairs, since it appears that we can no longer generalize across cases of syntactic displacement as having a common derivational source. Note, however, that the division into two modes of displacement does not simply introduce redundancy into the grammar: because of the way that the adjoining operation is defined, with its tight linkage to the creation of recursive syntactic structure, the kinds of displacement that can be derived using this operation are quite different in character from those generable by a (local) Move operation. While the Move operation is capable of reordering elements within a single elementary tree, displacement that results from adjoining cannot do so. The adjoining operation intercalates the lexical material contained in an auxiliary tree within the fixed structure (and order) of the tree that is targeted. Consequently, if two elements α and β in the same elementary tree stand in a particular precedence relation, say α precedes β, they must continue to do so even after adjoining applies, even if α is displaced away from β.[11]

If it turns out that unbounded displacements differ in their properties from local instances of movement, along the lines suggested by the division between Move and adjoining, this would constitute evidence in favor of the picture adopted here. In fact, there is at least one empirical domain where find precisely this pattern, namely non-verbal predications in English. Such predications, when they occur as small clause complements, are rigidly ordered, with subject preceding the predicate.

(25) a. I consider [Ted the cause of our problems]
b. *I consider [the cause of our problems Ted]

Yet, as is well-known, in the presence of the copula, such predications occur in both canonical and inverse orders, the latter exhibiting the reversal of subject and predicate.

(26) a. Ted is the cause of our problems
b. the cause of our problems is Ted

Moro (1997) assumes that the derivation of both kinds of copular constructions involves movement to the surface subject position: movement of the semantic subject derives the canonical order, while movement of the predicate derives the inverse order. Under this view, inversion is impossible in (25b) because the small clause, lacking a copula, does not provide the landing-site into which the subject or predicate can move. As a result, only the underlying subject–predicate order can surface.[12] This line of analysis leads us to the expectation that the addition of such a landing-site would render inversion possible. It is therefore suprising that if we make available a landing-site by passivizing the embedding predicate in (25b), inversion remains impossible.

(27) a. Ted is considered the cause of our problems
  b. *the cause of our problems is considered Ted

If the Move operation is implicated in both the derivation of inverse copula constructions like (26b) and raising passive constructions like (27b), this pattern is quite puzzling.[13] However, under the TAG architecture, it receives a straightforward explanation. Let us assume that the non-verbal predications in small clauses or copular constructions constitute the lexical core of individual elementary trees, with only the latter providing the functional structure necessary to provide a landing-site for inversion of the predicate. The verbal raising predicate *is considered* must, however, be generated as part of a separate elementary (auxiliary) tree, since it is headed by a separate lexical head. The examples in (27) will therefore be generated by adjoining this tree into the small clause tree, in a manner essentially identical to the raising derivation given in (9). Since inversion of the subject and predicate is not possible in the small clause elementary tree, as shown by the pattern in (25), it cannot obtain in the more complex structure. If we alter the complement of *consider* to include an infinitival copula, the pattern changes: now, not only is inversion possible within the complement, but also to the matrix subject.

(28) a. I consider Ted to be the cause of our problems
  b. I consider the cause of our problems to be Ted

(29) a. Ted is considered to be the cause of our problems
  b. the cause of our problems is considered to be Ted

This pattern follows directly, under the assumption that the infinitival copula is part of the functional structure of the DP predicate's elementary tree.

8.6 Deriving locality

Studies into the nature of filler–gap dependencies have been at the vanguard of theoretical development throughout the development of generative grammar (cf. the discussion in Chapter 18). The most significant issue in such studies has been the characterization and explanation of locality or island constraints, that is, the limits on the structures across which filler–gap dependencies can obtain. Work in the transformational tradition has derived such constraints through limitations imposed on a syntactic movement operation, such as Subjacency, or through representational constraints on the filler–gap dependency itself, such as Relativized Minimality.

As we observed earlier, the TAG-based system does not derive cases of filler–gap depencies in a uniform manner. Local displacement is derived from the application of a Move operation within an elementary tree, while long-distance movement results from adjoining. Consequently, it is simply impossible to derive locality from a derivational restriction on a single operation. A derivational view of locality fares no better: the derived tree is not the locus of syntactic constraints in the TAG framework, following the Fundamental TAG Hypothesis. This all leaves us with a vexing question: How can a TAG-based theory of syntax make sense of the well-attested locality restrictions on long-distance displacement? A failure to do so would constitute a substantial empirical deficiency.

It turns out that almost nothing needs to be added to TAG-based system of derivations already outlined to explain locality. As first discussed in Kroch (1987, 1989b) and studied in detail in Frank (2002), well-studied cases of syntactic locality in displacement follow as consequences of our derivational system, and do not require resort to additional stipulations. In this section, I will explore how this works in two kinds of cases: adjunct islands and relativized minimality effects (*wh*-islands and super-raising). Not only does this reduction of locality to properties of the TAG derivation lead to a simplification of the grammar, but it also suggests a deeper understanding of the nature of and reasons for syntactic locality, stemming from the properties of the recursive combinatory operations used to compose syntactic structure.[14]

8.6.1 Adjunct islands

As a first case of locality, let us consider cases of extraction from a well-known syntactic island, adjuncts. The following examples show such cases, involving two kinds of adjuncts, namely temporal adverbials and relative clauses.

(30) a. Who did you go to class [after you met]?
     b. What book did you visit a friend [who read]?

Such instances of extraction have been typically blocked because of some special property attributed to a syntactic category in an adjoined configuration, rendering it impenetrable to movement operations.

How might such examples be derived in TAG? By the θ-criterion, the displaced *wh*-element (more precisely a DP non-terminal into which the *wh*-phrase substitutes) must be part of the same elementary tree as the verb of which it is a thematic argument. For (30a), this means that elementary-tree-internal movement will give rise to an elementary tree of the following sort:[15]

(31)

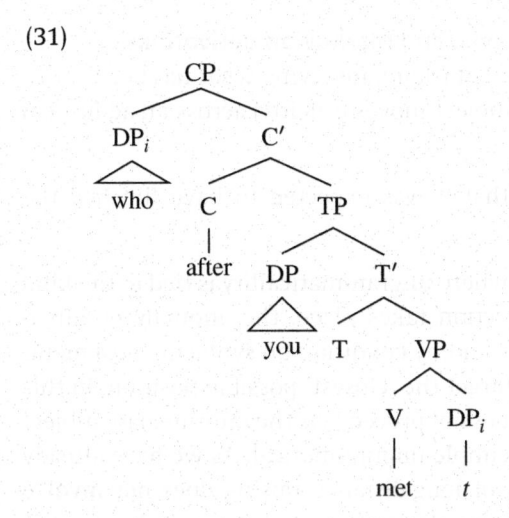

```
              CP
           /      \
         DPᵢ       C'
          |      /    \
         who   C       TP
               |     /    \
             after  DP    T'
                    |    /  \
                   you  T    VP
                           /    \
                          V     DPᵢ
                          |      |
                         met     t
```

Now, to derive (30a), we would need to exploit the following C'-recursive auxiliary structure:

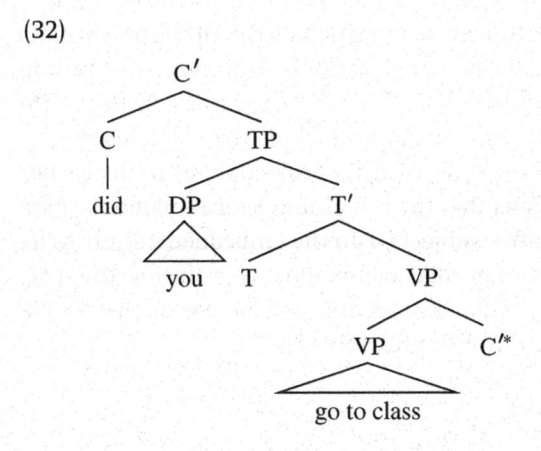

(32)

```
            C'
          /    \
         C      TP
         |    /    \
        did  DP    T'
             |    /   \
            you  T     VP
                      /    \
                    VP      C'*
                    |
                go to class
```

By adjoining this tree at the C' node in (31), we achieve the result of displacing the *wh*-phrase in (31) to the front of the sentence, yielding (30a). Though this derivation is impeccable from the TAG point of view, one of the elementary trees that is required runs afoul of the principles we have formulated concerning the nature of elementary trees. Specifically, in the tree in (32), the presence of the C' foot node violates the θ-criterion, since it is not assigned a role by the verb *go*. As we saw earlier in (5), one of the possible functions of adjoining is to introduce Chomsky-adjunction modification structures, and the θ-criterion in fact requires that it be used in such cases. This means, however, that we have arrived at an irremediable conflict: the θ-criterion demands that adjuncts adjoin into the structure that they modify, but displacement out of an adjunct is possible only if we adjoin the main clause into the adjunct.[16,17]

8.6.2 Super-raising, *wh*-islands, and Markovian derivations

Let us turn next to another kind of island, involving what has been called super-raising, where a raised subject moves (illicitly) across an additional clause.

(33) *the professor appears that it was expected to have finished the lecture

In contrast to adjunct islands, where ungrammaticallity is tied to the kind of domain out of which extraction takes place, the anomaly of super-raising has been linked to an economy condition on syntactic movement, namely that it should always target the 'closest' possible position. In this case, the fact that movement does not proceed via the intermediate subject (occupied by *it*) renders the example ungrammatical. As we have already observed, the TAG derivation of long-distance raising does not involve movement to positions in intermediate clauses. Consequently, there is simply no way to incorporate an explanation of the anomaly of (33) as a violation of a closest move condition.

Consider instead how (33) would be derived in TAG. By the θ-criterion, the elementary tree headed by *finished* must include the DP argument slots that will ultimately be filled by *the professor* and *the lecture* via substitution, since it is *finished* that assigns these DPs their thematic roles. By the CETM the *finished*-headed elementary tree will also include the extended projection of V, including at least the infinitival T's projection, as in the earlier raising derivations. This means that the remaining lexical material, spanning from the end of the matrix subject DP to the embedded infinitival *to*, must be added to the *finished*-headed elementary tree during the TAG derivation. Adjoining of the following recursive structure at the T'node of the *finished* tree would accomplish precisely this.

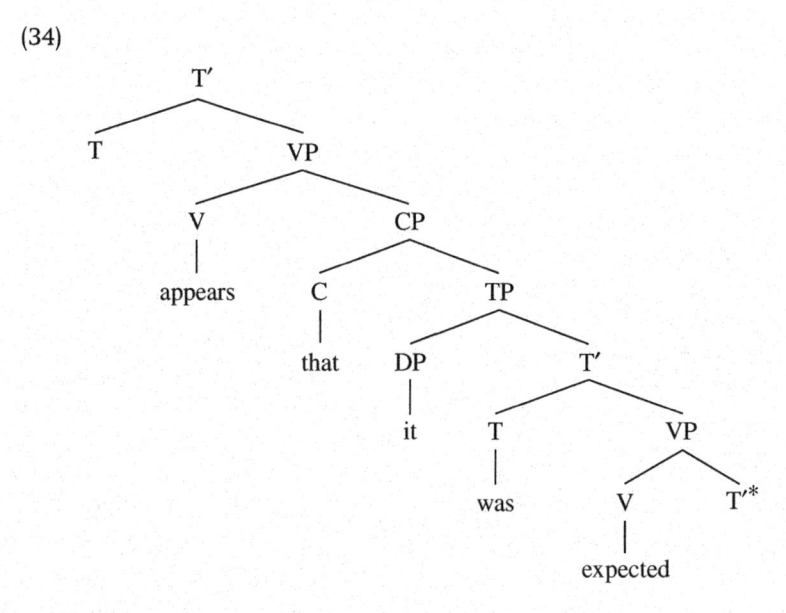

(34)

```
              T'
             /  \
            T    VP
                /  \
               V    CP
               |   /  \
           appears C   TP
                   |  /  \
                 that DP   T'
                      |   / \
                      it T   VP
                         |  /  \
                        was V   T'*
                            |
                        expected
```

The CETM tells us that this recursive structure cannot be an elementary tree, since it includes the extended projections of two predicates, namely *appears* and *expected*. This means that (34) must be derived through the combination of (two) elementary trees. Given the CETM, the most natural decomposition of this structure is into the following pair of elementary trees:

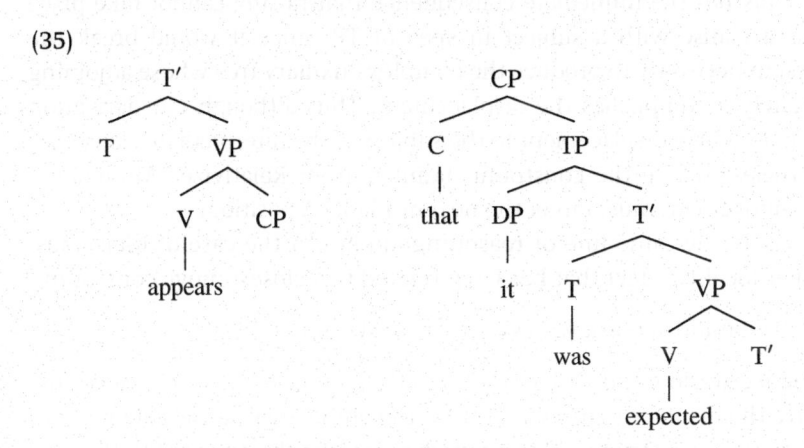

(35)

```
        T'                                CP
       / \                               /  \
      T   VP                            C    TP
         / \                            |   /  \
        V   CP                        that DP   T'
        |                                  |   / \
     appears                               it  T  VP
                                               |  / \
                                              was V  T'
                                                  |
                                              expected
```

The derivation could now proceed via the substitution of the *expected* tree into the CP complement node in the *appears* tree. The resulting derivation gives rise to the derivation tree in (36).

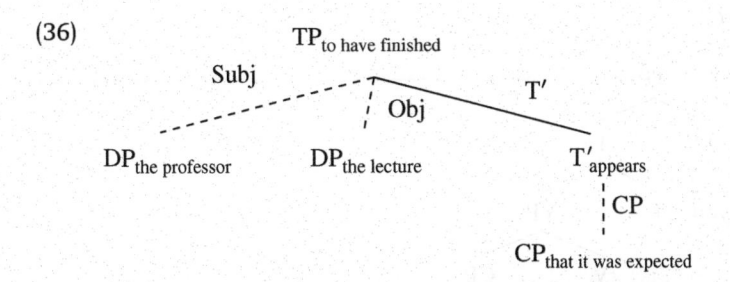

(36)

```
                    TP to have finished
         Subj    ⋰         ⋱           T'
       ⋰       ⋰  Obj         ⋱
  DP the professor  DP the lecture    T' appears
                                          ┆
                                          ┆ CP
                                          ┆
                                       CP that it was expected
```

Though this derivation tree looks strikingly like the one in (20), there is a crucial difference: this one does not abide by the Markovian property of TAG derivations. The offending operation involves the adjoining of the T'$_{appears}$ elementary tree into the *finished* tree. By the Markovian property, the well-formedness of this operation must be determinable by the properties of the two elementary trees that are participating in adjoining. However, the elementary tree being adjoined is not an auxiliary tree, and is therefore ineligible for this operation. Thus, even though the composite structure derived by substitution is recursive, it cannot function as an auxiliary tree for the purposes of the TAG derivation.

It is useful to consider what property of the displacement in super-raising results in the unavailability of a Markovian derivation. In the case of the well-formed derivation in (20), recursion at the T' level is a property of the auxiliary tree that is ultimately adjoined to accomplish displacement of the raised DP, as well as of the auxiliary tree that adjoins into it, extending the distance of the displacement. If any of the clauses are larger, such adjoining will no longer be possible, as we have seen, meaning that no clauses that intervene along the path of raising can include any structure above the level of T'. This has the immediate consequence that raising cannot take place across a clause with a subject in spec of TP, since it would break the recursion necessary to produce the complex auxiliary tree whose adjoining ultimately accomplishes the displacement. Thus although our derivation does not include displacement to the subject of the intermediate clause, we nonetheless derive the constraint, familiar from Relativized Minimality, that A-movement must target the next available A-position.

Precisely the same line of reasoning applies in the case of *wh*-islands, another locality effect that has been related to a closest move constraint.

(37) *What did you ask who said that we should bring?

By the θ-criterion and CETM, the TAG derivation of this sentence must involve the displacement of *what* from the embedded clause's elementary tree. Assuming a structure for *wh*-movement like the one in (11), this will involve the adjoining of the following structure at C' of the *bring*-headed elementary tree.

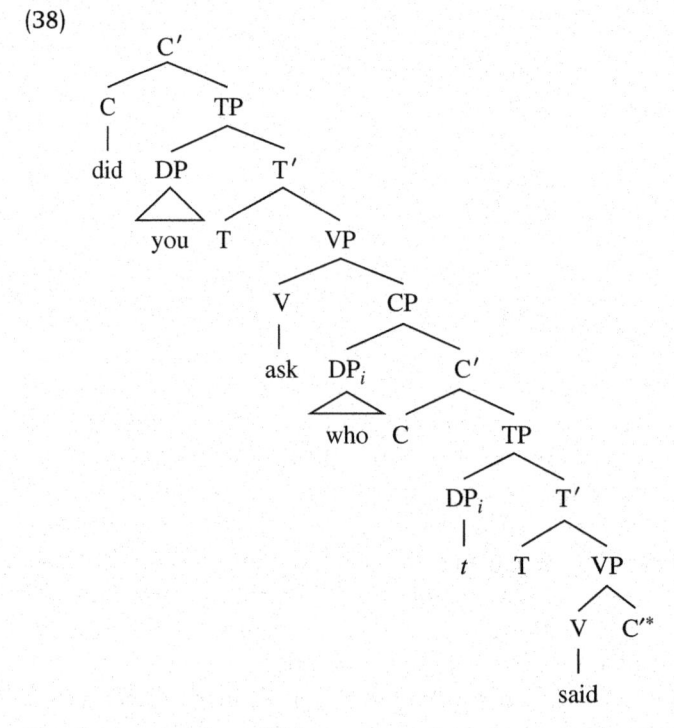

(38)

```
              C'
             /  \
            C    TP
            |   /  \
           did DP   T'
              /\   /  \
            you T  VP
                  /  \
                 V    CP
                 |   /  \
                ask DP_i C'
                    /\  /  \
                  who C  TP
                        /  \
                      DP_i  T'
                       |   /  \
                       t  T    VP
                              /  \
                             V   C'*
                             |
                            said
```

The decomposition of this structure forced upon us by the CETM results in two non-recursive structure, one spanning from C' to CP and the other from CP to C'. As a result, the combination of these structures can only proceed via substitution, and by the Markovian property, the result cannot serve as an auxiliary tree.

The TAG derivation of the locality effect of *wh*-islands can be overcome if we modify the structural position that the displaced *wh*-phrase occupies in its base clause. In the derivation of (37), I assumed that the *wh*-phrase *what* is located in the specifier of CP. Because the sister node of the specifier is C', displacement of this phrase required adjoining of a C'-recursive auxiliary tree. Suppose however we were to permit *wh*-phrases to reside in an 'outer' specifier position, whose sister is a full CP. If so, the structure that would need to be adjoined in, corresponding to (38), could be recursive on CP.

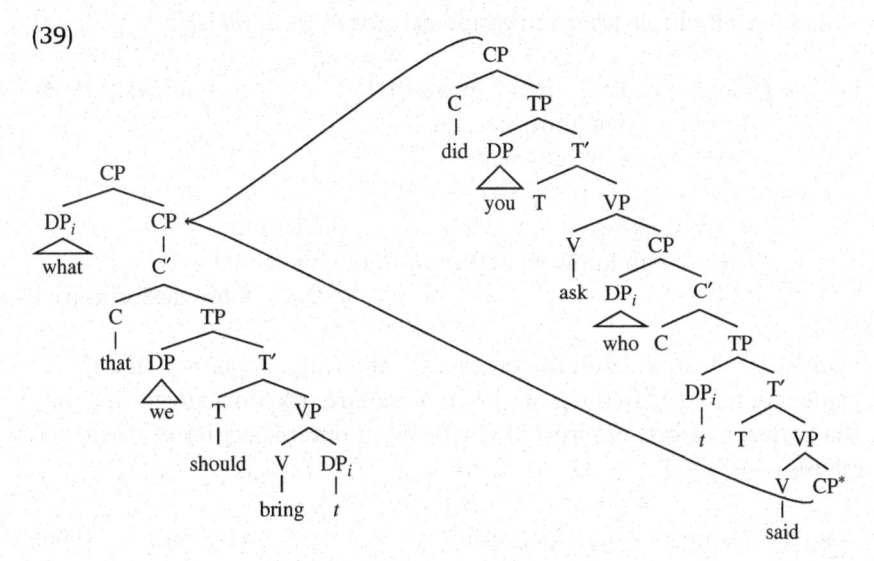

(39)

[Tree diagram showing CP structure with DP_i "what", CP with C' containing "that we should bring t", and a larger CP structure with "did you ask who C said" and trace DP_i, with CP* as the foot node.]

Under these structural assumptions, there is nothing blocking the TAG derivation, since a complex structure corresponding to (38) can be derived through adjoining and then be used to accomplish the displacement, in accordance with the Markovian property. The derivation tree for (37) would be as follows:

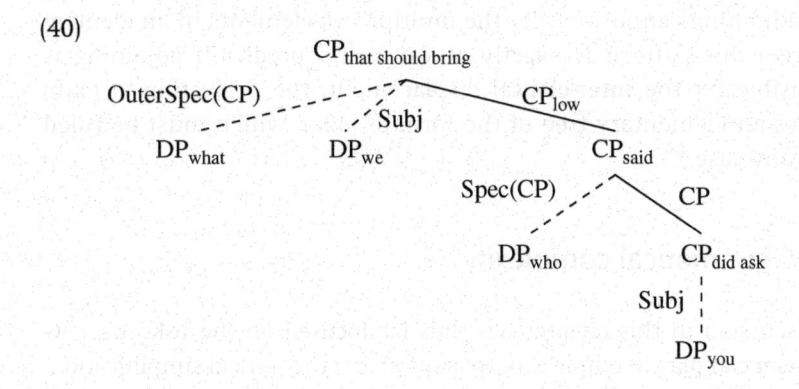

(40)

[Derivation tree with CP_{that should bring} at top, with children OuterSpec(CP) → DP_{what}, Subj → DP_{we}, and CP_{low} → CP_{said}, with Spec(CP) → DP_{who} and CP_{did ask} with Subj → DP_{you}.]

Here, *did you ask* adjoins at the root CP of the auxiliary tree *who said*. Since the latter is an auxiliary tree, this derived structure can undergo adjoining at the lower CP *what that we should bring*, deriving (37).

Of course, we want to rule out such a derivation for English, as extraction from *wh*-islands is not generally possible. As noted originally by Kroch (1989b), we can do this by prohibiting English *wh*-phrases from occupying such an outer specifier of CP. Kroch observes that this line of explanation makes the prediction that languages that do permit such specifiers, as evidenced by the possibility of multiple *wh*-fronting in a single clause, should tolerate *wh*-island-violating extractions. And indeed, this prediction appears correct. For instance, as the following examples show, Romanian allows both multiple *wh*-fronting and extraction from *wh*-islands.

(41) a. Cine despre ce   mi-a   povestit?   (Comorovski 1996)
      who about   what me-has told
      'Who told me about what?'
  b. Cine$_j$ știi   {despre ce$_i$ t$_j$ i-a   povestit t$_i$}?
      who you know about what him.DAT-has told
      'Who do you know what (he) has told him about?'
                                                                    (C. Dobrovie-Sorin, p.c.)

Strikingly, constraints on the ordering of multiple *wh*-phrases in a single clause are reflected in the patterns of *wh*-island extraction, suggesting that the path for extraction crucially involves an outer specifier of the lower clause.

(42) a. *Despre ce   cine ți-a vorbit?   (Comorovski 1996)
      about what who   you-has told
  b. *Despre ce$_i$ știi   {cine$_j$ t$_j$ i-a   povestit t$_i$}?
      about what you know   who   him.DAT-has told
      'What do you know who told him about?'
                                                                    (Comorovski 1996)

Since adjoining cannot reorder the multiple *wh*-elements in an elementary tree, this pattern is exactly as we would predict if adjoining is responsible for the inter-clausal displacement: the derivation of (42b) requires an elementary tree of the form of (42a), which must be ruled out in any case.[18]

8.7 Grammatical complexity

The discussion in this chapter has thus far focused on the role the TAG formalism can play in empirical explanation and theoretical simplification. While these are worthy goals in and of themselves, the use of TAG in syntactic theory is also motivated by questions of formal complexity. In this concluding section, I will briefly review the contributions that TAG makes in this connection.

More than half a century ago, Chomsky (1956, 1957) posed the question of how much formal power a grammar needs in order to capture linguistic regularities. By identifying the most restrictive system sufficient for the task of grammatical description, he hoped to uncover mathematically definable restrictions on human grammatical knowledge, restrictions which would constitute part of Universal Grammar. In order to assess the formal power of a grammar, he defined the notion of a *formal language* as a set of objects, most commonly a set of strings but also sometimes a set of more structured objects such as trees, graphs, or derivations. He then proposed to diagnose the formal power of a grammatical system in terms of the formal languages that it can define. One system is more restrictive than another, then, if it can define a more limited class of formal languages.

On the basis of the patterns of recursion found in center-embedded/nested sentences, where we find a mirror-image pattern between a sequence of verbs and their associated arguments, Chomsky presented a formal proof that regular grammars were inadequate as a model of grammar. Chomsky went on to argue that context-free grammars were inadequate on the basis of naturalness of explanation of phenomena involving displacement. Because of the purported inadequacy of context-free grammars, Chomsky adopted a more powerful system for grammatical representation, one incorporating grammatical transformations. Peters and Ritchie (1973) demonstrated, however, that such a move marked a death knell for the goal of deriving properties of Universal Grammar from formal restrictions, as transformational grammars impose essentially no restriction on what formal languages can be defined by a possible grammar.

Work in Generalized Phrase Structure Grammar (Gazdar et al. 1985) (cf. Chapter 7) resurrected inquiry into formally constrained models of syntactic knowledge, questioning Chomsky's abandonment of context-free grammars. The developers of GPSG added to the context-free formalism a system of features and metarules, thereby allowing a satisfying treatment of displacement, without increasing its formal power. As in the TAG framework, GPSG practitioners demonstrated that certain properties of grammar (e.g., the coordinate structure constraint) followed from the combination of properties of the formalism and independently necessary assumptions, and did not require additional stipulations. The GPSG enterprise was, however, cast into doubt by the work of Shieber (1985) and Culy (1985), who provided rigorous arguments against the linguistic adequacy of context-free grammars (or any formal equivalent). Their arguments centered on the existence of linguistic patterns that show cross-serial dependencies, where dependent elements come not in a mirror-image order, but in the same order as the elements on which they depend. To take Shieber's example, cross-serial dependencies are found in the ordering of verbs and nouns in Swiss

German embedded clauses, as the following example illustrates, with subscripts indicating verb–argument relations.

(43) ... das mer₁ em Hans₂ s huus₃ händwele₁ hälfe₂ aastriiche₃
... that we Hans.DAT the house.ACC have wanted helps paint
'... that we wanted to help Hans paint the house'

It can be easily shown that formal languages which enforce such dependencies cannot be generated by context-free systems, and hence they present an insurmountable obstacle to a context-free equivalent formalism like GPSG.

It appears, then, that Chomsky's move beyond context-free systems was formally justified. However, the enormity of the jump in power from context-free systems to transformational grammars was necessary only because of the nature of the hierarchy of grammars that Chomsky was exploring. This hierarchy lacks a class of grammars that constitutes a conservative step in expressive power beyond the formal languages definable by context-free grammars, what we can call the context-free languages.

Thirty years after Chomsky's early work, Joshi (1985) took up the investigation of formal constraints on grammar once again, attempting to define a class of *formal languages* that is sufficiently powerful to capture the regularities of natural language, and therefore more powerful than context-free, but still substantially restricted, thereby retaining the possibility of providing insight into the nature of Universal Grammar. In particular, Joshi defines a class of formal languages that he called the *mildly context-sensitive languages* (MCSLs), which is characterized by three properties:

(44) a. The MCSLs contain the context-free languages, but can also capture limited cross-serial dependencies of the sort necessary to characterize natural languages.
b. The MCSLs are parsable in polynomial time.
c. The MCSLs have the constant growth property: For every MCSL L there is a bound k such that for every sentence $w \in L$, there is another sentence $w' \in L$ such that $|w| < |w'| < |w| + k$.

The first property sets a lower bound on the complexity of MCSLs, requiring that they extend the context-free grammars, and be able to represent the kinds of dependencies found, for instance, in Swiss German.[19] The second and third properties impose upper bounds on the complexity of the MCSLs, guaranteeing that they are less complex than full context-sensitivity. Polynomial time parseability means that there is an efficient procedure for determining if a sentence is generated by a grammar and if it is, for assigning it a structural description. This ensures the processing of MCSLs will require limited computational complexity. The constant growth property demands that a MCSL must 'grow' in a simple fashion: longer sentences come into the language by adding units of fixed, bounded length, rather than through complex interactions with the material that came before.

Joshi puts forward the strong hypothesis that natural languages, understood in terms of their surface forms, fall entirely within the mildly context-sensitive class. The few arguments that have been advanced against this hypothesis (Radzinski 1991, Becker et al. 1992, Michaelis and Kracht 1997) have been found wanting (Joshi et al. 2000, Bhatt and Joshi 2004), suggesting that Joshi's hypothesis may well be correct. If so, it points to a severe and surprising computational restriction on possible grammars. Such a restriction would of course require explanation in any theory of syntactic knowledge.

One line of explanation for the mild context-sensitivity of human language could of course come from the properties of the formal system in which grammatical knowledge is represented. In this connection, it is interesting to observe that there is an interesting relationship between the formal languages generable by TAG and mild context-sentitivity. Note first that TAG can generate cross-serial dependencies of the Swiss German sort, using the following pair of trees:

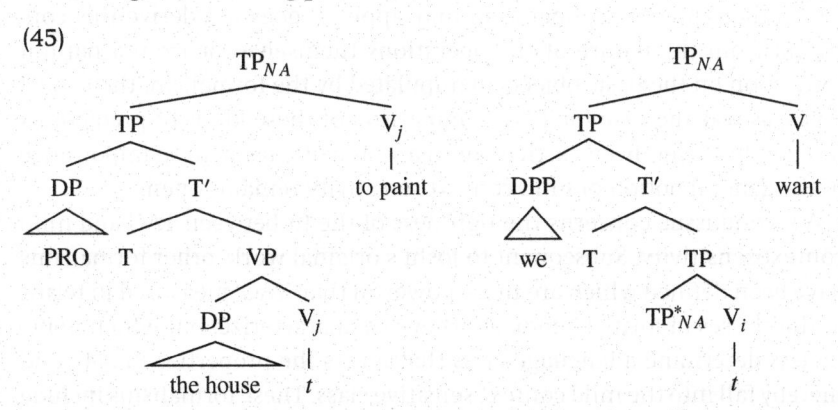

(45)

[Tree 1: TP_{NA} dominating TP and V_j; TP dominates DP (PRO T) and T' (VP); VP dominates DP (the house) and V_j (t); V_j = to paint]

[Tree 2: TP_{NA} dominating TP and V (want); TP dominates DPP (we) and T' dominates T and TP; TP dominates TP^*_{NA} and V_i (t)]

By adjoining the *we want* tree to the internal TP node (without an NA constraint) in the *to paint the house* tree), we derive the cross-serial ordering. This process can be iterated to construct unboundedly many such crossing dependencies.[20] Joshi (1985) points out that the formal languages definable by TAG, the Tree Adjoining Languages (TALs), also satisfy the other two properties in (44), namely they are parsable in polynomial time, and they abide by the constant growth property. Consequently, the TAG formalism can be seen as a candidate for a characterization of the mildly context-sensitive languages, and a syntactic theory that is couched in terms of the TAG formalism would provide an account of the limited complexity found in natural language.

As we have seen in this chapter, TAG contributes to syntactic theory not only in limiting its formal complexity, but also by providing explanations for constraints on grammatical dependencies. Given our current discussion, we might wonder whether it is the notion of mild context-sensitivity that is responsible for the derivation of such constraints on possible human grammars, or whether it is a more parochial property of the TAG formalism. This question is the topic of ongoing work, but there are a number of comments that can be made in this connection.

First, note that Joshi et al. (1991) establish that a number of independently proposed grammar formalisms, including Combinatory Categorial Grammar (CCG), Head Grammars, and Linear Indexed Grammars, are equivalent to TAG in their weak generative capacity. This means that the formal languages that these formalisms allow one to define are equivalent to the languages that are definable by TAG. This convergence on the one hand suggests a remarkable unanimity about the power that is necessary to characterize language. And yet, these formalisms do appear to differ in the predictions they make about the kind of patterns we should expect to find in the languages of the world, and the degree to which they allow us to derive substantive grammatical constraints from the formalism. For example, while TAG predicts that displacement from one syntactic domain to a higher one must proceed to the edge of the higher domain, CCG does not. Similarly, while CCG allows one to express the islandhood of adjuncts (Steedman 1996) in terms of a stipulated constraint on the contexts in which the type raising operation may apply, it does not derive this constraint from the nature of the operations themselves or from a natural restriction on the basic objects manipulated by the formalism, the lexical types, as was the case for TAG. Comparison of these kinds of predictions has not, however, been carried out in a systematic fashion, so importance of the general notion of mild context-sensitivity remains open.

A second issue concerns the tightness of the fit between TAG and mild context-sensitivity. Subsequent to Joshi's original work, other formalisms have been defined which are more powerful than TAG, measured in terms of the classes of formal languages they can characterize, but which nonetheless determine a language class that meets the properties in (44), and thereby fall into the mild context-sensitive class. These formalisms include Linear Context-Free Rewriting Systems, set-local Multicomponent Tree Adjoining Grammars, Multiple Context-Free Grammars, and Minimalist Grammars. The degree to which these formalisms impose interesting constraints on possible linguistic patterns is one which has received little study to date, though it is clear that they will not derive all of the TAG restrictions discussed in this chapter.

Finally, it is important to observe that the notion of mild context-sensitivity of a class of grammars concerns the notion of weak generative capacity, as it deals with questions of the formal languages it can define. As has often been pointed out, strong generative capacity, with its focus on the structural descriptions that a formalism assigns to sentences, is the much more interesting notion for linguistic theory. Strong generative capacity has been considerably more difficult to tackle formally. It currently remains open whether there is a notion comparable to mild context-sensitivity in the realm of strong generative capacity that could point to interesting limits on the kinds of grammatical structures we find.

Notes

1. Categorial grammar embraces the idea that hierarchy is fundamental, and posits operations that are responsible for the creation of hierarchical structure. However, it eschews an operation specifically designed to deal with displacement, instead enriching the class of operations that build hierarchical structure to accomplish the effects of displacement.
2. See Joshi and Schabes (1997) and Abeillé and Rambow (2000: Chapter 1) for more formally oriented introductions to the TAG framework.
3. One could alternatively take terminals to be the specification of a grammatical category (features) into which word forms are later inserted. In the elementary trees in previous work, I have adopted the former answer. Certainly, this choice aids readabilty, and I will continue it here, though the alternative deserves serious consideration.
4. Substitution of the DPs in this derivation does not yield a recursive result: there is no embedding of a node of one sort within another of the same sort in the resulting tree. As a result, one might argue that this operation is not tightly tied to the recursive property of syntactic structures. It is worth noting, however, that substitution is capable of creating recursive structures. For instance, the substitution of the clausal complement of a verb into an elementary tree would induce recursion. Because the other TAG operation, adjoining, can only introduce a single instance of recursion into a structural domain, substitution is necessarily implicated in recursive structures which are multiply recursive, such as sentences with clausal arguments in both subject and object positions.
5. It is also worth noting that such constraints are formally necessary to ensure that TAG has the closure properties to constitute what is called a full abstract family of languages (Vijay-Shanker 1987).
6. Adding a projection of v, in whose specifier the subject is assigned a role, would have no effect on the TAG derivation, and could be accommodated straightforwardly in the system being sketched here.
7. Nor does the absence of intermediate landing-sites impede our ability to account for other phenomena implicating successive-cyclic movement in A- and A'-movement, including for example scope reconstruction, complementizer agreement, and inversion (Frank 2002:81–89, 186–87).
8. This corollary leads us to be suspicious of instances of the existence of non-local dependencies that do not support such a factoring. In Frank (2004, 2006), I show that two such cases, Hungarian focus movement and cross-clausal agreement, are in fact better analyzed in other ways.
9. In order to license the foot nodes in modifier auxiliary trees like the adverbially headed auxiliary in (5), I assume that a modifier enters into a thematic relation with the element that it modifies, sufficient to satisfy the θ-criterion. However, to account for differences in projection,

I assume that this relation involves a different semantic relation, possibly along the lines of θ-modification (Higginbotham 1985) or predicate modification (Heim and Kratzer 1998). The set of thematic relations relevant to the θ-criterion will also need to be expanded to include a predication role, relevant in licensing the appearance of expletives in non-thematic subject position.

10. The question arises about whether this idiomatic tree obeys the CETM. Assuming we want to maintain this analysis of idioms, we will need to define lexical head in a way such that the entire idiom constitutes the extended projection of single lexical head.
11. See Frank (2010) for further exploration of this idea. This result recalls the proposal of Fox and Pesetsky (2005), under which only phase-local movement can accomplish reordering.
12. See Heycock (1995b) for discussion of a kind of small clause that does include additional functional structure, thereby rendering inversion possible.
13. Though see den Dikken (2006b) for a possible account.
14. The use of functional uncertainty in the LFG treatment of unbounded dependencies (Kaplan and Zaenen 1989) also posits a link between recursion and syntactic locality, with interesting connections to TAG, as Joshi and Vijay-Shanker (1989) point out.
15. For simplicity, I have assumed here that *after* is analyzed as a prepositional complementizer, forming part of the extended projection of the verb. If we take the preposition to constitute its own extended projection, the derivation is still blocked, but the argument to show why is somewhat more complex. See Frank (2002) for detailed discussion.
16. Truswell (2011) discusses a class of exceptions to the islandhood of adjunct clauses, which he argues to be correlated with the main and adjunct clauses having a single event structure (cf. Section 18.4). If his semantic characterization of these cases is correct, this would require a modification of the TAG θ-criterion to incorporate reference to event structure, and thereby allow frontier non-terminals corresponding to certain cases of adjuncts.
17. From this discussion, it would appear that the θ-criterion should also have the effect of ruling out adjunct *wh*-questions of the *When did you leave?* sort: the *wh*-phrase must apparently substitute into a non-projected non-terminal in the specifier of CP, yet this specifier is not part of a chain that is assigned a role in the tree. A number of paths might be followed to allow for an analysis of such cases. In one, we can deny the fact that such a specifier is illicit, allowing it to be licensed either by the predication role suggested in note 9 to account for expletive subjects, or possible by the presence of EPP features. See Frank (2002:281, n. 12) for some discussion. An alternative path might take the overt position of adjunct *wh*-phrases to be different from that

of argument *wh*-phrases: rather than being substituted into the specifier of CP, they would be adjoined to CP.
18. As is well-known, English does allow certain cases of extraction from *wh*-islands and other so-called weak islands. To account for such cases, and explain their sensitivity to referentiality/D-linking, one can exploit the Multi-Component version of TAG. For discussion and references, see Frank (2002: Sections 5.6–7)
19. Since the range of the cross-serial dependencies that needs to be captured is not made explicit in this statement, the statement in (44) does not strictly speaking constitute a definition for MCSLs. Nonetheless, from the point of view of providing a lower bound on the language class, this statement is useful.
20. See Kroch and Santorini (1991) for justification of this analysis and extensions.

Part III

Syntactic structures

9

Argument structure and argument structure alternations

Gillian Ramchand

9.1 Introduction

One of the major scientific results of Chomskian syntactic theory is the understanding that the symbolic representations of natural language are *structured*, by which I mean that symbols are organized in hierarchical constituent data structures, and are not simply linearly ordered strings or lists of memorized items. The semantic 'arguments' of predicates are expressed within natural language data structures, and therefore also form part of structured representations. This chapter is devoted to examining the major theoretical results pertaining to the semantics of verbal predicate argument relations and their systematic patterning in language. However, we will see that even isolating the logical domain of inquiry will involve certain deep questions about the architecture of grammar, and the relationship between listedness and compositional semantics.

Historically, the most important results in argument structure have come from those studying the properties of the Lexicon as a module of grammar, for a number of rather natural reasons as we will see. While this chapter will aim to give the reader a clear historical and ideological context for the subject matter and will document major influential strands of research, it will primarily concentrate on extracting the generalizations that I judge to be the lasting results of the past fifty years, and then secondarily, draw attention to the (still unresolved) architectural and theoretical issues that are specific to this domain.

Section 9.2 gives the perspective on the issues from the vantage point of the Lexicon, i.e. the practical problem of deciding how much and what kind of information is necessary for the listing of verbal lexical entries. It also serves as a kind of historical contextualization and background for the later sections of the article which describe the morphosyntactic patterns more generally. Section 9.3 gives a morphosyntactic overview of the patterns in argument structure related to SUBJECT selection. Section 9.4 does the same for the OBJECT position. While Sections 9.3 and 9.4 are basically about grammatical function, Section 9.5 reviews the correlations with one other important interacting syntactic phenomenon, namely case (see also Chapter 17). Section 9.6 explores the relationship between argument structure and the architectural interfaces, discussing in particular the interaction with discourse and cognitive facts (9.6.1), and the modular interaction between the Lexicon and the syntactic computation (9.6.2) in accounting for argument structure generalizations.

9.2 The View from the Lexicon

The history of isolating 'argument structure' as a distinct domain of inquiry in the modern era begins with notions of subcategorization and the specification of the information that a speaker knows when they know individual words (specifically, verbs) in their language. Thus, it was recognized early on that phrase-structure rules needed to be supplemented with a Lexicon that stated conditions of insertion for individual items, which included not just category membership but also context of insertion (Chomsky 1957, 1965). So, while the phrase-structure rule for VP might allow for optional NP, CP, or other kinds of complements to V, the lexical entry of an individual verb would ensure that it could only be inserted if the 'matching' phrase structure rewrite rule had been chosen. A toy example is shown in (1).

(1) Phrase Structure Rule: VP → V (NP/CP)
Lexical Entry for *hit*: V; ___NP
Lexical Entry for *deny*: V; ___CP
Lexical Entry for *dine*: V; ___

Variability in a particular verb's insertion possibilities could be captured in one of two ways: one could either list two distinct lexical entries with slightly different subcategorization frames (2i), or optionality could be built in to the subcategorization frame of a single entry as in (2ii).

(2) (i) Lexical Entry for *believe*$_1$: V; ___NP
Lexical Entry for *believe*$_2$: V; ___CP
(ii) Lexical Entry for *eat*: V; ___(NP)

Built into this system is the idea that a distinction needs to be made between lexical information that is relevant to the syntax, and that which is not. The lexical entry for *eat* above does not exhaust what the speaker knows when they know that word of English. A messy and sometimes conventional, sometimes idiosyncratic collection of conceptual information and associations goes along with each lexical item as well. Some of this information is implicated in judgments of infelicity, as opposed to straight up ungrammaticality. For example, the verb *eat* requires as its SUBJECT an entity which imbibes, or is at least living; an inanimate or abstract SUBJECT sounds nonsensical at worst, and poetic (requiring metaphoric interpretation) at best (3).

(3)   ♯ happiness ate the apple

Such information is often discussed under the heading of 'semantic selectional restrictions (s(emantic)-selection)' and not included in the formal lexical information about subcategorization for particular syntactic categories (c(ategory)-selection) (Chomsky 1965). Of course, the relationship between these types of information is potentially more complicated. In the case of argument selection, one possibility is that a lexical verb has a semantic selectional requirement, which, because of 'canonical realization rules' mapping from denotations to syntactic category, *translates* into particular c-selectional requirements (see Grimshaw 1979, 1981 for the idea that c-selection and s-selection are autonomous subsystems with 'canonical' mapping principles). This raises the question of whether c-selection needs to be stated independently at all – Pesetsky (1985) argues that they might be made to follow from independently needed statements about case assignment. However, more recent syntactic thinking casts doubt on the idea of the GB style 'Case Filter' as a primitive of grammar (rightly, I think), placing the burden back onto a basic notion of c-selection. There are two important ideas not to lose sight of here. First, the idea that some lexical information is relevant for syntactic behavior and some not remains an important truth, which should not be ignored as more detailed systems of argument classification are proposed. Specifically, distinctions in verb meaning must be encoded only insofar as they have systematic effects in the grammar. Second, some form of syntactic selection seems to be a fact of life, and cannot and should not be ignored when specifiying the grammar (Emonds 2000), hopefully reducible to selection for syntactic category of complement (Svenonius 1992).

To an important degree of approximation, the early systems of phrase-structure rule and lexical subcategorization frame worked very well, although they already raised the question of how to decide when separate lexical items were appropriate, or when the 'same' item was being used in two different ways. When two distinct alternants are available, as in the case of *give* (V; ___NP NP and V; ___NP PP) a single entry with optionality brackets does not suffice. If two lexical entries are given, how does one represent the fact that the two entries are related? In the case of the dative alternation, it was problematic that the alternation seemed to be *systematic* to a particular class of transfer predicates (see Oehrle 1976 for an important early study). Since the lexicon was supposed to be the repository of idiosyncratic memorized information, listing each transfer verb and its alternants individually raised the obvious spectre of the 'Missed Generalization.'

Indeed, missed generalizations were to be the driving force behind much of the early work on lexical argument structure: if thematic roles could be classified abstractly, and if patterns could be discerned across verb classes, then that was an obvious advance on mere listing. Such generalizations were noticed very early in the generative tradition (Gruber 1965, Fillmore 1968) and attempts were made to describe overarching principles that accounted for them. These generalizations could be stated in terms of general transformations as in Fillmore (1968), or in terms of a filter as in the case of the work of Gruber (1965). The publication of Chomsky's 'Remarks on Nominalization' (Chomsky 1970a) convinced many that there was another source or locus for stating generalizations/rules other than through transformations, and the tradition of capturing argument structure regularities in the Lexicon was born. Thus, alternations that were systematic could now be captured by rule, in this case 'Lexical Redundancy Rules' (Jackendoff 1972, 1975) since they represented a general pattern (apparently internal to the Lexicon). Although Chomsky himself did not advocate this move, it was a natural one for people to make, given the number of other generalizations that needed to be captured in the different realizations of related lexical items. I quote from Jackendoff (1975) here, to underline the point.

> Without transformations to relate *decide* and *decision*, we need to develop some other formalism. Chomsky takes the position that *decide* and *decision* constitute a single lexical entry, unmarked for the syntactic feature that distinguishes verbs from nouns. The phonological form *decision* is inserted into base trees under the node N; *decide* is inserted under V. Since Chomsky gives no arguments for this particular formulation, I feel free to adopt here the alternative theory that *decide* and *decision* have distinct but related lexical entries. (Jackendoff 1975: 640–41)

Thus, while Marantz (1997) is correct in pointing out that Chomsky's actual position in 'Remarks' may have been closer to the current Distributed Morphology (DM) idea of acategorial roots (see Section 9.6.2), the fact remains that the attack on over-powerful transformations provoked many linguists to seek a systematic alternative in terms of the lexicon, where the notion of selection/projection could be maintained and where generalizations of a different nature could be stated (specifically, argument structure generalizations). (We will return to a discussion of the DM position in relation to lexicalism in the final section of this chapter.) In fact, Jackendoff's solution for expressing the "relations between lexical entries" in terms of 'lexical redundancy rules' was not intended to be a transformational device, but rather the expression of the degree of redundancy between lexical entries that would be input to an economy metric that assessed the overall economy of the grammar which contained them.

The dominance of lexical theories in the domain of argument structure throughout the seventies and eighties is thus largely the result of contingent factors in the way the theory developed. It is important to realize that the very earliest work (cf. Gruber 1965 vs. Fillmore 1968) was divided about the place in the grammar where such generalizations should be located. I think those questions have resurfaced today, essentially because they were never really resolved. The major portion of the chapter however, will deal with outlining what we know about the actual generalizations themselves. Since much of that work is couched in a lexicalist framework, we need to first examine the tools that became current in the early stages of the theory. As we proceed, it will be important to keep separate the tools used in a specific type of theory, from the generalizations that they aim to express.

9.2.1 The rise and fall of thematic roles and thematic hierarchies

An early and important strategy for enriching the data structures of the Lexicon was the addition of thematic role labels, which were supposed to represent natural classes of participant which were relevant for syntactic patterning. One of the most important syntactic generalizations seemed to involved the choice of SUBJECT, but generalizations about case marking and choice of OBJECT vs. OBLIQUE were recognized early on as being relevant. Once thematic role labels are present in the data structures for individual lexical items, they can be input to statements that map directly to the syntax. Possibly the first thematic hierarchy was implicitly invoked by Fillmore (1968) in the service of stating a SUBJECT selection principle:

(4) if there is an A [= Agent], it becomes the SUBJECT; otherwise, if there is an I [= Instrument], it becomes the SUBJECT; otherwise, the SUBJECT is the O [= Objective, i.e. Patient/Theme]. (Fillmore 1968:33)

This essentially reduces to a SUBJECT selection principle which takes the highest role on the following hierarchy:

(5) Agent > Instrument > Patient/Theme

Thematic hierarchies were attractive to linguists because they were general structures which could be appealed to in the statement of a number of different syntactic generalizations. However, that appeal is dependent on there being a single such hierarchy, as opposed to different rank orderings depending on the phenomenon being investigated. Unfortunately, the consensus now seems to be that this simply is not the case. Levin and Rappaport Hovav (2005) list sixteen distinct thematic role hierarchies, organized by where Goal and Location are placed relative to the Patient/Theme roles, for example.

Indeed, Levin and Rappaport Hovav (2005) give a convincing deconstruction of the types and uses of thematic hierarchies over the years in which they had their heyday. They show that the different thematic hierarchies across researchers arise because a number of different factors. First of all, there is often a difference in scope or granularity involved, directly related to the type of syntactic phenomenon that is being accounted for. Thus, accounting for SUBJECT selection tends to provoke a different set of roles from the task of accounting for OBJECT selection or case marking. Also, researchers vary in whether they map the thematic hierarchy into syntactic relations in a top-down or bottom-up fashion, with or without fixed points, or in whether they believe that mapping to the syntactic representation is then input to further transformational rules or not. However, even after details of technical implementation are accounted for, it does not appear to be the case that a single hierarchy is relevant for all types of generalizations concerning the mapping to syntax. Rather, individual hierarchies are often simply convenient notations used to state one particular generalization in a particular domain, and are the statement of a pattern rather than an explanation of it. I refer the reader to Levin and Rappaport Hovav (2005) for more detailed exposition and examples.

An important dissenting voice to the thematic role and thematic hierarchy method of expressing the mapping to syntax came from Dowty (1989), who argued that the roles in use in the literature did not have clear definitions or entailments that were testable in a way that was replicable across researchers. In Dowty (1991), he argues further that the thematic roles need to be decomposed and that the primitives are really certain entailments which are 'prototypical' entailments of SUBJECT vs. OBJECT respectively. The choice of SUBJECT in Dowty's theory derives from which argument possesses more of the proto properties of SUBJECT than the others. Dowty (1991)'s list of proto-role properties is given below.

(6) **Dowty's proto-roles (1991)**
Contributing properties for the *Agent proto-role*
a. volition
b. sentience (and/or perception)
c. causes event
d. movement
e. referent exists independent of action of verb

Contributing properties for the *Patient proto-role*
f. change of state (including coming into being, going out of being)
g. incremental theme (i.e. determinant of aspect)
h. causally affected by event
i. stationary (relative to movement of Proto-agent)
j. Referent may not exist independent of action of verb, or may not exist at all.

Dowty's argument selection principle (Dowty 1991)
The argument of a predicate having the greatest number of Proto-agent properties entailed by the meaning of the predicate will, all else being

equal, be lexicalized as the subject of the predicate; the argument having the greatest number of Proto-patient properties will, all else being equal, be lexicalized as the direct object of the predicate.

General dissatisfaction with the thematic role approach made Dowty's system of proto-roles attractive to many linguists. The system was flexible, and even allowed for cross-linguistic disagreements in cases where the proto-role count was either even, or at least ambiguous. Moreover, the particular entailment properties that Dowty isolated seemed to be both easy to verify truth-conditionally, as well as have a general cognitive plausibility as primitives. Despite these advantages, it is important to realize that Dowty's system is essentially a retreat from a generative systematic treatment of argument structure patterns. The principle of argument selection given above cannot be seen as a fact about the synchronic computational system (since plausibly, grammars should not be able to 'count' (see Prince and Smolensky 1993) and are not actually subject to internal variability in cases of 'ties'). The Dowty principles above basically give up the idea that the generalizations we see should be represented in the core grammar – the principles he gives must have the status of general cognitive tendencies which ultimately underlie how various concepts tend to get lexicalized (memorized) in natural language (as the quote from Dowty's argument selection principle actually makes explicit).

I will say no more about the proto-role approach in this chapter, merely noting that its popularity is an important indicator of the failure of the thematic hierarchy approaches, and that it remains an alternative type of strategy for those who believe that argument structure generalizations lie outside of the grammar proper.[1] The logical conclusion of the Dowty approach takes us back to the method of listing and memorizing each lexical item separately, even when they look identical and exhibit argument alternations that seem to be systematic. This chapter, however, explores the opposite view, that argument structure generalizations tell us something real about the way that linguistic representations are structured (while still conceding that this is probably underwritten by our human cognitive tendencies).

The conclusion of Levin and Rappaport Hovav (2005) is that "it is impossible to formulate a thematic hierarchy which will capture all generalizations involving the realization of arguments in terms of their semantic roles" (p. 183). However, they do argue that *some* apparent thematic hierarchy effects arise because "embedding relations among arguments in an event structure are always respected in argument realization, with more embedded arguments receiving less prominent syntactic realizations" (p. 183). Thus, the dominant lexicalist position and general consensus seems to be moving toward more structured representations of lexical meaning: instead of role lists and an independent statement of ranking, we find event structure templates, or abstract representations of force dynamical interactions that exist in parallel to other kinds of conceptual information (Levin and Rappaport Hovav 1995, Pustejovsky 1995), or action tier (Jackendoff 1990a, Croft 1998), which are then projected onto the syntax.

9.2.2 Conditions on linking

In a lexicalist theory, the representation of lexical meaning must bear some relation to the syntactic structures those lexical items appear in. In the early days of subcategorization frames and an unstructured lexicon, this could simply be stated in terms of *matching*, since the information in the subcategorization grid was taken from the same vocabulary of symbols and relations as the information in the phrase structure. With the rise of structured lexical representations that utilize semantic primitives that are distinct from syntactic category labels and structures, such theories need 'mapping principles' to correlate the two types of representations. Thus, the history of argument structure is closely tied to the history of 'mapping principles' of various types, from very general and underspecified, to extremely specific.

The most general of these principles is the the Projection Principle, which merely says that the information encoded in the lexicon cannot be ignored or 'lost' during the course of a syntactic derivation; this will include information about category and thematic roles assigned in the classical theory. The Theta Criterion is specific to thematic role information and it enforces a one-to-one mapping between labeled argument positions in the lexicon and syntactically represented arguments.

(7) **The Projection Principle**
Representations at each syntactic level (i.e., LF, and D- and S-structure) are projected from the lexicon, in that they observe the subcategorization properties of lexical items.   (Chomsky 1981:29)

(8) **The Theta Criterion**
Each argument bears one and only one θ-role, and each θ-role is assigned to one and only one argument.   (Chomsky 1981:36)

However, even here we find differences. As Levin and Rappaport Hovav (2005) point out, mapping from thematic hierarchies can either work from the top down or from the bottom up, or directly rely on certain syntactic anchors for elements on the hierarchy. Thus, in Lexical-Functional Grammar (LFG), which takes grammatical functions (SUBJECT, OBJECT, OBLIQUE) to be primitives, the rules do not match up hierarchies so much as use distinguished positions on the hierarchy of thematic roles to map to independent syntactic primitives (Bresnan 2001; see also Chapter 6).

Another difference between theories of linking is the question of whether syntactic transformations can operate on the output of the linking rules or not, to create final syntactic relationships different from the initial ones. This state of affairs is commonplace in Government and Binding (GB)-like theories and their descendants which map to an *initial* structural position (D-structure), while it is not considered an option in LFG where mapping is directly to the F-structure[2] of the sentence, and where grammatical function does not get changed by syntactic rule. This leads to the classical conflict between the two theories with regard to stating a 'rule' in the lexical module, or as a syntactic movement/transformation (cf. Alsina 1992 vs. Baker 1988). I will not pursue this type of debate further in this chapter since it seems to bear more on an argument between LFG and GB than on the substantive issue of what the best statement of the semantic factors correlating with argument structure generalizations are, and on what constraints best express the alternation possibilities.

In general, linking theories tend to divide on whether they assume that the mapping to syntax is 'absolute' or 'relative.' In absolute systems, a particular thematic role or feature has an absolute syntactic correlate (a particular place in the phrase structure, or a particular syntactic feature); in relative systems, the mapping of a particular thematic role or feature to the syntax depends on what other thematic roles or features are also being mapped for that lexical item or construction. Pure hierarchy matching systems are essentially relativistic, but since the consensus in the argument structure literature seems to be that no single hierarchy has enough generality to provide a principled mapping theory for all the purposes required, I will say nothing further about them here.

Various absolute mapping principles have been proposed over the years, which have been very influential. The formalization of the intuition goes back to Relational Grammar and its Universal Alignment Hypothesis (UAH) (Perlmutter and Postal 1984), which states that there are universal principles of grammar which determine a nominal's initial syntactic representation in the relational structure, from its meaning. The intuition is expressed most famously in its GB version as Mark Baker's Uniformity of Theta Assignment Hypothesis (UTAH), which makes explicit reference to D-structure, but leaves open the nature of the structural relationships (assumed here to be phrase structural position) and thematic relationships (often assumed to be thematic role label, although this is not strictly necessary) involved.

(9) **The Uniformity of Theta Assignment Hypothesis (UTAH)**
Identical thematic relationships between items are represented by identical structural relationships between those items at the level of D-structure. (from Baker 1988:46)

This principle can be interpreted in many ways depending on the number and fine-grainedness of the thematic roles assumed. In a recent version of the UTAH and the roles that go along with it (Baker 1997), a very pared down set of abstract roles is correlated directly to particular syntactic positions at the bottom of the verbal phrase structure.

(10)

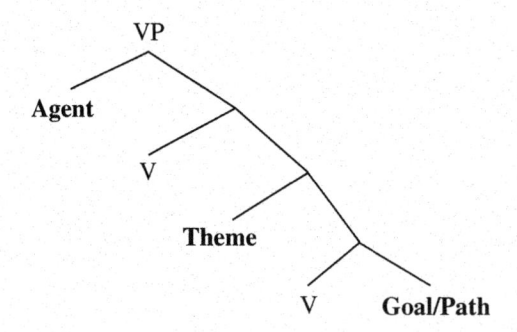

```
            VP
           /  \
       Agent   \
              / \
             V   \
                / \
            Theme \
                  / \
                 V   Goal/Path
```

The claim that there *is* a systematic mapping between structure and meaning is clearly consistent with a number of different proposals about what that mapping is. In other words it is not itself a theory of that mapping, but the statement of the assumption that such a mapping does indeed exist.[3] Thus, it is consistent with theories such as Tenny's Aspectual Interface Hypothesis (AIH) (discussed more fully in Section 9.4), among others (Tenny 1987, 1994). Interestingly, UTAH-friendly theories are also applicable to architectures which do not employ structured *lexical* representations, since the mapping between semantics and structure is assumed in more constructivist theories as well (e.g., Ramchand 2008).

In other cases, 'linking' principles impose certain architectural assumptions on the theory. In particular, the Projection Principle, while seemingly innocuous, requires that lexical alternations be underwritten either by highly underspecified lexical items, or by items that have first undergone modification by rule in the lexicon. Clearly, it was designed to disallow a system where syntactic rules could arbitrarily destroy lexically present information. However, such a system also disallows a model of partial projection of information to capture certain alternations (such as that proposed in, e.g., Ramchand 2008). Similarly, the Theta Criterion is designed to work with thematic role labels that label participants holistically, and not for more abstract feature decompositions. The one-to-one mapping that it enforces makes it necessary to posit coreference relationships as rules in the lexicon if 'roles' are to be fused under certain conditions.[4] Most importantly, these principles assume that the lexicon does contain information *to be* projected, an idea often denied in recent constructivist approaches (Marantz 1997, Harley and Noyer 2000, Borer 2005b). While the Theta Criterion (Hornstein 1990) and indeed the notion of a generative lexicon have come under fire in recent years (Borer 2005b, Ramchand 2008), it is important to keep sight of the fact that these two conditions together were designed to rule out generating such grossly offending forms as those in (11) below.

(11) a. *John hit
b. *Mary elapsed the time
c. *John ate dinner the fork

While this chapter does not wish to presuppose the existence of a structured lexical database with database internal rules, any rethinking of the grammatical architecture still needs to deliver these basic results.

This section has attempted to give some overview of the types of mechanisms and assumptions involved in the treatment of argument structure representation over the last thirty years. It is necessary to understand these various positions in reading any of the vast and important literature on this topic, which has contributed to our knowledge of the detailed empirical generalizations at stake. However, there will be certain strands of research that I will not follow up on in discussing the data in subsequent sections. This is because I believe that a certain consensus has been reached on a number of major points. Specifically, I will not assume that simple role lists or thematic hierarchies are adequate to the job of expressing the generalizations we see. I will assume rather that argument relations have an inherent structure to them, and that this is manifest in the syntactic representation. I will also not confine myself to the problem of SUBJECT selection, but look more generally at OBJECTS and PP arguments as well, touching on case, as another possible morphological correlate of argument structure generalizations in the syntax.

9.2.3 Accounting for lexical variability

Nominal projections bear certain semantic relations and bear participant roles in an eventuality described by a verb. The nature and structuring of those participants is what we have been referring to here as 'argument structure.' Argument structure, however, often implies a rigid structured representation that is lexically associated with a particular verb. In what follows, I will often use the more neutral terms 'participant relations' or 'event participancy' to refer to the relationship between a nominal entity and the eventuality that it participates in. The central empirical concern of the 'argument structure' literature is to uncover the morphosyntactic patterns that correlate with types of event participancy. This enterprise is often embarked on in conjunction with the separate (and sometimes confounded) architectural question of what a speaker knows when they know the limits and flexibilities of a verb in their language – the 'User's Manual' for each particular verb. The existence of pervasive lexical variability shows us that these are not at all the same question, and answering the first question with a rich listed representation as a 'lexical' entry is not sufficient. The existence of systematic regularities and rigidities in verbal meaning on the other hand, shows us that the strategy of ignoring the second question altogether, as in many radical constructivist accounts (Marantz 1997, Harley 1995, Borer 2005b), invoking convention and real-world knowledge to provide limits to verbal usage, is also not adequate. I give a brief overview here of the most discussed alternations and patterns that have been uncovered in the literature, since these constitute important data for answering both the empirical question, and the architectural question above.

The simplest argument alternation patterns noticed in the literature involved a single set of 'arguments' which offered a choice in realization possibilities. One important class of alternations involves variation in the choice of direct OBJECT. In the DATIVE/DOUBLE OBJECT ALTERNATION, the 'goal' argument can either be expressed as a *to*-PP alongside a 'theme' direct OBJECT (12a); or both participants can be expressed as DPs, with the 'goal' argument acquiring direct OBJECT status (as diagnosed by passivizability) (12b).

(12) DATIVE ALTERNATION:
 a. John gave the book to Mary
 b. John gave Mary the book

In the LOCATIVE ALTERNATION, either the 'location' (13a), or the 'located substance' (13b) can be the direct OBJECT with the other participant being expressed as a *with*-PP or a location PP respectively.

(13) LOCATIVE ALTERNATION:
 a. John smothered the toast with marmite
 b. John smothered marmite on the toast

In CONTACTIVE ALTERNATION (classified as the *with/against*-alternation by Levin 1993), either the contacted object can be the direct OBJECT with the instrument a *with*-PP (14a), or the instrument can be the direct OBJECT with the contacted object expressed as a locative PP (14b)

(14) CONTACTIVE ALTERNATION:
 a. John hit the table with the cricket bat
 b. John hit the cricket bat against the table

Alternations can also occur in two-argument verbs, where a DP OBJECT or SUBJECT argument can be realized alternatively as a PP OBLIQUE. Below we see the alternation between OBJECT and OBLIQUE (15) (better known as the CONATIVE ALTERNATION).

(15) CONATIVE ALTERNATION:
 a. John ate the apple
 b. John ate at the apple

The important thing about these alternations is that they do not simply involve individual lexical items. Rather, each alternation seems to be productively available for a wide class of verbs in each case, where the class of verbs has a recognizable semantic profile. Multiple listing of variants simply misses these generalizations. Instead, we must capture the patterns at the level of (lexical or syntactic) rule.

While the above alternations tempt the lexicalist to model them with a single argument list with different realization options, the CAUSATIVE-INCHOATIVE ALTERNATION is less straightforwardly a case of a single lexical entry, because the number of arguments is different in each version.

(16) CAUSATIVE-INCHOATIVE ALTERNATION:
 a. the window broke
 b. John broke the window

Moreover, even viewing the two alternants as related lexical items has provoked controversy over which of the two variants, the transitive or the intransitive, should be considered derived from the other. Authors like Levin and Rappaport Hovav (1995), Reinhart and Siloni (2004) and Chierchia (2004b) argue for deriving the intransitive variant from the transitive one, by means of argument supression. Other authors (Ramchand 2008, Davis and Demirdache 2000) build the transitive version from the intransitive one. In languages like English, there is no morphological difference between the alternants, but this is far from universal. Haspelmath (1993b) considers the alternation from a typological perspective and points out that there are languages where morphology is added to a transitive/causative form to give an intransitive (e.g., Slavic; Romance), as well as languages where morphology is added to the intransitive to give the transitive (e.g., Hindi; Indonesian). In English, however, the morphology does not give us any indication about which alternant, if any, is the derived form.

A lexical theory containing linking principles such as those described above essentially has three main options in dealing with such flexibility. The first option is to make the linking principles themselves flexible and non-deterministic. This is in a sense the option taken by Dowty (1991) and certain versions of LFG (cf. Bresnan 2001). The second option is to claim that the (a) and (b) sentences above involve the same underlying configurations, but at least one of them involves a non-trivial syntactic derivation. This, for example, is the option taken by Larson (1988a) in his treatment of the DATIVE ALTERNATION, and the solution advocated by Baker (1997). The extent to which this general strategy is plausible will depend on the syntactic principles required being independently justifiable, and not ad hoc additions to the syntactic toolbox merely to save the UTAH and its kin. The third strategy of course is to claim that the thematic roles in the (b) sentences are actually different from those in the (a) sentences (cf. Oehrle 1976, Pesetsky 1995, Harley 2000 for the double object construction). This is in fact the claim Baker (1997) makes for the

LOCATIVE ALTERNATION, although not for the DATIVE ALTERNATION. The success of this strategy revolves around resolving the tension between the need to use fairly abstract thematic labels to capture the natural classes which exist but which are nevertheless subtle enough to distinguish between thematic relationships in the closely related pairs above.

Further instances of argument structure variability are less easy to classify as 'alternations' *per se*, since they involve the addition of material or deletion of arguments, and do not simply manipulate a single 'role list.' Moreover, these instances of variability turn out to be pervasive, and not merely marginal characteristics of verbal behavior. It is the existence of variability such as the list of examples shown below for *eat* (17), which have persuaded many constructivists that the 'construction' is the domain of argument structure information, not the lexical item (Borer 2005b, Goldberg 1995). The examples of *siren* in (18) taken from Borer (2005b) are especially striking because the verb in question has been 'productively' formed from the nominal *siren*, making the memorization of multiple lexical items unlikely.

(17) CONSTRUCTIONAL VARIABILITY:
    a. John ate the apple
    b. John ate at the apple
    c. the sea ate into the coastline
    d. John ate me out of house and home
    e. John ate
    f. John ate his way into history

(18) a. the fire stations sirened throughout the raid
    b. the factory sirened midday and everyone stopped for lunch
    c. the police sirened the Porsche to a stop
    d. the police car sirened up to the accident
    e. the police car sirened the daylights out of me
                                                   (from Borer 2005b)

(19) a. Kim whistled
    b. Kim whistled at the dog
    c. Kim whistled a tune
    d. Kim whistled a warning
    e. Kim whistled me a warning
    f. Kim whistled her appreciation
    g. Kim whistled to the dog to come
    h. the bullet whistled through the air
    i. the air whistled with bullets
                             (from Levin and Rappaport Hovav 2005)

Levin and Rappaport Hovav (2005) point out that with this kind of phenomenon, once again, we are not just dealing with a single verb like *whistle*, but with a whole class of noise emission verbs in the case of (19) above. They also point out that many of the sentences in the above examples involve the *addition* of linguistic material. They use the term Event Composition for constructions of this type, avoiding the term 'complex predicate formation,' although some of these phenomena have been known under that label, or under specific construction labels such as 'the resultative construction.' These kinds of examples are important because they show that a static lexicon with a rigid mapping to syntactic structure is untenable – the kinds of syntactic transformations that one would need to convert one 'sentence type' to another would be way more powerful than any modern theorist would countenance, including both deletions and contentful additions (cf. Chomsky 1970a).

To drive home the point, consider the case of the resultative construction, shown below in (20). The (a) sentence contains a verb *break* which selects for a direct OBJECT, but in general *run* does not allow a direct OBJECT of this type. On a very basic distributional level, removing the adjectival predicate in (a) leaves a grammatical sentence, while removing it in (b) does not.

(20)   a. John broke the safe open
       b. Mary ran her shoes ragged

The paradox of the resultative construction thus resides in the failure of lexical statements about a verb like *run* to carry over to its behavior when different adjectival resultative predicates are present. In fact, the problem may occur in more subtle form for *all* resultatives, even the ones like (a) where it looks like there is no problem. For example, it has been argued that the semantic entailments over the direct OBJECT in a resultative construction are simply different from those found with the very same verb and OBJECT alone (Hoekstra 1988). If this is correct, then one might argue that the OBJECT in a resultative construction such as (20) above is *never* in a direct selectional relationship with the main verb (this is the position assumed by all 'small clause' analyses of the resultative construction; Kayne 1985, Hoekstra 1988, den Dikken 1995). Possibly, not all resultatives should be analyzed the same way, but even those analyses which maintain a selectional relationship between the verb and the direct OBJECT must find a way of 'adding' the entailments/selectional restrictions of the resultative secondary predicate (as in the 'complex predicate' analysis of the construction; Johnson 1991, Neeleman 1994a, Zeller 2001). Thus, not only does 'the safe' in (20a) get 'broken,' it also becomes 'open' as a result of the breaking. The resultative construction shows that generalizations over semantic role and syntactic behavior are not exclusively properties of a single lexical item, since the whole VP has to be taken into account. There seems to be an emerging consensus in the literature that sentences of this type require some kind of complex event structure, although whether these are built by systematic mechanisms (Carrier and Randall 1992, Levin and Rappaport 1998, Wunderlich 1997), or memorized as chunks (Goldberg and Jackendoff 2004) is still a matter of controversy. Among the theorists who choose to model the generalizations generatively and build up possible event structures using rules or constraints, it is a much debated architectural question whether that generative capacity should be located within a lexical module (Levin and Rappaport Hovav 1995 on 'template augmentation') or within the syntax proper (Ramchand 2008).

9.3 The view from morphosyntax: subject selection

Morphosyntactic representation is a hierarchically structured representation of individual signs. From this point of view, one should ask about which generalizations within the morphosyntax are correlated with the semantics of participant roles. Initially within the literature, argument structure properties were used to predict 'SUBJECT' selection, but in principle, argument properties have correlations with selection for other grammatical functions as well, such as 'OBJECT' and 'INDIRECT OBJECT.' Some theories assume that grammatical function in this sense is a primitive in its own right (e.g., Lexical-Functional Grammar), while other theories deconstruct these notions as positional ones in the morphosyntactic hierarchical representation.

Be that as it may, in the clear cases, there is general agreement on empirically isolating SUBJECT vs. OBJECT in natural languages, where many diagnostics coincide. Thus, even in languages with rather different typological properties, it has been argued that the notion of SUBJECT can be defined and has a number of recognizable properties within grammatical patterning. Keenan (1976) argues that the notion of SUBJECT is necessary to account for linguistic generalizations with regard to accessibility for relativization and agreement (see also Perlmutter and Postal 1984). SUBJECT also serves as the antecedent for reflexives, and it is the SUBJECT function that is deleted and referentially resolved in 'control' structures (see Chapter 16), the SUBJECT function is also the deleted element in 2nd person addressee imperatives (Keenan 1976). Generalizations about choice of SUBJECT therefore remain a robust source of evidence for argument structure, which have some potential for being compared crosslinguistically, even where details of morphosyntactic representation vary.[5]

In this section, I summarize what I take to be the major patterns and generalizations that have emerged from essentially forty years of research in this area. In doing so however, I include established alternations that are mediated by overt morphology side by side with those that are not. The general philosophy behind this choice is that from the point of view of syntax to meaning generalizations, it is artificial to make too sharp an a priori distinction between alternations that look like alternations in argument structure for a single lexical item, and alternations mediated by explicit verbal morphology.[6]

The SUBJECT position is an obligatory grammatical function in many of the world's languages, and it does not exclude any type of event-related participant in principle. Thus, 'Themes' and 'Patients' can end up in SUBJECT position in monotransitive verbs as easily as 'Agents' can. However, when there is more than one event participant, languages universally choose the 'Agent' argument as SUBJECT over the 'Theme' or 'Patient' if both are to be expressed as DPs. Having said that, there is still a wide variety of participant roles available to DPs in SUBJECT position, even in transitive verbs.

As a general crude summary, we can say that in dynamic eventualities (those that express some sort of change), a *causing* participant (one whose existence directly or indirectly, deliberately or inadvertently, is asserted to bring about the change in question) is privileged to hold the SUBJECT position, and this includes both inanimate and abstract causes, and facilitators like instruments.

In the case of stative verbs, the situation is a little more difficult to pin down: 'experiencers,' 'figures' of spatial relationships (cf. Talmy 1978, 2000), and 'topics' seem to be ways of characterizing the SUBJECTS of stative predications. In particular, Talmy (2000) defines Figure as the entity whose spatial location, or movement through space is at issue, while the Ground is the entity with respect to which that position or motion is defined.

(21) *The Figure–Ground asymmetry*:
The Figure is a moving or conceptually movable entity whose path, site, or orientation is conceived of as a variable, the particular value of which is the relevant issue.

The Ground is the reference entity, one that has stationary setting relative to a reference frame, with respect to which the Figure's path, site or orientation is characterized. (Talmy 2000)

However, this structural asymmetry can be seen in stative verbs as well, and one is tempted to the extend the definition of Figure/Ground from the purely spatial domain to encompass stative properties more generally: the Figure of a property predication is the entity whose degree of possession of a particular property is at issue; the Ground is the reference property, or property scale which the Figure is predicated to 'hold' to some degree. Clear intuitions in the spatial domain thus give rise to a natural analogy in the domain of more abstract properties, and Figure and Ground can be profitably used in these more general terms as the asymmetrical roles of a stative property ascription.

This predicational asymmetry corresponds to a syntactic one, with adpositional elements overwhelmingly, and possibly universally, selecting for Grounds as complements (see Svenonius 2007 for discussion), with the Figure as the implicit 'subject' of the relation (Talmy 2000, Svenonius 2007). Another commonly used label is the participant role of 'Holder' of a particular property (see Kratzer 1996 for the introduction of and use of this general role label). Fine grained differences in thematic role are not usually proposed for the stative SUBJECT position;[7] saliency and functional considerations seem to go into determining which entity in a static eventuality is chosen as the bearer of a property ascription. The bearer of a property ascription (Figure, or Holder) then contrasts with the non-SUBJECT participants in a static eventuality which provide additional information specifying the property being ascribed.[8]

It is important to emphasize that we should not expect to determine SUBJECT-hood deterministically from real world properties of a particular event. Rather, language users use language to structure an event and *give* it an interpretation in terms of predication. Thus, a natural language representation implies a particular choice of 'topic' or Figure for the static situation described. Similarly, there is no objective way of isolating the cause of a particular dynamic change in the world, although there *are* constraints on the cognitively natural ways in which human beings construe things as being caused. The claim here is that the morphosyntactic representation in the language carries reliable entailments about the assertion of the speaker and the way she is representing the force dynamics of the situation. Here, and in the discussion that follows, I reverse the standpoint of the traditional (lexicalist) position and ask not how meaning maps onto syntax (the direction of mapping that the UTAH and its kin regulate) but to what extent syntactic representations systematically deliver semantic entailments about event structure and role relations.

9.3.1 Causative–inchoative

Cross-linguistically, alternations between transitive and intransitive versions of lexical items sharing some core conceptual and morphological content are extremely common. As mentioned earlier, typological work (Haspelmath 1993a) shows that while some languages like English have verbs like *break* which alternate without any explicit morphology ('labile' verbs), other languages have explicit causativizing morphology (Indonesian, Japanese, Salish and the languages of the Indian subcontinent), while still others show decausativizing/reflexive morphology to create the alternation (e.g., *si* in Italian, *se* in French, *sja* in Russian).

An example of the causative–inchoative alternation in Hindi/Urdu is shown below, where the addition of the suffix *-aa* to the verbal root seems to 'add' a direct causer to the eventuality.

(22) a. makaan ban-aa
    house make-PERF.M.SG
    'the house was built'

    b. anjum-ne   makaan ban-aa-yaa
       Anjum-ERG house   make-*aa*-PERF.M.SG
       'Anjum built a house'   (from Butt 2003)

In Italian, on the other hand, we can find pairs where the intransitive/inchoative version of the verb shows up obligatorily with the marker *si* (which elsewhere functions as a reflexive clitic pronoun).

(23) a. il vento ha rotto   la finestra
         the wind has broken the window
         'the wind broke the window'

      b. la finestra *(si) è rotta
         the window REFL is broken
         'the window broke'   (from Folli 2001)

In English, as we have seen before, the alternation requires no morphology and verbs like *break* are classified as 'labile.'

(24) a. the wind broke the window
      b. the window broke

What is important to note about this alternation is that it is extremely common and pervasive cross-linguistically, and that the additional expression of a causer is what makes the difference between the transitive and the intransitive version. Thus, whether the alternation appears to be 'lexical,' as in English, or morphological as in Hindi/Urdu, or even analytic as in Romance, the pairing of causative and inchoative is linguistically natural and productively formed. Moreover, it is the causer that is always the external argument or SUBJECT in the verb's transitive version. No theory of argument structure can ignore this kind of relationship between events, or the idea of causer as a more prominent participant when it comes to SUBJECT selection. One might even argue that Causer or Initiator in a general sense is prototypically the most prominent participant in any event structure.[9]

As noted earlier, there is a debate in the literature concerning the direction of the causative–inchoative alternation. Levin and Rappaport Hovav (1995), Chierchia (2004a), and Reinhart (2002) all agree in deriving the inchoative alternant from a lexically causative base. For example, Levin and Rappaport Hovav (1995) argue that the transitive is the base form, and that the intransitive is derived by a lexical suppression of the Cause component in the item's lexical conceptual structure. Since not all transitive verbs with a Cause component actually have intransitive counterparts, a lexicon internal condition must be placed on the suppression mechanism. Basically, Levin and Rappaport Hovav argue that Cause may be suppressed precisely when the verb can be conceived of as being able to take place without any external causation.

However, since these verbs are the very ones where we can conceive of the event without a cause component, it seems unintuitive to insist that it must be present in the lexical representation. Reinhart (2002), who also takes the transitive-to-intransitive position, is forced to claim that intransitive unaccusative verbs with no transitive counterpart, do nevertheless have a transitive counterpart in the lexicon which is 'frozen' and never surfaces. In the case of English, a far more satisfying system emerges if we take the derivation to occur in the other direction: while very many causative transitives fail to have intransitive counterparts, only a very small number of unaccusatives, if any, fail to causativize. Under this view (espoused in Ramchand 2008), English is the morphologically non-overt counterpart of Hindi/Urdu, not of Italian. In fact, the only reason Levin and Rappaport Hovav (1995) and Reinhart (2002) run the derivation from transitive to intransitive is because their lexicalist assumptions do not sanction the idea that a syntactic formative can bear the semantics of causation and systematically add structural meaning to an underspecified lexical item. This is precisely what the causative morpheme, or Cause head in syntactic accounts, is intended to do. However, as discussed briefly in Section 9.2.3, there is no reason to suppose that the direction of derivation in one language is the same for another. If one takes overt morphology seriously, one would argue that the direction is from inchoative to transitive/causative in the case of Hindi/Urdu, and Salish (Davis and Demirdache 2000), and transitive/causative to inchoative in the case of Slavic and Romance. How exactly this is done in each language is an interesting question, but one which I put aside here – the generalization independent of these analyses is that there exists a linguistically privileged relationship between event descriptions and their direct causation counterparts, with a correspondingly privileged status of 'causer' for the SUBJECT position.

9.3.2 Passivization and Voice

What distinguishes Passive, and Voice alternations more generally, from the alternations discussed in the previous subsection is that they morphologically encode alternations of case and/or grammatical function. As we have seen, both case and grammatical function are logically separable from argument structure, but since they are demonstrably sensitive to argument structure properties they provide some of our best evidence for argument structure itself.

While the inchoative version of transitive–intransitive pairs discussed above involves the absence of the Cause argument, the passive is usually considered to be a morphological alternation which affects the *realization* of the arguments of a transitive verb and allows a previously non-SUBJECT argument to be promoted to SUBJECT position. In the passive, the previously external argument is not absent entirely, it is merely implicit or expressed in an oblique way. Passive occurs in just over 40 percent of the WALS (World Atlas of Language Structures) sample of languages. Passive is defined by the promotion to SUBJECT of the nominal that was the OBJECT of the corresponding Active, by the oblique or non-expression of the SUBJECT of the Active, and by the existence of explicit morphology on the Active form. An example from Swahili, using a morphological passive affix, is shown below (data and information from Siewierska 2008).

(25) a. Hamisi a-li-pik-a   chakula
       Swahili Hamisi 3SG-PST-cook-IND food
       'Hamisi cooked the/some food'

   b. chakula ki-li-pik-w-a   (na Hamisi)
      food   3SG-PST-cook-PASS-IND by Hamisi
      'The food was cooked (by Hamisi)'
                              (originally from Ashton 1947:224)

In English, as in many European languages, the passive is formed analytically from the perfective/passive participle and an auxiliary. The passive construction supports a *by*-phrase, unlike the inchoative constructions discussed in the previous section.

(26) a. the police arrested John
     b. John was arrested (by the police)

While these cases of passive involve both the demotion of the SUBJECT and the promotion of the OBJECT which then gets nominative case and passes the tests for SUBJECT, there are also languages where passivizing morphology appears on the verb and the agent is suppressed, but where accusative case is retained on the OBJECT. This is the case in Ukrainian (Sobin 1985), and accusative case is optional in Hindi, as the following examples from Hook (1979) (cited in Bhatt 2003) show.

(27) a. *Active*:
       ve   mujh-ko/*mẼ fauran   pehchaan l-ẽge
       they I.OBL-ACC/I immediately recognize take-FUT.MPL
       'they will recognize me immediately'
    b. *Passive, with accusative marking retained*:
       mujh-ko   fauran   pehchaan li-yaa   jaa-egaa
       me.OBL-ACC immediately recognize take-PFV PASS-FUT
       'I will be recognized immediately'
    c. *Passive, without accusative marking*:
       mẼ fauran   pehchaan li-i   jaa-ũgii
       I.F immediately recognize take-PFV.F PASS-FUT.1FSG
       'I will be recognized immediately'

In the (c) example, the single DP argument passes the tests for SUBJECT-hood in Hindi, as Bhatt (2003) shows, whereas in (b) it does not. Many languages also have impersonal passives of intransitive verbs, where there is no OBJECT to begin with, and where an expletive occupies SUBJECT position (see Afarli 1992). In these cases, passive is only possible with intransitives that have 'agent'-like SUBJECTs and not intransitives with 'patient-' or 'theme'-like SUBJECTS (Bhatt 2003 for Indo-Aryan; Afarli 1992 for Norwegian). This shows, in particular, that the most important function of passivizing morphology in these languages is the demotion of the external argument, and not the suppression of accusative case. Note that this operation, unlike the causative–inchoative alternation, seems to keep the basic argument structure intact but instead of the most prominent argument being promoted to SUBJECT, passive signals the syntactic demotion of that otherwise winning argument where it is either suppressed altogether or optionally expressed in the form of a *by*-phrase. In Baker *et al.* (1989), the presence yet syntactic inertness for SUBJECT-hood of the external argument is implemented in an analysis which argues that the participial ending itself in English is actually the incorporated external argument. Alternatively, to use recent Minimalist terminology, the expression of the external argument in a PP structure would remove that argument from the class of possible targets for the SUBJECT probing feature.[10]

As I have emphasized, the notion of SUBJECT, and also of nominative case (as I will discuss in Section 9.5) are logically distinct from argument structure roles (and from each other), by assumption. The question is whether we need a level of representation that encodes argument structure in addition to the morphosyntactically obvious things like case and agreement (cf. Jackendoff 1983, 1990a for the position that argument structure is encoded at a level of lexical conceptual structure distinct from syntax). We do need such a representation, if it is input to important generalizations about how verbs behave within and across languages.[11] Recall that the reason SUBJECT selection is important is that there seems to be a universal asymmetry in the relationship between event participancy and the choice of SUBJECT across verb types: 'causers' have priority over 'non-causers' within the same event, and the opposite alignment is never attested unless the 'causer' is unexpressed or licensed as an oblique.[12] This means that whatever syntactic mechanisms are responsible for choice of SUBJECT, they are fed in a systematic way by event structure/argument structure information. The existence of explicit morphology for 'demoting' external arguments shows that they have a special status in the systems of grammatical function.

I started this subsection with a sharp principled distinction between Passive and the inchoative or unaccusative version in a causative/inchoative alternating pair. The differences in English are clearly seen: in the inchoative there is no morphology different from the causative and the missing external argument cannot be expressed or invoked, it is simply missing; in the passive, explicit morphology creates the version without the external argument and the latter is implicitly present and/or can be expressed with a *by*-phrase.

(28) a. the ship sank (*to collect the insurance) / (*by the torpedo)
b. the ship was sunk (to collect the the insurance) / (by the torpedo)

The picture becomes more complicated, however, when cross-linguistic morphological patterns are taken into account. If we consider the whole range of sentence types where it has been argued that an internal argument of a related transitive appears to make it to SUBJECT position in a related intransitive, we find: (i) anticausatives (as in intransitive *break*, or *sink*); (ii) 'reflexive' interpretation of bodily function verbs (as in *shave*, and *wash*; (iii) dispositional middles as in *This bread cuts easily*; (iv) passives as in *The bread was cut by Mary*. Moreover, languages differ as to what morphological devices they use to build these meanings. As Alexiadou and Doron (2007) point out, some languages have a morphological 'middle' voice, side by side with the 'passive' voice, where the former is used for (i)–(iii) and the latter is used for (iv) (Classical Greek, Modern Hebrew); some languages have only a 'middle,' or 'non-active' voice which is used for all of (i)–(iv) (Modern Greek); yet others only have 'passive' which is used for (iv) while (i)–(iii) appear with active morphology (English). This morphological syncretism is not confined to members of the verbal paradigm. In the Romance languages, Slavic, and to some extent Germanic, clitic reflexives are also employed in all of the environments in (i)–(iii) (Kemmer 1993).

In the examples (29a–d) (from Alexiadou and Doron 2007), we see the non-active verbal morphology being used on lexical reflexives, intransitive members of the causative–inchoative alternation, middle and passive respectively.

(29) a. i Maria htenizete
the Maria combs-NACT
'Mary combs herself'
b. i supa kaike
the soup burnt-NACT
'the soup burnt'
c. afto to vivlio diavazete   efkola
this the book read-NACT easily
'this book reads easily'
d. i times   miothikan   apo to diefthindi
the prices lowered-NACT by the director
'the prices were lowered by the director'

Alexiadou and Anagnostopoulou (2004) argue for distinct constructions here, based on the fact that different PP adjuncts are acceptable in each case. In general, while the anticausative shows no evidence of a syntactically or semantically active 'causer' argument in the licensing of adjuncts and the control of purpose clauses, the passive construction does. The dispositional middle seems to be an intermediate case, with some researchers arguing that the external argument is syntactically active (Stroik 1992, Hoekstra and Roberts 1993) and others that it is not (Ackema and Schoorlemmer 1995, Lekakou 2005). All agree however that the middle differs from the anticausative in that the external argument is implicit or *semantically* present in the former, but not in the latter.

For our purposes here, it is relevant to note that the dispositional middle itself has additional properties that makes it relevant for a theory of argument structure. Unlike passive, the possibility of forming a dispositional middle is strongly dependent on the argument structure of the verb in question. This is the fact that Hale and Keyser (1987) set out to account for in their important early discussion of the construction. They argue that a necessary precondition for middle formation is that the internal argument to be promoted be the participant in the *central change subevent* of the verb's event structure (cf. also Jaeggli 1986 for the intuition stated in terms of an 'affectedness' constraint). This condition correctly rules out middles such as the ungrammatical (30) below, under the assumption that OBJECTs of verbs of contact are not represented as undergoers of a change, but as the final location of contact, and that stative verbs have no change event in their lexical representation at all.[13]

(30) a. *physics knows easily
b. *the wall hits easily

It is not possible here to do justice to the range of analyses offered for this cluster of phenomena, the differences among them, and the differences in morphosyntactic representation cross-linguistically. What this section has shown, however, is that there is remarkable cross-linguistic agreement on what criteria are in play when coding an argument as SUBJECT or OBJECT. 'Agents' and 'causers' make good SUBJECTS, and a language tends to employ explicit morphological devices when an 'undergoer of change' is expressed as the SUBJECT in preference to the 'agent' or 'causer.' The role of Holder or Figure is expressed as the SUBJECT of statives, and it is interesting that the notional object acquires this entailment in the dispositional middle. In many cases, the existence of identical morphology even blurs the simple division between passive as a grammatical function changing operation and causative–inchoative as an argument structure changing operation (and straddling the ambiguous case of the middle), as we saw above in Greek. Plausibly, what all these 'constructions' have in common is the fact that the argument that ends up as the SUBJECT *undergoes some change* as a criterion for the eventuality to hold. If this characterization is on the right track, then NonActive morphology in Greek is the morphological indicator of a generalization at the level of argument structure. It is also significant that special morphology is often required for 'undergoer of change' arguments to appear as SUBJECT of an underlyingly transitive relation.

9.3.3 Classes of intransitive

The unaccusative–unergative distinction (Perlmutter 1978) refers to the important grammatical difference in the behavior of monotransitive verbs, which is correlated with participant role. In brief, for some linguistic phenomena, 'theme/patient' SUBJECTS of single argument verbs behave more like the the OBJECTS of transitive verbs than the 'agent' SUBJECTS of single argument verbs do (even though both behave like grammatical SUBJECTS in a broad sense). To illustrate from Italian, (31) shows a classic example of an 'unergative' verb which has an agentive SUBJECT, while (32) gives and example of an 'unaccusative' verb which has a 'theme' SUBJECT.[14]

(31) Gianni telefona
    John   telephones
    'John is telephoning'

(32) Gianni arriva
    John   arrives
    'John is arriving'

In Italian, the SUBJECT of unaccusatives can be the nominal related to the *ne* clitic (roughly meaning 'of them') which cliticizes to the verb, and it shares this property with OBJECTS of transitive verbs.[15]

(33) a. *ne   telefonano   molti
       of-them telephoned.PL many
    b. ne   arrivano molti
       of-them arrived   many
       'many of them arrived'

In addition, when it comes to the formation of the periphrastic past tense, in many dialects the two different types select different auxiliaries to combine with the participle: roughly speaking, the unaccusative verbs tend to select *essere* 'to be,' while the unergatives select *avere* 'to have,' like transitives.

(34) a. Gianni ha telefonato
       Gianni has telephoned
       'Gianni telephoned'
    b. Gianni è arrivato
       Gianni is arrived
       'Gianni arrived'

Thus, the systematic existence of two types of monotransitive verbs shows that the notion of SUBJECT is not the only grammatically relevant distinction and that the semantic relationship of the participant to the event is also important for determining linguistic behavior. Unfortunately, as with thematic relations in general, the class of unaccusative verbs is not easily defined semantically. While there are some accounts that propose a purely semantic (i.e., non-syntactic) account of the two classes of intransitive (Van Valin 1990, Bentley 2006), most treatments in the literature attempt to relate the classes either to thematic role (Belletti and Rizzi 1988), or lexical semantic structure (Hale and Keyser 2002, Levin and Rappaport Hovav 1995), which in turn maps in a deterministic way to syntactic structure. Thus, most of these accounts assume that there is a structural difference between an unaccusative phrase structure and an unergative one, which underpins their different syntactic behavior.[16] The debate here mirrors the debate about argument structure more generally, with competing accounts of what semantic features of the participant relationship are criterial for class membership, and competing accounts of where the criterial semantic information resides: in the lexicon, (as in Levin and Rappaport Hovav 1995), in a derivational level of syntactic representation as in early GB and Relational Grammar accounts (Perlmutter 1978, Rosen 1984, Belletti and Rizzi 1988), or in a single syntactic phrase structural representation (McClure 1994, Borer 1998).

As has been known for a long time, many verbs actually show variable behavior with respect to the standard diagnostics: differences in telicity at the VP level affect the classification of that VP as either unaccusative or unergative with telicity correlating with an 'unaccusative' choice of auxiliary in Italian and many other languages (35) (Zaenen 1993, Folli 2003); differences in control or volitionality tend to push the verb in the other direction, toward more 'unergative' behavior (see Sorace 2000 for discussion).

(35) a. Gianni ha corso
Gianni has run
'Gianni ran'
b. Gianni è corso a casa
Gianni is run home
'Gianni ran home'

The existence of these effects threatened to undermine early accounts that relied on lexical specfication of verb types. However, as we have shown in this survey chapter so far, the existence of alternations and verbal flexibility is the normal pattern, not the exception. Any account of the behavior of verbal lexical items is going to have to deal with the fact that argument structures come in clusters of possibilities (with telic modulation and agentive modulation being extremely common). In this respect, the unaccusative vs. unergative classification is no different from the general situation of argument structure alternations.

Since the unaccusative–unergative distinction was discovered, it has been uncovered in many other languages and seems to be a pervasive fact: monotransitive VPs systematically fall into two natural classes, one of which has a more theme-like SUBJECT and the other of which has a more agent-like SUBJECT. It is important to reiterate that this is a formal linguistic distinction which can only be justified by language internal diagnostics and that these diagnostics can vary considerably from language to language. Another word of caution about the diagnostics is that since it is still an open question exactly what the structural distinction is between unergative and unaccusative structures, it can also sometimes be the case that different diagnostics are sensitive to different aspects of that structure. For example, it is not clear whether the structural representation of telicity is logically independent of whether a verb has a structural external cause or not. The two do not seem to go together in the normal intransitive case. In extreme cases, different diagnostics might pick out slightly different natural classes.

If we turn to English, we see that there is no equivalent of auxiliary selection or any equivalent of the the clitic *ne*, but there is still evidence that the two classes of verbs exist. As we have seen already, there is a class of verbs which systematically undergoes the causative–inchoative alternation. The intransitive member of those pairs have been called 'ergatives' by Hale and Keyser (1987),[17] but are probably more properly thought of as unaccusative. They clearly have a SUBJECT argument that is non-agentive and can be embedded under further causation.

(36) a. the glass broke
    b. John broke the glass

(37) a. Mary danced
    b. *John danced Mary

Correlating with this difference is the behavior of perfect participles when used attributively: perfect participles can attributively modify the argument that would have been the SUBJECT of an unaccusative verb, but not the SUBJECT of an unergative verb.

(38) a. the broken glass
    b. *the danced girl

In addition, resultative formation is possible with the direct OBJECT of a transitive verb, the SUBJECT of a passive, the single argument of a change of state verb (unaccusative, by hypothesis), but not the single argument of an agentive process verb (unergative, by hypothesis) (see Levin and Rappaport Hovav 1995 for discussion) (see examples in (39)).

(39) a. John broke the safe open
    b. the safe was broken open
    c. the safe broke open
    d. *Mary danced tired (on the reading: 'Mary danced until she became tired as a result')

Since it is an important cross-linguistic distinction, it is important to try to understand exactly what properties of participation in the event are relevant for making the difference. If we look at the abstract semantic ingredients of unaccusativity, we can see some clear patterns. In Italian specifically, Sorace (2000) shows that verbs in the so-called 'unaccusative' class range from verbs of change of location at one prototypical extreme (*cadere* 'fall'), through 'change of state' (*nascere* 'be born'), 'continuation of pre-existing state' (*sopravivere* 'survive') to even simple 'existence of state' (*esistere* 'exist') at the limit. 'Unergative' behavior on the other hand encompasses verbs of 'uncontrolled process' at the limit (*brillare* 'shine') through controlled motional processes (*correre* 'run') and finally controlled non-motional processes at the prototypical extreme (*lavorare* 'work'). Sorace claims that these semantic verb types form an implicational cline (the Auxiliary Selection Hierarchy (ASH)) which is reflected in variability judgments and various psycholinguistic behavioral effects, including some dialectal variation. However, while telic change of state[18] is the most prototypical unaccusative verb type and agent-controlled process is the most prototypically unergative verb type, it is important to realize that agency and telicity are not necessary conditions for unergativity and unaccusativity respectively. For example, Rappaport-Hovav and Levin (2000) show convincingly that it is not agency *per se* that determines class membership in English as either unaccusative or unergative, but some kind of 'internal causation.' They argue that intransitives such as 'glow,' 'stink,' and 'spew' pass the diagnostics for unergativity in Italian, Dutch, and Basque even though they do not possess arguments that bring anything about by agentive action. Similarly, *correre* 'run' shown above in (35) in Italian is presumably an action under the agentive control of the runner, but in its telic version, it qualifies as unaccusative in Italian. Correspondingly, telicity (in both English and Italian) is not a necessary condition for unaccusativity, since unbounded changes of state qualify as unaccusative (cf. examples below from English).

(40) a. the gap between the two planks widened slowly for many years
  (*atelic process*)
 b. successive winters widened the gap between the two planks for many years
  (*caused atelic process*)
 c. the widened gap proved a hazard for high-heel shoes (*participle formation*)

What agents and these other kinds of external argument have in common is that in each case the SUBJECT is an entity whose properties/behavior are responsible for the eventuality coming into existence. Thus, 'glow,' and 'stink' have an external argument which is responsible by virtue of inherent properties of incandescence or smelliness; for 'spew,' the particular SUBJECT is in some sense the source or cause of the spewing event by virtue of the fact that it has the requisite properties of kinetic energy;

volitional agents have intentions and desires that lead them to initiate dynamic events; instrumental SUBJECTS are entities whose facilitating properties are presented as initiating the event because they allow it to happen. It seems to be this sort of initiating or facilitating argument that is privileged when it comes to SUBJECT selection, when in competition with an argument that merely undergoes change. 'Unergative' verbs seem to have a representation that reflects an event structure that has just such an initiating or facilitating argument; 'unaccusative' verbs have a single argument that is not represented as an initiator in the event structure.[19]

9.4 The view from morphosyntax: object selection

While the history of argument structure started off with principles of SUBJECT selection, it can fairly be said that in the modern era, OBJECT selection and its semantic correlates have gained more and more prominence and stimulated much important work at the syntax–semantics interface. I have argued that initiation, broadly construed, was the key to many of the empirical argument structure generalizations that have been noted in the literature when it comes to SUBJECT selection. When it comes to OBJECT selection, the leading idea in the literature has been 'affectedness,' although this notion has been notoriously difficult to define, and it is caught up with notions of aspect and event measuring in a way that is sometimes difficult to disentangle.

It seems that what is crucial here is the notion of the argument 'undergoing' some sort of identifiable change/transition, whether it is with respect to its location or different kinds of property states. In the following three examples, we see that the DPs are equally respectable 'OBJECTS' regardless of whether the change is that of location (41a), state (41b), or material properties (41c) (see Ramchand 1997 and Hay et al. 1999).

(41) a. John pushed the cart
b. Mary dried the cocoa beans
c. Michael stretched the rubber band

The broad notion of Undergoer (after Van Valin 1990) seems to be the one responsible for class membership here, and includes OBJECTS of verbs of change of state like *dry*, as well as OBJECTS of verbs of translational motion like *push* and *drive*. In some very general sense, all of these OBJECTS count as 'affected,' since they *undergo* the change that is criterial of the event in question. Influentially, Tenny (1987, 1994) argued that aspect is the critical semantic information relevant to the establishment of OBJECT-hood and accusative case in the syntax (see also Section 20.3). In particular, she argues that only direct OBJECTS have the function of 'measuring out' the event. Leaving the notion vague for the moment, we note that there are a number of alternations in OBJECT choice which show that an intuitive difference in 'affectedness' is correlated with OBJECT-hood.

Consider the SPRAY-LOAD alternation in many languages, where the choice of OBJECT alternates, and where the argument that 'measures out' the event covaries with that choice (Jackendoff 1996a, Tenny 1994).

(42) a. John loaded the hay on the truck
b. John loaded the truck with hay

The semantic judgment here is that while the (a) sentence above describes an event which is is complete when all of 'the hay' has been loaded, the (b) sentence describes an event which is complete when 'the truck' is completely loaded.[20] The CONATIVE alternation shows a similar semantic shift, this time between the interpretation of a DP OBJECT (43a) as opposed to a DP embedded inside a prepositional phrase (43b). In the former case, the event of eating the apple is over once the apple itself is totally consumed; in the latter case, the eating event does *not* have a natural endpoint, and it is implied that the apple never gets fully consumed.

(43) a. John ate the apple
b. John ate at the apple

Correlations like these have given rise to syntactic theories which exploit features like [+telic] (van Hout 2000, Kratzer 2004) or [+quantity] (Borer 2005b) which are checked at some aspectual projection, bounding the event, and often at the same time being associated with accusative case. However, I think these theories are too strong. First of all it is important not to conflate the notions of 'affected argument,' 'measuring out,' and 'telicity.' I take telicity to refer to the notion of an inherent, or 'set temporal endpoint' (after Krifka 1989). As one can easily demonstrate, the mere existence of an Undergoer does not necessarily imply telicity, as the English examples in (44) show.

(44) a. the chocolate melted for hours   (atelic unaccusative)
b. John melted the chocolate for hours   (atelic transitive)

Verbs which have an argument that undergoes a gradual change (without attainment of a definite result) often display unaccusative behavior in the languages where the diagnostics are clear, indicating that they actually have internal arguments in the relevant sense (Sorace 2000, Rappaport-Hovav and Levin 2000).

However, once we have the notion of Undergoer, telicity does become a logical possibility since an object undergoing a change may undergo a determinate change to attain a final state, or the change can be given a determinate measure phrase, both of which will bound the event (see Hay et al. 1999 for an important discussion of the semantics of scales and measuring with regard to change of state verbs).

Thus, while Undergoer of a change and the achievement of a definite change of state often go together on a direct OBJECT, the two notions are logically separable. Ramchand (2008) calls the entailment type for the participant that achieves a change of state the Resultee. The following sentences from English show a pure Undergoer and a composite Undergoer-Resultee role respectively.

(45) a. John pushed the cart   (Undergoer; no transition to final state)
   b. John broke the stick
                        (Undergoer-Resultee; transition to final state)

The other distinction that needs to be made is that between OBJECTS whose quantizedness have a direct effect on the telicity of the resulting VP and OBJECTS that do not. The following examples make the point (this type of example was originally discussed by Verkuyl 1972).[21]

(46) a. John ate porridge for an hour / *in an hour (mass object; atelic VP)
   b. John ate five apples in an hour / ??for an hour
                                        (quantized object; telic VP)

The quantization property has been conflated with the 'affectedness' or Undergoer property in some of the literature, as a part of a general move to correlate OBJECT-hood with telicity. Basically, one prominent idea is that the OBJECT is the distinguished argument whose quantizedness gives rise to VP telicity, as opposed to SUBJECTS, whose quantizedness is irrelevant to telicity (MacDonald 2008). However, well-known examples already show that temporal boundedness is possible for a transitive VP even without a quantized OBJECT (47a), provided the verb itself is inherently telic; and temporal unboundedness is possible for a transitive VP *with* a quantized OBJECT (47b), especially for change of location verbs.

(47) a. the rocket re-entered breathable airspace in twenty minutes
                                        (mass object; telic VP)
   b. John pushed the cart for hours   (quantized object; atelic VP)

The quantization effect occurs in a class of verbs sometimes called 'creation/consumption' verbs and is due to a homomorphism between the run-time of the event and the material extent of the direct OBJECT (see Krifka 1987, 1992b for seminal work on this topic). The best we can say is that *if* we are dealing with a creation/consumption verb, then quantization of the internal argument corresponds to telicity of the VP. So, this is indeed a special property of internal arguments as opposed to external arguments, but it turns out to have rather restricted applicability.

The general notion of Undergoer as the holder of a changing property/location is a simple and powerful one, which covers a lot of central cases of direct OBJECTS. However, it does not accurately describe *all* the kinds of OBJECTS found cross-linguistically, even in English. In addition to Undergoers (and Resultees), we also find DP OBJECTS that are more accurately described as the DP Path travelled by a changing/moving entity. In (48a) we see a PP path argument of the motion verb *run* in English, and in (48b), we see a DP OBJECT filling the same semantic role.

(48) a. Mary ran along the beach
     b. John walked the trail

One of the exciting developments in the understanding of VP semantics is the deepening of our understanding of the notion of 'path' or 'scale,' which cross-cuts a number of distinct cognitive domains (see Schwarzschild 2002b on measures in general, Zwarts 2005 for spatial paths, Wechsler 2001 and Kennedy 1999a for gradable states). As Hay *et al.* (1999) point out, the case of creation/consumption verbs is simply a special case of some attribute of the OBJECT contributing the measuring scale that is homomorphic with the event. This property is shared by all paths, whether they are derived from the OBJECT as in the case of creation/consumption, whether they come from the scale that can be inferred from a gradable adjective, or whether it is a more obvious physical path as contributed explicitly by a PP with a motion verb. Dynamic verbs themselves combine with temporal information to create a temporal scale/path. All of these scales in different modalities combine in systematic ways in complex verb descriptions, a detailed discussion of which would take us too far afield here (but see the references cited above), but which often need to exploit the notion of homomorphism between one path/scale and another. When it comes to argument structure notions, I note only that a range of path-of-change related participants tend to make 'good' OBJECTS. In (49), we see examples of Undergoer, Undergoer-Resultee, Path, and even Measure in OBJECT position (although the latter type of OBJECT is notorious in not showing all the canonical properties of direct OBJECTS in some cases).

(49) a. John rolled **the cart** (Undergoer)
     b. John rolled **the cart** over (Undergoer-Resultee)
     c. John walked **the West Highland Way** (Path)
     d. John passed **two pleasant hours** in Mary's company last night (Measure)

Looking at the motion verb *push* below, we can clearly distinguish the Undergoer, from the Path, from the Measure of the path, where it is the Undergoer that is expressed as the direct OBJECT while the Path is a PP adjunct ('along the river') and the measure is a DP adjunct ('two miles').

(50) John pushed the cart two miles along the river

It is clear that Path in this sense is not a species of Undergoer at all, but complementary to it: in (50), the path describes the ground that the Undergoer traverses. However, what all of these cases have in common is that the internal argument is either part of the description of the path/scale of change itself or is the Undergoer of that change. I take this intuition to be the main result of the last fifteen years of research on the topic of 'affectedness' and the OBJECT position. In what follows, I will use the more specifically defined terms above (Undergoer, Resultee, Path) in place of 'affectedness' or 'measuring out' because the latter terms have been used to pick out sometimes contradictory notions in the literature. However, I believe that the generalizations arrived at here show a clear intellectual path starting with Verkuyl (1972), Krifka (1987), and Tenny (1987), preserving in particular the core intuitions of Tenny's research agenda when it comes to argument structure and the internal argument.

We need to say something here about the class of stative verbs, and in particular transitive stative verbs that have direct OBJECTS in some languages (like English) and take accusative case. The notion of affectedness is clearly irrelevant to non-dynamic predications, where nothing 'affects' anything else. Thus, we know right away that OBJECT-hood or accusative case cannot be in a one-to-one relationship even with the role cluster of Undergoer, Path, and Resultee.

(51) Katherine fears nightmares

(52) Alex weighs thirty pounds

In (52), and (51) above, the OBJECTS simply further specify or describe the state of affairs: 'the fear' that 'Katherine' has is 'of nightmares,' in (52), 'the weight' in question is the weight 'of thirty pounds.' The difference between the DP 'Katherine' and the DP 'nightmares' in (51) is a matter of predicational asymmetry: 'Katherine' is the theme or Figure of the predication (in the sense of Talmy 1978), i.e., the entity that the state description is predicated of; 'nightmares' is part of the description itself.

As we saw in the discussion of SUBJECT selection with regard to stative verbs, the difference between Figure and Ground (following Talmy 1978, 2000) is a potentially extremely important one when it comes to stative relationships, extrapolating from the example of prepositions in the spatial domain. If one extends the definition of FIGURE/GROUND from the purely spatial domain to encompass stative properties more generally, 'the nightmares' is part of the property description for 'fear' and is thus a Ground of that relation, while 'Katherine' is the Figure.

In our discussion of dynamic verbs above, the predicational asymmetry between Themes/Figures and Paths/Grounds was present as well, if we generalize the holders of static properties to the holders of dynamic properties as well. The Undergoer, the object in motion, or undergoer of a change is the holder of a changing property/location, and Paths are rhematic, being the part of the description of the path covered by the Undergoer. In Ramchand (2008), I argue that Paths are in fact in a distinct structural position from Undergoers. Specifically, Paths and Grounds of stative projections are in complement position (like the Grounds of prepositions), while Undergoers and Figures are 'subjects' of predication and are generated in the specifier position of phrase structural head that denotes that subevent description. If this is correct, then natural language builds in a close fit between hierarchical structure and predicational structure very generally.

To summarize, the notions of 'affectedness,' 'measuring out,' and 'telicity' have become associated with the internal argument position in much recent theoretical discussion. I have argued here that our current knowledge shows that there is indeed a privileged relationship between the internal argument and the path of change represented by the dynamic event. I have also tried to argue that arguments associated with the path of change description (aspectually internal arguments) still must be separated into at least three distinct notions – Undergoer, Path, Resultee – even within DP OBJECTs that bear 'accusative' case. It seems clear from the patterns discussed here that just as causation or initiation feeds the subsequent notions of nominative case and SUBJECT in a privileged way, being related to the path of change gives an argument privileged status when it comes to the OBJECT relation and accusative case. This special feeding relationship with grammatical OBJECT-hood is one which all theories of argument structure effects need to deliver. However, as I hope to have made clear, a single feature checking relationship between DP internal arguments and a feature such as [+telic] or [+quantized] is inadequate to the job. Further, when it came to stative verbs, a generalization of the Figure–Ground relation seemed to be the best macro-role account of the asymmetry between SUBJECT and OBJECT.

9.4.1 Applicatives

Just as overt morphology such as causative heads or Voice morphology can alter the natural choice of SUBJECT, cross-linguistically we find that certain kinds of morphology can appear on a verb to alter its OBJECT-taking abilities. In particular, applicative morphemes generally allow the promotion to OBJECT of an argument that was previously an OBLIQUE or prepositional element. The following examples from Bantu (Chichewa) are taken from Baker's (1988) book *Incorporation*, an early and extremely influential work on grammatical function changing. The applicative morpheme is shown in bold.

(53) a. mlimi   a-ku-dul-a   mitengo   (Chichewa)
       farmer SP-PRES-cut-ASP trees
       'the farmer is cutting the trees'
    b. mlimi   a-ku-i-dul-**ir**-a   mitengo nkhandwe
       farmer SP-PRES-OP-cut-**for**-ASP trees   fox
       'the farmer is cutting trees for the fox'   (Baker 1988:237)

In the (a) example, the direct OBJECT is 'trees' as diagnosed by its ability to undergo passive, and to trigger optional OBJECT marking agreeement on the verb. However, with the addition of the applicative morpheme -*ir*, the benefactive argument 'the fox' becomes the new direct OBJECT and takes over the syntactic properties associated with that role.

As Baker (1988) notes, it is extremely common cross-linguistically for languages to have applicative morphemes that can advance dative/ goal arguments in this way, and also benefactive/malefactive arguments (including Tzotzil (Mayan), Chamorro (Indonesian) and Tuscarora (Iroquoian), and the whole of Germanic (Indo-European) if the dative alternation is considered a member of this species despite the lack of overt applicative morpheme). If a language has only one possible kind of thematic relation that can be promoted to direct OBJECT-hood it is this one, and if it allows alternation without overt morphology it is with dative/goal arguments (Baker 1988). However, these are not the only 'oblique' relations that can be converted to OBJECT by the use of applicative morphemes. Less widespread, though common on the African continent, are applicative OBJECTs which bear underlying instrumental (54) and locative (55) relations.[22] (Once again the data here is taken from Baker 1988:238).

(54) a. fisi   a-na-dul-a   chingwe ndi mpeni   (Chichewa)
        hyena SP-PAST-cut-ASP rope   with knife
        'the hyena cut the rope with a knife'
     b. fisi   a-na-dul-**ir**-a   mpeni chingwe
        hyena SP-PAST-cut-**with**-ASP knife   rope
        'the hyena cut the rope with a knife'

(55) a. umwaana y-a-taa-ye   igitabo mu maazi   (Kinyarwanda)
        child   SP-PAST-throw-ASP book   in water
        'the child has thrown the book into the water'
     b. umwaana y-a-taa-ye-**mo**   amaazi igitabo
        child   SP-PAST-throw-ASP-**in** water   book
        'the child has thrown the book in the water'

Baker's (1988) analysis of these alternations involves the incorporation of an abstract preposition into the verb. The 'object' of the preposition is then left as a DP and receives case from the V+P complex, thus acting like the main OBJECT of the clause.

Applicative constructions, broadly construed, are those in which extra morphology on the verb allows a DP that was either not present before, or present in oblique form, to be expressed as the direct OBJECT. In certain languages, as we have seen in Bantu examples above, the morphology in question is specialized dedicated morphology. In many of the more familiar European languages on the other hand, adpositions or elements of the category P seem to be implicated in a wide variety of processes that add a DP to the direct arguments of a verb. This is not surprising, since small clause predications constructed with P-like material are some of the most productive ways of modifying argument structure relationships in the syntax (see Section 9.2 on accounting for variability). P-like elements show up as prefixal morphology in the Germanic, Slavic, and even Romance languages with concomitant changes in argument structure. The interesting question for us here is how the argument structure of the prepositional/adpositional elements integrates with the argument structure of the verb to create these 'applicative' structures.

As we saw in the discussion of Baker's work above, the derived object of an applicative construction in Bantu is argued there to be the Ground of a preposition-like relation (i.e., the complement of P). And indeed, a number of prefixed verbs in German and Slavic can also be argued to involve the promotion of the Ground element of P to the direct OBJECT position (Svenonius 2003). However, this is not the only possibility for prefixed verbs. Particles (which have been argued to be intransitive Ps; cf. Emonds 1985), introduce unselected OBJECTs of complex predications, but here the introduced element is most commonly the Figure of the P predication, at least in English. Thus, in languages where such a 'particle' incorporates, the derived OBJECT also turns out to be the Figure of the prepositional relation (once again, see Svenonius (2003) for a detailed examination of these different prefixed verb types across the Germanic languages).

In the examples from Russian below, I show a prefixed verb where the derived OBJECT is the Ground of the P-relation (a), and a prefixed verb where the derived OBJECT is the Figure of the P-relation as in a large, possibly a majority, of cases if Svenonius (2003) is correct.[23]

(56) a. Boris vy-brosil sobaku
Boris out-threw dog
'Boris threw out the dog'
b. samolet pere-letel granicu
plane across-flew border
'the plane flew across the border'
(from Ramchand 2005, Russian examples from E. Romanova, p.c.)

According to one prominent analysis of the the double object construction (Baker 1988, den Dikken 1995, and to some extent Larson 1988a), the goal argument is generated as the complement of a *to* preposition, and then it is a syntactic movement that gets it into a derived, structurally superior specifier position. Under this view, the double object version in fact as a kind of applicative where the applicative head for goals is systematically null in English (and many other languages).[24] Other analyses propose that the double object version and the dative version both involve small clause P predications embedded under the verb, but with different prepositions (a null P of possession, in the case of the double object version) (Pesetsky 1995, Harley 2000).

The study of applicatives is important because it allows us to decompose the contributions of different predicational elements. For the purposes here of understanding the nature of the OBJECT relation, it allows us to minimally compare DPs deemed ineligible for OBJECT-hood in the absence of applicative morphology, with their behavior and semantic properties in the presence of it. While there are many open issues here, both GROUNDS of Ps selected by the verb, and FIGURES of resultative predicates integrable with the verbal process, seem to be able to be promoted to direct OBJECT position of the verb itself, when given the appropriate morphological help.

More recently, the notion of applicatives and applicative heads has been further refined in the work of Pylkkänen (1999). Pylkkänen's work moves away from relating applicative formation to the behavior of P, and argues for a set of very abstract functional head types that introduce arguments in their specifier positions. The relation of the applied argument to the main verb depends in turn on the type of applicative head, and its position in the VP structure. In her analysis, there are two distinct types of applicative head: an inner applicative head that occurs between the verbal categorial head and the root, and an outer one which is situated between little v and the root.[25] The lower applicative head is said to mediate a predicational relationship between the original direct OBJECT and an applied argument (which is equivalent to the P_{poss} assumed by Pesetsky 1995 and Harley 2000 for the double object construction). Low applicatives in Pylkkänen's sense are thus dependent on the existence of the direct OBJECT for their introduction. Baker (1988) also points out that many applicatives that he treats in his analysis are possible only on originally transitive verbs, but he ascribes this to their ability to assign accusative case. Pylkkänen's analysis is quite different from Baker's in that it essentially gives a Figure or 'subject' of predication analysis for introduced OBJECT arguments. In other words, the applied argument is not the complement of a P relation in her analysis.[26] High applicatives for Pylkkänen are introduced outside the argument domain of the clause. Once again, they are arguments introduced in the specifier of a functional head, and semantically they apply to the event as a whole and do not just establish a relationship with an already present internal argument. Plausibly, malefactives and benefactives are of this category.

To summarize the results of this subsection, participant relations that are not straightforwardly related to the inner aspectual scale of a core verbal dynamic event, can nevertheless be 'promoted' to direct OBJECT position under certain syntactic and morphological conditions. The incorporation of P into the verb is one well-established way of making the complement of that preposition the derived OBJECT of the V+P complex. Baker (1988) has argued that the 'applicative' morphemes found in many languages should also be analyzed as instances of P incorporation. Applicatives have also be treated more recently as functional heads in their own right which introduce arguments of certain types in their specifier position. Interestingly, one of the common applicative types cross-linguistically, and one which often doesn't require explicit morphology, can plausibly be interpreted as Resultee addition (i.e., Figures of a resultative stative relation integrated with the verb), bringing them in line with the resultative construction and the particle shift construction in English more generally. Thus the pattern of unmarked alternations vs. morphologically mediated alternations confirms the pervasiveness of inner aspectual event mapping as the relation straightforwardly made available by a verb for the semantics of its direct OBJECT relation.

9.4.2 Antipassive

The antipassive construction is in some sense the analogue to the Passive discussed in Section 9.3, except that instead of removing the normal external argument from eligibility as SUBJECT, the antipassive 'demotes' the argument that would have been the direct OBJECT and expresses it as an OBLIQUE instead. (This is functionally an important construction in some ergative languages, where the absolutive argument controls certain syntactic behaviors.) The following examples are from Greenlandic Eskimo (originally from Sadock 1980, cited by Baker 1988).

(57) a. angut-ip   arnaq   unatar-paa   (Greenlandic Eskimo)
        man-ERG woman(ABS) beat-INDIC:3sS/3sO
        'the man beat the woman'
    b. angut   arna-mik   unata-**a**-voq
        man(ABS) woman-INSTR beat-**apass**-INDIC:3sS
        'the man beat a woman'

The resulting verbal form behaves like an intransitive verb, and the single remaining argument is marked with absolutive case. Greenlandic Eskimo is an ergative–absolutive language, but there are no attested instances of a productive piece of antipassive morphology on the verb in a nominative–accusative language (Dixon 1994, Manning 1996).[27] On the other hand, having both passive and antipassive morphemes is quite common for an ergative–absolutive language, as the further examples from Greenlandic Eskimo show (taken from Sells 2010). Like the antipassive examples in (57), the passive examples in (58) show intransitive agreement.

(58) a. angut-ip arnaq taku-vaa
man-ERG woman.ABS see-3SG:3SG
'the man saw the woman'
b. arnaq (anguti-mit) taku-tau-puq
woman.ABS (man-by) see-PASS-3SG
'the woman was seen (by the man)'

The passive and the antipassive further have in common that the 'demoted' argument appears as an 'optional' adjunct. In the absence of the adjunct, the demoted argument is felt to be semantically present, and according to Baker (1988), interpreted as a non-specific indefinite. Baker's (1988) analysis is that the antipassive morpheme is an incorporated OBJECT argument with vague/generic semantics, which pragmatically supports the existence of an adjunct phrase. This is directly contra the analysis in Marantz (1984) who argues that the oblique in the antipassive is a true argument of the verb. The debate is exactly paralleled by a similar debate concerning the *by*-phrase in passives, with researchers like Baker et al. (1989) analyzing the participial ending of the passive as an incorporated agent argument, and others like Collins (2005b) arguing that the *by*-phrase *is* the agent argument.

Antipassive therefore seems tightly bound up with case marking and grammatical function coding, a level that we have said is logically distinct from argument structure, but systematically fed by it. Both passive and antipassive use morphological means to disrupt the 'normal' mapping of argument structure to case or grammatical function. Thus the relevance of the antipassive to theories of argument structure is similar to that of the passive – understanding how this morphology works technically to affect the mapping to grammatical function is an important clue to the argument structure configurations and the way they connect to the syntax. But as with the passive, many of these issues remain unresolved, partly because our understanding of SUBJECT vs. OBJECT and case are still imperfect.

9.5 Case

So far I have assumed that the distinctions that we find in participant relations (which I have been calling 'argument structure') are logically distinct from grammatical function (which I have been calling SUBJECT and OBJECT). I further assume that distinctions of case are logically independent of the previous two modes of organization,[28] although this is another domain where argument structure effects are found across languages. Case and its interaction with argument structure have had a long history which I cannot hope to do justice to here.[29] I briefly summarize the main issues involved and refer the interested reader to the relevant literature.

When one considers the relationship to argument structure, or thematic role, there are three main categories of case that are normally distinguished in the literature: structural case, inherent case, and lexical or idiosyncratic case (see Butt 2006). Structural cases are those which clearly show an independence from thematic role, and which seem to be defined by their structural position in the phrase marker; inherent cases are related directly to semantic generalizations (whether one thinks of this in terms of traditional thematic role labels or not); lexical/idiosyncratic/quirky case is case that is assigned by the verb to the DP argument in a lexically idiosyncratic way that simply requires memorization (see also Woolford 1997, 2006). While the differences between these three categories of case are easy to state in theory, in practice it is somewhat more difficult to decide where each particular case phenomenon in a language lies in this typology.

Nominative case is the case found on SUBJECTS in nominative-accusative languages. It is clear that it does not correlate with thematic role (cf. 'John broke the window' vs. 'The window broke'). Accusative is also considered to be a structural case, as well as some instances of Genitive and Dative, and possibly some instances of ergative (see Chapter 17 for discussion). Instances of inherent case that are supposed to correlate with thematic role include the dative that occurs on ditransitive goals in Icelandic (Maling 2001) and German (Czepluch 1988) and on experiencer Subjects in Hindi/Urdu and indeed many South Asian languages (Mohanan 1994).

(59) eir   gáfu konunginum   ambáttina   (Icelandic)
      they gave king-the-DAT slave-girl-the-ACC
      'they gave the king the slave girl'
                              (from Maling 2002, cited in Woolford 2006)

(60) mujhe   is baat-kaa   bahut dukh   hai   (Hindi/Urdu)
      I.DAT   this.OBL thing-GEN great sadness be.PRES.SG
      'I am very sad about this thing'

As discussed in Chapter 17, many instances of inherent or semantically based case can be analyzed in a similar way to prepositions in languages with less rich case systems.

Instances of idiosyncratic case include special case forms required by certain prepositions, or on themes by particular verbs, where this simply has to be memorized on a case by case basis. In (61), we see the quirky accusative case marked SUBJECT of the Icelandic verb 'drift,' and in (62), we see the genitive marked OBJECT of the German verb 'remember.'

(61) bátinn   rak   á land   (Icelandic)
     the boat-ACC drifted to shore
     'the boat drifted to the shore'

(62) Peter gedachte   der gefallenen   Soldaten   (German)
     Peter remembered the-GEN.PL fallen-GEN.PL soldiers.GEN
     'Peter thought about / remembered the fallen soldiers'

Ergative case marking languages are distinguished by the fact that the single argument of monotransitive verbs receives the same 'case' as the internal argument of transitive verbs. This case is the 'unmarked' case in those languages and is generally given the label of Absolutive. This means that there is a distinguished case solely for the SUBJECT of transitive verbs, and this is the ergative case. I show examples from Dyirbal below, where 3rd person arguments show an ergative case-marking pattern.[30]

(63) a. yabu   banaga-nyu   (Dyirbal)
        mother.ABS return-NONFUT
        'mother returned'
     b. ?uma   yabu-?gu   bura-n
        father.ABS mother-ERG see-NONFUT
        'mother saw father'   (from Dixon 1994)

It has been claimed in some languages that ergative case is a semantically sensitive case, while others have argued that it is a structural case (Wunderlich 1997). Ergative case has also been argued to correlate with the thematic relation of agentivity in languages like Basque (Cheng and Demirdache 1993) and Hindi/Urdu (Mahajan 1994, Butt 1995). In Chapter 17, it is suggested that the disconnect between case and thematic role is more striking with ergative languages, since the SUBJECT of a transitive verb quite often has the 'same' thematic role as the SUBJECT of an intransitive ('unergatives'), yet they are case marked differently. However, the disconnect between case and thematic role is more striking with nominative–accusative languages when it comes to the direct OBJECT position, since the OBJECT of a transitive verb often has the 'same' thematic role as the SUBJECT of an intransitive ('unaccusatives'), and yet *they* are case-marked differently. Essentially, given the empirical fact that event structure does not match perfectly with structuring in the IP domain, any structurally defined case at this level is going to show mismatches with thematic structure.

As discussed in Chapter 17, Case Theory used to have an importance in the theory in the Government and Binding era (Chomsky 1981) that has largely been supplanted by a theory of Agree. An important generalization from that time, *Burzio's Generalization* (Burzio 1986), makes a direct correlation between having an external argument and the ability to assign accusative case. Burzio's Generalization is essentially a description of the fact that in nominative–accusative languages, the hierarchically superior argument moves to SUBJECT position, and claims further that Agents are not possible without (implicit, or incorporated) Themes. It is not clear how to assess the generalization for ergative–absolutive languages.[31]

The issue of structural case vs. inherent case takes on a different hue when we consider it in the light of the latest attempts to make semantic sense of such cases as nominative and accusative. Pesetsky and Torrego (2001) argue that structural case is *not* uninterpretable but that nominative is actually the nominal correlate of tense; Svenonius (2002a) and Pesetsky and Torrego (2004) argue that accusative is correlated with an aspectual event structure notion or lower tense node, respectively. More generally, as we have seen in Section 9.4, structural accusative case has been implicated in notions like specificity (Mahajan 1994), quantizedness, and 'measuring out' of the event (Kratzer 2004). Nominative and accusative failed spectacularly to conform to semantic role when our role list looked like traditional thematic role labels; as our semantic categories become more and more abstract, it is less clear whether those 'structural' cases really are so semantically innocent after all. From the point of view of argument structure, the question is whether the event structure hierarchies which involve notions like Cause/Initiator and Undergoer correlate reliably with these more abstract semantic notions, or whether they represent an even higher layer of abstraction of semantic structuring, or have no semantic consequences at all.

In sum, case has often been analyzed in such a way as to make it logically independent of argument structure facts. Structural case has been seen as a higher order level of grammatical organization, while lexical case has been relegated to the realm of memorized idiosyncrasy. However, there are a number of reasons to include case marking patterns in the empirical ground that forms the basis of our understanding of argument structure. First, there are many cases of case-marking patterns which have a reliable correlation with semantics. These need to be understood and established whether they reflect event participancy facts or something independent. Second, even the more abstract 'structural' cases may turn out to be correlated with semantic notions, once the categories are properly understood. Once again, it is important to understand whether this is a separate kind of semantic entailment or part of what we would want to include in our notion of argument structure.

9.6 Architectural issues: argument structure at the interfaces

The bulk of this review chapter has been devoted to giving a fresh look at the actual data and generalizations that are important to any successful theory of argument structure. Despite current theoretical disagreements, I think there is no doubt that there is now an impressive body of empirical work that has accumulated over the past forty years, and a considerable amount of progress in our understanding of basic patterns in both familiar and less well studied languages. While I have tried to put these discoveries in some kind of historical perspective, I have chosen so far not to emphasize the theoretical debates that surround the analysis of them. To a great extent, the patterns I have reported in this chapter are acknowledged by researchers of many different persuasions and form the basis of some kind of consensus about what is important.

Throughout this chapter, I have taken the position that what people refer to under the label 'argument structure' is the relational semantics of participancy between nominal projections and predicative projections. I have further taken the position that this level of semantic information is best described as a structured representation of event semantics involving notions of Cause, Change, and Result. The evidence that these factors are grammatically relevant comes from generalizations concerning SUBJECT or OBJECT selection, types of constructional alternation, and interactions with explicit morphology including case and verbal affixation.

While I believe the patterns that I have laid out are real, it should be clear that the mapping between 'argument structure' as I have construed it and the levels of case and grammatical function are by no means simple or one-to-one. Nevertheless, I have shown that there are clear patterns in the data that any theory will need to deliver. Constructing such a theory however, introduces its own complications due to the interaction of argument structure effects with other modules of the grammar. In the next two subsections, I outline the issues that arise in deciding on the division of labor between argument structure effects and other semantic factors on the one hand (9.6.1), and the division of labor between lexical specification and constructional effects on the other (9.6.2).

9.6.1 Other semantic factors, and the interface with pragmatics

There is ample evidence in the literature that there are other semantic factors that influence case and grammatical function that are not part of what I am considering as argument structure. I mention just a few of these factors here, since understanding them is logically required for a proper delineation of argument structure effects proper, although there is no space to do full justice to all the literature here.

First of all, there is substantial evidence when it comes to SUBJECT selection that many languages pay attention to the inherent semantic properties of the DPs in question to constrain suitability as SUBJECT. Animacy and related person hierarchies have thus been argued to have direct effects in the grammar of certain languages (e.g. Navajo (Hale 1972), Frishberg 1972); Mayan (Craig 1977, England 1991)), where it is essentially grammaticalized and operates as a hard constraint on the expression of arguments of the verb in the syntax or their relative prominence. For instance, in Navajo (Athapaskan) the possibility of reversing the arguments is constrained by their relative animacy on the hierarchy human > animal > inanimate (cf. Comrie 1989), and in cases of so-called differential OBJECT marking (DOM; cf. Aissen 2003), the relative prominence of OBJECTs in terms of animacy and definiteness is argued to interact with overt OBJECT marking; the higher an OBJECT is on these hierarchies, the more likely is it to be overtly case-marked. Animacy is an extremely salient factor in humans' cognitive awareness and organization. In addition to affecting how we process the world more generally, it has been found to be an important factor in linguistic processing, both in comprehension and production (Stowe 1989, Trueswell et al. 1994, Lamers 2005, inter alia). It is therefore important and interesting that these factors affect grammatical structuring. The position I take in this chapter is that since these are not relational notions of participancy, but are inherently part of the nominal's semantics, they do not fall under the rubric of 'argument structure.' However, they do compete with argument structure facts in determining syntactic behavior. It might even be argued that there are some languages that pay more attention to such cognitive determinants of relevance and saliency, and that argument structure *per se* plays only a minor role.

Even in languages where the grammar has not been argued to directly reflect animacy features (e.g., modern Germanic and Romance languages), its effects have been shown in the area of 'soft constraints.' For example, Øvrelid (2004) reports that in Norwegian, ninety-seven percent of the transitive clauses in a corpus are those in which the 'SUBJECT' ranks equal or higher than the 'OBJECT' in animacy, and shows that animacy together with definiteness plays an important role with respect to argument alignment. Thus, the very same pattern that gives rise to strict grammaticality vs. ungrammaticality in a Mayan language like Jacaltec (cf. Craig 1977), shows up as a strong functional tendency in a language like Norwegian. One major question that needs to be asked in this domain is whether the observed effects flow directly from a particular language's grammar ('direct' effects), or whether they flow from the general human cognitive system that the grammar is anchored to ('indirect' effects). On the architectural side, in theories of argument structure, animacy is not usually isolated as a feature *per se*, but shows up as part of the definition of roles like AGENT, or EXPERIENCER, or BENEFICIARY. The striking exception to this is Reinhart's 'Theta System' (Reinhart 2002), which explicitly uses the feature ±m (mental state) alongside ±c (cause) as the primary feature pair to classify arguments. There is no doubt that animacy interacts with argument structure in certain ways. For example, only animates can be volitional agents, and only animates can be experiencers. However, we have seen that the nature of the structuring according to event participancy does not make a distinction between abstract cause and intentional causer, and that the idea of experiencer as a thematic role often dissolves into different categories depending on whether the argument is being construed as 'affected' (undergoing a change) or 'possessional' (holding a particular kind of state). Although the issue is by no means settled, I have therefore put the issue of animacy aside here, given its non-*relational* nature, and in the hope that it will turn out to be an independent dimension of meaning.

Another recognized dimension of meaning is information structuring (see Chapter 23): topicality and obviation being important factors in the SUBJECT selection mechanisms of many languages for example (see Aissen 1997). When confronted with a particular language or phenomenon, it is important to be able to disentangle any effects of event structure from notions like topicality, or newness, or one risks misstating the generalizations. To illustrate with one recent prominent example, the dative alternation is one of the classics of the argument structure literature, spawning many different theories about the mapping between lexical semantics and structure, and the mapping between structure and meaning. However, recent corpus and experimental work on the dative alternation has shown that factors such as 'heaviness' and 'newness' are strong predictors of choice of alternant, with both 'heaviness' and discourse newness of the theme positively correlating with the use of the double object variant (Arnold et al. 2000, Bresnan et al. 2007). This recent work shows that alternations are less categorical than the earlier argument structure literature seemed to suggest (cf. Green 1974, Oehrle 1976, Pinker 1989), and mean possibly that the mappings between meaning and structure need to be stated more flexibly. Once again I put these issues aside as being beyond the scope of this chapter. Here I think it is clearer even than in the case of animacy that this dimension is a separate module which coexists with argument structure and its effects.

9.6.2 The lexicon vs. syntax

I end this chapter with a brief discussion of the non-lexicalist approaches to argument structure that have regained prominence over the past ten or fifteen years. I will also outline what I take to be the main issues at stake when it comes to the tension between the lexicalist intuitions of the seventies and eighties and the more constructivist agenda.[32]

As Levin and Rappaport Hovav (2005) discuss in their recent review monograph on argument structure, it seems clear that what is needed to capture the generalizations we find is some kind of structured representation, probably making core reference to notions of causation and embedding. In addition, the fact that argument structure manifestations in the syntax are so variable, but in systematic ways, shows correspondingly that those representations can be built up and manipulated in systematic ways also. Even if one agrees on all of this, there remains the architectural question of whether the lexicon itself should be conceived of as a module with some kind of rule-driven or generative capacity or not. The position taken by the constructivists is that meaning resides in structure, and that *syntax* makes structures, while the lexicon harbors only lists. For those lexicalists who entertain structured representations within the lexicon, they must face the question of redundancy, if the principles and vocabulary they espouse bear too close a resemblance to things that are already the proper business of syntax. Much hinges on how much structured meaning one allows in the syntax in the first place.

The resurgence of syntactic approaches to argument structure begins perhaps paradoxically with Larson (1988a), whose analysis of the double object construction actually employs a thematic role list and hierarchy. Larson's contribution is to advocate a system of VP shells, where the direct OBJECT and goal appear in specifier positions of those shells (depending on the alternant in question). This move essentially liberated researchers working on VP internal syntax by offering many potential positions and landing-sites, and opened up the idea of generating arguments (in particular, OBJECTs) in the specifiers of functional heads while still remaining in the domain of the VP.

The important substantive arguments for the syntacticization of argument structure come first from Ken Hale and Jay Keyser, however, in a series of articles beginning in the late eighties, culminating in the influential Hale and Keyser (1993) and subsequent monograph of collected and revised work (Hale and Keyser 2002). Hale and Keyser's intuition is that not all logically possible verbal meanings are actually instantiated in the grammar of natural languages because syntactic facts constrain how they are composed. This leads to the idea of a 'lexical syntax' ("the syntactic configurations projected by a lexical item"; Hale and Keyser 2002:1), which contains the structured decompositions of verbal meaning, built and constrained by the toolbox of grammar, to derive only the forms and patterns that actually exist. They initiated a theoretical programme which, while not complete, set the agenda for many working on argument structure for years to come. While Hale and Keyser were vague about the architectural status of their idea of 'lexical syntax' (sometimes implying that it was a level of syntax, and at other times calling it a lexical representation), their ideas have been most influential on later constructivists who advocate a strongly syntactic approach. The agenda is to use independently attested syntactic principles to understand the properties of the lexicon and how they interact with higher level syntactic facts.

Hale and Keyser also argue for many synthetic verb types in English, where lower predicational structure in the form of N, A, or P elements conflates into higher verbal heads constructing essentially derived argument entailments (denominal, deadjectival, and location/locatum verbs respectively). Deadjectival and denominal verbs arise from what I have described as Ground material being incorporated from complement position into the head. Thus, in Hale and Keyser (1993), the verb *dance* is covertly transitive: the nominal 'dance' can be thought of the complement of the generalized *do* process, which then 'incorporates' into the verbal head. In the case of the location verbs, such as *bottle*, the nominal in question is the complement of the PP (a Ground element which further describes the result state achieved by the undergoer of translational motion). In the case of locatum verbs (*saddle*), the 'incorporation' occurs from the complement position of an abstract possessional PP '$\emptyset_{with}$ saddle.' In the case of deadjectival verbs, the incorporation is from the AP scalar complement of the embedded small clause.

The intuition behind the Hale and Keyser account is that the correlation with selection (which determines the complement) and 'conflation' reflects a real syntactic generalization. In Hale and Keyser (2000), however, a distinction must be made between conflation and genuine syntactic incorporation (which had been assumed to be constrained by 'government'). The problem is that 'conflation' verbs are compatible with an overt DP in complement position.

(64) a. they are dancing a Sligo jig
      b. they shelved the books on the windowsill
      (Hale and Keyser 2002:49)

(65) *Conflation*:
Conflation consists in the process of copying the p-signature of the complement into the p-signature of the head, where the latter is 'defective.' (Hale and Keyser 2002:63)

The difference between 'conflation' and standard morphosyntactic instances of incorporation shows that the debate between a syntactic locus for these processes and a pre-syntactic one is not yet conclusive (see also Kiparsky 1997).

When there is great agreement on substantive content, the difference between a constructivist approach and a lexicalist one can seem more like notational variance. Thus, while lexicalists like Levin and Rappaport (1998) build structures using the vocabulary of labeled brackets and abstract conceptual 'constants,' Hale and Keyser build similar structures in the syntax and attach abstract structural semantic interpretation to syntactic functional heads. Thus both theoretical programs agree on the importance of the notion Cause and hierarchically structured representations, but disagree on whether the syntax and the lexicon use the same or different vocabularies. Compare the representations below, where (66) would be the Hale and Keyser version, and (67) the Levin and Rappaport style lexical representation.

(66)

```
        V₁
      (Cause)
         \
          \
       DP  \
       mud  \
             \
              V₂
            splash
                \
                 P    DP
                 |    △
                 on  the wall
```

(the pigs) splashed mud on the walls   (after Hale and Keyser 2002)

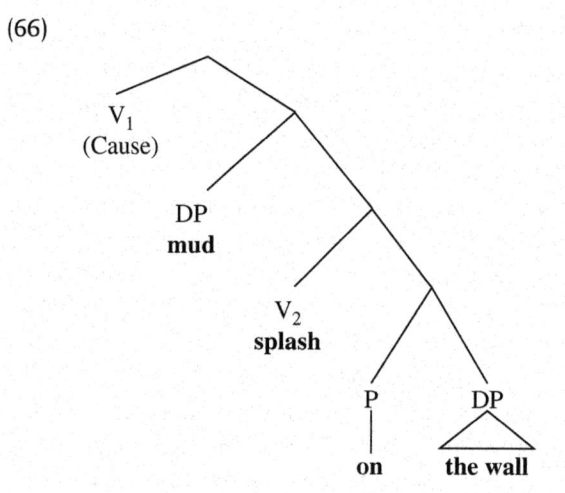

(67) *splash*: [x Cause [y TO COME TO BE AT z]]/ SPLASH
The variables x, y, and z get filled in by the the DPs 'the pigs,' 'mud,' and 'the walls' respectively in the syntax.
the pigs splashed mud on the walls   (after Levin and Rappaport 1998)

In such cases, the differences are conceptual and architectural and are not yet possible to decide conclusively. In other cases, the difference between lexical approaches and syntactic approaches also involve differences of substance and emphasis. One of the points that I hope to have convinced the reader of in this chapter so far is that while ideological and architectural differences are worth arguing about, one can still separate genuine empirical claims and advances from notational choices.

A further seminal paper in the syntactic treatment of argument structure is Kratzer (1996). Kratzer gives an argument based on compositional semantics that the external argument of a predicate cannot be represented as part of the lexical role list, but must be associated with the VP (verb plus OBJECT) as a whole to capture the pattern of selectional restrictions that we find. In doing so, she is essentially agreeing with and following up on data and argumentation in Marantz (1984), in which he shows that the internal argument of a verb can trigger a particular idiomatic interpretation that verb, but an external argument does not (but see also Horvath and Siloni 2002 for arguments against this view). The selectional restrictions on the external argument come from the Verb plus DP OBJECT combination as a whole. Kratzer invokes the recent trend in the logical semantics of events which separates the arguments from the verb itself and introduces them via separate relational predicates (usually thematic role labels are used for these relations but this is not necessary). Under the neo-Davidsonian view, as it is called (after Donald Davidson, who originally proposed an event argument for verbal predicates; Davidson 1967), verbs have only an event argument, while the DP arguments are related to that event variable by separate thematic relations (see Parsons 1990, Higginbotham 1985). A neo-Davidsonian schematic of the logical semantics for the arguments of a transitive verb like *destroy* is given below.

(68) $\exists e,x,y[\text{destroying}(e)\ \&\ \text{Agent}(x, e)\ \&\ \text{Patient}(y, e)]$

The difference here is that Kratzer (1996) argues that the empirical evidence supports severing the *external* argument from the verb, but not the internal ones. Schematically, again, the logic would look like (69) below.

(69) $\exists e,x,y[\text{destroying}(e,y)\ \&\ \text{Agent}(x, e)]$

Importantly, Kratzer's proposal is not just about some formal semantic interpretation language, because she assumes a tight mapping between syntax and semantics, she assumes that the logic above corresponds to a syntactic representation where the external argument is introduced in the specifier position of a functional head which lies outside the VP proper. She calls this projection VoiceP, and it bears some resemblance to the Hale and Keyser highest V head in introducing the external argument, although she does not give it the explicit semantics of Cause.

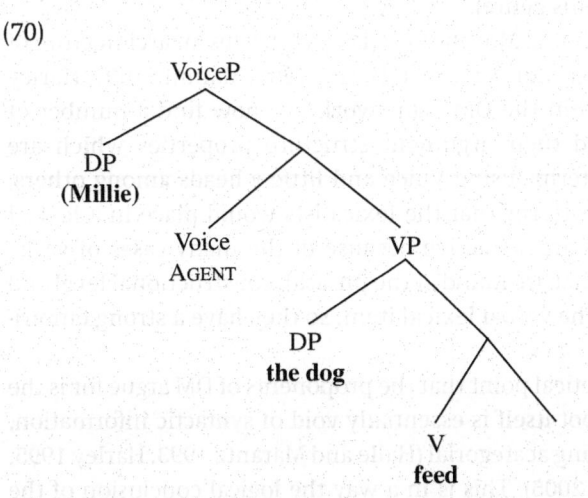

(70)

```
              VoiceP
             /      \
           DP        \
        (Millie)      \
                    Voice    VP
                   AGENT    /  \
                           DP   \
                        the dog  \
                                  V
                                feed
```

In Kratzer's semantics, the event description corresponding to the VP and the event description introduced by the Voice head (which essentially only has the function of introducing the external argument) are combined by event identification as part of the compositional semantics.

In an important set of arguments from distributive quantification, Schein (1993, 2003) shows compellingly that external argument and the internal argument *both* need to be logically independent of the verbal relation, giving rise to an even more decomposed representation (see Lohndal, 2012 for a discussion of Schein's arguments and his case against the classical Kratzerian position).

The modern tradition of syntacticizing argument structure takes elements from one or all of these works, although there is some disagreement about the scope and interpretation of these functional heads. The separation of the external argument is more widely represented in logical structure than the separation of the internal argument, where the latter is often treated as part of the verbal conceptual structure (Borer 2005b). Many researchers simply use little *v* heads (or their equivalent) which both introduce an external argument and have the semantics of cause (e.g., Ramchand 2008). Others use little *v* for Cause but add the external argument separately by means of a Voice head (e.g., Pylkkänen 1999). The situation is complicated by the fact that many authors assume that each of these functional heads can come in a number of different 'flavors,' with different featural and selectional properties (Folli and Harley 2004). Moreover, while Kratzer's semantics is very explicit and clear, it is not always so clear what the semantics for the various different types and flavors are, or how the pieces fit together compositionally in this later work. I think it is fair to say that currently there is no consensus on the number of types of little *v* heads, or the role of VoiceP as separate from it (see Alexiadou 2010, Schaeffer 2008, Folli and Harley 2004 for important examples of work in this genre).

The theory of Distributed Morphology (DM) advocates an architecture of grammar that is strongly non-lexicalist (Harley 1995, Marantz 1997, Harley and Noyer 1999). Within the DM framework, we now find a number of analyses of verbs and their argument structure properties which are couched in syntactic terms using Voice and little *v* heads among others, to capture semantic patterns that the lexicalists would place in a lexical entry. These accounts are attractive because of the many cases of variability and patterning that are found at the phrasal, constructional level and cannot be pinned on the verbal lexical item, so they have a strong empirical motivation.

An important theoretical point that the proponents of DM argue for is the idea that the verbal root itself is essentially void of syntactic information, even to the point of being acategorial (Halle and Marantz 1993, Harley 1995, Marantz 1997, Harley 2005). This is in a way the logical conclusion of the move toward introducing all argument structure and event structure features by means of functional heads. The proponents of the acategorial roots view argue that the root contains *only* conceptual information, and that all of the verb's syntactic behavior (including argument structure patterning, and even syntactic category) comes from the functional syntactic context that the root finds itself embedded in (see also, importantly, Borer 2005b).

The virtue of some of the syntactic work on argument structure is that it takes explicit account of morphology in addition to syntactic patterning in the manifestation of arguments. The real shortcoming of the syntactic work as I see it, is that it has largely ignored the issue of selection and subcategorization that the work on argument structure first started with.

In embracing the constructional patterns and the variable behavior of verbal lexical items, it is easy to underplay the fact that verbs actually do have a character and come with specific patterns of behavior. If we lived in constructivist heaven, every single conceptual verbal root would occur in all possible argument structure environments, given enough contextual support. Many constructivists argue that rigidities in verbal behavior come from frequency effects and/or conventionalization and are not really excluded by the grammar at all. They essentially deny that anything like 'selection' is necessary (see discussions, for example, in Borer 2005b and Lohndal 2012). However, as we have seen in this chapter, some verbs undergo the conative alternation and others do not (71); some verbs detransitivize and others do not (72); some verbs can undergo resultative augmentation and others do not (73).

(71) a. John ate at the apple
      b. John hit at the table
      c. *John destroyed at the city

(72) a. John broke the stick / the stick broke
      b. John ate the apple / *the apple ate
      c. John destroyed the city / *the city destroyed
      d. John hit the table / *the table hit

(73) a. John broke the vault open / into pieces
      b. John handed the letters in
      b. *John destroyed the city into cinders
      c. *John rejected Mary despondent

To ignore these issues and not address how the verbal root can constrain the syntactic functional environments that it can appear in, leaves a huge basic gap in descriptive adequacy as severe as the problems the lexicalists have with constructional variablity. It is of course possible to build in a notion of selectional frame within a DM architecture (see Harley and Noyer 2000 for an acknowledgment of the use of selectional templates in the post-syntactic component), but it runs the risk of reintroducing the lexicon by the back door.

To summarize the state of the architectural disagreements, I would argue that the established argument structure effects require a detailed hierarchically structured representation within an event semantics, although so far nothing hinges on this complex representation being part of the narrow syntax or part of a dedicated lexical module. The effects and the tools required appear to me to be syntactic in nature, once one believes that syntax maps in a transparent way to certain aspects of predicational semantics. However, this is just a hunch, and there is still a lot of work to be done to understand (i) the interaction of event structuring facts with the details of verbal morphology, case marking, and grammatical functions across languages, and (ii) the nature of the information on verbal roots so that they are underspecified enough to be flexible and yet specific enough to give rise to distinctive behaviors.[33]

I conclude with the claim that despite the great advances in understanding that have been made in (i) above, (ii), the 'Selection Problem' still looms as large as it ever did at the beginning of the generative enterprise. This chapter has thus come full circle, starting with a discussion of subcategorization frames (Chomsky 1957), and ending with a plea for linguists to revisit the serious and still unresolved problem of 'selection.'

Notes

1. According to this view, the Dowty list looks the way it does because of general human cognitive constraints on the mental representation of events, a not a priori implausible position.
2. F-structure is the data structure of LFG that represents grammatical function information such as SUBJECT and OBJECT separately from constituent structure or order (see Bresnan 2001 and Chapter 6 for details).
3. However, the UTAH in particular enshrines the correlation between form and meaning in one direction only – thematic relationships map deterministically onto syntax, but not necessarily in the reverse direction so that there can be a many-to-one relationship between thematic information and structural position. It is possible to go even further, with one-to-one mappings between phrase structure and meaning proposed by, e.g., Hale and Keyser (2000), a move that tends to be favored by the constructivists.
4. See for example, Reinhart's (2002) role coreference rules for lexicalized 'reflexives' such as *shave* or *bathe*, or the analysis of complex verbal forms where the 'affected argument' or PATIENT of one event is identified with the 'causer' or AGENT of an embedded event, as in Alsina and Joshi (1993) for Marathi causatives.
5. A brief comment about TOPIC is in order here. Many languages have been argued to be TOPIC prominent languages instead of SUBJECT prominent languages, although even in these languages is it often possible to distinguish the grammatical function of SUBJECT *in addition* to the discourse notion TOPIC (Li and Thompson 1976) (see also Chapter 23). Factors that distinguish TOPIC from SUBJECT include the fact that the former has a uniform discourse status in that it is always definite, unlike SUBJECT, and the fact that the SUBJECT bears a selectional relationship with the verb, whereas the TOPIC need not. In turn, it is the SUBJECT that is implicated in grammatical processes such as agreement, reflexivization, and passive within a particular language, and, crucially for us, it is the SUBJECT which is determined on the basis of the choice of verb (Li and Thompson 1976, Schachter 1976). Thus, SUBJECT can be distinguished from TOPIC and the former is the place where argument

structure generalizations can be sought. See also the discussion of the Voice systems of Austronesian languages in note 10.
6. It is true that *within* a particular language, one naturally assumes that morphology mediated alternations have a different status from flexibility alternations. However, when one looks cross-linguistically, both morphology mediated and non-morphology mediated alternations show substantial overlap in their effects. See the discussion of the 'causative–inchoative' alternation in the text.
7. But see Cinque (1990a) for an argument for a distinction between different types of stative verbs analogous to the unaccusative/unergative distinction.
8. One often also sees the traditional grammar term Rheme used for elements which are part of the description of the eventuality, in contrast to elements whose properties or changing properties are at issue (Themes).
9. This is consistent with the general consensus from the thematic role literature, where either Causer or Agent sit on top of the thematic hierarchy.
10. Another prominent case of voice alternations that comes to mind here is the voice system of the Austronesian languages, where explicit morphology changes the morphosyntactic representation of the arguments of a verbal predicate (Schachter 1976, Sells 2001a, Rackowski 2002). These systems are also potential sources of evidence for generalizations about argument structure prominence, but I put them aside in this chapter for reasons of space. Part of the problem with understanding the data revolves around resolving the difference between 'SUBJECT' and 'Topic' in these languages. If the morphological alternations involve choice of 'Topic,' then they are not likely to be relevant to argument structure. As Schachter discusses in an important early article (Schachter 1976), the promoted argument (the *ang-* marked argument in the case of Tagalog) is the only argument that can be relativized over, and is the only argument that can launch floating quantifiers (two classic 'SUBJECT' properties). On the other hand, it is the Actor argument, regardless of topic marking, which antecedes reflexives and is the referentially gapped DP in controlled clauses (two other classic 'SUBJECT' properties). In the end, the Austronesian languages may be more important for understanding the relationship between two different types of syntactically prominent position ('SUBJECT' vs. 'Topic') than for offering the simplest most direct evidence for argument structure hierarchies. I will therefore not discuss the relationship between Austronesian morphology and thematic role here, but the interested reader should see Rackowski (2002), Travis (2004), and Sells (2001a) for recent proposals.

11. It is a separate architectural question whether this representation is non-linguistic, as it is for Jackendoff (Jackendoff 1983, 1990a); linguistic, but in its own distinct module as in Levin and Rappaport Hovav (1995) and Williams (2003); or a subpart of syntactic representation itself as in most GB approaches to D-structure and in recent constructivist accounts.
12. While many languages show an ergative system of case marking which gives the non-causer priority in getting the unmarked case, and sometimes in triggering agreement, true *syntactic* ergativity is much rarer. Specifically, Anderson (1976) argues that when the syntactic diagnostics of SUBJECT-hood (such as relativization, antecedent of reflexive, controllee position in semantically controlled clauses, etc.) are examined, nearly all morphologically ergative languages turn out to have the same choice of ' SUBJECT' as nominative–accusative languages. In other words, the 'causer' argument is still the controlled position in non-finite clauses and seems to be hierarchically superior for the purposes of the Binding Theory. The only established case of a language which is syntactially ergative in addition to being morphologically ergative seems to be Dyirbal (Dixon 1972, 1994) where the absolutive case-marked argument is sytematically privileged with respect to relativization and control. This is nevertheless still not an exception to the generalization stated above unless it can be shown that the ergative case-marked argument (Agent, or Causer) in transitive verbs is not somehow oblique, or demoted.
13. In addition, the dispositional middle seems to have strong contextual constraints on it: it is only felicitous if the derived SUBJECT can be interpreted as bearing an inherent or (modalized) dispositional property facilitating that general event type. Thus, dispositional middles are derived statives (sometimes described in terms of genericity; see Condoravdi 1989), with a dispositional property ascribed to the notional object (Lekakou 2005). The 'property' reading is presumably related to the fact that the implicit agent receives a 'generic' or 'arbitrary' interpretation (Lyons 1995, Lekakou 2005).
14. The source of the labels unergative vs. unaccusative is complex, and the resulting terminology is confusing. Unaccusatives are so-called because, by hypothesis, they fail to assign accusative case, resulting in the promotion of a single internal argument to SUBJECT position. It is now generally used as a label for a class of verbs whose single SUBJECT argument has some properties in common with transitive OBJECTS, and is semantically more 'internal' (independently of what the correct analysis is). Unergative verbs are so-called because of a parallel argument for a hypothetical ergative–absolutive case-marking language. In such a language, the SUBJECT of a transitive verb gets special ergative case marking. However, with an unergative verb (which is intransitive by definition),

its SUBJECT is just as SUBJECT-like syntactically and semantically as the SUBJECT of transitives, but it would *not* get ergative case in an ergative case-marking language. Hence the term unergative. The term unergative as applied to verbs is now simply used to refer to intransitive verbs whose single SUBJECT argument shows no OBJECT-like properties, and is semantically more 'external.'

15. Subsequent work has cast doubt on the reliability of the *ne*-cliticization test as a diagnostic, with many authors pointing out a number of discourse factors that seem to cut across the distinction in argument structure (Levin and Rappaport Hovav 1995, Bentley 2004).
16. One problem often cited with the notion of unaccusativity is that translations of an unaccusative verb in one language do not always straightforwardly yield an unaccusative verb in another language, even where both languages make the distinction clearly (see Zaenen 1993 for the comparison between Italian and Dutch). However, this only appears to show that behavior cannot be predicted directly from the semantics of real-world situations, but that facts about situations in the world merely feed the way in which events are represented linguistically. Plausibly, only linguistic representations are symbolic and categorical; the real world is messy and open to different choices of representation in many cases.
17. Probably intended to be the opposite of 'unergative' in the context of the unergative–unaccusative distinction, this usage adds to the confusing cluster of terminological distinctions, being crucially different from the use of the term 'ergative' in ergative languages (which have a distinct ergative case for the SUBJECT of a transitive sentence). I stay away from this usage in what remains of this chapter, merely noting that it was the term originally used for the intransitive member of the verbs in English that show this transitivity alternation.
18. See also Section 20.3.
19. Once again, I state the semantic generalization in the direction from linguistic representation to entailments. The claim about the two different classes of intransitive is that they represent a decision about how a particular eventuality is presented: unergative VP structures contain the representation of a initiating argument; unaccusative VP structures do not. This claim explicitly denies that one can objectively determine event structure from observation of the real world, possibly a contentious point. Most relevantly for this chapter, however, the description of the correlation in this direction is deliberately silent about whether a particular *lexical* item is listed as being specific to one structure or the other.
20. Once again, the correlations here run from syntactic structure to semantic entailments, not from lexical item to semantic entailments. Note also that a speaker may choose to represent the event in either of

these two ways, depending on their communicative purpose, and what features of the event they care about.
21. One must be careful to distinguish this effect from the effect of indefinite plural DP participants, which can give rise to an atelic reading of the VP due to an indefinite number of event iterations distributed over the plural partiicipant. Crucially, this iterative effect shows up for both SUBJECTS and OBJECTS and even the OBJECTS of PPs within the verb phrase.
22. Baker (1988) claims however that this is the only productive case of locative applicatives that he knows of.
23. This kind of classification depends on being able to infer the argument structure of the prefix from the argument structure of the corresponding preposition. Such inferences can be tricky when the prefix is highly grammaticalized or bleached, but give quite consistent patterns when one confines oneself to physical events with clear positional entailments.
24. In Larson's (1988a) account, the *to* preposition, being a pure structural case marker, is absorbed in a kind of analogue of 'passive' and the syntactic movement is required to assign case to the stranded goal argument.
25. Little *v* is the name for the higher V label in a VP shells expansion (see Larson 1988a) of the verbal projection. The terminology comes from the Distributed Morphology tradition (see Harley 1995, Marantz 1997), where a lower case category label is also supposed to contribute syntactic category information to the whole projection. See Section 9.6 for further discussion of this framework.
26. In general, the modern neo-constructivists assume that *all* arguments are the specifiers of some functional head, so maybe the decision does not carry as much weight in those theories as in a more semantically specific theory.
27. The conative alternation, or the PP alternants of direct OBJECT DPs are an obvious candidate for the functional equivalent of an antipassive construction. These constructions, as we have seen, *are* common in nominative–accusative languages like Germanic. They are not strictly antipassive because they do not involve verbal morphology. They are also probably not functionally equivalent because demoting an argument from 'accusative' status is arguably not the same as demoting it from 'absolutive' status. Absolutives in ergative–absolutive languages have some SUBJECT-like properties, like controlling agreement. A complete understanding of the antipassive construction therefore depends on a fuller understanding of Absolutive case. The literature is far from consensual with regard to this particular question (see Legate 2008 for important discussion of the classification of case-marking systems and morphology).

28. In Chapter 17, Baker discusses the connection between case and agreement effects in some detail. While these two morphological phenomena are closely tied in some languages (e.g., English, Hindi), they are completely divorced in others (e.g., Burushaski). In the languages where the case and agreement interaction is set to 'no,' Baker argues that case assignment is probably best stated in terms of the 'relational' theory of case assignment (Marantz 1991), where the case assigned to a particular DP is dependent on what other DPs are present in a structural hierarchy (where I assume this structure is supposed to be in the first, vP phase). While this seems a useful description of the facts, it is not clear to me what the actual mechanism is. It seems clear, however, that it is intended to go beyond the syntactic tool of Agree in a Minimalist theory.
29. In some theories, case morphology is even proposed as one of the methods of 'linking' argument roles to the syntax (Kiparsky 1988, 2001). See Butt (2006) for discussions of the role of case theory with respect to argument structure in different linguistic theories.
30. As mentioned earlier, and summarized also in Chapter 17, many languages that show ergative case-marking patterns, show syntactic alignment effects that are identical to that of nominative–accusative languages. This often includes agreement effects as well as the other well-documented effects of SUBJECT-hood cross-linguistically.
31. In the modern theory, Burzio's Generalization is restated as a property of little v in the phrase structure: a little v which theta-marks an agent, assigns accusative case (or, alternatively, initiates an Agree relation with a DP that it c-commands); the other type of little v, which does not theta-mark an agent, does not (cf. Kratzer 1996). However, in the absence of a deep understanding of why these two properties should be correlated, the restatement here (for the languages that show the correlation) is just as much of a description as Burzio's orginal observation.
32. I use the term 'constructivist' here for the research position that sees meaning as residing in structure, but where that structure is produced by a generative module. This is in contrast with Construction Grammar (Goldberg 1995) whose proponents believe in attaching meaning to 'constructions' but where these are listed just like lexical items. (See also Section 3.4.)
33. Ramchand (2008) is an attempt to build such a system using only categorial features on verbal roots, but it is by no means the only way to do it.

10

The syntax of predication

Caroline Heycock

10.1 Introduction

Predication is typically thought of as a (linguistic) semantic notion: the construction of a proposition from two components, a subject and a predicate. Syntactically, this corresponds to the idea that a clause – or any other structure that will be interpreted as a proposition – has an essentially bipartite structure. One, typically nominal, expression has a special status as the subject, and the remainder of the clause, typically but not necessarily built around a verbal expression, functions as the predicate. Different researchers have very different approaches to the status of predication as a syntactic concept; this chapter attempts to outline the main ways in which predication has been analyzed in the generative syntactic literature. The discussion here is limited to 'primary' predication; the topic of secondary predication has been given a recent extensive overview in Rothstein (2006).

10.2 What is predication?

The notion that a proposition has a fundamentally bipartite structure derives ultimately from Aristotle (for some recent summary discussion, see Rothstein 2001 and den Dikken 2006b). Most current theories of semantics are, however, built not on Aristotelean logic but rather on the system developed from Frege's work, so that a transitive verb, for example, will translate as a 2-place predicate which combines with two arguments, neither of which is privileged over the other. It is of course possible to 'Curry' or 'Schönfinkelize' n-place predicates to yield functions taking their arguments one-by-one, so that there will always be one argument that is combined last – thus reinstating an asymmetry of sorts. Generally, however, the need to do this does not follow from any inherent property of the semantic system, but rather from having to interpret an independently motivated syntactic structure.

If proposition-denoting constituents do have a bipartite structure, this is therefore an important empirical finding about the *syntax* of natural language. This point has been made perhaps most strongly and consistently by Susan Rothstein (Rothstein 1983, 2001), who argues that predication is a syntactic primitive (see in particular Chapter 1 of Rothstein 2001 for a detailed exposition and motivation for this view). Some other researchers in this area have taken what appear to be directly opposed views about the basis for a subject–predicate structure: for example Åfarli and Eide (2000) are very explicit that they take predication to be a fundamentally semantic requirement that then has to be represented in the syntax, stating:

> ... we will not derive [the requirement for subject–predicate structure] from predication in the standard syntax-based manner of Rothstein (1983); Chomsky (1986b); Heycock (1994b), but in a full-blooded semantic manner ... (Åfarli and Eide 2000:27)

But the distinction between the two positions – predication as a semantic primitive that is represented in the syntax, and as a syntactic primitive that is interpreted in the semantics – is much less clear than it may appear at first sight. Thus, for example, although Åfarli and Eide (2000) are explicit about wanting to derive the necessity of the syntactic structure they propose for predication from the semantics,[1] they say about the predicational operator head that they adopt from Bowers (1993):

> There is no intrinsic reason why that operator should be a predication operator, however, but our claim is that that is in fact the case. Thus, that is a contingent fact about the human language faculty. As a consequence, the formation of a proposition invariably opens up an argument position, which has to be filled somehow. (Åfarli and Eide 2000:29)

Since the requirement for the predication head to build up a proposition is a structural requirement, and cannot be derived from any other property of the semantic system, it is not clear why it should be assumed to be a contingent fact about the linguistic semantics, rather than a contingent fact about syntax, that it has to exist. This is a fundamental question, but one that depends for its answer as much on the overarching theoretical question of how much of 'semantics' is in fact part of the syntactic system as on specific empirical facts concerning predication.

10.3 The interpretation of predication

Syntactic structure has to be interpreted. Although we are here concerned with the syntax of predication, proposals – or in some cases just assumptions – about the semantics of predication cannot be entirely set aside, not least because what syntactic structures are considered to instantiate predication in some cases depends on what the semantics of predication are taken to be.

10.3.1 Predication as a type of theta-role assignment

One of the seminal works on the syntax of predication is Williams (1980). For Williams, predication is a mode of θ-role assignment: assignment of a θ-role to an argument merged outside the maximal projection of the θ-assigning head. Thus *subject* is defined in Williams (1983a:287) as follows:

(1) *Subject as external argument*
    The subject of a predicative phrase XP is the single argument of X that is located outside of the maximal projection of X.

Since 'argument' here means an element assigned a θ-role, for Williams all subjects are assigned θ-roles that are projected up from the head of their XP predicate. One consequence of this definition of predication is that Williams allows for clauses – and indeed propositions, which for him are not necessarily represented as clauses or as constituents of any kind – not to have subjects at all. Thus for Williams expletive subjects are explicitly not subjects of predication – an expletive is "an inert element which does not count as a subject" (Williams 1980:221) – so they must be required for some other reason:

(2) *It* occurs in the [NP, S] position if an external argument does not have
    to appear there.   (Williams 1983b:441)

Williams does not himself pursue further the question of why [NP,S] ($\approx$ SpecTP) is necessarily generated/filled (or indeed how to deal with expletives in other positions). Various attempts have been made to account for this by principles other than predication: see Section 10.4.1 below.

The take on predication in Napoli (1988, 1989) also ties predication to a relation close to, but not identical with, θ-role assignment. Ramchand (1997), too, follows Williams in taking subjects of predication to be 'external arguments' (for Ramchand, crucially external to the projection of Aspect). Such external arguments may bear one of two 'general external roles' depending on whether the predicate has internal aspectual structure or not (p. 191). However, drawing on ideas from Carlson (1977), Kratzer (1995), and Diesing (1989, 1992), Ramchand (1997) further introduces what appears to be an additional layer of predication where either an entity (in the case of an individual-level predicate) or an event variable (in the case of a stage-level predicate) is singled out as what the predication is 'about.' Thus for Ramchand, in a sentence like (3) under a non-generic interpretation of the bare plural, *kittens* is the external argument of the predicate *available*, but there is a higher predicational structure whose subject is the event variable, so that the sentence is 'about' the event, which is "the semantic 'subject' of the predicational structure" (p. 198).

(3) kittens were available

This notion of predication as an 'aboutness' relation (also appealed to in the work of Rizzi, as discussed below) is borrowed from the definition of topic that stems from the work of Reinhart (1981b); the relation between the concepts of 'subject' and 'topic' is a complex one that remains underexplored. For discussion of the relation between subject and topic, see Chapter 23 on Information Structure.

10.3.2 Predicates and properties

An alternative view of the semantics of predication that has much influenced syntacticians, in particular Bowers (1993, 2001), and those who have adopted his syntactic analysis (including for example Bailyn 1995, Adger and Ramchand 2003), is that developed by Gennaro Chierchia (Chierchia 1984, 1985, Chierchia and Turner 1988). Under this view, syntactic predicates correspond to properties, which can appear in two guises: as the familiar propositional functions (functions from individuals to propositions) or as individuals themselves (the 'individual correlates' of properties). Chierchia argues that the existence of these two guises or 'modes of being' for properties is what allows us to attribute properties to properties, as for example (4) in (Chierchia 1985:418); what we are doing is attributing a property *qua* propositional function to a property *qua* individual.

(4) a. wisdom is hard to find
     b. the property of being wise is hard to find
     c. {being wise / to be wise} is crazy
     d. wearing black ties is a passing fad
     e. being crazy is crazy

For Chierchia, a non-finite predicate corresponds, not to a propositional function, but to its individual correlate; finiteness has the effect of taking the individual and returning the unsaturated propositional function which can then be predicated of a subject. Bowers (1993) adopts Chierchia's general proposal, but rejects the idea that finiteness is what turns an individual correlate into a propositional function: instead this is the role of a dedicated functional head (see Section 10.6 below).

The idea that finiteness is responsible for taking properties-as-individuals and yielding properties-as-predicates does not seem to be tenable – or at least it would come at the high cost of denying that predication obtains in the bracketed sequences in (5):

(5) a. I consider [Julia radical]
    b. I consider [it obvious that she is right]
    c. with [the boss on holiday], her staff can do what they want
    d. that makes [your objections irrelevant]
    e. they made [him leave]

This is a cost that syntacticians have typically been unwilling to countenance (although it may be the position of, e.g., Rizzi and Shlonsky 2007); the proposal that there is a dedicated predicational head avoids this. Nevertheless, one feature of the 'neo-Chierchian' take on predication is that the constituents that appear as the complement to the predication head, and that therefore, by hypothesis, themselves denote properties-as-individuals, never seem to be able to have properties attributed to them directly as might be expected:[2]

(6) a. I regard Julia as wise
    b. {wisdom / being wise / *wise} is a desirable attribute

Conversely, when the kind of nominalizations that Chierchia took as denoting the individual correlates of properties occur in 'predicate' positions, even with a putative overt instantiation of the predication head such as *as* in (7b,c), the result is never that the corresponding property is predicated of the subject. There is nothing syntactically wrong with (7a–c), but they don't mean that the property of wisdom is attributed to the subject:

(7) a. I consider John wisdom ≠ I consider John wise / to have the property of wisdom
    b. I regard John as wisdom ≠ I regard John as wise / having the property of wisdom
    c. I regard that behaviour as wisdom ≠ I regard that behaviour as wise / having the property of wisdom

The interpretation of examples like these shows that if *wisdom* is the individual correlate of *wise*, the propositional function can nevertheless not be obtained by applying to it the predicational operator; it seems that the only propositional function that can be created is *being identical to the property of {wisdom/being wise}*, that is, it seems that something like Partee's (1987:127) *ident* typeshifter has to take the nominalized property to yield a different predicate.[3] In sum, we never seem to be able to peel away the predicative layer and pull out the individual correlate of the property which by hypothesis is underneath, suggesting at least that either properties-as-individuals or the predication operator are more indirectly represented in the syntax than initially suggested.

Rothstein does not adopt property theory, but shares with the approach of Chierchia the idea that the XP that constitutes a predicate does not immediately correspond to a function that can take the subject as its argument to yield a proposition (or rather to yield a set of events, which is what she takes the denotation of an IP to be). Instead such an XP is a saturated expression, although the thematic role associated with the external argument, if there is one, is associated with an unbound variable. So again a further operation ('predicate formation' – which introduces a lambda that binds the free variable) is required to take this saturated expression and yield a function that take a single argument.

10.4 Evidence for predication

10.4.1 Expletives

Expletive or pleonastic subjects constitute perhaps the strongest argument that there is a need to invoke a notion of predication independent of θ-role assignment, and more specifically that the requirement that propositions be built from a subject and a predicate is syntactic rather than semantic, since by hypothesis expletives contribute nothing to the semantics.[4] So for example Rothstein (2001) says "the crucial evidence for [the requirement that a clause consist of a subject combining with a predicate] comes from sentences where the subject argument is a pleonastic, a 'dummy' DP which adds no semantic information to the sentence, as in [(8)]" (p. 38):

(8) a. it seems that John is late
 b. it turned out that my keys were in my pocket
 c. it is unlikely that the child will sleep this afternoon

It is of course the case that syntactic structures containing expletives still have to be interpreted; the typical move for the pronominal expletive that occurs in the examples in (8) is to have it denote a minimally informative pronoun, an element with no properties, ⊥ (Sag 1982, Dowty 1985, Gazdar et al. 1985, Chierchia 2004b, Rothstein 2001).

There have been various attempts to nullify this argument for a syntactically motivated relation of predication. In the 1980s and early 1990s Fukui (1986), Fukui and Speas (1986), and Authier (1991) argued that the occurrence of a constituent in the specifier of IP (given the assumption that all the arguments of a verb are generated within the VP) is forced by case assignment to that position, so that predication need not be invoked – and, indeed, that the 'subject position' is not always required. In Heycock (1994b:48ff.) the counterargument was made that this would not explain for example the ungrammaticality of (9e):

(9) a. it is important that students are unionized
 b. it is important for students to appear to be unionized
 c. it is important to appear to be unionized
 d. it is important for it to appear that students are unionized
 e. *it is important to appear that students are unionized

The grammaticality of (9c) shows that the infinitival complement to *important* need not be introduced by *for*, which is typically assumed to be responsible for the accusative case assignment to the embedded subject in an example like (9b). Under the accounts that attempt to derive the distribution of expletives from the assignment of case, the presence of *for* in (9d) is what explains the appearance of the expletive in this example. But then (9e) should be grammatical: case-assigning *for* is absent, and so is the expletive subject of the infinitival. Rather it appears that the explanation has to go the other way: the expletive in (9d) is not present because the case assigner *for* requires it, rather the case assigner *for* has to be present so that the expletive can appear.[5]

In a different vein, Postal and Pullum (1988) argue that there are cases of expletives in subcategorized positions, for example as in (10). If this is the correct analysis of these examples, it would follow that expletives must be allowed to occur independently of predication; although this would not exclude the possiblity that predication is a requirement that might be satisfied by an expletive, by making this only one motivation for the existence of expletives, it would clearly weaken the argument.

(10) a. I figured it out to be more than 300 miles to Tulsa
 b. I regret it very much that we could not hire Mosconi
 c. Elmer regards it as suspicious that no primitives are defined
 d. they never mentioned it to the candidate that the job was poorly paid
 e. dish it out; does it; have it at with NP; fight it out with someone; etc.

Rothstein (1995, 2001) discusses these cases in some detail, and argues that they fall into two broad categories: cases in which the pronoun is indeed expletive, but where it is in fact not (merged) in an internal argument position but as the subject of a small clause (which may then move to a higher position) (10a), and cases in which the pronoun is merged as an internal argument, but is not in fact an expletive, but a semantically contentful pronoun (10c–e).

While Rothstein rejects the idea that *it* in the structures in (10c–e) above is an expletive, she does claim this status – again, with supporting arguments – for all the cases in (11):[6]

(11) a. it rained, it snowed, and it got colder and colder
 b. it is unlikely/possible/certain that we'll arrive on time
 c. it was widely believed that the earth was flat
 d. it {seemed/turned out/appeared} that John had already arrived
 e. it is easy to please John

In the literature, a distinction is often drawn between the case in (11a) ('weather,' 'ambient,' or 'meteorological' *it*) and at least the cases in (11b, c) – *pace* Rothstein's arguments about the ambiguity of (11c) – where the *that* clause could also appear in subject position ('extraposition' *it*). We may further separate out the case in (11d); there does not seem to be an accepted term for this class; let us call it 'non-extraposition' *it*. The construction in (11e) will be discussed separately in Section 10.4.2.1.

Contrary to Rothstein's conclusions, many researchers follow the lead of Bolinger (1973) in taking weather *it* to be at least a 'quasi-argument.' The main evidence for this is the possibility for weather *it* to control PRO in examples like (12) (see Napoli 1988 for a more detailed discussion of these cases and futher references):

(12) it rained, before PRO snowing

Rothstein rejects this argument for two reasons. First, the same behaviour is shown by 'true' pleonastics, as in (13a), where Rothstein is clearly assuming that extraposition *it* is uncontroversially a true pleonastic (Rothstein 2001:69). (13b), based on an example from Reeve (2009), is of a similar type:

(13) a. at first, it seemed improbable that we would arrive at all, before becoming more likely that we would just be very late
      b. it became clear, after having been explained to us many times, that we were wrong

This argument has, however, been turned on its head by other researchers: Bennis (1986), for example, argues that in Dutch the equivalent of extraposition *it* is not an expletive, precisely because it can appear in this context (see also Hoekstra 1983, Vikner 1995), and this is also the argument that Reeve makes for English. Examples of non-extraposition *it*, however, seem significantly less acceptable in this context. Such cases were indeed originally contrasted with the behaviour of weather *it* (Chomsky 1981:323):

(14) it seemed that John was wrong without [*PRO/it seeming that Mary was right]

Rothstein's second argument that weather *it* (and extraposition *it*) are expletives despite their apparent ability to control PRO is that their co-occurrence with PRO subjects seems very limited, suggesting – Rothstein avers – that the adjunct in (12) and (13) may be some other construction entirely, without a PRO subject at all. Rothstein's own examples are not all probative because at least some cases of failure of control by a putative expletive pronoun could be attributed to a requirement for control by an animate in the context given, hence the neuter pronoun would fail whether or not it was expletive. But it is possible to construct examples like the following, where (15a) shows that control by an inanimate is possible, but control by weather *it* and extraposition *it* (15a–c) still seems degraded, although in my judgment not quite to the extent of non-extraposition *it* (15d):

(15) a. if a house$_i$ is going to last, PRO$_i$ not {to be/being} built on sand is a prerequisite
b. ??if it$_i$ is going to freeze, PRO$_i$ not (to be) snowing is a prerequisite
c. ??if it$_i$ is going to be obvious that we're the right people, PRO$_i$ {to be/being} evident that we know what we're doing is important
d. * if it$_i$ is going to be obvious that we're the right people, PRO$_i$ {to seem/seeming} that we know what we're doing is important

One further argument that expletives are licensed by predication (and that extraposition *it* is an expletive) is that they are impossible in nominalizations, where it can be assumed there is no predicational structure (Rothstein 1983, Abney 1987):[7]

(16) a. *its likelihood that Julia will arrive on time is a relief
b. *its rain bothered us
c. *its appearance that Julia has already left is a relief

In sum, while the distribution of expletives remains a strong motivation for a syntactic position required by predication, the status of some of the most commonly cited examples of *it* as an expletive is not uncontroversial; the clearest case in English of an expletive use of *it* is when it appears with *seem*, *turn out*, or *appear*, the least clear is weather *it*, and extraposition *it* lies somewhere between the two.

Svenonius (2002b) discusses weather *it* and extraposition *it* (it appears that he may include examples with *seem* / *appear* / *turn out* under the same heading, although this is not completely clear) and concludes that they may all in fact be thematic:

> ... the only reasonably clear case of an expletive is the impersonal one, represented by two types. One type is the historically locative *there* in English, *er* in Dutch, and *der* in Danish and some dialects of Norwegian and Swedish (in the latter spelled *där*). In the other Germanic languages, the existential expletive is generally identical to the neuter pronoun (Svenonius 2002b:7)

However, it should also be noted that even the first of these, at least (*there* in English) is not uncontroversial: a number of authors, including among many others Williams (1984), Rothstein (2001) and Landman (2004), have argued that *there* is a contentful expression; Moro (1991, 1997) develops a proposal that *there* in English, and its counterpart *ci* in Italian, are predicates that 'invert' with (move leftward past) their subjects, as a particular case of the inverse predication construction discussed below in Section 10.7.3. As Svenonius (2002b) notes, that may leave the expletive that appears in impersonal passives (a construction missing from Modern English, of course) as the only completely uncontested case.

10.4.2 Non-thematic subjects

10.4.2.1 The *tough* construction

The second phenomenon that has motivated claims that predication is a relation independent of θ-role assignment is the existence of non-expletive subjects that do not occupy θ-positions (and hence are, it is argued, licensed by virtue of being the subjects of predication). The classic example is *tough*-movement, as exemplified in (17), where *Kathryn* in (17b), occupies the same position that is occupied by the expletive *it* in (17a):

(17) a. it is tough to diagree with Kathryn
 b. Kathryn is tough to disagree with

Rothstein (2001) adds to these the type of example in (18):

(18) this book is for you to read

The *tough* construction has been much discussed since Chomsky (1964a), Rosenbaum (1967) (for a recent overview, see Section 3.1 of Hicks 2009b). Chomsky (1977) demonstrated that it shows many of the characteristics of *wh*-movement, and his proposal that in examples like an empty element moves from a θ-position within the infinitival clause to some position at its edge has been widely adopted ever since.

(19) Julia is easy Op$_i$ PRO to admire t$_i$

As Chomsky himself noted, however, any derivation of this kind gives rise to problems for the licensing of the lexical subject; the null operator that is merged as the object of *admire* will get the relevant θ-role, but the general properties of *wh*-movement do not allow the 'sharing' or 'transmission' of this θ-role to the lexical subject.

Adopting the basic insight from Chomsky's proposal, a number of researchers have proposed that the A' movement of a null operator from within the infinitival creates a predicate, and that the predication relation between this and the subject is enough to license that subject, even in the absence of θ-role assignment (see, for example, Browning 1987, Heycock 1993, 1994b, Rothstein 2001, Rezac 2004, Landau 2009). This approach attributes to predication the capacity to license not only syntactic positions, but also arguments, on a par with θ-role assignment.

There have been a number of attempts to find alternatives to allowing predication to license the subject in the *tough* construction; that is, to provide accounts under which the subject is assigned a θ-role. Various authors have argued that the *tough* adjective or nominal itself assigns a thematic role to the subject; so that the θ-role assigned to *John* in (20a,b) is the same, and the infinitive clause is merely some kind of adjunct:

(20) a. John is {unpleasant/difficult/awkward}
 b. John is difficult to dislike

Versions of this kind of analysis can be found in, e.g., Lasnik and Fiengo (1974), Schachter (1981), Wilder (1991), Williams (1983b), and Hornstein (2001). However, detailed arguments against such analyses have been given in Perlmutter and Soames (1979), Heycock (1994b), Goh (2000a, 2000b) and most recently Hicks (2009b). Hicks (2009b) himself provides an account where the subject DP is assigned a *theme* θ-role by a null operator; this aspect of his proposal is however both theoretically and empirically questionable (on the one hand, it is surprising that a null operator should be able to assign a θ-role, and on the other, there is no evidence for a consistent θ-role to the subject, *pace* the cited observation from Postal 1974 that the infinitival clause has to be agentive). As it stands, then, there is as yet no convincing argument that the subject of *tough*-predicates are licensed by θ-role assignment rather than by predication.

Particularly in the context of *tough* movement it is worth recalling that the proposal that non-expletive noun phrases may be licensed by predication alone is less radical in the context of Minimalism than it was in the context of earlier generative frameworks. If predication can license arguments, it has always been clear that this must happen after a certain amount of movement has taken place (either of the subject, or of a null operator creating a derived predicate, or both). In a framework where θ-role assignment has to be established at a level of D-structure, this makes licensing by θ-role assignment and licensing by predication seem quite distant from each other. But once the θ-Criteron as a condition on D-structure has been abandoned, licensing by θ-role assignment and licensing by predication become much closer; this was of course essentially one of the empirical arguments that was given in Chomsky (1993) for abandoning D-structure.

10.4.2.2 Other non-thematic subjects

Heycock (1993, 1994b), Rezac (2004), and Landau (2009) propose that evidence for licensing by predication is to be found also in the construction in (21), sometimes referred to as 'copy raising,' although this terminology is unhelpful in that it presupposes an analysis which is clearly unsustainable for at least some cases to which it is often applied.

(21) Julia sounds like she is the woman for the job

Crucially, the cases that are relevant for this argument are those where the subject is not assigned a thematic role by the verb *sound* or its equivalents, that is to say, where it is not interpreted as the 'perceptual source' (Asudeh and Toivonen 2012). In the absence of further context, (21) is ambiguous in this regard, but it is possible to construct more revealing examples. Thus while it is plausible that *her cat* is an argument of *sound* in (22a), this contrasts with the interpretation in (22b), (see Heycock 1994b:287ff. for discussion):

(22) a. Julia can hear a terrible meowling from under the tree. Her cat sounds like it is in a lot of pain.
b. I read the letter where Julia told me about her new pets. Her cat sounds like it must have been very expensive.

In Heycock (1993, 1994b) it is argued that in these cases there is no null operator creating the predicate, both because such an analysis would treat the pronouns in the embedded clauses as resumptive pronouns with a distribution that they do not display elsewhere in English, and because some examples do not even contain a pronoun:

(23) a. that book sounds like everyone should own a copy
b. from what you say, your car sounds like you need a new clutch
c. that family sounds like the gene pool is way too shallow

Landau (2009), however, rejects examples like (23a–c) and argues for an operator + resumption analysis of the cases in (22), thereby making the construction more similar to the *tough* construction.[8] Whether or not operator movement is always involved, however, these analyses all treat this construction as again exemplifying predication as a licensing mechanism on a par with θ-role assignment.

In Fukuda (1991), Heycock (1993, 1994b), and Namai (1997) it is in addition claimed that the 'multiple subject' construction found in Japanese (as well as other languages) involves recursive predication, the 'outer' subjects being licensed as subjects of predication. The following well-known examples are from Kuno (1973b); note that the multiple subjects are not marked with the topic marker *wa* but with the nominative *ga*.

(24) a. John-ga   otoosan-ga sinda
John-NOM father-NOM died
John [has the property that] his father died
b. bunmeikoku-ga   dansei-ga   heikinzyumyoo-ga   mizikai
civilized countries-NOM males-NOM average life span-NOM short
'civilized countries [have the property that] the average lifespan of males there is short'
c. New York-ga   koosoo-kentiku-ga   ooi
New York-NOM high-rise buildings-NOM plentiful
'New York has many high-rise buildings'

A more detailed discussion of the Japanese multiple subject construction can be found in Vermeulen (2005), which gives a differentiated account depending on whether or not the subject binds a possessor argument (as it does in (24a–b) but not in (24c)); for the cases where the subject binds a possessor Vermeulen again argues that it is licensed by predication in the same way as a *tough* construction.

10.5 Where is predication?

The *Projection Principle* of Government and Binding (GB) Theory essentially stated that syntactic structure is projected from the lexicon, in particular from thematic grids (see Section 9.2.2). It was 'extended' in Chomsky (1981) by the requirement that clauses must have a subject. This is couched as a universal syntactic principle that the immediate constituents of S are NP, Infl, and VP. Although it was stated that "the Projection Principle and the requirement that clauses have subjects are conceptually quite closely related" (Chomsky 1982:10), justifying putting them together as the *Extended Projection Principle* (EPP), no detailed exploration was given there as to the nature of the posited conceptual relationship.

Within the GB/Principles and Parameters/Minimalist framework it is natural to attempt to try to derive from other properties of features of the grammar the requirement that clauses have subjects (a requirement that came to be referred to as the EPP, the 'core' case of the Extended Projection Principle involving the projection of argument structure being essentially taken over by the Principle of Full Interpretation). As discussed in Section 10.4.1, one proposal was that the occurrence of a constituent in the specifier of IP is forced by case assignment to that position. Borer (1986, 1989), on the other hand, proposed that the requirement that clauses have subjects derived not from case, but from agreement, specifically agreement with the functional head Infl[ection], according to the following rule (Borer 1986, (47)):

(25)   Coindex NP with INFL in the accessible domain of INFL.

For this account the principal problem is the occurrence of expletives in small clauses where there is no independent evidence for the existence of Infl (Stowell 1983, Heycock 1994b:51ff., Rothstein 2001:75ff.); for example, as discussed extensively in Gee (1977), Higginbotham (1983b), Safir (1993), and Felser (1998), English 'bare' infinitive perception verb complements can include expletive *there*, even though this type of infinitive is generally held not to include any head higher than Aspect (Felser 1998). The much-cited example in (26) is from Gee (1977). More recently, Åfarli and Eide (2000) make the same point with the Norwegian examples in (27):

(26)   I have never seen there be so many complaints from students before

(27)   a. vi ser [xp det [som positivt at   du vil komme]]
          we see   it   as   positive that you will come
          'we see it as positive that you want to come'
       b. vi har gjort [xp det [kaldt i   rommet]]
          we have made   it   cold in room-the
          'we have made it cold in the room'

One version of the subject requirement that survives into some Minimalist analyses is probably most closely related to Borer's view, as it is envisaged to be the result of some feature on the functional head T[ense] that its specifier has to be filled. As pointed out in Åfarli and Eide (2000), such updates of Borer's proposal of course share the problem just discussed.

A slightly different variant of this approach is to be found in recent work by Luigi Rizzi (Rizzi (2005b, 2006b, 2007, Rizzi and Shlonsky 2007, and see also Cardinaletti 2004). In these works it is proposed that there is a distinct projection instantiating predication, SubjP, situated in the left periphery of the clause, above Tense but below Fin[iteness]. For Rizzi, the most important property of the SpecSubjP position is that it is a 'criterial' position; a phrase with a matching feature must move there in the same way that it is proposed movement is forced to the specifiers of heads bearing, e.g., Topic, Focus, or Q features. And, crucially, once a phrase moves to such a criterial position, it is frozen in place; this is how Rizzi derives the asymmetry between subjects and objects in their freedom to move. Importantly, though, the 'Subj Criterion' may be satisfied by expletives (whether overt or unpronounced); this yields one way for the thematic subject to be extracted (by 'skipping' this position; see in particular Rizzi and Shlonsky 2007). Like Ramchand (1997) (see the text above example (3) above), Rizzi proposes that predication is interpreted in topic-like terms of 'aboutness,' and that if a contentful phrase does not occupy SpecSubjP the clause is interpreted as 'presentational.' Given that the typical way for English to allow subjects to be extracted is by 'skipping' the criterial SpecSubj position, this appears to predict – in Rizzi and Shlonsky's system – that any such 'aboutness' interpretations should be lacking if a subject is extracted (the representation of, e.g., *Who did they say was intelligent?* would be identical to the representation of *Who did they say was available?* in having no copy of the extracted subject in the embedded SpecSubj). However, in general in these articles the focus is much more on the derivation of the restrictions on subject extractions than on the interpretation of the Subj head.

The other most frequent claim about the locus of predication, whether stated directly or indirectly, is that a constituent that translates as a proposition must have the form of a subject–predicate. The existence of small clauses that may lack tense is of course not a problem for such an approach; the issue that arises instead is whether the requirement is itself in origin a semantic rather than a syntactic one, as discussed above – although, as also discussed earlier, in either case the requirement is itself structural. Stowell (1983), for example, concluded that "the requirement for a subject is not a special property of any particular syntactic category, but rather is a general requirement imposed by the theory of predication: every clause must contain both a subject and a predicate" (p. 298). Although 'clause' is usually a syntactic term, it is fairly clear from the context that what Stowell has in mind here is a constituent that is interpreted as a proposition, and his article was a seminal one for the proposal that such proposition-denoting constituents could be of differing syntactic categories (hence the title of his article: 'Subjects across Categories)'.[9]

As discussed earlier, most generative syntacticians thus assume the existence of 'small clauses': proposition-denoting constituents that do not contain a finite verb, or any verb at all, even in languages where matrix clauses normally must contain a verb; the examples are repeated here.

(28) (a) I consider [$_{SC}$ Julia radical]
    (b) I consider [$_{SC}$ it obvious that she is right]
    (c) with [$_{SC}$ the boss on holiday], her staff can do what they want
    (d) that makes [$_{SC}$ your objections irrelevant]
    (e) they made [$_{SC}$ him leave]

Thus predication structures seem to come in at least two sizes: full finite clauses and tenseless small clauses.[10] Further, with the general adoption of some version of the hypothesis that the subject of a 'full' clause is not merged above Tense but within the projection of the lexical head (the 'VP-internal subject hypothesis'), every full clause is potentially built around a small clause:

(29) (a) [$_{TP}$ Julia$_i$ is [$_{SC}$ t$_i$ radical]]
    (b) [$_{TP}$ he$_i$ has [$_{SC}$ t$_i$ left]]

One possible way of approaching this is to drop the idea that predication obtains at the TP level, so that in a simple clause like (29b), for example, the only instance of predication will be the structure below Tense. This is the approach of Moro (1990) and Bowers (1993, 2001), for example. An alternative is to assume that there may be multiple layers of predication within even a single clause: this kind of approach is adopted in Heycock (1994b), perhaps also in Ramchand (1997), and, in a very different way, in den Dikken (2006b).

In Heycock (1994b) it is proposed that a clause like (29b) involves both VP and TP predicates, and that in a V2 language where there may be further movement to the specifier and head of CP in a declarative, there may be a further instance of predication at CP (as proposed originally in Rizzi (1990c). The proposal in den Dikken (2006b) goes even further in this direction, proposing that topics in English also are related to the rest of the sentence (the comment) by predication (pp. 27f.), and that covert movement of a focused element to the specifier of a focus head also sets up a predication relation between the focus and the presupposition (p. 28). On the other hand, den Dikken appears to assume less layering of predication in any given sentence than might appear possible in his system. For example, although the light verb v and Tense are both potentially 'RELATOR' heads that induce or mediate predication relations in his proposal (see below), the assumption for a simple clause appears to be that VP is necessarily a predicate and that whichever functional head (v is treated as such at least for these purposes) takes VP as a complement will establish the predication relation (p. 24):

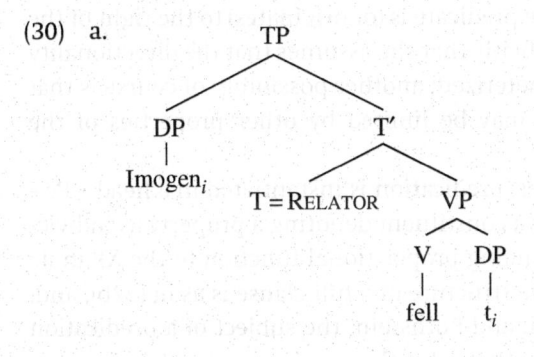

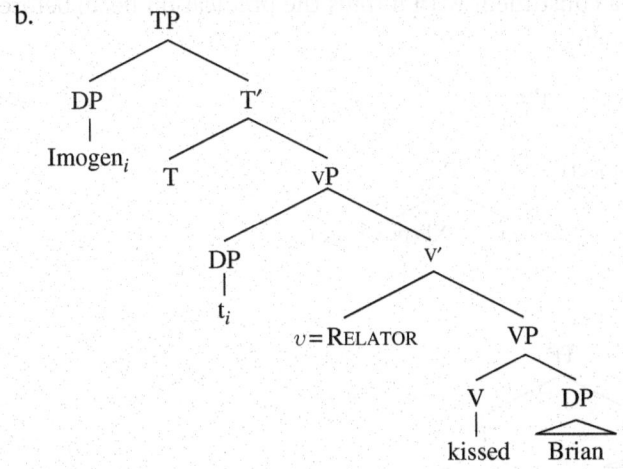

(30) a.
```
              TP
             /  \
            DP   T'
            |   /  \
         Imogenᵢ T=RELATOR  VP
                          /  \
                         V    DP
                         |    |
                        fell  tᵢ
```

b.
```
              TP
             /  \
            DP   T'
            |   /  \
         Imogenᵢ T   vP
                    /  \
                   DP   V'
                   |   /  \
                   tᵢ v=RELATOR  VP
                                /  \
                               V    DP
                               |    △
                             kissed Brian
```

Den Dikken also proposes predication as the relation holding between manner adverbials and clauses, and as a relation that can obtain within various types of nominal, as discussed briefly in Section 10.6 below. Notice that of course as additional cases of predication are proposed, the notion of 'subject' of predication is correspondingly extended. Thus, if topics and foci are also subjects of predication,[11] all of the boldfaced elements in (31) are subjects in this extended sense:

(31) **John**, **we** gave only **books**

10.6 Syntactic representation

Within the generative tradition, agreement has alternated between being thought of as a relation and as a functional category that participates in relations. The same is true for predication. For Williams and Rothstein, for example, predication is a relation that holds in a particular configuration (mutual c-command) between subject and predicate. Given that mutual c-command is by definition a symmetrical relation, this configuration by itself says nothing about directionality. Both authors only analyse in any detail structures in which the predicate is (or originates) to the right of the subject. Rothstein states explicitly that she assumes that the directionality of predication may be parameterized; another possibility of course is that the possible configurations may be limited by other properties of the individual grammar.

For Bowers (1993), however, predication is instantiated in a head – Pr – that takes as its complement a constituent denoting a property as individual and applies the corresponding propositional function to the XP in its specifier. Thus for Bowers the structure of a full clause is as in (32b), and, contrary to Williams, Napoli, and Rothstein, the subject of a predication always forms a constituent with it (plus the predication head) before any further movement.

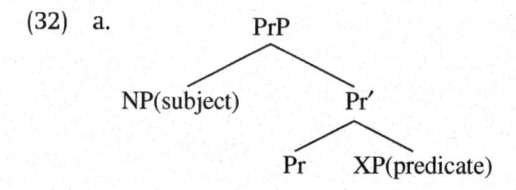

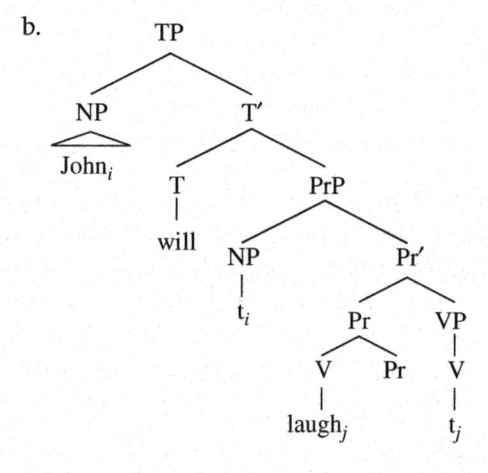

(32) a.

```
            PrP
           /   \
   NP(subject)  Pr'
                / \
              Pr   XP(predicate)
```

b.

```
              TP
             /  \
           NP    T'
           |    /  \
         John_i T    PrP
                |   /   \
              will NP    Pr'
                   |    /  \
                   t_i Pr   VP
                      /  \   |
                     V   Pr  V
                     |       |
                  laugh_j   t_j
```

For Bowers – and, as we will see below, in an even more radical way for den Dikken – the predicational head may be realized in a number of different guises even within a single language. In a full clause and in many small clauses in English it has no phonetic realization; in some small clauses though it is lexicalized as *as*.

As discussed in Bowers (2001:310), a number of other authors have identified other overt realizations of the predication head in other languages, including Russian (Bailyn and Rubin 1991, Bailyn 1995, 2002),

Norwegian and German (Eide and Åfarli 1999),[12] Japanese (Nishiyama 1999), and Scottish Gaelic (Adger and Ramchand 2003). There are also various different assumptions about the exact properties of the predication head. From now on unless the discussion is very specifically about Bowers's papers I will refer to the predication head as Pred (the terminology of Svenonius (1994a).

Den Dikken proposes, like Bowers, that predication has to be instantiated as a functional head, which he calls the 'RELATOR,' that establishes a relation between a subject and a predicate in its specifier and complement, but with two differences.[13] First, there is no single RELATOR category, instead den Dikken proposes that any functional head can have the RELATOR 'role': for example, as we have already seen above, Tense can function as the RELATOR, as can v, or Top[ic], or various other functional heads. Thus, although den Dikken refers to the RELATOR as "an abstract functional connective" that can be "realized" by various elements, it appears to be more like a feature that can (optionally) be part of the content of a functional head, or may in some cases constitute the only content (this is the analysis for *as*, for example, in *I regard her as my friend*, as proposed by Bowers (1993)).

The second difference between den Dikken's RELATOR and Bowers's Pr head – and most other variants of Pred in other people's work – is that for den Dikken a RELATOR head may, other things being equal, take the predicate as either its complement or its specifier, and the subject consequently either as the specifier or the complement. Cases that den Dikken analyses as reverse predication[14] include the substructures in (33);[15] the idea of treating the kind of nominal in (36) as an instance of nominal-internal predication originates with the analysis in Napoli (1989); it is taken further in den Dikken's work, culminating in den Dikken (2006b).

(33) a. [[$_{Predicate}$ a big creature] [for=RELATOR [$_{Subject}$ a butterfly]]]
 b. a [[$_{Predicate}$ big] [Ø=RELATOR [$_{subject}$ butterfly]]]

(34) a. Brian was kissed by Imogen
 b. Brian$_i$ was [[$_{Predicate}$ kissed t$_i$] [by=RELATOR [$_{Subject}$ Imogen]]]

(35) a. je laisse/fais embrasser Brian à   Imogen
    I let/make kiss   Brian to Imogen
    'I let/make Imogen kiss Brian'
 b. je laisse/fais [[$_{Predicate}$ embrasser Brian] [à=RELATOR [$_{Subject}$ Imogen]]]

(36) [[$_{Predicate}$ an idiot] [of=RELATOR [$_{Subject}$ a doctor]]]

In fact den Dikken argues that the phrase *an idiot of a doctor* is ambiguous between being a case of reverse predication, as illustrated in (36), and involving movement of a predicate-complement over a c-commanding subject; this latter analysis is argued to be the only one available for cases like *a jewel of a girl*; see Section 11.8.8.

Although this ambidirectionality seems like a major difference between den Dikken's approach and that of Bowers and most other researchers on the syntax of predication, it is important to bear in mind that there is a prior difference in that for all those who assume that the semantics of predication involves a function applying to an entity to yield a truth value, at least (33) and (36) would not be straightforwardly analyzable as predications, regardless of directionality.

Den Dikken takes the position that predication is completely independent of θ-role assignment. With regard to the light verb v that may act as the RELATOR, he insists that "it [must be] clearly understood that this light v is just an instantiation of a general-purpose functional head that helps establish predication (2006b: 255)," and stresses the general independence of predication from θ-role assignment.

> [A] head H is a θ-assigner or a mediator of predication but never both at the same time – an approach, in other words, that strictly divides the labor of θ-assignment and mediation of predication relationships. (p. 22)

Given that in his analysis the light verb v that acts as the RELATOR in a clause with an unergative or transitive verb is also the head that introduces the 'external argument,' this analysis is also in the tradition that asserts that predication can license arguments – not only expletives – that receive no θ-role.[16]

10.7 Copular constructions

10.7.1 Small clauses in copular constructions

The acceptance of 'small clauses' as instances of predication gives rise to the question of why these do not occur as matrix clauses in English and a number of other languages, in contrast to the situation in, for example, Hebrew (for Hebrew, see among others Doron 1983, Rapoport 1987, Sichel 1997, and Rothstein 2001). A typical proposal – or assumption – is that in English a matrix clause must contain an instance of Tense, and that Tense in this language only selects for VP, rather than, say, AP or NP (see Déchaine 1993 for detailed discussion).[17] The copula *be* is then treated as an essentially meaningless verbal head that selects a small clause, the subject of which then raises for reasons of case or some requirement that SpecTP be filled (see Rothstein 2001, however, for an interesting deviation from this position and a proposal about the semantic contribution of *be*). If a small clause is headed by Pred then this is generally taken to be the locus of the 'main' predication in the clause.

(37) he$_i$ is [$_{PredP}$ t$_i$ [$_{Pred'}$ Ø [$_{AP}$ right-wing]]]

Examples like (38) suggest, however, that even under the assumptions of Bowers (1993, 2001) or den Dikken (2006b) it must at least be possible for another layer of predication to be superimposed, since for both of these authors *as* is taken to be a predicate head in the construction *regard NP as XP*:

(38) a. they regard him as being right-wing
 b. they regard [PredP him$_i$ [Pred' [Pred as] [VP being [PredP t$_i$ [Pred' [Pred Ø] [AP right-wing]]]]]]

10.7.2 Predicative and equative copular constructions

It has been observed by a number of different authors at different times that contrary to what the type of analysis of copular clauses sketched above seems to predict, the types of subject–predicate relations that are possible in small clauses seems to be a subset of those that occur in full copular clauses.

One type of copular clause in English that does not correspond to a well-formed small clause is the *equative* or *equational* type, where it seems that two individuals (or possibly other types of entity) are being equated, rather than a property being predicated of an individual:

(39) a. A: I like Richard Bachman's stuff, but I can't stand that Stephen King.
 B: But Richard Bachman is Stephen King!
 b. War is war.

The simplest move is to posit ambiguity for *be*, with one instance – equative/equational *be* – taking two referential arguments (see among many others Bowers 1991, Zaring 1996, Mikkelsen 2005, and for rather different takes on equative *be*, Sharvit 2003, Heller 2005).[18] In a very important pair of papers on the semantics of nominals and of copular constructions, Partee (1986, 1987) proposes instead that the equative reading arises through the application of the typeshifter *ident* to an individual-denoting nominal, which yields an equative predicate. The copula can then be given a uniform meaning in both 'equative' and 'predicative' sentences, as in each case it simply applies its complement predicate to the subject:

(40) ident: $j \rightarrow \lambda x[x = j]$

Partee states that she takes the possibility of appearing with *consider* diagnostic for predicative status, and notes the ungrammaticality or marginality of proper names in this position:

(41) Mary considers that {an island/*?Schiermonnikoog}

But it is not clear from the proposal how such cases are in fact to be allowed in copular sentences but excluded in small clauses.

One possibility that has been partially explored is the hypothesis that although small clause complements to verbs like *consider* have been assumed to be pure examples of predication, in fact there may be more than one type of small clause (for very different proposals that involve this hypothesis or something like it, see, e.g., Heycock 1994a, Carnie 1997, Pereltsvaig 2007, Citko 2008). Without pursuing this further, it may be noted with respect to examples like (41) that *consider* seems to require small clauses with predicates that are in some sense gradable, which might itself rule out (at least certain cases of) equatives in this context:[19]

(42) a. John is in {London/a good mood}
     b. I consider John in {??London/a good mood}

It remains at present an open question what the best syntactic analysis of 'equative' predications should be, and indeed is disputed whether the category even exists.[20]

10.7.3 Specificational or inverse copular constructions

Equative sentences are one type of copular sentence that are not straightforward to derive by embedding a small clause under a semantically transparent copula and allowing the subject of that small clause to raise. The second type is one that has attracted far more attention in the last thirty-five years, ever since the publication of Higgins (1973): specificational sentences. A good definition of such sentences presupposes an analysis, but they have at least two very salient characteristics: the nominal that appears in what appears to be the canonical predicate position appears to be 'more referential' than the nominal that appears in the canonical subject position, and the information structure is fixed, with the postcopular nominal obligatorily focused. Some typical examples are given in (43):

(43) a. the cause of the riot was the announcement of a pay freeze
     b. her favourite author was Joseph Heller
     c. one thing you might consider is psychotherapy
     d. the culprit was Jennifer

In the syntactic literature since Higgins, and particularly in the last two decades, probably the most widely adopted analysis of specificational sentences is that they are a variant of predicative copular sentences in which the subject–predicate relations are inverted by leftward movement of the predicate over its subject.[21] Variants of this analysis have been proposed and defended by a number of syntacticians and (rather fewer) semanticists, including Blom and Daalder (1977), Williams (1983b), Partee (1986) (but see the subsequent Partee 1999, which abandons this analysis for English, largely on the basis of the arguments discussed below with respect to (50)–(54)), Heggie (1988a), Moro (1988, 1997), Verheugd (1990), Heycock (1994a, 1994b), Guéron (1992, 1993), Mikkelsen (2004, 2005), and den Dikken (2006b).

Although it was not the first proposal to treat specificational sentences as inverted predications (predecessors include Blom and Daalder 1977, Williams 1983b, Heggie 1988a, 1988b, Partee 1986), the most detailed and influential treatment of this kind is that of Andrea Moro (Moro 1991, 1997, 2000), who gives detailed exemplification and analysis of various aspects of this construction. These include not only the issue of predicate-like interpretation of the initial noun phrase discussed above, but the limited extraction possibilities of and from the postcopular phrase, and the agreement pattern in Italian where, unlike English, agreement is consistently with the postcopular nominal.

(44) a. I don't know who$_i$ the culprit was t$_i$ (if it wasn't Jennifer)
  b. *I don't know [which student]$_i$ the culprit was t$_i$
  c. *I don't know what$_i$ the cause of the riot was their announcement of t$_i$

(45) il colpevole sono io
  the culprit   am   I
  'the culprit is me'

Subsequently, a number of resesarchers have further observed that reference back to the subject of a specificational sentence is done with the singular neuter pronoun *it* rather than with the expected gendered pronoun (Büring 1998, Heycock and Kroch 2002, Mikkelsen 2002, 2004, 2005):

(46) a. Ahab is the best man for the job, isn't he/*it?
  b. The best man for the job is Ahab, isn't *he/it?

Mikkelsen in particular argues that this pattern is explained if the initial nominal in a specificational sentences is a predicate, since crosslinguistically predicates typically pronominalize with the least specified singular pronoun (e.g., masculine singular *lo* in Italian, masculine singular *le* in French, neuter *es* in German). In English, in fact, pronominal reference to predicates is rare (typically ellipsis is used instead), but as Mikkelsen points out, the use in examples like (47) is a candidate:

(47) Laura is a hardworking woman, even if she doesn't look it

It should be noted, however, that in specificational sentences the initial pronoun may and in some cases must be plural, which never seems possible for pronouns in predicate position:

(48) a. The winners were Federer and Williams, {weren't they/*wasn't it}?
  b. Federer and Williams were the winners, even though they don't look {*them/it}

This points perhaps to a solution more along the lines suggested in Romero (2007), who treats the initial nominal in a specificational sentence as a concealed question in the sense of Heim (1979).[22] Although she only mentions the fact that this explains the neuter gender, it turns out that in these cases too we get obligatory marking for number. *Guess* and *announce* are verbs whose complement DP is a concealed question:

(49) a. John guessed the winner of the Oscar for best actress before I guessed {it/*her}
b. John guessed the winners before the committee announced {*it/them}

Thus while the pronominalization facts argue against treating specificational sentences as an equation of individuals, as argued for example in Heycock and Kroch (1999), they do not straightforwardly support the analysis of the initial nominal as a predicate.

It was mentioned at the beginning of this section that a second characteristic of specificational sentences is that they have a fixed information structure, with the postcopular NP obligatorily focused, as noted already in Higgins (1973). Most accounts of specificational sentences have not, however, succeeded deriving this property.[23] Mikkelsen, however, builds this into her account. Essentially she argues that concerns of locality would normally prevent the predicate from being attracted to clausal subject position when an eligible subject is available, so that we should expect predicate inversion to be blocked. She allows the subject position in English to be optionally endowed with an uninterpretable Topic feature, however: if the predicate is the closest element with a matching feature the small clause subject will not count as an intervenor (as it does not have the relevant feature content to be attracted itself). Hence inversion can only take place if the inverted predicate is topical, leaving the small clause subject, or some part of it, as the only available candidate for focus.

The predicate inversion analysis of specificational sentences has proved very compelling, particularly for the explanation that it provides for the extraction asymmetries noted above, but it is not without its critics. For Heycock and Kroch (1999) the main failing is that it overgenerates. In particular, they argue that when the predicate of a small clause is clearly predicative, and an equative interpretation is ruled out, the result of predicate inversion is simply ungrammatical. Crucial examples – because they involve predicates which have the syntactic form of definite DPs, uncontroversially licit as occupants of the clausal subject position – are the type given in (50)–(53). In (50) and (51) and the predicates have the form of definite noun phrases, but they still cannot be inverted to form acceptable specificational sentences, as shown in (52) and (53).

(50) John is the one thing that I want a man to be – honest

(51) A: There are sympathetic nurses and callous nurses; which kind of nurse is Mary?
B: Mary is the first kind of nurse.

(52) *The one thing that I want a man to be – honest – is John

(53) A: There are sympathetic nurses and callous nurses; give me an example of the second kind of nurse.
B: Mary is the second kind of nurse.
B': *The second kind of nurse is Mary.

It should be noted that, for example, (52) contrasts minimally with (54). The initial *wh*-clause appears to be identical, again denoting a predicate – but in this case it is equated with another predicate, and as a result the sentence is fully grammatical:

(54) The one thing that I want a man to be is honest

It should also be observed that in (53) *the second kind of nurse* is discourse-old for Speaker B, and that the context sets up the other DP as a focus, so that there seems no reason why *the second kind of nurse* should not be able to bear a Topic feature. This makes it hard to see how these cases could be dealt with by Mikkelsen's proposal to limit this kind of overgeneration by the discourse properties of the elements in question.[24] Explaining why inversion is limited to predications that are in some sense equative therefore remains as a challenge for this approach.

10.8 A' movement of predicates

Predicates can undergo various kinds of A' movement, including topicalization and *wh*-movement:

(55) a. tall$_i$ he most certainly is not t$_i$
b. What$_i$ do you think I am t$_i$? Stupid?

Birner (1992) analyzes in depth a further type of predicate movement which involves in addition postposing of the subject. Birner herself is more concerned with the pragmatics than with the syntax of this construction, although she notes that the initial phrase in this construction does not behave like a subject in that it does not undergo Subject–Aux inversion.

(56) a. under his ragged nails was the mechanic's permanent, oil-black grime
b. co-sponsoring the event along with the Archdiocese of Denver was Citizens for Responsible Government, which has backed pro-life ballot initiatives in Colorado
c. even rarer, according to these experts, is the kind of wholesale fraud that Pennsylvania authorities have alleged in the Crafton case
d. not the least of Upali's enemies is Sri Lanka's prime minister, Ranasinghe Premadasa

(57) *Is not the least of Upali's enemies Sri Lanka's prime minister, Ranasinghe Premadasa?

Further arguments that this construction involves A′ movement of the predicate are given in Heycock and Kroch (1998). The existence of this construction in English does mean that examples of 'predicate inversion' in English have to be checked carefully to determine whether they have to be analyzed as instances of this kind of A′ movement, or can be classed with specificational sentences. A related point concerning superficial ambiguity between predicate inversion as discused above and A′ movement of predicates is discussed with respect to Danish – and the discussion can be replicated for other V2 Germanic languages – in Mikkelsen (2002).

In an influential paper, Huang (1993) points out that topicalized VPs and other predicates show different reconstruction effects with respect to binding than do fronted arguments.

(58) [Which pictures of himself$_{i/j}]_k$ did John$_i$ think Bill$_j$ liked t$_k$?

(59) a. [criticize himself$_{*i/j}]_k$ John$_i$ thinks Bill$_j$ never will t$_k$
b. [proud of himself$_{*i/j}]_k$ John$_i$ thinks Bill$_j$ will never be t$_k$

Essentially Huang's argument is that the coreference possibilities of noun phrases within a fronted predicate are constrained differently to those within fronted arguments because fronting the predicate will always involve fronting the trace of the subject in its specifier. Huang's article was written at a time when there was much debate about the exact position of VP-internal subjects (see Section 11.6.2); his idea was that this evidence showed that such subjects must be generated as specifiers of VP, rather than in an adjoined position. Bowers (2001) argues that the postulation of a predicate head in all cases of predication makes it possible to retain Huang's analysis despite the evidence from examples like *I consider her Mary's best friend* that the subject of, for example, a nominal predicate cannot be generated in the specifier position of the nominal. Assuming the idea of a predicate head, the structure of the fronted predicates in (59) must therefore be roughly as in (60):[25]

(60) a. [$_{PredP}$ t$_j$ [$_{Pred'}$ criticize$_v$ [$_{VP}$ himself$_j$ t$_v$]]]$_k$ John$_i$ thinks Bill$_j$ never will t$_k$
b. [$_{PredP}$ t$_j$ [$_{Pred'}$ Ø [$_{AP}$ proud of himself$_j$]]]$_k$ John$_i$ thinks Bill$_j$ will never be t$_k$

The postulation of a predicate head that is distinct from the lexical verb or adjective, however, introduces a degree of freedom into the system that was not present when Huang was writing. Thus some further argument needs to be given to guarantee that PredP, rather than just AP, fronts in (60b), for example. And in fact, if *as* really is the instantiation of Pred, it seems that we actually have direct evidence that the smaller constituent can front; but the binding possibilities are limited in the way that Huang observed.[26]

(61) a. *as a genius, I would hesitate to regard him
b. ?a genius, I would hesitate to regard him as

(62) How proud of himself*$_{i/j}$ does Bill$_i$ regard John$_j$ as?

Thus it seems that either the status of *as* may need rethinking, or an alternative analysis of the binding facts is required (see Heycock 1995a for one proposal).

10.9 Conclusion

The syntax of predication was heavily discussed in the 1980s and 1990s, much inspired by the pioneering work of Edwin Williams, Susan Rothstein, and John Bowers. In subsequent years work on the topic became perhaps less prominent, although there has been a steady flow of work particularly on copular constructions, above all the specificational cases dissected so thoroughly by Roger Higgins in the 1970s, and then brought back to attention most notably through the work of Andrea Moro. There are of course many topics within this area that have been only touched on in the briefest way in this chapter, including the syntax of secondary predication (Rothstein 2006), and the possibility of analysing the syntax of certain complex nominals in terms of predication, as proposed in Napoli (1989) and den Dikken (2006b). Predication as a syntactic licensing relation sat uncomfortably within earlier generative frameworks, for the reasons discussed above; the Minimalist abandonment of D-structure has opened the way for a better integration of the theory of predication into syntactic theory more generally, as the renewed interest in (still controversially) non-thematic subjects has demonstrated.

Notes

1. Åfarli and Eide (2000) adopt from Bouchard (1995) the idea that semantics writ large divides into three subcomponents, only one of which, 'Grammar Semantics,' directly affects syntactic form; the requirement that propositions are structured into subject and predicate is hypothesized to be part of Grammar Semantics.
2. The notable exception to this generalization is when the property attributed is syntactically complex, with a gap in a predicate position (see Williams 1990 and Heycock and Kroch 1999 for some discussion of these cases):

   (i) a. wise is a good thing to be *e*
   b. wise is what I want to be *e*

3. This is closely related to the argument made in Williams (1982:286), about the external argument of event nominalizations as opposed to the verbs from which they are derived. Williams makes the point that when a noun like *desiccation* is used predicatively, as in (i) (interpreted as *I consider that to be desiccation*), the subject of this predicate is not the thing undergoing *desiccation*, although that would be the subject of the corresponding verb:

   (i) I consider that dessication

   As Williams says, "[(i)] says that that is an act of dessication, not a thing undergoing dessication".

4. But see remarks above for Williams's very different view of the relation of expletives to predication.
5. Examples like (9d) also posed a problem for the idea that case had the function of making θ-roles 'visible' (Chomsky (1986b), since by hypothesis the expletive has no θ-role.
6. In fact she argues that (11c) is ambiguous, with the pronoun an expletive on only one reading (Rothstein 2001:68)
7. It should be observed that *it* expletives of various kinds are possible in gerunds (Baker 1985, Abney 1987). Abney gives the following examples and judgments (pp. 113f.):

   (i) a. we would prefer its not raining just now
       b. ? (I'm happy about) its being likely that John will finish soon
       c. ??(I was surprised at) its seeming that John might not win

   For a discussion of the failure of *there* to occur in any kind of nominalization see Abney (1987).

8. Hicks argues that the possibility of having a quantified subject distinguishes *tough*-predicates from these cases (p. 543). But Lappin (1984) provides several acceptable examples with quantified subjects in the course of his discussion of scope in this construction, including (ia,b); (c) is an attested example from the Web (http://extras.denverpost.com/broncos/mail1007.htm, last accessed 22 December 2010).

   (i) a. everyone seems as if he is working hard
       b. no one seems like she wants to go to Antarctica
       c. When a team is winning, everyone seems like he is a leader. When a team is losing, no one seems like he is stepping forward.

   Hicks also points out that *there* expletives can occur in this construction, while they cannot occur as the subject of *tough*-predicates. The occurrence of *there* in 'copy-raising' constructions is very limited, however, and it has been argued in Potsdam and Runner (2001), Rezac (2004) and Landau (2009) that it is evidence for a distinct subconstruction – see Landau (2009) for discussion.

9. Edwin Williams and Susan Rothstein are notable dissenters from this view of the syntax of predication, since both are explicit in arguing that a predicate does not necessarily form a constituent with its subject; the effect of this is most evident in their (differing) treatments of secondary predication.
10. In fact there are various different types of tenseless verb-headed predicates in English, which do not have the same distribution as each other, and none of which have the same distribution as other predicates:

    (i) a. I consider Julia {radical/a genius/at the peak of her career/to be ruthless/*be ruthless/*being ruthless}
    b. with Julia {radical/a genius/at the peak of her career/*to be ruthless/*be ruthless/being ruthless}, ...
    c. we should let Julia {*happy/*a happy person/*in ignorance/*to stay/stay/*staying}

11. It should be noted, however, that den Dikken leaves it open whether in a Focus–Presupposition relation the subject of predication is the Focus or the Presupposition.
12. Eide and Åfarli (1999) differ from Bowers in their analysis of main clause predication, proposing that Pr does not have its own projection but is part of the make-up of the verb itself.
13. These are the two main syntactic differences between Pr and the RELATOR head; semantically they appear also to be different. As mentioned above, for Bowers predication is crucially involved in the building of propositions from properties and individuals. Although at times den Dikken also seems to think of predication in this way, for example stating that "a predicate is a function (in simple cases, such as *Imogen sneezed*, from individuals to truth values" (p. 17), he also states as a tentative hypothesis that predication corresponds to set intersection; this is quite different to the assumptions of other work on the syntax of predication, including Bowers's.
14. Note that den Dikken reserves the term *reverse* predication for configurations where the predicate is merged as the specifier of a RELATOR head; he distinguishes between this and *inverse* predication, where a predicate-complement moves to the left of the subject.
15. Den Dikken also includes (ia,b) as cases of reverse predication, but does not discuss them further:

    (i) a. we have [[$_{Predicate}$ a fool] [as=RELATOR [$_{Subject}$ our president]]]
    b. we have [[$_{Predicate}$ a fool] [for=RELATOR [$_{Subject}$ a president]]]

    It is not obvious that one would want to conclude that the first nominal is the predicate in these examples; varying the DPs suggests that the first nominal can refer to an individual, while the second cannot.

(ii) a. we are happy to have {you/that woman/Julia} {for/as} our president
   b. *we were unhappy to have a fool {for/as} that president

16. For Bowers the Pr head is necessarily present in a full clause, so it may either acquire a subject DP in its specifier position through merge (in the case of an unergative or transitive verb) or move (in the case of an unaccusative, for example). In Bowers (1993) it is proposed that the verb moves to Pr in order to be able to assign a θ-role to the external argument (Bowers claims that the absence of look-ahead means that it is predicted that this will also happen in cases where there is no external θ-role to be assigned (p. 600)); in Bowers (2001) he states only that he remains "agnostic as to where θ-roles are assigned" (p. 302).

17. Of course, if Tense selects for PredP, this dependence will have to be captured in some other way.

18. A citation that might seem to be missing here is Russell (1919) Chapter XVI, which contains the stentorian quote:

    The *is* of 'Socrates is human' expresses the relation of subject and predicate; the *is* of 'Socrates is a man' expresses identity. It is a disgrace to the human race that it has chosen to employ the same word 'is' for these two entirely different ideas – a disgrace which a symbolic logical language of course remedies.

    As Moro (1997) points out, most linguists today would consider both of the examples that Russell cites to be instances of predicative copula constructions, with *is* having the same (lack of) meaning in both; see Matushansky and Spector (2005), however, for a treatment of indefinite noun phrase 'predicate' constructions in French as instances of equatives.

19. The '??' judgments really indicate pragmatic infelicity; these examples can generally be coerced into some kind of reading where being in London or being Swedish is presented as being a gradable, subjective property.

20. Note that mere reversibility of the two nominals is not sufficient evidence that a construction equates two entities, given the type-ambiguity of nominal phrases in English at least; see among others Williams (1994), Heycock and Kroch (1999), and den Dikken (2006b, 2006d) for discussion.

21. Although it is commonly assumed that specificational structures necessarily involve the copula, in fact this is not quite true (Heycock 1994a):

    (i) a. I had thought the culprit must be Jack. But if the murder actually took place at 9pm, not 10, that would make the culprit Joe.
       b. I had hoped the winner would be Laura. But if the number was 15 rather than 50, that would make it Amy.

22. The idea that the initial phrase in a specificational pseudocleft is interpeted as a question (or, for some authors, in addition has the syntactic form of a question) has a long history: see in particular Faraci (1970), Ross (1972b, 1985, 1997, 2000), den Dikken et al. (2000), Schlenker (2003b), and Romero (2005).
23. In den Dikken (2006b) it is argued that the only difference as far as focus is concerned between specificational sentences in English and 'garden-variety transitive sentences,' which as he points out typically feature focal stress on the final element in the VP, is that in specificational sentences focus cannot project: "The postcopular/postverbal subject's focal stress is the consequence of its finality in the sentence; the fact that focus does not project beyond the subject seems to be a reflex of the fact that the subject noun phrase of a Predicate Inversion construction is basically 'frozen' in the syntax" (pp. 82–83). But while it is certainly typical for English sentences to have stress on the final element, the characteristic of a specificational sentence is that this final focus is not just typical but actually required, even though generally English allows focus to be assigned relatively freely, including to constituents in phrase-initial position.
24. The problem of overgeneration is even more acute in the analysis in den Dikken (2006b), where the predicate in a specificational sentence is a null pro-predicate modified by a reduced relative clause with a gap in subject position. (ib) shows the structure of the predicate that is fronted in (ia), the only pronounced part of which is *the best candidate*.

    (i) a. the best candidate is Brian
         b. [NULL PRO-PREDICATE [$_{CP}$ Op_i [C [$_{RP}$ t_i [Ø = RELATOR the best candidate]]]]]

    This amounts to the proposal that the predicate in a specificational sentence is a reduced free relative, roughly corresponding to the (non-reduced) *who is the best candidate*. The problem then is that not even the category of the predicate embedded within the reduced relative should be able to affect the ability of the larger inverted predicate to occupy subject position: we would expect, for example, (iia) to be as grammatical as (iib):

    (ii) a. *I think that annoying is his attitude
         b. I think that what is annoying is his attitude

25. The structure in (60a) follows Bowers's proposal that the verb head-moves to Pred and that the object is the specifier of VP.
26. A similar problem arises for the argument that the problem of 'unlike category coordination' in the case of predicates is solved by the

postulation of a predication head, as in (ia), since 'unlike categories' can coordinate just as well under *as*:

(i) a. Julia$_i$ is [[$_{PredP}$ t$_i$ Ø a fool] and [$_{PredP}$ t$_i$ Ø unsafe in company]]
b. I regard Julia as [[$_{DP}$ a fool] and [$_{AP}$ unsafe in company]]

Of course there are possible analyses of unlike category coordination which would render (ib) unproblematic; see in particular Bayer (1996).

11

Lexical categories and (extended) projection
Norbert Corver

11.1 Syntactic structures as projections of lexical properties[1]

One of the most fundamental properties of human language is its hierarchical organization. A linguistic expression like (1a) is not merely a linear sequence of words, as in (1b), but is organized in a part–whole manner; i.e. two words (parts) may combine into a larger unit (whole), which in turn may combine with another word to form an even larger unit (whole), which again may combine with another lexical item to form an even larger syntactic unit, and so forth and so on. This part–whole organization of linguistic expressions is referred to as phrase structure or constituent structure (Carnie 2008).

(1) a. three beautiful pictures of Sue
 b. [three] [beautiful] [pictures] [of] [Sue]
 c. [three [beautiful [pictures [of [Sue]]]]]

Evidence for this phrase structural organization of linguistic expressions comes from constituency behavior: parts (constituents) that form a whole (a larger constituent) behave as a unit syntactically. For example, the unit can be displaced to another syntactic position, as exemplified in (2a) for the linear string *of whom*; it can be pronominalized by a single word, as illustrated in (2b) for the string *pictures of Sue*, and in (2d) for the string *three beautiful pictures of Sue*; or it can undergo ellipsis (see Chapter 19), as shown in (2c) for the sequence *beautiful pictures of Sue*.[2]

(2) a. [Of whom] did John see [three beautiful pictures –]?
 b. John saw [three beautiful *pictures of Sue*] and Bill saw [three ugly ones]
 c. John saw three *beautiful pictures of Sue* and Bill saw [four –]
 d. John saw [*three beautiful pictures of Sue*] and I saw [them] too

An important insight, already familiar from traditional and structuralist grammars under the name of endocentricity, is the idea that a phrasal unit like *three beautiful pictures of Sue* is organized around a core lexical item, the so-called head of the phrasal construction. It is this head which determines the categorial nature of the entire construction. Or to put it differently, the nominal head (the noun *pictures* in (1b)) projects its categorial feature onto the larger units in which it is contained: that is, the larger constituents *pictures of Sue*, *beautiful pictures of Sue* and *three beautiful pictures of Sue* are all syntactic objects that are *nominal* in nature. In short, the categorial property *noun* that is associated with the lexical item *pictures* is projected onto the larger phrase-structural units. These phrase-structural units may therefore be called nominal projections.

The idea that a property of a syntactic structure (e.g. the categorial nature of a phrasal constituent) is projected from a property of a lexical item plays a central role in generative syntax. As a matter of fact, this idea has been generalized to the extent that a syntactic structure in its entirety is essentially projectable from the properties of its constituent lexical items. In other words, a syntactic structure is a phrase structural manifestation of the lexical properties associated with the lexical items that constitute the building blocks for the syntactic structure.

This projection or "structuralization" (Chametzky 2000) of lexical information is explicitly stated in Chomsky's (1981:29) Projection Principle:

> Representations at each syntactic level (i.e., LF, and D- and S-structure) are projected from the lexicon, in that they observe the subcategorization properties of lexical items.

In this formulation, made within the theoretical confines of the Government and Binding framework (see Chapters 2 and 4), projection regards the subcategorization property of a lexical item, i.e. the lexical property of c(ategorial)-selection. For example, the lexical entry of a verb like *meet* contains the c-selection property that *meet* takes an NP-complement, as in *(John) met her*. Chomsky's Projection Principle expresses that each syntactic representation (i.e. D-structure, S-structure, and LF) associated with the linguistic expression *John met her* must represent the lexical information that *meet* takes an NP as its complement.

In the Minimalist Program (Chomsky 1993, 1995c; see Chapter 4), where a linguistic expression is associated with two interface representations, LF and PF, the role of the Projection Principle in the mapping between lexicon and syntax is clearly present as well:

> Another natural condition is that outputs consist of nothing beyond properties of items of the lexicon (lexical features) – in other words, that the interface levels consist of nothing more than arrangements of lexical features. (Chomsky 1995c: 225)

According to this statement, linguistic expressions are nothing but structural arrangements (i.e. projections, structuralizations) of lexical information. This formulation implies that no new (i.e. non-lexical) informational properties, such as referential indices or hierarchical bar level information, may be introduced in the course of the derivation of a linguistic expression. Chomsky (1995c:225, 228) calls this constraint regarding the information present in syntactic structures the Inclusiveness Condition.

If any syntactic object is a structural projection of lexical information associated with lexical items, it is obviously crucial to have a clear view of the types of lexical items that are contained within the lexicon and the lexical information that is associated with them. A central dichotomy in the (syntactic) categorization of lexical items is that between lexical categories (also called content words or major, substantive, or open-class categories), on the one hand, and functional categories (also called function words or minor/closed-class categories), on the other hand. Lexical categories are often characterized as being those lexical items which have a relatively 'specific' or 'detailed' semantic content and as such carry the principal meaning of a linguistic expression. They name the objects (N: *picture, wine*), events (V: *to sleep, to eat*), properties (A: *beautiful, angry*), and locations/directions (P: *behind, to*) that are at the heart of the message that the sentence is meant to convey.³ Another important lexical property of lexical categories is their argument structure or thematic grid: i.e. the information how many arguments the head licenses and what semantic role (agent, theme, goal, etc.) each receives. For example, the verb *buy* in *John bought a house* is a two-place predicate, which assigns an agent role to the subject *John* and a theme role to the direct object *a house*.

As opposed to lexical categories, functional categories have a more 'abstract' meaning and fulfill an essentially grammatical function within a linguistic expression; in a sense they are needed to glue the content words together (Muysken 2008).⁴ The abstract meaning of the functional lexicon comprises such properties as tense (e.g. the past tense bound morpheme *-ed*, as in *kill-ed*), (in)definiteness (the articles *a, the*), and degree (the degree words *too, how*). Importantly, there is a certain connection between the lexical system and the functional system: For example, tense goes with verbs (*will sleep*), (in)definiteness goes with nouns (*a/the picture*), and a degree word like *too* goes with adjectives (*too angry*).

Some characteristic properties that have been noticed for functional categories are listed in (3), which is adapted from Abney (1987). It should be noted that none of the listed properties is necessary or sufficient to attribute functional status to a lexical item.⁵

(3) *General properties of functional heads*
   a. They constitute closed lexical classes.
   b. They lack descriptive content.
   c. They can be sisters to only one kind of category
   d. They are generally phonologically and morphologically dependent.
   e. They are usually inseparable from their sister projection.

The dichotomy between lexical categories and functional categories raises a number of questions from the perspective of syntactic projection of lexical information, such as:

(a) Which lexicon-properties are associated with lexical categories (LC) and how are they projected onto a syntactic structure Σ?
(b) Which lexicon-properties are associated with functional categories (FC) and how are are they projected onto a syntactic structure Σ?
(c) How is the knowledge about the 'connection' between the lexical system and the functional system (e.g. the knowledge that *the* goes with N and *will* with V) represented in the lexicon and how is this lexical information projected onto syntax?
(d) To what extent are functional projections (i.e. syntactic structures that project from the properties of a functional category) structurally the same as lexical projections (i.e. syntactic structures that project from the properties of a lexical category)?
(e) To what extent is there cross-categorial similarity as regards the 'grammatical role' of the functional projections that are associated with the lexical categories (V, N, A, P)?
(f) Is projection of lexical information cross-linguistically uniform, or do languages display cross-linguistic variation in this respect?

In this chapter I will present answers to some of these questions, as they have been given in the generative literature. There are two general answers that I would like to mention here already, since they are characteristic of the current generative-syntactic conception of phrasal architecture and the nature of syntactic projection. The first answer regards questions (d) and (e): much generative research on syntactic projection takes the view that projection is symmetric (i.e. parallel) across syntactic categories. According to this view, the structuralization of lexical properties (i.e. the way in which lexical information is mapped onto syntactic structure) is fundamentally the same in verbal, nominal, adjectival, and prepositional phrases.

The second answer which I would like to already mention here regards question (c). It is generally assumed these days that the projection of a lexical category – the so-called lexical projection – is structurally contained within the projection of a functional category.[6] This conception of projected structure – sometimes referred to as the Functional Head

Hypothesis (Grimshaw 1991) – is represented in (4a), where FP stands for one or more functional projections on top of the lexical projection LP. Importantly, this conception of phrasal projection is different from the one held in earlier stages of generative grammar, according to which the functional projection(s) was/were taken to be part of (i.e. embedded within) the lexical projection; see (4b), which represents the so-called Lexical Head Hypothesis.

(4) a. [$_{FP}$ Spec [$_{F'}$ F [$_{LP}$ L]]]
    b. [$_{LP}$ [$_{FP}$ F] [$_{L'}$ L XP]]

The Functional Head Hypothesis in (4a) in combination with the symmetry hypothesis is at the basis of Grimshaw's (1991) notion of extended projection, which captures the phrase structural 'unity' of the lexical layer and the dominating functional layer(s); see Section 11.7 for details. The functional head F and its phrasal projection FP in (4a) are considered to be extended projections of the lexical head L and its projection LP. Given the four lexical categories V, N, A, and P, the following four extended projections can now be distinguished, where F(P) stands for one or a sequence of functional projections:

(5) a. [$_{FP}$ F [$_{VP}$ V]]   (extended verbal projection)
    b. [$_{FP}$ F [$_{NP}$ N]]   (extended nominal projection)
    c. [$_{FP}$ F [$_{AP}$ A]]   (extended adjectival projection)
    d. [$_{FP}$ F [$_{PP}$ P]]   (extended adpositional projection)

This chapter is organized as follows. Section 11.2 discusses the projection of phrasal structure and shows how the theory of phrase structure developed from a system of construction specific phrase structure rules to a system of general X-bar theoretic principles that govern the projection of syntactic structure. In Section 11.3, some further X-bar theoretic issues are dealt with, more specifically: the featural definition of syntactic categories, and the bar level property (i.e. hierarchical levels of projection). Section 11.4 discusses a number of phrase structural properties, including (multi-)dominance, precedence, binary branching, and multiplanar phrase structure. Section 11.5 shows how the Functional Head Hypothesis applies to the clausal system, leading to a conception of phrase structure in which the lexical projection VP is embedded within the functional projections IP and CP. Section 11.6 then discusses the projection of thematic information within the lexical projection, the regulating roles of the Theta Criterion and the Extended Projection Principle, and, finally, the so-called VP-internal Subject Hypothesis. Section 11.7 deals with the nature of functional categories and the concept of extended projection. Sections 11.8, 11.9 and 11.10 discuss, respectively, the extended nominal projection, the extended adjectival projection, and the extended adpositional projection. Section 11.11 concludes this chapter.

11.2 Phrasal projection: from PS-rules to X-bar Theory

In early generative grammar (cf. Chomsky's 1957 *Syntactic Structures* and Chomsky's 1965 *Aspects of the Theory of Syntax*), the phrase structures of a language L are generated by so-called phrase-structure rules or PS-rules (see Chapter 2, and also Carnie 2008 for discussion). Those rules have the format in (6), where X is the name of the phrase defined, and Y, Z, and W are either phrases – and therefore in need of phrase-structure definitions themselves – or the names of lexical categories such as Noun, Verb, Adjective, and Preposition.

(6) X → Y Z W ...

This format may be instantiated by phrase-structure rules like (7) and (8), which can generate a phrase structure representation like (9). The phrase structure rules in (7) are syntactic rules: they build a phrase structure; the phrase structure rules in (8) are lexical rules: they assign lexical items (*met, John, from, et cetera*) to syntactic categories (V, N, P, etc.).[7]

(7)   a. S → NP VP
      b. VP → V NP
      c. NP → (DET) N (PP)
      d. PP → P NP

(8)   a. V → met/ –NP
      b. P → from/ –NP
      c. N → John
      d. N → man
      e. N → Brazil
      f. ART → the

(9)   [$_S$ [$_{NP}$ [$_N$ John]] [$_{VP}$ [$_V$ met] [$_{NP}$ [$_{DET}$ the] [$_N$ man [$_{PP}$ [$_P$ from] [$_{NP}$ [$_N$ Brazil]]]]]]]

Within the 'lexical' phrase structure rules in (8), two types of lexical rules can be distinguished: context-sensitive rules and context-free rules.[8] The former are instantiated by (8a–b): these rules indicate that V and P can be lexicalized by *meet* and *from*, respectively, only when they are followed by an NP. In other words, there must be an NP in their structural context. The reason for adding this context-sensitive information is that one does not want *meet* to be inserted in a VP which consists solely of a V (i.e. **John met*). The context-free rules (8c–f) do not provide such a structural context requirement.

In the 1970s and 1980s, the phrase-structure component, as exemplified in (7)–(8), was largely "dismantled" (Stowell 1981; see also Fukui 2001 for discussion), for a number of reasons. The phrase-structure rule system was considered to be descriptively too rich, redundant, and explanatorily inadequate (i.e. it did not give any insight into what Chomsky 1986b calls Plato's problem, i.e. the logical problem of language acquisition). For example, it was noticed that reference to context in phrase-structure rules is restricted to rules such as (8) that assign lexical items to their syntactic categories (Chomsky 1986b:81). The phrase-structure system could be simplified by separating the lexicon from the syntax. This separation led to a reduction in the variety of phrase-structure rules. More specifically: there is only one type of phrase-structure rule, viz. the context-free one. Lexical phrase-structure rules like (8) were abandoned entirely and context-sensitive information was stated in so-called subcategorization frames that were part of the lexical entry of a word. For example, the lexical entries of the verb *meet* and the preposition *from* contained the following subcategorization (i.e., c(ategorial)-selection) information:

(10) a. *meet*, [_NP]
b. *from*, [_NP]

But even a situation in which the phrase-structural component contains only context-free rules like (7) turns out to be non-optimal. Much of the information expressed by the phrase-structural rules in (7) is also available in the lexicon. For example, the information that a V can combine with an NP, as expressed by the phrase-structure rule in (7b), is also available in the lexicon. The subcategorization frame associated with the verb *meet*, for example, already expresses this contextual information; see (10a). With the aim to avoid redundancy in the expression of information, it has been proposed that phrase-structure rules expressing head–complement structure should be eliminated from the phrase-structure system altogether. Thus, (7b) and (7d) could be simplified to:

(11) a. VP → V
b. PP → P

The fact that an NP-complement must be present in a phrase-structural representation like (9) now follows from the interaction of two things: first, the subcategorization information in the English lexicon that the verb *meet* takes an NP-complement as a lexical property; second, the Projection Principle, which requires that lexical properties be represented structurally in syntactic representations (i.e. "structuralization of lexical information").

Even with the elimination of the head–complement structure from phrase-structure rules (i.e. the move from (7b,d) to (11)), redundancy remains within the system of context-free phrase-structure rules in (11). Furthermore, a generalization is missed (see also Chapter 2). The redundancy expressed is the fact that each phrasal constituent VP, PP, and NP contains a head of the same categorial type. Thus, VP contains a verbal head, PP a prepositional head, and NP a nominal head. The generalization that the head node shares its categorial properties with the phrasal node containing it – traditionally known as the endocentricity property – is a deep and general property of human language which needs to be singled out from the construction specific phrase-structure rules in (11) and (7c) and be stated as a general phrase-structure principle of human language. This is what Chomsky (1970a) did when he proposed his so-called X-bar Theory of phrase structure. According to this theory, the phrase-structure component of human language consists of the following two basic phrase-structure rules, which are considered to be principles of Universal Grammar:

(12) X-bar Theory
    a. X′ → X YP   (the head–complement phrasal structure)
    b. X″ → [SpecX′] X′   (the specifier–head phrasal structure)

The symbol X in (12) is a variable ranging over the lexical categories N, V, A, and P. The symbol X′ (called "X-bar", although typographically it is often represented by a prime rather than a bar) represents a phrasal constituent consisting of the head X and a complement. X″ (X-double bar) contains the X′-constituent and the so-called specifier of X′. It is useful to know that X″ is equivalent to XP, where P stands for *Phrase*. It should also be mentioned here that in Jackendoff's (1977) seminal study on English phrase structure an X-bar Theory is proposed which went up to X-triple bar; I will come back to this in Section 11.3.

An important consequence of the formulation in (12) is that headedness no longer needs to be stipulated in separate construction-specific phrase-structure rules (i.e. separate phrase-structure rules for NP, VP, PP in (7)/(11)). According to the X-bar principles in (12), when the verb *meet* becomes syntactically active and "structuralizes", so to speak, it "structuralizes" according to the laws of X-bar Theory. That is, it projects its categorial property of being a V onto its phrasal projections (V′ and VP). In other words, the categorial property of the head determines the categorial property of the phrase (X′ and X″).

The universal phrase-structural principles in (12) also immediately rule out imaginable phrase structures like (13), which could in principle be generated by the PS-rules in (14).

(13)   a. [$_{VP}$ [$_P$ from] [$_{NP}$ Brazil]]
      b. [$_{PP}$ [$_{NP}$ Brazil]]

(14)   a. VP → P NP
      b. PP → NP

As noted by Lyons (1968), these structures are not automatically excluded by the context-free phrase-structure rule format in (7), which only needs to satisfy the requirement that the input symbol to the left of the arrow is a single non-terminal symbol and the output to the right of the arrow is a non-null string of non-terminal symbols. Thus, the context-free phrase-structure rule system is too permissive, i.e. it generates syntactic structures that are not allowed in human language. The X-bar format of phrase-structure rules, on the contrary, immediately rules out the illegitimate syntactic structures in (13): The VP in (13a) and the PP in (13b) must be projections of the heads V and P, respectively.

Besides giving us a notion of "possible phrase structure rules", X-bar theory, as represented by the rules in (12), expresses the idea of phrase-structural parallelism (i.e. symmetry) across different categories. The "X" in (12) is a variable that ranges over the class of lexical categories V, N, A, and P. This implies that the phrasal projections VP, NP, AP, and PP are similar (symmetric) in their internal structural organization.[9] Chomsky (1970a) argues that this parallelism permits a generalized formulation of grammatical functions (e.g. subject, object) and the rules of subcategorization. For example, the notion of "object of" is associated with the head–complement relationship; that is, objects are dominated by X'. Thus, the complements *the city* and *(of) the city* in (15a) and (15b) fulfill the grammatical function of "object". Likewise, *destroyed* and *destruction* are subcategorized for (i.e. categorically select) an NP, where *of* is often taken to be a case realization or case marker inserted late in the derivation (see Chomsky 1981). The patterns in (16) and (17) provide a further illustration of the idea that subcategorization information (*in casu*: selection of PP in (16) and selection of a clause, S', in (17)) is cross-categorially associated with the complement position of the head.[10]

(15) a. the enemy [$_{V'}$ [$_V$ destroyed] [$_{NP}$ the city]]
 b. the enemy's [$_{N'}$ [$_N$ destruction] [of [$_{NP}$ the city]]]

(16) a. John [$_{V'}$ [$_V$ relies] [$_{PP}$ on Mary]]
 b. John's [$_{N'}$ [$_N$ reliance] [$_{PP}$ on Mary]]
 c. John is [$_{A'}$ [$_A$ reliant] [$_{PP}$ on Mary]]

(17) a. [John [$_{V'}$ [$_V$ claimed] [$_{S'}$ that Bill was unhappy]]]
 b. [John's [$_{N'}$ [$_N$ claim] [$_{S'}$ that Bill was unhappy]]]

Although the parallel grammatical function of *the enemy* and *the enemy's* in (15) is intuitively quite clear, a uniform mapping of the grammatical function of "subject of" onto a phrase-structural position (e.g. [Spec, X']) was not straightforward in the earliest conception of sentential structure. Sentences did not quite fit into the X-bar schema as given in (12); they were generated by the PS-rule in (18), which, given its non-endocentric nature, clearly is not in accordance with the rules of X-bar theory:

(18) S → N'' V''

As we will see in Section 11.6, further developments in phrase-structure theory and theta theory – more specifically, the so-called VP-internal subject hypothesis (Kitagawa 1986, Koopman and Sportiche 1991) – led to the identification of [SpecLP], where L equals V, N, A, P, as the structural position associated with the thematic notion external argument.[11] In other words, [SpecLP] was considered to be a structural position to which a theta-role can be assigned (i.e. a so-called theta-position).

Chomsky's original conception of the notion specifier is very different from the one associated with the VP-internal subject hypothesis. Chomsky (1970a:52) proposes "to refer to the *phrase* associated with N', A', V' in the base structure as the 'specifier' of these elements". The specifier position is the phrase-structural position in which functional material can be found. In other words, the specifier position is associated with non-argumental rather than argumental (i.e. thematic) material. More specifically, [SpecN'] is analyzed as the determiner, [SpecV'] as the auxiliary, [SpecA'] as the modifying element *very*, and [SpecP'] as the modifying element *right*.

(19) a. [$_{NP}$ the [$_{N'}$ reliance on his parents]]
b. [$_{VP}$ will [$_{V'}$ rely on his parents]]
c. [$_{AP}$ very [$_{A'}$ reliant on his parents]]
d. [$_{PP}$ right [$_{P'}$ above the door]]

Chomsky's (1970a) proposal of X-bar theory triggered the appearance of a great number of studies that tried to lay bare the phrasal syntax of NP (Selkirk 1970, 1977), AP (Bowers 1975, Bresnan 1973, 1977, Hendrick 1978), PP (Emonds 1976, Hendrick 1976, van Riemsdijk 1978), and clauses (Hornstein 1977). A major landmark in the generative study of phrasal structure is Jackendoff (1977), which takes a cross-categorial X-bar theoretic perspective on English phrase structure. These studies showed among others: (i) that the specifier can also sometimes be occupied by lexical categories (e.g. N, A), as exemplified in (20); (ii) that the specifier can be occupied by similar elements cross-categorially, which is a sign of symmetry; see, for example, (21) (cf. van Riemsdijk and Williams 1986); (iii) that the specifier can be phrasal, as illustrated by the examples in (22).[12]

(20) a. [$_{NP}$ [$_{NP}$ the boy's] [$_{N'}$ reliance on his parents]]
b. [$_{AP}$ [$_{AP}$ quite heavily] [$_{A'}$ reliant on his parents]]
c. [$_{PP}$ [$_{AP}$ quite high] [$_{P'}$ above the door]]

(21) a. [more [water]]
b. [more [beautiful]]
c. [more [in the picture]]

(22) a. [[so much more] water than expected that they needed to build bigger dams]
b. [[so much more] beautiful than me that I feel like an old man]
c. [[so much more] into ESP than the others that we should invite him for a talk]

In view of these phenomena, the architecture of phrasal categories can schematically be represented as follows, where FP is the phrasal projection of a functional head F and XP is the complement of L.[13] Importantly, the functional projection FP is contained within the lexical projection LP.

(23) [$_{LP}$ FP [$_{L'}$ L XP]]

As we will see in Section 11.5, this conception of phrase structure – the so-called Lexical Head Hypothesis – has shifted to one in which we have the reverse embedding relation; that is, the lexical projection LP is contained within the functional projection FP.

I would like to conclude this section on phrase-structure rules and X-bar Theory with the following remark. Originally, X-bar Theory, as formulated in (12), was a set of constraints on the formal properties of phrase-structure rules. Stowell (1981) presents a different perspective by taking X-bar Theory as a constraint on syntactic structure. That is, the (phrase-structural) form of the syntactic object that results from the "structuralization" of lexical information (e.g. projection of subategorization and thematic information) is evaluated by the X-bar requirements.[14]

11.3 On features and projections: categorial features and bar levels

This section discusses some further 'featural characteristics' of X-bar structures, starting with the featural definition of syntactic categories. As was noted in the previous section, the endocentricity requirement, as part of X-bar Theory, states that a phrase (X', X'') bears the same category as its head. For example, if the head is of the categorial type N, then the phrasal projections X' and X'' are also of the categorial type N (i.e. N' and N''). Chomsky (1970a) proposes that the four basic syntactic categories N, V, A, and P are actually not atomic syntactic categories. Rather, they are considered to be feature complexes, with [+/–N] (substantive) and [+/–V] (predicative) as the epistemologically basic concepts in the definition of syntactic categories:[15]

(24) a. N = [+N, –V]
      b. V = [–N, +V]
      c. A = [+N, +V]
      d. P = [–N, –V]

An advantage of this feature compositional analysis of syntactic categories is that it allows the expression of cross-categorial similarities among syntactic categories. For example, the two syntactic categories that can have an NP as their complement in English, verbs and prepositions, can now be referred to with the single designation [–N]; see (25). Reinterpreted in terms of case theory, the [–N] categories are the only categories that are able to assign structural case to their NP-complement (cf. Stowell 1981).

In short, with a system of features it becomes possible to characterize natural classes of syntactic categories which share a certain grammatical behavior.[16]

(25) a. she [$_{[-N,+V]}$ kisses] [$_{[+N, -V]}$ Peter]   (she kisses Peter)
   b. [$_{[-N, -V]}$ with] [$_{[+N, -V]}$ Peter]   (with Peter)
   c. *[$_{[+N, -V]}$ pictures] [$_{[+N, -V]}$ Peter]   (*pictures Peter)
   d. *[$_{[+N,+V]}$ afraid] [$_{[+N, -V]}$ Peter]   (*afraid Peter)

Another potential source of support for a system of categorial features comes from the conception of neutralization (Muysken and van Riemsdijk 1986, Stowell 1981). The feature system permits the existence of categories that have an 'in-between' status by being specified for a single feature. For example, it has been argued by Aoun (1981) and van Riemsdijk (1983) that the distinction between A and V may be neutralized to [+V] in some languages.

A second featural characteristic of X-bar structures concerns the bar-level property, which designates the phrasal projection type. That is, how many distinguishable bar levels (i.e. levels of phrasal projection) does the syntactic projection of a head have? In Chomsky's (1970a) original X-bar theoretic statements (see (12)), two bar levels are distinguished: X' (the intermediate projection) and X'' (the maximal projection). This conception of phrase structure, however, does not accommodate constituents that act as modifiers, like the attributive adjective *smart* in (26a); cf. Stuurman (1985:202), and also Section 2.4.2 According to Jackendoff's (1977:53) Uniform Three-Level Hypothesis, there are three levels of phrasal projection: X', X'', and X'''. As shown in (26b), the attributive AP (i.e. A''') *smart* can now be accommodated as a sister to N' (see Chapter 13 for discussion of adjectival modification).

(26) a. a smart student of physics
   b. [$_{N'''}$ [$_{Art'''}$ a] [$_{N''}$ [$_{A'''}$ smart] [$_{N'}$ student [$_{P'''}$ of physics]]]]

The possibility of adding (in principle, infinitely) many modifiers to a phrase – for example, attributive adjectives modifying a noun – has led to an alternative phrase-structural analysis which takes X'' to be the maximal projection level and X' to be a recursive node. For example, the nominal expression in (27a) receives the X-bar analysis in (27b). Evidence that the addition of each attributive adjective adds an extra N'-layer comes from the phenomenon of *one*-pronominalization: on the assumption that this pro-form takes constituents for its antecedents, in (28) *one* is recursively coreferential with a N'-projection.[17,18]

(27) a. a smart young Dutch student of physics
   b. [$_{N''}$ a [$_{N'}$ smart [$_{N'}$ young [$_{N'}$ Dutch [$_{N'}$ student of physics]]]]]

(28) a. he is a [smart young Dutch student of physics]$_i$ and Bill is another one$_i$

b. he is a smart [young Dutch student of physics]$_i$ and Bill is a stupid one$_i$
c. he is a smart young Dutch [student of physics]$_i$ and Bill is a smart young English one$_i$

In Muysken (1983), the bar-level property, which represents the hierarchical level of projection, is reinterpreted in terms of features, more specifically: [+/−maximal] and [+/−projection]. This feature definition leads to a system with three projection types: head ($X_{[-max,-proj]} = X^0$), the intermediate iterative category X′ (= $X_{[-max,+proj]}$), and the maximal category XP (=$X_{[+max,+proj]}$). This featural definition of projection types predicts a fourth type of category, viz. $X_{[+max,-proj]}$. This fourth type of category is possibly instantiated by particles (e.g. *away* as in *John threw the ball away*) and clitic pronouns (e.g. French *le* in *Jean le voyait* 'Jean him$_{clitic}$ saw'); see Chomsky (1995c:249) and Section 4.2.4.2. These categories can be bare, in the sense they do not (or not necessarily) have a complement and specifier structure, but nevertheless display phrasal behavior.[19]

A further step toward the dismantling of the X-bar theoretic notion of bar level was undertaken by Speas (1985, 1990) and Fukui (1995). Rather than interpreting the notion of bar level by making reference to a certain rule (e.g. X′ → X YP in (12a)) or in terms of 'projection' features (e.g. $X_{[-max,+proj]}$), these studies suggest that the bar-level property is a derived property, rather than a primitive one, which can be read off the tree; that is, the bar-level property of a constituent is determined by the structural relation this constituent bears to other constituents in the tree. In other words, the bar-level property of a constituent is a relational property of that constituent, and not an inherent one. This relational notion of bar level is implemented as follows in Speas's analysis. First of all, she proposes that phrasal structure is generated by means of a single rule mechanism, called Project Alpha, which projects (i.e. generates) phrasal structure up from a head. This rule states the following:

(29) Project Alpha
A word of syntactic category X is dominated by an uninterrupted sequence of X nodes.

This uninterrupted sequence of projections of X is called the 'Projection Chain of X'. The maximal and minimal categories of this chain are defined in terms of their hierarchical position relative to other nodes in the tree. A maximal projection (XP) is the node of some category X that is immediately dominated by some other category; the minimal category (X) is the node that dominates nothing. The (intermediate) categories between the XP and the X are undefined for 'bar level' (and as such, according to Speas, invisible to syntactic computation).[20] To illustrate this relational notion of bar level, consider the following structure:

(30) John [$_V$ [$_V$ met] [$_N$ a [$_N$ smart [$_N$ young [$_N$ Dutch [$_N$ student]]]]]]

The uninterrupted sequence of N-projections (making up *a smart young Dutch student*) constitutes the projection chain. The most deeply embedded N-constituent (in italics) is the minimal category (*student*). The highest N-constituent (in italics) is the maximal category (*a smart young Dutch student*), since it is immediately dominated by a different categorial projection, viz. a V-category.

This relational notion of bar level has as a consequence that vacuous projections (i.e. projections that do not branch) are ruled out. Thus, bare nouns, adjectives, prepositions, etc. – that is, words that take neither a complement nor a specifier – have a simple single-node structure. That is, instead of the (partially) labeled bracketings in (31a), we have the labeled bracketings in (31b):[21]

(31) a. [$_{N''}$ [$_{N'}$ [$_N$ he]]] left the [$_{A''}$ [$_{A'}$ [$_A$ angry]]] dog [$_{P''}$ [$_{P'}$ [$_P$ inside]]]
    b. [$_N$ he] left the [$_A$ angry] dog [$_P$ inside]

The relational notion of bar level (i.e. level of projection), as proposed by Speas and Fukui, is also characteristic of Chomsky's (1995b) theory of Bare Phrase Structure (see also Chapters 2 and 4), which in less formal terms states the following: "Given a phrase marker, a category that does not project any further is a maximal projection XP and one that is not a projection at all is a minimal projection X^0; any other is an X', invisible at the interface and for computation" cf. Chomsky (1995b:396).[22] The computational mechanism that generates syntactic structure on the basis of the lexical items that constitute the input to syntax – the so-called numeration – is the operation Merge. Merge takes a pair of syntactic objects (SO_i, SO_j) – where SO can be a lexical item or a phrase built by the computational system – and replaces them by a new combined syntactic object (SO_{ij}); see Chomsky (1995c:226). The SO whose categorial property is projected onto the newly created syntactic object constitutes the head of the syntactic projection.

11.4 Dimensions of phrase structure representation

So far, it has been argued that a linguistic expression is essentially a structural arrangement (i.e. projection/structuralization) of lexical information which is associated with the constituent lexical items that make up the linguistic expression. This structural arrangement constitutes a phrase structure (also called constituent structure), which can informally be characterized as a syntactic object which is hierarchically organized. This hierarchical organization is defined in terms of the phrase-structural relation of dominance, which is essentially a containment relation (i.e. 'top to bottom' or 'bottom to top', depending on one's perspective), and is traditionally known as embedding. Besides the hierachical dimension of dominance (i.e. hierarchical arrangement), there is also a linear dimension, so-called precedence (i.e. linear arrangement), associated with phrase structure; that is, the hierarchically ordered phrase structure must be mapped onto a linearly ordered sequence of words. For example, the prepositional phrase *right above me* (as in *The picture hangs right above me*) displays the following linear order at the (sound) surface: *right* < *above* < *me*, where < stands for 'linearly precedes'. It is generally assumed that dominance is a fundamental ordering relation of syntactic structure. Opinions differ on whether precedence is a fundamental ordering relation which is 'grounded' in syntax. In what follows, I will briefly discuss some of the issues that concern the nature of phrase structure and its ordering dimensions.

11.4.1 The hierarchical dimension of linguistic expressions

For my discussion, I will use the linguistic expression *right above me*. The phrase-structural organization of this expression can be characterized as follows (see also (19d)): the prepositional lexical item *above* and the nominal lexical item *me* combine to form the larger syntactic object (i.e. phrase structure) *above me*, which is analyzed as a prepositional phrase structure under an analysis in which it is the categorial property 'P' which projects onto the larger phrasal constituent.[23] The phrasal structure *above me* combines in turn with the constituent *right*, which yields the even larger prepositional phrase structure *right above me*. This phrase-structural organization can graphically be represented by means of a tree structure (also called phrase marker), as in (32a), or a labeled bracketing, as in (32b):[24]

(32) a.

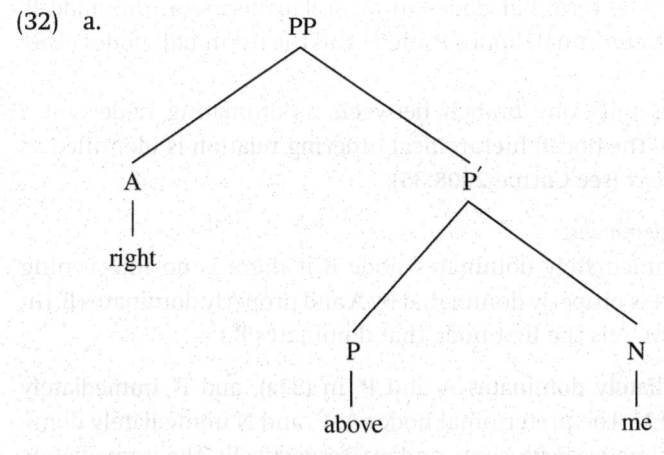

```
           PP
          /  \
         A    P'
         |   / \
       right P   N
             |   |
           above me
```

b. [PP [A right] [P' [P above] [N me]]]

The tree structure in (32a) contains eight nodes (i.e. constituents): the words *right*, *above*, and *me* are the so-called terminal nodes. These are nodes with no branches underneath them; in other words, they do not contain smaller constituents. These terminal nodes are connected, respectively, to the following categorial head nodes: A, P, and N, which are so-called preterminal nodes. The preterminal nodes P and N form a larger (phrasal) constituent together, which is graphically represented by the 'meeting' of two branches, i.e. the connecting lines in the tree structure, in a single node, viz. P'. The prepositional label of this phrasal node results from the projection of the 'prepositional' categorial feature of the preterminal node. The phrasal constituent *above me* combines with the adjectival node *right*, which yields the even larger prepositional constituent (i.e. node) *right above me*. When we leave the structure as it is in (32a), PP can be characterized as the root node (i.e. the node which does not have any branch on top of it) and A, P, N, and P' as the intermediate nodes (i.e. a node which is neither a root node nor a terminal node). PP, P', P, A, and N are all non-terminal nodes. According to Chomsky (1955, 1957), labels on phrase markers are to be understood as defining the 'is-a' relations between portions of the terminal string and non-terminal symbols. Thus, the terminal string *right above me* has the following 'is a' relations in the phrase marker in (32a): (i) *right above me* is a PP; (ii) *above me* is a P'; (iii) *above* is a P; (iv) *right* is an A; (v) *me* is a N.[25]

Within the small tree structure in (32a), we can identify various dominance relationships between the nodes in the tree, where dominance can informally be defined as follows (see Carnie 2008:29):

(33) *Dominance*
Node A dominates node B if and only if A is higher up in the tree than B and if you can trace a line from A to B going only downwards.

According to this definition, the (root) node PP dominates the nodes A, P', P, and N and the terminal nodes in (32a). Furthermore, the node P' dominates the (preterminal) nodes P and N and the (terminal) nodes *above* and *me*.

When there is only one branch between a dominating node and a dominated node, the (local) hierarchical ordering relation is identified as *immediate dominance* (see Carnie 2008:35):

(34) *Immediate dominance*
Node A immediately dominates node B if there is no Intervening node G that is properly dominated by A and properly dominates B. (In other words, A is the first node that dominates B.)

Thus, PP immediately dominates A and P' in (32a), and P' immediately dominates P and N. The preterminal nodes A, P, and N immediately dominate the terminal nodes *right*, *above*, and *me*, respectively. The immediately dominating node is called the mother node and the immediately dominated node is called the daughter node. For example, P' is the mother of P and N, and P and N are daughters of P'. Having the same mother node, the nodes P and N can further be characterized as sister nodes.

The notion of dominance also enables us to give a more precise definition of constituency (see Carnie 2008:37):

(35) *Constituent*
A set of nodes exhaustively dominated by a single node.

Exhaustive dominance holds between a set of daughter nodes and their mother node. Only when the mother node dominates the entire set (and only that set) can we say that the mother node exhaustively dominates the set. Thus, the preterminal nodes P and N are exhaustively dominated by a single node and consequently form a constituent, viz. P'. The nodes A and P, on the contrary, are not exhaustively dominated by a single mother node and therefore do not form a constituent.

11.4.2 The linear dimension of linguistic expressions

Although there is little controversy about the question as to whether syntactic objects are organized along the dominance (i.e. top-down) axis of syntactic trees, there has been more controversy about the question as to whether syntactic objects are organized along the precedence (i.e. left–right) axis.[26] That is, is linear order of constituents encoded in phrase-structural (i.e. syntactic) representations? And if it is, how is it 'regulated'? In a grammar model containing phrase-structure rules, as in early generative models, not only the (immediate) dominance relation between the mother node and the daughter nodes but also the linear precedence relation(s) between the daughter nodes could easily be expressed. For example, a phrase structure rule like (36) expresses that P' contains two daughter constituents and that these daughter constituents have the linear relation 'P precedes N'.[27]

(36) P' → P N

Within the Principles and Parameters tradition (Chomsky 1981), it is typically assumed that the dominance dimension and the precedence dimension are separate from each other, although both are still regulated in syntax.[28] Following the lead of Stowell (1981), who proposes that phrase-structure rules are category neutral and govern the general hierarchical form of phrases in a particular grammar, attempts have been made to regulate the linear order of constituents in terms of general (parameterized) principles. One such parameter is the headedness parameter, which parameterizes the direction of headedness – head initial (e.g. VO) versus head final (e.g. OV) – in the X-bar schema (Travis 1984, 1989, Fukui 1993). Thus, English has the rule in (37a), while Japanese has the rule in (37b).[29]

(37) a. X' → X (WP)
b. X' → (WP) X

Koopman (1984) and Travis (1984) have further suggested that the linearization of the head and its complement might be reduced to parameterized principles that belong to other parts of the grammar, specifically Case Theory (see Chapter 17) and Theta Theory (see Chapter 9). They propose that each of these theories has a parameter of directionality of assignment; that is (i) case is assigned either leftward or rightward, and (ii) theta roles are assigned either leftward or rightward. In a language like English, the case directionality parameter and the theta directionality parameter are set the same way, viz. rightward. In Japanese, a rigid head-final language, they are both set as leftward. Interestingly, Koopman and Travis argue that there are languages in which theta-directionality and case-directionality are set differently. Chinese, being one of those languages, has leftward theta-role assignment but rightward case assignment. This non-uniform directionality results into different linearization patterns for V and its selected object: if it is a prepositional object (i.e. PP), it precedes V, given the fact that V assigns its theta-role to the left. Since PP does not need case, it stays in a preverbal position. If it is a nominal object (i.e. NP), however, the NP starts out in a preverbal position, where it receives its theta-role, but ends up after (rightward) movement in a postverbal position in order to receive (rightwardly assigned) case. Schematically, this yields the linearizations in (38), where t represents the trace of the displaced NP:

(38) t_i/PP V NP$_i$

An important landmark in the generative study of hierarchical phrase structure and linearization is Kayne's (1994) *The Antisymmetry of Syntax*. In this study, Kayne tries to establish a formal relationship between the hierarchical organization of a syntactic structure projected from words and the linear ordering of that string of words. More specifically, he claims that precedence (a linear relation between two lexical items A and B) can be determined by asymmetric c-command (a hierarchical relation between A and B). That is, a lexical item corresponding to a node A linearly precedes a lexical item corresponding to node B if and only if A asymmetrically c-commands B.[30] One important consequence of the antisymmetry approach (discussed further in Section 2.4.2, Section 4.2.1, and in Chametzky 2000 and Carnie 2008) is that the claim that underlyingly all sentences in all languages are ordered as SVO (or better: specifier-head-object) implies that any non-SVO order must be a derived order.[31]

In Chomsky (1995c:334ff.), it is argued that the hierarchical dimension and the linear dimension of linguistic expressions are truly separate from each other: the former is taken care of by the syntactic component (say, Merge and projection), the latter by the phonological component. This position is also taken in Berwick and Chomsky (2011): taking language (i.e. I-language) to be at the interface with the Conceptual–Intentional system (i.e. the system of thought) and the sensorimotor system (i.e. the system involved in the externalization of thought, for example, by means of sound), they argue that it is just hierarchy and structure which is relevant for the system of thought. The linear dimension of language is a property of the sensorimotor system: we speak linearly when we externalize our thoughts by means of sound (see also Hornstein 2009:55ff.).

11.4.3 Branching, multi-dominance, and multiplanar structure

An important X-bar theoretic question about phrase-structure representation concerns the branching nature of phrasal projections. More specifically, are phrasal projections binary branching (i.e. does any mother node maximally have two daughters?), or can they also be ternary, quaternary, *et cetera* branching (i.e. can a mother node have more than two daughters?). In studies such as Jackendoff (1977) and Chomsky (1986a:3), the latter position is taken. Chomsky formulates this in terms of the X′-schemata in (39) (see also Section 2.4.2, and note 11 there), where the Kleene star (*) stands for zero or more occurrences of some maximal projection. A consequence of this analysis is that internal theta roles (e.g. goal and theme in a sentence like *John sent her a letter*) are assigned under sisterhood with the head (V).

(39) a. $X' = X \, Y''^*$
 b. $X'' = Y''^* \, X'$

In Kayne (1981, 1994), the binary branching hypothesis is adopted: a constituent branches maximally into two subconstituents.[32] Or to formulate it from a bottom-up perspective: a new constituent is added one at a time to the existing syntactic structure generated so far by the computational system. An obvious consequence of this binary-branching hypothesis is that a predicate which has two internal theta-roles in its thematic grid cannot assign both roles under sisterhood. That is, an internal role can also be assigned to the specifier position.[33] Notice, finally, that the operation Merge (Chomsky 1995c), which turns a pair of syntactic objects into a new syntactic object, automatically results in a binary-branching syntactic representation.

Another question concerning phrase-structure representation regards the 'dimensionality' of constituent-structure representation. As noted in Sections 11.4.1 and 11.4.2, our (written) tree representations of linguistic expressions typically have two dimensions: a hierarchical (dominance) dimension and a linear one (precedence). In such a 'standard' tree representation, a node (i.e. constituent) is typically dominated by a single mother node. It has been argued, though, that for certain linguistic expressions we might have to relax this constraint on multi-dominance.[34] These expressions typically involve a mismatch between an expected syntactic form and an available linear order. One such expression is the Right Node

Raising construction in (40a), where the direct object noun phrase *soccer* seems to belong to both *loves*, the transitive verb of the first conjunct, and *hates*, the transitive verb of the second conjunct. That is, a single constituent satisfies the requirements (*in casu*, assignment of a theta-role to an internal argument) of two different positions in the syntactic tree. One approach toward this pattern of constituent-sharing has been in terms of trees in which a single node (*soccer*) is simultaneously dominated by more than one mother node (the VP of the first conjunct and the VP of the second conjunct). This pattern of multi-dominance is represented in (40b). As indicated, the representation of multi-dominance in a single tree structure leads to 'line crossing': that is, the branch connecting the first conjunct's VP and the NP *soccer* crosses three branches.

(40) a. Bill loves and Mary hates soccer
 b.

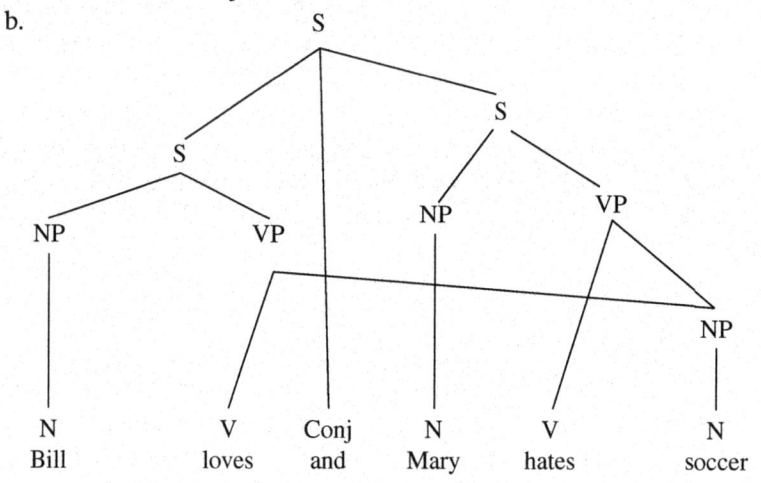

```
                              S
                 _____/|_____
                /             |            \
               S              |             S
              / \             |            / \
            NP   VP           NP          VP
            |   /|\           |          /| 
            |  / | \          |         / |
            | /  |  \         |        /  |
            N V  Conj         N        V      NP
                                              |
                                              N
           Bill loves and    Mary    hates   soccer
```

Alongside phrase-structure representations in which 'multi-dimensionality' is represented in a single constituent structure (as in (40b)), there have also been approaches in which sentences (i.e. strings of words) are assigned multiple planes of constituent representation.[35] These multiple planes are typically motivated by situations in which one and the same linear string displays constituency behavior that matches different hierarchical properties (see Carnie 2008:189ff.).[36] In Haegeman and van Riemsdijk (1986), for example, it is proposed that a string like (41a), can be organized along two phrase-structural dimensions: the basic constituency structure (i.e. the top plane) represents the lexical knowledge that *counted* selects a full preposition *on*, which heads a PP. The bottom plane results from reanalysis of *count* and *on* into a single complex verb: [$_V$ *counted on*]. In this reanalyzed constituent structure, *Mary* is the direct object of the complex verb. It is this bottom tree which is input to operations like passivization: being the object of the complex passive verb *counted-on*, the underlying direct object NP *Mary* can be moved to the subject position of the clause, yielding the 'pseudo-passive' *Mary was counted on*.

(41) a. John counted on Mary
     b.

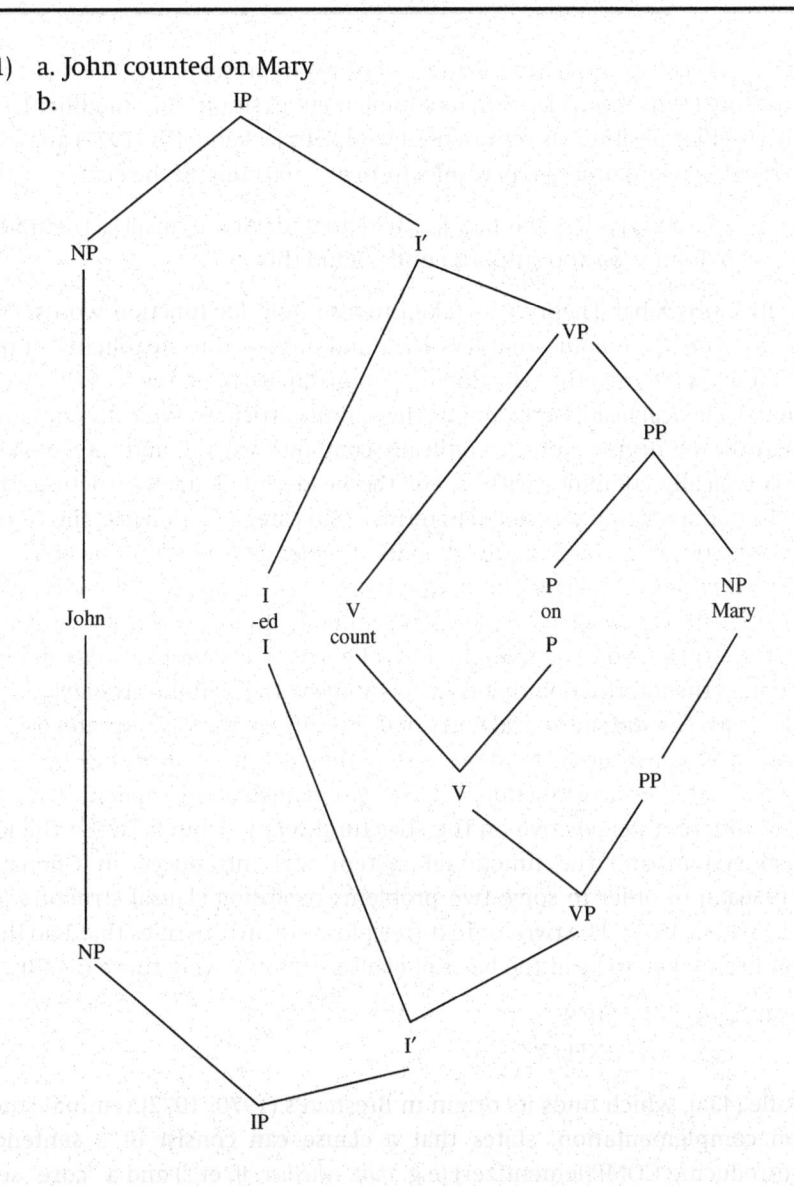

[Tree diagram: IP dominating NP (John) and I'; I' dominating I (-ed) and VP; VP containing V (count) and PP; PP containing P (on) and NP (Mary); with additional lower projections showing V, PP, VP, NP, I', IP]

11.5. Toward the Functional Head Hypothesis

In Chomsky (1970a), the specifier position of the lexical projections NP, VP, AP, and PP was taken to be the locus of a phrasal functional category. In Jackendoff (1977), the phrasal status of the specifier system is articulated very explicitly. For example, determiners such as *the*, *a*, *those*, and *which* are analyzed as Art''' (X''' being the maximal projection in Jackendoff's system) and degree words such as *as*, *so*, *too*, and *how* as phrases of the categorial type Deg'''. Empirical support for the phrasal status of these functional elements came from projections in which, besides the head position, also one or both of the satellite positions (i.e. the specifier and complement) are occupied by material. For example, the degree word *too* (represented as the syntactic category Deg) takes a clause in its complement position and a modifier *far* in its specifier position, as represented in (42). In Jackendoff's (1977) analysis, its surface word order (42b) results from extraposition of the clause:

(42) a. John is [$_{AP}$ [$_{DegP}$ far [$_{Deg'}$ [$_{Deg}$ too] [to understand this]]] [$_{A'}$ [$_A$ stupid]]]
b. John is far too stupid to understand this

In short, X-bar Theory was taken to also hold for function words. One thing which was somewhat less clear and discussed less explicitly in this analysis concerned the selectional relationship between the function word and the lexical head. For example, the definite article *the* typically combines with N, the degree word *too* typically combines with A, and the auxiliary *will* typically combines with V. For the head–complement structure, this selectional relation was stated in terms of subcategorization (e.g. the verb *to meet* is subcategorized for an NP in its complement position, the adjective *dependent* for a PP, etc.). The nature and 'directionality' of the selectional relationship between a lexical category and its function word(s) remained more implicit. For example, the lexical entry of a noun like *father* did not contain the information that it can combine with a definite article *the*, as in *the father*. Nor did the lexical entry of *the* specify that it was 'subcategorized' for an N'-constituent. In short, the nature of the relationship between lexical category and functional category remained quite implicit.

A different perspective on the structural relationship between the lexical system and the functional system was introduced in Chomsky (1986a:3) in order to solve two problems regarding clausal structure (cf. Hornstein 1977). The two context-free phrase-structure rules that had thus far been taken to be at the basis of clause structure were those in (43):

(43) a. S' → COMP S
b. S → N'' (INFL) V''

Rule (43a), which finds its origin in Bresnan's (1970, 1972) seminal study on complementation, states that a clause can consist of a sentence-introducing COMP(lementizer) (e.g. *that, whether, if,* etc.) and a "core" sentence S (see (44a)).[37] This COMP also functions as a landing-site for fronted *wh*-phrases, as in (44b):

(44) a. I wonder [$_{S'}$ whether [$_S$ John recognized her]]
b. I wonder [$_{S'}$ who$_i$ [$_S$ John recognized t$_i$]]

Rule (43b), still present in Chomsky (1981), generates a syntactic structure in which the subject N'' is located outside of the maximal projection of V, as in (45a). It differs in this respect from the subject of the noun phrase, which, as shown in (45b), occupies the Spec-position of N.

(45) a. [$_S$ the enemy will [$_{V''}$ [$_{V'}$ [$_V$ destroy] [$_{NP}$ the city]]]]
b. [$_{N''}$ the enemy's [$_{N'}$ [$_N$ destruction] [of [$_{NP}$ the city]]]]

The two phrase-structure rules in (43) are problematic from an X-bar theoretic perspective: Although (43a) has the appearance of an X'-rule, with S being contained within S', it is clear that S is not a true head (X°) from which S' projects; S contains phrasal material. In other words, this rule does not conform to the endocentricity requirement that a phrase be projected from a head. Also the status of COMP, which is taken to be a head, is unclear. If COMP is a head, how can you move phrasal material to it? The phrase-structure rule (43b) is also problematic from an X-bar theoretic perspective: the sentential structure (i.e. S) is not endocentric; S does not project from a head. If we take endocentricity (i.e. headedness) to be a universal property of phrase structure, including structure projected from functional categories (cf. Jackendoff 1977), then the phrasal structure generated by rule (43b) is illegitimate.

All these phrase-structural problems at the clause level were solved by taking a new perspective on clausal phrase structure: more specifically, it was proposed that the X-bar system extends to functional categories such as C and I in the following way.

(46) a. $[_{I''}$ N'' $[_{I'}$ I $[_{VP}\ldots V\ldots]]]$ (S = I'')
     b. $[_{C''}$ Spec $[_{C'}$ C $[_{IP}\ldots I\ldots]]]$ (S' = C'')

According to the structure in (46a), the functional category I projects in accordance with the X-bar theoretic rules: I takes VP as its complement and takes the subject N'' as its specifier (cf. Stowell 1981, Huang 1982a, Pesetsky 1982b, Chomsky 1986a).[38] The same goes for the functional category C, which takes IP as its complement and uses its specifier position as the landing-site for fronted *wh*-phrases (cf. Chomsky 1986a). An important outcome of this conception of clausal architecture is the fact that the lexical projection VP is contained within the functional layers of the clause: IP and CP. In this respect, it crucially differs from earlier conceptions of phrase structure, like the ones presented in Chomsky (1970a) and Jackendoff (1977).

The structural analysis in (46) has a number of advantages. First of all, the selectional relation between a functional head and a lexical phrase can be stated more elegantly: the functional head takes the selected phrase in its complement position, quite analogously to the c-selectional relation between a lexical head and its complement. In other words, the (subcategorization) information that C c-selects IP and that I c-selects VP is projected onto a head–complement structure. Second, and related to this, we can get rid of context-free phrase-structure rules entirely (see Stowell 1981). In other words, the elimination of the base component can be extended to syntactic objects involving functional material. Third, the structural analysis in (46) makes it possible to account for a number of word order phenomena in terms of 'natural' movement operations. That is, the functional system creates syntactic positions (viz. [SpecFP] and F) which serve as natural landing-sites for phrasal (i.e. XP) movement and head (X-zero) movement. More specifically, we can assume a concept of structure preservation along the lines of Emonds (1970): heads move to head positions, XPs to XP-positions (see also Chomsky 1986a). For example, *wh*-movement can now be interpreted as movement of a wh-phrase to the specifier position of CP (cf. (47a)), and the Germanic Verb-Second phenomenon (cf. den Besten 1983, Koster 1975) can be analyzed as movement of the finite verb to C, coupled with movement of some phrasal category to [SpecCP], as in Dutch (47b). Finally, the placement of Romance main verbs in a pre-adverb position, as exemplified in (47c), can now be explained in terms of raising of the main verb to the functional head I (cf. Pollock (1989), extending proposals by Emonds (1978); see also Belletti (1990)). In short, the Functional Head Hypothesis, represented in (46) for the clausal system, allows for an elegant account of a variety of word order phenomena in the sentential domain.

(47) a. I wonder $[_{CP}$ [which president]$_i$ $[_{C'}$ C $[_{IP}$ she admires t_i]]]
   b. $[_{CP}$ [waarschijnlijk]$_j$ $[_{C'}$ bewondert$_i$ $[_{IP}$ zij t_j deze president t_i]]]
       probably   admires   she   this president
      'she probably admires this president'
   c. je crois $[_{CP}$ que $[_{IP}$ Jean $[_{I'}$ embrasse$_i$+I $[_{VP}$ souvent $[_{VP}$ t_i Marie]]]]]
      I believe that Jean   kisses   often Marie
      'I believe that Jean often kisses Marie'

In summary: from the perspective of the Functional Head Hypothesis, the clause has the general form in (48).

(48) $[_{CP} \ldots [_{C'}$ C $[_{IP} \ldots [_{I'}$ I $[_{VP} \ldots [_{V'} \ldots V \ldots]]]]]]$

Each structural layer (VP, IP, CP) is associated with a particular type of information: VP is the configuration in which thematic information (theta-roles) is assigned (see Chapter 9), IP is the structural domain associated with tense and event structure (see Chapter 20), and CP, finally, is the structural domain in which discourse and illocutionary properties are represented (see Section 11.11; see also Chapter 12 for more elaborate discussion of the functional structure of the sentence).

11.6. The projection of thematic information

11.6.1. The Theta Criterion, the Projection Principle, and the Extended Projection Principle

In Section 11.1, the notion of projection was characterized as the 'structuralization' of lexical properties of a lexical item. For example, the categorial property V of the lexical item *(to) meet* is structuralized in the sense that it is passed on to the phrasal projections of the lexical head V: V' and V''.

Another lexical property associated with V is its so-called argument structure, i.e. the thematic properties associated with a lexical head (see Chapter 9 for more discussion). For example, the argument structure of the transitive verb *to meet* (see (49a)) expresses that it has two thematic roles (theta-roles) to assign: theme and agent. As illustrated in (49b), the former is assigned to the direct object (the so-called internal argument), the latter to the subject (the so-called external argument); see Williams (1980).[39]

(49) a. to meet, <agent, theme>
 b. He<agent> met her<theme>

Besides transitive verbs like *to meet*, English (and human language, more generally) distinguishes other types of verbs, among which: unergative (intransitive) verbs (50a), unaccusative (intransitive) verbs (50b), and ditransitive verbs (50c). The argument structures of these verbs are given in (51).

(50) a. he<agent> slept
 b. he<theme> grew
 c. he<agent> showed her<goal> the slave<theme>

(51) a. to sleep, <agent>
 b. to grow, <theme>
 c. to give, < agent, goal, theme>

Given the fact that lexical information is projected onto syntax, the question arises how this is done for argument structure. That is, how does the thematic information as part of the lexical entry of a lexical item structuralize? The guiding intuition is that the theta-roles as specified in the argument structure of the verb match up with the syntactic constituents (e.g. noun phrase, clause) – also referred to as 'arguments' – as part of the syntactic structure. This matching condition is stated in terms of the so-called Theta Criterion (cf. Freidin 1978, Chomsky 1981:36):

(52) *Theta Criterion*
 (i) Each argument bears one and only one theta-role, and
 (ii) each theta-role is assigned to one and only one argument.

The first statement of this criterion rules out illegitimate sentences like (53):[40]

(53) a. *he slept [the man]
 b. *he slept [that John was afraid of cats]

Since the intransitive verb *sleep* can take only one argument (here *he*), then by the Theta Criterion, the second NP in (53a) or the clause in (53b), cannot also be construed as one of its arguments.

The second clause of the Theta Criterion in (52) applies to sentences like those in (54). (54a) cannot mean: 'He recommended Sue to herself.' That is, the noun phrase *Sue* cannot be associated with two thematic roles (say, theme and goal). Likewise, (54b) cannot mean: 'John recognized himself in the mirror.' That is, the noun phrase *John* cannot be associated simultaneously with the thematic roles agent and theme.

(54) a. *he recommended Sue
 b. *John recognized in the mirror

Within the Government and Binding framework (Chomsky 1981), D-structure is considered to be the 'core' representation of theta-properties. It has been proposed, however, that theta-properties must also be satisfied at the levels of S-structure and LF. This restriction is known as the Projection Principle and can be formulated as (55):

(55) *Projection Principle*
Lexical structure must be represented categorially at every syntactic level, i.e. D- structure, S-structure, and LF.

The Projection Principle requires that the lexical information that a verb like *recognize* assigns the theme theta-role to an argument-NP in its complement position be represented not just in the D-structure representation but also in the S-structure representation and the LF-representation. An important consequence of this principle is that displacement of an argumental noun phrase to another syntactic position, as in (56b–c), does not result in the disappearance of that noun phrase from its original position. The Projection Principle demands that something be left behind there, a so-called trace, thus satisfying the lexical property of *recognize* that it has a theme theta-role to assign. (On traces as copies of the moved constituent, see Section. 4.2.4.1.)

(56) a. Bill recognized Sue$_{<Theme>}$
 b. Who$_i$ did he recognize t$_{i<Theme>}$?
 c. Sue$_i$ was recognized t$_{i<Theme>}$.

A second important consequence of the Projection Principle is that it prohibits certain transformational operations. For example, it prohibits a displacement process that exchanges two noun phrases, leaving no traces (cf. van Riemsdijk and Williams 1986). Thus, the exchange depicted in (57) is excluded because the theta-role assignments would be different in the two syntactic structures.

(57) Bill$_{<Agent>}$ recognized Sue$_{<Theme>}$ →   (D-structure)
 Sue$_{<Agent>}$ recognized Bill$_{<Theme>}$ (S-structure)

A third consequence of the Projection Principle is that absence of an internal theta-role in the thematic representation of a verb results obligatorily in the absence of a direct object NP in the syntactic structure. It is even impossible to just insert an expletive (i.e. semantically empty) pronoun *it* as a complement of the verb.

(58) *Bill slept it (meaning: 'Bill slept')

(58) shows that an object position is not projected structurally if there is no 'thematic base' for it. Subject positions differ from object positions in this respect. Clauses must have a subject position, i.e. even if there is no 'thematic base' for the projection of a subject position. Evidence for the obligatory presence of a subject position comes from the examples in (59):

(59) a. it seems that John speaks Swahili
 b. *seems that John speaks Swahili

The raising verb *seem* does not have an agent role in its thematic representation. Its theta grid only contains a theme-role, which is assigned to the complement clause *that John speaks Swahili*. Even though there is no external theta-role available for projection onto a subject position in syntax, the subject position must be present in the syntactic representation. This is clear from the obligatory presence of the expletive pronoun *it*.

The two principles – the Projection Principle in (55) and the requirement that clauses have subjects – together constitute what is called the Extended Projection Principle (EPP) in Chomsky (1981). It should be noted here that in the literature the term Extended Projection Principle is usually applied in a metonymic kind of way, to refer just to the second requirement. (For discussion of the generalized EPP of recent Minimalist work, see especially Chapter 5.)

The question obviously arises as to why clauses must have a subject (i.e. [SpecIP]). Chomsky and Lasnik (1993/1995:55) speculate that this obligatoriness of the subject position (also referred to as the EPP-property) should be interpreted "perhaps as a morphological property of I or by virtue of the predicational character of VP (Williams 1980, Rothstein 1983)"; see also Chapter 10. In Rizzi (2006b), the EPP-property is reinterpreted as a manifestation of what he calls 'the Subject Criterion', the general idea being that there is a functional layer in the higher functional field of the clause where the subject-predicate relationship is established; on this, see also Chapter 12.

Let me end this section with a brief remark on the structuralization of thematic information in Chomsky's (1993, 1995c) Minimalist framework, according to which there is no D-structure representation (see also Section 4.2.1). This means that there is no separate syntactic representation where thematic information is structuralized and which forms input to the 'transformational component'. According to Chomsky (1995c:313) thematic information is projected onto syntax as a property of Merge. For example, when a verb like *meet* merges with the nominal object *him*, the former discharges its theme role to the latter within the local configuration just created. In other words, the theta-relatedness of a predicate and an argument is a 'base property'. This 'base' connection between Merge and thematic discharge blocks structures in which a

DP-argument receives its thematic role after having been displaced to some syntactic position (e.g. raising from the complement of V to [SpecVP]) or in which a predicate discharges its thematic role after having been raised to some structural position (e.g. theta-role assignment to [SpecIP] after V has raised to I).[41]

11.6.2. The VP-internal subject hypothesis

In the earlier conceptions of clause structure, subjects – as opposed to objects, which are typically realized as complements of V – are realized in a position outside of the VP (whence Williams's 1980 distinction between external argument versus internal argument). According to the PS-rule in (43b), the subject is interpreted as the NP immediately dominated by S, and according to the reanalysis of S as IP, the subject can be identified as the specifier of IP (see (60a)). In the course of time, this VP-external analysis of the subject has been replaced by a VP-internal analysis (i.e. the subject as the specifier of the lexical projection VP, as in (60b)), which in turn has been replaced by an analysis in which the subject is associated with the specifier of a so-called 'small' vP on top of the lexical projection VP, as in (60c).

(60) a. [$_{IP}$ John [$_{I'}$ will [$_{VP}$ [$_{V'}$ recognize her]]]]   (VP-external hypothesis)
 b. [$_{IP}$ – [$_{I'}$ will [$_{VP}$ John [$_{V'}$ recognize her]]]]
                                (VP-internal subject hypothesis)
 c. [$_{IP}$ – [$_{I'}$ will [$_{vP}$ John [$_{v'}$ v [$_{VP}$ recognize her]]]]]   (light vP-hypothesis)

In Kitagawa (1986) and Koopman and Sportiche (1991), the traditional view that the subject of the clause corresponds to [SpecIP] is abandoned. Instead they propose, building on Stowell's (1981) claim that subjecthood is a property of the specifier position of a lexical phrase, that the clausal subject originates in [SpecVP], as is represented in (60b). The surface order *John will recognize her* (where the subject precedes the tensed auxiliary) is then obtained by movement of the agent-NP *John* to [SpecIP]:

(61) [$_{IP}$ John$_i$ [$_{I'}$ will [$_{VP}$ t$_i$ [$_{V'}$ recognize her]]]]

A conceptual argument in support of the VP-internal subject hypothesis is the fact that the lexical projection VP can now be identified as the sole syntactic domain of thematic role assignment by V. That is, all theta-roles in a head's theta grid are discharged within the maximal projection of that head. At the empirical level, a number of arguments have been adduced in support of the VP-internal subject hypothesis. I will mention two of them here (see Section 10.8, for a possible third, based on the binding facts of predicate fronting constructions). First, on the basis of the structure in (60b) a straightforward account can be given of the floating quantifier phenomenon, exemplified in (62b); see Sportiche (1988). Under the assumption that the quantifier *all* and the nominal expression *the boys* form a constituent underlyingly, the floating pattern can be derived by just moving the nominal expression and leaving the quantifier stranded, as in (62c). In the non-floating pattern in (62a), the entire complex phrase *all the boys* is moved from [SpecVP] to [SpecIP].

(62) a. [all the boys] will recognize her
      b. the boys will all recognize her
      c. [IP [the boys]i [I' will [VP [all [ti]] [V' recognize her]]]]

Second, the VSO-order of Celtic languages like modern Irish (cf. McCloskey 1991) can be straightforwardly accounted for under the VP-internal subject hypothesis: the word order in the embedded clause in (63) follows from head movement of V-to-I in combination with a subject that remains *in situ* (i.e. in [SpecVP]).

(63) sílim   [go   dtuigeann   Bríd   Gaeilge]
      think.PRES.1.SG COMP understand.PRES   Bridget Irish
      'I think that Bridget understands Irish'   (Irish; Tallerman 2005)

While there is general agreement that the subject argument originates in a syntactic position lower than [SpecIP], it has been proposed that this 'base position' of the subject agument is not as low as [SpecVP]. Instead, it is assumed that the verbal structure involved in the assignment of thematic roles is composed of two layers: one verbal layer (i.e. lexical VP) in which internal argumental roles such as theme and goal are assigned and another layer, so-called *v*P (cf. Chomsky 1995c), in which the external role (agent) is assigned (see (60c)).[42] It is *v* that assigns the external theta-role (agent) to the subject-NP in [Spec*v*P].

Splitting the agent off from the VP – and thus reintroducing the VP-external hypothesis, although in a more local way – has a number of advantages. First of all, it enables us to capture Marantz's (1984) observation that while we find V+O idioms, there are no S+V idioms.[43] That is, the verb and the object can form a meaning unit together, expressing a metaphorical meaning, whereas S+V typically cannot. This is exemplified in (64), where (64a) has a literal meaning and (64b–c) the metaphorical meaning:

(64) a. throw a ball
      b. throw a party
      c. throw a fit

If agents are tied to the verb less closely, then this might be expressed structurally by placing the subject in a verbal layer (*v*P) separate from the verbal layer containing the internal arguments (VP).

Another possible argument in support of the structure in (60c), featuring *v*P, comes from the analysis of ditransitive constructions such as (65) and (66). In fact, the *v*P analysis has its origin in the analysis of this construction type by Larson (1988a).

(65) a. John showed [Sue] [a book]
     b. John showed [a book] [to Sue]

In (65a), we have the word order goal–theme, whereas in (65b) we have the order theme–goal, where the goal is realized as a PP. As noted by Barss and Lasnik (1986), the goal–theme order and the theme–goal order display the binding asymmetries in (66) and (67), respectively. As shown in (66a), the goal-NP is able to act as an antecedent for the reflexive pronoun (the theme-NP); the reverse binding pattern is not allowed (see (66b)). In (67a), it is the theme-NP which acts as a binder for the reflexive pronoun contained within the goal-PP; the reverse binding relation yields an ill-formed pattern.

(66) a. John will show Sue$_i$ herself$_i$ (in the mirror)
     b. *John will show herself$_i$ Sue$_i$ (in the mirror)

(67) a. John will show Sue$_i$ to herself$_i$
     b. ??John will show herself$_i$ to Sue$_i$

Larson (1998) shows that under a split-VP analysis these binding facts can be straightforwardly accounted for in terms of the structural relation c-command, which is generally taken to be involved in binding relations involving reflexives (Reinhart 1976; see Chapter 15).[44] These binding facts suggest that the goal-NP *Sue* in (66a) and the theme-NP *Sue* in (67a) asymmetrically c-command the reflexive pronoun. The structures in (68) (for (66a)) and (69) (for (67a)) ensure this. With the presence of an extra verbal layer (in Larson's analysis an additional projection VP, in Chomsky's a *v*P), we can accommodate both the theme and the goal within the VP in such a way that one (specifier of VP) c-commands the other (complement of V). As indicated by the (b)-examples, the surface order is accomplished by moving the lexical verb to the functional head *v* (with movement of the *v*P-internal subject to [SpecIP] in addition).

(68) a. [$_{IP}$ – [$_{I'}$ will [$_{vP}$ John [$_{v'}$ e [$_{VP}$ Sue [$_{V'}$ show herself]]]]]] →
     b. [$_{IP}$ John$_i$ [$_{I'}$ will [$_{vP}$ t$_i$ [$_{v'}$ show$_j$ [$_{VP}$ Sue [$_{V'}$ t$_j$ herself]]]]]]

(69) a. [$_{IP}$ – [$_{I'}$ will [$_{vP}$ John [$_{v'}$ e [$_{VP}$ Sue [$_{V'}$ show to herself]]]]]] →
     b. [$_{IP}$ John$_i$ [$_{I'}$ will [$_{vP}$ t$_i$ [$_{v'}$ show$_j$ [$_{VP}$ Sue [$_{V'}$ t$_j$ to herself]]]]]]

11.7 Functional categories and extended projections

With the clausal domain being split up into an enclosed lexical layer (VP), which itself may be further split up into a VP and a *v*P, and an enclosing functional layer (i.e. IP and CP), the question arises how in spite of this 'divided' syntactic structure, the unity or connection among these layers is preserved. Intuitively, VP-IP-CP feel like they belong together. And empirically as well, this relatedness of the three layers is felt, for example by the fact that the lexical category Verb can be associated via head movement with the functional head positions I (see French (47c)) and C (see Dutch (47b)).

Abney (1987:57–58) tries to capture this connection between the lexical layer (e.g. VP) and the functional layers (IP, CP) in terms of his notion of s(emantic)-projection, which he distinguishes from c(ategory)-projection. C-projection is simply the usual notion of syntactic projection: V c-projects to VP, I c-projects to IP, and C c-projects to CP. S-projection "is the path of nodes along which its descriptive content is 'passed along'". With this statement, Abney expresses that the descriptive content of the lexical category V is projected from the lexical head onto the members of the lexical projection line (V', VP) and the members of the functional projection lines (I, I', IP; C, C', CP). The notion of S-projection is more precisely defined as follows by Abney (1987:57, his example (47)), where Abney (p.56) uses the notion of f-selection to indicate "the syntactic relation between a functional head and its complement".[45]

(70) b is an S-projection of a iff
    a. b = a, or
    b. b is a c-projection of an s-projection of a, or
    c. b f-selects an s-projection of a.

When we now consider the syntactic structures in (71a) and (71b), the nodes V, V', and VP represent the C-projection of the lexical head V and the nodes V, V', VP, I, I', IP, C, C', CP represent the maximal S-projection of V.

(71)   a. [$_{CP}$ Spec [$_{C'}$ C [$_{IP}$ Spec [$_{I'}$ I [$_{VP}$ Spec [$_{V'}$ V YP]]]]]]
      b. [$_{CP}$ Spec [$_{C'}$ **C** [$_{IP}$ Spec [$_{I'}$ **I** [$_{VP}$ Spec [$_{V'}$ **V** YP]]]]]]

While Abney tries to capture the 'unity' of the lexical projection VP and the functional projections IP and CP in terms of the more semantically oriented notion of 'projection of descriptive content', Grimshaw (1991) takes a somewhat more syntactic approach by characterizing the 'unity' of the three layers VP, IP, and CP in terms of their shared categorial identity (see also Haider 1988, van Riemsdijk 1990, 1998). That is, the functional heads I and C (and also their phrasal projections) are of the same categorial type as the lexical category: they are all verbal, i.e. [+V,-N] according to Chomsky's (1970a) characterization of syntactic categories in terms of primitive features [+/-V] (predicative) and [+/-N] (substantive); see Section 11.3. What distinguishes the functional heads I and C from the lexical head V is their functional status, which is encoded as a value for the functional feature F. As shown in (72), F0 is assigned to the lexical category, F1 to the lowest functional category, and F2 to the next highest functional category, and so forth and so on. Importantly, a category label is now a pair consisting of a categorial specification and a functional specification. This compositional nature of the categorial labels expresses the idea that functional categories are relational entities: I and C are functional categories by virtue of their relationship to the lexical category V.

(72) a. [+V,-N] F0 (= lexical category V)
    b. [+V,-N] F1 (= functional category I)
    c. [+V,-N] F2 (= functional category C)

In accordance with the idea of categorial projection, the phrasal projections of V (i.e. V' and VP) are also categorially specified as in (72a). The projections I' and IP have the specification in (72b), and C' and CP the one in (72c). Grimshaw uses the term 'perfect projection' to refer to a maximal projection which projects from a category which it shares both categorial and functional features with. Thus, VP is a perfect projection of V and V'; IP is a perfect projection of I and I'; and CP is a perfect projection of C and C'. Note that this notion of perfect projection corresponds to Abney's notion of C-projection. Grimshaw introduces the notion of extended projection to refer to a maximal projection which projects from a category which it shares categorial features with (e.g. [+V,-N]). Thus, IP is an extended (verbal) projection of V, V', VP, I, and I'; and CP is an extended (verbal) projection of V, V', VP, I, I', IP, C, and C'.

For further discussion of the architecture of the extended verbal projection, I refer to Chapter 12. Each of the four lexical categories (A, N, P, and V) has its own extended projection. In Sections 11.8–11.10, I will give a characterization of the other three extended projections.

11.8 On the functional structure of the extended nominal projection

11.8.1 From NP to DP

In early phrase-structural analyses (Chomsky 1970a, Selkirk 1970, Jackendoff 1977), nominal expressions such as *the analysis of the problem* and *John's analysis of the problem* were commonly analyzed as maximal projections of a lexical head N. In conformity with the X-bar theoretic principles, N combines with a complement (*(of) the problem*) forming an N'-level phrase, which in turn combines with the specifier (in our examples, the determiner *the* or the prenominal possessor *John's*) yielding the maximal level NP.

(73) [NP the/John's [N' [N analysis] [PP of the problem]]]

As shown in (73), a determiner like *the*, analyzed as phrasal Art''' in Jackendoff (1977), and the prenominal lexical possessor-NP *John's* are taken to occupy the same position, viz. [SpecNP]. This similarity in distribution may be somewhat surprising given the fact that ArtP and NP are quite different syntactic objects: one is a projection of a functional head, the other of a lexical head.

In the 1980s, an alternative conception of nominal expressions came to the fore: the so-called D(eterminer)P(hrase)-hypothesis. According to this view, nominal expressions are DPs rather than NPs. That is, the lexical projection NP does not enclose the functional projection (ArtP/DP) in its spec-position; rather, the functional projection DP encloses the lexical projection NP. Schematically:

(74) [$_{DP}$ Spec [$_{D'}$ D [$_{NP}$ Spec [$_{N'}$ N Compl]]]]

One of the earliest proposals arguing in favor of this phrase-structural architecture of nominal expressions was made in Brame (1982:321), who makes the following statement: "I think it is a mistake to think of N as the head of an NP. One should think in terms of DPs, i.e. determiner phrases, not in terms of NPs"; see also Hellan (1986).[46] Abney (1986, 1987) is one of the first to further develop the DP-hypothesis in (74), which has the conceptual advantage of drawing a parallel with the phrase-structural make-up of clauses: verbs project to a lexical projection VP and project further to extended verbal projections such as IP and CP; analogously to this, nouns project to a lexical projection NP and project further to the nominal projection DP.[47] Importantly, D is no longer defective with respect to X-bar Theory: just like C and I, it can take a complement and a specifier.

In what follows I will reproduce some arguments that have been given in the literature in support of the DP-hypothesis and the extended nominal projection more generally.[48]

11.8.2 Agreement: DP ≈ IP?

At the empirical level a variety of arguments have been adduced in support of the DP-hypothesis. A first, morphosyntactic piece of evidence in support of the DP-hypothesis comes from the expression of agreement (see Chapter 17). More specifically, there are languages in which agreement morphology in the clausal domain and the nominal domain is expressed in a similar way (see Szabolcsi 1983 for Hungarian, and Kornfilt 1984 for Turkish). As noted in Abney (1987), this morphological parallelism can be captured straightforwardly under a DP-analysis, which ascribes a structure to nominal expressions that is more closely parallel to IP than the traditional NP-structure. One language which Abney (pp. 37–53) discusses to illustrate this parallelism is Yup'ik, a Central Alaskan Eskimo language. As shown in (75a), the agreement relationship between the ergative subject and the verb is marked morphologically by the agreement suffix -t. (75b) shows that this same agreement marking is attested on the possessor and the possessed noun in a possessive nominal expression:

(75) a. angute-t   kiputa-a-t   (Yup'ik)
       man.ERG(PL) buy-OM-SM
       'the men bought it'
    b. angute-t   kuiga-t
       man-ERG(PL) river-SM
       'the men's river'

The identical morphological expression of the agreement relationship in the possessive nominal domain and the clausal domain in Yup'ik suggests that there is a common configurational structure which underlies this agreement relationship. If agreement involves a Spec-head relationship between the functional head I^0 and the subject noun phrase in the clausal domain, then this same structural relationship should be at the basis of the agreement relationship in the nominal domain. The DP-hypothesis provides this configuration, with [SpecDP] being the locus for the agreeing possessor and D being the locus for the agreeing suffix which ultimately gets associated with the possessed noun via N-raising to D. Schematically, and abstracting away from the syntactic representation of the object marker:

(76) a. [IP angute-t [I' [I -t] [VP kiputa-a]]]   (75a)
     b. [DP angute-t [D' [D -t] [NP kuiga]]]   (75b)

11.8.3 Gerunds: solving an X-bar theoretic problem

Abney (1987) argues that English nominal constructions of the type *John's analysis of the problem* have the structure in (77), with the so-called Saxon genitive noun phrase *John's* occupying [SpecDP]; see Abney (1986) for an analysis in which *'s* is located in D.

(77) [DP John's [D' D [NP analysis of the problem]]]

As Abney points out, the structural analysis in (77) provides a straightforward account of gerundive nominal expressions like *John's analyzing the problem*. Observe, first of all, that the traditional NP-analysis of gerunds, given in (78a), is not congruent with the requirements of X-bar Theory: it violates the X-bar theoretic requirement that a phrasal node be headed by an X^0 category (i.e. a head) of the same categorial type. In (78a), there is no noun (N) heading NP. Under the DP-hypothesis, gerunds receive a phrase-structural analysis which is compatible with X-bar Theory. The functional node D takes the lexical projection VP as its complement – which is the 'special' property of gerundive nominals – and has the DP *John's* in its specifier position.

(78) a. [NP [NP John's] [VP analyzing the problem]]
     b. [DP [DP John's] [D' [D ø] [VP analyzing the problem]]]

As noted by Fukui and Speas (1986), a further strengthening of the parallelism between the clausal domain and the nominal domain can be obtained by adopting the NP-internal subject hypothesis, on a par with the VP-internal subject hypothesis (see Section 11.6.2): that is, the external argument of a nominal head, just like that of a verbal head, starts out in the Spec-position of the lexical projection, i.e. NP, and reaches its surface position after displacement to [SpecDP], as depicted in (79a). A conceptual advantage of this analysis is that we have a maximally uniform mapping of theta-roles onto syntactic structure: both in the verbal domain and in the nominal domain, arguments start out within the lexical projection (NP, VP). As exemplified in (79b), the external argument of a gerundive nominal expression starts out in [SpecVP] and ends up in [SpecDP] after displacement.

(79) a. [DP John's$_i$ [D' [D Ø] [NP t$_i$ [N' analysis [of the problem]]]]]
     b. [DP John's$_i$ [D' [D Ø] [VP t$_i$ [V' analyzing the problem]]]]

11.8.4 Subextraction: DP ≈ CP?

Whereas Abney draws a parallel between nominal D(P) and verbal I(P), Szabolcsi (1987, 1994), basing her analysis on Hungarian, takes a somewhat different position, though one which still supports the idea that nominal expressions are DPs rather than NPs. Instead of equating nominal D with I(nflection), which she takes to be suffixed directly onto N (i.e. [N N+I]), she argues that D(P) is an analog of C(P). The central insight here is that [SpecDP], just like [SpecCP], functions as an escape hatch for subextraction. In other words, cross-categorial parallelism involves here the phenomenon of subextraction (see Corver (2006b)), i.e. displacement of a constituent out of a larger, containing phrase. Evidence for this escape hatch function of [SpecDP] in Hungarian comes from the extraction of dative-marked possessors out of possessive nominal constructions. Before showing this, I should note that Hungarian has two types of possessive nominal expressions (cf. Szabolcsi 1987, 1994): one in which the possessor bears nominative case and one in which it bears dative case. Interestingly, the former appears in a post-article position, whereas the latter occurs in a pre-article position:

(80) a. a   Mari   kalap-ja
        the   Mari-NOM   hat-POSS.3P.SG.
     b. Mari-nak   a   kalap-ja
        Mari-DAT   the   hat-3P.SG.
     'Mary's hat'

As shown in (81), the dative-marked possessor, as opposed to nominative-marked one, can in Szabolcsi's appropriate terms, run away from its nominal home. Szabolcsi interprets this as evidence for the fact that the possessor cannot be extracted out of the noun phrase directly from the base position (i.e. the position associated with nominative case), and that subextraction from the noun phrase is only possible if the possessor can proceed through the specifier of DP, which is associated with dative case.

(81) *[Mari]$_i$ Peter látta   [DP a   [t$_i$ kalap-já-t]] ?
     Mari-NOM   Peter saw   the   hat-POSS.3P.SG-ACC
     'Peter saw Mary's hat'

(82)   [Mari-nak]$_i$ Peter látta [$_{DP}$ t'$_i$ a [t$_i$ kalap-já-t]] ?
       Mari-DAT Peter saw   the   hat-POSS.3P.SG-ACC
       'Peter saw Mary's hat'

The two symmetric views on the role of D, i.e. D ≈ I (Abney) and D ≈ C (Szabolcsi), have resulted in phrase-structural analyses of the nominal system in which there is both a functional layer corresponding to clausal IP and a functional layer corresponding to clausal CP. This structural representation is given in (83), where AgrP is the nominal counterpart of the extended verbal projection IP, and DP the nominal counterpart of CP (see Giusti 1991, Cardinaletti and Giusti 1992; cf. also Delsing 1993, 1998, Schoorlemmer 1998, who use the label PosP rather than AgrP).

(83) [$_{DP}$ Spec [$_{D'}$ D [$_{AgrP}$ Spec [$_{Agr'}$ Agr [$_{NP}$ Spec [$_{N'}$ N XP]]]]]]

The Hungarian nominal expression in (84) and the Italian one in (85) exemplify this structural representation.

(84) a. az   én kalap-om
        the I hat-1P.SG
        'my hat'
     b. [$_{DP}$ [$_{D'}$ az [$_{AgrP}$ én$_i$ [$_{Agr'}$ -om [$_{NP}$ t$_i$ [$_{N'}$ kalap]]]]]]

(85) a. la   sua   casa
        the his/her   house
        'his/her house'
     b. [$_{DP}$ [$_{D'}$ la [$_{AgrP}$ sua$_i$ [$_{Agr'}$ Agr [$_{NP}$ t$_i$ [$_{N'}$ casa]]]]]]

11.8.5 Noun phrase internal word order and N-to-F movement

An important line of (syntactic) argumentation in support of the DP-hypothesis comes from word order phenomena within nominal expressions. As is well-known from the clausal system, (cross- or intra-linguistic) word order variation may result from the application of overt verb movement to a higher (i.e. c-commanding) functional head such as I or C. As argued by Pollock (1989), who builds on Emonds (1978), for example, the word order contrast between Romance (86) and Germanic (87) results from the presence versus absence of overt V-to-I movement:

(86) a. Jean mange souvent des   pommes   (French)
        Jean eats   often   ART.PL   apples
     b. [$_{IP}$ Jean [$_{I'}$ mange$_i$+I [$_{VP}$ souvent [$_{VP}$ t$_i$ des pommes]]]]

(87) a. John often eats apples
     b. [$_{IP}$ John [$_{I'}$ I [$_{VP}$ often [$_{VP}$ eats apples]]]]

If L-to-F movement (i.e. movement of a lexical head to a functional head) applies in the extended verbal projection and is at the basis of various word order phenomena, then – from the perspective of cross-categorial symmetry – the same type of operation would be expected to be active in the nominal domain and to be at the basis of certain word order patterns.

Ritter (1988, 1991) provides evidence for the existence of N-to-D movement in her analysis of word order phenomena within the so-called construct state (CS) construction in Hebrew. As shown in (88), the CS noun phrase differs in a number of respects from the so-called free state (FS) noun phrase. First of all, the CS cannot co-occur with a definite article (i.e. *ha-ahavat dan et acmo).[49] Second, the subject *dan* must be bare; i.e. the genitive case that is associated with it cannot be realized prepositionally by means of *shel* (*ahavat shel dan et acmo).

(88) a. ahavat   dan   et   acmo   (CS)
        love   Dan   ACC   himself
        'Dan's love of himself'
     b. ha-ahava shel dan   et   acmo   (FS)
        the-love of   Dan   ACC   himself
        'Dan's love of himself'

Besides these differences, the two constructions in (88) share an important property: the subject *dan* is able to act as an antecedent for the reflexive object. Importantly, the following expressions in which the reflexive is the subject and *dan* the object are ill-formed.

(89) a. *ahavat acmo   et   dan
         love   himself   ACC   Dan
     b. *ha-ahava shel   acmo   et   dan
         the-love of   himself ACC   Dan

The examples in (89a) and (89b) suggest that both in the CS noun phrase and in the FS noun phrase, the subject asymmetrically c-commands the object. Ritter argues that this subject–object asymmetry follows from a SNO base pattern (i.e. Subject + Noun + Object), with S being in the specifier position of the lexical projection NP and O being in the complement position. The surface order NSO is then derived by the application of N-to-F movement. In the FS-construction, the lexical head *ahava* raises and adjoins to an intermediate functional head NUM (the locus of number features), as depicted in (90a); the subject *dan* is case-marked by the dummy case marker *shel*. In the CS-construction, the lexical noun *ahavat* raises via the intermediate functional NUM-head to the functional D-head, to which it gets adjoined; see (90b). It is assumed that this phonetically empty D-head assigns genitive case rightward under adjacency with the case-receiving subject. Ritter argues that this situation is obtained by moving the subject to [SpecNumP].

(90) a. [$_{DP}$ [$_{D'}$ ha [$_{NumP}$ [$_{Num'}$ ahava$_i$ [$_{NP}$ shel+dan [$_{N'}$ t$_i$ et acmo]]]]]]   (FS)
     b. [$_{DP}$ [$_{D'}$ ahavat$_i$ [$_{NumP}$ dan$_j$ [$_{Num'}$ t′$_i$ [$_{NP}$ t$_j$ [$_{N'}$ t$_i$ et acmo]]]]]]   (CS)

Evidence that the lexical noun raises to a higher functional head (NUM in FS and D in CS) comes from the distribution of attributive adjectives. Consider, for example, the distribution of the attributive adjective *ha-gadol* in the following possessive noun phrases:

(91) a. beyt   ha-mora   ha-gadol   (CS)
        house   the-teacher   the-big
        'the teacher's big house'
     b. *beyt ha-gadol ha-mora

(92) a. ha-bayit   ha-gadol   shel   ha-mora   (FS)
        the-house   the-big   of   the-teacher
     b. *ha-bayit   shel   ha-mora   ha-gadol
        the-house   of   the-teacher the-big
        'the teacher's big house'

Starting from the assumption that attributive APs are base-generated as left-branch modifiers adjoined to NP, Ritter (1991) argues that the word orders in the a-sentences result from the application of raising of the noun to a higher functional head: D in (91a), and NUM in (92a).[50]

Another illustration that certain noun-phrase internal word order phenomena receive a straightforward account if one adopts an N-to-F head movement analysis comes from the distribution of attributive adjectives in the nominal domain (see also Chapter 13). As noted by Cinque (1994), there is a contrast between Germanic languages and Romance languages as regards the placement of certain attributive adjectives with respect to the noun. More specifically, in Romance, certain adjectives occur in postnominal position, whereas their Germanic counterpart occurs in prenominal position:

(93) a. the Italian invasion of Albania   (English)
     b. *the invasion Italian of Albania

(94) a. *l'italiana invasione dell'Albania   (Italian)
     b. l'invasione italiana dell'Albania

In these examples, the AP *Italian/italiana* is a 'thematic' AP which expresses the external theta-role of *invasion/invasione* (cf. Kayne 1981, Giorgi and Longobardi 1991). The PP *of Albania/dell'Albania* occupies the complement position of N. English (representing Germanic) and Italian (representing Romance) differ from each other in the placement of the Noun with respect to the attributive AP. Cinque argues that this contrast follows from the presence of N-to-F movement in Italian and its absence in English. Schematically:[51]

(95) a. [$_{DP}$ the [$_{FP}$ [$_{F'}$ F [$_{NP}$ Italian [$_{N'}$ invasion [of Albania]]]]]]
     b. [$_{DP}$ l' [$_{FP}$ [$_{F'}$ invasione$_i$ [$_{NP}$ italiana [$_{N'}$ t$_i$ [dell'Albania]]]]]]

Cinque (1994) notes that certain attributive adjectives must occur prenominally in Italian (see (96a)). For those cases, he assumes that N raises to an intermediate F-head. That is, N-movement does not necessarily move the N-head to the highest F-projection.

(96) a. la terribile invasione italiana dell'Albania
 b. *l'invasione terribile italiana dell'Albania

(97) [DP la [AgrP terribile [Agr' invasione_i [NP Italiana [N' t_i [dell'Albania]]]]]]

Using a pre-DP-framework, Grosu (1988) argues for Romanian that N moves to D, when D is an enclitic definite article (see also Dobrovie-Sorin 1988, Cornilescu 1995, Giusti 1994, 1997, 2002 for discussion of this phenomenon in a variety of Balkan languages). This is exemplified in (98). (98a) shows that when an indefinite article is present in D, the word order is basically the same as in Italian, with some adjectives in prenominal position and others in postnominal position. When the enclitic definite article *ul* is present, the noun can occur as the leftmost element within the noun phrase (see (98b)). The noun then functions as a host for the enclitic article.

(98) a. un frumos baiat român   (Romanian)
  a nice   boy Romanian
  'a nice Romanian boy'
 b. baiatul frumos (cel roman)
  boy-the nice   (the Romanian)
  'the nice (Romanian) boy'

The N-initial word order in (98b) can be captured straightforwardly under a head movement analysis which raises the lexical noun via the intermediate Agr-heads to D.

(99) [DP [baiat]_i-ul [AgrP frumos [Agr' t''_i [AgrP cel roman [Agr' t'_i [NP t_i]]]]]]

Just like Romanian, the Scandinavian languages exhibit postnominal enclitic definite articles, as illustrated in (100) (see also Section 13.4.3). Analogously to the Romanian N-initial pattern in (98b), one might propose to derive the Scandinavian word order pattern N-Art_def via N-to-D raising (Delsing 1988, Taraldsen 1990). However, the nominal expression in (100), which features both a pre-adjectival determiner and a postnominal enclitic article (also known as the double definiteness phenomenon), suggests that N-raising does not move as a high as D but rather to the head position of a lower determiner projection, which hosts the enclitic article.[52]

(100) a. hus-et   (Norwegian)
   house-the
   'the house'
  b. det store hus-et
   the big house-the
   'the big house'

Although, as opposed to Romanian, the Italian common noun *invasione* is not able to raise all the way up to D (see (96b)), there are nominal expressions in which the noun *can* raise as high as D. Longobardi (1994) argues that Italian proper names display this N-to-D movement behavior. The evidence for this is given in (101). In (101a), the proper name occurs with a definite article and is preceded by the adjectival possessive pronoun *mio*. (101b) shows that the nominal expression is ill-formed if the D-position is not realized. Interestingly, in (101c) we also have a nominal expression without an article, but now it is well-formed. As suggested by the word order, the D-position has been lexicalized via head raising of the proper name *Gianni* to D, the locus of referentiality.

(101) a. [Il   mio   Gianni] mi   ha   finalmente telefonato
         the   my   Gianni me   has finally   called
     b. *[Mio   Gianni] mi   ha   finalmente telefonato
          my   Gianni   me   has finally   called
     c. [Gianni mio]   mi   ha   finalmente telefonato
         Gianni my   me   has finally   called

In short, various word order phenomena within nominal expressions of different languages receive an interesting account in terms of noun phrase-internal head movement, if one adopts the functional head hypothesis for the nominal domain.

11.8.6 Islandhood

Another potential line of support for the DP-hypothesis comes from island phenomena (see Chapter 18). In Corver (1990), it is argued that the islandhood of certain nominal expressions can be accounted for in terms of the Subjacency Condition (Chomsky 1973; see Chapter 18) if one adopts a DP-hypothesis. According to this locality condition, a displaced constituent may not cross more than one bounding node, i.e. 'barrier' in terms of Chomsky's (1986a) *Barriers* theory, by means of a single movement step. A category YP counts as an '(inherent) barrier' if it is not L-marked, i.e. if it does not stand in a theta-government relation with respect to a lexical head (e.g. V); see Chomsky (1986a:13) for discussion of L-marking. Furthermore, a category ZP can also become a barrier by inheritance; namely, when it dominates a category YP which is a barrier. Given the syntactic configuration in (102), direct removal of a constituent XP from within the lexical projection NP (or any other maximal projection dominated by DP) to a position external to DP yields a violation of the Subjacency Condition: XP crosses YP, which is an inherent barrier since it is not L-marked by the functional category D, and it crosses DP, which inherits barrierhood from the dominated projection YP.[53]

(102) *....XP$_i$ ... [$_{DP}$ Spec [$_{D'}$ D [$_{YP}$ ... t$_i$ .... N....]]] (base order of XP and N irrelevant)

Corver (1990, 1992) shows the islandhood of the DP-configuration on the basis of examples like (103), where an attributive AP is extracted from within the noun phrase. Culicover and Rochemont (1992) do the same for subextraction of adjunct-PPs; see (104):

(103) a. Peter kissed [an extremely pretty girl]
 b. *[Extremely pretty]$_i$ Peter kissed [$_{DP}$ [$_{D'}$ a [$_{YP}$ t$_i$ girl]]]

(104) a. Peter kissed [a girl with red hair]
 b. *[With red hair]$_i$ Peter kissed [$_{DP}$ [$_{D'}$ a [$_{YP}$ girl t$_i$]]]

Corver (1990, 1992) further notes that so-called Left Branch Condition effects (cf. Ross 1967a; see also Chapter 18) can be captured quite easily if one adopts a DP-analysis for nominal expressions. For example, the ill-formedness of the pattern in (105a) directly follows under a phrase-structural analysis in which *who* is in a Spec-position and *-s(e)* in a functional head position (say D), as in (106). Subextraction of *who+-se* involves fronting of a non-constituent, which is impossible (see also Chomsky 1995c:263). Subextraction of *who* is also ruled out under the assumption that the clitic element *-s(e)* cannot be stranded (see (105b)).[54,55] The only possible displacement is the one in (105c), where the entire noun phrase is pied-piped.[56]

(105) a. *Whose did you kiss *sister*?
 b. *Who did you kiss *-se* sister*?
 c. *Whose sister* did you kiss?

(106) You kissed [$_{DP}$ *who* [$_{D'}$ *-se* [sister]]]

11.8.7 DPs as arguments

Szabolcsi (1994) tries to further strengthen the analogy between C and D by arguing that they fulfill a similar semantic role: they both act as subordinators in the sense that they enable the clause or the nominal expression to act as arguments (i.e. theta-role bearing constituents; see also Longobardi 1994, Stowell 1989). That is, C turns the proposition (IP) into a (sentential) argument, just as D turns the nominal predicate (NP) into an argument. Empirical support for this subordinating function of D and C comes from the fact that both elements are typically absent in root (i.e. non-argumental) contexts. This is exemplified in (107a–b) for Italian: declarative main clauses, as opposed to embedded clauses, are typically not introduced by a subordinating complementizer like *che*. Likewise, vocative nominal expressions (108b), as opposed to argumental noun phrases (108a), typically lack an (in)definite article.

(107) a. *che abbia telefonato Gianni
       that has telephoned Gianni
       'Gianni has made a phone call'
    b. credo che abbia telefonato Gianni
       I-think that has telephoned Gianni
       'I think that Gianni has made a phone call'

(108) a. ho incontrato *(un/il) grande amico di Maria ieri
       I-have met (a/the) great friend of Maria yesterday
    b. caro amico, vieni a trovarmi
       dear friend, come to visit-me

As noted by Longobardi (1994), a bare NP is also possible in Italian as a nominal predicate (i.e. a non-argument) in copula constructions:

(109) a. Gianni è tenente
       Gianni is lieutenant
       'Gianni is a lieutenant'
    b. Gianni è grande amico di Maria
       Gianni is great friend of Maria
       'Gianni is a great friend of Maria's'

Importantly, Longobardi (1994) observes that certain nominal expressions that lack an article may nevertheless function as arguments. As we have already seen in (101c), for example, proper names in Italian are typically bare. Longobardi proposes that, although these nominal expressions are articleless on the surface, there is a silent D present heading a DP. He proposes that the lexical noun raises to D for reasons of referentiality. Sometimes, this head movement step becomes visible, for example, when the noun crosses an adjectival possessive pronoun, as in (101c). The derived structure of *Gianni mio* is given in (110).

(110) [$_{DP}$ [$_{D'}$ Gianni$_i$ [$_{AgrP}$ mio [$_{Agr'}$ t'$_i$ [$_{NP}$ t$_i$]]]]]

11.8.8 A note on 'dummy' *of* and single extended projection

In Grimshaw (1991), the notion of extended projection refers to a maximal projection which projects from a category which it shares categorial features with. Thus, in (111a), the DP *a truck* is an extended projection of the noun *truck*. In the slightly more complex pattern *a truck with pipes* in (111b), the nominal expression consists of multiple extended projections, viz. (i) the DP *pipes*, which projects from the noun *pipes* and arguably contains a phonetically empty D representing the plural indefinite article, (ii) the PP *with pipes* headed by *with*, and (iii) the DP *a truck with pipes*, which projects from the noun *truck*.

(111) a. he unloaded [$_{DP}$ a truck]
b. he unloaded [$_{DP}$ a truck [$_{PP}$ with [$_{DP}$ pipes]]]

When we consider the nominal expression *a truck of pipes* in (112), one might be tempted, in view of the superficial similarity, to assign it a structural analysis similar to the one in (111b). It has been argued, though, that this so-called (pseudo)partitive construction constitutes a single extended projection (van Riemsdijk 1998, Vos 1999), with *pipes* being the truly lexical category and the word *truck* being a so-called *semi-lexical* head; i.e. a head which is neither a truly lexical head nor a truly functional head (see note 5; see also Corver and van Riemsdijk 2001, Löbel 2001, Stavrou 2003). The lexical noun and the semi-lexical noun are 'connected' to each other by means of the dummy (i.e. semantically empty) preposition *of*. Importantly, *truck* designates a quantity. Thus, (112) can informally be paraphrased as: 'He unloaded pipes, and the amount of pipes was equal to a truck(load).'

(112) he unloaded [a truck of pipes]

Another type of binominal construction that has been investigated quite extensively in the generative literature is the so-called N of N construction in (113), which also features the connecting element *of* (see Ruwet 1982, Kayne 1994, den Dikken 2006b, Bennis *et al.* 1998; see also Section 10.6):

(113) John hated [that idiot of a policeman]

In Kayne (1994), den Dikken (2006b) and Bennis *et al.* (1998), it is argued that the noun *idiot* starts out as a (small) clause-internal predicate nominal and reaches its surface position as a result of DP-internal predicate movement. In Kayne's analysis, the predicate nominal moves to the Spec-position of a prepositional D *of* (see (114a)); in den Dikken's (2006b) analysis the predicate nominal moves to the Spec-position of some functional head (a so-called 'linker'), which spells out as what he calles the 'nominal copula' *of*.[57,58]

(114) a. [that [$_{D/PP}$ [$_{NP}$ idiot]$_j$ [$_{D/P'}$ of [$_{IP}$ a policeman [$_{I'}$ t$_i$ t$_j$]]]]]
b. [$_{DP}$ that [$_{LP}$ [$_{NP}$ idiot]$_j$ [$_{L'}$ R$_i$+L (= *of*) [$_{RP}$ a policeman [$_{R'}$ t$_j$]]]]]

In the spirit of Kayne (1994), and following den Dikken's (2006b) implementation of the predicate movement analysis of the N of N construction, Corver (1998, 2003) proposes the derived structure in (115) for a nominal expression like *a truck of pipes* in (112). That is, the quantity designating noun starts out as a predicate nominal and reaches its surface position as a result of DP-internal predicate movement:[59]

(115) [$_{DP}$ a [$_{LP}$ [$_{NP}$ truck]$_j$ [$_{L'}$ R$_i$+L (= *of*) [$_{RP}$ pipes [$_{R'}$ t$_i$ t$_j$]]]]]

11.8.9 Conclusion

Since Abney (1986, 1987), much generative syntactic research has been devoted to laying bare the architecture of the extended nominal projection by in depth investigation of the internal syntax of nominal expressions in a great variety of languages. In this section, I have only discussed a small number of the functional layers whose existence within the extended nominal projection has been argued for in the generative literature. I will end this section by simply listing, without any further discussion, some of the other functional layers that have been argued to be part of the extended nominal projection:[60] (i) Kase Phrase (KP) (Bittner and Hale 1996a); (ii) Quantifier Phrase (QP) (Cardinaletti and Giusti 1992, Shlonsky 1991); (iii) Classifier Phrase (ClP) (Cheng and Sybesma 1999), (iv) Divider Phrase (DivP) (Borer 2005a) (v) Word Marker Phrase (WMP) (Bernstein 1993b) (vi) Gender Phrase (GenP) (Picallo 1991); (vii) FP hosting attributive adjectives (Cinque 1994) (viii) Topic Phrase (TopP) (Giusti 1996, Aboh 2004b); (ix) Focus Phrase (FocP) (Giusti 1996, Aboh 2004b, Corver and van Koppen 2009). If the noun-phrase internal distribution of adnominal adjectives follows the pattern of adverbial distribution along the lines of Cinque's (1999:106) Universal Hierarchy of Clausal Functional Projections, then adnominal adjectives will appear as specifiers of distinct functional projections. According to this approach, the extended nominal projection contains a universal hierarchy of AP-related functional projections including, for example, SizeP (*small*), ShapeP (*round*), ColorP (*white*), OriginP (*German*), as in *a small round white German car* (see Scott 2002, and also Chapter 13).

11.9. On the functional structure of the extended adjectival projection

11.9.1 From AP to DegP

In the wake of Chomsky's (1970a) X-bar Theory, generative linguists started to explore the internal structure of adjectival expressions (cf. Bowers 1975, Selkirk 1970, Bresnan 1973, Jackendoff 1977). It was observed that certain adjectives, just like verbs, can take PPs or clauses as their complement (see (116)). Furthermore, the specifier position of AP was identified as the locus for elements such as functional degree words (*how, too, that, so, more, less*), adjectival modifiers (*extremely, terribly*), and measure phrases (*ten feet*). As indicated in (116b), the projection of the comparative morpheme *more* contains the *than*-phrase; this *than*-phrase surfaces in the right periphery of the adjectival structure as a result of AP-internal extraposition.[61]

(116) a. John is [$_{AP}$ [$_{DegP}$ (far) too] [$_{A'}$ proud of Mary]]
b. John is [$_{AP}$ [$_{AP}$ [$_{DegP}$ (far) more t_i] [$_{A'}$ proud of Mary]] [than Bill is]$_i$]
c. John is [$_{AP}$ extremely [$_{A'}$ proud of Mary]]
d. that fence is [$_{AP}$ ten feet [$_{A'}$ high]]

The adjectival structures in (116) represent what Grimshaw (1991) calls the Lexical Head Hypothesis, i.e. the lexical head A is the head of the entire adjectival projection and the functional categories associated with A are located in [SpecAP]. The alternative analysis, representing the Functional Head Hypothesis, takes the entire adjectival construction to be a maximal category DegP, which is headed by the functional head Deg that takes the lexical projection AP as its complement. In Grimshaw's terms, DegP is an extended projection of the adjective. Schematically:

(117) [DegP Spec [Deg' Deg [AP Spec [A' A YP]]]]

From a conceptual point of view, the DegP-hypothesis in (117) seems to be the null hypothesis: if the lexical domain is closed off by a functional projection in the nominal and verbal systems, one would, for reasons of cross-categorial symmetry, expect the same to hold for the adjectival system (cf. Abney 1987, Grimshaw 1991, Corver 1990, 1991, 1997a, 1997b).[62] In what follows, I will discuss some of the empirical arguments that have been given in support of the DegP-hypothesis, and the functional head hypothesis more in general.[63]

11.9.2 Accommodation of lexical items

Abney (1987) notes that under a DegP-hypothesis it is possible to accommodate the variety of adjectival specifiers under a two-bar X-bar Theory. As shown in (118), degree words like *how* and *so* can co-occur with other specifying elements like *very* and *utterly*. Under a traditional AP-analysis, as in Chomsky (1970a), the co-occurrence of these items is unexpected, since functional degree words and adverbial degree modifiers are assumed to be located in one and the same structural position, namely [SpecAP]. Under a DegP-analysis, the two elements can be accomodated: one item is located in Deg, the other in [SpecAP].[64]

(118) a. Fred was [so **utterly** confused that he fell off the podium]
       b. [*How* **very** long] he can stay under water!

(119) a. [DegP [DegP [Deg' so [AP utterly [A' confused]]]] that he fell off the podium]
       b. [DegP [Deg' how [AP very [A' long]]]]

Corver (1990), building on Bresnan's (1973) proposal that a lexical and structural distinction should be made between quantifier-like degree words (Q^0; e.g. *enough, more, less*) and determiner-like degree words (Deg^0), accommodates the sequence of degree words in (118) by placing *so/how* in Deg and *utterly/very* in the spec-position of a functional projection QP, which is the complement of the functional Deg-head.[65] This leaves [SpecAP] available for the external argument of the adjective (e.g. *Fred* in (118a)).

(120) a. [DegP [DegP [Deg' so [QP utterly [Q' Q [AP confused]]]]] that he fell off the podium]
       b. [DegP [Deg' how [QP very [Q' Q [AP long]]]]]

11.9.3 Word order phenomena and head movement

In Corver (1990, 1991, 1997a, 1997b), it is noted that the formation of analytic comparative forms like *taller* is problematic if one adopts a traditional AP-analysis in which *-er* is located in [SpecAP]. Under such an analysis, the analytic form is derived either by moving the bound morpheme rightward to the adjectival head or by moving the adjectival head leftward to the specifier position and adjoining it to *-er*. Clearly, the two movement patterns violate the ban against movement to a non-c-commanding position (see (121a)). Under the Functional Head Hypothesis, the comparative forms can be straightforwardly derived by means of head-to-head movement, as illustrated in (121b). Note that the bound morpheme *-er* is analyzed here as a functional Q-head (rather than a Deg-head) (see Bresnan 1973 and Corver 1997a,1997b).

(121) a. [AP [DegP -er] [A' [A tall]]]
      b. [QP [tall$_i$+[Q -er]] [AP t$_i$]]

Another word order pattern that may provide support for an A-to-F (where F = Deg/Q) raising analysis comes from the phenomenon of *enough*-inversion (see Bresnan 1973, Jackendoff 1977), which is illustrated in (122). As opposed to degree words such as *less, more, too, et cetera*, the degree word *enough* occurs in a post-adjectival position.

(122) a. John is [fond *enough* of Sue (to marry her)]
      b. John is [*less* fond of Sue (than Bill is)]

Traditionally, the obligatory inversion pattern in (122a) has been interpreted as resulting from a rightward shift of the quantifier, from the specifier position of AP to a position in between the adjective and the complement of the adjective (Maling 1983). Such a displacement operation, however, involves lowering, which is generally taken to be an illegitimate syntactic operation. Under a functional head analysis, the phenomenon of *enough*-inversion may be reinterpreted as a leftward head movement operation adjoining the adjective to the quantifier-like degree word *enough*, as in (123) (see Corver 1997a, 1997b).[66]

(123) [[QP [Q fond$_i$+[Q enough]] [AP t$_i$ of Sue]] [PRO to marry her]]

Also in other languages such inversion patterns are attested. In Welsh, for example, the degree word *iawn* 'very' occurs in a position in between the adjective and the PP-complement, just like English *enough* in (122a).[67] This inverted word order is given in (124). The post-adjectival placement of *iawn* may be analyzed in terms of head movement of the adjectival head to a higher functional position, say Deg, as is represented in (125), where I take *iawn* to occupy the specifier position of QP (compare English (120b)).

(124) rydyn   ni'n   falch   iawn   o Mair
      are.1.PL we-PRED   proud   very   of Mary
      'we are very proud of Mary'

(125) [DegP [Deg′ falch$_i$ [QP iawn [Q′ t′$_i$ [AP t$_i$ of Mair]]]]]

Zamparelli (1993) discusses the Italian word order facts in (126) and proposes that the word order in (126b), where the nominal measure phrase follows the adjective, is a derived order. More specifically, the adjectival head *alto* has moved to a functional head position which c-commands (and precedes) the measure phrase. The derived structure, slightly adapted here, is represented in (127) (see also Corver 2009).

(126) a. Gianni è [molto   alto]
         Gianni is much   tall
         'Gianni is very tall'
      b. Gianni è [alto due metri]
         Gianni is tall two meters
         'Gianni is two meters tall'

(127) [DegP alto$_i$ [QP [due metri]$_j$ [Q′ t′$_i$ [AP t$_i$ t$_j$]]]]

Another word order pattern that is suggestive for the presence of a functional layer on top of the lexical projection AP is the adjectival construct state construction as found in languages such as Modern Hebrew (128) and Standard Arabic (129); cf. Siloni (2002).

(128) a. rina   yefat   mar'e.   (Modern Hebrew)
         Rina   beautiful   look
         'Rina is good-looking'
      b. shney   bakbukim   mle'ey   máyim
         two   bottles   full   water
         'two bottles full of water'

(129) r-rajul-u   l-jamiil-u   l-wajh-i   (Standard Arabic)
      the-man-NOM   the-beautiful-NOM   the-face-GEN
      'the beautiful-faced man'

As discussed in Siloni (2002), the adjectival expressions in (128)–(129) display the characteristic properties of construct state constructions. First of all, they are head initial. Second, the adjective directly precedes a noun phrase, i.e. without the mediation of any (dummy) prepositional element. Third, phonological alternations are found between construct state forms (e.g. *yefat* in (128a)) and free state forms (e.g. *yafa*, as in *yalda yafa*, girl beautiful, 'a beautiful girl'). Fourth, the nominal expression that directly follows the adjective carries genitival case, as is shown morphologically by the Standard Arabic example in (129). In view of the parallelism between the nominal construct state construction and the adjectival one, it seems likely that the latter receives a similar structural analysis. This would mean that the nominal expression raises from within the lexical projection AP to a specifier position of some intermediate functional projection FP, and that the adjectival head raises to the head of DegP, the projection that closes off the extended adjectival projection. Schematically:

(130) [$_{DegP}$ yefat$_j$+Deg° [$_{FP}$ mar'e$_i$ [$_{F'}$ t$'_j$ [$_{AP}$ t$_j$ t$_i$]]]]

11.9.4 Displacement and islandhood

Another type of argument in support of the DegP-hypothesis comes from islandhood. As noted in Corver (1990), the non-extractability of degree words, which used to be accounted for in terms of Ross's (1967a) Left Branch Condition, follows immediately under an analysis in which the degree word is a functional head taking AP as its complement. Being a head (i.e. Deg°), displacement of the degree word to, for example, [SpecCP] is blocked for the same reason that displacement of C° or D° to [SpecCP] is blocked: movement of a zero-level category to [SpecCP] violates the structure preservation requirement on substitution operations (cf. Chomsky 1986a). Interestingly, left-branch phrasal modifiers *can* be removed from within the extended adjectival projection. For example, the left-branch adjunct DegP *hoe erg* in (132) can be extracted out of the adjectival projection and move to [SpecCP].[68] Under a lexical head analysis, the contrast between the left-branch extraction in (131a) and (132a) remains unexplained: both involve removal of a left-branch maximal category from [SpecAP]. As shown by (131b) and (132b), pied-piping yields a well-formed structure in both cases.[69]

(131) a. *Hoe$_i$ is Jan   [t$_i$ verslaafd aan slaappillen]?   (Dutch)
           how is Jan   addicted to sleeping-pills
           'How much addicted to sleeping pills is John?'
       b. [Hoe verslaafd aan slaappillen] is Jan?

(132) a. Hoe erg$_i$ is Jan [t$_i$ verslaafd aan slaappillen]?
           how much is Jan   addicted to   sleeping-pills
       b. [Hoe erg verslaafd aan slaappillen] is Jan?

The following subextraction facts from English can be accounted for along the same lines: subextraction of the left-branch constituent *how* involves removal of a Deg-head, whereas subextraction of *how heavily* involves subextraction of a phrasal constituent. Again, pied-piping of the entire adjectival phrase is permitted with both patterns.

(133) a. *How$_i$ do you think he is [t$_i$ dependent on his sister]?
       b. [How dependent on his sister] do you think he is?

(134) a. [How heavily]$_i$ do you think he is [t$_i$ dependent on his sister]?
b. [How heavily dependent on his sister] do you think he is?

Another type of 'displacement argument' in support of the DegP-hypothesis is based on the Dutch subextraction phenomenon in (135), involving wh-movement of a measure phrase contained within the specifier position of the Degree Phrase.

(135) a. [Hoeveel cm   te   klein]$_i$ denk je   dat   ze t$_i$ was?
        how-many cm   too   small   think you that   she   was
        'How many centimeters too small do you think she was?'
b. *Hoeveel cm te denk je dat ze klein was?
c. [Hoeveel cm]$_i$ denk je dat ze [t$_i$ te klein] was?

(135a) shows that the entire adjectival phrase can be fronted to [SpecCP]. (135c) illustrates that movement of just the measure phrase (MP) is permitted as well. The relevant example which favors the DegP-hypothesis is (135b). Here the sequence 'measure phrase – degree word' is extracted, yielding an ill-formed sentence. Under a phrase structural analysis like (136), the ill-formedness is directly explained by the fact that non-constituents cannot be input to wh-movement. Under the Lexical Head Hypothesis, represented in (136a), the ill-formedness of (135b) remains a mystery. If you can move the lower MP and if you can pied-pipe the entire adjective phrase, why should movement of the entire Degree Phrase (a maximal category) out of [SpecAP] be blocked?

(136) a. [$_{AP}$ [$_{DegP}$ hoeveel cm te] [$_{A'}$ klein]]   (Lexical Head Hypothesis)

b. [$_{DegP}$ [hoeveel cm] [$_{Deg'}$ te [$_{AP}$ klein]]]

(Functional Head Hypothesis)

11.10 On the functional structure of the extended adpositional projection

11.10.1 The syntactic structure of locative and directional adpositional phrases

In the 1970s, a number of studies appeared that showed that, just like verb phrases and noun phrases, prepositional phrases can have a complex internal structure which is built by phrase structure rules like (137) that accord with the rules of the X-bar Theory of Chomsky (1970a) (see Jackendoff 1973, 1977, Hendrick 1976, Emonds 1976).

(137) a. P' → P XP
b. PP → Spec P'

Jackendoff (1973, 1977) points out for English that the complement position can be occupied, for example, by phrasal categories such as NP (138a) and PP (138b). In the latter case, the prepositional head is typically a directional P and the complement a locative PP. Jackendoff further points out that the specifier position is the locus for elements such as *right* and *far* and for noun phrases designating a measure; see (139).

(138) a. John stood [PP [P′ [P behind] [NP the gate]]]
b. a great howl of pain emerged [PP [P′ [P from] [PP behind the barn]]]

(139) a. John stood [PP right/far/two meters [P′ [P behind] the gate]]
b. a great howl of pain emerged [PP [P′ [P from] [PP right/far/two meters [P′ [P behind] the barn]]]]

Similar structures are given for Dutch by van Riemsdijk (1978) in his seminal study of the syntax of Dutch adpositional phrases. An important observation he makes about the Dutch adpositional system is that there is a class of pronouns – the so-called R-pronouns – which systematically precede the adposition.[70] Compare, for example, the patterns in (140):

(140) a. Marie stond toen [vlak achter het hek] (Dutch)
Marie stood then right behind the gate
b. Marie stond toen [vlak achter hem/haar/*het]
Marie stood then right behind him/her/it
c. Marie stond toen [vlak er achter] / [er vlak achter]
Marie stood then right there behind / there right behind
'Marie stood right behind it'

In (140a), the adposition *achter* precedes its nominal complement, the full noun phrase *het hek*. In other words, *achter* is pre-positional here. In (140b), the pre-position *achter* combines with the pronominal complements *hem* and *haar*. As indicated, the neuter singular pronoun *het* is not permitted in this position. Instead we have the post-positional pattern in (140c), where *achter* is preceded by the R-pronoun *er*. In other words, the different syntactic placement of the pronoun correlates with a change in morphological form. As indicated, the R-pronoun can occur in a position in between the modifier *vlak* and the postposition (*vlak er achter*) or in a left-peripheral position within the PP (*er vlak achter*). In order to capture this word order variation, van Riemsdijk (1978:87) proposes a PS-rule like (141), which permits a [+R] position both to the left and to the right of the modifier *vlak*:[71]

(141) P″ → [+PRO,+R] – [N‴, A‴, P‴, M] – [+PRO, +R] – P′

Van Riemsdijk (1978) further makes the important observation that the R-pronoun, as opposed to the full NP and the non-R-pronouns, can leave its prepositional home: the postposition can be stranded after subextraction of the R-pronoun. The specifier thus functions as an escape hatch for extraction, analogously to the specifier positions of extended projections discussed previously in this chapter (see Sections 11.8.4 and 11.9.4)

(142) a. Marie stond er$_i$ toen [$_{PP}$ t$'_i$ vlak achter t$_i$]
Marie stood there then right behind
'Marie stood right behind it then'
b. Daar$_i$ stond Marie toen [$_{PP}$ t$'_i$ vlak achter t$_i$]
There stood Marie then right behind

11.10.2 Extended adpositional projections: word order and subextraction

Taking the perspective of cross-categorial symmetry, a number of studies have appeared since the 1990s which apply the Functional Head Hypothesis to the adpositional system. According to this view, the adpositional architecture consists of a lexical projection PP which is dominated by one or more layers of functional projections. Following Grimshaw (1991), this adpositional architecture can be characterized as an extended adpositional projection. Schematically, where FP stands for one or more functional projections on top of the lexical PP (see van Riemsdijk 1990, Zwarts 1992).

(143) [$_{FP}$ Spec [$_{F'}$ F [$_{PP}$ Spec [$_{P'}$ P XP]]]]

One of the first studies taking this functional head perspective on the adpositional system is Koopman (2000). Building on van Riemsdijk's (1978) observations about the Dutch adpositional system, she argues that the extended projection of a locative adposition can consist of functional projections such as PlaceP, DegP$_{(Place)}$ and CP$_{(Place)}$;[72] see also den Dikken (2010a) for Dutch, and Svenonius (2010) for English.[73]

(144) [$_{CP}$ Spec [$_{C'}$ C$_{(Place)}$ [$_{DegP}$ Spec [$_{Deg'}$ Deg$_{(Place)}$ [$_{PlaceP}$ Spec [$_{Place'}$ Place [$_{PP}$ Spec [$_{P'}$ P$_{loc}$ DP]]]]]]]]

The positions [SpecPlaceP] and [SpecCP] are the loci for Dutch R-pronouns, with the latter Spec-position being the structural position from where R-pronouns can leave their prepositional home (i.e. the escape-hatch position). The projection DegP contains modifying material such as the lexical item *vlak* (see (140)), which is taken to be a lexicalization of the Deg-head, and the measure phrase *twee meter*, which, being a maximal category XP, occupies [SpecDegP]. The strings *(daar) vlak (daar) achter* ('right behind it') and *(daar) twee meter (daar) achter* ('two meters behind it') are given in (145) and (146), respectively:

(145) a. [$_{CP}$ Spec [$_{C'}$ C$_{(Place)}$ [$_{DegP}$ Spec [$_{Deg'}$ vlak [$_{PlaceP}$ daar$_i$ [$_{Place'}$ Place [$_{PP}$ Spec [$_{P'}$ achter t$_i$]]]]]]]]
b. [$_{CP}$ daar$_i$ [$_{C'}$ C$_{(Place)}$ [$_{DegP}$ Spec [$_{Deg'}$ vlak [$_{PlaceP}$ t$'_i$ [$_{Place'}$ Place [$_{PP}$ Spec [$_{P'}$ achter t$_i$]]]]]]]]

(146) a. [CP Spec [C' C(Place) [DegP twee meter [Deg' Deg [PlaceP daar$_i$ [Place' Place [PP Spec [P' achter t$_i$]]]]]]]]
b. [CP daar$_i$ [C' C(Place) [DegP twee meter [Deg' Deg [PlaceP t'$_i$ [Place' Place [PP Spec [P' achter t$_i$]]]]]]]]

Evidence for the placement of *vlak* (or *pal* 'right') in Deg comes from the phenomenon of P-incorporation. As noted by den Dikken (1995:108), an intransitive adposition cannot be incorporated into a verb when it is modified by a bare modifier like *vlak* (see (147)). This incorporation process is possible, however, when the adposition is modified by a phrase like *twee meter* (see (148)). If *vlak* occupies Deg, as in (145), P-incorporation is blocked for reasons of locality: the lexical head P is too distant from V, since the Deg-head *vlak* is an intervening head c-commanding the lexical adposition. When Deg is empty, the adposition can move through this extended functional position on its way to V.

(147) a. ... dat Jan de bal [vlak over] heeft geschoten
... that Jan the ball right over has shot
'... that Jan shot the ball right over'
b. *..dat Jan de bal [vlak t$_i$] heeft [[over]$_i$+geschoten]
(no P-incorporation)

(148) a. ... dat Jan de bal [twee meter over] heeft geschoten
... that Jan the ball two meter over has shot
'... that Jan shot the ball two meters over'
b. ...dat Jan de bal [twee meter t$_i$] heeft [[over]$_i$+geschoten]
(P-incorporation)

Koopman further argues that the CP$_{(Place)}$-level is the (functional) phrase structural level which determines the external syntactic behavior of the extended prepositional projection. For example, this phrase structural level is accessible to displacement operations such as wh-movement and scrambling.

In line with Jackendoff's (1990a) conceptual meaning analysis of locative and directional PPs, Koopman (2000) proposes that the extended projection of directional adpositions contains a PathP on top of (some projection of) PlaceP (see also van Riemsdijk and Huybregts 2007, den Dikken 2010a, Svenonius 2007). This yields the following representation, which is an extended projection of lexical P:

(149) [PathP Spec [Path' Path [CP Spec [C' C(Place) [DegP Spec [Deg' Deg(Place) [PlaceP Spec [Place' Place [PP Spec [P' P XP]]]]]]]]]]]

As discussed by van Riemsdijk (1978) and as shown in (150), Dutch distinguishes three types of directional PPs on the surface: prepositional, postpositional, and circumpositional.[74]

(150) a. *Prepositional directional PP*
    Jan is met z'n auto [in het water] gereden
    Jan is with his car in the water driven
    'Jan drove into the water with his car'
  b. *Postpositional directional PP*
    Jan is met z'n auto [het water in] gereden
    Jan is with his car the water in driven
    'Jan drove into the water with his car'
  c. *Circumpositional directional PP*
    Jan is met z'n auto [onder het viaduct door] gereden
    Jan is with his car under the railway arch through driven
    'Jan drove under the railway arch with his car'

Koopman argues that all three extended directional adpositional projections involve displacement of a lower extended projection of P into [SpecPathP] (see den Dikken 2010a for adaptations and refinements of Koopman's analysis). More specifically, CP$_{(Place)}$ moves to [SpecPathP] in order to derive the prepositional pattern in (150b) and the circumpositional one in (150c). The displacement process is most clearly visible in the circumpositional pattern, where *door* lexicalizes the functional Path-head. As shown in (153a–b), CP$_{Place}$ moves to SpecPathP, after the lexical P *onder* has raised to the functional head Place. Koopman argues on the analogy of these circumpositional patterns that prepositional directionals display the same derivation, as shown in (151a–b).[75] Thus, these directionals are prepositional on the surface but hidden postpositional structures at a more abstract level. Consider, finally, the derivation of postpositional PPs like (150b). As depicted in (152a–b), a PlaceP (rather than CP$_{(Place)}$) is moved to [SpecPathP], after the lexical P has undergone head movement via Place into Path.[76]

(151) a. [$_{PathP}$ Spec [$_{Path'}$ Path$_\emptyset$ [$_{CP(Place)}$ C [$_{PlaceP}$ in$_j$ [$_{PP}$ t$_j$ het water]]]]]
   b. [$_{PathP}$ [$_{CP(Place)}$ in het water]$_k$ [$_{Path'}$ Path$_\emptyset$ t$_k$]]

(152) a. [$_{PathP}$ Spec [$_{Path'}$ in$_j$ [$_{PlaceP}$ Spec [$_{Place'}$ t'$_j$ [$_{PP}$ Spec [$_{P'}$ t$_j$ het water]]]]]]
   b. [$_{PathP}$ [$_{PlaceP}$ t'$_j$ het water]$_k$ [$_{Path'}$ in$_j$ t$_k$]]

(153) a. [$_{PathP}$ Spec [$_{Path'}$ door [$_{CP(Place)}$ C [$_{PlaceP}$ onder$_j$ [$_{PP}$ t$_j$ de brug]]]]]
   b. [$_{PathP}$ [$_{CP(Place)}$ onder de brug]$_k$ [$_{Path'}$ door t$_k$]]

As is clear from the above discussion, various word order patterns can be accommodated if one adopts a more articulate structure of the adpositional system.

11.10.3 Agreement in postpositional phrases

Another phenomenon that has been interpreted as evidence for a more articulate adpositional structure comes from the phenomenon of adpositional agreement. In Kayne (1994:49), the following statement is made about this phenomenon: "Kenneth Hale (personal communication) notes that although there are languages like Navajo, with obligatory agreement between an adposition (postposition) and its lexical complement, prepositional phrases in SVO languages never, as far as he knows, show such agreement." Kayne argues that the observation that adpositional agreement is attested with postpositional phrases but not with prepositional ones follows from his theory of antisymmetry (see Section 11.4.2, above; also, Section. 1.1.3, and Section. 2.4.2), according to which 'complements' to the left of a head are actually in a specifier position of a functional head.[77] In other words, the agreement relationship between the nominal element and the adposition is associated with a Spec-head configuration. Schematically, where α represents the feature for which the adposition, which raises to Agr, and the nominal element agree.

(154) $[_{\text{AgrP}} \text{DP}_{k/\alpha} [_{\text{Agr}'} \text{P}_i + \text{Agr}_\alpha [_{\text{PP}} t_i\ t_k]]]$

A language which nicely shows this relationship between a postpositional configuration and adpostional agreement is Hungarian. As noted in Marácz (1989:362), Hungarian displays what he calls 'dressed' adpositions: i.e. postpositions which are inflected for person–number agreement when they select a personal pronominal complement.[78] This is exemplified in (155). As shown in (156), adpositional agreement is absent when the nominal argument is a full noun phrase.

(155) a. (én) mögött-*em*
          I   behind-AGR.1.SG
          'behind me'
       b. (te) mögött-*ed*
          (you) behind-AGR.2.SG
          'behind you'
       c. (ő) mögött-*e*
          (he) behind-AGR.3.SG
          'behind him'
       d. mi-mögött-*ünk*
          we-behind-AGR.1.PL
          'behind us'

(156) a   fiú   mögött(*-*e*)
       the boy   behind(*-AGR.3.SG)
       'behind the boy'

Under the assumption that case and agreement checking exploits the Spec-head configuration, the derived structure of (155a) can now be represented as in (157):

(157) $[_{\text{AgrP}} \textbf{én}_k [_{\text{Agr}'} [[\text{mögött}]_i + [_{\text{Agr}} \textbf{em}]] [_{\text{PP}} t_i\ t_k]]]$

From the fact that a degree modifier like *pont* ('precisely') precedes the agreeing pronoun, we may conclude that the AgrP-projection is located below DegP under an extended adpositional structure like the one proposed by Koopman (2000).

(158) János [pont   én mögöttem]   állt
       János precisely I behind.AGR.1.SG stood
       'János stood precisely behind me'

11.10.4 Axial and deictic projections

I will conclude this section on the extended adpositional projection with two further functional projections that have been identified for this domain: AxPart and DeixP (see Svenonius 2006). Svenonius argues that the functional projection AxPartP is attested in the extended projection of 'complex prepositions' like *in front of* in (159a), to which he assigns the 'decomposed' syntactic structure in (159b):

(159) a. John stood [*in front of* the house]
       b. [PlaceP [Place in] [AxPartP [AxPart front] [KP [K of] [DP the house]]]]

The element *in* corresponds to the functional head Place, the abstract noun-like element *front* is a functional head Ax(ial)Part, and *of* is a genitival case, which is structurally represented by the functional projection KP.[79,80]

Svenonius (2006) further argues that the extended adpositional projection may contain a Deictic projection, a layer of functional structure which expresses degrees of proximity to a deictic center. Evidence for such a functional layer comes, for example, from Persian which exhibits a distal marker in the adpositional structure (see Pantcheva 2006):[81]

(160) dær 10 metri-ye   un   birun-e   xane   (Persian)
       at   10 meters-EZ   DIST outside-EZ   house
       'there, 10 meters outside the house'

11.11 Projection and symmetry: some concluding remarks

The central topic of this chapter was the projection of syntactic structure. A syntactic structure is essentially a phrase structural manifestation (a 'structuralization') of the lexical properties (features) that are associated with the lexical items that constitute the building blocks for the syntactic structure. In other words, lexical information as specified in the lexical items of the lexicon is projected onto a syntactic structure. A fundamental distinction in the lexicon is that between lexical categories (content words) and functional categories (function words). According to the current generative-linguistic conception of phrase structure, this distinction is reflected in the structuralization of lexical information. The projection of the lexical category (N, V, A, P) constitutes the lowest structural domain of a so-called extended projection. The sequence of functional projections is built on top of the lexical projection and consequently constitutes the higher domain of the extended projection. The projection of the lexical category (V, N, A, P) is the domain in which thematic (s-selectional) information gets structuralized. This structuralization of thematic information (i.e. the mapping of theta-roles onto syntactic arguments) is evaluated by the Theta Criterion. The structuralization of category-selectional information (i.e. the subcategorization property) applies both at the level of lexical categories (e.g. the verb *meet* takes a DP as its complement) and at the level of functional categories (e.g. the complementizer *that* takes a TP$_{[+finite]}$ as its complement). Functional categories, as opposed to lexical categories, have the lexically specified ability of attracting a designated property to their specifier position (i.e. the displacement property of human language). In the clausal domain, for example, the functional head T is lexically specified for needing a constituent (typically a DP) in its specifier position (i.e. [SpecTP]). This requirement, known as the Extended Projection Principle (EPP), can be satisfied by displacement (Internal Merge) of an argumental DP into this position, but also by inserting (External Merge) an expletive element in this position. Importantly, the EPP-property, which is a feature lexically associated with T, gets structuralized, i.e. is projected in syntax. Likewise, the EPP-property of other functional categories may get structuralized via displacement or base insertion of lexical material.

A major guideline of generative syntactic research has always been the quest for symmetry. In this chapter, we saw several illustrations of this, among which: (i) the uniform X-bar theoretic format for the phrase-structural organization of the lexical categories N, V, A, and P; (ii) the extension of the X-bar theoretic format to functional categories; and (iii) the uniform binary branching organization of phrase structure. All this suggests that the projection of lexical items onto syntactic phrase structure applies in a cross-categorially uniform way. A further illustration of this 'symmetry of projection' comes from the structuralization of the functional/lexical dichotomy: for all extended projections, it is assumed that the lexical structural layer is hierarchically embedded within the functional structural layer.

This question about the symmetry of projection raises two further questions, which were already mentioned in Section 11.1 but have not been explicitly addressed so far:

1. To what extent is there cross-categorial similarity as regards the 'grammatical role' of the functional projections that are associated with the lexical categories (V, N, A, P)
2. Is projection of lexical information cross-linguistically uniform, or do languages display cross-linguistic variation in this respect?

Let us begin with question (1). This question addresses the issue of whether the various layers of information as represented in the four extended projections (i.e. extended N, V, A, and P) are similar in type. The general research program on extended projections tends to adopt the position that, at a more abstract level, the same types of information are attested across the various extended projections and that the structural organization of these 'informational layers' is highly similar (see among others Abney 1987, Szabolcsi 1987, Cinque 2002). It seems uncontroversial that the extended projection of the lexical category V includes, as its core, the following three functional projections (see Chomsky 2002, den Dikken 2010a):

- a projection for aspectual information
- a projection for temporal-deictic information
- a projection for expressing illocutionary force

The aspectual projection (AspP) encodes information about the delimitedness/boundedness versus non-delimitedness/unboundedness of an event.[82] The temporal-deictic projection (TP) encodes information about how the event is situated in time: 'present', 'past', and 'future'. The Force projection (CP) encodes illocutionary properties such as 'declarative', 'interrogative', 'exclamative', etc. It is generally assumed that these information types are distributed across the clause (i.e. the extended verbal projection) in the following organized way:

(161) $[_{CP} \ldots C \ldots [_{TP} \ldots T \ldots [_{AsP} \ldots Asp \ldots [_{VP} \ldots V \ldots]]]]$

The organization of information within the other extended projections (Ext-NP, Ext-PP, Ext-AP) seems to be quite similar (cf. den Dikken 2010a): NumP has been interpreted as the nominal correspondent of verbal AspP (Ritter 1991), with the mass/count distinction being parallel to the *delimited/non-delimited* distinction in the verbal domain. Personal deixis ('me', 'you', 'other') can be interpreted as the nominal counterpart of verbal Tense ('present', 'past', 'future'). And, as hinted at by many studies on the DP-hypothesis, D can be analyzed as the informational equivalent of C (cf. among others Szabolcsi 1994, Bennis et al. 1998).

As den Dikken (2010a) notes, this structural organization of information can also be identified in the extended adpositional projection. The 'verbal-aspectual' distinction between delimited versus *non-delimited* events has its 'spatial' equivalent at the level of locative P (Koopman's PlaceP) and directional P (Koopman's PathP). For example, both *walk into the house* and *walk around the house* involve a path-denoting PP, but while the former path is bounded, the latter is not (see also Zwarts 2005). As noted by Tortora (2008), locative PPs also display this spatial-aspectual distinction: the Italian PP *sopra il tavolo* 'on the table' expresses that the figure is at a specific point on the table (punctual, bounded location), whereas in the PP *sopra al tavolo* 'on to-the table' the figure is spread out all over the table (non-punctual, unbounded location). As further argued by den Dikken, the extended adpositional system also contains a projection for encoding spatial deixis (see also Svenonius 2010). This projection structuralizes the distinction between 'here' ('at the speaker') and 'there' ('not at the speaker') in the locative domain, and between orientation 'toward the speaker' and 'away from the speaker' in the directional domain. In a language like German, these deictic–spatial distinctions can be nicely expressed by means of the following particles: *hier* [proximal, place], *da/ dort* [distal, place], *her* [proximal, path], *hin* [distal, path] (see van Riemsdijk and Huybregts 2007). Finally, as noted by Koopman (2000), the extended adpositional projection is topped off by a functional projection which, just like CP and DP, is 'accessible' to external-syntactic operations like *wh*-movement and scrambling and provides an escape-hatch position for subextraction operations.

If aspectual, deictic, and force layers can be identified in the extended verbal, nominal, and adpositional projections, then arguably we should be able to identify these informational layers also in the extended adjectival projection. One might argue, for example, that the aspectual dimension is found in the extended adjectival expressions in (162), which feature a gradable adjective whose degree is specified in different ways. In (162a), the measure phrase *five feet* identifies a specific point on the scale of 'degrees of tallness'. In other words, the degree is 'punctual and bounded'. This bounded reading is also found in a comparative form like (162b), where the measure phrase designates the size of the gap that spans from today's pile of snow up to yesterday's pile of snow (see Schwarzschild 2005). Interestingly, the degree expressed by a comparative form like *taller* can also be unbounded. This is the case in (162c), where the modifier *ever* specifies the unboundedness of the degree of tallness.[83]

(162) a. the pile of snow was [five feet tall]
b. today's pile of snow is [two feet taller than yesterday's]
c. the piles of snow grow [ever taller] in his garden

The presence of a deictic–degree dimension within the extended adjectival projection is suggested by the occurrence of adjectival expressions like (163), in which the demonstrative elements *this* and *that* refer to a degree of tallness.

(163) a. the fish was [this big] (accompanied by a gesture indicating the size)
b. Was the fish really [that big]?!

Finally, just like the other extended projections, the extended adjectival projection is closed off by a functional projection which, just like CP and DP, is 'accessible' to external-syntactic operations and provides an escape hatch position for subextraction operations (see, for example, the subextraction patterns in (132a) and (134a); see also Corver 2000 on subextraction in Romanian).

Let me finally say a few words about the second question mentioned above, i.e. the question as to whether the projection of lexical information onto syntax is cross-linguistically the same or different. Or, to put it differently, is the lexical information associated with lexical items structuralized uniformly across languages or do languages differ in this respect? In the history of generative syntax, different answers have been given to this question for the various types of projection we have discussed in this chapter. For example, as for the projection of phrasal structure, it has been proposed by Hale (1981) and Farmer (1984) that a distinction should be made between configurational languages (e.g. English) and non-configurational languages (e.g. Warlpiri; see also Chapter 6). The former project a hierarchical (X-bar) structure in which argumental phrases are in an asymmetric relation to the verb (e.g. the subject is in a more prominent position with respect to the verb than is the direct object), whereas the latter project a flat structure in which argumental phrases are in a hierarchically symmetric relation to the verb – essentially, they are all complements to the verb – and are freely ordered with respect to each other. In Hale (1981), the non-configurationality property is expressed by means of the following rule, which essentially states that linguistic expressions are formed by stringing words together:

(164) E → ...W*...

Other linguists have argued that non-configurationality is only apparent. Saito (1985) and Hoji (1986), for example, have shown that an apparently non-configurational language like Japanese actually has a hierarchical syntactic structure in which the subject-argument and the direct object-argument are hierarchically distinct.[84] According to this view, all languages are uniform as regards the projection of hierarchical structure.

Also with respect to the projection of thematic information, different views have been presented: a very influential view has been Perlmutter and Postal's (1984) Universal Alignment Hypothesis, according to which the mapping between theta-roles and syntactic argument positions is based on a universal hierarchy (see also Baker's (1988) Uniformity of Theta Assignment Hypothesis). There have been different views, however, according to which theta-roles are not (necessarily) mapped onto fixed syntactic positions. For example, this has been argued for by researchers who advocate a base-generation approach toward the phenomenon of scrambling (see e.g. Bayer and Kornfilt 1994, Neeleman 1994b, Neeleman and Reinhart 1998). According to this base-generation analysis, the thematic roles associated with a lexical head (e.g. V) may be assigned to different syntactic 'satellite' positions within the verbal projection. In other words, there is not a designated syntactic position onto which a specific theta role is projected.

Another potential dimension of variation regards the notion of extended projection. More specifically, do all languages display the same projection levels or may languages differ in this respect? In Corver (1990, 1992), for example, it is proposed that nominal expressions in Slavic are NPs (i.e. lexical projections) rather than DPs, and that this accounts for the possibility in those languages of subextracting left branch specifying elements (cf. Ross's 1967 Left Branch Condition). Languages that do not permit left-branch extraction (e.g. English) typically have a DP-layer on top of the NP-projection. This DP-layer creates a barrier for subextraction. Thus, according to this view, languages may differ in the architecture of the extended nominal projection (say, bare NP versus extended DP) (see also Fukui 1988, Baker 2003, Bošković 2005a). Other researchers, however, have argued that these asymmetries in left-branch subextraction should not be related to a difference in extended projection. More specifically, all languages project a DP-level on top of the lexical projection NP (see, for example, Progovac 1998, Rappaport 2001). In other words, according to this view, extended nominal projections are cross-linguistically uniform.[85]

Even though views may differ on whether languages may vary in their ways of projecting lexical properties onto syntactic form, there arguably is consensus on one important thing: projection of lexical knowledge onto syntactic structure is a core mechanism of human language.

Notes

1. I would like to thank Marcel den Dikken and an anonymous reviewer for useful comments on a previous draft of the chapter.
2. *Ellipsis* is used here as a descriptive term; that is, I abstract away from whether it involves deletion of lexical material or 'insertion' of a silent pronoun ONE. See Ross (1967), Jackendoff (1977), Lobeck (1995) for discussion.
3. It should be noted that the parallel between category and sense is by no means perfect. This can be easily illustrated on the basis of the category 'noun'. The noun *examination*, for example, can have different interpretations. In a sentence like *The examination was on the table* it refers to a concrete entity (object reading); in the sentence *The examination of the patients took a long time* it refers to an event (Grimshaw 1990); and, finally, in the sentence *Those things on the table are examinations* it designates a property.
4. Emonds (2000) expresses the distinction between lexical items of the 'lexical type' and lexical items of the 'functional type' in terms of a bifurcated lexical model. The former lexical items are located in what he calls the 'Dictionary', the latter in the so-called 'Syntacticon'.
5. The distinction between lexical categories (content words) and functional categories (function words) is a central one in studies on the

syntactic categories of natural language. As with all types of categorization, there are elements which cannot be put straightforwardly under one of the two classes. Certain lexical items display ambiguous behavior: they share properties with lexical categories and at the same time they display functional characteristics. One of the first generative syntacticians who drew attention to what he called the 'squishiness' of syntactic categories was Ross (1972a, 1973). Emonds (1985:162–191) also addresses the question of gradience on the lexical-functional dimension. He points at the existence of closed classes of grammatical formatives that are subclasses of the lexical categories N, V, A, and P. In informal terms, these subclasses can be characterized as the most frequently used and least semantically specified members of each lexical category. Emonds calls these 'in between' subclasses "grammatical nouns, verbs, adjectives and prepositions". Some examples of the category 'grammatical noun' are: *one, self, thing, place, way*. See also Corver and van Riemsdijk (2001), who use the descriptive term 'semi-lexical categories' for such lexical items.

6. Although structural containment of the lexical projection within the functional projection (see (4a)) is arguably the norm, there are cases in which a projection of a lexical category L1 is immediately contained in another lexical category L2. The quintessential phenomena are incorporation (see Chapter 9) and restructuring. An illustration of the former phenomenon is given in (ia) from Mohawk, where the noun 'meat' directly combines with the verb 'eat' to give the complex verb 'to meat-eat' (*waha'wahrake'*); see Baker (1988, 2001). Notice that in the plain pattern in (ib) the (projection of the) lexical category is structurally contained within the functional projection DP, which has *ne* as its functional head.

(i) a. owira'a   waha'wahrake'   (noun incorporation pattern)
    baby   meat-ate
    'the baby ate some meat'
  b. owira'a   wahrake'   ne   o'wahru.   (plain pattern)
    baby   ate   the   meat
    'the baby ate the meat'

7. The '()' in phrase structure rule (7c) indicates that the presence of *DET* and *PP* in the nominal structure is optional.
8. Chomsky's original conception of phrase structure rules was entirely context-free (which led to the introduction of subcategorization). See Chapter 2 and Lasnik (2000) for systematic discussion of the early developments of phrase structure grammar.
9. See Emonds (1985) for an asymmetric analysis of phrasal projection: N, A and P project to the double-bar level, while V projects to V'''.
10. The clausal category labeled S', which in the 1970s and (part of) the 1980s was used to represent a clause introduced by a subordinating

conjunction like *that* (Bresnan 1972), immediately contains a category COMP and a 'lower' clausal category S (see (43) in Section 11.5). As we will see below, the S/S' notation is not perfectly X-bar theoretic, despite the fact that it seems to invoke an X-bar theoretic notion.

11. For the notions external argument and internal argument, see Williams (1981b, 1995) and also Chapter 9.
12. The *than*-phrase is often taken to originate in the complement position of the degree word *more*. Its surface position outside of the functional projection DegP results from extraposition (see e.g. Jackendoff 1977 for discussion).
13. I abstract away here from the possibility of having a lexical phrase in the specifier position, as in (20).
14. The idea that phrase structure theory might be interpreted as a set of well-formedness conditions goes back to McCawley (1968a), predating the introduction of X-bar Theory.
15. See Jackendoff (1977) for a feature analysis of syntactic categories in terms of the features [+/−S] (i.e. (im)possibility of a category to have a subject) and [+/−O] (i.e. (im)possibility of a category to have an (NP-) direct object). For further discussion of the featural basis of syntactic categories, see among others Muysken and van Riemsdijk (1986), Reuland (1986) and Baker (2003).
16. One may be skeptical about the usefulness of cross-categorial similarities stated in terms of a shared feature. It is just as easy to find cross-categorial generalizations that are not thus statable. For example, P (i.e. [−N, −V]) and A (i.e. [+N,+V]) are the possible adnominal adjuncts. Also, some generalizations pick three out of four categories: thus, N, A, and P are united in not having tense. See van Riemsdijk (1978:112ff.) for discussion.
17. The (X-bar theoretic) notion of adjunct is often used to refer to YPs that are both daughter of a single-bar level category (X') and sister to a single-bar level category (X'); see Carnie (2008:122). A specifier is a daughter of a maximal category (X'') and sister to a single-bar level category (X'). A complement, finally, is a sister to the head (X). For the sake of completeness, it should be noted here that the notion of adjunct is also sometimes used to refer to a phrase YP that is Chomsky-adjoined to the maximal category XP, as in: [$_{XP}$ YP [$_{XP}$ Spec [$_{X'}$ X Compl]]] (see Carnie 2008:151 for discussion).
18. In more recent conceptions of phrase structure, attributive APs have been associated with specifier positions of functional projections (see Chapter 13 for discussion).
19. For analyses that assume that pronominals can have a phrasal structure, see among others Cardinaletti and Starke (1999), Corver and Delfitto (1999), and Déchaine and Wiltschko (2002).

20. In (28), *one*-pronominalization is given as an argument for X′-recursion. Obviously, from Speas's point of view, *one*-pronominalization has to be dealt with differently (if pronominalization is a rule of the syntactic computation).
21. In Kayne's (1994) antisymmetry framework, vacuous projection of hierarchical structure is possible.
22. Chomsky's (1995c:228) Inclusiveness condition rules out the representation of bar level information, for example as primes (X′, X″), in syntactic structures. According to the inclusiveness condition, "no new objects are added in the course of computation apart from re-arrangements of lexical properties".
23 In the tree structure in (32), the categorial label (e.g. P) and the lexical item (e.g. *above*) are represented as separate objects (i.e. nodes). This expresses the view that the word and the categorial value are separate levels of phrase structure. As an alternative, one might take the categorial value to be a property of the word. In that case, the word *above* and the categorial label P would be properties of information which constitute a single (terminal) node (i.e. there is no branch connecting them), as in (i); see Carnie (2008:27ff.) for discussion. In the tree diagrams in (40b) and (41b), this alternative analysis is used.

(i)   P
      above

24. I have simply represented here the simplex constituent structures *right* and *me* as A and N, respectively.
25. It should also be noted here that Chomsky's original conception of phrase structure was set-theoretic rather than graph-theoretic (Chomsky 1957:27–29, 1975a:183). See also Lasnik (2000:29ff.) for insightful discussion of Chomsky's early notion of set-theoretically defined P-marker and the 'is a' relation. Also, in Lasnik and Kupin (1977), it is argued that trees (i.e. graph-theoretic representations of phrase structure) are not adequate representations of phrase structure. In Chomsky's (1995c:241ff.) Bare Phrase Structure Theory, the set-theoretic conception of phrase structure representation is explicitly present.
26. See Sections 1.1.3, 2.4.2, and 4.2.1 for related discussion of issues related to linearization.
27. As noted in Carnie (2008:40), the easiest way to define precedence is by appealing to the most local of dominance relations (immediate dominance) in combination with the orderings of elements: sister constituents are always ordered left to right on a single line in a tree structure. For example, the preposition *above* sister-precedes the noun *me* in (32a), since the former precedes the latter on the same horizontal line. Importantly, this linear ordering might result from

ordering specifications in phrase structure rules or other generative principles of linearization.

28. See also Gazdar and Pullum (1981) for a rule formalism which separates these two dimensions within Generalized Phrase Structure Grammar (see Chapter 7): I(mmediate)D(ominance)-rules regulate dominance relations and L(inear)P(recedence)-rules regulate precedence relations.

29. The parameter should also be defined for the specifier-X' relation:

   (i) a. XP → X' (YP)
        b. XP → (YP) X'

30. Asymmetric c-command is the structural relationship that holds between an aunt node and its niece nodes: A asymmetrically c-commands B if A c-commands B but B does not c-command A. For example, in the tree representation (32a), the adjectival node *right* asymmetrically c-commands the nodes *above* and *me*. Symmetric c-command typically involves a sisterhood relationship: A symmetrically c-commands B, if A c-commands B and B c-commands A; see Kayne (1994:4ff.) for discussion. Reinhart's (1976:32) original definition of the c(onstituent)-command relationship is given in (i); see Carnie (2008:49ff.) for discussion.

   (i) *C-command*
        Node A c-commands node B if neither A nor B dominates the other and the first branching node dominating A dominates B.

31. Another consequence of Kayne's theory of the antisymmetry of syntax is that the essentials of X-bar Theory can be derived. In other words, X-bar Theory is not a primitive component of Universal Grammar.

32. See also Larson's (1988a) Single Complement Hypothesis, according to which maximal projections (XP) are limited to one complement and one specifier per phrase.

33. As in Larson's (1988a) analysis of ditransitive constructions. Of course, this follows only if there *are* in fact predicates that assign two internal theta-roles. In den Dikken (1995), for example, an analysis of ditransitive constructions is proposed which takes the verb to select a single (small clause) complement within which one internal (Goal) and one external (Theme) role are assigned by a separate predicate (P).

34. See, among others, Sampson (1975), McCawley (1982, 1989), Blevins (1990) for tree structures which feature multi-dominance and/or line crossing.

35. This amounts to a relaxation of the constraint that trees have a single root.

36. Hale (1983) gives a multi-planar analysis of Warlpiri sentences, which are characterized by relatively free word order. He suggests that one plane of syntactic organization (so-called 'L-syntax') represents the

basic predicational structures of the clause, while the the other plane of syntactic organization (so-called 'S-syntax') reflects the surface-constituent relations.

37. Chomsky (1973:244, (54)) mistakenly attributes to Bresnan (1970) the phrase structure rule S → COMP S'. Bresnan herself has the familiar rewrite rule in (43a): she give[s] two basic arguments justifying the phrase structure rule S' → COMP S, that is, establishing that COMP is a node in deep structure (Bresnan 1970:303).
38. The idea that the sentence category (S) is to be analyzed as the X-bar projection of I(nfl) is anticipated in Jeanne (1978).
39. The idea that particular theta roles map onto particular syntactic positions in the sentence is expressed in Relational Grammar by the so-called Universal Alignment Hypothesis (see Perlmutter and Postal 1984). According to this hypothesis, theta roles are mapped directly into argument position based on the following hierarchy: *Agent > Theme > Experiencer > Others*. Baker (1988) adopts this idea into the Government and Binding theory in the form of the Uniformity of Theta Assignment Hypothesis (UTAH). See also Larson (1988a). Chapter 9 presents a more elaborate discussion of argument structure.
40. It should be noted that *sleep* CAN actually take a complement in resultatives, as in *He slept his head off* and *He slept himself into a mental breakdown*. The contrast between these and (53b) indicates that apparently small clauses differ from full clauses (which is something that still counts as a bit of a problem for the Small Clause hypothesis).
41. In the literature, there are proposals in which such things *are* possible. In Hornstein (2001), for example, it is proposed that theta-features can drive displacement operations, which means that movement to theta-positions is possible. See Section 4.2.1 for relevant discussion.
42. This 'small vP' layer has alternatively been called PredP (Bowers 1993) and VoiceP (Kratzer 1995).
43. There are apparent exceptions to the statement that S+V idioms do not exist. For example, in the expression *A little birdie told me that...*, which is used if someone does not want to say where he got some information from, the subject *a little birdie* and the verb *tell* seem to form an idiom. Marantz (1984), though, has argued against these being counterexamples to his generalization.
44. Jackendoff (1990b) countered Larson's translation of the Barss and Lasnik binding asymmetries into c-command asymmetries, saying that they reflect a linear asymmetry, not one that should be couched in terms of c-command. See den Dikken (1995) for an alternative structural analysis which also tries to capture the Barss and Lasnik asymmetries in terms of the c-command relationship.
45. According to Abney (1987:56), "f-selection corresponds semantically to the 'passing on' of the descriptive content of the complement".

46. Postal's (1969) proposal that pronouns in English are actually determiners (compare *the linguists* and *we/us linguists*) also hinted at the idea that nominal expressions are actually determiner phrases.
47. See Larson (1991a, 2013) for an alternative view of the projection of the D(eterminer)-system. In line with the analysis of natural language quantification as involving generalized or restricted quantifiers (Barwise and Cooper 1981), he adopts the relational view of determiners: i.e. determiners (e.g. definite articles) express relations between predicates. Thus, they take predicates as their arguments. According to this view, D is not analogous to I or C, but rather to a predicate category such as V. For example, the determiner *the* is analyzed as a dyadic predicate. A nice illustration of this dyadic nature comes from the nominal expression in (ia), in which the presence of the modifying relative clause is dependent on the definite article. Larson takes the relative clause to be a predicate in the complement position of *the*. As shown in (1b), the specifier positions of *the* is occupied by the nominal predicate *Paris*. The surface order is derived by raising of the determiner *the* to a higher D-position (see (ic)), analogously to the verb raising operation in VP-shell structures.

(i) a. the Paris that I like   (Compare: *the Paris)
   b. [$_{DP}$ Paris [$_{D'}$ [$_D$ the] [$_{CP}$ that I like]]]
   c. [$_{DP}$ *pro* [$_{D'}$ the$_i$ [$_{DP}$ Paris [$_{D'}$ t$_i$ [$_{CP}$ that I like]]]]]

The pro-predicate in (ic) is licensed by the higher D and receives a value from its syntactic configuration at LF.
48. For discussion of the internal architecture of the extended nominal projection, see also Corver (1990), Valois (1991), Bernstein (1993a, 2001), Zamparelli (1995), Alexiadou and Wilder (1998b), Vangsnes (1999), Longobardi (2001), Cinque (2002), Coene and D'Hulst (2003), Roehrs (2006), Alexiadou et al. (2007), Leu (2008).
49. The *-t* ending on *ahavat* marks the construct state form.
50. For further discussion of the construct state, see Siloni (1996, 1997). See Shlonsky (2004) for an analysis of Hebrew construct state noun phrases in terms of phrasal movement.
51. A problem with the N-to-F head movement analysis for Romance is that, when there are multiple attributive modifiers, this head movement hypothesis predicts that the modifiers should all line up postnominally in the same order in which they line up prenominally. This, however, is not the distributional pattern we find, as shown by the example in (ib), which is the French counterpart of the English nominal expression in (ia):

(i) a. a beautiful round table
   b. une   table   ronde   magnifique   (French)
      a   table   round   beautiful
   'a beautiful round table'

It is more likely, therefore, that some sort of snowballing or roll-up phrasal movement is involved in the derivation of the French word order in (ib). That is, starting from the underlying pattern *une magnifique ronde table*, the surface order is derived by first moving the phrase *table* to a position preceding *ronde* (yielding *une magnifique table$_i$ ronde t$_i$*) and subsequently moving the phrase *[table$_i$ ronde t$_i$]* to a position preceding the attributive adjective *magnifique* (yielding: *une [table$_i$ ronde t$_i$]$_j$ magnifique t$_j$*). See Cinque (2005) and Laenzlinger (2005) for an analysis of the ordering of attributive adjectives in terms of roll-up phrasal movement; see also Section 13.5.

52. See Delsing (1993), Santelmann (1992), Kester (1992), Vangsnes (2001), Embick and Noyer (2001), and Julien (2002, 2005) for discussion of N-raising and the double definiteness phenomenon in Scandinavian languages (and see Section 13.5, on double definiteness in Greek). See Hankamer and Mikkelsen (2005) for a lexical approach toward forms like *huset* in (100a).

53. Crucially, this analysis only works if [SpecDP] is not available as an escape hatch for subextraction; possibly, there are restrictions on the types of categories that can land in [SpecDP]. Arguably, [SpecDP] *is* available as an escape hatch for subextraction of possessors in a language like Hungarian, which permits dative possessor extraction (see (82)). Under such an analysis, XP first moves to [SpecDP] and, consequently, crosses only a single barrier, viz., YP in (102), which is permitted by the Subjacency Condition. Since XP has landed in [SpecDP], it is no longer possible for DP to inherit barrierhood from YP. Consequently, XP can move out of [SpecDP] to the (nearest) DP-external position without violating the Subjacency Condition. DP does not count as a barrier, since it is L-marked by the lexical category V.

54. Kayne (2002b) also argues that *who* and *-se* do not form a constituent and consequently cannot be removed from within the noun phrase. Interestingly, Kayne (2002b, note 37) notes the contrast in (i):

    (i) a. **Whose were you talking to sister?
        b. ??Who were you talking to's sister?

    In (ia), a string which does not form a constituent is fronted, yielding a strongly ungrammatical sentence. In (ib), a constituent (*who*) is subextracted, leaving the clitic element *-se* behind. Stranding the clitic element yields a less unacceptable sentence.

55. See den Dikken (1998) and Bernstein and Tortora (2005) for an analysis according to which the possessive *-s(e)* and the contracted copula *-s*, as in *Who's coming for dinner?*, are the same thing.

56. An important presupposition is here that *-s(e)* does not attach to *who* in syntax. That is, attachment of the clitic to its host takes place in phonology.

57. RP in (114b) stands for Relator Phrase, which is a functional head that mediates a predication relationship between a predicate (e.g. *idiot*) and a subject (e.g. *a policeman*).
58. See also Doetjes and Rooryck (2003) and Uriagereka (2008) for discussion of DP-internal predicate movement.
59. See Martí-Girbau (2010) for a DP-internal predicate movement analysis of (pseudo-)partitive constructions in Catalan.
60. Some of these functional projections are not supposed to be unique to *nominal* extended projections. For example, FocP, TopP, and RP are functional layers whose presence has also been argued for in the extended verbal domain. See Rizzi (1997) for FocP and TopP (also Chapters 12 and 23), and den Dikken (2006b) for RP.
61. In this section, I will not discuss the syntax of degree clauses like *than Bill is* in (116b) and like *to serve on a submarine* in (i). Nor will I discuss the syntax of consecutive clauses like the one in (118a).

    (i) John is [too tall to serve on a submarine]

    For analyses (some adopting the Lexical Head Hypothesis, others the Functional Head Hypothesis), see among others the following studies: Baltin (1987a), Larson (1988b), Corver (1990), Rothstein (1991a,1991b), Rijkhoek (1998), Kennedy (1999b, 2002), Lechner (1999), White (1997), Heim (2000), Bhatt and Pancheva (2004).
62. See Larson (1991a/2013) for an analysis of degree words as elements that express relations between predicates. See note 47 for a similar analysis of determiners.
63. See Corver (2000, 2009) for an analysis of certain pre-adjectival degree modifiers in terms of predicate movement. That is, the degree modifier is taken to start out as a post-adjectival predicate and ends up in its surface position as a result of predicate movement within the adjectival system, quite along the lines of predicate movement in the nominal domain (see Section 11.8.8).
64. For the sake of dicussion, I will assume here that the consecutive clause is adjoined to DegP.
65. See Doetjes (1997, 2008), Neeleman *et al.* (2004), Corver (2000, 2005) for discussion of the various types of degree expressions and their syntactic placement.
66. As an alternative, one might propose that *fond* raises to Deg (via Q), with *enough* being in the specifier position of QP:

    (i) [$_{DegP}$ [$_{Deg'}$ fond$_i$ [$_{QP}$ enough [$_{Q'}$ t'$_i$ [$_{AP}$ t$_i$ of Sue]]]]]

    Both (123) and (i) give an account of the phenomenon of *enough*-inversion which is compatible with general constraints on movement; more specifically, the moved element ends up in a position from where it c-commands its original site.

67. This inversion pattern is not attested with all degree words. Tallerman (1998), for example, notes the following contrast:

    (i) a. dyn   balch iawn   (Welsh)
            man proud very
            'a very proud man'
        b. llyfr rhy ddrud
            book too expensive
            'a too expensive book'

68. In Corver (1997b) it is suggested that the phrasal modifier originates in [SpecQP].

69. As noted in Hoekstra and Jordens (1994) and van Kampen (1997), *wh*-movement in Dutch child language may shift a left-branch element like *hoe*, leaving behind the adjectival projection. This is exemplified in (i), which is taken from van Kampen (1997:116); see also Section 24.3.1.

    (i) ik weet niet *hoe* het *lang* is   (Emma 3;1/Laura 3;6)
       I   know not how it   long is
       'I don't know how long it is'

As shown in (ii), subextraction of a left-branch constituent is also permitted from within the nominal domain in Dutch child language ((ii) taken from van Kampen 1997:116):

    (ii) *Welk*   wil   jij   *boekje*?   (S. 2;9)
        which   want you   booklet
       'Which booklet do you want to read?'

Interestingly, instances of left-branch subextraction are also found in adult language systems. For example, Italian permits subextraction of *quanto* from within an adjectival projection (Rizzi 1990a) and Polish allows subextraction of a *wh*-determiner (Corver 1992):

    (iii) *Quanto* è   *alto*?   (Italian)
         how   is   tall
        'How tall is he?'
    (iv) *Jaki*   wykreciłes   *numer*?   (Polish)
        which (you)dialed   number
       'Which number did you dial?'

The question obviously arises as to how to account for these differences in left-branch subextraction behavior. Some researchers have tried to relate it to presence versus absence of a certain functional layer (e.g. DP in the case of nominal expressions) within the extended projection (see e.g. Corver 1990, 1992, Zlatić 1997, Bošković 2005a). Others have argued that it should not be related to a difference in projection of functional structure but rather to the availability as an escape hatch of the Spec-position of the relevant functional projections (DP, DegP) (see e.g. Progovac 1998, Rappaport 2001). See Corver (2006b) for a general discussion of subextraction behavior.

70. They are called R-pronouns because they share the consonant *r* in their phonology: *er* (there), *daar* (there), *hier* (here), *waar* (where), *ergens*, (somewhere), *nergens* (nowhere), *overal* (everywhere). It should be noted that sharing the consonant *r* is hardly an efficient defining property of R-words: the Dutch personal pronoun *haar* 'her' also includes an *r*, but it does not fall within the class of R-pronouns; it must follow P, as in *achter haar* 'behind her', and not **haar achter* (her behind).

71. M in (141) stands for 'modifier' (possibly phrasal).

72. $CP_{(Place)}$ is used on analogy with the CP-layer in the extended verbal domain. It is the functional layer which provides the escape hatch for subextraction from the extended adpositional projection.

73. See also Asbury et al. (2008) for discussion of the syntax and semantics of adpositional PPs in a broad variety of languages. Other studies on the internal architecture of the adpositional system are among others: Helmantel (2002), Botwinik-Rotem (2004), and Asbury (2008).

74. I will abstract away from the distribution of degree words and measure phrases in this discussion of directional adpositional phrases. See Koopman (2000) and den Dikken (2010a) for discussion.

75. Koopman points out that the phonologically empty Path-head of the directional extended prepositional phrase gets incorporated into the lexical head that selects the PathP. Importantly, not all lexical heads are able to function as a host for this incorporated null Path-head. In other words, there is a selectional relationship between the lexical head and directional pre-PP. For example, while the verb *rijden* 'to drive' in (150) can function as a host for an incorporated zero Path-head, the pre-PP *in de kamer* can only have a locative meaning when it combines with the verb *lopen* 'walk', which suggests that *lopen* cannot function as a host for an incorporated null-Path head. See also den Dikken (2010a) for discussion.

76. See van Riemsdijk (1990) for an alternative analysis in which the postpositional element in Dutch post- and circumpositional phrases is a functional P (i.e. p), which takes a lexical PP-complement to its left. The postpositional pattern *het water in* is derived by movement of the lexical P to the functional p-head, as in (ib). In the circumpositional pattern *onder het viaduct door*, the functional head is occupied by *door* (see (ic)).

(i)   a.   [$_{pp}$ [$_{PP}$ P NP] p]
      b.   [$_{pp}$ [$_{PP}$ t$_i$ het water] in$_i$]
      c.   [$_{pp}$ [$_{PP}$ onder het viaduct] door]

77. The reviewer of this chapter points out a curious case of 'agreement' in Malagasy: adpositions may carry tense/aspect inflection, apparently. Randriamasimanana (1999:510) gives the following example:

(i) N-andeha t-any   Antsirabe I   Paoly   (Malagasy)
     PAST-go PERF-to   Antsirabe ART Paul
     'Paul went to Antsirabe'

78. Besides 'dressed' adpositions, Marácz distinguishes 'naked' adpositions. The two types of adpositions display different morphosyntactic behavior. For example, the noun phrase of a dressed P displays nominative case (a default case, according to Marácz 1989). Naked Ps, on the contrary, assign a lexical case to their nominal complement (e.g. instrumental, allative, superessive, ablative).

(i) a. János   mögött   (dressed P)   (Hungarian)
        John-NOM   behind
        'behind John'
     b. János-on   át   (naked P)
        John-SUPER over
        'over John'

79. Jackendoff (1996b:14) gives the following description of the notion of 'axial part'.

> The 'axial parts' of an object – its *top, bottom, front, back, sides,* and *ends* – behave grammatically like parts of the object, but, unlike standard parts such as a *handle* or a *leg*, they have no distinctive shape. Rather, they are regions of the object (or its boundary) determined by their relation to the object's axes. The up–down axis determines top and bottom, the front–back axis determines front and back, and a complex set of criteria distinguishing horizontal axes determines sides and ends.

80. As pointed out by the reviewer of this chapter, Finnish seems to provide a good illustration of the 'nominal flavor' of AxPart: The 'nominal flavor' element takes case inflection like a regular noun. This is exemplified in (i):

(i) a. pöydän a-lla (table-GEN top-ADESSIVE; 'on top of the table')
     b. pöydän a-lta (table-GEN top-ABLATIVE; 'off the top of the table')
     c. pöydän a-lle (table-GEN top-ALLATIVE; 'on to the top of the table')

For discussion of adpositional patterns having a 'nominal flavor', see also Aboh (2010), Noonan (2010), and Terzi (2010).

81. EZ in (160) stands for *ezafe*, i.e. the marker that shows up in so-called *ezafe*-constructions (see Ghomeshi 1997).
82. 'Delimitedness' (also called 'boundedness') refers to the property of an event's having a distinct, definite endpoint in time (see Verkuyl

1993, Tenny 1994). For example, sentence (ia) describes a delimited event since the destroying of the car requires a certain amount of time and has a definite endpoint, as is clear from the (un)acceptability of the temporal adjunct-PPs. Sentence (ib) does not describe a delimited event, since the pushing of the car is something that can go on for an indefinite period of time.

(i) a. they destroyed the car in an hour / *for an hour
b. they pushed the car for an hour / *in an hour

83. This unbounded degree can also be expressed by iteration of the comparative adjective (see (ia)) or, when we have a free comparative morpheme, by iteration of the comparative morpheme itself (see (ib)):

(i) a. the piles of snow grow [taller and taller] in his garden
b. Mary became [[more and more and more] intelligent]

Note that iteration of the comparative adjective is not possible when a 'single' degree of tallness is designated:

(ii) *today's pile of snow is [two feet *taller and taller* than yesterday's]

84. See also Adger *et al.* (2009) for a configurational analysis of Kiowa, a language that appears to be highly non-configurational on the surface.

85. The question as to whether nominal projections are cross-linguistically uniform or not is also a topic of discussion in the literature on the East Asian Altaic languages (Japanese, Korean). See Fukui (1988) for the view that Japanese nominal expressions lack a DP-layer, and see Park (2008) and Furuya (2008) for analyses in defense of a DP-layer in languages such as Korean and Japanese.

12

The functional structure of the sentence, and cartography

Luigi Rizzi

12.1 The head of the sentence

The modern study of the structure of the sentence started when the question of the headedness of sentences was asked. Classical X-bar Theory (Chomsky 1970a) had laid the ground for a systematic study of the internal structure of phrases, understood as projections of lexical heads. What was the head of the sentence? The lexical verb looked like a plausible candidate, but clearly the sentence potentially contained more material than a single X-bar schema could integrate: a possible sequence of auxiliaries and modals, adverbials of various kinds, and the subject. It thus seemed natural to assume, around the late 1970s, that the sentence could be headed by a non-lexical, or functional head, potentially realized by a non-lexical verb like an auxiliary, copula, or modal. This hypothesis was part of a much larger trend to assign a more central role, in syntactic structures and computations, to the functional lexicon, now understood as providing the basic scaffolding for the insertion of the contentful lexical items and their projections.

The first proposal, adopted in *Lectures on Government and Binding* (Chomsky 1981), was to assume a single abstract functional head, Inflection (Infl, or I), expressing morphosyntactic properties typically associated to verbal inflections or non-lexical verbs: tense, mood, the expression of agreement with the subject, etc. Through the further assumption that X-bar Theory applies uniformly to functional and contentful (lexical) categories (Chomsky 1986a:4), the assumed clausal structure was something like the following:

(1)
```
              IP
           /      \
         NP        I'
         |       /    \
         N      I      VP
        John   will   /    \
                     V      NP
                    see     |
                            N
                           Mary
```

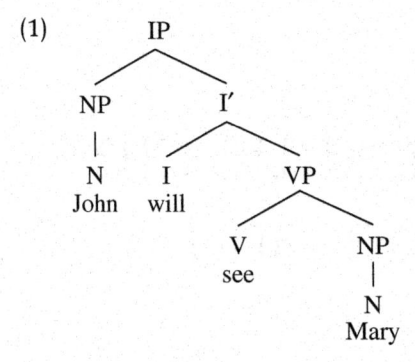

Immediate positional evidence in favor of distinguishing at least two verbal positions in the clausal structure was offered by the co-occurrence of functional and lexical verbal elements in a fixed order (*will see*), and by the fact that they occur on opposite sides of certain adverbs like *often*, which seem to demarcate the two positions:

(2) a. John will often [see Mary]
    b. John has often [seen Mary]
    c. John often [sees Mary]

Comparative evidence corroborating the view that functional verbs are independent heads, rather than specifiers of lexical verbs, was provided by the reinterpretation in X-bar theoretic terms of Greenberg's (1963) observation that auxiliaries and other functional verbs display a head-like behavior across languages in that they tend to conform to the head–complement order of the language: so VO languages like English show the order Aux–VP, while OV languages like Japanese show the order VP–Aux (of course there could be exceptions, as disharmonic head–complement orders are attested: Biberauer, et al. 2008).

12.2 V-to-I movement

Focusing on one of the main functions of I, the expression of tense, one could observe that in some languages the tense marker is exactly where structural hypothesis (1) predicts it to be, a particle in between the subject and the predicate. This happens e.g. in many Creole languages (with present expressed by a zero particle):

(3) a. im nuo   dat   (Jamaican Creole: Durrleman 2008)
       he knows that
    b. im en   nuo   dat
       he PAST know that
    c. im wi   nuo   dat
       he FUT know that

Many other languages seem to function differently, with the tense marker expressed by a morphological ending glued to the lexical verb, as in the following Italian example:

(4)   Gianni incontr+erà Maria
      Gianni meet+FUT   Maria

Here, as in many other cases, linguists have followed an intuition of uniformity, and formulated the hypothesis that the syntactic representation of (4) is essentially identical to (1), i.e., in terms of tree structure:

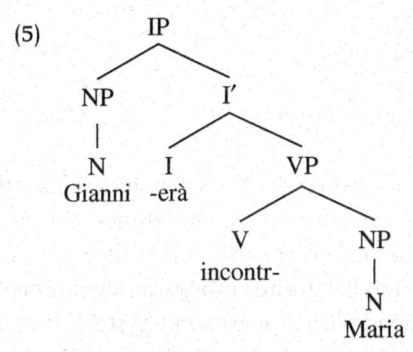

(5)
```
            IP
           /  \
         NP    I'
         |    / \
         N   I   VP
       Gianni -erà / \
                  V   NP
               incontr- |
                        N
                      Maria
```

The two structures do not differ syntactically, but morphologically: the future tense marker is an autonomous word in English, and an inflectional morpheme in Italian and many other languages. Something must happen in the derivation of (4) as the temporal affix and the lexical root are not complete words, and cannot survive alone. In order to meet morphological well-formedness, the lexical root moves to I, creating the complex word *incontr+erà* (cf. Emonds 1978 on the French equivalent).

This movement operation is not simply a formal trick to align syntax and morphology: it predicts that certain changes in word order should be produced by the movement of the verbal root. If an adverb like *often* marks the edge of the VP, verb movement should change the adverb–verb order. The contrast between English and Romance languages like French or Italian is illuminating in this respect:

(6) a. ils ont souvent rencontré Marie   (Pollock 1989, Emonds 1978)
     b. they have often met Mary

(7) a. *ils souvent rencontrent Marie
     b. they often meet Mary

(8) a. ils rencontrent souvent Marie
     b. *they meet often Mary

The adverb occurs in between I and V in both languages (the exact position is not critical here), as in (6). In French the verb moves to I to pick up the inflection (as in (9); the inflection is audible with other verb classes: *disent,* mettent, prennent 'they say, put, take', etc.), and this gives rise to the order V+I - Adv - O, as in (8)a. In English the lexical verb remains in the VP, hence it is preceded by the adverb in the surface order, as in (7)b:

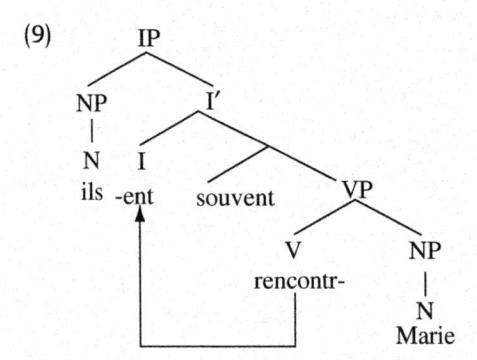

(9)
```
              IP
            /    \
          NP      I'
          |      / \
          N     I   \
         ils  -ent   VP
                    /  \
                   V    NP
               rencontr- |
                         N
                        Marie
```

It was observed that the difference between the two languages is plausibly not arbitrary but linked to a salient morphosyntactic difference: the richer inflectional paradigm of French verbs versus the more impoverished English paradigm (just -s and -ed for English finite verbs vs. a richer morphological specification of tense and mood with at least some systematic manifestations of agreement, audible also in Modern French). This suggested the conjecture of a direct causal role played by the morphology: the rich verbal inflection has the capacity to attract the lexical verb, while a more impoverished morphology is unable to attract the verb, which remains in its initial position in the VP (but see Sections 12.3 and 12.4 for further discussion).

This conjecture is supported by diachronic evidence. Roberts (1993) shows that V-to-I movement is still attested in Shakespearian English. e.g., the following examples taken from *Hamlet* show that the lexical verb could raise past the negative adverbial *not*:

(10) a. I know *not* ...
 b. go *not* to Wittenberg
 c. I speak *not* to him

Roberts connects this state of affairs to the richer inflectional paradigm of verbs at this stage, e.g., with distinct overt second and third person agreement morphemes: *cast, castest, casteth*. The weakening of the inflectional paradigm has the consequence, in this view, of determining a syntactic change, the loss of verb movement for lexical verbs.

12.3 Modern English -s, -ed

This approach raises the question of how in Modern English the residual finite inflections *-s/-ed* can be placed on the lexical verb which has remained VP-internal.

(11) John often sees Mary

A time-honored approach, which in fact introduced the crucial positional difference between functional and lexical verbs, is Chomsky's (1957) Affix Hopping (see also Chapter 2): a weak inflection, unable to attract the verb, moves downward (past the adverbial in a case like (12)) and attaches to the verb which remains in its VP-internal position (see Bobaljik 2001, Lasnik 1999a for different versions of this idea).

(12) John -s often see Mary ➔ Affix hopping ➔
      John ___ often see-s Mary

One problem with this analysis is that it involves a lowering operation, which is generally banned elsewhere. Moreover, it is not clear how it could express the difference between adverbials like *often*, which permit the process, and the negative adverbial *not*, which bans it and requires *do*-support to ensure the proper attachment of the affix to a verbal element (a process also required in questions and a few other constructions):

(13) a. *John ___ not sees Mary
      b. John does not see Mary

One possible alternative would be to adopt, at least for English-type languages, the analysis presented in Chomsky (1995c), according to which the verb is inflected in the numeration, so that the complex forms *sees, smoked*, etc. enter syntax already formed. The correctness of the affix is checked through a search operation (Agree), connecting I (endowed with the relevant tense and agreement features) and the inflected verbal form:

(14) John I [see-s Mary]
      └─────────▲
           Search

Why is this operation blocked by *not*, while other adverbials do not seem to interfere? While many technical solutions to this problem have been proposed, I would like to sketch out here a possible new line of analysis, inspired by the study of the clausal cartography and locality, and still falling within the narrow range set by Chomsky's (1957) seminal approach. One crucial ingredient is Cinque's (1999) approach to the clausal cartography, according to which adverbials are uniformly merged in the specifier position of dedicated functional heads: Neg for *not*, and X (presumably an aspectual head; see below) for *often*. So we have:

(15) John I [not Neg [see-s Mary]]

(16) John I [often X [see-s Mary]]

The question then reduces to why Neg blocks Agree connecting I and the verbal inflection in view of checking/licensing it, while X does not interfere. I would like to suggest that Neg is specified [+V] (on categorial features, see Chapter 11), an assumption justified by the fact that Neg appears to be a possible insertion site for the functional verb *do*.[1] X in (16) is not a verbal insertion site, hence by parity of reasoning it lacks such a specification. Then, if I searches the structure for a [+V] element, the search operation will be intercepted by Neg$_{+V}$ in (15) and will not reach *see-s*, which will remain unchecked, thus giving rise to the ungrammaticality of (13a). The only option here will be to leave the lexical verb uninflected and to insert an inflected *do* in Neg: it will be successfully searched for by I and will move to it, like other functional verbs (auxiliaries, copula: *John has not seen Mary, John is not happy*), thus yielding (13b).

In (16), X (by assumption not specified [+V], as it is not a verbal insertion site) will not interfere in the search from I to *see-s*, hence Agree and checking will proceed, yielding the well-formed (11). The contrast (11)–(13a) is thus derived from locality, as a particular case of the intervention effects that are subsumed under Relativized Minimality (Rizzi 1990a, 2004a; see also Chapter 18) or Minimal Search (Chomsky 2000b). A similar analysis can be given for the obligatory *do*-insertion with main-clause interrogatives, under the assumption that such constructions require a Q-head (see also Section 2.3) in the inflectional space, with characteristics analogous to the Neg head:

(17) John I [Q$_{+V}$ [see-s Mary]]

Here a search from I cannot reach *see-s* because of the intervention of Q$_{+V}$. The only option is to leave V uninflected and insert *do* under Q, which will then undergo checking and movement.[2] A similar analysis can be given for emphatic *do*-insertion.

What about languages with richer inflection like French? Many options come to mind. A natural hypothesis is that morphologically richer and more impoverished languages use two fundamentally different modes of association of inflections to verbal roots: the 'lexicalist route' may be restricted to English-type languages, hence it may be the defining characteristic of the verbal morphosyntax of languages with 'weak inflection' (see Chapter 17 for relevant discussion). On the other hand, languages with richer verbal inflection would normally use the 'syntactic route,' hence have affixes generated in the inflectional space, and attract the verbal root as assumed in Section 12.2. A significant change in the verbal paradigm may correlate with a shift from the syntactic to the lexical mode of association (see the end of Section 12.4).

12.4 The microcomparative study of Scandinavian

The close connection between syntax and morphology is confirmed by other cases of microcomparison (see also Chapter 24), cases in which the compared varieties are close enough historically to control for the possible interfering effect of other parametric properties. One domain which has been extensively investigated in this connection is the comparison between Icelandic and the Continental Scandinavian languages, which have innovated in several respects. While Icelandic presents a well-developed verbal paradigm, with distinct agreement forms, Danish (much as Swedish and Norwegian) has fully eliminated the specifications of agreement from the verbal paradigm:

(18) Icelandic (*heyra* 'hear')
present: heyr-i, heyr-ir, heyr-ir, heyr-um, heir-ið, heyr-a
preterite: heyr-ði, heyr-ði-r, heyr-ði, heyr-ðu-m, heyr-ðu-ð, heyr-ðu

(19) Danish (*høre* 'hear')
present: hør-er
preterite: hør-te

As expected, Icelandic requires movement of the finite verb to I across the negative marker, as in (20), while Danish keeps the finite lexical verb in the VP, as in (21) (we have to look at embedded clauses to control for the interfering effect of Verb Second in these languages).

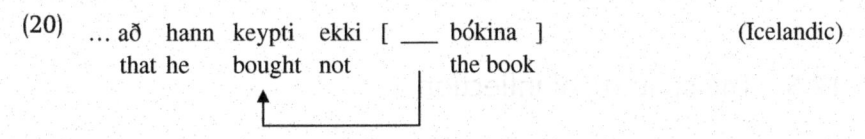

(20) ... að hann keypti ekki [___ bókina]   (Icelandic)
       that he bought not   the book

(21) ... at han ikke [købte bogen]   (Danish)
       that he not bought the book

Platzack (1987) also shows that seventeenth-century Swedish had a well-developed verbal paradigm and V-to-I movement, and both properties were lost in the subsequent development of the language. Jonas (1996) shows that Faroese, morphologically half-way between insular and continental Scandinavian, with an impoverished but still attested morphological agreement, appears to be in a transitional state as far as V-to-I is concerned, with movement in one variety and lack of movement in another (but see Heycock et al. 2010).[3]

Various linguists have tried to make the notion of 'morphological richness' relevant for the triggering of V-to-I movement precise. One idea has been to calculate richness on the basis of the number of distinct inflectional morphemes in core paradigms: Roberts (1993), Vikner (1995), Rohrbacher (1999). Another idea has been to look at the number of inflectional morphemes which can co-occur: Modern English allows only one morpheme, ruling out the possibility of co-occurrence between distinct tense and agreement morphemes (*call-s, call-ed, *call-ed-s* vs. Italian *parl-av-ano*: Bobaljik 2001). Biberauer and Roberts (2005) also take into account the morphosyntactic differentiations in the tense system. See also Holmberg and Platzack (1995).

The difficulty of identifying a natural threshold of morphological richness systematically holding across languages for the triggering of verb movement has led some researchers to skepticism on the validity of the hypothesis that head movement may be morphologically driven (Ackema 2001, Bobaljik 2002b). Perhaps, inflectional morphological specifications do not cause verb movement; rather, morphology is a reflex, not a cause, of verb movement, which is triggered independently (as Bobaljik argues). In fact, different functional motivations and formal implementations of verb movement have been proposed, quite independently from morphological properties. For instance, Koster (2003) analyzes verb movement in the inflectional space as 'partial movement' of the carrier of T (the inflected verb) to its scope position in the C system, a movement fully implemented in the generalized V-2 languages. Be it as it may, the fact remains that microcomparative studies of Romance and Germanic have uncovered many cases supporting a close syntax-morphology connection of the kind illustrated above. The extension of the scope of such observations to other language groups, as well as the directionality of the causal relation (does morphological richness trigger head movement, or is it just a reflex of verb movement triggered for independent reasons?) remain open issues.[4]

12.5 The splitting of inflection

The distinction between lexical and functional heads in the clausal domain stemmed from various kinds of theoretical and empirical considerations:

(22) a. the idea that structure only arises through the projection of heads, and X-bar schemata are uniform across all kinds of syntactic heads, lexical and functional;
 b. the observation that in some languages tense is expressed by an autonomous function word, providing direct evidence for a functional head of the sentence;
 c. the idea that inflectional morphological affixation could take place in the syntax through head movement;
 d. the necessity of integrating into the structure more elements analyzable as specifiers (subjects, adverbials of various sorts), leading to the identification of distinct positions occupied by the verb across paradigms and languages.

As of the mid-1980s it became clear that the same logic and arguments that motivated the distinction between lexical and functional heads would lead to the postulation of richer functional structures. The first impulse came from Pollock (1989), who observed that a system with a single inflectional head would be insufficient to accommodate the (at least) four different positions that a lexical verb can occupy in French:

(23) a. X_4 ne X_3 pas X_2 complètement *comprendre* la théorie ...
       ne   not   completely   understand the theory ...
   b. X_4 ne X_3 pas *comprendre* complètement X_1 la théorie ...
       ne   not understand completely   the theory ...
   c. X_4 il ne *comprend*   pas X_2 complètement X_1 la théorie
       he ne understands not   completely   the theory
   d. Ne *comprend*-il X_3 pas X_2 complètement X_1 la théorie?
       ne understands he   not   completely   the theory
                                                  (Pollock 1989)

Granting that the infinitival verb can occur in its VP internal position adjacent to its object, as in (23a), the finite verb can raise across the negative element *pas*, as in (23c), and further raise to C in interrogatives like (23d); but the possibility of an additional position for the non-finite verb higher than an adverbial like *complètement* but lower than *pas*, as in (23b), remains unaccounted for. Assuming X_1 to be the basic position of the lexical verb in the VP and X_4 to be C, the node I had to be split at least into the two nodes X_2 and X_3 to accommodate this paradigm (but see Iatridou 1990 for an approach not involving a split Infl). As the verbal inflection typically expresses tense and agreement with the subject, it was natural to assume that the two clausal heads X_2 and X_3 would be labeled T and Agr(eement). Pollock's initial assumption was that the two heads would occur with T on top, but shortly after that proposal, Belletti (1990) gave arguments in favor of the opposite ordering: Agr–T.

It may be argued that the string of verbal prefixes appearing in agglutinative languages like the Bantu languages provides direct evidence for the ordering of the sequence:

(24)   njuchi zi-na-wa-lum-a   alenje   (Chichewa)
       bees   AgrS-Past-AgrO-bite-ASP hunters   (from Baker 1988)

Here the agreement in class with the subject (subject agreement or AgrS) precedes the specification of tense, which in turn precedes other specifications like agreement with the object. In inflectional languages, the tense morpheme, when isolable, occurs closer to the root than agreement, hence the order is root-T-Agr:

(25)   parl-o   parl-av-o   parl-er-ò
       speak-pres-Ips   speak-imp-Ips   speak-fut-Ips
       parl-i   parl-av-i   parl-er(a)-i
       speak-pres-IIps   speak-imp-IIps   speak-fut-IIps
       parl-a   parl-av-a   parl-er-à
       speak-pres-IIIps   speak-imp-IIIps   speak-fut-IIIps

Belletti (1990) argued that this ordering is a consequence of the syntactic ordering Agr T and of the successive association of the affixes to the verbal root through head movement. Starting from

(26) ... [$_{Agr}$ -o] ... [$_T$ -av-] ... [$_V$ parl-] ...

the verbal root first moves to T, creating the intermediate form *parl-av-*, and then proceeds to Agr creating the complex morphological form *parl-av-ano*. In other words, if the order Agr–T is postulated, affixation of the verb in the inflectional space proceeds in accordance with Baker's Mirror Principle:

(27) Mirror Principle: the order of affixes in inflectional morphology reflects the order of syntactic heads (the most internal affix is the lowest one in syntax)   (Baker 1985)

Other agreement projections expressed in the functional structure of the clause were postulated. If nominative case assignment takes place in the high Agreement projection delimiting the IP (AgrS), it was natural to think of accusative case assignment as provided by a lower object agreement (or AgrO) projection, overtly expressed in examples like (24). Kayne (1989a) had provided a groundbreaking analysis of past participle agreement with a moved object in French, on which the subsequent analysis of agreement processes was modeled with the necessary modifications. Participial agreement was initially assimilated to AgrO (Chomsky 1993), but it soon became clear that a distinct Agr projection had to be postulated, specifically associated to the aspectual properties expressed by the participial morphology. See Belletti (2001a) for a general assessment of agreement projections in the clausal structure.[5]

12.6 Cartographic projects

Around the mid-1980s, syntactic studies had assumed clausal representations like the following, based on the idea that all categories are headed and uniform X-bar schemata are projected by both lexical and functional elements.

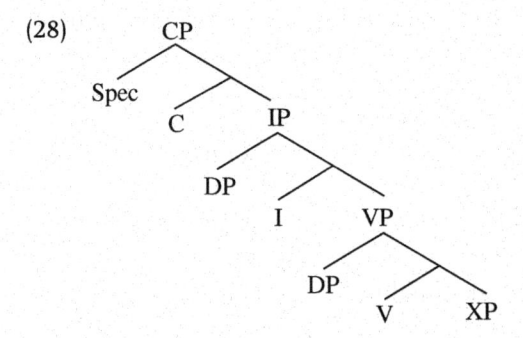

(28)

```
          CP
         /  \
      Spec   \
              C   IP
                 /  \
                DP   \
                    I   VP
                       /  \
                      DP   \
                          V   XP
```

The splitting of the inflectional space, linked to a systematic syntacticization of inflectional morphology and a renewed attention to adverb syntax, determined a very fast growth of the assumed functional structure. It was as if new analytic energies had suddenly been liberated by the demonstration that one could go beyond representations with heads restricted to concrete words, and it was possible and profitable to identify syntactic entities at a finer level of granularity. Researchers were fascinated by the explanatory results made possible by the splitting of words and inflections, and also puzzled by the fact that the new trend gave the impression of an ever-increasing complexity of syntactic representations: Where would one find the bedrock of primitive syntactic elements?

The aim of drawing realistic maps of syntactic structures, doing justice to the richness and articulation of syntactic representations, gave rise to the cartographic projects. One initial leading idea was to try to complement the trend of bottom-up, problem-related discovery of the functional structure which had started with Pollock (1989) with a more top-down, global perspective, trying to make a rough estimate of the upper limit of the structural complexity (as in Rizzi 1997 for the CP system, Cinque 1999 for the IP system; see Cinque & Rizzi 2010a for a general overview of this line of research and the main empirical results).

The fundamental guideline of cartographic studies is that syntactic representations are locally simple, ideally in a rather radical sense:

(29) Some guidelines:
- simple heads: one (morphosyntactically relevant) property is expressed by one feature, which in turn defines one functional head;
- simple projections: a head can take a single complement (because of binary branching: Kayne 1984) and a single specifier: no adjunction, no multiple Specs, no multiple complements.

Such guidelines do not preclude the possibility of complex heads expressing conglomerates of properties, such as verbs inflected for tense, agreement, and other properties, nouns carrying number, gender, and case morphology, etc.; but such complex entities do not come out already assembled from the lexicon, they are assembled through the syntactic operation of head movement. If the elementary heads that enter into syntactic computations are simple, the assembly of their projections also respects basic principles of simplicity and uniformity. Adjunction to a maximal projection, an operation hard to tease apart from movement to a specifier position (Kayne 1994), should ideally be dispensed with. Multiple complements and multiple specifiers could only arise if more heads were involved, possibly glued together into a single morphological word through head movement.[6]

The guiding assumption then is that syntactic structures respect conditions of optimal local simplicity: complex words and syntactic configurations are created through syntactic computations, with the recursive application of Merge and Move. The optimal satisfaction of local simplicity thus leads to a higher global complexity of syntactic representations, with rich functional structures, reiterated applications of Merge, movement of heads and phrases.

The projects of drawing detailed structural maps started with certain zones of the syntactic tree in Romance and Germanic (Rizzi 1997, 2004c, Cinque 1999, 2002, Belletti, 2004b, 2009) but quickly showed a strong cross-linguistic vocation extending to Finno-Ugric (Puskás 2000), Semitic (Shlonsky 1997), West African (Aboh 2004a), Bantu (Biloa 2008), Creole (Durrleman 2008), East-Asian (Tsai 2007, Endo 2007), Austronesian (Pearce 1999), Classical languages (Salvi 2005), etc.

12.7 Cartography and adverb syntax

The basic cartographic guidelines have immediate consequences for the study of adverb syntax: if phrasal adjunction is not an available option, adverbs must be situated in the Spec position of functional heads. (See Chapter 13 for a more detailed discussion of adverb syntax.)

This is the line pursued with great systematicity in Cinque (1999). One crucial observation is comparative: certain properties of modality, tense, aspect (see Chapter 20), etc., which some languages express through adverb phrases, are expressed in other languages by particles, or by affixes attached to the verb. These seemingly different devices manifest fundamentally uniform properties, Cinque observes: in particular, the order of elements is essentially uniform across languages. An example from Cinque (1999:91) can be provided. In English, habitual (*usually*) and frequentative (*often*) adverbs, similar but not identical in meaning (according to Comrie 1976, 'habitual' describes a situation which is characteristic of an extended period of time, while 'frequentative' indicates the mere repetition of a situation) can co-occur in the fixed order habitual–frequentative:

(30) a. John is usually often obliged to stay home
 b. *John is often usually obliged to stay home

In the Austronesian language Rapanui, the two properties are expressed by aspectual particles *pura* and *vara*, occurring in a fixed order:

(31) Rapanui (Austronesian):
 pura vara tu'u mai a Nau
 HAB FREQ come toward Pers.Sing. Nau
 'Nau usually often comes here'

In the Papuan language Yareba the two properties are expressed by suffixes occurring in the fixed order V-... FREQ-HAB-..., which, by the Mirror Principle, also shows the syntactic order HAB > FREQ:

(32) Yareba (Papuan):
yau - r   - edib - eb - a - su
sit   CM   FREQ HAB PRES 3ms
'he habitually repeatedly sits down'

Cinque straightforwardly captures the cross-linguistic generalization in the following way. The functional structure of the clause includes projections for habitual and frequentative aspects in a fixed order:

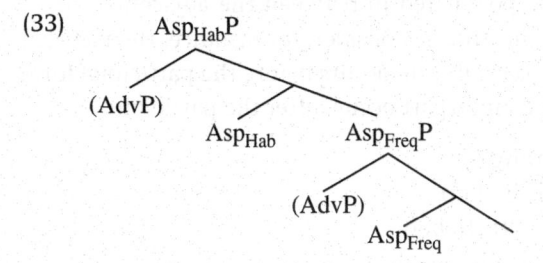

(33)
```
          Asp_Hab P
         /        \
     (AdvP)        \
              Asp_Hab   Asp_Freq P
                       /         \
                   (AdvP)         \
                              Asp_Freq
```

Some languages (English) do not overtly express such aspectual heads, and the properties may be expressed by appropriate adverbials occurring in the respective Spec positions; other languages (Rapanui) overtly realize the heads through aspectual particles; other languages (Yareba) express the two aspectual heads as suffixes, which end up occurring on the inflected verb in the mirror image of their syntactic order, under the Mirror Principle.

In conclusion, Cinque argues, there is a uniform hierarchy of aspectual heads as in configuration (33), which may be expressed in rather different forms in different languages according to the particular morphological choices of the language, which may opt for no head marking at all (in which case the interpretive properties may be express by adverbials occurring in the respective Spec positions), or head marking as particles or affixes.

Cinque then extends and generalizes this line of reasoning from aspectual properties to properties of modality, tense, mood (see Chapter 20), and voice, thus arriving at a single universal hierarchy in which the functional structure of clauses is organized. The hierarchy is illustrated by (mostly) English adverbs in what follows (for further refinements see Cinque 2006, which uses the functional structure for a novel analysis of restructuring phenomena):

(34) [*Frankly* Moodspeech act [*fortunately* Moodevaluative [*allegedly* Moodevidential [*probably* Modepistemic [*once* T(Past) [*then* T(Future) [*perhaps* Moodirrealis [*necessarily* Modnecessity [*possibly* Modpossibility [*willingly* Modvolition [*inevitably* Modobligation [*cleverly* Modability/ permission [*usually* Asphabitual [*again* Asprepetitive(I) [*often* Aspfrequentative(I) [*quickly* Aspcelerative(I) [*already* T(Anterior) [*no longer* Aspterminative [*still* Aspcontinuative [*always* Aspperfect(?) [*just* Aspretrospective [*soon* Aspproximative [*briefly* Aspdurative

[*characteristically* (?) [? Asp_{generic/progressive} [*almost* Asp_{prospective} [*completely* Asp_{completive(I)} [*tutto* Asp_{PlCompletive} [*well* Voice [*fast/early* Asp_{celerative(II)} [*completely* Asp_{SgCompletive(II)} [*again* Asp_{repetitive (II)} [*often* Asp_{frequentative(II)} ...

In some cases, it is possible to give straightforward evidence for the idea that adverbials indeed are in the Spec of dedicated heads rather than simply adjoined to particular projections in a fixed order: through a careful comparative study of closely related varieties, it is sometimes possible to show that head positions must be postulated in between the adjacent pairs of adverbials occurring in specific orders. Consider, for instance, the fact that in French the sequence *tout bien* 'all well' occurs before the participial form of the verb, while its Italian counterpart occurs after the participle:

(35) a. Jean a   tout bien rangé
       Jean has all   well tidied up
     b. Gianni ha sistemato tutto bene
       Gianni has tidied up all   well

In Cinque's analysis the fixed order between *tout* and *bien*, *tutto* and *bene* follows from the fact that the two elements occur in the Specs of two strictly ordered functional projections, completive aspect and voice, respectively.

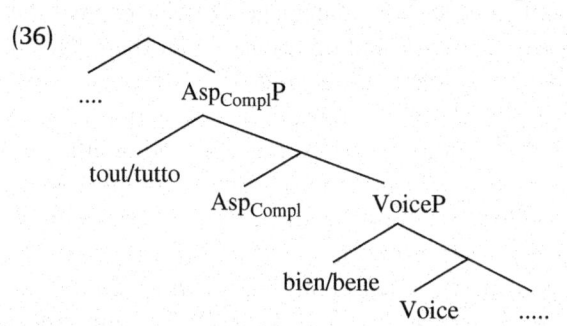

(36)

```
        ....   Asp_Compl P
              /        \
         tout/tutto
                Asp_Compl    VoiceP
                           /        \
                      bien/bene
                                Voice   .....
```

In Italian the participial verb raises to a higher functional head, while in French it remains in Voice, or in an even lower position (Guasti and Rizzi 2002 suggest that this difference may be related to the different morphological realization of participial agreement, more robust in Italian than in French). Cinque also shows that there is a language splitting the *tutto bene* sequence, while keeping the ordering of the two elements constant. In Logudorese Sardinian the past participle must be higher than *bene*, while it may remain lower than *tutto*, or move past it:

(37) a. apo mandigadu bene (*bene mandigadu)
       'I have eaten well'
                                    (Logudorese Sardinian; Cinque 1999:46)
     b. apo tottu mandigadu (mandigadu tottu)
       'I have eaten all'

In terms of (36), the participial form in Logudorese can then remain in Asp$_{Compl}$, or move to a higher position. If each adverbial element sits in the specifier of an independent dedicated head, the intermediate case of Logudorese, in between French and Italian, is immediately expected: the same structure (36) is common to the three languages, and what varies is the position of the verbal element: lower than the subsequence (36) in French, higher than (36) in Italian, while in Logudorese the verbal element can stop in the intermediate Asp position. If *tutto* and *bene* were adjoined to a single projection in a fixed order in a more impoverished structural representation, a case like Logudorese would require a substantially different analysis, while it is immediately expected and integrated in a uniform analysis given (36).

Cinque's approach has raised a very lively debate, with different viewpoints expressed on the nature of adverbial positions and the ordering constraints (see Nilsen 2003, and Cinque's rensponses to various critical appraisals in Cinque 2004; see also Cinque and Rizzi 2010a for a general assessment). A critical feature of his approach is that it has the capacity to express in a straightforward manner the uniform order of elements emerging from the comparative study, the variation in morphological means notwithstanding. One important issue that this approach raises (as much as any alternative) is the determination of the ultimate roots of the universal functional hierarchy. It is hard to see much of an alternative to the conjecture that the ordering must be grounded in the semantics of tense, mood, aspect, and the other functional specifications of the clause, in ways that are not, at the moment, well understood. In a system like (34), such properties should be naturally expressible as s-selectional (semantic selectional; Grimshaw 1979) requirements of the system of functional heads involved.

The respective ordering of two adverbials can be straightforwardly determined in many cases, such as (30) or (35). In other cases things may be more difficult because independent reasons may prevent the co-occurrence of the two adverbials. Suppose, for instance, that we intend to determine whether *pas*, the adverb expressing clausal negation in French, occupies the same position as other negative adverbials such as *plus* (anymore). Both possible orders are in fact ungrammatical:

(38) a. *ils   n'ont   pas   plus   téléphoné
         they ne have not   anymore telephoned
     b. *ils   n'ont   plus   pas   téléphoné
         they ne have anymore not   telephoned

It could be that *pas* and *plus* compete for the same position; alternatively, their co-occurrence could be prohibited for some independent reason. A good independent reason in fact exists in this case: *pas* cannot co-occur with other negative quantifiers (except marginally to express contradictory negation), i.e., it does not enter into negative concord (Haegeman

1995, Haegeman and Lohndal 2010; see Chapter 21), a property which could independently exclude its co-occurrence with *plus*, even if the two elements occupied distinct positions:

(39) *Jean n'a pas vu personne
   'Jean has not seen nobody'

Cinque (1999:5) argues that in such cases one can establish the order indirectly: if one can establish that A precedes B, and B precedes C, one can conclude by transitivity that A precedes C, even if A and C cannot co-occur for independent reasons. A third element permitting us to implement this reasoning in the case at issue is the adverb *déjà* 'already,' which necessarily follows *pas* and precedes *plus*:

(40) a. si tu n'as *pas déjà* (*déjà pas*) mangé, tu peux le prendre
      'if you have not already eaten, you can take it'
   b. a l'époque, il ne possédait *déjà plus* (*plus déjà*) rien
      'at the time, he already didn't possess anything any longer'

Through transitivity, *pas* < *déjà*, *déjà* < *plus*, therefore *pas* < *plus* (where '<' denotes 'precedes'). Independent evidence for this conclusion, Cinque shows, is provided by the comparison with Italian *mica*. This negative adverbial is akin to *pas* in that it also expresses sentential negation (irrelevantly for the current argument, with an added presuppositional flavor[7]), but it is consistent with another negative quantifier, with which it enters into negative concord:

(41) non ho mica visto nessuno
   'I haven't *mica* seen no one'

And in fact, *mica* can co-occur with Italian *più* 'anymore' in the fixed order *mica* < *più*:

(42) Gianni non ha mica più (*più mica) telefonato
   'Gianni hasn't *mica* anymore telephoned'

So, Italian straightforwardly shows the ordering which cannot be seen directly in French, but can be indirectly argued to hold in this language as well.

Independent evidence of a different kind, and internal to French, for the ordering *pas* < *plus* is provided by the interaction with verb movement, Cinque shows. In contemporary French, a lexical verb cannot raise past *pas* (such examples are still found in Voltaire's French):

(43) a. *ne dormir pas
         ne sleep   not
   b. ne pas dormir
         ne not sleep

On the other hand, the lexical verb can optionally raise past *plus* :

(44) a. ne dormir plus
    ne sleep anymore
  b. ne plus dormir
    ne anymore sleep

This straightforwardly follows if *plus* occupies a position lower than *pas*, and the infinitive verb can move past *plus*, while it cannot reach the head position higher than *pas* (presumably corresponding to the position which carries agreement in the finite paradigm) :

(45) [_ [pas _ [plus ... dormir]]]
      ↑   ↑_____|
      *   OK

Notice that this argument, just as the one based on (36)–(37), requires that adverbials do not simply pile up adjoined to projections in a fixed order: they must be specifiers of independent functional heads which may be targeted by verb movement, otherwise there would be no room for verb movement stopping in between two ordered adverbials in cases like (36) and (43)–(44). So these analyses provide support for the 'simple projections' guideline of the cartographic projects.[8]

12.8 The cartography of the left periphery: the Force-Fin system

The traditional approach to the complementizer system assumed a single X-bar layer headed by C. Elementary distributional considerations suggest that this view is oversimplified (see also Chapter 11): different 'complementizer-like' elements clearly occupy distinct structural positions. For instance, prepositional complementizers introducing control infinitives like *di* in Italian, *de* in French, etc. are considered the non-finite counterpart of finite complementizers (Kayne 1984: Chapter 5):

(46) a. ho deciso che partirò
       'I decided that I will leave'
    b. ho deciso di partire
       'I decided *di* to leave'

Nevertlesess, *che* and *di* occupy different positions with respect to a topic in the Clitic Left Dislocation construction (on which see below). *Che* necessarily precedes the topic, while *di* follows it:

(47) a. ho   deciso che, a Gianni, gli   parlerò domani
       (I) have decided that to Gianni (I) to-him will-speak tomorrow
       'I decided that, to Gianni, I will speak tomorrow'

b. ho deciso, a Gianni, di parlargli domani
      'I decided, to Gianni, *di* to speak tomorrow'

Could it be that *di* should be reanalyzed as being part of the inflectional system, rather than of the complementizer system? No, there are good reasons supporting the classical analysis of *di* as a complementizer: for instance it is incompatible with a *wh*-element, much as other bona fide complementizers (the Doubly-Filled COMP effect[9]).

(48) a. ho deciso di partire
        'I decided *di* to leave'
     b. ho deciso dove andare
        'I decided where to go'
     c. * ho deciso dove di andare
        'I decided where *di* to go'

Moreover, while *di* typically occurs with control, it is inconsistent with raising, as other manifestations of the C system typically are (e.g., raising is typically impossible from indirect questions, which require a C system; on control and raising, see Chapter 16). Both cases are illustrated with *sembrare* 'seem' which takes both control complements (introduced by *di*, with the dative experiencer acting as the controller) and raising complements (bare):

(49) a. Gianni sembra [t essere stanco]
        'Gianni seems to be tired'
     b. mi sembra [di [PRO essere stanco]]
        'it seems to me to be tired = It seems to me that I am tired'
     c. * Gianni sembra [di [t essere stanco]]
        'Gianni seems to be tired'

So the classical analysis that looks upon *di, de,* etc. as non-finite complementizers (Kayne 1984) seems to be well substantiated. But if this is correct, (47) shows that *di* is a complementizer occurring in a position distinct from, and lower than, the finite complementizer.

In the system first presented in Rizzi (1997) it is proposed that the complementizer system is a rich structural zone delimited by two heads and their projections: the upward delimitation is provided by Force, expressing the illocutionary force, or, more neutrally, the clausal type (as in Cheng 1991) of the sentence. Force expresses the information that a higher selector needs: whether the sentence is a declarative, or an interrogative, or an exclamative, etc. The downward delimitation is provided by Fin(iteness), a head expressing the finite or non-finite character of the clause. The space delimited by Force and Fin can be used to host positions dedicated to expressing properties of scope and discourse semantics: the scope of interrogative, relative, exclamative, comparative, etc. operators, and positions dedicated to discourse-related properties such as topicality and focus (on scope, see Chapter 22; on discourse functions, see

Chapter 23). Often, only one of the two positions is lexicalized. In finite clauses in Romance and Germanic, Force is typically lexicalized by elements such as *che, que, that, dass, dat, at*, etc. (with Fin lexicalized by the prepositional complementizers *di, de*, etc. in Romance, *for* in English, etc.). In Irish the element translated as 'that', *go*, apparently lexicalizes Fin, hence it follows left-peripheral material, such as the preposed adverbial in (50):

(50) is doíche   [faoi cheann cúpla lá [go bhféadfaí imeacht]]
      is probable at-the-end-of couple day that could   leave
                                                    (Irish: McCloskey 1996)

Roberts (2004) argues that in Welsh both Force and Fin may be lexicalized by separate particles, *mai* and *a*, which surround the string of topics, foci, and preposed adverbials, as in

(51) dywedais i [mai 'r dynion fel arfer a [werthith y ci]]
      said   I C the men as usual C will-sell the dog
                                                    (Welsh: Roberts 2004)

Both heads may occasionally be simultaneously filled also in other languages, e.g., in embedded Verb Second configurations such as embedded negative inversion in English (52) ('residual Verb Second' in this case), in which *that* expresses the declarative force, and the modal moves across the subject to Fin (and possibly to a higher Foc position).

(52) John said [that [in no case would [he do that]]]

12.9 Some interpretive and formal properties of topic and focus

The space delimited by Force and Fin contains positions dedicated to properties of scope-discourse semantics: different kinds of operators taking scope over the clause, and positions expressing informational properties and relevant for the organisation of discourse: *in primis*, topic (typically expressed in Romance by the Clitic Left Dislocation construction: Cinque 1990b) and left-peripheral focus (a position which is specialized for contrastive focus in Romance, hence typically involving a final negative tag expressing the contrast, and inconsistent with a resumptive clitic, which is required by the topic with direct objects).

(53) a. il suo libro, lo dovresti leggere   (Topic–Comment)
         'his book, you should read it'
      b. IL SUO LIBRO dovresti leggere, non il mio (Focus–Presupposition)
         'HIS BOOK you should read, not mine'

Topic and focus constructions are characterized by special properties at the interfaces with sound and meaning. At the former interface, they are marked by special prosodic contours which make them easily detectable from the speech signal (for a recent discussion see Bocci 2009; see also Chapter 23). At the interface with semantics and pragmatics, topic and focus are key ingredients for the expression of informational properties. They are connected, respectively, to given and new information, in ways that may be complex and partially variable across languages.[10]

The interface properties of topic and focus can be highlighted by creating mini-discourse contexts and checking the appropriateness of the different constructions. Consider for instance the fact that the new information in a question–answer pair cannot be expressed by a topic, as in (54)A':

(54) Q: Che cosa hai dato a Gianni?
'What did you give to Gianni?'
A. gli ho dato il tuo libro
'I gave to him your book'
A': # il tuo libro, glielo ho dato
'your book, I gave it to him'

On the other hand, a topic can take up the information given in the question, and make it prominent (most naturally if there is a choice to be made in the set of the given referents, as is explicitly required by the parenthesized part of the question in the following dialogue):

(55) Q: Che cosa hai fatto col mio libro? (e con quello di Piero?)
'What did you do with my book? (and with Piero's?)'
A: il tuo libro, lo ho dato a Gianni (quello di Piero non lo ho più visto)
'your book, I gave it to Gianni (Piero's I haven't seen it anymore)'

So the topic is an element selected from the presupposed, background information and made prominent (see C. Roberts 2010 on the interpretive properties of topics):

(56) "Among the elements of the background, I select X (Topic) and tell you about it that Y (Comment)"

As for focus, in Standard Italian (and many Romance languages and dialects), the left-peripheral focal position cannot correspond to simple new information focus, which is normally expressed in sentence-final position; rather, it expresses new information which somehow falls outside the range of natural expectations, with which it is contrasted. For instance, it can be felicitously used to correct a previous statement:

(57) A: so che ieri hai letto un articolo per preparare l'esame ...
'I know that yesterday you read an article to prepare for the exam ...'
B: Scherzi ? UN LIBRO ho dovuto leggere (non un articolo).
'You kiddin'? A BOOK I had to read, not an article.'

Contrastive focus in this sense strongly invites a negative tag, explicitly denying the "natural expectation" (in cases like (57B), correcting the previous statement); new information focus does not normally occur with (and certainly does not require) a negative tag excluding alternatives.

There is a parameterization here: the Sicilian dialect (and the regional varieties of Italian spoken in Sicily and other southern regions) uses a clause-initial position also for new information focus (Cruschina 2008):

(58) A: Chi scrivisti? (Sicilian)
'What did you write?'
B: n'articulu scrissi
'an article I wrote'

Foci can be definite or indefinite. In fact, focus is new information in a relational sense: what is new is not (necessarily) the referent of the focused element (which may well be very prominent in the previous discourse), but the fact that it participates with that particular theta role in the event that is described. Consider for instance the following modification of (57):

(59) a. so che hai dovuto leggere due capitoli dell'ultimo libro del Prof per preparare l'esame ...
'I know that you had to read two chapters of the professor's latest book to prepare for the exam ...'
b. Scherzi ? TUTTO IL LIBRO ho dovuto leggere.
'You kiddin'? THE WHOLE BOOK I had to read.'

Here the professor's book is prominent from the context, and the new information is that the whole book is the patient of *read*. So, a definite focus is perfectly natural (see also Section 12.10 for a larger comparative perspective on these notions).

12.10 The criterial approach to topic, focus and scope-discourse semantics

In this section I would like to focus on a particular approach to scope-discourse semantics which fits well with the cartographic perspective illustrated in the previous sections. In much current work in theoretical syntax, A' movement has a clear functional motivation: it is a way to express properties of scope-discourse semantics in configurational terms (see also Section 3.3.3). More precisely, an A′ chain is a way to associate two kinds of interpretive properties to an element: properties of argumental semantics (theta-roles for arguments or, more generally, s-selectional properties), and properties of scope-discourse semantics (Chomsky 2004), the scope of operators, topicality, and focus. So, in a question like *which book did you read?*, the expression *which book* is interpreted both as the thematic patient of *read*, and as a *wh*-operator with scope over the main clause, hence yielding a main interrogative.

How is a given position characterized as 'dedicated' to a particular scope-discourse property? One view that is particularly congenial to the cartographic projects is the so-called criterial approach (Rizzi 1991/1996, 1997). According to it, scope-discourse properties are expressed by dedicated functional heads, which assign to their dependents interpretive roles such as topicality, focus, etc. (much as thematic properties are assigned by lexical elements to their dependents). So, a question, a topic–comment and a focus–presupposition sentence would have the following representation, with a functional head of the appropriate quality mediating a specifier (the *wh*-operator, the topic, the focus) and a complement (the scope domain, the comment, the presupposition, respectively):

(60) a. Which book   Q   should you read <which book>?
     b. this book   TOP   you should read <this book>
     c. THIS BOOK   FOC   you should read <this book>

Such a structural approach to scope-discourse semantics is supported by the fact that in some languages the system of criterial heads is overtly expressed by specific particles. So, Q can be realized as *of*, the same particle designating yes/no-questions in certain Dutch varieties, as in (61a), and many languages use overt particles marking topic and focus, such us *yà* and *wè*, respectively, in the West African language Gungbe:

(61) a. ik weet niet [wie *of* [Jan ___ gezien heeft]]
        I know not   who Q   Jan   seen   has
                                          (Dutch varieties: Haegeman 1996)
     b. ùn sè [dò [dàn   ló *yà* [Kòfi hù   ì]]] (Gungbe Aboh 2004a)
        I heard that snake the TOP Kofi killed it
     c. ùn sè [dò [dàn   ló *wè* [Kòfi hù ___]]] (Gungbe Aboh 2004a)
        I heard that snake the FOC Kofi killed

It seems natural to make the working hypothesis that in all languages such positions are structurally expressed by functional heads, which in some languages are overt and in other languages lack a morphological and phonetic content, a low level parameterization. Topic and focus structures can then be assumed to involve the following syntactic configurations, triggering the interpretive routine indicated under each elementary tree:

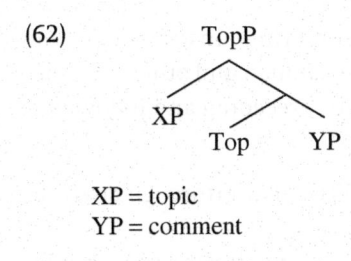

(62)
```
         TopP
        /    \
       XP    /  \
            Top  YP
```
XP = topic
YP = comment

(63) 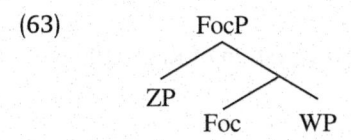
```
         FocP
        /    \
       ZP    /  \
            Foc  WP
```
ZP = Focus
WP = Presupposition

It is important here to disentangle two related but distinct issues which arise in the study of the interface between syntax and pragmatics. One has to do with the question whether there are structurally defined positions which are interpreted at the interface as expressing certain discourse-related functions. The other issue relates to the nature of the syntactic labels of the dedicated heads and projections. Such representations as (60)–(63) assume labels that transparently express the relevant discourse function. Other approaches (for instance, the recent proposal of López 2009), while accepting the view that syntax expresses dedicated positions for given discourse functions, assume a system of syntactic heads which are interpretively opaque, but can be associated to interpretively transparent features. In fact, the very first (pre-cartographic) version of the criterial approach (Rizzi 1991/1996) was phrased in such terms, with an interpretively opaque C head which could be specified by interpretively transparent features such as +wh (or +Q), etc. The advent of richer cartographic representations made it possible to directly postulate a system of interpretively transparent heads. Essentially the same development took place in the study of the clausal structure, with the splitting of an interpretively opaque inflectional head into interpretively transparent heads expressing tense, mood, aspect, etc.

It should be clear that the view embodied in such representations as (60)–(63) is controversial: different viewpoints on the informationally opaque or transparent character of syntactic representations are expressed, e.g., in López (2009) and Cinque and Rizzi (2010a). In the remainder of this section I will continue to adopt the transparent view, which is supported by languages in which special morphemes express the relevant heads, as in (61); but it should be borne in mind that the issue is very much the focus of current theoretical debate (a detailed defense of the transparent view is offered in Rizzi 2010).

Criterial positions can co-occur, respecting ordering constraints that can vary to some extent from language to language. Italian and other Romance languages permit a multiplicity of topics, both preceding and following a unique focus position:

(64) credo che, nella riunione di oggi, QUESTO, al direttore, gli dovreste dire, non qualcos'altro
'I believe that in today's meeting, THIS, to the director, you should say, not something else'

So we have the following representation, in the system of Rizzi (1997):

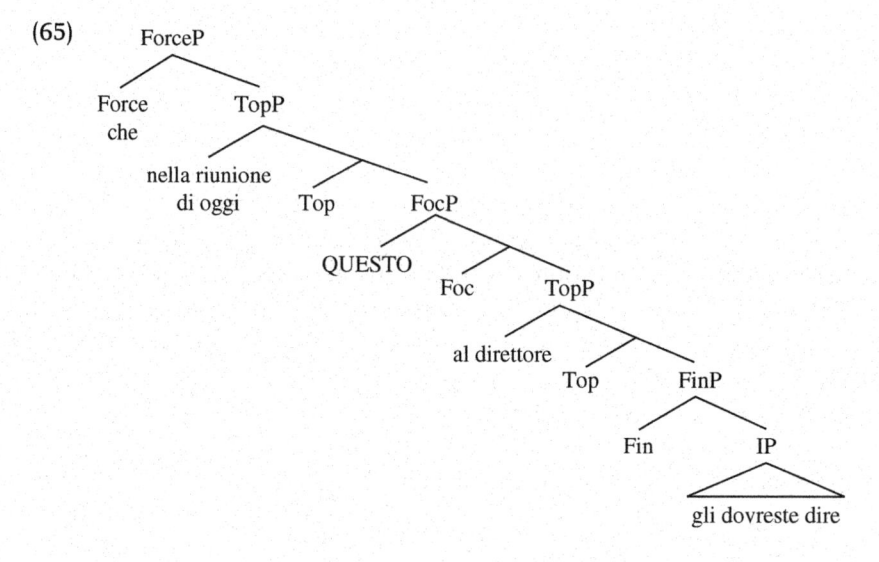

(65)
```
        ForceP
       /      \
    Force     TopP
    che      /    \
      nella riunione
         di oggi   \
                  Top   FocP
                       /    \
                   QUESTO    \
                           Foc   TopP
                                /    \
                         al direttore \
                                     Top   FinP
                                          /    \
                                        Fin    IP
                                              /  \
                                         gli dovreste dire
```

Subsequent work has suggested that it is possible to introduce a finer typology of topics, with distinct interpretive properties correlated to distinct topic positions. Benincà and Poletto (2004) isolate 'scene setting' topics (introducing the scene in which the event takes place), typically higher than other topics; Frascarelli and Hinterhölzl (2007), Bianchi and Frascarelli (2009) distinguish between 'aboutness,' 'contrastive,' and 'familiarity' topics, the latter being restricted to the lower topic position.

The exploitation of the left periphery for scope-discourse can vary across languages as a function of various constraints and parameterizations. For instance, generalized Verb Second languages such as German normally admit a single left-peripheral specifier (topic, or focus, or a preposed adverbial, or the local subject) as a function of the V2 constraint.[11]

A rather common pattern in non-V2 languages is illustrated by Gungbe, which admits the fixed order topic–focus, with both topic and focus unique:

(66) ... dò   Kòfí yà   gànkpá mè wè   kpònòn   lé sú - ì   dó
      ... that Kofi Top PRISON IN Foc policemen Pl shut him there
                                                    (Gungbe: Aboh 2004a)

Two parametric properties seem to distinguish the topic system of a language like Gungbe from the Italian/Romance system: on the one hand, topic is recursive in Italian (i.e., a Top head can select a TopP), and unique in Gungbe; on the other hand, a topic position lower than Focus is possible in Italian but excluded in Gungbe (and in many other languages: Haegeman 2010).

Other cross-linguistically variable co-occurrence restrictions between left-peripheral elements are found. For instance, in Hungarian the Top layer seems to be contingent upon the presence of a lower Foc layer (or on a lower layer hosting a quantifier), a constraint which is satisfied in (67a), but not in (67b) (Puskás 2000; see also Brody 1990, É. Kiss 1987):

(67) a. Attilát   EMŐKE   szereti
        Attila-ACC EMŐKE-NOM loves
     b. *Attilát   Emőke   látta az esküvő előtt
        Attila-ACC Emőke-NOM saw the wedding before

Such cross-linguistic differences appear to be expressible as parameterized selectional properties of the left-peripheral heads.

While the uniqueness or recursive character of topics apparently is a matter of parameterization, a left peripheral focus seems to be unique systematically:

(68) a. a Maria, il tuo libro, glielo devi date
        'to Maria, your book, you should give it to her'
     b. *a MARIA (,) IL TUO LIBRO devi dare (non a Giulia, il disco)
        'to Maria your book you should give, not to Giulia the record'

In fact, structures like (68b) could be excluded for principled reasons. Consider the interpretive routine associated with focus (63): the complement of the Foc head is interpreted as the presupposition; if the Foc projection was recursive, we would inevitably end up with the lower focus which is internal to the presupposition of the higher focus, and this would give rise to an interpretive clash.[12] If this is right, Foc recursion may well be excluded in principle.[13]

12.11 The position of *wh*-interrogatives and the special status of *why*

Interrogative *wh*-operators typically target the Foc projection as their landing site in the left periphery of the clause. Straightforward evidence for this is provided by the fact that in languages with overt focus markers like Gungbe *wh*-elements bear the Foc marker in questions.

(69) Été   wè Séná xìá ___ ?
     What FOC Séna read ___?

The same conclusion can be reached in a more indirect way in languages lacking an overt focus marker. In Italian, *wh*-interrogative elements are incompatible with the activation of a left-peripheral focus, while they can naturally co-occur with a topic:

(70) a. A Gianni, che cosa gli hai detto?
          'To Gianni, what did you say?'
      b. *A GIANNI che cosa hai detto? (non a Piero)
          'To Gianni what did you say? (not to Piero)'

This pattern of incompatibility also follows from the hypothesis that an interrogative *wh*-phrase targets the unique SpecFoc position. This very simple positional analysis requires some auxiliary hypotheses to account for certain differences between contrastive focus and *wh*-constructions. Syntactically, *wh*-elements require inversion (this is true of bare *wh*-elements, while lexically restricted *wh*-elements may occur in uninverted structures, at least marginally), while a contrastive focus is natural, in many varieties of Italian, without inversion:

(71) a. *Che cosa Gianni ha detto?
          'What Gianni said?'
      b. Che cosa ha detto Gianni?
          'What said Gianni?'

(72) QUESTO Gianni ha detto (non quello che doveva dire)
      'this Gianni said, not what he was supposed to say'

There are differences also at the interface levels: *wh*-questions obviously do not involve any explicit contrastive interpretation, and are not marked by the very salient intonational contour which characterizes contrastive focus.

A standard criterial analysis of the obligatory inversion with questions is the following. The C-system must be endowed with a Q feature for the structure to be properly interpreted as a question. The Q feature is expressed in the IP (under T, or as an independent head in the vicinity of the T head; the reason of this connection between T and Q is not clear at the moment), and this is the defining characteristic of languages with inversion in interrogatives; the movement of the inflected verb, or of a verbal chunk (Rizzi 2006c), across the subject has the effect of endowing the C-system with Q (languages not involving inversion in interrogatives, such as Modern Hebrew or Brazilian Portuguese, presumably have the Q feature/head directly generated in the C-system).[14]

A notable exception to the obligatoriness of inversion is with *wh*-element *perché* (why) and other reason adverbials (*for what reason*, etc.):

(73) a. *Come Gianni ha parlato?
   'How Gianni spoke?'
   b. *Dove Gianni è andato?
   'Where Gianni went?'
   c. Perché Gianni è partito?
   'Why Gianni left?'

Perché can be preceded and followed by a topic, and can be followed (but not preceded) by a focus:

(74) a. A Gianni, perché, queste cose, non gliele avete dette?
   'To Gianni, why, these things, you didn't say them to him?'
   b. Perché proprio QUESTO gli hai detto, e non qualcos'altro?
   'Why exactly THIS did you tell him and not something elese?'
   c. *Proprio QUESTO perché gli hai detto, e non qualcos'altro?
   'Exactly THIS why did you tell him, and not something else?'

These distributional properties suggest that *perché* does not target the same landing site as the other *wh*-elements, Foc. On the basis of this kind of evidence, it is proposed in Rizzi (2001a) that *perché* is externally merged in the Spec of a higher dedicated head, Int(errogative), occurring in a position higher than Focus, and also used for the markers of (embedded) yes/no-questions like Italian *se*, English *if*, etc. If Int, contrary to Foc, is inherently endowed with the Q feature, inversion is not required in this case.

Very different types of evidence can be found across languages for the special status of the equivalent of *why* with respect to other *wh*-elements. Colloquial French allows *wh-in-situ*, but *pourquoi* cannot be naturally left *in situ*, as is expected if it is externally merged directly in the left periphery:

(75) a. Il est parti quand?
   'He left when?'
   b. ?*Il est parti pourquoi?
   'He left why?'

The same kind of evidence comes from the reluctance of *why* to occur *in situ* in multiple questions in English (Lasnik and Saito 1992):

(76) a. Why did you buy what?
   b. ?*What did you buy why?

Kayne and Pollock (1978) observed that *pourquoi* does not naturally license Stylistic Inversion in French. This also follows if the licensing of Stylistic Inversion requires an IP internal variable, as Kayne and Pollock argued:

(77) a. Quand est parti Jean?
   'When left Jean?'
   b. ?*Pourquoi est parti Jean?
   'Why left Jean?'

In Japanese (and Korean) *wh*-elements *in situ* are perturbed by the presence of a quantificational subject, which presumably determines an intervention effect (Relativized Minimality) affecting covert movement to their LF scope position, as in (78a). But Ko (2005a) observes that *naze* 'why' is not affected by a quantificational subject, as in (78b). This is expected if *naze*, contrary to other *wh*-elements, is externally merged already in its scope position in the left periphery (and, irrelevantly, the subject is scrambled past it to obtain the word order in (78b)).

(78) a. *Daremo /Hanako-sika nani-o yoma-nakat-ta no?
 anyone / Hanako only what read-not-past Q
 b. Taroo-sika naze sono hon-o yoma-nakat-ta no?
 Taroo only why that book read-not-past Q

McCloskey (2002, and previous work) observes that in Modern Irish there is a special complementizer, *aL*, signaling A'-movement to its Spec, and another complementizer, *aN*, signaling external merge in its Spec (see also Section 18.10). For instance, the first occurs with relatives with a gap, derived through movement, and the second occurs with resumptive relatives, presumably involving no movement:

(79) a. an ghirseach a ghoid na siogai ___
 the girl aL stole the fairies ___
 'the girl that the fairies stole away ___'
 b. an ghirseach a-r ghoid na siogai i
 the girl aN stole the fairies her
 'the girl that the fairies stole her away'

McCloskey then shows that while other *wh*-adjuncts ('how long', etc.) co-occur with the movement complementizer *aL*, the equivalent of *why* co-occurs with the external merge complementizer *aN*, supporting the hypothesis that no movement is involved in this case:

(80) a. Ca fhad a bhi tu ann?
 how long aL were you there?
 b. Cen fath a-r dhuirt tu sin?
 what reason aN said you that?

In Standard English, *why* requires inversion, which suggests that it is treated like any other *wh*-element.[15] An interesting hint regarding the special status of *why* is offered by language acquisition. Thornton (2008) observes that while obligatoriness of inversion with other *wh*-elements is essentially acquired at the age of three, learners of English continue to systematically produce uninverted sentence with *why* till much later. Thornton also shows that uninverted *why* clauses in child English have properties analogous to Italian *perché* clauses (compatible with a lower focus, a lower topic, etc.). Thornton concludes that the language learner is indeed exploring, for a sizeable period of time, a corner of UG which is not target consistent, but is utilized by a number of adult languages, including Italian. We cannot address here the important question of what internal pressure leads the child to explore so systematically a grammatical option not supported by experience. Suffice it to say, in the present context, that these acquisition data underscore how natural it is to assign a special status to *why* questions, a status which emerges in very different forms in different languages, and is explored by the child even in the absence of supporting evidence.

12.12 Other left-peripheral positions

Adverbials can be preposed to the lower part of the left periphery without giving rise to a proper topic or focus reading or prosody. Moreover, a preposed adverbial differs from a preposed argument in that it does not affect further movement:

(81) a. the book that, tomorrow, I will give to Mary
 b. ??the book that, to Mary, I will give tomorrow

Actually, in certain cases a preposed adverbial has a facilitating effect on movement:

(82) a. * this is the man who I think that will sell his house next year
 b. this is the man who I think that, next year, will sell his house
 c. * this is the man who I think that, his house, will sell next year

(82a) is a familiar case of *that*-trace violation (Taraldsen 1978, Pesetsky 1982a); (82b) shows that a preposed adverbial interpolating between the complementizer and the subject trace alleviates the violation (Bresnan 1977, Culicover 1991): the 'anti-adjacency' (Rizzi 1997) or 'adverb' (Browning 1996) effect. (82c) shows that topicalization of an argument does not have any such ameliorating effect: in fact, quite independently from *that*-trace contexts, movement across an argumental topic gives rise to a degraded result in English (as (81b) shows). For these and other reasons, it is proposed in Rizzi (2004a) that adverbs may be highlighted by being preposed to the Spec of a dedicated head Mod(ifier), located in the lower part of the left-peripheral structure and distinct, formally and interpretively, from Top and Foc (see Rizzi 2009c for an analysis of antiadjacency that capitalizes on the particular position of Mod).

On the opposite, upper side of the periphery, Saito (2010) has recently proposed, building on Plann (1982), that a special head should be identified designating a "paraphrase or report of direct discourse." This special marker is overtly expressed in Spanish indirect questions exhibiting a double complementizer, according to Plann's analysis:

(83) te preguntan que para qué quieres el préstamo
'they ask you that for what you want the loan'

Saito shows that the 'report' head *to* in Japanese can co-occur with the interrogative Force marker *ka* and with *no*, which he interprets as a possible realisation of Fin in Japanese sentences like the following:

(84) Taroo-wa [$_{CP}$ kare-no imooto-ga soko-ni ita (no) ka (to)] minna-ni
     Taroo-TOP he-GEN sister-NOM there-in was *no* *ka* *to* all-DAT
     tazuneta
     inquired
     'Taroo asked everyone *if* his sister was there'   (Saito 2010: (41))

Saito (2010) then arrives at a partial cartography of the Japanese right periphery as in (85a), corresponding to the mirror image (85b) in head-initial languages:

(85) a. ...] Fin] Force] Report]
     b. [Report [Force [Fin ...

The parallelism (which, as far as I can tell, holds independently of whether or not head-final languages are to be analyzed in antisymmetric terms à la Kayne 1994) is further enhanced, Saito observes, by the observation that a sequence of topics can occur in a hierarchical position sandwiched in between Force and Fin, much as in familiar head-initial languages.

12.13 Conclusion

The study of the functional structure of the clause has considerably changed the theoretical and descriptive study of natural language syntax. First, it has renewed the study of the interface between inflectional morphology and syntax, through the systematic implementation of a program which has its roots in *Syntactic Structures* (Chomsky 1957); second, it has drawn new attention to the analysis of adverbs and adverbial positions, which is now fully integrated in the study of the clausal structure; third, it has renewed the study of the interface between syntax and pragmatics, with a detailed analysis of the syntactic positions dedicated to particular discourse-related functions. The structural maps of the different zones of the clause have also provided a model for pursuing on a large scale and on a fully systematic basis the project of a detailed cartography of syntactic structures, also encompassing the other types of phrasal categories (e.g., Cinque, 2002 on DPs, Cinque and Rizzi 2010b on PPs).

Notes

I would like to thank Guglielmo Cinque, Marcel den Dikken, and an anonymous reviewer for very helpful comments on a preliminary version of this chapter.

1. It is plausible to assume that *do* is inserted under Neg, or under the head bearing +Q in interrogatives, as a 'last resort' strategy, i.e., when no functional verb is independently available for the expression of such features as +Neg, or +Q; I will not try to develop here a full analysis of the distribution of *do*-support encompassing emphatic environments, *do* in negative imperatives, etc.
2. That Q (and related specifications) may be expressed in the inflectional space is independently supported by the existence of languages manifesting forms of a special '*wh*-agreement' on the verbal inflection in various *wh*-constructions (Chung 1998).
3. More recent work on dialectal varieties of Continental Scandinavian has led to a reassessment of the issues, while still confirming the strict connection between morphological richness and syntactic behavior. See, e.g., Koeneman and Zeijlstra (2010) and references cited there.
4. It should be noted that the issue of whether or not syntax is driven by the richness of morphology and the existence of two routes, lexical and syntactic, for the association of roots and affixes, are at least partially independent issues. See also Guasti and Rizzi (2002) for related but independent cases in which movement and morphological richness appear to be related.
5. On the position(s) that the subject can occupy in the functional structure, see Cardinaletti (2004), Shlonsky (1997), Rizzi and Shlonsky (2007), and, on subject clitics in dialectal varieties, Poletto (2000), and Manzini and Savoia (2005).
6. The idea that more structure is involved in multiple complement constructions than meets the eye was foreshadowed by much important work on ditransitive constructions: Larson (1988a), Kayne (1984: Chapter 9), Hoekstra (1984), den Dikken (1995). See Chapters 9 and 11 for relevant discussion.
7. The markers of clausal negation can appear at different levels of the functional structure in different languages. For a detailed description, with special reference to Romance varieties, see Zanuttini (1997); and Zeijlstra (2004) and Moscati (2010).
8. It is sometimes proposed in the literature that head movement may not be part of core syntax, and take place in the PF component. This assumption (on which see also Chapter 5, for a negative assessment) may affect the argument given in the text if head movement is seen as a mere (non-structure-preserving) reshuffling of elements in the PF

component. Other versions of head movement as a post-syntactic process (e.g., Chomsky 2001a:37) still maintain that the targeted position is a head position, hence are consistent with the argument above.

9. The effect may hold even more strongly with *di* than with the finite counterpart *che*: many dialectal varieties in Romance and Germanic permit the sequence (equivalent to) *wh – che*, but I am not aware of any variety admitting (the equivalent of) *wh – di*. This may illustrate a genuine difference between the two types of complementizer, but it could also be a consequence of the relative rarity, across varieties, of infinitival questions.

10. On the interface between syntax and discourse, seminal contributions are Erteschik-Shir (2007), Reinhart (1981b, 1997, 2006), Vallduví (1992), and, on focus, Rooth (1992a). See López (2009) for a recent, comprehensive approach to the matter.

11. It is proposed in Rizzi (2006c) that a 'bottleneck' arises in the Fin projection of generalized V2 languages. This restriction allows only one element to escape from the IP and reach its appropriate scope-discourse position in the left periphery. This approach makes it possible to maintain that the left peripheral zone of V2 languages is as richly articulated as in non-V2 languages, and the syntax–pragmatics interface is equally transparent. See Müller and Sternefeld (1993) for an early proposal assuming an articulated periphery in V2; and Grewendorf (2002).

12. One might observe that the lower topic phrase in representations like (65) is part of the presupposition of the contrastive focus. If the lower topic head also defines a topic–comment structure, shouldn't one expect an interpretive clash to arise here as well, with a comment which is in the presupposed part? Evidently, no clash arises in this case, as the structure is fine. One possible line of analysis here could consist in denying that a comment necessarily expresses new information; in fact, a statement articulated as topic–comment can be reiterated, as in the following mini-dialogue:

(i) A: il tuo libro, lo ho letto
 'Your book, I read it'
 B: E' vero, il mio libro. lo hai letto ... (però non ci hai capito niente!)
 'It's true, my book, you read it ... (but you didn't understand a thing!)'

If the association of the comment with new information is typical, but not necessary and absolute, then no interpretive clash is predicted to arise in (65).

13. Belletti (2004a) argues that the functional structure of the clause also includes a 'low periphery,' associated to the *v*P and endowed with

topic and focus positions. Such discourse-related positions then appear to be associated to both phasal categories, in the sense of Chomsky (2001).

14. In embedded contexts, the co-occurrence of Foc and Wh is marginally possible in Italian:

   (i) a *A GIANNI che cosa hanno detto, non a Piero?
       'TO GIANNI what did they say, not to Piero?'
       b ?mi domando A GIANNI che cosa abbiano detto, non a Piero
       'I wonder TO GIANNI what they said, not to Piero'

   Evidently, embedded questions have an additional position to host the wh-operator, lower than Foc. Presumably, a Q head can occur in the left periphery if it is selected by a higher verb:

   (ii) mi domando [A GIANNI Foc [che cosa Q [abbiano detto ___ ___]]]

   The lack of inversion in embedded questions in English can presumably be treated analogously: if Q can be generated in the C system, T to C becomes unnecessary, because the C system is already endowed with Q. If an application of movement is unnecessary, in a system constrained by economy, it is impossible: movement takes place only when it is necessary.

15. Or perhaps, more minimally, that *why* is externally merged in SpecInt in English, too, but Int lacks Q in this language, so that inversion is required.

13

Adverbial and adjectival modification

Artemis Alexiadou

13.1 Introduction

Adjectives and adverbs are generally considered as "highly complex and significantly less studied than other major categories" (McNally and Kennedy 2009:1). These authors reiterate similar such statements found in other recent collections or overviews on related matters (see, e.g., Alexiadou 2002a, Delfitto 2006, the introduction in Lang et al. 2003, and more recently Maienborn and Schäfer 2011). The reason why linguists are intrigued by the behavior of these elements has to do primarily with the puzzles these pose for both syntax and semantics, and the ways these components interact with one another which make it problematic to articulate a comprehensive theory of modification.

In this chapter, I will address some of the issues that have been in the center of the discussion on adjectival and adverbial modification, and point out a number of sources where the reader can find further information on the specific question he/she is interested in. The chapter is structured as follows. Section 13.2 is devoted to a discussion on the lexical status of modifiers. Section 13.3 presents certain distributional and semantic classifications of adjectives and adverbs that have been proposed in the literature. Section 13.4 discusses a number of proposals concerning the licensing of modifiers. Section 13.5 focuses on one influential proposal that adjectives and adverbs are specifiers of designated functional projections and the problems this faces. Section 13.6 concludes.

13.2 Lexical status

Although by now there is a relatively rich literature on adjectives and adverbs, it is surprising that it is still very difficult to come up with a definition of what these elements actually are. Criteria that work for one language prove ineffective for other languages regardless of whether they are syntactic, morphological, or semantic. Perhaps what we could consider a consensus in the literature is the view proposed in, e.g., Croft (1991) and Bhat (1994) that adjectives (and adverbs) are the prototypical modifiers in natural languages.

A first issue concerns the question whether adjectives and adverbs belong to the universal set of lexical categories. For instance, Dixon (1982, 2004) points out that the category of adjectives does not exist in the same way in all languages (see also Croft 1991, Beck 1999). Beck, in particular, shows that languages with few or no adjectives are a typological commonplace and that therefore there is something marked about the adjective class compared with noun or verbs, but cf. Baker (2003).

Attempts have been made to offer a categorial specification of adjectives in terms of binary categorial features [±N/V] (Chomsky 1970a, Déchaine 1993, and others; see Chapter 11). Recently, however, Baker (2003) has emphasized that the standard view of categories is under-developed, and leaves us ill-equipped to do typological work.

(1) illustrates the classification proposed in Chomsky (1970a) in terms of [±N/V] categorial features. The distribution of these features gives the following four major categories:

(1) a. +N, -V = noun
 b. -N, +V = verb
 c. +N, +V = adjective
 d. -N, -V = adposition (preposition and postposition)

Clearly, (1) has nothing to say about adverbs: from this perspective adverbs are not defined as a lexical category.

In a recent study, Baker (2003) argues in detail that from the four elements above only the first three constitute universal lexical categories, the fourth one being functional. Nouns, verbs, and adjectives can be defined as follows: nouns have a referential index, verbs have specifiers/subjects, and adjectives basically lack both these properties. Nothing is said, once again, concerning the characterization of adverbs.

The puzzle about the status of adverbs becomes even more complex once one realizes that these seem to belong to different lexical categories. For instance, they can be related to adjectives, e.g., *hard, fast*, to nouns, e.g., *yesterday* (2a) (see Larson 1985; cf. McCawley 1988), prepositions, e.g., *upstairs, before* (2b) (see Jackendoff 1972), and perhaps even determiners, e.g., *now, there*, etc. (2c) (see Delfitto 2006, Leu 2008).

(2) a. he arrived yesterday
 b. Mary found the book upstairs
 c. he is now receiving a big package

However, the category that adverbs seem to be most related to is that of adjectives. This is so for the following reasons:

(i) In a number of languages adverbs are not morphologically distinct from adjectives:
   (3) a. he is a fast runner
       b. he runs fast

(ii) Very often adverbs are transparently derived from adjectives via the addition of a particular suffix, e.g. -ly in English:
   (4) a. she is a beautiful dancer
       b. she dances beautifully

(iii) Adverbs, as argued explicitly by Jackendoff (1972), seem to have a similar distribution within the clause to the one adjectives have within the noun phrase. Jackendoff observed that exactly like adjectives appear in English between the determiner and the noun, adverbs appear in the clause between the subject and the main verb:
   (5) a. the red book
       b. John often eats rice

In the late 1980s/early 1990s, it was observed that there are a number of closer distributional co-properties common to adjectives and adverbs (see also the discussion in Section 13.5). For instance, in noun phrases containing a derived nominal, the order of prenominal adjectives typically matches that of the adverbs in a clause headed by the corresponding verb. Assuming the hierarchy in (6a) the examples in (6b–f) and (7) below illustrate that the hierarchy among adverbs in the clause is replicated by adjectives in the noun phrase (Valois 1991, Cinque 1999, Alexiadou 1997; here '>' denotes 'higher on the hierarchy than,' which in the linear string translates into precedence).

(6) a. SPEAKER-ORIENTED > SUBJECT-ORIENTED > FREQUENCY > COMPLETION > MANNER
    b. he probably quickly left   speaker-oriented > manner
    c. he cleverly always leaves on time subject-oriented > aspect
    d. he probably cleverly left on time
                                          speaker-oriented > subject-oriented
    e. he probably completely changed his mind
                                          speaker-oriented > aspect
    f. he often completely changed his mind   frequency > completion

(7) a. his probable quick departure
    b. his probable complete change of mind
    c. his clever complete change of mind
    d. his probable quick change of mind

Such remarks have led a number of researchers to assume that adjectives are integrated syntactically in the nominal domain in the same way that adverbs are integrated in the clause, a point I will be discussing in some detail in this chapter, especially in Sections 13.4 and 13.5.

In order to account for the distributional similarities between adjectives and adverbs, and for their differences, Emonds (1985) proposed the following: adverbs have a defective distribution, and this relates to Case Theory. In his analysis, adjectives are case-marked, while adverbials are not, and for this reason they are confined to specific positions (but cf. Larson 1987).

In the more recent literature, and especially in research done within the framework of Distributed Morphology, the perspective on categories differs radically. Specifically, the claim is being advanced that lexical categories as such do not exist as primitives. What used to be considered as lexical items are in a certain sense compositional, as they are put together in the syntactic derivation by combining a categorizing, functional, head and a root, as in (8a) below. Roots have no grammatical category, but they can never appear 'bare'; they must always be categorized by virtue of being in a local relationship with one of the category-defining functional heads, following the assumption in (8b), based on Embick (2010; see also Marantz 1997):[1]

(8) a. [Functional Structure [Root]]
 b. **CATEGORIZATION ASSUMPTION**:
 Roots cannot appear without being *categorized*; Roots are categorized by combining with category defining functional heads.

The most widely discussed categorizing heads are *v*, *n*, and *a*. However, *a* is mostly used as an 'adjectivizer,' leaving again the problem of classification of adverbs without an answer. Can we claim that both adverbial and adjectival affixes realize *a*? If so, what is then the difference between adjectives and adverbs? Does it reduce to differences in distribution, as already assumed in the 1970s and 1980s? From this perspective, the adverb *probably* could be decomposed as in (9), assuming that *-able* realizes *a* (Embick 2010). However, it is not clear how the two *a*-heads differ from one another. One could argue that *-ly* realizes a higher functional head.

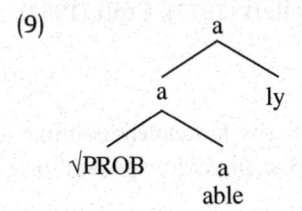

(9)
```
            a
           / \
          a   ly
         / \
      √PROB  a
             able
```

13.3 Distributional and semantic classes of modifiers

For both adjectives and adverbs, a major classification that has been proposed amounts to suggesting that these modify either the lexical layer, mostly, or the functional layer, mostly. For instance, beginning with adverbs, a first classification splits them into predicate operators and sentence operators (Thomason and Stalnaker 1973). This split roughly corresponds to the familiar distinction between VP and S(entence) adverbs. However, it has been pointed out that the classification into VP and S modifiers is not sufficient and that it should be extended in view of the fact that certain adverbs modify V, others modify the VP, others modify units larger than VP but not as large as S, and finally others modify units as large as S.

In the same spirit, McConnell-Ginet (1982) distinguishes three types of adverbs depending on their distribution, which subsume several semantic subtypes. First, there are VP-internal adverbs which operate on the verb before this combines with its arguments (10a); see also the discussion later in this section. These are generally manner adverbs. Second, there are VP-external adverbs which operate on higher predicates that take the VP as their complement. They are instantiated by agent-oriented adverbs (10b). Finally, there are S-adverbs: they operate on the sentence. These are primarily modal (10c) and pragmatic adverbs, e.g. *fortunately*.

(10) a. John wrote the letter carefully
    b. the police intentionally arrested the criminal
    c. probably, John left the room

McConnell-Ginet argued that adverbs of the type in (10a) are semantic arguments of the verb, in that they augment its interpretation, echoing Davidson's (1967) treatment of adjuncts (see also examples (22), and (23) below). In the syntactic literature, this idea finds an implementation in Larson (1988a), where it is argued that (some) adverbs are complements of V (see also Grimshaw and Vikner 1992, and the discussion in Section 13.4.4). VP-internal adverbs belong to the following groups: instrumental modifiers: *with a key*, goal modifiers: *to shore*, benefactives: *for anyone listening*, source modifiers: *from my informants*, and locatives: *on the edge*. One could group all of these under the label circumstantial adverbials.

Different classifications are offered by Laenzlinger (1998) and Ernst (1998), who build on work by Bartsch (1976), Bellert (1977), Croft (1984), and others. These are exemplified below:

(11) a. S-adverbs:
    1. pragmatic adverbs, i.e. evaluative adverbs: *fortunately*; conjunctive adverbs: *however*; formal adverbs: *precisely*; speaker oriented adverbs: *frankly*
    2. domain adverbs: *logically*
    3. modal adverbs: *probably*
    4. subject-oriented adverbs: passive sensitive adverbs: *deliberately*; agent-oriented adverbs: *violently*
    5. event adverbs: time: *yesterday*; location: *here*
    6. aspectual adverbs: frequency: *frequently*; motion: *slowly*

b. VP adverbs:
aspectual adverbs: assertive adverbs: *always*; quantificational adverbs: *much*; degree adverbs: *almost*
circumstantial: verb oriented: *correctly*; object oriented: *entirely*

(12) speech-act: *frankly, honestly, simply*
modal: *probably, maybe, surely*
evidential: *clearly, apparently*
evaluative: *luckily, apparently*

agent-oriented: *politely, stupidly*
mental-attitude: *happily, willingly*
manner: *loudly, tightly*

When we now turn to adjectives, we observe that event/derived nominals are modified by adjectival categories that are related to adverbial classes, e.g., speaker-oriented, subject-oriented, manner, and thematic adjectives (see, e.g., Valois 1991). Moreover, in the context of derived nominals, we also find ambiguities in the adjectival interpretation that are similar to what has been observed for the verbal clause and the adverbial counterparts of the adjectival modifiers. This is briefly illustrated below.

In the Italian examples (13a–b), the adjective *brutale* is ambiguous between two interpretations:[2]

(13) a. la stupida aggressione brutale/italiana all'Albania
 the stupid attack brutal/of-Italy to-the Albania
 the stupid Italian attack on Albania in a brutal manner
 b. la loro brutale aggressione all' Albania
 the their brutal attack in-the Albania
 their brutal attack on Albania

In (13a), the adjective is postnominal and it has a manner-like interpretation. But in (13b), the adjective is prenominal and expresses the speaker's evaluation about the event of attacking ('it was brutal on their part to attack Albania'). This is reminiscent of the pattern in (14): the sentence-final adverb receives a manner interpretation, while the preverbal placement leads to a strong preference for the subject-oriented interpretation:

(14) a. John read the book carefully
 b. John carefully read the book

Matters are different, however, when we turn to (non-derived) object nominals. These are modified by cardinal, ordinal, quality, size, shape, color, and nationality adjectives (see Sproat and Shih 1987, Cinque 1994).

From a semantic point of view, an important classification of modifiers is in terms of intersectivity. In other words, modifiers are classified as being ±intersective. Let me first illustrate this distinction for the domain of adjectives, summarizing crucially Kamp and Partee (1995), and then show how this can be extended to adverbs:

(15) **The intersectivity hypothesis**
Given the syntactic configuration [$_{CNP}$ Adj CNP], the semantic interpretation of the whole is ‖ Adj ‖ ∩ ‖ CNP ‖ (set intersection, predicate conjunction)

An intersective adjective is for instance the adjective *carnivorous*. (16a) has the interpretation illustrated in (16b):

(16) a. a carnivorous mammal
b. ‖ carnivorous mammal ‖ = ‖ carnivorous ‖ ∩ ‖ mammal ‖
{x | x is carnivorous and x is a mammal}

Normally, an adjective that can be interpreted as in (16b) is labeled predicative.

The group of non-intersective adjectives comprises a number of different subtypes. First, we have so-called subsective adjectives, as in (17). The interpretation of (17a) is that *John is good as a lawyer*. This modification says nothing about his qualities as a person.

(17) a. John is a good lawyer
b. ≠ John is good and John is a lawyer
c. = John is good as a lawyer
d. ‖ good N ‖ ⊆ ‖ N ‖

Second, we have adjectives that are neither intersective nor subsective. These are called plain, as they have no entailments at all. An example is given in (18):

(18) a. John is a former senator
b. ≠ John is former and John is a senator
c. = John was formerly a senator
d. ‖ former N ‖ ⊄ ‖ N ‖
e. ‖ former N ‖ ≠ ‖ former ‖ ∩ ‖ N ‖

Finally, there is a fourth group of adjectives that are neither intersective nor subsective. These are labeled privative, as they entail the negation of the noun property. Adjectives such as *fake* are typical examples of this class:

(19) a. fake pistol
b. ≠ this is fake and this is a pistol
c. ‖ fake ‖ ∩ ‖ N ‖ = ∅

Note here that although *fake* can appear in a predicative position, it is clearly non-intersective. This raises the question whether one can equate the ±intersective distinction with the ±predicative one.

It has been pointed out in the literature that several adjectives are ambiguous between an intersective and a non-intersective/subsective interpretation. Consider the following example, based on Bolinger (1967) and Larson (1998a):

(20) a. Olga is a beautiful dancer
      b. Olga is a dancer and [Olga] is beautiful
      c. Olga is beautiful as a dancer

The reading in (20b) is intersective, while the reading in (20c) is non-intersective and subsective. In (20c), the adjective *beautiful* applies to Olga *as a* dancer. To account for these two interpretations, Larson (1998a) proposes that a noun like *dancer* includes in its semantic structure two arguments. The adjective *beautiful*, a predicate, can be predicated either of the event argument *e* or of the external argument (x), in which case the intersective reading arises.[3]

(21) a. an event argument (e) which ranges over events and states;
      b. an argument (x) which is a variable ranging over entities.

Note that the ±intersective distinction often correlates with the type of adjective found within the DP. For instance, most color (*red*) and size (*round*) adjectives are intersective.[4] Qualitative adjectives such as *careful* tend to be subsective. Modal adjectives such as *potential* are plain, and temporal adjectives such as *past* are privative.

Adverbs sometimes allow a similar treatment. Consider example (22), taken from Fromkin et al. (2000:385, their example (35)):

(22) the witches by the cauldron laughed in the forest

In (22), the PP *in the forest* provides a restriction on *laughed* just as the PP *by the cauldron* restricts the set of witches referred to.

In fact, (23) is a similar example going back to Davidson (1967):

(23) Jones buttered the toast in the bathroom with the knife at midnight

According to Maienborn and Schäfer (2011), if Davidson was right and verbs introduce a hidden event argument, then intersective adverbial modifiers can be analyzed as simple first order predicates that add information about this event.

These authors correctly point out that Davidson's proposal accounts for the typical entailment patterns that characterize intersective adverbials directly on the basis of their semantic representation. That is, the entailments in (23'a–d) follow from (23') simply by virtue of the logical rule of simplification.

(23') Jones buttered the toast in the bathroom at midnight
       a. Jones buttered the toast in the bathroom and Jones buttered the toast at midnight
       b. Jones buttered the toast in the bathroom
       c. Jones buttered the toast at midnight
       d. Jones buttered the toast

The data in (22) and (23/23') include VP adverbials, i.e. manner and circumstantial adjuncts. It is rather hard to see how this approach extends to other classes, though see Maienborn and Schäfer (2011) for references. Clearly, S-adverbials such as modal, subject-, and speaker-oriented ones would be analyzed as being non-intersective.

Finally, as was the case with adjectives, adverbs can also be ambiguous between an intersective and a non-intersective interpretation. This was illustrated with example (14) above. On the manner interpretation a restriction is provided on the event of reading; on the subject-oriented one this is not the case.

13.4 Licensing of modifiers

13.4.1 Adjunction

An important issue in syntactic theory is how to best account for the integration of modifiers into the domain these modify (see also Chapters 10, 12). Generally, the representations in (24) are taken to illustrate the relationship of modification. In both examples, a modifying expression, an adjective and an adverb respectively, is adjoined to the phrase it modifies:

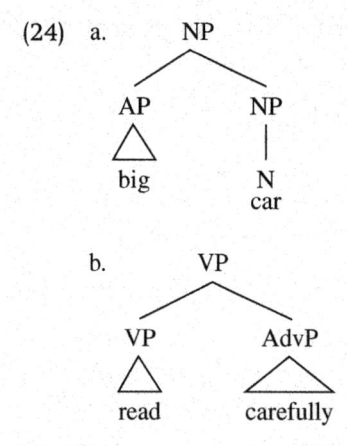

(24) a. NP
         ╱ ╲
        AP   NP
        △ |
       big   N
             car

b. VP
    ╱ ╲
   VP   AdvP
   △   △
  read carefully

Modifiers are not selected by the NP or VP they modify, and their category is not determined by the element heading the NP or the VP. In syntactic theory, in order to integrate modifiers into the structure, the mechanism of adjunction (left or right) was created. Standardly, adjuncts are assumed to adjoin to the maximal projection (Chomsky 1986a), and are generally considered as satellites to it, since they are not obligatory.

In most versions of the Principles and Parameters theory, a clear distinction is made between adjuncts and specifiers (see Section 2.4.2). In particular, given the abstract representation in (25), X indicates the head of the constituent XP. The head X combines with a constituent, ZP, which is referred to as the complement of X. The combination of X and its complement is X', the intermediate projection of X. X' combines with another constituent, YP, referred to as a specifier, to form XP, the maximal projection.

(25)
```
        XP
       /  \
     YP    X'
 [specifier] / \
            X   ZP
          [head] [complement]
```

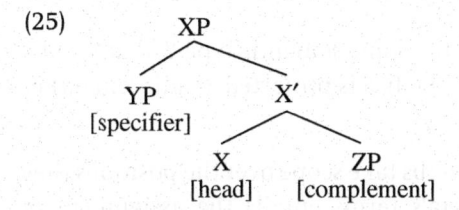

As mentioned above, phrases can be added to XP through adjunction. For instance, adjunction of WP to XP creates an additional projection of the same category and bar-level, as in (26).

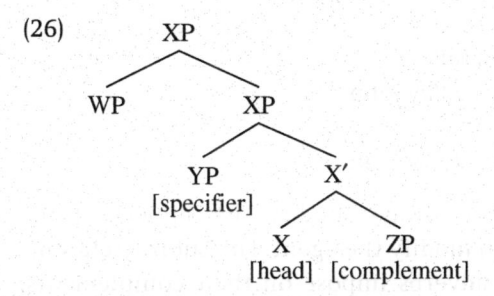

(26)
```
          XP
         /  \
       WP    XP
            /  \
          YP    X'
      [specifier] / \
                 X   ZP
              [head] [complement]
```

With the introduction of adjunction into the theory of phrase structure the problem arose how one can restrict it. Kayne (1994) proposed that there is no difference between specifiers and adjuncts, in fact all specifiers are adjuncts to XP and each phrase can have only one specifier (see Section 12.6).

In Chomsky (1995c), the distinction between adjuncts and specifiers is preserved; however, it becomes clear that the definition of adjuncts is not a straightforward matter (see Section 4.2.4.2). On the other hand, several researchers (see, e.g., Lebeaux 1988 and more recently Uriagereka 2002) have suggested that adjuncts are in their (own) dimension. Specifically, they are added derivationally without ever being attached to the phrase marker.

A number of researchers, influenced or inspired by Kayne (1994), have argued that adjectives and adverbs are actually specifiers of functional projections (Alexiadou 1997, Cinque 1994, 1999, 2010, Laenzlinger 1998, 2005; see also Chapter 12). The idea is that adjectives and adverbs are specifiers of specialized categories which appear in a specific order (FP1 < FP2 < FP3, where '<' denotes precedence), and that the APs with the relevant features are, according to standard theoretical assumptions, in specifier–head agreement with the corresponding head F^0. I will discuss this approach in detail in Section 13.5 below.

Prominent scholars advancing an adjunction approach to modifiers include Sportiche (1988) and Zubizarreta (1987). Sportiche (1988) proposes that the distribution of adverbs is governed by the following principle:

(27) Adjunct projection principle
If some semantic type X modifies some semantic type Y, and X and Y are syntactically realized as a and b, a is projected as adjacent either to b or to the head of b.

Zubizarreta (1987) assumes that adverbs take scope over the positions they modify. Modification in Zubizarreta's terms entails the assignment of adjunct theta-roles, which are invisible to the Theta Criterion (see Chapters 9, 11). These differ from argument theta-roles in that they are not assigned at deep structure. Evidence for this comes from the orientation of subject-oriented adverbs and manner adverbs in active and passive sentences:

(28) a. John intentionally killed Bill
b. Bill intentionally was killed by John
c. John killed Bill intentionally
d. Bill was killed intentionally by John

While subject-oriented adverbs always modify the subject of the clause, manner adverbs (28c–d) modify the agent. For Zubizarreta, this follows from the restrictions adverbs impose on their complements. Manner adverbs are acceptable only if they adjoin to VP that contains an Agent.

13.4.2 Predication

For both adjectives and adverbs predicative analyses have been proposed. (For general discussion of predication, see Chapter 10.) In the case of adjectives, this is represented primarily by viewing them as predicates within reduced relative clauses, an analysis that goes back to the early days of generative grammar, see Jacobs and Rosenbaum (1968). Kayne (1994) revived this analysis and suggested that it holds for all adjectives, and here is how: relative clauses are CP complements of an external determiner D (see also Chapter 11, note 47). D comes to be associated with its head nominal by movement of that nominal up from its base position inside the relative clause (the 'head-raising' analysis). Adjectives are generated as predicates within the CP. The noun is analyzed as the subject of the predicative AP, see (29):

(29) [$_{DP}$ D [$_{CP}$ [$_{IP}$ NP   AP]]]
         the   book red

Alexiadou and Wilder (1998a) point out, however, that not all adjectives are amenable to such an analysis. In particular, only predicative adjectives may modify nouns this way. In other words, it is predicted that adjectives that cannot be used predicatively (in copular sentences, etc.) should not be able to enter the structure in (29), suggesting that there are at least two sources for adjectival modification (see Bolinger 1967, Sproat and Shih 1987, Cinque 1994).

Alexiadou and Wilder (1998a) and Cinque (2010) appeal to the distinction between direct and indirect modification to be discussed in Section 13.5. They both claim that the reduced relative clause analysis is best suited for indirect modification. While Alexiadou and Wilder are inconclusive on the source of direct modification, Cinque adopts the adjectives-as-specifiers analysis. On this view, all indirect modifiers are introduced via reduced relative clauses, while direct modifiers occupy specifier positions within the extended projection of the noun.

It should be noted here that Cinque's analysis departs from the specific execution proposed by Kayne in that it claims that the relative clauses in question are internally headed. The universal structure he proposes is as in (30) below. Crucial to this proposal is that N-movement is 'replaced' by XP movement, a proposal also made by other authors (see, e.g., Alexiadou 2001a, Laenzlinger 2005, Shlonsky 2004). See Section 13.5 for some arguments against head movement in the nominal domain.

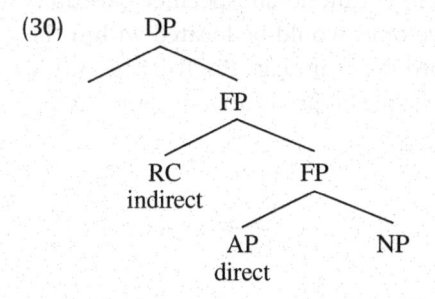

(30)
```
            DP
           /  \
              FP
             /  \
           RC    FP
        indirect /  \
                AP    NP
              direct
```

Direct modifiers are APs in specifier positions, while indirect modifiers are reduced relative clauses located in specifier positions located above the direct modifiers. In order to account for the cross-linguistic variation in word order in Germanic and Romance, which will be discussed in detail in Section 13.5, Cinque proposes that in Germanic, in the normal case, nothing happens. The structure above gives the correct linear order.

But what about the limited cases of postnominal indirect modifiers in English, e.g., *the stars visible* (see Section 13.5)? In this case, one must assume that NP raises to a projection higher than the relative clause in (30). In general, XP raising is assumed to account for the Romance facts, which have direct modifiers preceding indirect modifiers. According to Cinque, these involve a more complex derivation illustrated in (31). First the NP raises to the Specifier of FP2 and then FP2 undergoes remnant movement to a position higher than FP1. Obligatory NP raising takes place in Italian over classificatory adjectives and adjectives of nationality. Optional NP raising takes place over adjectives of size, shape, and color:

(31)

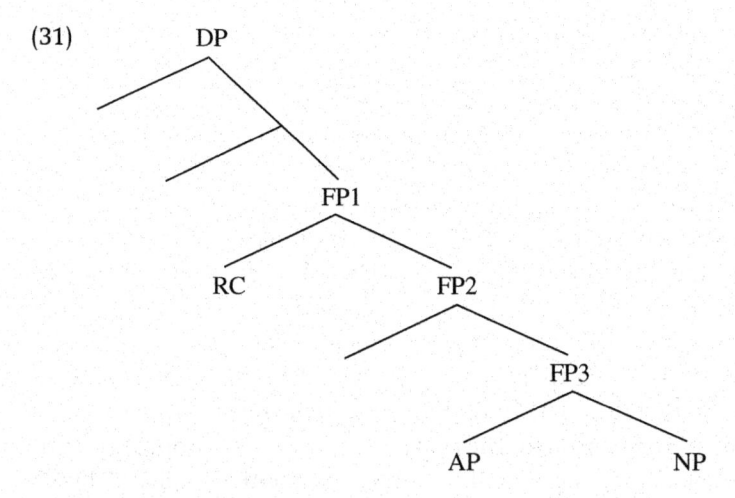

```
            DP
           /  \
          /    \
                FP1
               /   \
              /     \
             RC      FP2
                    /   \
                   /     \
                          FP3
                         /   \
                        AP    NP
```

How can the Kaynian analysis capture the above facts? In my opinion, there are two possible paths to follow. On the original Kayne (1994) analysis, where the subject of the predicative small clause is an NP, adjectives that are not predicative would occupy functional specifier positions between DP and CP, while predicative ones would be located within the CP. In order to derive the correct word order in, e.g., English one would have to make sure that the AP raises from the predicative position above the other adjectives:

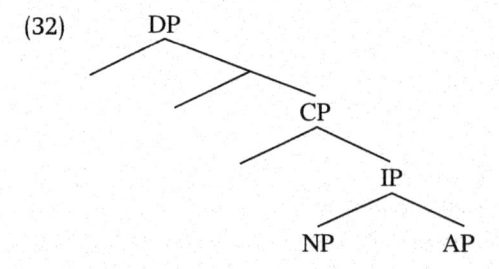

(32)

```
       DP
      /  \
     /    \
           CP
          /  \
         /    \
               IP
              /  \
             NP   AP
```

An alternative would be to assume that the subject of predication is a DP and not an NP (Alexiadou and Wilder 1998a). On this analysis, one could argue that direct modifiers are specifiers within the DP and the correct word order in English is derived via raising of the predicative AP to SpecCP. As for the Romance data, again one would have to assume some version of a remnant movement analysis.

Turning now to adverbs, Roberts (1987:72f.) develops a predication analysis of adverbs based on the assumption that adverbial licensing is based on a predication relation and selectional restrictions on predicates.

(33) a. (cleverly), John (cleverly) kissed Mary (cleverly)
b. (quickly), John (quickly) kissed Mary
c. (evidently), John (evidently) kissed Mary
d. John (easily) kissed Mary (easily)

The distribution of adverbs in the above examples is regulated by their selectional restrictions. *Cleverly* is a two-place predicate selecting as its argument both the subject and the predicate; *quickly* is a one-place predicate that selects either Infl or the VP. *Evidently* selects the whole sentence, and *easily* is predicated of the verb. This, however, raises the question which adverbs are predicational. Ernst (2002) suggested that predicational adverbs are largely those representing these non-quantificational adjectival predicates, such as *probably, significantly, wisely*, and *loudly*. This set contains both manner and sentence adverbs; see also Haumann (2007), who offers a critical overview of the recent literature on adverbs.

Den Dikken (2006b) presents a different take on adjectival and adverbial modification as predication. The core idea in this work is that "all predication relationships are syntactically represented in terms of a structure in which the constituent denoting the subject and the predicate are dependents of a connective or RELATOR that establishes the connection, both the syntactic link and the semantic one between the two constituents" (den Dikken, 2006b:11). (34) corresponds to the representation of all predication relationships, which are not taken to be directional. In other words, in (34) the predicate can also be generated in Spec RELATORP, with the subject being the complement of the RELATOR:

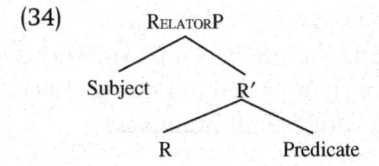

(34) RELATORP
      /   \
   Subject   R'
             / \
            R   Predicate

Consider now the treatment of *Olga dances beautifully*: in this structure *beautiful* is the predicate in the complement of the RELATOR and the proposition *Olga dances* is its subject. *-ly* is the lexicalization of the RELATOR head. In this sense the string *Olga dances beautifully* receives an analysis parallel to its close counterpart *Olga dances like a beauty*. Both *like* and *-ly* lexicalize the RELATOR head, which according to den Dikken captures the historical connection between the two. For den Dikken, *beautiful* is generated as the complement of the RELATOR head, which takes the VP in its specifier (cf. Larson 1998a).

Considering adjectives that are ambiguous between intersective and non-intersective readings, den Dikken proposes the following. Consider (35a):

(35) a. Olga is a beautiful dancer
     b. [RP Olga [RELATOR = be [RP [AP beautiful] [RELATOR [NP dancer]]]]]

dancer originates in the complement position of the RELATOR. There is a two-way relationship between *dancer* and *beautiful* in (35b) above. The AP is predicated of the noun phrase thanks to the fact that it is connected to the extended noun phrase via the RELATOR, and at the same time the extended noun phrase restricts the adjective due to the fact that the noun phrase is the complement of the RELATOR head.

Perhaps the analysis in Sportiche (1998) and Barbiers (1995) could be seen as earlier executions of a related idea; see also Costa (1998) and Nilsen (1998). Specifically, Sportiche proposed that syntactic adjunction is not an available option. Rather, adjectives and adverbs are dominated by a projection whose head takes the modifiee of the adjective or the adverb as an argument, that is as a complement, as in (36a) or sometimes as a specifier, as in (36b). The general intuition is that adjectives and adverbs bear the same kind of relation to their modifiee that determiners bear to their noun phrases or predicates to their arguments. On this account, the variable position of the adverb *stupidly* receives the following structural representations and as a result two distinct interpretations, cf. also example (14):

(36) a. John will stupidly answer
 [$_{AdvP}$ [$_{Adv'}$ [stupidly] [$_{VP}$ answer]]]
 b. John will answer stupidly
 [$_{AdvP}$ [$_{VP}$ answer] [$_{Adv'}$ [$_{Adv}$ stupidly]]]

13.4.3 Head feature licensing

It has also been proposed that both adjectives and adverbs occupy head positions in the extended projection of the NP and VP, respectively. For instance, Abney (1987) and Delsing (1993) both argued that adjectives are syntactic heads between D and N. One argument provided in favor of this view has to do with a set of facts from Danish discussed in Delsing (1993) (see also Section 11.8.5). Consider the following pair of examples:

(37) a. hus-et
 house-the
 b. det gamle hus
 this old house

In (37a) the suffixed article attaches to the noun; in (37b) however, in the presence of an adjective, the article has to be spelled out by an independent morpheme. To account for the pattern in (37a), Delsing proposed that N raises to D. In (37b) the intervention of an adjective blocks this movement, as it would lead to a violation of the Head Movement Constraint (see also Chapter 18).

A number of problems have been raised for the analysis of both adjectives and adverbs as heads. Beginning with adjectives, it has been observed that in many languages prenominal adjectives can take complements, thus challenging their head status. A particularly clear counterargument is provided by Svenonius (1994b) and I briefly summarize it here. Consider (38):

(38) some barely hot black coffee

In (38) the degree adverb *barely* modifies the adjective *hot* and not the adjective *black*. The intended interpretation is that the coffee is *barely hot* not that it is *barely black*. Under the head analysis, *barely* is associated with an AP dominating the projection *hot black coffee*. This structure, however, gives the wrong interpretation, namely *barely* modifies *hot black coffee*. Example (38) is not problematic for the specifier and adjunction analyses, since under these analyses *barely* can be taken to be adjoined to the AP headed by *hot* in the specifier/adjunct position, leading to the correct interpretation of the string above.

Turning to adverbs, Travis (1988) proposed that adverbs are not maximal projections, but rather heads. An argument in favor of this view is that adverbs seem to be defective in that most adverbs cannot take complements, but see (39c–d from Jackendoff 1977):

(39) a. fearful of Bill
b. *fearfully of Bill
c. that his company is going out of business is unfortunate for Bill
d. unfortunately for Bill, his company is going out of business

The distribution described by Travis holds for adverbs in preverbal position and makes an analysis of this class as heads plausible, at least in a language such as English, which lacks V-movement. But if we consider data from other languages, such as French, a head analysis of adverbs can no longer be maintained. As has been observed and discussed extensively in the literature, in French, the finite verb in a subordinate clause obligatorily precedes adverbs, while in English the finite verb obligatorily follows adverbs (Emonds 1978, Pollock 1989; see also Chapter 12):

(40) a. John [$_{VP}$ often eats tomatoes surprises most people]
b. *Jean [$_{VP}$ souvent mange des tomates surprend tout le monde]

Under the assumption that in both language groups the adverb is attached at the same site, this pattern suggests that in the first group the verb has undergone head movement outside the VP, while in the second group the verb remains in the VP.

13.4.4 Complementation

Another view holds that modifiers can also be complements. This has primarily been argued with reference to adverbs, not adjectives. On this analysis, adverbs are projected in the innermost complement position of VP shells. Larson (1988a) is the representative proposal in this connection; see also Rivero (1992) and Alexiadou (1997), who relativize Larson's claim to a subset of adverbs.

The data discussed in Rivero (1992) and Alexiadou (1997) concerning incorporation of adverbs in Modern Greek (though cf. Smirniotopoulos and Joseph 1998 for a different analysis) seem to support the idea that at least some adverbs can be analyzed as being defective, i.e., not full XPs. Rivero (1992) observed that in Greek the adverb–verb complex cannot be interrupted by clitics or other adverbs. The only adverbs that can undergo incorporation are manner adverbs and certain aspectual ones of the type that could be seen as innermost complements of V; see Alexiadou (1997).

(41) a. kaloefage
    well.ate.3SG
    'he ate well'
  b. *kalo to-efage
    well it-ate.3SG
  c. *kalo-sinithos-efage
    well-usually-ate.3SG

In the next section, I will discuss an influential approach to modifiers, which views them as specifiers of designated functional projections (see Chapter 12).

13.5 Adverbs and adjectives as specifiers

An influential view holds that both adverbs and adjectives are specifiers of designated functional projections in the verbal and nominal extended projections, respectively. The phenomenon that this analysis is based on involves multiple modification and to some extent is seen in combination with the head vs. XP movement issue to account for linear order effects.

Beginning with adjectives, it has been observed by Sproat and Shih (1987) that typically observe strict ordering restrictions. For instance, prenominal adjectives in English and other languages follow an ordering of the type illustrated in (42) (where '<' denotes precedence). This ordering is stated on the basis of hierarchically organized semantic classes of adjectives:

(42) a. QUANTIFICATION < QUALITY < SIZE < SHAPE/COLOR < PROVENANCE
  b. numerous/three beautiful big grey Persian cats
  c. lovely little round Greek cats

Scott (1998), and see also Svenonius (2008), gives arguments for additional internal orderings among adjectives that belong to one category in (42a).

For Sproat and Shih (1987, 1991), the adjective ordering should be stated not as a linear ordering among various types of adjectives but rather as their relative linear proximity. The authors relate the linear orders observed above to two further types of modification, namely direct and indirect modification. In direct modification, the adjective modifies the head noun directly, and the scales described above govern the ordering of adjectives that are integrated via direct modification. On the other hand, in indirect modification, the adjective indirectly modifies the noun, meaning that it is part of a relative clause. Indirect modification is not subject to linear ordering effects.

These authors discuss this distinction in Chinese, where the two types of modification differ morphologically. Specifically, in Chinese, adjectives modifying nouns in direct modification must obey the ordering in (42), as shown by the examples in (43). The linearization of multiple APs can be violated, but only when these are accompanied by the particle *de* (43d).

(43) a. xiâo lü huãping
       small green vase
   b. *lü xiâo huãping
       green small vase
   c. xiâo-de lü-de huãping
       small-DE green-DE vase
       small green vase
   d. lü-de xiâo-de huãping
       green-DE small-DE vase

The particle *de* is also a relative clause marker. This supports Sproat and Shih's claim that indirect modification is modification by relative clauses:

(44) fēi-de nião
     fly-DE bird
     the birds which are flying

The general claim by these authors is that direct modification is characterized by (45), while indirect modification is characterized by (46).

(45) Direct modification
   a. is subject to ordering restrictions
   b. permits intersective and non-intersective modifiers

(46) Indirect modification
   a. is not subject to ordering restrictions
   b. permits intersective (predicative) modifiers only

An influential proposal on how to deal with linear ordering effects is the one proposed by Cinque (1994).[5] According to Cinque's (1994) analysis, adjectives are specifiers of specialized projections and across languages inserted in a prenominal position. Since in many languages of the world the surface order of adjectives with respect to the head noun is that they follow the head noun, it is claimed that this is derived by head movement of the noun to a higher functional projection. Let me illustrate this with two examples. Consider first the Germanic vs. Romance contrast. As is well known, in, e.g., French certain adjectives can follow the head noun (47a), while in, e.g., English all adjectives precede the head noun (47b):

(47) a. un joli gros ballon rouge
     b. a beautiful big red ball

Assuming that both in French and in English the adjectives are generated prenominally, the fact that in French the adjective *rouge* follows the head noun is accounted for by the fact that the noun has moved to the head of the projection hosting the adjective *big* in this language. Thus the difference in linear order in the two languages relates to the availability of noun movement in French and the absence thereof in English (see Bernstein 1993a and others):

(48) a. Germanic [$_{DP}$ D [$_{FP}$ AP F [$_{FP}$ AP F [$_{NP}$ N ...]]]]
b. Romance [$_{DP}$ D [$_{FP}$ AP [$_F$ N$_n$] [$_{FP}$ AP [$_F$ t$_n$] [$_{NP}$ t$_n$ ...]]]]

A second example for N movement is Welsh, where it is argued that the head noun moves higher than all the specifier positions where the adjectives are located:

(49) cwpan mawr gwyrdd Sieineaidd
    cup   big   green   Chinese
    'a big green Chinese cup'   (Rouveret, 1994:213)

However, both the analysis of adjectives as specifiers of designated functional heads and the account in terms of head movement have been criticized, and the latter has been revised by a number of authors. The point concerning the adjectives in specifier hypothesis is more general and it arises the same way in the context of adverbs, though the literature has been more concerned with bringing counterarguments for the domain of adverbs and less so for the domain of adjectives. The core question raised is the following: Why should one assume that the linear order is given by the syntax, hence postulating a number of functional projections in the absence, in most cases, of overt morphological evidence for such projections? It could very well be, as Sproat and Shih (1987, 1991) suggested, that there is a "cognitive and semantic basis" for the ordering. In other words, the source for adjective ordering could lie outside of the core grammar.

Turning now to head movement, a number of authors (Lamarche 1991, Alexiadou 2001a, Bouchard 2002) have pointed out that this makes a number of wrong predictions. For instance, it fails to predict the fact that adjectives stack postnominally in Romance in the mirror image order of the stacking of prenominal adjectives in Germanic. As Cinque (2010) argues in detail, if this Germanic/Romance contrast is to be derived via movement, then it must be phrasal, snowballing/roll-up movement (see Chapter 11, note 51). In this chapter, I cannot summarize all the evidence presented against the N-movement approach. It can be found in Alexiadou et al. (2007) and in Cinque (2010). I will limit myself to the discussion of two points.

First, the noun-movement analysis predicts existence of unexpected scope effects (Svenonius 1994b, Bouchard, 2002). As these authors point out, the noun movement analysis predicts that a postnominal adjective should not be able to take scope over a prenominal one. In examples like (50) below, however, this seems indeed to be possible:

(50) e' un *giovane* scrittore *assai noto* di romanzi gialli
he is a very well-known young writer of detective stories
(assai noto > giovane)   (from Cinque 2010)

Second, this analysis cannot provide a common basis for the interpretive differences between pre- and postnominal adjectives in Germanic and Romance. These data, taken from Larson (1998a), form the core of the argumentation against noun movement in Cinque (2010). Consider the following examples, again taken from Cinque (2010):

(51) a. the visible stars include Aldebaran and Sirius   (ambiguous)
   1. the stars that are generally visible   individual-level
   2. the stars that are visible now   stage-level

   b. the stars visible are Aldebaran and Sirius
   1. # the stars that are generally visible   individual-level
   2. the stars that are visible now   stage-level

As observed in Bolinger (1967) and discussed several times in the literature after him, the prenominal adjective in (52a) is ambiguous between two readings; following Svenonius (1994b), the two readings are classified as individual-level vs. stage-level. On the other hand, the postnominal adjective in (52b) has only one interpretation, the stage-level one.

In Italian, Cinque notes a mirror image effect.

(52) a. le invisibili stelle di Andromeda sono molto distanti
                                                      (unambiguous)
   1. the stars that are generally visible   individual-level
   2. # the stars that are visible now   stage-level

   b. le stelle invisibili di Andromeda sono molto distanti (ambiguous)
   1. the stars that are generally visible   individual-level
   2. the stars that are visible now   stage-level

In Italian (and Romance in general), it is the postnominal adjective that is ambiguous, while the prenominal one is not ambiguous and receives only the individual-level interpretation. The two readings can in fact co-occur in both language groups, and when they do, they are strictly ordered (Larson 1998a), as shown in (53) (where '<' denotes precedence):

(53) a. stage-level < individual-level < N
      indirect modification < direct modification N
      every VISIBLE visible star

   b. N < individual-level < stage-level
      N < direct modification < indirect modification
      una posizione invidiabile INVIDIABILE
      a   position enviable   enviable

Cinque discusses a number of other ambiguities, which all show the general pattern just sketched above. A second one is the so-called restrictive vs. non-restrictive ambiguity. It is widely assumed that adjectives can modify a noun in two ways, as restrictive or as non-restrictive modifiers. Kamp (1975:153) pointed out that an adjective modifying a noun restrictively helps identify the individual that is the referent of the noun phrase. If, on the other hand, the adjective modifies the noun non-restrictively, then it does not provide information that is relevant to the reference of the noun. In other words, non-restrictive modification expresses a property of the referent that is taken to be evident in the context in which the sentence is uttered.

Consider the following German example, taken from Umbach (2006:152). As the author states, "the prominent interpretation of the NP *unschuldige Passagiere* 'innocent passengers' is such that the modification by *unschuldige* 'innocent' is non-restrictive. According to this interpretation passengers in the context of an aircraft hijacking are generally viewed as innocent and are contrasted with kidnappers. There is also a restrictive interpretation of *unschuldige Passagiere* such that kidnappers are regarded as non-innocent passengers, which is, however, a more marked reading":

(54) Ein Abschuss eines gekaperten Flugzeuges, in dem sich
a shooting down of a hijacked aircraft on which REFLEXIVE
neben den Entführern unschuldige Passagiere befinden, ist
in addition to the hijackers innocent passengers are, is
und bleibt verboten.
and remains illegal
'shooting down a kidnapped aircraft that has innocent
passengers on board in addition to the kidnappers is and remains illegal.'

The distinction between restrictive and non-restrictive modification can be brought about either via intonation or via word order. In the following example, taken from Umbach (2006:152), we can observe that since according to what we know about the world flowers are always colorful, the modifier has to be interpreted non-restrictively. If, however, we place focus on the modifier, we would induce a restrictive interpretation triggering a set of alternatives. So it turns out that the non-restrictive interpretation requires the modifier to be deaccented.

(55) in Annas Garten sind bunte Blumen, aber kein Gemüse und
in Ann's garden are colorful flowers, but no vegetables and
keine Bäume
no trees
'in Anna's garden there are colorful flowers, but no
vegetables and no trees'

In German, adjectives can never appear in postnominal position. In English, where this is sometimes possible, as noted by Bolinger (1967), prenominal adjectives can be ambiguous between a restrictive and a non-restrictive interpretation, whereas postnominal adjectives can only be understood restrictively (see also Larson and Marušič 2004):

(56) a. all of his **unsuitable** acts were condemned (ambiguous)
b. 'all of his acts were condemned; they were unsuitable'
(non-restrictive)
c. 'all of his acts that were unsuitable were condemned'
(restrictive)

(57) a. every word **unsuitable** was deleted (unambiguous)
b. #'every word was deleted; they were unsuitable' (non-restrictive)
c. 'every word that was unsuitable was deleted' (restrictive)

In Romance, this difference shows up in a different manner; in fact we get a mirror order effect. As Cinque (2010) discusses at length, it is the prenominal position that is unambiguously interpreted as non-restrictive, while the postnominal one is ambiguous between a restrictive and a non-restrictive interpretation.

(58) a. le **noiose** lezioni di Ferri se le ricordano tutti (unambiguous)
the boring lectures of Ferri SE them remember all
b. 'everybody remembers F's classes, all of which were boring'
(non-restrictive)
c. #'everybody remembers just F's classes which were boring'
(restrictive)

(59) a. le lezioni **noiose** di Ferri se le ricordano tutti (ambiguous)
the lectures boring of Ferri SE them remember all
b. 'everybody remembers F's classes, all of which were boring'
(non-restrictive)
c. 'everybody remembers just F's classes which were boring'
(restrictive)

In languages like Greek, as argued by Kolliakou (2004) and others following her, a restrictive interpretation arises via the presence of two determiners within the same noun phrase (the 'double definiteness effect'; see also Chapter 11, note 52).

(60) a. o diefthindis ipe oti i kali erevnites tha apolithun
the director said that the efficient researchers will be fired
b. o diefthindis ipe oti i kali i erevnites tha apolithun
the director said that the efficient the researchers will be fired

(60a) has two readings. According to reading 1, only the efficient researchers will be fired; on reading 2, the efficient researchers happen to be part of the larger group that will be fired. (60b) is not ambiguous: it only has reading 1. In support of this, note that adjectives that do not have restrictive readings are out (61); Alexiadou and Wilder (1998a), Kolliakou (2004):

(61) a. o platis Irinikos   b. *o platis o Irinikos
     the wide Pacific   the wide the Pacific

The important observation here is that the noun-movement analysis cannot capture these facts. Ideally, one would want to claim that the adjectives are situated in the same position within the noun phrase across languages. But assuming a noun-movement analysis for the Romance data cannot explain this pattern. Moreover, as English is not generally assumed to have noun movement, the postnominal position of the adjective must have a different source. According to one view, this is best analyzed in terms of reduced relative clauses; see Section 13.4.2.

Turning now to adverbs, it has also been noted that when more than one adverbial modifies the clause (62–63), these seem to appear in a particular linear order (Cinque 1999, Alexiadou 1997, based on observations by Jackendoff 1972, Travis 1988; '<' once again denotes precedence).

(62) a. SPEAKER-ORIENTED < SUBJECT-ORIENTED < FREQUENCY < COMPLETION < MANNER
     b. he probably quickly left   speaker-oriented < manner
     c. he cleverly always leaves on time   subject-oriented < aspect
     d. he probably cleverly left on time
                                              speaker-oriented < subject-oriented
     e. he probably completely changed his mind
                                              speaker-oriented < aspect
     f. he often completely changed his mind frequency < completion

(63) Speech Act < Evaluative
     a. honestly I am unfortunately unable to help you
     b. *unfortunately I am honestly unable to help you
        Evaluative < Evidential
     c. fortunately, he had evidently had his own opinion of the matter
     d. *evidently, he had fortunately had his own opinion of the matter
        Evidential < Epistemic
     e. clearly John probably will quickly learn French perfectly
     f. *probably John clearly will quickly learn French perfectly
        Epistemic < Past tense
     g. probably he once had a better opinion of us
     h. once he probably had a better opinion of us
        Past tense < certainly
     i. he was then certainly at home
     j. *he was certainly then at home

In an impressive typological study, Cinque (1999) argues that the ordering of adverbs in a clause is determined by a universal hierarchy and proposes that this hierarchy is itself unambiguously determined by phrase structure, with the adverbs occupying unique specifiers of functional projections, along the lines of (64) below (see also Section 12.7):

(64) [frankly Mood speech act [fortunately Mood evaluative
[allegedly Mood evidential [probably
Mood epistemic [once T (Past) [then T (Future) [perhaps
(Mood irrealis) [necessarily Mood
necessity [possibly Mood possibility [Mood obligation [Mood
ability/permission [usually
Asp habitual [again Asp repetitive [often Asp frequentative I
[intentionally Mood volitional
[quickly Asp celerative [already T (anterior) [nolonger Asp
terminative [still Asp continuative
[always Asp perfect? [just Asp retrospective[soon Asp
proximative [briefly Asp durative
[characteristically (?) Asp generic/progressive [almost Asp
prospective [completely Asp
sgCompletive I [tutto Asp Pl Completive I [well Voice [fast
Asp Celerative II [again Asp repetitive
II [often Asp frequentative II [completely Asp sgCompletive II

The argument is based on the relative order of adverbs with respect to functional heads and the proposal is that the set of functional projections in (64) is licensed either by a functional element in the head position, or via an adverb in the Spec position. When both co-occur we have the familiar version of spec–head agreement.

Cinque (1999) as well as Alexiadou (1997) and Laenzlinger (1998) are the main representatives of the syntactic approach to linear order. For this approach, the linear order follows from the order of functional projections. The adverb is interpreted at the point of its insertion in the structure.

However, Haider (2000) among others points out that on this view, the adverbial hierarchy seems to be coded twice, first in the principles of syntactic structuring and second in the algorithm for the construction of semantic representations. For this reason, alternatives have been proposed to counteract this redundancy. For instance, Haider argues that the relative order of adverbials is characterized as an interface effect of the mapping of syntactic domains on type domains in the structure of the semantic representation.

Ernst (2002) advances a proposal where linear order of adverbs is largely a function of the interaction of compositional rules for the various adjuncts, plus their lexico-semantic requirements. He assumes that there are different ontological entities like 'events,' 'propositions' and 'facts' into which the clause is divided and adverbs can apply to. These ontological categories are in a hierarchical arrangement (65a) and can undergo type-conversion (see Nilsen 2004 for criticism). Ernst proposed that the semantic composition of a clause is governed in part by the Fact-Event-Object (FEO) Calculus, which takes semantic entities to be of certain types and puts constraints on how certain of these types combine, events and propositions in particular. The main constraint of the FEO Calculus is in (65b):

(65) a. SPEECH ACT > FACT > PROPOSITION > EVENT > SPECIFIED EVENT
 b. Main Constraint on the FEO Calculus: Any FEO type may be freely converted to any higher FEO type, but not lowered.

On the empirical side, the specifiers approach has received a lot of criticism (see most prominently Ernst 2002, 2007, Nilsen 2004, and references therein). Let us consider one of these arguments. It has been observed that the relative order between two adverbs is not always rigid, and that this provides a clear argument against the 'functional specifier' approach. Such data are discussed in Ernst (2002) and Nilsen (2004) and are illustrated below. (66) shows that, contrary to what (64) would predict, adverbs can occupy a variety of positions with respect to each other:

(66) a. she frequently was suddenly (being) rejected by publishers
 b. she suddenly was (being) frequently rejected by publishers
 c. on Wall Street, Enron was already allegedly going bankrupt
 d. on Wall Street, Enron was allegedly already going bankrupt

In a system such as Ernst's, this variability is explained in terms of the FEO calculus. But an alternative, advanced in Cinque (2004), is that *frequently/often/rarely*/etc. occur in two distinct positions, one above and one below *wisely, suddenly, already, willingly* (and other adverbs).

(67) she rarely was suddenly (being) (frequently) rejected by the publishers (frequently)

If there are two positions available for certain adverbs, in principle one would expect that these could be filled simultaneously. While such examples sound rather marked with frequency adverbials, they sound much better with adverbs like *stupidly, rudely*, etc. These, depending on interpretation (manner or subject-oriented), occupy different positions in the structure of the clause, cf. (14) above.[6] The two theories are summarized and compared to one another in the contributions to Alexiadou (2004); see also Ernst (2007).

13.6 Conclusions

The aim of this chapter has been to offer an overview of certain issues that have been extensively discussed in the literature on the syntax of adjectival and adverbial modification. As is clear from this summary, the proper analysis of these elements is still very much a matter of debate. Often the debate is related to a more general one surrounding the status of adjunction in generative grammar, a process for which no consensus seems to have been found.

In conclusion, it can be said that antisymmetry-based approaches to modification opened up a very fruitful way to deal with this issue that led to a number of fine-grained descriptions of the behavior of adjectives and adverbs across languages as well as significant cross-linguistic comparisons. Thus, adjectives and adverbs can no longer be considered as less-studied categories, though they might still be more complex than nouns and verbs.

Notes

1. Alexiadou (2002b) discusses the categorization issue within the framework of Distributed Morphology. Note here that other frameworks that dispense with lexical categories, such as Borer (2005a), do not discuss the issue of categorization of adjectives/adverbs.
2. The class of denominal adjectives such as *italiana* contains adjectives called relational ones. These were discussed by Bartning (1976), Levi (1978), Kayne (1984), Grimshaw (1990), and Giorgi and Longobardi (1991); cf. Fábregas (2007) and Alexiadou and Stavrou (2011) for recent treatments in the spirit of Distributed Morphology. Adjectives of the type in (13a) are labeled ethnic adjectives and they are listed among thematic adjectives, since they seem to bear a theta-role assigned to them by the noun they modify. One should distinguish between (13a) and (i) below, where the relational adjective modifies a common/object noun:

    (i) her Italian bag cost a fortune

    The adjective in (i) assigns to the noun a property which is related to some origin and is intersective. Such denominal adjectives pattern with classificatory adjectives, as they are used to (sub)classify the denotation of the noun (Bosque and Picallo 1996); specifically, they denote (sub) kinds, e.g., types of bags. On the other hand, the adjective in (13a) is not intersective.
3. The ±intersective distinction is related to the distinction between intensional and extensional modifiers. Adjectives interpreted intensionally modify the sense or intension of the noun (Bolinger 1967, Higginbotham 1985, Demonte 1999:58). An adjective that is not intensional is extensional – it modifies the x that falls in the extension of the noun. Extensional adjectives "help to determine the particular individual which is the intended referent of the description in which the adjective occurs" (Kamp 1975:153). The term non-intersective is almost synonymous to the term intensional: an intensional adjective does not

combine with a noun to yield a co-extensive modified nominal expression For instance, an adjective like *present* (or *former*) in (18)) is intensional, and thus the string the *present senator* means 'the one who is currently a senator,' and not the 'senator who is present.'

4. Size adjectives seem to be able to carry what can be referred to as relative interpretations, in the sense that the property which they assign to the noun is not assigned in any absolute terms, they are interpreted with respect to a certain standard. Consider in this context the use of *big* in expressions such as *a big butterfly* and *a big elephant*. A *big butterfly* denotes an entity that is big 'for a butterfly,' and not an entity that is big in any abstract or absolute sense. A *big elephant* denotes an elephant that is judged as big only when compared to other elephants – i.e. to members of the same class. Though such adjectives are intersective, and not subsective, in order to account for their particular interpretation, Larson and Segal (1995) introduce the notion of 'comparison class,' which is part of the adjective's lexical structure. It takes the form of a *for*-PP: 'a small elephant is small for an elephant but big when compared to a butterfly.' See Higginbotham (1985), and Alexiadou et al. (2007) for an overview.

5. As will be discussed later in this section, Cinque (2010) revised this analysis. See also Section 13.4.2.

6. The question that arises is of course whether these adverbs are multiply listed in the lexicon or any adverb can be in principle inserted in any position. Neither option seems very attractive. On the one hand, multiple listing would lead to an explosion of the lexicon. On the other hand, it has been pointed out that adverbial distribution is not unprincipled.

Part IV

Syntactic processes: their nature, locality, and motivation

14

Economy of derivation and representation

Samuel D. Epstein, Hisatsugu Kitahara,
Miki Obata, and T. Daniel Seely

14.1 Background: Government and Binding Theory, Principles and Parameters

14.1.1 The motivation for and the beauty of GB theory

Chomsky's Government and Binding theory (Chomsky 1980a, 1981, 1982) is often and aptly characterized as a radical departure from pre-existing theories of the human capacity for acquiring knowledge of syntax.[1] Virtually all traditional approaches assume that languages are rule governed. The formal diversity of the rules postulated in order to capture the diverse set of cross-linguistic and cross-construction syntactic phenomena represented a serious impediment to the central goal of linguistic theory (as Chomsky 1955/1975: Introduction and subsequent work by Chomsky characterizes it), namely to explain the human capacity to acquire any possible human (I-)language on the basis of linguistic input consisting of continuous acoustic disturbances or (for signed languages) retinal images of hand shapes, locations, and, orientations changing over time. That is, the quest for descriptive adequacy (in the sense of Chomsky 1964b) precluded the construction of an explanatorily adequate theory. (For background on levels of adequacy, see Section 3.2.5.)

This central problem was identified and addressed by the search for a more restricted unified, universal theory of 'possible human syntactic rule system.' This was attained by determining and formulating general constraints on all rules (e.g. Ross 1967a, Chomsky 1965, 1973). Another, slightly different, approach was to impose constraints not on the formulations of rules themselves, or on their collective mode of application (e.g., rule ordering) but rather by formulating constraints on representations appearing at certain levels of representation.

This search for a more constrained explanatorily adequate and unified theory of syntax ultimately developed into what was the 'radical departure' advanced by GB theory. The theory pursued the hypothesis that human knowledge of language (more specifically, syntax) consisted not of a system of rules but of constraints on output at one or another of the levels of representation postulated in GB (DS, SS, PF, LF). With such constraints on representation incorporated into the theory, the logic was that the diverse, unconstrained, language-specific, and construction-specific transformational rules could be significantly simplified. The transformational component of UG was hypothesized to consist of Move Alpha (Chomsky 1981, 1982) or Affect Alpha (Lasnik and Saito 1992); and the set of phrase-structure rules was simplified by the postulation of X-bar Theory (Jackendoff 1977), which in effect expressed a constrained theory of 'possible PS rule' with X-bar Theory assumed to be expressed as a constraint on phrase-structure representations, in part facilitating the wholesale elimination of PS rules (see also Chapters 2 and 11). This shift from rules to principles (constraints on representation) was intended to overcome all the explanatory difficulty associated with the postulation of formally diverse, language-specific and construction-specific rules. In addition, stipulated rule orderings were to be reducible to the more general, architectural, ordered set of levels of representation postulated in GB theory (the so-called T- or Y-model; see Section 2.3).

In postulating neither language-specific nor construction-specific rules, the theory no longer directly accounted for 'sentence relatedness' (e.g., the relation between active and passive sentence) by a rule mapping the representation of one kind (actives) to the representation of the other kind (passives). Rather, the theory was attractively rendered far more distant from the data, with deeper deductive structure, more complex forms of argument, and more abstraction. That is, the GB theory was modularized, consisting of separate components and principles each dedicated to monitoring certain formal subproperties of syntactic representations (see Section 4.1). Each of these modules contained an overarching constraint on a level of representation which ensured the well-formedness of certain subproperties of each syntactic representation, despite the fact that the simplified rules massively overgenerate since they themselves incorporate no constraints and hence bear no empirical burden. Thus, 'sentences' are analyzed as decomposable complex macrostructures, knowledge of which is the epiphenomenal manifestation of the satisfaction of the various dedicated principles. A sentence is what you get if and only if the unconstrained rules apply in such a way as to produce a representational output or outputs which satisfy each of the dedicated representational constraints of the theory as differentially applied to the various levels of representation (e.g., the Theta Criterion applying at DS, the Case Filter applying at SS).

This system of level-ordered filters and constraints also explained at a certain level why there existed transformational movement rules at all: they were necessitated because the demands of DS and the demands of SS were not simultaneously satisfiable, given the unification of theta and case assignment under the single (binary local) relation government. That is, in order to satisfy Theta Theory at DS in [__*was believed John to steal*], John must, under government theory, be in the semantic position, subject of *steal*. But in order to satisfy Case Theory, with case also assigned under government, *John* had to occupy the subject position of ___*was believed*. Thus the demands of theta and case, both unified under government, required *John* to be in two different positions, thereby explaining the very existence of movement transformations such as these.

As Chomsky (1981:13) puts it, "[t]he objective of reducing the class of grammars compatible with primary linguistic data has served as a guiding principle in the study of generative grammar since virtually the outset, as it should, given the nature of the fundamental empirical problem to be faced – namely, accounting for the attainment of knowledge of grammar – and the closely related goal of enhancing explanatory power." Yet "[e]arly work in transformational grammar permitted a very wide choice of base grammars and of transformations. Subsequent work attempted to reduce the class of permissible grammars by formulating general conditions on rule type, rule application, or output that would guarantee that much simpler rule systems, lacking detailed specification to indicate how and when rules apply, would nevertheless generate required structures properly. For example X-bar theory radically reduces the class of possible base components, various conditions on rules permit a reduction in the category of permitted movement rules and conditions on surface structure, S-structure and LF allow still further simplification of rules and their organization." However, as Chomsky warns from the very outset, "reduction in the variety of systems in one part of the grammar is no contribution to these ends if it is matched or exceeded by proliferation elsewhere."

14.1.2 Beauty and the beast

Despite the logic and historical continuity underlying the birth of GB theory and despite its explanatory and empirical cross-linguistic successes, there were perceived to be problems, of perhaps a new kind, confronting the explanatory depth of this theory. Grappling with the specific problems perceived to be inherent in GB coupled with a continued commitment to explanation is what led to the transition to the Minimalist Program (see Chapter 4, and also the introduction to Epstein and Seely 2002a for discussion of the rationale for and – we believe, misplaced – opposition to this program), aspects of which are discussed in the following subsections. For reasons of space, we will simply list some illustrative central problems confronted by GB theory, as were recognized by numerous researchers.

14.1.2.1 The theory of syntactic relations

The single syntactic relation in GB theory, government, although unifying the modules and principles of Universal Grammar, suffered from a number of potential problems. As Epstein (1999) observes, unification is in fact not attained, since the 'is a' (immediate domination) relation is not subsumed under government. This problem relates to the levels postulated in GB. First, D-structures exhibiting the 'is a' relation are built (all at once). Only then are government relations defined on these entirely built-up structures. This raises another problem. Since government is defined, it is unexplained – i.e., why is *this* definition on representations relevant and not other equally definable representational relations? Moreover, government is not primitive, but (by the time of Chomsky 1986a) is a highly complex definition incorporating a number of (similarly unexplained) sub-definitions of more primitive concepts and relations, including m-command, maximal projection, 'excludes,' '(immediately) dominates,' barrier, blocking category, L-marking, theta-marking, and sisterhood (see Epstein 1999:322 for discussion).

In addition, though theories of binding (Chomsky 1981; Chapter 15, this volume) and ECP (Lasnik and Saito 1984, 1992, Chomsky 1986b; Chapter 18, this volume) were sought which appealed only to this single notion of government, it was arguably the case that the relations required by the principles of these modules had to be more permissive, allowing binary relations (e.g., binding relations and ECP-enforced antecedent–trace relations) to span larger domains that appeared irreducible to the very local relation of government. In addition, it was recognized that government in its initial form was a head to non-head relation, while the relations imposed by the theories of binding and ECP were seemingly relations between two maximal projections.

14.1.2.2 The principles

Although Vergnaud's Case Filter (see Chapter 17, (66)) and early formulations of the ECP represent pioneering improvement over the similarly pioneering generalized filters of Chomsky and Lasnik (1977) (e.g., the that-*t* filter or the *for-to* filter), these filters, like the government relation, were nonetheless defined, hence not explained. As with the axioms of any theory, we must ask 'Why?': First, why is there a Case Filter at all? Second, why is the Case Filter an S-structure condition, and not a DS, LF, or PF condition – or even an everywhere principle (as was the Theta Criterion, given the Projection Principle)? Why does it apply to NPs and not some other specific category? And why should (or how can) phonetic content be relevant to a non-PF, i.e., an S-structure (syntax-internal) condition? Finally, why should it apply to the non-natural class +phonetic NP and *wh*-trace (Freidin and Lasnik 1981)? This situation reflects precisely the concern to which Chomsky (1981:13) alluded, as noted at the end of Section 14.1.1, above: simplification of one component (the rule system) is to some degree subverted by proliferation elsewhere, in the stipulative and diverse formalism incorporated into the output filters.

14.1.2.3 Technicalia

Since Fiengo (1977) and Chomsky (1973, 1975b), there was another proliferation concern. The rules were simplified, but in order to feed the correct application of S-structure representational principles, traces, indexing on traces, and chains were proposed as representational constructs (see, e.g., Sportiche 1983, Rizzi 1986b). The concern then was that – to use Chomsky's (1995c:224) term anachronistically – these kinds of postulates might constitute 'coding tricks,' non-explanatory technicalia that bear significant degrees of the empirical burden, thereby covering the data formally without providing the desired kind of explanatory insight regarding the phenomena under analysis.

14.1.2.4 Levels of representation

As early as Chomsky (1986b) it was recognized that S-structure was a 'suspect' level of representation since it was entirely internal to the syntax and unlike DS, LF, and PF had no interaction with interface systems. Moreover, as Chomsky (1986b) noted, since it is the central level in the T/Y-model, i.e., the only level that is the output of the DS-to-SS mapping, yet also the input to both the PF and LF components, it ought to be deducible from the demands imposed by the other three components it mediates between. This raised the question of whether the stipulated level-ordered architecture with its four levels of representation, to which the principles were assumed to apply, might all be eliminable, and an entirely level-free theory of UG developed (see Epstein *et al.* 1998, Epstein 1999, Uriagereka 1999). (See Lasnik 2002 and the references cited there for discussion of these works in historical context, both their relation to earlier cyclic proposals in standard theory, notably Jackendoff 1972 on semantic cyclicity and Bresnan 1971b on phonological cyclicity, as well as the subsequent development of 'minimized,' hence level-free, current phase-based models.)

14.1.2.5 Language variation and parameters

It was not clear why GB researchers found the parameters they did, or why these parameters exhibited what might be a version of the formal diversity previously exhibited by specific rules. This diversity was not an impediment to learnability as long as the values of each parameter were determinable by (linguistic) experience (the nature of which is determined by UG). However, simplicity, elegance, and similar considerations led to the question of why we find parameterization of, e.g., head-first vs. head-last, +/–null subjects, and parameterization of bounding nodes for Subjacency. Why should *these* be the loci of parameterization?

Of course if levels of representation are eliminated, there will then be no place at all for the (stipulated) filters on, or principles constraining, levels of representation to apply. Furthermore, parameters *in* the formulation of these constraints on levels of representation would be similarly undermined. If the principles and their parameterized instantiations in core grammars cannot be applied at levels of representation, we could incorporate the constraints back into the rules, which they had previously been factored out of; but this would only lead us back to the very questions we began with and which rightly motivated GB, such as "Why do we find *these* specific rules and not others?" If Epstein (2003/2007) is on track, the Minimalist Program breaks this vicious circle by postulating that both the purely principle-based approach and the purely rule-based approach were, by virtue of their purported purity, on the wrong track. Rather, the Minimalist hypothesis is that both approaches were in part on the right track in that there exist both rules and constraints on representation. The constraints on representation, however, are constraints on the independently motivated interface representations, the (arguably) ineliminable representations of sound (PF) and meaning (LF). Ideally, the constraints are entirely natural, not stipulative technicalia, but reducible to some form of Chomsky's (1986b) Full Interpretation, which requires that every element in an LF representation must be semantically interpretable and every element in a PF representation must be phonologically interpretable. For example, case-features, lacking semantic content, must be eliminated from the representation sent to LF, but retained in the representation sent to (or spelled out at) PF. The rules are not devoid of empirical content (as was Move Alpha or Affect Alpha) but have a definite form, yet one which is reduced to a bare minimum. For example, Merge A and B forming C = {A, B}, which is arguably unifiable with Move (Kitahara 1995, 1997). This eliminates construction and language specificity from the rules and by Occam's Razor reduces rules to their minimal (binary) form. With recursive application of (bare minimum) rules postulated, the possibility arises in such a derivational system that natural, general, and perhaps not even specifically linguistic (see, e.g., Chomsky 1965:59, 1998, 2005) constraints on computational efficiency might be invoked to explain modes of rule application (derivations) previously stipulated as either rule (ordering) constraints or formal technical conditions on syntax-internal levels of representation. Thus ideally the minimal rules (or single rule, Merge) apply in the most computationally efficient way (derivational economy) in order to satisfy the minimal (and natural) bare output conditions on interface representations (representational economy). Parameterization of principles (e.g., the Null Subject Parameter) must then be reduced to independently necessary, minimal, and constrained morpho-featural cross-linguistic variation in the lexicon (see Borer 1984b, Fukui 1986; and Chapters 4 and 25).

14.2 The 1990s: The (re-)emergence of economy guidelines

Since Chomsky (1981), the main concern in the field had been to determine what kind of linguistic principles are genetically determined and how (some of) those principles of UG are parameterized. Some of the postulated UG principles follow the spirit of 'least effort' or economy in that they "legislate against 'superfluous elements' in representations and derivations" (Chomsky 1991b:418). The Principle of Full Interpretation (discussed in Chomsky 1986b), for example, requires representations at D-structure, PF, and LF to be minimized, i.e., they can contain no superfluous elements, while economy of derivation requires that derivations have as few steps as possible (see, e.g., Chomsky 1991b). This section is devoted specifically to addressing the concept of economy – how the most economical derivations and representations are generated.

14.2.1 Economy of derivation: a least effort condition

When there are multiple possible derivations all deriving the same representational output, economy conditions compel the grammar to perform the most economical one.[2] But how is economy to be quantified, characterized, or measured?

Let us consider verbal inflection formation as a case study, following Chomsky (1991b).

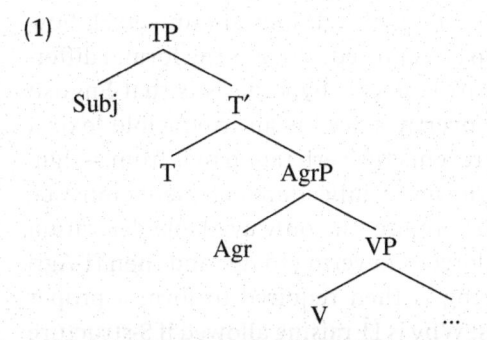

(1)
```
         TP
        /  \
     Subj   T'
           /  \
          T    AgrP
              /    \
            Agr     VP
                   /  \
                  V    ...
```

Given that verbal morphology on T and on Agr must be combined with V (Lasnik 1981b) by S-structure in (1), there seem to be two logical solutions to meeting the SS demand: either V moves to T/Agr or T/Agr moves to V. The former involves V-raising to Agr, and then the V-Agr complex subsequently raises to T. The latter possibility involves T-lowering to Agr and then to V. Notice, however, that the lowering operation creates improper chains: the traces left behind by T and Agr are unbound. These representations then have to be 'repaired' to create proper chains in the LF representation, to which the Chain Condition is assumed to apply. Chomsky (1991b) suggests that by applying LF-raising of V, which is already combined with T and Agr by lowering, proper chains are formed. In both the lowering and the raising derivations, T and Agr can be amalgamated with V and the resulting amalgam appears at T. Hence, the two derivations compete for most economical. Now the question is which derivation is more economical: the derivation with only raising or the derivation with both lowering and subsequent 'repair'-raising.

Chomsky (1991b) suggests that in terms of least effort, the V-raising derivation is preferred over the T/Agr-lowering option in that the former (with only raising) involves fewer derivational steps than the latter (with both lowering and raising). The idea is that fewer transformational rule applications are more economical. As a concrete illustration of this, consider French and English V-movement data. According to Pollock (1989), French verbs obligatorily undergo overt movement in finite clauses while English main verbs remain *in situ* in overt syntax (see also Chapter 12):[3]

(2) a. John often kisses Mary
    b. *John kisses often Mary

(3) a. Jean embrasse souvent Marie
       Jean kiss   often   Marie
    b. *Jean souvent embrasse Marie

In English the verb must not precede the VP-adverb in (2) while in French (3) it must. In the English case, verbs never move across VP-adverbs in the mapping to S-structure/PF representation, i.e., there is no overt V-movement (of main verbs). If economy conditions are universal, how is this cross-linguistic variation to be captured? What is the formal difference between French and English? Pollock's hypothesis is that English main verbs cannot raise to Agr overtly since, as an irreducible lexical property, English 'opaque' Agr prevents the verb raised to it from assigning its theta-role at S-structure. However, inflectional elements must be attached/affixed by S-structure. Therefore, the only available derivation for the English case is that T undergoes lowering to Agr and then [T-Agr] lowers to V. Subsequent LF-raising is then required to form a proper chain. Now a new question arises: Why is LF raising allowed if S-structure raising to Agr was claimed to be a Theta Criterion violation? Chomsky's (1991b) answer is that at LF, Agr, having no semantic interpretation, deletes, as required by economy of representation. Therefore, the LF-raised English V is not in fact attached to an Agr at LF, and as a result, the theta-role can be assigned. Thus, English lowers and then raises yet this satisfies economy of derivation since it is the most economical derivation consistent with (i) the requirement that Infl/Agr affixes be attached at S-structure, (ii) the assumption that English Agr blocks theta-role assignment by a verb attached to it, (iii) the application of the Theta Criterion throughout the derivation, and (iv) the hypothesis that well-formed chains cannot include unbound traces. In the French case, on the other hand, V can raise from post-adverbial position to pre-adverbial position by S-structure. In principle, it could do so only by raising or by overt lowering followed by subsequent overt raising. In the spirit of least effort, overt raising without prior overt lowering is the derivation which is chosen since it involves fewer derivational steps and satisfies all requirements. In summary, all languages obey economy of derivation, apparent differences deriving from irreducible lexical properties of the language's functional categories, such as Agr. Thus it appears that the fact that "raising is necessary if possible" (Chomsky 1991b:426) follows from the economy condition. This is one of the case studies exemplifying the idea that fewer derivational steps ('least effort') are more economical.

Nevertheless, there are some cases where the 'fewer-is-more-economical' hypothesis does not work straightforwardly, necessitating further elaboration of economy guidelines. Thus, consider the fact that the English *yes/no* question in (4b) involves *do*-support.

(4) a. John kissed Mary
    b. Did John kiss Mary?

The derivation of (4b) should, like all derivations, observe the least effort requirement. In this case, however, inflectional morphemes are not amalgamated with V via V-raising, but instead the inserted *do* 'supports' these morphemes. Here it seems that only the raising operation is possible, much like in French: while the main verb *kiss* remains *in situ*, Agr raises to T and then [T-Agr] raises to C resulting in (4b). If the same analysis is applied to a past-tense declarative case, however, an unwanted output is obtained. Compare (5) with (4a):

(5) *John did kiss Mary   (*did* unstressed, non-contrastive)

If *do*-insertion renders T/Agr-lowering to V and subsequent LF-raising unnecessary as it does in (4b), there is no apparent reason why (5) should be ungrammatical. The derivation for (4a) contains many steps of movement made by lowering and LF-raising: two steps for lowering and two steps for LF-raising. Meanwhile, (5) requires only *do*-insertion and one step made by Agr-movement to T. If an economical derivation is determined only by the number of derivational steps, the derivation for (5) survives and blocks (4a). With respect to this puzzling problem, Chomsky (1991b) suggests an additional economy condition: UG principles are less costly than language-specific rules (such as English *do*-support). Chomsky (1991b:427) writes: "We may think of them [=UG principles], intuitively, as 'wired-in' and distinguished from the acquired elements of language, which bear a greater cost." How is this relevant to least effort conditions? Chomsky states that UG principles can be applied whenever necessary but language-specific rules are applied as 'last resorts' to avoid violations that are not otherwise avoidable. In this analysis, applying only UG operations, which are allowed to apply wherever possible, requires less effort than applying language-specific rules.

Successive-cyclic *wh*-movement (see Chapter 18) reveals another issue confronting economy of derivation, which we briefly mention here and develop further in Section 14.3. It has long been hypothesized that long-distance *wh*-movement is carried out by iterative application of (short) movement operations. However, such successive cyclic movement includes many more derivational steps than would a single one-fell-swoop movement to the final landing site. Under the 'fewer-is-more-economical' condition, long movement in a one-fell-swoop manner should be preferable to short movement by iterative application of the movement operation. Intermediate steps of *wh*-movement have been claimed to be "morphologically observable" in some languages (e.g., see McCloskey 1979, 2002 for Irish; Torrego 1984 for Spanish; but see den Dikken to appear and Section 18.10). In spite of involving many more derivational steps, it appears that successive short movement must somehow be the more economical option than long movement. This issue will be addressed in Section 14.3 (see also Zwart 1996).

14.2.2 Economy of representation: eliminating superfluous elements

As discussed in the last section, syntactic derivations are not allowed to contain any superfluous derivational steps. Chomsky (1991b:437) suggests in addition that correspondingly "there can be no superfluous symbols in representations." Chomsky's (1986b, 1991b) Principle of Full Interpretation (FI) "holds that an element can appear in a representation only if it is properly 'licensed'" (Chomsky 1991b:437). FI is a principle relating syntactic computation to the derived representations accessed by other/external systems. The three levels interfacing with other systems, D-structure, PF, and LF, are naturally assumed to exhibit representations observing FI. D-structure representations which are assumed to interface with the lexicon satisfy FI by obeying X-bar Theory, so that elements selected from the lexicon have to project structure in accordance with the X'-schema; otherwise, the lexicon cannot be linked to the computational system. Since PF is the interface to the external systems controlling pronunciation (or gesture for signed language) and perception, "each symbol is interpreted in terms of articulatory and perceptual mechanisms in a language-invariant manner" (p. 438). Similarly, for LF representations, "every element that appears at LF must have a language-invariant interpretation in terms of interactions with the systems of conceptual structure and language use" (p. 438). Thus, in the event that a syntactic representation contains a superfluous symbol, FI forces the symbol to disappear before reaching the interface levels. This is intended to underlie an explanatory account of the conditions under which certain deletion operations apply. That is, they apply 'in order to' delete superfluous elements prohibited from an interface level representation. (See Epstein 2003/2007 for relevant discussion of this mode of explanation.) Let us consider in more detail what a legitimate LF representation is.

Chomsky and Lasnik (1993) suggest that a chain is an LF legitimate object only if the chain is uniform. There are three types of uniform chains. First, let us consider A-chains, in which all positions in the chain are A-positions.

(6) John seems to like the car
LF: [$_{TP}$ John [$_{VP}$ seems [$_{TP}$ t_2 to [$_{VP}$ t_1 [$_{VP}$ like the car]]]]]

John undergoes A-movement from the embedded [SpecvP] to the matrix [SpecTP] via the embedded [SpecTP]. Since each position *John* occupies throughout the derivation is an A-position, the resulting chain (*John*, t_2, t_1) is uniform with respect to the A-property, so is LF-legitimate. The second type of chain is an A'-chain, in which all positions in the chain are A'-positions as in (7). In (7), the extracted element *how* is an adjunct, so that the launching-site and all other landing-sites are A'-positions. The resulting chain (*how*, t_3, t_2, t_1) is thus uniform with respect to A/A'-properties, hence it is a LF-legitimate chain as it is.

(7) How do you think that Sue fixed the car?
LF: [$_{CP}$ how do [$_{IP}$ t_3 you think [$_{CP}$ t_2 that [$_{IP}$ Sue fixed the car t_1]]]]

The third type of chain is another kind of A'-chain, called an 'operator-variable' chain, illustrated in (8).

(8) What do you think that Anna bought?
LF: [$_{CP}$ what do [$_{IP}$ t_3 you think [$_{CP}$ t_2 that [$_{IP}$ Anna bought t_1]]]]

In (8), the extracted *wh*-phrase *what* is an argument, so that the launching-site is an A-position. However, the landing sites are all A'-positions, so that the chain formed (*what*, t_3, t_2, t_1) is not uniform with respect to A/A'-properties. If the LF-representation retained this illegitimate object, the semantic interpretation of (8) could not be executed given FI, one aspect of which is assumed to be chain uniformity. Therefore, there is a need to apply a repair operation – a 'last resort' operation that yields fully interpretable representations. To 'save' the representation, Chomsky (1991b) and Chomsky and Lasnik (1993) assume that the generalized operation Affect α (subsuming Move, Delete, Insert) discussed in Lasnik and Saito (1992) is applied only as a last resort operation to satisfy FI. In this case, the deletion operation is applicable to the intermediate traces in order to transform the illegitimate chain (*what*, t_3, t_2, t_1) into the legitimate chain (*what*, t_1), a two-member chain composed of a semantically interpretable operator and variable. This application of deletion is the only way to save the representation in this case. Again, the idea is to explain empirically motivated rule application as opposed to stipulating when it must and must not apply in order to yield correct predictions.

Worth mentioning here is a tension between economy of derivation and economy of representation inherent in this analysis. While Affect α is applied as a last resort in order to render a representation legitimate, its application increases the number of derivational steps. In other words, here, the more economical representation (one satisfying FI) is derived by a more costly derivation: more work is needed to produce less representation. In order to allow such derivations, economy of derivation should be taken to apply the fewest operations necessary to yield representations satisfying FI. Perhaps this marks the beginning of the idea that the syntax operates in service to the interface conditions.

14.3 Toward the Minimalist Program

Since the introduction of Chomsky's (1993) Minimalist Program, the ban on superfluous elements (in derivations and in representations) has been applied also to the entire architecture of UG. One of the characteristic manifestations is the elimination of S-structure (first alluded to in Chomsky 1986b) and of D-structure as well. The goal of Minimalist architecture is to include within it only what is 'conceptually necessary,' namely, the lexicon and the interfaces CI and SM; non-interface, entirely syntax-internal levels of representation such as S- and D-structure should be eliminated if possible. Chomsky (1993:3) argues: "each language will determine a set of pairs (π, λ) (π drawn from PF and λ drawn from LF) as its formal representations of sound and meaning, insofar as these are determined by the language itself." In other words, there are no representations which have nothing to do with the ineliminable aspects of sound and meaning and the derivational system works only for the purpose of generating these fully interpretable representations. Those representational products produced by the computational system give fully interpretable instructions to the external systems. Also, these representations serve as inputs to the performance systems: PF-representation for the articulatory–perceptual system and LF-representation for the conceptual–intentional system. In this sense, PF/LF-legitimate objects can be defined as objects which can give appropriate instructions to the performance systems. Given this architecture, all the conditions (including FI) which have been applied to representations are now recaptured as interface conditions, imposed by the external systems needing instructions. If an LF-representation includes something superfluous, the representation naturally receives a defective interpretation in the C-I system.

Also, in order to execute more economical derivation, not only are 'fewer steps' and 'shorter moves' postulated but also the new concepts Procrastinate and Greed play important roles. The former states that

LF-movement is less costly than overt movement, so movement should be postponed to LF if possible. The latter, called 'self-serving last resort,' requires that the application of an operation to α is allowed only when morphological properties of α are not otherwise satisfied, enabling us to explain not only when operations do apply but also when operations do not apply.

The Minimalist Program provides us with clearer grounds regarding how/why linguistic representations are highly constrained under the spirit of least effort and also goes toward more restricted derivational procedures. By doing so, a higher level of explanation is attained in that the application and non-application of operations is not stipulated but rather is deduced from general economy conditions which are neither language-specific nor construction-specific and (following Chomsky 2005) are perhaps not uniquely syntactic or even linguistic by hypothesis but instead reflect general efficiency guidelines (least effort) and are formulated in service to interface interpretability (economy of representation).

14.3.1 The advent of checking theory

Chomsky (1993) develops the first version of the 'checking' theory of case and agreement (see also Chapter 17); and the analysis represents a milestone in Minimalist theorizing: the deduction of GB's Case Filter from far more general interface conditions, and the unification of case and agreement as specifier–head relations.

What motivates checking theory and what are its central assumptions? One major development in Chomsky (1993) is the elimination of GB's most central and unifying relation, government. For Chomsky (1993:6), "[i]n a minimalist theory, the crucial properties and relations will be stated in the simple and elementary terms of X-bar theory." The structural relation of government played a central, unifying role in GB theory – for example, theta-roles and case were assigned under government. Thus, if the complex definition of government is dispensed with on Minimalist grounds, all operations and principles that appeal to government "must be reformulated" (p. 6). How can this be accomplished?

A major concern of Chomsky (1993) was the *re*formulation of Case Theory. Within GB, case assignment was configurationally diverse hence non-unified in that, say, NOM was assigned to Spec TP, while ACC was assigned from a head to its complement, or in the instance of ECM, to the specifier of a head's complement. Alternatively, Chomsky (1995c:173) takes a "narrower approach" whereby "all these modes of structural Case assignment [are] recast in unified X-bar-theoretic terms, presumably under the Spec-head relation." Adopting, and elaborating, the split-Infl analysis of Pollock (1989), Chomsky (1993) assumes the basic clausal structure of (9):

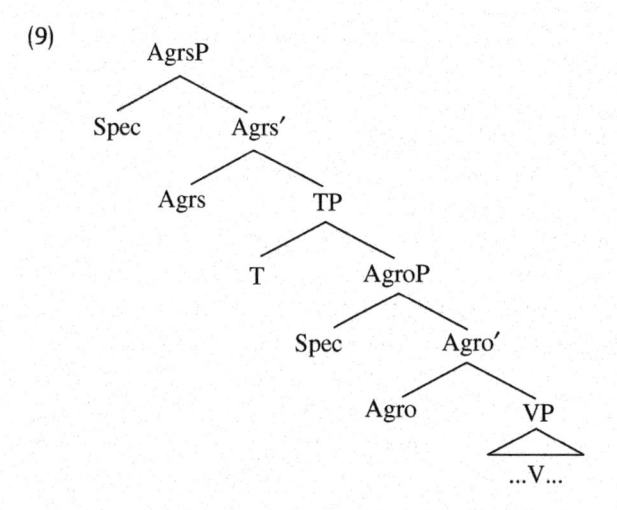

(9)
```
           AgrsP
          /     \
       Spec    Agrs'
              /    \
           Agrs    TP
                  /  \
                 T   AgroP
                     /    \
                  Spec   Agro'
                         /   \
                       Agro   VP
                              /\
                             ...V...
```

The Agr ('o' for Object and 's' Subject were just mnemonic, not theoretical) heads bear the standard phi-features, while T bears tense. Chomsky (1993) proposes that agreement and structural case are "manifestations of the Spec-head relation" (p. 7). The elimination of government in favor of the "fundamental relations of X-bar theory" is a form of methodological Minimalism: to the extent that X-bar Theory is independently motivated, the relations available from it come for free, and hence are to be preferred on conceptual grounds to (complex) relations such as government that are descriptively defined on phrase markers.

The traditional way to interpret agreement and structural case is as a form of feature assignment from one category to another. Some functional category lexically bears phi-features, for example, and 'gives them over' to a lexical head (to a Verb, for instance) under the right structural licensing conditions; similarly for case: a head such as finite T, or a transitive V, lexically 'has' case and 'gives it over' to a local NP. The alternative developed in Chomsky (1993), and still assumed in modified form in more recent Minimalist work (see below), is not one of feature assignment, but rather of feature checking (see also Chapter 17): a lexical head such as V and N enters the derivation not as a bare root but rather "with all of its morphological features, including Case and phi-features" (p. 29). Agreement features are assumed to be an 'intrinsic property' of categories such as V (and, for example, Adj), while case is intrinsic to N. Rather than being assigned inflectional features in the syntax, lexical categories such as V and N must now have their intrinsic inflectional features checked against a functional category with matching features. Checking can take place only in the restricted licensing configurations of the primitive X-bar relations. This, in turn, motivates a series of derivational operations, specifically head and phrasal movement. The intent is to try to deduce instances of obligatory movement of a category X from the requirement that X have its features checked, which requires X to get into the relevant checking relation.

Simplifying somewhat, let us consider subject agreement and nominative case checking, in, say, *He eats cheese*. The NP/DP *he* (specifically, its head) will have an intrinsic, lexically specified case feature which it bears as it enters the derivation: *he*[nom]. Likewise the head *eats* is fully inflected as *eats*[Agrs, Tns]. For convergence, the intrinsic inflectional features of these lexical categories must be checked. There are two checking relations available, head–head, and spec–head. Since it is itself a head, the relevant checking relation for *eats*[Agrs, Tns] is head–head, and thus this Verb will raise to Agrs in (9), where the relevant local configuration is represented in (10):

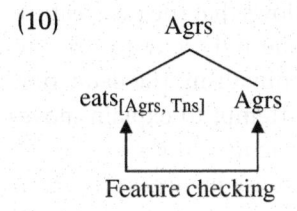

(10)
```
            Agrs
           /    \
  eats[Agrs, Tns]  Agrs
       ↑           ↑
       └───────────┘
        Feature checking
```

Here Agrs, which bears phi-features, checks against the Agrs features of *eats*; if the phi-features of the two heads are identical (i.e., if they 'match'), then checking is successful and as a result, Agrs (or each semantically uninterpretable feature within it) 'disappears' – a prerequisite to semantic (LF) well-formedness. If the features of the two elements are not identical, then Agrs cannot delete and the derivation fails to converge at LF. Next, the Agrs+*eats*[– , Tns] complex raises to T in order to check the Tns feature of *eats* against the matching Tns feature of T. Head movement involves just this sort of checking, and it is motivated by the need for convergence at the interfaces. Under checking theory, and on the assumption that only the primitive relations of X-bar Theory constitute the available checking relations, head movement is motivated by the need for convergence at the interfaces.

Chomsky (1993) assumes that the NP, *he* in our representative examples, includes "intrinsic" case and phi-features "and that these too must be checked in the appropriate position" (p. 29). Chomsky assumes that +tns T checks nominative case. Thus, the subject NP raises to spec TP for nominative case checking. We will explore in the next section more recent developments related to which element 'benefits' from checking: the mover or a category in a primitive relation to the landing site.

So far, we have sketched the basic ideas of checking theory as proposed in Chomsky (1993). A number of important developments within the Minimalist Theory emerged. One is a deduction of the Case Filter (with case and agreement unified under the specifier–head relation). In Chomsky (1993) the motivation for NP movement to Spec T is essentially the need for feature checking: if the features are not checked by matching features in a primitive X-bar configuration, then the derivation fails to converge at the interfaces. The Case Filter then becomes "an interface condition" (p. 29). This leading idea develops in Chomsky (1995c) into a generalized theory of the interface interpretability of features. The case feature of an NP is not interpretable at the LF interface; this is assumed to be a fact about the structural case feature – evidenced by there being no obvious semantic distinction between *he/him* in virtual minimal pairs such as *I believe he left* and *I believe him to have left* (see also Chapter 17). Given economy of representation, which "we may take ... to be nothing other than FI [Full Interpretation]", it follows that "every symbol must receive an 'external' interpretation by the language-independent rules" (p. 200). Since case is not interpretable at LF, and since, crucially under checking theory, case is an intrinsic feature of N (NP), it follows that the case feature must be checked (assuming that checking is the only way to execute feature deletion). Here we see a milestone of Minimalism: the deduction of the Case Filter. Again, the central goal is to attempt to explain movement, and eliminate purely syntax-internal (S-Structure) filters.

But Chomsky (1993) also has other important consequences relevant to economy. Under checking theory "we need no longer adopt the Emonds-Pollock assumption that in English-type languages I lowers to V" (p. 195) as discussed in detail in Section 14.2. Rather, "V will have the inflectional features before Spell-Out in any event, and the checking procedure may take place anywhere, in particular, after LF movement. French-type and English-type languages now look alike at LF" (p. 195). In both French and English, then, V will raise up to and through the functional projections (AgrO, AgrS, Tns) in order that V's intrinsic inflectional features be checked under the head–head relation. In French, such head movement is overt, i.e., before Spell-out (yielding *Jean embrasse souvent Marie* 'John kisses often Mary', (3a)); in English, it occurs after Spell-out, it is covert (yielding *John often kisses Mary* (2a) at PF).[4] Chomsky (1993), adopting ideas of Pollock (1989) and of Chomsky (1991b), postulates that this overt–covert distinction can be derived in terms of 'feature strength' (see also Chapter 4). Agr is strong in French-type languages; Agr is weak in English-type languages. This notion of strength is an early form of interpretability of features at the interfaces (more fully developed in later Minimalist work). The strong checking features of Agr are 'visible' at PF. These strong features furthermore are *not* PF legitimate. In effect, then, strong features force overt movement. If Agr bearing strong features has not participated in checking, then its strong features are not deleted and hence make their way to PF inducing a PF crash. If the features are checked, they 'disappear' since 'they have done their job.' Thus, since Agr's checking features are strong, 'overt' movement follows from the interface conditions. The Agr checking features in English are weak (in contrast to French), which means that they are not visible to PF and so do not cause a problem there.[5] An interesting question that now emerges is why overt raising is barred in English. Since Agr is weak in English, V need not raise, but this does not in and of itself entail that V cannot raise. Here is precisely where economy of derivation enters. According to Chomsky (1995c), a natural economy condition is that LF movement is cheaper than overt movement. This principle is called 'Procrastinate.' Basically, the idea is that if an operation need not apply now, then it must not apply now; operations apply only when the time comes that they must, hence as late as possible, never prematurely. Hence, English overt V-raising is barred by this economy of derivation condition.

14.3.2 The tension between different notions of economy and a possible resolution

At this stage in the historical development of economy conditions, a tension between different notions of economy emerges. Chomsky (1993) notes two notions of derivational economy. Relative to the movement operation, one notion is that movements should be as short as possible. Thus, in Minimality cases like Superiority, Superraising, the Head Movement Constraint, and *wh*-islands (cf. Rizzi 1990a, and Chapter 18), the generalization seems to be that the shortest move is preferred. In (11), an example of Superiority, movement of $whom_1$ is shorter than movement of $whom_2$ (in terms of intervening categories or paths) and thus the shorter move (11a) is preferred via economy.

(11) a. $Whom_1$ did John persuade t_1 [to visit $whom_2$]?
    b. *$Whom_2$ did John persuade $whom_1$ [to visit t_2]?

"Looking at these phenomena in terms of economy considerations, it is clear that in all the 'bad' cases, some element has failed to make 'the shortest move'" (Chomsky 1993:14).

Another natural notion of economy, however, is 'fewest derivational steps,' as discussed in Section 14.2, where one derivation is compared to another based on the number of operations (or instances of an operation) that have applied: the derivation with the fewest operations (necessary for convergence) is preferred. Such a notion of economy is featured in Chomsky (1993) in an early Minimalist analysis of word order variation between French and English, as detailed in Section 14.2 above.

Chomsky (1993) notes a tension between these two notions of economy: "if a derivation keeps to shortest moves, it will have more steps; if it reduces the number of steps, it will have longer moves" (p. 15). In Chomsky this tension is resolved by taking "the basic transformational operation to be not Move alpha but *Form Chain*" (p. 15). Consider (12):

(12) __ seems [__ to be likely [John to win]]

Under standard successive-cyclic A-movement, construed in classic derivational terms, (12) would involve two instances of movement: First, *John* moves to spec of intermediate T, yielding (13), and second, *John* in intermediate position moves to matrix spec T, yielding (14).

(13) __ seems [John to be likely [t to win]]

(14) John seems [t to be likely [t to win]]
     ↑_____↑_____|

Each of these two movements is the shortest possible; but making such short moves entails that there are more derivational steps. The Form Chain approach, on the other hand, effectively eliminates derivation-internal steps. Form Chain takes (12) as input and directly gives (14) as output, all at once. Thus, in mapping (12) directly to (14), only one relevant operation has applied, i.e., there has been just one application of Form Chain. Form Chain is representational to the extent that there is no internal structure in the mapping of (12) to (14); the operation Form Chain takes (12) as input, the lights go out and when they are back on again (14) is present. Form Chain then has one step. Shortest move is translated to keep links of a chain minimal, where the chain is formed all at once.

14.3.3 Global economy vs. local economy

Another important issue that arises in considerations of economy is whether economy is viewed as global, involving an entire derivation or comparisons between multiple derivations, or local, involving comparison of just some restricted set of operations internal to a single derivation at a single derivational point. As noted in Collins (1997), early economy principles were global. They involve comparison of alternative derivations with the same starting point (the same initial lexical array or numeration) and the same convergent endpoint. Consider, for example, Kitahara's (1995) formulation of 'Fewest Steps' in a derivation:

(15) *Shortest Derivation Requirement*
    Minimize the number of operations necessary for convergence.

Collins (1997) notes that (15) is global in the sense that the number of steps of alternative derivations (from the same numeration (Chomsky 1995c) or to a single convergent interface representation) are compared. (15) is also global "in that it involves reference to the notion of convergence" (Collins 1997:5). Basically, we need to know where the derivation is going, what its output will be (specifically, a convergent object at both interfaces), and then select the derivation among the available competitors that involves the fewest steps.

Collins argues for an alternative conception of economy: local economy. The basic idea is that economy is evaluated based on immediately available syntactic objects within a derivation, and not on the entire derivation. "During a derivation at any step the decision about whether to apply an operation (in an optimal derivation) is based on the syntactic objects to which the operation is applying" (Collins 1997:4). Last Resort is proposed as a principle of local economy. Last Resort states that:

(16) An operation OP involving alpha may apply only if some property of alpha is satisfied.

Thus, head movement can apply only if features of the head get checked as a result, likewise for phrasal movement. Minimality is then stated in terms of operations that satisfy Last Resort:

(17) *Minimality*:

An operation OP (satisfying Last Resort) may apply only if there is no smaller operation OP' (satisfying Last Resort).   (Collins 1997:9)

Collins argues that the only economy conditions are local ones, like (16) and (17) above, and much subsequent literature in Minimalism adopted this locality approach.

14.4 From local economy to efficient computation

Since Collins (1997), the focus of Minimalist inquiry has been shifted to the elimination of principles with 'look-ahead properties' in favor of those that keep to local economy, and the attempt of such elimination has formed the basis for our understanding of the principles of efficient computation. In this section, we trace the development of the principles of local economy and of efficient computation.

14.4.1 Competitors under local economy

In Chomsky (2000b) and his subsequent work, principles with 'look-ahead properties' have been reformulated in terms of 'local calculations,' under which competitors are no longer entire derivations associated with the same lexical array LA, rather competitors are alternative possible operations applied at a single point internal to a single derivation.[6] The decision as to which operation is the most efficient one can be made using only information available at that particular choice point in the derivation. Under this interpretation of local economy, Chomsky (2000b:101) defined Move as the composite operation that combines Merge and Agree, and he demonstrated that preference for simpler operations over more complex ones captures the 'last resort' character of Move. Consider (18):

(18) a. *there is likely [$_{TP}$ someone to be $t_{someone}$ in the room]
  b. there is likely [$_{TP}$ t_{there} to be someone in the room]

Each derivation involves the stage [T [*be someone in the room*]], where T requires that something occupy Spec-T.[7] At this point, Merge of expletive *there* in Spec-T and Move of *someone* to Spec-T are (in principle) available, but preference for simpler operations over more complex ones selects Merge of *there* in Spec-T over Move of *someone* to Spec-T, because "Move is more complex than its subcomponents Merge and Agree" (Chomsky 2000b:101). Thus, the 'last resort' character of Move (observed when constructing the embedded TP in (18b)) follows naturally from the local calculation.

This analysis, however, would make a wrong prediction. Consider (19):

(19) a. I expected [$_{TP}$ someone to be $t_{someone}$ in the room]
      b. *I expected [$_{TP}$ t_I to be someone in the room]

Here too, each derivation involves the stage [T [*be someone in the room*]], and two options, Merge of *I* in Spec-T and Move of *someone* to Spec-T, are (by hypothesis) available to narrow syntax; but if so, preference of simpler operations over more complex ones would select Merge of *I* in Spec-T over Move of *someone* to Spec-T, yielding the wrong result, namely (19b), along with the inability to generate (19a). Chomsky (1995c:313) took the contrast in (19) to indicate that an argument merged into a non-theta-position becomes an illegitimate object, violating the Principle of Full Interpretation, and thereby causing the derivation to crash. He suggested that at the stage in question, the crashing fate of Merge of *I* in Spec-T is calculated; hence, Move of *someone* to Spec-T – a more complex operation than Merge of *I* in Spec-T (which will crash the derivation later at the CI interface) – is allowed to take place. Chomsky (2000b:103), however, presented an alternative analysis with no 'look-ahead' calculation. He took the contrast in (19) to indicate that Merge of an argument in non-theta-position is not available to NS as a legitimate competitor operation at the corresponding stage. He proposed the following theta-theoretic condition (where pure Merge is Merge that is not a subpart of Move):

(20) Pure Merge in theta-position is required of (and restricted to) arguments.

Under (20), Merge of *I* in Spec-T in (19) is not an allowable or possible operation (by definition); hence it is not a competitor. As desired, (19b) is simply underivable and is blocked without any reference to the 'look-ahead' calculation, while (19a) is now derivable as desired. If operative complexity matters for Minimalist design, this alternative analysis is arguably preferable to the one with the 'look-ahead' calculation.[8]

Under (20), Merge of *there* in Spec-T in (18) is still permitted as a legitimate competitor operation (since *there* is not an argument), and this option is selected by preference of simpler operations over more complex ones. Note that this particular choice is logically possible only if *there* is an item present in the LA.

As shown above, the initial choice of LA plays a crucial role, but this cannot be the whole story. Consider (21):

(21) a. there is a possibility [$_{CP}$ that someone will be $t_{someone}$ in the room]
      b. a possibility is [$_{CP}$ that there will be someone in the room]

(21a) is now seemingly paradoxical. The derivation of (21a) contains *there*, and recall, inserting *there* is less complex than moving *someone*, yet in (21a), we see that Move of *someone* to Spec-T in the embedded CP is possible. It should not be, given that insertion of *there* is a simpler operation filling Spec-T. So somehow, when building the embedded CP, in particular Spec-(embedded)T, Move can be preferred over Merge – the exact opposite of what was motivated above, namely Merge over Move.

Chomsky (2000b:106) presented a straightforward solution to this problem. The basic idea is that structures are built bottom-up, cyclically, in chunks called 'phases' (see also Section 18.9), each associated with its own separate lexical subarray SA. So first we form SA={*that, will, be, someone, in, the, room*}, needed to generate the embedded CP. Expletive *there* is absent from this SA. Consequently, insertion of *there* is not an option, since *there* is absent from the SA (formed to build the embedded CP). Thus, movement of *someone*, in fact, satisfies Merge over Move, since we had nothing to merge in Spec-T, when movement to Spec-T took place.

Formally, Chomsky proposed that a subarray SA_i is extracted from LA and placed in the workspace of narrow syntax. As SA_i is exhausted, narrow syntax may proceed if possible, or a new SA_j may be extracted from LA and placed in the workspace, allowing narrow syntax to proceed as before. Under this proposal, narrow syntax accesses only part of the entire sentential LA at each stage of the derivation, thus contributing to the reduction of operative complexity.

In short, given the postulation of SA, (21a) and (21b) do not compete. In the derivation of (21a), the (embedded) CP is constructed from SA_i containing no expletive; hence, Move of *someone* to Spec-(embedded)T is the only option available to narrow syntax at the corresponding stage. In the derivation of (21b), the (embedded) CP is constructed from SA_j containing an expletive; hence, Merge of *there* in Spec-(embedded)T is selected over Move of *someone* to Spec-(embedded)T at the corresponding stage, because Merge (of *there* in Spec-(embedded)T) is simpler than Move (of *someone* to Spec-(embedded)T). Notice there is no optionality involved in the derivations of (21). Importantly, optionality has to be eliminated if we adopt the Strong Minimalist Thesis, i.e., narrow syntax is a computationally efficient satisfier of the interface conditions, though the option of having an expletive is available to the formation of lexical arrays and subarrays.

14.4.2 Phase-based cyclicity

The notion SA received more prominence when the cyclicity condition was reformulated. Chomsky (2000b:106) assumed that SA should determine a natural syntactic object SO. Such an SO is taken to be 'propositional' – either a verb phrase *v*P (in which all theta-roles are assigned) or a full clause CP (including tense and illocutionary force). With this assumption, he proposed that (i) SA contains an occurrence of *v* or C, exactly one occurrence if it is restricted as narrowly as possible, and (ii) a SO derived in this way by choice of SA is a phase of a derivation, i.e., vP and CP are said to be phases. Given (i) and (ii), Chomsky (p. 108) formulated the Phase Impenetrability Condition (PIC) as a very strong cyclicity condition:

(22) In phase α with head H, the domain of H is not accessible to operations outside α, only H and its edge are accessible to such operations.

Upon the completion of α, the PIC prohibits any head outside α from affecting lexical items inside the complement domain of H.[9] Furthermore, as discussed by Chomsky (2000b:132), if H itself is no longer accessible after a new SA is extracted and a lexical item of this SA is merged with α, then PIC ensures that, upon the completion of α, all lexical items inside the complement domain of H become 'syntactically inert,' undergoing no further syntactic operation.[10]

This phase-based analysis of cyclic derivation sheds light on the old problem posed by two apparently contradictory notions of economy: "if a derivation keeps to shortest moves, it will have more steps; if it reduces the number of steps, it will have longer moves" (Chomsky 1993:15; see Zwart 1996 for relevant discussion). Given phase-based cyclic derivation, movement must always target the edge of the minimal phase containing the mover's departure site; hence one-fell-swoop movement crossing a phase is not a possible operation (see also Sections 18.8 and 18.9). Consequently, under this formalism there is no choice between fewest moves vs. shortest move; the latter are required.

14.4.3 Uninterpretable features and syntactic operations

Under the phase-based analysis of cyclic derivation, what happens inside a phase cycle has been at the center of investigation.

In the early stage of Minimalist theorizing, the presence of semantically uninterpretable features (like structural case or phi-features on T) was recognized as a serious problem, and why they exist became one of the core questions. To answer this question, the Minimalist Program pursued the intuition that they are implemented for movement, where movement is, by hypothesis, required to satisfy FI; this pursuit substantiated the view that movement is carried out in the interest of deleting those (otherwise useless, but by hypothesis offending) uninterpretable features.

Let us take a concrete case. Consider (23):

(23) [$_\alpha$ an unpopular candidate] T-was elected t_α

In Chomsky (2000b, 2001), there are three kinds of uninterpretable features: the set of phi-features on T (identifying T as a target of movement), the EPP-feature of T (requiring that something be overtly merged with the projection headed by T), and the case-feature of *an unpopular candidate* (identifying α as a category for merger that satisfies EPP). The probe–goal system (itself constrained by Minimal Search, not illustrated here but hypothesized also to be optimal) is then proposed as a device to yield (23) by deleting all three kinds of uninterpretable features. In (23), for the phi-set of T, there is only one choice of matching features, namely, the phi-set of *candidate*. Now, locating *candidate* as a goal, the phi-set of T, functioning as a probe, erases under phi-matching, and the case-feature of the goal erases as a reflection of such phi-matching. The operation Agree carries out such erasure of the uninterpretable features on probe and goal, and Merge (moving the goal of T's probe to Spec-T) satisfies the EPP-feature of T. Thus, the combination of Agree and Merge dislocates α to Spec-T and eliminates all three kinds of uninterpretable features (listed above), and it does so inside the phase. Notice that in this phase, there is no competing operation that could carry out the same task; hence, narrow syntax has no option but to select the composite operation Move (combining Agree and Merge).

In Chomsky (2007, 2008), however, it is proposed that T does not inherently bear phi-features; rather, it gets them in the course of the derivation, from the C that selects T, via feature inheritance. This proposal entails that T bears phi-features when selected by C. Under this proposal, the combination of Agree and Merge still dislocates α to Spec-T and eliminates all three kinds of uninterpretable features, but it does so necessarily after Merge of C with 'spec-less' TP.[11]

Here, more detailed analysis of the deletion of uninterpretable features is needed. Prior to the deletion of uninterpretable features, they must receive some value; otherwise, their phonetic interpretation cannot be explained. We get *he* or *him* in English depending on the structural conditions for case valuation. Likewise, specifications of the phi-features on English T (phonetically realized as -s or as Ø) are syntactically determined.

The assumption is then that structural case and phi-features on T "are unvalued in the lexicon, thus properly distinguished from interpretable features, and assigned their values in syntactic configurations, hence necessarily by probe-goal relations" (Chomsky 2007:18). Under this assumption, prior to Agree, such uninterpretable features are (by definition) offending features at the two interfaces; hence, they cannot be transferred. Once valued by Agree, they may yield a phonetic interpretation, but they will never yield a semantic interpretation.[12] Thus, even if they are valued by Agree, they still lack a semantic interpretation, and so they must be deleted, i.e., not transferred to the semantic component, where their appearance would violate FI. But such deletion cannot take place after they are valued by Agree, because "the uninterpretable features, and only these, enter the derivation without values, and are distinguished from interpretable features by virtue of this property" (Chomsky 2001:5); hence, in the eyes of Transfer, after valuation, they are indistinguishable from their interpretable counterparts, which are (by definition) undeletable. Thus, Chomsky (2007:19) concludes that they must be valued at the phase level where they are transferred, and such derivationally valued features are deleted when transferred to the semantic component, but they remain intact when transferred to the phonological component.[13]

14.4.4 Principles of efficient computation

In Chomsky (2007, 2008), the simple definition of Merge has been maintained, and the observed properties of Merge have been (largely) derived from local efficiency considerations, reformulated as principles of efficient computation.

Merge is defined as "an operation that takes n syntactic objects (SOs) already formed, and constructs from them a new SO" (Chomsky 2008:137), and "arguably restriction of computational resources limits n for Merge to two" (p. 138). The binary limitation, $n=2$, yields Kayne's (1981) unambiguous paths – the binary-branching structures that Chomsky's (2000b) Minimal Search and Kayne's (1994) LCA-based linearization operate on. Binarity is understood to be a property of Merge deducible from a general principle of efficient computation (not a specifically linguistic property stipulated in the definition of Merge).

Another principle of efficient computation is the No Tampering Condition (NTC): "Merge of X and Y leaves the two SOs unchanged" (Chomsky 2008:138). Given NTC, Merge does not alter X or Y; rather, it places the two SOs in a set.[14] Furthermore, Merge of X and Y results in 'syntactic extension,' forming a new SO={X, Y}, not 'syntactic infixation' embedding X within Y, for example. One desirable consequence of NTC is that Merge invariably applies to the edge; hence, the empirical content of Chomsky's (1993) Extension Condition (largely) follows from NTC.

The Inclusiveness Condition is another natural principle of efficient computation: "no new objects are added in the course of computation apart from rearrangements of lexical properties" (Chomsky 1995c:228). Given the Inclusiveness Condition, Merge does not add bar levels, traces, indices, or any similar technicalia (invoked in GB theory) throughout a derivation.

Assuming Merge to be the sole structure-building operation of narrow syntax, Chomsky (2005, 2007, 2008) argues that Move should reduce to an instance of Merge.[15] Suppose X is merged to Y (introducing the asymmetry only for expository purposes). There are (in principle) two possible positions where X originates: either X originates external to Y (External Merge, EM) or X originates internal to Y (Internal Merge, IM). But they are simply two instances of the same operation Merge; and in both cases, Merge yields a new SO={X, Y}. Now, given NTC, IM necessarily yields two copies of X: one external to Y (in the landing-site position) and the other within Y (the departure site), as in [X [$_Y$ ... X ...]]. Thus, there is no need to stipulate a rule of formation of copies (or remerge), and Chomsky's (1993) copy theory of movement then follows from "just IM applying in the optimal way, satisfying NTC" (Chomsky 2007:10); it is a consequence of NTC-compliant execution of IM.

To generate a derivation, Merge must be able to find SOs, and how Merge gets access to SOs is also constrained by the principles of efficient computation. In the simplest case, only the label (i.e., head) of the full SO – either the root SO thus far constructed or the atomic SO not yet merged – can be accessed to drive further operations. Suppose X and Y are two separate full SOs. Then, their labels x and y can be accessed with "no search" (Chomsky 2000b:132); they are 'directly accessible' to narrow syntax. Suppose X is internal to Y (where Y is the root SO thus far constructed). Then, the accessed label y of Y, functioning as a probe, carries out the task of finding X as its goal. This probe–goal search, which reduces operative complexity by restricting the searchable domain of the probe to just its complement domain, is taken to be part of the generalized computationally efficient principle, Minimal Search (Chomsky 2007:9).[16]

Minimal Search is arguably the outgrowth or development and refinement of 'derivational c-command' (Epstein *et al.* 1998, Epstein 1999, Epstein and Seely 2006), under which c-command is not stipulatively defined on output representations, but is rather deduced from the bottom-up iterative application of binary Merge during the course of the derivation. Thus, it is natural, for example, that upon the merger of T with [*a man outside*], T minimally searches precisely the SO it was merged with, namely [*a man outside*], and this search by T finds (or matches) the phi-features of *man* and values the unvalued phi-features on T as 3rd person, masculine, singular, ultimately pronounced /iz/ as in *There is a man outside*. Interestingly, Epstein *et al.* (1998: Section 4.8) noted that c-command seems to be a necessary condition for a syntactic relation or phenomenon, but they also noted it is not sufficient – and wondered why. Specifically, c-command is an unbounded relation that can span multiple clauses, yet we see no syntactic relations spanning such distances. Under Chomsky's PIC-based analysis, coupled with Minimal Search, it is explained why 'c-command within a phase' (a.k.a. Minimal Search) is derivationally deducible and c-command relations strictly bounded by PIC.

As shown above, it is reasonable to maintain the simple definition of Merge and to derive the observed properties of Merge from principles of efficient computation such as the binary limitation, NTC, the Inclusiveness Condition, and Minimal Search.

14.5 Summary and conclusion

In this chapter, we have reviewed the central notions of economy, including aspects of their history, motivation, modern form, and empirical content. There are two notions of economy: economy of representation and economy of derivation. As for the former, the goal is to minimize the theoretical constructs postulated, appealing only to those concerning irreducible lexical features (i.e., atoms), the products of their combination, and the 'conceptually necessary' interface requirements (of sound and meaning) demanding interpretability of representations. As for economy of derivation, the goal is to deduce stipulated technical constraints on rules to independently motivated, ideally not linguistic-specific, principles of efficient computation. Indeed, the Strong Minimalist Thesis regarding syntax, phonology, and semantics might be encapsulated as computationally efficient satisfaction of natural interface conditions. Interestingly, the theory is neither rule-based (as was Standard Theory) nor filter-based (as was GB Theory), but rather is mixed. There are simple, minimal rules (perhaps even just one, viz. Merge) the application of which is constrained by general principles of minimal computation; any effort must be motivated by the 'functional' (see, e.g., Epstein 2003/2007) goal of satisfying minimal, natural, interpretability requirements of the interfaces. This program is consistent with Einstein's conception of "the grand aim of all science, which is to cover the greatest possible number of empirical facts by logical deduction from the smallest possible number of hypotheses" (Einstein 1954:282), committed to the view that "our experience hitherto justifies us in believing that nature is the realization of the simplest conceivable mathematical ideas" (Einstein 1934:274).

Notes

1. For an excellent recent overview of Government and Binding Theory, see Lasnik and Lohndal (2010); see also Chapters 2 and 4, and Chomsky and Lasnik (1993).
2. For the purposes of this section, we will assume that multiple derivations compete for most economical only if they result in identical output representations. See Section 14.4 for discussion of competitor sets.
3. As Pollock (1989) observes, V-movement in French is optional in infinitival clauses. In English, on the other hand, finite auxiliaries such as *be* and *have* behave like obligatory raising verbs in French. That is, the issue is not only French vs. English. Following Lasnik (1981b), Chomsky (1991b) makes a distinction between these languages in terms of the strength of Agr: strong Agr, which French has, can accept any element while weak Agr, which English chooses, can only accept 'light' elements, e.g. finite auxiliaries. This chapter does not go into detailed discussion of French infinitives and English auxiliaries but rather seeks to present the verb movement facts as an illustration of the properties of economy.
4. Note that the overt/covert distinction with V-raising is analogous to Huang's (1982a) theory of overt vs. covert *wh*-movement: derivations are universal, but the specific point in the derivation at which PF-interpretation applies is parameterized, with few options (before

vs. after spell-out). But for the MP there is no S-structure and hence no parameters can involve S-structure (hence no 'apply before/after S-structure'). For Chomsky, only properties of functional categories can be parameterized, leading to the notion of feature 'strength.'

5. As Chomsky (1995c) notes, the weak vs. strong distinction is stipulative. However, this stipulation involves features of functional categories, and is thus consistent with the Borer (1984b) and Fukui (1986) hypothesis that such features, the atomic, i.e., irreducible elements of the theory, are the loci of parametric variation.

6. Chomsky (1995c:225) extended lexical arrays to numerations, in order to distinguish independent selections of a single lexical item. A numeration is defined as a set of pairs (LI, i), where LI is an item of the lexicon and i is its index, understood to be the number of times that LI is selected. In his later work, however, Chomsky (2000b:114) noted that this extension can be eliminated by leaving the removal of an item of LA when accessed in computation as an option. We leave this issue open and proceed with a simpler concept, namely LA. The choice between the two concepts, however, does not affect our discussion.

7. We ignore *to* here, since it is not relevant for our discussion.

8. Notice that here we see 'look-ahead' being avoided by recasting a representational constraint (on LF) as a constraint on rule application (see Section 14.1).

9. Suppose α is HP=[XP [H YP]]. Then, YP is the complement domain of H, and XP is the edge of H.

10. Chomsky (2001) slightly modified the formulation of the PIC. Under the modified version, the PIC applies to α as soon as α is embedded within a distinct phase. In his recent work, however, Chomsky (2007, 2008) adopts his (2000b) version of PIC (given in (22)). We leave this issue open and proceed with a restrictive version, namely PIC formulated as (22). The choice between the two versions, however, does not affect our discussion.

11. This 'feature-transmitting' property of C (allowing T to inherit features from C) is then assigned to phase heads generally: C and v. See Epstein *et al.* (to appear b) for precise presentation of step-by-step derivations in this theory. See also Epstein *et al.* (to appear a) for an attempt to explain on the basis of feature inheritance (i) why it is that the phase-head complements, VP and TP, are what gets spelled out, and (ii) why these complements are spelled out when they are.

12. That is, while case and agreement seem to be syntactically determined processes with phonetic reflexes, the claim is that there are no corresponding syntactically determined 'semantic feature valuation' operations, e.g., where an animacy feature is valued in proximity to some other animacy feature. See Epstein *et al.* (2010) for relevant discussion.

13. As concerns the timing of valuation and transfer, see Epstein and Seely (2002a), Epstein et al. (2010), and Richards (2007).
14. Empirically, for example, Merging *the* and *dog* together to form a DP does not alter *the* or *dog*, though we can imagine and formulate combinatorial systems in which such Merger could change the meaning of *dog*, the meaning of *the*, their syntactic category membership, their lexical phonology, etc.
15. Note that in Chomsky (2005, 2007, 2008), Move is no longer the composite operation that combines Agree and Merge.
16. Given this interpretation of Minimal Search, the label cannot probe into its own specifier.

15

Syntax, binding, and patterns of anaphora

Ken Safir

15.1 Introduction

In this chapter, I present what is understood about the portion of our innate human language faculty that permits us to understand the patterns of anaphoric possibilities permitted by linguistic forms and sentences that contain them. Although semantic issues intrude constantly, the primary focus of this chapter is on the consequences of the pattern of anaphora for syntactic theory.

An *anaphoric relation* is typically said to hold whenever we relate the semantic value (or reference) of a linguistic form to the value of some previous or anticipated mention.[1] The syntactically determined distribution of possible anaphoric readings raises what Chomsky (1986b) called 'Plato's problem' in a particularly poignant way. Native speakers have a great deal of knowledge about where anaphoric relations can and cannot hold, knowledge that is not sufficiently explained by the meaning of words or their exposure to the contexts in which they are spoken. Although the patterns of anaphora differ across languages in ways that we are still discovering, much of the variation seems systematic and some generalizations about anaphoric patterns are robust. As a result, linguistic theory has devoted a great deal of attention to anaphoric relations over the last fifty years and the analysis of anaphoric patterns has frequently influenced the direction of syntactic theorizing.

My goal is to give a portrait of a moment in our understanding of these matters. In so doing, I will flag central discoveries and advances and present the major theoretical proposals and the concerns that motivate them. My coverage of the issues will not be complete or comprehensive and my theoretical biases will emerge frequently, but I hope that my presentation of the state of the art will provide a sense of the trajectory of the research in this domain of inquiry and draw attention to some open issues that we may hope the next generation of linguists will better understand. For reasons of space, my presentation will be empirically thin, but references are provided for those who are inclined to explore the issues in deeper detail.

Part of the art of every science is to narrow larger questions into smaller ones that permit feasible research programs, and so the divisions in this chapter are designed to refine the questions that must be explored. Section 15.2 lays out some boundary conditions for the syntax/semantics interface that anaphora questions inevitably invoke, while introducing questions surrounding obviation and the distribution of non-local, non-obligatory anaphora. In Section 15.3 we explore Chomsky's (1981) Binding Theory, the challenges it faced, and the strategies used to defend it. The families of theories that have been offered as more explanatory alternatives to the Binding Theory are sketched and evaluated in Section 15.4. Section 15.5 explores the richness of anaphoric morphology and its consequences for the syntax of anaphora and is followed by a brief conclusion.

15.2 The interface between syntax and interpretation

As a bit of convenient terminology, let us say that in any circumstance where two linguistic forms A and B are understood to pick out the same entity in a discourse that A and B are coconstrued. Because there are a variety of coconstrual relations, and not all of them are regulated by syntax, it is necessary to begin by distinguishing coconstrual types that bear on the syntactic pattern of anaphora and those that do not.

One key distinction between coconstrual relations, stemming from work by Evans (1980) and Reinhart (1983), is that between coreference and bound variable anaphora. In (1a) and (1b), the pronouns are coconstrued with their antecedents, *every Republican* and *George*, respectively, where italics in the examples indicate that two terms are to be coconstrued.

(1) a. *every Republican* loves *his* mother
    b. *George* loves *his* mother

In (1a) the value for the pronoun varies with that assigned to the subject bound by the universal quantifier, such that each loving Republican is matched with his own mother. In (1b) it is possible to regard *his* as a bound variable to the subject position, such that its value varies with that of the subject, but since the subject picks out a unique individual, *his* can be no one but *George*. Alternatively, *his* could be 'merely coreferent' with *George*, such that the two terms happen to pick out the same individual in discourse, a reading that is sometimes called 'accidental coreference.' The bound reading is distinguishable from an otherwise coconstrued one in ellipsis environments like (2a–b).

(2) a. *every Republican* loves *his mother* and George does, too
    b. *George* loves *his* mother and Bill does, too

Example (2b) is ambiguous, keeping constant that *George* and *his* in the first conjunct are coconstrued, whereas (2a) has only the bound interpretation, namely, one where every Republican loves his own mother and George is another own-mother-lover. By contrast, (2b) also allows an interpretation where Bill loves George's mother. The bound reading interpreted in ellipsis contexts is called the sloppy reading, whereas the one that keeps the value in the first conjunct as a constant is called the strict reading.

The usual way in which the sloppy reading is treated in the semantics is to treat the pronoun as bound by a lambda abstract over the VP as in (3) so that the second conjunct is interpreted as copying the value for the VP (see, for example, Heim and Kratzer, 1998, and especially Büring, 2005, for an extensive and more nuanced treatment of semantic binding).

(3) [$_{TP}$ every Republican [$_{T'}$ Tns [$_{VP}$ λx (x love x's mother)]]] and
    [$_{TP}$ George [$_{T'}$ Tns [$_{VP}$ λx (x love x's mother)]]]

Whatever the subject is for the first conjunct, whether it is quantified or not, if the lambda abstraction is a property of it, then the same lambda abstraction is a property of the subject in the second conjunct, in this case, *George*. The strict reading is the more problematic one, insofar as coconstrual in the first conjunct *requires* coconstrual under a strict or sloppy reading in the second conjunct. As a case in point, (2b) allows a strict or sloppy reading, but it does not allow a reading where *Bill* loves anyone other than his own mother or George's mother (if *George* is coconstrued with *his* in the first conjunct). To insure that the strict reading is the only other reading, not just accidentally the same one, some device must reliably assure coconstrual in the case of the strict reading. There is controversy about how this is to be achieved and how much has to be represented in the syntax, a matter to which we return (see Fox, 2000, on 'parallelism,' and references cited there).

Not every form has the same potential to be a bound element. Proper names do not permit bound variable readings because their relations to referents are fixed (but see note 3). Descriptions are generally classed with names in this respect, though for definite descriptions, the matter is more complex in ways that we will not delve into here (except in passing). Forms that must always have an antecedent in the sentence are generally called syntactic anaphors (in this chapter, just 'anaphors'). Pronouns can be free to pick out any previous or anticipated mention as their antecedent, but as we have just seen, they can also be bound. What is striking about this classification, and most significant from the syntactic point of view, is that it is insufficient to predict the class of possible, impossible, and/or limited coconstruals unless the structural geometry of sentences is taken into account.

There are at least three ways in which syntactic configuration influences possible coconstruals. C-command plays a role in the distribution of bound variable coconstruals, c-command and locality play a role in the distribution of anaphors, and c-command plays a role in a form of non-coconstrual called obviation, to which we turn shortly.

Consider first how the classical Binding Theory of Chomsky (1981) (henceforth, BT), addresses the questions related to anaphors and obviation. The BT is stated on the notions 'bound' and 'free,' which in turn depend on what it means for two nominals to be co-indexed.

(4) The Binding Theory
Principle A. An anaphor is bound in its binding domain.
Principle B. A pronoun is free in its binding domain.
Principle C. A name must be free.

(5) a. X binds Y if X c-commands Y and X and Y are coindexed.
b. If Y is not bound it is free.

(6) X c-commands Y if the node immediately dominating X also dominates Y and X does not dominate Y.[2]

The 'binding domain' introduces a locality restriction on anaphors which essentially limits the application of Principles A and B to clausemate or coargument contexts, but we reserve discussion of the issues surrounding the locality restrictions for Section 15.3. For this section we concentrate on what form(s) of coconstrual the BT regulates.

If we take 'bound' to be bound as a variable and 'free' to be not bound as a bound variable, then much depends on whether or not a pronoun can be coconstrued with an antecedent it is not bound by. We have seen for strict readings that coconstrual without variable binding is necessary. Thus Principle B predicts that a pronoun like *him* (7) in can be coconstrued with *George* as long as *him* is not a bound variable.

(7) *George loves him.

This is the wrong result, however, since (7) does not have the status of (1b), which, for the strict reading, is a successful coconstrual that is not a bound reading (as illustrated in (2b)). BT contemporary definitions of binding domain, to which we will soon return, were devised to insure that the subject would be local to the direct object and not the possessor of a nominal, so as to prevent (1b) from falling under Principle B. However, the problem now is that if the strict reading is not a bound reading in the antecedent clause of (2b), then the theory needs to distinguish not only bound coconstrual and not-bound coconstrual, but some sort of enforced non-coconstrual, or obviation. Principle B must insure that a pronoun is not only free but obviative with respect to potential binders in its local domain.

I will return to Principle B in subsequent sections, but for the rest of this section I concentrate on (4c), known as Principle C in the literature (which is a restatement of a principle proposed by Lasnik 1976), because most of the discussion of obviation in the literature has centered around the interpretive force of Principle C.

Principle C predicts that (8a) is excluded, because the pronoun *he* binds *the CEO*, on the assumptions (a) that definite descriptions (other than pronouns and anaphors) are treated as names, (b) that (all) coconstrual = coindexing, and (c) that *he/Jones* c-commands *the CEO*.[3]

(8) a. *he/Jones* has been said to have criticized *the CEO*'s mother
 b. *his/Jones'* accountant has been said to have criticized *the CEO's* mother
 c. *He/Jones* is in a lot of trouble. We believe that *the embattled CEO* will soon be arrested.

Where the pronoun does not c-command, as in (8b), or when it is not in the same sentence as the name (8c), Principle C does not block coconstrual, although examples like (8b) and (8c) are subject to discourse effects, and 'backwards' anaphora cases like (8b) (with the pronoun) are sometimes regarded as degraded.[4] The issue that arises for Principle B now arises again: Should coindexation in the BT refer to any coconstrual, or to some limited set of coconstrual relations, such as bound variable anaphora?

Grodzinsky and Reinhart (1993), following Reinhart (1983), take the position that coindexation, insofar as it is necessary at all, only notates bound variable relations. They argue further that Principle C effects (obviation) follow from an independently necessary restriction on bound anaphora, which I informally restate in (9b) and the pragmatically interpreted principle in (10).[5] The significance of (9a) is to insure that *wh*-traces (or traces of quantifier raising) are defined as variables which, given (9b), are potential antecedents for pronouns and anaphors bound as variables.

(9) a. An empty category is a variable if it is A'-bound by a quantifier.
 b. A pronoun or anaphor that is interpreted as a variable must be A-bound.
(10) Rule I: NP A cannot corefer with NP B if replacing A with C, C a variable A-bound by B, yields an indistinguishable interpretation.

Rule I is designed to favor bound variable anaphora as the best form of coconstrual whenever it is possible, and it is possible wherever a pronoun or anaphor can be A-bound (by (9b)). The effect of Rule I is as follows: If the speaker could have used a pronoun eligible for a bound interpretation (and hence the favored form of coconstrual), but instead the speaker uses something other than a pronoun, then the hearer must assume that the speaker does not intend to express coreference. Pronouns are almost always available in positions where names are c-commanded by their purported antecedents, and while pronouns and anaphors are possible bound variables, names and non-pronominal descriptions are assumed not to be.[6] Thus in (8a), *the CEO* could be replaced by *his* under coconstrual with *he/Jones*, and the result would satisfy the condition on bound anaphora in (9a–b), so the use of a name, *the CEO*, in place of a bound variable is illicit, unless there is some different manner of coconstrual intended (i.e., a coconstrual that is distinguishable from a bound variable interpretation).

Thus Rule I purports to derive Principle C, but it does so by distinguishing bound variable anaphora from other sorts of coconstrual which are assumed to be intrinsically less favored. Moreover, it assumes that there is a level of comparison between representations where one coconstrued interpretation is determined to be distinguishable from another, a matter to which I return in Section 15.4.2. The key effect of this approach, however, is to treat obviation differently from other coconstrual relations, in that obviation, unlike bound variable anaphora, is a pragmatic effect based on structural/representational options.

One advantage of treating Rule I as a pragmatic inference is that some apparent counterexamples to Principle C (raised by Evans 1980, and Reinhart 1983) appear tractable if we assume that coindexing of BT and Rule I only records bound anaphora, and that 'mere coreference' and obviation are not indicated in the grammar at all. For example, (11a–c) were taken to be problematic for BT Principle C since coconstrual persists where Principle C predicts name should be free (which, when Principle C was introduced, was intended to result in obviation).

(11) a. John is Bill
 b. If everyone loves Jack, then I suppose it's safe to say that (even) Jack loves Jack
 c. I know what Max and Jane have in common. Jane thinks Max is terrific and Max thinks Max is terrific.

Copular constructions like (11a), where *John* and *Bill* must be coconstrued even though *John* c-commands *Bill*, are no longer a problem, because *Bill* is not construed as a bound variable of *John* or the sentence would not be informative. The point of (11a) is to unite information about John and Bill such that what have been taken to be two distinct discourse referents should be understood as one. Since this form of asserted coconstrual could not have been expressed by a bound variable, Rule I does not predict obviation. Turning to (11b), the point of the deduction is to elucidate the set of Jack-lovers, not the set of self-lovers. Substitution of the last *Jack* by a reflexive would yield an interpretation where Jack is a self-lover (a bound reading), but this is not the point the speaker is making, rather the speaker asserts that Jack is included in the larger set of Jack-lovers, not the larger set of self-lovers (see Safir 2004a:27). A similar point can be made for (11c), in that the sentence is enumerating the members of the set of people who think Max is terrific (not people who regard themselves as terrific), and Max is a member of that set. Moreover, the latter two readings are confirmed not to be bound variable readings by the ellipsis test – only strict readings are possible (i.e., where Mary loves Bill in (12a) and Alice does not think Max is terrific in (12b)). (See Chapter 19 for more discussion of ellipsis.)

(12) a. if everyone loves Bill, then I suppose it is safe to say that Bill loves Bill, and that Mary does, too
b. Max and Jane have something in common that they don't share with Alice. Jane thinks Max is terrific, and, of course, Max thinks Max is terrific, but Alice doesn't.

Thus the 'obviative' effect of Principle C is not one inducing non-coreference nor disjoint reference (see Safir 2004a:45–48, contra Lasnik 1976, 1981a:151–52), but the result is a pragmatic inference of expected non-coconstrual induced by a syntax-based condition. The obviative effect can be overcome in the right context, such as in (13), where *even* is taken to adjust expectations, i.e., even the individual least likely to hate Bill's mother hates Bill's mother.

(13) a. even *Bill* hates *Bill's* mother
b. *crazy *Bill* hates (crazy) *Bill's* mother

Though other approaches treat the syntax-based condition differently (see Section 15.2.1), and some treat the pragmatic effect differently (e.g., Koster 1997), the obviated reading (expected non-coconstrual), and thereby the conditions by which it is neutralized, is part of what is syntactically induced by whatever achieves the interpretive result of Principles B and C.

To briefly summarize, I have distinguished two forms of coconstrual, bound variable interpretation and coconstrual without bound variable interpretation ('mere coreference,' as in cases of backwards coconstrual like (8)). I have also delved into one form of non-coconstrual, obviation. Principle C is an attempt to bring c-command to bear to predict patterns of obviation. In place of Principle C, Grodzinsky and Reinhart (1993) relate the c-command condition on bound variable anaphora to the obviation effects through a pragmatic inference rule, Rule I. Thus obviation is treated as a pragmatic effect triggered by (a) a syntactic condition on bound variable anaphora and (b) a preference for bound variable readings over other forms of coconstrual.

15.2.1 C-command and bound variable readings

The syntactic cornerstone of Reinhart's approach is (9), which licenses a semantic bound variable reading for the pronoun only when it is syntactically A-bound by a variable. On the assumption that a trace of *wh*-movement is a variable (by (9a)), this condition derives crossover effects (first observed by Postal 1971), such as that in (14a) (which cannot mean 'the man who praised himself left town'). Postal noted that the *wh*-phrase had 'crossed over' the pronoun while moving leftward in (14a–b), but not (14c).

(14) a. *the man *who he* praised *t* left town
 b. ??the man *who his* mother praised *t* left town
 c. the man *who t* praised *his* mother left town

Wasow (1979) distinguished violations of cases like (14a) from (14b) as cases of strong crossover vs. weak crossover, respectively. In strong crossover examples like (14a), (9) is violated *and* the coconstrued pronoun c-commands the trace. Weak crossover cases like (14b), which Wasow regarded as resulting in weaker unacceptability, also violate (9), but the pronoun does not c-command the trace.[7] By contrast, (14c), which satisfies (9), permits a bound reading.

The distribution of crossover effects has been taken to be a very important diagnostic of movement-generated structures since Chomsky (1977), and thus has played an important role in syntactic argumentation. The crossover effect diagnostic was used to justify covert syntactic movement of *in situ* quantifiers to scopal positions (quantifier raising, as in May 1977, and much subsequent work), leaving a trace that counts as a variable by (9a). Thus in (15a–b), *everyone* moves to establish scope over the clause, as in (16a–b), respectively, but in doing so, the same configuration as in (14b) obtains for (15a) as represented in (16a), where *t* does not bind *his*. Once again, (9) predicts a weak crossover effect.

(15) a. ??*his* mother loves *everyone*
 b. *everyone* loves *his* mother
(16) a. *everyone* [[*his* mother] loves *t*]
 b. *everyone* [*t* loves *his* mother]

Unfortunately for (9), bound variable readings for pronouns are also possible in contexts where c-command does not hold, and sloppy readings are supported, as in (17a), an inverse linking case (see May 1977) and the possessive construction in (17b), which allows sloppy readings even without a quantified antecedent, as (17c) shows.

(17) a. someone in *every Chinese city* loves *its* weather, but no one in any Siberian city does
 b. *everyone's* mother loves *him*, but no one's accountant does
 c. Some people have mothers who love them. *George's* mother loves *him*, but I don't know if Bill's mother does.

One strategy in the face of apparent counterevidence is to defend (9) by making ancillary assumptions. Thus Kayne, (1994:23–24), assumes that adjoined positions to DP c-command out of DP, though somewhat arbitrary assumptions about the A/A' distinction must be posited. Büring

(2005:180–81) argues that these cases are instances of 'donkey pronoun' anaphora, as in 'Most men who own *a donkey* beat *it*' (even though universals in the position of *a donkey* do not permit this sort of anaphora, in contrast to (17a), e.g., 'Most men who own *every donkey they feed* beat *it*' is unacceptable) (see also Tomioka 1999).[8] If (9b) is undermined, then the ability of Rule I to predict Principle C effects (obviation) is also undermined.

Higginbotham (1983a, 1985) and Safir (2004a:32) take a different tack, abandoning (9) and generalizations like it in favor of the view that bound variable anaphora is possible wherever a pronoun is in the scope of the quantifier that binds it, but crossover occurs whenever the Independence Principle is violated (using here Safir's interpretation of Higginbotham's idea).

(18) The Independence Principle
 If x (or z containing x) c-commands y, then x cannot depend on y.

Insofar as pronouns must depend on variables to be interpreted as bound variables, pronouns coconstrued with *wh*-traces must depend on those traces. In (14a), the pronoun c-commands the trace it depends on, violating (18), while in (14b), the pronoun is contained in a nominal that c-commands the trace, again violating (18). This approach captures the crossover effects insofar as bound variable readings are blocked, but the condition also allows for bound variable readings in cases like (17b), where the quantifier (or its trace after QR) does not c-command the pronoun bound as a variable.

At this point it is important to distinguish dependent identity readings, bound variable readings, and mere coreferent readings. A dependent identity reading is one where a pronoun depends for its value on another entity in discourse. The coconstruals in (11a–c) are not dependent identity readings. The broad prediction of (18) is that dependent identity is supported wherever (18) is not violated.

Quantifier-bound readings are a special subset of dependent identity readings where the antecedent is a variable (or a quantifier *in situ*, depending on the account). Since a pronoun must also be in the scope of a quantifier that binds it, some contexts where (18) is not violated still do not permit bound variable anaphora. Insofar as the scope of quantifiers does not extend across independent sentences, dependent identity pronouns are not bound by quantifiers extra-sententially, as illustrated in (19a). On this account, strict readings, such as the one possible for (19b), are dependent identity readings permitted across sentences by the Independence Principle.

(19) a. John loves *everyone*. *Mary likes *him/them* too.
 b. A: *John* loves *his* mother
 B: So what, Bill does, too

Recall that in (19b), either a strict reading (Bill loves John's mother) or a sloppy one (Bill loves his own mother) is possible, but here the cross-sentential anaphora is not 'mere coreference,' but dependent identity, enforced by the parallelism that licenses ellipsis generally. Thus the typology of coconstrual readings includes dependent identity cases that are not quantifier-bound, those that are, and mere coreferent readings, which are not dependent identity cases. VPs with bound readings antecede sloppy readings in ellipsis contexts, but they can also license strict readings by dependent identity with the pronoun of the first conjunct, since (18) is not violated. When the antecedent of the elided VP has a quantifier-bound pronoun, however, the strict reading fails because quantifier scope fails, not because of (18). This predicts that if a quantifier has scope (determined by c-command at LF) over both the ellipsis site and the VP that licenses it, even readings that are locally strict can involve bound variables.

(20) *every boy* claims that *he* loves *his* puppy and that St Francis does too

The sloppy reading of (20) is one where St Francis loves his own puppy, but the strict reading, where St Francis loves each boy's puppy, is also a quantifier-bound reading (i.e., it is not 'accidental,' contra Hicks, 2009a:122), enforced by the same parallelism constraint independently required in every account. Most accounts will yield the same semantic result, but only if it is admitted that strict readings involve an enforced identity reading that is not achieved by mere coreference.[9]

15.2.2 Representing dependent anaphora

In the history of generative grammar, the way that the relation between coconstrued terms has been notated has often been taken to be a substantive issue with consequences for syntactic form. It is clear, at the minimum, that we must know whether or not *Velma* and *her* are coconstrued and not merely coreferent in order to know whether or not (21) is acceptable, or if the morphologically distinct *herself* is necessary.

(21) *Velma* praised *herself/her*

As a matter of non-theoretical notation, we have notated coconstrual with matching italics, but in what follows we consider some other ways that coconstruals have been notated and/or distinguished.

Indices were employed to mark coconstrual from the earliest work on anaphora in the generativist tradition (e.g., Ross 1967b), but coindexation became part of posited mental representations only when traces (particularly, Chomsky 1977) and the definition of binding (in (5)) became part of the theory. Interpretive schemas for indices were proposed (Chomsky 1980a, 1981, Lasnik 1981a:125–33, Fiengo and May 1994). On some accounts, a phrase could bear an index '*i*' whether or not any other phrase in the structure bore *i*, and DPs, if they happened to have the same index, would covary for coconstrual. Phrases that do not bear the same index are treated as not coconstrued (e.g., Chomsky 1980a) or, as Fiengo and May (1994) put it, there is no linguistic commitment to whether they are coconstrued or not. Some indexing systems, like that of Fiengo and May, distinguished forms of coconstrual, such as bound variable coconstrual, in the sloppy reading for VP ellipsis, and coreferent coconstrual, in the case of the linguistically enforced strict reading for VP ellipsis.

As part of the Minimalist Program, Chomsky (1995c) rejects the idea that indices are properties of nominals in syntax at all. There are two motivations for this position. The first is that indices violate the Inclusiveness Condition, a theory-internal requirement within Minimalism that no new grammatical entities may be introduced into the derivation that are not in the initial numeration (where the numeration is the set of forms that are the input to a derivation). The second motivation is based on the view that the actual reference of a nominal is not a syntactic property of the nominal, but only syntactically regulated coconstrual relations between nominals must still be expressed. Higginbotham (1983a, 1985) proposes an alternative to indices that meets the second criterion (but is still inconsistent with inclusiveness). Dependent nominals are related to their antecedents by an intrinsically asymmetric notation, as in (22).

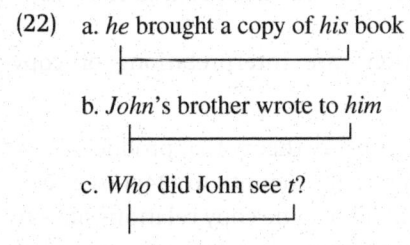

(22) a. *he* brought a copy of *his* book
      |⎯⎯⎯⎯⎯⎯⎯⎯⎯⎯⎯⎯⎯⎯⎯⎯|

      b. *John's* brother wrote to *him*
         |⎯⎯⎯⎯⎯⎯⎯⎯⎯⎯⎯⎯⎯⎯⎯⎯|

      c. *Who* did John see *t*?
         |⎯⎯⎯⎯⎯⎯⎯⎯⎯⎯⎯⎯|

This way of representing dependency never attributes a syntactic property to any nominal, except in relation to its antecedent. The value for *his* is thus a function of the value assigned to *he* in contexts where (22a) is uttered, but there is no syntactic commitment as to the value of *he*.[10] In the same fashion, *him* depends on *John's* in (22b). Note also that movement relations, which propagate an index in indexing approaches, must be converted in this approach to dependency arrows. However, something special must apply to convert copies of quantifiers to dependent variables in any theory, as discussed below.

In the arrow approach, every dependent identity relation is notated by an arrow connecting the antecedent with the dependent nominal. Thus mere coreference, as opposed to dependent identity, is invisible to syntax, apart from the (neutralizable) expectation of non-coconstrual induced by obviation, as mentioned above. Restrictions on coconstrual are expressed as restrictions on the distribution of arrow relations rather than the BT notion of binding.

Every theory requires some representation of bound coconstrual accessible to syntax or the interpretation of tree geometry, or there would be no way for syntax to regulate these relations. Although the arrow notation eliminates indices as properties of nominals, neither indices nor arrows satisfy Chomsky's inclusiveness restriction, nor is it clear that any existing proposal for indicating coconstruals relevant to the evaluation of syntactic configurations can satisfy inclusiveness.[11]

15.2.3 Coconstrual as movement

With the objective of reducing identity relations in syntax to a bare minimum, Kayne (2002a) and Hornstein (2001), amongst others, have suggested that the identity relation involved in coconstrual at a distance is the same one that is involved when a constituent is displaced, i.e., dependent coconstrual is generated by movement. On the assumption that relations between where a constituent begins and where it lands are copy relations (as in Chomsky 1995c), as all coconstrual-as-movement (CAM) theories do, the hypothesis space can be summarized as in (23).

(23) a. All dependent identity relations are interpretations of copy relations.
b. Some dependent identity relations are interpretations of copy relations.
c. No dependent identity relations are interpretations of copy relations.

We can regard (23c) as a non-starter, since every theory that produces (24b) must achieve an interpretation of (24a) that amounts to (24c) (see, e.g., Chomsky 1976a and Fox 2003), and so at least some copy relations have to be translated into dependency relations.

(24) a. Which person did John see?
b. *which person* [did John see *which person*]
c. 'for which x, x a person, John see x'

Thus (24) is enough to establish that at least (23b) is supported. To support (23a), however, coconstruals like those in (25) must all be movement induced, since they are bound variable readings, as illustrated by the success (indeed, the necessity) of the sloppy identity interpretation.

(25) a. *every boy* likes the coach who flatters *him*, but not every father does
b. *most people* know what *they* want to do, but Bill doesn't

Since *wh*-movement is impossible from the position where the pronouns in (25a–b) are found, CAM accounts must posit a form of movement unlike any other known, or they must accept (23b). If coconstrual is only partially determined by the distribution of possible movements, then the argument from parsimony for the CAM theories disappears (see Safir, 2008:346, for a stronger statement). Thus both movement and some other (unbounded) relation of coconstrual must be weighed as analytic options for any given phenomenon.

Further reasoning about the relation between movement and coconstrual requires further assumptions. The copy relation that results from movement operations in Minimalist theorizing is an indistinctness relation (occurrences are not distinguishable by virtue of their internal properties since only one object is involved). Pronouns are in a dependent identity relation as indicated by the availability of strict and sloppy readings for pronouns represented in (26).

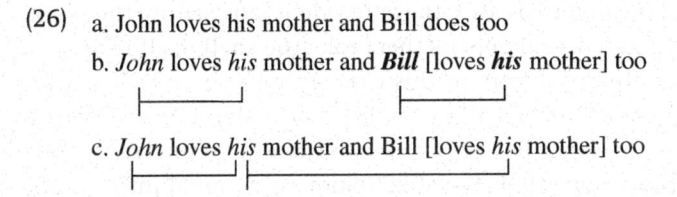

(26)   a. John loves his mother and Bill does too
       b. *John* loves *his* mother and ***Bill*** [loves ***his*** mother] too
       c. *John* loves *his* mother and Bill [loves *his* mother] too

As will be demonstrated later (see examples (73–74)), reflexives permit both strict and sloppy readings in a productive class of ellipsis contexts as well, so if pronouns are in dependent identity relations, then English reflexives are too (but see Section 15.5.2 for some indistinctness cases). Thus the attempt to represent coconstrual as nothing more than the copy relation fails to express the necessary range of dependent identity relations, at least without further elaboration.

Hornstein (2001), extending an analysis he proposes for obligatory control (see Chapter 16), defends the position that relations between copies generated by movement are what instantiate core cases of A-binding phenomena (on the assumption that movement from a theta-position to another theta-position is possible). He proposes, for example, that reflexives surface as a result of how copies are (or are not, in the case of obligatory control) spelled out in certain syntactic contexts. This proposal is discussed in Section 15.4.3.

Not all CAM theories have the same commitments. On Kayne's (2002a) CAM theory, antecedent–trace relations are not necessarily treated as a copy relation (it is not crucial), but the key idea is that all coconstrual begins as a sisterhood relation between the elements coconstrued, and then one sister, the one understood as the antecedent, moves out, as in (27)

(27)   a. [believes that [*John he*] is smart]
       b. [*John* [believes that [[*t he*] is smart]]]

This theory does not address differences between mere coreference and dependent identity and so it is not clear how strict and sloppy readings would be distinguished. Moreover, the theory makes radical assumptions, including that CAM requires movement out of islands, across different sentences, and across speakers in a dialogue.[12]

(28) A: *Markus* is irritating
   B: You should give [t *him*] a chance.
(29) *Wilson* remembers the first person **who** [t *he*] met **t** in Wilkes Barre
(30) *Arliss* praises [t *himself*]

Kayne treats the two sentences in (28) as if conjoined and he derives coconstrual between *him* and *Markus* by movement of *Markus* from [*Markus him*] in the second sentence into the subject position of the first sentence. The same sort of derivation applies to (29), where the surface position of *Wilson* is achieved by movement out of [*Wilson he*], which starts in the relative clause subject position, and moves to matrix subject position. In (30), as in the first two cases, the antecedent moves from the 'shell' into a theta-position where it gets its theta-role (the shell itself receives a theta-role in its initial position), in this case stranding a reflexive. Thus movement preserves coconstrual on the basis of underlying sisterhood, but 'CAM-movement' must be able to violate islands, be intersentential, and, following Hornstein (1999), be able to move a nominal into a theta-position, an operation forbidden in Chomsky (1981).

Kayne's theory is thoroughly consistent in that all coconstrual regulated by syntax is notated in the same way, i.e., all coconstrual relations begin as sisterhood relations that are extended by movement of the antecedent out of a shell, but the price for syntax is high. Although Kayne's CAM theory has not been adopted whole by anyone else at this writing, some CAM subextraction analyses have been inspired by it.[13]

15.2.4 Summary

Any plausible theory of anaphora must distinguish relations of dependent identity, pronouns bound as variables, and obviation, and should account for the syntactic restrictions that hold of these forms of coconstrual. Pronouns must be in the scope of the quantifiers that bind them, where scope and binding are regulated by c-command, though there appear to be dependent identity cases that hold where c-command does not. The contributions of syntax and pragmatics were distinguished for Principle C effects: a name cannot depend on any nominal that c-commands it and is in an obviative relation with its c-commanders. Obviation can be understood as the presumption that coconstrual between Y and X is unexpected, unless some discourse context overcomes the presumption. Obviated dependent identity coconstruals, however, are not recoverable in the same way. If Grodzinsky and Reinhart's (1993) approach is defensible, then Principle C follows from the constraint on bound variables in (9) and a pragmatic rule, Rule I, but the status of (9b) has been challenged by the alternative accounts of Safir and Higginbotham.

The question was raised as to whether indices or arrows are the best notation to characterize the relevant relations that syntax must be sensitive to, but neither indices nor arrows reduce to any other necessary relation, such as movement. Attempts to reduce dependent coconstrual to the distribution of movement copies fall short in present formulations, both insofar as indistinct copies must be converted to quantifier-variable dependencies, and because a radical extension of possible movement relations would be required to cover bound pronoun anaphora.

15.3 Binding Theory and local domains

The locality restrictions on anaphora have played a major role in the development of syntactic theory, especially since the early 1970s. Chomsky (1976a), for example, argues that the syntactic restrictions that regulate relations between antecedents and the pronouns, reciprocals, and reflexives they can be identified with are the same restrictions as those that hold between subject positions and their traces in passive and raising constructions derived by movement. In particular, the Specified Subject Condition and the Tensed-S Condition were taken as applying generally to rules of grammar, including movement (see Chapter 18) and restrictions on local coconstruals. This apparent unification continues to play a role in syntactic theorizing.

15.3.1 Classic Binding Theory

The constraints on rules of the 1970s were rethought in Chomsky's (1981) Binding Theory (BT) in terms of locality domains conditioning possible coconstrual relations, relations that are otherwise freely possible – i.e., not created by rules of grammar. Coconstrual relations were reduced to the three BT principles in (4) and the locality constraints of the 1970s were recast as the binding domain.

(31) Binding domain: The binding domain for α is the minimal IP containing the governor of α and a SUBJECT accessible to α.
(32) The class of anaphors includes reflexives, reciprocals, and A-traces. Typical phenomena captured by BT Principles A and B are exemplified in (33a–e).
(33) a. the men love *themselves/each other/*them*
 b. *the men* expected [$_{CP}$ that [$_{IP}$ *they/?*each other/*themselves* would be happy]]
 c. *the men* expected [$_{IP}$ *themselves/each other/*them* to be happy]
 d. *the men* expected [$_{IP}$ me to love *them/*each other/*themselves*]
 e. *they/*themselves/*each other* implicated *themselves/each other*

The notion SUBJECT simply requires that an IP is only a binding domain if it has a structural subject (overt or PRO) or a finite tense (we ignore 'accessibility', but see Section 15.2.3.3). In a simple clause, as in (33a), the application of Principles A and B is straightforward, insofar as *the men* locally binds the anaphors, *themselves* and *each other*, satisfying Principle A, but *them*, if bound by *the men*, violates Principle B. With the advent of abstract Case Theory, (33a) and (33b) are distinguished because in (33b), the case of the subordinate subject is provided within the subordinate clause (nominative assigned by [+tense]). By contrast, the source of accusative case in (33c) is the matrix 'Exceptional Case-Marking' (ECM) verb *expect* given the sort of infinitival complement *expect* can take (as a special lexical property, it is posited to take an IP infinitive). If a case assigner is a governor, then the binding domain for the pronouns and anaphors in (33c) is taken to be the matrix clause, where local binding permits anaphors but not pronouns. In (33d), the bound anaphors/pronoun are assigned case (and governed) by the subordinate verb *love*, and thus cannot access the higher domain including *the men* in the matrix clause, with predictable results. Examples like (33e) do not permit anaphors to be in subject position because they are not bound.[14]

For the data described so far, a version of binding domain for α based on case governors would be sufficient, whereby the binder must be in the same IP (clause) as the minimal IP which contains its case assigner, but such a definition would not then extend to (34a–c).

(34) a. *Karl* was killed *t*
 b. *Sarah* seems [$_{IP}$ *t* to be guilty]
 c. *Excalibur* was expected [$_{IP}$ *t* to be heroic]

In the theory of abstract case, every overt nominal phrase (DP or NP, depending on developments in X' Theory; see Chapter 11) must be case-marked, and in movement theories of passive and raising, movement can thus be motivated as a search for case (see also Chapter 17). Passive verbs are posited not to assign accusative, so *Karl* must move from object position, where it gets its patient theta-role, to subject position, dethematized by a lexical operation, where it can get nominative case. The infinitival subject of the complement of *seem* and of passivized ECM *expect* moves for the same reason, but in all three examples, the trace is thus caseless. Therefore binding domain cannot be defined as the clause containing the case assigner if it is to extend to the trace of A-movement.

'Government' was introduced into the definition of binding domain to permit the generalization of anaphoric domains to apply to both raising verb complement subjects, passive objects, and ECM verb complement subjects. Definitions of government were various, and are not pertinent here, but it is enough to say that a head (X^0) was understood to govern anything immediately dominated by one of its projections, as well as the head of its complement, but could only govern into the specifier of its complement if the complement were IP (e.g., not CP or DP). Thus in the schematic diagram in (35) Y governs ZP, XP, X' and X, but not RP or WP, unless XP is in fact IP, in which case Y would also govern RP.

(35) a.
```
        YP
       /  \
      ZP   Y'
          /  \
         Y    XP
             /  \
            RP   X'
                /  \
               X    WP
```

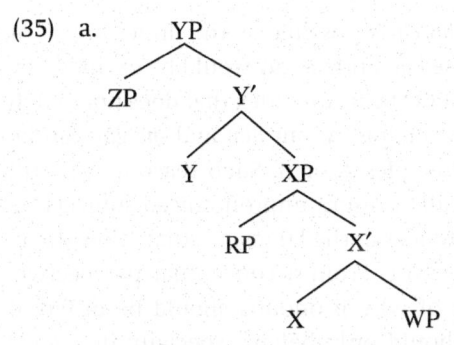

b. Elsbeth expects [$_{IP}$ him to leave]

It was assumed that a case-assigning head must govern the assignee, but raising and passive verbs, which do not assign case, would still govern the traces that follow them, since a complement NP (DP in later work) is a daughter of V', and the trace of raising is the specifier of an IP complement of the raising verb. In (35b), if the complement of *expect* is an IP (as XP is the complement of Y in (35a)), then *expect* governs the Spec of IP (=RP) and assigns it accusative case. In (34c), passivized ECM *expect* governs the subject trace in its infinitive complement, just as a raising verb does.

The achievements of the BT were considerable, including the unification of Case Theory and BT under government, the reduction of locality restrictions on A-movement to Principle A, and deriving the PRO Theorem (which proved chimeric, but that is discussed in Chapter 16). Combined with a theory of (non-)coconstrual representation, BT was a comprehensive theory of anaphora with wide empirical coverage, and it stimulated a flood of cross-linguistic study exploring its predictions. For subsequent work that has sought to improve on its empirical predictions and/or reduce its theoretical assumptions, BT has served as the point of departure (as it is in this chapter).

Moreover, BT effects have played an important role in diagnosing other constructions and detecting the existence of empty categories. For example, the existence of structurally represented null antecedents has largely been supported by the BT effects that are correctly predicted if the null categories are posited.

(36) to praise *himself/him/the guy* would embarrass *John*

While the object of *embarrass*, *John*, can be coconstrued with any of the forms after *praise*, the possible interpretations of the one doing the implicating is notably restricted. If the 'praiser' is understood to be John, only *himself* is possible. If the praiser is not John, then it is possible for *him* and *the guy* to correspond to John. These results are exactly what is expected if a structurally present null subject of the infinitive is assumed to be present, such that it c-commands the direct object of *praise*.

(37) a. [$_{CP}$ [$_{IP}$ [$_{CP}$ [$_{IP}$ PRO$_i$ to praise himself$_i$/*him$_i$/*the guy$_i$]]would upset John$_i$]]
    b. [$_{CP}$ [$_{IP}$ [$_{CP}$ [$_{IP}$ PRO$_j$ to praise *himself$_i$/him$_i$/the guy$_i$]] would upset John$_i$]]

If PRO bears index *i*, then only *himself* is possible as the direct object of *praise* to satisfy Principle A, because *him* and *the guy* would be excluded by Principles B and C, respectively. If PRO bears an index that does not match that of *John*, then *himself* fails by Principle A, but *him* and *the guy* can be coconstrued without violating Principles A or B. Such reasoning is still considered diagnostic of syntactically present unpronounced subjects, as it is for null subjects of tensed sentences in the languages that allow them.

BT faced many challenges, however. From a conceptual perspective, there was no principled account of why pronouns should be different from anaphors, why pronouns should only behave specially in a local domain, and why the local domain in which pronouns behaved specially should happen to be the same one in which anaphors had to be bound. The notion 'syntactic anaphor' risked circularity, since anything respecting Principle A could be treated as one. The last question bore on the status of A-movement – should A-trace be an anaphor or should anaphors be unified as A-traces? The theories discussed in Section 15.4 address most of these questions.

Other questions addressed the level of application of the BT. Most accounts assumed that BT applied at LF, after reconstruction,[15] but Belletti and Rizzi (1988) argued that Principle A, as opposed to Principles B and C, should apply at any point in a derivation where it could be satisfied, on the basis of examples like (38a), and others have appealed to (38b).

(38) a. pictures of each other would please the boys
b. the men wondered which pictures of each other the journalist would publish

Belletti and Rizzi argued that psych predicates like *please* derive from an underlying structure where *pictures of each other* originates in a position c-commanded by *the boys*, and that binding in the pre-movement position is enough to satisfy Principle A, which would not be satisfied at S-structure. Conversely, movement of *which pictures of each other* in (38b) brings the anaphor close enough to its antecedent only after movement. Binding by Principle A at the first opportunity covers both cases. Under the copy theory of movement, the point can be put differently, insofar as at least one copy of an anaphor must be bound at LF. However, some would dismiss evidence based on anaphors embedded in *picture*-nominals, which may be more freely bound for other reasons (see Section 15.3.3). The matter remains open.[16]

The BT formulation of binding domain also faced many empirical challenges. As attempts were made to apply BT to other languages, it was discovered that forms taken to be anaphors could be sensitive to a variety of domains, both smaller and larger than in English. Questions were raised about the complementary distribution of pronouns and anaphors, suggesting that the domains for anaphors and pronouns could differ (even in English; see Huang 1983). Some languages have anaphors that require that their antecedents be subjects (see, for example, Safir and Sikuku, forthcoming, on reflexive markers in Lubukusu, a Bantu language, where what counts as a subject is explored) or not be subjects (Scandinavian pronoun-SELF; see Hellan 1988). Finally, the notion 'anaphor' itself received scrutiny, as attempts were made to account for the varieties of anaphoric forms, both in languages with morphologically impoverished distributions of anaphors, and those with richer anaphor morphologies and more highly articulated locality distributions (see Sections 15.3.2–15.3.3 for discussion and references concerning the variety of locality domains and Section 5 concerning the morphological varieties of anaphors). Thus the elegance and generality of BT appeared threatened by the richness of typological variation.

15.3.2 Defending the classic BT

There were two main responses to the empirical challenge posed by the existence of variation in the structural distance permitted between antecedents and anaphors. One response was to increase the set of binding domains parametrically available, while the other was to insist on a single domain and derive divergence from it from other interfering factors.

Manzini and Wexler (1987) (M&W) is an exploration of the first strategy. They proposed a parameterized set of locality domains for binding (drawing from Yang, 1983), one fitting inside another, and that the lexical entry of an anaphor specifies which domain it is bound in. M&W propose the set binding domains (governing category) in (39) (details suppressed).

(39) γ is a governing category for α iff γ is the minimal category that contains α and a governor for α and has
    a. a subject; or
    b. an INFL; or
    c. a Tense; or
    d. a 'referential' Tense; or
    e. a 'root' Tense.

The difference between English *herself* in (40a) and Italian *sè* in (40b) illustrates the difference between (39a) and (39b). While (40a) is an instantiation of (39a), since only the genitive is a possible antecedent for *herself* in English (for most speakers), (40b) instantiates (39b) insofar as the genitive of the nominal and the matrix subject are both possible antecedents (in Manzini's dialect).

(40)   a. *Mary saw [a/*Bill's description of herself]*
      b. *Alice guardò i ritratti di sè di* **Mario**
        '*Alice* looked at **Mario**'s portraits of *her*/**him**'

Scandinavian simplex SIG-type forms, which can be bound from a higher clause across infinitival (−tense) subjects, instantiate (39c), logophorically interpreted Icelandic *síg*, which can be bound across subjunctive ('non-referential') clauses, instantiates (39d), and Chinese *ziji*, which can be bound across any intervening clause, instantiates (39e). There is no obvious reason for this particular list of domains as opposed to some other, but M&W note an empirical generalization about the relation between domains, namely, that the positions for anaphors in each domain is a subset of the next larger domain such that a < b < c < d < e.

M&W maintain that binding domains are learnable because they respect the Subset Principle, which provides an acquisition strategy that a child can exploit to reliably arrive at the right setting for an anaphor based solely on positive evidence. If a child tacitly assumes, at least initially, that the domain for every anaphor is the smallest one, then every time she hears the anaphor used with an antecedent outside the most local domain, she posits a larger domain for the anaphor in question. Thus a child acquiring the anaphor *sè* in Italian will initially assume that *sè* is locally bound, but exposure to a sentence like (40b) will then reveal that the domain is wider. In the absence of evidence for an expanded domain, the initial assumption of a local domain prevails (hence the English setting, (39a), for *herself*). The inverse of this reasoning is employed for pronouns. Pronouns are initially assumed to be disjoint from potential antecedents in the widest possible domain; each pronoun coconstrued with a more local antecedent is evidence the child should assume a smaller obviation domain for pronouns.

(41) a. *Melba* thinks that *she* is smart
     b. *Melba* lifted *her* book
     c. *Melba forgave *her*

If a child hears (41a–b), it is evidence that the domain in which pronouns can be coconstrued with an antecedent is rather small, but unless the child hears (41c), which she would not hear in English, she will assume (41c) is not possible,

Although the M&W approach was an important step in the direction of integrating acquisition data into the theoretical discussion of the patterns of anaphora,[17] it faced a number of difficulties, not least that it did not easily accommodate anaphoric distributions where one domain is not the subset of the other, as in the Norwegian pattern in (42).

(42) a. vi fortalte *Jon* om *ham selv*/*ham/*seg/*seg selv
        'we told *John* about *himself*'
     b. *Jon* fortalte meg om *ham selv/*ham/*seg/*seg selv*
        '*Jon* told me about *himself*'

The anaphor *seg selv* is subject sensitive and favors coargument interpretation, which means that it can only have a local subject antecedent, whereas *ham selv* can only have a local non-subject antecedent, i.e., their domains are complementary. Thus *Jon* in (42a) is not a possible antecedent for *ham selv*. It is possible to introduce distinct subset calculations for non-overlapping domains at the price of weakening the theory (see Safir 1987). Moreover, positing locality domains as properties of lexical items affords lexical stipulation a wide-ranging descriptive power over structures in syntax. Alternatives to this approach aim to predict the domain of an anaphor from independently necessary aspects of its feature matrix as they interact with general principles, not by using the lexicon to stipulate the locality syntax of any item.[18]

Another approach to parametric variation of binding domains sought to show that anaphors that appear to have domains larger than those of English differ only in that they permit abstract movement of anaphors into the local domains of their antecedents. Lebeaux (1984b), Chomsky (1986b), Pica (1987), Battistella (1989), and Huang and Tang (1991), amongst others, developed accounts along these lines. Example (43a) is Chinese from Cole and Sung (1994), and a schematic version of such an analysis (not precisely theirs) for *Lisi* as antecedent is in (43b).

(43) a. Lisi$_i$ kanjian neige taoyan ziji$_{i/j}$ de ren$_j$
 Lisi see that dislike ZIJI rel person
 Lisi$_i$ saw the person who$_j$ dislikes him$_i$/himself$_j$
 b. Lisi kanjian [$_{DP}$ neige [$_{CP}$ taoyan ziji de] [$_{NP}$ ren]]
 Lisi *ziji*-T *t*-V [D [*t*-C ... *t*-T *t*-V *t* ...] NP]

BT Principle A applies after covert head movement of *ziji* into the matrix clause and so the local binding domain of BT holds in (43) just as it does for English pronoun-*self*. The more local interpretation ('the person' antecedes) is derived if *ziji* moves only to the lower T.

Covert movement approaches thus preserve the classic BT binding domain in the face of linguistic variation by raising anaphors into the local binding domain (to highlight analyses of this class, I will call raising an anaphor into a higher locality domain a 'hoisting' analysis). For example, if ECM complement subjects were to raise into the higher clause,[19] then hoisted pronouns and anaphors could be locally bound by the matrix subject, respecting (31). Lasnik (1999a:197) shows that ECM complement subjects do indeed behave as if in the higher clause because they can be controllers for adjuncts construed with the clause of the selecting verb (see also Sections 4.2.3 and 16.2.3).

(44) a. the DA proved [*two men* to have been at the scene of the crime] during *each other's* trials
 b. the DA [$_{VP}$ *two men* [$_{VP}$ proved [$_{IP}$ *t* to have ....]] [PRO during *each other's* trials]]

If control antecedents must c-command PRO, then *two men* only c-commands in (44b), but that is only possible, Lasnik argues, if an ECM complement subject can be raised into the clause of its antecedent. However, as pointed out in Safir (2004a:149–50), if the analysis in (44b) and (45b) is correct, the binding domain for English, if not generally, could be smaller than the domain that regulates A-traces, casting doubt on the BT assumption that A-traces and anaphors have the same domain.

(45) a. *the DA* proved *himself* to be incompetent by behaving irrationally
 b. *the DA* [$_{VP}$ *himself* [$_{VP}$ proved [$_{IP}$ *t* to be incompetent]] ...

Safir (2004a) argues further not only that long-distance binding of anaphors is made possible by covert raising into a local domain, but that every covert hoisting analysis should correspond to a form of bounded overt movement, such movement attaching a clitic to a predicate that does not select it (see, in particular, Lee-Schoenfeld, 2004, for German), or operator movement that is restricted to pass through tenseless clauses (as in the case of *tough*-movement).

(46) a. Clausemate domain (e.g., the reflexive marker in Bantu languages; see Mchombo, 2004, and Safir and Sikuku, forthcoming, for exploration of clausemate status in Lubukusu)
 b. A-movement domain (extends to edge of subordinate IP and/or DP) (as in (45)). (e.g., English *each other*)
 c. Clitic-binding domain (potentially out of PP) (e.g., German *sich*)
 d. Tenseless operator domain (across infinitives) (e.g., Scandinavian SIG see Hellan, 1988, and Hindi APNAA, see Davison, 2000)

Safir criticizes Cole and Sung (1994), who propose unbounded covert head movement through tensed clauses and across islands (as in (43)), a covert hoisting analysis that relies on a sort of movement that has no attested overt counterpart. As we show in Section 15.3.3, distributions corresponding to (39d,e) in the M&W classification should not be domains for anaphors at all, but fall under other generalizations.

Another potential advantage for hoisting analyses is that they can account for (anti-)subject orientation (Pica 1987), on the assumption that the landing-site of such movements is higher than the object and lower than the subject (e.g., head-adjunction to T, as in (43b)). Then the only c-commanding antecedent in the local domain is the subject. Movement of a reflexive to a Romance proclitic position, for example, would have this effect. Pica (1987), Hestvik (1992), and Avrutin (1994) also propose hoisting analyses for the anti-subject orientation of pronouns in Danish, Norwegian, and Russian, respectively, although the assumption that pronouns must move to be disjoint from a local antecedent seems insufficiently motivated. The hoisting analysis remains an attractive one for many anaphors, if not for pronouns, though independent evidence for the covert movements of anaphors beyond analogy to overt movement types is sparse.

15.3.3 Local anaphors and non-local anaphora

An important empirical challenge to locality and complementarity concerns the fact that, in some of the world's languages, forms which are bound in the more local domains, like (39a–c) or (46a–d), can also be virtually free, if certain semantic and pragmatic conditions are satisfied. For example, forms classed as anaphors because they can be locally bound when pronouns cannot, can in some languages, like Chinese, be anteceded not only across tensed sentences and islands (43a), but also by non-c-commanding or even non-sentence-internal antecedents (47). Similar facts hold in widely dissimilar languages (see, e.g., Safir, 2004a:173–78, for examples from the literature and for further discussion).

(47) *Zhangsan* zhe ren yi-xiang hu-li-hu de guo shenghuo. Jushuo you yihui lian *ziji* fan-le-fa dou bu zhidao.
'Zhangsan has always been absentminded. It was said that *he* once broke the law without even knowing it.'

In Safir (2004a), forms of this kind are called unbounded dependent forms (UD-forms), forms that require an antecedent but are unrestricted by locality. UD-forms when locally bound tend to show interpretive contrasts with constructions where it is anteceded outside the bounded domain (see, e.g., Huang and Liu 2001:168–72). For example, non-local UD-forms are sensitive to discourse factors like point of view (or logophoricity, see below) while their locally bound versions are not. Thus UD-forms are cross-classified as local anaphors, on the one hand, and pronoun-like dependents on the other, permitting a distribution that amounts to the union of both domains of bound anaphora. Some UD-forms, like pronouns but unlike anaphors, even permit split antecedents (not *ziji*; but see Safir, 2004a:177–78 for Turkish, Malayalam, and Japanese examples from the literature). If non-local UD-forms are pronoun-like, overlapping distribution with pronouns outside their locality domains will lead to false counterexamples to the claim that pronouns and anaphors are in complementary distribution. It remains an open question whether there is any way to predict which anaphors are likely to be cross-classified as UD-forms.[20]

Another class of contexts that are apparent counterexamples to the complementary distribution of anaphors and pronouns are pronoun-*self* forms in English that behave like UD-forms in examples like (48a–c) (see Zribi-Hertz, 1989, Pollard and Sag, 1992, 1994, Baker, 1994, amongst others).

(48) a. in *John's* perspective, pictures of *himself* kissing porn stars are not bad publicity
b. *John* insists that the press would never have expected any superstar other than *himself* to play with such an injury
c. *John* admitted that Mary and *himself* make a good couple

However, most of the counterexamples posed can be classed as cases where pronoun-*self* is systematically 'exempted' from local binding. Some theories that address these cases, such as Reinhart and Reuland (1991:297–98), Safir (1992, 1997), Reuland (2001a), and Reinhart (2006), rely on the intuition that some anaphors are exempted from locality altogether in domains where there is no possible candidate for a local antecedent.

The execution of these theories is different, but for Reinhart and Reuland, an anaphor in a conjunction, as in (48c), is not itself an argument of a predicate, hence not susceptible to their Principle A. Safir points out that some anaphors cannot have a coargument antecedent by virtue of what the predicate means, as in (48b), where 'x other than x' is a contradiction. Other predicates, such as *picture*-nominals, have no local structural antecedent (48a). Thus (48a–c) are exempted from local binding requirements. Reuland (2001a, 2001b) takes a different tack, arguing that all anaphors are unbounded unless something forces them to be bound locally (e.g., local SELF-adjunction to a predicate). The domain of exempt anaphors is thus essentially unrestricted, as in the case of UD-forms.

Both exempt anaphors and UD-forms are typically conditioned by semantic and pragmatic factors that are related to point of view, or logophoricity, a term introduced by Hagège (1974) and widely employed since Clements (1975) to characterize a class of morphologicaly distinct pronouns or agreement markers that are used when the antecedent is the subject (usually) of a propositional attitude verb. Languages differ as to whether there is lexical specificity of the predicates that trigger the effect, whether narrative point of view (sometimes called 'logophoric center') is sufficient to license the logophor, or if special syntax is involved. Reuland and Sigurjónsdóttir (1997), for example, show that the Icelandic *síg* embedded in subjunctives is logophorically conditioned, but *síg* is not so conditioned in infinitival domains. Thus the M&W locality domain in (39d) appears to be a logophoric domain. From this perspective, Icelandic *síg* is an anaphor that happens to be cross-classified as a logophor.

Moreover, an anaphor may be cross-classified as a logophor, but logophors do not have to be anaphors. Gokana, for example, uses agreement affixes for this sole purpose (Hyman and Comrie 1981), Ewe uses a special pronoun (Clements 1975), and Amharic uses 1st person pronoun morphology (Schlenker 2003a). One key feature of logophoric forms is that when they are bound, the antecedent is understood to be aware of self-reference. Compare the Yoruba example (from Adésolá 2004) in (49a), which employs a pronoun otherwise limited to binding by focus, and an Icelandic subjunctive example (49b) with *sín*.

(49) a. Olú gbàgbó pé ilé rè/òun ti wó
    Olu believe that house he(w)/he(s) ASP fall
    'Olu believes that his house has collapsed'

b. Ödipus hélt að móðir sín hefði aldrei hitt föður hans
Oedipus thought that mother his had-Subj-past never met father his
'Oedipus thought that his mother had never met his father'

With respect to the contrast in (49a), Adésolá remarks, "a strong pronoun is used when self-reference is intended by the reported speaker (or believer), while a weak pronoun is used when the reported speaker (or believer) does not know that he was in fact referring to his own house." The weak pronoun does not have to refer to Olu, but the strong one must. The same sort of fact is illustrated for Icelandic *sín* in (49b), which requires the interpretation that what Oedipus thinks is that the woman he, Oedipus, took to be his mother had never met his father. But (49b) cannot mean that Oedipus thinks that the woman who has never met his father is in fact his own mother. The English translation allows for the possibility that the person that only the speaker of (49b) knows to be his (Oedipus's) mother has never met Oedipus's father (see Safir 2005:162, for discussion). Finally, the Yoruba strong form *òun* does not behave as an anaphor in local domains: not only can it appear in tensed subject positions and have split antecedents, but if it is bound by a clausemate logophoric pronoun, *òun* must be embedded in a reflexive (the Yoruba reflexive 'BODY-of-pronoun' with a weak pronoun is *ara rè*, but it is *ara òun* when bound by a local subject *òun* (see Adésolá 2004:171, fn. 100).

(50) Olu ro   pe oun ti   korira ara oun ju
     Olu thinks that he(s) (has) hated himself too.much

Thus the logophoric domain in (39d) is not the extended domain of anaphors, unless a given anaphor happens to be cross-classified as a logophor.[21]

The only other point to add here is that exempt anaphors and UD-forms also appear to prefer logophoric environments, but at this writing there are no point-by-point comparisons of, say, Yoruba logophoric contexts and those contexts where exempt anaphors are found in English.

15.3.4 Twilight of the Binding Theory

Thus BT faced many challenges, both theoretical and empirical. The empirical challenges of domain variation and (anti-)subject-orientation were initially met by parameterization of locality domains that weakened the universality of the local domain. Strategies that preserved the generality of local domains include the hoisting analyses, the cross-classification of anaphors with logophors and UD-forms and exemption of anaphors in certain structural contexts.

Moreover, the BT turns out to be the first of several theories designed to predict complementary distributions of the pattern of anaphora, and so the strategies pioneered to explain real or apparent breakdowns in complementary distribution in defense of BT turn out to have outlived that theory. Four such strategies are typically applied, including (i) positing different structures for superficially similar strings (e.g., '*John* saw a snake near *him/himself*'), which is often addressed in terms of differences of thematic structure with associated predicates (as in Reinhart & Reuland e.g., 1993:663–64, 686–88) or in terms of embedded PRO 'subjects' for PPs (e.g., Hestvik 1991); (ii) positing distinct coconstrual relations (e.g., bound vs. merely coreferent interpretation, as in Grodzinsky and Reinhart, 1993); (iii) positing cross-classification (e.g., anaphors and logophors or UD-forms); and (iv) permitting anaphors with no local candidate antecedent to be exempted from locality requirements. Appeals to these strategies usually interact with special assumptions about morphology (see Section 15.5).

It is primarily the theoretical shortcomings of BT, however, that drive new approaches. As Minimalist thinking about the architecture of grammar emerged with Chomsky (1995c) and earlier, BT began to look too rich in the number of principles involved, too isolated from other principles of grammar, and too stipulative about anaphorhood and locality. By focusing attention on these issues, BT set the stage for new thinking about the patterns of anaphora.

15.4 Alternatives to Binding Theory

Most alternatives to BT aimed at reducing the number of principles involved by deriving the BT principles from independently necessary generalizations, on the one hand, and developing a more plausible model of the lexical properties that might account for the empirical diversity of anaphoric domains and pronoun distributions, on the other. Few alternatives to the BT present a comprehensive account of all the issues raised so far, but many contain a leading idea or two that differ from central concepts in BT in ways we will explore. Thus some of the counter-theories may seem incomplete, but research on a variety of fronts has led to hybrid accounts that careful readers of current literature may trace to parts of some of the theories discussed in this section.

15.4.1 Predication-based theories

The classic BT does not appear to address one of the most widespread methods of forming reflexive sentences in the world's languages, namely, affixation to a transitive verb in such a way that the resulting predicate lacks an overt object (both languages exemplified in (51) are SVO and 'RFM' is the gloss for 'reflexive marker').

(51) a. Jean se regarde. (French)
   Jean SE looks.at
   b. Yohani mwâyílángire (Kinande)
   Yohani mo-a-a-yi-langir-e
   John   PST-SM.c1-TM-RFM-see-FV
   Both: 'John saw himself'

While it is possible, within the BT approach, to analyze some of these constructions as instances where marking on the verb controls and in some way identifies a null object anaphor, the overlap with passive constructions in many languages (see Section 15.5.4) suggests the possibility that the affix is responsible for reducing the valency of the verb it attaches to. If there is an operation that renders a predicate reflexive, then the natural strategy from a theoretical point of view is to use it to replace, as much as possible, what must otherwise be said about anaphora. Indeed the locality of Principles A and B provides a suggestive target, because locality of anaphoric relations could potentially *follow* from the necessarily local relations that a predicate enters into with its arguments.

One of the most influential approaches since classic BT is that of Reinhart and Reuland (1993) (henceforth, R&R), who claim that the local character of Principles A and B derives primarily from the fact that reflexivity is a property of predicates, on the one hand, and from the assumption that local binding is restricted by conditions on chains. Core principles of their system are presented in (52–53).

(52) Condition A: A reflexive-marked syntactic predicate is reflexive.
(53) Condition B: A reflexive semantic predicate is reflexive-marked.[22]
(54) A predicate is reflexive if two of its arguments are coindexed.
(55) A predicate P is reflexive-marked iff either P is lexically reflexive or one of P's arguments is a SELF anaphor.

The rough correspondents of Principles A and B in this theory are (52) and (53), respectively. In (56), the argument reflexive (*himself*) marks the predicate as reflexive (pronoun-*self* is [+REFL]), so the sentence is interpreted accordingly, but *John praised him* cannot be interpreted reflexively because it is not reflexive marked (independent pronouns are [–REFL]).

(56) *Paul praised himself/*him*

Since *Paul* and *him* are coarguments of *praise*, they are part of the semantic *praise* predicate and (53) applies. Reflexive marking, insofar as it applies to the predicate introduced by the verb, might be most naturally expected to be instantiated as a verbal affix, and indeed R&R suggest covert affixation of the -*self* portion of pronoun-*self*. They do not, however, treat French *se* as a reflexive marker, but instead assume, on analogy with Dutch *zich*, that *se* is a vestigial object. Dutch *zich* contrasts with *zichzelf* in that *zich* is primarily used with inherently reflexive verbs, as in (57a).

(57) a. *hij* wast *zich*
he wash.past ZICH
'he washed'
b. *George* bewondert *zichzelf/*zich*
George admired ZICH-SELF/ZICH
'George admired himself'

Verbs like this are intrinsically marked with a null reflexive affix in the R&R account, so Dutch has a null SELF morpheme attached to the verb. The appearance of the *zich* object is treated as a vestige of case expression since (53), stated on semantic predicates, does not crucially require the presence of an object.

R&R (1993:675–81) contrast the Principle B effects that derive from (53) with the Principle A effects that apply to syntactic predicates, which are defined in a way that matches the domain for BT Principle A.

(58) The syntactic arguments of P are the projections assigned theta-role or Case by P.
(59) *Esther* expects *herself* to win

In (59), *herself* forms a syntactic predicate with its antecedent because *herself* is assigned accusative case by *expect* on the Exceptional Case-Marking analysis (which we will not review here), even though *Esther* and *herself* are not semantic coarguments. The [+REFL] property of pronoun-*self* is adequate to satisfy (52).

There are still pronoun obviation effects handled by BT Principle B that are not handled by (53), however, and these receive a different treatment.

(60) a. *Esther* expects *herself/*her* to win
b. *Sam* seems to *himself/*him* to be smart

Since *Esther* and *her*, on the one hand, and *Sam* and *him*, on the other, are not coarguments, (53) does not rule them out. R&R propose that these cases fall under the Chain Condition.

(61) Chain Condition: A maximal A-chain $(a_1, \ldots, a_1)$ contains exactly one link – a_1 – that is both [+R] and case-marked.

The marking [+R] means that a nominal can be independently referential, whereas if it is [-R], then it must be part of a chain (see Sections 15.4.4, 15.5.2 and note 32 on classification as [-R]). In English ECM and raising environments like (60a–b), pronoun-*self* is treated as [-R, +REFL], so it can reflexivize the syntactic predicate *expect* while being in a chain with *Esther*. Since *her* is not part of the semantic predicate *expect*, however, Principle B does not apply to it, but here the Chain Condition does the work; *her* cannot participate in a chain with *Esther* because simple pronouns are [+R]. Similarly in (60b), Principle B does not apply to *her* and instead (61) blocks chain formation, but it is not obvious how *herself* can satisfy its [+REFL] feature, since *seem* has no subject theta-role.

Forms like Dutch *zich*, insofar as they appear with inherently reflexive predicates, are now captured by the fact that *zich* is both [-R] (not referential) and [-REFL]. In such cases, the verb is lexically reflexive-marked by a null [+REFL] and the [-R] feature of *zich* permits it to form a chain with the subject while being available to absorb Accusative Case.

(62)   hij heeft *zich/*zichzelf*   geschaamd
       he has   ZICH/ZICH-ZELF felt.ashamed
       'he was ashamed'

In languages like French, *se* is also [-REFL, -R], but *se* is used productively to form reflexive readings for transitive verbs, and so it is necessary to assume that a more generally applied null reflexive affix is available in French.

One of the enduring contributions of this approach, for those who think it is on the right track, is that it seems better adapted to address those languages where reflexivity is a verbal affix (e.g., French *se* is so treated, blurring the line between clitics and affixes), since it is the predicate that is marked and not an argument of the predicate, as in English. Additional machinery to account for inherent reflexivity appears to be necessary in any approach (see Section 15.5.3).

The main work of the Chain Condition, which departs from GB-era assumptions in that it permits chains with more than one theta-role, is to rule out pronouns in (60a–b); Principle C effects are redundantly handled by Rule I anyway, and (53) rules out all the coargument cases redundantly (see Safir 2004a:19–21). The Chain Condition is then taken to predict (a) the contrasts between [+REFL, +R] elements and [-REFL, +R] elements in contexts like (60), and (b) the differential effects in acquisition experiments that, according to R&R, distinguish between pronouns obviated by the Chain Condition and those obviated by (53) (as in cases where the distribution of *zich* and *zichzelf* overlap). However, this theory must also introduce the [-R] feature to A-traces so that they can participate in chain locality, which, if traces are really copies, is a very unnatural move. We shall return briefly to contrasts between [+/-REFL] anaphors in Section 15.5.2. Finally, the Chain Condition faces problems similar to those faced by BT whenever the domain of anaphora does not match the domain of A-movement (e.g., subjects can bind possessor anaphors in Scandinavian, but productive possessor raising to subject is not possible).

What the predication-based approach insures for future work, however, is that coargument relations must play a distinct role from broader locality in any adequate account of anaphoric effects. This has consequences for both the typology of anaphors and the typology of anaphoric patterns, depending on whether a given pattern relies on argument anaphors, affixal markers, or other forms that evoke distinctions between coarguments, on the one hand, and other broader local coconstruals, on the other.

15.4.2 Competition-based theories

Competition-based theories of anaphora take the complementarities in the distributions of pronouns and anaphors and/or those in the distribution of dependent forms and names to be the result of competitions, either between forms for bound interpretations, between derivations, or between levels of grammar. Unlike BT, which assumes that the domains of Principles A and B just *happen* to be the same, these theories see Principle B effects as the result of a lost competition. Potential counterexamples to such theories arise where forms are not in complementary distribution, which we briefly return to, with the discussion of Section 15.3.2-15.3.3 in mind.

Theories that treat forms as the competitors typically assume that a 'less anaphoric' form cannot be coconstrued with the antecedent if a 'more anaphoric' form is available. Theories of this kind must (a) determine which forms are available to enter competition to be dependent on a given antecedent, (b) provide a ranking of some sort that at least values syntactic anaphors over pronouns for the dependent reading, and (c) systematically determine the outcome of a competition in semantic, syntactic, and/or morphological terms.

Reinhart's Rule I could be thought of as the first principle of this kind, insofar as pronouns and anaphors outcompete names/descriptions in bound reading contexts, with the determination that names are not to be coconstrued with the antecedent when a pronoun is available. With respect to local anaphora, Reinhart's principle made no prediction, since Reinhart assumes that both pronouns and anaphors could be bound as variables (see Grodzinsky and Reinhart, 1993:75 fn.3) – that is why R&R addresses local anaphora with their predicate and chain theory.

A number of linguists have explored competition approaches to address locality effects (see, for example, Bouchard 1984, Levinson 1987, 1991, Hellan 1988, Pica 1986, Burzio 1991, 1996, Richards 1997a, Williams 2003 and Safir 2004a, amongst others), and I reproduce here a few of arguments that have been made in support of such an approach. Burzio (1989), the first explicit theory of this kind, points out that if something like Principle A limits the availability of syntactic anaphors, Principle B follows as the elsewhere case, such that pronouns are excluded where syntactic anaphors are possible.

(63) a. Parish praised *himself/*him*
  b. *Thora* thinks that *she/*herself* is smart
(42) a. vi fortalte *Jon om ham selv/*ham/*seg/*seg selv*
    'we told *John* about *himself*'
  b. *Jon* fortalte meg om **ham selv/*ham/*seg/seg selv*
    '*Jon* told me about *himself*'

Hellan (1988) argues that *selv*-forms outcompete *seg* and simple pronouns. For (42), repeated here, the both *seg* and *seg selv* must have a local subject antecedent, but *selv* forms always outcompete *seg* for productive coargument reflexive readings, so (42b) employs *seg selv*. Since *seg* and *seg selv* are subject-oriented, they cannot be anteceded by *Jon* in (42a). This leaves pronoun-*selv* as the winner in competition with the simple pronoun for binding by the local non-subject antecedent *Jon*. *Seg* can, among other contexts, be a long-distance anaphor reaching beyond more local infinitival subject antecedents, but anywhere *seg*, *seg selv*, or *ham selv* cannot appear, a pronoun is possible.

Moreover, if Principle B effects arise from lost competitions, then it is predicted that pronouns can be interpreted as reflexive in a language that has a lexical gap for dedicated syntactic anaphors altogether. Levinson (1987) points out that this is arguably the case for Old English (64).

(64) hi   gecyston hi
     3ppl kissed   3ppl
     '*they* kissed *them/themselves/each other*'

Burzio points out further that in languages where the anaphor is restricted to 3rd person, 1st and 2nd person pronouns express the reflexive reading, in contravention to BT Principle B, as in French (65a) and Norwegian (65b).[23]

(65) a. je me/*se vois
        I me   see
        'I see myself'
     b. jeg skammer meg/*seg
        I   shame   me/SIG
        'I am ashamed'

Thus a gap in the paradigm for reflexive forms for 1st and 2nd person is predicted to result in what would be violations of Principle B.

Those determined to defend Principle B could assume that 1st and 2nd person object pronouns in these languages are homonyms or syncretisms with anaphors, and that the same holds on a grander scale for Old English, but such a position fares poorly if examined over a range of cases. For example, the Danish subject-oriented 3rd person local possessive anaphor *sin/sine*, which agrees with the possessum, is in complementary distribution with a singular pronoun, as predicted for both BT and competition theories where the possessor is in the same domain as its antecedent.

(66) a. *John laeste sin/*hans artikel*
        'John read *his* article'
     b. *John og Mary laeste *sin/deres artikler*
        'John and Mary read *their* paper'

However, Pica (1984) notes that Danish *sin/sine* cannot have a plural antecedent (though its Norwegian counterpart can). In this context, the 3rd person plural pronoun, which does not normally have to be bound at all, must be used for the local anaphoric interpretation. Competition theory predicts that the pronoun is optimal in the absence of a plural form. Note, however, that cross-classification of the possessive as an anaphor in a non-competitive theory is not sufficient; Danish plural possessive pronouns would also have to be stipulated not to be locally anti-subject oriented, especially in the absence of a hoisting analysis (see Safir 2004a:72).

This latter point dovetails with another argument made by competition theorists, namely, that anti-subject orientation appears to be found only in languages that have subject-oriented anaphors. Thus, as Safir (2004a:85) points out, if subject orientation is required in a given language, as it is for the 3rd person SIG/SIN forms in Danish and Norwegian, the anti-subject-orientation of pronouns is predictable, as in the case of the pronouns in compound anaphors. Danish *sig selv* forms are subject-oriented, so less dependent pronoun-*selv* forms, which are also necessarily local,[24] are correctly predicted to be anti-subject-oriented. Anti-subject-oriented forms may turn out to be all and only those potentially bound forms that have lost to subject-oriented competitors.[25]

There several sorts of theories that employ a competitive principle evidenced as a choice of form. Levinson (1987, 1991) and Huang (2000: Chapter 4) argue that the competitive principle involved reduces to Gricean implicatures, Burzio (1989, 1991) appeals to an economy principle of morphology, and Safir (2004a, 2004b) argues for a category of competitive algorithms related to interpretation at the interfaces of which the competitive principle is one. We consider each of these briefly in turn.

Levinson (1987) argues that the competition effect can be reduced to Gricean pragmatic implicatures, on the assumption that if one meant to express local coconstrual, one would have used the required local form for it (assuming a version of Principle A for local anaphors), not the form that can be used non-locally as well (an appeal to the Maxim of Quantity of Grice's, 1989:26, i.e., make your contribution to conversation as informative, and only as informative, as is required), unless one did not intend the locally bound reading.[26] Y. Huang's (2000; Chapter 4) version of the Gricean account begins with the assumption that the Principle B effect arises from a disjoint reference presumption for the arguments of a predicate (which is also an alternative proposed in Levinson, 1991), originating as a usage preference, as in Farmer and Harnish (1987), or even from world knowledge, due largely to the way the world stereotypically is (Y. Huang 2000:216) (see note 40). Principle A effects arise from overcoming the disjoint reference presumption by enforcing the most informative interpretation (which is the most specific one – an anaphor has only one possible antecedent). The use of the morphologically least specified element available falls under Huang's minimal-effort-inclined 'I-implication.' The maxim of quantity

'Q-implicates' that if the most informative form is not used, then the most specific interpretation was not intended, i.e., if a pronoun is used where an anaphor could have been, or when a name is used where a pronoun could have been, then coreference was not intended. He also suggests that there are distinctions between anaphors on the referentiality scale: *gap* >> *self* >> *self self* >> *pronoun-self*.[27] The self-directed predicates (see note 40), like *dress* or *wash*, use the most economical form (nullity) because less morphological effort is needed for predicates that favor the most specific reading (e.g., predicates like *John dressed*, as opposed to predicates he regards as other-directed, e.g., *John praised *(himself)*).

Several points of concern arise for theories of this kind. First, the pragmatic principles do not distinguish bound from coreferent readings without referring to syntax. Even if we add that a bound interpretation outranks a coreferent one, Huang would predict obviation cases like '*His mother never criticizes John*,' because, without reference to c-command, *his* should be disjoint from *John* by Q-implication, contrary to fact because '*Everyone's mother loves him*' permits binding. Moreover, Huang never fully addresses the syntactic limitations on the distribution of non-coargument anaphors, such as the ECM contexts in (35), or for any of the bounded, but extended, binding domains in (39). For forms that can be bound across infinitive subjects for example, like *síg* in Icelandic or Hindi *apnaa*, some syntactic locality condition has to be stated, and so the distribution of these forms cannot be derived from the use of an anaphor to overcome unmarked predicate disjunction.

Burzio's (1989, 1991) competition account is formulated in terms of economy and does not depend on pragmatic maxims.

(67) Morphological Economy: A bound NP must be maximally underspecified.

In keeping with the idea that anaphors are maximally underspecified elements (an assumption critiqued in Section 15.5.1), Burzio's principle insures that a pronoun will not be possible where an anaphor is permitted, and if semantic content other than features constitutes further specification, then names are more specified than pronouns. The more underspecified an anaphor is, the less discriminate it is with respect to what can antecede it, such that it defeats pronouns in more contexts. Thus the anaphor cognates *sig* (Danish), *zich* (Dutch), and *sebja* (Russian) can all be anteceded by singular 3rd person antecedents, but *sig* cannot be anteceded by plurals or non-3rd person, while *zich* can be anteceded by singulars or plurals, but not non-3rd person, and *sebja* can be anteceded by any person or number. Thus *sebja* defeats independent pronouns of all persons, *zich* defeats all 3rd person independent pronouns, and Danish *sig* defeats only 3rd person singular independent pronouns. The underspecification is consistent with Burzio's formulation of Anaphor Agreement.

(68) Anaphor Agreement: The morphological form of a dependent cannot have an agreement feature that conflicts with its antecedent.

Burzio's reliance on the notion that anaphors are featureless and participate in 'pseudo-agreement' is too strong. After all, English reciprocals require local antecedents (apart from picture nominals), but they are neither featureless, nor is their lexical content completely accidental (see Section 15.5.3). Burzio (1991) moved away from (67) because anaphors like pronoun-SELF in English permit SELF to be inflected for number, so he later amended (67) to be sensitive to 'Referential economy,' on the assumption that SELF-forms are 'referentially' weak by comparison with pronouns. This weakened the elegance of the theory in ways that other such hierarchies inherit. However, Burzio did not address the difference between bound and coreferent readings at all, and this limits the extension of his theory to Principle C effects, for example.

Safir (2004a) offers a more comprehensive competitive approach which treats the core phenomenon as a competition of forms to represent an interpretation in a specific syntactic context. Like Burzio (1989) and Levinson (1987), he assumes a form of Principle A, like Y. Huang (2000), he assumes a ranking of forms (69) that extends to anaphors as well, but he adds the syntactic competitive principle in (70), from which he derives the effects of Principles B and C by obviation resulting from lost competition.

(69) Most Dependent Scale: anaphoric.pronoun-SELF >> pronoun-SELF >> anaphoric.pronoun >> independent pronoun >> r-expression

(70) Form-to-Interpretation Principle (FTIP) (simplified):
If x c-commands y and z is not the most dependent form available in position y with respect to x, then y cannot be directly dependent on x.

In its details, the competition pits numerations differing only by choice of dependent form to represent a particular dependent reading, e.g., **The boys love them** does not support the identity-dependent reading because replacing *them* with *themselves* will also permit a successful derivation (on global competitions of this kind see below). As to the ranking in (69), 'pronoun' is a form consisting only of features (no semantically identifiable root) and a pronoun is independent if it can occur in any context without an antecedent. Scandinavian SIG is an anaphoric pronoun because it meets the description of a pronoun and is never independent. On this account, compounds containing a relational anaphoric stem (e.g, SELF or some body part, as discussed in Section 15.5.1) are more dependent than forms without them. Forms containing anaphoric pronouns are more dependent than those that have potentially independent pronouns. Finally potentially independent pronouns are more dependent than r-expressions. Terms more dependent than 'independent pronoun' must have a local antecedent (= Principle A).

The assumption that x-SELF forms are more dependent than SIG forms permits the competitive approach to derive the behavior of anti-local anaphors, such as Norwegian *seg*, which must be bound, but cannot be locally bound (unless the verb is inherently reflexive). When a local anaphor competes against another broader bounded anaphor, the broader-bounded anaphor cannot be used in the more local domain (see Richards, 1997a, and Safir, 2004a, for arguments of this kind). Rather than stating an anti-locality restriction on *seg*, for example, the competition theory predicts that *seg* will not be used where more dependent (x-SELF) forms are available. Conversely, for inherent reflexives, the x-SELF forms are independently blocked (see Section 15.5.2), and so once again, the SIG form fills in as the next most dependent form.

Complementarity is only required (in the form of obviated coconstrual) when the antecedent c-commands, so where the antecedent cannot be a binder, as in '*His* mother never criticizes *John*,' pronouns are not syntactically required to be in complementary distribution with names. The availability of a form for competition is determined by its specification in the lexicon, e.g., its φ-features (determining if it can agree), designation as anaphor or pronoun (determining whether it must be locally bound), presence of a non-pronominal stem (determining its place on the hierarchy of anaphors), and whether it is subject to raising that causes subject orientation (it is unclear what determines this).

It is not always fully appreciated that competition plays a prominent role in most post-BT theories. Reuland (2001a), a theory primarily based on predication relations and Agree, suggests that there is a hierarchical processing advantage to establishing coconstrued readings by one method as opposed to another, such that predication is the most efficient way, binding is less efficient, and what we have called 'mere coreference' is least efficient (see also Reinhart, 2006). These approaches, in the tradition of Reinhart (1983) and Grodzinsky and Reinhart (1993), thus rely on competitions between components for the representation of coconstruals to induce obviation (determining somehow, in ways never fully spelled out, whether or not coconstruals represented in different components are distinguishable or not). By comparison with CAM approaches or Safir's approach, which require global comparisons within a component, Reuland (2001b:352–54) requires a supra-global comparison, not just of possible derivations, but of connections made in different components to specifically evaluate anaphoric relations. The latter issue is addressed in Reinhart (2006), where more explicit assumptions about 'reference set computation' are explored, and a program for research into the cost of such computations is outlined.

Hornstein (2001, 2007) argues that it is not components or morphological forms but syntactic derivations that compete. Safir's FTIP also requires comparisons of derivations, but the competing derivations are limited to those based on the numeration and interpretation at LF, where only a more dependent form can be substituted in the numeration and re-computed to determine whether or not a more dependent form than the given one was available. If the more dependent form that is substituted into the LF numeration permits a convergent derivation, then the thematic position of the form in the given sentence is obviated. Hornstein (2007), revising his earlier copy-covering pronoun-insertion analysis (Hornstein 2001:170–72, 178), argues that pronouns and reflexives have no lexical features, so the numeration that initiates a derivation does not contain them.[28] A derivation on a numeration that inserts a pronoun is independently determined as less valued than one introducing a reflexive because the latter is derived by movement, thus the competition is not between numerations, but within the numeration. Apart from technical details that this approach must address (e.g., the copy must be suppressed, the morphology of anaphors is not arbitrary, etc.; see Safir, 2008, for further issues), the notion that movement is more economical is rejected in Chomsky (2004), who proposes that the existence of movement is a necessary consequence of Merge if Merge applies to a term already in the derivation (Internal Merge); there is no intrinsic economic contrast between External and Internal Merge. Unless Chomsky's proposal is rejected, the economy argument has to be recast.

All of these approaches, however, assume a competition for the most efficient formation of an anaphoric relation, and are not weighted against other requirements of a derivation (i.e., only the success of anaphora is measured). Safir's algorithm is the most syntactically explicit, but the conditions governing the competition do not follow from the general design of the grammar, a result the Reinhart/Reuland approach and the CAM approach aim to achieve, whatever their shortcomings.[29] However, all of these theories appeal to competition based on global (or supra-global) comparisons at least in part, especially for obviation, even if predication, movement, or agreement are the featured mechanisms. In this respect, none are fully consistent with the general Minimalist strategy of Chomsky (1995c:227–28), which rejects global comparison as too powerful a theoretical device.

15.4.3 Locality in coconstrual-as-movement theories

CAM theories begin from the intuition that the distribution of anaphora can be reduced to independently necessary conditions on movement, as discussed in Section 15.2.3. The idea that A-traces are anaphors like reflexives and reciprocals dates from BT Principle A, but CAM theories reverse priority to propose that whatever enforces this locality relation on movement (e.g., phase theory from Chomsky, 2000b, 2001) makes Principle A unnecessary.

The idea that movement and coconstrual are generated by the same device begins as early as Lees and Klima (1963). The CAM approach was revived in Hornstein (1999), wherein it is proposed that obligatory control can be derived by movement if the Theta Criterion is abandoned, that is, if movement from one theta-position into another theta-position is permitted, with the result that the moved constituent bears two theta roles.

(71) a. [tried [[Thomas] to climb the hill]]
      b. [*Thomas* [tried [[*Thomas*] to climb the hill]]]

Even the mechanism of movement in search of case, or some successor idea, can be employed to motivate the movement, leaving a theory of copy pronunciation (see Sections 4.2.4.1, 5.2.2.3, 16.2.1, and 16.2.4) to eliminate the lower copy, just as would be expected in a raising construction, except that, for raising predicates, no second theta-role is acquired by the moved DP. Hornstein's account of obligatory control remains controversial, as discussed in Chapter 16, but whatever its prospects, his extension of the same analysis to derive Principle A is primarily what we are concerned with here.

Hornstein, unlike Kayne, assumes that the copy left by movement is spelled out as an anaphor in local contexts. This also represents a change from an indistinctness relation to a dependency relation, as discussed earlier, but apart from these issues, and movement from one theta-position into another, which the control analysis already proposes, the theory does reduce the distribution of reflexives to contexts where this sort of derivation can apply. The appearance of the reflexive form is a spell-out required to realize the case of the lower copy, and this is a departure from Hornstein's (1999) PRO analysis, where PRO is assumed to originate in a caseless position.

(72) a. praised Maury[+Case, +θ]
      b. *Maury*[+Nom, +θ1] praised *Maury*[+ACC, +θ2]
      c. *Maury* praised *himself*

Hornstein (2007) suggests that Principle B is derived by derivational competition (see Section 15.5.2), on the assumption that pronouns cannot appear where a movement derivation is possible, and a movement derivation will result in reflexive morphology as the spell-out of the lowest cased copy. One problem with this account is that local English reflexives can receive strict readings in certain VP ellipsis contexts (see, for example, Hestvik 1995, Kennedy and Lidz 2001, Safir 2004b:30), but PRO requires a sloppy reading.[30]

(73) a. Marcia expected herself to be more successful than Alice did
      b. Marcia expected to be more successful than Alice did
(74) a. Bush considers himself above the law, but we don't

b. Legislators have been known to pay themselves more liberally than most voters would
c. Attorney Shaw had to represent himself, since no other competent lawyer was willing to

While (73a) allows a reading where Alice did not expect Marcia to be so successful, Alice's expectations of success in (73b) are uniquely reflexive.[31] The coargument-bound reflexives in (74a–c) all support strict readings. This strikes at the heart of the parallel between the CAM PRO analysis and the one for morphological anaphors.

It is also notable that CAM approaches cannot derive the distribution of reciprocals the same way as reflexives, since reciprocal morphology carries with it meaning that is not found in its antecedent. Where reflexives are anteceded by reciprocals, a single movement derivation would have to leave different morphological residues with different meanings.

(75) *The boys* expect *each other* to trust *themselves*

Hornstein (2001:187) treats *each other* as an adverbial remnant of movement (see also Kayne, 2002a as in Section 15.2.3), but it is then unclear why such remnants cannot be left by *wh*-movement (e.g., *Which men did Mary see [which men [each other]]).

These problems for the CAM theory of anaphors as residues are not all that arise (see Safir, 2003, 2008, for further critique), but even those mentioned here seem to seriously cloud the prospects for this approach.

15.4.4 Agreement-based theories

In Chomsky (2000b), the Agree relation is introduced as a relation between a probe (normally a syntactic head) and a goal (normally a DP), such that the head values its features by association with the goal. The central intuition of Agree-based theories of anaphora is that the Agree relation can effect coconstrual and that the locality relation required by Principle A can therefore reduce to the locality restrictions on Agree (see Section 18.12), namely, phases, the descendants of barriers (Chomsky 1986a). Since the antecedent is not normally a head, however, the probe must somehow facilitate or establish coconstrual between the antecedent and the goal.

Part of the reason for introducing Agree is to account for instances where movement does not appear to occur, but locality restrictions still hold on agreement relations (see Chomsky 2000b:125, 2001:16, 2004:116; also Section 18.12). The Agree relation is modeled as a computationally restricted search into the complement of a head, such that locality will be determined by more general limitations on efficient computation. In practice, the locality boundaries of searches (which block Agree relations) are expressed as phases. The phases are taken to be CP and vP, where 'v' is the head that, for all transitive and unergative verbs, assigns external argument theta-roles in its SPEC (e.g., the V *hit* assigns a patient theta-role to its object and then V raises to v where the external argument of *hit* is assigned to the Spec-vP). The edge of a phase is material that is merged to [v XP] or [C XP] (as well as v and C, respectively). Movement to the phase edge permits edge material to avoid immediate spell-out and interpretation, which occurs for the complement of v and C as soon as a new head is merged above the edge of the phase. The inability of a head in one phase to look into a closed phase is called the Phase Impenetrability Condition (PIC) (see Chapter 18).

Reuland (2001a, 2005a, 2005b) is the first proposal to appeal to properties of Agree to characterize anaphoric relations and, Reuland argues, to use it to derive Principle A from general economy conditions and conditions on how structures are interpreted. The account of Reuland (2005a) is designed essentially as follows: when two arguments of a predicate are the same in the relation λx (x Pred x), the two arguments become indistinguishable and reduce to a one place predicate, λx (x Pred) (as is possible for verbs like *wash*, given a rule of thematic merger, see Section 15.5.3, but not *kill*), if they are too close to one another (see also Lidz, 2001a, 2001b, 2001c). If a probing head can connect the two variables of a predicate within a phase, the reduction cannot be stopped, and results in ill-formedness if the predicate requires more than one argument. Thus certain variables have to be 'protected' from coargument binding within the phase to remain distinct, but must still form a relation via a chain to effect bound anaphora. The distinctness of variables is protected by embedding anaphors inside predicate shells, e.g., the *zich* of *zichzelf* is protected by the *zelf* portion, which, as a relational predicate, provides the status of a separate argument structure (see Jayaseelan, 1997, for the related idea that pronouns in complex anaphors are protected from Principle B). This correctly predicts that, within a phase, *zich* without *zelf* can be an argument anaphor if it is embedded in a PP or a small clause subject. Thus the local distribution of complex anaphors is a consequence of the protection mechanism, not BT Principle A and not R&R's (52). Since only forms that have incomplete feature specifications can enter into chains (essentially the [+/−R] distinction), pronouns will not be able to form chains on this account, although they could be logically bound, were it not for obviation where a chain-binding derivation is available.

At its best, Reuland's agreement-based theory derives Principles A and B from the assumption of variable indistinctness, the argument structure of predicates, the protection effect when chain-susceptible elements are embedded in relational structures, the processing efficiency hierarchy for forming anaphoric relations, and the assumption that only elements with incomplete feature complexes can agree in chains (in place of any primitive anaphor/pronoun distinction).

Reuland (2001a) does, however, rely on rich assumptions about chains (three kinds are appealed to) in order to model the appropriate effects, but it is not clear that chains of any sort have independently motivated status in Minimalism. The pronoun/anaphor distinction that captures Principle B effects relies on an assumption about the context-dependency of number features (see Reuland 2001a:464–65, 468), a non-standard assumption at best, and the role of covert [+SELF] morphemes (as protectors) continues to play a role, even for non-coarguments, e.g., ECM complement subjects, where protection should be unnecessary.[32] Reuland (2005a) gives a more schematic presentation where the role of chains is diminished, but whether the translation of Agree into dependency relations will capture the right interpretations (such that anaphors can permit strict and sloppy readings for examples like (2b) or (19)) is not established. If Principle A can truly be derived, Agree-based theories have a leg up on any theory that must stipulate Principle A, including R&R, although the manner in which pronouns are disqualified from chains in this theory remains suspect, and with it the derivation of Principle B, which other competition theories do derive.[33]

Another Agree account, Kratzer (2009), proposes that the head that probes for Agree is to be interpreted as an operator that combines with its complement to form a property. That property is predicated of the specifier of the probe (the antecedent), thus permitting semantic binding to be read directly from syntactic probe–goal relations. Recall, however, that Agree was originally formulated as a relation between a probe head and a c-commanded phrase (a goal) that values the probe, as in cases where T probes the subject below it to effect subject–verb agreement. The latter is not an antecedent–anaphor agreement relation, however. The two relations are necessarily distinct for Icelandic cases like (76) (from Zaenen et al. 1990:102) where T agrees with a vP internal nominative, but antecedent–anaphor relations hold between a dative subject and a genitive anaphor.

(76) henni þykir broðr sinn/*hennar leiðinlegar
   she-DAT thinks brother.NOM SIN.GEN/her.GEN boring
   'she finds her brother boring'

Thus there are two visible agreement relations, subject–verb and SIN with possessum, and neither effects anaphora (indeed, it appears anaphors never agree with verbs, see Section 15.5.1). For Agree to be translated into binding, the binder and the bindee must be connected by Agree, but either the probe is the dative subject, not a head, or the probe mediates relations between its specifier and something in its complement. Davison (2001:54–55) has made the same argument on the basis of Hindi data.

Given our demonstration that the anaphoric relation cannot reliably piggyback on other Agree relations, a special class of anaphor-agreement inducing heads will need to be structurally represented in Kratzer's theory to capture semantic binding and no morphological evidence for such heads currently exists (see also Safir, 2010; Appendix A, for further discussion). Heinat (2006) overcomes this difficulty, however, arguing that whatever is merged at the apex of the tree involves 'Minimal Search,' including phrasal nodes (compare Chomsky, 2004:113). Moreover, Heinat proposes to distinguish pronouns and reflexives by virtue of whether a non-categorial stem is directly merged with N or D. In the former case, N provides valued phi-features which subsequent merger of D can probe and be valued by, but if D is directly merged to a stem, then D will lack valued phi-features, which only Agree with a probing DP merged later. The (interesting) morphological details aside, it is curious that Heinat assumes all bound variable relations are formed by Agree. Heinat does not offer any account of how pronouns can be bound variables (e.g., 'Everyone loves *his* mother'), and so it is not clear why whatever device achieves these relations cannot provide a bound relation in local contexts for a pronoun. Appeal to some sort of competitive account between Agree and this device, as in Reuland's theory, is conceivable, but out of the spirit of Heinat's approach. Unfortunately, this leaves no account of the obviative effect of Principle B at all.[34]

In the Agree-based approach of Hicks (2009a), by contrast, it is assumed that Principle B is derived as an economy effect ('featural economy'), whereby contexts where variable binding could have been induced by Agree cannot be induced by the mechanism for non-local bound pronouns. Hicks contends that the competition in question does not amount to a global comparison, but some of his nuanced assumptions about features that are assigned integers as values are anaphora-specific, and instances of featural economy that do not pertain to anaphora are not explored.

Other Agree-based proposals are likely to appear as long as Agree restricted by phases is the premier locality relation in Minimalist theorizing and as long as there is hope of deriving Principle A (see, for example, Rooryck and vanden Wyngaerd 2011), but the conversion of Agree relations into interpretive relations, the derivation of Principle B effects by obviation, and the potential proliferation of Agree relations are challenges to regard carefully in the new work that will emerge.

15.4.5 Where we are

How should we evaluate future work in this area going forward? Certainly, there is no satisfactory return to the BT principles, all of which the accounts mentioned here have tried to derive from other principles or generalizations that are posited to be independently necessary. It seems likely that Principle C effects will be derived from lost competition with (component representations or derivations containing) a subclass of bound pronouns and that Principle B effects will largely reduce to lost competitions with (derivations containing) anaphors. Attempts to derive Principle A (and preserve derived obviation for Principle B effects) in CAM and Agree accounts remain attractive in principle, but a convincing account of the technical details, one that does not ultimately clutter central principles, remains elusive. As we shall see in Section 15.5, the richness of the empirical patterns observed remains an ongoing challenge for every current theory.

All the approaches just described must assume a semantic interface that makes use of the syntax to predict (non-)coconstrual, a pragmatic interface that produces expectations, at minimum, and, in some cases, a morphological interface can insert a form that supports the syntactically established (non-)coconstrual. Future accounts will need to capture distinctions made in Section 15.2 regarding how coconstrual relations come to be represented and interpreted, no matter what the approach. Moreover, it will be necessary to guard against appeals to interface conditions if they simply restate stipulations in the syntax in other accounts. It is possible that elements of all the theoretical strategies introduced here will play a role in the theory that ultimately accounts for the possible patterns of anaphora.

15.5 Morphology, variation, and interpretation

The internal structure of anaphors and pronouns turns out to bear an important relation to the class locality relations they can enter into and the possible interpretations they can have. Beyond contrasts between locally free pronouns, on the one hand, and locally bound anaphors, on the other, different types of anaphors, distinguishable by their morphology and the semantic contributions of their lexical stems, can contrast with one another, even in the same language, both with respect to locality and interpretation (e.g., as illustrated for Norwegian). Moreover, many languages have several sets of pronouns, distinguished in their distribution on the basis of their morphology and antecedency. This section briefly explores the contribution of morphological factors to some of the theoretical questions raised by the varieties of locality and interpretation. The theoretical question that arises is whether there are syntactically determined bounds to variation in this domain and whether the general principles proposed to account for anaphoric patterns will dissolve into morphologically driven provisos. In the best case, central principles will be universal and "the apparent linguistic diversity across languages can in fact be reduced to the respective lexical properties of the different linguistic entities" (Pica 1991:133).

15.5.1 Pronouns vs. anaphors

Burzio (1989) observes that if a syntactic anaphor is a form that must have a local antecedent, then Principle A is a tautology. Burzio suggests that what is crucial to anaphors is underspecification of features, either person, number, gender, or case, an idea embraced by Reinhart and Reuland (1991, 1993) and later Reuland and Reinhart (1995) for case. The suggestion is that underspecified forms cannot refer, and so must have a closer connection to their antecedents, whereas pronouns with a full set of person, number, and gender features (phi-features) and case can refer independently, and thus can appear in a sentence without an antecedent. The Russian anaphor *sebya*, for example, is not distinguished for number, person, or gender and accordingly can be anteceded by any sort of antecedent, but potentially independent pronouns in Russian are distinguished for phi-features.

There are several difficulties for underspecification-based accounts, however. First of all, English anaphors are distinguished for person, number, and gender on the pronouns that are associated with *-self*. Morever, *-self* can itself be inflected for number (e.g., *themselves, yourselves*), and the paradigm of pronouns associated with *-self* in standard English is idiosyncratic (genitive pronouns combine 1st and 2nd person, accusative with 3rd person masculine singular), which suggests that the properties of the forms must in some respects be taken as a whole. Furthermore, proper names in English are unspecified for gender (e.g., 'Marion Morrison' is the birth name of the actor known as John Wayne), and they are obviously not anaphors (but see note 3). If we restrict the underspecification criterion for anaphors to forms that do not have other semantic content, then the fact that body part anaphors like Yoruba *ara rè* 'BODY-of-pronoun,' which can have the literal meaning when used non-anaphorically, becomes accidental, as it does for all 'relational anaphors' (see below), leaving no obvious retreat for the underspecification view. German 1st and 2nd person object pronouns are bound locally, but do not appear defective for case in any obvious way (but see Reuland and Reinhart 1995). Reuland (2001a) abandons the deficient case account for a deficient number specification, but see note 32 for a critique. Finally, null arguments of tensed sentences that are interpreted as independent pronouns without sentence internal antecedents are common in the world's languages, not just in heavily inflected null-subject languages, but in languages without overt inflection, such as Chinese and Japanese.

It is generally true that strictly anaphoric forms can never be used for deixis, even for pronoun-*self* in English (excepting Hibernian English, where pronoun-*self* appears to act as a pronoun).

(77) *Look! It's himself! (Accompanied, perhaps, by pointing gesture)

Many forms that are not anaphors are also inappropriate for deixis, such as unstressed pronouns and clitic pronouns when they are distinct from full forms in a given language, but it does appear that nearly all the forms that require local binding also fail the deixis test.

In short, there is no current theory that predicts that the class of locally bound things will have all and only the morphological properties that anaphoric forms can have, because neither underspecification nor failure of deixis are sufficient conditions to identify an anaphor and only failure of deixis is a necessary one (but see Keenan, 2007, for semantic tests designed to empirically isolate anaphors).

Although GB-era syntax treated pronouns and anaphors as necessarily non-overlapping classes (to derive the distribution of PRO, an approach now abandoned), most assume now that some pronouns are anaphoric. Descriptively, pronouns are nominal forms that have no semantic root and have only feature content. Pronouns are independent if they do not require an antecedent sentence-internally, and are treated as anaphoric if they require a c-commanding antecedent. Thus forms like French *se* and Dutch *zich* are pronouns, but anaphoric insofar as they must be bound. The French verb-affixed clitic *le* 'him' or the tonic pronoun *lui* are independent pronouns. Moreover, pronoun paradigms often include anaphoric forms (e.g., the pattern *me/te/se* and *mon/ton/son* for French, where only *se* happens to be anaphoric, or *mich/dich/sich* for German). There are some languages that distinguish amongst pronoun classes for topicality vs. contrast, by emphasis or stress, or by logophoricity or else they permit one class of pronouns to be bound as variables, but not others. We will not explore these differences between non-anaphoric pronoun classes here, but see Cardinaletti and Starke (1999), Déchaine and Wiltschko (2002), and Safir (2004a:185–90) for discussion of the relation of the internal structure of pronouns to their potential for deixis and bound variable interpretation.

Another distinction between pronouns and anaphors is that pronouns typically permit split antecedents (e.g, Bouchard 1984), but anaphoric forms almost never do. This is very difficult to test for coargument antecedents since pragmatically plausible three-argument verbs need to be employed, but the prediction can be tested for English possessive reciprocals, as shown in (78). In Hindi (Davison 2000), the tense-bounded anaphor *apnii* in (79) can have Ram or Shyam as its antecedent (and plural antecedents), but not both.

(78) a. *Alice* introduced **John** to **each other's** accountant(s)
  b. *Charlotte* introduced **Emily** to **their** accountant
(79) *raam-nee **syaam-see apnii** gaaRii-kii marammat kar-nee-koo kah-aa
  Ram-ERG Shyam-with SELF vehicle-of repair do-INF-DAT say-PF
  'Ram told Shyam to repair self's vehicle'

Apparent counterexamples to this claim seem to involve anaphors cross-classified as UD-forms (see Section 15.3.3).

A last distinction is that in many languages, such as Italian, anaphors cannot be partners for subject–verb agreement (Rizzi 1990b, Woolford 1999), whereas pronouns (bound or not) can so participate.

(80) a. *a loro   interessano solo se stessi
       to them.DAT interest.3pl only themselves
       'They are interested only in themselves'
    b. a me   interessano solo loro
       to me.DAT interest.3pl, only them.NOM
       'I am interested only in them'

Some long-distance anaphors can apparently appear in nominative positions, but most of those cases seem to pass tests for UD-forms, as discussed in Section 15.3.3, or else subject–verb agreement is absent. The phenomenon suggests some sort of obviated agreement, perhaps a matter that can be addressed by an Agree-based theory of anaphora (because it is too exactly what is not expected), but the questions surrounding it remain open.

15.5.2 Differences between types of anaphors

Once we agree on how pronoun behavior and anaphor behavior are to be distinguished, a matter that is not fully settled (e.g., see Section 15.3.3), we are still left with considerable variation amongst the forms that are classed as anaphoric or that require local anaphoric interpretation. This variation extends across a number of dimensions, including principally those below:

(81) a. Surface position of the anaphoric marker: These include predicate affixes that induce reflexive readings (prefixes to verb stems in Narrow Bantu), clitic forms that show some interpretive, syntactic, or morphological independence from the predicates they attach to (as in Romance, where clitics can climb), independent forms that appear in argument positions (as in Germanic) and adjunct, typically adverbial, forms (e.g., *he did it himself*). In some languages, markers can also occur in discontinuous combination (e.g., as in French *Ils se voient l'un l'autre*, 'They see each other,' where *l'un l'autre* appears to be an adjunct).
    b. Morphological complexity of the anaphoric marker: Some anaphors are taken to be simple underived roots that do not inflect, as is frequently the case for affixal markers, but also for many argument markers (e.g., Scandinavian SIG). Other markers consist of decomposable parts, including more than one stem (e.g., Dutch *zich+zelf*), or a stem–affix analysis (e.g., Lubukusu AGR-*(b)eene*) or both (e.g., English pronoun-*selv(es)*).
    c. Semantic atoms in the anaphoric marker: Some stems (semantic atoms) have stable meanings when external to an anaphor, and these meanings fall into very limited semantic categories that occur cross-linguistically, including body parts (e.g., Yoruba *ara* 'body'), OWN (Lubukusu *(b)eene*), or SAME (French *même*), most

typically for reflexive readings, OTHER, ONE-ONE, and similar forms for reciprocals. Other languages have a stem that has no identifiable meaning, and others still have forms that qualify as pronouns.

d. Interpretive class of the anaphoric marker: There are many variations on anaphoric readings (e.g., reciprocal, reflexive, distributive/non-distributive, dual/plural), or non-anaphoric readings that cluster with anaphoric ones (see Section 15.5.4). Whether or not proxy readings (see further below) or *de se* readings (see note 21) or other aspects of point of view are permitted or implied also comes into play.[35]

e. Agreement on the marker: These include agreement with an antecedent, and/or with an external modified nominal (e.g., Norwegian *sin(e)*, a possessor that agrees in gender with its head noun), and internal agreement amongst parts of complex markers (difficult to tell from antecedent agreement with both internal parts, as in English *themselves*).

The main issues are whether or not the bounds of all this variation can be predicted, whether there are causal factors that determine whether any properties of (81a–e) vary together, and if values for (81a–e) play a role in predicting possible syntactic locality domains, possible UD-form or exempt anaphor distributions, and/or syntactic subject-orientation.

The most general approaches will either predict the morphological properties of forms bound anaphorically based on their syntactic configuration, or they will predict the syntactic configurations in which forms can be anaphoric on the basis of their internal morphological properties (or both). CAM theories, for example, should strive to predict the morphological properties of bound elements based on how the derivation has been constructed, whereas competition approaches should show that internal properties of morphological forms should predict the competitions they can enter into to support anaphoric readings; their distributions are the outcomes of those competitions. Safir proposes that the forms in question can be marked in the lexicon as anaphoric (subject to Principle A effects), but all other properties of lexical items are not anaphora-specific (e.g., the size of the binding domain should depend on non-anaphoric properties). R&R's predication approach assumes that nominals are specified for features that matter for predicate and chain formation, and the distribution emerges from whether or not chains or predicates can be formed including the form with the relevant specifications (i.e., [+/−R, +/−SELF]). Heinat (2006) proposes that the internal structure of a form, whether the non-categorial root combines first with N or with D, determines susceptibility to Agree (and thus binding). However, all theories will seek to capture families of anaphors classified by internal properties that appear to act in a general way.

One internal property of anaphors that has been linked to syntactic distribution is (81b), noted by Faltz (1977) and treated by Pica (1987) as a firm correlation presumed to hold both cross-linguistically and language-internally (in languages with more than one anaphor).

(82) Complex (multimorphemic) anaphors are restricted to the most local domains, while anaphors bound at greater distance are always simplex.

For example, the Scandinavian SIG-type anaphors can be bound at a distance across infinitives, but the complex SIG-SELF forms cannot be. In theories like R&R, the locality of SIG-SELF would be reduced to the locality SELF-movement to form a reflexive predicate, for example. The bounded, but not very locally bounded, simplex forms are then hypothesized by Pica (1987) and others to be susceptible to long-distance head movement (which, as pointed out in Section 15.3.2, is not attested overtly). There are, however, counterexamples to the generalization, as pointed out by Huang (2000:96), including complex anaphors that can be long-distance bound and some that are only long-distance bound, but see Safir (2004a:274, fn. 46) for discussion. Moreover, if Kayne (2000a) is right, the *m/t/s* pronominal paradigms of Romance and Germanic are internally complex (e.g., French *me/te/se, moi/toi/soi*, etc.) so the generalization about simplex forms, insofar as it can be maintained at all, might be restated as involving forms without non-pronominal stems in their internal morphology.

For example, Safir (1996, 2004a) distinguishes between relational anaphors, those based on meaningful stems, and pronominal ones, and goes on to investigate whether the internal structure or the residual meaning of (often somewhat semantically bleached) stems helps to determine their interpretations and distributions, based on the competitions they enter into. Thus it appears that body-part anaphors (e.g., pronoun-SELF/HEAD/FACE/BODY) are rarely used for reciprocal meaning unless there is no explicitly reciprocal form in the language, but anaphors based on OTHER are never reflexives.[36] Although Schladt (2000) provides a broad survey of the stems employed for reflexive anaphors, not enough empirical research has explored these questions (e.g., with respect to SAME and OWN-based anaphors). These issues are important insofar as they provide a testing ground for the ability of the different theories in Section 15.4 to accommodate and/or predict patterns of lexicalization and distribution for both relational anaphors and pronominal ones.[37]

Recent literature summarized in Safir (2004a:112–14, 124–35) has puzzled over contrasts between the ability of different anaphor types to represent proxy readings.

(83) at the wax museum opening, *Castro* expected *himself/PRO* to be dressed in a uniform

The pronoun-*self* form permits two interpretations, one where Castro-person expects Castro-person to be so dressed, and one where Castro-person expects Castro-statue to be so dressed, but PRO in place of pronoun-*self* only permits the person-person reading, not the person-statue reading. Thus, as Jackendoff (1992) was the first to point out, reflexive identity can hold between non-coextensive denotations. The fact that the overt form in English is required for this interpretation does not permit us to test differences between anaphors in this respect, but Norwegian does, where the proxy relation is person-literary work instead of person-statue.

(84) a. Yeats leste seg selv på engelsk og så gjorde Hamsun det på norsk
 'Yeats read SIG-SELF in English and then Hamsun did in Norwegian'
 b. siden han visste at Le Carré var flerspråklig, bad Grisham Le Carré om ikke å lese seg på tysk
 'knowing Le Carré was a polyglot, Grisham asked Le Carré not to read SIG in German' [SIG = Grisham's writing]
 c. Le Carré synes at folk skulle lese ham kun på engelsk
 'Le Carré thinks that people should only read him in English'

Safir (2004a:132, 169) points out that Norwegian *seg* cannot support proxy interpretations locally, where *seg* is only possible for inherent reflexives, but *seg selv* supports the proxy reading where it is available. Where *seg selv* is not available (e.g., non-locally) and *seg* is, *seg* can support a proxy reading (84b). Finally, where *seg* is not available, a pronoun supports the proxy reading. Safir argues that SELF forms cannot be obligatorily indistinct from their antecedents in languages that have an alternative that can be indistinct, so Norwegian-*selv* forms are not available to represent necessarily indistinct interpretations (like (65b)). Where indistinctness is not required, *seg selv* wins the competition to represent this reading, but it is not an intrinsic property of *sig* that it cannot support a proxy reading, as (84b) shows. Thus the competitions that anaphors and pronouns enter into are determined by their internal properties, but their empirical distributions are determined by the competitions they win.[38]

Other instances of the syntax of anaphora reaching down into the morphology of anaphors must be omitted here for reasons of space (but see Sections 15.4.3–15.4.4), but this is enough to illustrate that the agenda of any explanatory theory of anaphoric relations will be responsible for a theory of the morphological forms that effect those relations.

15.5.3 Reciprocal anaphora

The distribution of reciprocal readings is a topic too broad for discussion here, involving as it does a range of possible reciprocal readings (see

Büring, 2005:203–220, for a formal semantic treatment and references) and a wide range of possible morphological expressions (see in particular Frajzyngier and Curl 2000b, and Nedjalkov 2007). On the other hand, reciprocals have not received the same attention in the syntax of generative grammar (as opposed to the semantics) that reflexives have and so explicit syntactic analyses are relatively few.

There have been decompositional analyses of the English reciprocal *each other*. Perhaps the best known is Heim *et al.* (1991), which treated *each* as a quantifier (a 'range argument') which adjoins to the antecedent ('the distributor') and binds the relational argument place of *other* (which is adjoined to VP), i.e., each member of the set of the antecedent is other than each of the other members of that set when paired in the two-place tricking relation.

(85) [$_{IP}$ [$_{DP}$ [$_{DP}$ the boys]$_j$ each$_k$] [$_{IP}$ t$_j$ [$_{VP}$ [$_{DP}$ t$_k$ other]$_l$ [$_{VP}$ tricked t$_l$]]]]

The clause-boundedness of quantifier raising predicts the absence of long-distance reciprocals, which is generally true. However successful the syntactic analysis was for *each other* (see Everaert 2000, and Williams 1991), it did not appear to generalize to reciprocals in other languages, either because different lexical stems are involved (e.g., in Lubukusu, Agr-*eene khu beene* 'Agr-own on/to/for own', as discussed in Safir and Sikuku, forthcoming), or a dedicated reciprocal affix is monomorphemic and located on a predicate (such as the verb extension *-an-* in the Narrow Bantu languages) or realized in root reduplication (e.g., Amharic), or the marker that can be interpreted as reciprocal is polysemous, either affixal (e.g., French clitic *se*) or in argument position (Yoruba *ara rè* 'body 3ps. pronoun'), or in some combination that permits disambiguation (e.g., French *se* and the adjunct *l'un l'autre* 'the one the other') (see, in particular, Nedjalkov 2007: Chapter 3).

BT predicts that reflexives and reciprocals would have the same domain, and though this is true for English in interesting cases, such as (86a), an ECM environment, it is not true for possessors like those in (86b), where reciprocals are possible and reflexives are not (see Everaert, 2000, for discussion).

(86) a. the boys expect *each other* to be honorable
b. the boys read *each other's/their/*themselves* books

From a competition theory perspective, the binding domain may apply to reflexives and reciprocals in the same way, but that domain would then have to include the possessor position, since possessor reciprocals have access to antecedents in the minimal clause that includes the possessum. The lack of a possessive form for *himself* would be treated as a gap in the local domain that is filled by a pronoun.[39]

With respect to affixal reciprocals, Reinhart and Siloni (2005) argue that the predicate-based theory of reflexivity can be extended to account for reciprocals, and contend further that there is covariation in the derivation of affixal reciprocals and reflexives in the languages that have both. They argue that, like affixal reflexives, affixal reciprocals (or inherent reciprocals without an affix, e.g., *the boys argued*) can be formed either in the lexicon or in the syntax by a rule that merges two thematic arguments of a predicate into one argument position. Their Lex-Syn parameter then requires that if affixal reflexives are formed uniquely in the lexicon in language L (i.e., thematic merger reduces transitive argument structures to intransitive ones), then affixal reciprocals are only formed in the lexicon (and vice versa), but if the affixal reflexive is formed in the syntax, then affixal reciprocals must be too (and vice-versa). Dutch is a lexicon language (where *zich* is treated as a case-absorbing clitic and there is no abstract SELF-affixation, contra R&R) as is English (e.g., *John washed*, where there is no overt affix), such that predicate formation is uniquely in the lexicon, whereas they argue that predicate formation for reciprocals and reflexives is part of the syntactic component in languages like French and German.

The predictions made by this ambitious theory require careful comparative analyses. Chichewa and Kinande, for example, are Bantu languages which have both a reflexive marker and a reciprocal marker expressed in their verbal morphology. Mchombo (2004) argues that Narrow Bantu reciprocals are formed in the lexicon (e.g., they interact with derivational affixes and can form nominalizations), but reflexive markers are syntactic, an adverse prediction for Reinhart and Siloni, if true. Mutaka and Safir (2007) argue that Kinande morphology shows that inherent reflexives are not derived from transitive counterparts, but rather that transitive counterparts are fashioned from inherent reflexive lexical entries. Although these facts appear to compromise the Reinhart and Siloni approach in two ways, closer analysis is necessary to see if these challenges are fatal. From the theoretical perspective, however, thematic merger stipulated to apply to coarguments is a departure from minimalist practice, since application of the rule in the syntax is not subsumed under Merge or Agree.

The brief remarks in this section serve only to show that exploration of the syntax of reciprocals holds the promise of informing future work on both the theory of locality in syntax and the theory of predicate–argument structure.

15.5.4 Polysemy

One class of issues that arises in many languages concerns the polysemous properties that some anaphoric markers bear. It is notable in these discussions that the markers that are most polysemous are affixal markers, not argument markers. While argument markers may be polysemous for reciprocal/reflexive and reflexive/emphatic or all three (e.g., Gungbe *pronoun-dé-Num*), polysemy for reflexive with passive, anti-causative, middle, etc., does seem rare for argument reflexive markers but is widely attested for clitics or verbal affixes (see Heine, 2000, for a survey of African anaphoric markers). Discussions of how grammaticalization processes might tend to produce such patterns of polysemy, such as Heine's, suggest nominal origins for reflexives that phonologically reduce even as the range of functions they cover increases. Kemmer (1993) and Lichtenberk (2000), amongst others, have explored some suggestive semantic generalizations about typical clusters of polysemy.

Theories of emphatic reflexives, some of which depend on scalar implicatures or evoked alternatives, relate argument position reflexives to adverbial reflexives (e.g., '*John* went to the store *himself*'), reasoning as follows: if most predicates are *other-directed*, then adding an emphatic SELF marker (or some other stem) reverses the expectation of other-directedness, hence local reflexives are complex (see König and Siemund, 2001:60–62, and Gast, 2006, for further discussion and references; compare the disjoint reference presumption discussed in Section 15.4.2 and Reuland's account of resistence to indistinguishability in Section 15.4.4).[40] It has been argued that complex reflexives arise historically in this fashion, as grammaticalization of adverbial reflexives creates argument reflexives (e.g., Keenan, 2002, but see also van Gelderen, 2000a, 2000b, and Rooryck and vanden Wyngaerd, 2011, section 5.2.3 for the history of English).

Within generative syntax, the polysemy of reflexively interpreted affixes is usually treated as originating in the way the predicate–argument structure of predicates interacts with general properties of the syntax. Several attempts have been made to relate reflexive interpretations to unaccusativity (e.g., Marantz 1984, Grimshaw 1990), that is, reflexives are analyzed as structures where no thematic role is assigned to the subject and the apparent subject is moved from (or from within) object position. The affix iteself (*se* in (87)) is analyzed as a marker indicating de-linking of the logical subject, or as an anaphor corresponding to the logical subject that frees up the syntactic subject position for *les filles* to move into it (see, e.g., Pesetsky 1995, Sportiche 1998).

(87) a. [les   filles] se voient   [t]
       the.pl girls SE see.pres.3pl
       'the girls see *themselves/each other*'
   b. [un veston de laine] se lave [t] facilement.
       a   jacket of wool SE wash easily
       'a wool cardigan washes easily'
   c. [la   branche] s' est casseé [t]
       the branch SE is broken
       'the branch broke'

Insofar as middles (87b), decausatives (87c), and passive structures (not shown) have been analyzed as unaccusative structures, the advantage of this approach is that polysemous markers can be argued to arise naturally on the basis of the kinds of syntax that they have in common.

Other generativist approaches to polysemy rely more on lexical manipulation of argument structure and/or interpretation and keep the syntax of affixal reflexives unergative. Reinhart and Siloni (2004, 2005) argue at length that the unaccusative analysis for reflexives in languages like Dutch and French fails too many of the diagnostic tests for unaccusativity to be viable and instead propose the rule of thematic merger discussed in Section 15.5.3. Lidz (2001a:312) argues that some 'reflexive' affixes, such as the one he discusses in Kannada, are actually just markers indicating a "mismatch between the representation of the thematic relations in a sentence and the lexical-aspectual decomposition of the verb in that sentence." He argues that different linking mismatches arise in reflexive and decausative sentences, but since both involve a mismatch of the thematic/lexical–aspectual mapping, the relevant affix appears. Steinbach (2002) also rejects the unaccusative analysis and combines linking rules in the lexicon with transitive syntax and the assumption that weak reflexives are only optionally interpreted as arguments (strong ones must be) to derive the polysemy of the German middle marker (reflexive, anti-causative, middle) from semantic interpretation (drawing on Reinhart, 2002).

Rooryck and vanden Wyngaerd (2011) return to the ergative analysis of inherent reflexivity by arguing that these verbs take a clause-like inalienable possessor complement (RP), containing a subject-like possessum and prepositional object complement possessor. Instances of dative subjects in German like (88a) are derived from the complement structure in (88b).

(88) a. Jan hat sich den Fuss verletzt (German)
Jan has REFL the.ACC foot hurt
'Jan hurt his foot'
b. ___ T [vp verletz [RP [RP [DP den Fuss] R [PP P [DP sich]]] R [PP P [DP Jan]]]]

Through a series of head incorporations, the R and P nodes do not surface morphologically, but they contribute to the ability of the unaccusative verb to assign accusative case to *den Fuss*, (based on the internal structure for these relational phrases proposed by den Dikken, 2006b, and references cited there). *Jan* raises to Spec-T where it antecedes *sich*. By this means, the ergative analysis is preserved, accounting for the lack of volitional agentivity, even though verbs taking complements of this sort can still assign accusative case. Rooryck and vanden Wyngaerd then set out to counter the arguments proposed by Reinhart and Siloni against an ergative approach to reflexivity in French and Dutch, in particular, while extending the analysis to other constructions that employ the same marker. I set aside further discussion for reasons of space, but this is enough to indicate that the ergative reflexive analysis as an approach to polysemy remains in play.

15.5.5 Some open questions

The enormous variety of anaphoric forms, their distributions, and their interpretations certainly remains a descriptive and theoretical challenge for future work. We now know a great deal about the varieties of anaphora, thanks to large-scale comparative work by Faltz (1985), which is his pioneering 1977 dissertation, Geniušiene (1987), Y. Huang (2000), Kemmer (1993) (on the polysemy of many anaphoric markers), many of the essays in Frajzyngier and Curl (2000a, 2000b), Nedjalkov (2007) (an enormous compendium of work on reciprocals), and countless smaller studies reporting on anaphora in the world's languages.

It is notable, however, that most of these works focus on classes of forms or classes of constructions and do not compare the full pattern of anaphora in one language with its full pattern in another. For competition theories, this is a shortcoming, because forms with identical domain restrictions will have different overt distributions depending on what other forms compete with them within one language as opposed to another, and close analysis of syntactic contrasts between languages will reveal non-anaphoric properties that influence anaphoric patterns. The detailed monographs that facilitate such comparison, such as those by Everaert (1986) on the anaphoric pattern in Dutch, or Hellan (1988) for Norwegian, are relatively rare. In this respect, future work on the morphological variety of anaphoric markers is more likely to make progress when a range of highly detailed works on particular languages permit rich cross-linguistic comparison.[41]

15.6 Directions for future research

Minimalist approaches to syntax suggest that the theory of anaphora should be an epiphenomenon of one or a few syntax generating principles that interact with interface properties (perceptual-articulatory, conceptual-interpretive) to permit the class of human languages that are possible. The diversity of anaphoric patterns on the surface seems to require many distinctions within our knowledge of grammar, but every ancillary device to create a richer classification takes us further from the Minimalist ideal, unless there is independent evidence that the device in question can be attributed to an independently necessary property of the syntax or the interfaces. The 'narrow syntax' itself seems to contain Merge and Agree constrained by properties of the lexicon and competitive principles that are couched in the language of economy or optimal computation. All of the successors to BT have appealed to some or all of these devices, but whatever the right devices are, the best outcome in the long run would be for the theory of anaphora to disappear as an independent entity.

However, we must be wary of approaches that translate unsolved problems into Minimalist terms and declare victory. The right theory must explain why coconstrual is sensitive to syntax at all, and so some form of coconstrual must be expressed in derivations or representations (e.g., turning indices into features with integers as values, as in Hicks, 2009a, does not remove indices from the theory, except on a theory-internal interpretation of inclusiveness). Agree theories look promising as accounts of why local anaphor binding is sensitive to c-command, but the right theory of coconstrual must explain how local Agree is interpreted as variable binding. No approach to obviation for Principle B or C effects has escaped some version of a competition theory, typically appealing to global or supra-global comparisons. Moreover, if it is true that bound variable pronouns are sensitive to scope, rather than c-command licensing, as argued here, then Principle C effects, which are c-command sensitive only, do not follow from the condition on variable binding. The theoretical works reviewed here have addressed many of these issues, though many questions remain open. If the recent range of book-length treatments of the anaphora questions are any indication (e.g., Heinat 2006, Hicks 2009a, Reuland 2011 and Rooryck and Wyngaerd, 2011), we can be certain this will remain an active area of research for a long time to come.

Notes

I would like to thank Marcel den Dikken, Matthew Barros, Sara O'Neill, and an anonymous reviewer for comments that improved the final draft. This chapter was written with the support of NSF BCS-0919086.

1. This chapter only addresses anaphora between nominals, most typically involving nominals interpreted as entities, rather than events, propositions, or states of affairs. Although spatial, modal, and temporal anaphora deserve more attention from syntacticians, they are set aside here for reasons of space.
2. The notion 'c-command' as stated here is Reinhart's (1976) version, a descendant of earlier notions (see Lasnik, 1981a:1–36, for the history). Some definitions eliminate symmetric c-command (e.g., Kayne, 1975, who relates it to precedence) and some definitions are derivationally based (e.g., Epstein et. al., 1998). Others reject a pure structural statement in favor of prominence of thematic roles (e.g., Pollard and Sag 1994; but see Safir 2004a:140–45), but all theories assume if X

c-commands Y, then X c-commands Z if Z is dominated by Y, which is crucial to the unbounded character of c-command.
3. As Lasnik (1981a:149–67) has pointed out, there are languages (e.g., Thai) in which names can be quite generally c-commanded by a coconstrued name, and these constitute counterexamples to Principle C as stated. He points out, however, that even in these cases, the c-commander cannot be a coconstrued pronoun. For other languages where names appear to be bound, see Mortensen (2003) and Lee (2003).
4. Backwards anaphora is often regarded as degraded without an appropriate pragmatic context (e.g., Safir 2004b:53). Kayne (2002a:150) cites literature claiming that it is unacceptable in some languages.
5. The difference between A- vs. A′-binding was originally stated in terms of positions assigned theta-roles vs. positions not assigned theta-roles, respectively. With the expansion of functional structure, the distinction had to be restated (see Chomsky, 1995c:64, who with Howard Lasnik introduces the notion 'L-related') in order to preserve the distinction between binding by predicate arguments vs. binding by elements that are not predicate arguments (e.g., and adjuncts, quantifiers), but the idea is that certain positions are defined as quantification or discourse-related, and others as case- or predicate-related, and only binding from the latter sorts of positions is A-binding. Most of the discussion in this chapter is about A-binding.
6. It is possible for some descriptions to act as locally A′-bound variables in relative clause resumption contexts, e.g., *Do you remember **that third-grader** who, even after all we did, we couldn't imagine how **the little bastard** was ever going to pass?*, but as Lasnik points, out, epithets, unlike pronouns, cannot be A-bound, e.g., **Every third grader** wonders how **he**/*the little bastard* is going to pass. See Kayne (2002a:140) and Dubinsky and Hamilton (1998), however, for some interesting counterevidence. See also notes 3 and 13.
7. The literature on crossover effects is deep and wide and will not be explored here. See Safir (2004b) and Büring (2005) for references and a literature review as well as particular theories, but weak crossover effects continue to inspire new research.
8. Barker (2012) details a much wider range of violations of (9), including examples like (i–iii), where the quantifier takes extra-wide scope (but notice that (18) is not violated).
    (i) the scope of *each book* has expanded on that of *its* predecessor
    (ii) when the game ended, the amount of wealth that *each person* had accrued was added to *their* overall score
    (iii) after unthreading *each screw*, but before removing *it*, make sure the boards will remain aligned, so you can replace *it* later
9. Büring (2005:116) gets the strict reading from the assumption that independent pronouns (as opposed to names and descriptions) have

indices, that the overt VP and elided VP "must be syntactically identical, *including indices*" (emphasis Büring), and the proviso that "No LF representation may contain both semantically bound and free occurrences of the same pronoun" ("No spurious indices"). The role of syntactic indices, which are interpreted as coreference, insures the strict reading is the only alternative to the sloppy one here. He later shows that neither syntactic indices nor the spurious indices proviso are needed if we adopt Rooth's (1992b) focus theory of ellipsis, in which the referential values of pronouns will have to match if the entailments of focus domains do – an approach that is most definitely *not* mere coreference (see also Fox, 2000, on parallelism). See Büring's discussion of what the elimination of syntactic indices would mean for assignment functions (pp. 135–37). More problematic for elimination of syntactic, as opposed to semantic, binding are cases like "*Only John* voted for *himself*" (Heim 1993), which allow a strict/sloppy-like distinction where there is only one focus domain. Büring (p. 141) suggests syntactic indices may still be needed to satisfy Principle A and provide for the strict reading. Safir (2004a:111) addresses a similar issue with *even* and concludes syntactic antecedence is crucial.

10. If *he* is assigned an index in the semantic or discourse representation, that is a separate matter that the syntax of these forms does not address (unless we follow the proposal Büring rejects for syntactic indices on pronouns; see note 9). Thus whether or not there are indices in semantics (see, e.g., Jacobson 1999, Pollard 2005) is a question largely orthogonal to the one addressed here. Since the focus here is on syntax, accounts of discourse anaphora do not receive any serious attention here, but see Ariel (1990) for an influential study.

11. It is also not clear that the notion 'numeration' needs to be part of linguistic theory (see Safir 2010:44), and if so, inclusiveness may not be definable in a useful way. Hicks (2009a: Chapter 4) proposes a special class of features to which integers corresponding to antecedent values are assigned, which appears only to smuggle indices into the feature system (a concern he considers, but does not, in my opinion, allay) in order to satisfy inclusiveness.

12. Both Kayne (2002a) and Hornstein (2001) allow 'sideways movement' (see Bobaljik and Brown 1997; and also Section 16.2.4), which permits B, a subconstituent of A, to move (Merge) to C, where C is not a node dominated by or dominating A. Although both Hornstein and Nunes (2004) claim advantages for parasitic gap and across-the-board structures, this increase in the options for movement allows for many more possible coconstruals, a proposal critiqued in Safir (2003, 2008).

13. For example, Aoun et al. (2001) argue that a form of subextraction from what is superficially a resumptive epithet accounts for differences between interpretations of epithet resumptives embedded in islands

and those that are not. See also Boeckx (2003). A variant of Kayne's approach is advocated in Zwart (2002).
14. It is usually assumed that reverse binding, where an anaphor is in a position that c-commands its antecedent, is impossible, but see Anagnostopoulou and Everaert (1999), for an account of some plausible cases. See also discussions of backwards control in Chapter 16.
15. Reconstruction describes constructions where subparts of a displaced constituent behave as if they were still present in the position from which they were displaced, e.g., 'Which pictures of *his mother* did John say that *every boy* should be proud of?' Most speakers can answer 'The ones of her as a bride', which is a relational bound variable interpretation of *his* (the mothers vary) where *every boy* appears to have scope over *his*, even though *his* appears to be outside the scope of *every boy* after displacement, but not before. I avoid the rich literature surrounding reconstruction effects for reasons of space, but see Safir (2004b) and Sportiche (2006) for discussion and recent references.
16. See Hicks (2009a: Chapter 3) for extensive discussion of Principle A as an anywhere condition as opposed to its application uniquely at LF.
    In the 1970s and 1980s, examples like (i) and (ii) were part of the pattern to be captured by binding domains, and attempts to distinguish elements contained in thematic subjects from thematic subjects themselves were attempted (for a summary, see Lasnik, 1981a:1–36).

    (i)   *the men* said that pictures of *themselves* would be on sale
    (ii) *the men* said that there would be pictures of *each other* on sale
    (iii) **the men* said that *each other/themselves* were guilty

    These examples also involve *picture*-DPs, however, and are now not typically treated as core locality phenomena. See Section 15.3.3 for discussion.
17. Acquisition studies have made important contributions to the study of anaphora, but I have little to say about them for reasons of space. (See Chapter 25 for discussion of acquisition, including some anaphora-related issues.) Issues surrounding the emergence of Principle B effects and the nature of obviation have been especially influential. See especially Thornton and Wexler (1999), Reinhart (2006), and Elbourne (2005), for references and discussion. For a recent account of how other psycholinguistic evidence bears on anaphora, see Burkhardt (2005).
18. Dalrymple (1993:39–40), suggests incorporating an even more elaborate listing of domains that adds subject-orientation within an LFG approach (see Chapter 6). See Safir (2004a:60) for discussion.
19. Postal (1974) was an early advocate of this view, which, in Minimalist approaches, is interpreted as movement from complement SpecIP position to a case-marked, but non-thematic position in (functional projections just above) the matrix VP (e.g., Lasnik and Saito 1999).

20. In some languages, anaphors cross-classified as UD-forms can also be bound by 'subcommanding' antecedents. These are typically possessors of nominals c-commanding the UD-form and they are required to encode point of view (e.g., 'John's letter says ... UD-form,' but not 'John's car crushed UD-form'). These cases may fall together with non-commanding antecedents that are logophorically conditioned, rather than a special class. See Y. Huang (2000:119–20) for animacy considerations and Huang and Liu (2001:170–72) who argue that such cases are true, locally conditioned, anaphoric binding.

21. The literature on logophoricity has grown considerably in recent years. See Koopman and Sportiche (1989) for the first influential syntactic analysis, and see Culy (1994, 1997) and Y. Huang (2000:172–204) for some of the cross-linguistic generalizations. For the literature on Yoruba and a broader account, see Adésolá (2004). Sells (1987) and Kuno (1987) explored aspects of point of view associated with logophoricity, and much recent work has addressed the semantic 'awareness' effect described in the text, interpreted by many (e.g., Chierchia 1989, Cole et al. 2001, Schlenker 2003a Anand 2006) as *de se* in the sense of Lewis (1979). Schlenker, for example, favors an analysis whereby the indexicality of 1st person pronouns which pick out the utterer in context (see note 23) are shifted to pick out the attitude-holder, an analysis that is appealing for languages, like Amharic, that permit 1st person pronouns to act as logophors, but is not morphologically justified in most languages. See also Safir (2004c) for a syntactic A'-binding analysis based in part on Baker (1998) (but see Reuland, 2001b, for another view), an evaluation of the claim that the readings are *de se* (for a different view, see Giorgi, 2007), as well as a critique of the shifted indexical analysis.

22. Bouchard (1984:58), was the first to suggest that reflexive predicates must be morphologically marked. Williams (1980, 1994) also proposes a predicate-based theory. He argues, for example, that the unacceptability of 'John is *his* cook' vs. 'John likes *his* cook' (see Higginbotham, 1983a) is a Principle B violation insofar as *his cook* is predicated directly of *John*, and is not an argument of *is* (as opposed to *like*). Such cases are amenable to an Agree account if *be*, as opposed to *like*, does not establish a phase in these cases.

23. It is probably not an accident that 1st and 2nd person pronouns are most likely to lack anaphoric forms, since they normally pick out the utterer and the addressee, respectively, in the moment of speech, and so the bound reading is normally extensionally equivalent to one where the utterer is selected by each 1st person mention, for example (see note 32). Differences, however, persist between anaphoric and pronominal indexicals. In (i), from Safir (2004c:110), *myself* requires a bound reading to the subject and *me* does not permit it (Heim, 1993, points out related ambiguities for 'Only I think I will win').

(i) If I were (anyone of) you, I wouldn't be talking to myself/me
(ii) I can defend myself more effectively than other people can

Moreover, 1st person reflexives can get both strict and sloppy readings, as in (ii) (see also Rullmann, 2004). The literature on indexicality, though relevant, is too rich to treat responsibly here. See Schlenker (2003a) and Higginbotham (2009) for discussion and references.

24. In Safir (1997), it is shown the exempt anaphor phenomenon is evidenced for Scandinavian pronoun-SELF forms, but not for SIG or SIG-SELF forms. This may be an indication that exempt anaphors require certain internal structure (or perhaps must contain a non-anaphoric pronoun). Büring (2005:242) notes that Serbo-Croation *sebe* cannot act as an exempt anaphor, but Reuland and Koster (1991:24) provide an example that Dutch *'mzelf* can be so interpreted.

25. This claim is based on 'strict subject orientation' as described in Safir (2004a:170–73).

26. For a critique of Levinson's accounts, see Safir (2004a:62–66).

27. Y. Huang does not specify what counts as SELF in a language, but he seems to contrast, e.g., Dutch *zich/zichzelf* as SELF/SELF-SELF, which is an insufficient analysis of the morphology, and a glossing practice critiqued in note 36.

28. Except for the derivational aspect, Hornstein's approach recalls that of Everaert (1991), who proposed that pronouns and anaphors could be inserted into representations where binding and locality determine the features that the forms would have to have, with appropriate selections from the lexicon. A version of this strategy might be feasible within a Distributed Morphology approach and some recent Agree-based accounts have taken this tack (e.g., Heinat 2006, Hicks 2009a, and Rooryck and vanden Wyngaerd, 2011).

29. There has also been an attempt to model anaphoric distributions in the Optimality Theory (OT) framework (Burzio 1998, Wilson 2001, Fischer 2004), where all syntactic outputs are regulated by a competition between ranked constraints. In this way of thinking, no special competitive principle is necessary since the whole grammar is built that way. Global comparison in the OT competition has its disadvantages for semantic-interpretation-based constraints, however. For example, the GEN principle cannot put *John expects himself to win* in competition with *John expects him to win*, or else *John expects him to win* would not be a possible sentence of English under any interpretation. In other words, a fully specified bound reference interpretation must be part of what GEN provides and any forms that are used to represent a specified bound meaning must be faithful to that reading – and inviolably so. The OT calculation must, in effect, build the syntax from a representation that has the complete semantics encoded in it,

such as predefined scope for quantifiers binding variables, etc. or else add a new competition after the derivation is built. No work in OT has taken this consequence seriously, so I will not examine approaches of this kind further.

30. The mistaken claim that anaphors only permit strict readings is often cited (e.g., Hicks 2009a:120), but what has been shown in the literature is that some anaphors in some contexts favor only bound readings, as Hicks acknowledges on the same page in his fn. 23. This is a fundamental problem for theories, like that of Hicks, that tie anaphorhood to sloppy readings only through a special bound variable property of anaphors.

It is notable that pure reciprocal forms appear never to permit strict readings in ellipsis contexts, e.g., *The girls hate each other more than the boys do.* It is not clear what a truly reciprocal interpretation anteceded by *the girls* would mean, but neither can this be taken to mean 'The girls hate each other more than the boys hate *them*.' Anecdotal evidence suggests this is true cross-linguistically.

31. Fiengo and May (1994) suggest that nominals represented in the interpretation of elliptical VPs can be treated as pronominals (they call it 'vehicle change'; see also Section 19.2.2.3), even if their parallel overt antecedents are not.

(i) Mary thinks she likes *Bill*, but *he* doesn't think she does [like *him*]

If *Bill* had to be present in the ellipsis site, we would expect a Principle C violation, but vehicle change to a pronoun makes it possible. See Safir (2004b:29–30) for an account of strictly interpreted reflexives as vehicle-changed pronouns in ellipsis sites. Büring (2005:138–41) argues both readings should be possible, and he considers a range of preferences for reflexives in ellipsis contexts.

32. These assumptions all raise questions, if not eyebrows. Number can indeed be context independent, e.g., 'Pants that clean themselves are in high demand,' where the plurality of *pants* is not context-sensitive. Reuland assumes that anaphors are underspecified for number, like *zich*, which he treats as the factor that allows them to form chains (but compare Danish SIG/SIN forms, which are inherently singular and form chains). In languages like German, however, where 1st and 2nd person otherwise independent object pronouns, *mich* and *dich*, are used for local reflexive readings, Agree must treat these pronouns as lacking grammatical number (on the view that each use of them must pick out the same utterer/addressee in context), hence they are [–R] so they must form chains. On the other hand, they must then be capable of heading chains without number, since they can also be independent when they are not local (unlike Danish SIG/SIN, but like 1st and 2nd person pronouns in Danish, which can be independent). See note 23.

33. I do not have space, or the final version of Reuland (2011), to review for this chapter, but in his book-length treatment, Reuland further develops many of the themes of his earlier work and ties them together into a comprehensive framework, which readers are recommended to consult.
34. Heinat (2006:17) does not address the fact that the absence of a bound variable reading does not imply disjoint reference without further assumptions.
35. Some of the point of view issues pertain to predicates, not to anaphors bound in those predicates, but anaphors may have the effect of adjusting point of view, e.g., in reciprocal sentences, there are opposite viewpoints for any two participants. See Frajzyngier (2000a, 2000b) and Kuno (1987).
36. There is a general tendency in cross-linguistic reporting to gloss reflexive morphemes, or at least morphemes that in part of their distribution are bound locally, as 'SELF,' even when there is no indication that the word has any semantic stem in it, or even if it has a different semantic stem. Progress in this area will require much greater attention to these empirical details.
37. One recurrent semantic connection in the choice of anaphoric atoms is inalienable possession, insofar as body parts are typically inalienably possessed and OWN asserts possession. As noted in Safir (1996), the metonymic use of body part anaphora is idiomatic, and so the relational content of inalienable possession is employed to produce an identity marker (see also Reinhart and Reuland 1991). As early as Helke (1971), parallels have been drawn between inalienable possession idioms (e.g., '*They* held *their* breath') and reflexives, and in this respect possessor raising and or datives of possession should also be part of the locality discussion, but are omitted here for reasons of space. See Rooryck and vanden Wyngaerd (2011) for an approach to anaphoric patterns that relies heavily on connections between inalienable possession and reflexivity.
38. See Reuland and Winter (2009) for a different analysis.
39. Non-local pronouns typically do not support a reciprocal reading, even where reciprocals are not possible, as in (i)

(i) the boys knew that *they/*each other* were planning escapes

However, coargument coconstrual for 1st and 2nd person plural in German allow both reflexive and reciprocal readings (see Safir 2004a:93). In languages that have argument position anaphors that are bound across intervening infinitival subjects, such as Norwegian or Hindi, there is no reciprocal interpretation at a distance. See note 30.
40. Although the emphatic analysis of complex reflexives is attractive insofar as it guides interpretation, there is reason to doubt that there is a presumption that predicate arguments are disjoint (as in Huang

2000) or that other-directedness is a general case. Rather, some predicates exhibit self-directedness, such as English *wash, dress, stretch*, and so can be intransitive and reflexively understood, and some predicates are other-directed, such as *argue, kiss* (see Dimitriadis 2008a, 2008b for a semantic analysis) or adjectives like *(dis)similar to*, or exception predicates like *everyone excepting Bill* (see Safir 1992, 1997). These directed predicates, typically few in number in the languages that have them, tend to show special morphology (or the lack of it) and tend to belong to the same small semantic classes across many languages. Most predicates, however, are not obviously directed one way or the other, i.e., English verbs like *praise, introduce, kill, love*, etc. do not seem to have any presupposed directedness at all.
41. The work of the Afranaph Project (ongoing) seeks to fill this gap by providing comprehensive descriptions of patterns of anaphora within particular languages, but that research is still in its infancy.

16

Raising and control

Maria Polinsky

Compare the following two sentences:

(1) John is likely [___ to apply for this job]

(2) John is planning [___ to apply for this job]

Semantically and structurally they show interesting similarities and differences. Both involve an obligatory interpretive dependency between an overt argument NP in the matrix clause and a lower unpronounced argument in the complement clause, represented atheoretically as a gap. The difference between these two constructions is an instance of the well-known distinction between raising (1) and control (2), two phenomena that have been at the forefront of linguistic theory starting with Rosenbaum (1967), Postal (1970, 1974), Jackendoff (1972: Chapter 2), Chomsky (1973), Bach (1979), and Bresnan (1972, 1982). This chapter will examine these phenomena and survey the basic approaches to them in linguistic theory. Given the prominence of raising and control in the linguistic literature it is impossible to do justice to all the rich work on their syntax – the reader should view this chapter as an introduction to the existing approaches and is advised to consider further readings presented at the end of the chapter.

The chapter is structured as follows: In Section 16.1, we will survey the basic properties of raising and control structures. Section 16.2 presents the current Minimalist views on raising and control. Section 16.3 shows the main approaches to raising and control in unification-based lexicalist theories. Section 16.4 uses the material from previous sections to deliberate on the inventory of silent categories employed in modern syntactic theories. Section 16.5 outlines some remaining issues in the syntax of raising and control and presents further directions that stem from the main issues discussed in this chapter.

16.1 Basic properties of raising and control constructions

16.1.1 Raising to subject

Raising is somewhat limited by lexical idiosyncrasies of a given language; in English it is possible with predicates like *seem, appear, happen, be likely, be apt, turn out, begin* but not similar predicates like *be possible* (see Davies and Dubinsky 2004: Chapter 1 for a list of typical raising predicates). Cross-linguistically, the set of lexical items that license raising must be determined empirically in each case, as it may vary from language to language in semi-predictable ways. Nevertheless, it is the case time and again that similar lexical items can be used as raising and control predicates across languages; for instance, modal and aspectual verbs are often raising predicates, and verbs of intention and desire are typical control predicates (Stiebels 2007, 2010). Furthermore, an interesting generalization about raising and control has to do with the fact that one and the same lexical item can alternately participate in raising and control. Thus, as we will see below, *begin* is sometimes a raising predicate and sometimes a control predicate. These empirical facts cast some doubt on the prospects of a straightforward lexical classification of words/predicates in terms of raising vs. control.

Returning to our example (1), this construction can alternate with a construction that has the expletive subject *it*:

(3)   a. the police appeared to the protesters [___ to stay calm]
      b. it appeared to the protesters that the police stayed calm

The co-occurrence with the expletive (as well as with idiom chunks, cf. (4) and (11) below, where a raising-to-object verb appears) is an indication that raising verbs do not assign an external theta-role to their argument, thus patterning just like other unaccusative verbs.[1] This is also shown by co-occurrence with idiom chunks:

(4)   the cat appears to be out of the bag

The only difference between raising verbs and unaccusatives such as *fall* or *arrive* is that the latter take a DP complement, whereas raising verbs take a clausal complement (we will discuss the actual category of that complement in Section 16.2).

The DP that can undergo raising (*the police* in our example) is interpreted within the embedded clause. The position of that DP is relevant for anaphoric relations (see Chapter 15); compare the difference in binding between (5a) where the silent subject of the infinitive determines the place and interpretation of the reciprocal, and (5b), where the reciprocal is bound by the matrix subject:

(5)   a. Bruce Wayne and Batman seemed to Vicki Vale [___$_i$ to hate each other$_i$]
      b. Bruce Wayne and Jack Napier$_i$ seemed to each other$_i$ [___ to be easy to defeat]

Another empirical generalization is that the subject-to-subject raising construction is scopally ambiguous. Thus, the sentence in (6) has two readings:

(6) someone from Chicago is likely to win a Nobel Prize
  i. there is someone in Chicago who is likely to win a Nobel Prize (*someone* scopes over *likely*)
  ii. it is likely that there is someone from Chicago who will win a Nobel Prize (*likely* scopes over *someone*)

The interpretation in (6ii) is only possible in a raising construction, not in a control construction. Note that there is no ambiguity if the indefinite expression cannot be interpreted as the implicit subject of the infinitival clause:

(7) Milton Friedman seemed to someone from Chicago to be a Nobel Prize winner (scopally unambiguous with respect to *seem* and *someone*)

Finally, raising cannot skip intermediate clauses and has to create a dependency between the subject of an embedded clause and the subject of the immediately dominating clause:

(8) *Kim$_i$ seemed [for Pat to believe [___$_i$ to know the answer]]

To summarize our empirical observations, raising to subject has the following properties:

(9) a. it targets only the subject of the embedded clause
  b. it cannot skip clauses
  c. it shows lack of selectional restrictions (idiom chunks can raise)
  d. it exhibits reconstruction for binding and scope

16.1.2 Raising to object

Consider now the pair in (10):

(10) a. everyone expected that Argentina would win the World Cup
  b. everyone expected Argentina to win the World Cup

The DP *Argentina* is clearly the subject of the embedded clause in (10a) but it can also appear as the object of the matrix verb (10b). In both cases, however, its thematic interpretation comes from the predicate of the embedded, not the matrix clause. Just as with raising to subject, the matrix verb does not impose selectional restrictions on the relevant DP – thus, idiom chunks can raise:

(11) a. Who would expect the pot to be calling the kettle black in this case?
  b. John believed the shit to have hit the fan
  c. Mary showed the cat to be out of the bag

Only subjects of the embedded clause can undergo raising to object, just as was the case with raising to subject.

Although semantically the DP in the raising to object construction is interpreted within the embedded clause, structurally it behaves as if it is in the matrix clause – for instance, it can be the subject of the passive featuring the matrix verb, as in (12); see also (47), below.

(12) Argentina was expected (by everyone) to win the World Cup

Furthermore, the raised object can be separated from the infinitival clause by the intervening material which clearly belongs with the matrix clause, e.g.:[2]

(13) a. the chairman expected his earnings foolishly to show increases
b. she made Jerry out to be famous

For the adverbial *foolishly* to be interpreted with the matrix verb (which is the only interpretation that makes sense) it has to be in the same clause as that verb; this means that the material preceding it, including the raised DP, should also belong with the matrix clause. Likewise, the particle verb *make out* has to be represented in the same clause, therefore the DP separating the verb and the particle is also in that clause.

However, there is also contradictory empirical evidence, which is unexpected under the conception that the raised DP belongs in the matrix clause. Compare the following contrast (see Chomsky 1973, Postal 1974, Runner 1998 for an extensive discussion):

(14) a. Which artist$_i$ do you admire [paintings by ___$_i$]?
b. ?/*Which artist$_i$ do you expect [paintings by ___$_i$] to sell the best?

Subextraction out of a regular object in (14a) is unproblematic, but subextraction out of the raised object in (14b) is marginal at best, and many native speakers reject this extraction altogether. This contrast is surprising if both clauses have the same syntactic structure and differ only in complexity. Worse still, regular objects can always participate in *tough*-movement, illustrated in (15b), but raised objects cannot (16b) (Chomsky 1973:254, Postal 1974, Langacker 1995, Runner 2006):

(15) a. it was easy for Jones to force Smith to leave
b. Smith was easy for Jones to force to leave

(16) a. it was easy for Jones to expect Smith to leave
b. *Smith was easy for Jones to expect to leave

Assuming that *tough*-movement should take any object and transform it into a subject, these facts are surprising, and the judgments on the offending sentences are even more robust than in the case of subextraction. Altogether, there seems to be interesting evidence that the subject of the infinitival clause raises to the object of the matrix clause, but there are also contradictory data suggesting that the position of the raised object is somehow different from its more typical counterpart.

16.1.3 Control: subject and object control

Just as raising involves an interpretive dependency between an overt, fully lexically specified DP in one clause and a silent (missing) argument of another clause, so does control,[3] as illustrated in (17) for subject and (18) for object control:

(17) the police intended to stay calm

(18) the police appealed to the protesters to stay calm

In (17), the subject of intending and the implicit subject of the infinitival clause *to stay calm* have the same denotation: the police; this is an instance of subject control. In (18), the object of the matrix clause (*the protesters*) identifies the implicit subject of the infinitival clause; this is an instance of object control.

Like raising, control can only apply to subjects of embedded clauses, and like raising, it can create an interpretive dependency between the embedded subject and matrix subject or matrix object. It also obeys locality – no intermediate clauses can occur between the matrix and the embedded control clause.

Control and raising have several principal differences, however. First, control predicates impose selectional restrictions on their arguments, which means that expletives or idiom chunks cannot participate in control chains, cf. the contrast between (19) and (20):

(19) there is likely to be a riot

(20) *there decided to be a riot

Second, control and raising differ with respect to passivization. If the embedded clause of the raising construction is passive, it is truth-conditionally equivalent to the active infinitival clause (21); under control, there is no such equivalence: (22a) denotes a different state of affairs than (22b). The contrast between (21) and (22) follows from the fact that control but not raising predicates impose selectional restrictions on their arguments. In (22a) *implored* theta marks *the players*, while in (22b) it theta-marks *Maradona*, so that it is unsurprising that the two sentences should have different meanings. Since *expected* does not theta-mark *the players* and *Maradona*, truth-conditional equivalence is preserved.

(21) a. the public expected the players to hug Maradona =
      b. the public expected Maradona to be hugged by the players

(22) a. the public implored the players to hug Maradona ≠
      b. the public implored Maradona to be hugged by the players

Also related to selectional restrictions is the property that control arguments typically have to be sentient and volitional:

(23) the governor decided to withdraw the resources from the program

(24) *the crisis decided to withdraw the resources from the program

Unlike raising, control constructions do not show evidence of reconstruction; the only reading of (25) is that there is a particular individual who decided to run the race, thus *someone* takes wide scope:

(25) someone decided to run the race

Next, raising and control constructions differ in their ability to nominalize: nominalizations of raising constructions are impossible, whereas control structures nominalize freely, thus:[4]

(26) a. *the police's appearance (to the protesters) to stay calm
     b. *Kim's consideration of Pat to be a good role model

(27) a. the police's intention to stay calm
     b. the police's appeal to the protesters to remain calm

Control, unlike raising, allows for differences in interpretation depending on the uniqueness of the controller, i.e., the degree to which the missing argument in the referential dependency has to be identified with the overt argument in that dependency (Jackendoff and Culicover 2003). For instance, the subject of the infinitive has to be identified with the object of the matrix clause in (28), may be partially identified with it in (29), and cannot be identified with it at all in (30):[5]

(28) the author$_i$ decided [___$_i$ to withdraw the paper]

(29) the chairman$_i$ agreed [___$_{i+k}$ to meet tomorrow]

(30) it is not recommended [___ "anyone" to swim here]

Some researchers view the distinction between unique and non-unique control (variable control) as a continuum; the position on that continuum is determined by the semantic properties of a particular control verb and the overall event structure of the relevant construction. Such a position is particularly well articulated by Culicover and Jackendoff in a series of papers (Culicover and Jackendoff 2001; Jackendoff and Culicover 2003) and their book *Simpler Syntax* (2005). Other researchers view the distinction as categorical – it can be couched in terms of obligatory and non-obligatory control, cf, for example, Williams (1980), Chomsky and Lasnik (1993), Hornstein (2001, 2003), among others. Generally, there are two main conditions on obligatory control: uniqueness of the controller and locality of the relation between the controller and the controlee. The uniqueness can be derived either from the lexical properties of a given control predicate (which seems to be the predominant view in the literature cf. Stiebels 2010) or in a purely syntactic way, as will be shown in Section 16.2.4 below.

Related to the phenomenon of variable control is the phenomenon of control shift (Růžička 1983, 1999, Comrie 1984, 1985a, Farkas 1988, Wegener 1989, Sag and Pollard 1991, Panther 1993, Petter 1998, Stiebels 2007, 2010): control predicates that take at least three arguments (including the clausal complement) shift from subject to object control or vice versa.[6] Control shift is better illustrated in German than in English; for instance, *versprechen* 'promise' allows shift from subject to object control, *bitten* 'ask' shifts in the opposite direction, cf.:

(31) a. Maria$_i$ verspricht Peter$_k$ [___$_k$ zur Party gehen zu
       M   promises   Peter   to party go.INF to
       dürfen]
       be.allowed. INF
       'Mary promises Peter to be allowed to go to the party'
    b. Maria$_i$ bat   Peter$_k$ [___$_i$ zur Party gehen zu
       M   asked Peter   to party go.INF to
       dürfen]
       be.allowed. INF
       'Mary asked Peter to be allowed to go to the party'

Unlike control, raising constructions do not allow for shift or variable antecedents of the silent element of the dependency – compare the German examples in (31) with their raising counterpart (and its English translation) where no shift from the subject to object is ever possible (see also (7) above).

(32) Maria$_i$ schien Peter [___$_i$ zur Party gehen
     M   seemed Peter   to party go.INF
     zu   dürfen]
     to   be.allowed. INF
     'Mary seemed to Peter to be allowed to go to the party'

In another principled difference, object control allows subextraction, while subject to object raising does not – compare (33a-b):[7]

(33) a. Which senator did she persuade the staff of to give her an internship?
     b. *Which senator did she expect that staff of to give her an internship?

Given interesting similarities and differences between raising and control, one of the crucial questions addressed by syntactic theories is whether the similarities outweigh the differences and the two constructions should receive a unified syntactic account.[8] This question has been resolved differently in different theoretical frameworks, and the next two sections present a brief overview of the main conceptual arguments to the two phenomena as well as a brief sketch of the respective theoretical models.

16.2 Raising and control in generative grammar

16.2.1 Raising

The account of subject raising in formal grammars is probably the most straightforward and has undergone little change since the seminal work by Rosenbaum (1967). The main idea is that the structure consists of two clauses, the matrix and the infinitival clause, which is a TP.[9]

The subject DP of the embedded clause moves from the argument position in which it receives an interpretation to a non-theta-position. This movement is necessitated by the EPP of the matrix clause, thus:

(34) a. [TP[DP e] seem/appear/be likely [TP Bruce Wayne to defeat Jack Napier]]
 b. [TP [DP Bruce Wayne$_i$] [VP seem/appear/be likely [TP ~~Bruce Wayne$_i$~~ to defeat Jack Napier]]]

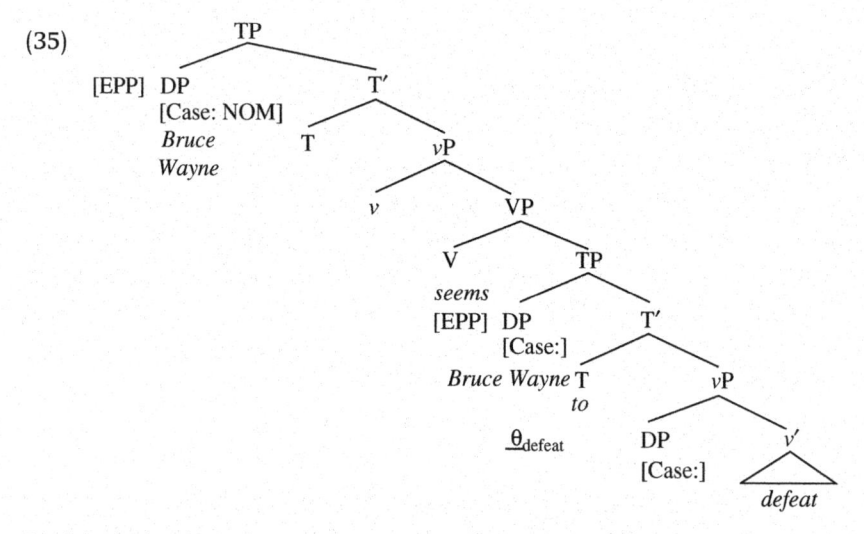

(35)
```
            TP
           /  \
   [EPP] DP    T'
   [Case: NOM]/  \
   Bruce     T    vP
   Wayne         /  \
                v    VP
                    /  \
                   V    TP
                 seems /  \
                  [EPP] DP  T'
                  [Case:]  /  \
                  Bruce Wayne T  vP
                            to /  \
                         θdefeat  DP  v'
                              [Case:] \
                                      defeat
```

In this derivation, the DP *Bruce Wayne* first merges in the specifier of the embedded vP, satisfying the external theta-role of the verb *defeat*. It then moves to the embedded spec, T to satisfy its EPP requirement. Infinitival T heads are unable to check case, so the case feature of this DP still remains unchecked; it then moves to the specifier of the matrix T, where it receives case and satisfies the EPP requirement of the matrix clause.[10]

As we have seen in Section 16.1, the higher verb does not select for its external argument. This argument undergoes A-movement from the complement clause. Evidence in support of such movement from the embedded to the matrix position comes from binding and connectivity effects (reconstruction), cf. examples (5) and (6) above. The understanding of the mechanism of movement has undergone changes over the history of generative approaches. In the Principles and Parameters framework, the moved element was represented by an NP-trace. The Minimalist Program (Chomsky 1995c, 2000b, Nunes 1995) has returned to an old view (as presented in Chomsky 1955/1975) that movement (Internal Merge) consists of two distinct operations, a copying of the item being displaced and a second, deletion operation that eliminates some copies (see also Sections 4.2.4.1, 5.2.2.3, and 15.4.3).

This copy-and-delete approach to movement is particularly relevant in the case of inverse or backward raising, where the lower, not the higher copy of a movement chain is pronounced. Such raising has been attested at least in some languages (Haddad 2010; Potsdam and Polinsky 2012). We will return to the backward pattern in Section 16.2.4, but here it is crucial to note that its analysis would be difficult without the copy-and-delete approach to movement.

The crucial components of the syntax of raising are therefore as follows:

(36) a. the construction is biclausal with the embedded TP
b. the higher verb does not assign a theta-role to its external argument
c. the subject DP undergoes raising to satisfy the EPP on matrix T

16.2.2 Control: PRO

In this section, we consider the various proposals that have been made regarding the nature of control complements, the distribution and interpretation of PRO, and the correct way to analyze control within the Minimalist Program. Like raising, control structures are biclausal, but the standard assumption about control structures is that the embedded clause is larger than in raising – it is typically assumed to be a CP. Some attempts have been made to argue that it is actually smaller (for example, Ghomeshi 2001 and the lexicalist analyses discussed in Section 16.3 below), while an intermediate position is taken by those who claim that some, but not all control complements are smaller than a CP (Wurmbrand 2001, Landau 2001). However, care should be taken to distinguish control from restructuring, which involves much smaller complements (Rizzi 1978a, 1982a; Wurmbrand 2001, among many others).[11]

The most well-established approach to control was developed within the framework of Government and Binding Theory (Chomsky 1982). In this approach, the unpronounced element in control structures is the base-generated empty category PRO:

(37) The police$_i$ tried [PRO$_i$ to uphold the rules]

Theta Theory forces the presence of PRO in the complement subject position. The Theta Criterion in (38) requires bi-uniqueness between arguments and theta-roles (see also Chapters 9 and 11). As a result, every argument position must be filled at deep structure, prior to any transformational operations.

(38) Theta Criterion (Chomsky 1981)
a. each argument bears exactly one theta-role
b. each theta-role is assigned to exactly one argument

With respect to the Control structure in (37), the two agent theta-roles of *try* and *uphold* must each be assigned to distinct arguments, the overt DP and PRO, respectively. PRO's presence in the embedded clause's subject position is independently required by the Extended Projection Principle, which stipulates that all clauses must have subjects (Chomsky 1982; see Chapter 11, this volume).

Case Theory (see Chapter 17) then restricts PRO's distribution (Manzini 1983, Koster 1984, Huang 1989, Martin 2001). PRO only appears in the subject position of some infinitives and does not alternate with an overt noun phrase. In some earlier analyses, it was assumed that the subject position of control infinitivals was caseless, therefore, overt noun phrases simply could not be licensed there. In the approach developed by Chomsky and Lasnik (1993), infinitivals assign a special 'null Case,' and only PRO is capable of having null Case.

Finally, Control Theory governs the actual interpretation of PRO. As a first approximation, PRO's controller is the closest c-commanding noun phrase, in accordance with Rosenbaum's (1967) Minimal Distance Principle (see Larson 1991b and Landau 2001, 2004 for a detailed discussion):

(39) Minimal Distance Principle (MDP)
PRO's controller is the closest c-commanding potential antecedent.

Crucially, referential PRO must have a controller, co-indexed with a c-commanding antecedent. If it does not have a controller, PRO receives an arbitrary interpretation, indicated with PRO_{arb}; we are now in a position to rework the example of non-unique control from above:

(40) It is not recommended [PRO_{arb} to swim here] (=(30))

The central assumptions of this approach are summarized as follows:

(41) PRO Control assumptions
a. every argument receives exactly one theta-role (Theta Criterion)
b. PRO bears null Case (is Caseless)
c. PRO must be bound for a referential interpretation

Within the Minimalist Program, the most successful analysis of control that retains PRO belongs to Landau (2001, 2004, 2006, 2008). He modifies Chomsky and Lasnik's approach to PRO by eliminating null Case (41b). He argues that PRO can bear lexical case just as any overt DP can; the crucial evidence for that claim comes from case concord in languages such as Icelandic, Hungarian, and Russian, where an element associated with PRO inside the embedded clause can show its case.[12] Crucially, the case of PRO is determined by language-specific principles, and it can be either structural case as in German (42), or quirky case as in Icelandic (43):

(42) Hans   hat   die   Zeugen   gebeten   [PRO$_{NOM}$ (German)
    Hans   had   the   witnesses   asked
    einer   nach   dem anderen   einzutreten]
    one.NOM   after   the other   step_in.INF
    'Hans asked the witnesses to step in one after the other'
                                            (Landau 2006:155, (1d))

(43) stràkanir   vonast til [að PRO$_{ACC}$ vanta   (Icelandic)
    the_boys.NOM   hope for   lack.INF
    ekki   alla   í   skólann]
    not   all.ACC in   the_school
    'The boys hope not to be all absent from school'
                                            (Landau 2006:155, (1a))

The other crucial component of Landau's analysis of control follows from the elimination of null Case. Since case varies by language and can no longer be maintained as the critical part of the analysis of control, either empirically or theoretically, the distribution of PRO needs to be accounted for in a different way. Landau's solution is to achieve such an account using agreement: the distribution of PRO is determined by the specific values of [T] and [Agr] on the T and C heads of the embedded clause (Landau 2004, 2006). The distribution of these features is inherently tied with the distribution of independent ([+T, +Agr]) and dependent tense, both of which have been explored in the semantics literature. In syntax, semantic tense is indexed by the morphological feature [T] on C⁰ and T⁰ (see also Chapter 20). For complement clauses, the matrix verb may impose selectional restrictions on the complementizer's [T] feature. If a matrix verb does not impose selectional restrictions on the embedded C⁰ head, that head has independent tense. If the embedded C⁰ is subject to selectional restrictions from the matrix verb, its semantic tense can either be the same as the matrix tense (anaphoric tense) or remain *partially* independent of it (dependent tense). The latter is the case with irrealis complements, found under Hebrew finite control (Landau 2004) or in English *for*-complements (Bresnan 1982c). Landau's proposal is that the scale of finiteness is tied to the value of the uninterpretable [T] and [Agr] features on the embedded C⁰ and T⁰ heads.

(44)   a. independent tense: no [T] on C⁰ (∅)
       b. dependent tense: [+T] on C⁰
       c. anaphoric tense: [−T] on C⁰

When the C and T heads are positively specified for the features T and Agr (thus, are [+T, +Agr]) they always select a lexical DP; however, any other feature composition leads to the selection of PRO. The difference between a lexical DP and PRO is also encoded featurally; they differ in the value of the interpretable feature [R] (referential), with DP being [+R] and PRO, [−R]. The formal implementation of these rules is as follows (with Landau's 2004, 2006 notation slightly simplified):

(45) a. R-assignment rule
   For $X^0_{[\alpha T, \beta AGR]} \in [T^0, C^0, ...]$:
   i. $\emptyset \to [+R]/X^0_{[—]}$ if $\alpha = \beta = +$
   ii. $\emptyset \to [-R]$/elsewhere
b. Specifying [R] on DPs:
   i. lexical DP, *pro* → [+R]
   ii. PRO → [-R]

Thus, a feature-based algorithm predicts the distribution of PRO in a variety of clausal complements. Landau (2006:162) himself acknowledges the stipulative nature of this algorithm but defends it by contending that any theory of control needs stipulative mechanisms in some of its components, be that Case or associations of functional heads with particular features required in the Minimalist Program.

16.2.3 Raising to object

The raising to object construction has probably received the most attention in the theoretical literature, with two competing analyses on the market: Exceptional Case Marking (ECM) and true raising.

According to the ECM account (Chomsky 1981), the 'raised' object is never part of the main clause: it is syntactically and semantically in the embedded clause throughout the derivation, thus:

(46)   ┌─ECM─┐
Kim expects [vP ~~expects~~ [VP ~~expects~~] [TP Pat to offer help]]

However, the raising predicate in the main clause has an exceptional ability to case mark this embedded argument (hence exceptional case marking); this ECM ability is specified on the relevant verbs in the lexicon. The main objections to this account for English have to do with the incorrect predictions it makes with respect to word order (cf. examples (13a–b) above). In addition, there is a difference in c-command between the sentences that involve 'raising,' however understood, and their counterparts in which the DP in question is without doubt inside the embedded clause. To illustrate this difference, consider the following examples (see also Sections 4.2.3 and 15.3.2):

(47) a. the DA proved none of these defendants to be guilty during any of the trials
b. *the DA proved that none of these defendants was guilty during any of the trials

In (47a), the negative polarity item *any* is licensed by the c-commanding expression *none of these defendants*; NPI licensing is clause-bound, which supports the idea that the negated expression is clausemates with the NPI.

In (47b), where the negative phrase is clearly enclosed within the embedded clause, NPI licensing is impossible (cf. Lasnik and Saito 1991, Runner 1998). Such a difference in licensing presents another formidable obstacle to the idea that the accusative object remains inside the embedded complement throughout the derivation.

Although ECM is hardly ever used anymore to account for subject-to-object raising in English, new versions of the ECM account have been proposed for Algonquian (Bruening 2001) and some Austronesian languages (Davies and Dubinsky 2004).

In the alternative to ECM, which we will refer to as the true raising analysis,[13] the subject of the embedded clause undergoes overt raising out of that clause and takes the object position of the matrix verb. This account maintains that the 'raised' object is the subject of the embedded clause at D-structure (or at the point of first Merge), hence also at LF. Its presence in the lower clause allows for its interaction with that clause's material, reconstruction and binding. On the other hand, the analysis maintains that the subject of the embedded clause actually raises into the matrix clause – because of that, it can interact with the material of the higher clause, which accounts for the examples such as (13a–b) that remain problematic for the ECM analysis.

However, the true raising to object analysis runs into problems with respect to extraction facts, noted in (14a–b) above – such sentences, where subextraction would target a subject island, are explained under the ECM account. The following observations can be made with respect to this problem. First, the judgments on the offending examples are far from crisp, and it may well be that the problem is not categorical but just has to do with the overall complexity of the structures under consideration. If so, this is no longer a syntactic issue. But assuming that the judgments are robust, there are two possible solutions proposed by researchers: the CED account and the Subjacency account (see Chapter 18).

Under the CED, or rather neo-CED account (Nunes and Uriagereka 2000, Bošković 2001, 2008a, Stepanov 2007), the key idea is that phrases which have undergone movement are frozen for further extraction, in keeping with the standard freezing accounts (Wexler and Culicover 1980, Rizzi 2006b). The modification pursued by proponents of the neo-CED approach is that subjects always undergo such movement whereas objects do not. This explains why subjects that have been raised to the object position are frozen for extraction. However, most standard accounts of phrase structure also include objects moving outside of the VP, for instance, for case, and this creates a further complication unresolved by the neo-CED account.

Under the Subjacency account (Davies and Dubinsky 2003), the crucial difference between subjects raised to object position and regular objects is in their category: regular objects can be NPs, but subjects that raise to the object position have to be DPs. As independent evidence for the difference between DPs and NPs, DPs are typically islands for movement (Longobardi 1994, 2005; Giorgi and Longobardi 1991), whereas NPs are transparent. This contrast is called upon to explain the differences in extraction. The question, of course, is what this would follow from. A possible explanation may come from the interface between syntax and information structure.[14] What subjects in the structural subject position and in the Object Shift position have in common is that they end up in positions that give rise to a topic reading, which is only available for DPs; objects, while *allowed* to undergo Object Shift, are not generally *forced* to undergo it, so they are different from ECM-subjects in not being required to be full DPs.

To see this, consider that SpecTP is generally conceived of as an A-bar, *topic* position. Since topics must be referential (Gundel 1974/1989, Reinhart 1982, among many others), this in turn means that they must be DPs. For the accusative subject of ECM constructions (for which it is not clear that it is ever in a SpecTP position), the account would have to be different: it would likely capitalize on the fact that Object Shift has information-structural effects similar to movement to SpecTP, in particular, topicality (cf. Diesing 1996, Neeleman and Reinhart 1998, Erteschik-Shir 2007: Chapter 3, among others).

16.2.4 Raising and control as movement

So far, the approaches reviewed here distinguish between raising and control, assigning them very different derivations and silent elements: raising verbs take a TP complement and involve a trace of movement, control verbs take a CP and have a special lexical item, PRO, whose behavior is determined by a number of syntactic principles outlined above. However, with the advent of the Minimalist Program, one of the explicit goals was to scrutinize the various underlying tenets of the Principles and Parameters theory and retain only those that seem truly indispensable.

Three developments in particular played a role in the change of analytical approaches to raising and control: the reconceptualization of movement as copying and deletion (internal merge), already discussed above; the reformulation of the Theta Criterion (an argument must be assigned at least one θ-role under Full Interpretation, and an argument may be assigned more than one θ-role),[15] and the abandonment of null Case. Taken together they effectively allow syntactic theory to dispense with PRO, which has long been considered stipulative (Hornstein 1999). The push is to derive its effects with independently needed mechanisms.

Adopting these assumptions leads to a relatively radical reconceptualization of control (O'Neill 1995, Hornstein 1999, Manzini and Roussou 2000). The control relation can be derived via A-movement. The analysis thus unifies raising and control, which now differ minimally in whether or not the higher predicates assign a θ-role to the raised NP. On Hornstein's analysis, a control structure is derived in the following manner (irrelevant details omitted):

(48) [TP the police_i [VP tried [TP ~~the police~~_i to [VP uphold the rules]]]]

In the lower subject position, the NP *the police* is assigned the agent θ-role of *uphold*. It then raises to the higher subject position and is assigned the agent θ-role of *try*. The driving forces behind the movement are the need to have θ-roles assigned and the Extended Projection Principle.

This approach (see also the discussion in Chapter 15 of coconstrual-as-movement analyses) has several conceptual advantages over the Principles and Parameters analysis. Most obviously, it eliminates PRO and null Case. It also eliminates the need for the Minimal Distance Principle to specify PRO's controller. Instead, the locality effects of the Minimal Distance Principle derive from well-known constraints on the locality of A-movement (Rizzi 1990a).

One of the strongest arguments in favor of the movement approach to control is empirical; it comes from the phenomenon of backward or inverse control. Under inverse control, the lower (embedded) member of the control chain is spelled out and the higher constituent is not expressed, thus, using a schematic representation:[16]

(49) ~~DP_i~~   Control Predicate [CP DP_i ... Infinitive]

To illustrate this phenomenon, consider the following pair of sentences from the Austronesian language Malagasy (Potsdam 2009):[17]

(50) a. inona no   naneren' i Paoly azy_i   [ho atao ___i]?
        what FOC   force.CT Paul   3SG.ACC   do.TT
     b. inona no   naneren' i Paoly ___i   [ho atao-ny_i]?
        what FOC   force.CT Paul   do.TT-3SG
     'What did Paul force him/her to do?'

The two sentences are truth conditionally equivalent and can be shown to represent obligatory control. In (50a), the overt element of the control chain is pronounced in the matrix clause, and in (50b), in the embedded clause (the silent members of the control chain are indicated by co-indexed gap symbols). However, quantifier float, extraction facts, and Condition B effects all point to the presence of a silent copy of the third singular (he/she) in the matrix clause in (50b), thus (unnecessary details of the derivation are omitted and English words are used to represent the Malagasy data):

(51) [TP [T' forced [vP Paul [v' v⁰ [him [TP do he something]]]]] something]
                          [ACC]   [NOM]
                          θ_force   θ_do

By assumption, the control complement is a TP; the DP *he* starts out as the external argument of that complement clause where it checks the theta-role of the verb *do* and receives the nominative case (unlike English, this is a case position). The DP *he* then moves to the higher clause and there receives a second theta-role, that of the internal argument of *force*. The movement is driven by the need to satisfy this theta-role feature on the higher verb. In this position, the controller also has its case feature revalued as accusative. In both structures, (50a) and (50b), the spelled-out copy has all its features valued, which accounts for the possibility of an alternation. The Principle of Chain Reduction (Nunes 2004), which we will discuss later, is responsible for the deletion of one of the copies (see also Sections 4.2.4.1, 5.2.2.3, and 15.4.3). The outstanding difficulty of this analysis is in the multiple case-checking, which, however, is a broader problem.

The Malagasy data are particularly compelling because Malagasy is not a pro-drop language. One might entertain the possibility that the structure of (50b) is something like (52) with a null pronominal as object, and Condition C is either circumvented due to scrambling (see Cormack and Smith 2004 for a similar proposal with respect to Korean) or is simply inoperative in Malagasy. However, even if one were to try to work around Condition C, they would run into the empirical problem that there is no evidence of object pro-drop elsewhere in Malagasy.

(52) inona no naneren' i Paoly pro_i [ho atao-ny$_i$]?
    what FOC force.CT Paul 3SG.ACC do.TT-3SG

Turning now to the PRO-based analysis of backward control, we see that it is fraught with problems because PRO is not c-commanded by its antecedent and cannot be licensed (or has to have an arbitrary interpretation, which is contrary to fact). The movement analysis of control, which treats the two elements as parts of a movement chain, has no problem with such a structure. The choice of a particular copy for deletion may be determined by language-specific properties or may be optional if both copies have all their features checked (Potsdam 2009). In addition to backward control, there is also initial cross-linguistic evidence for backward raising (in Northwest Caucasian, see Polinsky and Potsdam 2006, Potsdam and Polinsky 2012; and in Arabic, Haddad 2010), which reiterates the similarities between the two structures. However, the issue of copy deletion/retention is still very much an open one, and it remains to be seen if the constraints on such deletion can avoid the risk of overgeneration. Even if the choice of a copy for deletion allows for some arbitrariness, one would need to explain why it is usually the lower copy that gets deleted.

While the unification of control and raising under a movement analysis is supported by inverse structures, this analysis still needs to overcome a number of empirical and theoretical challenges, and we will now turn to some of those, namely non-obligatory control, adjunct control, and control inside nominals.

Under the movement analysis of control, a special analysis is needed for cases which involve arbitrary PRO, as in (29) above. Their analysis is achieved by appealing to the difference between movement and pronominalization; the key idea is that only obligatory (unique) control involves movement, whereas arbitrary control is non-obligatory and involves pronominalization. Thus:

(53) a. we decided [~~we~~ to swim here]
            (Obligatory control (OC), A-movement)
      b. it is not recommended [*pro* to swim here]
            (Non-obligatory control (NOC), pronominalization)

On the conceptual level, this distinction has the advantage of appealing to two processes – pronominalization and movement – that are independently known to be needed in grammar. Further motivation for this distinction comes from the fact that obligatory and non-obligatory control show recurrent principled differences summarized below:

(54) properties of OC versus NOC[18]

	OC	NOC
a. unique controller	yes	no
b. strict reading under ellipsis	no	yes
c. paraphrasable with a pronoun	no	yes
d. allows a non-local antecedent	no	yes
e. allows a non-c-commanding antecedent	no	yes
f. allows split antecedents and partial control	no	yes

The example in (55a) illustrates that obligatory control does not permit PRO to have a non-local antecedent (54d) and does not permit partial control (54f), whereas non-obligatory control allows both, as (55b) shows. The contrast between (55a) and (55b) also demonstrates that non-obligatory control can have a non-c-commanding antecedent (54e):

(55) a. Mary$_i$ said that her professor$_j$ decided [___*$_{i/j}$ to apply for a grant]
      b. Mary$_i$ said that her professor$_j$ wondered whether [___$_{i/j}$ to apply for a grant]

However, while the movement theory of control treats these differences as stemming from the syntax of the two structures, a more semantically driven approach (e.g., Jackendoff and Culicover 2003) accounts for them in non-syntactic terms. The idea behind Jackendoff and Culicover's proposal is that once more fine-grained semantic distinctions among control predicates are introduced, the possibility of exhaustive vs. partial control would follow from the lexical interpretation of the relevant predicates.

Next, the movement analysis of control also needs to account for control into adjunct clauses (adjunct control). What needs to be explained here is how the controller is determined and why movement out of adjuncts is permitted. Adjunct clauses always show subject control, cf.:

(56) Kim$_i$ [$_{VP}$ interviewed the applicants$_j$ [$_{CP}$ before ___$_i$ hiring them$_j$]]

Subject control into such adjunct clauses is predicted under the Minimal Distance Principle (see (39) above) if we take it that the adjunct clause is outside the VP and closer to the subject. However, according to Minimalist assumptions, the adjunct clause is in fact inside the VP, which seems to make the incorrect prediction that the controller should be the object. In addition, adjunct control is a problem for the movement analysis of control on account of the fact that it would have to involve movement out of an adjunct, in apparent violation of the CED.

Note that there is disagreement in the literature concerning whether adjunct control instantiates OC or NOC. An example of a proposal that places adjunct control in the latter category is Kawasaki (1993), who considers most adjunct clauses to be PPs with a CP complement. Building on Borer (1989), Kawasaki proposes that such control structures always involve pro as a subordinate subject. This empty category is licensed by non-finite T^0 inside the CP adjunct, and a functional head Agr identifies its content. If C^0 is empty, Agr raises to CP and inherits the phi-features of an antecedent. These phi-features are later copied onto *pro*. For example, in (57), anaphoric Agr raises to C^0 leaving a trace behind. It inherits the phi-features of *John* and copies them onto *pro*.

(57) [$_{CP}$ [$_{IP}$ John$_i$ felt old [$_{PP}$ after [$_{CP}$ Agr$_i$ [$_{IP}$ *pro*$_i$ t$_i$ seeing himself$_i$ in the mirror]]]]]

In sentences like (58) and (59), on the other hand, Agr cannot be co-indexed with a c-commanding antecedent. Here, Agr is [+Topic Oriented], referring to a non-commanding antecedent, an NP that is mentioned or implied earlier in discourse. If Kawasaki's proposal is along the right lines, adjunct control should not be classed as a case of obligatory control, and hence need not be analyzed as involving A-movement by those who advocate the movement theory of control.

(58) Suddenly the pirates$_i$ showed up from behind the rocks. [$_{PP}$ After [$_{CP}$ Agr$_i$ [$_{IP}$ *pro*$_i$ robbing the passengers]]], the ship was sunk.

(59) [$_{PP}$ after [$_{CP}$ Agr$_i$ [$_{IP}$ *pro* pitching the tents]]], darkness fell quickly
(adopted from Kawasaki 1993:172–74 (23a) and (24))

Williams (1992) divides adjunct control into two types: logophoric and predicative. In logophoric adjunct control, the controller of the unpronounced subject in the adjunct is implicit, probably mentioned earlier in discourse, as in (58). Predicative adjunct control, on the other hand, involves a grammatical controller. Hence for Williams, logophoric adjunct control is a case of NOC, while predicative adjunct control involves OC. Within the movement theory of control, only predicative control is treated as involving movement, whereas NOC is considered to involve pronominal rather than logophoric elements in the unpronounced position. The adjunct in predicative adjunct control structures is an unsaturated predicate (with an open subject position) that may be predicated of the subject in the matrix clause. That means that sentence (60a) has the structure as in (60b), where co-indexation between the adjunct and the matrix subject stands for predication. This analysis is also adopted by Landau (2001:176–78; 2007b:304).

(60) a. Tom escaped after kissing Mary
 b. Tom$_i$ escaped [after ___$_i$ kissing Mary]$_i$

Thus, earlier analyses of adjunct control treat all such cases, or at least a subset thereof as non-obligatory control. Within the movement approach to adjunct control, the proposal is to assimilate adjunct control to obligatory control and still to apply movement. This entails a reconsideration of some conceptions of movement. The key mechanism employed in this approach is that of sideward movement (Nunes 2004). Movement is a compositional process that can be broken into the operations of Copy, Merge, Form Chain, and Chain Reduction. In addition, Nunes claims that the output of movement has to be subject to the Linear Correspondence Axiom (LCA: Kayne 1994; see Sections 2.4.2 and 11.4.2). The LCA is responsible for the ordering of elements spelled out at PF. Movement can be sideward in that a copied element can merge with another phrase marker, different from those which dominate it in its original position. Crucially, on this approach, the two copies no longer have to be in a c-command relation, so the problem of extracting out of adjuncts is overcome.[19] Haddad (2009a, 2009b, 2011) provides a careful application of the general principles of sideward movement to adjunct control in Dravidian and Assamese. In this work, he shows that sideward movement correctly derives three types of adjunct control: forward adjunct control, backward adjunct control, and copy control.

The movement analysis of control would also appeal to sideward movement for the analysis of control by objects of prepositions:

(61) John prayed [$_{PP}$ to Athena] to take care of herself/*himself
 (Culicover and Jackendoff 2001:509, (47b))

(62) Kennedy's challenge [$_{PP}$ to NASA] to put a man on the moon by 1970
 (Pesetsky 1991:134, (519c))

(63) it is requested [$_{PP}$ of you] to leave your bags in a locker

Control inside nominals has been a long-standing problem for all control theories. Particularly germane to the controversy over control as movement is the observation that raising within nominals is impossible (Culicover and Jackendoff 2001), although this is challenged in Sichel (2007). If Culicover and Jackendoff are right, then as with adjunct control, the next step is to establish whether control within nominals involves OC or NOC. Note also that in recent work, Sichel (2010) has argued that a number of empirical facts about control into nominals are related to the syntax and semantics of nominals themselves and therefore, some properties of derived nominals may be irrelevant for the typology of control.

Finally, the movement analysis of control plays down the principled differences between control and raising discussed in Section 16.1. In addition to reconstruction, nominalizations, and interaction with *tough*-movement mentioned above, there is also a significant developmental difference: children acquire control structures earlier and with more ease than they learn raising (Hirsch and Wexler 2007), which is unexpected if both phenomena have the same syntax. In the discussion of the movement theory of control it is important to bear in mind, however, that it is a *movement* theory of control and not a *raising* theory of control (Boeckx and Hornstein 2010). Although this theory makes control similar to raising, it does not necessarily identify the two phenomena. While raising (in the familiar sense of the term) involves movement to a non-theta position, 'control' would involve movement into a theta-position. The literature arguing against the movement theory of control has often fallen prey to the temptation to think that this theory identifies raising and control.

Overall, the decision whether to pursue a unified analysis of raising and control or to keep them separate has been the subject of lively debate in generative grammar.[20]

16.3 Lexicalist approaches to raising and control

In unification-based theories (Lexical-Functional Grammar or LFG (see Chapter 6, especially Section 6.3.2), and Head-Driven Phrase Structure Grammar or HPSG (see Chapter 7)), raising and control are minimally different in whether or not the matrix predicate imposes selectional restrictions on the functional controller argument. Structure sharing is a major mechanism used for constraining the range of structures generated under control and raising verbs. Structure sharing serves as a kind of co-indexing that means an entire syntactic item is identical to some other item indexed ('tagged') the same way. LFG and HPSG share the following critical assumptions concerning raising and control:

(64) a. the relation of raising and control is specified lexically
　　　b. the two members of the referential dependency are represented by one syntactic entity
　　　c. this syntactic entity is identified with the subject of the complement clause
　　　d. the identity of controller and controlee is established in argument structure
　　　e. the embedded clause is an infinitival VP (XCOMP in LFG)

In LFG (Bresnan 2001, Falk 2001), obligatory control is accounted for in terms of the so-called functional control or functional predication relation (anaphoric control, which roughly corresponds to non-obligatory control above, has different properties). A control predicate takes a thematic subject and a VP-type embedded construction (XCOMP) as its argument. For instance, a lexical entry for *try* will be partially represented as:

(65)　*try*: (↑PRED) = 'try ⟨(↑SUBJ) (↑XCOMP)⟩'

A crucial assumption about the embedded predicate is that it does not have an overt subject (hence the characterization of this embedding as an *open function*). Functional Control serves to link the unfilled subject position of the open function (XCOMP) and the subject of the matrix predicate; this linking is defined in the lexicon (Bresnan 1982c, 2000, Zaenen and Engdahl 1994) by stating that the subject of the embedded predicate is also the subject of the matrix verb:

(66)　*try*: (↑PRED) = 'try ⟨(↑SUBJ) (↑XCOMP)⟩'
　　　　(↑SUBJ) = (↑XCOMP SUBJ)

Another crucial assumption is that the functional controller must f-command[21] the controlee, therefore it must be less deeply embedded in the functional structure. This indicates that LFG predicts forward but not backward control because backward control would require that the f-command assumption be abandoned or modified. In modifying the theory, Sells (2006) proposes to accommodate backward (inverse) relationships by introducing the notion of subsumption, which should replace equality used otherwise to account for functional control.

(67)　Subsumption
　　　a. SUBJ ⊆ XCOMP SUBJ (information only flows down from subject; whatever information subject has in the upper clause, it also has in the embedded constituent but not vice versa)
　　　b. SUBJ ⊇ XCOMP SUBJ (information only flows up to subject; whatever information subject has in the embedded clause, it also has in the upper constituent but not vice versa)

Under subsumption, the direction of structure sharing can be reversed, which would allow for backward control and raising. The direction is dependent on c-structure, which in turn allows for both possibilities documented in a given language. The restrictions on subsumption may be language specific and should be provided as part of the lexical information of a given verb. The overall result is welcome in that it captures the relevant empirical facts; however, it remains to be seen if this analysis can avoid overgeneration. It is also not clear how to connect the availability of backward patterns noted in the literature with other structural properties of languages such as word order or headedness (see Polinsky and Potsdam 2006 for a discussion).

In HPSG, raising and control remain more apart – raising is treated as true unification, while control is achieved by the identity of indices. In neither structure is there a structural position in the embedded clause containing a trace or a *pro*; recall that the embedded clause is just the infinitival VP.

Sag et al. (2003) and Runner (2006) show the advantages of handling object raising and control in HPSG terms. To account for raising to object and object control constructions in a uniform way, they propose general constraints on the verbs which license raising to object and object control constructions; these constraints are again specified in the lexicon:

(68) *object-raising verb lexeme*: ARG-ST < NP, <, [SYN[VAL[SPR< <>]]]>

(69) *object-control verb lexeme*: ARG-ST<NP, NP_i , [SYN[VAL[SPR<NP_i>]]]>

A raising to object verb such as *believe* or *expect* will be typed as an object-raising verb lexeme. The constraint in (68) places restrictions on what items appear in the argument structure (ARG-ST) of a lexeme of that type. This constraint states that the argument structure of this class of lexemes contains three phrases. The first is a DP (NP). The second item in the argument structure is indicated by the tag <. Another tag of the same nature is on the third argument on this type's argument structure; thus, the second argument and the specifier (SPR) of its third argument are structure-shared. Separate independently motivated constraints in the grammar restrict the category of the second phrase to an NP.

An object control verb like *persuade* will be typed as an object-control verb lexeme and will be subject to the constraint in (69). It is identical to the constraint on object raising verbs in (68) except that the item in the argument structure is an NP co-indexed with rather than structure-shared with the specifier of the third argument. In contrast to structure-sharing (tagging), co-indexation proper in HPSG indicates intended reference (in binding as well as in control).

Thus, on the HPSG account, the sentence structures for object raising and object control look identical:

(70) Kim [$_{VP}$ expected Pat [$_{VP}$ to run the race]]

(71) Kim [$_{VP}$ persuaded Pat [$_{VP}$ to run the race]]

The main difference resides in the different relationships between the object of the matrix clause (*Pat*) and the lexical subject of the embedded verb, although only in argument structure representations: in (70) they are the same NP, and in (71), they are co-indexed, which implies a looser relationship due to the fact that they both have their own thematic roles.

Within the framework of Cognitive Grammar (Langacker 1995), raising and control are treated in a similar way: despite apparent differences in the implementation and technical aspects, Cognitive Grammar shares with LFG and HPSG the idea of function sharing and of lexical specification. As in LFG,

Cognitive Grammar does not divide raising and control into separate phenomena in need of different analyses; instead, they are treated as part of a continuum – this is called for to explain situations where one and the same verb can have both control and raising uses, as is the case with many aspectual predicates (cf. Perlmutter 1970 Davies and Dubinsky 2004), cf.:

(72)   a. more progress can begin to be made in this direction
       b. the soldiers began to dismantle the fort

Cognitive Grammar identifies the relationship between the sentences which have a referential dependency (73a), (74a) and their 'non-raised' counterparts (73b), (74b) without a referential dependency as that of partial synonymy and emphasizes principled differences between them.

(73)   a. Don is likely to leave
       b. we expect Don to leave

(74)   a. that Don will leave is likely
       b. we expect that Don will leave

Simplifying things somewhat, the choice of a 'raised' or 'non-raised' version depends on semantics and pragmatics, in particular, on information structure. If the focus of the utterance is on the event denoted by the entire sentence, a non-raised sentence is more likely, whereas if the subject of the embedded clause is informationally prominent then the 'raised' version is chosen. In this way, Cognitive Grammar differs from other approaches in that it attempts to identify the conditions governing the use of raising versus control sentences.

16.4   Raising, control, and the typology of empty categories

As this overview of raising and control phenomena has shown, there are a number of approaches to the structures outlined in Section 16.1. Since the work on raising and control has been at the forefront of linguistic theorizing for decades, the literature is full of rich empirical evidence that needs to be accounted for in theories of raising and control. Not only do these data raise questions concerning the appropriateness of a particular theory and the prevalence of syntax or semantics, they also have a bearing on the inventory of silent categories in modern syntax.

   The range of empirical facts considered here allows at least some theories to recognize the following inventory of silent categories:

(75)   silent elements in control and raising structures
       a. *pro* (null pronominal)
       b. PRO
       c. trace of A-movement (movement to an argument position)
       d. A-bar bound trace (interpreted as a variable)

Although we have not discussed A-bar bound trace so far we include it because it plays an important role in the overall typology of silent categories and also because there are treatments of NOC and arbitrary control in terms of operator movement and A-bar bound variables (cf. Lebeaux 1984a, 2009).

The distribution of the null pronominal is well regulated by the principles of Binding Theory, Principle B in particular (see Chapter 15). As shown above, the null pronominal is mostly observed in cases where there is no unique controller – some theories of NOC feature *pro* as the null subject.

The distribution of PRO was subject of the PRO Theorem in the Principles and Parameters framework. However, after some of the fundamental principles of generative syntax were revised in the Minimalist Program, the distribution of PRO can no longer be explained by the same rules. The most articulated account of PRO's distribution can be found in the work by Landau (see Section 16.2.1 above). The main conception behind the distribution of PRO now has to do with the referential status of DPs as linked to the features T and Agr on the higher functional heads of the clause, T and C.

Finally, the distribution of NP-movement in argument positions is regulated by the principles of Relativized Minimality and locality as described in Chapter 18.

A fundamental question concerning the distribution of silent elements has to do with the nature of the relationship between the constituent that has independent reference and the silent (or partially spelled-out) constituent whose reference is dependent on the former. There are essentially three ways of achieving that: predication, binding, and Landau's approach based on Agree. Here we restrict our attention to the first two.

Under the predication approach to control (which can also be extended to raising), there is a dependency between the element that has full referential content (controller) and the embedded complement, which represents a predicate. Thus, (76) below is interpreted as meaning 'In all worlds where the police's intentions hold, the police have the property of staying calm.'

(76) the police intended to stay calm (=(17))

Predicational approaches to control were initially proposed in semantic analyses (Bach 1979, 1982, Chierchia 1984, Dowty 1985).

In syntax, the predicational approach to control stems from Williams's work (Williams 1980, 1985, 1987), which presents a particularly careful examination of predication and argues that referential dependencies involved in control are a subset of the more general class of predication relations. Predication is established at a special grammatical level (Predicate Structure), which means that it is partially independent of the actual projected arguments and can potentially involve implicit arguments. The crucial requirements on predication are twofold (see also Chapter 10): the logical subject of the predication relation has to be external to the predicate, and the relation itself has to be local. Locality is implemented by the requirement that the DP predicated of must be in a mutual c-command relation with (a) the predicate or (b) another predicate that immediately contains it, which lets in the matrix VP. This disjunctive formulation allows us to account for adjunct control (c-command relation between the subject and the predicate) and complement control (sub-requirement (b)).

The predication relation thus crucially depends on the presence of an external argument, which serves as a variable vertically bound by its maximal projection (Williams refers to that as a kind of lambda abstraction). For his approach, it is not critical that the role be realized as a syntactic node in the phrase structure – the only crucial requirement is that such a role be understood as present and can act as a bound variable. While some researchers criticize this approach as too general or weak (see Landau 2011), it provides an important foundation for the establishment of predication relations.

The binding approach to control treats the silent element in the complement clause as a null anaphor. The locality of control is achieved by limiting the binding domain to the clause immediately dominating the embedded complement clause. Such an analysis can easily account for obligatory control and, as long as the adjunct clause is adjoined low, for adjunct control as well. A major challenge to such an approach comes from non-obligatory control, where this binding condition is violated. To preserve the overall conception of control as binding, Manzini (1983, 1986) proposed that an anaphor without a governing category be bound in its domain-governing category. This entails that a silent element without a binding domain is exempt from binding. Manzini's binding approach works in the following manner:

(77) a. complement clauses always have a binding domain, the matrix clause (hence, these clauses instantiate obligatory control)
b. subject clauses lack a binding domain because the clause immediately dominating them has no accessible subject (hence, non-obligatory control)

Other binding approaches to control have analyzed the silent element in non-obligatory control as a pronoun (Bouchard 1984, Koster 1984, Hornstein 2003).

Both approaches, viz. predication and binding, successfully account for the bulk of control phenomena and can be extended to raising. However, they face problems with adjunct control (especially if the adjunct clause is not in the VP). In addition, the binding approach to control requires a substantial reconsideration of independently established binding generalizations.

Lebeaux (1984a) presents an interesting attempt to combine the advantages of both approaches without a more significant readjustment of the theoretical machinery involved.

16.5 Beyond the scope of this chapter

This chapter has presented the empirical foundations of raising and control constructions and has outlined major theoretical approaches to these constructions, with a focus on syntactic analyses. The debate between the syntactic and semantic approach to raising and control has been going on for decades, and although each side may claim victory, their true success has to do with uncovering a broader range of natural language phenomena that need to be accounted for by any theory of raising and control. The range of phenomena that a successful theory of raising and control has to account for is much broader. For instance, an important phenomenon that we have not discussed here is that of copy raising (78) (see also Section 10.4.2.2) and its rarer counterpart, copy control:[22]

(78) a. there looks like there could be a different solution
b. Richard seems like he is in trouble

Under copy raising, first introduced on the linguistic scene by Rogers (1974), both elements of the dependency are pronounced or partially pronounced, and the crucial question, which still evokes significant debate, has to do with the possibility of analyzing this construction as true raising or as a completely different phenomenon (see Potsdam and Runner 2001, Asudeh and Toivonen 2012, Landau 2011, Haddad 2009a, and further references therein).

Another important question has to do with the relation between raising and *tough*-movement illustrated in (79):

(79) this professor is tough to please

The initial analysis of this construction, proposed by Rosenbaum (1967), identified it as an A-movement operation, a type of object-to-subject raising. The raising analysis of *tough*-movement was also developed by Brody (1993) and Hartman (2009); all these analyses emphasize that the matrix predicate does not assign an external theta-role, which is typical of raising. Other researchers however have pointed out the presence of A-bar effects in *tough*-movement (Chomsky 1977, 1981, Rezac 2006, Hicks 2009b and references therein). The debate on *tough*-movement and its place in the family of raising and control constructions is still ongoing.

Another important area of inquiry that has been particularly productive lately is that into finite control – a control structure where the embedded complement is finite. Compare subject and object finite control in Persian, with the finite predicate of the embedded clause appearing in the subjunctive (see Hashemipour 1988, 1989, Ghomeshi 2001, Karimi 2008 for details):

(80) a. Kimea$_i$ tasmim gereft   [(ke) ___$_i$ be-r-e]
     Kimea decision took.3SG that   SBJN-go-3SG
     'Kimea decided to go'
   b. mâ Kimea$_i$-ro   marjbur kard-im [(ke) ___$_i$ be
     1PL Kimea-ACC force do-1PL   that   to
     sinamâ be-r-e]
     movies SBJN-go-3SG
     'We forced Kimea to go to the movies'

In the Principles and Parameters framework, which had the PRO Theorem, an account of finite control was quite challenging. With the development of other approaches, syntactic and lexicalist, and with the dissociation between PRO and case, finite control has emerged as an interesting possibility which may or may not require a unified account. Aside from Persian, finite control has been documented in Greek (Terzi 1991) and other Balkan languages (see Terzi 1993, Landau 2004, and references therein), where it is motivated by language-specific properties (Balkan languages lack infinitives), in Arabic (Haddad 2010), and in Malagasy (Potsdam and Polinsky 2007).

Some other areas of inquiry include (i) the phenomenon of partial control just briefly touched upon above (see Landau 2001, Stiebels 2010, Snarska 2009, Madigan 2009, among others); (ii) the special status of *promise* and *threaten* (Langacker 1995, Larson 1991b, Hornstein 2003); and related to that, (iii) Visser's Generalization (Visser 1973, Bresnan 1982c, Bach 1980, Rudanko 1989, van Urk 2010), according to which object control structures have corresponding passives, while subject control structures do not, as shown in (81) and (82):

(81) a. Pat persuaded Kim to run the race
    b. Kim was persuaded by Pat to run the race

(82) a. Kim promised Pat to run the race
    b. *Pat was promised by Kim to run the race

Within syntactic theories, the approach to raising and control has a bearing on the structure of embedded clausal complements (see the differences across frameworks concerning the size of such complements in control and raising), the inventory and nature of silent elements, and the need for a distinction between raising and control altogether.

Notes

I am grateful to Youssef Haddad, Hazel Pearson, Eric Potsdam, Greg Scontras, and Barbara Stiebels for helpful discussions of this work. I owe my deepest gratitude to Marcel den Dikken and an anonymous reviewer for their thorough and thought-provoking comments on an earlier version of this work. Whatever errors and omissions are left in this chapter is entirely my responsibility.

1. Some researchers (Bennis 1986, Moro 1997) disagree with the characterization of the proleptic *it* as a true expletive and consider it either an argument or a (pro)predicate. A reader who shares their concerns may be more convinced by the behavior of idiom chunks (4), (11), and the expletive *there* (19)–(20).
2. For further discussion of this phenomenon, see Postal (1974), Johnson (1991), Ernst (2002), Runner (2006).
3. Also known as Equi(-NP-Deletion) in the earlier generative literature.
4. An anonymous reviewer reminds us that this claim has been disputed in Postal (1974) and Sichel (2007). Postal points out that with a gerundive complement, nominalization of *appear* is acceptable, as shown in

    (i) The police's appearance of staying calm.

5. Partial control and non-obligatory control do not have grammatical counterparts in the realm of raising constructions (see also Landau 2001).
6. It has on occasion been pointed out that control shift is not a property of control as such because it can be mimicked in finite contexts, with overt pronominal subjects. Thus, (i) is matched by (ii), and (iii) by (iv):

    (i) John promised Mary to leave
    (ii) John promised Mary that **he** would leave
    (iii) John promised Mary to be allowed to leave
    (iv) John promised Mary that **she** would be allowed to leave

    The parallel is further supported by the fact that in both infinitival and in finite clauses *be allowed to* shifts back to subject control if an adjunct is added to the lower clause that makes the subject a more natural antecedent:

    (v) John (talking on the phone to Mary about the fact that he would once again have to work late) promised her to be allowed to leave once **he** had read all of the documents on his desk
    (vi) John (talking on the phone to Mary about the fact that he would once again have to work late) promised her that **he** would be allowed to leave once he had read all of the documents on his desk

    This last point actually suggests that the fluidity of antecedent choice seems to be largely determined by pragmatics/context or world knowledge. If so, control shift may not need to be accounted for in syntax.
7. See Runner (2006) for further discussion and references therein.
8. Another large question addressed by researchers has to do with the need to account for these constructions primarily in semantic terms

or primarily in structural terms. We will not be concerned with the former option here, but an interested reader may consult the work by Farkas (1988), Ružička (1999), Culicover and Jackendoff (2003), and Stiebels (2007, 2010), who address control phenomena primarily in semantic terms. See also note 6 above.
9. Some researchers, however, propose that the raising complement may be larger, a CP (Karimi 2008). This would be consistent with the conception that the features of T are entirely derivative of C's features, hence TP should be unable to exist in the absence of a local C (cf. Chomsky 2008).
10. Another possibility of course is that movement to the spec,T position of the infinitival clause does not take place at all (cf. Baltin 1995, Wurmbrand 2007). The overall derivation presented here does not change significantly if that specifier position is skipped.
11. The idea that control complements are VPs (thus, small) was prominent in the more semantically oriented approaches (Bach 1979, Chierchia 1984, Dowty 1985) and is still present in lexicalist theories, which will be discussed in Section 16.3.
12. See Stenson (1989), Sigurðsson (2004) on case-marked PRO in Icelandic, and also Harley (2001) on case-marked PRO in Irish.
13. The earliest version of the true raising analysis belongs to Rosenbaum (1967) and was further developed in Postal (1974). In later work, it was defended by Authier (1991), Johnson (1991), Koizumi (1995), Runner (1998, 2006), among others.
14. I would like to thank Marcel den Dikken for pointing out this possibility to me.
15. See Brody (1993), Bošković (1994), Chomsky (1995c).
16. Backward subject control has been attested in Tsez (Polinsky and Potsdam 2002), Jakaltec (Craig 1974), Greek and Romanian (Alexiadou et al. 2010). See Fukuda (2008) for an overview.
17. The glosses are slightly modified compared to the original document.
18. We set aside two further properties that might be used to distinguish OC and NOC – partial control and the possibility of split antecedents – due to the ongoing controversy over how to handle these cases. For a detailed discussion of partial control, see Landau (2001: Chapter 2); his claim is that partial control can be reduced to obligatory control with a PRO. A large part of the controversy surrounding partial control has to do with the empirical data which vary significantly across speakers. This is not entirely surprising given that partial control examples usually require some contextual setting (Landau 2001:27 Jackendoff and Culicover 2003) but the full range of empirical data representing partial control is not yet clear.
19. De Vries (2009) develops Nunes's ideas further and proceeds to unify regular and sideward movement as different instances of remerge.

20. The interested reader should consult Landau (2003, 2006, 2008), Boeckx and Hornstein (2003, 2004, 2006a, 2006b, 2010), Kiss (2006), and Bobaljik and Landau (2009) for a lively debate between the PRO-camp and the control-as-movement camp.
21. f-command in LFG is a relationship which determines asymmetric binding from one element to another. It is roughly comparable to c-command in the Principles and Parameters framework and Minimalist Program and corresponds to o-command in HPSG.
22. See Polinsky and Potsdam (2006) for some discussion of copy control.

17
Agreement and Case

Mark C. Baker

17.1 Introduction: definitions and orientation

Core cases of agreement can be characterized as morphological marking on the central verb of a clause that reflects some features of a noun phrase in that clause. For example, finite verbs in both English (Indo-European (IE)) and Kinande (Bantu) change in morphological form depending on whether the subject is singular or plural:[1]

(1) a. the <u>woman buys</u> fruit each day in the market
    b. the <u>women buy</u> fruit each day in the market

(2) a. <u>aba-kali ba-[a]-gul-a</u> eri-tunda   (Kinande)
      2-woman 2S-T-buy-FV 5-fruit
      'the women bought a fruit'
    b. <u>omu-kali a-gul-a</u> eri-tunda
      1-woman 1S-T-buy-FV 5-fruit
      'the woman bought a fruit'

Many extensions from this core are possible and attested in languages of the world. For example, a verb might agree with the features of some noun phrase other than the subject, such as the direct object or the indirect object. Or a different syntactic category might agree with the features of a nearby noun phrase, such as a possessed noun with its possessor, or a preposition with its complement. In addition, adjectives, determiners, and other 'modifiers' inside a noun phrase can agree with the head noun. This too happens in both IE languages like Spanish and Bantu languages like Kinande. There are some impressionistic differences between the sort of agreement that shows up on verbs and the kind that operates within a noun phrase, so that the distinct term *concord* is sometimes used for the latter phenomenon, to distinguish it from the former. However, the two also have much in common, and both are included in the scope of this chapter.

One can imagine generalizing the notion of agreement further, to situations in which a given word shows morphological changes that depend on some grammatical category in the sentence other than a nominal. For example, one can imagine one verb in a structure agreeing with another verb in its tense marking, as may happen in (for example) serial verb constructions in some languages. Another striking example is the Kayardild language of Australia, in which everything in the verb phrase must match morphologically the tense value of the verb (Evans 1995). Such generalizations of the notion of agreement would be very welcome from the standpoint of generative theory, because they might help to show the full scope and properties of the fundamental agreement relation. However, few such cases have been studied in any depth in the generative literature. I thus exclude them from discussion in this chapter, while acknowledging that the restriction to agreeing with NPs may prove to be arbitrary.

Core instances of case marking can be characterized as morphological marking on a noun phrase that reflects some aspect of its grammatical relationship to the central verb of the clause. For example, pronouns in English take different forms depending on whether they function as the subject of a finite verb or as its object. Similar differences are seen more robustly on noun phrases of all sorts in languages like Japanese:

(3) a. I found them in the park
    b. they found me in the park

(4) John-ga   Mary-ni   hon-o   yatta   (Kuno 1973b:5)
    John-NOM   Mary-DAT   book-ACC   gave
    'John gave Mary a book'

Like agreement, the notion of case marking can profitably be extended from verb-headed clauses to other kinds of categories. For example, many languages have a special case (genitive) that marks an NP as relating to a nearby noun within a larger NP – the relationship of possessor, for example. Similarly, case marking on a NP can show that that NP is the grammatical object of a particular adposition, or that it is the complement of an adjective. These phenomena also fall within the scope of this discussion.

One might also consider extending the notion of case marking, such that the case-marked item need not be an NP or similar category. One can imagine, for example, a verb like *make* determining something about the form of the verb that heads its complement in a sentence like *I made Chris run home*. Such dependencies might be considered a form of case marking in a broadened sense; see, for example, Fabb (1984) for an extension along these lines. This too would be a theoretically welcome development, but relatively little is known about it, and I do not consider such extensions further here.

Agreement and case can be seen as being in a sense opposites of each other. When an NP is the subject of a finite verb and the features of that NP influence the form of the finite verb, that is agreement. When an NP is the subject of a finite verb and the features of the finite verb (i.e., its finiteness) influence the form of the NP, causing it to be nominative, that is case assignment. Case and agreement are also functionally similar in that they are (along with word order) two of the most important devices that natural languages use to express what grammatical functions and/or thematic roles noun phrases have with respect to the verb. In this way, they are functionally analogous and in some instances complementary. This is reflected in Johanna Nichols's (1986) influential distinction between head-marking languages and dependent-marking languages. Head-marking languages are roughly languages that are rich in agreement, and dependent-marking languages are roughly those that are rich in case assignment. This functional similarity is one reason why it makes sense to treat the two topics in the same chapter.

There is also a stronger, although more controversial reason for discussing agreement and case together. Some generative linguists have posited a particularly tight theoretical relationship between the two, such that they are both morphological manifestations of a single abstract relationship holding between a lexical item and a nearby noun phrase (Chomsky 2000b, 2001) (a view with its origins in George and Kornfilt 1981). This view aspires to capture the fact that, in many IE languages at least, a verb agrees with a given noun phrase only if that noun phrase bears nominative case. This is true of English, but it is even more striking in, for example, Hindi. In Hindi, the case on the subject varies with the tense–aspect of the clause: subjects in imperfective clauses are nominative, whereas subjects in perfective clauses are ergative. This goes hand in hand with a difference in agreement. The verb agrees with the subject in imperfective clauses but not in perfective clauses (Mohanan 1995:83), as shown in (5). Facts like these are common and suggest that case and agreement are indeed closely related topics.

(5) a. Anil   kitaabẽ   becegaa
       Anil.M(NOM) book-F.PL   sell-FUT.M.SG
       'Anil will sell (the) books'
    b. Anil-ne   kitaabẽ   becīī.
       Anil-ERG   book-F.PL   sell-PERF-F.PL
       'Anil sold (the) books'

There are many other reasons why case and agreement have been major topics of interest within generative syntax. Both are common cross-linguistically. Almost exactly 50 percent of languages sampled have case marking on full NPs (92/190) according to Comrie (2005). Agreement is even more common: 78 percent (296/378) of languages have some form of agreement with noun phrases marked on verbs, according to Siewierska (2005). Combining these two sources using the 'composer' feature of the *World Atlas of Language Structures* (Haspelmath et al. 2005) indicates that only some 11 percent of languages (21/188) have neither. So these are not obscure features of natural languages. At the same time, it is clear that neither is universal. Since they are aspects of grammar that seem central to some languages but that other languages seem to do perfectly well without, they raise important questions about parameterization and the nature of cross-linguistic variation. Finally, Chomsky (2000b, 2001) has given added prominence to these topics by positing Agree as one of only two primitive syntactic operations, on a par with the fundamental operation Merge, and even more basic than Move.

Both topics also have intrinsic intellectual interest for their own sakes. It can be a fascinating challenge to try to work out the exact case-marking and agreement rules for particular languages, and see how they relate to each other and to other aspects of the syntax. We can take this then to be the central question that the theories of agreement and case are concerned with, and it provides the primary focus for this chapter.

17.2 The syntax of agreement

Let us begin by considering agreement in more detail. Virtually all generative treatments begin with subject–verb agreement, for reasons that are easy to understand. First, this is the most common kind, being found in almost 75 percent of languages sampled (266/378 in Siewierska 2005, 79/108 in Baker 2008b), whereas object agreement is only found in some 50 percent (54/108 in Baker 2008b). Second, there seems to be a typological (near-) universal, such that a language does not have agreement with direct objects unless it also has agreement with (at least some) subjects (e.g., Croft 1990:106).[2] Third, subject agreement is the only kind found in the most accessible and best-studied languages (e.g., IE), where generative linguists have typically started. The question arises, then, what is the true nature of agreement, such that grammatical subjects do agreement particularly well.

17.2.1 The fundamental nature of agreement

17.2.1.1 What undergoes agreement?
As a preliminary to answering this, we need to be more precise about just what syntactic element is agreeing with the subject. It may not be the verb, precisely, because not all verbs agree in IE languages. Rather only tense-marked, finite verbs agree, as in (6).

(6) a. I expect Mary to come/*comes
    b. I hope that Mary comes/*come

Similarly, in auxiliary-plus-participle constructions containing more than one verbal element, subject agreement in IE languages appears only on the auxiliary verb – the same one that is inflected for tense:

(7) a. Mary is/was coming
    b. *Mary are/were comings

Moreover, in *do*-support contexts in English, where the tense factor is separated from the verb root by some other syntactic category, agreement always shows up along with tense on the dummy verb root *do*, not on the main verb:

(8) a. Mary does not help   *Mary do not helps
    b. Does Mary help?   *Do Mary helps?
    c. John helps and Mary does too   *John helps and Mary do too

For reasons such as these, generative linguists often factor the finite verb into two distinct syntactic elements, Tense and Verb, which may or may not become fused into a single word in the course of a grammatical derivation (Chomsky 1957, 1981). Once this move is made, it is clear that it is the Tense node that agrees with a noun phrase in English and related languages, not the Verb node proper, in a structure something like (9). Generalizing on this case, it is common to think of agreement not being a property of lexical categories *per se*, but of the functional categories that are associated with them and often are realized as morphemes on them. We will see other examples of this below.

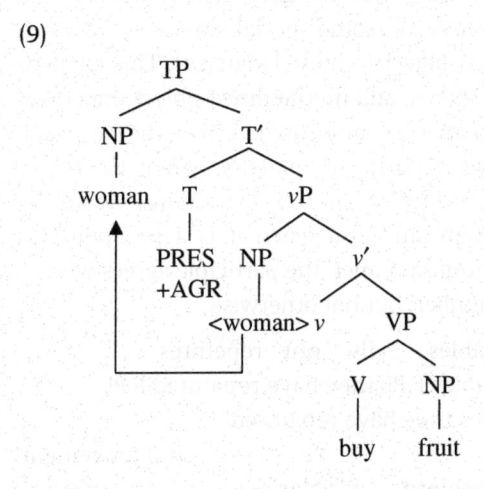

(9)

```
                TP
              /    \
            NP       T'
            |      /   \
          woman   T     vP
                  |    /  \
                PRES  NP    v'
                +AGR  |    /  \
                   <woman> v   VP
                              /  \
                             V    NP
                             |    |
                            buy  fruit
```

17.2.1.2 What is the structural condition on agreement?

The next question, then, is why it is the subject NP that Tense typically agrees with, rather than some other NP in the clause, such as the direct object. Considering (9), two natural hypotheses spring to mind, given the widespread assumption that the subject originally starts somewhere in the (greater) verb phrase and then moves to the specifier of the phrase headed by Tense in a Subject-Tense-Verb-Object language like English (Koopman and Sportiche 1991). If one thinks of agreement as taking place after movement, then the natural condition is that a head can only agree with the NP that is its specifier in the sense of X-bar theory (see especially Chapter 11) – the Spec–Head Agreement Hypothesis (SHAH). The object does not move to SpecTP, so T cannot agree with it, on this view. Alternatively, if one thinks of agreement as taking place before movement, then one has to think of T as scanning downward through the structure, looking for something to agree with. Why then does T agree with the subject rather than the object? Presumably because the subject is higher than the object: the subject c-commands the object, but not vice versa. Therefore, if one thinks of T as beginning at its own position and searching further and further downward in the structure for something to agree with, then it will encounter the subject before the object. Agreement with the subject is then established before the object is even seen. This is the Agree Hypothesis (AGRH). Both hypotheses account for the primacy of subjects over objects when it comes to agreeing with Tense in a reasonably simple and natural way.

17.2.1.3 Motivation for Specifier–Head agreement

Historically speaking, the SHAH is the older of the two views. It dominated generative research from about 1985–1999, ever since Chomsky (1986a) first regularized the role of Tense within the X-bar system. Its popularity was fueled by Kayne's (1989a) influential study of agreement in French and Italian. Kayne pointed out that there are some special situations in which the verb does agree with its direct object in these languages. This happens only if (i) the verb is a participial form, and (ii) the direct object undergoes some kind of movement, so that it appears before (higher than) the participial verb. Depending on the language/variety, this happens when the object undergoes *wh*-movement and when the thematic object becomes the surface subject as a result of passivization (and also when it is a pronoun that cliticizes to T). When these conditions are met, the participle agrees with its thematic object in gender and number, but not otherwise:

(10) a. je sais combien de tables ils ont repeintes
I know how.many of tables.F.PL they have repainted.F.PL
'I know how many tables they have repainted'
(*wh*-movement)

b. cette table a été repeinte par Marie (passive)
this table.F has been repainted.F by Marie
'this table has been repainted by Marie'

c. ils ont repeint/*repeinte la table (no movement)
they have repainted/*repainted.F the table.F
'they have repainted the table'

Kayne's interpretation of this paradigm was based on (a version of) the SHAH. Unmoved objects are not the specifiers of any category; rather they are the complements of the verb. If all agreement is Spec–Head agreement, then it follows that such objects cannot be agreed with – not by T or by anything else. But movement is local, and typically needs to proceed via intermediate landing-sites in order to respect locality conditions (see Chapter 18). Such landing-sites will generally be specifiers (or adjoined positions, if those are different).[3] The moved objects in (10) hence plausibly occupy specifier positions at intermediate points of the derivation. In those positions, they could very well trigger agreement on the head of the phrase they are the specifier of. More specifically, Kayne assumed that the structure of sentences like these contained a head we may call Ptpl, similar to Tense, but lower in the structure. Moved objects can pass through the specifier of this Ptpl head, and hence trigger agreement on Ptpl, as shown in (11). The Ptpl head then fuses with the verb root to derive the inflected participle in much the same way that Tense fuses with the auxiliary to form the finite auxiliary.

(11) a. they have [Ptpl [$_{VP}$ painted the table]]   (no agreement possible)

   b. [$_{NP_i}$ How many tables] they have [t$_i$ Ptpl [$_{VP}$ painted t$_i$]]
                                                          (spec–head agreement)

The success of this theory in explaining why objects are like subjects for agreement purposes if and only if they move gave much credit to the SHAH.

Other data that helped establish the SHAH included studies of Bantu languages such as Swahili and Kilega in works like Kinyalolo (1991). Kinyalolo points out that in Kilega it is sometimes possible to move something other than the thematic subject into the SpecTP position, before the finite verb. If the thematic subject moves there, that is what T (realized as a prefix on the finite verb) agrees with (12a). But if a locative expression moves to SpecTP (the so-called locative inversion construction), then T agrees with the fronted locative, not the thematic subject, as shown in (12b). Some central Bantu languages even allow the thematic object to move to SpecTP under certain conditions. When this happens, T agrees with the fronted object, as shown in (12c).

(12) a. mutu   t-á-ku-sol-ág-á   maku wéneéné   (p. 29)
   1.person NEG-1S-drink-HAB-FV 6.beer alone
   'a person usually does not drink beer alone'
   b. mu-zízo   nyumbá mu-á-nyám-é bána wálúbí   (p. 17)
   18-10.that 10.house 18S-T-sleep-FV 2.child one.day.period
   'there will sleep children in those houses tomorrow'
   c. maku ta-má-ku-sol-ág-á   mutu   wéneéné   (p. 29)
   6.beer NEG-6S-drink-HAB-FV 1.person alone
   'no one usually drinks beer alone'

The generalization is clear: whatever occupies the SpecTP position is what triggers agreement on T. Another, fairly similar example motivating the SHAH was Classical Arabic, where the verb shows full agreement in

SVO order, when the subject arguably moves to SpecTP, but reduced agreement (in gender only) in VSO order, when the subject does not move to T (Koopman and Sportiche 1991, Fassi Fehri 1993).

17.2.1.4 Motivation for downward probing Agree

Chomsky (2000b, 2001) caused a fundamental shift in how these questions are looked at, away from the SHAH and toward the AGRH. Part of his motivation for this had to do with abstract considerations within the Minimalist Program, not necessarily having to do with 'on the ground' facts about agreement paradigms. He wanted to replace Move as a primitive syntactic operation, so as to explain why it seems to function as a last resort, preempted by other syntactic operations. He therefore identified both Merge and Agree as essential components of the composite operation Move. In essence, this made X agreeing with Y a *precondition* for Y moving to the specifier of X, rather than a *result* of that movement. This perspective also cohered with other theoretical concerns about the cyclicity of derivations, the key role of c-command, and the desire to make conditions as simple as possible. For example, Chomsky (1995c) has suggested that the notion of specifier does not even exist as a primitive of the theory within the Minimalist Program. If not, then it is no longer attractive (or even possible?) to stipulate within the theory of agreement that a head agrees with its specifier but not its complement.

But Chomsky's new AGRH does link up with certain empirical facts that did not fit so well with the SHAH. For example, in English the thematic subject can sometimes be left in its lower position, with SpecTP being filled with the semantically empty place-holder (expletive) *there*. When this happens, Tense can still agree with the thematic subject in the same way that it does when the subject actually moves to SpecTP position:[4]

(13) a. five linguists are/*is in the room
b. there are/??is five linguists in the room
c. five linguists seem/*seems to be in the room
d. there seem/??seems to be five linguists in the room

The fact that Tense still agrees with the NP *five linguists* in (13b,d) looks like a serious blow to the SHAH. The AGRH offers a more unified account, according to which T always scans downward through the structure, agreeing with the closest NP. It so happens that that NP does subsequently move up to SpecTP in many instances, but that is a partially separate issue, and agreement is not contingent on it – at least in English.[5]

The AGRH's edge increases when one realizes that similar instances of surface-downward agreement are found even when something other than an expletive is in SpecTP position. For example, locative inversion exists in English as well as in Kilega, but in English the verb agrees with the postverbal NP, not with the raised locative:[6]

(14) (Mary said that) on the table were put peanuts

Inasmuch as (12) seemed decisive for the SHAH, (14) seems compelling for the AGRH. Moreover, since *on the table* is a meaningful element, one cannot simply delete it before LF or insert it at PF to fix the problem without losing something essential to the meaning of the whole. The same point can be made even more forcefully with Hindi examples like (5b). (5b) shows that the subject is marked with ergative case in the perfective aspect, and under these conditions T agrees with a bare NP object. The object clearly cannot occupy SpecTP without driving out the subject, and the subject is not semantically vacuous, hence not deletable.[7] Here it seems that T agrees with an NP that could never be in its specifier at any level of representation – as allowed by downward Agree.

Facts like these still do not put the matter beyond debate, however. One might say that the locative in (14) moves overtly to SpecTP and then is reconstructed back into its original position, or that it moves to a clause-initial position other than SpecTP (cf. note 6), and then the NP moves to SpecTP covertly. Or there could be a complex sequence of movements, such that the object in (5b) is in SpecTP at one crucial point of the derivation, before further movements separate them again. Indeed, some linguists still argue in favor of SHAH instead of the AGRH (Koopman 2005) or in addition to it (Franck *et al.* 2006). However, the SHAH has become a minority view.

17.2.2 Further conditions on the Agree relationship

Implicit in the discussion so far have been two conditions on Chomsky's relation of Agree. The agreeing head must search 'downward,' through its c-command domain for something to agree with, not 'upward,' or 'sideways' to positions with which there is no c-command relationship. Second, the agreeing head must agree with the closest element it finds with the relevant features – for example, with the subject rather than the object in structures that have both. This second condition has been called the intervention condition. Systems derived from Chomsky (2000b, 2001) also make use of two other conditions: what we can call the activity condition, and the phase condition.

17.2.2.1 The activity condition

The activity condition says that in order for an NP to be eligible for agreement, it must have an unvalued uninterpretable feature of its own. In practice, this means that the NP must have an unvalued case feature, since the other features of the noun (number, gender, person) are considered to have a semantic interpretation on noun phrases.[8] The intuition here is that both members of the Agree relation must have some deficiency that gives them a motive for participating in Agree. The practical effect is that a head like T cannot agree with an NP that has already received case from some other source. For example, T cannot agree with a subject in Icelandic when the subject has an idiosyncratic dative case marking that certain predicates (verbs and adjectives) require (lexical case; see below). In contrast, T can perfectly well agree with a subject which does not have a lexically specified case, one which T is free to assign nominative case to when it agrees with it.

(15) a. stelpunum   hafði   verið illt   (Sigurðsson 2002:707–708)
        girls.the.DAT had(3.SG) been bad.NOM.N.SG
        'the girls had been feeling bad'
     b. stelpurnar   höfðu   verið illar
        girls.the.NOM had(3.PL) been bad.NOM.F.PL
        'the girls had been angry'

Chomsky also uses the activity condition to explain why T cannot agree with the object of a prepositional phrase in an English structure like (16).

(16) *there seem to some linguists that agreement is a fascinating topic
     (Compare: it seems to some linguists that agreement is a fascinating topic)

The NP *some linguists* receives case from the preposition *to* in this sentence (see below), so it is not eligible for T to agree with, even though it is the first NP that T would find as it searches downward through its c-command domain.[9]

17.2.2.2 The phase condition and long-distance agreement

In addition to the intervention and activity conditions, Chomsky posits what we might call a phase condition on the operation of Agree. For example, this accounts for the fact that T can agree with an NP inside its clausal complement in (17a) but not in (17b):

(17) a. there seem [to be five linguists in the room]
     b. *there seem [that five linguists are in the room]
        (Compare: it seems [that five linguists are in the room])

Five linguists is the closest NP to the matrix T in both examples. However, Chomsky assumes that finite clauses (and transitive verb phrases) are phases (see Chapter 18). A phase is a self-contained chunk of syntactic structure, which is derived independently and then becomes largely or completely inert to manipulation within a larger syntactic unit. One consequence of this inertness is that the subject of the finite clause becomes invisible to Agree initiated by something in the higher clause (see Section 18.12). This accounts for the ungrammaticality of (17b). In contrast, infinitival clauses with a defective T node and no complementizer like the one in (17a) are not phases. As a result, T can agree with *five linguists* in this sentence. The phase condition on agreement is taken to be a corollary of a much more general restriction, the so-called Phase Impenetrability Condition, which is also supposed to hold of movement and many other syntactic relationships (ideally all).[10]

The phase condition has helped provoke important new research into the topic of so-called long-distance agreement (LDA) in a variety of languages. Some languages do seem to permit a functional head in a matrix clause to agree with an NP contained inside an embedded clause, in contrast to what we see in (17b). One rather well-documented case of this is the Caucasian language Tsez (Polinsky and Potsdam 2001:584):

(18) enir [užā   manalu   b-āc'ułi] b-iyxo
     mother boy.ERG bread.III.ABS III-ate   III-know
     'the mother knows that the boy ate the bread'
                                        (or r-iyxo, agreeing with CP)

Nevertheless, most of the literature claims that Chomsky's phase condition is actually valid for such cases, and serves to explain some subtle conditions on LDA constructions. For example, Polinsky and Potsdam argue in detail that LDA with an embedded argument in Tsez is only possible if the NP is topicalized (perhaps covertly) within the embedded clause. On the one hand, if 'bread' in (18) is explicitly marked as a topic by the suffix -n, then agreement with it on the matrix verb becomes obligatory (p. 610). On the other hand, if something other than the absolutive argument 'bread' is the topic of the lower clause – such as 'yesterday' in (19) – then LDA with 'bread' becomes impossible:

(19) *enir [huł   už-ā   manalu   b-āc'-ru-łi] b-iyxo
                                                          (p. 636)
     mother yesterday(TOP) boy.ERG bread.III.ABS III-ate   III-know
     'the mother knows that yesterday the boy ate the bread'
                                                        (OK: r-iy-xo)

Topicalization arguably moves the relevant NP to the edge of the embedded CP phase, so that it is not part of the frozen chunk, so that the topic remains visible for agreement with the matrix verb. Similar accounts have been proposed for Algonquian languages like Passamaquoddy and Innu-Aimûn (Bruening 2001, Branigan and MacKenzie 2002). And there seem to be other kinds of (apparent) LDA as well, for example, 'restructuring' cases where the embedded clause is really only a VP, hence not a phase (see Bhatt 2005 on Hindi, Bobaljik and Wurmbrand 2005a on Itel'men). See Polinsky (2003) for a good overview of the various analytic options available for explaining different kinds of LDA, as well as Frank (2006) and Etxepare (2006) on the possibility of indirect local agreement.

17.2.2.3 Summary: conditions on Agree
In summary, then, the recent Chomskian theory of Agree has essentially the following structure, consisting of four main conditions, with plenty of room to flesh out the relationships among them and other details in different ways.

(20) F agrees with XP only if (XP has the features F is seeking, and):
  a. F c-commands XP. (the c-command condition)
  b. There is no YP such that YP comes between XP and F and YP has the sought-for features. (the intervention condition)
  c. F and XP are contained in all the same phases. (the phase condition)
  d. XP has an unvalued case feature. (the activity condition)

17.2.3 Agreement on other categories

17.2.3.1 Object agreement

So far our focus has been on agreement between the finite verb and the subject. Typological evidence shows that this is the most common kind of agreement, but not the only kind. The second most common kind, found in roughly 50 percent of the languages of the world, is agreement between the verb and an object and/or an indirect object. Simple examples from Swahili are given in (21), based on the analysis of Riedel (2009).

(21) a. ni-li-mw-ona   mwanawe   (Riedel 2009:46)
        1sS-PAST-1O-see   1.child.POSS.3S
        'I saw his child'
     b. tu-li-vi-pot-ez-a   vi-tabu   vy-ote   (Vitale 1981:17)
        1pS-PAST-8O-lose-CAUS-FV 8-book   8-all
        'we lost all of the books'

This kind of agreement is less well understood, in part because it does not exist overtly in the best-studied languages. However, ideas about the relationship between case and agreement have led generative linguists to assume that object agreement happens covertly even in languages like English, because agreement with the object is the vehicle for assigning accusative case to that object. This is taken to be parallel to the relationship between agreement with Tense and nominative case assignment (see also below).

It is therefore widely assumed that the Chomskian account of subject–verb agreement generalizes to verb–object agreement as follows. Basic clause structure includes some other functional head that can initiate agreement, similar to T but lower in the structure. In particular, this additional functional head is below *v*P, but above VP. As such, it is at all stages of the derivation lower than the subject, which originates in Spec*v*P. Therefore, as it probes downward through its c-command domain, it encounters the object first, and the result is object agreement. Like T, this functional head usually fuses with the verb, so object agreement is typically on a morphologically complex verb form, not on a free standing functional category. The derivation is schematized in (22).

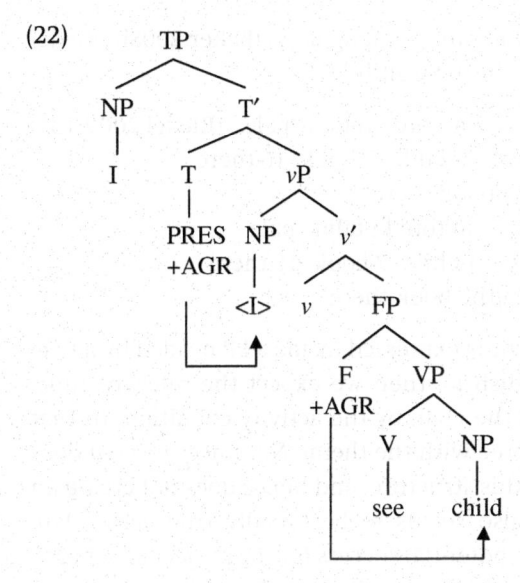

(22)
```
            TP
           /  \
         NP    T'
         |    /  \
         I   T    vP
             |   /  \
           PRES NP   v'
           +AGR |   /  \
               <I> v    FP
                       /  \
                      F    VP
                    +AGR  /  \
                         V    NP
                         |    |
                        see  child
```

More specifically, this account predicts that object agreement should be agreement with the *highest* object, whenever there is more than one, as in double object constructions involving verbs like 'give,' 'show,' and 'send.' Standard tests that involve anaphora, binding, and quantifier scope imply that the higher object is very often the goal NP if there is one (Barss and Lasnik 1986, Larson 1988a, Marantz 1993), as shown in (23). The expectation, then, is that, whenever this is true, the inflected verb will agree with the goal NP rather than the theme NP in a double object construction, following reasoning articulated in Boeckx and Niinuma (2004). This holds despite the fact that object agreement with the theme argument is normal in a single object construction.

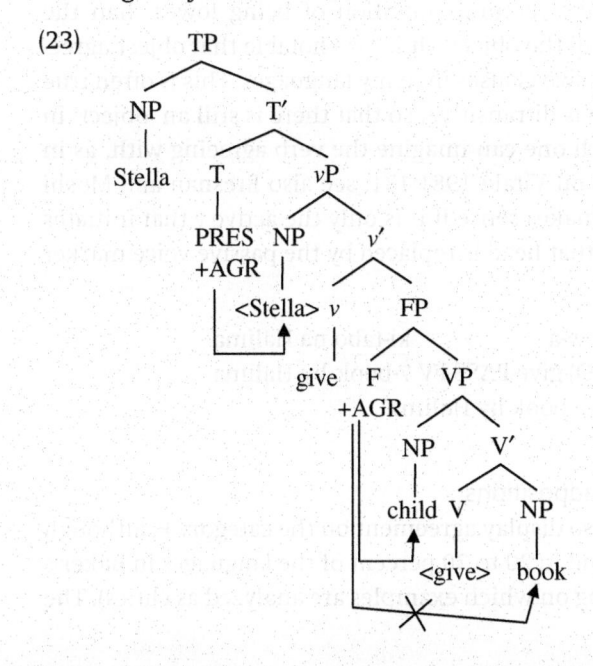

(23)
```
              TP
             /  \
           NP    T'
           |    /  \
         Stella T    vP
                |   /  \
              PRES NP   v'
              +AGR |   /  \
                <Stella> v  FP
                         |  /  \
                       give F   VP
                           +AGR /  \
                               NP   V'
                               |   /  \
                             child V   NP
                                   |    |
                                <give> book
```

This is correct for quite a wide range of languages (Baker 2008b, Riedel 2009); (24) is a sample contrast from Swahili.[11]

(24) a. Stella a-li-m-pa   m-toto ki-tabu pale   (Riedel 2009:131)
        Stella 1S-PAST-1O-give 1-child 7-book 16.there
        'Stella gave the child a book there'
     b. *Stella a-li-ki-pa   m-toto ki-tabu pale
        Stella 1S-PAST-7O-give 1-child 7-book 16.there
        'Stella gave the child a/the book there'

In contrast, if the goal argument is expressed inside a PP headed by a true preposition analogous to English *to*, then we expect the relevant functional head not to agree with the goal, by the activity condition. In that circumstance, the head can agree with the theme NP, since the goal does not c-command the theme in this structure, and hence does not create an intervention violation. This also seems to be broadly true across languages.[12] This then looks like a potential success for the project of generalizing the theory of Agree from subject agreement on T to object agreement in this way.

What more precisely is the head F that undergoes object agreement? There are many proposals about this in the literature. Two notable possibilities include saying that it is an (inner) aspect head (Travis 1991) or saying that it is a dedicated agreement head which has no independent semantic content (Chomsky 1991b, Koizumi 1995). But the most widespread view is that the head that agrees with the object is the transitive *v* itself – the same head that assigns a thematic role to the subject. This head has the advantage of being independently motivated and making a semantic contribution to the structure (unlike a special AgrO head; cf. Chomsky 1995c), and it meets the structural condition of being lower than the subject but higher than all the objects. It is also notable that object agreement is impossible in passive clauses in many languages. This is often true even when the base verb is ditransitive, so that there is still an 'object' in the passive version which one can imagine the verb agreeing with, as in (25) from Swahili (based on Vitale 1981:131; see also Bresnan and Moshi 1990). This curious fact makes sense if it is only the active *v* that initiates object agreement, since that head is replaced by the passive voice marker in the passive version.[13]

(25) Fatuma a-li-(*ki)-p-ew-a   ki-tabo na Halima
     Fatuma 1S-PAST-(7O)-give-PASS-FV 7-book by Halima
     'Fatuma was given a book by Halima'

17.2.3.2 Agreement on adpositions

Natural languages can also display agreement on the category P, although this is less common, found in 20 to 30 percent of the languages in Baker's (2008b) survey (depending on which examples are analyzed as clitics). The best example in IE languages is Welsh, in which many Ps agree with their object when the object is a pronoun.

(26) soniais I amdan-o ef (Harlow 1981:220, 249)
talked I about-3sM him
'I talked about him'
amdanaf (i); amdanat (ti); amdani (hi); amdanynt (hwy), etc.
about-1s me about-2s you about-3sF her about-3p them

Generalizing the Agree account to this situation seems quite straightforward. P probes downward and agrees with the first relevant category it finds, namely its own NP complement, which does not have case apart from the P (so it is active). In typical PP structures, there is no other NP that could cause an intervention effect, nor any CP boundary that qualify as a phase, so there is nothing to disrupt the agreement. Notice also that P apparently agrees with its complement in (26), not its specifier. This is possible additional support for the AGRH over the SHAH.[14]

17.2.3.3 Agreement on complementizers

Agreement on complementizers is also found occasionally, although it is not very common. The main cases known in IE languages are from dialects of Dutch and German. In these languages, C agrees with the subject of its TP complement, as in (27).

(27) kvinden **dan** die boeken te diere zyn (West Flemish)
I-find that-PL the books too expensive are (Carstens 2003)
'I find that those books are too expensive'

This is compatible with the AGRH (but probably not with the SHAH; see van Koppen 2005), in that the subject is in the c-command domain of C, is not contained in any phase smaller than the CP as a whole, and is the highest NP in TP, hence the first thing C encounters probing downward. The main new question that these examples pose concerns the activity condition. T also agrees with the subject here, which should value the subject's case as nominative and make it inactive for agreement with C. The leading intuition, however, is that C and T are very closely related categories, so they might not even count as different heads for purposes of case and agreement (see, for example, Chomsky's 2008 proposal that T inherits its agreement features from C). See Carstens (2003), van Koppen (2005), and references cited there for further discussion.

17.2.3.4 More on object agreement: sensitivity to specificity

One might think that the existence of object agreement also supports the AGRH over the SHAH, since the targets of object agreement seem to be like the complements of Ps and the targets of C agreement in being below the agreeing head, as taken for granted in (22). But there is a complicating factor. Unlike other forms of agreement, object agreement is often related to the specificity of the agreed-with nominal. For example, Zulu verbs are said to agree with their (highest) object only if that object is specific (Doke 1963:299):

(28) a. ngi-leth-el-a   umfundisi incwadi
      1sS-bring-APPL-FV   teacher.1   book
      'I am bringing a teacher a book'
    b. ngi-ya-m-leth-e-la   umfundisi incwadi
      1sS-DISJ-1O-bring- APPL-FV   teacher.1   book
      'I am bringing the teacher – the one who told me to do so – a book'

Similarly, subjects of all kinds trigger subject agreement in Amharic, but only specific objects trigger object agreement (Baker, to appear). Why should this be?

In fact, the contrast in (28) is reminiscent of an important contrast in the literature on the syntax–semantics interface. Diesing (1992) shows that the position of the object and its interpretation are interrelated in German. When the direct object appears relatively close to the verb, after certain particles and adverbs (presumably its base position), it is interpreted as an indefinite expression with a narrow scope existential interpretation. In contrast, when it appears farther from the verb, before these particles and adverbs (a moved position), it is given a specific interpretation (Diesing 1992:107–108). Diesing's influential interpretation of these facts is that the VP is the domain for a certain kind of semantic interpretation: it is the domain of existential closure, where material is not interpreted presuppositionally. NPs that are generated inside this domain and stay there receive weak/non-specific indefinite readings at LF; NPs that move outside this domain (by 'object shift') receive strong/specific readings at LF.

Diesing's phenomenon seems rather similar to the one seen in (28),[15] except that what correlates with semantic specificity in Zulu is agreement rather than word order. We can relate the two if we say that (28b) also has the object NP move to a higher position, outside VP. However, there is no net effect of this movement on word order in Zulu, because the verb happens to move to a higher position still – presumably T (Baker 2008b:198–200). This verb movement restores the V-O order that was initially reversed by object shift. The resulting structures would thus look something like this:

(29)   a. [$_{TP}$ I Tense [$_{FP}$ (*AGR$_i$ +)bring [$_{VP}$ teacher$_i$ <bring> book]]]
           ↑_____| verb movement
         NP is in VP, domain of existential closure, doesn't trigger agreement

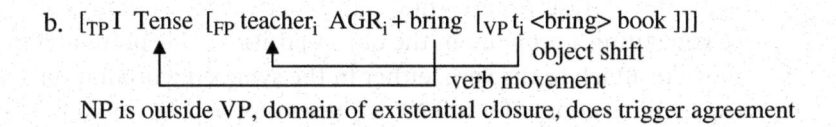

b. [$_{TP}$ I Tense [$_{FP}$ teacher$_i$ AGR$_i$ + bring [$_{VP}$ t$_i$ <bring> book]]]
                    ↑   ↑ | object shift
                    | |_____|
                    |_____ verb movement
       NP is outside VP, domain of existential closure, does trigger agreement

So apparently scrambling/object shift feeds object agreement in some languages.

A proponent of the SHAH might take encouragement from this paradigm. When the object shifts out of VP, receiving a 'strong' interpretation, it lands in the specifier of a functional head (there being no movement into complement positions). The moved NP could then trigger agreement on this functional head, in accordance with the SHAH. In contrast, the unmoved NP could be in a complement position; hence it will not trigger agreement according to this view. (Indeed, this analysis of Zulu is conceptually very similar to Kayne's analysis of French, discussed in connection with (10) and (11) above.)

In contrast, a proponent of the AGRH might try to use the phase condition (20c) to explain this pattern. In addition to CPs, transitive verb phrases count as phases in Chomsky's conception. Suppose then that the lower functional head that initiates non-subject agreement (F) is outside this phase, whereas the base position of the direct object is inside this phase. Then F cannot agree with the object unless object shift/scrambling takes that direct object out of the VP phase (or to its edge), resulting in a strong/specific interpretation on the object NP. In contrast, there is (in standard treatments) no phase boundary between T and the base position of the subject, in SpecvP. Therefore agreement between T and the subject is not contingent on the subject moving anywhere, along with whatever semantic factors might be associated with such movement. There are clearly some important details still to work out in this sketch. For example, it seems to imply that either the head involved in object agreement is higher than normally assumed (above *v*P) or that the phase boundary is lower than normally assumed (VP rather than *v*P) (see Fox and Pesetsky 2005, and Chapter 18, note 37). But it is a potentially promising alternative way to capture the relationship between object shift, interpretation, and agreement that can be observed in some languages with overt object agreement.

17.2.3.5 Object agreement versus pronominal cliticization

These issues regarding object agreement relate to a huge analytical problem that besets work in this domain: the problem of distinguishing true agreement with an object from the cliticization (or incorporation) of an object pronoun to the verb. In their purest forms, the two are very different conceptually. In an agreement analysis, a full NP is generated in the object position and a functional head picks up features from that NP via Agree. The NP in question could be a null pronoun, perhaps licensed by the Agree relation, but that is simply a special case; it could also be a full NP argument. In contrast, a pure cliticization derivation would necessarily involve generating a pronoun in the object position. This pronoun would then move to attach to the verb, either in the syntax (incorporation) or at PF (simple cliticization). If a full NP is present as well, it would be some kind of dislocated adjunct, generated in a position other than the true object position, but licensed by binding the object pronoun (cf. *That girl, I really like her*). These two analyses are contrasted schematically in (30).

(30) a. [Subject Tense [$_{FP}$ F [$_{VP}$ Verb   NP/pronoun]]]
     |_____↑ Agree

   b. [Subject Tense [$_{FP}$ F [$_{VP}$ pronoun$_i$+Verb t$_i$]]] (NP$_i$)
                                  ↑ | mov't
                                  |_____| (syntax or PF)

But conceptually distinct as these two analyses are, they can be quite difficult to tease apart empirically, given that the position and interpretation of an NP that has undergone object shift may not be much different from the position and interpretation of an NP that is a dislocated adjunct. For example, both would be constrained to be definite or specific rather than non-specific, according to Diesing's Mapping Hypothesis. As a result, there are debates that go back and forth as to whether a particular morpheme is an object agreement or a cliticized pronoun in the literatures on many language families, including Romance, Bantu, Hungarian, Amharic, and others. Typically both sides in these debates bring up many relevant considerations, and taken on their own each article may seem quite convincing. But they are also not compatible with each other, and different considerations can pull in different ways. To make matters even more complex and interesting, there are also intermediate theories that combine aspects of the pure agreement theory and the pure cliticization theory as outlined above. These include Sportiche's (1997) proposal that clitics in Romance head Clitic Phrases, which enter into Agree-like relations with associated DP arguments, and the 'big DP' hypothesis of Uriagereka (1995) and others, which claims that what is cliticized to the verb is not the whole pronominal argument of the verb, but only its D head. As the space of theoretical possibilities expands in this domain, the challenge of finding decisive empirical arguments to show which is correct for which language becomes even greater.

In one sense, it is not surprising that these analyses are hard to tease apart. Indeed, this analytical ambiguity is presumably a source of language change, with pronoun cliticization often leading to the innovation of new agreement systems in languages that did not previously have them. But linguists need to piece together the big picture on this matter, so that we will be able to construct more reliable typologies of object agreement (not mixing in instances of cliticization), and so that we can see exactly how it compares to other kinds of agreement.[16] Indeed, similar issues also arise for other kinds of agreement, such as distinguishing subject agreement and subject clitics (see, for example, Culbertson 2010 on French). However, in the domain of subject agreement the issues seem a bit easier to resolve empirically, perhaps because true subject agreement is less often related to definiteness of the subject, as discussed briefly above.

17.2.4 Agreement parameters

The discussion of object agreement in Zulu can also lead us to consider systematic cross-linguistic variation in the area of agreement.

The most obvious and uncontroversial type of variation is variation in the range of heads that participate in agreement across languages. For example, finite T agrees (with the subject) in English and Kinande, but not Japanese; transitive v agrees (with the object) in Swahili but not English; P agrees in Welsh but not English; C agrees in West Flemish but not in standard Dutch, and so on. This is the familiar sort of variation in the features of individual categories listed in the lexicon – the typical kind of cross-linguistic variation that one expects to find in the Minimalist Program (Chomsky 1995c).

But comparing the Bantu languages with the IE languages might point to a more subtle kind of cross-linguistic variation in agreement as well, where languages differ not only in which heads agree, but in how they agree. We saw that the relationship of object agreement to definiteness in Zulu was just what would be expected on the SHAH. There are, however, other languages in which it does seem possible to have object agreement with an indefinite object inside the VP. One is Nahuatl:

(31) [$_{VP}$ Ø-quim-itta cōcōhua] in   pilli.   (Launey 1981)
       3sS-3pO-see   snakes   DET child.
       'the child saw (some) snakes'

Recall also that subject agreement in inversion constructions in Kilega gave support for the SHAH (see (12)), whereas inversion constructions in English gave some of the best evidence for the AGRH (see (14)). There might then be a substantive difference between the two language families on this point. Perhaps, then, instead of pooling all the data together and debating which is the universal condition on agreement, we need to consider the possibility that each might be right for different languages, or even for different constructions in the same language. For example, perhaps something like the SHAH is true for the Bantu languages, whereas the AGRH is true for IE languages.

Two ways of stating such a parameter have been proposed in the literature. One version has been worked out most fully by Carstens (2005). She maintains the idea that agreement happens by a head probing downward in a pre-movement structure, even in Bantu languages, just as in Chomsky

(2000b, 2001). What is special about the Bantu languages, she claims, is that they are also subject to a principle like (32).

(32) If F agrees with X, then X must check an EPP feature of F. (Bantu)[17]

This is, in essence, the exact converse of the traditional SHAH. The SHAH said that if X moves to SpecFP, then X and F agree. (32) says that if F agrees with XP, then XP must move to the SpecFP position. It therefore accounts for the core difference between Bantu agreement and IE agreement without changing the basic mechanics of Agree.

Baker (2008b: Chapter 5) develops a slightly more radical view of the parameter in question. He says that, although the agreeing head can c-command the agreed with NP in IE, the agreed with NP must c-command the agreeing head in Bantu. In effect, he takes the c-command condition on Agree (20a), makes it more symmetrical as in (33a), and then parameterizes it as in (33b).

(33) *Direction of Agreement Parameter (DAP)*
F agrees with XP only if (XP has the features F is seeking, and):
a. F c-commands XP or XP c-commands F.   (IE value)
or
b. XP c-commands F   (Bantu value)

This also accounts for the core differences in subject agreement and object agreement between Bantu languages and IE languages in a unified way. (Baker claims that (33) is better than (32) because it also applies to agreement on adjectives; see next section.)

What is particularly interesting about this parameter is that it seems to apply to a language as a whole. So far we have seen that the difference shows up both in subject agreement and object agreement, but arguably the same difference is seen even with agreement on P and C across the two language families. We saw in (26) that Ps in Welsh can agree with their unmoved (pronominal) objects. Ps in Kinande (34) and Kilega (Kinyalolo 1991:111) can also agree with their objects, but only if that object has moved out of PP – by way of SpecPP, we may assume – by passive or by cleft formation.

(34) a. Kambale a-ka-kanay-a   na-(*bo) abas-syakulu
Kambale 3sS-PRES-speak-FV with-2 2-old.people
'Kambale is speaking with the old people'
                                    (no Agr on P with NP in situ)

b. aba-syakulu si-ba-li-kan-ibaw-a   na-bo
2-old.people NEG-2S-PRES-speak-PASS-FV with-2
'old people are not spoken with'
                                    (Agr on P with moved NP)

Similarly, (27) shows that Cs in West Flemish agree downward with the subject of their TP complements. Cs can also agree in some Bantu languages, but what they agree with is quite different: Cs in Bantu appear to agree upward, with the subject of the matrix clause.

(35) mo-n-a-layir-ire   Kambale **in-di**   a-gul-e   ama-tunda
      AFF-1sS-T-convince-EXT Kambale.1 1sS-that 1S-buy-SUBJ 6-fruits
      'I convinced Kambale that he should buy fruits'
                                                              (Kinande)

Diercks (2010) studies this type of agreement in detail, and argues that it is really agreement with a null operator in SpecCP that is controlled by the matrix subject; this operator is similar to the one used in many generative accounts of logophoric pronouns in African languages (see Chapter 15). In all these various constructions, then, IE languages allow a head to agree with something it c-commands, whereas the Bantu languages only allow a head to agree with something that c-commands it (or with its Specifier, depending on the execution). This seems then be to a general property of languages as wholes (a 'macroparameter'), not a lexical property of particular heads in a language (a 'microparameter'; see also Chapter 25). Baker (2008b: Chapter 5) claims that this is confirmed by his broader survey of 108 languages, in which, out of sixty languages that show agreement on more than one syntactic head, sixteen consistently require that all the heads be c-commanded by the agreed-with NP, forty-three consistently permit all their heads to agree downward, and only two appear to be inconsistent in this respect. This then seems to be systematic syntactic variation, rather than lexical variation – a syntactic parameter in the original sense of Chomsky (1981) (see esp. Chapters 24 and 25, this volume, on the nature of parameters). Yet at the same time, not quite everything fits into this picture as neatly as it should. For example, the object agreement found on participles in French (see (10) above) seems to be a type of agreement that needs to be upward in a language (family) that otherwise permits agreement to be downward. More work is thus needed to establish what the robust crosslinguistic patterns are in this domain.

17.2.5 Concord

Yet another syntactic category that agreement is sometimes found on is the adjective, as illustrated in (36). These Spanish examples show that adjectives can in general agree both when they appear in predicate position and when they appear as attributive modifiers (although there are languages in which an adjective may agree when it is in one of these positions but not the other). Predicate adjectives agree with the subject of predication, whereas an attributive adjective agrees with the noun that it modifies:

(36) a. l-as   mujer-es   son   alt-as
         the-F.PL woman.F-PL are.3pS tall-F.PL
         'the women are tall'

b. l-as   mujer-es   alt-as   arriva-ron
the-F.PL woman.F-PL tall-F.PL arrive-PAST.3pS
'the tall women arrived'

Entirely similar patterns are found in the Bantu languages, among others (Baker 2008b:14–21). This kind of agreement seems rather different from subject–verb agreement in several ways. First, the morphemes are different: third person plural agreement on a verb in Spanish is indicated by -(ro)n, for example, whereas third person plural agreement on an adjective is indicated by -os or -as, depending on whether the noun is masculine or feminine. Second, the features that are agreed with are somewhat different: both adjectives and verbs agree in number, but only verbs have distinct forms that agree in person as well. So a verb agreeing with a first person plural subject in Spanish would bear the suffix -mos, distinct from -n, whereas an adjective agreeing with a first person plural pronoun would continue to bear -os or -as. Third, the contexts where agreement happens seem different: adjectives take part in NP internal agreement as shown in (36b), whereas verbs generally do not. Finally, one can have multiple adjectives agreeing with the same nominal, when two adjectives modify a single noun, but one cannot (in English) have two verbs agree with the same subject (see (17b) and (48)). This cluster of differences has made some linguists think that adjectives participate in concord, rather than true agreement – a formally different morphosyntactic relation.[18] If it exists, concord would also apply to other categories inside a nominal – articles, demonstratives, quantifiers, etc. – and it might cover feature matching in additional features – e.g., case as well as person, number, and gender in languages where case is marked overtly.

17.2.5.1 Concord on adjectives as Agree

But there are important similarities between the two types of agreement as well, which suggest that we should not be too hasty in distinguishing them. The fact that adjectival agreement and verbal agreement happen in somewhat different syntactic environments might simply follow from the fact that adjectives and verbs appear in systematically different environments, as a result of their fundamental difference in category (see, for example, Baker 2003). So if a finite verb can never be used as an attributive modifier inside a complex NP, then it is not surprising that finite verbs never undergo NP-internal agreement the way that adjectives do; they simply never get the chance. It is perfectly possible that many of the other apparent differences between verbal agreement and adjectival agreement can also be explained away in this manner.

Indeed, Baker (2008b: Chapter 3) constructs an argument that concord on adjectives should be reduced to agreement in Chomsky's sense. He begins by constructing truly minimal pairs, in which a raising adjective like *likely* is used in predicate position, following a copula, where it is maximally similar to the sentences with raising verb *seems* that motivate the characteristic details of Chomsky's theory of Agree (see Section 17.2.2). When such sentences are constructed in a language where adjectives show agreement, such as Icelandic, the two kinds of agreement turn out to be parallel in every respect. Crucial test sentences include the Icelandic equivalents of the following:

(37) a. there are likely to be some communists on the school board
b. it is clear to some women that it had rained
c. it is likely that some women are in the room

The matrix adjective can agree with the subject of the non-finite clause in (37a), but not with the object of a PP in (37b), or with the subject of a finite clause in (37c). This is exactly parallel to the behavior of agreement on the verb *seem* in English, as reviewed in Section 17.2.2 above (and to the behavior of agreement on the copula in (37a–c)). We can conclude then, that 'concord' here is subject to the same restrictions as verbal agreement is, including the activity condition, the phase condition, and the intervention condition.

It seems clear, then, that we want to have the same theory of agreement apply to adjectives like 'likely' in Icelandic as applies to T in English. But 'likely' can also be used attributively, in expressions like 'a likely outcome.' When it is, it agrees in number and gender with the modified noun, using the same morphemes as when it is used in predicative environments, including raising constructions. Putting the pieces together, then, we want the same theory to apply to verbs and to raising adjectives, the same theory to apply to raising 'likely' and to attributive 'likely,' and the same theory to apply to attributive 'likely' and to other attributive adjectives. Baker (2008b) thus concludes that we should have a single theory of agreement that covers all these special cases.

This is not to say that Chomsky's theory of Agree might not need some tweaking so that it applies properly to adjectival structures as well as verbal structures. Baker (2008b) claims that two adjustments are necessary. First, suppose that the structure of an adjectival predication is (an elaboration of) (38) (as argued in Baker 2003).

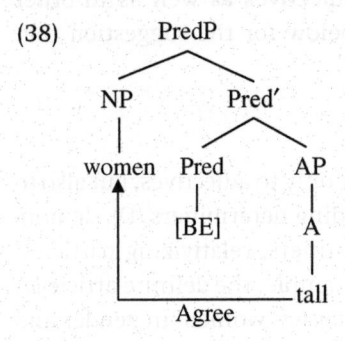

(38)
```
            PredP
           /    \
         NP     Pred'
         |      /   \
       women  Pred   AP
              |      |
             [BE]    A
              ↑      |
              |_____tall
                Agree
```

If so, then the c-command condition on agreement as Chomsky stated it cannot be entirely correct, because the adjective does not c-command the NP it agrees with at any level of representation. Baker therefore generalizes this condition, so that either element of the Agree relation can be the higher one, as stated in (39).

(39) F agrees with XP only if F c-commands XP or XP c-commands F.

Note that (39) is the same as the IE setting of the agreement parameter in (33). The Bantu setting of (33) is more restrictive, but it also correctly allows agreement in a structure like (38). Predicate adjectives thus provide additional evidence that upward Agree is possible.

Baker also claims that Chomsky's activity condition should be generalized so as to work for adjectival constructions. Normally a T or v must agree with an NP that has an unvalued case feature, and the agreement results in that NP's case feature becoming valued as nominative or accusative. But adjectives do not determine the structural case of the NP that they agree with in this way. On the contrary, (40) shows that adjectives take on the case of the NP that they agree with, where the NP's case is determined by its relationship to Tense and the verb – another type of agreement/concord:

(40) a. María   er   góð   (Thráinsson 1979:361)
        Maria.NOM is good.F.SG.NOM
        'Maria is good'
     b. ég tel   Maríu   vera góða
        I   believe Maria.ACC to.be good.F.SG.ACC
        'I believe Maria to be good'

In this light, Baker suggests that the activity condition be generalized as follows:

(41) F agrees with NP X only if F determines the case feature of NP (case assignment) or NP determines the case feature of F (case concord).

It is plausible to think, then, that with a small number of adjustments such as these, the Agree theory will apply to adjectives as well as to other syntactic categories. (See Section 17.3.4.2 below for the suggestion that (41) is also parameterized, much as (39) is.)[19]

17.2.5.2 Other kinds of concord

The traditional notion of concord applies not only to adjectives, but also to other expressions inside the nominal, including determiners (D), demonstratives, possessive pronouns, certain quantifiers, relativizing particles, and so on, depending on the language. For example, the definite article *las* in (36) from Spanish agrees with the noun *mujeres* 'women' in gender and number, using the same inflectional suffixes that the agreeing adjective does (-*a-s*). There would seem to be little difficulty in generalizing the theory of Agree to these functional heads. For example, a D c-commands its NP complement, there is no closer NP to D, and no phase boundary separates them. The only question would concern the activity condition, since Ds do not usually assign case to their NP complements.[20] But the generalized version of this condition in (41) works here too, since Ds match their NP complements in case, as seen clearly in languages like German and Greek. Given that Ds share case with their NP complements, they can agree with them in number and gender as well. One may reasonably hope that this analysis will extend to all instances of concord within a complex NP, but there may be other structures that need to be considered more carefully in order to prove this in full detail.

We have been exploring the possibility that concord falls under the same theory as agreement. Is there a separate notion of subject–predicate agreement in addition? Some linguists have thought so. However, now that agreement on adjectives and tensed verbs (including copulas) has been dealt with, there is little for subject–predicate agreement to do. The most obvious case that remains is predicate nominal sentences, where the predicate often seems to agree with the subject in number, as shown in (42).

(42) a. Mary is a linguist/*linguists
b. they are linguists/*a linguist

But there is reason to believe that this is not really agreement in the syntactic sense. Rather it follows for semantic reasons: a group of people cannot be a single linguist, nor can a single person be multiple linguists. The way of individuating people and the way of individuating linguists is too similar for these mismatches in number to be possible. When the methods of individuating are sufficiently distinct, then it is possible for the predicate nominal to have a different number value than its subject, as shown in (43).

(43) a. they are a committee which has been charged with investigating abuses
b. these clouds are a sign of rain
c. the biggest problem we have is locusts

There is no syntactic rule enforcing agreement between the subject and the predicate here, just a general issue of semantic compatibility that must be respected.

The overall thrust of this discussion is that it seems likely – although far from certain – that all the major types of agreement in phi-features can be attributed to a single formal relation of Agree, along the lines of Chomsky's original proposal, but with a few adjustments. One phenomenon that needs further consideration, however, is case concord: the fact that a predicate and its subject must often agree in case (as in (40)). In languages with overt case inflection, the predicate in examples like (42) and (43) often (though not always) agrees with the subject in case, even when there is no necessary agreement in number and gender features. This might ultimately motivate a kind of feature matching (i.e., concord, agreement) that is partially distinct from Agree.

This also reminds us to consider case marking more carefully in its own right.

17.3 Case assignment

In addition to changing perspective on the structural conditions on agreement, Chomsky (2000b, 2001) also inverted the relative importance of agreement and case within generative syntax. Throughout the 1980s (following Chomsky 1981), case assignment and the Case Filter – a requirement that all NPs be assigned case somehow (see (66)) – were seen as among the most important syntactic conditions, determining the distribution as well as the form of noun phrases, triggering syntactic movement, and so on. But given Chomsky's (2000b) promotion of Agree to primitive status, together with controversies about how adequate the 1980s-style explanations were, the role of case theory is now often backgrounded, and case is seen as an additional side effect of the primary relation of Agree, as discussed above. Nevertheless, there are important points to be made about case assignment itself, and there are some hints that the relationship between case assignment and agreement might not always be as tight as current theory claims. If so, then case assignment continues to be a topic of investigation in its own right.[21]

17.3.1 Case theory: some hard cases

With regard to the basic task of deciding what morphological form of an NP appears where and why, the challenge for a case theory (similar to agreement theory) is to explain why case marking *largely* goes along with grammatical function and thematic role, but yet is not *perfectly* correlated with either. For example, it is largely true that accusative case marks the direct object, and that is presumably part of why it is useful to have such a thing in natural human languages. However, it is not always true. (44) shows two sentences in which the subject of the embedded clause (at least in terms of thematic role, perhaps also structurally in terms of occupying SpecTP) is in accusative case:

(44)   a. I expect him to win   (compare: I expect that he will win)
         b. I would prefer for her to go first
                                 (compare: I prefer that she goes first)

Conversely, the underscored noun phrase has the same thematic role in (45a) and (45b) – the role of theme. Nevertheless, it is accusative in the first and nominative in the second:

(45) a. the navy sinks them in the harbor
                                    (speaking of a particular kind of ship)
     b. they sink in the harbor

It is facts like these that make case theory non-trivial, showing that there is more to it than a one-to-one mapping between the morphological form of a NP and its thematic role or grammatical function.

17.3.2 Conditions on case assignment

17.3.2.1 Government

In the Government-Binding era, the condition generally put on case assignment was government: a syntactic head X could assign case to an NP Y if and only if X governed Y (Chomsky 1981). Government in turn was thought to be something like mutual c-command: X governs Y if and only if X c-commands Y and Y c-commands X (Aoun and Sportiche 1983). This condition allows a transitive verb to assign accusative case to its complement (the direct object) and a P to assign case to its complement, as desired. But government needs to be slightly broader than this, to allow T to assign nominative case to the subject in SpecTP, and to allow the verb *expect* to assign accusative case to the subject of its non-finite complement in sentences like (44a).[22] It proved challenging to allow these case assignments in a principled way, without letting in too much, and also maintaining a notion of government that was useful in other syntactic domains, such as the theories of movement and anaphora. Definitions of government became increasingly complex (see Rizzi 1990a for one example of this line of work at its best) – hence less elegant and plausible as basic principles of grammar. This led Chomsky (1993) to abandon the notion of government altogether, as part of his inauguration of the Minimalist Program (see Chapters 4, 14). This in turn gave syntacticians a motive to try to make more out of the connection between case assignment and agreement.

17.3.2.2 Agree as the source of restrictions on case assignment

We have already seen that Chomsky (2000b, 2001) has a case condition built into his rule of Agree (the activity condition). Indeed, he takes case on the NP and agreement on the functional head to be two morphological effects of the same Agree relation. Agree only takes place, on his conception, if both the functional head and the NP have an unvalued feature. Once Agree happens, the person–number–gender features of the functional head take on values that match those of the NP (agreement), while the case feature of the noun takes on a value determined by the agreeing functional head. If the functional head is Tense, the value of the NP's case feature in English is nominative; if the functional head is transitive *v*, the value of the NP's case feature is accusative. These rules work well in simple structures. For example, the subject of the finite clause is usually nominative for the same reason that the subject is usually what T agrees with: the subject is the first NP that T can find by looking downward. Similarly, the object of the clause is usually accusative because (by hypothesis) it is the first NP that *v* finds looking downward.

(46) [$_{TP}$ She PRES [$_{vP}$ <she> *v* [$_{VP}$ see him]]]

        Agree, NOM   Agree, ACC

This view also extends to the data in (44), which show the limits of the simplest linking rules. Although morphological case does not line up perfectly with thematic role or grammatical function in these examples, it is correlated with agreement. The accusative subjects in (44) appear when the clause has a non-finite T (the infinitive marker *to*) that does not undergo agreement, whereas nominative subjects appear in clauses that have finite Ts that do undergo agreement. In (44a), the T of the embedded clause does not have unvalued phi-features, therefore it cannot enter into an Agree relation with the DP *he/him*, so it does not value the case feature of that DP as nominative. The next relevant functional head working upward through the sentence is the transitive *v* associated with the matrix verb *expect*. This searches its c-command domain for something to agree with, and the first NP it finds is *he/him*. It thus agrees with *him* and values its case feature as accusative. This Agree relation is not realized on the *v* itself in poorly inflected English, nor is it realized morphologically on a full NP like *John*, but it is realized on a pronoun, resulting in *him* rather than *he* in (44a). The structure is given schematically in (47).[23]

(47) [$_{TP}$ I PRES [$_{vP}$ <I> *v* [$_{VP}$ expect [$_{TP}$ him   to [$_{VP}$ win]]]
                                                                    (no Agr)

        Agree, NOM   Agree, ACC

This important structure is known as the Exceptional Case-Marking (ECM) construction (see also Section 16.2.3), 'exceptional' because the matrix verb induces accusative case on an NP that is not its object in a structural or thematic sense (it is not the complement of *expect*, nor does *expect* assign it a thematic role). Such structures have played a large role in generative theory precisely because the normally tight correlations between position, thematic role, case, and agreement come apart exactly here. Therefore, they have provided a powerful laboratory for teasing out what relates most closely to what.

The Agree approach to case assignment also gives some traction on why the theme argument gets accusative case in (45a), but nominative in

(45b). Note that there is also an agreement difference: Tense (realized on the finite verb) agrees with the theme argument in (45b) but not in (45a). Nor is it mysterious why agreement works in this way: in (45a) a second NP is generated in the structure, expressing the agent of the event of sinking. Given that this NP is above the theme but below T, T will Agree with it, and cannot Agree with the theme, by the intervention condition. In contrast, there is no agent NP in (45b). The theme is the only NP present, hence it is the first NP T finds to Agree with. There is no issue of intervention, so T readily Agrees with the theme NP in this structure.[24] Then, by hypothesis, the same relationship that puts person–number–gender features on T assigns nominative case to the NP it Agrees with. It thus follows that the theme argument is nominative in (45b) but not in (45a).

Overall, then, Chomsky's theory of Agree can legitimately be understood as being a theory of case assignment just as much as it is a theory of agreement, despite the fact that its name emphasizes the agreement side of the relation.

17.3.2.3 Burzio's Generalization

There is a little more to say about the contrast in (45), however. We also need to take into account the lexical properties of the v node. We know why the theme NP does not get nominative in the (45a) version, but why can it get accusative? By hypothesis, this is because it enters into Agree with a different head, v, which gives its own characteristic case value to the NP it agrees with. But then why can't the theme NP also get accusative from v in (45b), as well as or instead of getting nominative from T? If anything, v should get the first chance to Agree with NP and assign it case, assuming that the derivation proceeds in bottom-up fashion, with lower heads like v inserted before higher heads like T and then processed immediately. To address this, Chomsky and others assume that there is a different sort of v – or perhaps no v at all – present in (45b). Indeed, it is the job of v also to theta-mark the subject, so the fact that a thematic subject is present in (45a) but not in (45b) shows that the v has different lexical properties in the two structures. We can then assume that the v that theta-marks a subject also initiates Agree (with the object, as it turns out), whereas the v that does not theta-mark a subject does not initiate Agree. This is a contemporary account of an observation that goes back to the early 1980s, known as Burzio's Generalization (Burzio 1986), which states that the theta-role assigning properties of a verb and its case-assigning properties are interrelated (see also Section 5.4.5).[25] See Kratzer (1996) for another version of this approach.

At one level, this is a perfectly reasonable thing to say about v. It is formally no different from saying that finite T undergoes agreement, but non-finite T does not – something that we can observe rather directly in (44). Why then shouldn't v also subdivide into Agreeing and non-Agreeing versions? But at a deeper level, this stipulation still seems a bit arbitrary, since it is not clear from a formal viewpoint why there should be covariation between the agreeing property of v and its theta-role assigning property. After all, there is no intrinsic relation between Agreement and theta-marking for T: T never takes part in theta-marking, whether it agrees or not. So it seems that the Agree theory has a plausible way to *encode* Burzio's Generalization, locating it in the lexical properties of a particular syntactic category (v), but it has no deep *explanation* for Burzio's Generalization.

17.3.2.4 More on the relationship of case and agreement

An additional interaction between case and agreement that Chomsky intends his system to capture is that one cannot have two full person agreements with the same argument in English. This can be seen in subject-to-subject raising constructions, as in (48).

(48) a. *John seems – has solved the problem
      b. John seems – to have solved the problem
      c. it seems (that) John has solved the problem

In English one also cannot have ECM with an NP that has undergone agreement:

(49) a. *I believe [her has solved the problem]
      b. I believe [her to have solved the problem]
      c. I believe [(that) she has solved the problem]

Both patterns follow from Chomsky's activity condition on Agree, in much the same way that (17b) arguably does. Agreement in the lower clause between T and the subject values the case of the subject as nominative. NPs that have all of their features valued are not active for Agree. Hence, neither T (in (48a)) nor v (in (49a)) in the matrix clause can Agree with NP; agreement turns out to be unique. It also follows that neither the matrix T nor the matrix v can assign case to the embedded subject, because case assignment depends on Agreement. Hence, an NP can only be case-marked once within this set of assumptions.[26] (However, there are languages that differ from English in this respect, including Burushaski and many Bantu languages; I return to this briefly in Section 17.3.4.2 below.)

17.3.3 Types of case

So far our discussion has focused on nominative and accusative case – the two clearest examples of structural case, so-called because which NPs get these cases depends on aspects of the syntactic structure. However, richly inflected languages typically have additional cases as well, anywhere from two or three to nearly twenty (e.g., Estonian, Lezgian) or even more.[27] How then do these additional cases fit into the picture?

17.3.3.1 Genitive case

Consider first genitive case, the case often found on an NP inside a larger NP, for example a possessor. The Agree theory can be extended to this case fairly readily, by saying that there is an agreeing functional head, the (possessive) determiner, inside the complex nominal. This determiner Agrees with the possessor NP, and thereby values its case as genitive. This agreement is not seen overtly in English, but it is seen clearly in many other languages. (50) is an example from Turkish in which both agreement on the D+Noun combination and genitive case on the possessor are realized morphologically:

(50) ben-im kitab-ım; Hasan-ın kitab-ı (Kornfilt 1997:230)
I-GEN book-1sP Hasan-GEN book-3sP
'my book' 'Hasan's book'

Indeed, in Turkish, the relationship between genitive case and possessive agreement on N is parallel to the relationship between nominative and agreement on V across the board.

17.3.3.2 Case assigned by adpositions

The Agree approach might also be extended to case assignment to the objects of prepositions and postpositions. One can say that P has agreement features, which probe downward to find the nearest NP, agreeing with it and valuing its case feature. The case assigned by P might be dative in a language like German (51a), which distinguishes more cases (Emonds 1985:226–27), or 'objective' (not morphologically distinct from accusative) in a language like English (51b), which makes fewer distinctions.

(51) a. mit einem Computer 'with a.DAT computer' (German)
b. I voted for her in the last election

Normally, the NP that P agrees with and case marks will be the complement of P, but there may also be instances of P case marking the subject of its clausal complement, as in (44b), or in a construction like *With [her helping us], we can relax*. (Alternatively, if *for* in (44b) is taken to be a pure complementizer, then this is an instance of C assigning case downward to an NP via Agree.) It is worth bearing in mind, however, that the case assigned by Ps seems more irregular than the case assigned by Tense or v: it varies substantially from one P to another even in the same language. For example in a language like German or Russian, one P might assign accusative case (*für* 'for'), another genitive (*während* 'during'), and yet another dative case (Emonds 1985:226). So case assigned by Ps might be lexical case rather than structural case, as defined below.[28]

17.3.3.3 Semantic cases

Consider next the various cases other than nominative and accusative that are found inside clauses without an overt P: dative case in German to show the goal of motion, ablative case in Latin to show the source of motion, instrumental case in Greenlandic to show the instrument, still more exotic cases like the 'postelative' of Lezgian to express 'from behind' (Haspelmath 1993a:74), and so on. The number of such cases available in a language varies considerably, from four (German) to eighteen (Lezgian) or more. These cases seem to behave somewhat differently from the core structural–grammatical cases nominative and accusative. For these cases, the thematic role that an NP has and its morphological marking are closer to being in a one-to-one correspondence. Moreover, these cases do not tend to appear and disappear on NPs depending on structural factors like how many NPs there are or whether the clause is finite or non-finite the way that nominative and accusative do. These cases are thus treated differently in virtually every developed case theory, and they are known as semantic or inherent cases.

Indeed, in many approaches the semantic cases are analyzed essentially as Ps. When the marker of being a source is realized as a separate word, like *from* in English, it is called a preposition; when it is realized as an affix on the noun, it is traditionally called a case, like *-aj* in Lezgian (*sew-re-w-aj* 'from the bear'). But the one-word/two-word distinction is probably not very significant within generative syntax – as we have already seen concerning the relationship between Tense and verb in Section 17.2.1.1.

This relationship between semantic case and P can be developed in at least three ways. First, one can say that the P is phonologically null but assigns a special case like dative or ablative to its NP complement (Emonds 1985, McFadden 2004). This is the most likely analysis for many Germanic and Slavic languages. Second, one can say that the P is overt, it assigns phonologically null Case to NP, but then fuses with the NP at PF. This is the likely analysis for Hungarian (see den Dikken 2005: Section 4.2.3). Third, both elements could be spelled out overtly. This is probably the source of the bimorphemic and even trimorphemic cases found in languages with particularly large case systems, such as Finnish, Estonian, and Lezgian. (52) is a Lezgian example.

(52) rak'-ar.i-qh-aj   k'waC.i-n ses-er   ata-na   (Haspelmath 1993a:94)
 door-POSTEL   foot-GEN sound-PL come-AOR
 'from behind the door came the sound of footsteps'

Having a postelative case may seem very exotic, but the difference between Lezgian and English largely dissolves when one realizes that it decomposes into a morpheme meaning 'from' (*-aj*), a morpheme meaning 'behind' (*-qh*), and an oblique case morpheme (*-ari*) that is an element in all the complex cases. What we really have here is the same [$_{PP}$ P [$_{PP}$ P [NP]]] structure as in the English translation, with the lower P assigning oblique case to its NP complement, and both Ps combining with the noun to form a single word.

This being said, the exact boundary between inherent and structural case is not always crystal clear. This is true especially for the borderline cases, dative, genitive, and sometimes instrumental, which (depending on the language) seem to have some semantically predictable uses and other more grammatical uses. For example, dative case marks goals and beneficiaries in many languages (semantically predictable case) but it can also mark the lower agent of a morphological causative construction (structural case?). Whether one of these types of dative case reduces to the other, or whether one needs to accept that there really are two kinds of dative case, has not been settled.[29]

17.3.3.4 Lexical case

Yet another category of case is so-called lexical case. This kind of case is determined not by syntactic position (like structural case) or by thematic role (like semantic case), but by idiosyncratic lexical properties (see Woolford 2006 for discussion). A classic example is dative subjects in Icelandic (e.g., (15a), a more typical example of which is (53).

(53) henni   leiddust   þeir   (Taraldsen 1995:307)
      her.DAT   was.bored.by.3pS   they.NOM
      'she was bored with them'

There is a definite tendency for verbs that take experiencer subjects rather than true agents to have lexical dative subjects in Icelandic and other languages, but the matter varies idiosyncratically in ways that seem not fully predictable. Other non-agentive verbs in Icelandic demand that their subject be accusative or genitive, for example. Yet others ('love,' 'hate') take subjects with nominative case, assigned by T under agreement in the usual way. And the details vary significantly from language to language.

In some languages but not others, NPs with lexical case behave grammatically very much like subjects and objects that bear structural case, while in others they do not. Icelandic and German are otherwise similar languages that seem to differ in just this way; see Zaenen et al. 1985 and much subsequent literature. NPs with lexical case that behave like subjects and objects, as in Icelandic, are sometimes said to have quirky case. There is a very large and complex literature on these and related matters, with much debate about what quirky case means for case theory more generally.

17.3.4 Ergativity and parameters of case assignment

This brings us to the topic of ergative–absolutive case–marking systems, such as the one in Hindi mentioned briefly above (see also Section 5.4). In some languages, the relationship between case and thematic-role/syntactic position seems even less direct than in the European languages. Among these are the so-called ergative languages such as Basque and Hindi. The characteristic feature of ergative languages is that the subject of a transitive clause bears a distinct case (ergative), whereas the same case marking (called absolutive, or sometimes nominative) is used for both the subject of an intransitive clause and the object of a transitive clause. (54) gives a typical example from the Caucasian language Lezgian.

(54) a. stxa   k'wal.i-z xta-na   (Haspelmath 1993a:5)
        brother(ABS) house-to return-AOR
        'the brother came back home'
     b. wax-a   stxa   k'wal.i-z raqur-na
        sister-ERG brother(ABS) house-to send-AOR
        'the sister sent the brother home'

In many pairs, the subjects of transitive and intransitive verbs will have the same thematic role (e.g., agent, as in (54)), but different case marking. Conversely, the object in (54b) has a different thematic role from the subject in (54a), but the same case marking. So the mismatches between case and position or grammatical function are even more salient in these ergative languages than in the standard nominative–accusative language. General discussion of the topic of ergativity can be found in Dixon 1994.

17.3.4.1 Generative approaches to ergativity

Although the mismatch between thematic role and case marking in (some) ergative languages seems inescapable, one could imagine that case and syntactic position or grammatical function are still well aligned. This would be true if 'brother' is really the subject in (54b) as well as in (54a), even though that is not true of the English translation. This in turn would imply that the mapping between thematic roles and syntactic positions is fundamentally different in an ergative language than it is in an accusative language like English: the theme argument can be assigned to the subject position, and the agent argument to the complement of V position. This view was proposed in generative terms by Marantz (1984) for the Australian language Dyirbal, described by Dixon (1972); it is also approximately the idea that seems to be present in some functionalist approaches, including Dixon's. But considerations first raised by Anderson (1976) show that this is not true, at least for the large majority of ergative languages. In general, word order, control, binding, and other syntactic relations are what one would expect if the syntactic positions/grammatical functions were the same in ergative languages as in accusative languages. For example, it is the agentive subject that is controlled in English infinitival constructions like *Chris tried [PRO to examine the doctor]*. If the theme argument were truly the subject in ergative languages, one would expect them to have the equivalent of *Chris tried [the doctor to examine PRO]* – meaning what an English speaker means by *Chris tried to be examined by the doctor*, but with no hint of passive in the embedded clause. But this is not what typically happens in ergative languages: rather the element that is controlled in a non-finite clause (if any) is the same as in English. Overall, then, it seems that only case and perhaps agreement are different in most ergative languages, not all of syntax.[30] So ergativity is primarily a problem for the theory of case itself to address.

Generative analyses of ergative case patterns have changed significantly over the years with changes in the overall framework (Bok-Bennema 1991, Murasugi 1992, Bobaljik 1993). Probably the most widespread view at present subsumes ergative case to inherent or lexical case, rather than structural case (see also Chapter 5). In essence, this means that ergative case subjects like (54) in Lezgian are similar to quirky dative subjects like (53) in Icelandic. For example, Woolford (2006) claims that a transitive *v* assigns ergative case directly to its subject in SpecvP. This DP is then inactive for Agree, so T agrees with the object instead in a language like Hindi, assigning it nominative case. In an intransitive clause, ergative case is not assigned by *v*; T then agrees with the highest NP, the subject, as usual. The result is that the object of the transitive clause gets the same case (nominative) as the subject of the intransitive clause. Case and agreement are correlated in Hindi, as usual, once ergative is removed from the picture as being a different kind of case. Moreover, there is some lexical idiosyncrasy to ergative marking in Hindi and Basque, as one might expect on this view: these languages have a few intransitive verbs that have ergative subjects, and a few transitive verbs that do not – either because the theta-role of the subject is different, or as a purely idiosyncratic lexical stipulation. So it is plausible to say that Hindi is like Icelandic except that there are more verbs with lexical case subjects in Hindi. Lezgian could be analyzed in the same way, except that Agree between T and the absolutive NP is not overt in this language, just as Agree between T and the nominative NP is not overt in Japanese, under standard assumptions (see (4)).[31]

One should perhaps not get too comfortable with always treating ergative as an inherent or lexical case, though. Even in Hindi, it is not clear why ergative varies with the aspect of the clause, as shown again in (55). If ergative is an inherent case, which is tied closely to a particular thematic role or lexical item, we do not expect this variation.

(55) a. Anil kitaabẽ becegaa (=(5))
Anil.M(NOM) book-F.PL sell-FUT.M.SG
'Anil will sell (the) books'
b. Anil-ne kitaabẽ becĩĩ
Anil-ERG book-F.PL sell-PERF-F.PL
'Anil sold (the books)'

Furthermore, there are other ergative languages (Greenlandic, Chukchi, Shipibo) in which the distribution of ergative case seems perfectly regular: ergative shows up on all and only the subjects of two-argument verbs, never appearing on the subject of an intransitive, and never failing to appear on the subject of a transitive (Bobaljik 2008). Ergative case in Greenlandic or Chukchi may then be different from ergative case in

Hindi or Basque, behaving more like a structural case. So it is not clear that Woolford's proposal generalizes to all ergative languages.

17.3.4.2 Case and agreement in ergative languages

There are also ergative languages in which the relationship between case and agreement, which is so close in Hindi, breaks down entirely. Burushaski is a clear example, as analyzed by Baker (2008b:169–70, 204). In this language, T agrees with the thematic subject regardless of whether its case is ergative or nominative/absolutive. Similarly, transitive v agrees with some absolutives – those one would consider direct objects – but not with those that are agentive intransitive subjects (data from Willson 1996).

(56) a. acaanák <u>hilés</u>   <u>i-ír-imi</u>   (p. 19)
     suddenly boy.ABS 3.M-die-PAST.MsS
     'suddenly the boy died'   (T agrees with ABS 'boy')
   b. <u>hilés</u>-e **dasin** **mu**-yeéts-<u>imi</u>   (p. 17)
     boy-ERG girl.ABS FsO-see-PAST.MsS
     'the boy saw the girl'
                       (T agrees with ERG 'boy'; v agrees with ABS 'girl')

This lack of a relationship between case and agreement is a general property of Burushaski, holding also of object agreement initiated by v. (57) shows that object agreement is possible with dative objects as well as with nominative/absolutive ones:

(57) a. (u:ṇ)   <u>gu</u>-yɛts∧-m   (v agrees with NOM/ABS object)
       you-ABS 2sO-see-1sS   (Lorimer 1935)
       'I saw you'
   b. <u>u:ṇər</u>   hik tr∧ṇ <u>gu</u>-čič∧-m   (v agrees with DAT object)
       you-DAT one half 2sS-give-1sS   (Lorimer 1935)
       'I shall give a half to you'

Interestingly, there is also no uniqueness of person agreement in Burushaski of the kind that Chomsky derived for English from his Agree theory (see (48)). Both the main verb and the auxiliary (raising) verb agree in person with the subject argument in Burushaski:

(58) ja   be.∧d∧pi.ɛn ɛt-a   b-a   (double agreement with subject)
     I.ERG discourtesy do-1sS be-1sS   (Lorimer 1935)
     'I have committed a discourtesy'

Burushaski confirms indirectly that Chomsky was right to see these case-agreement phenomena as interrelated in English; it shows this by way of contrast. But it also shows us that it is not universally true that case and agreement are two sides of the same coin. Baker (2008b: Chapter 5) thus claims that there is a second major parameter that governs the behavior of agreement in languages of the world, stated as follows:

(59) *The Case Dependence of Agreement Parameter (CDAP)*:
F agrees with DP/NP only if F values the Case feature of DP/NP or vice versa.

In Hindi, the CDAP is set to yes (see (55)); in Burushaski it is set to no. This parameter is not only relevant to ergative languages: Baker claims that it also distinguishes IE from Bantu, given that Bantu languages also allow person agreement on every verb in auxiliary-plus-main verb constructions (Kinyalolo 1991, Carstens 2001, Baker 2008b), unlike IE.

17.3.5 Dependent case

We now face a new question: If ergative and absolutive case do not come from agreement with heads like T and *v* in Burushaski, where do they come from? What determines the case of NPs in languages where case and agreement are more or less independent?

There is an alternative approach to structural case assignment that might make a contribution here. Marantz 1991 presents a view of case assignment in which functional heads have little or no direct impact. What is crucial to accusative case assignment in his proposal is not that there be a particular functional head nearby, like transitive *v*, but rather that there be a second NP higher than the NP to be assigned accusative – namely the subject. This can be stated as in (60a).[32] (This precise formulation is from Baker and Vinokurova 2010.)

(60) a. If there are two distinct argumental NPs in the same phase such that NP_1 c-commands NP_2, then value the case feature of NP_2 as *accusative* (unless NP_1 has already been marked for case).
b. If there are two distinct NPs in the same phase such that NP_1 c-commands NP_2, then value the case feature of NP_1 as *ergative*.
c. Otherwise, mark NP as nominative/absolutive.

One attractive property of Marantz's system is that it works just as well for ergative languages as for nominative–accusative languages. Ergative languages are simply those that choose to mark morphologically the higher of the two NPs in a local domain (e.g., a single clause) rather than the lower one, as stated in (60b). Then the subject of a transitive clause gets specially marked, rather than the object. Nominative/absolutive case is simply a default case that is assigned to anything that is not marked accusative by (60a) (in a nominative–accusative language) or ergative by (60b) (in an ergative–absolutive language). See Baker and Vinokurova (2010) for some detailed arguments that (60a) is a more accurate rule for accusative case assignment in the Turkic language Sakha than the Chomskian view where accusative case is assigned by agreement with a designated functional category; see also Baker (to appear) on Amharic.

Another attraction of Marantz's system is that it extends nicely to so-called tripartite case systems like Nez Perce. What is special about Nez

Perce is that it has three distinct structural cases: nominative, for the subject of intransitive verbs; ergative, for the subject of transitive verbs; and accusative, for the object of transitive verbs. This is shown in (61). (See Woolford 1997 and Deal 2010 for data and alternative analyses.)

(61) a. hi-páay-na háama   Nez Perce   (Rude 1986:126)
      3S-arrive-ASP man
      'the man arrived'
   b. háama-nm hi-**néec**-'wi-ye   **wewúkiye-ne**   (Rude 1986:127)
      man-ERG   3S-pO-shoot-ASP elk-ACC
      'the man shot the elk(pl)'

Nez Perce then is simply a language in which both (60a) and (60b) are in use within the same grammar. And if Legate (2008) is right (see note 31), this kind of case system is more widespread than is usually realized, so accounting for it theoretically is important.

17.3.6 Differential argument marking

So far we have assumed that the case marking borne by each grammatical function is relatively uniform in a given language. However, this is not always true. The data in (62) from the Turkic language Sakha is a fairly typical case in point. Here one can observe that sometimes the object is marked accusative, with the suffix -*y*, and sometimes it is morphologically unmarked, just as nominative subjects are in this language.

(62) a. Masha salamaat-y   türgennik sie-te   (*salamaat)
        Masha porridge-ACC   quickly   eat-PAST.3sS   (porridge)
        'Masha ate the porridge quickly'
     b. Masha türgennik   salamaat sie-te   (#salamaat-y)
        Masha quickly   porridge eat-PAST.3sS   porridge-ACC
        'Masha ate porridge quickly'

More specifically, when the object is interpreted as definite or specific, it is marked with the accusative suffix; when it is interpreted as a non-specific indefinite it is not marked accusative. This is an instance of what is known as differential object marking. A seminal discussion of the phenomenon in various languages is Aissen (2003).

It is notable that the semantic distinction between an accusative NP and a bare NP in Sakha is very reminiscent of Diesing's (1992) semantic difference between moved and unmoved direct objects in German, discussed in Section 17.2.3.4. The connection seems even greater when one notes that the unmarked word order for accusative objects in Sakha is different from that of caseless objects: caseless objects must be immediately adjacent to the verb (62b), whereas accusative objects most naturally come before adverbs or VP-internal PPs (62a). So we have evidence that object shift exists in Sakha, and it has the same kind of effect on the interpretation of NPs as in German. This object shift also seems to feed accusative case assignment. We can capture this using Marantz's notion of dependent case, if we say that the local domain that must have two NPs in it for case marking to happen is not the clause, but rather the phase. Recall that transitive verb phrases are a type of phase. If the object stays in VP, there is only one NP in the VP phase and one in the CP phase, so (60a) does not apply, and both NPs are left unmarked for case. In contrast, if the object moves out of VP, then it escapes the VP phase as well as the domain of existential closure. Now there are two NPs in the larger CP phase, and (60a) marks the lower one accusative. This then is an account of one sort of differential object marking, summed up graphically in (63). We see that object shift can feed accusative case assignment, much as it feeds agreement in languages like Zulu (see (28)).

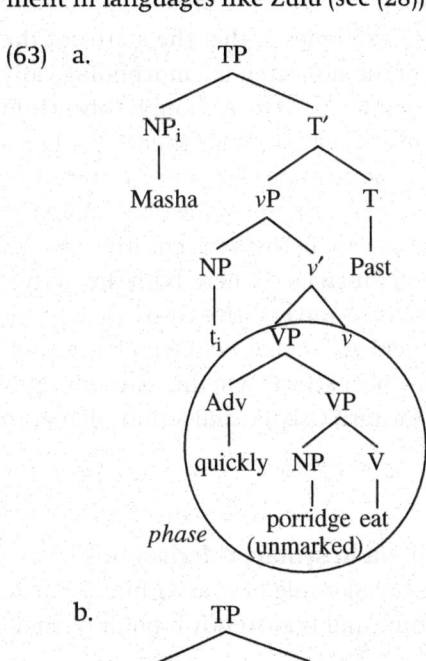

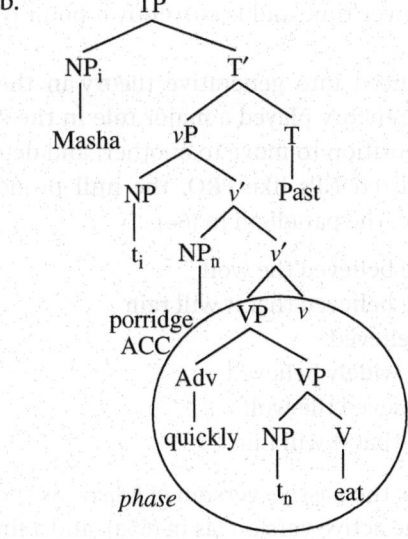

(63) a.

[Tree diagram: TP with NP$_i$ (Masha) and T'; T' branches to vP and T (Past); vP contains NP (t$_i$) and v' (VP, v); VP contains Adv (quickly) and VP (NP porridge, V eat). The phase circle encloses the lower vP/VP region, labeled "phase" and "(unmarked)".]

b.

[Tree diagram: TP with NP$_i$ (Masha) and T'; T' branches to vP and T (Past); vP contains NP (t$_i$) and v'; v' branches to NP$_n$ (porridge ACC) and v' (VP, v); VP contains Adv (quickly) and VP (NP t$_n$, V eat). The phase circle encloses the lower VP region, labeled "phase".]

A further fact about Nez Perce supports this view. (64) shows that if the object is indefinite in Nez Perce it is not marked for accusative case and the verb does not agree with it. In contrast, (61b) shows that if the object is definite, then it is marked accusative and is agreed with. Thus we see that object shift can feed case and agreement in the same language. (Nez Perce is a language with very free surface word order, so it is not clear if object shift can be detected via surface word order as well.)

(64) háama   hi-'wí-ye   wewúkiye   (Rude 1998:552)
     man.NOM 3S-shoot-ASP   elk.NOM
     'the man shot an elk'

The other striking thing about these examples is that the status of the object also affects the case marking of the subject: it is a morphologically bare nominative form in (64), but ergative in (61b). Although this would be somewhat mysterious in a purely Agree-based case theory (T agrees with the subject in both examples), it makes perfect sense in terms of dependent case assignment. The movement that puts the object into the same phase as the subject inevitably feeds both the accusative rule in (60a) and the ergative rule in (60b) in languages where both are active. This supports the idea that accusative case and ergative case can be exact opposites within the same system.[33] Other languages in which the specificity and/or surface position of the object affects whether the subject is marked ergative or not include Ika, Eastern Ostyak, and Kanuri (Baker to appear).

17.3.7 On the role of case assignment in syntactic derivations

In closing, let us briefly consider the broader role of case within syntactic theory. This also has changed over time and is currently a point of some controversy.

When case was first introduced into generative theory in the early 1980s, it was thought that case theory played a major role in the syntax, forcing NPs generated in one position to move to another, and determining the distribution of specialized NPs like PRO, the null pronominal anaphor. Consider, for example, the paradigm in (65).

(65) a. Little Red Riding Hood believed the wolf
     b. Little Red Riding Hood believed that it will rain
     c. the wolf was widely believed
     d. that it would rain was widely believed
     e. *it/there was widely believed the wolf
     f. it was widely believed that it will rain

Why can't the NP *the wolf* follow the passive version of *believe*, as shown in (65e)? Such an NP can follow the active version, as in (65a), and a finite CP can follow both the active version and the passive version, as shown in (65b,f). Why then must *the wolf* move to the subject position in order to get a grammatical outcome, as in (65c)?

It was thought in the 1980s and beyond that this could be derived from Case Theory. The line of thinking went as follows (based on a letter of Jean-Roger Vergnaud to Chomsky, incorporated into Chomsky 1981). In Greek, noun (phrases) must always be inflected for some case or another: one has *anthrop-os* 'man-NOM,' *anthrop-on* 'man-ACC,' etc., but never *anthrop* 'man.' There must therefore be (morpho)syntactic rules that say which forms are used where in Greek. These rules or principles are the core domain of case theory, as we have been discussing. Suppose, however, that there are gaps in these rules – syntactic positions to which no case assignment rule applies. A noun like *anthrop* 'man' could not be used in such a position, because one would not know which form to use. However, phonologically null NPs do not have inflectional endings. Hence, one might expect that they could be used in such positions where overt NPs cannot be. Moreover, argument-type categories other than NP, such as CP and PP, are not inflected for case either. Therefore they too might be usable in caseless positions. Finally, Vergnaud and Chomsky assume that English is really just like Latin and Greek in these respects: its paradigm for the word 'man' is *man* (NOM), *man* (ACC), *man* (DAT), and so on – but there is no form for caseless 'man' in English any more than there is in Greek.

This then gives a way of thinking about the paradigm in (65). We can say that part of the difference between the passive form *was believed* and the active verb *believed* is that only the latter assigns accusative case. The complement of the passive verb is thus one of these caseless positions. It can be occupied by a CP (65f), or by a null NP such as the trace of *the wolf* (65c), but it cannot be occupied by the overt NP *the wolf*, there being no such form. (65e) is then a violation of the Case Filter, stated as in (66).

(66) *Overt NP if NP does not receive case.

In contrast (65c) is grammatical because here the overt NP *the wolf* is in SpecTP position, a position that is assigned nominative by the finite T.[34] The conclusion was that Case Theory can explain why movement is required in some situations but not others.

Although this form of explanation has not been entirely rejected by generative linguists, there is now much uncertainty about whether it is the best way to explain facts like these. Doubt has crept in for several reasons, many of them enumerated by Marantz (1991) and McFadden (2004). For example, one needs another condition anyway, the so-called Extended Projection Principle (EPP), to regulate the distribution of expletives. The EPP says roughly that the SpecTP position must be filled (in English). This is needed in order to say why the pronoun *it* is required in (65f), why one cannot just say *Was widely believed that it will rain*. Moving the complement of the verb to SpecTP position in (65c,d) is another way to satisfy this condition. Therefore, if one were to say that for some reason no suitable expletive place-holder is available in (65e), or that NP-movement takes priority over expletive insertion for some principled reasons, then the EPP would be enough to force movement in this example, and the Case Filter in (66) might no longer be needed for this. Moreover, the case-theory story threatens to unravel if the case system has any sort of default case-assignment mechanism, which gives case to NPs not otherwise case marked. Yet most theories do in fact make use of some such mechanism, such as default nominative assignment for hanging topics and other isolated NPs (cf. (60c)). Finally, Marantz and others point out that quirky case-marked NPs in Icelandic move to SpecTP positions in passives and unaccusatives, and must be controlled PRO in infinitives, just as in English. This holds true even though one would know perfectly well from the lexical entry of the verb what case form the relevant argument of the verb should have (e.g. dative). Because of considerations like these, some generative linguists have abandoned the Case Filter entirely, and indeed do not assign any role to case in the syntax, claiming that there is nothing to case theory beyond determining what form a particular NP will have at PF (see also Bobaljik 2008).

But there are still some residues of the 1980s account to be dealt with. First, the EPP is hardly anyone's favorite primitive principle itself; conceptually it might be more desirable to explain it in terms of something like the Case Filter, rather than the other way around (see, for example, Bošković 2002c). Second, questions remain about the subject position of non-finite verbs. Another major use of the Vergnaud–Chomsky Case Filter was to explain paradigms like (67).

(67) a. [that Chris will declare bankruptcy] is unfortunate
b. [*Chris to declare bankruptcy] would be unfortunate
c. [(PRO) to declare bankruptcy] would be unfortunate
d. [for Chris to declare bankruptcy] would be unfortunate

The subject of the clause in brackets can be an overt NP if the T is finite (67a), or if the prepositional complementizer *for* is included (67d). However, if neither of these elements is present, then the subject of the clause can only be the null pronominal anaphor PRO (here meaning roughly 'one, people in general'), as shown in (67b) versus (67c) (on PRO, see Chapter 16). In classical Vergnaud–Chomsky terms, this followed from the Case Filter. Finite T is a case assigner, marking the subject in (67a) nominative; *for* is a case assigner, marking the subject in (67d) accusative, as we have seen. But there is no case-assigning category nearby in (67b,c) so *Chris* is not case-marked, in violation of (66); thus only (67c) is possible. This paradigm is quite different from the one in (65), in that it does not involve movement or the distribution of expletive pronouns. Thus there is little chance that (67) can be explained by the EPP in a similar way.[35] Critics of the Case Filter can with some justice point to gaps and stipulations in the classical account of (67), but it is not clear that anything significantly better has come to the fore. (See also Baker and Vinokurova 2010, who find a role for the Case Filter in the details of Sakha.)

17.4 Conclusion

This last discussion illustrates on a small scale what is an overall theme of the chapter as a whole: that agreement and case are lively areas of ongoing inquiry, an integral part in one way or another of the larger generative enterprise. We have seen some of the key data that generative theories have concerned themselves with in these domains, and some of the leading ideas that have been used to address that data. We have also gotten a taste of how thought has progressed in recent years on these topics, some of what has been gained, and some hints as to what remains to be done in these ever-fascinating areas.

Notes

1. Abbreviations used in the glosses of examples include: ABS, absolutive; ACC, accusative; AFF, affirmative; AOR, aorist; APPL, applicative; ASP, aspect; CAUS, causative; DAT, dative; DET, determiner; ERG, ergative; EXT, aspect extension; F, feminine; FUT, future; FV, final vowel; GEN, genitive; HAB, habitual; III, gender class (Tsez); M, masculine; N, neuter; NEG, negative; NOM, nominative; PASS, passive; PAST, past; PERF, perfective; PL, plural; POSS, possessive; POSTEL, postelative; PRES, present; PTPL, participle; SG, singular; SUBJ, subjunctive; T, tense; TOP, topic. Arabic numerals refer to noun class in Bantu languages; otherwise combinations of a numeral (1, 2, 3), lower-case letter (s, p), and upper-case letter (S, O) express the person, number, and grammatical function of an agreement marker.
2. This does not show up as clearly in Siewierska (2005), who gives a small but non-negligible list of languages with only P (patient, roughly object) agreement (24/378). This could be an artifact of her not distinguishing cliticized pronouns from agreement; see Section 17.2.3.5 for some relevant discussion.
3. Traditional X-bar Theory distinguishes three kinds of positions: specifiers, complements, and adjoined positions. In some versions (e.g., Chomsky 1993), adjoined positions form a natural class with specifier positions, such that they too can be agreed with. An alternative, then, is to say that the trace of the moved phrase is adjoined to PtplP in (11b) – as Kayne (1989) actually assumed for rather technical reasons, which I do not discuss here. However, it is currently somewhat uncertain whether

4. The contracted singular form *there's* is notably better than *there is* in (13b), especially in informal and unguarded speech; see Sobin (1997), among others. If examples like (13b,d) are removed from consideration as being marginal and explicitly learned 'viruses', as Sobin suggests, the weight of the evidence might switch back to the SHAH. However, I believe that Sobin's data are consistent with the judgments in (13) being solid and grammatical, with messiness entering in only when the subject is a conjoined NP.
5. The facts in (13) were of course known prior to Chomsky (2000b), but they were thought not to be a problem for the SHAH because one could say that the NP *five linguists* moves *covertly* to the SpecTP position where it undergoes agreement. There have been various ways of caching out the notion of 'covert movement' at different stages of the theory, but they all capitalize on the fact that SpecTP is occupied by expletive *there*, a meaningless element that does not necessarily need to be present at LF. See Chomsky (1986b) for one early version, and Bobaljik (2002a) for a more recent one. Facts like (13) thus do not necessarily kill the SHAH, but they do make the AGRH seem simpler and more straightforward.
6. Den Dikken (2006b:98–102) argues that the PP is not actually in SpecTP in (14), but rather an empty category is. But the fact remains that the overt NP *peanuts* is *not* in SpecTP, and yet seems to be agreed with, prima facie evidence for the AGRH. Also relevant here is Diercks's (2010) study of Lubusuku, which has two distinct forms of locative inversion, one in which T agrees with the fronted locative as in Kilega (12b), and one in which it agrees with the postverbal subject as in English (14).
7. Chomsky (2000b) made this point using dative subject constructions like (53) in Icelandic. However, the two constructions are treated similarly in many generative accounts; see below for some discussion.
8. However, interesting alternatives exist. For example, Carstens (2011) argues that it is the gender feature, not a case feature, that makes nominals eligible for agreement in Bantu languages, in an effort to capture the fact that the relationship between case and agreement seems different in those languages. Markman (2009) proposes another variant, claiming that agreement must delete some feature (s) on the agreed with nominal: if the nominal has case features (as in IE), those are affected, but if a nominal does not (Bantu, Mohawk), then its phonological features are deleted, leading to a kind of non-configurationality.
9. Questions have been raised in the literature about how the activity condition relates to the intervention condition. In particular, does an NP that is not active for agreement because it does not have an unvalued case feature still prevent T from agreeing with a more remote NP? Chomsky (2000b, 2001) says that agreement is blocked in these circumstances, based on data from dative subject constructions in Icelandic (see

Schütze 1997) – the so-called 'defective intervention effect.' But it is controversial whether this is a robust phenomenon. First, the Icelandic facts themselves turn out to be quite complex and somewhat variable across speakers and constructions (Bobaljik 2008, Sigurðsson and Holmberg 2008). Second, the empirical situation is complicated by the fact that many other languages, superficially similar to Icelandic, do allow full agreement between T and a nominative NP of any person in the presence of a dative experiencer, including German, Russian, and Greek. Therefore, theoretical discussion of this phenomenon is ongoing.

10. Note that there may be some redundancy between the activity condition and the phase condition. (17b) can also be ruled out by the activity condition, given that *five linguists* has its case valued as nominative by the embedded T. Conversely, (16) could be ruled out by the phase condition condition if PPs are on the list of categories that count as phases (see Baker 2008b:44 n. 16 for a possible advantage to this).

11. Note that the top-down logic of Boeckx and Niinuma's claim about how object agreement should behave within this theory of agreement is valid even if the particular phenomenon that they were discussing (honorific marking in Japanese) is not properly subsumed to agreement – a controversial matter.

12. See for example Baker (to appear) on Amharic. However complex and largely open issues can arise when the goal is described as bearing dative case, rather than being a bare NP or an obvious PP. It can be far from obvious what the structure of such goals is and how the principles of agreement apply to them, and languages may differ in this respect. Further complexities arise in languages (Basque, Southern Tiwa, etc.), where the verb agrees with three arguments rather than two. Here much depends on whether one analyzes the language as having a third agreeing functional head in the structure (cf. Adger and Harbour 2007 on Kiowa), or whether there are only two agreeing heads but one of them agrees more than once (e.g., Baker (2008b:94–102) on Nahuatl). One also must be particularly careful to distinguish object agreement from cliticized pronouns when considering these matters; see Section 17.2.3.5 for some discussion.

13. However, languages may vary on this point. For example, Amharic does permit object agreement on the passive of a ditransitive verb (Baker, to appear). It is conceivable, then, that there is a dedicated AgrO head in Amharic, whereas this is conflated with transitive *v* into a single head in Swahili, Mohawk, Nahuatl, etc.

14. However, some have proposed analyses in which NP moves to SpecPP so as to agree with P, and P then moves to some higher head to restore the observed P-NP order in Welsh (see Koopman 1993 and Kayne 1994:50). These more complex analyses would be consistent with the SHAH.

15. It remains, however, to be seen if the semantic distinction between agreed-with and unagreed-with objects in (say) Zulu is *precisely* the

same as the semantic distinction between moved and unmoved objects in Germanic. Often the descriptive literature on languages with object agreement is not detailed enough to clearly distinguish specificity from definiteness. This is an important topic for further research.

16. Preminger (2009) and Nevins (2010) are two recent attempts to propose criteria for distinguishing agreement from cliticization in the general case. But see Baker (to appear) for some doubts about the applicability of their criteria to instances of object agreement in particular.

17. For some discussion of the EPP and EPP features, see Chapter 4.

18. This is characteristic of the HPSG literature, for example Wechsler and Żlatić (2003), but Chomsky has occasionally suggested the same thing in passing remarks. On HPSG, see Chapter 7.

19. Another apparent difference between agreement on adjectives and agreement on verbs is that verbs can agree with NPs in person as well as number and gender (the latter seen in Semitic and Bantu, although not in IE), whereas adjectives do not. This has been taken to be a consequence of there being two different kinds of agreement – concord agreement and index agreement – in the HPSG literature. Baker (2008b), however, argues at length that this difference is explicable in terms of independently motivated differences in the structural configurations that adjectives and verbs appear in. According to him, a category can only agree with an NP in person if a projection of that category merges directly with the agreed-with NP (the Structural Condition on Person Agreement). Note that the adjective does not merge with the subject in the typical adjectival structure in (38), whereas T does merge with the subject in the typical clausal structure in (9). Baker goes on to show that in more specialized structures in which T does not merge with the NP it agrees with, T like A loses the ability to agree in person as well as number.

20. Although perhaps determiners can sometimes assign case to their complements, depending on their lexical properties: some quantifiers in Russian take NP complements in genitive case, for example.

21. In the 1980s, 'Case' (with an initial capital 'C') referred to 'abstract/structural case' (case assigned in particular structural configurations, and not necessarily morphologically explicit; see Section 17.3.7, below), as distinct from 'case,' which referred to (overt) morphological case. Throughout this handbook, this distinction is not orthographically expressed, in line with more recent practice in the field.

22. The adjustments need not be particularly complex, however. For example, T governs the subject in SpecTP if the notion c-command is replaced by m-command in the sense of Chomsky (1986a:8). Moreover, this together with Kayne's (1994) treatment of specifiers as adjuncts could be used to account for Exceptional Case-Marking examples like

(44a) in terms of government as well (Marcel den Dikken, personal communication). Hence, a return to some form of government within Minimalism is not inconceivable.

23. Note that for this account to work we must also say that the nonfinite clause in (47a) is not a phase, so that Agree between v and NP does not violate the phase condition. Chomsky claims that finite CPs are phases, but non-finite TPs not immediately contained in CP are not.

24. Note that the phase condition on Agree implies either that the verb phrase in an 'unaccusative' structure like (45b) is not a phase (Chomsky's view), or else that the theme argument moves out of the verb phrase prior to Agree taking place (also sufficient, at least for this example).

25. Various counterexamples to Burzio's generalization have been pointed out in the literature; see, for example, Sobin (1985) on the Ukrainian passive. This suggests that the principles involved may not be absolute, but it does not take away the burden of explaining those (many) situations in which it is true – for example, why *Sink them in the harbor is impossible as an equivalent to (45b) in English.

26. This reasoning only goes through if the agreeing functional head does in fact value the case features of the agreed with NP. An adjective agreeing with a given NP does not prevent further agreement with that NP precisely because the adjective does not assign case, according to Chomsky (cf. (40)). He suggests that this is because the adjective agrees only in number and gender but not in person, but see Carstens (2001) for a critique of this aspect of Chomsky's proposal. Various slightly non-standard systems also exist in which an NP can be assigned case more than once, with one case overwriting the other.

27. Comrie (1981b) says that one dialect of Tabasaran has fifty-three cases – although many of these can be morphologically decomposed, as discussed for Lezgian below.

28. Part of the reason why the case assigned by P is so variable probably has to do with the fact that the historical origins of Ps can be quite variable. For example, Ps can be derived from or contain a relational noun (e.g., *beside* in English); these are often the ones that take genitive complements. Other Ps can be derived historically from verbal participles (cf. *concerning, during* in English); these are prone to assigning accusative case. How much of this history should be recapitulated in the synchronic formal analysis is uncertain. In some IE languages, the same P can take an accusative NP or a dative NP, depending on whether the meaning is directional or locational; see Caha (2009:167–75) for an interesting recent analysis.

29. See, for example, Baker and Vinokurova (2010) for discussion of dative case in the Turkic language Sakha, which is relevant to these questions.

30. There is, however, some research in the tradition of Keenan and Comrie's (1977) Accessibility Hierarchy that may point to another syntactic difference: in some ergative languages, the object (absolutive) but not the subject (ergative) nominal can be extracted, whereas this pattern is not typically found in accusative languages. See Campana (1992), among others, for references and analysis in generative terms. See also Bittner and Hale (1996b) for a comprehensive and nuanced generative approach to ergative languages.

31. Building on Woolford's view, Legate (2008) argues that at least some of the ergativity phenomenon may in fact be a mistake, the result of syntacticians being somewhat naive about morphology. She argues that, in many ergative Australian languages and others, transitive objects receive accusative case from the verb and intransitive subjects receive nominative case from T, much as in accusative languages. The difference is simply that these two cases are not spelled out with different morphemes at PF in the ergative languages (although inherent ergative on a transitive subject is). Her crucial argument depends on case concord inside NPs, where one element of the NP (e.g., a pronoun) does happen to manifest a nominative–accusative distinction. The concord phenomenon then suggests that this case must therefore be present more widely.

32. An important predecessor to this view is the 'Case in Tiers' approach of Yip et al. (1987). However, Marantz's version extends more readily to tripartite case systems like Nez Perce's in (61). Marantz's idea also corresponds quite directly to the insight of Comrie (1981a:117–20), who claims that the communicative function of case is to distinguish the NPs in clauses that have more than one.

33. See Deal (2010) for a different analysis of these facts within a nonstandard agreement based theory.

34. Of course, some particular version of the case marking rules must be used along with such an account. The rules in question could be either 1980s era rules of the form 'an active verb (but not a passive verb) assigns ACC to an NP that it governs' or contemporary rules of the form 'active v Agrees, but passive v does not Agree.' This form of explanation can be agnostic as to the exact mechanisms of case assignment.

35. Note also that *unfortunate* is not a predicate of obligatory control, so there is no reason to think that PRO in (67c) is needed for lexical semantic reasons, as could be the case for the complement of a verb like *try*, in partially similar examples like *Chris tried PRO/*John to win.*

18
The locality of syntactic dependencies

Marcel den Dikken and Antje Lahne

18.1 Introduction

One of the central properties of human language is recursion: a finite number of symbols can be reassembled into hierarchical structures by means of self-embedding, thus yielding a potentially infinite number of different sentences, and sentences of infinite length (Chomsky 1957). This might lead one to expect that syntactic dependencies, such as filler–gap dependencies and reference relations, are unbounded, too. Almost from its inception, however, syntactic theory of Chomskyan orientation has recognized that syntactic dependencies can span only a limited portion of structure, and that apparent long-distance dependencies typically consist of a succession of local dependencies. This property of syntactic dependencies is called *locality*. The earliest generative work on locality concentrated primarily on filler–gap dependencies (Chomsky 1964b, Ross 1967a); but referential dependencies (Chomsky 1973; see Chapter 15) and predication relations (Williams 1980; see chapter 10) were quickly shown to obey locality restrictions as well. Locality is thus a pervasive property of syntactic dependencies:

Locality as a property of syntactic dependencies
Syntactic dependencies of all types are confined to a limited portion of structure.

Because of its universality, locality is one of the pivotal issues for any formal theory of grammar. Two research questions are central in the pursuit of a principled theory of locality: (a) How is locality motivated and defined? (b) How big are locality domains? These questions will be at the forefront throughout the discussion in this chapter.

Some of the early generative locality principles addressed both referential and filler–gap dependencies; few have succeeded in unifying the locality conditions imposed on these two types of dependencies (but see the 'generalized binding' approach of Aoun 1986). At present, a fully general theory of syntactic locality is non-existent. In this chapter, we will focus on the locality of filler–gap dependencies, quintessentially represented by *wh*-movement, and sketch a historical perspective on its development.[1]

The historical development of the generative-syntactic theory of locality is not a linear one – but at the same time, it is also emphatically not the case that, as the Stoics said, *panta rhei kai oudhen menei* ('everything flows and nothing stays'): the development of the theory has proceeded through a succession of cycles, with every completion of a cycle marking increased empirical coverage but typically also a more complex theory, opening the search for a leaner theory that strives to eventually attain a higher level of empirical adequacy than its predecessor.

The exact definition of the local domain in syntax (whether it be called 'cyclic node,' 'bounding node,' 'barrier,' or 'phase') has varied substantially throughout the history of generative grammar; and the extent and density of successive-cyclic movement derivations is also a matter of long-standing debate. As a result, there is to date no broad consensus on the core issues in the theory of the locality of filler–gap dependencies. Certain clear trends can be discovered, however, as we will show in this chapter.

Throughout the development of the theory of locality, we find a basic split between two notions – what we will call *absolute* and *relative* barriers for syntactic dependencies. Absolute barriers are formed by a node in the tree that will not have any movement go beyond it. Examples of this type of barrier are Ross's (1967a) island constraints, Chomsky's (1973) Subjacency Condition, and Huang's (1982a) Condition on Extraction Domain. Chomsky (1986a) presents an algorithm for the computation of such absolute obstacles (transparently termed 'barriers'[2]), and the cyclic Spell-out theory of current Minimalism seeks to derive absolute barrierhood from ideas about the relationship between syntax and the sound and meaning interfaces, via the Phase Impenetrability Condition.

Historically older than the absolute barriers approach is the notion of a relative barrier. The basic idea here is that syntactic dependencies between a filler and a gap are blocked by the intervention of a closer element of the same type (usually a potential antecedent for the gap). Examples are the Superiority Condition (Chomsky 1973), the theory of Relativized Minimality (Rizzi 1990a), and the Minimal Link Condition (Chomsky 1995c), all ultimately successors to the A-over-A Principle (Chomsky 1964b).

Though at different stages the theory has tended toward either absolute or relative barriers, it seems unlikely that all empirical phenomena would fit into a single type of explanation. The two conceptions are not incompatible. It is therefore reasonable to expect principles of both types to co-exist, with some locality effects being exponents of absolute barrierhood whereas others are derived by principles invoking relative barriers. Moreover, it is possible that some of the locality effects that have been tackled in syntax (e.g., the many 'selective islands' discovered thanks to Relativized Minimality) are better accounted for in the semantic component (see Szabolcsi and den Dikken 2003 and references cited there). The central task of the syntactic theory of locality is to model the division of labor in such a way that overlaps in explanation between principles of absolute and relative barrierhood, and between principles of syntax and semantics, are avoided.

18.2 Locality in early Chomskyan generative grammar

18.2.1 The A-over-A Principle

In generative syntax, the study of locality restrictions on syntactic dependencies (especially filler–gap or movement dependencies) finds its origin in Chomsky (1964b), where a condition is introduced (later to be called the 'A-over-A' Principle, where 'A' is a variable for a particular kind of constituent) that accounts for the fact that a *wh*-fronting sentence of the type in (1b) lacks one of the readings of its supposed underlier, (1a). The sentence in (1a) is three-ways ambiguous, supporting all of the syntactic parses given in (2a–c), paraphrased below the structures.[3] The *wh*-fronting construction in (1b) supports two of these readings, but is unable to have the gerundial phrase construed as a reduced relative clause (as in (2c)).

(1) a. Mary saw the boy walking toward the railroad station
    b. Who did Mary see walking toward the railroad station?

(2) a. [$_{IP}$ Mary$_i$ [$_{VP}$ [$_{VP}$ saw [$_{DP}$ the boy]] [$_{SC}$ PRO$_i$ [$_{VP}$ *walking toward the railroad station*]]]]
    ('Mary saw the boy as she was walking toward the railroad station')
    b. [$_{IP}$ Mary [$_{VP}$ saw [$_{SC}$ [$_{NP}$ the boy] [$_{VP}$ *walking toward the railroad station*]]]]
    ('Mary saw that the boy was walking toward the railroad station')
    c. [$_{IP}$ Mary [$_{VP}$ saw [$_{NP}$ [$_{NP}$ the boy] [$_{RRC}$ (...) [$_{VP}$ *walking toward the railroad station*]]]]]
    ('Mary saw the boy who was walking toward the railroad station')

Chomsky (1964b:931) argues that the fact that in (2c) the NP *the boy* cannot be replaced with *who* and undergo *wh*-fronting by itself is due to the fact that there is a larger constituent of category NP that is eligible for *wh*-fronting in this structure: *the boy walking toward the railroad station*. The theory imposes "a general requirement that the dominating, rather than the dominated, element must always be selected" in configurations of this type. Chomsky formulates the condition informally as one that "asserts ... that if the phrase X of category A is embedded within a larger phrase ZXW which is also of category A, then no rule applying to the category A applies to X but only to ZXW," and he suggests that this condition "when appropriately formalized, might then be proposed as a hypothetical linguistic universal" (p. 931).

Chomsky (1964b) does not name the condition just described. The name by which it is generally known, the A-over-A Principle, is due to Ross (1967a[1986]:10). It applies to (2b) under specific assumptions (embedded in our structure in (2c)), at least one of which is now generally rejected: that the restrictive relative clause is merged with the determiner+noun constituent *the boy* as a whole. It has been generally understood at least since McCawley (1981) that restrictive relatives are in the scope of the definite article, hence should not be merged with a constituent containing the definite article; what we need instead is something like (2c′) (which adopts the DP hypothesis; see Section 11.8).

(2c′) [IP Mary [VP saw [DP the [NP [NP boy] [RRC (...) [VP *walking toward the railroad station*]]]]]]

With the reduced relative clause taken to combine just with *boy* (with *the* merging with the constituent *boy walking toward the railroad station*), *the boy* is not a constituent in the structure in (2c′), hence ineligible for *wh*-movement in the form of *who*. The A-over-A Principle thus does not seem necessary for deriving the lack of a reduced relative clause reading for *walking toward the railroad station* in (1b) – which was the original impetus for the development of the condition. Nor does it seem, with hindsight, to be operative in the derivation of the cases to which Chomsky (1973:235) applies the condition (which are all based on a particular understanding of the passive transformation that is no longer current).[4]

Furthermore, the principle makes a number of incorrect empirical predictions. As Ross (1967a) shows, there are well-formed examples that are ruled out by the A-over-A Principle. A grammatical example involving movement of a *wh*-element out of an NP is given in (3a). On the other hand, there are ill-formed sentences that are not excluded by the A-over-A Principle, such as example (3b). The ungrammaticality of (3b) is not strictly speaking an A-over-A effect, as the dominating category is different from the moved category (AP-movement from an NP); however, the effect seems to be of the same type: the presence of a higher, more inclusive category blocks movement of a more deeply embedded category.

(3) a. Who would you approve of [NP my seeing [NP *ec*]]?
    b. *[AP How intelligent] do you have [NP a *ec* sister]?

The A-over-A Principle is thus both too strong and too weak. There are two ways of proceeding in such a situation: we could either revise the principle in such a way that it makes empirically correct predictions, or abandon it and replace it with a different constraint or set of constraints (Ross 1967a [1986]:2).

The first route is taken in Chomsky (1968, 1973), where the A-over-A Principle is reformulated with reference to cyclic nodes, as in (4):

(4) *A-over-A Principle* (Chomsky 1968, 1973)
If a transformation applies to a structure of the form $[_\alpha \ldots [_A \ldots] \ldots]$ where α is a cyclic node, then it must be so interpreted as to apply to the maximal phrase of the type A.

With cyclic nodes understood to be NP and S/IP, the fact that the gerundial noun phrase in (3a) itself contains a cyclic node S/IP (on the assumption that the gerund is contained in a fully clausal structure, of which *my* is the subject; see (5)) allows (3a) to satisfy the A-over-A Principle as desired: *who* is indeed the largest phrase of type A (i.c. NP) within the locally containing cyclic node α (i.c. S/IP) to which the *wh*-movement transformation could apply.

(5) Who would you approve of $[_{NP} [_{S/IP}$ my seeing $[_{NP} ec]]]$?

This revision covers (3a), but now subject extraction out of complex gerunds cannot be derived anymore: in **whose would you approve of seeing John?*, the element *whose* originates as the subject of the cyclic S/IP node inside the complex gerundial NP *whose seeing John*, so lifting the NP (=A) out from under S/IP (=α) ought to be legitimate; but in point of fact, it fails. This problem is solved in Chomsky (1973:235, fn. 10) by additionally adopting Ross's (1967a[1986]:127) Left Branch Condition in (6) to secure the ban on movement of left-branch constituents out of NP in the general case.[5]

(6) *The Left Branch Condition*
No NP which is the leftmost constituent of a larger NP can be reordered out of this NP by a transformational rule.

Chomsky (1973:235) mentions a second possible revision of the A-over-A Principle, which is, however, not developed any further. The idea here is that the A-over-A Principle "does not establish an absolute prohibition against transformations that extract a phrase of type A from a more inclusive phrase of type A. Rather, it states that if a transformational rule is nonspecific with respect to the configuration defined, it will be interpreted in such a way as to satisfy the condition."

A further reformulation of the A-over-A Principle is proposed in Bresnan (1976). The basic idea of Bresnan's approach is that the A-over-A Principle is not sensitive to categorial information, but to the *kind* of transformation taking place. The element that undergoes a syntactic operation (such as the *wh*-movement transformation) is always the maximal (i.e., most inclusive) portion of structure that can undergo this particular transformation. A possible undergoer of a particular transformation T is one that satisfies all requirements imposed on T. For the case of *wh*-movement, there is a requirement according to which the *wh*-phrase must be the leftmost item of the moved constituent. It is thus possible that there is a more inclusive element of the same category which cannot undergo T, as it does not fit the requirements imposed on T – this is exactly what is going on in the previously problematic example (3a). Bresnan's version of the A-over-A Condition correctly derives the grammaticality of this example: *who* is the maximal item that can undergo the *wh*-movement transformation; the higher, more inclusive noun phrase *my seeing who* cannot be *wh*-moved, as it does not meet the requirement imposed on the *wh*-transformation that says that the *wh*-phrase must be the leftmost item of a *wh*-moved constituent.[6] Furthermore, as Bresnan's formulation of the A-over-A Condition does not lean on categorial information, it also applies to and correctly derives examples like (3b). This formulation is the first instance in the generative literature of what has come to be known as Relativized Minimality (see Section 18.6).

18.2.2 Ross's Island Conditions

Ross (1967a), on the other hand, takes the alternative route and gives up the general A-over-A Principle, replacing it not with one 'weaker principle' but with a series of construction-specific constraints which proscribe, for each of these structures separately, the formation of filler–gap dependencies across them. Ross's highly influential work effectively drew the curtain on the A-over-A Principle at this particular stage in theory development, and led the theory to take a decidedly taxonomic turn toward very specific constraints with small application domains. The locality constraints proposed by Ross are listed in (7). (We will return to each of these in what follows.)

(7) a. *the Complex NP Constraint* (CNPC; Ross 1967a:70)
No element contained in a sentence dominated by a noun phrase with a lexical head noun may be moved out of that noun phrase by a transformation.
I spoke to [the man who kissed Mary]
*Who did you speak to [the man who kissed ec]?
b. *the Coordinate Structure Constraint* (CSC: Ross 1967a:89)
In a coordinate structure, no conjunct may be moved, nor may any element contained in a conjunct be moved out of that conjunct.
I kissed [Mary and Sue]
*Who did you kiss [Mary and ec]?
c. *the Sentential Subject Constraint* (Ross 1967a:134)
No element dominated by an S may be moved out of that S if that node S is dominated by an NP which itself is immediately dominated by S.
[that he kissed Mary] was surprising
*Who was [that he kissed ec] surprising?
d. *the Right Roof Constraint* (Ross 1967a:185; term from Perlmutter and Soames 1979)
An element cannot move rightward out of the clause in which it originates.

they had expected [that they would find the treasure said to have been buried on that island] since 1932

*they had expected [that they would find ec] since 1932 *the treasure said to have been buried on that island*

e. the Left Branch Condition (LBC; Ross1967a:114) (see (6))

The new category-specific constraints have strong descriptive power: they cover all cases previously derived by the A-over-A Principle as well as those cases for which the A-over-A Principle makes the wrong predictions. From a conceptual point of view, however, they are inferior to the A-over-A Principle, as they do not conform to an important desideratum of generative grammars: grammatical constraints should be category-neutral and as general as possible (Chomsky 1968:46f.). The A-over-A Principle is not subject to this critique, as it is not specified for particular categories. In current theorizing, the A-over-A Principle has prevailed; a derivative of it, the Minimal Link Condition (Chomsky 2000b:123, 2001:27), is now widely considered to be in effect. The constraints proposed in Ross (1967a) are generally not evoked anymore nowadays; they have, however, proven highly valuable for theory development, as the detailed study that led to their postulation also led to the discovery of many new facts. Furthermore, their names have survived as descriptive terms for the effects they accounted for (e.g., 'CNPC effects,' 'LBC effects').[7]

18.2.3 The *Wh*-Island Condition and the Tensed-S Condition/ Propositional Island Condition

Ross (1967a[1986]) does not contain the *Wh*-Island Condition. As a matter of fact, Ross (1967a: Chapter 2) demonstrates that a general constraint barring *wh*-movement across another *wh* (as in Chomsky 1964a: 43–44) would be somewhat too strong: (8a–d), involving infinitival embedded questions, are "all more or less acceptable"; and even when the embedded question is finite (9)/(10), *wh*-extraction from it often leads to a relatively acceptable result (Ross 1967a[1986]:19–20):

(8) a. he told me about a book which I can't figure out whether to buy *ec* or not
b. he told me about a book which I can't figure out how to read *ec*
c. he told me about a book which I can't figure out where to obtain *ec*
d. he told me about a book which I can't figure out what to do about *ec*

(9) a. he told me about a book which I can't figure out why he read *ec*
b. ? he told me about a book which I can't figure out whether I should read *ec*
c. ??he told me about a book which I can't figure out when I should read *ec*

(10) Which books did he tell you {?whether/??when} he wanted to read *ec*?

Ross notes the general difference between infinitival and finite questions, finding the former "by and large more acceptable" than the latter ("for some reason that is obscure to me"). Ross (1967a[1986]:154) explicitly does not assume (contra Dean 1967) that subordinate clauses are generally opaque. But Chomsky (1973:238) does declare all tensed S-nodes islands – as per the Tensed-S Condition (renamed the Propositional Island Condition (PIC) in Chomsky 1977):

(11) *Tensed-S Condition/Propositional Island Condition (PIC) – version 1*:
No rule can involve X, Y in the structure ... X ... $[\alpha$ ... Y ... $]$ ... where α is a tensed clause.

Only so-called 'bridge verbs' (Erteschik-Shir 1973) can lift this condition. The most prominent approach to this phenomenon is that the sentential complements of bridge verbs, unlike those of factive and manner-of-speaking verbs, provide an 'escape hatch' for extraction (Chomsky 1973; see Haegeman 2006, de Cuba 2007 for recent discussion).[8] Thus, "an item can 'escape' from a tensed sentence if it has been moved into the COMP position on an earlier cycle and is moving into the COMP position on the present cycle" (Chomsky 1973:243–44). Condition (11) is then reformulated as (12):

(12) *Tensed-S Condition/Propositional Island Condition (PIC) – version 2*:
No rule can involve X, Y in the structure ... X ... $[\alpha$ ... Y ... $]$ ... where Y is in COMP and X is not in COMP, or Y is not in COMP and α is a tensed S.

So movement can relate X and Y across a tensed clause as long as both X and Y are in COMP. This forces a successive-cyclic 'COMP-to-COMP movement' derivation for *wh*-movement.[9]

18.2.4 The Subjacency Condition

The revised Tensed-S Condition in (12) can be further generalized. The first formulation of this generalization, the Subjacency Condition, is formulated in Chomsky (1973) as follows:[10]

(13) *Subjacency Condition*:
No rule can involve X and Y, with X superior to Y, if Y is not subjacent to X.

The Subjacency Condition has the effect that a single movement step must not cross more than one cyclic or bounding node. This principle remained in effect throughout the 1970s and 1980s.

The Subjacency Condition captures Ross's Complex NP Constraint and the *Wh*-Island Condition under a single rubric: movement out of a complex NP crosses two cyclic/bounding nodes (NP and S/IP), and so does movement out of a *wh*-question (two S/IP-nodes are traversed in one fell swoop; escape-hatching movement is not possible because the COMP position of the embedded *wh*-question is occupied).[11] It also derives some Left Branch Condition effects, the ungrammaticality of **whose did you read article?* being due to the fact that NP and S/IP are crossed in one go. However, the Left Branch Condition, in its most general formulation, does not just proscribe extraction of left-branch constituents of noun phrases: it also rules out movement of left branches of complex adjectival projections (as in **how do you think I am tall?*, contrasting with *how tall do you think I am?*), which is something the Subjacency Condition has nothing at all to say about (because AP is not declared a cyclic/bounding node). Thus, a number of Left Branch Condition effects cannot be derived by means of the Subjacency Condition.[12] On the other hand, Subjacency is too strong in deriving a general prohibition on extraction from noun phrases, which is empirically not borne out — sentences like *who did you read an article about?* are grammatical.

The remaining constraints introduced by Ross (the Coordinate Structure Constraint, the Right Roof Constraint, the Sentential Subject Constraint) cannot be directly derived from the Subjacency Condition as it stands either. The Coordinate Structure Constraint bans extraction of or from a single conjunct in a coordinate structure, but, as Ross notes, so-called 'across the board' extraction from (though not of) all conjuncts does deliver a grammatical output (*who did you [meet ec] and [have lunch with ec]?*). This empirical state of affairs, with its sensitivity to extraction from one or all conjuncts, and to the distinction between full extraction and subextraction, is inherently such that the Subjacency Condition cannot derive it. Successfully accommodating the effects of the Coordinate Structure Constraint in an explanatory theory of constraints on filler–gap dependencies has proven a major challenge.[13]

The Right Roof Constraint is unusual in being specific to *rightward* movement: rightward movement is highly local, resisting filler–gap dependencies across even a single finite clause – even if that clause is demonstrably transparent to leftward movement. The Subjacency Condition could only account for the effects of the Right Roof Constraint if leftward movement but not rightward movement can make use of the 'escape hatch' COMP. This is exactly what Drummond *et al.* (2010) argue to be the case, seeking to derive the ban on escape-hatching rightward movement from Fox and Pesetsky's (2005) theory of cyclic linearization, in conjunction with the assumption that escape-hatch positions systematically *precede* the rest of the locality domain. Movement of α to the escape-hatch position of the locality domain ß would result in a linearization instruction to the PF component that α be spelled out to the *left* of ß; but subsequent extraposition of α to a position to the *right* of ß would deliver a conflicting linearization statement.

The Sentential Subject Constraint, which bans extraction from sentential subjects, is impossible to accommodate under the Subjacency Condition. Movement should be able to proceed via the COMP position of sentential subjects to the matrix COMP position without violating Subjacency: only the matrix S/IP-node would be crossed in the movement process. In addition, it is not just *sentential* subjects that are opaque: subjects of finite clauses in general, even nominal ones, resist subextraction:

(14) a. *Who was [that he kissed ec] surprising?
b. *Who was [the sudden appearance of ec] surprising?

This general Subject Condition effect should be accounted for by the theory of locality. Subjacency as it stands seems at first to accommodate the ill-formedness of (14b) straightforwardly: NP and S/IP are crossed under movement. But this is deceptive: recall from our discussion of the Complex NP Constraint above that if extraction from NP were to generally proceed in one fell swoop, the theory would wrongly rule out all subextraction from NP categorically, even in cases in which it leads to a grammatical result. And as we pointed out at the beginning of this paragraph, (14a) is not accounted for by the Subjacency Condition without additional assumptions about the distribution of escape-hatching movement.[14] It is clear, therefore, that the Subject Condition does not fall out from the Subjacency Condition as it stands.

18.2.5 The Condition on Extraction Domain

There is a further restriction on filler–gap dependencies (one not discovered by Ross) that the classic Subjacency Condition also does not account for: the fact that extraction from adjuncts is often degraded:

(15) a. ?Who did you leave town [before talking to ec]?
b. *To whom did you leave town [before talking ec]?

The facts in (15) show that adjuncts are robustly opaque to extraction of PPs (even complement–PPs, as in (15b)) whereas they are quite easily traversed by NPs.

Huang (1982a) brought the Subject Condition and the Adjunct Condition together in the Condition on Extraction Domain.

(16) *Condition on Extraction Domain* (CED; simplified version; Müller 2010)
    a. Movement must not cross a barrier.
    b. An XP is a barrier iff it is not a complement.

As it stands, the Condition on Extraction Domain is problematic. It merely codifies the empirical facts, and does not cover all of them, failing, for instance, to make the desired distinction between (15a) and (15b). A a number of attempts have been made to derive the CED from independently motivated principles or basic properties of syntactic derivations, and to reconcile the CED with the adjunct extraction facts. Important studies include Kayne (1984), Chomsky (1986a), Cinque (1990b) and Manzini (1992). See Müller (2010) for a critical overview.

In Section 18.3, we will elaborate on the topic of adjunct island effects, introducing the theory of barriers (Chomsky 1986a), and, in Section 18.4, two alternatives to it: the LF pied-piping account by Cinque (1990b), and Truswell's (2011) Single Event Grouping Condition. Subsequently, in Section 18.5, we will come back to subject/object asymmetries.

18.3 Locality in the theory of barriers

Adjuncts, in contrast to subjects of finite clauses, are not generally resistant to subextraction. Chomsky (1986a:32, 66) notes the sensitivity of the Adjunct Condition to the categorial nature of the extracted material (attributing the observation to Adriana Belletti), seen in (15). He suggests an account couched in terms of the theory of barriers – a theory that marks the first significant development in generativist theorizing about locality in syntax since the introduction of the Subjacency Condition.

The theory of barriers is an attempt at integrating the theories of bounding and government, which had been developed independently and employed discrete toolkits. Central in this theory is the algorithm for the computation of barriers – the new name for cyclic or bounding nodes. Opaque domains are no longer stipulated in the form of a list of nodes (NP and S/IP for English, NP and S'/CP for Italian; Rizzi 1982a), as in the classic Subjacency Condition, but computed via (17).[15]

(17) in the configuration [... α ... [γ ... β ...]], where γ is a category that excludes α and dominates β, γ is a *barrier* for a relationship between α and β iff (i) or (ii) or (iii):
 a. γ is a Blocking Category; γ ≠ IP
 b. γ immediately dominates a Blocking Category that dominates β
 c. γ is the immediate projection of a governor for β that is closer to β than α is (Minimality)

Any category that does not receive a θ-role from a lexical category under government is a Blocking Category for material that it dominates. A Blocking Category is inherently a barrier, *unless* it happens to be an IP, which by stipulation is exempt from inherent barrierhood (17a). In addition to inherent barrierhood, the theory also recognizes the possibility of a node γ acquiring barrierhood *via inheritance* from a Blocking Category that γ immediately dominates (17b). This notion of inheritance barrier is crucial to Chomsky's (1986a) account of the Wh-Island Condition, which we will not discuss in any detail here. A third way for a category to be a barrier (specifically for government) is via the 'minimality' clause in (17c), which we will return to in Sections 18.5 and 18.6.

Inherent barrierhood (17a) has the interesting property of identifying subjects and adjuncts as a natural class: neither is governed by a lexical category, hence both are Blocking Categories and therefore, in turn, inherent barriers for extraction. The Subject and Adjunct Conditions, previously unified at a descriptive level in the CED, are thus derived on principled grounds. But while subjects are absolute islands, adjuncts often allow extraction of noun phrases from them, as we saw in (15). Chomsky (1986a) seeks to derive this independently, from a new theory of adjunction.

The starting point is the structural constellation in the first line of (17), wherein a dependency between α and β cannot be formed if γ is a Blocking Category for β. But Chomsky argues that even when no escape hatch like COMP (rechristened 'SpecCP' in Chomsky 1986a, which extends the X-bar schema to all functional categories) is available, barrierhood can be voided via intermediate adjunction to the barrier γ. This constellation is illustrated in (18).

(18) $[\ldots \alpha \ldots [_\gamma \delta [_\gamma \ldots \beta \ldots]]]$

Here, γ consists of two segments. Both segments γ exclude α, but only the higher segment γ dominates δ; the lower segment γ does not dominate δ. Crucially, condition (17) is understood in such a way that 'a category γ' means 'all segments γ.' Thus, according to (17), since δ is neither dominated nor excluded by γ in (18), a syntactic dependency can be formed between α and δ (crossing only the higher segment of the category γ) and between δ and β (crossing only the lower segment of γ). Since neither of the two dependencies crosses the category γ as a whole, and since only categories can be barriers (by definition), it follows that even if γ is itself not L-marked, extraction from γ can succeed in (18).

In order to ensure that inherent barriers cannot be voided via adjunction as a matter of course, it must be assumed that intermediate adjunction is not freely available. Chomsky (1986a:6) posits that it is restricted in such a way that it must never target an argument. This condition accounts for the ban on subextraction from subjects. Adjuncts, not being arguments, should in principle be able to host intermediate traces of movement. And this is why (15a) is relatively acceptable: the *wh*-NP *who* adjoins to the *before*-PP on its way out. But in the case of (15b), intermediate adjunction must be impossible. The key difference between (15a) and (15b) is that the extracted material in the latter is a PP. So if movement from the adjunct, which is itself also a PP, proceeded via intermediate adjunction to the adjunct in the case of (15b), we would derive an intermediate representation featuring one PP adjoined to another:

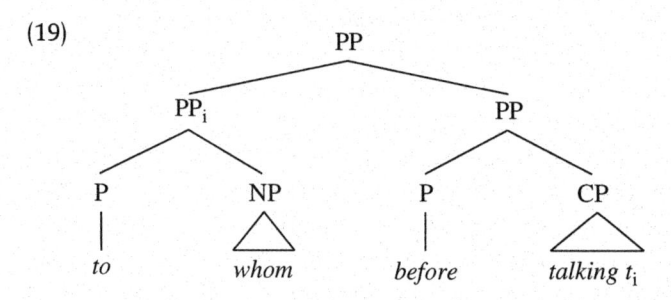

(19)

```
                      PP
                 ┌─────┴─────┐
               PP_i           PP
              ┌─┴─┐          ┌─┴─┐
              P   NP         P   CP
              │   △          │   △
              to  whom     before talking t_i
```

This kind of configuration is ruled out, according to Chomsky, for independent reasons: the X-bar schema (see especially Chapter 11) would be unable to figure out which P is the head of the complex PP in (19). With (19) ruled out as an intermediate step in the derivation of (15b), fell-swoop extraction from the adjunct will be forced in this case, ultimately resulting in a violation of the Subjacency Condition. However, there is a caveat to this solution. In the *Barriers* theory (unlike in its successor, the Minimalist Program; see Chapter 4), indices play a significant role. The PP on the left edge of the complex PP-structure in (19) bears an index, and does not propagate this index to the complex PP as a whole. Thus, the system should be able to recognize the head of the complex PP irrespective of the categorial status of the complex PP's dependents.[16] Indeterminacy regarding headedness is thus unlikely to be the real root of the problem, at least within the *Barriers* theory.

18.4 LF pied-piping of islands

An alternative approach to the NP/PP dichotomy has been proposed by Cinque (1990b).[17] This approach capitalizes on the distribution of so-called resumptive pronouns: while argumental NPs are well known to be able to bind resumptive pronouns (as in (20a)), PPs cannot do so (see (20b)):

(20) a. the keys that I can never remember where I put *them*
 b. *the place that I can never remember which keys I put *there*

Cinque (1990b) proposes that filler–gap dependencies between a nominal filler and a gap in an argument position within a so-called 'strong' island involve null resumption (i.e., no movement), whereas other filler–gap dependencies are derived via movement.[18]

Without further modification, this analysis predicts that binding-based filler–gap dependencies across islands never exhibit island effects. This is not borne out: even when the filler is nominal, argumental, and referential, it cannot always establish an A'-dependency with a gap across an island:

(21) a. ?Who did John leave town [before talking to *ec*]?
 b. *Who did John leave town [before saying *ec* would win the election]?

Moreover, island-violating dependencies of the type in (21a) are not completely unbounded. We find residual, and robust, island effects as soon as more than a single island is traversed: (22) shows that an A'-dependency involving a referential argument-NP spanning *two* islands is entirely ungrammatical (regardless of the particular combination of islands chosen; see also Longobardi 1984, Chomsky 1982, 1986a for relevant observations):

(22) a. *Who did John try to leave town [before being arrested [after talking to *ec*]]?
　　b. *Who did John try to leave town [before talking to someone [who had met *ec*]]?

To take care of these facts, Cinque (1990b) proposes that resumption-based dependencies, though not involving movement in overt syntax, nonetheless *are* movement dependencies at LF: the resumptive is not moved directly, but rather pied-piped by a higher constituent. In cases like (21a), the entire adjunct-PP headed by *after* legitimately LF-moves toward *who*, rendering the sentence grammatical. Likewise, for both cases in (22), the pied-piped constituent is the projection of the adjunct containing the pro-form (i.e., the projection of *after* in (22a); the relative clause in (22b)). Crucially, however, the lower adjunct in (22) is itself contained in a larger adjunct-PP, out of which it cannot be moved. The possible alternative – pied-piping the *before*-PP – is prohibited: the pied-piping domain cannot be extended beyond the lower adjunct, as it is ungoverned. This account extends to (21b): since *ec* in (21b) is in the subject position of a finite clause (a *non-canonically governed* position), a pied-piping domain cannot be established above it.[19] Thus, A'-dependencies, even those involving an argumental nominal filler, can never cross more than one island at a time.[20]

But in the case of adjunct islands, crossing even a single one is sometimes fatal, even in the case of *wh*-dependencies involving nominal *wh*-expressions. Thus, while in (23) the gerundial adjuncts are perfectly transparent to the establishment of nominal *wh*-dependencies across them, in (24) the same *wh*-dependencies, in apparently the same structural environments, fail.

(23) a. What did John {arrive/drive Mary crazy} [whistling *ec*]?
　　b. Which book did John design his garden [after reading *ec*]?

(24) a. *What did John {work/paint this picture} [whistling *ec*]?
　　b. *Which letter did John break a glass [before/after writing *ec*]?

Truswell (2011) provides important insight into the conditions under which *wh*-dependencies across single adjuncts are grammatical, and under which they are not. We will present the gist of Truswell's analysis here as a postlude to our discussion of adjunct islands.

Truswell shows that the islandhood of adjuncts is conditioned by semantic factors: extraction from adjuncts is possible if the syntactic material spanned by the movement dependency can be interpreted as forming a single event.

(25) *The Single Event Grouping Condition* (Truswell 2011:157)
　　An instance of *wh*-movement is legitimate only if the minimal constituent containing the head and the foot of the chain can be construed as describing a single *event* grouping.

For the case of extraction from gerundial adjuncts, a grammatical output results if the two events expressed by the adjunct and the matrix clause plausibly entertain a contingent relation. Thus, for instance, in the version of (23a) with *drive Mary crazy*, there is a causal relation between matrix clause and embedded clause: the most salient interpretation of this example is *What is x such that John whistling x caused Mary to go crazy?* But in (24b) there is nothing about John's breaking a glass that makes it sensible to think of it as being contingent on his writing a letter prior or subsequent to it. Consequently, (24b) is unacceptable.

18.5 Subject/object asymmetries revisited: the Empty Category Principle

At this point, we return to subject/object asymmetries. As (21b) showed already, subjects of finite clauses resist being severed from their antecedents by a strong island, which makes them different from objects, which, when nominal and referential, can generally cross an island without much difficulty (in English). Another respect in which subjects and objects famously differ is their sensitivity to lexical complementizers in filler-gap dependencies involving them:

(26)   a. Who do you think (that) John invited *ec*?
       b. Who do you think (*that) *ec* invited Mary?

(27)   a. Who would you prefer (for) John to invite *ec*?
       b. Who would you prefer (*for) *ec* to invite Mary?

This 'complementizer-trace effect' (sometimes referred to as 'that-trace effect', but the effect is not specific to the finite complementizer *that*, as (27) shows) has been prominent on the syntactic research agenda for several decades (see also Sections 3.2.4 and 12.12). The standard Chomskyan approach to 'complementizer-trace effects', at least since Chomsky (1981), has been couched in terms of a condition on the trace left behind by movement — the Empty Category Principle (ECP), which demands that a trace be properly governed. Proper governors can be either θ-governors or antecedent-governors. Since traces in subject positions are never θ-governed, their only hope is to find a local antecedent. According to Chomsky, the complementizer in C obstructs the desired relationship of antecedent-government between the trace in subject position and its closest antecedent because the complementizer is a *closer governor* of the subject trace. Thus, by the minimality clause of the definition of a barrier in (17c), above, the complementizer's immediate projection (C') prevents the subject trace from being properly governed, which causes the variants of (26b) and (27b) that contain a lexical complementizer to violate the ECP.[21]

18.6 Relativized Minimality

What Chomsky (1986a) proposes is a definition of minimality (often referred to as *rigid* minimality) according to which a head that serves as a closer governor for β will *always* count as an intervener for the establishment of a (government) relationship between β and some more distant governor α – *regardless* of the nature of the (government) relationship between α and β: this head will intervene in the establishment of both head-government (a relationship between a head and a phrase) and antecedent-government (usually a relationship between a phrase and a phrase, or between a head and a head).

This definition of minimality is compatible with the overall theory of Chomsky (1986a).[22] There is, however, a logical alternative according to which the intervention effect is relativized to the nature of the relationship involved: intervening heads interfere with relations between heads; intervening elements in A-positions interfere with relations between phrases in A-positions; and intervening elements in A'-positions interfere with relations between a phrase in an A'-position and its trace. This is the central insight of Rizzi's (1990a) reinterpretation of minimality, known as Relativized Minimality:

(28) Relativized Minimality
in a configuration [... α ... γ ... β ...], where α c-commands γ and γ c-commands β, γ blocks a relationship between α and β iff γ is of the same type as α, where 'of the same type' is understood as:

a. if α is a head, γ is a head
b. if α is a phrase in an A-position, γ is a phrase in an A-position
c. if α is a phrase in an A'-position, γ is a phrase in an A'-position

Relativized Minimality provides an immediate syntactic account of a variety of well-known locality effects.[23] Thus, it derives the Head Movement Constraint (HMC) of Travis (1984), which says that a head is not allowed to move across another head (but recall Note 11, on long head movement):

(29) a. John will be invited
b. Will John be invited?
c. *Be John will invited?

Though (as we know from *is John invited, too?*) the auxiliary of the passive is in principle eligible for Subject–Aux Inversion, it cannot undergo the process in (29c); instead, the modal *will* must be the auxiliary that inverts with the subject, as in (29b). Relativized Minimality derives this straightforwardly: *will* c-commands *be*, and is of the same type as *be* (both are heads), thus preventing *be* from raising to C past *will*.

The ban on 'super-raising,' illustrated in (30), also falls out directly from Relativized Minimality. In the process of raising from the lower clause (demarcated by the brackets) into the subject position of the higher clause (an A-position), the NP *John* must cross the intervening subject of the lower clause (another A-position), occupied by expletive *it/there*, in the sentence in (30b). The ensuring Relativized Minimality violation is responsible for the ungrammaticality of the sentence. No violation is incurred in (30a), where A-movement can proceed successive-cyclically without skipping any A-positions along the way.

(30) a. John seems [to be invited]
      b. *John seems [that it/there will be invited]

Neither in ruling out (29c) nor in accounting for (30b) does Relativized Minimality improve upon the empirical coverage of earlier Principles and Parameters theory: as Baker (1988) demonstrated, the HMC falls out from the ECP (see also Chomsky 1991b); and 'super-raising' can be accommodated by Principle A of the Binding Theory. The real empirical gain of Relativized Minimality is that it accounts for a wide variety of intervention effects found in the realm of A'-dependencies – a much wider array than had previously been discovered. Relativized Minimality thus played an important heuristic role as well, opening up what has proved to be a highly fertile field of study.

It is easy to verify that the *Wh*-Island Condition falls out from clause (28c): the *wh*-constituent in the lower clause in (31) c-commands the trace of the *wh*-constituent in the higher clause, and sits in a position that is of the same type (an A'-position) as the position occupied by the *wh*-constituent in the higher clause.[24] But not only *wh*-phrases in embedded SpecCP positions interfere with A'-dependencies involving *wh*-phrases: a negation or some other type of 'affective operator' (in the sense of Klima 1964) in the matrix clause does, too (see Chapter 21). Ross (1984) first noted the harmful effect of a negation on the formation of *wh*-dependencies (see (31c)), and referred to it as an 'inner island' effect. In addition to sentential negation, (31d–f) show that lexically negative verbs, downward-entailing quantifiers such as *few*, and focus particles (*only*) also break the link between *how* and its trace in the lower clause.[25]

(31) a. *How* do you think [that he behaved *ec*]?
      b. **How* do you wonder [why he behaved *ec*]?
      c. **How* don't you think [that he behaved *ec*]?
      d. **How* did he deny [that he behaved *ec*]?
      e. **How* do few people think [that he behaved *ec*]?
      f. **How* does only Mary think [that he behaved *ec*]?

For Rizzi (1990a), these are all effects of Relativized Minimality: in each case, there is an operator (sometimes an abstract one, as in the case of lexically negative verbs) in an A'-position intervening harmfully between the *wh*-phrase in the matrix SpecCP and its trace in the lower clause.

Relativized Minimality is founded on the following insight, which also underlies the traditional Binding Theory (see Chapter 15): a dependent element β that seeks to engage in a local relationship of type R with a c-commanding element higher up the tree will try to establish this relationship with the closest available element α with which this relationship can in principle be engaged; if β cannot successfully establish that relationship with α, it is not granted any further opportunities, and the derivation is terminated. Such an approach works very well for dependencies that are blocked by interveners which have key properties in common with the desired antecedent. Thus, in *John considers Mary proud of himself*, the anaphor cannot pick out *John* as its antecedent because *Mary* is closer and 'accessible'; and similarly, in *how do you wonder why he behaved?*, the empty category cannot be associated to its antecedent *how* because *why* is closer and 'accessible.'

There are cases, however, in which the intervener is not, at first sight, a closer potential antecedent for β. Ross's 'inner island' (*how strongly do(*n't) you think inflation will rebound?*) is such a case: a negation is apparently a harmful intervener for the adjunct *how*, but it is difficult to imagine negation as a closer potential antecedent for the trace of *how*. From Rizzi's point of view, negation (γ) must be 'of the same type as' α to break the relationship between α and its trace β. Starke (2001) develops this into a feature-class approach to Relativized Minimality-type intervention effects (see also Rizzi 2004a): elements γ that are in the same feature class as α qualify as harmful interveners for the establishment of a dependency between α and β. Starke devises a geometry of features, and places 'wh/focus' and 'neg' in the same feature class (the class of quantificational features), so that that the negation qualifies as a γ that breaks the relation between a *wh*-phrase α and its trace β.

Starke's (2001) feature geometry fine-tunes the empirical coverage of Relativized Minimality. It is Starke's stated aim to show that such an approach can unify both weak islands and strong islands under the general rubric of Relativized Minimality (see Starke 2001 for further details). But the strong islands involved in the Subject Condition and the Adjunct Condition remain difficult to recast as involving intervention by a closer potential antecedent.

18.7 The early Minimalist approach to locality: The Minimal Link Condition and equidistance

The beginning of the 1990s marked the return to intervention-based locality constraints. Another constraint which was formulated at this time, and which is one of the most important constraints nowadays, is the Minimal Link Condition. The background against which this constraint was developed is the newly introduced idea that all syntactic operations are driven by features:

(32) Last Resort (Chomsky 1991b, 1995c)
Movement must result in feature checking.

With this in mind, let us go back to the two relative locality principles we have encountered, the A-over-A Principle and the Superiority Condition (on the latter, see also Section 4.25). Both can be reformulated in terms of feature-driven syntax, as in (33) (where [*F*] stands for a feature of a probe that is looking for a match to get itself valued and checked):

(33) a. F-over-F Principle
In a structure $\alpha_{[*F*]} \ldots [\beta_{[F]} \ldots [\gamma_{[F]} \ldots] \ldots] \ldots$, movement to [*F*] can only affect the category bearing the feature [F] that is closest to [*F*].
b. Superiority Condition
In a structure $\alpha_{[*F*]} \ldots [\ldots \beta_{[F]} \ldots [\ldots \gamma_{[F]} \ldots] \ldots] \ldots$, movement to [*F*] can only affect the category bearing the feature [F] that is closest to [*F*].

The difference between these two principles is that the A-over-A (now F-over-F) Principle makes a statement about competing categories, where one dominates the other, while the Superiority Condition makes a statement about competing elements, where one m-commands the other. Now that the principles are reformulated in terms of features, it becomes clear that they are actually two subcases of one natural class of phenomena, which are better derived from a unified principle. The unification is known as the Minimal Link Condition (MLC), which is given here in its generalized version:

(34) *Generalized Minimal Link Condition* (e.g. Fitzpatrick 2002)
In a structure $X_{[*F*]} \ldots [Y_{[F]} \ldots [Z_{[F]}]]$, movement to [*F*] can only affect the category bearing the feature [F] that is closest to [*F*].

How exactly the minimal link is determined depends on the definition of closeness, which is delegated to a separate condition. Closeness is usually determined in terms of path length, which in turn is defined in terms of the cardinality of the nodes crossed by the dependency. Ideally, each node that is crossed counts as one 'mark' in the determination of the length of the path. It has been shown, however, that this is not the case: the counting is apparently selective. There are a number of well-established notions of closeness: one has it that the specifier and the complement of a head α are equally close (=*equidistant*) to α (Pesetsky and Torrego 2001); another says that the specifier of α is closer to α than any category that is further embedded in the complement of α (Pesetsky 1982b, Collins 1997); and a third maintains that elements at the edge of the complement of α are equidistant to α (Chomsky 2001).

There is one important difference between Rizzi's Relativized Minimality and Chomsky's (1995c: Chapter 3) MLC-based approach to locality. In the Relativized Minimality framework, harmful intervention cannot be canceled. Under the MLC approach this is not necessarily the case. Chomsky (1995c: Chapter 3) adds a provision whereby (narrow-) syntactic head movement renders a closer and a more remote constituent of the same type equidistant:[26] movement of a head X whose specifier is β to a higher head Y whose specifier is γ makes β and γ members of the same minimal domain, and thereby equidistant from α, which is now allowed to take γ as its antecedent without incurring a violation of the MLC.

(35) [$_{YP}$ γ Y [$_{XP}$ β X ... α ...]]

The MLC approach can therefore be seen as a relaxation of the Relativized Minimality approach. It remains tightly constrained, however: since head movement is itself subject to a strict locality condition (a head can only move up to the next-higher head, and cannot subsequently 'excorporate' from the complex head created by head movement), this theory guarantees that it is only the specifiers of two projections that are *immediately* embedded one inside the other can be rendered equidistant. The *Wh*-Island Condition is therefore still derived by absolute locality: the specifier of the embedded CP and the specifier of the matrix CP cannot be made equidistant by domain-extending head movement.

For the other Relativized Minimality effects discussed in Rizzi (1990a) and work done in its wake, the relaxation of Relativized Minimality proposed by Chomsky (1995c: Chapter 3) has no adverse consequences either. There is, in effect, precisely one case for which this relaxation of Relativized Minimality does have repercussions: the case of NP-movement past the local A-position into the next available A-position in the tree. This is precisely the context in which apparent violations of 'strict' Relativized Minimality do indeed seem to manifest themselves. One such case, discussed by Guasti (1993), is the passive, depicted in (36). Here an NP originating within V' moves past the implicit external argument of the passive (*pro* or PRO, located in SpecVP) into SpecIP, in apparent violation of Relativized Minimality. Guasti circumvents this by capitalizing on the idea that movement must target the closest *potential* landing-site. The specifier position of VP in a passive is a θ-position, and (by the Theta Criterion) θ-positions are by their very nature never potential landing-sites for movement. SpecVP in (36) is therefore ignored in the search for the closest potential landing site.[27]

(36) [$_{IP}$ John$_i$ was [$_{VP}$ ec$_j$ [$_{V'}$ invited ec$_i$]]]

The second, more worrisome, case of apparently non-local NP-movement presents itself in Chomsky's (1995c: Chapter 3) analysis of Object Shift. In (37), movement of the object across the base position of the subject could be given 'Guasti's fiat'; but subsequent movement of the subject across the *derived* position of the object (which happens overtly in languages like Icelandic and Japanese; (37) is an English gloss) cannot – the position skipped in this movement step is plainly a potential landing-site.

(37) [$_{IP}$ Mary$_j$ [I [$_{AgrOP}$ John$_i$ [AgrO [$_{VP}$ ec$_j$ [$_{V'}$ *invited* ec$_i$]]]]]]

Here domain-extending head movement of AgrO to I comes to the rescue, rendering SpecAgrOP and SpecIP equidistant. Whenever the object raises overtly to a VP-external A-position, it is now predicted that the verb must leave the VP and be subsequently pied-piped by onward raising of AgrO to I.[28]

18.8 From barriers to phases

Early Minimalist work tends to concentrate on locality effects of the type captured in terms of (some version of) Relativized Minimality. Chomsky's (2001, 2008) 'derivation by phase' model of locality is predicated on the premise that there are fixed points in the syntactic structure-building process at which the structure created up to that point is handed over to the interpretive components. This marks a return to the barriers theory of Chomsky (1986a), this time with a conceptual anchoring.

The basic idea underlying phases is that syntactic computation does not operate on large portions of structure. Rather, the operation space available is restricted to a small 'window' (see, e.g., Chomsky 2000b, 2001, 2008; Epstein and Seely 2002b). This line of thought ultimately goes back to Miller (1956), who, in reviewing a number of contemporary psychological experiments, observes that working memory capacity seems to be limited to around seven items ('chunks') such as words, letters, or digits.

In the barriers theory, the demarcation point of this 'window', or locality domain, is formed by heads or phrases that act as barriers in that the material below them, though present, is opaque to (i.e., not accessible for) syntactic operations crossing the window. The barriers theory contains two stipulative ingredients: (a) the opaque nature of structure parts below a barrier, and (b) the identity of barriers. From these we can distill two questions which lie at the basis of any theory of grammar: (i) How is locality motivated? (ii) How large are locality domains?

In facing these questions, the task is to develop a grammar model in which locality is motivated, and locality domains are determined in a principled fashion. This led to the reformulation of locality domains in terms of phases. The motivation for locality is now approached from a psychological perspective on grammatical theory in which topmost priority is given to the desideratum that grammar be an optimally designed, efficient computational system; i.e., derivations must be as simple as possible. For Chomsky (2000b, 2001; see also Epstein and Seely 2002b, Richards 2004), this primarily means that the number of syntactic objects that have to be processed at a time during computation must be minimal. This is assumed to be ensured by regularly transferring parts of the structure to the interfaces, PF and LF (cyclic spell-out). More deeply embedded items thus 'vanish' from the current derivation; they cannot be accessed at later points.

Where are the boundaries of locality domains? In minimalist models, cyclic spell-out typically works in such a way that the complement of designated syntactic heads X (called phase heads) is transferred when the XP is completely built up. What remains accessible after transfer is therefore the head X and its edge, i.e., the residue outside of X', comprising specifiers of X and adjuncts to XP. The domain that is spelled out cannot comprise X, as it is needed for selection and head movement (Chomsky 2000b). Hence, the necessary size of the operation space comprises the space between the currently created node of the category Y and the next lower phase head X, including X itself. The effect of cyclic spell-out is formalized in terms of the Phase Impenetrability Condition (PIC).

(38) *Phase Impenetrability Condition* (Chomsky 2000b:108, 2001:13)
The domain of a head X of a phase XP is not accessible to operations outside; only X and its edge are accessible to such operations.

18.9 The size of syntactic domains

Having addressed question (i) from Section 18.8 ('How is locality motivated?'), let us proceed to discuss question (ii), concerning the size of locality domains. A number of different answers have been given to this question. The existing approaches can be classified according to two criteria: on the one hand, phase heads can be semantically or structurally defined; on the other hand, phases can be static or dynamic. A semantic definition of phases derives the phase head status from a semantic property of certain heads. In structural phase definitions, phase head status is the result of a structural configuration; theories of this type often declare each phrase a phase. In static phase approaches, being a phase head is a fixed property of certain heads. Dynamic approaches, on the other hand, treat phases as entities of variable, and syntactically manipulable, size: the phase head property can be shifted upwards in the tree.

In the conventional approach, only C and v (the 'light verb' selecting the root-VP) are assumed to be phase heads, whereas other heads (except perhaps for D/N) are not (Chomsky 2000b:106, 2001:12; Matushansky 2003). The rationale behind this assumption is that C and v are the heads of the propositional categories CP and vP.[29] These categories are independent at LF as a designated semantic type can be associated with them: vP, a full (verbal) argument structure, is the minimal category that is assigned a truth value;[30] CP, a full clausal entity including tense and illocutionary force, is the highest type associated with a truth value. Thus, phases are semantically complete; but they are not necessarily internally convergent (i.e., syntactically complete): not all features are necessarily valued within the phase. This approach is thus a semantic-static phase theory.

Syntactic objects that are transferred to LF are semantically complete (in the sense just described), and objects that are transferred to PF as a unit are phonetically isolable. The latter property should give us a straightforward diagnostic for phasehood. Phonetic isolability implies that the objects in question should be able to be clefted, extraposed, right-node raised, used in *though*-constructions, or in predicate fronting (Matushansky 2003; see also Abels 2003). However, the diagnostic and its outcome are problematic in two ways. First, it is in fact the *complements* of the phase heads (in the conventional view: IP, VP), not the phases themselves, that Chomsky takes to be the parts of structure that are transferred to the interfaces; so phonetic isolability would diagnose phase-head complements rather than phases (Nissenbaum 1998, Abels 2003). Second, LF-independence does not appear to completely overlap with PF-independence (Bošković 2002c, Matushansky 2003, Boeckx and Grohmann 2006, Marušić 2005). Not all elements that are semantically complete are phonetically isolable; and vice versa, not all elements that are phonetically isolable are semantically complete. The former is illustrated by clefting: while the contrast in (39a–b) (Rizzi 1982b) seems to confirm that CP is a phase while IP is not, the ungrammaticality of (39c) (Matushansky 2003) would seem to call into question the phasehood of vP. Moreover, while clefting IP fails, pseudoclefting it is successful (as in *what John did// bought was* [$_{IP}$ *he bought a book*]; see den Dikken, et al. 2000 for detailed discussion).

(39) a. it is [$_{CP}$ to go home every evening] that John prefers
      b. *it is [$_{IP}$ to go home every evening] that John seems
      c. *it is [$_{vP}$ doubt that Desdemona was faithful] that Othello did

That phonetic isolability is not necessarily in sync with semantic completeness is also shown forcefully by Right Node Raising. The fact that there must be a pause before the 'raised' material signals PF independence. But both CPs and TPs are right-node raisable, as the examples in (40) show (Bošković 2002c:182, Abels 2003:63; the examples in (40a–b) are from Postal 1998, but the observation goes back at least to Bresnan's 1974 (35c)).[31]

(40) a. John believes, and Peter claims, [$_{CP}$ that Mary will get a job]
      b. I know when, but I don't know where, [$_{IP}$ Amanda met Steve]
      c. I have been wondering whether, but would not positively want to state that, [$_{IP}$ your theory is correct]

Another research line links locality domains to segmental and prosodic PF-effects (Truckenbrodt 1995b, Kratzer and Selkirk 2007, Ishihara 2004,

2007, Legate 2003, Dobashi 2003, Scheer 2008, 2009a, 2009b, Pak 2008, Kahnemuyipour 2009). The basic idea here is that a structural unit that is spelled out also behaves as a prosodic unit at PF. There is controversy as to where this effect presents itself: Kratzer and Selkirk (2007) argue that prosodic constituency is aligned with the *left* edge of spell-out domains (that is, the highest phrase within a spell-out domain is a prominent prosodic phrase); Feldhausen (2008) presents evidence from prosodic phrasing of Catalan Clitic Left and Right Dislocation that at least for the vP, prosodic constituency is aligned with the *right* edge of the syntactic structural unit. (The choice of left or right edge may be a matter of parametric variation.) Ishihara (2004, 2007), on the other hand, argues that the whole structure part that is spelled out forms a prosodic constituent. An important finding of this line of research is that the CP and possibly the vP, but no other syntactic phases (including DP), leave phonological traces. Words, on the other hand, are phonological but not syntactic barriers/phases (Scheer 2009a).

An alternative to the LF- and PF-centric approaches to phases summarized above is an approach that can be classified as 'structural'. Representatives of this approach are theories that assume that each phrase is a phase: phrasal movement has to proceed through the edge of each XP on its path. This idea goes back to Manzini (1994), who unifies the conditions on head movement and XP movement under one locality condition. Manzini's analysis is based on the notion of 'minimal domain' defined in (41):

(41) *Minimal domain*
The minimal domain (X) of a head X consists of all and only the elements that are immediately contained by, and do not immediately contain, a projection of X.

The minimal domain (X) of a head X thus contains X itself, X's specifier, X's complement, and all adjuncts to X^n. Movement is constrained by a locality condition according to which movement from a minimal domain (X) to a minimal domain (Y) is possible iff (X) and (Y) are adjacent:

(42) *Locality*
For all i (where $i=1-n$), let an item A_i be in (X_i). Given a dependency $(A_{i=1}, \ldots, A_{i=n})$, for all i, (X_i) and (X_{i+1}) are adjacent.

(42) has the effect that movement must proceed through every phrase along the path to its final landing-site. Other systems working along the same lines are Takahashi (1994), Agbayani (1998), and Sportiche (1998). There are several implementations of this idea in phase-based systems (see Müller 2004a, Epstein and Seely 2002b, Lahne 2008). In these phase-based approaches, there is no distinction between phase heads and non-phase heads: each phrase head is a phase head; each phrase is a phase.

While the approaches reviewed so far in this section take phases to be immutable, a number of phase models share the basic assumption that phases are not fixed entities, but dynamic in the sense that phasal domains are extendable (i.e., Spell-out can be delayed) under certain conditions. Analyses of this type are Uriagereka (1999), Svenonius (2001a, 2001b), den Dikken (2007), Gallego (2005), and Gallego and Uriagereka (2006). All of these are representatives of the semantic-dynamic phase model: they agree with Chomsky in taking the defining property of phases to be some semantic property, but disagree in allowing phasehood to shift. For Svenonius (2001a, 2001b), phases are not predefined entities of fixed size; rather, the system transfers any entity as soon as it is convergent. The defining property of a phase is internal convergence, which is defined in terms of completeness:

(43) *Completeness*
An XP is complete if it contains no unvalued features. Unvalued features of an item X are valued only at X's final landing site.

In den Dikken (2007), the original phase-defining property is semantic completeness as in the Chomskyan standard, with the difference that only simple predications (*v*Ps and other small clauses) are inherent phases. Thus, CP is not inherently phasal, though it can become a derived phase as a result of *v*-to-I-to-C movement.

A major insight steering the semantic-dynamic phase model is that syntactic head movement triggers the expansion of the phase. This idea goes back to Chomsky (1986a), where V-to-I movement has the effect that the derived I+V complex L-marks its VP complement, thereby lifting VP's barrierhood. The most prominent formulation of the basic idea is the definition of a barrier in Baker (1988):

(44) *Barrier* (Baker 1988)
An XP is a barrier between α and β iff XP excludes α and includes β and either (a) or (b) holds:
(a) XP is not selected;
(b) X is distinct from Y, where Y is the next higher maximal projection that dominates α.

Let us briefly show the effect (44) has on the barrier status of VP (in the original architectural setting without *v*P). VP is selected by I; hence, condition (44a) will not identify VP as a barrier. Whether VP is a barrier or not is therefore dependent on (44b) – specifically, the second part of (44b), the distinctness condition. Distinctness is defined in such a way that X is distinct from Y iff no part of Y contains the index of X. Now consider what happens when V-to-I movement takes place: then V is no longer distinct from I, as I now wholly contains V, including V's index. So whenever verb movement takes place, (44b) is not met, and VP is not declared a barrier. In this sense, head movement opens up barriers.

Two chronologically parallel phase-based implementations of Baker's (1988) insight are presented in Gallego (2005) and Gallego and Uriagereka (2006), and in den Dikken (2007). The former concentrate on CED effects, with *phase sliding* chosen as the name for movement of a phase head leading to upward percolation of phase properties to the category to which it moves. In den Dikken (2007), the properties of predicate inversion, ditransitive constructions, parts of Holmberg's Generalization, quantifier scope freezing, and the non-island status of highest-subject *wh*-constructions are derived from phase extension, the name given to idea that an XP which is not an inherent phase (i.e., a predication) acquires phase status when the head of an inherent phase moves to X. Under phase extension, the projection of the moving phase head loses its inherent phasal status. Under phase sliding, v stays a phase head and contributes this property to the new level, so that IP becomes a phase although I does not become a phase head.

(45) a. *Phase sliding*
Movement of a phase head leads to 'upward percolation' of phase properties to the category to which it moves. Thus, in a language with v-to-I movment, the phase is I, not v.
b. *Phase extension*
Syntactic movement of the head H of a phase α up to the head X of the node γ dominating α extends the phase up from α to γ; α loses its phasehood in the process, and a constituent on the edge of α ends up in the domain of the derived phase γ as a result of phase extension.

In their output representations, these dynamic phase models converge in interesting ways with the analysis of long A'-dependencies emerging from work adopting the formalism of Tree Adjoining Grammar (TAG) – see especially Frank (2002, 2006) and Chapter 8. The TAG approach does not postulate an intermediate trace of the A'-moved constituent in the specifier position of the complement-CP or on the edge of the matrix VP/vP. In long-distance A'-dependencies, the matrix clause forms an 'auxiliary tree' recursive on C' that is adjoined into the elementary tree (a simple CP) that harbors the (local, CP-internal) A'-dependency. Movement to SpecCP within the elementary tree must proceed via the vP-edge (if vP is a taken to be a phase and if a stopover on its edge is needed to void it), but in the auxiliary tree representing the matrix C', there can be no vP-adjoined trace because this auxiliary tree does not represent an A'-dependency at all.

Within the realm of movement-based accounts of filler–gap dependencies, the mainstream Chomskyan position, characterized by stopovers on the edges of all vPs and CPs, involves the most densely successive-cyclic derivations, whereas the TAG-based derivation features the smallest number of intermediate steps that a principled theory of locality can countenance. Any deviation from the minimum would have to be motivated on the basis of empirical evidence. We turn to this next.

18.10 Empirical evidence for locality domains: reflexes of successive-cyclic movement

There are a number of empirical observations that can be taken to provide evidence for the size and location of locality domains. In the background throughout is the idea that the existence of locality domains enforces long movement to proceed via successive-cyclic application of local movement steps. The motivation for intermediate landing-sites is that elements that are needed later on must be made available at each domain edge – otherwise, they would not be accessible anymore at later stages of the derivation. On the other hand, there are also economy considerations which need to be considered: a derivation must not contain more movement steps than necessary. While long dependencies must have a local representation (a trace or copy of the moved constituent) in every locality domain that is traversed, only *one* 'touchdown' per domain is necessary. In other words, an element that forms a long dependency has exactly one local representation in every domain that is crossed. If there are empirical reflexes of successive-cyclic movement, then these can be turned into diagnostics for the size of locality domains.

There are a wide variety of data that have been taken as evidence for the view that long-distance dependencies involve intermediate representations of the moved item. They are usually referred to collectively as 'reflexes of successive-cyclic movement' or 'path effects'. The data can be divided into three basic types:

- Semantic effects: long-moved elements are interpreted in intermediate positions (connectivity effects,[32] elliptic repair, pair-list readings; see Barss 1986, Lebeaux 1988, Chung, Ladusaw and McCloskey 1995, Fox 2000, Merchant 2001, Agüero-Bautista 2007).
- Morphological effects: long-distance movement affects the form of lexical items between and only between extraction site and final position (changing verbal agreement markers, changing complementizers; McCloskey 1979, Clements 1984, Chung 1998, McCloskey 2001).
- Syntactic effects: long-distance movement affects the syntactic environment between and only between the extraction site and the 'final destination' of the movement (head and XP movement, e.g., verb inversion and extraposotion; see Kayne and Pollock 1978, Torrego 1984, Ortiz de Urbina 1989, Henry 1995, Müller 1999), or the moved item is multiply pronounced (*wh*-copying, partial *wh*-movement; see du Plessis 1977, Cole 1982, McDaniel 1989, Wahba 1992, Thornton 1995, Horvath 1997, Fanselow and Mahajan 2000, McCloskey 2000, Felser 2004, Bruening 2006, Barbiers *et al.* 2009).

Since their discovery, path effects have been the topic of a lively debate – largely due to the fact that empirical material presented as evidence for a particular theory of the size of syntactic domains often turns out, when viewed from an impartial point of view, to allow for several different conclusions (see den Dikken 2010b). Successive-cyclic movement involving intermediate touch-downs at their edge has been proposed for each of the core categories: C (Lebeaux 1988, Barss 1986, Chung 1998, Müller 1999, McCloskey 2002), I (Bošković 2002c, Merchant 2001), v (Fox 2000, Legate 2003, Sauerland 2003, Agüero-Bautista 2007), V (Lahne 2008), and D (Svenonius 2004, Heck and Zimmermann 2004). However, even though the empirical observations are widely recognized, there is controversy as to their analysis.

First of all, there has been some controversy over the status of passive and unaccusative v. In Chomsky's (1995c: Chapter 4) original proposal, passive or unaccusative v does not mark the edge of a locality domain – if it did, agreement between I and the argument NP would be blocked in expletive-associate constructions like (46), as the NP is not accessible anymore at the point at which I is merged (Chomsky 2000b:108; 2001:12f.). Thus, only C and unergative/transitive v (called 'v*') are declared ('strong') phase heads, by virtue of their bearing uninterpretable phi-features (Chomsky 2008).

(46) [$_{IP}$ there [$_{I'}$ I [$_{vP/VP}$ arrived [$_{NP}$ a man]]]]

This view is challenged in Legate (2003) and Sauerland (2003), on the basis of the claim that the edge of passive and unaccusative v is a reconstruction site, just as is the edge of transitive v.[33] Den Dikken (2006c) in turn argues that the data discussed in Legate (2003) and Agüero-Bautista (2007) can also be taken as evidence for intermediate movement to the edges of I and V, respectively.

The status of IP as an intermediate landing-site for successive-cyclic movement is likewise controversial. Abels (2003) argues against the edge of IP as an intermediate landing-site (a view partly revoked in Abels and Bentzen, to appear). Furthermore, Fox and Lasnik (2003) suggest that the data discussed in Merchant (2001) are not a reflex of movement to the edge of IP (as proposed by Merchant), but, on the contrary, a reflex of a non-successive-cyclic movement step skipping the edge of IP.

There is also controversy concerning path effects in the C domain. Lahne (2008) analyzes the morphological path effects found in Chamorro and Irish as well as verb inversion not as effects occurring at the edge of C, but at lower edges. Rackowski and Richards (2005) propose that successive-cyclic movement in Tagalog does not proceed via the C domain, a view strengthened in den Dikken (to appear) on the basis of data from Hungarian and Chamorro as well as wh-scope marking and wh-copying (see Chapter 22).

18.11 Anti-locality

The discussion of locality in this chapter so far has been focused on establishing that there is an *upper* limit on the distance covered by syntactic operations. There appears to be a *lower* limit as well: syntactic operations, most prominently movement, must not be too local. This has come to be known as anti-locality. Chomsky's (1986a:49–50) Vacuous Movement Hypothesis (VMH) is probably the first explicit acknowledgment of the idea that there is something special about movement that covers a very short distance. The VMH, in Chomsky's own formulation, does not actually rule out movement that effects no change in the linear string (Chomsky merely states that "vacuous movement is not obligatory at S-Structure"); but later work has tended toward interpreting the VMH as a ban on string-vacuous movement. That such an interpretation is desirable is suggested by the fact that objects but not subjects can be topicalized:[34]

(47) a. [$_{IP}$ John [$_{VP}$ likes Mary]]
 b. [$_{IP}$ Mary$_i$, [$_{IP}$ John [$_{VP}$ likes t$_i$]]]
 c. *[$_{IP}$ John$_i$, [$_{IP}$ t$_i$ [$_{VP}$ likes Mary]]]

Subjects are generally assumed to be located at the edge of IP, and (English-style) topicalization is usually treated as adjunction to IP. If this is correct, the ill-formedness of (47c) indicates that an anti-locality constraint is at work: a ban on movement from the specifier position of some XP to an adjunction position to the same XP (Bošković 1994, 1997). Saito and Murasugi (1999)[35] analyzed this as an economy effect, a ban on superfluous steps. It is formalized in the following way:

(48) *Constraint on Chain Links* (Saito & Murasugi 1999, quoted from Bošković 1997)
A chain link must be at least of length 1. A chain link from α to β is of length n iff there are n nodes (X, X', or XP, but not segments of these) that dominate α and exclude β.

The ill-formedness of examples like (47c) can now be derived: the adjunction of a specifier of X to XP results in a chain link of length 0, as there is no node that dominates t_i but excludes *John$_i$* (the lower IP node does not count as a distinct node, as it is a segment of IP).

A second anti-locality effect is the presumed prohibition on 'comp-to-spec' movement: the complement of X must not be moved to the edge of X (Abels 2003, Pesetsky and Torrego 2001).

(49) a. *[$_{XP}$ [α] X [t$_α$]]
 b. [$_{XP}$ [α] X [$_{YP}$ Y [t$_α$]]]

And Grohmann (2003) examines at length a third type of anti-locality effect, the ban on 'domain-internal dependencies': thus, an element that has been merged as the complement of V cannot move within the verbal domain to be used as the subject:

(50) a. *[$_{vP}$ John$_i$ [$_{VP}$ likes t$_i$]]
 b. [$_{vP}$ John [$_{VP}$ likes himself]]

Anti-locality effects in general are derived by Grohmann by assuming that clauses are partitioned into three domains, so-called prolific domains: the Theta-domain is the part of the derivation where thematic relations are created (VP/vP); the Phi-domain is the part of the structure where agreement is established (IP); the Omega-domain is the part where discourse information is encoded (Grohmann 2003). The Condition on Domain Exclusivity states that a syntactic object X can occur only once within a domain unless the different occurrences are phonologically realized differently.

This condition explains a number of things. First, it accommodates the fact that TPs are immobile as the complement of C, as shown in (51c):

(51) a. nobody believes that this will happen
b. that this will happen, nobody believes
c. *this will happen, nobody believes that

Similarly, while VPs are mobile in principle, it appears that they cannot be moved away leaving a v behind. To see this, we first need to look at (52). This example shows that an anaphor contained in a topicalized noun phrase can be bound by a new binder in the matrix clause.

(52) a. John$_i$ said that Bill$_j$ likes [pictures of himself$_{i/j}$]
b. John$_i$ said that [pictures of himself$_{i/j}$], Bill$_j$ likes

But as Huang (1993) was the first to stress, this effect cannot be replicated for an apparent case of VP topicalization:

(53) a. John$_i$ said that Bill$_j$ would never [criticize himself$_{*i/j}$]
b. John$_i$ said that [criticize himself$_{*i/j}$], Bill$_j$ never would

Huang (1993) argues that the cause of the different behavior of examples like (53) is that the fronted constituent contains a trace of the external argument, which invariably wins as the binder for the anaphor. To preserve this kind of account in the current standard approach to the syntactic projection of argument structure, in which the external argument is base-merged as the specifier of v (Bowers 1993, Chomsky 1995c, Kratzer 1996, etc.), we will need to ensure that what is topicalized in (53b) is necessarily the vP, not the VP (which does not contain the external argument). To ensure that topicalization of the 'big' VP, with stranding of v, is impossible, we can then invoke Grohmann's Condition on Domain Exclusivity.[36]

18.12 On the locality of Agree(ment)

That movement operations are constrained by some form of absolute barrier is, as we have seen, a recurrent theme in generative syntax. Until recently, this conclusion would have carried over without further ado to all feature-checking relationships: the assumption that constituents have to move if they are to establish feature-checking relationships with functional heads was entirely standard in Principles and Parameters theory. This changed with the arrival of Agree. This operation allows a functional head F to check features of constituents in its c-command domain, without any movement of these constituents being necessary as long as they are not separated from F by a lower phase head. With the introduction of Agree emerged a question that had hitherto been non-negotiable: Are feature-checking dependencies subject to the same locality restrictions as movement dependencies or not? Some recent work has explicitly addressed this question, with specific reference to Agree relations involving case- and phi-features (on which, see Chapter 17). We can distinguish two different but fundamentally converging outlooks on the question: one line of thought argues that Agree relations can span distances that Move cannot, the other that Agree relations cannot span distances that Move can. We will highlight Bošković (2007a) as a representative of the former line, and Bobaljik and Wurmbrand (2005a) of the latter.

Bobaljik and Wurmbrand (2005a) present an argument based on the surprising lack of scope ambiguity in certain kinds of constructions with restructuring infinitives as evidence that Agree relations are sensitive to absolute barriers of a particular sort, but not to the ones that interfere with movement. Alongside phases (the absolute barriers obstructing Move), they set up 'agreement domains' – local domains across which Agree relationships cannot be established. Agreement domains differ from phases in being determined contextually rather than rigidly: a VP can be an agreement domain, but not intrinsically so; it is one only if it is selected by a lexical verb. In being mere VPs, agreement domains are also smaller than phases – hence Agree relations are sometimes more local than movement dependencies.

Bošković (2007a), on the other hand, investigates contexts in which Agree seems to hold across the boundaries of locality domains. This phenomenon is called long-distance agreement. The etiology of long-distance agreement is such that the verb of a root clause agrees with an argument of an embedded clause (for data, see Polinsky and Potsdam 2001, Khalilova 2007, Grosz and Patel 2006, Bhatt 2005, among others). Bošković concludes that the PIC intrinsically does not apply to dependencies that do not affect the linear string (e.g., Agree relations).

Bobaljik and Wurmbrand and Bošković would thus appear on the surface to have very different concerns. But they are united in the belief that Agree is not subject to the PIC. Bošković (2007a) goes further than Bobaljik and Wurmbrand (2005a) in offering a rationale for the apparent insensitivity of Agree relations to the PIC. His explanation is based on a particular outlook on the role that phases, and thereby the PIC, play in grammar. He embraces Fox and Pesetsky's (2005) argument to the effect that phases are linearization domains and that therefore material that extracts from a phase must typically do so via a touch-down on the edge of the phase in order to prevent a linearization conflict.[37] Based on this, Bošković concludes that the PIC is intrinsically silent on dependencies (such as Agree relations) that do not affect the linear string. More generally, he asserts that phases and PIC have no direct relevance for the locality of syntax: phases constrain syntactic derivations only *indirectly*, forcing successive-cyclic movement in contexts in which linearization conflicts would otherwise result.

Empirically, the cases that Bošković addresses fall into three separate classes. One is formed by cases that have been argued in the literature to be compatible with Agree being subject to the PIC in one way or another (initially, as in Polinsky and Potsdam 2001, by maneuvering the goal of Agree onto the edge of the phase, but more recently either with an appeal to clause union/restructuring, as in Boeckx 2004, Bhatt 2005, Bobaljik and Wurmbrand 2005a, or in terms of 'cyclic Agree,' as in Stjepanović and Takahashi 2001, Legate 2005, Boeckx 2007b, Keine 2008; see Richards 2008 for an overview). A second class involves cases that are likely to have been misanalyzed as instances of long-distance agreement (see Bobaljik 2008 for evidence that the key datum from Chukchi involves prolepsis). And a sizeable third group of examples involves a construction (the English *there*-expletive construction) whose syntax remains very much a matter of debate entirely independently of the agreement properties it has (see Hoekstra and Mulder 1990, Moro 1997, Sobin 1997, Schütze 1999, den Dikken 2001, and references there; see also the end of Section 10.4.1 and Section 17.2.2.2). It is highly likely that the various cases of 'long-distance Agree' do not form a homogeneous set. It seems not unlikely that reasonable ways can be found to keep them under the purview of the PIC.

Though both Bobaljik and Wurmbrand (2005a) and Bošković (2007a) exempt Agree from the PIC, both also recognize that Agree relations are not immune to locality constraints: Bošković argues that Agree is sensitive only to relative barriers ('intervention effects'),[38] while Bobaljik and Wurmbrand design a dedicated type of absolute barrier for Agree. Kariaeva (2009) develops the latter's theory further and shows that agreement domains should in fact be defined relative to the type of agreement involved: VP is an agreement domain for relations involving case, while concord relations of the type examined by Kariaeva (involving long-distance concord relationships in discontinuous noun phrases in Ukrainian) are obstructed by projections of nouns rather than verbs. Thus, barriers for agreement relations become a species of relative barriers.[39]

As Bobaljik (2008:317) points out, "[t]here are no clear cases in the literature of agreement reaching deeper into a finite clause than to the primary topic of that clause." Unless relative barriers can be shown to weed out all undesirable long-distance Agree relations stretching beyond an embedded topic, it is likely that some appeal to absolute barrierhood will continue to be necessary in the context of Agree. If so, the null hypothesis remains that the kinds of absolute barriers that Agree recognizes are the same that movement dependencies are also constrained by.[40]

18.13 Concluding remarks: types of locality

A central theme throughout this chapter, and indeed, throughout the history of generative syntax, has been the fact that syntactic dependencies can be obstructed in two basic types of ways: via the intervention of a closer potential antecedent for the gap (relative barriers; locality by intervention) or via the intervention of an opaque node in the tree (absolute barriers; locality by impenetrability). This dichotomy can be traced back to the beginning of theory development: the earliest locality condition, the A-over-A Principle, is a locality principle of the first type, while the island constraints proposed in Ross (1967a) can be seen as locality principles of the second type. A peculiarity of the historical development of the generative approach to locality restrictions is the fact that it has oscillated between the two types of barrier, at times giving pride of place to the former, and at other times concentrating on the latter.

- Locality by intervention: A-over-A Principle, Superiority Condition, Strict and Relativized Minimality, Minimal Link Condition, Shortest Path, Fewest Steps, equidistance
- Locality by impenetrability: All island constraints, Subjacency, Condition on Extraction Domain, *Barriers*, Phase Impenetrability Condition, etc.

The explanatory range of these two types of locality constraints overlaps. For example, as Müller (2004a, 2006) notes, the effect of the MLC is limited by the Phase Impenetrability Condition, as the MLC presupposes search space, while one of the conceptual reasons for phases is to reduce the derivational complexity and thus relieve active memory by limiting the search space (Chomsky 2004). For the following constellation, the MLC predicts that an operation cannot involve X^0 and G_2 due to the presence of the higher possible goal G_1. However, this result is also delivered by cyclic spell-out: if Y^0 is a phase head, then G_2 is inaccessible to X as it is already spelled out when X is merged (Müller 2006, Rizzi 2006a).

(54) $[_{X'} X^0 [_{YP} [G_1] Y^0 [_{ZP} [G_2]]]]$

Current Minimalism has found its way back to *Barriers* and, ultimately, Ross's constraints on movement in its emphasis on absolute barriers for filler–gap dependencies. On the other hand, Relativized Minimality as well as the earliest 'Minimalist' theory of locality (the one of Chomsky 1993) are concerned with relative or 'interventionist' barriers, and in this respect fit in the tradition of the very earliest perspective on locality ever unfolded in the Chomskyan line: the A-over-A Principle (where 'A' is a variable for a particular kind of constituent). The two lines of research on locality (the absolute and relative ones) have not, to date, resulted in a unified perspective on syntactic locality. Whether such a unified perspective is possible or even desirable is a question to which future research should make a major contribution.

Notes

1. See Chapter 10 for discussion of the locality of predication relations, and Chapters 15 and 16 for the locality of binding and NP-movement dependencies. We will talk about the locality of head-movement dependencies in passing in note 11 (where Travis's 1984 Head Movement Constraint is mentioned and critiqued) and also in Section 18.6, in the context of Relativized Minimality. Other locality constraints on syntactic dependencies, which often do not fit very straightforwardly under the rubric of syntactic locality theories, are addressed elsewhere in this handbook. Thus, for the Immediate Scope Constraint (Linebarger 1980), at work in the licensing of polarity items, see Section 21.3.3 and for the locality constraints on LF-dependencies, including Quantifier Raising, see Sections 22.2.1 and 22.2.2. Rizzi (1982a) suggested the possibility of parametric variation in the demarcation of local domains (see the end of Section 25.2), an issue we will mention in passing in the second paragraph of Section 18.3.
2. 'Barrier' in the narrow sense denotes a syntactic boundary within Chomsky's (1986a) theory of barriers; throughout this chapter, we will also use this term as a generic, framework-independent expression for impenetrable syntactic boundaries.
3. For the parse in (2a), we adopt an analysis in which the gerundial VP is part of a VP-adjoined small clause with a null subject (PRO) controlled by the matrix subject (on control, see Chapter 16). The label 'SC' in (2a) and (2b) stands for 'small clause,' and is used here for expository convenience. Similarly, the label 'RRC' in (2c), which represents a restrictive relative clause, is used pre-theoretically. For discussion of small clauses and their internal structure, see the chapter on predication (Chapter 10); for discussion of relative clauses, see Section 13.4.2 (and also Chapter 11, note 47). The structure in (2c) does not adopt the DP hypothesis (see Section 11.8), and assumes that restrictive relatives are adjuncts to NP – this is important in order for an 'A-over-A' account of the type proposed by Chomsky to be implementable (see the main-text discussion that follows).
4. Chomsky's (1973) examples are given in (i)–(iii). They are supposed to be derived via applications of Passive that demote a subpart of the subject

and promote the object into the position vacated by the demoted subpart of the subject. But passivization is not an operation performed on grammatical functions: it is an operation on the passivized verb's thematic grid. It is impossible, therefore, to affect only a subpart of the verb's external argument by passivization and leave the rest intact. The b-sentences are thus underivable entirely independently of the A-over-A Principle.

(i)   a.   John and Bill saw Mary
       b.   *John and Mary was seen by Bill
(ii)   a.   John's winning the race surprised me
       b.   *John's winning I was surprised by the race
(iii)   a.   the man who saw Mary bought the book
       b.   *the man who saw the book was bought by Mary

5. The Left Branch Condition (on which, see also Section 11.8.6 and 11.9.4) would follow directly from a strict interpretation of the A-over-A Principle not making reference to cyclic nodes, such as the informal definition given in Chomsky (1964b:931) quoted in the paragraph below (2), above. But as (3b) demonstrates, such a strict interpretation of the principle is too strong. Note that the ungrammaticality of *whose would you approve of seeing John? will also follow, without an appeal to the Left Branch Condition being necessary, if whose is not a constituent – see Kayne (2000b:109) and also note 54 of Chapter 11 on the relative contrast between **whose were you talking to sister? and ??who were you talking to 's sister?

6. The requirement that the wh-element must be leftmost inside a wh-moved constituent is not surface true (these are reports [the height of the lettering on the covers of which] the government prescribes), so it will need to be conjoined with a theory of pied-piping. On pied-piping and the constraints thereon, see Ross (1967a), Heck (2008), Jayaseelan (2010), and references there.

7. From the outset of our discussion of Ross's island constraints, it will be good to bear in mind that Merchant (2001) has argued, basing himself on observations that in part go back to Chung et al. (1995), that several of Ross's constraints are PF islands – that is to say, the island violations are violations of some PF constraint, not a syntactic constraint. He makes this argument on the basis of the fact that the island violations in question disappear under PF-ellipsis in contexts of sluicing (see Chapter 19 for more discussion). Thus, the CNPC violation that is in effect in the non-elliptical version of (ia) (i.e., the version that includes at PF all of the material struck out in the example) is entirely absent in its elliptical counterpart (lacking the struck-out material). Similarly, the Left Branch Condition is lifted under ellipsis in (ib), as is the Subject Condition in (ic), as well as the ban on extraction out of embedded questions instantiated by (id) (which, as we stress at the outset of the

next section, was not among Ross's original set of constraints), and even the ever elusive ban on extraction of a conjunct (one part of the CSC), as shown in (ie).

(i) a. they want to hire someone who speaks a Balkan language, but I don't know which (Balkan language) ~~they want to hire someone who speaks t~~
b. she bought a big car, but I don't know how big ~~she bought t a car~~
c. a biography of one of the Marx brothers is going to be published this year – guess which (Marx brother) ~~a biography of t is going to be published this year~~
d. she asked if somebody was going to fail Syntax I, but I can't remember who ~~she asked if t was going to fail Syntax I~~
e. they persuaded Kennedy and some other Senator to jointly sponsor the legislation, but I can't remember which one ~~they persuaded Kennedy and t to jointly sponsor the legislation~~

8. It should be stressed, however, that Erteschik-Shir (1973) explicitly did not pursue an approach along such lines. For her, the opacity of complements of non-bridge verbs and the transparency of complements of bridge verbs is a function of the information-structural properties of the matrix verb: bridge verbs are usually not focused, allowing their clausal complements to be focused; on the other hand, non-bridge verbs, such as manner-of-speaking verbs like *mumble* and *lisp*, usually attract the focus themselves, depriving their clausal complement of this discourse function. From Erteschik-Shir's general hypothesis that only focus domains are visible for extraction, it then follows that, in the typical case, complements of non-bridge verbs, not being focus domains, will be opaque. This predicts that whenever the information packaged by the non-bridge verb is not discourse-new, focus should be able to shift to its complement, rendering the latter transparent – and indeed, Erteschik-Shir points out that *who did John mumble/lisp that he had seen?*, which is severely degraded out of context, improves significantly in a discourse context in which John's mumbling/lisping has been mentioned previously. No syntacticization of the type mentioned in the main text would straightforwardly be able to account for this effect of discourse. (See Chapter 23 for more discussion of the syntax/discourse interface.) Aside from Erteschik-Shir's (1973, 2007) own information-structural approach, a sentence-processing theory (see Chapter 26) of strong and weak islands such as the one proposed in Kluender (1992, 1998) may be able to accommodate the effect.
9. A-movement dependencies generally cannot be established across Tensed-S boundaries either ('super-raising': *the problem seems that there has been solved*). This follows from (12), but it also falls out independently from the Specified Subject Condition of Chomsky

(1973), or its binding-theoretic successor Principle A in later work (see Chapter 15). We have simplified Chomsky's (1973) definition in (12) by eliminating the reference to the Specified Subject Condition, which will play no role in what follows. For brief remarks on the Specified Subject Condition, see also Sections 3.3.3 and 15.3.

10. The term 'subjacent' is a conflation of 'subordinate' (the antonym of 'superior' in the definition in (13)) and 'adjacent'. It is defined as follows: "let us say that if X is superior to Y in a phrase marker P, then Y is 'subjacent' to X if there is at most one cyclic category C Y such that C contains Y and C does not contain X. Thus, if Y is subjacent to X, either X and Y are contained in all the same cyclic categories (and are thus considered at the same level of the transformational cycle) or they are in adjacent cycles" (Chomsky 1973:247).

11. Empirically, the *wh*-island effect in (i), which involves two *wh*-clauses, is very similar to the so-called 'superiority' effect seen in multiple *wh*-questions that involve just a single clause (see (ii)) – and Chomsky's use of the adjective 'superior' in the definition of Subjacency in (13) seems to strengthen the parallel. The patterns in (i) (Subjacency) and (ii) (Superiority), though appearing at first to be each other's inverses, match almost perfectly on an analysis of *wh-in-situ* in pair-list questions according to which the *in-situ wh*-constituent undergoes LF movement toward the *ex-situ* one (the standard GB approach to wh-in-situ; see especially May 1985, and also Section 22.2.2, which in addition addresses the question of whether *wh-in-situ* is subject to Subjacency). (We say 'almost perfectly' because Superiority effects with *when* and *where* are often absent (Kuno and Robinson 1972:474; Quirk et al. 1966, 1985) while *wh*-island effects with *when* and, to a somewhat lesser extent, *where* are robust.) Once the *in-situ wh*-constituent is assumed to move across the *ex-situ* one in (ii), all the ungrammatical examples in (i) and (ii) can be seen to involve illegitimate movement of a subject or adjunct *wh*-constituent across another *wh*-element, as schematized underneath the examples.

(i) a. *Who do you wonder what/why ate?
b. ?What do you wonder who ate?
c. *Why/how do you wonder what he ate?[* on a 'downstairs' reading for why/how]
d. ?What do you wonder why/how he ate?
[wh_1 ... [wh_2 ... ec_1 ...]] ungrammatical for $wh_1 \in$ {subject, adjunct}

(ii) a. Who ate what?
b. *What did who eat?
c. Why/how did he eat what?
d. *What did he eat why/how?
[wh_1 wh_2 [... ec_1 ...]] ungrammatical for $wh_1 \in$ {subject, adjunct}

In spite of the empirical similarity between *wh*-island and *wh*-superiority effects, however, Chomsky's (1973) account of the two phenomena runs along rather different lines. While the *wh*-island effect in (i) comes under the rubric of the Subjacency Condition in (13), for the superiority effect in (ii) Chomsky proposes a separate condition, given in (iii). Support for Chomsky's decision to formulate Subjacency and Superiority as independent conditions comes from the fact that in languages such as German, the two phenomena go separate ways: German often exhibits no Superiority effects, but Subjacency effects are consistently strong.

(iii) Superiority Condition
No rule can involve X,Y in the structure ... X ... [... Z ... -WYV ...] ... where the rule applies ambiguously to Z and Y and Z is superior to Y

The Superiority Condition, while formulated generally, has very limited empirical effects. In the domain of NP-movement, any putative superiority violation will minimally violate one other principle of the theory as well: thus, *John was Mary killed*, an attempt at raising the object in a passive without demoting the subject, violates the Case Filter, as does the 'super-raising' case *John seems/is likely it/there to be invited*, in which the expletive is not in a case position (that expletives, including *there*, need to be in case positions (at least in English) is evident from the ungrammaticality of sentences such as *[it to seem that John is sick] would be unlikely* and *[there to be someone sick] would be unfortunate*); and familiar 'super-raising' cases such as *John seems that it/there will be invited* or *John is likely for it/there to be invited* violate the Tensed-S Condition (though not, interestingly, its successor, the Subjacency Condition: only one S-boundary is crossed, which should be allowed). Although head movement does seem to obey superiority in English (*been John has invited?* – Travis's 1984 Head Movement Constraint), instances of 'long head movement' have been reported in the literature on the Balkan languages and medieval Romance and Breton (Rivero and Lema 1989, Rivero 1993, Borsley et al. 1996) that suggest that there is no absolute ban on moving one head across another head (see also Chomsky 1991b for an argument that the HMC is false except where it reduces to the ECP). Even for *wh*-movement, cross-linguistic investigations have unearthed data that seem to indicate that superiority is not systematically in effect; but in this context the literature has generally gravitated toward the position that apparent superiority violations arise on a principled basis, as a consequence of differences among languages in the ways they perform multiple *wh*-fronting (see Richards 1997b and references there).

12. For important discussion of the Left Branch Condition, see Corver (1992) and Bošković (2005a). On parameterization in the realm of

LBC effects (specifically in the context of noun phrases), see the discussion in Chapter 25 of the NP/DP parameter.

13. See Munn (1993), Johannessen (1998), and references there for detailed discussion of coordination constructions and the restrictions on extraction from them. Ruys (1992) and Fox (2000) address the questions posed by coordinate structures with respect to quantification and scope (see Chapter 22). Chaves (2012) perhaps comes closest to providing an integrated account of the restrictions on extraction from coordinate as well as subordinate constructions, embedded within the framework of Head-Driven Phrase Structure Grammar (HPSG); see Chapter 7 for general discussion of HPSG.
14. Denying (as does Koster 1978b) that 'subject sentences' exist, and treating them as topics instead, is one possible approach to (14a). But it would not extend to (14b).
15. The definitions in (17) are ours, but do not differ substantively from those in Chomsky (1986a). Later in this chapter as well, definitions are generally phrased in our own words.
16. A blanket ban on adjunction of likes to likes is equally unlikely to be feasible: for serial verb constructions, for instance, structures have been proposed (e.g., in Déchaine 1993, Veenstra 1996, and references there) in which one constituent of category V is adjoined to another constituent of category V.
17. Important precursors are Perlmutter's (1972) original proposal that all extractions leave invisible resumptive pronouns, and Obenauer's (1984) argument that all successful extraction from islands involves null resumptives (see also Postal 1998).
18. Rizzi (2001b) extends this resumption-based account for argumental nominal fillers to the realm of so-called 'weak' or 'selective' islands. On the strong/weak island dichotomy and the typology of weak islands, see Szabolcsi and den Dikken (2003). For Cinque (1990b), strong islands can at best contain a(n argumental) nominal gap, weak islands in addition allowing PP-gaps as well. By this diagnostic, adjunct islands are strong (recall (15a–b)) whereas (non-finite) *wh*-islands, for those speakers for whom (ia) is grammatical, are weak. Postal (1998) arrives at a somewhat different dichotomy, between 'locked' and 'unlocked' islands.

   (i) a. *this is a topic about which John asked [whether to talk *ec*]
       b. ?this is a topic which John asked [whether to talk about *ec*]

19. The extent of the pied-piped constituent (called a g-projection in Cinque 1990b, following Kayne 1984) is formally computed according to (i):

   (i) *g-projection* (Cinque 1990b:140; based on Kayne's 1984 notion of connectedness)

a. γ is a g-projection of α iff (i) or (ii):

   (i) γ is a regular X′-projection of α or of a g-projection of α
   (ii) γ immediately dominates β, a canonical head-governor of a (g-)projection of α

b. β is a canonical head-governor if β is a head that is a governor and {precedes its governee in a VO language/follows its governee in an OV language}

20. Cinque (1990b) himself does not present a connectedness account of (21b). Instead, he seeks to derive its ungrammaticality from the requirement that pro be formally licensed by a governing head (see Rizzi 1986a). Specifically, Cinque proposes that C is not an appropriate licenser of resumptive *pro* (Cinque 1990b:120), whence the ungrammaticality of (21b) with *ec = pro*.

21. There is little consensus in the literature on the question of whether the 'complementizer-trace effect' should be given a syntactic account, and even less on the question of why these sentences are perfect without the complementizer. (See Bayer et al. 2011 for recent discussion and references.) Note that the minimality-based solution just sketched is actually unformulable in the theories of Chomsky (1981) and (1986a), as both adopt a definition of government according to which the subject of a finite clause is always locally governed by I(nfl): I assigns nominative case to the structural subject position under government in both Chomsky (1981) and (1986a) (the latter adopting the Aoun and Sportiche 1983 'm-command' definition of government, allowing I to govern its own specifier). For non-finite I, assumed not to be a governor, this problem does not arise.

22. Note, in particular, that in this theory, heads can serve as antecedent-governors for phrasal traces: such is the case in Chomsky's 'extended chains' account of NP-movement, where the trace of the raised NP in a sentence like *John is considered ec intelligent* is antecedent-governed by the trace of the auxiliary *is*. See Chomsky (1986a:75–77) for details. Since Chomsky allows heads to serve as actual antecedent-governors for phrasal traces, there is nothing peculiar, within the theory laid down in Chomsky (1986a), about heads interfering with antecedent-government relationships between two phrases (as in his account of the 'complementizer-trace effect').

23. Relativized Minimality as such cannot account for 'complementizer-trace effects' – an ancillary constraint on the licensing of traces is required: the head-government requirement of Rizzi (1990a). Since 'complementizer-trace effects' are not locality effects in the sense of the discussion in this chapter, we will not elaborate on them here.

24. We are illustrating the *Wh*-Island Condition with the aid of a case of adjunct extraction: recall that filler–gap dependencies involving

referential nominal arguments are usually grammatical across islands, thanks to the fact that they can be formed without movement from the island taking place. Rizzi (1990a) adopts Cinque's (1990b) null resumption approach to such dependencies.

25. This is not an exhaustive list of 'harmful interveners' – for more detailed discussion and references to the primary literature on intervention effects, see Szabolcsi and den Dikken (2003).

26. We note that equidistance here has been formulated in the contemporary probe-centred approach to movement. We should also point out that the idea that local domains for particular syntactic processes can be extended via the application of head movement is older than Minimalism. See the text around (44), below, for discussion.

27. See Collins (2005a, 2005b) for an alternative approach to this problem, couched in terms of 'smuggling,' i.e., movement past the apparent intervener of a larger constituent (the V' in (36), or the VP in a v-VP structure) that contains the noun phrase that is to be raised to matrix subject.

28. This derives the core of Holmberg's Generalization, the fact that overt Object Shift correlates with overt verb movement. But as Fox and Pesetsky (2005:22) point out, Chomsky's (1995c: Chapter 3) account of Holmberg's Generalization does not capture the fact that Object Shift is also licensed when a past participle by itself undergoes movement into the left periphery of the clause (as in *kysst har jag henne inte* 'kissed have I her not'). Fox and Pesetsky's own analysis of Holmberg's Generalization in terms of preservation of relative linear order (see also note 37, below) does account for this.

29. With phases defined as propositional categories, and with locality defined in terms of phases as in (38), current syntactic theory has in effect made its way back to the Propositional Island Condition of Chomsky (1977). It is interesting to note, therefore, that the acronyms for the Phase Impenetrability Condition and the Propositional Island Condition are the same.

30. There has been some controversy over the phase-head status of passive and unaccusative *v*. See the discussion in Section 18.10, below, for details.

31. Denying phasehood to IP continues a tradition that goes back all the way to the 'birth' of IP in Chomsky (1986a), where IP is explicitly exempted from inherent barrierhood (by stipulation; recall (17a)): if IP were allowed to be an inherent barrier in the theory of Chomsky (1986a), adjunction to IP would become necessary to extract material from IP; but if IP-adjunction were *generally* possible in this theory, the account of virtually all island effects would be entirely lost.

32. We insist on the term 'connectivity effects' rather than 'reconstruction effects', which is often used in the literature as a synonym for the former. But while 'connectivity' is a theory-neutral term, 'reconstruction'

crucially implicates movement and (intermediate) copies/traces. That it is unlikely that all connectivity effects can be analyzed in terms of reconstruction is shown perhaps particularly clearly by Sharvit (1999), with reference to connectivity effects in specificational sentences. Sharvit advocates a semantic, non-reconstruction-based account of anaphor connectivity.

33. Their conclusion is thus that *v* is always a phase head. A potentially interesting consequence of this conclusion is that the 'spine' of the derivation consistently becomes a regular sequence of the type 'phase head – non-phase head – phase head – non-phase head' (C – I – *v* – V); see Chomsky (2000b, 2001), Richards (2007).

34. The *Barriers* theory should also proscribe successive-cyclic movement of subjects proceeding via an intermediate step of string-vacuous topicalization, for otherwise, the ECP-based account of the *that*-trace effect would evaporate: if the subject of a subordinate finite clause were allowed to topicalize prior to undergoing *wh*-movement to SpecCP, **the man who Bill thinks that likes Mary* could be derived without an ECP violation being incurred (with the subject's trace in SpecIP being properly antecedent-governed by the intermediate trace in the IP-adjoined position, which is itself subject to deletion at LF and hence in no need of licensing).

35. The manuscript version of this work, circulated in 1993, was the major stimulus for a wave of discussion of anti-locality in the literature.

36. The contrast between (52) and (53) is also brought up in Section 10.8, where empirical evidence for the need for an alternative to Huang's (1993) approach is mentioned. Heycock (1995a) is one such alternative. See also den Dikken (2006c:32).

37. We say 'typically' because escape-hatching movement is not required precisely when fell-swoop movement out of the phase produces no linearization conflict – which is the case when the material relative to which the moved constituent is linearized within the local phase also leaves the phase and lines up *vis-à-vis* the moved element in such a way that the underlying order is perfectly restored. See Fox and Pesetsky (2005) for an application of this idea in the context of Object Shift. Den Dikken (2007:16) points out that their analysis of Scandinavian Object Shift depends on the attribution of phasehood to 'big' VP, which is unlikely to have that status on conceptual grounds. For discussion of linearization, see also Sections 1.1.3, 2.4.2, 4.2.1, and 11.4.2.

38. Richards (2008) overlooks the role of relative barriers ('intervention effects') when he says that there is evidence that the PIC does constrain Agree coming from the fact that *there are likely that it seems to be several men in the garden* is as bad as its super-raising counterpart (**several men are likely that it seems to be in the garden*): the expletive subject *it* is a (defective) intervener for a long-distance Agree

relationship between *are* and *several men* independently of whether the PIC is in effect.
39. Kariaeva (2009) also strongly confirms that agreement domains constrain agreement and concord relations but not movement dependencies.
40. This is also the perspective of Chomsky (2000b), where Move is parasitic on the prior establishment of an Agree relation.

Part V

Syntax and the internal interfaces

19

Ellipsis phenomena

Jeroen van Craenenbroeck and Jason Merchant

19.1 Introduction

Ellipsis phenomena – or deletions, in traditional generative terms – involve a number of cases where otherwise expected material goes missing under some conditions. As is usual, we will restrict our attention to just a few cases of what could in principle fall under St Isidore's definition of ellipsis;[1] in particular, we present and examine cases of missing sentential material, predicate material, and nominal material, known roughly as clausal ellipsis, predicate ellipsis, and nominal ellipsis, respectively.

How to formulate a condition ensuring 'recoverability of deletion' has been a central question since the dawn of generative grammar. It was addressed in passing in Harris (1957), Lees (1961), and Smith (1961), and is the subject of discussion at some length in Chomsky (1965: esp. pp. 177–84). In this chapter, we review a number of phenomena with a bearing on this question, and show that the great strides that have been made in understanding a wide variety of data and in their analytical coverage point the way to a deeper understanding of the nature of syntax and its component parts. In particular, ellipsis data are profitably used as a centerpiece of arguments that syntax is not surfacist (or 'lexical' in Chomsky 1965's sense). Put differently, there is strong evidence suggesting that ellipsis sites contain an abstract – i.e., unpronounced – syntactic representation. Viewed from this perspective, the 'recoverability of deletion' question becomes one of identity: to what extent and in what way is the abstract syntactic structure of the ellipsis site identical to the overt syntactic structure of its antecedent?

A second question, one with a much less elaborate research tradition, concerns ellipsis licensing. As discussed in detail by Lobeck (1995) (though see also Zagona 1982 for an early predecessor), even when deletion is perfectly recoverable, it does not necessarily yield a well-formed result:

(1) *John read the long book and I read the short [NP e].

Regardless of whether one assumes the ellipsis site (marked *e* in (1)) to contain abstract syntactic structure, and regardless of whether one takes syntax or semantics (or a mix of both) to define the anaphoric relation between an ellipsis and its antecedent, it seems clear that the elided NP in (1) is sufficiently recoverable. In spite of this, however, ellipsis is disallowed. This shows that on top of recoverability, there is a second well-formedness condition on ellipsis, one that commonly goes by the name of licensing, to the effect that not every phrase is elidable. Generally speaking, ellipses seem to group at the clausal, predicate, and nominal level, yielding clausal ellipsis, predicate ellipsis, and nominal ellipsis, respectively. It is these three broad subtypes that we will focus on in the next three sections. For each type we first discuss the evidence for postulating abstract syntactic structure inside the ellipsis site. Based on these findings, we then turn to recoverability, in particular focusing on morphosyntactic discrepancies between antecedent and ellipsis site, while the final part of each section deals with licensing.[2]

19.2 Predicate ellipsis

19.2.1 The main types of predicate ellipsis

Predicate ellipsis can be roughly defined as a type of ellipsis in which the main predicate of the clause is missing – often together with one or more of its internal arguments – but in which the inflectional domain and the canonical subject position are outside the scope of the ellipsis and hence remain unaffected. The examples in (2) illustrate the main ellipsis phenomena that fall under this rubric.

(2) a. John likes candy, but Bill doesn't __ (Verb Phrase Ellipsis)
    b. she'll read something to Sam, but she won't __ to Bill
                                                              (Pseudogapping)
    c. John will eat candy and Bill will do __, too   (British English *do*)
    d. Jan   wil   niet meedoen, maar hij moet __. (Modal Complement
       John wants not participate but   he must   Ellipsis)
       'John doesn't want to participate, but he has to'
    e. Ben will be in the garden, though he'd rather not be
                                                          (Predicate phrase ellipsis)

Without a doubt the most famous member on this list is Verb Phrase Ellipsis (henceforth VPE). It is fair to say that this construction – particularly in its English incarnation – has dominated the literature on ellipsis in the first few decades of generative grammar. Accordingly, the literature on VPE is vast and we cannot do full justice to it here, but key publications include Hankamer and Sag (1976), Sag (1976), Williams (1977), Zagona (1982), Hardt (1993), Fiengo and May (1994), Lobeck (1995), Fox (2000), and Johnson (2001).

Pseudogapping was first identified and named by Stump (1977) (see also Levin 1978, 1979 for early discussion). While he argued that 'pseudogaps' involve a process different from VPE, ever since Jayaseelan (1990) it has become standard practice to analyze this construction as VPE with additional extraction of a VP-internal constituent (in (2b) the PP *to Bill*) to a position outside of the ellipsis site. This is the account proposed by Johnson (1996), Lasnik (1999b, 1999c, 2001a), Kennedy and Merchant (2000), Takahashi (2003, 2004), Gengel (2007), Merchant (2008a), and Aelbrecht (2010) (though see Hardt 1993, Lobeck 1995 for a differing view), the main debate in this strand of literature centering around (a) identifying the type of movement responsible for extracting the remnant out of the ellipsis site, and (b) identifying the exact size of the ellipsis site (an issue we return to below).

The examples in (2c) and (2d) are more recent additions to the predicate ellipsis spectrum. The former is a British English construction that is on the surface identical to VPE, but for the presence of a non-finite form of the verb *do* next to the ellipsis site (see Chalcraft 2006, Haddican 2007, Aelbrecht 2010, Thoms 2010, and Baltin 2010), while Modal Complement Ellipsis (cf. (2d)) only differs from VPE – again, on the surface – in that the licensing verb is obligatorily a (deontic) modal. It is attested in Dutch, German, French, Spanish, and Italian, and discussed by Dagnac (2010) and Aelbrecht (2010).

Example (2e) illustrates a kind of predicate ellipsis that is rarely discussed. It concerns cases where a non-verbal predicate (which could be a PP, AP, DP, or some other category) has gone missing. If examples such as these genuinely involve PP/AP/DP/...-ellipsis, they differ noticeably from the other examples in (2), all of which involve the deletion of a verbal projection (see below for discussion). Another option, though, would be to assume that (2e) involves VP-deletion as well, but with prior extraction of *be* to a position outside of the ellipsis site (along the lines of Thoms 2010). It should be clear that more research is needed on this subtype of predicate ellipsis.

Having introduced the central characters of this section on predicate ellipsis, we now turn to the evidence suggesting that the ellipsis site in all these constructions contains unpronounced syntactic structure.

19.2.2 Unearthing the unspoken VP
In line with the existing research tradition on ellipsis, we primarily focus on VPE in this section, turning to the other types of predicate ellipsis only if they yield different empirical results or if they add an additional perspective on the issue under investigation. As pointed out in Section 19.1,

ellipsis can be used as a prime counterargument against the claim that syntax is surfacist or non-abstract. In this section we present two strands of research corroborating that statement. The logical structure of these two case studies is identical: if an ellipsis site contains unpronounced syntactic structure, it should partake in the same morphosyntactic processes that one also finds in non-elliptical syntax. The processes we focus on here are agreement and movement.

19.2.2.1 Agreement

Phi-feature agreement between the subject and the finite verb (see Chapter 17) has taken center stage in generative theorizing since its inception and continues to do so today. In current Minimalist work this phenomenon is argued to be the result of an Agree-relation between a Probe (T°) carrying uninterpretable and/or unvalued phi-features and a Goal (the subject-DP) endowed with the interpretable/valued counterparts of those features (see Chomsky 2000b et seq.), and while there are definitely alternatives around (see, e.g., Bobaljik 2008), what all proposals to date have in common is that both the host and the target of agreement have to be syntactically represented in order for the relation between the two to materialize. Consider in this respect the examples in (3).

(3) a. I didn't think there would be many linguists at the party, but there were/*was
    b. I didn't think there would be a linguist at the party, but there *were/was

The verb *was/were* agrees with the unpronounced associate DP inside the ellipsis site (*many linguists* in (3a) and *a linguist* in (3b)), thus strongly suggesting that the understood meaning of the elided VP is syntactically present as well. While these facts were already observed by Ross (1969), they have featured only sporadically in the ellipsis literature (cf. in particular López 1995 and van Craenenbroeck 2010a).

19.2.2.2 Movement

Ellipsis sites can be extracted out of. If they contain an unpronounced but otherwise fully regular syntactic representation, this is precisely as expected. The (lack of) transparency of ellipsis sites for syntactic movement operations has become a lively research topic in recent years, so we can only present the main lines of the debate here and refer to the original papers for details. In this section we first discuss the three main types of movement (X°, A, A′), then we highlight the special position pseudogapping has in this debate, and finally we turn to ellipsis sites that cannot be (or can only partially be) extracted out of.

Head movement of the main verb out of VPE-sites yields so-called V-stranding VP-ellipsis. It is attested in Irish, Hebrew, Portuguese, Galician, Russian, Swahili, and Ndenduele (see McCloskey 1991, 2004,

Ngonyani 1996, Sherman (Ussishkin) 1998, Doron 1999, Goldberg 2005, Martins 1994, 1996, Santos 2009, Gribanova 2009, Schoorlemmer and Temmerman 2010). Some examples are given in (4) and (5) (Goldberg 2005:2).

(4) Q: Šalaxt etmol et ha-yeladim le-beit-ha-sefer?
      send.2sg yesterday ACC the-children to-house-the-book
   A: Šalaxti.
      send.1sg
   'Q: Did you send the children to school yesterday? A: I did.'
                                                                                                               (Hebrew)

(5) dúirt mé go gceannóinn é agus cheannaigh   (Irish)
   said I that buy it and bought
   'I said I would buy it and I did.'

A central issue surrounding the phenomenon of V-stranding VPE is the so-called Verbal Identity Requirement.[3] It concerns the generalization in (6) (Goldberg 2005:171), which is illustrated by the Irish example in (7) (Goldberg 2005:168):

(6) Verbal Identity Requirement
   The antecedent- and target-clause main Vs of VP ellipsis must be identical, minimally, in their root and derivational morphology.

(7) *Léigh mé an dách níor thuig.
   read[PAST] I the poem but.not[PAST] understand[PAST]
   INTENDED: 'I read the poem, but didn't understand it'

In spite of the fact that the verb *thuig* 'understand' has raised out of the ellipsis site and hence is perfectly recoverable, V-stranding VPE is not allowed. As stated in the generalization in (6) the verb in the antecedent has to be identical to the verb in the elliptical clause (modulo inflectional morphology, see also below, Section 19.2.3). What makes this pattern even more striking is the fact that such a stringent identity requirement on material that has been extracted out of the ellipsis site appears to be absent in the case of phrasal (A- or A'-) extraction. In (8a) the DP *Mary* has undergone subject raising out of the complement of *seem*, while (8b) illustrates a case of topicalization (the DP *tomatoes* having moved from the object position of *like*). We return to such cases in more detail below.

(8) a. John seems to be happy, but Mary doesn't
   b. potatoes I like, but tomatoes I don't

To date, there is no comprehensive account of the Verbal Identity Requirement (though see the references mentioned above for various possible approaches). As such, it remains one of the (many) open questions in the field of ellipsis.

A-movement out of VPE-sites is widely attested. VPE occurs productively in passives, unaccusatives, and raising constructions. Some representative examples are given below.

(9) a. John was arrested, and Bill was too
b. John arrived at the party before Nika did
c. John seems to be happy, but Mary doesn't

Likewise, A'-extraction out of an elided VP is also possible. This is illustrated below for *wh*-movement (10a), topicalization (10b), relativization (10c) and QR (10d).

(10) a. I know which books you like and which ones you don't
b. potatoes I like, but tomatoes I don't
c. give me the books you like and the ones you don't[4]
d. a nurse will examine every patient and a doctor will too

$(\forall > \exists, \exists > \forall)$

This topic has sparked a lot of research in recent years. Roughly speaking, it is centered around two issues. The first concerns characterizing the conditions under which A'-extraction out of VPE-sites is allowed, while the second focuses on locality restrictions on the movement operations involved. As for the former, it was first observed by Sag (1976) that A'-extraction out of an elided VP is subject to a fairly stringent focus requirement. In Schuyler's (2002:18) phrasing, "there must be a contrastively focused expression in the c-command domain of the extracted phrase." This explains why there is a contrast between the examples in (11) (the a-example is adapted from Merchant 2008b):

(11) a. *they attended a lecture on a Balkan language, but I don't know which they did
b. ED attended a lecture on carpenting, but I don't know what MARY did

While in (11a) there is no contrastive focus in between the ellipsis site and the moved *wh*-phrase, in the grammatical (11b) the subject is focused and A'-extraction out of the VPE-site is allowed. This issue has been taken up in various ways by Williams (1977), Evans (1988), Fiengo and May (1994), Schuyler (2002), Kennedy (2002), Takahashi and Fox (2005), Merchant (2008a), and Hartman (2010). The consensus nowadays is that the ill-formedness of (11a) is due to the violation of a constraint dubbed 'MaxElide' by Merchant (2008b), which states that in the case of A'-extraction out of an ellipsis site,[5] the biggest possible constituent should be elided. In (11b) focus on the subject prevents anything bigger than the VP to be elided, but in the absence of such focus (as in (11a)) MaxElide requires that clausal ellipsis (in particular sluicing, see below, Section 19.4) take place instead of VPE.

The second research question related to A'-extraction out of VPE brings us right back to the core issue of this section, i.e., the claim that there is unpronounced syntactic structure inside ellipsis sites. To the extent that this is true, it not only predicts that elided VPs should be able to host traces of movement, but also that such movement operations should be subject to the same locality restrictions as their non-elliptical counterparts, even if the relevant locality domain is situated entirely inside the ellipsis site. The data in (12) (taken from Merchant 2008b:143-44) show that this prediction is borne out.[6]

(12) a. *Abby DOES want to hire someone who speaks GREEK, but I don't remember what kind of language she DOESN'T
b. *BEN will be mad if Abby talks to Mr Ryberg, and guess who CHUCK will
c. *they got the president and 37 Democratic Senators to agree to revise the budget, but I can't remember how many Republican ones they DIDN'T

Compare these examples to their full, non-elliptical counterparts:

(13) a. *Abby DOES want to hire someone who speaks GREEK, but I don't remember what kind of language she DOESN'T want to hire someone who speaks
b. *BEN will be mad if Abby talks to Mr Ryberg, and guess who CHUCK will be mad if Abby talks to
c. *They got the president and 37 Democratic Senators to agree to revise the budget, but I can't remember how many Republican ones they DIDN'T get the president and to agree to revise the budget

The fact that the VPE-examples in (12) are as ungrammatical as the non-elliptical data in (13) represents – in Culicover and Jackendoff's (2005:11 n8) terms – "impressive evidence of the reality of the invisible structure." None of the examples in (12) overtly contains an island. The fact that they are nonetheless ill-formed then strongly suggests that the offending syntactic representation is covertly present (see Sag 1976, Haïk 1987, Postal 2001, Lasnik 2001a, Fox and Lasnik 2003, Kennedy and Merchant 2000, Merchant 2001, 2008b, and Kennedy 2003 for additional discussion).[7]

Summarizing this section so far, we have shown that VP-ellipsis sites allow for extraction via X°-, A- and A'-movement, thus corroborating the claim that they contain unpronounced syntactic structure. In so doing, we have focused exclusively on VP-ellipsis. In the remainder of this section we turn to the other types of predicate ellipsis outlined in (2) and discuss to what extent they have featured in the extraction debate. Pseudogapping occupies a specific position in this respect. Recall that this construction is commonly analyzed as VPE with prior extraction of a VP-internal constituent out of the ellipsis site. To the extent that this analysis is on the right track, the very existence of pseudogapping provides evidence in favor of postulating invisible structure. At the same time, however, a number of researchers (see Jacobson 1992, Hardt 1993, Lobeck 1995) have argued against the extraction analysis of pseudogapping and moreover, have argued that what looks like extraction from VPE-sites is in fact pseudogapping with a fronted remnant. Put differently, in an example like (10a) (repeated below), the trace of *wh*-movement would in fact be outside of the ellipsis site.

(14)   I know which books you like and which ones$_i$ you don't ___ t$_i$

The relevance of this analysis for the topic of this section should be clear: if the *wh*-phrase does not originate inside the ellipsis site, an important argument in favor of abstract syntactic structure falls away. As Johnson (2001) points out, however, the analysis sketched in (14) is rendered unlikely by a number of empirical differences between pseudogapping and A'-extraction out of VPE-sites. First of all, while the former is incompatible with preposition stranding, the latter is not.

(15)   a. *Sally will stand near Mag, but he won't Holly
       b. ?I know which woman FRED will stand near, but I don't know which woman YOU will

Second, pseudogapping cannot remove part of a noun phrase, but A'-extraction can:

(16)   a. *while Holly didn't discuss a report about every boy, she did every girl
       b. I know which woman HOLLY will discuss a report about, but I don't know which woman YOU will

Third, while the locality restrictions on pseudogapping are more akin to those found in Dutch scrambling, A'-extraction shows the hallmarks of regular successive-cyclic movement:

(17)   a. *while Doc might claim that O. J. Berman had read his book, he wouldn't the paper
       b. I know which book DOC might claim O. J. Berman had read, but I don't which book PERRY might

It seems fair to conclude, then, that A'-extraction out of VPE-sites cannot be reduced to pseudogapping. As a result, the argument in favor of abstract syntactic structure stands.

Our reasoning so far took the form of a one-way implication: the possibility of extraction implies the presence of unpronounced structure. In much of the literature on this topic, however, the inverse implication is – explicitly or implicitly – also assumed to hold. For example, null complement anaphora (see below, Section 19.4) licenses none of the extraction options available to VP-ellipsis and as a result is assumed not to contain any internal structure (see Depiante 2000 and references mentioned there; cf. also van Craenenbroeck 2010a for relevant discussion):

(18) a. *Which films did he refuse to see, and which ones did he agree?
b. *these films he refused to see and those he agreed
c. *I know the films he refused to see and the ones he agreed
d. a movie executive refused to see every film, and an intern agreed
$$(\exists > \forall, *\forall > \exists)$$

Recent work on Modal Complement Ellipsis (MCE) and British English *do* (BE *do*), however, has called this second implication into question (cf. in particular Aelbrecht 2010 and Baltin 2010). What is remarkable about these types of predicate ellipsis is that they allow some, but not all extractions. Relevant examples (culled from the references just mentioned) are given in (19) and (20).

(19) a. die broek moet nog niet gewassen worden, maar hij mag
those pants must yet not washed become but he may
wel al (Dutch)
PRT already
'those pants don't have to be washed yet, but they can be'
b. ?*ik weet niet wie Kaat WOU uitnodigen, maar ik weet wel
I know not who Kaat wanted invite but I know AFF
wie ze MOEST
who she had.to
'I don't know who Kaat WANTED to invite, but I do know who she HAD to'

(20) a. John might seem to enjoy that, and Fred might do___too
b. *although we don't know what John might read, we do know what Fred might do___

As these data show, both MCE and BE *do* allow for A-movement (passive in (19a) and subject raising in (20a)) out of the ellipsis site, but A'-extraction yields an ill-formed result.[8] From the point of view of the two-way implication discussed above, such mixed behavior is unexpected: an ellipsis site should either be transparent for all types of movement, like VP-ellipsis, or for none at all, like null complement anaphora. Without going too deeply into the details of their account, what both Aelbrecht and Baltin argue is that MCE and BE *do* contain a full-fledged (but unpronounced) syntactic structure, and that the limited extraction possibilities illustrated above are due to the timing of the ellipsis operation. Roughly speaking, the ellipsis process operative in MCE and BE *do* happens at a point during the syntactic derivation when A-movement has, but A'-movement has not yet taken place. As a result, it bleeds the latter and the mixed data pattern in (19)/

(20) arises. More generally, what this means is that the absence of extraction can no longer be taken to be a diagnostic for the absence of syntactic structure inside an ellipsis site. In particular, it could well be that even null complement anaphora involves abstract syntax, but that the timing of the ellipsis process in this specific construction precludes any movement operation from targeting material inside the ellipsis site.

19.2.2.3 Summary

In this section we have reviewed a body of work on predicate ellipsis that, even though very diverse, converges on the conclusion that (VP-)ellipsis sites contain abstract syntactic structure. As pointed out in Section 19.1, this conclusion naturally leads one to a particular formulation of the question of recoverability: To what extent and in what way is the abstract elliptical structure identical to the overt syntax of the ellipsis antecedent? This forms the main focus point of the next section.

19.2.3 Syntactic or semantic identity?

The 'recoverability of deletion' question typically presents itself as one of division of labor: it is clear that the ellipsis site and its antecedent have to be identical in some sense for the deletion to be recoverable, but the question is which component of the grammar – and accordingly, what type of representation – is used for measuring this identity. While answering this question is non-trivial and a lot of research efforts have been devoted to it, it is clear that what is *not* at stake is surface identity, be it of a phonological or a morphological nature. Put differently, it is not the case that a phrase has to be string-identical to another one in order for it to be elidable. This is poignantly illustrated in the following example (adapted from Arregui et al. 2006), which shows that mere homophony (in this case, of *right* and *write*) does not suffice to render an ellipsis site recoverable:

(21) *Injustices, he rights, but books he doesn't __

Less 'exotic' examples of surface mismatches show that morphological identity is not required either. Consider the following pair (from Merchant 2009a):

(22) a. Emily played beautifully at the recital and her sister will __, too
b. Emily played beautifully at the recital and her sister will play beautifully at the recital, too

As the non-elliptical example in (22b) illustrates, the elided verb in (22a) is not surface identical to its counterpart in the antecedent clause (simple past vs. infinitive). In spite of this lack of morphological identity, however, this instance of VP-ellipsis is perfectly recoverable. This shows once more that surface identity is not what makes ellipsis recoverable.

The two obvious candidates for measuring identity are syntax and semantics, i.e., some researchers have argued that ellipsis sites and their antecedents have to be identical in structure (see Chomsky 1965, Ross 1969, Sag 1976, Hankamer and Sag 1976, Williams 1977, Hankamer 1979, Chao 1987, Rooth 1992a, Lappin 1992, Fiengo and May 1994, Lappin 1996, Chung et al. 1995, and many others), while others maintain that identity of meaning is what is required (see Dalrymple et al. 1991, Hardt 1993, 1999, Kempson et al. 1999, Asher et al. 1997, 2001, Ginzburg and Sag 2000, Merchant 2001, Hendriks 2004, Hendriks and Spenader 2005, and many others), with still others arguing for a combination of both (see Kehler 2002, Chung 2006, Merchant 2007, and van Craenenbroeck 2009). One of the standard ways of distinguishing between such proposals involves looking at mismatches between an ellipsis site and its antecedent. Semantic theories of ellipsis resolution predict that variations of form are allowed as long as they do not affect the interpretation, while syntactic theories predict that any deviation in syntactic structure – even if semantically vacuous – should lead to a recoverability failure. In this section we focus on four types of ellipsis-antecedent mismatches.[9]

The first set of data builds on the examples in (22). As was pointed out by Warner (1985) and further discussed by Lasnik (1995) and Potsdam (1997), the type of morphological mismatch illustrated in (22) is disallowed with auxiliaries:

(23) a. *Emily was beautiful at the recital and her sister will __, too
 b. Emily was beautiful at the recital and her sister will be beautiful at the recital, too

While the switch from simple past in the antecedent to infinitive in the ellipsis site proceeds without hiccups in the case of a lexical verb like *play*, with a functional verb like *be* ungrammaticality ensues. As such, these data represent a case where it is variability in form rather than meaning that determines ellipsis possibilities. Lasnik (1995) argues that the distinction between (22a) and (23a) is due to the fact that functional verbs enter the derivation fully inflected, while lexical ones acquire their inflection in the course of the derivation. This means that while there is a stage in the derivation at which the simple past and the infinitive of *play* are syntactically identical, this is not the case for *was* versus *be*. Viewed from this perspective, then, the morphological mismatch data in (22)/(23) constitutes an argument in favor of a syntactic identity theory of ellipsis resolution. This line of reasoning has been called into question, however, by Potsdam (1997), who argues that the distinction between (22a) and (23a) is not one of (lack of) syntactic identity or lexical vs. functional verbs, but rather concerns the fact that the antecedent for ellipsis contains a(n X°-) trace in (23a) but not in (22a). Assuming that the presence of such a trace disrupts (syntactic or semantic) identity between antecedent and ellipsis site, it follows that VPE is licensed in (22a), but not in (23a), and the argument favoring the syntactic theory disappears. While Potsdam does not offer an explanation for the identity disrupting behavior of X^0-traces – and note that XP-traces *are* allowed in ellipsis antecedents, see (8b) – the data in (24) do suggest that he is on the right track: when the antecedent is headed by a non-finite – i.e., non-moved – auxiliary, morphological mismatches are (much more) acceptable:

(24) a. Of course, if we had wanted to ___, we could have been great. But we didn't need to ___.
b. Of course, if we had wanted to be great, we could have been great. But we didn't need to be great.

It seems fair to say, then, that at the current state of research, the relevance of the data in (22)–(24) for the recoverability question remains unsure.

The second set of mismatch data concerns one of the – if not *the* – prototypical cases of form variation without (truth-conditional) semantic import: active–passive mismatches. As was explicitly and extensively discussed by Hardt (1993) (though see also Sag 1976, Dalrymple *et al.* 1991, Fiengo and May 1994, Johnson 2001, Kehler 2002, Frazier 2008, Arregui *et al.* 2006, Kim *et al.* 2011, and Merchant 2007, 2008a), the fact that such mismatches are allowed – under certain yet to be fully understood circumstances – constitutes prima facie strong evidence for a semantic identity account of ellipsis.

(25) a. passive antecedent + active ellipsis site
this problem was to have been looked into, but obviously nobody did ___
b. active antecedent + passive ellipsis site
the janitor should remove the trash whenever it is apparent that it needs to be ___

In both of these examples, the ellipsis site differs syntactically but not semantically from its antecedent, strongly suggesting that it is semantics rather than syntax that regulates identity under ellipsis. As was pointed out by Merchant (2007), however, this clear picture dissolves as soon as the data in (25) are contrasted with those in (26).

(26) a. passive antecedent + active ellipsis site
*Joe was murdered, but we don't know who
b. active antecedent + passive ellipsis site
*someone murdered Joe, but we don't know who by

What these examples show is that clausal ellipsis – in this case sluicing, see below (Section 19.4) for discussion – does not allow for active–passive mismatches. From the point of view of a semantic identity theory, either active and passive are semantically identical or they are not. If the former, then both (25) and (26) should be as good as (25); if the latter, they should both be as bad as (26). The fact that they display mixed behavior is very hard to account for from a semantic perspective. Syntactically, however, the contrast can be made sense of: suppose the functional head responsible for active and passive voice (Voice° in Merchant's analysis) is included in a clausal ellipsis site, but sits outside of a VPE-site. That means that in the case of VPE, antecedent and ellipsis site are syntactically identical (i.e., neither active nor passive), while in the case of sluicing they are not, thus accounting for the contrast between (25) and (26). Although Merchant's analysis is not uncontested (see in particular Arregui et al. 2006, Frazier 2008 for an alternative account in terms of processing), it constitutes one of the strongest arguments for syntactic identity to date.[10]

A third type of mismatch was first noted by Bresnan (1971a) and Sag (1976:157ff.) and has recently been discussed by Merchant (to appear b). It concerns the behavior of negative polarity items (see Chapter 21) under ellipsis (examples taken from Merchant to appear b):

(27) John didn't see anyone, but Mary did
 a. ... but Mary did see someone
 b. *... but Mary did see anyone
 c. $\exists x.see(Mary, x)$

(28) John saw someone, but Mary didn't
 a. ≠ ... but Mary didn't see someone
 b. = ... but Mary didn't see anyone
 c. $\neg\exists x.see(Mary, x)$

While one can easily argue that the semantics of *someone* and *anyone* are identical – both of them corresponding to an existentially bound variable – it is less clear if their syntax is as well. To the extent that it is not, these data constitute an argument for a semantic identity theory of ellipsis. Merchant (to appear b) illustrates what the syntax of polarity items (and determiners more generally) would have to look like in order for the data in (27)/(28) to be amenable to a syntactic identity account. In particular, the determiner-part of *someone/anyone* (i.e., *some/any*) has to be syntactically underspecified for polarity (both of them receiving the following feature specification: D[Indef; Pol: __]). As a result, they are syntactically identical and can be interchanged under ellipsis.[11] The head responsible for differentiating *some* from *any* ($\Sigma°$ in Merchant's account) is situated outside of the ellipsis site and hence does not enter into the recoverability issue that is at stake here.[12] While this account of polarity arguably has a high degree of abstractness, there are more ellipsis data suggesting that a lexical decomposition of determiners is sometimes required (Johnson 2001:(107), cited in Merchant to appear b, see also Jacobs 1980, Giannakidou 2000, Potts 2000 for related discussion):

(29) I could find no solution, but Holly might
 a. ≠ ... but Holly might find no solution
 b. = ... but Holly might find a solution

Given that VPE is allowed here, the determiners *a* and *no* have to be identical. This would follow if both of them enter the derivation unspecified for polarity, with a higher head valuing their polarity feature. Syntactic identity would then be calculated over the pre-valued representation. Summing up, polarity mismatches under ellipsis can either be seen as an argument in favor of the semantic identity theory of ellipsis, or they offer a unique window on the sub-word syntax of polarity items.[13,14]

The fourth and final type of mismatch under discussion here concerns pronoun/name-equivalences under ellipsis dubbed 'vehicle change' by Fiengo and May (1994). An example is given in (30).

(30) a. they arrested Alex$_i$, even though he$_i$ thought they wouldn't __
      b. *they arrested Alex$_i$, even though he$_i$ thought they wouldn't arrest Alex$_i$

If the VP-ellipsis site in (30a) were completely identical to its antecedent, this example would violate principle C of the Binding Theory just as the non-elliptical (30b) does. The fact that it is well-formed, then, suggests that the proper name *Alex* has 'transformed' – hence the metaphor 'vehicle change' – into the pronoun *he*, thus avoiding the binding violation. The basic premise of these data is the same as that of the polarity facts in (27)/(28): while one can easily argue that the denotation of *Alex* and *he* is identical under the relevant assignment function, syntactically there seems to be a substantial difference between these two DPs. Even Merchant's (to appear b) syntactic account of polarity items introduced above would be to little or no avail here. Specifically, one is hard-pressed to find a common, unspecified syntactic core for *he* and *Alex* such that an Agree- or checking-relation with a higher functional head can turn the first into a pronoun and the second into a proper name. As such, vehicle change presents a strong argument for a semantic identity theory of ellipsis resolution.

All in all, the jury is still out on which module of the grammar is responsible for measuring the identity between a (predicate) ellipsis site and its antecedent. Both positions have their advocates, arguments, and counterarguments, and this promises to be a fruitful area of research for many years to come.[15]

19.2.4 Licensing and cross-linguistic variation in predicate ellipsis

Recoverability is only one side of the ellipsis coin: even if they are perfectly (syntactically and semantically) recoverable, only VPs in specific syntactic environments can be elided. Consider a relevant contrast in (31).

(31) a. *Moby Dick* was being discussed and *War and Peace* was being __ too
      b. *Moby Dick* was discussed and *War and Peace* was __ too

In these examples the same VP is targeted by deletion. Moreover, this VP is recoverable, as there is a salient antecedent in the first clause that is entirely (syntactically and semantically) identical to the ellipsis site, and yet VP-ellipsis is only allowed in the complement of *was*, not in that of *was being*. This issue is known as the licensing question, and contrary to the puzzles discussed above it has received only a limited amount of attention in the literature; while most of the early studies on VPE noted that the construction was limited to specific syntactic contexts, hardly any of them any addressed the question of why that should be the case. The most significant contribution in this area is Lobeck (1995), but licensing is also addressed in Zagona (1982, 1988a), Johnson (2001), Merchant (2001), van Craenenbroeck (2010a), Aelbrecht (2010) and Thoms (2010). Lobeck argues that ellipsis sites are empty pronominals (*pro*) that have to be head-governed (essentially following the ECP). In the case of VP-ellipsis, the relevant head governor is T°. This means that we find VPE whenever T° is lexically filled, i.e., in the complement of modals, infinitival *to*, and the auxiliaries *have*, *be*, and *do*:

(32) a. Rudy can't jitterbug, but Debby can __
 b. Rudy can't jitterbug, but he wants to __
 c. Rudy hasn't jitterbugged, but Debby has __
 d. Rudy is jitterbugging, but Debby isn't __
 e. Rudy likes jitterbugging, but Debby doesn't __

Moreover, whenever a lexical verb raises to T°, it should license ellipsis as well. This is borne out by possessive *have* in British English ((33), data from Thoms 2010), and by the cases of V-stranding VPE discussed in Section 19.2.3.

(33) a. I haven't a copy of *Lolita*
 (OK in British English, * in American English)
 b. Rab has a copy of *Lolita* and Morag has __ too
 (OK in British English, * in American English)

As (33a) shows, British English differs from American English in allowing possessive *have* to raise across negation (to T°), while the b-example illustrates that verb raising of this type correlates with VPE-licensing. On closer inspection, however, this simple picture breaks down in a number of cases. First of all, negation can also license VPE (data from Potsdam 1997 and Johnson 2001):

(34) a. John's happy, but I'm not __ [16]
 b. I consider Bill intelligent and I consider Sally not __
 c. Ted hoped to vacation in Liberia but his agent recommended that he not __

Second, infinitival VPE (i.e., VPE licensed by infinitival *to*) is subject to an additional set of restrictions. Roughly put, it has to be 'close enough' to a higher lexical head (a requirement both Zagona 1988a and Lobeck 1995 implement in terms of head movement of *to* to some higher position). The data in (35)–(37) show the lack of infinitival VPE in adjunct clauses, subject clauses and (certain) infinitival *wh*-questions (all examples are from Johnson 2001).[17]

(35) *Mag Wildwood came to read Fred's story and I also came to __

(36) a. *You shouldn't play with rifles, because to __ is dangerous
b. you shouldn't play with rifles, because it's dangerous to __

(37) a. *Mary was told to bring something to the party, so she asked Sue what to __
b. John wants to go on vacation, but he doesn't know when to __

Third (and as was already illustrated in (32a)), VPE cannot be governed by an auxiliary in the *ing*-form (Johnson 2001):[18]

(38) Doc Golightly is being discussed and Sally is being __ too

Fourth and finally, some but not all epistemic modals can license VPE (the relevant distinction being necessity vs. possibility, cf. Gergel 2009):

(39) a. *Mary must be a successful student, and they say Frances must __ too[19]
b. ?Mary must be a successful student, and they say Frances may __ too

If the epistemic necessity modal is not adjacent to the ellipsis site, however, the contrast with possibility modals disappears and ellipsis licensing is allowed:

(40) A: I wonder if Mary has already talked to that employee. B: She must have __ because his desk is empty.

All in all, then, the licensing contexts of VPE in English constitute a fairly diversified group, and there is no unified account of them to date. One that comes reasonably close is that of Thoms (2010). He proposes that ellipsis is a side-effect of copy deletion in movement chains. In a nutshell, if for whatever reason the lower copy in a movement chain fails to be deleted, ellipsis of the sister of the higher copy can serve as a Last Resort rescue strategy in order to ensure that the structure can be linearized. This means that ellipsis is dependent on movement, i.e., every ellipsis site has been moved out of, or to put it in terms of licensing: ellipsis is licensed by movement.[20] Thoms cogently extends his account to epistemic modals and *ing*-forms (presenting non-movement accounts for both of them) and to negation (which he argues moves to a focus position), but he is forced to set aside infinitival VPE. However, the more fundamental problem with his account (one that Thoms himself also acknowledges) is that it overgenerates. If ellipsis is contingent on movement, then every movement operation should in principle be able to license ellipsis, contrary to fact. For example, given that in Dutch main verbs raise out of the VP (due to the V2-requirement of this language), we expect to find V-stranding VPE, but we do not:

(41) *Jan eet appels en ik eet ook __
John eats apples and I eat also
INTENDED: 'John is eating apples and I am too'

More generally, what the example in (41) shows is that ellipsis licensing is directly related to cross-linguistic variation; a head licensing ellipsis in one language might not do so in another. For example, the different types of predicate ellipsis introduced at the beginning of this section are all assumed to have different licensors. Modal Complement Ellipsis in Dutch, German, French, Italian, and Spanish is only licensed in the complement of root modals (Aelbrecht 2010, Dagnac 2010; the Dutch example in (42c) is from Aelbrecht 2010):

(42) a. Jan wil helpen, maar hij kan niet
John want help but he can not
'John wants to help, but he can't'
b. *Jan heeft geholpen, maar Marie heeft niet
John has helped but Mary has not
INTENDED: 'John has helped, but Mary hasn't'
c. *Jan zou liever niet te laat komen, maar hij wil wel
John would rather not too late come but he wants AFF
eens
sometimes
INTENDED: 'John would rather not be too late, but it sometimes happens that he is'

Similarly, Aelbrecht (2010) argues that British English *do* is licensed by the auxiliary *do* rather than by T° or modals (though see Baltin 2010 for an opposing view). It is important to realize that a difference in ellipsis licensor frequently means a difference in size of the ellipsis site. For instance, British English *do* is argued to involve VP-deletion (Aelbrecht 2010, Baltin 2010), VP-ellipsis deletion of *v*P (Merchant 2007), pseudogapping deletion of VoiceP (Merchant 2008a) and MCE deletion of an even bigger portion of the clausal structure (Aelbrecht 2010). While these differences are sometimes put to good analytical use (see above on the Aelbrecht/Baltin analysis of the limited extraction possibilities in MCE and BE *do*), one cannot help but feel that a generalization is being missed by treating all these cases of predicate ellipsis separately. In this respect we agree with Johnson (2008:3) that the field of ellipsis still bears too many signs of the construction-specific days of generative grammar; a unified account of the four types of predicate ellipsis discussed here would be a first step toward rectifying that situation.

19.3 Clausal ellipsis

19.3.1 The main types of clausal ellipsis

Clausal ellipsis can be defined as a subspecies of ellipsis whereby an entire clause is missing, including the canonical subject position and the agreement domain, but often to the exclusion of one or more clause-internal constituents. As we will see in this section, those constituents are usually argued to have moved to the left periphery of the clause prior to deletion. Clausal ellipsis comprises at least the following subtypes:

(43) a. Ed killed someone, but I don't know who (sluicing)

b. Ed is eating, but I don't know what (sprouting)

c. Ed gave a lecture, but I don't know what about (swiping)

d. Jef eid iemand gezien, mo ik weet nie wou da (spading)
Jef has someone seen but I know not who that
'Jef saw someone, but I don't know who'

e. A: What did you buy? B: A boat. (fragment answers)

f. John likes sandals and Mary stiletto heels (gapping)

g. Ed likes stiletto heels and Maggy too (stripping)

h. Ed wanted Bill to help Mary, but he refused
(null complement anaphora)

As already indicated by the naming convention, the first four constructions on this list form a unit, with the first one, sluicing, as the most basic (and well-known) type. The term sluicing refers to the phenomenon whereby an entire constituent question is missing, except for the *wh*-phrase.[21] It was first discovered (and named) by Ross (1969), and has since been analyzed by van Riemsdijk (1978), Chao (1987), Lobeck (1991), (1995), Chung et al. (1995), Romero (1998), Ginzburg and Sag (2000), Lasnik (2001a), Merchant (2001), and Culicover and Jackendoff (2005), among several others. Sprouting is a subtype of sluicing (first discussed in depth by Chung et al. 1995, but mentioned in most of the literature on sluicing) whereby the sluiced *wh*-phrase has no overt correlate in the antecedent clause: while in (43a) *who* in the elliptical clause corresponds to *someone* in the antecedent clause, there is no such overt correlate for *what* in (43b). In swiping constructions a *wh*-PP has been sluiced, but the canonical order of preposition and *wh*-phrase (the former preceding the latter: *about what*) has been inverted. Swiping is an acronym (coined by Merchant 2002) for 'Sluiced Wh-word Inversion with Prepositions In Northern Germanic' and it is analyzed by Ross (1969), Rosen (1976), van Riemsdijk (1978), Lobeck (1995), Chung et al. (1995), Kim (1997), Culicover (1999), Richards (1997b, 2001), Merchant (2002), Culicover and Jackendoff (2005), Hasegawa

(2007), Hartman and Ai (2007), Hartman (2007), and van Craenenbroeck (2010a). Finally, spading is a type of sluicing whereby the sluiced *wh*-phrase is followed by a demonstrative pronoun. It is exemplified here for dialectal Dutch, but has been attested in Frisian, French, Czech, Northern Norwegian, Serbo-Croatian, and certain dialects of German. Spading is briefly noted for Frisian by Hoekstra (1993) and discussed in depth by van Craenenbroeck (2010a), who also coined the name (which is an acronym for 'Sluicing Plus A Demonstrative In Non-insular Germanic').

Fragment answers are subsentential XPs with the same propositional content and assertoric force as utterances of fully sentential syntactic structures. The literature on this topic is vast and can be roughly divided into two camps. A first set of researchers (Hankamer 1979, Morgan 1973, 1989, Stanley 2000, Reich 2002, 2003, Brunetti 2003a, 2003b, Merchant 2004, Valmala 2007, Ludlow 2005) argue that fragments are derived from a fully clausal source via ellipsis, while others (in particular van Riemsdijk 1978, Hausser and Zaefferer 1978, Yanofsky 1978, Carston 2002, Ginzburg and Sag 2000, Jackendoff 2002, Barton 1990, Stainton 1995, 1997, 1998, 2005, 2006a, 2006b) attempt to derive the properties of fragments without appealing to ellipsis.

Gapping and stripping are often considered to be two of a kind: both of them have to be directly coordinated with their antecedent and they seem to differ only in the number of constituents remaining after ellipsis: one (accompanied by a polarity element) in the case of stripping and more than one in the case of gapping.[22,23] Once again, the literature on this topic is quite extensive (Sag 1976, Neijt 1979, Pesetsky 1982b, Kim 1998, Depiante 2000, Hoji 1987, 1990, Fukaya and Hoji 1999, Hoji and Fukaya 2001, Fukaya 2002, 2007, Chao 1987, Reinhart 1983, 1991, McCawley 1991, Coppock 2001, Hankamer 1979, Hartmann 2000, Hudson 1976, Jackendoff 1971, Lin 2002, Ross 1970, Steedman 1990, Depiante 2000, Ackema and Szendrői 2002, Johnson 2009), with some more recent work (see in particular Johnson 2009) arguing that gapping does not involve ellipsis at all, but rather is a subspecies of across-the-board movement.

Null complement anaphora (NCA) is the odd man out in this list in that it involves the deletion of an entire clausal complement without there being any 'survivors,' i.e., clause-internal XPs that surface next to the ellipsis site. As pointed out above (in Section 19.2.2.2), the elliptical constituent in cases of NCA is commonly considered to contain no internal syntactic structure, and as such is assumed to be more akin to null pronominals (or deep anaphora in Hankamer and Sag's 1976 terminology).[24] For discussion of NCA, see Shopen (1972, 1973), Hankamer and Sag (1976), Grimshaw (1979), Sæbø (1996), and Depiante (2000).

Space limitations prevent us from discussing all the types of clausal ellipsis listed in (43) in detail. We will focus on sluicing (and its subtypes) and fragment answers in the remainder of this section. The logical structure of the section is the same as that of the previous two: we first present evidence in favor of the hypothesis that ellipsis sites contain unpronounced syntactic structure and then focus on recoverability and licensing.[25]

19.3.2 Clausal ellipsis as movement + deletion

Just as was the case with predicate ellipsis, extraction out of clausal ellipsis sites counts as strong evidence in favor of postulating an abstract syntactic structure for such constructions, the idea being that this structure has to be present in order to host the foot of the movement chain. When it comes to the different types of movement, however, differences begin to emerge between predicate and clausal ellipsis. First of all (and unsurprisingly), A-movement out of clausal ellipsis sites is unattested. Given that the landing-site of such A-movement is contained inside the ellipsis site, any movement beyond that position would not be A-movement. The second difference, however, is less obvious: it turns out that there are no known cases of head movement out of clausal ellipsis sites. Consider in this respect the sluicing data in (44).

(44) A: John has invited someone from his office.
      B: Really? Who (*has)?

(45) [CP Who [C' has [TP he t$_{has}$ invited t$_{who}$?]]]

Under the – fairly standard, cf. Merchant (2001) for discussion – assumption that sluicing involves TP-deletion, the perfective auxiliary *has* should raise out of the ellipsis site and occur to the right of the sluiced *wh*-phrase, contrary to fact. It thus looks like head movement is being bled by ellipsis.[26] A particularly striking case in this respect involves clausal ellipsis in *yes/no*-questions in Hungarian (van Craenenbroeck and Lipták 2008). As shown in (46), in embedded *yes/no*-questions the finite verb obligatorily bears the interrogative suffix *-e*; this suffix cannot attach to any constituent other than the verb (see (47), with *-e* attached to the preverbal focus *János*), which van Craenenbroeck and Lipták take to be an indication that the verb undergoes head movement to the interrogative head hosting the suffix.

(46)   kiváncsi vagyok, hogy   JÁNOS ment-**e** el
       curious I.am   COMP János went-Q PV
       'I wonder if it was János who left'

(47) * kiváncsi vagyok, hogy   JÁNOS-**e** ment el
       curious I.am   COMP János-Q went PV
       'I wonder if it was János who left'

Under ellipsis, however, the *e*-suffix *can* attach to a preverbal focus; in fact, this is the only option in this context:

(48)   János meghívott egy lányt, de nem tudom   hogy ANNÁT*(-e)
       John invited   a   girl but not I.know that Anna-Q
       'John invited a girl, but I don't know if it was Anna'

Van Craenenbroeck and Lipták take this to mean that while the interrogative head hosting the *e*-suffix is outside of the ellipsis site and hence remains overt, the movement operation combining the finite verb with this suffix has been bled by ellipsis. The interaction between head movement and ellipsis has sparked some discussion in the literature (see Merchant 2001:62–74, Lasnik 1999b, 1999c, 2001a, Boeckx and Stjepanović 2001, Baltin 2002, van Craenenbroeck and Lipták 2008, Schoorlemmer and Temmerman 2010, Thoms 2010), and though some of these papers focus on the intriguing discrepancy between predicate ellipsis (where in the case of V-stranding VPE head movement out of an ellipsis site is fine, see above) and clausal ellipsis, a unified account of all these cases is still lacking. As a result, the interaction between head movement and clausal ellipsis does not provide any conclusive evidence for postulating unpronounced syntactic structure.

As far as A'-movement is concerned, however, things are different. As pointed out above, one of the possible ways of analyzing clausal ellipsis with one or more XP-remnants is by assuming that those XPs have moved into the left periphery of the clause prior to the ellipsis process. To the extent that such an account is successful, all the subspecies listed in (43) – with the exception of NCA – bear witness to the abstractness of syntax in elliptical constructions. In order for this line of reasoning to go through, however, the postulated movement operations would have to bear the hallmarks of regular, non-elliptical A'-movement. One such characteristic is locality. As it turns out, fragment answers (49a), sprouting (49b), contrast sluicing (49c), and adjunct sluicing (49d) are indeed sensitive to island restrictions (data in (49a–c) from Merchant 2009a):[27]

(49) a. A: Did each candidate$_2$ agree on who will ask him$_2$ about TAXES (at tonight's debate)?
   B: *No, about FOREIGN POLICY.
b. Tony sent Mo a picture that he painted, but it is not clear with what
   = <Tony sent him the picture t$_{with\ what}$>
   ≠ <Tony sent him a picture [that he painted t$_{with\ what}$]>
c. she knows a guy who has five dogs, but I don't know how many cats
   = <he [=the guy who has the five dogs] has t$_{how\ many\ cats}$>
   ≠ <she knows a guy who has t$_{how\ many\ cats}$]>
d. they were looking for a man who could solve the problem in a certain way, but I don't know how
   = <they were looking for a man t$_{how}$>
   ≠ <they were looking for a man [who could solve the problem t$_{how}$]>

The fact that these familiar locality restrictions show up in ellipsis contexts constitutes very strong evidence for a movement+deletion-analysis of clausal ellipsis and hence for the existence of unpronounced syntactic structure.

This important conclusion is sometimes overshadowed by the (admittedly puzzling) fact that sluicing with indefinite correlates is *not* sensitive to islands. Some representative examples are given in (50).

(50) a. they want to hire someone who speaks a Balkan language, but I don't remember which
b. every linguist$_1$ argued with a philosopher who took issue with one of his$_1$ claims, but I can't remember which one of his$_1$ claims

Data such as these have received a fair amount of attention in the literature (Ross 1969, Chung et al. 1995, Merchant 2001, 2004, 2006, Fox and Lasnik 2003, Culicover and Jackendoff 2005, Temmerman 2010), with some authors arguing against a movement account (and in some cases also against the existence of abstract syntactic structure), while others have taken these data as an indication that island violations are to be situated in the PF-component (and as a result, they can be undone by not pronouncing the violation; see also Chapter 18, note 7).[28] That said, a full account of all relevant cases of island (in)sensitivity is still lacking.

Aside from locality, the second main strand of argumentation in favor of unpronounced syntactic structure inside ellipsis sites comes from connectivity effects between the extracted remnant and the postulated elided structure. We discuss three types of connectivity here: preposition stranding, case matching, and binding (for additional arguments, see in particular Merchant 2004 and Agüero-Bautista 2007). As for preposition stranding, Merchant (2001) first observed that there is a close correlation between elliptical and non-elliptical syntax in this respect:

(51) Preposition Stranding Generalization (PSG)
A language *L* will allow preposition stranding under sluicing iff *L* allows preposition stranding under regular *wh*-movement.

In order to see this generalization in action, consider the data in (52)–(55). The second example shows that English is a language that allows preposition stranding under regular, overt *wh*-movement. Similarly, in sluicing (see (52)), when the correlate of the sluiced *wh*-phrase is a PP (in this case *with someone*), that *wh*-phrase can either surface as a PP or as a DP. In the latter case, it has stranded its preposition inside the ellipsis site in a manner completely parallel to the overt movement operation in (53). The Greek data in (54)–(55) on the other hand, display the opposite pattern: Greek allows preposition stranding neither in overt nor in elliptical syntax.

(52) Peter was talking with someone, but I don't know (with) who

(53) Who was Peter talking with?

(54) i   Anna milise me kapjon, alla dhe ksero *(me) pjon
    the Anna spoke with someone but not I.know with who
    'Anna spoke with someone, but I don't know with who'

(55) *Pjon milise   me?
    who she.spoke with
    INTENDED: 'Who did she speak with?'   (Greek; Merchant 2001:94)

Merchant shows that this two-way correlation holds in twenty-five languages (seven of which allow preposition stranding).[29] Under the assumption that ellipsis sites contain no internal syntax, such a correlation would be coincidental and unexpected. As such, the PSG represents a strong argument in favor of the analysis of sluicing under discussion here.

The second type of connectivity effect was already observed by Ross (1969), but is further worked out and elaborated upon by Merchant (2001, 2004). It concerns the fact that in languages with morphological case marking, sluiced *wh*-phrases bear the exact same case that they would in non-elliptical *wh*-questions (compare (56a) with (56b)). Under the assumption that this structure is also present (but remains unpronounced) in sluicing, this correlation follows naturally. In the absence of such abstract structure, however, this case matching requires additional theoretical machinery (see, e.g., Ginzburg and Sag 2000, Culicover and Jackendoff 2005, Progovac et al. 2006).

(56) a. er will jemandem schmeicheln, aber sie wissen nicht,
      he wants someone.DAT flatter   but they know not
      {*wer   / *wen   / wem}   (German)
      who.NOM / who.ACC / who.DAT
      'he wants to flatter someone, but they don't know who'
   b. er will jemandem schmeicheln, aber sie wissen nicht,
      he wants someone.DAT flatter   but they know not
      {*wer   / *wen   / wem}   er schmeicheln will
      who.NOM / who.ACC / who.DAT he flatter   wants
      'he wants to flatter someone, but they don't know who he wants to flatter'

Third, both sluiced *wh*-phrases and fragment answers show binding connectivity with material inside the elliptical clause. Some representative examples are given below.

(57) a. every professor$_i$ wanted to talk about one of his$_i$ books, but I don't remember which one of his$_i$ books
   b. A: What does every professor$_i$ want to talk about?
      B: One of his$_i$ books.

In both of these examples the pronoun *his* in the ellipsis remnant can acquire a bound variable reading, with the DP *every professor* as the binder. Under the standard assumption that such binding requires c-command at one stage of the derivation, and given that no such relation is established between the pronoun and the overt DP *every professor* in the antecedent, variable binding must take place inside (the unpronounced syntactic structure of) the ellipsis site.

Summing up, even though the absence of head movement out of clausal ellipsis sites and the island insensitivity of certain types of sluicing are puzzling from the point of view of an abstract syntax analysis of ellipsis, there is ample evidence from locality and connectivity suggesting that this abstract structure nonetheless exists. We now turn to the recoverability condition on this unpronounced structure.

19.3.3 Recoverability: clefts and no new words

The question of whether the identity relation between an ellipsis site and its antecedent is syntactic or semantic in nature once again hinges on the type of discrepancies one finds between the two. Some of these mismatches have already been discussed and/or are identical to those found for predicate ellipsis. For example, the fact that no active–passive mismatches are found in sluicing (see above, example (26)) constitutes prima facie evidence for a syntactic identity requirement (though see the discussion in Section 19.2.3 for a more nuanced view). Similarly, vehicle change and category mismatches are attested in clausal ellipsis, just like they are in predicate ellipsis. At the same time, however, certain types of mismatches are specific to clausal ellipsis. In part this is simply related to the fact that the ellipsis site is bigger, and as a result, there are more elements that can diverge. For instance, a sluicing site can differ from its antecedent in finiteness (data from Merchant 2001):

(58) a. decorating for the holidays is easy if you know how
      = how <to decorate for the holidays>
      ≠ *how <decorating for the holidays>
   b. I'll fix the car if you tell me how
      = how <to fix the car>
      ≠ how <I'll fix the car>
   c. I remember meeting him, but I don't remember when
      = when <I met him>
      ≠ *when <meeting him>

In all of these cases there is a clear syntactic difference between the structure of the antecedent and that of the ellipsis site, but semantically they seem to be completely parallel. As such, discrepancies like these constitute evidence against a syntactic identity account for ellipsis.

Another type of mismatch that is specific to clausal ellipsis concerns sprouting. Consider the data in (59).

(59) a. she was eating, but I don't know what
b. she solved the puzzle, but I don't know where/when/how
c. she finished her homework, but I don't know with whose help

At first sight, the antecedent clause and the sluiced clause are not syntactically identical in (59a). In particular, while the latter contains a trace/copy of the moved *wh*-phrase *what* in object position, the former features the intransitive use of the verb *eat*. Semantically, however, the two clauses are equivalent: there is a mutual entailment relation between *she was eating* and *she was eating something*. Just as was the case with the polarity item mismatches in Section 19.2.3, we can proceed in two ways at this point: either we take sprouting to favor the semantic theory, or we refine the syntax such that ellipsis site and antecedent become syntactically isomorphic. In this particular case, what this would mean is that implicit arguments such as the understood object of *eat* have to be structurally represented. While this might seem like a small (yet not uncontroversial) price to pay, example (59b) suggests that not only arguments, but also null adjuncts have to have a syntactic representation. That is, every clause comes with syntactically represented place, time, and manner variables.[30] To the extent that one is not willing to go down that road, the data in (59a–b) support the semantic theory of ellipsis resolution. However, (59c) shows that this theory is not without its problems either: given that there is no obvious semantic equivalence between finishing one's homework and finishing one's homework with someone's help (the former not entailing the latter), the semantic theory would wrongly predict sluicing not to be an option here. Whether or not the syntactic theory would fare any better depends on whether the manner variable in the antecedent can count as syntactically identical to the trace of *with whose help* in the ellipsis site. At any rate, it is clear that sprouting poses non-trivial problems for the recoverability theory of ellipsis.

As Chung (2006) has pointed out, these problems are worsened when one considers the absence of preposition stranding under sprouting. The relevant data are in (60) and (61).

(60) a. *they're jealous, but it is unclear who
b. *Joe was murdered, but we don't know who
c. *last night he was very afraid, but he couldn't tell us what

(61) a. they're jealous, but it is unclear of who
b. Joe was murdered, but we don't know by who
c. last night he was very afraid, but he couldn't tell us of what

As the examples in (61) show, it is perfectly possible to sprout a *wh*-PP. Moreover, as was discussed in the previous section, English is a language that allows preposition stranding under sluicing (see (52) and surrounding text). When these two are combined, however, as in (60), sharp ungrammaticality ensues, or in the words of Chung (2006:82), languages "allow a preposition to be stranded in (the elided IP of) sluicing, *as long as the remnant has an overt correlate in the antecedent IP*" (original italics). Let us consider what this means for semantic and syntactic identity theories of ellipsis. Note that the prepositions in (60)–(61) are of a purely grammatical nature, i.e., they make no semantic contribution to the sentence. Hence, stranding them inside the ellipsis site should not affect the semantic identity relation between the ellipsis and its antecedent, and a semantic theory would wrongly predict the examples in (60) to be as good as those in (61). However, the same holds for the syntactic approach: in order to accommodate the data in (61) this theory has to allow for implicit PP-arguments to be structurally represented in the antecedent, but that same mechanism would ensure syntactic isomorphism between ellipsis site and antecedent in (60) as well. In short, the contrast between (60) and (61) can be captured straightforwardly by neither the semantic nor the syntactic recoverability theory of ellipsis. What Chung proposes is that these facts should be handled by a(n additional)[31] lexical requirement, which she phrases as follows:

(62) Every lexical item in the numeration of the sluice that ends up (only) in the elided IP must be identical to an item in the numeration of the antecedent CP.

In other words, an ellipsis site cannot contain any 'new' words, words that are not already present in the antecedent. As far as we know, this is the only compelling case where a lexical requirement on ellipsis has been proposed. How it should be integrated into the syntactic and semantic theories discussed elsewhere in this chapter is an open question.

The final type of mismatch we focus on here concerns the use of clefts or copular clauses as the underlying structure for sluicing – sometimes incorrectly referred to as pseudosluicing; see note 34 for terminological clarification. Consider again the basic spading example in (43d) (repeated below).

(63) Jef eid iemand gezien, mo ik weet nie wou da
Jef has someone seen but I know not who that
'Jef saw someone, but I don't know who'

Van Craenenbroeck (2010a) argues at length that the example in (63) derives from the cleft in (64) rather than from the regular *wh*-question in (65).

(64) Jef eid iemand gezien, mo ik weet nie wou da   da was da Jef
     Jef has someone seen   but I know not who that that was that Jef
     gezien eit
     seen has
     'Jef saw someone, but I don't know who it was that he saw'

(65) Jef eid iemand gezien, mo ik weet nie wou da Jef gezien eit
     Jef has someone seen   but I know not who that Jef seen   has
     'Jef saw someone, but I don't know who Jef saw'

The evidence in support of this claim comes from a series of empirical correspondences between spading and clefts, which set them apart from regular *wh*-questions. Consider for example the data in (66)–(68):

(66) A: Jef ei   nie alliejn Lewie gezien. B: Nieje? Wou nog?
        Jeff has not just   Louis seen   no   who else
     'A: Jeff hasn't just seen Louis. B: No? Who else?'

(67) *Wou <nog> was da   <nog> da Jef gezien ou?
      who else   was that else that Jeff seen had

(68) A: Jef ei   nie alliejn Lewie gezien. B:* Nieje? Wou <nog>
        Jeff has not just   Louis seen   no   who else
     da   <nog>?
     that   else

While sluiced *wh*-phrases can be modified by *nog* 'else' (66), such modification is disallowed both in clefts (67) and in spading (68). Moreover, the same data pattern emerges with respect to case marking, modification by negation and affirmation, multiple *wh*, non-overt antecedents, and exhaustivity. All of these empirical parallelisms follow straightforwardly under the assumption that a spaded example such as (63) is the elliptical version of the cleft in (64). To the extent that this is on the right track, however, spading poses a substantial problem for the syntactic identity theory of ellipsis: given that the antecedent clause in (63) does not contain a cleft, it is not syntactically isomorphic to the ellipsis site in any straightforward sense – for one, it is monoclausal, while the cleft structure in the ellipsis site is biclausal. Semantically, however, the two structures are identical (see van Craenenbroeck 2010a:56–62 for detailed discussion). In short, the fact that a cleft can be sluiced under identity with a non-cleft structure provides strong evidence in favor of a semantic recoverability condition on ellipsis.

Interestingly, clefts have been argued to underlie certain non-spading variants of sluicing as well. As was already pointed out by Merchant (2001:100–102), the Preposition Stranding Generalization does not seem to be equally strong in all languages. In fact, some of them at first sight present downright counterexamples for the PSG. Spanish is a case in point:

(69) *¿Qué   chica rubia   ha hablado Juan con?
     what   girl   blonde   has talked Juan with
     INTENDED: 'What blonde girl did Juan talk to?'

(70) Juan ha hablado con una chica rubia, pero no sé   cuál
     Juan has talked with a girl blonde but not know which
     'Juan talked to a blonde girl, but I don't know which'

While (69) shows that Spanish is a non-preposition stranding language, the second example illustrates that under sluicing preposition stranding does appear to be an option. As such, these data directly contradict the PSG. However, a number of authors have proposed – not just for Spanish, but for similar facts in French, Italian, Polish, Brazilian Portuguese, and English – that what underlies the sluice in (70) is not a regular *wh*-question with concomitant preposition stranding, but rather the cleft (or copular clause) in (71) (see Vicente 2008, Szczegelniak, 2005, 2008, Rodrigues *et al.* 2009, van Craenenbroeck, 2010a:115, 2010b; and see Almeida and Yoshida 2007 and Sag and Nykiel 2008 for an opposing view):

(71) Juan ha hablado com una chica pero no sé   cuál   es *pro*
     Juan has talked with a   girl but not know which is it
     'Juan talked to a girl, but I don't know which girl it was'

Supporting evidence for this analysis once again comes from empirical parallelisms between clefts or copular clauses on the one hand and P-stranding sluicing on the other. For instance, while a sluiced *wh*-phrase in Spanish can generally be modified by *más* 'else,' this is not possible when a preposition has been stranded (see (72)), which matches the absence of *más*-modification in clefts, shown in (73).

(72) Juan ha hablado con una chica rubia,   pero no sé
     Juan has talked with a girl blonde but not know
     *(con) qué   chica más
     with   what   girl   else
     'Juan talked to a blonde girl, but I don't know to what other girl'

(73) *Juan ha   hablado con una chica rubia, pero no sé
     Juan has talked with a girl blonde but not know
     qué   chica más es *pro*
     what   girl   else is it
     *'Juan talked to a blonde girl, but I don't know to what other girl it was'

The relevance of these data for the 'recoverability of deletion' issue is the same as that of spading: apparent PSG-violations in non-preposition stranding languages show that sluicing can elide a cleft or copular structure in the absence of such a structure in the antecedent, thus lending strong support to semantic identity theories of ellipsis resolution.

Summing up, while some of the antecedent–ellipsis mismatches found in clausal ellipsis are parallel to those attested in predicate ellipsis, others are quite specific. Most notably, sprouting seems to pose problems for both the syntactic and the semantic theory of ellipsis identity (and in favor of a lexical recoverability requirement), while spading and apparent PSG-violations present a strong case against syntactic isomorphism.

19.3.4 Licensing: the *wh*/sluicing-correlation

Lobeck (1995:54–62) and Merchant (2001:54–61) point out that sluicing (in English) is restricted to – i.e., only licensed in – constituent questions. That is, there is no IP-deletion in declaratives (74a), *yes/no*-questions (74b), infinitival declaratives (74c), or relatives (74d) (examples from Merchant 2001:56–59).

(74) a. *it was painted, but it wasn't obvious that __
 b. *the Pentagon leaked that it would close the Presidio, but no-one knew for sure whether/if __
 c. *Sue asked Bill to leave, but for __ would be unexpected
 d. *somebody stole the car, but they couldn't find the person who __

Lobeck is an advocate of the so-called proform analysis of ellipsis, i.e., she assumes sluiced clauses contain a null IP-proform that acquires internal syntactic structure by copying in the antecedent clause at LF. What the data pattern in (74) shows, Lobeck argues, is that this IP-proform has to be properly head-governed by a C°-head that is endowed with a strong [+wh]-specification. Merchant on the other hand encodes the distribution of sluicing in a Minimalist, PF-deletion based analysis of this construction. According to him, the sole distinction between an elliptical clause and its non-elliptical counterpart is the presence in the former of a feature, dubbed [E], with the following specifications:

(75) a. the syntax of [E]: E[$u$wh*,uQ*]
 b. the phonology of [[E]]: $\phi_{IP} \to \emptyset/E$ __
 c. the semantics of [E]: [[E]] = λp : e-GIVEN(p) [p]

Of interest to us here is the requirement in (75a).[32] It represents Merchant's version of the licensing requirement on sluicing, and tries to capture the data pattern in (74) by stating that [E] itself has to check certain syntactic features, in particular [+wh,+Q]. Given that it can only check these features in a local relationship with the C° found in constituent questions, this is the only context where the syntactic requirements of [E] will be met, and accordingly, where sluicing will take place.

The downsides of the Lobeck/Merchant-approach are (a) that it is specific to sluicing, and (b) that it is specific to English(-type languages).[33] In particular, given that they by definition occur in non-interrogative contexts, fragment answers require a different head governor in Lobeck's view and a different [E]-feature in Merchant's analysis. Moreover, languages in which the *wh*-phrase does not move all the way up to specCP require an [E]-feature with a different syntactic feature specification. Consider in this respect the Hungarian sluicing example in (76).

(76) János meghívott egy lányt, de nem tudom   hogy kit
     John invited   a   girl but not know-1SG that who
     'John invited a girl, but I don't know who'

As is well known, *wh*-phrases in Hungarian target a preverbal focus position in the low left periphery (a position typically identified as specFocP; see É. Kiss 1987 et seq.). The relative position of the complementizer *hogy* 'that' and the sluiced *wh*-phrase *kit* 'who' in (76) suggests that sluicing can take place from this low focus position as well. That means that in Hungarian the [E]-feature does not have [+wh,+Q] as its syntactic specification, but rather [+Foc]. Van Craenenbroeck and Lipták (2005, 2006, 2009) pursue this line of reasoning and propose the following generalization:

(77) **The *wh*/sluicing-correlation**
     The syntactic features that the [E]-feature has to check in a language L are identical to the strong features a *wh*-phrase has to check in a regular constituent question in L.

The intuition behind (77) is that the type of clausal ellipsis a language has is completely determined by the type of *wh*-movement it has. In languages patterning like English (e.g., Dutch, German, French), *wh*-phrases move all the way up to specCP to check [+wh,+Q]-features and accordingly, this is also the feature specification of [E], and sluicing is only found in constituent questions. In Hungarian-type languages (e.g., Russian, Romanian, Serbo-Croatian, Bulgarian, Polish), on the other hand, *wh*-phrases only check a [+Foc]-feature. The [E]-feature inherits this specification, and any constituent that checks a focus- (or more generally, an operator-)feature is predicted to license clausal ellipsis. The data in (78)–(80) show that this is borne out for foci, quantifiers, and *is* 'also, even'-phrases:[34]

(78) János meghívott valakit   és azt   hiszem, hogy Bélát
     János PV-invited someone and that-a think   that Bélá
     'János invited someone and I think it was Béla whom he invited'

(79) tudtam, hogy János meghívott néhány embert,
     knew   that János PV-invited some   people
     de nem tudtam, hogy mindenkit
     but not knew   that everyone
     'I knew that János invited some people, but I didn't know that he invited everyone'

(80) tudtam, hogy János meghívott néhány embert, de nem
knew that János pv-invited some people but not
tudtam, hogy Marit is
knew that Mari also
'I knew that János invited some people, but I didn't know that he invited Mari, too'

The generalization in (77) thus not only encodes the cross-linguistic difference between English and Hungarian sluicing, it also leads to a unified view on regular, *wh*-sluicing, and the non-interrogative instances of clausal ellipses in (78)–(80). In fact, even within English the *wh*/sluicing-correlation might allow for a unified account of various types of clausal ellipsis. Under the assumption (argued for by den Dikken and Giannakidou 2002 and den Dikken 2003) that *wh*-phrases in English target specCP in embedded questions but specFocP in matrix questions, the generalization in (77) predicts that English should allow non-*wh*-sluicing, but only in matrix contexts. This ties in nicely with the fact that fragment answers cannot be embedded:

(81) A: What did Ernie buy?
B: a. A banana.
b. *Bert said that a banana.

Although clearly more work needs to be done in order to work out the full cross-linguistic picture (see in this respect also Temmerman 2010), it is fair to say that the research into the cross-linguistic syntax – i.e., licensing – of clausal ellipsis is more detached from its construction-specific roots than predicate ellipsis is.

19.4 Nominal ellipses

In many languages, a head noun or nominal phrase can be missing from a nominal expression. That it or some stand-in for it is nevertheless still present and active in the syntax is apparent from the fact that such missing nouns can still control agreement on all the usual targets for agreement by nouns (adjectives, determiners, verbs, etc.), as in the following Spanish examples (from Eguren 2010), where material marked by <> is elided:

(82) a. antes bebía cerveza alemana y ahora solo bebo
before I.drank beer.f.sg German.f.sg and now only I.drink
<cerveza> española
beer.f.sg Spanish.f.sg
'I used to drink German beer before, and now I only drink Spanish beer'

b. al principio llegaron   estudiantes de físicas y   luego
at.the start arrived.3pl students   of physics and later
llegaron   <estudiantes> de químicas
arrived.3pl students   of chemistry
'At the start students of physics arrived, and later students of chemistry arrived'

It is important to distinguish such nominal ellipses from nominalizations of adjectives (or numerals, etc.). Some of the typical tests are the following (from Giannakidou and Stavrou 1999):

(83) Tests for distinguishing nominal ellipsis from nominalizations
  a. Does X need a nominal antecedent, or can it be used out of the blue? (Ellipses – unlike nouns – tend to need overt linguistic antecedents, though not always.)
  b. Does X form a comparative (or superlative[35])? If yes, then it is ellipsis.
  c. Does X have the full range of meanings found in uncontroversially adjectival uses? (Nominalizations, like lexical compounds, often acquire or are restricted to a subset of the expected range of meanings.)
  d. Does X form a plural with plural nominal morphology (where this differs from adjectival desinences)? If not, then it is ellipsis.

For example, *poor* in English is a nominalization by most of the above tests: it needs no antecedent, it does not form a comparative, and it does not have the full range of meanings found when used as a modifier of nouns. (The last test does not give a meaningful result in this case, as the nominalization is a collective, which triggers plural agreement on predicates and cannot be pluralized or used as a predicate itself: *He is a poor*.)

(84) a. the poor deserve our help
  b. *if you have money, you should help the poorer (than you)
  c. A: Look at the poor kitty stuck in the tree!
     B: *That's no poor – he lives there.
  d. *The poors are everywhere in this town!

An especially well-studied area of nominal ellipsis comes from the Romance languages, which show an important pattern of variability with respect to the kinds of antecedents that can identify nominal ellipses, and the forms of co-occurring determiners that appear with ellipses. A typical example comes from Spanish, as discussed in Depiante (2001), in which a special form of the indefinite determiner appears (the same one that appears in partitives; see especially Sleeman 1996 for discussion):

(85) a. un muchacho lindo
       a guy   good-looking
    b. *uno muchacho lindo

(86) (Viste a algunos muchachos?) (Did you see some guys?)
    a. *vi   a   un (lindo)
       I.saw ACC a (good-looking)
    b. vi a uno (lindo)
    c. uno de los muchachos
       one of the guys'

Such facts led Alexiadou and Gengel (2008) to conclude that the nominal ending -o/-a, normally appearing on the noun (such as *muchach-o*), is an independent head (a classifier) in the syntax. When the noun fails to raise to the head hosting the ending (where it normally hosts the affix), it can exceptionally attach instead to the indefinite determiner, just as was the case for the Hungarian marker -e discussed in Section 19.3.2 above:

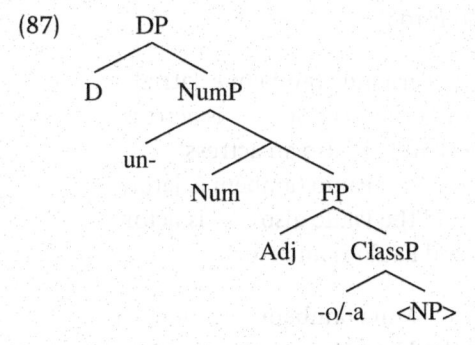

(87)   DP
              / \
             D   NumP
            un- /   \
               Num   FP
                    / \
                  Adj ClassP
                       /   \
                     -o/-a <NP>

Other researchers (see Kester 1996 for one example), maintaining traditional lexicalist assumptions about the forms of the articles, propose constraints to regulate the appearance of these exceptional determiners.

19.4.1 Featural identity in nominal ellipsis

One important generalization that seems to emerge from the literature[36] is the surprising fact that some nouns behave like adjectives in predicate position: that is, in predicate positions, number and gender on some (but not all) nominals can vary.

The basic facts were first discussed for Spanish; they are partly reproduced here. Gender on *predicate* nominals may be ignored, but only sometimes: when the nominal takes its gender as a result of agreement with a controller outside the ellipsis site, its value can vary in the pair (as in (88a) from Masullo and Depiante 2004), while if the nominal has a lexically specified (inherent) gender, this is impossible:

(88) a. Juan es un   buen   abogad-o y María también (es un-a
        Juan is a.m.sg good.m.sg lawyer-m.sg and Maria also   (is a-f.sg
        buen-a   abogad-a)
        good-f.sg lawyer-f.sg)
    b. *Juan es un   buen   tío   y María también (es un-a
        Juan is a.m.sg good.m.sg uncle.m.sg and Maria also   (is a-f.sg
        buen-a tía)
        good-f.sg aunt.f.sg)

A full paradigm is given from Brazilian Portuguese, as discussed in Nunes and Zocca (2005), Bobaljik and Zocca (2009), and Nunes and Zocca (2010) (the same facts hold in Greek as well):

(89) a. o João é médico   e   a Maria também é [médica]
        the João is doctor-masc and the Maria also   is doctor-fem
        'João is a doctor and Mary is too'
    b. a Maria é médica   e   o João também é [médico]
        the Maria is doctor-fem and the João also   is doctor-masc
        'Maria is a doctor and João is too'

(90) a. ? o Paulo é ator e a Fernanda também é [atriz]
          the Paulo is actor and the Fernanda also   is actress
          'Paulo is an actor and Fernanda is also an actress'
    b. ??a Fernanda é atriz e   o Paulo também é. [ator]
          the Fernanda is actress and the Paulo also   is actor
          'Fernanda is an actress and Paulo is an actor'

(91) a. *o Drácula é conde e a Mina também é [condessa]
          the Dracula is count and the Mina also   is countess
          'Dracula is a count and Mina is a countess'
    b. *a Mina é condessa e o Drácula também é [conde]
          the Mina is countess and the Dracula also   is count
          'Mina is a countess and Dracula is a count'

These researchers identify the three classes of predicative nouns given in Table 19.1: *lawyer*-type nouns (allowing gender switches in both directions), *uncle*-class nouns (allowing gender switches in neither direction),

Table 19.1. Classes of nouns under NP-ellipsis

Class	masc antecedent fem ellipsis	fem antecedent masc ellipsis
Abogado 'lawyer' /médico 'doctor' (m↔f) nouns	yes	yes/?
tio 'uncle' /princess (invariant) nouns	*	*
actress (m→f) nouns	yes	*

and *actress*-type nouns (allowing gender switches in only one direction, from masc to fem).

In these languages, the masculine is unmarked by two other tests for gender markedness:

(92) a. as médicas = a group of female doctors only
b. os médicos = a group of male doctors, or a mixed group

(93) a. Tem um médic-o na figura? Tem, a Maria.
have a doctor-masc in.the picture have the Maria
'Is there a doctor in the picture? Yes, there is Maria.'
b. Tem uma médic-a na figura? #Tem, o João.
have a doctor-fem in.the picture have the João
'Is there a doctor-fem in the picture? #Yes, there is João.'

One possibility for accounting for this pattern of data is to claim that certain nouns behave as predicate adjectives when used in predicate positions, whether because they undergo a lexical process that changes their category or because their nominal feature set simply is the same an adjectival one: for a recent example of the latter idea, see Zamparelli (2008), who claims that "nouns that form bare predicates have an impoverished set of features (in particular, no set value for gender), and can be licensed by entering in an agreement relation with the subject of the predication" (p. 101). Zamparelli identifies several classes of nouns that behave this way, and these are the ones that allow for a bare use (without indefinite article), which he calls 'role' nouns: in particular nouns denotings professions, family relations, other relations, compounds with *capo*, and nouns indicating nationality (*Pole, Italian, Swede*), and perhaps adherence (*Muslim, Catholic, atheist*).

(94) a. Carlo è (un) insegnante (Italian)
Carlo is (a) teacher
b. Marta è (una) {parente / cugina } di Marco
Marta is (a) relative cousin of Marco

Another possibility for analyzing these differences would be to claim that gender is invariant on *tío, tía*, but that on nouns like *abogado, abogada*, the suffix is a classifer morpheme (in predicate use) or a gender marker (in non-predicate use). Though gender and noun class systems have much in common, they are distinct (see Corbett 1991 for some discussion of the differences). In particular, Corbett notes that the same noun may appear with different classifiers yielding different interpretations. For example, Rice (2000), following Poser (1996), argues that what are traditionally called 'genders' in Athabaskan languages are in fact noun class markers; in Carrier, for example, there are three morphemes that appear on the verb that seem to depend on an NP argument: *d-, n-,* ø. But some nouns, such as the word for 'rope,' sometimes do not trigger the marker (despite the fact that this marker does occur on this verb with other nouns):

(95) a. tł'u **di**-n-cha (Rice 2000:327)
rope **sticklike**-perfective.viewpoint-be.big
'the rope is thick'
b. tł'u n-yiz̲
rope perfective.viewpoint-be.long
'the rope is long'

Applying this to the ellipsis cases, then, would lead us to conclude that the 'gender' affixes are systematically ambiguous: adjectival-like agreement suffixes (like noun classifiers in Athabaskan) when in predicates, and true gender elements when in arguments.

Finally, Nunes and Zocca (2010) suggest the following analysis, in brief.

(96) a. Juan is an [abogad-[ϕ:_]] and Maria too is an [abogad-[ϕ:_]]
b. Juan is a [tí-[ϕ:masc]] and Maria too is a [tí-[ϕ:fem]]
c. Brad is an [Agr$_\phi$ act-∅] and Angelina is too an [Agr$_\phi$ act-∅]
Angelina is an [Agr$_\phi$ act-fem] Brad is too an [Agr$_\phi$ act-∅]

None of these approaches deal very satisfactorily with the fact that in argument positions, however, only number can vary; gender does not vary in any class of noun. This is illustrated here with data from Spanish from Masullo and Depiante (2004) (the facts appear to be the same in Portuguese and Greek).

(97) a. Juan visitó a su { tío |abogado} y Pedro visitó
Juan visited ACC his uncle.m.sg lawyer.m.sg and Pedro visited
a los <{ tíos | abogados}> suyos
ACC the.m.pl uncle.m.pl lawyer.m.pl his.emph.m.pl
'Juan visited his {uncle | lawyer}, and Pedro visited his ({uncles| lawyers})'
b. *Juan visitó a su {tío |abogado} y Pedro visitó
Juan visited ACC his uncle.m.sg lawyer.m.sg and Pedro visited
a la <{ tía | abogada}> suya
ACC the.f.sg aunt.f.sg lawyer.f.sg his.emph.f.sg
('Juan visited his {uncle | lawyer}, and Pedro visited his ({aunt | lawyer})')

This ban on gender variation is not about the *form*; gender-variable nouns with invariant form (such as *testigo* 'witness,' *dentista* 'dentist,' *estudiante* 'student,' *poeta* 'poet,' and the like) also fail to alternate between genders in argument position (while still able to alternate in number):

(98) a. el testigo no se presentó a la audiencia
the.masc witness not self attended to the hearing
'the witness did not attend the hearing'

    b. la   testigo no se presentó a la audiencia
       the.fem witness not self attended to the hearing
                                        (Masullo and Depiante 2004)

(99) a. el fiscal   interrogó   al   testigo del   crimen
       the prosecutor interrogated ACC.the.masc.sg witness to.the crime
       y   el juez a   la   testigo del   robo
       and the judge ACC the.f.sg witness to.the robbery
   b. *el fiscal   interrogó   a   la testigo   del   crimen y
       the prosecutor interrogated ACC the witness.fem to.the crime   an
       el juez interrogó   al   <testigo> del   robo
       the judge interrogated ACC.the.masc witness   to.the robbery
   c. el   fiscal   interrogó   a   los   testigos del   crimen
       the prosecutor interrogated ACC the.m.pl witnesses to.the crime
       y   el juez   interrogó   al   <testigo> del   robo
       and the judge interrogated ACC.the.m.sg witness   to.the robbery
   d. el   fiscal   interrogó   al   testigo del   crimen y
       the prosecutor interrogated ACC.the.m.sg witness to.the crime   and
       el juez interrogó   a   los   <testigos> del   robo
       the judge interrogated ACC the.m.pl witnesses to.the robbery

The generalization seems to be the following (see Merchant 2011 for discussion):

(100) **Gender and ellipsis generalization** When gender is variable (as on determiners, clitics, adjectives, and some nominals under certain conditions), it may be ignored under ellipsis. When gender is invariant (on nouns in argument positions, and on some nominals in predicative uses), it may not be ignored under ellipsis.

This echoes Chomsky's (1965:179–180) remarks: "the features added to a formative by agreement transformations are not part of the formative in the same sense as those which are inherent to it." Chomsky formulates his condition on erasure operations (including ellipsis, and relativization) as follows:[37]

(101) a term X of the proper analysis can be used to erase a term Y of the proper analysis just in case the inherent part of the formative X is not distinct from the inherent part of the formative Y. (Chomsky 1965: 182)

As Chomsky notes, this condition unfortunately cannot distinguish cases of erasure under ellipsis (in his case, in comparatives) from erasure of the internal head in relative clauses (where all features must match); he leaves this as an unsolved problem.

19.4.2 The role of agreement in licensing NP-ellipsis

A final topic that has attracted significant interest in the literature on NP-ellipsis is the role of agreement on elements outside the ellipsis site. Both Lobeck (1995) and especially Kester (1996), among others, look at this question in some detail. As Kester (1996) points out, NP-ellipsis in Dutch is licensed by adjectives with overt morphological agreement (found with common gender nouns in all declensions, and with neuters only in 'definite' environments):

(102) 'indefinite' adjectival declension (after *een* 'a,' *geen* 'no,' etc.)
    a. ik heb een groen-e fiets en jij een zwart-e
       I have a green-AGR bike.COM and you a black-AGR
       'I have a green bike and you have a black one'
    b. *ik heb een groen konijn en jij een zwart
       I have a green rabbit.NEUT and you a black
       'I have a green rabbit and you have a black one'

(103) 'definite' adjectival declension (after *de/het* 'the,' Ø)
    a. ik heb de groen-e fiets en jij de zwart-e
       I have the green-AGR bike.COM and you the black-AGR
       'I have the green bike and you have the black one'
    b. ik heb het groen-e konijn en jij het zwart-e
       I have the green-AGR rabbit.NEUT and you the black-AGR
       'I have the green rabbit and you have the black one'

Corver and van Koppen (2009) propose an analysis of these facts that takes the morpheme *-e* not to mark (just) agreement, but focus (see also Gengel 2007, but cf. Eguren 2010 for some objections). They provide three reasons to doubt that *-e* is merely an agreement morpheme. First, they show that in colloquial Dutch, one can sometimes find *-e* on an adjective modifying an elided *neuter* noun after the indefinite article:

(104) over konijnen gesproken ... (talking about rabbits ...)
                                                          [colloquial Dutch]
    %ik heb gisteren een zwart-e _ zien lopen
     I have yesterday a black-e see run
     'I saw a black one running yesterday'

Second, although an agreeing form can sometimes signal a semantic difference, as with *groot/grote* meaning variously 'great' and 'large' as in (105a), in NP-ellipsis contexts such as (105b), the obligatory *-e* fails to resolve the ambiguity: just in this case, the 'agreeing' form can have either reading.

(105) a. ik heb gisteren een { groot / grot-e} pianist horen spelen
        I have yesterday a big / bige pianist hear play
        'I heard a great / large pianist play yesterday'
                                                            (colloquial Dutch)

b. ik heb gisteren een echt grot-e _ horen spelen
      I have yesterday a real big-e hear play
      'I heard a truly great / large one play yesterday'
                                          (colloquial Dutch)

Finally, participles ending in *-en* (a 'strong' ending) used as attributive adjectives do **not** take adjectival inflection, unless accompanied by NP-ellipsis:

(106) a. het doorbakken(*-e) konijn
         the well.baked- e   rabbit
      b. het doorbakken*(-e) _
         the well-baked-e

These differences indicate, according to Corver and van Koppen (2009), that *-e* realizes a Focus head in the nominal domain, yielding the following structure for NP-ellipsis, with an E feature on the Focus head licensing deletion of its complement.

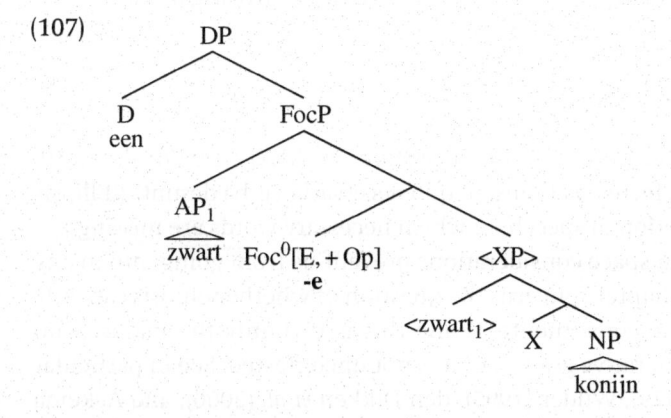

(107)
```
              DP
             /  \
            D    FocP
           een   /  \
              AP₁    \
             /  \     \
          zwart  Foc⁰[E,+Op]  <XP>
                  -e         /   \
                       <zwart₁>   \
                                X   NP
                                   konijn
```

19.4.3 Concluding remarks

Just as we have seen for predicate and clausal ellipses, there remain many open questions concerning ellipsis in the nominal domain. Addressing such questions further leads us to consideration of topics such as the nature of *pro* (which some recent work has suggested does not exist as such, its putative effects reducible instead to ellipsis of pronouns; see Takahashi 2008a, 2008b for a recent approach) and of null nouns and *one*-anaphora (see Panagiotidis 2003a, 2003b, for important recent discussion).

19.5 Conclusion

A major reason ellipsis continues to garner such sustained interest is its location on the frontlines of any debate about the division of labor between syntax and semantics: as such, the analysis of elliptical phenomena can play a crucial role – pro or con – in arguments about the nature of syntactic representations, the role of syntax in meaning, and in the putative sometime absence of syntax from the mechanisms that generate propositional content even in the narrowest sense.

We have concentrated here on the traditional three kinds of ellipsis studied in generative linguistics – predicate, clausal, and nominal ellipses – but we by no means intend to imply that these phenomena are exhaustive of the domain. Indeed, they are not: there are a number of other phenomena that have an equal claim to the label 'ellipsis' and to our theoretical attention, including a wide variety of other 'missing' elements or other cases where the narrow propositional content appears to be richer than traditional theories of lexical and compositional meaning would seem to derive. The question of whether and, if so, how the analysis of such areas of enriched content and contextualism should influence our understanding of the phenomena discussed in this chapter is just one of the many reasons these domains remain rich and productive areas of investigation.

Notes

1. See the *Etymologiarum, Liber I 'De grammatica'*, ch. XXXIV 'De Vitiis', sec. 10: "Eclipsis est defectus dictionis, in quo necessaria verba desunt" ('Ellipsis is an incompletion of speech, in which necessary words are missing').
2. An issue which space considerations prevent us from going into in any detail in this chapter concerns the question of whether ellipsis can only target syntactic constituents. While this is certainly the mainstream position in generative grammar, it is not uncontested. See in particular Hankamer (1979), Wilder (1995), den Dikken *et al.* (2000), and Ackema and Szendrői (2002) for accounts of non-constituent deletion.
3. One could argue that the very identification of V-stranding VPE also represents a central research issue in this area. In particular, as has been argued in detail by Goldberg (2005), one should take care to distinguish V-stranding VPE from (possibly multiple) null arguments, a task that proves to be especially tricky in languages with extensive pro-drop. See Otani and Whitman (1991), Hui-Ju Grace (1998, 2002), Kim (1999), and Goldberg (2005: Chapter 2) for discussion.
4. A special case of relativization out of a VPE-site concerns Antecedent Contained Deletion (ACD), illustrated in (i).

   (i) John read every book I did

   The literature on ACD is too vast for us to do justice to it here. See in particular Bouton (1970), Sag (1976), May (1985), Baltin (1987b), Hornstein (1995), Kennedy (1994, 1997b), Merchant (2000a, 2000b), and Fox (2002) for discussion.

5. Though see Hartman (2010), who argues MaxElide also holds for X°- and A-movement.
6. Note that in each of these examples the focus requirement discussed in the text surrounding (11) is met. This means that the ill-formedness of the data in (12) is not due to a violation of MaxElide.
7. For completeness' sake, we should add that some – in particular, clausal – types of ellipsis have been argued to *repair* island violations. We return to such cases in Section 19.3.2 below.
8. The data pattern for BE *do* is more complex than is suggested here. See Baltin (2010) for refinement and discussion.
9. One type of mismatch that we will not discuss is the occurrence of sloppy readings (see Chapter 15) under ellipsis. On the one hand, this phenomenon can be dealt with successfully in both syntactic and semantic identity theories, while on the other (and more importantly), sloppy readings also show up in contexts where no ellipsis is involved (see Hobbs and Kehler (1997 for a quick overview), which suggests that the analysis should not be ellipsis-specific either (a point that was already made very convincingly by Tancredi 1992; see Merchant, to appear, for discussion).
10. In the context of this section on predicate ellipsis it is worth noting that pseudogapping and modal complement ellipsis add additional complexity to the debate on active–passive mismatches. The former does not allow such mismatches at all, which Merchant (2008a) takes to be an indication that pseudogapping deletes a larger chunk of the verbal domain – in particular, a constituent including the Voice°- head – than VP-ellipsis. MCE on the other hand, allows mismatches with a passive antecedent and an active ellipsis site, but not in the other direction (Aelbrecht 2010). Although no account of these data has been proposed to date, they do fit the general pattern that passive-to-active mismatches are judged better than active-to-passive ones (cf. in particular Arregui *et al.* 2006, Frazier 2008).
11. As for why the wide-scope reading in (28a) is disallowed, see Fox (2000).
12. It is worth pointing out that this kind of solution is unformulable on a Postal (2000)-style approach to *any*-NPIs, according to which the negation that licenses them originates within the noun phrase (i.e., '*not +any* N'). This means that if one could argue that syntactic identity is required for ellipsis, this would also allow one to argue against a Postalian approach to NPIs. See Section 21.3.2.2 for further discussion. Many thanks to Marcel den Dikken for drawing our attention to the incompatibility between the account presented here and that of Postal.
13. Note that the behavior of minimizers under ellipsis (see (i)) differs from that of the polarity items discussed in the main text. As Merchant (to appear b) shows, it is not the case that minimizers are ungrammatical

when they are not licensed by negation. Rather, they receive their literal, non-idiomatic reading. Given that the same holds in non-elliptical contexts (see (ii)), these examples should not be classified as antecedent–ellipsis mismatches.

(i) John didn't sleep a wink, but Mary did __
(ii) John didn't sleep a wink, but Mary did – in fact, she slept all morning!

14. The same fate befalls category mismatches between antecedent and ellipsis site. Consider the following example (from Hardt 1993):

(i) David Begelman is a great laugher, and when he does __, his eyes crinkle at you the way Lady Brett's did in *The Sun Also Rises*

The NP *laugher* acts as antecedent for the elided VP *laugh*. As such, this example appears to constitute evidence for a semantic identity theory of ellipsis. However, Johnson (2001) analyzes these examples as involving deverbal nouns, which contain a VP at some level of representation, and it is this VP that antecedes the instance of VPE in the complement of *does*.

15. One type of mismatch between ellipsis and antecedent that we had to leave out due to space limitations concerns split antecedents. As was pointed out by Webber (1978), a VPE-site can take the conjunction of two preceding VPs as its antecedent:

(i) Sally wants to sail around the world, and Barbara wants to fly to South America, and they will _ , if money is available

The elided VP here refers to 'sail around the world and fly to South America' even though that conjoined VP is not part of the preceding discourse. Accordingly, examples such as these have been taken to constitute evidence for a semantic identity theory of ellipsis. See Baltin (2010) and Elbourne (2008) for additional discussion.

16. Note that in this example it is not the verb that serves as ellipsis licenser. As discussed by King (1970) among many others, contracted auxiliaries cannot license VPE:

(i) *John is not happy, but I'm _

17. As a reviewer points out, the facts are even more complicated than is suggested here. In particular, in subject infinitives with a lexical subject, infinitival VPE *is* allowed:

(i) for Fred to leave early wouldn't surprise me, but for Pete to _ certainly would

18. There is disagreement in the literature on whether an *ing*-form can license VPE when it is not adjacent to the ellipsis site (see also (40) for the relevance of adjacency). Aelbrecht (2010) claims that it cannot on

the basis of examples such as that in (i), while Sag (1976:26) presents (ii) as well-formed.

(i) *I hadn't been thinking about it, but I recall Morgan having been _
(ii) Which bothers you more: John's having been arrested for drug dealing, or Bill's having been _?

19. One of our reviewers disagrees with this judgment and points out that for him/her VPE in the complement of epistemic *must* is well-formed.
20. To be more specific, Thoms argues that only A′- and X°-movement can license ellipsis, see the original paper for details.
21. Though see below, Section 19.3.4, for a refinement re. non-interrogative sluicing.
22. Traditionally, gapping is claimed to allow only two remnants, but for several languages this seems to be too strict, see, e.g., Aelbrecht (2007) on gapping in Dutch. Whatever the exact number, though, it should be clear that gapping is only allowed with a highly limited number of remnants.
23. It might not be intuitively clear to what extent gapping constitutes clausal ellipsis – rather than, for example, simple deletion of the main verb. While the latter analysis was clearly prominent in the earliest literature on this topic, ever since Sag (1976) and Pesetsky (1982b) it has become fairly standard to analyze gapping as involving movement of the remnants to the left followed by deletion (or across-the-board (ATB) movement, see below) of the rest of the clause. That gapping has to target more than just the main verb is also suggested by examples such as (i):

(i) John wanted to begin to sell candy and Bill _ apples

24. Hankamer and Sag (1976) made a distinction between deep and surface anaphora, the former being base-generated, the latter derived transformationally via deletion. Deep anaphora included *do it*, sentential *it*, NCA, and *one*-pronominalization, whereas surface anaphora were exemplified by VPE, sluicing, stripping, gapping, conjunction reduction, and *so*. Criteria for distinguishing between the two types of anaphora included the ability to appear without a linguistic antecedent (deep anaphora), the requirement that the anaphor be strictly syntactically identical to its antecedent (surface anaphora), and the requirement that the antecedent be a syntactic constituent (surface anaphora).
25. Comparative constructions are also a fertile breeding ground for ellipsis, with a wide variety of ellipsis types attested in reduced clausal comparatives; there is widespread agreement that there is, however, no particular operation of Comparative Ellipsis different from the other ellipsis processes described in this chapter (see Lechner 2004, Corver 2006a, and Merchant 2009b). Accordingly, we do not devote

any attention specifically to comparatives in the main text of this chapter.

26. As pointed out by Merchant (2001:62ff.) the data discussed here fall under the broader generalization formulated in (i):

   (i) Sluicing-COMP generalization
   In sluicing, no non-operator material may appear in COMP.

   Given that (i) does not explicitly refer to (head) movement, it also correctly rules out cases of Doubly-Filled COMP or second-position clitics in sluicing contexts. To the extent that (48) is an example of sluicing, however, (and see below, Section 19.3.4, for discussion that it is), the *e*-suffix is in violation of the Sluicing-COMP generalization.

27. Similar locality effects are found in gapping and stripping, see Johnson (1996, 2009), Coppock (2001), Winkler (2005), Lechner (2001), Merchant (2009a).

28. Island violations are not the only contexts of so-called elliptical repair. See van Craenenbroeck and den Dikken (2006), Richards (2001: Chapter 4), Lasnik (to appear), and in particular Merchant (2008b:152–53) for further cases.

29. Recently, a number of (apparent) counterexamples to the PSG have been reported in the literature. These facts will be addressed in the next section.

30. We leave *why*-sluices out of the discussion here, as this *wh*-phrase might be base-generated in the left periphery (see Culicover 1991, Reinhart 1981a, Rizzi 1990a), in which case it would play no role in determining the degree of identity between antecedent and ellipsis site.

31. Note that the requirement in (62) is not meant to replace syntactic or semantic identity. As the example in (i) shows, the mere requirement that an ellipsis site cannot contain any 'new' words vastly overgenerates:

   (i) *John likes Sue, but I don't know why ~~Sue likes John~~

32. The phonology of [E] in (75b) is fairly straightforward: it instructs whatever PF or post-PF mechanism is responsible for phonological realization not to parse its complement. The semantics of [E] in (75c) encodes the identification or recoverability requirement on the elided phrase (see above, Section 19.3.3). Roughly, an expression is e-GIVEN when it has an appropriate, salient antecedent. What the formula in (75c) says, then, is that semantic composition cannot proceed if the complement of [E] is not e-GIVEN. In other words, only phrases that have an appropriate, salient antecedent (i.e., whose content is recoverable from this antecedent) can be elided.

33. Additionally, neither Lobeck nor Merchant can account for *why* the distribution of sluicing is as in (74). Although this is an issue that has not been satisfactorily answered yet, relevant discussion can be found in Romero (1998) and Hartman (2007).
34. The correlation in (77) also predicts that *wh-in-situ* languages should not allow for any clausal ellipsis. This ties in nicely with Merchant's (1998) claim that what looks like sluicing in Japanese in fact does not involve clausal ellipsis, but arises through the combination of pro-drop and copula drop in a copular clause with a *wh*-phrase as predicate. Merchant dubs this phenomenon 'pseudosluicing,' see the original paper for details, and cf. also Merchant (2001:115-20), van Craenenbroeck (2010a:79-81) for related discussion.
35. In English, the superlative itself licenses NP-ellipsis, so this form is not a reliable test in this language; see Kester (1996).
36. A literature that space prevents us from doing any sort of justice to here; see for example Ritter (1988), Bernstein (1993a), Picallo (1991), Sleeman (1996), Kester (1996), Panagiotidis (2003a, 2003b), Alexiadou and Gengel (2008), Marchis and Alexiadou (2008), Corver and van Koppen (2007, 2009), Depiante and Hankamer (2008), Barbiers (2005a), Brucart (1987, 1999), Depiante and Hankamer (2008), Giannakidou and Stavrou (1999), Depiante and Masullo (2001), Kornfeld and Saab (2002), Nunes and Zocca (2005).
37. For some speakers, apparently these contrasts carry over into the adjectival domain as well. Chomsky (1965), in the long footnote 35 (pp. 233-234.), cites Vaugelas:1647 as follows:

> Vaugelas (1647, pp. 461-462) maintains that such a *façon de parler* cannot be considered either "absolument mauvaise" or "fort bonne," and suggests that it be avoided when masculine and feminine forms of the Adjective differ. Thus, a man speaking to a woman should not say *je suis plus beau que vous*, but should rather ("pour parler régulièrement") resort to the paraphrase *je suis plus beau que vous n'êtes belle*, although it would be perfectly all right for him to say *je suis plus riche que vous*.
>
> It need hardly be added that French *riche* is an adjective that shows no gender distinctions.

20

Tense, aspect, and modality

Karen Zagona

20.1 Introduction

Tense, aspect, and modality are grammatical categories that occur as functional heads in clause structure. They are traditionally grouped together by virtue of their semantic cohesion and their frequent morphological clustering or fusion. Syntactically, however, the functional heads that comprise these categories are layered throughout clause structure. Tense is restricted in its syntactic distribution, and is relatively uniform in its effects on clause operations (agreement and EPP). Aspect and modality morphemes are more varied in their lexicalization and in their syntactic distribution. Aspect morphemes can occur in low and high positions in the predicate (vP phase), and modal elements of different types can occur in a variety of positions in clauses.

Tense, aspect, and modality are also similar in their sensitivity to features of other constituents in the syntactic context, including those of predicates and arguments, adjuncts, and other functional heads such as negation and force. Tense, aspect, and modality all specify propositions in relation to a context of evaluation. For tense and aspect, the context is temporal. For modality the context is an external experiencer or source of judgment about the proposition.

Aspect situates an event relative to a temporal frame, and identifies topographic features of the event relative to the frame, such as whether its beginning and endpoints are included within the temporal frame, whether the event consists of a single state or multiple states, and whether or not some state persists once the event ends. The details of aspectual meaning depend on the level of clause structure where it is encoded and the grammatical features of predicates, arguments, and adjuncts of vP. **Tense** usually specifies a temporal relation (such as precedence or simultaneity) between a time interval of vP and an external time. In the simplest cases (non-embedded clauses and non-narrative contexts), the external time of evaluation is that of the speaker's context ('speech time'). In embedded contexts the evaluation time may be controlled by the event in the matrix clause. In narrative, a previous sentence may provide the antecedent. **Modality** signals the evaluation of a proposition with respect to an external judgment. As with aspect, modality is encoded in several ways cross-linguistically as well as language-internally. The nature of the judgment expressed by a modal constituent (in particular, the epistemic/deontic distinction) depends on its own features and on the position in which it is encoded in a clause. There are several subcategories of modality, including verbal mood morphology (subjunctive, indicative), modal verbs or particles (of possibility or necessity, for example), and evidential markers, which specify a source of information about a situation.

This chapter will focus on tense, aspect, and modality in clauses. These three categories occur systematically and predictably in clause structure, and there is a close connection between the structural configuration in which they appear, their status as functional categories, and systematic features of their meanings. Their structural and grammatical properties are closely tied to their meanings, and may be the sole basis for them (as opposed to meanings that are encoded in lexical roots). This is indicated in the domain of tense by research on agrammatic aphasia, which shows that deficits of fluency in tense morphology are accompanied by deficits of comprehension (Varlokosta et al. 2006, Faroqi-Shah and Dickey 2009). There are significant parallels between clauses and nominals with respect to tense, aspect, and modality. One parallel is the semantic similarity between the atelic/telic distinction for events and the mass/count distinction for nominals (Krifka 1989). A second parallel is that, like clauses, nominals can contain adjuncts that modify events, such as duration adverbials (*the examination of papers for three hours*). It has been argued that nominals that have event interpretations contain verb phrases as well as the functional categories that are associated with temporal interpretation, such as aspect, voice, and tense (van Hout and Roeper 1998, Alexiadou 2001b). In non-event nominals, the appearance of such adjuncts is optional and sensitive to features of individual roots, and probably not related to functional heads in DP.[1] However, it must be borne in mind that there are languages in which morphemes that are at least superficially identical to tense morphemes appear within DP. There is ongoing investigation with respect to whether the semantic value of these morphemes is the same in the nominal field as in clauses; Alexiadou (2009) argues that some cases of DP-internal tense morphology may have a determiner-like function rather than a tense function. A related issue is that of potential commonalities between the functional heads in the left periphery of clauses and DPs (Wiltschko 2003, Lecarme 2004, Tonhauser 2007, Nordlinger and Sadler 2008, Alexiadou

2009). Wiltschko (2003) argues that in at least one language, finite relations in clauses are not temporal locations of events; and conversely, DPs in some languages appear to mark temporal relationships distinct from those of clausal tense (Lecarme 1996, 1999, Nordlinger and Sadler 2004).

20.2 Tense

Research in generative syntax has focused on describing the morphosyntactic encoding of features related to temporal meaning, and on accounting for the general properties of tenses that occur in natural language ('possible' versus 'impossible' tenses). This section outlines empirical generalizations that have been discussed and their generative syntactic description. Section 20.3 will discuss aspect, and Section 20.4, modality and Mood.

The discussion begins in Section 20.2.1 with an overview of semantic approaches to tense, to motivate background assumptions about what the syntax needs to represent. Section 20.2.2 gives an initial sketch of how the key features are encoded in clause structure, and Sections 20.2.3 and 20.2.4 show how tenses in main clauses and embedded clauses are analyzed.

20.2.1 Semantics of tense

In finite clauses, tenses specify an ordering relation between times. Consider the tenses shown in (1):

(1) a. the train arrived
    b. the train will arrive

In these sentences, the arrival-time of the train is understood as occurring before or after another time. Pre-theoretically, we understand these sentences as involving a relationship between two times: (i) the time of the event of the train's arrival, and (ii) the time at which the sentence is thought or said or heard. One approach to tense that has been widely adopted in truth-conditional semantics is based on tense logic, which analyzes times as introduced by tense operators (Prior 1967) or quantifiers (Dowty 1979, Montague 1973). That is, there is a distinction between entities that are referred to by propositions (sentences), and constructs that are purely formal, such as operators, logical connectives, and truth values, which exist within the formal language of evaluation. Times are introduced in the formal language. This is illustrated by the semantic rule for interpretation of a Past operator in (2):

(2) Where ϕ is a sentence, PAST (ϕ) is true at time t iff there is a time t' such that $t' < t$ and ϕ is true at t'. (Enç 1987)

As this rule shows, times are introduced as part of the semantic language that represents the truth conditions that correspond to the sentence operator PAST. This rule provides 'instructions' for the evaluation of truth of the proposition. The sentence whose truth is evaluated is itself atemporal (*the train (to) arrive*).

A second approach to tense semantics is the 'referential approach,' which is based on the claim that languages do refer to times, which therefore should be analyzed as entities. Under this assumption, tenses are one form of reference to times. This has been found to provide a more adequate description of tenses themselves, as well as their interactions with one another and with other constituents. The referential approach is widely presupposed in generative syntactic analyses of tense. A number of arguments have been advanced in support of it.

(i) Pronominal property of tenses
Partee (1973) showed that the kind of reference that is assigned to times is akin to that of pronouns. The sentence *I didn't turn off the stove* does not mean that there is no time in the past when I have turned off the stove, but that there is some contextually salient time (such as just before I left home today) when I didn't turn it off. In this respect, tenses are like personal pronouns, whose reference is contextual.

(ii) Non-scopal property of tenses
The tense logic approach predicts that tense should take scope over all sentence constituents, and should show scope interactions with other quantifiers. These systematic interactions are not observed. The nominals in (3) and (4), for example, do not show the predicted readings:

(3) a. all rich men were poor children   (Enç 1987)
    b. every fugitive is now in jail

(4) the college student invented a time travel machine
                                        (Musan 1999:621)

In these sentences, the subject is temporally independent of the tense. In (3a), the time at which men are rich is different from the time at which they were poor children; in (3b), the time of being in jail is not the same as the time of being a fugitive. In (4), the inventor of the time machine could have been a student at the time of the invention, but other readings are possible as well, such as that the inventor is now a college student (Musan 1999).[2] Subordinate clause tenses lack predicted scope interactions as well:

(5) the teacher saw the child who is crying

(6) a child was born who would be king
                                        (Giorgi and Pianesi 1997)

In example (5), the tense of the relative clause is independent of the main clause. (5) cannot mean that the child's crying is cotemporaneous with the time of the main clause event. In (6), neither tense can take scope over the other; the past time of being born is not within the scope of the future time of being a king, nor is the time of being a king within the scope of the past time of the relative clause.

(iii) Syntactic context and tense interpretation

The syntactic context of a clause influences its tense. In particular, when past tense is embedded under past tense, the interpretation of the embedded tense is sensitive to whether the clause is a complement or adjunct. In complement clauses, past tense may be interpreted relative to the event in the main clause; in adjunct clauses, past tense is not interpreted relative to the main clause event. This contrast in the dependence/independence of the embedded tense is illustrated in (7) versus (8):

(7) a. yesterday John met the woman who was elected two years ago
b. two years ago John met the woman who was elected yesterday

(8) a. yesterday John said that Mary was elected two years ago
b. *two years ago John said that Mary was elected yesterday

The events in the relative clauses in (7) are not interpreted relative to the past time in the main clause. The interval of the woman's being elected can be understood to precede the main clause event, as in (7a), or follow it, as in (7b). In complement clauses such as (8) however, the past tense is interpreted relative to the main clause. The complement tense can precede the main clause event, but not follow it. To convey the meaning that (8b) attempts, *was elected* must be replaced by a future form *would be elected*. Complement clauses are one environment in which there is also formal agreement between tenses in the two clauses, which will be discussed below in connection with sequence of tense. The point to be made here is that the tense logic approach does not predict that structural distinctions should influence the operation of the semantic rules for tenses. This phenomenon remains a mystery, and it would be necessary to appeal to some independent set of rules or principles to account for these facts. On the referential approach, it is to be expected that referential dependencies occur and are sensitive to structural relationships. Several analyses have been proposed, and it may be said that the appeal of the referential approach is that it allows an examination of similarities between these phenomena and other syntactic dependencies that influence (co-)reference.

(iv) Non-recursion of tenses.
Tense logic allows tense operators to be 'stacked,' as shown in (9):

(9) a. [P [P [John leave]]]   (= John had left)
    b. [P [P [P ... [John leave]]]]   (= John had had had ... left)

This predicts that alongside the past perfect tense (9a), there should be a tense such as (9b) that occurs in some languages: a past of a past of a past (Hornstein 1981). This prediction is not supported; tenses of the form (9b) do not appear to be possible. This implies that, even if a tense logic approach to the semantics of tense were shown to be correct for independent reasons, it would still be necessary to develop a grammar of tense as part of the theory of UG, to explain what tenses can be acquired in natural language (possible versus impossible tenses).

Within the referential theory of tense, two frameworks for representing times syntactically have been proposed. One is based on ternary tense structures, implementing the framework of Reichenbach (1947); the other is a binary system, the Tense Anchoring account of Enç (1987). Reichenbach (1947) analyzes tenses as composed of three times and two possible relations between them. The primitives of the system are three times: S, (Speech time), R (Reference time), and E (Event time). These three times are present in all tenses, and are either simultaneous or in a precedence relation (indicated by ',' and '_' respectively). These primitives derive tenses such as those in (10):

(10) Tenses:
   a. S, R, E   present
   b. R, E_S   past
   c. S_ R, E   future
   d. E_ S, R   present perfect
   e. E_ R _ S   past perfect
   f. S _ E _ R   future perfect

In simple tenses, R and E are cotemporaneous; consequently it appears that only two times are part of the interpretation. In compound perfect tenses, R and E are in a precedence relation. This is brought out by the ambiguity of the adverbial *at 3:00* in (11), which can specify either R or E:

(11) John had eaten at 3:00
   (i) $E_{(at\ 3:00)}$ _ R _ S
   (ii) E_ $R_{(at\ 3:00)}$ _ S

An important aspect of Reichenbach's approach is that it predicts the impossibility of recursion of tenses. Hornstein (1981, 1990) provides a syntactic analysis of tense based on the Reichenbach approach, and provides further arguments for the realization of times in clause structure. Hornstein argues that rules of adverb interpretation, of sequence of tenses, and of temporal clause interpretation operate on basic tense structures like (10), and their operation is subject to syntactic constraints, a result which provides independent syntactic evidence for the referential theory of tense. Many generative analyses of the syntax of tense are 'neo-Reichenbachian,' in the sense that some properties of Reichenbach's system are modified or abandoned on the basis of syntactic generalizations. For Reichenbach, all tenses are ternary structures; generative studies have mapped the components of tenses to distinct positions in clause structure (Guéron and Hoekstra 1988, Zagona 1988b, 1990, Giorgi and Pianesi 1991, 1997, Stowell 1996, Demirdache and Uribe-Etxebarria 2000, Thompson 2005). The Speech time is realized in the left periphery or in TP; Reference time is realized in an Aspect Phrase above vP, while E is a feature of the v/V projections (see Thompson 2005). One consequence of this mapping is that ordering relations are viewed as local, pair-wise relations: between S and R, and between R and E. A further revision of Reichhenbach's system concerns the status of Event time, which is argued not to participate directly in tense relationships, but rather to do so indirectly. Demirdache and Uribe-Etxebarria (2000) argue, for example, that there is a distinction between the event time and 'asserted time'; with the latter notion being relevant for tense ordering relations. The question has also been raised whether there is motivation for a distinction between 'event' and 'Event time.'[3] Revisions to Reichenbach's approach have made the system more constrained in some respects and less so in others. For example, by mapping the Times S, R, and E to specific syntactic positions in clause structure, it is possible to restrict ordering relations to pairs of times, and consequently, fewer tenses are predicted to exist in UG: there are no possible tenses in which S is ordered relative to E (*E _ S _ R), since S and E are not in a local syntactic relation, on the assumption that in clause structure, R intervenes between S and E. On the other hand, a principled mechanism is needed to account for restrictions on recursion of Times, in order to block sequences like *John had had left. Demirdache and Uribe-Etxebarria (2000) argue that the relevant restriction is semantic. (See Section 20.3.2 below.)

The Tense Anchoring approach of Enç (1987) provides a different basis for restricting the occurrence of Times, essentially by associating them with specific functional categories in clause structure. Enç posits two temporal indices, one in C and one in Tense. This system is neutral with respect to the treatment of perfect tenses, which might be analyzed either as biclausal tense structures or as an aspectual relationship. Under Minimalist assumptions, the syntax does not use indices as a formal device for identifying reference, and the discussion that follows will focus on elaborating the features that are encoded in specific heads, and their contribution to tense, aspect and modality.

Summarizing, the referential approach to tense has been widely adopted in the generative literature on the syntactic side of tense semantics, because it both more accurately describes certain features of tense meaning, and provides a way of analyzing contextual properties of tenses, and the distinction between possible and impossible tenses. Referential approaches to tense include (i) Tense Anchoring, which is the starting point for the present discussion and (ii) work in the tradition of Reichenbach (1947).

20.2.2 Tense in clause structure

Assuming the correctness of the referential approach to tense, times should have grammatical representation in clause structure, and the question arises as to what features are needed for time reference and where in clause structure they are encoded. We take as a point of departure the pre-Minimalist analysis of Tense Anchoring (Enç 1987), which provides representations for past and present tense. Leaving aside aspectual relationships within the verb phrase, tense interpretations are based on a relationship between two times: (i) the time of an event, and (ii) a tense anchor whose default interpretation is 'speech time.' The Tense Anchoring analysis represents these times as referential indices on the complementizer and INFL, the inflectional head of the clause, as shown in (12b) and (13b):

(12) a. the train arrived
  b. [$_{CP}$ C_i [$_{IP}$ DP [$_{I'}$ [$_{INFL}$ $PAST_j$] VP]]]

(13) a. Mary is in London
  b. [$_{CP}$ C_i [$_{IP}$ DP [$_{I'}$ [$_{INFL}$ $PRES_i$] VP]]]

The referential indices in (12b) and (13b) correspond to the times referred to: the index on INFL is the time of the event, and the index on C is the anchor time.[4] Principles of Tense Anchoring specify the nature of the anchor: in main clauses the anchor is indexical ('Now'). Semantic rules for tense interpret [PAST] and [PRESENT] times in relation to the anchor.

The goal of the following discussion is to explore how these descriptive generalizations can be captured under current assumptions as to the role of functional categories in the grammar, and on current understanding of the structure of finite clauses. One important development in the analysis of clause structure is the finding that there are functional categories in the left periphery of the clause in addition to CP (see Chapter 12). Of particular relevance is what Rizzi (1997) refers to as Finite Phrase, which specifies values for finiteness and for mood. Incorporating mood features into the analysis of tense will provide a more detailed picture of temporal relationships and their interaction with 'marked' modality of different varieties. The complementizer phrase (CP) of earlier frameworks will be referred to here as ForceP (Rizzi 1997), since it is the category that determines clause typing (declarative, interrogative). The three syntactic categories whose features bear crucially on tense and modality are thus Tense Phrase, Finite Phrase, and Force Phrase:

(14) [ForceP Force [FinP Fin [TP Tense vP]]]

In order to describe the syntactic underpinnings of tense interpretation, the relevant features of each of these categories need to be discussed. It will be shown that each of these categories may be associated with more than one feature that contributes to tense interpretation. In some cases, these features may be treated as separate heads for ease of exposition.

The assumptions of phase-based Minimalist syntax (Chomsky 2008) are presupposed here. One relevant assumption is the Inclusiveness Condition, which prohibits introduction of elements in the syntax that are not drawn from the lexicon. It is generally accepted that lexical properties are represented as features, so the relationships expressed above in terms of co-indexing, insofar as they reflect syntactic relationships, should be recast in terms of relationships between features; it will be assumed that in the syntax, this is carried out via the operation Agree. Another assumption is that Agree is triggered by unvalued features of phase heads, which are the heads of CP (=ForceP) and vP. Fin and Tense are assumed to be dependent phase heads, which means that they inherit their functional category status from the phase head. It is assumed that Agree effects feature valuation and deletion. Feature valuation determines the spelled out form of the feature. For example, the past tense inflection on the verb *arrived* is an uninterpretable tense feature on v, valued by Tense as 'past.' The value given the feature by Agree determines its form, but the meaning of 'past,' if it is present in the sentence, is not attributable to the verbal morphology, but to interpretable tense and mood features elsewhere in the clause.

In Sections 20.2.2.1–20.2.2.3, the relevant features of Tense, Finite, and Force Phrases are introduced. Features are shown in small caps, the interpretability or uninterpretability of the feature is shown by *i* or *u* preceding it, and values are shown after a colon: [iPERSON:1] is an interpretable person feature whose value is 'first'; [uPERSON:] is an uninterpretable person feature; after Agree, it is valued: [uPERSON:1]. A line through such a feature indicates that it is marked for deletion and does not contribute to semantic interpretation: [~~uPERSON:1~~].

20.2.2.1 Tense

Tense merges with vP and in general has the effect of specifying a temporal location of its complement, the vP event. It is generally assumed that Tense is interpretable, and that its values 'past' and 'present' (and perhaps 'future') provide the temporal reference for vP. However, the ability of Tense to situate an event before the evaluation time is not a property of Tense by itself but depends on indicative mood as well. Iatridou (2000) notes that past tense morphology is systematically used in counterfactual conditional clauses in languages with past subjunctive morphology:

(15) a. if it weren't raining, we could go outside
b. if Mary knew the answer, she would be the only one

The events of the conditional clauses are not interpreted as past counterfactuals but as present ones. Iatridou proposes that what we call a past tense morpheme provides a skeletal meaning of exclusion. If it is interpreted temporally, it excludes speech time; if not interpreted temporally, it excludes the actual world. In other words, subjunctive mood does not establish a time-ordering mode of evaluation; indicative mood does so, in which case the exclusion feature is interpreted as a preceding time. As a first approximation:

(16) a. Indicative mood + exclusion → temporal precedence
b. Indicative mood + inclusion → temporal overlap
c. Non-indicative mood + exclusion → excludes speaker's world
d. Non-indicative mood + inclusion → includes speaker's world

English indicative tenses (16a) and (16b) have temporal interpretations; (16c) is counterfactual, and (16d) may describe unrealized events, such as in volitional contexts (*They insisted that he arrive early*).[5]

One conclusion that can be drawn from the preceding discussion is that Tense Phrase as a category is not, strictly speaking, a 'time phrase' but rather an abstract 'location phrase.' Mood features determine whether or not Tense features are interpreted as a Time:

(17) Indicative Mood selects: Tense [iTIME:include/exclude]

Because temporal inclusion/exclusion is one instance of the more general notion of exclusion/inclusion as discussed above, it is possible that other alternative features and feature values could be proposed. However there is some evidence that for English, at least, a [Time] feature is always present in finite tense, even when its temporal value is not licensed by indicative mood. In that context, it is an uninterpretable feature – a formal Tense feature that is valued by agreement, but does not contribute an independent temporal relation for purposes of semantic interpretation:

(18) Non-indicative Mood selects: Tense [uTIME:include/exclude]

This 'defective' Tense feature is valued by a time feature elsewhere in the structure, and is then deleted. This situation is illustrated by temporal adjunct clauses and sequence-of-tenses contexts in complement clauses.[6] Temporal adjunct clauses require formal agreement in past/non-past features with the modified clause:

(19) John played baseball when Mary played/*plays soccer

It will be shown below (Section 20.2.4.1) that temporal adjunct clauses that are introduced by temporal prepositions such as *before, after, when,* and *while* are missing features of the left periphery of the clause, and consequently do not have specified mood and Tense features. The mood and Tense features of the adjunct clause are valued by those of the modified clause. Certain complement clauses allow the option of an unvalued Tense feature. Sequence-of-tenses contexts such as (20) illustrate:

(20) John believed yesterday that Fred was ill
    (i) Fred was ill before yesterday   ('shifted' reading)
    (ii) Fred was ill yesterday   ('simultaneous' reading)

On the 'shifted' reading, the complement clause has a semantic past tense, because Fred's being ill is interpreted as preceding the main clause event, which is itself prior to speech time. On the 'simultaneous' reading, however, the embedded clause event is a formal past tense only; it is not associated with a past meaning. On the 'simultaneous' reading, the form that the tense takes is one in which TenseP agrees with its external evaluation time: the main clause event time. This phenomenon is observed in English as well in the form of finite modals, particularly future modals *will/would*. In embedded clauses, *would* indicates futurity relative to a past time:

(21) a. Mary said last week that John will play soccer Friday
     b. Mary said that John would play soccer Friday

The form *will* in (21a) indicates that the event of playing soccer is situated subsequent to speech time, so *Friday* must be understood as a future day; in (21b) the event of playing soccer is situated after the main clause event, so in this context *Friday* is understood as subsequent to the matrix event, and that could be before or after speech time.

An important prediction of this approach is that, because the [TIME] feature in these dependent contexts is deleted once it is valued, the event in such a context is not 'anaphoric' to the [TIME] feature that values it. Instead, the absence of an interpretable [TIME] feature results in other features of the context contributing to temporal interpretation. This prediction is borne out in the cases that will be discussed below for English.

20.2.2.2 Finite Phrase

Finite Phrase is a relational predicate that mediates between the proposition (syntactically, the *v*P) and its external evaluation (syntactically, the ForceP). It conveys that there is an external situation with respect to which the proposition is judged, and specifies the mechanism or modality of that evaluation. It interacts with Force to convey the factuality or other status of the proposition relative to some external perspective; in main clauses that perspective is usually that of the speaker. As discussed above in

Section 20.2.2.1, the temporal interpretation of present tense and past tense are attributable to indicative mood. Finite Phrase is then hypothesized to have a feature [MOOD] that specifies whether the proposition is evaluated temporally or in some other way. 'Indicative' is a temporal-ordering value of mood:

(22) Indicative: [iMOOD:ordering] (=temporal ordering)

As discussed above, the temporal ordering value of [MOOD] selects Tense with an interpretable value for exclusion/inclusion, as shown in (17). With respect to other possible values for [MOOD], other values can be grammatically differentiated. For example, the Lamas Kechwa variety of Quechua has a desiderative mood suffix (Sánchez 2006). It is possible that such values as 'volition,' 'possibility,' 'necessity,' and 'subsequence' could be inherently valued on [MOOD]. For English, however, there is little evidence that those subcategories are grammatically differentiated. This suggests that non-indicative mood is unvalued:

(23) Non-indicative: [uMOOD:]

Its values are determined by phrases that have interpretable mood features, including verbs, modal auxiliaries, certain adverbs, and negation. The [MOOD] feature by itself is uninterpretable; it is valued and deleted; semantic values for modality are provided by a constituent that has interpretable modal features, and in the absence of such a constituent, the derivation fails. *Mary leave* has no interpretable modal feature to value [uMOOD].

It should be noted that [uMOOD] in (23) could in principle be valued as indicative – as a 'temporal ordering' modality, by another constituent. Whether such situations exist is an open question. A phenomenon that appears amenable to such analysis is discussed in Sybesma (2007). Sybesma notes that in Dutch, what appears superficially to be a past tense morpheme is infelicitous in isolation, such as in out-of-the-blue contexts. This is shown by the contrast in (24) (examples, glosses, and notes from Sybesma 2007:582):

(24) a. ik woon in Rotterdam
      1s live in Rotterdam
      'I live in Rotterdam'   (perfect; present tense only)
   b. #ik woonde in Rotterdam
      1s live.PST in Rotterdam
      'I lived in Rotterdam'   (very odd/infelicitous in isolation)
   c. ik woonde in 1989 in Rotterdam
      1s live.PST in 1989 in Rotterdam
      'I lived in Rotterdam in 1989'   (perfect; past tense only)

Unlike English, which allows past tense freely in out-of-the-blue contexts, Dutch requires a temporal adverb, as shown by the contrast between (24b) and (24c). This is explained if the past morpheme in (24b), (24c) is an [exclude] feature, which acquires a temporal precedence interpretation only if the ordering value of Fin is valued by a constituent with an intrinsic temporal ordering value.[7]

20.2.2.3 Force Phrase

The main property of Force Phrase is specification of clause typing. The feature that encodes values for clause typing is hypothesized to be [ACT]. One motive for this choice is Cinque's (1999) generalization that clause-typing features of Force represent speech acts. This is brought out by adjuncts that modify the manner of assertion:

(25) [ForceP [ACT:declarative] *frankly, confidently*] …

Another property of Force Phrase is that it encodes information about the relationship that the speaker has to the proposition (Giorgi 2010, Delfitto and Fiorin 2011). One role that the speaker has is as the default source of judgment. The adverbs in (25) are speaker-oriented, which implies that they are predicated of the speaker. The speaker is therefore assumed to be an implicit agent or source argument of the declarative or other speech act encoded in Force. Another role that the speaker has is as the default center of deixis for the proposition with regard to person features and time. In a main clause declarative the speaker is (a) the agent of declarative force, (b) the referent for first person, and (c) the spatio-temporal point of reference 'here' and 'now' for the 'actual world.' In embedded clauses, the speaker does not always fulfill all these roles. This is illustrated by the contrast between a main clause such as (26a) and quoted and reported speech contexts (26bc):

(26) a. I have the grocery list
b. John said: "I have the grocery list"
c. John said he had the grocery list

In the main clause declarative (26a), the speaker fulfills all three roles: agent of declarative force, referent for first person, and spatio-temporal point of reference for the 'actual world' of evaluation of the proposition. In (26b) and (26c), the speaker does not fulfill all these roles. In the quoted clause (26b), the main clause subject *John* fulfills all three roles: the source of declarative force, the reference for 1st person and the spatio-temporal reference point for present tense. In (26c) the speaker provides only the reference for first person; the source of the embedded declarative judgment is the matrix subject, and the spatio-temporal reference point is the matrix predicate *said*. The time of the embedded clause event is interpreted in relation to the time *said*.

For tense interpretation it is necessary to provide an account of the conditions under which the evaluation time for the proposition is speech time, versus those in which it is determined by a linguistic antecedent, as in (26b–c). To accomplish this, a description of 'speaker' must be provided. This should include a nominal first person feature, along with a deictic location of the nominal. A category Deixis is proposed to describe entitites that are identified spatio-temporally. The speaker in this context is [iPERSON:1]; speech time is [iTIME:1].

(27) a. Deixis: [iPERSON:1]   (=implicit speaker)
     b. Deixis: [iTIME:1]   (=implicit speech time)

The implicit speaker and speech time provide the center of deixis for interpretation of person features and times. In main clause declaratives, the act of assertion is predicated of the speaker; the speaker is the implicit agent or source of declarative force. In embedded clauses, declarative force can be dissociated from the speaker and speech time, and linked instead to a linguistic antecedent. This seems to occur when the value of Force is itself determined in part by the matrix clause. In quoted speech, the matrix verb fully determines the embedded clause Force, as well as the center of deixis for person and time reference. In that context, unvalued deixis features are perhaps valued by features of the main clause verb. In other embedded contexts, such as reported speech in (26c), the embedded clause force is dissociated from deixis features. In such contexts, the matrix predicate may semantically select a non-deictic Force Phrase. We must make concrete an implementation of how main clauses are interpreted with reference to speech time. This can be accomplished by agreement between uninterpretable features of Force and the interpretable features of the Deixis phrase:

(28)   [$_{ForceP}$ [ACT:decl]   [$_{Deixis}$ [iPERSON:1], [iTime:1] ...]]
       [uTIME:1]
       [uPERSON:1]

The agreement between the declarative force feature and the speaker feature gives rise to an interpretation on which the speaker is the agent of declarative force and the spatio-temporal location of the speaker is the temporal reference for the speech act: the speech time. In embedded contexts, suppose a certain verb selects a CP that has no specified deixis property. In this context, the uninterpretable [Time] and [Person] features of Force Phrase will be valued in the matrix clause, by features of the matrix event:

(29)   [$_{ForceP}$ v+V   [ACT:decl]]
       [uTIME:exclude]   [uTIME:exclude]
       [uPERSON: 3sg]   [uPERSON: 3sg]

There is evidence that the conditions under which the features of Force get valued have other consequences for the interpretation of the clause. In particular, whether Force features are valued by deixis features or not influences the availability of backwards pronominalization:

(30) a. John$_i$ will be late, he$_i$ said   (Speaker's assertion)
    b. *John$_i$ would be late, he$_i$ said   (John's assertion)
    c. he would be late, John said   (John's assertion)
    (Reinhart 1975: 136)

In (30a), the preposed complement clause is the speaker's assertion, its tense is evaluated relative to speech time, as is shown by the future-from-'now' meaning of *will*. This clause does not reconstruct to complement position, as is indicated by possible coreference of *John, he*. In (30b–c), the preposed clause is the subject's assertion, rather than the speaker's; it is temporally evaluated relative to the matrix subject's time of report, as is shown by the future-of-past value of *would*. The impossibility of coreference between *John* and *he* shows that the preposed clause must reconstruct to complement position. The difference in reconstruction effects can be explained in terms of a difference in valuation of the [uPERSON] and [uTIME] features of the complement clause Force Phrase. These features are valued *in situ* by the main clause *v*. Once they are valued, the clause is inert and unable to undergo movement. Reordering of the clause is to an A'-position or is outside the narrow syntax.

20.2.2.4 Summary

To summarize, the functional categories that provide the basis for interpretation of tense are Tense Phrase, Finite Phrase, and Force Phrase, and the Deixis category that specifies the center of deixis for person, time, and world of evaluation. The categories, features, and feature values are shown in (31)–(34):

(31) Category: Features:
    a. Tense [iTIME:include] (in indicative mood=temporal overlap)
        [iTIME:exclude] (in indicative mood=temporal precedence)
        [uTIME]
    b. Finite [iMOOD:ordering] (Indicative mood)
        [uMood]   (Non-indicative mood)
    c. Deixis [iPERSON:1]   (speaker; center of deixis)
        [iTIME:1]   (speech time; center of temporal deixis)
    d. Force [iACT:declarative]
        [uPERSON]
        [uTIME]

Section 20.2.3 below will show how these features derive properties of tense in simple main clauses; embedded clauses are discussed in Section 20.2.4.

20.2.3 Main clauses: past, present, future

This section shows how the features encoded on Force, Fin, and Tense provide the syntactic ingredients to describe tense-related phenomena in main clauses.

20.2.3.1 Past tense

To derive the meaning of past tense for (32a), functional heads are specified for the values shown in (32b). Note that subject–verb agreement is ignored; the phi-features of the left periphery reflect the agreement of Force with deixis features, as discussed above in Section 20.2.2.3.

(32) a. the train arrived
 b. (i) v [uTENSE]^8 (Agree: valued by Tense)
  (ii) Tense [TIME: exclude]
  (iii) Fin [MOOD: ordering]
  (iv) Deixis [iPERSON:1] [iTIME:1]
  (v) Force [ACT: decl] [uPERSON] [uTIME]
                                                        (Agree: valued by Deixis)

To derive a main clause declarative such as (32), Tense first merges with vP. (Further details of this relationship will be discussed below in Section 20.2.3.2 and in Section 20.3 on Aspect). The Agree relation between Tense and v values the [uTENSE] feature of v. Fin then merges with TP; its [MOOD] feature is valued as temporal ordering (indicative). Tense and Mood together derive the meaning 'precede' for the temporal location of the event. Force and Deixis are then merged with FinP, establishing the external evaluation for the proposition. ForceP has a declarative value, meaning that there is a speech act of assertion of the proposition. The Deixis Phrase encodes features that specify the center of deixis. The uninterpretable [Person] and [Time] features of Force mean that Force phase does not intrinsically specify the entity responsible for assertive force; by Agree, it is valued as a deictic source: the speaker, and the speech time. Recall from Section 20.2.2 that past time is a contextually salient time, as in Partee's example: *I didn't turn off the stove*. This follows from the way in which the meaning of the indicative past tense is constructed, as a (temporal) location that is anchored to the speaker's time of assertion. In a negative sentence such as Partee's, a temporal location in the past is established in the same way. Clausal negation does not scope over the times in Tense and in Force. Only the polarity of the event is altered.

Once the CP phase operations are complete, the phase is spelled out and interpreted. The meaning relationships that are available at the conceptual interface include the ordering of events (speech act event and vP event) via the ordering of times, and the anchoring of the event relative to the time of assertion.

20.2.3.2 Present tense

Present tense has a [TIME] feature with the value [include]. This is illustrated in (33), where speech time is temporally included within the state:

(33) States: Time of the state includes the anchor
 a. Sue likes Fellini
 b. the train remains in the station[9]
 c. a bronze pig sits near the entrance to the market

The derivations for these sentences are the same as those discussed above for past tense; the only difference is the value of the [TIME] feature of Tense:[10]

(34) a. *Sue like Fellini*
 b. (i) v [uTENSE]
   (ii) Tense [TIME: include]
   (iii) Fin [MOOD: ordering]
   (v) Deixis [iPERSON:1] [iTIME:1]
   (iv) Force [ACT:decl] [uTIME][uPERSON]

In (34), indicative mood and the inclusion value of Tense combine to produce the meaning of temporal overlap; in the context of speech time, this gives the meaning of present tense.

Non-statives are only compatible with present tense under certain conditions. If the event is interpreted as a single episode, it is usually incompatible with present tense, as in (35); non-single episode readings such as those in (36) are possible:[11]

(35) a. *a panda eats leaves at this very moment
 b. *the baby walks (as I speak)
 c. *Sue reads a novel at this moment

(36) a. a panda eats leaves (generic)
 b. Sue studies at the library (frequentative, habitual)
 c. the baby walks (modal: ability)

The ungrammaticality of present tense single-episode non-statives implies that there is some clash between the inclusion value of Tense and the transitions that comprise non-stative events. Since a 'transition' involves a change of states over time, it may be that precedence relationships are a component of the interpretation of non-stative episodes. This form of sequentiality may in turn be constructed from the same features that produce precedence in the tense/mood system, namely [ordering] and [exclusion]. The unacceptability of the sentences in (35) would then involve a clash between the [inclusion] feature value for Tense and an [exclusion] value for ordering subevents of vP:[12]

(37) *[TIME: include] + [v[exclude] ...]

This clash arises when the event involves a single episode. When it does not involve a single episode, as in the interpretations in (36), the transitional character of the relationship between subevents that comprise individual events of eating, studying, or walking is masked by other factors. In particular, the present time interval does not correspond to the run-time of any single event. For example the modal reading in (36c) describes an interval at which there is a *capacity* for the baby's walking (deontic modality). The essential difference between (35) and (36) is that for the single-episode interpretations, the present time interval inherits the finite partitions that are introduced by the event-internal exclusion feature; for the readings in (36), it does not. The mechanism that blocks the inheritance of event-internal features by the present time interval is grammatical aspect. Traditional descriptions of aspect distinguish between perfective and imperfective values of aspect. Perfective aspect refers to events from a transitional perspective, by specifying the onset and termination points of the situation. Stated differently, perfective aspect makes definite reference to the first and last moments of the event, so temporal ordering and precedence are components of perfective interpretation. Imperfective aspect lacks this component of interpretation. Imperfective interpretations can diverge from perfective in several ways, according to the number and definiteness of the events referred to, their polarity, modality, and other modifiers. Indefinite plural and generic events are interpreted as imperfective. (See Section 20.3 below.) It appears, then, that the contrast between (35) and (36) follows from the perfective/imperfective value of grammatical aspect rather than from the stativity or non-stativity of the events. This is supported by the fact that non-stative events are possible in the present tense if overt imperfective morphology or an imperfective adverb is added (*A panda is eating leaves; A panda always eats leaves*). It appears that in the absence of such items, null aspect is interpreted as perfective:

(38) a. stative *v*P + null aspect → imperfective aspect
b. non-stative *v*P + null aspect → perfective aspect

The ungrammaticality of the sentences in (35) can then be characterized in terms of a clash between the underlined feature values:

(39) *[MOOD:ordering] [TIME: include] [ASPECT: ordering, exclude] (i.e., perfective)

In many other languages the simple present tense with null aspect has imperfective readings, such as an ongoing single-episode.[13] This is illustrated for Spanish in (40).

(40) (en este momento/frecuentemente) Susana lee una novela
at this moment/often Susana read.PRES.3s. a novel
'Susana is reading a novel at this moment'
'Susana reads novels often'

This shows that the generalization (38b) is a language-particular feature of English, rather than a universal. In Spanish, null morphology is not valued by agreement with the verb. (See Section 20.3.1.)

Summarizing the discussion of this section, to derive a present tense interpretation, the [TIME] feature of Tense is valued as [include], interpreted as temporal inclusion of speech time. It was shown that present tense has co-occurrence restrictions with aspectual features of the verb phrase. These restrictions are due to incompatibility between a sequentially interpreted transitional event and [TIME:include]. Such an account supports the analysis of present tense as specified for a certain temporal value, since if it were lacking in any temporal feature specification, it would not be expected to display co-occurrence restrictions of any type.

20.2.3.3 Future

There is little consensus about the status of future as a tense. It is sometimes analyzed as a simple tense on a par with past and present (Hornstein 1990, Demirdache and Uribe-Etxebarria 2000); other studies argue that it involves a secondary relation of aspect or modality that is dependent on past/present tense.[14] It will be assumed here that future reference is not constructed in the same way as past and present; in fact, the analysis outlined above is not amenable to three-way tense distinctions. As discussed above, past and present are derived compositionally from a value for [include/exclude], in combination with an ordering value of [MOOD]. Future reference is often constructed with modal or aspectual morphology as a secondary relation relative to speech time. It will be assumed that future reference generally derives from an unvalued [Mood] feature that is valued by [SUBSEQUENCE], a feature that is introduced in different ways across languages. As Comrie (1985b) and others observe, one difference between future time and present/past time is that events located at future times are speculative, capable of being changed by intervening events. They are not definite or immutable, and as such, they cannot be part of the knowledge base of the speaker; consequently their truth or existence cannot be asserted. Such events are inherently irrealis, and it is expected that languages that have mood distinctions categorize future as non-indicatives. The discussion below will look at two types of morphology that license this type of interpretation: modal WOLL in English, and Russian aspectual morphology.

English *will* and *would* are often analyzed as an abstract modal WOLL with future value that combines with present or past tense, deriving *will* or *would* (Abusch 1985, Ogihara 1995, Condoravdi 2001, Copley 2002, Wurmbrand 2007):

(41) a. [TIME:include] + WOLL → *will*
    b. [TIME:exclude] + WOLL → *would*

The analysis of *will/would* as spelling out a time feature accounts for their modification by temporal adjunct clauses, which agree in past/present value with the modified clause. The basic pattern of agreement that is characteristic of temporal adjunct clauses is shown in (42):

(42) a. when the train arrived, Fred met Mary   Past/Past
b. *when the train arrived, Fred meets Mary   *Past/Present
c. *when the train arrives, Fred met Mary   *Present/Past

Similarly, a main clause that contains *will* or *would* triggers agreement that follows the same pattern: the tense of the adjunct clause agrees with the form of WOLL as predicted by the features of (43):

(43) a. *when the train arrived, Fred will meet Mary   *Past/will
b. when the train arrived, Fred would meet Mary   Past/would
c. when the train arrives, Fred will meet Mary   Present/will
d. *when the train arrives, Fred would meet Mary   *Present/would

The structure is shown in (44):[15]

(44)

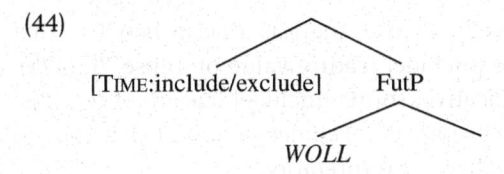

      [TIME:include/exclude]   FutP

                           WOLL

In a future sentence such as *Mary will leave*, a present time feature + WOLL is spelled out as *will*; in a future-of-the past context such as *John said that Mary would leave*, a past time feature + WOLL is spelled out as *would*.

Notice that the [TIME] feature in (44) cannot be the feature of TP, since TP specifies the temporal location of its complement, the vP event. The [TIME] feature that combines with WOLL is the evaluation time. This is illustrated by (45):

(45) a. John said (last week) that Mary would leave the next day.
b. John said (yesterday) that Mary would leave in three days.

In both sentences in (45), the embedded clause event is subsequent to its evaluation time, the time of the main clause event *John said*. The spell-out of WOLL as *would* is determined by an exclusion feature value for the evaluation time, not the event of Mary's leaving. This is confirmed by the fact that Mary's leaving can be interpreted as either before or after speech time. Therefore the [TIME:exclude] feature that combines with WOLL to derive *would* is the feature of the external [TIME] feature of ForceP, which is in turn valued by agreement with *said*:

(46)

    John said [$_{CP}$ Force[ACT:decl][u TIME: exclude] [Fin Tense [$_{FutP}$ WOLL vP]]

The TenseP in such sentences lacks an interpretable value for past or present location of the event, since the temporal location of the event is determined by WOLL, not by Tense. This suggests that [MOOD] is also unvalued, since indicative mood is a temporal ordering value, which selects valued Tense. Furthermore, the future event is not asserted to exist; WOLL provides subsequence value: [MOOD:subsequence]. This is also supported by the fact that future constructions with WOLL pattern differently from indicative present tense with respect to combining with non-stative single episode events. It was shown in Section 20.2.3.2 above that English present tense is incompatible with non-stative, single-episode events. However, when present tense combines with WOLL a single-episode interpretation is possible:

(47) a. the carpenter builds a chair (*single ongoing present event)
b. the carpenter will build a chair (single future event)

In both derivations, Tense has the feature [TIME:include]. In (47a), null grammatical aspect is interpreted as perfective, as discussed above (see (38)). When vP merges with present tense, there is a clash between the [exclude] feature of vP and the [include] feature value of Tense. In (47b) however, the clause is non-indicative, so the [include] feature of tense is not interpreted as temporal inclusion. An [exclude] feature of vP in a non-indicative context has an 'unrealized' interpretation.[16]

In Russian, perfective aspect combines with non-past tense to derive future interpretation. Past tense is identified morphologically by the suffix -l (Dormer 2009:36 & ff.) If -l is absent, the determination of present versus future reference depends on the perfective/imperfective features of the verb phrase. Future reference occurs with either a perfective verb, as in (48), or an auxiliary *bud-* 'be' followed by an imperfective verb, as in (49):

(48) a. Ivan šjët (Present)
Ivan sew.3SG
'Ivan sews(impf)/is sewing(impf)'
b. Ivan vyšjet (Future)
Ivan embroider.3SG
'Ivan will embroider(pfv)'

(49) a. Ivan budet šit' (Imperfective)
Ivan be.3SG sew.IMPF
'Ivan will sew(impf)'
b. *Ivan budet vyšit' (Perfective)
Ivan be.3SG embroider.PFV
INTENDED: 'Ivan will embroider(pfv)'

Dormer (2009) argues that these have in common a [+bounded] feature at the level of verb phrase aspect. Perfective verbs have a temporal endpoint, and auxiliary *bud-* is argued to be perfective also.[17] Future interpretation is analyzed as the endpoint of an interval that begins with present time. The imperfective aspect of (48a) lacks a bounded feature, so the event is not understood as the endpoint of the present interval. If the assumptions outlined above are adopted, it would be assumed that the [+bounded] feature of *v*P is an exclusion feature, since perfective events are understood as sequences of changes of state. These aspectual features may serve the same function as English WOLL, which is to value non-indicative mood as sequential. The exclusion feature of *v*P in combination with unvalued mood is interpreted as a predicted event rather than as one whose existence is taken as factual; the [Mood] feature of the clause appears to be valued by the ordering feature of Aspect phrase. Russian can then be assumed to have the same ingredients for future as English: non-indicative mood and an ordering feature. These combine to derive the meaning of an unrealized time. The two languages differ in the lexical source of the ordering feature that values non-indicative mood: in English, it is a feature of the specialized modal WOLL; in Russian it derives from interpretable ordering features in the aspect system.

20.2.3.4 Summary
The syntactic features that were introduced in Section 20.2.2 were applied here to describe basic tenses in English. In main clauses, indicative past tense refers to a time that does not include the speech time, and is in a precedence relationship with it. Present tense consists of indicative mood and an inclusion value of Tense. The assumption that present tense is specified with an inclusion feature was claimed to account for the inability of single-episode, change-of-state readings to be located in the present tense in English, with unmarked aspect. Future tense is analyzed as a non-indicative mood feature that that is valued as subsequence. There is variation in how this feature can be valued, illustrated by English modal WOLL and by Russian and perfective aspectual features.

20.2.4 Embedded clause tenses
The behavior of Tense in embedded clauses is affected by a variety of factors, including the argument/adjunct status of the clause, features of subordinating prepositions, and features of the functional heads in the clause itself. Adjunct clauses are discussed in Section 20.2.4.1, and the phenomenon of sequence-of-tenses (SOT) for complement clauses is examined in Section 20.2.4.2.

20.2.4.1 Adjunct clauses
As discussed in Enç (1987), English relative clause tenses behave like main clause tenses: tense is evaluated relative to speech time:[18]

(50) the students met the linguist who taught/teaches/is teaching/will teach morphology

(51) a. last week the students met the linguist who gave a guest lecture on morphology yesterday
b. yesterday the students met the linguist who gave a guest lecture on morphology last week

In (50), the main clause contains a past event, and the relative clause can be any past or non-past tense. The sentences in (51) show that, when both clauses contain a past tense, there is no specific ordering relation between the past events. The adverbs *yesterday* and *last week* can be reversed, showing that the main clause event does not serve as a temporal anchor for the relative clause, nor does the relative clause restrict the reference of the main clause event. However other types of adjunct clauses do not all show the same degree of formal and semantic independence. It has already been shown in Section 20.2.3 that temporal adjunct clauses agree with the matrix clause in Tense. Compare the temporal clauses in (52) with the non-temporal adjuncts in (53):

(52) a. Sue arrived when Fred left/*leaves/*will leave
b. Sue plays the piano after Mary does a flute solo/*did a flute solo

(53) a. Mary bought her piano where Fred works
b. Sue will win because she practiced all winter

The non-temporal adjuncts in (53) allow different tense and mood features in each clause. Temporal adjuncts, however, show agreement with the modified clause in the past/non-past value of tense. This formal agreement is not attributable to temporal anaphora, however, since the events of the two clauses are not always interpreted as cotemporaneous. Several factors affect their relationship, including features of the subordinating preposition and aspectual features of the predicates. The prepositions *while* and *as* impose overlapping interpretations; *before* and *after* impose sequential order, and *when* permits both, according to the aspectual features of the predicates:[19]

(54) a. Mary sang when Sue played the piano
(overlapping or sequential events)
b. Fred was a student when Mary graduated (overlap)
c. Fred graduated when Mary was a student (overlap)

In (54a), both events are non-stative; the unmarked interpretation is that the events are sequential; although temporal overlap is possible, the adjunct clause event is understood as beginning first. The sequential relationship is more salient if the *when*-clause is preposed: *When Sue played the piano, Mary sang*. Stative predicates impose an overlapping interpretation; in (54b) the stative is in the main clause, and in (54c) it is in the *when*-clause. Imperfective morphology also produces an overlapping interpretation: *Mary was singing when Sue played the piano; Mary sang when Sue was playing the piano*.

Structurally, temporal adjunct clauses can be analyzed as bare Finite Phrases, lacking both Force features and values for tense and mood:

(55) [when [$_{FinP}$ Fin[uMood] [$_{TP}$ [uTime] vP]]]

The tense and mood features of the adjunct are valued by agreement with those of the modified clause. The temporal clause is finite, so it has case and agreement features that are expected in finite clauses. However, the temporal location of the event is 'relativized' – predicated of the [TIME]/[MOOD] features of the matrix clause. This analysis accounts for the fact that the realis/irrealis status of the event of the temporal clause is determined by the matrix clause, as shown by comparison of (56a–b) with (56c):

(56) a. John will leave after Harry has arrived
b. John may leave when Harry has arrived
c. John will/may leave now that Harry has arrived

In (56a) and (56b), the matrix clause is non-indicative, with mood valued by the modals *will* and *may*. The event of the temporal clause is likewise non-indicative, interpreted as a predicted or possible event, not as one that has occurred or is occurring. In this respect, the evaluation of temporal clause events differs from that of indicative main clause events (*Harry has arrived*.) To derive an indicative interpretation for an event in a temporal adjunct clause, as in (56c), the clause takes a different form, with an overt complementizer and no temporal preposition. Clauses introduced by *now that* have independent tense, as can be seen by the absence of obligatory agreement with the modified clause: *John will arrive now that Harry left; John is happier now that he will be playing shortstop*. The analysis in (55) also predicts that modals *will* and *would* should not occur in temporal adjunct clauses, since they spell out both WOLL and the external [TIME] feature of ForceP (evaluation time). If it is correct that temporal clauses have no ForceP, the associated [TIME] feature is also absent, so no modal is possible.[20] Another indication that temporal clauses are not specified for tense is that they allow single-episode interpretations of present tense with unmarked aspect: *Sue will play the piano when Mary arrives*; in matrix clauses, **Mary arrives* is not a possible single episode, due to the clash between perfective aspect and present tense, as discussed above in Section 20.2.3.2. The absence of a valued [TIME] feature of TenseP accounts for the fact that no tense/aspect clash occurs in temporal clauses.

20.2.4.2 Complement clauses: sequence of tenses (SOT)

It was noted in Section 20.2.2 above that in complement clauses, past tense does not always have a precedence interpretation. This is illustrated by (20), repeated below as (57):

(57) John believed yesterday that Fred was ill
  (i) Fred was ill before yesterday   ('shifted' reading)
  (ii) Fred was ill yesterday   ('simultaneous' reading)

On the 'shifted' reading, the complement clause past tense does have a precedence interpretation. The time of Fred's illness precedes the main clause predicate, which in turn precedes speech time. On the 'simultaneous' reading, the events of the two clauses are cotemporaneous. To account for the shifted reading, it is usually assumed that the embedded clause has a past tense that is anchored by the main clause event time rather than by speech time. On the Tense Anchoring approach, the embedded clause COMP time is analyzed as bound by the main clause event time:

(58) [COMP$_i$ [INFL$_j$ [$_{vP}$ John believed [COMP$_j$ INFL$_k$ [Fred was ill]]]]]

In (58), the embedded CP is co-indexed with the main clause INFL, so the evaluation time for the complement clause is interpreted as anaphoric to the time *believed*. The embedded INFL contains a past tense, which is interpreted as preceding its local anchor.

To capture these generalizations within the framework outlined in this chapter, it can be assumed that the embedded clause has tense and mood features that are the same as those of indicative past tense in main clauses; the difference lies in the features of ForceP, which in turn affects the evaluation time of the clause. Recall that, in main clauses, the time feature of the Force Phrase is valued by the time feature in Deixis. In SOT contexts such as (57), the time feature of ForceP is valued by the matrix clause event. This is not unexpected, in that the speaker is not the source of assertion of the truth of the complement clause proposition; the speaker reports the matrix subject's belief with regard to it. This implies that *believe* selects a CP whose world of evaluation is not described as being the speaker's world. That is, the Force Phrase of that clause lacks deixis features; the uninterpretable time and person features of Force are therefore valued in the next phase up, by *v*. The matrix subject is interpreted as the source of evaluation of the proposition, and the time of its evaluation is the matrix event. The relevant feature specifications in the derivation are shown in (59)–(60):

(59) Embedded clause:
  a. vP: [*Fred was ill*]
  b. Tense [TIME:exclude] (values [uTIME] and [uMOOD] features of vP)
  c. Fin [MOOD:ordering]   (indicative mood)
  d. Force [iACT:decl][uTime][uphi]
                                       (force and related features are unvalued)

(60) Main clause:
   a. V, v [uTENSE]
   b. Tense [iTime:exclude]
   c. Fin [iMood:ordering]
   d. Deixis [iPERSON:1] [iTIME:1]
   e. Force [ACT:decl] [uTIME][uPERSON]

The absence of deixis features in the embedded clause leaves the Force Phrase with unvalued features. The main clause vP provides the formal features which, via Agree, identify the main clause event as source of the embedded clause world of evaluation; the matrix TenseP and MoodP in turn provide the interpretable features that establish the time of evaluation.

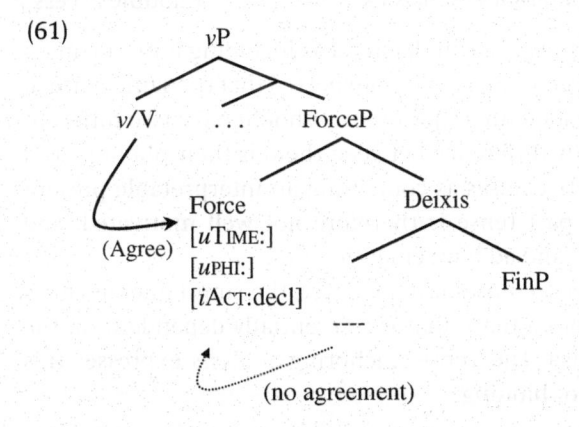

(61)

```
                vP
              /    \
          v/V       ...    ForceP
                          /      \
              (Agree)  Force      Deixis
                      [uTIME:]    /    \
                      [uPHI:]           FinP
                      [iACT:decl]
                              ----
                      (no agreement)
```

In summary, a shifted reading arises because the embedded clause has no deixis features. Consequently, the implicit agent of the assertion is not valued as speaker, and instead has a linguistic antecedent that is determined by agreement with the main clause v, which has [TIME] and [PERSON] features. The matrix vP thereby provides the source of evaluation for the embedded clause declarative force.

Turning now to the simultaneity reading, this is the reading that gives rise to the traditional term 'sequence of tenses' (Latin *consecutio temporum*), because it appears that the embedded clause is semantically a present tense that is spelled out as past in the context of the main clause past. In (57) for example, if John believed yesterday that Fred was ill at that time, the relevant temporal relationship appears to be one of inclusion, and the most obvious source for this interpretation would be a present tense (*Fred is ill*) whose evaluation time is 'shifted' to the past – the matrix event time. What is also suggestive of a present tense in the embedded clause is the fact that the simultaneous interpretation requires imperfective aspect. If the embedded clause event is non-stative single episode, the simultaneous interpretation is not available: *John believed that Mary wrote the letter* does not mean that he believed that she was writing it at the time. This suggests present tense because, as was shown above in Section 20.2.3.2, non-statives give rise to perfective readings of null aspect, and present tense is incompatible with perfective aspect. Nevertheless, analyzing the tense in question as a present tense is problematic. One difficulty is that there is no independent motivation for a morphophonological rule that spells out present indicative tense with past morphology. Furthermore, if the embedded clause contained a present tense, it would be expected, contrary to fact, that in these contexts WOLL should be spelled out as *will*, and that temporal clause modifiers should contain present tenses. An argument against a present tense analysis is that, in the same context, a present tense that is actually spelled out as present tense has a different interpretation, namely the 'double access' interpretation illustrated in (62):

(62) John said (yesterday) that Fred is sick   ('double access')

The interval of Fred's being sick is understood as including both the main clause past event and speech time.[21] It is unexpected that the same tense in the same context (embedded under past tense) should have two different interpretations if the only difference between them is their phonological form. The analysis of SOT clauses as containing an interpretable present tense pronounced as a past tense is therefore not well motivated, and requires ad hoc spell-out and ad hoc semantic rules.

Referential approaches to tense have analyzed the simultaneous interpretation as deriving from a tense that is referentially dependent on the tense of the Matrix clause. The Tense Anchoring analysis expresses this generalization in terms of binding:

(63) a. John said (yesterday) that Fred was ill (then)
      b. [COMP$_i$ [INFL$_j$ [John said [COMP [INFL$_j$ [Fred was ill]]]]]]

The embedded tense is bound by the main clause tense. On the approach presented in this chapter, it is expected that the Force Phrase can get its temporal reference from the main clause event, as discussed above. If the embedded clause contains an indicative past tense, it is not expected that the event time should also be anaphoric to the main clause event. In fact, the embedded clause event is not strictly anaphoric to the time of the main clause. There is no mechanism motivated elsewhere that would derive an anaphoric interpretation. In fact, the generalization that is needed is not really anaphora. In (63), for example, the duration of the main clause event is not the same as that of Fred's being ill. The two events are indirectly related to each other. A similar situation was shown to hold in the interpretation of temporal adjunct clauses. It was shown above in Section 20.2.4.1 that temporal adjunct clauses lack independent values for tense and mood, and that those features are valued by agreement with the modified clause, accounting for the identity of formal features. Once valued, those features are deleted. The semantics of the temporal clause follow from other properties of the context, including aspect and features of the subordinating preposition. It appears that embedded finite clauses in SOT contexts allow a similar structure, although they differ from temporal clauses in that they contain a CP layer, as shown by the availability of complementizers. The embedded clause in (63a) is then assumed to have either an indicative tense, deriving a 'shifted' interpretation, or a bare FinP with uninterpretable Tense. As shown in (64), the [TIME] and [PHI] features of ForceP are again valued by the matrix event; since TP does not have a valued time feature, the *v*P of the embedded clause is valued by agreement with ForceP:

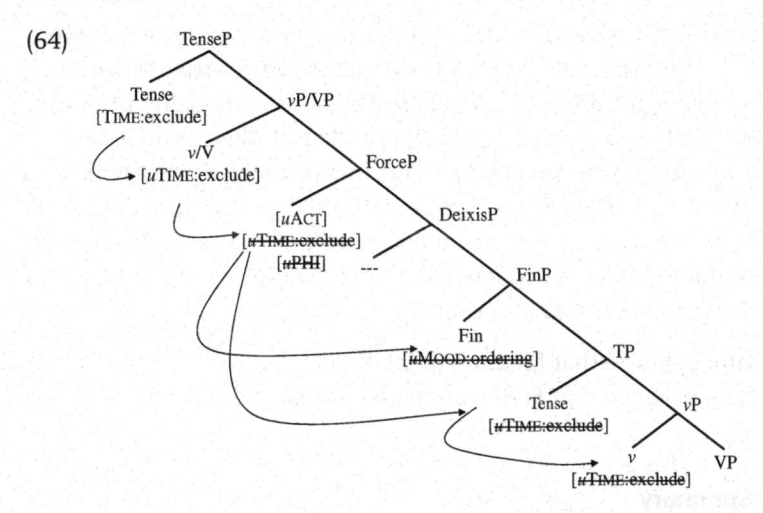

(64)

[Tree diagram showing: TenseP with Tense [TIME:exclude] and vP/VP; v/V [uTIME:exclude]; ForceP with [uACT], [uTIME:exclude], [uPHI]; DeixisP; FinP; Fin [uMOOD:ordering]; TP with Tense [uTIME:exclude] and vP; v [uTIME:exclude] and VP]

The embedded clause verb has past form, due to agreement with the evaluation time, which in turn agrees with the matrix verb. Each of the instances of Agree in (64) occurs elsewhere in the grammar. In the matrix clause in (64), agreement between Tense and *v* values the uninterpretable tense feature of the verb, as occurs in main clause past and present tenses. Agreement between the matrix *v* and the [TIME] feature of ForceP was discussed above for the shifted interpretation of past under past. This is typical of argument clauses, including both subject and complement clauses. Agreement between the evaluation time and the *v*P of the lower clause is needed for temporal clauses, as discussed above. Agreement between Tense and Force is also motivated for the spell-out of *WOLL* and other modals in subordinate contexts, as discussed above in Section 20.2.3.3. Such clauses are also 'bare' finite clauses in the sense that their modality and temporal properties are determined by other constituents, not by Tense and Finite heads.

As SOT contexts show, bare finite clauses with a CP layer (Force Phrase) are not by definition irrealis; their modality is determined by the syntactic context, according to the features of constituents that value the [MOOD] feature of the clause. In this respect SOT differs from temporal clauses. In the latter, an irrealis matrix clause always imposes an irrealis interpretation on the temporal clause, as shown in (65):

(65) a. John will hit the ball when Bill pitches it
　　　b. Fred said last year that John would hit the ball when Bill pitched it

In these temporal adjunct clauses, the event of Bill's pitching the ball is not factual but rather predicted, as determined by agreement of non-indicative mood features between the two clauses. In SOT contexts however, the complement clause can be independent of the mood of the matrix clause:

(66) a. John will believe that Fred is ill
　　　b. Mary said that John would believe that Fred was ill

This difference may be related to the presence of ForceP in the SOT complement clause. Since the embedded clauses in (66) have assertive force, albeit a defective one, with unspecified deixis features, the modality of evaluation is potentially independent. In Temporal clauses, there is no independent force and therefore in principle no independent deixis, hence no independent tense. The distinction is supported by the distribution of modals: it was shown above that modals are generally not licensed in temporal adjunct clauses, a fact that was attributed to the absence of Force. In SOT contexts, modals occur freely:

(67) a. John believed that Fred might be ill
　　　b. John believed that Fred would leave the next day

20.2.5 Summary

The syntax of tense has been shown above to involve interactions among features on the three main functional heads Force, Finite, and Tense. In addition, a Deixis cluster of features was proposed to represent the center of deixis for the 'actual world' of evaluation. Each of the three functional heads was analyzed as varying between interpretable feature values and the absence of any specified value. When features are unvalued, agreement with other constituents is necessary to value and delete the uninterpretable feature. In these contexts, constituents in the syntactic environment can provide a variety of values. This approach provides a sketch of how time reference is anchored to the speaker and speech time, and how embedded clauses construct displaced evaluation.

20.3 Aspect

The term 'aspect' refers to two different layers of temporal information in the predicate phrase: (a) the classification of events according to their temporal properties (stative/non-stative, punctual/durative, telic/atelic); and (b) grammatical aspect, a temporal framework within which the event is located or described. The temporal framework provided by grammatical aspect typically has properties that are distinct from those of the event itself.

For example, an event: *to cross the street* has an onset, an internal stage of movement, and an endpoint. Grammatical aspect can bring into focus either the entire event or just one part of it, such as its internal process stage, or its onset or its result state: *John crossed the street* focuses on the whole event, including its beginning and end; *John was crossing the street* focuses on the process. Grammatical aspect represents the event from an external perspective, and is referred to as 'viewpoint' aspect (Smith 1992/1997). The discussion below will consider how grammatical aspect can be given a phase-based analysis. Section 20.3.2 discusses perfect tenses.

20.3.1 Grammatical aspect

Informally, tense is described as establishing a relationship between the time of an event and an evaluation time, as was discussed in Section 20.2 above. However, there are many contexts in which it is clear that the run-time of an event is not the same as the interval of the finite tense ordering relationship. This is illustrated by the contrast between (68a) and (68b–d):

(68)   a. Bill wrote a poem
       b. Bill was writing a poem (when I arrived)
       c. Bill had written a poem (when I arrived)
       d. Bill used to write poems

In (68a), the interval that is located in the past is just the duration of the event of Bill's writing a poem. It encompasses the entire event, including its beginning and endpoints. In (68b), only a portion of the event of writing a poem is asserted as located in the past. The sentence asserts only that the process of writing was ongoing, but the endpoint may or may not have been reached. That is, the time frame for the event is narrower than the event. In (68c) and (68d), a time frame that is larger than the interval of Bill's writing a poem is located in the past. These sentences all refer to events that have similar intrinsic temporal characteristics: an onset initiated by an agent, a process of activity involving the creation of poems, and the potential for an endpoint (or *telos*). The subevents of the situation are shown in (69):

(69)   (pre-event) [$_{\text{EVENT}}$ Onset [Process] Endpoint] (post-event)

Grammatical aspect introduces an interval that matches up to the run-time of the event in various ways, as shown in (70)–(73): The time asserted by the speaker as holding in the past in (68a–d) is shown underlined below:

(70)   a. Bill wrote a poem
       b. Asserted interval: (pre-event) [**Onset [process] Endpoint**] (post-event)

(71) a. Bill was writing a poem
b. Asserted interval: (pre-event) [Onset **[process]** Endpoint] (post event)

(72) a. Bill had written a poem
b. Asserted interval: (pre-event) [[**Onset [process] Endpoint] Post event time**]

(73) a. Bill used to write poems
b. Asserted interval: [... **[Event]** .. **[Event]** ... **[Event]** ...]

The time introduced by grammatical aspect, which corresponds to the time asserted by the speaker, is referred to as the Assertion Time (the time that corresponds to states and events that are asserted by the speaker; Klein 1995) or the Reference Time in the sense of the Reichenbach framework (Section 20.2.1). It is described in Smith (1992/1997) as Viewpoint Aspect, because it characterizes the situation in a manner that reflects the speaker's viewpoint on it, rather than just the intrinsic temporal properties and duration of the event.

The classification of Assertion Times according to their distinctive temporal properties is described along two dimensions. One is the Perfective/Imperfective distinction. Perfective aspect includes the boundaries of the event in the Assertion Time, as in (70a); imperfective aspect corresponds to all other temporal relationships between the asserted time and the run-time of the event, including progressive aspect. In sentences whose predicates involve transitions (change of state), perfective and imperfective aspect behave differently with respect to time adverbs and temporal adjunct clauses. Time adverbials pick out different points in the event:

(74) a. at 1:30, Sue ate lunch   (Onset = at 1:30)
b. at 1:30, Sue was eating lunch   (Internal stage = at 1:30)

In (74a), the punctual adverbial identifies the onset of the event; in (74b) it identifies a point internal to the event. Similarly, *when*-clauses identify either the onset or an internal stage of an event:

(75) a. when we got home, Sue ate lunch
b. when we got home, Sue was eating lunch

A second dimension for classifying Assertion Times is proposed in Demirdache and Uribe-Etxebarria (2000), based on ordering relations between Assertion Times and the event. They argue that the same primitives and temporal relations that underlie tense construal also apply to aspect, and that primitive temporal relations are predicates 'before,' 'within,' and 'after'; when encoded in Tense Phrase, these relations produce tense interpretations (past, present, future); in an aspect phrase, the same primitive relations produce aspectual interpretations: prospective aspect, progressive aspect, and perfect (or retrospective) aspect:

(76) a. Sue was writing a poem   (progressive aspect: [Within])
     b. Sue had written a poem   (perfect aspect: [After])[22]
     c. Sue was going to write a poem   (prospective aspect: [Before])

To derive these readings, Demirdache and Uribe-Etxebarria propose parallel analyses of Tense and Aspect; while Tense establishes an ordering relationship to an external Utterance Time anchor, Aspect establishes an ordering relation to an external Assertion Time (AST-T) anchor. Demirdache and Uribe-Etxebarria's structure is shown in (77):

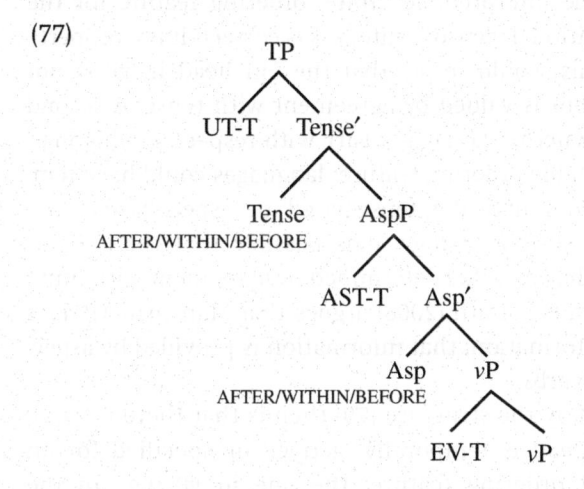

(77)
```
                TP
               /  \
           UT-T    Tense'
                  /   \
              Tense    AspP
         AFTER/WITHIN/BEFORE
                        /  \
                    AST-T   Asp'
                           /   \
                         Asp    vP
               AFTER/WITHIN/BEFORE
                                /  \
                             EV-T   vP
```

The choice of semantic feature for Aspect determines the readings of prospective, progressive, and perfect aspect. The alternation between perfective and imperfective aspect is analyzed by Demirdache and Uribe-Etxebarria (2007) in terms of an Aspect head that is morphologically unspecified for a 'before/after/within' temporal relation, and instead establishes a referential dependency between Assertion Time and Event Time, shown by co-indexation in (78):

(78) [$_{AspP}$ AST-T$_i$ Asp [$_{vP}$ EV-T$_i$ ...]]

The co-indexing of Assertion Time and Event Time arguments has two possible semantic effects. One is anaphoric binding, where Event Time is anaphoric to Assertion time; this derives the perfective reading. The second is variable binding, where the Assertion Time binds some time at which the event holds; this could correspond to an interval larger than or smaller than the run-time of the event itself. This allows both progressive readings as well as habitual readings.

This approach could be represented in a phase-based clause structure by extending the temporal relations discussed in Section 20.2 to vP to account for aspectual relationships. Tense and Aspect would be analyzed as parallel sequences of a Fin/Time heads:

(79) a. CP: [$_{CP}$ v_{Force} ... Fin ... [TIME] (=Tense)]
    b. vP: [— ... Fin ... [TIME] (=Aspect) ... v ...]

Just as the Fin head in the CP phase encodes features that specify the modality of the relationship between the speech act (Force) and the propositional content of the clause, the Fin head in the vP phase might encode the relationship between the external time, TENSE, and the internal time (Aspect). One question that arises for the proposed structure in (79b) is whether it also has an interpretable ordering feature, or whether only one of these heads bears the interpretable 'finite' ordering feature for the entire clause. If the traditional view of finiteness is correct, it is a property of an entire clause. This would imply that the Fin head in vP is not independently valued, but is valued by agreement with tense. A second issue to be explored is whether languages vary with respect to which Fin head bears the interpretable ordering feature; languages could have temporal ordering that is grammatically 'tense-based' or 'aspect-based.' In a language that lacks tense morphology, it is possible that the [MOOD] feature in the CP phase has its value determined by agreement with finite aspectual morphemes in vP. Smith (2008) argues that Mandarin TP does not encode temporal information; that information is provided by aspectual morphemes and adverbs.

The possibility raised by the structure (79) then is that there is variation as to which Fin head is temporally 'active,' or specified for an interpretable temporal ordering feature: the one in vP (i.e., in the Aspect system), or in CP (in the Tense system). Furthermore, it could be that this variation is not determined once-and-for-all in a grammar, but instead is specific to certain paradigms. As illustration, there is some evidence that English and French differ with respect to whether present tense is specified as an [Inclusion] feature at the level of Tense or at the level of Aspect. It was proposed for English in Section 20.2.3.1 that there is a present tense, specified as an interpretable [Include] value of Tense, while unmarked Aspect is uninterpretable, valued by agreement with features of the verb. In French, grammatical Aspect is not determined by agreement with the verb, since a progressive interpretation is possible for active verbs with unmarked aspect. On the other hand, Tense may not be inherently specified for an ordering value. It is observed by Laca (2005) that French present tense is neutral, allowing both perfective and imperfective readings (from Demirdache and Uribe-Etxebarria 2007):

(80) à 1h30, Cécile déjeune
      'at 1:30, Cecile eats'
      (i) at 1:30, Cecile starts eating
      (ii) at 1:30, Cecile is eating

The ambiguity observed in (80) is what is expected for a tense that is morphologically unspecified for an ordering value. Similarly, a compound perfect with present tense morphology is ambiguous between a present perfect and a past (perfective) event:

(81) Jean a   lu   ce livre
      J. have.PRES.3s read.PRT that book
      'John read/has read that book'

One interpretation of (81) – the 'perfect' reading – refers to a state that holds at speech time; the other (perfective) interpretation is of a past event. This systematic ambiguity is expected if French present tense is not specified for an [Include] feature, but instead inherits its value by agreement with aspect values of vP.[23]

Summarizing, the interval that is in an anchoring relation to Speech time in main clauses is not the run-time of the event, but is an 'asserted time.' To describe the relationship between the Assertion Time and Event Time, a second Fin/Time sequence was postulated in the vP phase. These heads provide a position for encoding the features related to Aspect, which relates the event time to the Asserted time of Tense. Variations in the distribution of interpretable temporal features between CP and vP may account for variation in temporal systems across languages.

20.3.2 Perfect tenses

The parallel treatment of Tense and Aspect discussed in Section 20.3.1 provides a straightforward means of accounting for sentences like (82b), with compound perfect tense, where Event Time is understood as preceding the Assertion Time:

(82) a. John arrived at 3pm
      b. John had arrived at 3pm

In the simple past tense, the time of John's arrival is unambiguously 3pm; in the compound perfect, John's arrival is ambiguous between 3pm and a time prior to 3pm. The two readings of the past perfect illustrate that Assertion Time and Event Time can have an independent ordering relation, as proposed by Demirdache and Uribe-Etxebarria's analysis, and as analyzed in the Reichenbach framework, discussed in Section 20.2.1. Adapting this generalization to a phase-based representation, the features of Tense and Aspect would be as shown in (83):

(83)   a. CP: [$_{CP}$ Force ... Fin[MOOD:ordering] ... [TIME:exclude]
             (=TENSE)]
          b. vP: [—   ... Fin[MOOD:ordering] ... [TIME:exclude]
             (=ASP) ... v ...]

The event interval excludes the Assertion Time, which in turn excludes the anchor (speech time).

A phase-based analysis of the relation between Assertion Time and Event Time might also provide a natural explanation for the non-recursion of tenses. It is generally assumed, particularly in the literature based on the framework of Reichenbach (1947) that Tense–Aspect combinations of certain types, such as (84b), are impossible in all languages:

(84) a. John had been laughing
     b. *John had had laughed

The Reichenbach framework accounts for this generalization in a principled way, since it claims that all tenses are composed of exactly three times. The phase-based account based in (79) predicts that just the times that are 'visible' for interpretation at the edge of the phase can participate in relations at the next phase up; other temporal relations can be present, but will not enter into relations at higher levels of structure. This could provide a means of accounting for apparent exceptions to the ban on recursion of tenses noted by Demirdache and Uribe-Etxebarria (2000, 2007). They cite examples from Breton, and from the *passé surcomposé* in French, as in (85) (Demirdache and Uribe-Etxebarria 2007):

(85) quand j'ai   eu   dansé,
     when have-PRES-1SG   have.PAST-PART   dance.PAST-PART
     je me suis désaltéré
     I quenched my thirst

A further issue for the analysis of perfect tenses concerns whether perfect morphology encodes a second precedence relation or not. To illustrate, a present perfect sentence such as *Sue has eaten lunch* would be analyzed on the Reichenbach approach as encoding a precedence and a simultaneity relation: R,E_S; since E is associated with R, it should precede speech time. However, there is some degree of variability of interpretation of compound perfect tenses, both cross-linguistically and language-internally. Language-internally, interpretation can vary according to the choice of adverbs and the aspectual characteristics of the verb. This is shown by the contrast between stative and eventive predicates in (86):

(86) a. Sue has stayed at the library
     b. Sue has eaten lunch

The stative present perfect can either mean that there was one past non-specific instance of Sue's staying at the library, or that there is a state of affairs that started at some indefinite time in the past and persists in the present. The non-stative perfect lacks the 'persistent' reading; (86b) can only mean that the event of eating lunch is finished. As was discussed in Section 20.3.1, an interpretable indicative tense has a consistent semantic effect; absent an interpretable value, other factors, including grammatical aspect, determine temporal relations between events that are in construction with one another. If perfect tenses were intrinsically specified for an ordering relation, the 'shifted' reading should always occur, regardless of the aspectual class of the verb or other factors.[24] The restriction of this reading of non-statives suggests that the vP Fin phrase is not intrinsically specified as an ordering head:

(87) vP: [$_{AspP}$ – Fin[uMOOD] Aspect[TIME] [v+V]] (=Ev-T)

The Fin Phrase [MOOD] is valued by Agree and deleted. Because it is unvalued, the event time is not intrinsically ordered relative to Assertion Time. This is an instance of neutral aspect, in the sense of Demirdache and Uribe-Etxebarria (2000), as discussed above in Section 20.3.1. It is predicted under that analysis that both perfective and imperfective readings are available. This prediction is borne out for English. The possibility remains that in other languages, the Fin phrase is activated in vP.

20.4 Modality and mood

Modality and mood are relational categories that express a mode by which a proposition is anchored to the external context of evaluation. To introduce modality and mood it is useful to take as a point of departure the unmarked temporal modality of indicative declaratives. As discussed above in Section 20.2.2, in indicative clauses the [MOOD] feature of FinP has a temporal value; this means that FinP specifies a temporal relationship between the proposition and its external source of evaluation. The features of ForceP, DeixisP, and FinP identify the time of evaluation as the time of the speaker's assertion. By contrast, semantically 'marked modality' indicates a departure from this relationship, for example to express attitudes about the occurrence of an event that has not yet occurred, such as a wish, demand, or fear that the event be realized. It can also express variations in the context of evaluation. Palmer (2001) reports that in Central Pomo, a language indigenous to northern California, a declarative morpheme takes different forms to indicate whether the assertion is the speaker's, or is based on a report by someone else, or is assumed to be general knowledge. Additionally, in some languages the source of evidence for the assertion can be grammatically marked, according to whether the reported event was seen by the speaker, heard by the speaker, or was based on the speaker's personal experience. These distinctions reflect a modality system referred to as evidentiality, which might be analyzed as adjuncts of the Force Phrase.[25] Another type of marked modality reflects the speaker's degree of certainty about the situation, as is found with certain uses of English modals, as in: *John may be finishing that book already*. Marked modality also identifies potential or hypothetical ones as opposed to existing ones.

These various types of marked modality indicate the range of meanings that fall under the notional concept of modality; what is particularly relevant for the syntax is how the functional features of the clause give rise to these interpretations. In this chapter, it has been assumed that indicative mood is the interpretable, valued form of the mood feature, and that indicative mood identifies events as existing, occupying spatio-temporal coordinates in the speaker's actual world. A clause that bears the unvalued form of the feature gets its interpretation by the presence of an item that has intrinsic modal value. In this situation mood is licensed via Agree. The discussion below examines two situations in which grammatical morphemes reflect systematic mechanisms of valuation of mood. The first is the finite English modals, which introduce two types of modality: epistemic and deontic. The second is Spanish subjunctive clauses, which introduce marked modality of different types in Romance languages and English.

20.4.1 Epistemic and deontic modal verbs

Epistemic modality expresses the speaker's judgment about the factual status of the proposition; deontic modality expresses judgments from sources other than the speaker. These readings are illustrated in (88), (89):

(88) Sue may organize the project
    (i) speaker's judgment of possibility of the event
    (ii) subject has permission (from someone unspecified) to perform the event

(89) Sue must leave at noon
    (i) speaker's judgment of necessity of the event
    (ii) subject has obligation (from someone unspecified) to perform the event

Although languages vary in the syntax of their modal morphemes, there appears to be a cross-linguistic generalization that epistemic modals are always outside the scope of the clausal event time, while deontic modals need not be. In French and Spanish, for example, modals are fully inflected verbs, yet Borgonovo and Cummins (2007) show that even when inflected for past tense, epistemic modals are interpreted at holding at speech time, not in the past:

(90) Epistemic readings:
    a. Pedro debía   estar en casa   (Spanish)
       Pedro must-Past-Imp be-INF at home

    b. Pierre devait   être   à la maison   (French)
        Pierre must-Past-Imp be-INF at home
        'Peter must have been at home'

(91) Deontic readings:
    a. Pedro debía   pagar   la cuenta   (Spanish)
        Pedro must-Pastimperf. pay-INF the bill
    b. Pierre devait   payer   la facture   (French)
        Pierre must-Pastimperf. pay-INF the bill
        'Peter was supposed to pay the bill'

For the English finite modals, many studies have likewise noted that epistemic modals hold only at the anchor time of the clause (Stowell 2004, von Fintel and Iatridou 2003, Boogaart 2004), while deontic modals are not always so restricted. This is shown by Stowell (2004):

(92) a. Jack's wife can't be very rich   (speech time impossibility)
        'it is not possible that Jack's wife is very rich'
    b. Jack's wife <u>couldn't</u> be very rich   (speech time impossibility)
        '<u>it is not possible</u> that Jack's wife is very rich'
        *'<u>it was not possible</u> that Jack's wife was very rich'
                                                              (past impossibility)
(93) a. Carl can't move his arm   (speech time ability)
    b. Carl couldn't move his arm   (past ability)

On the assumptions discussed in previous sections of this chapter, the inability of epistemic modals to be located in the past implies that epistemic readings of modals lack an indicative temporal ordering value for [MOOD]. It has been shown above that morphological past tense only has a temporal precedence interpretation in the indicative mood – that is, a [MOOD] feature with a temporal ordering value, which in turn licenses a temporal value of the [TIME] feature of ForceP. It may be that epistemic modals are ones whose 'subject' is the interpretable [1sg] feature of the DeixisP, since epistemic interpretations report or assert the speaker's judgment about the possibility or necessity of the event. On deontic interpretations, the possibility for, or obligation to perform the event is conferred or granted by someone unspecified. Since the conferring of permission or obligation is an event that is separate from the speaker's judgment about the proposition, it can in principle occur at a different time from the evaluation time.

As noted above, epistemic and deontic modals do not seem to differ in their distribution in clauses or in their inflectional morphology. Their differences in interpretation are therefore expected to be due to their interactions with features of FinP, ForceP, and DeixisP. The English finite modals merged in the same position as *WOLL*, as analyzed in Section 20.2.3.3 above:

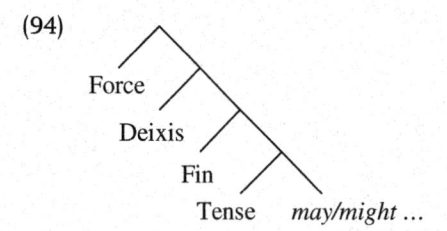

(94)
```
        Force
           \
          Deixis
             \
             Fin
               \
            Tense  may/might ...
```

The discussion below will explore the idea that the epistemic/deontic distinction is akin to the distinction between *will* and *would*. It was shown in Section 20.2.3.3 that the two forms of *WOLL* spell out features 'past' or 'present' plus the value of WOLL. It will be recalled, however, that what appeared to be a past/present feature is the time of evaluation of the clause, not the event time. To account for the contrast between epistemic and deontic modals with respect to temporal reference, it is hypothesized that they differ with respect to whether they are licensed in relation to the speaker feature of Deixis Phrase or not. A modal that is licensed in relation to the speaker feature is interpreted at the spatio-temporal coordinates of the speaker. A modal that is otherwise licensed, can have other temporal coordinates in embedded clauses such as SOT contexts.

20.4.1.1 Epistemic modality

A key distinction between epistemic and deontic interpretations concerns whether the modal expresses a judgment of the speaker or another entity. To capture this distinction, it can be supposed that modals can be predicated of the Deixis Phrase, which encodes the interpretable feature [*i*1PERSON] or 'speaker.' Finite modals also have an uninterpretable Time feature that is valued by the external evaluation time of the clause.

(95) Modal[uDeixis] + [uTime:Include] → epistemic interpretation

Since the clause is non-indicative, it has no interpretable Tense ordering feature. The modal values the [uMOOD] feature of the clause, and its [uDeixis] feature is valued by Deixis, as shown in (96):

(96) a. Sue may organize the project
      b.

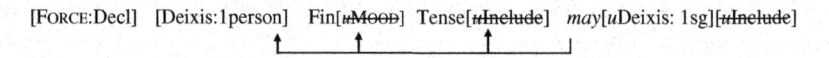

   [FORCE:Decl] [Deixis:1person] Fin[uMOOD] Tense[uInclude] *may*[uDeixis: 1sg][uInclude]
         ↑   ↑   ↑   ↑

In this derivation, the modal *may* values the [MOOD] feature of FinP. This differs from indicative clauses, where anchoring is a temporal location of the event in relation to the anchor. It also agrees with the uninterpretable tense feature of Tense Phrase. Although *may* is formally a present tense, it is a formal tense only valued by agreement. By the same token, a 'past' form of a modal such as *could* is understood as a possibility with respect to a past time of evaluation, as in (97):

(97) Carol said that Sue could organize the project

The [Time] feature of Tense Phrase agrees with the evaluation time of the clause, which in turn is the time of the matrix event. This accounts for the lack of a past epistemic reading of (92b) above. In that context *could* does not refer to a past impossibility because there is no temporal ordering feature specified in the embedded Fin phrase. The analysis predicts correctly that in SOT contexts, an epistemic modal has a 'simultaneous' interpretation, not a shifted interpretation:

(98) John believed (at noon) that Carl could move his arm (at 11am)
    a. Possibility for the event to occur (epistemic; at noon/*at 11am)
    b. Ability of Carl to move his arm (deontic; at noon/at 11am)

An epistemic reading of the embedded clause can only be understood as implying a possibility that existed at noon, not a possibility that existed prior to noon. On the deontic (ability) reading of the modal, the ability could be either at noon or prior to noon. The explanation for the forced simultaneous reading in the embedded clause follows from the fact that simultaneous readings in SOT contexts are also instances of an unvalued [MOOD] feature, as discussed above in Section 20.2.

The past/non-past alternations – *can/could*, for example – are thus expected not to reflect real temporal distinctions on an epistemic interpretation. The contrast between the exclude/include values of Tense was analyzed above as having a temporal value only in the context of indicative mood, that is, where FinP has an ordering feature. Otherwise, its value may be fixed by a linguistic antecedent, as in SOT contexts, or by pragmatic factors. In at least some instances, the contrast could indicate the extent to which the speaker is the source of the modal judgment. For example, *Carl can move his arm* suggests that the speaker is affirming the possibility, while *Carl could move his arm* suggests a possibility that the speaker is reporting, but is not necessarily committed to. Perhaps for this reason only the latter is compatible with a conditional clause, which specifies external sources under which the possibility holds.

20.4.1.2 Deontic modality

It was suggested above that deontic interpretations of modals do not reflect the speaker's judgment about the event, but a possibility (permission) or obligation granted by some other entity. As they are not related to the evaluation of the clause, but to the description of the event, it is natural that they are not linked to the speaker, and can be temporally independent of the evaluation time. This was shown to be the case above for French and Spanish in (90), and for English in examples like (99):

(99) a. Carl can move his arm (present ability)
  b. Carl could move his arm (present or past ability)

Deontic modals appear to be like other auxiliary verbs in that they may have interpretable tense features, which implies that they are compatible with indicative mood as well as non-indicative. Their readings are then determined by the mood of the clause, which in turn determines whether the tense feature is interpretable (an 'event time') or not. Relevant features are shown in (100):

(100) FinP   Tense
  a. [Mood:order] [iTime:Include] *can* → present ability
  b. [uMood:]   [uTime:Include] *can* → ability at speech time
  c. [Mood:order] [iTime:Exclude] *could* → past ability
  d. [uMood]   [uTime:Exclude] *could* → ability; at non-deictic evaluation time

In (100a), the inclusion feature relates the ability to speech time via the present event time; in (100b), the tense feature is uninterpretable, valued by agreement with the time of evaluation, which is in turn linked to the DeixisP as discussed previously. This interpretation is pragmatically indistinguishable from epistemic possibility, but is derived from different grammatical relations. In (100c), the indicative mood and exclusion value of tense give *could* a past interpretation; finally in (100d), the [exclude] feature of mood does not imply precedence but rather non-deictic source of evaluation. Since deontic modals can have a true temporal past tense, it is expected that they allow 'shifted' interpretations in SOT contexts:

(101) John believed at noon that Carl could move his arm (the day before).

As expected, the embedded clause in (101) can describe an ability of Carl that held before the time of John's belief about it. This reading is possible based on the features in (100c), since the embedded clause has a temporal ordering value for [Mood]. This follows the expected pattern in SOT contexts, where the embedded clause allows both ordering and non-ordering modalities.

Note that not all putative 'past' forms of modals behave like *could*. There is no difference between *may* and *might* with respect to present/past interpretation:

(102) a. John could move his arm yesterday
  b. ?*John might move his arm yesterday
  c. *John should move his arm yesterday

The difference between *could*, on one hand, and *might* and *should*, on the other, raises the question of which behavior is typical of deontic modals. Although further examination of this question is needed, it will be supposed here provisionally that *could* represents the typical pattern, since, as was shown above for French and Spanish, deontic modals generally allow past interpretations. There is also some reason to question whether *might* and *should* are past forms. Unlike *could*, they do not work perfectly in contexts of obligatory tense agreement. As noted in Section 20.2.2.1, *when*-clauses agree with the clause they modify in [past/non-past]:

(103)   a. John left when he could/*can
        b. John left when he ??might/*may

To conclude, epistemic and deontic modals differ in their semantic and grammatical relationship to the features of the left periphery that specify the external mode of evaluation of the proposition. Epistemic modals convey a possibility or necessity whose source is the speaker; deontic modals report a judgment that is independent of the speaker's evaluation of the clause, and consequently, like other auxiliary verbs, deontic modals are compatible with both indicative and non-indicative modalities.

20.4.1.3   A note on raising/control and modals

The analysis of English finite modals outlined above analyzes both the epistemic and deontic modals of English as grammatical formatives, in the sense that they are merged in the functional structure of the CP-TP phase, and are not analyzed as argument-taking predicates. This analysis is at odds with an approach to the epistemic/deontic contrast on which these differences in interpretation arise from raising versus control structures (see Chapter 16). Certain modals do imply an additional semantic role on their deontic readings – particularly modals of permission and obligation: in *John should collect the samples*, the obligation reading implies that unspecified people judge John as obligated to perform the event. Epistemic readings are usually judgments attributed to the speaker, not others.

Despite the capacity for root modals to imply additional participants, the contrast does not appear to be amenable to an analysis in terms of a raising/control distinction, at least for the English finite modals discussed above. For English, the finite modals do not seem to have any valency effects. The putative argument of the root modal is never realized as an overt argument (*To them, John may organize the project*). Furthermore, Wurmbrand (1999) shows that deontic modals are compatible with expletives:

(104)   a. there may be singing but no dancing on my premises
        b. There must be a solution to this problem on my desk, tomorrow morning!

20.4.2 Subjunctive mood

In English, verbal morphology often expresses values for Tense without regard to whether the Fin head has an ordering value or not. In other languages, verbal morphology can overtly encode different feature values of [Mood] and [Force]. Mood distinctions can be illustrated for Spanish subordinate clauses, where unmarked (Indicative) mood is used for subordinate declaratives:

(105) a. Juan dice que María llegó
 Juan say.PRES.3s that Maria arrive.PAST-IND.3s
 'Juan says that Maria arrived'
 b. Juan dice que María llega
 Juan say.PRES.3s that Maria arrive.PAST-IND.3s
 'Juan says that Maria is arriving'.

In (105), the embedded clause is declarative and has an independent tense: the embedded verb can be inflected for past or present, independently of the tense of the main clause.

One context in which Spanish complement (and adjunct) clauses require subjunctive mood is where the complement is a future (unrealized) goal relative to the main clause predicate. This includes complements of verbs of volition, wishing and fearing, illustrated by the main clause *querer* 'want' in (106):

(106) a. Juan quiere que vayamos al cine
 Juan want.PRES.3s that go.PRES-SUBJ.1pl to-the cinema
 'Juan wants that we go out to the movies'
 b. *Juan quiere que fuéramos al cine
 Juan want.PRES.3s that go.PAST-SUBJ.1pl to-the cinema
 'Juan wants that we go to the movies'

The subjunctive complement cannot refer to an event that occurred at a time prior to the matrix predicate. The obligatory subjunctive mood and its subsequence interpretation are accounted for by the absence of an independent ordering value on the embedded Fin head. Indicative is impossible because the clause has volitional rather than declarative force, and the modal relation determined by the force of the volitional verb is subsequence. The [Force] and [Mood] features of the subordinate clause are valued by the matrix volitional verb. Main clause wishes also use subjunctive morphology, with an overt complementizer:

(107) Que lleguen pronto
 that arrive-PRES.SUBJ.3pl soon
 'May they arrive soon'

The force of (107) may be the same as that of the complement of volitional verbs, further distinguishing these clauses from indicative ones.

Subjunctive morphology is also called for in contexts where the matrix verb attenuates or negates the assertive force of the complement. This includes complements of emotive verbs, which presuppose their complements, and verbs of doubt and uncertainty.

(108) Juan está   contento de que María haya llegado
      Juan be.PRES.3s happy   of that Maria have PRES-SUB.3s arrived
      'Juan is happy that Maria has arrived'

In each of these subjunctive contexts, the matrix verb provides features that affect the force of the embedded proposition. Subjunctive morphology signals that the embedded proposition is not asserted by the speaker; the alternative mechanism of evaluation is determined by the matrix verb. Its interpretable features value the mood feature of the embedded clause.

On the hypothesis that subjunctive mood encodes [uMOOD], valued by modal elements in the clause, it is expected that cross-linguistic variations in lexical resources should produce variations in the mechanisms for valuing [uMOOD]. This was illustrated above in Section 20.3 with respect to how future interpretations are constructed in English and Russian. It is also supported by cross-linguistic differences in the semantic domains that require subjunctive mood. Since [uMOOD] is valued by a range of modal elements, different combinations of features may have distinct morphological reflexes. Spanish and Italian, for example, differ with respect to which verbs of mental attitude select subjunctive. Across Romance languages it is common for verbs of belief to take an indicative complement, while its negation can take subjunctive. An exception is Italian, where verbs of belief take subjunctive complements, as discussed in detail by Giorgi and Pianesi (1997, 2000). More general discussion of predicate types that take subjunctive clauses is found in Quer (1998).

Notes

1. Larson (1998) argues that temporal modifiers in DP can modify an event argument as well as a noun, as in (i), which is ambiguous between readings in (ii):

   (i) my former restaurant
   (ii) a. [DP my [Poss [former [restaurant]]]] (my thing that is formerly a restaurant)
       b. [DP my [former [Poss [restaurant]]]] (a restaurant that is formerly mine)

   Reading (iib) is parallel to clausal past tense: *I had a restaurant*.

2. Musan (1999) also shows that different types of nominals have different properties with respect to independence of tense, which further confirms the independence of nominals from restriction by tense.
3. Guéron (2004) argues that within the verb phrase, events are analyzed spatially, and time relations are introduced external to VP. Larson (2003) argues that adverbials of duration such as *for two hours* modify events directly, not time-of-events.
4. The category IP in (12) and (13) corresponds to Tense Phrase together with agreement features.
5. Another syntactic context in which Tense features potentially have an atemporal interpretation is in nominals. Alexiadou (2009) argues that Tense morphology in nominals may function to mark specificity rather than temporal relationships.
6. For discussion of non-temporal past tense forms see also Palmer (2001) and Lecarme (2008).
7. Sybesma draws a parallel between Dutch and Chinese, which lacks overt tense morphemes. This would imply that both languages have Fin Phrase and Tense Phrase. They differ from English in lacking a morpheme with an intrinsically valued ordering feature in Fin Phrase. An alternative explanation for the Dutch pattern in (24) is that the requirement for an adverbial anchor may due to requirements of aspect.
8. For ease of exposition the uninterpretable [TIME] and [MOOD] features of *v* are shown as [TENSE].
9. Some stance verbs are not fully acceptable in the present tense without modification, such as addition of an adjunct like *still*, or locative inversion:

   (i) still, the train remains in the station
   (ii) in the station stands/sits the train

   Although the reason for the contrast is unclear, it may be related to the compatibility of stance verbs with both stative and non-stative contexts. Clause-initial phrases such as in (i) and (ii) may license a stative interpretation.
10. Present has been analyzed in terms of several different relations: temporal inclusion, simultaneity, and temporal anaphora (Demirdache and Uribe-Etxebarria 2000, Hornstein 1990, Zagona 1988).
11. Sentences with performative verbs (*I pronounce you the winner*) are exceptional; they have an ongoing present interpretation in the present, although they are not stative. Another exception is eyewitness reports, such as sports reports: *Beckham gets the ball. He shoots ... and scores.* (Example due to Marcel den Dikken, p.c.)
12. The ban on present morphology with change of state predicates is overridden in contexts such as conditionals and temporal adjuncts:

(i) if Sue prints the article ... (future)
(ii) when Sue prints the article ... (future)
(iii) before/After Sue prints the article ... (precedence/subsequence)

13. Whether or not a language admits a progressive interpretation in the present tense without morphological marking could potentially be analyzed in terms of different default values for unmarked aspect, or alternatively, in terms of an unvalued Aspect head in vP, which is valued by different mechanisms. English unmarked aspect ([uAspect:], uninterpretable aspect) seems to be valued by verbal features, while Spanish unmarked Aspect is sensitive to Tense. For related discussion see Giorgi (2010: 113ff.).

14. For analysis of the syntax and semantics of the future, see Fleischman (1982), Hornstein (1990), Enç (1987, 1996), Demirdache and Uribe-Etxebarria (2000), Abusch (2004), Verkuyl (2008).

15. For discussion of this representation see Cinque (1999), Wurmbrand (2007), Verkuyl (2008).

16. Like *will*, other modals are compatible with both stative and non-stative events. However the temporal interpretation of the event is determined by the verb, not by the modal:

(i) a. John may be at home (present state)
     b. John will be at home (future state)

This shows that *will* has an [order] feature that *may* does not have. When *may* combines with non-statives, the event has a future interpretation *John may build a chair*. The [order] interpretation derives from the verb, not the modal.

17. According to Dormer (2009:113–15) *bud-* is historically derived from a form of the verb *byt^j* 'to be' in Old Russian, which had perfective and imperfective paradigms; *bud-* was the perfective stem. In Modern Russian, the imperfective forms have been lost, while the perfective forms based on the *bud-* stem remain intact. In Modern Russian, *bud-* retains the distribution of a perfective verb. It occurs in the 'injunctive' construction, 'let's X,' in the finite form that is found with perfective verbs:

(i) davaj   bud-em   pis-at'
    let-INJ BUD-1PL(PFV)   write-INF(IMPF)
    'let's write'

In Romance languages, what appears to be a future tense is also constructed from an infinitive with present form of a perfective verb, as in French: *ir-ai* 'go+have+1.sg'; and Spanish *cantar+(h)e* 'sing +have+1sg.'

18. Under certain conditions, relative clause tenses have a temporal anchor distinct from the speaker's time of utterance. *Tomorrow I'll*

find some people who finished the marathon and I'll interview them. The past tense in the relative clause is evaluated relative to the main clause event time (=tomorrow). For related phenomena in Japanese relative clauses, see Makihara (2005) and references cited.

19. Another point of variation in how temporal clauses are interpreted concerns the choice of events that stand in the ordering relation. Temporal clauses introduced by *before* and *after*, for example, admit long-distance ordering relations:

    (i) I saw Mary in New York [before [she claimed [that she would arrive]]]

    The time of seeing Mary in New York may precede either the time *claimed* or the time of Mary's arrival. For discussion and different approaches, see Larson (1990), Thompson (2005).

20. Temporal clauses do allow modals under certain conditions, although these seem generally to be deontic interpretations, with the time feature representing an event time, as in: *Sue didn't drive when she could take the bus*; *The students write well before they can speak fluently*.

21. Descriptively, the 'double access' reading appears to involve an ordinary main clause indicative present tense, but where the source of the embedded clause declarative force is still interpreted as the main clause subject, with an implicit temporal restriction on the assertion. Verbs of saying differ from verbs of attitude with respect to whether they allow present tense embedded under past. See Giorgi and Pianesi (2000) for discussion.

22. Demirdache and Uribe-Etxebarria interpret the temporal predicate as locating its specifier relative to its complement. In the perfect, and in past tense, the anchor is temporally after the event; in future and prospective aspect, the anchor is before the event.

23. In infinitives, English perfect morphology has a perfective past reading, as shown in (i):

    (i) to have read a book yesterday would please Sue

    This suggests that infinitives have and unvalued [TIME] feature that can be valued by the ordering/exclusion feature of the participle.

24. Iatridou, Anagnostopoulou and Izvorski (2001) show that the aspectual features of participles vary across languages, and are responsible in part for the range of readings of perfect tenses from language to language.

25. Data for Central Pomo, as well as detailed discussion of evidentiality and modality in general, can be found in Palmer (2001).

21
Negation and negative polarity

Hedde Zeijlstra

21.1 Introduction

A universal property of natural language is that every language is able to express negation, i.e., every language has some device at its disposal to reverse the truth value of the propositional content of a sentence. However, languages may differ to quite a large extent as to how they express this negation. Not only do languages vary with respect to the form of negative elements, but the position of negative elements is also subject to cross-linguistic variation. Moreover, languages also differ in terms of the number of manifestations of negative morphemes: in some languages negation is realized by a single word or morpheme, in other languages by multiple morphemes.

The syntax of negation is indissolubly connected to the phenomenon of (negative) polarity. In short, and leaving the formal discussion for later, negative polarity items (NPIs) are items whose distribution is limited to a number of contexts, which in some sense all count as negative. NPIs surface in various kinds of environments and may also vary in terms of the restrictions they impose on their licensing contexts and the type of licensing relation. Therefore, studying NPIs provides more insight not only into the nature of such context-sensitive elements, but also into the syntax of negation itself.

Finally, it should be mentioned that the distinction between negative elements and NPIs is not always that clear-cut. In many languages negative indefinites, quite often referred to as n-words (after Laka 1990) appear to be semantically negative in certain constructions, while exhibiting NPI-like behavior in other configurations. The same may also apply to negative markers in some languages.

This chapter aims at providing an overview of the most important recent findings and insights gained in the study of the syntax of negation and polarity. Section 21.2 deals with the syntax of negative markers;

Section 21.3 discusses the syntax and semantics of (negative) polarity items. Section 21.4 will focus specifically on negative concord (i.e., the phenomenon where multiple instances of morphosyntactic negation yield only one semantic negation), with special emphasis on the ambivalent nature of n-words. Section 21.5, finally, concludes.

One final note: the syntax of negation is complex and touches upon a multitude of phenomena, many of which cannot be discussed here in detail, or even at all, for reasons of space. Absence of discussion of such contributions should not be viewed as an indicator of their (lack of) importance.

21.2 The syntax of sentential negation

In this section I provide a brief overview of the range of variation that the expression of (sentential) negation cross-linguistically exhibits and what its underlying syntax is. First, in Section 21.2.1, I introduce the distinction between sentential and constituent negation, after which I continue by describing the range of variation that is cross-linguistically attested with respect to the expression of sentential negation (Section 21.2.2). Section 21.2.3 deals with the syntactic status of negative markers and, finally, in Section 21.2.4 their syntactic position is discussed.

21.2.1 Sentential and constituent negation

Before discussing the various ways in which sentences can be made negative, one important distinction needs to be made. Take for instance the following minimal pair, dating back to at least Jackendoff (1972).

(1) a. with no clothes is Sue attractive
    b. with no clothes Sue is attractive

Although both cases involve the same negative constituent (*with no clothes*), (1a) and (1b) crucially differ in their readings. Whereas (1a) denies Sue's attractiveness, (1b) entails it, albeit under special circumstances. Also, syntactically (1a) and (1b) are different, in the sense that (1a) triggers verbal movement to C^0, whereas (1b) does not. Since in (1a) the entire sentence is felt to be negative, and in (1b) only the PP *with no clothes*, it is said that (1a) constitutes an instance of sentential negation, whereas (1b) exhibits constituent negation.

Klima (1964) was the first to offer a number of diagnostics for sentential negation, such as (among others) continuations by positive question tags or *either* phrases; sentences involving constituent negation, by contrast, can only be followed by negative question tags or *too* phrases.

(2) a. With no clothes is Sue attractive, is/*isn't she?
    b. With no clothes Sue is attractive, isn't/*is she?

(3) a. with no clothes is Sue attractive, and/or Mary either/*too
    b. with no clothes Sue is attractive, and/or Mary too/*either

Klima's tests have given rise to a number of criticisms. These criticisms initially concerned the diagnostics, though not the distinction between sentential and constituent negation itself. First, the criteria are language-specific and therefore do not naturally extend to other languages; second, the Klima tests also take semi-negative adverbs, such as *seldom* or *hardly*, to induce sentential negation (see (4)), even though such elements do not reverse the polarity of the sentence: (4) does not deny that John drives a car.

(4) John seldom drives a car, does he?

Finally, the alleged mutual exclusiveness between sentential negation and constituent negation was called into question. Take for instance (5):

(5) Not every professor came to the party, did they?

Not every professor clearly forms a constituent (a negative DP). Although examples like (5) are often analyzed as constituent negation (cf. Payne 1985, Cirillo 2009), the diagnostics point in the direction of sentential negation. It is, thus, a question whether exhibiting constituent negation is actually incompatible with expressing sentential negation. Rather, what seems to be the case is that sentential negation should be considered a scopal notion, rather than a notion in terms of syntactic structure. Then, (5) is simply an instance of constituent negation that is also able to express sentential negation.

Following a research tradition that essentially goes back to Jackendoff (1969, 1972), Lasnik (1975) and many others, Acquaviva (1997) argues that the notion of sentential negation should be defined in semantic rather than syntactic terms. Specifically, Acquaviva argues that sentential negation is the result of negating the quantifier that binds the event variable. In terms of neo-Davidsonian event semantics (Davidson 1967, Parsons 1990), representations of sentential negation must be represented as in (6):

(6) John didn't drive
    $\neg \exists e[drive(e) \& Agent(j, e)]$

Currently, most scholars treat sentential negation à la Acquaviva (cf. Herburger 2001, Zeijlstra 2004, Penka 2007). Note, though, that adopting this kind of perspective on sentential negation does not necessarily preclude the validity of syntactic approaches to the analysis of sentential negation, as it is generally assumed that existential closure of the predicate containing the event variable takes place at the level of the vP boundary (cf. Diesing 1992, Ladusaw 1992, Herburger 2001, Zeijlstra 2004, 2008, Penka 2007).

21.2.2 Ways of expressing sentential negation

The distinction between sentential and constituent negation paves the way for one of the central questions that this chapter is about: what are the syntactic properties of the expression of sentential negation?

Languages exhibit a fair amount of cross-linguistic variation with respect to the way sentential negation is expressed. However, closer inspection reveals some remarkable correspondences as well. Let me discuss two of them.

First, as has been noted by Horn (1989) in his seminal work on negation, the expression of a negative sentence is always marked in comparison to its affirmative counterpart. There is no language in the world in which affirmative sentences are marked and negative ones are not (see also Dahl 1979, Payne 1985). In this respect negative and affirmative sentences in natural language are not symmetric but rather asymmetric in nature (for a discussion on this asymmetric view on the positive–negative distinction, see also Ladusaw 1996).

Second, various strategies for expressing negation turn out to be universally absent. For instance, no language in the world is able to express negation solely by means of word order shift, a strategy that is often exploited to express other grammatical functions, such as interrogatives (cf. Horn 1989; Zeijlstra 2009).[1]

This leaves open a syntactically limited set of possible expression strategies: sentential negation must be expressed overtly (i.e., it cannot be left unspecified), and marking cannot occur merely by way of a word order shift. This means that every instance of sentential negation must be expressed by some negatively marked, overt element, with variation lying only in the type, position, and number of such markers.

Elaborating on Zanuttini's (2001) state-of-the-art overview, three major classes of negative elements expressing sentential negation can be identified.

The first class of strategies concerns negative verbs. In languages like Evenki (a Tungusic language spoken in Eastern Siberia) special auxiliaries can negate a sentence. Alternatively, in many Polynesian languages (e.g., Tongan) negative verbs even select an entire clause (in a way similar to the English *it is not the case that* ... construction). Examples are shown in (7).[2,3]

(7) a. bi ə-ə-w dukuwūn-ma duku-ra (Evenki)
   I NEG-PAST-1SG letter-OBJ write-PART
   'I didn't write a letter'
  b. na'e 'ikai [CP ke 'alu 'a Siale] (Tongan)
   Asp neg [ASP go ABS Charlie]
   'Charlie didn't go'

The second class of expression strategies is constituted by languages that make use of negative markers that participate in the verbal inflectional morphology. An example is Turkish, where sentential negation is expressed by means of a negative morpheme *me* that is located between the verbal stem and the temporal and personal inflectional afffixes.

(8)　John elmalari ser*me*di　　　　　　　　　　　　　　(Turkish)[4]
　　　John apples　like.NEG.PAST.3SG
　　　'John doesn't like apples'

The final class of expression strategies exploits negative particles to express sentential negation. Negative particles come about in different forms. Following Zanuttini (1997, 2001) and Zeijlstra (2007), one can distinguish the following two kinds of negative particles: negative markers that attach to the finite verb and those that do not.

The first type of these negative particles are negative markers that when expressing sentential negation must be attached to the finite verb.[5] Czech *ne* and Italian *non* are two examples:

(9)　a. Milan *ne*volá　　　　　　　　　　　　　　　　　(Czech)
　　　　 Milan NEG.calls
　　　　 'Milan doesn't call'
　　　b. Gianni *non* ha telefonato　　　　　　　　　　　(Italian)
　　　　 Gianni NEG has called
　　　　 'Gianni didn't call'

In both examples the negative marker shows up in a position to the immediate left of V_{fin}. It must be noted though that these markers exhibit different phonological behavior. Italian *non* is a separate morphological word, which for syntactic reasons precedes the finite verb, whereas in Czech the negative marker is also phonologically attached to V_{fin}. The examples above thus show that this first class of these negative particles is not homogeneous.[6]

The second class of negative particles is characterized by the fact that, in contrast with the first class, their syntactic position does not depend on the surface position of the (finite) verb. Movement of the finite verb does not trigger displacement of the negative marker. In this respect, the distributional position of these negative markers is similar to that of aspectual adverbs, as is shown for German *nicht* 'not' and *oft* 'often' in (10) and (11).

(10)　a. Hans kommt *nicht*　　　　　　　　　　　　　　(German)
　　　　 Hans comes NEG
　　　　 'Hans doesn't come'
　　　b. ... dass Hans *nicht* kommt
　　　　 ... that Hans NEG comes
　　　　 '... that Hans doesn't come'

(11) a. Hans kommt *oft* (German)
    Hans comes often
    'Hans often comes'
  b. ... dass Hans *oft* kommt
    ... that Hans often comes
    '... that Hans often comes'

A final remark needs to be made about the occurrence of multiple negative markers. Many languages allow more than one negative marker to appear in negative clauses. Catalan for example has, apart from its preverbal negative particle *no*, the possibility of including a second additional negative particle *pas* in negative expressions. In Standard French the preverbal negative particle *ne* must even be accompanied by the negative particle *pas*.[7] In West Flemish, finally, the negative particle *nie* may optionally be joined by a negative particle *en* that attaches to the finite verb (12).[8]

(12) a. *no* serà (*pas*) facil (Catalan)
    NEG be.FUT.3SG NEG easy
    'it won't be easy'
  b. Jean *ne* mange *pas* (French)
    Jean NEG eats NEG
    'Jean doesn't eat'
  c. Valère (*en*) klaapt *nie* (West Flemish)[9]
    Valère NEG talks NEG
    'Valère doesn't talk'

Jespersen (1917) had already observed that examples like the ones in (12) reflect a widespread diachronic development of languages. Languages like English, Dutch, Latin, and many others all changed from languages with only a clitic-like negative marker through intermediate stages as in (12a-c) to a stage in which negation is expressed only by means of a postverbal negative marker. This process is known as Jespersen's Cycle (after Dahl 1979) and has been formulated by Jespersen as follows:

> The history of negative expressions in various languages makes us witness the following curious fluctuation; the original negative adverb is first weakened, then found insufficient and therefore strengthened, generally through some additional word, and in its turn may be felt as the negative proper and may then in course of time be subject to the same development as the original word. (Jespersen 1917: 4)

A number of analyses have been presented to account for the range of variation that is attested cross-linguistically (both synchronically and diachronically) with respect to the expression of sentential negation, of which a number will be discussed in the next section. However, it must be noted that this range of variation is not unique to negation. It shows close resemblance to, for instance, the range of variation that tense, aspect, and mood markers exhibit, as well as their similar diachronic developments (cf. Hopper and Traugott 1993, Roberts and Roussou 2003, van Gelderen 2009).

21.2.3 On the syntactic status of negative markers

The question now arises as to what is the exact syntactic status of the different types of negative particles that have been discussed above, and to what extent they can be analyzed in formal syntactic terms.

Pollock (1989), based on an intensive study of the distinction between French auxiliaries and lexical verbs, argues that negative particles, such as French *ne* and *pas*, are base-generated in a particular functional projection, dubbed NegP, that intervenes between TP and AgrsP. The finite verb, on its way to T⁰, then picks up the negative marker *ne* leaving *pas* behind in its specifier position.

(13) [$_{TP}$ Jean ne-mange [$_{NegP}$ pas ~~ne-mange~~ [$_{AgrP}$ ~~mange~~ [$_{vP}$ ~~mange~~]]]]

The idea that negative markers are hosted in some functional projection in the clausal spine has strongly shaped the study of the syntactic status of negative markers, the primary question being which particles may head such a negative phrase and which ones may not.[10]

Zanuttini (1997, 2001) already applies a number of diagnostics to prove that those markers that always show up in the proximity of the finite verb are syntactic heads that have the entire *v*P in their complement. One such diagnostic concerns clitic climbing. In (14b) it can be seen that the presence of the French negative marker *ne* blocks movement of the clitic *la* from a position within an infinitival complement of a causative verb to a position adjoining the matrix auxiliary. The example in (14c) makes clear that this blocking effect is due to the intervening clitic-like negative marker *ne*, as clitic movement over *pas* is not illicit. Zanuttini follows Kayne (1989b) in arguing that this must be due to *ne* being an intervening head blocking antecedent government of the trace, although this analysis does not crucially rely on Kayne's explanation, as in other frameworks intervening heads are also taken to interfere with clitic movement as well (see Pollock 1989, Travis 1984).

(14) a. Jean la$_1$ fait manger t$_1$ à Paul (French)[11]
     Jean it makes eat to Paul
     'Jean makes Paul eat it'
   b. *Jean l$_1$'a fait ne pas manger t$_1$ à l'enfant
     Jean it.has made NEG NEG eat to the child
     'Jean has made the child not eat it'

c. Jean *ne*   l₁'a   *pas*   fait   manger t₁ à Paul
      Jean NEG   it.has NEG   made   eat   to Paul
      'Jean hasn't made Paul eat it'

Another diagnostic, also presented in Zanuttini (1997), concerns blocking of verb movement. Paduan, an Italian dialect from Veneto, requires the C⁰ head to be overtly filled in *yes/no* interrogatives.[12] In positive interrogatives, the verb moves from V⁰ to C⁰. As a consequence of the Head Movement Constraint (Travis 1984), such movement would be illicit if another overtly filled head intervened. Hence, if the Paduan negative marker *no* is an intervening head, V-to-C movement is predicted to be excluded in Paduan *yes/no* interrogatives. This prediction is indeed borne out, as shown in (15).

(15) a. Vien-lo?   (Paduan)
          comes-he
          'Is he coming?'
      b. *Vien-lo   no
          comes-he NEG?
          'Isn't he coming?'

Zanuttini's analysis that those negative particles that attach to the finite verb must be heads of some functional projection in the clausal spine is further proved by Merchant (2006), who developed another diagnostic: the so-called *why not* test. Merchant argues that the English *why not* construction must be analyzed as a form of phrasal adjunction and therefore it is predicted that this construction is only allowed in those languages in which the negative marker is phrasal as well.

(16) [YP [XP why] [YP *not*]]

As Merchant shows, this prediction is borne out for many of the languages with a negative particle, illustrated by examples from Italian and Greek in (17), where the negative particle heads NegP and thus cannot participate in 'why not' constructions:

(17) a. *Perche non?   (Italian)
      b. *Giati dhen?   (Greek)
          why NEG
          'Why not?'

In those languages, in order to express something meaning 'why not,' the construction 'why no' ('no' as in 'yes/no') must be used:

(18) a. Perche *no*?   (Italian)
      b. Giati *oxi*?   (Greek)
          why   no

This observation holds for all languages where the negative marker itself is not taken to be phrasal, except for those languages where the negative marker is phonologically identical to the word for 'no,' such as Spanish and Czech.

(19) a. ¿Porqué *no*? (Spanish)
 b. Proč *ne*? (Czech)
    why NEG/no

The three diagnostics just discussed all show that those negative particles that attach to the finite verb must be taken to be syntactic heads within the clausal spine. It is only natural, then, to assume that those negative particles whose sentential position is in principle independent of the surface position of the verb should be taken as phrasal elements, i.e., not as elements occupying a head position in the clausal spine (leaving open the question whether these elements are then specifiers of NegP or not). This assumption indeed appears to be correct.

If negative adverbs are XPs they should not block head movement and 'why not' constructions should be acceptable.[13] Both predictions are correct. V2 languages such as Dutch, German, or Swedish exhibit V2 in main clauses. This implies that the verb has to move over the negative adverb to C^0 in a negative sentence, as is shown for Dutch and Swedish below and has already been shown for German in (10):

(20) a. ...om Jan *inte* köpte boken (Swedish)
    ...that Jan NEG bought the book
    '...that John didn't buy the book'
 b. Jan köpte *inte* boken
    Jan bought NEG the book
    'Jan didn't buy the book'

(21) a. ...dat Jan *niet* liep (Dutch)
    ...that Jan NEG walked
    ...'that Jan didn't walk'
 b. Jan liep *niet*
    Jan walked NEG
    'Jan didn't walk'

From these results it follows that the negative adverbs in (20)–(21) behave like maximal projections. It is then also expected that these elements are allowed to adjoin to 'why' in the 'why not' constructions. This expectation is confirmed as well, as shown in (22).

(22) a. Why   *not*?   (English)
 b. Warum *nicht*?   (German)
 c. Waarom *niet*?   (Dutch)
 d. Varför *inte*?   (Swedish)
    why   NEG
    'Why not?'

So, to conclude, the distinction between the two types of negative particles can be naturally reduced to a distinction in syntactic phrasal status.

The next question that arises is whether negative markers that are instances of the verbal morphology, such as the Turkish negative marker *me*, which precedes tense, mood, and person affixes and follows reflexive, causative, or passive affixes, are fundamentally different from markers that attach to V_{fin}. Can it be the case that they are both base-generated in some Neg^0 position in the clausal spine and only differ with respect to their morphophonological properties? This question is not restricted to the realm of negative markers, but concerns the comparison between inflectional and non-inflectional morphemes in general. Traditionally, inflected verbs have been considered to be the result of a head movement process where the verb 'picks up' its affixes (cf. Baker 1985a, Pollock 1989). In this sense, the underlying syntactic structure of sentences with a non-phrasal negative particle and an inflectional negative marker may be identical.

Such a view (present, for instance, in Pollock 1989) is currently in dispute, however, casting doubt on the idea that inflectional negative markers are plain syntactic heads, and has been replaced by either lexicalist accounts, where lexical items enter the derivation fully inflected (cf. Chomsky 1995c et seq.), or Distributed Morphology-based approaches where the formal features in the verbal tree are post-syntactically spelled out as either inflectional morphemes or separate words (cf. Halle and Marantz 1993 and subsequent work). Under lexicalist approaches, inflectional markers must be different from syntactic heads; other approaches question the idea that syntactically inflectional markers are fundamentally different from syntactic heads: they are only the result of different mechanisms in the spell-out process. But even under lexicalist approaches the presence of an inflectional morpheme is connected to a corresponding syntactic head to which the inflectional morpheme stands in an Agree relation.

Thus, in principle, nothing forbids a unified treatment of non-phrasal negative particles and inflectional negative markers (i.e., all negative markers whose sentential position is dependent on the position of the finite verb) in terms of elements connected to some head position in the clausal spine. However, before we can draw any definite conclusions, detailed discussion will be required of the way that inflectional markers should be treated syntactically. Such a discussion exceeds the study of negation and is therefore beyond the scope of this chapter.

21.2.4 On the syntactic position of negative markers

The fact that negative markers can be heads of a particular functional projection (dubbed NegP) leads to two further questions: (i) What is the syntactic position of this NegP with respect to other functional projections in the clausal spine? and (ii) Is this negative projection also present in languages that lack an (overt) negative head or do these phrasal negative markers occupy specifier/adjunct positions of other projections?

Pollock (1989) proposed that NegP is located below TP and above AgrP, but the exact position of negation within the clausal spine has been the subject of quite extensive discussion (cf. Belletti 1990, Laka 1990, Zanuttini 1991, Pollock 1993, Haegeman 1995, amongst many others).

Most of these proposals point out that nothing a priori forces the position of the negative projection to be universally fixed. Ouhalla (1991a), for instance, shows that in Turkish, negative affixes are in between the verb and tense affixes, whereas in Berber, negation is in the outer layer of verbal morphology, as is shown in (23).[14]

(23) a. *ur*-ad-y-xdel Mohand dudsha (Berber)[15]
 NEG.FUT.3MASC.arrive Mohand tomorrow
 'Mohand will not arrive tomorrow'
 b. John elmalar-i ser-*me*-di (Turkish)
 John apples like.NEG.PAST.3SG
 'John doesn't like apples'

Assuming that both inflectional negative markers are hosted at Neg⁰, Ouhalla argues that the position occupied by NegP in the clause is subject to parametric variation along the lines of his NEG Parameter (24), which puts NegP either on top of TP or on top of VP.[16]

(24) NEG Parameter
 a. NEG selects TP
 b. NEG selects VP

According to Ouhalla, the different values of this NEG Parameter are also reflected by the differences in the expression of sentential negation in Romance languages and Germanic languages. For him, in Romance languages NegP dominates TP while it does not do so in Germanic languages.[17,18]

The idea that the position of NegP is more flexible than initially suggested by Pollock (1989, 1993) was further adopted by Zanuttini (1991, 1997). She claims, much in line with the later cartographic approach initiated by Rizzi (1997) and Cinque (1999) (see Chapter 12), and based on various Italian dialect data, that different negative markers in Romance varieties may occupy different positions in the sentential structure and that universally at least four different NegPs are available (see also Benincà 2006, Poletto 2000, 2008, Manzini and Savoia 2005, for a discussion of negation in various Italian dialects):[19]

(25) [$_{NegP1}$ [$_{TP1}$ [$_{NegP2}$ [$_{TP2}$ [$_{NegP3}$ [$_{AspPperf}$ [$_{AspPgen/prog}$ [$_{NegP4}$]]]]]]]]

In Zanuttini's work, different types of negative markers have different syntactic and/or semantic properties, such as sensitivity to mood (in many dialects/languages a different negative marker appears if the sentence displays irrealis mood) or the ability to induce sentential negation without the support of other negative elements (which Italian *non* is able to, but French *ne* is not).

Zanuttini's proposal has also met with criticism. Whereas her proposal is essentially right in arguing that more positions should be available for negative markers, she does not make it clear why these positions should have to be part of a universal syntactic template. The fact that the distribution of negation appears to be richer than a fixed NegP position suggests does not necessarily constitute an argument in favor of an even more fine-grained fixed structure. It might just as well indicate that the syntactic distribution is relatively free and only constrained by independently motivated syntactic or semantic restrictions.

This is essentially the argument that Zeijlstra (2004) puts forward. He argues that the minimal (semantic) requirement for a negative marker to express sentential negation is that it outscopes *v*P to ensure that sentential negation is yielded (see Section 21.2.1), and that this constraint determines the cross-linguistic range for variation. Similarly, Zeijlstra (2006), following Han (2001), argues that negation may never be interpreted in a position at least as high as C^0 in main clauses (as otherwise negation would outscope operators with the illocutionary force of a speech act). These two assumptions thus require negative markers to occupy a position somewhere in the syntactic middle field without alluding to any syntactic principle (except one that states that semantic scope reflects syntactic structure; see May 1977). Finally, Zeijlstra argues that semantic differences between different positions (or types) of negative marker should also result in different scopal effects, i.e., the syntactic position of a negative marker is (relatively) free, but if the negative marker is included in different positions, different semantic effects are expected to arise.

Zeijlstra's line of reasoning is in line with a series of approaches put forward by (amongst others) Ernst (2002), Svenonius (2001c), and Nilsen (2003), who argue that, generally, the fixed orders of adverbials (see Chapter 13), arguments, discourse particles, etc. does not reflect a prefabricated syntactic template, but rather results from the fact that alternative orders would lead to semantic anomaly. Consequently, following the anti-cartographic nature of these approaches (mostly notably Nilsen 2003), Zeijlstra argues that, whereas negative head markers must head a NegP of their own, negative specifiers do not necessarily do so. For languages like Dutch and German, Zeijlstra assumes that their adverbial negative markers (*niet* and *nicht*, respectively) occupy adjunct positions of *v*P and he claims that a negative projection is even lacking in the clausal spine.

Zeijlstra's more flexible analysis of the sentential locus of negation and negative markers has been adopted by Penka (2007), Cirillo (2009), and Breitbarth (2009). Breitbarth (2009), and also Haegeman and Lohndal (2010), argue that an important consequence of Zeijlstra's approach is that only negative markers may occupy a Neg⁰ position. As obvious as this may sound, closer inspection reveals that this has serious repercussions for the analysis of negative markers that cannot express sentential negation without additional support by another negative marker, as illustrated in (12b–c) and repeated as (26a–b) below.

(26) a. Jean *ne* mange *pas* (Standard French)
Jean NEG eats NEG
'Jean doesn't eat'

b. Valère (*en*) klaapt *nie* (West Flemish)
Valère NEG talks NEG
'Valère doesn't talk'

As Breitbarth, and Haegeman and Lohndahl, observe, West Flemish *en* is never able to render a sentence negative by itself.[20] It is only optionally available in sentences that have already been made negative by other overt negative elements. For that reason, *en*, strictly speaking, cannot be taken to carry some negative feature, which in turn can project Neg⁰. Instead, they argue that *en* carries a weak polarity feature that constitutes a Polarity Phrase (PolP). Similar arguments have been proposed for the Afrikaans sentence-final negative marker *nie* (Oosthuizen 1998, Biberauer 2008a) and French *ne* (Zeijlstra 2009). For the latter Zeijlstra argued that French *ne*, being an element that may only survive in (semi-)negative contexts without contributing any semantic negation, should actually be considered a plain NPI. This already shows the intricate relationship between negation and negative polarity, the topic of the next section.

21.3 Negative polarity items

The previous section has illustrated that the expression of sentential negation is subject to a number of both syntactic and semantic constraints. However, the syntax of negation is not restricted to the syntax of negative markers and other negative elements only. As has briefly been touched upon at the end of the previous section, some elements do not induce semantic negation by themselves, but at the same time only survive in contexts that, in one way or another, are negative. Such elements are generally referred to as negative polarity items (NPIs), although other names surface as well (e.g., 'affective items'; see Giannakidou 1999).

The most well-known examples of NPIs are formed by the English *any*-series, although many more can be given, e.g., English *yet*, *need*, *either*, or *lift a finger*:

(27) a. we *(didn't) read *any* books
b. I have*(n't) been there *yet*
c. I *need**(n't) do that

d. I *(didn't) read the book, and John *(didn't) *either*
e. nobody/*somebody *lifted a finger*

NPI-hood is by no means restricted to English. To the best of my knowledge, all languages have some NPIs at their disposal (see also Haspelmath 1997 for a non-exhaustive list of languages that display NPIs) and many languages exhibit a typology of NPIs, often at least as rich as that of English.[21]

As has been pointed out by Giannakidou (1999), the term 'NPI' in most cases is a misnomer, as most so-called NPIs are licensed in contexts that are not strictly speaking negative as well, such as restrictive clauses of universal quantifiers, *yes/no*-questions, or contexts introduced by *at most N* constructions or semi-negative adverbs, such as *hardly*.

(28) a. every student who knows *anything* about linguistics, will join the event
b. Do you want *any* cookies?
c. at most three students did *any* homework
d. John hardly likes *any* cookies

NPIs have received wide attention by scholars in syntax, semantics, and pragmatics, and they have constituted a fruitful and popular research area over the past thirty years. As Ladusaw (1996) points out in his seminal overview article, the study of the behaviour of NPIs has been dominated by four research questions: (i) the licenser question; (ii) the licensee question; (iii) the licensing (relation) question; and (iv) the status question.

The licenser question aims at determining what counts as a proper NPI licensing context. The licensee question asks why certain elements are only allowed to occur in particular contexts and what distinguishes them from polarity-insensitive elements. The licensing (relation) question addresses what kind of constraints the relation between the NPI licenser and its licensee is sensitive to. Finally, the status question addresses the status of sentences containing unlicensed NPIs: Are such sentences bad for syntactic semantic and/or pragmatic reasons? Note that the status question is very tightly connected to the licensee question. If it is, for instance, a syntactic property of NPIs that they require a higher negative(-like) element, then a sentence containing an unlicensed NPI is grammatically ill-formed; on the other hand, if NPIs come along with a pragmatic effect that causes them to only be felicitously uttered in negative(-like) contexts, then, by contrast, a sentence containing an unlicensed NPI may still be grammatical. The four questions thus reduce to three core questions (see also Giannakidou 2001, 2010, 2011 who in a slightly differently formulated way also presents these questions as core questions in the study of polarity).

The study of NPI-hood is, however, not restricted to these questions. At least two additional phenomena merit discussion as well.

First, some NPIs, such as English *any*-terms, not only survive in negative or semi-negative environments, but may also appear in positive contexts inducing a so-called free-choice reading. An example is given in (29) below.

(29) *any* student of linguistics should read *Syntactic Structures*

In (29), *any* is not interpreted as a plain indefinite but receives an interpretation that at least at first sight behaves more like a universal. The central question in the study to NPIs that can also induce free-choice readings, such as *any*, is whether such elements are lexically ambiguous between an NPI and a free-choice item, or whether these different interpretational (and distributional) properties follow from one and the same underlying semantic denotation.[22]

Another thorny phenomenon concerns the alleged mirror image of NPI-hood. Some elements, like English *some* or *rather*, may only appear in positive contexts. Take for instance (30):

(30) a. I didn't drink some wine   ($\exists > \neg$; *$\neg > \exists$)
     b. I am (*not) rather ill

Some cannot survive in a negative context. (30a) only has a reading where *some* outscopes the negation ('there is some wine that I didn't drink'); the reading where *some* takes scope under the negative marker is blocked. *Rather*, in (30b), cannot occur in a negative context at all. Elements with this property, such as *some* and *rather*, are referred to as positive polarity items (PPIs). At the same time, as we will see, NPI and PPI do not always behave on a par, raising the question as to whether NPI-hood and PPI-hood are indeed two sides of the same coin, or actually constitute inherently different phenomena.

This section is set up as follows. In Sections 21.3.1–21.3.3, I address the three questions that originate from Ladusaw (1996), the licenser question, the licensee/status question, and the licensing question. In Sections 21.3.4 and 21.3.5 I focus on free choice and PPI-hood, respectively.

21.3.1 The licenser question

As the examples (27)–(28) have already shown, NPIs are only licensed in particular contexts, some truly negative, some not. The question thus arises as to what properties constitute NPI licensing environments.

The first and still one of the most important and influential proposals that tries to reduce all NPI licensing contexts to one single semantic property, is Ladusaw's (1979) proposal, based on Fauconnier (1979), that all NPI licensers are downward entailing (DE), where DE is defined as follows:

(31) δ is downward entailing iff $\forall X \forall Y (X \subseteq Y) \rightarrow ([[\delta]](Y) \subseteq [[\delta]](X))$[23]

To illustrate what is meant here, let's look at the examples in (32) and (33). In (32a) the first sentence entails the second one but not the other way round (32b). This is due to the fact that the set of red shirts is a subset of the set of shirts. The entailment goes from a set to its supersets.

(32) a. Mary is wearing a red shirt → Mary is wearing a shirt
b. Mary is wearing a shirt ↛ Mary is wearing a red shirt

In DE contexts, entailment relations are reversed. This is shown for the negative contexts in (33) where the only valid inferences are now from a set to its subsets.

(33) a. nobody is wearing a red shirt ↛ nobody is wearing a shirt
nobody is wearing a shirt → nobody is wearing a red shirt
b. John is not wearing a red shirt ↛ John is not wearing a shirt
John is not wearing a shirt → John is not wearing a red shirt

However, DE-ness is not restricted to negative contexts. Also, the first (but not the second) argument of a universal quantifier,[24] semi-negatives, such as *few*, and *at most N* constructions are DE and license NPIs.

(34) a. every student went to bed → every linguistics student went to bed
b. few people sing → few people sing loudly
c. at most three students left → at most three students left early

Although this proposal is to be considered a milestone in the study of NPIs, it faces several serious problems as well, as has often been addressed in the literature (see the detailed discussions below for references). The three most important ones are the following: (i) not every NPI is licensed in the same sets of DE contexts; (ii) some NPIs can be licensed in non-DE contexts as well; and (iii) successful NPI licensing does not depend only on the logico-semantic properties of the NPI licensing context.

With respect to (i), it can be observed that some NPIs are subject to different licensing conditions than others. For instance, whereas English *any*-terms seem to be fine in all DE contexts, the Dutch counterpart to *any*, i.e., *ook maar*, is ruled out in DE contexts like *niet iedereen* ('not everybody'):

(35) a. nobody / not everybody ate *anything*
b. [niemand / *niet iedereen] heeft ook maar iets gegeten (Dutch)
nobody / not everybody has PRT PRT something eaten
'nobody / not everybody ate anything'

Van der Wouden (1994), elaborating on Zwarts (1995), argues that DE should be thought of as some layer of a negative hierarchy, where the true negation (*not*) forms the highest layer, followed by so-called anti-additive elements (*nobody, nothing, no*), followed by the next layer, being DE-ness.[25] NPIs, then, differ with respect to which layer of negativity is qualified to license them. English *any* is licensed in DE contexts (and thus in all negative contexts), others only in anti-additive contexts (such as

Dutch *ook maar*) and some NPIs can only be licensed by the sentential negative marker.[26]

Although these observations are all empirically correct, it should be noted that even this classification should be subject to further modification. For instance, Hoeksema (1999) shows that Dutch NPI *hoeven* cannot occur in the first argument of a universal quantifier, which is DE but not anti-additive, even though it can occur in other non-anti-additive DE contexts such as *weinig* ('few'):

(36) a. *iedereen die *hoeft* te vertrekken, moet nu opstaan
       everybody who needs to leave   must now get.up
       'everybody who needs to leave, must get up now'
   b. weinig mensen *hoeven* te vertrekken
       few people   need   to leave
       'few people need to leave'

With regard to (ii), Giannakidou (1997, 1999 et seq.) shows that just as DE-ness is not always a sufficient condition for NPI licensing, it is not always a necessary condition for it either. For instance, *yes/no*-questions are not DE, even though they license NPIs (see van Rooij 2003) and similar observations have been made for comparatives and superlatives (cf. Hendriks 1995, Schwarzschild and Wilkinson 2002, Giannakidou and Yoon 2010).[27] Also, Greek *tipota* 'anything' can be licensed under modals meaning 'may' or 'want' or in subjunctive clauses (Giannakidou 1997, 1999, 2000).[28] Apparently, DE-ness does not seem to be the weakest layer of negativity and therefore Giannakidou proposes, following Zwarts (1995), to further extend the hierarchy of negative contexts by an other layer of negativity: non-veridicality (defined as in (37)).

(37) A propositional operator F is non-veridical if *Fp* does not entail or presuppose that *p* is true in some individual's epistemic model (after Giannakidou 1997, 1999, 2010, 2011).

To clarify this, *perhaps* in (38a) is a non-veridical operator whereas *unfortunately* in (38b) is veridical, since a speaker uttering (38a) does not take the sentence *John is ill* to be necessarily true, whereas a speaker uttering (38b) does do so.

(38) a. perhaps John is ill
   b. unfortunately John is ill

Non-veridicality can be seen as an additional layer of negativity (even weaker than DE-ness) and may account for those cases where NPIs, such as English *any* terms, may appear in non-DE contexts.[29] However, at the same time, NPIs like *any* may not appear in all non-veridical contexts, such as most modal contexts:

(39) *perhaps John read *any* books

In order to account for this, Giannakidou alludes to the difference between licensing and anti-licensing: she argues that Greek *tipota* 'anything' may occur in all non-veridical contexts, i.e., non-veridical contexts license *tipota*; by contrast, English *any* is said to be banned from all veridical contexts, i.e., veridicality anti-licenses *any*. This leaves open the possibility that *any* is still banned in some non-veridical contexts.

In connection with (iii), we should note that under the Ladusaw–Zwarts–Giannakidou approach, NPI licensing is only dependent on the logico-semantic properties of the licensing context. This is, however, not always the case. For instance, conditionals only allow NPIs under particular pragmatic conditions as discussed by Heim (1984) and von Fintel (1999). Linebarger (1980, 1987) and Giannakidou (1999) provide additional examples where contexts that are clearly non-DE or non-veridical still license NPIs if they come along with a particular negative implicature, as is shown below:

(40) exactly four people in the room *budged an inch* when I asked for help[30]

The source of licensing in (40) cannot be reduced to the semantic properties of its position at LF, but seems to lie in the fact that for the speaker the number of assistants is smaller than expected/hoped for.

The last example suggests that not only semantic but also pragmatic conditions apply to NPI licensing.

21.3.2 The licensee question

Perhaps even more important than the question as to what licenses an NPI is the question as to what property an NPI has such that it can only occur in this particular type of context. It is exactly this question which has dominated the study of NPI licensing over the past ten to fifteen years.[31]

Two types of approaches have been formulated to address this question. For some scholars, NPI-hood reduces to some semantic and/or pragmatic requirement that means that NPIs can only be felicitously uttered in negative contexts of some sort (DE, anti-additive, or non-veridical). For others, the answer should lie in syntax, i.e., NPIs come along with some syntactic feature that forces them to appear in negative environments only.

21.3.2.1 Semantic and/or pragmatic approaches

The first major contribution in the first direction is the widening + strengthening account by Kadmon and Landman (1993). Their account consists of two steps. First, they propose that NPI indefinites, such as English *any* terms, differ semantically from plain indefinites in the sense that NPIs are domain wideners. Such domain-widening indefinites extend the domain of reference beyond the contextual restrictions that plain indefinites are subject to. Take (41), which contains Kadmon and Landman's original examples:

(41) a. I don't have potatoes
b. I don't have any potatoes

Whereas (41a) entails that, in a particular domain, the speaker does not have potatoes, (41b) suggests that the speaker does not even have a single old potato in some corner in the kitchen.

The second step in Kadmon and Landman's line of reasoning is that they claim that sentences containing NPIs like *any* must be stronger than sentences containing a plain indefinite. (41b) is stronger than (41a): the set of situations where (41b) is true is a clear subset of the set of situations where (41a) is true, so (41b) entails (41a). The strengthening requirement is thus met. However, the fact that (41b) is stronger than (41a) is due to the presence of the negative marker: given that negation is DE, removal of the negation in the examples in (41) would reverse the entailment relation. Therefore, without the presence of the negation, a sentence like (41b) would actually be weaker than the sentence without *any*. Uttering (41b) without the negation would thus violate the pragmatic strengthening condition. This is exactly what, for Kadmon and Landman, rules out sentences containing unlicensed NPIs.

The idea that NPIs come along with widening and strengthening effects, which are responsible for the fact that they can only be felicitously uttered in DE contexts, has been adopted and implemented in various ways. Krifka (1995), for instance, argues that the strengthening condition follows as an implicature as sentences with a weak reading generally bring along an implicature that the stronger reading is ruled out. In this respect, he focuses on elements denoting minimal amounts and explains that especially those elements are prone to become NPIs.

Lahiri (1998) connects the NPI property to NPI *even*, arguing that the underlying structure under NPIs is something like 'even a(n) N,' based on data from Hindi, where the word for *even* is overtly present in indefinite NPIs:

(42) a. koii bhii (Hindi)[32]
one even
'anybody'
b. koii bhii nahiiN aayaa
one even not came
'nobody came'

A problem, already acknowledged by Krifka (1995) and also present in Giannakidou (2011), is that under the Kadmon and Landman approach NPIs pose strengthening restrictions on the contexts that they can appear in, without such restrictions being encoded in their lexical representations. Therefore it remains unclear what enforces the fact that sentences containing NPIs must be stronger than those with a plain indefinite.

In order to ensure that NPIs are always subject to a strengthening requirement, Chierchia (2006) proposes that NPIs are domain wideners that carry an additional, syntactic feature that requires that NPIs must appear under the direct scope of an abstract strengthening operator that states that any stronger scalar alternatives of the sentence containing the NPI are false.

Furthermore, Chierchia argues, along the lines of Kadmon and Landman and Krifka, that strengthened domain wideners always yield a semantic contradiction unless they appear in DE contexts. If that is correct, it immediately follows that NPIs are doomed in any contexts other than DE ones.[33]

Giannakidou (1997, 2001, 2010) points out that despite the current popularity of the widening + strengthen approach outlined above, it still faces several problems.

First she shows that pragmatic infelicitousness and semantic contradictions are generally not judged as being ungrammatical, as shown in (43) below (taken from Giannakidou 2011).

(43) a. the king of France is my brother
     b. John was born in NY, and he was not born in NY

However, the judgments on unlicensed NPIs are much stronger: speakers generally feel them to be ungrammatical.

Also problematic, she argues, is that Kadmon–Landman type of analyses only apply to indefinite NPIs. Although most NPIs are indefinites, not all of them are. For instance, NPIs like *either* or *need* are not. Concerning the latter, as Iatridou and Zeijlstra (2010) have shown, deontic modal NPIs are actually always universal and never existential. This suggests that, though not necessarily on the wrong track, the original approach is insufficient: it is not the only way to explain why NPIs are banned from certain contexts. It should be noted, however, that most NPIs denote scalar endpoints, suggesting that scalarity still underlies NPI-hood.[34]

The third problem for Giannakidou is that widening + strengthening approaches do not naturally extend to those cases where NPIs are licensed in non-veridical, non-DE contexts, such as *yes/no*-questions.

In order to solve this final problem, Giannakidou (2010, 2011) exploits another type of account, arguing that even within the domain of indefinite NPIs a distinction must be drawn between those NPI indefinites that appear in DE contexts only (and could potentially be analyzed as having their NPI property derived from their domain widening effects) and those that do not.

For her, this latter type of NPI is lexically deficient for referentiality. She assumes that NPIs like Greek *kanenas* 'anybody,' which are fine not only in downward-entailing contexts, but also in all kinds of other non-veridical contexts, can only be uttered felicitously when they do not have to refer to some entity in the real world. Therefore, these elements are expected to not appear in veridical contexts.

21.3.2.2 Syntactic approaches

Although currently many scholars assume that the ill-formedness of sentences containing unlicensed NPIs is due to pragmatic and/or semantic reasons, others have argued that those are ungrammatical as a result of some syntactic constraint.

The tradition that takes NPIs to come along with a syntactic requirement that they be licensed by a (semi-)negative operator goes back to Klima (1964), and has been presented in more modern frameworks by Progovac (1992, 1993, 1994), who takes NPI licensing to be some special instance of syntactic binding, and by Laka (1990), who relates NPIs to the obligatory presence of an affective phrase (ΣP).

Postal (2000), followed by Szabolcsi (2004), introduces a revival of Klima's theory and claims that NPIs such as English *any* underlyingly carry a negation, suggesting a syntactic representation of *any* as (44).

(44) *any*: [$_D$ NEG [SOME]]

In a negative sentence containing *any*, the negation moves out of *any* to a higher position where it is realized as an overt negator; in semi-negative sentences this negation may incorporate in other elements.

Den Dikken (2006a) adopts the essence of Postal's analysis, but modifies it in more Minimalist terms by assuming that NPIs carry an uninterpretable negative feature that must be checked against a negative head in the clause.[35] Independently, and for different reasons, Neeleman and van der Koot (2002) and Herburger and Mauck (2007) reached this conclusion as well.

The main problem for such purely syntactic approaches, however, is that it is hard to understand why most types of NPIs that are attested always denote some endpoint of a scale. In principle, if NPI licensing is an instance of syntactic feature checking, all kinds of elements should be able to act as NPIs, whereas the distribution of most if not all NPIs seems to be restricted semantically.

Herburger and Mauck (2007) try to overcome this criticism by arguing that the scalar endpoint property is a necessary, but not a sufficient condition for NPI licensing. For them, it is indeed a pragmatic and/or semantic property whether some element may be a candidate for becoming an NPI, but that it is only the presence of some uninterpretable negative feature that turns an element into an NPI.

21.3.3 The licensing question

Finally, all cases discussed so far show that all NPIs must stand in a particular relation to their licensers. Ladusaw (1979) suggests that, since the licensing requirement involves a scopal semantic property, this relation basically boils down to a scope requirement at LF: all NPIs must be within the scope of a DE operator at LF.

However, as Ladusaw (1979) notes, this constraint on the licensing relation may be a necessary but not a sufficient condition. NPIs, generally speaking, may not precede their licenser, even if this licenser outscopes the NPI at LF. Hence Ladusaw (1979) argues that the c-command relation must hold not only at LF, but also at surface structure. This now explains why (45) (taken from Ladusaw 1996) is ruled out.[36]

(45) *he read any of the stories to none of the children

But, Linebarger (1980) points out that the NPI licensing relation must be more severely constrained. Concretely, she claims that NPIs must not only be outscoped by a DE operator at LF, but no scope-taking element may intervene between the NPI and its licenser either, a claim dubbed the Immediate Scope Constraint (ISC). Take the following minimal pair (again from Ladusaw 1996):

(46) a. Sam didn't read every child a story ¬>∃>∀; ¬>∀>∃
     b. Sam didn't read every child any story ¬>∃>∀; *¬>∀>∃

Although (46a) is ambiguous between a reading where the existential scopes over the universal and a reverse reading, this second reading is ruled out in (46b). This directly follows from the ISC, as the NPI then would not be directly outscoped by a DE operator.[37]

In the more recent literature on the NPI licensing relation, two phenomena have further refined our understanding of the licensing relation. Both phenomena are instances of NPI licensing where an NPI is not directly outscoped by its licenser at LF.

The first phenomenon concerns the difference between direct and indirect licensing (Linebarger 1980, Giannakidou 1999). As discussed at the end of Section 21.3.1, NPIs are sometimes fine in non-DE contexts as long as these contexts introduce some negative implicature. The relevant example was (40), repeated as (47) below.

(47) exactly four people in the room *budged an inch* when I asked for help

Obviously, the well-formedness of (47) does not follow under the above-sketched ISC analysis.

For Linebarger, examples such as (47) show that NPI licensing actually takes place indirectly. In short, she states that what is responsible for NPI licensing is that a sentence containing some NPI gives rise to an implicature that contains a negation directly outscoping this NPI. For sentences already containing a negation this follows straightforwardly; for other DE operators this implicature needs to be paraphrased in some way such that it contains a negation (e.g., *few X* implies *not many X*). For (47), the required negative implicature should contain a paraphrase such as 'not as many people as I expected.' Note that as long as a formal computation procedure of such implicatures is lacking, this type of account cannot make exact predictions.[38]

Giannakidou (1999, 2006a) occupies an intermediate position between Ladusaw's and Linebarger's proposals. She takes NPI licensing to be a relation that takes place at LF between an NPI and a non-veridical operator and which is subject to the ISC.[39] But she also allows NPI rescuing, where a sentence containing NPI that lacks a non-veridical licenser at LF may be rescued from ill-formedness, if the sentence still gives rise to a negative implicature. This mechanism is close to Linebarger's account, with the difference that for Linebarger all NPI licensing functions in this way, whereas for Giannakidou it is a secondary mechanism: Giannakidou thus allows NPI licensing to take place at two distinct levels.[40]

The second phenomenon concerns another instance of rescuing and is known as parasitic licensing (den Dikken 2006a). Take the following example, from Hoeksema (2007).[41]

(48) ik hoop niet dat je *(ooit)   meer   van mening verandert
      I hope not that you ever(NPI) anymore(NPI) of   opinion change
      'I hope that you will never change your opinion anymore'

Ooit and *meer* are both NPIs, with the crucial difference that *ooit* may be licensed by an extra-clausal negation, but *meer* may not. However, the licensing of *meer* may be rescued if the clause containing *meer* also contains properly licensed *ooit*. In this sense, the licensing of *meer* is parasitic on *ooit*-licensing.[42]

21.3.4 NPIs and free choice

In this subsection and the following one I address two facts that are closely related to negative polarity: free choice and positive polarity.

Free-choice (FC) items are elements that express indifference or arbitrariness (in some form) with respect to a possible referent. Take the examples in (49):

(49) a. I'll have *whatever* you'll be having
      b. *Irgendjemand* hat angerufen   (German)[43]
         FC.person   has called
         'some person called'
      c. *any* cat hunts mice

In all these examples the speaker does not seem to impose any restrictions on the set of possible referents induced by the free-choice element.

Interestingly, in many languages many words display both NPI and FC effects, for instance Serbo-Croatian *ko bilo* 'anybody,' Malagasy *na inona na inona* '(lit.) or what or what, i.e., anything' (Paul 2005), and English *any* (being the most stereotypical example). English *any* may surface, as exemplified above, in (a limited number of) positive contexts, as long as it acts as a FC item.

Given the above, an immediate question that arises is whether English *any* and other elements that may manifest both FC and NPI behavior are lexically ambiguous or have a single lexical representation.

For Kadmon and Landman (1993), domain widening is a property of both FC and NPIs. Just as *I don't have any potatoes* has a stronger reading than *I don't have potatoes*, Kadmon and Landman argue that (49c) is stronger than *A cat hunts mice*. Whereas the generic with the indefinite allows exceptions, the FC example is more restrictive in this sense. Since the same effect that drives NPIs to be subject to certain licensing constraints is responsible for the FC effects, Kadmon and Landman take FC *any* and NPI *any* to be a single lexical item. On similar grounds, Chierchia (2006), Aloni and van Rooij (2007), and van Rooij (2008) also opt for a unified analysis of FC and NPI *any*.

The major problem for analyses that argue for such a unified account is that FC *any* often seems to yield a universal rather than an indefinite reading. This is shown in (50), taken from van Rooij (2008), where both examples convey that all students in Mary's class are working on NPIs, not just some, albeit it that the example containing *any*, but not the one with *every*, comes along with a sort of 'and that's not an accident' implicature.

(50) a. any student in Mary's class is working on NPIs
b. every student in Mary's class is working on NPIs

For Dayal (1998, 2004) this has been a motivation to radically break with the idea that FC *any* is an indefinite and to analyze it instead as a universal quantifier. FC and NPI *any* in her view are homophonous.

A problem (indicated by Giannakidou 2001) with analyses that are based on a treatment of FC *any* as a universal quantifier is that the universal reading of FC *any* is not always manifest. Clearly, the example below does not mean 'pick *every* card.'

(51) pick any card

Thus for Dayal, it is necessary to derive the indefinite reading of FC *any* from an underlying universal semantic representation, and the reader is referred to Dayal (1998, 2004) for the specifics of her proposal based on the so-called *vagueness requirement*, which demands that when uttering FC elements, the speaker must, in some sense, be ignorant or indifferent about the truth of the entire utterance.

Dayal's proposal has been criticized by those who seek a unified treatment of FC and NPI *any*, but also by those who take FC and NPI *any* to be both indefinite but nonetheless not identical. The most elaborated proposal along these lines is Giannakidou (2001), also outlined in Giannakidou (2011), Giannakidou and Quer (1997), and Giannakidou and Cheng (2006). Giannakidou builds on the insight that both FC and NPI *any* are in some sense restricted to appearing in non-veridical contexts only, but that FC *any* is furthermore subject to a condition that bans it from episodic contexts.

Perhaps the most pressing question in the context of FC items is what the exact semantic effect is that FC generally contributes. For relevant discussion of this question in the recent literature, the reader is referred to Kratzer and Shimoyama (2002), Jayez and Tovena (2005), Menendez-Benito (2005), and Aloni (2006).

21.3.5 NPIs and PPIs

A final phenomenon that needs to be addressed concerns positive polarity items (PPIs). While English *any*-terms require some DE or non-veridical licensing context, PPIs, by contrast, are known to be illicit in negative contexts.

At least four different types of PPIs have been discussed in the literature. The first type is represented by the English *some* series and their counterparts in other languages (Jespersen 1917, Baker 1970b, Progovac 1994, van der Wouden 1994, Giannakidou 1997, 2010, 2011, Haspelmath 1997, Szabolcsi 2004, amongst many others). The second class consists of high scale elements, such as *rather* (cf. Krifka 1995, Israel 1996). The third class of PPIs contains speaker-oriented adverbs and has been thoroughly discussed by Nilsen (2003) and Ernst (2009). The final class of PPIs concerns deontic modals, which obligatorily outscope negation, such as English *must* (cf. Israel 1996, Iatridou and Zeijlstra 2009, Homer 2010). For an overview of all types of PPIs, the reader is referred to van der Wouden (1994) and Israel (2007); for acquisition studies of the relative scope of PPIs and negation, see Section 25.6.4.

Each type is exemplified in (52). Note, though, that contrary to most NPIs, PPIs in negative sentences do not always render a sentence ill-formed, but rather disambiguate them. Therefore, in (52a) and (52d), the sentences are not ruled out, but rather the readings with the PPI taking scope under the negation are excluded.

(52) a. John didn't see somebody
      * 'John saw nobody'
      √'there is somebody John saw'
   b. I am (*not) rather ill
   c. they (*don't) possibly like spinach
   d. Mary mustn't leave
      * 'Mary doesn't have to leave'
      √'it's obligatory that Mary leaves'

What PPIs thus show is that they cannot scope below negation. In that sense, they appear to be the mirror image of NPIs, and various proposals have tried to understand the behaviour of PPIs in terms of anti-licensing (Ladusaw 1979, Progovac 1994, amongst others). On the other hand, it has recently been claimed by many, most notably by van der Wouden (1994), Szabolcsi (2004), Ernst (2009), and Giannakidou (2011), that PPIs behave rather differently from NPIs and therefore should call for a different theoretical treatment.

Szabolcsi (2004), who pursues Postal's (2000) idea that NPIs underlyingly carry some negation or negative feature, proposes that PPIs like *some* actually have two underlying negative features. Since two negations cancel each other out, *some* can naturally survive in positive sentences/environments. In negative contexts, though, one negative feature is taken care of by the presence of an overt licenser, leaving the PPI behind with an unlicensed negation. Therefore, the PPI in a negative context makes the sentence bad.

Evidence for this analysis comes from the fact, already noted by Jespersen (1917) and discussed in Baker (1970b), that PPIs, surprisingly, are fine under the scope of two DE/negative operators, strikingly an environment where NPIs are generally licensed as well:

(53) I don't think that John didn't call anyone/someone $\neg > \neg > \exists$

These facts indeed indicate that PPIs are not simply the mirror image of NPIs. The reader is referred to Giannakidou (2011a) for a critical assessment of these facts, although she ultimately reaches the same conclusion as Szabolcsi, namely that PPI-hood must not be explained as the result of anti-licensing requirements.

A different line of reasoning is explored by Nilsen (2003). Following Krifka (1995), Nilsen argues that the pragmatic and semantic effects that Kadmon and Landman take to be responsible for NPI-hood naturally extend to PPI-hood.[44] This idea is also manifest in Ernst (2009), who, whilst arguing against Nilsen's scale-based analysis of PPI-hood, endorses the idea that the PPI status of speaker-oriented adverbs ultimately reduces to speaker commitment and is therefore pragmatic/semantic in nature.

Some recent observations by Iatridou and Zeijlstra (2010) also point in the direction of a unified source for PPI- and NPI-hood. These authors try to account for the scopal relations that deontic modals display with respect to (sentential) negation in terms of negative and positive polarity. They argue that whereas English *have to*, *can*, and *may* are polarity-neutral, other universal modals are either PPIs (*must*) or NPIs (*need*).[45] Interestingly, though, neither PPIs nor NPIs show up in the domain of existential deontic modals, suggesting that if in one particular domain NPIs surface, PPIs are also likely to be found there, and vice versa. This makes it likely to assume that whatever mechanism is responsible for the occurrence of NPIs in a certain domain also applies to PPIs.

21.4 Negation or negative polarity: negative concord

Although the distinction between negative elements (as discussed in Section 21.2) and NPIs (as discussed in Section 21.3) appears to be straightforward – negative elements are semantically negative, NPIs are not – it turns out that things are not always that clear. In this section, I present one such case. Take the following Italian examples:

(54) a. Gianni *non* ha telefonato   (Italian)
        Gianni NEG has called
        'Gianni didn't call'
    b. *nessuno* ha telefonato
        n-body has called
        'nobody called'

In (54a) the semantic negation is introduced by *non*. The sentence without *non* simply means 'Gianni called.' In (54b) *nessuno* acts like a negative quantifier, such as English *nobody*, and thus induces the semantic negation. However, if the two are combined in a sentence, only one semantic negation is yielded, whereas from compositional perspective two semantic negations would be expected:

(55)   Gianni *(non)* ha telefonato a *nessuno*
       Gianni NEG has called   to n-body
       'Gianni didn't call anybody'

The phenomenon where two (or more) negative elements that are able to express negation in isolation yield only one semantic negation when combined is called 'negative concord' (NC) after Labov (1972), and has been discussed extensively in the past decades.

NC is exhibited in a large variety of languages. Within the Indo-European language family almost every variety of the Romance and Slavic languages and a number of Germanic languages (Afrikaans, West Flemish, Yiddish, and some Dutch and German dialects) as well as Albanian and Greek exhibit NC.

NC comes about in different forms. In some languages, for example Czech, a negative marker obligatorily accompanies all negative indefinites (or n-words, as Laka 1990 refers to negative indefinites in NC languages), regardless of their number and position. Those languages are called Strict NC languages, following terminology by Giannakidou (1997, 2000). In other languages, so-called Non-strict NC languages, such as Italian, NC can only be established between n-words in postverbal position and one negative element in preverbal position, either an n-word or a negative marker. Examples are below:

(56) a. Milan *(ne-)*vidi *nikoho*   (Czech)
        Milan NEG.saw n-body
        'Milan doesn't see anybody'
    b. dnes *(ne-)*volá *nikdo*
        today NEG.calls n-body
        'today nobody calls'

    c. dnes *nikdo* *(*ne-*)volá
       today n-body NEG.calls
       'today nobody calls'

(57) a. Gianni *(*non*) ha telefonato a *nessuno*   (Italian)
     Gianni NEG has called   to n-body
     'Gianni didn't call anybody'
    b. ieri   *(*non*) ha telefonato *nessuno*
     yesterday NEG has called   n-body
     'yesterday nobody called'
    c. ieri   *nessuno* (*non*) ha telefonato (a *nessuno*)
     yesterday n-body NEG has called   to n-body
     'yesterday nobody called (anybody)'

The reader should note that this typology of NC languages is not exhaustive. In languages like Bavarian and West Flemish NC is allowed to occur, but it is not obligatory (den Besten 1989a, Haegeman 1995). In French and Romanian the combination of two n-words gives rise to ambiguity between an NC reading and a reading with two semantic negations, standardly referred to as a double negation reading (cf. de Swart and Sag 2002, Corblin *et al.* 2004, de Swart 2006, 2010, Falaus 2009).

The central question in the study of NC concerns the apparent violation of semantic compositionality in examples like (55). How is it possible that two elements that induce semantic negation when used by themselves yield only one negation when combined?

In the literature, two approaches have been dominant: (i) the negative quantifier approach, where every n-word is taken to be semantically negative and where the missing negation in (55) results from some semantic absorption mechanism dubbed quantifier resumption; and (ii) the approach that takes n-words to be semantically non-negative NPI-like indefinites and where the semantic negation in (54b) is only covertly present. In the remainder of this section I briefly discuss and evaluate these two main approaches.[46]

21.4.1 The negative quantifier approach

One proposal, which takes all negative elements to be semantically negative, goes back to Zanuttini (1991), Haegeman and Zanuttini (1991, 1996), and Haegeman (1995) and is further formalized by de Swart and Sag (2002). According to these scholars, NC readings are the result of a process of negative absorption, analogous to *Wh* absorption as proposed by Higginbotham and May (1981). Take (58).

(58) Who loves who?

This sentence can be interpreted as 'which pairs <x,y> are love-pairs?' The process responsible for this reading is so-called quantifier resumption (cf. van Benthem 1989, Keenan and Westerstahl 1997), which turns a pair of quantifiers binding a single variable into a single quantifier binding a pair of variables. Applying this to negation, a sentence containing two negative quantifiers (like (59)) should then be able to undergo quantifier resumption as well and yield a reading 'There are no pairs <x,y> that are love-pairs,' which is an NC reading.

(59) nobody loves nobody

However, (59) does not yield an NC reading. Under this quantifier resumption approach, languages cross-linguistically vary with respect to whether they allow quantifier resumption to apply to sentences containing more than one negative quantifier or not. NC languages are then languages where quantifier resumption must then take place, whereas in languages that lack NC it should not be allowed.[47] Also, under this approach negative markers must be considered negative quantifiers as well, otherwise the NC reading of (55) cannot be accounted for.

The power of the quantifier resumption approach is that it can explain why two negative elements together may yield an NC reading, thus tackling the compositionality problem. However, it leaves open the question as to why certain languages should exhibit NC in the first place. Why, for instance, can the negative marker *non* not be left out in (55)? For de Swart and Sag (2002), these questions are independent from the question as to what semantic mechanism derives NC readings in the first place (see de Swart 2010 for an answer to these independent questions in terms of Optimality Theory).

21.4.2 The NPI approach

The reader will have noticed that the English translations of the NC examples all contained NPIs. For instance, the Italian example in (55), repeated in (60a), has the same semantics as the English one in (60b).

(60) a. Gianni *(non) ha telefonato a nessuno   (Italian)
      b. Gianni has*(n't) called anybody

In this example *nessuno* and *anybody* share two important properties: (i) they are interpreted as indefinites; and (ii) they must be licensed by negation (*non* and *n't*, respectively). The similarities between NPIs and n-words do not end with these two properties. A third striking parallel between NPIs and n-words is that both can appear in constructions which are DE but not anti-additive. This is shown in the following Spanish example taken from Herburger (2001).

(61) dudo que vayan a encontrar *nada*   (Spanish)
      doubt that go to find n-thing
      'I doubt that they will find anything'

Here the verb *dudo* 'doubt,' which is DE (but not anti-additive), is able to establish an NC relation with *nada*. Examples such as this form a major problem for theories that take n-words to be negative quantifiers. Without adopting additional machinery it is impossible for the verb and the quantifier to undergo resumption together.

Given these strong similarities between NPIs and n-words (or polarity and NC), and in order to solve problems introduced by (61), several scholars have proposed that n-words are in fact special kinds of NPIs. If the lexical semantics of elements such as Italian *nessuno* is actually *anybody* instead of *nobody*, the proper readings in (60) and (61) follow immediately. However, such an approach faces one immediate problem. If n-words are semantically non-negative, how can the readings of sentences such as (54b) (repeated as (62) below), where a single n-word induces semantic negation, be derived?

(62) *nessuno* ha telefonato (Italian)
     n-body has called
     'nobody called'

In an influential proposal by Ladusaw (1992), n-words are said to differ from plain NPIs in the sense that they are self-licensing, i.e., if nothing else licenses n-words, NPIs license themselves. But how is this mechanism of self-licensing implemented within a particular syntactic framework? Zeijlstra (2004, 2008), following a proposal by Ladusaw, argues that NC is an instance of syntactic agreement, where n-words are said to be semantically non-negative indefinites, carrying uninterpretable negative features that agree with a semantic negation. In cases of self-licensing the semantic negation is then left phonologically abstract.

Another approach that is based on Ladusaw's conjecture is Giannakidou (2001), where it is argued that self-licensing amounts to ellipsis of the negative marker. This account, however, applies to Strict NC languages only.

21.5 Concluding remarks

In this chapter I have tried to sketch the major developments in the study of the syntax of negation and the study of negative polarity, and the ways these two phenomena can be taken to be connected. The major goal of this chapter has not been to present how certain problems can be solved, but rather to demonstrate what the important questions are that have arisen over the past decades. At the same time, I hope this article reveals that substantial progress has been made over the past ten to fifteen years in the study of negation and polarity.

Concerning the syntax of negation, the various studies of the syntactic properties of negative markers (most notably Zanuttini's analyses of negative markers in Romance varieties) led to a much better understanding of what constrains the cross-linguistic variation that languages exhibit with respect to the expression of sentential negation. At the same time, many more languages, especially outside the family of Indo-European, need to be investigated to provide a more complete picture.

In the study of negative polarity, we now not only much better understand which properties constitute NPI licensing contexts, we have also seen answers to the question of why certain elements are sensitive to negative polarity in the first place. For instance, the Kadmon and Landman (1993) style of reasoning, especially in Chierchia's (2006) implementation, shows that it is possible to derive NPI-hood in terms of domain widening and strengthening. Many important questions, however, are still open. One of them is the question how the NPI property follows for non-indefinite NPIs, such as English *need*. Another open question is why certain NPIs require a different type of licensing environment than other NPIs.

Notes

1. This does not mean that the word order in an affirmative sentence is always the same as in a negatively marked sentence (see Laka 1990 for examples from Basque).
2. Data from Payne (1985), cited in Zanuttini (2001).
3. For many more examples of negative auxiliaries, see Miestamo (2005).
4. Example from Ouhalla (1991a), also cited in Zanuttini (2001).
5. This type of negative particle has been referred to by Zanuttini (1997) amongst others as preverbal negative markers, as these negative markers generally left-attach to the finite verb.
6. See Zanuttini (1997) for a more fine-grained overview of different kinds of preverbal negative markers based on a survey of Romance microvariation (mostly Northern Italian dialects), including a comparison between preverbal negative markers and other clitics. See also Poletto (2008) for a further refinement.
7. In colloquial French, though, this negative marker *ne* is often dropped.
8. Another well-studied language that exploits multiple negative markers to express sentential negation is Tamazight Berber (cf. Ouhalla 1991a, Ouali 2005).
9. Example taken from Haegeman (1995).
10. In more recent Minimalist work, the head–phrase distinction is no longer taken to be syntactically primitive, but a pure reflex of featural projection (a head contains a feature that is still able to project; a phrase does not); see the discussion of Bare Phrase Structure in Chapters 2 and 4. This, however, does not affect the diagnostics and dichotomy discussed in this chapter.
11. Examples (14a–b) are from Kayne (1989b), cited in Zanuttini (2001).
12. Cf. Benincà & Vanelli (1982), Poletto (2000), Poletto and Pollock (2001).

13. Though it should be noted that these diagnostics are less straightforward under remnant movement approaches to verb movement (cf. Nilsen 2003, Müller 2004b, Bentzen 2007).
14. See also Ouali (2005) for a discussion of Berber negation.
15. Example taken from Ouhalla (1991a).
16. Ouhalla uses the term 'parameter' in the traditional sense. Note, though, that it is unclear how such a parameter can be implemented under the Borer–Chomsky conjecture that takes parametric variation to be stated in terms of lexical features of functional categories (Borer 1984a, Chomsky 1995c). See also Chapters 4 and 25.
17. See also Laka (1990), who argues that a broader Polarity Phrase (PolP), which also hosts negative markers, merges in English below IP but above IP in Romance languages.
18. However, Haegeman (1995) argues that, at least in West Flemish, NegP is located above TP.
19. It must be noted, though, that Cinque (1999) excludes negation from the adverbial hierarchy because of its freer distribution.
20. Except for a small number of fixed constructions, such as '*k en weet* (I en know 'I don't know') in Ghent Dutch (cf. Haegeman 1995).
21. In the remainder of this chapter, for illustration purposes only, I mostly focus on English NPIs, though.
22. Note that not every NPI or free-choice element exhibits this schizophrenic behavior, nor is it the case that every free-choice item is an NPI.
23. Definition adopted from van der Wouden (1994).
24. Quantifiers denote relations between two arguments: a nominal and a verbal argument. For instance, in *every student sings*, *student* is the first argument and *sings* is the second. NPIs may only occur in the first argument (as shown in (28a)). In the second argument, which is not DE, NPIs may not show up: **Every student who knows about linguistics, will join* any *event*.
25. A function f is anti-additive iff $f(A \vee B) \Leftrightarrow (f(A) \wedge f(B))$. E.g., *no student* is anti-additive, since *no student drinks or smokes* is truth-conditionally equivalent to *no student drinks and no student smokes*. *Not every* is not anti-additive *as not everybody drinks and not everybody smokes* does not entail that *not everybody drinks or smokes*.
26. An example of the latter category would be Dutch idiom *voor de poes*: *zij is *(niet) voor de poes* 'she's pretty tough,' cf. van der Wouden (1994).
27. But see Nilsen (2003) for a discussion of these claims.
28. It is important to stress that not only Greek but many other languages as well exhibit NPIs that can be licensed in all kinds of non-veridical, but non-DE contexts; examples are Chinese (Lin 1996), Hindi (Lahiri 1998), Salish (Matthewson 1998), Navajo (Fernald and Perkins 2007), and Romanian (Falaus 2009).
29. See Zwarts (1995) for a proof that all DE contexts are non-veridical.
30. Example taken from Ladusaw (1996).

31. I follow Ladusaw (1996) in calling this question the licensee question. Others have referred to it differently, e.g., as the 'sensitivity question' (Giannakidou 1997) or the 'compostionality question' (Giannakidou 2011a).
32. Example taken from Lahiri (1998).
33. The reason why an unlicensed strengthened domain widener yields a semantic contradiction is the following. Just as (41b) is stronger than (41a), (41b) without the negative marker *not* (*I have any potatoes) should be weaker than (41a) without the negative marker (*I have potatoes*). Given the presence of the abstract strengthening operator, uttering *I have any potatoes* would entail that *I have potatoes* is false. But if it is not the case that I have potatoes, it also follows that I don't have any potatoes. Therefore, unlicensed NPIs (for Chierchia, unlicensed strengthened domain wideners) yield a semantic contradiction. Since entailment relations reverse in downward entailing contexts, this contradiction no longer appears under negation. Therefore (41b) does not yield a contradiction and is fine.
34. Chierchia (2006 et seq.) goes even further than this and argues that this is the case for all NPIs.
35. Den Dikken does not claim, though, that NPIs always carry an uninterpretable negative feature. For English *any*, for instance, den Dikken assumes that it is are lexically ambiguous between NPIs carrying such a negative feature and 'plain NPIs' that just have the property that they need to be licensed by a DE/non-veridical operator at LF, suggesting that there are actually two different grammatical types of NPI licensing: syntactic and pragmatic/semantic licensing.
36. However, as has been pointed by Ross (1967a), Linebarger (1980), and Uribe-Etxebarria (1996), NPIs sometimes appear outside the scope of their licenser at surface structure, as shown below. The example is from Linebarger (1980).

    (i) a doctor who knew anything about acupuncture wasn't available

37. Interestingly enough, modals do not count as interveners between NPIs and their licensers (witness the well-formedness of *Nobody may read any book*) (cf. von Fintel and Iatridou 2007).
38. The lack of a formal procedure for implicature computation makes this type of analysis extremely vulnerable to overgeneralization, as almost every sentence brings in negative implicatures (cf. Krifka 1995).
39. Giannakidou is less committed to Ladusaw's claim that NPIs must be outscoped by their licenser. For Greek n-words, for instance, Giannakidou (2000) assumes that these are universal quantifying NPIs that must (directly and immediately) outscope a non-veridical operator.
40. In order to distinguish between licensing in the broad sense (all types of NPI licensing) and LF licensing of NPIs, Giannakidou refers to the former as NPI sanctioning.

41. For more examples, see den Dikken (2002, 2006a) and Postal (2000).
42. Parasitic licensing shows some striking resemblances with secondary triggering (after Horn 2001), where unlicensed NPIs may be rescued by virtue of the presence in the local environment of another, properly licensed NPI.
43. Taken from Kratzer and Shimoyama (2002)
44. Israel (1996), on different grounds reaches a similar conclusion.
45. The observation that English *must* is a PPI is due to Israel (1996) and has also been entertained by Homer (2010).
46. Other approaches have been formulated as well. Herburger (2001), for instance, argues that n-words are lexically ambiguous between negative quantifiers and NPIs. For a detailed discussion of the existing accounts of NC, the reader is referred to Zeijlstra (2007, 2008). For a similar discussion on the relation between negative concord and NPI licensing, the reader is also referred to Penka and Zeijlstra (2010).
47. De Swart and Sag (2002) argue that evidence for this position comes from languages like French and Romanian, where sentences with two negative quantifiers are actually ambiguous and can have an NC and a non-NC reading. For them, in these languages quantifier resumption optionally applies.

22
The syntax of scope and quantification

Veneeta Dayal

22.1 Introduction

The initial breakthrough in our understanding of natural language quantification came with Frege's insight that quantifiers are operators prefixed to an open sentence, binding a variable inside it. An examination of predicate logic formulae highlights features of the logical calculus that continue to be of relevance in current thinking on the topic of quantification:

(1) a. $\forall x \, [\text{student}(x) \rightarrow \text{study}(x)]$
    b. $\forall x \, \exists y \, \text{like}(x,y)$
    c. $\exists y \, \forall x \, \text{like}(x,y)$

A quantifier has scope over the formula to which it is attached: [student(x) → study(x)] in (1a), for example, is the scope of $\forall$. When a quantified formula itself includes a quantifier, the relational dimension in quantification emerges. We can then talk about wide or narrow scope: $\forall$ has scope over $\exists$ in (1b), and $\exists$ over $\forall$ in (1c). The syntax of predicate logic also allows for complex interactions between quantifiers and other scopal expressions, such as negation and intensional operators.

Though Frege's approach captured many important insights about natural language, the problem of deriving the appropriate logical forms from sentences of English grammar was not dealt with. The challenge of bringing natural language syntax in closer alignment with logical structure was first successfully met in Montague's analysis of English (Montague 1974; see also Dowty et al. 1981). There are two related aspects of his analysis that are significant. The theory of generalized quantifiers, with its ability to quantify over properties, allows for a unified account of all types of quantifiers. These include proper names, universals, definites, indefinites, and complex quantifiers built on them, as well as quantifiers that cannot be captured by first order predicate logic, like *few* and *most*. It also allows for a compositional treatment of noun phrases. Thus *every student* has a denotation that is built up from the meanings of its constituents: it denotes the set of properties that include the common noun set in its denotation. This is a significant departure from predicate logic, where the components of meaning associated with the noun phrase are dispersed over the formula.

Montague claimed an inherent logical structure for English, positing semantic transparency of the kind seen in predicate logic formulae. The disambiguated structures in (2b) and (2c), for example, are abstract derivational histories of the sentence in (2a). The semantics he provides for such structures adequately captures the ambiguity of (2a):

(2) a. every student likes some book
 b. [every student$_i$ [some book$_j$ [he$_i$ likes he$_j$]]]
 c. [some book$_j$ [every student$_i$ [he$_i$ likes he$_j$]]]

Generalized quantifier theory, unlike predicate logic, makes it possible to interpret quantifiers *in situ*. This is particularly straightforward in the case of quantifiers in subject position. In addition to (3b), where the universal forms an operator–variable chain with the pronoun in subject position, a syntactic analysis without such a relation is also possible (3c). (3b) and (3c) have the same truth conditions, they are true if and only if the property *sang* is one of the properties denoted by *every child*. In (3b), an open sentence has to be converted into a predicative term and then applied to the function denoted by the quantifier (see also Chierchia and McConnell-Ginet 1990 and Heim and Kratzer 1998). In (3c), the denotation of the predicate can combine directly with the denotation of the subject:

(3) a. every child sang
 b. [every child$_i$ [he$_i$ sang]]
 c. [every child [sang]]

It is also possible to interpret quantifiers in object position directly by having transitive verbs take generalized quantifiers as their first argument. This involves some complexity in the interpretive procedure but Montague argues that the complexity is desirable, particularly in the case of intensional verbs.

Montague's system, then, represents significant advances in the analysis of natural language quantification. Nevertheless, it inherits the weakness of overgeneralization inherent in Frege's approach. Not every possible structural analysis of a natural language sentence correlates with intuitively available readings for that sentence. The study of quantification within the generative tradition since Montague can be characterized as a search for principled ways of regulating scopal dependencies and interactions. The goal has been to find ways to derive all and only the set of logical representations that accord with speakers' intuitions about possible readings.

In Section 22.2 I trace some of the major landmarks in our understanding of scope and scope interaction since Montague's seminal work, focusing primarily on quantified noun phrases and wh expressions. In Section 22.3, I discuss the phenomena of quantifier split and quantifier float, showing how the challenges posed by syntactic deviations from the normal form of quantification have been addressed in research on the topic. Finally, in Section 22.4 I turn to the scope marking and copy constructions, illustrating their special properties by comparing them to regular *wh*-extraction.

22.2 The syntax of scope

Montague's account of the proper treatment of quantification is the theoretical baseline for further developments in syntactic and semantic theories of scope. In reviewing these developments, our primary focus will be on the syntactic literature. We will refer to semantic proposals along the way, where they are relevant for the syntactic theory under discussion. (For discussion of the acquisition of scope, see Section 25.6.4.)

22.2.1 Quantifier scope and Logical Form

May (1977, 1985) marks a crucial point in the study of scope within the Government and Binding tradition (Chomsky 1981, 1986a). The following principles governing scope, proposed in May (1985), highlight the original contribution of his approach:

(4) a. *The Condition on Quantifier Binding*: Every quantified phrase must properly bind a variable.
 b. *Condition on Proper Binding*: Every variable in an argument position must be properly bound.
 c. *C-command*: α c-commands β iff every maximal projection dominating α dominates β, and α does not dominate β.
 d. *Scope Principle*: Mutually c-commanding quantifiers can take scope in either order.

By requiring a strict correspondence between operators and variables, vacuous quantification is ruled out. Furthermore, these conditions effectively make Quantifier Raising obligatory, resulting in logical structures isomorphic to predicate logic formulae. While their interpretive import is essentially the same as that of Montague's derivational analyses, the significance of May's account is that it builds in syntactic constraints on scope, analogous to those observed in overt forms of displacement, such as topicalization and *wh*-movement. The existence of such constraints gives theoretical bite to the notion of an abstract level of analysis by making explicit claims about the way it is derived. Logical Form (with capital letters; LF) within generative syntax draws its inspiration from the notion of logical form (in small letters;

LF) in the philosophical tradition, but is distinct from it. LF refers to a level of syntax intermediate between surface form and semantic interpretation, lf to representations of the logical calculus. As a syntactic construct, LF provides a means for addressing the challenge of overgeneralization that besets quantification theory.

Conceiving of Quantifier Raising (QR) as a syntactic rule provides a general explanation for some of the restrictions on quantifier scope that had been observed earlier. As discussed by Rodman (1976), for example, [$_{PP}$ *in every corner of the room*] can take scope over [$_{DP}$ *a bone*] in (5a) but not (5b). This follows since the universal quantifier is inside a complex DP and cannot move to a position above the existential:

(5) a. there is a bone in every corner of the room
    b. #there is a bone which is in every corner of the room

Similarly, the bound variable readings in (6) are predicted to be blocked. To get the desired reading in (6a), QR would have to occur out of a coordinate construction. This can be subsumed under the general label of locality violations (see Chapter 18) and whatever principles of syntax rule out the formation of overt dependencies in such constructions can be tapped to rule out the creation of problematic covert dependencies at LF. Similar considerations apply to (6b), where a bound variable reading would require the quantifier to move over a variable to its left, a weak crossover (WCO) violation.

(6) a. *every girl$_i$ is here and she$_i$ wants to study
    b. *his$_i$ mother loves every boy$_i$

May puts the rule of QR to use in explaining other complex paradigms. (7a)-(7b), with a universal and a *wh*-expression, display a subject–object asymmetry. When the universal is in subject position and the *wh* binds a trace in object position (7a), a pair-list answer can be given, with individual students matched up with objects purchased (7c). When the *wh* binds a subject trace and the universal is in object position, as in (7b), such an answer is not possible:

(7) a. What$_i$ [did every student buy t$_i$]?
    b. Who$_i$ [t$_i$ bought every book]?
    c. John bought *Namesake*, Bill bought *Anna Karenina*, and Sue bought *The Idiot*

(7b) can only be answered by naming an object such that every student bought that object, the individual answer. This is, of course, in contrast to sentences with ordinary quantifiers where no subject–object asymmetry is observed with respect to scopal interaction. May's explanation rests on the assumption that the scope domain of QR is IP, not CP. That is, locality is assumed to be a distinctive feature of QR. This yields the following potential LF's for (7):

(8) a. [$_{CP}$ what$_i$ [$_{IP}$ every student$_j$ [$_{IP}$ t$_j$ buy t$_i$]]] (LF for 7a)
 b. *[$_{CP}$ who$_j$ [$_{IP}$ every book$_i$ [$_{IP}$ t$_j$ buy t$_i$]]] (LF for 7b)
 c. [$_{CP}$ who$_j$ [$_{IP}$ t$_j$ [$_{VP}$ every book$_i$ [$_{VP}$ buy t$_i$]]]] (LF for 7b)

In (8a) the *wh* and the universal mutually c-command each other. The IP dominating the universal does not count as a maximal projection, it is merely a segment of another maximal projection. According to the Scope Principle in (4d), the scope order of the two quantifiers is open. If the *wh* takes wide scope it yields the individual answer, if the universal takes wide scope it yields the pair-list answer. In order for this to happen in the case of (7b), an LF like (8b) would need to be derived. This is not a well-formed LF since there is an ECP violation with respect to the subject trace, which is neither lexically governed by the verb nor locally governed by its antecedent. An LF like (8c), which has the universal adjoined to VP, does not violate ECP but neither does it create the conditions under which the Scope Principle could apply. The *wh* obligatorily takes scope over the universal and the pair-list answer remains unavailable.

May's appeal to VP adjunction has independent motivation. He points to the ambiguity of sentences involving ellipsis (see Chapter 19), discussed by Williams (1977). In (9a), QR of the universal to IP yields the distributed reading, while QR to VP yields the collective reading. This contrasts with (9b) which has only the collective reading. This is as expected if QR to IP is blocked when a *wh*-operator binds a subject trace. The only remaining option is adjunction to VP, resulting in the collective reading:

(9) a. Max saw everyone before Bill did
 b. Who saw everyone before Bill did?

Among the other scopal phenomena for which May's account provides an explanation are cases such as (10). (10a) is a case of inverse scope where a universal inside the complex DP takes scope over the existential. This is accounted for by allowing adjunction to DP. (10b), a raising construction, differs from the control construction in (10c), in allowing the universal inside the embedded clause to take scope over the existential in a higher clause (on raising vs. control, see Chapter 16). In order to account for this, May admits the possibility of quantifier lowering in (10b), as part of the general option that moved expressions have to reconstruct to their position of origin (see Barss 2001 and Sportiche 2006). Once this happens, the Scope Principle ensures that the two quantificational expressions can interact and the relevant reading emerges:

(10) a. some politician from every city will attend the convention
 b. some politician$_i$ is likely [t$_i$ to address every rally in John's district]
 c. some politician$_i$ wants [PRO$_i$ to address every rally in John's district]

May's conception of QR as a syntactic operation subject to constraints regulating WCO and island violations entails that proper names and definites, which do not show sensitivity to these effects, can be interpreted *in situ* without the benefit of covert movement. This is in line with the flexible approach to DP interpretation (Partee and Rooth 1983, Partee 1987), which takes the basic meaning of proper names and definites to be at the level of entities, while allowing them to shift to generalized quantifier interpretations when necessary.

There had been attempts to regulate scope possibilities directly on surface structures, most notably in Reinhart (1979), but they had not been particularly successful (see Chierchia and McConnell-Ginet 1990 and Szabolcsi 2001 for discussion). May's approach, which taps syntactic principles regulating movement in deriving Logical Form, is the first serious attempt that made substantive headway in limiting scopal interactions. It is worth keeping in mind, though, that his Logical Forms are not semantically transparent. Due to the *Scope Principle*, a single LF can map on to two lfs. For example, [IP everyone$_i$ [IP someone$_j$ [IP t$_i$ saw t$_j$]]] corresponds to $\forall x \, \exists y \, saw(x,y)$ and $\exists y \, \forall x \, [x \, saw \, y]$. This is a departure from Montague's structural analyses, which provided disambiguated structures for interpretation.

22.2.2 Extensions of the theory to *wh*-movement

There have been several extensions and refinements of the theory of quantifier scope and Logical Form since May. Huang (1982a) was the first to test its cross-linguistic applicability, focusing primarily on Chinese, a *wh-in-situ* language. His core claims can be illustrated with the following:

(11) a. Lisi mai-le   sheme (ne)
        Lisi buy-ASP what   Q
        'What did Lisi buy?'
    b. ni   xiang-zhidao [Lisi zeme mai-le   sheme]
        you wonder   Lisi how bought-ASP what
        'For what object x, you wonder how Lisi bought x?'
        *'For what manner x, you wonder what Lisi bought in that manner?'
    c. ni   zui   xihuan [piping   shei de shu]
        you most like   criticize who REL book
        'For which x, you like the book that criticizes x?'

As (11a) demonstrates, *wh*-expressions remain in their base positions at S-structure. Additionally, there is a morpheme optionally identifying the clause as interrogative. Huang treats *wh-in-situ* as moving at LF in order to be interpreted. Under this view, fronting and non-fronting languages differ only in the level at which movement takes place. He shows that in a context like (11b) where the matrix verb selects a +WH complement, it is possible for the object *wh-in-situ* to be interpreted with matrix scope, but not the adjunct. The availability of a wide-scope reading for the embedded object reveals an important property of LF movement that Huang argues for, namely the insensitivity to syntactic islands. This is further shown by the possibility of a direct question interpretation for (11c), where the *wh*-expression is contained inside a complex DP. Huang argued that movement at LF differs from overt movement in not being constrained by Subjacency, only by ECP. This is a non-trivial claim and has been challenged by Choe (1984), Nishigauchi (1986), Pesetsky (1987), and Dayal (1996).

Nishigauchi argues that although the Japanese counterpart of (11c) does have a direct question interpretation, the Japanese translation for (11b) can only be understood with both embedded *wh*'s taking narrow scope:

(12) a. Tanaka-kun-wa [Mary-ga doko-de dono hono-o katta]-ka
Tanaka -TOP Mary-NOM where which book-ACC bought Q
sitte-imasu ka
know Q
'Does Tanako know where Mary bought which book?'
*'For which book x, does Tanako know where Mary bought x?'
b. kimi-wa [dare-ga kai-ta] hono]-o yomi masi-ta ka
you-TOP who-NOM write book-ACC read Q
'For which x, you read the book that x wrote?'

Nishigauchi takes the data as evidence that the scope of *wh-in-situ* is constrained by Subjacency. He adopts the unselective binding approach to *wh*-expressions and captures the facts by requiring *wh-in-situ* to be bound by the closest Q-operator (see also Pesetsky 1987). The apparent wide scope interpretation of (12b), he suggests, is due to local movement of the *wh-in-situ* to a DP adjoined position. Binding of the *wh* by the Q operator becomes possible after large scale pied-piping of the DP.

A different approach to these facts is proposed by Watanabe (1992). He keeps to the view that LF *wh*-movement is not subject to Subjacency, positing S-structure movement of an abstract *wh*-element in Japanese to account for the *wh*-island effect noted by Nishigauchi. As shown in (13), a wide-scope reading for *dono hono-o* 'which book' is not possible in Japanese because the null operator associated with it would have to cross a *wh*-island in order to reach the matrix Spec position:

(13)

[$_{CP}$ OP$_i$ [Tanaka [$_{CP}$ OP$_j$ [Mary [t$_j$ doko] [t$_i$ dono hono] bought] Q] know] Q]

Watanabe's proposal introduces an interesting division among *wh-in-situ* expressions. They can either have invisible operator movement at S-structure or they can move covertly at LF. The former is marked by island sensitivity, the latter is not. Watanabe's view of Japanese *wh* is based on morphological considerations as well. According to him, the postulation of a null *wh*-operator that moves to associate with the overt Q morpheme fits in with the fact that the same expressions are interpreted as simple indefinites when there is no Q morpheme. In these cases, there is no null operator inside the noun phrase. For a recent account that relies on the role of interpretation in addressing these facts, see Shimoyama (2001).

Dayal (1996), like Pesestky and Nishigauchi, also argues against Huang's claim that LF movement of *wh-in-situ* is immune to Subjacency restrictions, but does so using facts that were previously thought to be evidence for such movement:

(14) a. Which student knows where Mary bought which book?
 b. [which student$_i$ [t$_i$ knows [which book$_j$ where$_k$ [Mary bought t$_j$ at t$_k$]]]]
 c. [which book$_j$ which student$_i$ [t$_i$ knows [where$_k$ [Mary bought t$_j$ at t$_k$]]]]

As noted originally by Baker (1970a), the question can be answered by naming a single individual who knows the details of Mary's shopping or by a list pairing individuals and books. The first answer is thought to be derived by the LF in (14b), the second by the LF in (14c). Dayal (1996), taking her cue from Kuno and Robinson (1972), argues against this position on the basis of wide-ranging cross-linguistic evidence.

Languages like Hindi do not allow wide-scope interpretations for *wh-in-situ* inside finite complements, as shown by (15a). Yet the counterpart of (14a) admits pair-list answers. Languages like Bulgarian which obligatorily front all *wh*s, as shown in (15b), do so as well, even though the embedded *wh* is stuck in the embedded Spec position. Finally, an intervening clause of the kind seen in (15c) rules out the possibility of pair-list answers even though the intervening clause does not present an island:

(15) a. anu jaanti hai ki   uma-ne kyaa   khariida
 Amu knows   that Uma   what bought
 'Anu knows what Uma bought'
 b. koj znae kakvo kade e kupila Mariya
 who knows what
 c. Which student$_i$ [t$_i$ said [that John knows [where Mary bought which book]]]?
 d. [[where did Mary buy which book]$_j$ [which student]$_i$ [t$_i$ knows the answer to t$_j$]]

Dayal argues that the scope of *wh-in-situ* is local, just like that of quantified expressions. The effect of wide scope is achieved when there is a particular *wh*-configuration – there should be a *wh*-expression in the matrix clause and there should be a multiple *wh*-question as a complement of the matrix verb. The embedded multiple *wh*-question in such cases can be interpreted as a second order question. This family of questions can interact with the *wh*-expression in the immediately higher clause and yield a pair-list answer. As shown schematically in (15d), questions like (14a) are treated as multiple questions pairing values for *which student* with values for questions of the form: *where did Mary buy book-x? where did Mary buy book-y?* (see Dayal 2005 for further details).

This approach effectively explains the correlation between a local triangular constellation of *wh*-expressions and the possibility of multiple-pair answers, and proposes a more straightforward characterization of LF as obeying locality. On the other hand, it entails explanations that require a move away from simple first order semantics for *wh*-questions. As such, approaches that look for ways to regulate long-distance LF movement of *wh-in-situ* continue to have currency (see, in particular, Richards 1997b).

22.2.3 Further refinements of the theory of quantifier scope and Logical Form

In this section I will briefly discuss three further developments in syntactic accounts of quantifier scope. Aoun and Li (1989) noted that quantified expressions in Chinese do not show the same scopal properties as English. That is, the counterpart of the classic *Someone loves everyone* has only one interpretation, the one that respects the surface order. They propose the following to capture scope effects:

(16) a. Scope Principle: A quantifier A has scope over a quantifier B if some part of A's A'-chain c-commands some part of B's A'-chain.
b. Minimal Binding Requirement: A variable must be bound by the most local A' binder.

(17) a. [$_{IP}$ someone$_i$ [$_{IP}$ t$_i$ [$_{VP}$ everyone$_j$ [$_{VP}$ loves t$_j$]]]]
b. [$_{IP}$ someone$_i$ [$_{IP}$ t$_i$ [$_{VP}$ everyone$_j$ [t$_i$ loves t$_j$]]]]

In (17a), *everyone* cannot have scope over *someone* since it does not c-command any member of the latter's chain. The universal is prevented from adjoining to IP by the Minimal Binding Requirement. This results in a fixed scopal relation. This, according to them, is the situation in languages like Chinese. Alternatively, a subject may originate inside VP, as shown in (17b), resulting in a configuration where both quantifiers c-command some member of the other's chain. Crucially, in this case there is no violation of the Minimal Binding Requirement since the VP internal trace is an NP trace, not a variable. This is the source of the scopal ambiguity seen in English.

Aoun and Li's approach is successful in accounting for the fact that sentences like (18a) have only a clause-bounded reading for the universal while sentences like (18b) allow the universal to take wide scope over the *wh* in matrix spec. This assumes, of course, that pair-list answers are a result of wide scope of the universal over the *wh*:

(18) a. some student thinks that every professor is a genius
b. What do you think everyone brought to the party?

Since the *wh* originates in the embedded object position, its trace will be c-commanded by the universal, which can then take scope over it. The main results of their theory carry forward to the revised version of Aoun and Li (1993). Their work has been influential in prompting a closer look at scope freezing effects, particularly in double object constructions, and requiring that scope theories be held up to a high empirical standard. Like Huang's approach to LF, Aoun and Li's theory is informed by a serious attention to cross-linguistic differences in quantifier scope possibilities.

Another major development in the theory of quantifier scope is Hornstein (1995), who considers the idea of QR as a free adjunction operation to be problematic within the assumptions of the Minimalist framework. He proposes that all phenomena for which QR is posited can be as well or better accounted for by A-movement to Spec positions of functional projections within IP. In particular, subjects move to Spec of AgrS and objects to Spec of AgrO. It is assumed that one member of each chain must delete, and depending on whether the head or the tail of the chain is deleted, different scopal relations are obtained:

(19) a. someone loves everyone
b. [$_{AgrSP}$ someone [$_{AgrOP}$ everyone [$_{VP}$ (someone) [$_{VP}$ loves (everyone)]]]]
c. [$_{AgrSP}$ (someone) [$_{AgrOP}$ everyone [$_{VP}$ someone [$_{VP}$ loves (everyone)]]]]
d. *[$_{AgrSP}$ someone [$_{AgrOP}$ (everyone) [$_{VP}$ (someone) [$_{VP}$ loves everyone]]]]
e. *[$_{AgrSP}$ (someone) [$_{AgrOP}$ (everyone) [$_{VP}$ someone [$_{VP}$ loves everyone]]]]

Hornstein adopts the Mapping Hypothesis of Diesing (1992), which requires presuppositional expressions to move out of the VP. Under the view that universals are presuppositional, the LFs in (19d) and (19e) are ruled out. The LFs that respect the Mapping Hypothesis, (19b) and (19c), deliver the two readings associated with (19a).

Of course, this has consequences for universals in subject position:

(20) a. everyone loves someone
b. [$_{AgrSP}$ everyone [$_{AgrOP}$ someone [$_{VP}$ (everyone) [$_{VP}$ loves (someone)]]]]
c. [$_{AgrSP}$ everyone [$_{AgrOP}$ (someone) [$_{VP}$ (everyone) [$_{VP}$ loves someone]]]]
d. *[$_{AgrSP}$ (everyone) [$_{AgrOP}$ someone [$_{VP}$ everyone [$_{VP}$ loves (someone)]]]]
e. *[$_{AgrSP}$ (everyone) [$_{AgrOP}$ (someone) [$_{VP}$ everyone [$_{VP}$ loves someone]]]]

The LF in (20b) where the lower members of both chains are deleted, as well as (20c) in which the higher member of the object chain is deleted, yield the subject wide-scope reading. (20d) and (20e), LFs in which the higher member of the subject term is deleted, violate the Mapping Hypothesis. This means that there is no LF in which *someone* can take scope over *everyone*. Hornstein derives the $\exists\forall$ reading as a subcase of the available $\forall\exists$ reading. Among the situations that make (20b) or (20c) true are those in which the same individual happens to be loved by everyone.

Hornstein also extends his account to differences in scope possibilities in raising vs. control constructions (see Chapter 16, where Hornstein's 1999 more recent approach to control as involving movement is also discussed), as well as the interaction of scope facts with Binding Theory (see Chapter 15):

(21) a. someone is likely to meet everyone
 b. [$_{AgrSP}$ someone is likely [$_{AgrSP}$ someone to [$_{AgrOP}$ everyone [$_{VP}$ someone meet (everyone)]]]]

While the existential can take scope in any of the three positions in this case, if there is a pronoun in one quantified expression that is bound by the other, scope possibilities are reduced in order to meet the demands of variable binding. Hornstein achieves several interesting results. He can derive the effect of QR while adhering to Minimalist assumptions about grammar, he can derive the locality associated with QR without stipulation, and he can capture an array of rather complex facts about scope. Even so, there have been serious challenges to his theory. Kennedy (1997a), in particular, argues against Hornstein's analysis of Antecedent Contained Deletion (ACD) and maintains that QR cannot be dispensed with.

Fox (1995) brings a fundamentally different perspective to the theory of Logical Form, claiming that movements regulating quantifier scope are regulated by semantic calculations. That is, LFs are not evaluated with respect to absolute standards of well-formedness but rather enter into competition with each other. To illustrate, consider the two possibilities for (22a) admitted by May's account:

(22) a. some student admires every professor
 b. [$_{IP}$ some student$_i$ [$_{IP}$ t$_i$ [$_{VP}$ every professor$_j$ [$_{VP}$ admires t$_j$]]]]
 c. [$_{IP}$ every professor$_j$ [$_{IP}$ some student$_i$ [$_{IP}$ t$_i$ admires t$_j$]]]

While (22c) involves a longer movement for the universal than (22b), and is therefore a costlier operation, it is justified because the two outputs are semantically distinct. If the matrix quantifier were a proper name or another universal quantifier, however, considerations of economy would rule out adjunction to IP since there would be competition between a less and a more costly operation for the same semantic output.

The payoff of this approach is that it provides a natural explanation for some well-known problems in the theory of syntactic scope. Fox can successfully account for the fact that although the universal in standard cases of ellipsis loses its potential for wide scope, as demonstrated by (23a), it is able to take wide scope when there is a quantified subject in the ellipsis sentence (23b):

(23) a. some student admires every professor and John does too
      b. some student admires every professor and some administrator does too

(24) a. *[[every professor$_j$ [some student admires t$_j$]] and [every professor$_j$ [John admires t$_j$]]]
      b. [[every professor$_j$ [some student admires t$_j$]] and [every professor$_j$ [some adminstrator admires t$_j$]]]

In the case of (23a), the LF with wide scope for the universal is ruled out because it has no semantic impact on the elided sentence after material from the antecedent is reconstructed in the ellipsis site (24a). In (23b), however, there is a difference between QR to VP and QR to IP, so the LF with universal wide scope is admitted (24b). Fox's approach marks a shift in the relation between syntax and semantics within the generative syntactic tradition. They are no longer considered autonomous components of grammar since semantic output regulates syntactic operations.

There are, of course, many other important proposals that have been made which I must set aside in the interests of space, referring the reader to Szabolcsi (2001) and É. Kiss (2006), among others, for a more extensive survey.

22.2.4 The checking theory of scope

The theories that we have looked at so far all have two properties in common. One, scope possibilities are determined by general principles governing syntactic dependencies rather than by properties of the particular quantifier. That is, the locus of explanation is the chain, not the members of the chain. Two, they all assume a semantics in which the operator binds an individual variable inside IP. The theories we will now consider represent significant departures with respect to these two dimensions.

A significant shift from the quantifier-blind approach is presented in Beghelli and Stowell (1997). Building on Liu (1990) and Szabolcsi (1997a), they take the fact that gaps in attested scope orders correlate with semantic classes of quantifiers seriously and reassess the standard assumption of the same scope for all quantifiers. They argue instead for an articulation of the landing-site of quantifiers, claiming that different classes of quantifiers have designated landing sites based on their inherent semantic properties:

(25) a. [RefP GQP [CP WhQP [AgrSP CQP [DistP DQP [ShareP GQP [NegP NQP [AgrOP CQP VP]]]]]]]
b. QP-Types:
Interrogative QPs (WhQPs): *which N, what, etc.*
Negative QPs (NQPs): *nobody, no N, etc.*
Distributive Universal QPs (DQPs): *each* and, to some extent, *every*
Counting QPs (CQPs): *few, fewer than five, between six and eight, etc.*
Group-Denoting QPs (GQPs): *a N, two N, the N, etc.*

The basic idea is that movement of DPs is triggered by the demands of feature checking. Movement is to the Spec position of the relevant functional projection with the particular feature, as shown in (25a). It follows that for any given set of quantifiers in a sentence, the set of possible readings will be that subset which conforms to the scope hierarchy.

Beghelli and Stowell depart from standard assumptions in the generative syntax tradition in taking definites to also be scopal expressions. Along with indefinites, they can take widest scope, with a function roughly equivalent to a Topic. Additionally, a definite with a pronoun that is externally bound, or an indefinite, can take scope in ShareP, below WhQs and universal quantifiers. Finally, indefinites may be interpreted in situ. The system allows for the ambiguity observed in natural language while imposing non-trivial limitations on it:

(26) a. each/every student read two books
b. two students read every/each book

(27) a. some/one of the students visited more than/fewer than three girls
b. every student visited more/fewer than three girls

The sentences in (26) are ambiguous because there are two positions at which *two books* / *two students* can be interpreted, Spec of RefP which is higher than DistP, the landing site for the universal, or at Spec of ShareP, which is lower. The sentences in (27), on the other hand, are unambiguous because *more than / fewer than three girls* must be interpreted in Spec of AgrO, which is below the positions at which the quantifiers in subject position can be interpreted (see also Szabolcsi 1997a).

Beghelli and Stowell introduce some further complexity into the system, in order to increase empirical coverage. For example, they include the possibility of interpreting *a N* and bare plurals, but not numeral NPs, as variables in the sense of Kamp (1981) and Heim (1982). This accounts for the contrast between (28a), originally due to Hirschbühler (1982), and (28b). *An American flag*, but not *five guards*, can be reconstructed below AgrAP, in its thematic position, and yield an inverse scope reading:

(28) a. an American flag was hanging in front of two buildings
b. *five guards stood in front of two buildings

Beghelli and Stowell address at some length the scope properties of the universals *each*, *every*, and *all (the)*. They classify the first two as strongly distributive. The data in (29) are predicted because the distributive semantics of *each* and *every* brings out the variation needed for the relevant reading of *a different boy* to emerge:

(29) a. each boy / every boy / *all the boys read a different book
b. a different boy read every book / each book / * all the books

Note that the schema in (25) predicts that *wh*-expressions can scope under Group Denoting NPs like *a N, two N, the N* but not under Distributive QPs *each* and *every*. We know, however, that the latter allow pair-list readings and if such readings arise from the quantifier scoping over *wh*, as often assumed, some modification of the schema is required. This question is taken up by Beghelli (1997) who argues that *wh*-expressions can reconstruct to positions lower than DQP, into Spec of ShareP or their case positions. He also follows Szabolcsi (1997a) in allowing universal quantifiers to be interpreted not only as generalized quantifiers but also as set-denoting terms. When they denote sets, they remain *in situ*. This gives rise to the following LF schema for questions with quantifiers:

(30) $[_{CP} [Q\text{-}Op_i + t_i] [... [_{AgrXP} [\text{every N}]_{k/i} ...] ... [_{AgrYP} \{WhQP\}i ...] ...]]$

Beghelli takes the Q-operator in (30) to unselectively bind the reconstructed *wh*-phrase as well as the universal in its path. Subject–object asymmetries are captured because a universal in object position lies outside the path of the Q-operator and the reconstructed subject *wh*-phrase that it binds.

In the interest of space, we must set aside further issues regarding pair-list readings addressed by Beghelli (see also Szabolcsi 1997b). We will also not discuss scope interaction between quantifiers and events and between quantifiers and negation (on the latter, see Chapter 21). We conclude by noting that the checking theory of scope represents a genuinely new approach to the problem of restricting QR. It gains strong empirical support from languages like Hungarian, studied by É. Kiss (1991), which transparently reflects in overt syntax the articulation of the scope domain proposed by Beghelli and Stowell for English. Kilega (Kinyalolo 1991), Chinese (Bartos 2000), and Palestinian Arabic (Khalaily 1995) have been claimed to be further instances of such languages. It still remains somewhat mysterious, however, why cross-linguistic variation in the domain of quantification is negligible compared to variation in the domain of *wh*-movement, where *wh-in-situ* and obligatory multiple fronting mark two ends of a spectrum that includes several mixed cases as well.

22.2.5 *Wh*-expressions and skolem functions

So far we have considered accounts in which quantification involves a chain between an operator (represented by the DP, *every student, which boy*, etc.) and an individual variable (represented by a trace *t*). We now turn to accounts which depart from this view. In this section we will discuss Chierchia (1993), who argues for a functional trace to deal with subject–object asymmetries in questions with quantifiers. In the next, we will consider Reinhart (1997, 1998), who argues for choice functions over properties to account for unexpected wide-scope effects for *wh-in-situ* and indefinites.

Chierchia (1993) builds on the view in Engdahl (1986) and Groenendijk and Stokhof (1984) that *wh*-expressions can quantify over functions from individuals to individuals (see Cooper (1983) and Hintikka (1986) for uses of functions in the semantics of definite and indefinite noun phrases). The domain of quantification for the *wh*-expression, then, is not a set of individuals $\{a, b\}$, for example, but rather a set of functions, say $\{f_1, f_2, f_3, f_4\}$, from some set of individuals, $\{c,d\}$ to $\{a,b\}$: $f_1=\{c\to a, d\to b\}$, $f_2 = \{c\to b, d\to a\}$, $f_3 = \{c\to a, d\to a\}$, $f_4 = \{c\to b, d\to b\}$. This means that the individual *a* can be referred to directly or via a function such as $f_2(d)$.

Chierchia argues for a syntactic reflex of this semantic option and uses it to explain the subject–object asymmetry in questions with quantifiers. *Wh*-expressions can optionally quantify over functions and when they do, their trace is doubly indexed. In (31b), for example, the subscripted i-index identifies the trace with the *wh*-operator *which book*, which quantifies over functions. The NP *book* provides its restriction by requiring the output of the function to be a book, for any argument y, as indicated in the underlined part of (31c). The superscripted a-index on the trace, which is bound by the c-commanding argument *every student*, is an individual variable. Intuitively, the a-index corresponds to the pronoun in functional answers, such as *Everyone read his favorite book* or *Everyone read her recently purchased novel*, and may be taken as having a pronominal character:

(31) a. Which book did every student read?
b. [which book$_i$ [every student$_j$ [t$_j$ read t$_i^j$]]]
c. $\lambda p\ \exists f\ [[\ \forall y[\underline{book(f(y))}] \wedge p =\ ^\wedge\forall x[student(x) \to read(x, f(x))]]$

(32) a. Who read every book?
b. [who$_i$ [every book$_j$ [t$_i^j$ read t$_j$]]]

Since the quantification is over variables whose possible values are functions to a set of books, an appropriate answer would name the function that picks out the proposition relating students and the book they read. That is, a wide-scope *wh*-expression need not name a single book that every student read. Variation in interpretation is possible without the universal actually taking scope over the fronted *wh*-expression because the functional trace is interpreted not as an individual but as a skolemized function $f(x)$, with x bound by the universal, as discussed above.

Let us see now how Chierchia exploits the syntax of the functional variable to explain the absence of a functional reading for (32a): *Its author read every book*. As shown in (32b), the i-index of the *wh*-trace is bound by the *wh*-expression *who*. In order for the universal term to bind the a-index of the trace, it must QR to a c-commanding position. This configuration, however, results in a WCO violation since the a-index has a pronominal character. Thus, Chierchia successfully accounts for a hitherto unnoticed subject–object asymmetry with respect to functional answers. The next step is to tie this in with the familiar subject–object asymmetry in pair-list answers.

The pair-list answer can be thought of as simply the graph of the function, as in Engdahl's original account, in which case the scope relations remain as represented for functional answers. It can also be argued to build on the functional representation, by extracting a set from the quantificational term and, in essence, distributing the question over members of that set. One reason for doing so is that all quantifiers can yield functional answers but the set of quantifiers that admit pair-list answers is restricted. For example, *every* and *each* allow for pair-list answers, *no* and *most* do not, while there is some debate about whether numerals like *two* or *three* do. What formal properties of quantifiers are relevant depends on what the core empirical facts are taken to be. I refer the reader to Chierchia (1993), Dayal (1996), and Szabolcsi (1997b) for detailed discussion of this point. For present purposes it suffices to note that taking the question to be formed out of sets extracted from the quantifier requires giving the quantifier scope outside C^0, the point at which the propositional core $p= IP$ is determined but not necessarily over the *wh*-quantifier.

An important aspect of Chierchia's account of questions with quantifiers is that it focuses on the relationship between the *wh* and the quantifier in their base positions, rather than at their landing-sites, to explain the contrast in judgment between sentences like (31a) and (32a). One advantage of doing so is that it can apply to pair-list answers to multiple *wh*-questions, which had been noted to have features in common with questions with quantifiers (É. Kiss 1993). Comorovski (1996) and Dayal (1996) both adopt the functional approach for multiple *wh*-questions to explain subtle subject–object asymmetries that cannot be explained by theories like May's that depend on the structural divide between CP for *wh*-movement and IP for QR. Dayal modifies Chierchia's analysis, based on a closer examination of the types of pairings allowed in pair-list answers.

An alternative to Chierchia's account is Krifka (2001), who argues that pair-list answers to questions like (29a) involve wide scope over the *wh* and gives a semantics for them in terms of speech acts. He explains the restriction to universal terms as being due to the semantics of quantifying into question acts. Krifka's explanation for the asymmetry turns on the notion of topic-hood, but it is worth noting that he leaves unaddressed the correlation between the structures that allow pair-list answers and those that allow functional answers. It is also worth pointing out that the correlation with WCO configurations pointed out by Chierchia is not easily subsumed under Krifka's approach. Still, he makes a forceful argument for wide scope for the universal term in such cases, partially resurrecting May's approach as involving distinct scope relations between the *wh* and the quantifier and providing a new perspective on its interpretation. It is not clear to what extent it could be extended to multiple *wh*-questions.

22.2.6 The choice function account of *wh*-expressions and indefinites

We turn now to the role of choice functions in theories of scope. Reinhart (1997, 1998) argues that LF movement of *wh-in-situ* does not fit in with Minimalist assumptions about structure building. She proposes that they should be interpreted in their base positions via choice functions, which are functions from properties to individuals. If $\{a,b\}$ is the extension of a property, it is possible for a choice function $f_1\{a,b\}$ to pick out a and another choice function $f_2\{a,b\}$ to pick out b. Intuitively, f_1 and f_2 might correspond to descriptions like *the one on the left* or *the one most recently purchased*. Reinhart's use of choice functions can be illustrated with the following multiple *wh*-question in English:

(33) a. Which student read which book?
 b. [which student$_i$ [t$_i$ read which book]]
 c. $\lambda p \, \exists f \, \exists x [\text{student}(x) \wedge \text{CF}(f) \wedge p = x \text{ read } f(\text{book})]$

While the fronted *wh* quantifies over individual students in the standard way, the *wh-in-situ* is interpreted with a functional variable in argument position. The functional variable is bound from above C^0, where the propositional core of the question is determined. That is, from the position where normal *wh*-expressions take scope. The function takes the set of books as argument and returns an arbitrarily chosen member of that set. It thus delivers the same result as quantification over individuals, but without resorting to covert movement.

One immediate consequence of admitting two forms of scope taking for *wh*-expressions is that it allows for a distinction in the scopal properties of moved *wh* and *wh-in-situ*. This makes it possible to maintain standard syntactic restrictions on movement because non-moved *wh*, which are associated with non standard scope effects, only *appear* to violate syntactic constraints. They are, in fact, interpreted by the alternative mechanism of choice functions. In (34a), for example, *which philosopher* can be interpreted inside the island, with the functional variable being bound by existential closure at the matrix level. This is shown in (34b):

(34) a. Which linguist will be offended if we invite which philosopher?
 b. $\lambda p \, \exists x \, \exists f \, [\text{linguist}(x) \wedge p = [\text{invite}(we, f(\text{philosopher})) \rightarrow \text{be-offended}(x)]]$
 c. $\lambda p \, \exists x \, \exists y \, [\text{linguist}(x) \wedge p = [[\text{philosopher}(y) \wedge \text{invite}(we, y)] \rightarrow \text{be-offended}(x)]]$

Reinhart compares the choice function approach to the earlier attempt to preserve the integrity of LF movement by utilizing unselective binding in such cases (Pesetsky 1987 and Nishigauchi 1986). She points out that the semantics of conditionals yields the wrong results for the unselective binding analysis of (34a). A proposition that picks a non-philosopher such as *Donald Duck* would count as a possible answer under this approach, as shown in (34c). Since *we invite Donald Duck* would make the antecedent false, the whole conditional would be true. The choice function approach, on the other hand, because the choice is made from the common noun set, appropriately restricts answers to those that pair linguists with philosophers.

Dayal (2002) notes, however, that the answer to (34a), while it names two individuals, one for the fronted *wh* and one for the *wh-in-situ*, does not allow for the pair-list answer typical of multiple *wh*-questions. Highlighting the fact that we have no direct intuitions about the scope of *wh*-expressions and that we must rely almost entirely on the diagnostic of possible answers to determine their scope, she argues that such variations in the nature of possible answers must be carefully considered (see also Pesetsky 2000 and Bošković 2002a for more on this distinction; see also Section 22.4.1).

The second application of choice functions, argued for by Reinhart, is in the domain of indefinites (see also Winter 1997). Choice functions provide a simple way of explaining an indefinite's propensity for unexpected wide scope readings. (35a), for example, has a natural interpretation in which the indefinite in the antecedent of the conditional refers to a specific individual. Fodor and Sag (1982), in their classic paper, had attributed this to a lexical ambiguity between a referential and a quantificational meaning. Among their primary arguments for the referential possibility was that indefinites either obey the same constraints as other quantifiers or they take widest scope. Crucially, they claimed that a sentence like (35b) does not have an intermediate scope reading, with *a student of mine* taking scope below *every professor* but above *the rumor*:

(35) a. if a relative of John's dies, he will inherit a fortune
b. every professor heard the rumor that a student of mine had been called before the dean

Subsequent studies have shown that intermediate scope readings are, in fact, available (Farkas 1981, Partee and Rooth 1983, King 1988, among the earliest). In (36a), for example, the choice of topic can vary with students. Such intermediate scope readings have prompted the relativization of choice functions to c-commanding arguments, as shown in (36b). Here the variable over choice functions is parameterized to an individual. This is essentially the procedure of skolemization, discussed in connection with the functional approach to questions with quantifiers:

(36) a. every Ph.D. student knows [most of the articles [that have been written on some topic]]
b. [every Ph.D. student$_i$ [knows [(f$_i$(topic))$_j$ [most of the articles [written on t$_j$]]]]]

The use of choice functions in analyzing indefinites goes back to Hintikka (1986) and it continues to be of interest to semanticists (see Ruys 2006 and references cited there). Among the issues that are being debated is whether the variable over choice functions should be existentially bound at the matrix position or remain free, how the parameterization of the function should be calibrated, and how choice functions interact with other phenomena, such as distributivity, donkey anaphora, ACD, etc.

An alternative position on the scope of specific indefinites is advocated by Schwarzschild (2002a), who takes them to be existential quantifiers with distinguishing features. He proposes that their domain of quantification is a singleton. This aligns them with definites, the appearance of extraordinary wide scope being a case of scopelessness: if there is only one (singular or plural) entity in a set, the reading remains unaffected whether it takes scope over or under some other scopal expression. Schwarzschild further suggests that the property responsible for turning the domain of an indefinite into a singleton is 'private.' Roughly speaking, the referent of a definite is familiar to both hearer and speaker, while that of a specific indefinite is familiar only to the speaker.

To sum up, the general consensus is that the unusual scope effects associated with indefinites do not warrant a relaxation of constraints on quantifier raising. This contrasts with *wh-in-situ* where there continues to be a range of views on their movement possibilities.

22.2.7 Section wrap-up

In this section I have touched on the major developments in syntactic theories of scope, all of which include a notion of operator–variable chains of the type seen in predicate logic. In concluding this section, I would like to briefly mention approaches that do not share this commitment. Recall from the introduction that Montague's analysis of English does not force the creation of an operator–variable relation (cf. (3c)). There are two major developments of this idea that have currency in present analyses of quantification.

The first approach abjures the creation of operator–variable chains in syntax, introducing such dependencies directly in the semantics. Cooper (1983) proposed a procedure for interpreting a quantificational expression *in situ* by positing a variable in argument position and storing the quantificational force for unpacking at a higher point in the derivation. This general procedure, which goes by the name of Cooper-storage, allows for distinct readings depending on the order in which quantifiers are brought out of storage to bind the variables they are associated with. The significance of this procedure is that it allows for a viable semantic account of scope and scopal ambiguities, without postulating an abstract level of syntax. Cooper-storage is therefore of particular significance for theories of grammar that compute meaning directly on surface structure. Note, of course, that Cooper-storage has to build in some syntactic sensitivity in order to account for locality-related effects. This somewhat reduces its distance from accounts that tie in such sensitivity with Logical Form.

The second approach represents a more radical departure from the accounts we have been looking at. It not only does away with operator–variable chains in syntax, it does not appeal to such dependencies even in the semantics. In a series of papers, Jacobson (1999, 2000 for example) has laid out a program showing how direct compositionality can be delivered by a 'variable free' semantics, which dispenses with the task of interpreting variables and shifts the burden of explanation to principles of semantic combination.

I have kept the discussion of non-movement and/or variable-free accounts of quantifier scope brief because they have not had significant impact on the development of syntactic theory within the Chomskian tradition. In the rest of the survey we will continue to limit ourselves primarily to analyses of scope phenomena that assume movement and variable binding. It is worth keeping in mind, however, that there are no semantic imperatives forcing the creation of operator–variable chains and semantically viable alternatives are available in the literature.

22.3 Quantification at a distance

In the previous section I gave an overview of the main developments in the theory of scope, focusing on quantified noun phrases that have their normal constituent structure. There are, however, constructions in which expressions that can plausibly be analyzed as parts of a single constituent appear at a distance from each other. One such case is *combien*-(sub)extraction, another is quantifier float. These two constructions are the focus of the present section.

22.3.1 Quantifier higher than restriction

The following data is illustrative of *combien*-(sub)extraction, which alternates with full DP fronting in French. What makes this construction theoretically interesting is that the alternation is not always available. An intervening adverb, for example, blocks *combien*-split:

(37) a. [Combien de livres]$_i$ as-tu   (beaucoup) consulté t$_i$?
       how many of books   have-you a lot   consulted
    b. Combien$_i$ as-tu   (*beaucoup) consulté [t$_i$ de livres] ?
       how many have-you a lot   consulted of books
       'How many books have you consulted?'

On the basis of data such as these, Obenauer (1984) argued that the adverb had a blocking effect because of its similarity to the extracted element, an idea that proved central to the development of Relativized Minimality (Rizzi 1990a; see also Chapter 18).

Further striking effects are revealed when the extraction is over islands. There is a clear contrast between full DP and determiner subextraction, reminiscent of argument–adjunct asymmetries, in the case of *wh* and negative (or 'inner') islands:

(38) a. ?[Combien de problèmes]$_i$ sais-tu   [comment [PRO résoudre t$_i$]]?
       how many of problems   know-you how   to-solve
    b. *Combien$_i$ sais-tu   [comment [PRO résoudre [t$_i$ de problèmes]]]?
       how many know-you how   to-solve   of problems
       'How many problems do you know how to solve?'

(39) a. [Combien de voitures]$_i$ n'a-t-il pas conduit t$_i$?
    b. *Combien$_i$ n'a-t-il   pas conduit [t$_i$ de voitures]?
       how many   NEG-has-he not driven   of cars
       'How many cars didn't you drive?'

The unacceptability of (38b) and (39b), however, can be mitigated in D-linked contexts, in the sense of Pesetsky (1987). If there is a pre-established set of entities to which the relevant phrase refers, normal constraints on movement are relaxed. Thus referentiality has to be recognized as an independent factor in the licensing of chains. These insights about *combien*-split have proved critical in refining our understanding of islands and the nature of A-bar dependencies (Cinque 1990b; see also Section 18.4).

Combien-(sub)extraction has also been significant in advancing the theory of reconstruction. Consider in this connection (40a), which has full DP extraction with the predicates *composer* and *chanter*, and (40b) and (40c) which have subextraction with those predicates:

(40) a. Combien de chansons vas-tu   composer/chanter?
       how many of songs   will-you compose sing
    b. Combien vas-tu   composer de chansons?
       how many will-you compose of songs
    c. Combien vas-tu   chanter de chansons?
       how many will-you sing   of songs

There are two potential readings here: the referential reading (*how many songs are there that you will sing/compose them*) and the cardinal reading (*for what number x, will you sing/compose x-many songs*). Given the lexical semantics of the predicates, both readings are available with *chanter* but only the latter with *composer* in (40a). The subextraction versions, however, have only cardinal readings with both predicates, suggesting that cardinal readings generally involve interpreting the restriction in the base position (Dobrovie-Sorin 1994, Heycock 1995a). We can infer from this that reconstruction is possible in (40a), and furthermore, that raising of the stranded element in (40b–c) does not happen at LF.

These conclusions are corroborated by similar effects in English. (41b) represents the referential reading of (41a), where a particular set of books exists and Mary said "read them to me." (41c) represents the cardinal reading, where a particular number is such that that Mary said "read me x number of books," without insisting on particular books:

(41) a. How many books did Mary ask you to read?
b. How many books are there such that Mary asked you to read them?
c. For what number x, did Mary ask you to read x-(number of)-books?

The referential reading is obtained by interpreting *how many books* in Spec of matrix CP, the cardinal reading by reconstructing the NP to the base position and leaving the *wh*-determiner in surface position (see Cresti 1995, Heycock 1995a, Kroch 1989a, among others, for further discussion).

Another interesting aspect of *combien*-subextraction, one that looks ahead to the topic of the next subsection, is discussed by de Swart (1998b):

(42) a. Combien de chansons les enfants ont-ils tous chanté(s)?
 how many of songs the children have-they all sung
b. Combien les enfants ont-ils tous chanté de chansons ?
 how many the children have-they all sung of songs

(42a) is ambiguous. On the wide reading the set of songs (and consequently the number of songs) is the same for all the children. On the narrow reading, the choice of songs can vary with the children, though not the number. (42b), under *combien*-split, has only the latter reading. De Swart's work also shows that *combien*-extraction over interveners is acceptable if the intervener can get out of the way by taking scope over *combien* (see, however, Obenauer 1994 and Sportiche 2006 for a somewhat different take on these facts).

The *combien*-split construction, then, has been extremely important in the development of syntactic theories of movement and reconstruction, providing direct empirical evidence for them. It has also been important in the development of interpretive accounts for quantifiers that allow the quantifier to occur at a higher level in the structure than its restriction. It is worth highlighting that the conclusion we come to from *combien*-split is that a restriction can be interpreted lower than the site at which it surfaces but it cannot be interpreted higher than its surface position, even if the quantificational element in it has moved to that site. That is, reconstruction can be of full DPs or just of the inner NP but QR is limited to full DPs, it cannot raise NPs to the site of their quantificational associate.

22.3.2 Restriction higher than quantifier

Floating quantifiers ostensibly present the opposite situation, with the restriction appearing in a structurally higher position than the quantifier. However, the aptness of this characterization depends on the approach one adopts. Consider the following paradigm, which shows the universal at a lower position than its associate DP. The variants in (43b) have essentially the same meaning as (43a):

(43) a. all the students / each of the students / both the students have read the book
  b. the students (all/each/both) have (all/each/both) read the book
  c. [the students$_i$ [([$_{DP}$ all/each/both t$_i$)] [have [$_{VP}$ [$_{DP}$ all/each/both [$_{DP}$ t$_i$]] read the book]]]]
  d. [the students$_i$ [(all/each/both) [have [(all/each/both) [$_{VP}$ t$_i$ read the book]]]]]

There are, broadly speaking, two approaches to this construction. One takes the universal to be a constituent of the subject DP which originates inside VP, as shown in (43c) (Sportiche 1988, Miyagawa 1989, Déprez 1989). If movement targets the large DP, we get the sentence in (43a). If it targets only the inner DP, we get the sentences in (43b), with stranding of the universal at the base or at intermediate positions in the movement chain. The alternative approach takes the floating quantifier to be an adverbial of a sort, as shown in (43d) (Dowty and Brodie 1984, Bobaljik 1995, Doetjes 1997, Brisson 1998). In this approach, there is no direct syntactic connection between the sentence in (43a) and those in (43b). Specific analyses of these sentences, of course, often involve more nuanced positions within this spectrum.

Floating quantifiers are attested in a number of languages. An example from French, already foreshadowed in our discussion of *combien*-split, is given below:

(44) a. (toutes/*tous) les femmes sont (toutes/*tous) arrivées
     all   the women   have all   arrived
  b. (*toutes/tous) les hommes sont (*toutes/tous) arrivés
     all   the men   have all   arrived
  'all the women/men have arrived'
  'the women/men have all arrived'

As we can see, the quantifier shows distinct agreement patterns, depending on whether the associate nominal is feminine or masculine. The point of note is that this remains so whether the quantifier appears as part of the associate DP, or as a floating quantifier. This follows straightforwardly from the movement approach to the phenomenon, while it appears, at least on the face of it, to be a problem for the adverbial approach.

To sum up, then, the advantages of the movement/stranding approach are the following: it can account straightforwardly for the positions at which floating quantifiers appear by tracking the path of DP movement, it predicts semantic uniformity for the members of the paradigm, and it explains the agreement patterns in languages where such distinctions are manifested.

The adverbial approach, on the other hand, can point to the fact that the correlation between the positions for floating quantifiers and DP movement is not absolute. There are positions through which DP movement is known to occur but floating quantifiers are disallowed there. Most significantly, the object in passive and unaccusative constructions cannot have a floating quantifier in its base position, as seen in (45) and (46). In fact, Bobaljik (1995) notes that the predictions of the movement/stranding approach also fail with unergatives.

(45) a. all / each of / both the suspects have been arrested
b. the suspects$_i$ have (all/each/both) been arrested *all/*each/*both t_i

(46) a. all / each of / both the children have arrived
b. the children$_i$ have (all/each/both) arrived *all/*each/*both t_i

In sentences with several auxiliaries, floating quantifiers are unacceptable at lower levels, suggesting that (45)–(46) may be part of a more general ban on occurrence lower down in the tree:

(47) the vegetables (all) will (all) have (all) been (*all) being (*all) roasted for an hour by the time you arrive

Furthermore, the adverbial approach can show that floated *all* interacts with adverbs (Fitzpatrick 2006). In (48a), *bravely* has both a subject-oriented and a manner reading. In (48b) it only has a subject-oriented reading. Fitzpatrick also notes the possibility of iteration of the kind shown in (49):

(48) a. the gladiators all bravely fought the lions
b. the gladiators bravely all fought the lions

(49) a. all/both of the students have each been asked to fill out the form in pencil
b. both of the teams have all been asked to turn in their projects tomorrow

The question for the adverbial approach is how to capture the relation between the quantifier and the DP associate. One option, proposed by Doetjes (1997), is that the quantifier has in its scope a null pro that is in a binding relation with the DP typically thought to be the associate. This points the way for solving potential problems for the approach, such as the agreement patterns seen in (44).

There is also the issue of finding a way to align the meanings of floating and non-floating versions. Brisson (1998), for example, treats the floating quantifiers *all/both* as subject-oriented adverbs that do not contribute to the truth conditions of the sentence but rather interact with a distributive operator to strengthen the meaning of a definite noun phrase. While a definite DP can countenance some exceptions in predication (that is, it is not a *strict* universal), modification by a floating quantifier ensures that every member of the associate's restriction participates in predication. Note that the distributive operator under this view does not enforce distributivity, but only regulates it so that statements with definites, with or without the modifier, can have collective, intermediate distributive, or total distributive readings.

As would be obvious, the phenomenon of floating quantifiers is theoretically as well as empirically intriguing and there is a substantial literature on the topic. Fitzpatrick (2006) points out that prior approaches force a choice between the two approaches. He argues, on the basis of the well-known facts as well as on novel cross-linguistic data, for a dichotomy in the class of floating quantifiers. According to him, floating quantifiers of the sort we have discussed are adverbial, but there are floating quantifiers in languages that originate inside the associate. He takes the first kind to be distinguished by the fact that it is associated with A-chains, as noted by Déprez (1989). They get the analysis in (50), incorporating Doetjes's proposal of a null pronominal element:

(50) [$_{DP}$ the students]$_1$ have [$_{VP}$ [all pro$_1$] [$_{VP}$ t$_1$ had their lunch]]

Fitzpatrick claims that the second kind of floated quantifiers is associated with A'-chains, and can be illustrated by Japanese examples like (51a). (51b) shows an intermediate stage of the derivation where *hon-o san-satu* has been scrambled to the intermediate CP level, followed by stranding, as shown in (51c):

(51)
a. [$_{CP}$ hon-o John-ga [$_{CP}$ san-satu Mary-ga [$_{CP}$ gakusei-ga yonda to] ita to] book-ACC John-NOM 3-CL Mary-NOM student-NOM read C said C omotteiru]
thinks
'John thinks that Mary said the students read three books'
b. [$_{CP}$ John-ga [$_{CP}$ [[hon-o san-satu]$_i$ Mary-ga [$_{CP}$ gakusei-ga t$_i$ yonda to] itta to] omotteiru]]
c. [$_{CP}$ hon-o$_j$ John-ga [$_{CP}$ [[t$_j$ san-satu]$_i$ Mary-ga [$_{CP}$ gakusei-ga t$_i$ yonda to] itta to] omotteiru]]

Fitzpatrick provides independent semantic motivation for his proposal by showing differences between the two types with regard to exhaustivity. His account, as we can see, expands the empirical coverage of theories of floating quantifiers but it remains to be seen if it will hold up to further scrutiny.

22.3.3 Section wrap-up

Although the unselective binding and choice function approaches to quantification surveyed in Section 22.2 involve syntactic distance between the quantifier and the restriction, they cannot be characterized as quantification at a distance since the syntax of the noun phrase remains intact. It contributes the common noun denotation, a restriction on a variable or the argument to a function, while the quantificational force comes from elsewhere. Similarly, the type of quantification seen in Japanese where quantificational morphemes mark the scope site and regular indefinites the restriction, cannot be characterized as quantification at a distance since one morpheme simultaneously associates with more than one nominal phrase.

The constructions we have considered in Section 22.3 are fundamentally different in that two expressions that could plausibly be thought of as forming a constituent, surface in different parts of the structure. They thus represent cases of quantification at a distance and, as we have seen, have the potential to track possibilities for movement and reconstruction. Whether analyses agree on the nature of the dependency involved, they all agree that these constructions are significant for syntactic theories of movement and scope.

22.4 *Wh*-scope marking and *wh*-copying constructions

In this section, we turn to *wh*-scope marking and *wh*-copying constructions, constructions that exemplify two non-standard ways of forming long-distance *wh*-dependencies (see also Section 25.4.2). Since background assumptions about standard long-distance extraction play a crucial role in analyses of both constructions, we will at various points allude to extraction; but I refer the reader to Chapter 18 for a more focused discussion of it.

22.4.1 The diagnostic of specification in answers

Wh-dependencies vary in interesting ways across and even within languages. In order to appreciate the issues surrounding the various strategies, it is important to note a fundamental difference between indicators of scope for regular quantificational DPs and those for *wh*-expressions. Natural languages typically do not show quantifier scope overtly (though there are some, such as Hungarian). It is much more common to find *wh*-scope being overtly represented. Thus in languages like English or Bulgarian, questions are distinguished from declarative statements by fronting of *wh*-expressions, which we take as marking the scope of that *wh*. As indicated in Section 22.2.2, the issue of determining scope arises primarily in the case of *wh-in-situ*, in languages like Chinese or Hindi that do not have overt movement, or languages like English that allow fronting of only one *wh*-expression. In the case of quantifiers, the issue of scope is settled by probing intuitions about the truth conditions associated with particular structures. In the case of questions, however, this diagnostic does not apply. Instead, we must take recourse to indirect means, using the possibility/requirement of specifying values for *wh*-expressions as the indicator of scope. As such, it is important to understand the diagnostic before applying it to constructions where syntactic position may appear less than transparent.

Consider (52a) and its possible answer in (52b). This can be derived in a Karttunen/Hamblin-style semantics for questions under a representation like (53a), where the *wh* is fronted at LF, leaving behind a trace in argument position. This is interpreted as in (53b), resulting in denotations naming books directly, as in (53c). Alternatively, it can be interpreted *in situ*, as in (54a), using the choice function analysis of Reinhart (1997, 1998), discussed in Section 22.2.6. Here the *wh-in-situ* is bound by an existential quantifier over functions that gives it scope outside the propositional core. The resulting interpretation refers to books via functions, as shown in (54c). In either case, one can derive intuitively acceptable answers such as (52b):

(52) a. Which student bought which book?
 b. Bill bought W&P, Sue bought *Aspects*

(53) a. [$_{CP}$ which student$_i$ [$_{IP}$ t$_i$ bought which book]]
 LF→ [$_{CP}$ which book$_j$ which student$_i$ [$_{IP}$ t$_i$ bought t$_j$]]
 b. $\lambda p \, \exists x \, \exists y \, [\text{student}(x) \, \& \, \text{book}(y) \, \& \, p = \text{bought}(x,y)]$
 c. {Bill bought W&P, Bill bought *Aspects*, Sue bought W&P, Sue bought *Aspects*}

(54) a. [$_{CP}$ which student$_i$ [$_{IP}$ t$_i$ bought f(which book)]]
 b. $\lambda p \, \exists x \, \exists f \, [\text{student}(x) \, \& \, p = \text{bought}(x, f(\text{book}))]$
 c. {Bill bought f_1(book), Bill bought f_2(book), Sue bought f_1(book), Sue bought f_2(book)}

Extrapolating from this, it seems reasonable enough to take the next step and claim that if an answer to a question specifies values for a *wh*-expression, that *wh*-expression must take scope outside the propositional core in C^0. However, this step is not valid. As noted originally by Kuno and Robinson (1972), both versions of (55a), the one with a *wh*-expression and the one with the definite, allow for a pair-list answer specifying values for individuals and books:

(55) a. Who knows where Mary bought these books/which book?
b. [$_{CP}$ which book$_j$ who$_i$ ... [$_{CP}$ where$_k$ [$_{IP}$ ...t$_j$ ... t$_k$ ...]]]
c. [$_{CP}$ these books$_j$ who$_i$ ... [$_{CP}$ where$_k$ [$_{IP}$ ... t$_j$ ... t$_k$ ...]]]

If one takes the pair-list answer as evidence of matrix scope for *wh*, as in (55b), one would have to take a similar stand on the definite (55c), a move most linguists would not want to make. There are, in fact, differences between possible answers to the two questions that have been discussed in subsequent literature (see Dayal 1996), which I will not delve into here. The point of relevance for us is that Kuno and Robinson's argument remains relevant and serves as a corrective against an unquestioning reliance on specification as evidence of scope for *wh*-expressions. It is particularly significant in framing our survey of the research on *wh*-scope marking.

22.4.2 *Wh*-scope marking

A *wh*-scope-marking construction, also known as partial *wh*-movement, instantiates a *wh*-dependency of a particular kind. There is a fixed *wh*-expression, corresponding typically to *what* in the matrix, and one or more *wh*-expressions in an embedded clause (56a). Examples from German and Hindi are given in (56b) and (56c), respectively:

(56)
a. [... WHAT ...([... WHAT ...)[... wh$_1$ ... (wh$_n$) ...]]]
b. Was denkst du (was Peter glaubt) mit wem Maria gesprochen hat?
   what think you what Peter believes with who Maria spoken has
   'Who do you think (Peter believes) Maria has spoken to?'
c. Anu kyaa kahtii hai (ravi kyaa soctaa hai) uma kis-se baat kar rahii hai?
   Anu what says   Ravi what thinks   Uma who-with talk doing is
   'Who does Anu say (Ravi thinks) Uma is talking to?'

If the embedding is deep, the matrix *wh*-expression is repeated in each of the intermediate clauses. In fronting languages the *what*-expression is in SpecCP, otherwise it remains *in situ*. The embedded clause *wh*-expressions likewise obey the standard question formation strategies of the language. As one can see, even though every clause in the chain has a *wh*-expression the embedding predicates are not +wh selecting. That is, *ask* or *wonder* are not good embedding predicates, but *say*, *believe*, or *think* are. Embedding predicates also cannot be in the negative (see Fanselow 2006 for a recent survey).

In a variant of this construction, the clauses are independent as shown in (57a), with a prosodic contour that clubs them together. German (57b) is a variant of (56b) with V2 in every clause, a matrix clause feature. The English example in (57c) has inversion in all the clauses, again a feature of matrix clauses. Note that there is no acceptable embedded version for the English (57c):

(57)
a. [[... WHAT ...] ([... WHAT ...]) [... wh$_1$ ... (wh$_n$) ...]]
b. Was denkst du? (Was glaubt Peter?) Mit wem hat Maria gesprochen?
   what think you what believes Peter with who has Maria spoken
c. What do you think? (What does Peter believe?) Who has Maria spoken to?

Unless otherwise specified, the discussion in this section applies to both versions of the strategy, embedded and sequential scope marking.

To complete the picture, the last clause in a *wh*-scope marking construction can be a multiple *wh*-question, assuming that the language allows multiple *wh* in simple questions:

(58) a. Was denkst du wem Karl welches Buch gegeben hat?
        what think you who Karl which book given has
        'Who do you think Karl has given which book to?'
     b. Anu kyaa kahtii hai kaun kis-se baat kar rahaa hai?
        Anu what says who who-with talk doing is
        'Who does Anu say is talking to who?'

Now, coming to the diagnostic of specification, we find that an answer to a scope marking question specifies values for all and only the *wh*-expressions in the most deeply embedded clause / last question in the sequence, not for the preceding *what*-expression(s). If we take specification of values to be an indicator of scope, a plausible analysis for scope marking is one that gives the embedded *wh*-expression(s) scope at the level of the highest clause and makes the matrix (and intermediate) *wh*-expressions semantically irrelevant. This is what lies behind the first analyses of this construction, van Riemsdijk (1982) for dialects of German, Hiemstra (1986) for Frisian, and McDaniel (1989) for Romani. Hiemstra's approach gives an idea of the extent to which the diagnostic of answers has influenced the analysis of scope marking.

Hiemstra views *wh*-movement as movement of a *wh*-feature (see also Cheng 2000). Languages differ with respect to what is involved in this movement. If the whole feature matrix of the *wh*-phrase is moved, including the phonetic matrix, we get long-distance *wh*-movement of the English kind. If only the *wh*-feature moves, it needs to be spelled out at the landing-site as the most unmarked *wh*-expression of the language: *was* in German, *wat* in Frisian, *mit* in Hungarian, *kyaa* in Hindi, etc. This is the scope marking construction. If person–number features of the *wh*-phrase are also moved, we get the copy construction to be discussed in the next section. In every case, the answer is predicted to specify values for the same *wh*-expression, the one that originates in the (most deeply) embedded clause and lands by LF in the highest Spec position.

The appeal of such an approach, dubbed the direct dependency approach in Dayal (1994), is undercut by the existence of scope marking in languages like Hindi in which covert *wh*-extraction out of finite clauses is not attested. It is also undercut by the discovery of sequential scope marking of the kind exemplified by (57) in English and German (Dayal 1996, Reis 2000). Rejecting the view that specification of values entails matrix scope, the indirect dependency approach (Dayal 1994, 1996, 2000) develops an account taking *what* to be a bona fide *wh*-quantifier over propositional variables. That is, the matrix question or the first question in the sequence, like any question, asks for information: *What does Bill think?* The next question provides the restriction on the variable: *Where did Mary go?* Answers to the first question are constrained by the set of propositions denoted by the second question. Embedding has consequences for binding-theoretic effects but the basic computation regarding the role of successive clauses remains the same in embedded and sequential versions of the construction.

A hybrid analysis has been proposed by Mahajan (2000), Fanselow and Mahajan (2000), and independently by Horvath (1997). It shares with the indirect dependency approach the view that the embedded clause is the complement of the matrix *wh*-expression and posits an LF where this complement raises up to its base position. However, it shares with the direct dependency approach the view that the matrix *wh* is semantically an expletive and is replaced by the *wh*-expressions in the complement at interpretation. One might say that the syntax of this approach aligns with the indirect dependency approach but its semantic assumptions are those of the direct dependency approach.

The choice between these approaches to scope marking has been debated extensively since the mid-1990s. Von Stechow (2000) and Beck and Berman (2000) propose a cross-linguistic division among languages with respect to the nature of the dependency. They suggest that direct dependency is appropriate for languages like German and indirect dependency for languages like Hindi. In fact, Bruening (2004) argued on the basis of Passamaquoddy that the two types of dependencies could co-exist in a single language. A cross-linguistic divergence between direct and indirect dependency languages, however, no longer seems to be the prevalent view. Many of the arguments for it are countered in Dayal (2000), based partially on a more nuanced presentation of the German facts in Reis (2000). Fanselow (2006) notes a general shift in favor of indirect dependency in recent analyses of the phenomenon. Stepanov (2001), Klepp (2001), Legate (2002), and Felser (2004) are some examples of this trend, as is Bruening (2006), who reverses his position on Passamaquoddy and comes out unequivocally in favor of the indirect dependency approach for scope marking.

22.4.3 The *wh*-copying construction

The *wh*-copying construction, though it shares some similarity with *wh*-scope marking, differs from it in significant ways (see Felser 2004 for a detailed discussion):

(59) a. [... wh$_1$ ...([... wh$_1$ ...)[... wh$_1$ ...]]]
   b. Wer denkst du (wer glaubt Peter) wer kommt?
      who think you who believes Peter who comes
      'Who do you think (Peter believes) will come?'

There can be only one *wh*-expression in the most deeply embedded clause and it is this *wh*-expression that occurs in the higher clause(s). A non-embedded, sequential variant of this construction has not so far been reported. Furthermore, there is no *wh*-copying construction corollary of the scope marking structure in (60), due to Höhle (2000), with a conjoined question in embedded position:

(60) Was meint er wann sie kommt und wen sie mitbringt?
      what thinks he when she comes and who she brings
      'What does he think when is she coming and who is she bringing?'

On the basis of such facts, Dayal (2000) suggests copying involves single chain formation under a direct dependency type of configuration, aligning it with extraction, while scope marking creates an indirect dependency between a *wh*-expression and a complement clause. More in depth analyses of the copying construction have been provided where the relationship with extraction has been explicitly articulated on the basis of morphosyntactic differences between the two.

The most intriguing difference between the copying construction and extraction has to do with restrictions on the type of *wh* allowed in the former. It is generally assumed that only monomorphemic *wh*-expressions are acceptable. This is captured in Hiemstra's account, discussed in the previous section, by taking the copying construction to be the spell-out of a structure in which only the person–gender–number features of the *wh*-expression move. Rett (2006) provides an alternative account for this fact. According to her, *wh*-expressions can simply contribute a variable (as *wh*-pronominals) or be generalized quantifiers (as *wh*-determiners). She shows that when a *wh*-quantifier only contributes a variable, iteration of *wh*s with a final existential binder is not problematic. When a *wh*-expression is a generalized quantifier, iteration leads to vacuous quantification. Thus, the copying construction that requires *wh*-expressions in intermediate positions is only compatible with *wh*-pronominals. This does not apply to extraction where the *wh*-quantifier leaves *wh*-traces in intermediate positions.

Hiemstra's and Rett's accounts do not predict the following paradigm from van Kampen (1997, 2009), discussed in den Dikken (to appear). While full DPs are barred from occurring in every Spec position, it is possible to have them in one of the Spec positions:

(61) a. Welke jongen denk je wie ik gezien heb?
 which boy think you who I seen have
 (colloquial and child Dutch)

b. Wie denk je welke jongen ik gezien heb?
 who think you which boy I seen have *(colloquial Dutch)*

c. *Welke jongen denk je welke jongen ik gezien heb?
 which boy think you which boy I seen have
 'Which boy do you think I saw?'

Den Dikken's analysis of the paradigm in (61) rests on the view that long-distance dependencies of any kind do not result from movement but arise from a relationship of agreement between a scope marker in a higher clause and an actual *wh* in the lower clause. This is shown schematically in (62):

(62) a. SM ... [$_{vP}$ v [$_{VP}$ V [$_{CP}$ XP C ... X̶P̶ ...]]]
 b. SM ... [$_{vP}$ S̶M̶ [$_{vP}$ v [$_{VP}$ V S̶M̶ [$_{CP}$ XP C ... X̶P̶ ...]]]]
 c. SM$_i$ ... [$_{vP}$ S̶M̶ [$_{vP}$ v [$_{VP}$ V S̶M̶ [CP XP$_i$ C ... X̶P̶ ...]]]]

(62a–b) represents scope marking while (62c) represents so-called extraction and *wh*-copying. The crucial difference is that only the latter shows concord. The relevant differences between extraction and copying construction depend on whether concord is partial or full. A full concordial relationship, where the matrix scope marker spells out all the features of the embedded *wh* (which remains silent), characterizes extraction. Partial concordial relationship characterizes the copying construction. Approaching the paradigm in (61) from this perspective, he analyzes (61b) as resulting from concord restricted to the N-features (number and animacy) but leaving out the quantificational D-features. (61c) is ruled out because full concord forces deletion of the lower *wh*-expression. Although den Dikken does not address (61a), his analysis of these structures presents a genuinely novel approach to the phenomena. While it successfully addresses the morphosyntactic differences in chain formation between the three constructions, it needs to be ascertained if it can also successfully address the semantic differences that have been noted between scope marking, on the one hand, and extraction and the copying construction, on the other.

22.4.4 Section wrap-up

Thornton and Crain (1994) report an acquisition study that provides interesting corroboration of the division between *wh*-scope marking and *wh*-copying constructions. According to them, English-speaking children initially manifest both constructions, but with the acquisition of extraction, the copying construction is lost while scope marking is retained. With the discovery of sequential scope marking, we now have reason to believe that scope marking is available in English and may well be available universally. It follows, then, that there is no reason to expect children to lose this construction. That the copying construction should be replaced by extraction is to be expected in a language where the adult grammar does not have the copying construction (see Dayal 2000). (For more discussion of acquisition, see Chapter 25.)

While much of the work in the domain of long-distance *wh*-dependency has focused on the nature of quantification involved, closer attention to the discourse contexts that favor one strategy over another might prove useful in shedding further light on the variation between them. Similarly, a diachronic study might also be helpful in this regard. The studies surveyed here provide a solid theoretical and empirical foundation for approaching these constructions from pragmatic and/or historical perspectives.

22.5 Conclusion

There are several important aspects of grammar relevant to the topic of this survey that have not been adequately covered here. These include negation (see Chapter 21), prosody (see Chapter 23), scope-taking adjuncts (see Chapter 13), and tense, aspect, and modality (see Chapter 20). This survey has focused on significant developments in the theory of quantification and scope since Frege's original insight about the logic of quantification and Montague's demonstration of the compositional relationship between natural language syntax and logical representation. There have been many innovations in the theory geared toward restricting the overgeneralization inherent in the system of scope taking, either by constraining movement of quantified phrases and/or by positing alternatives to treatment of noun phrases as generalized quantifiers over properties of individuals. These innovations have sometimes been driven by theoretical imperatives but their evaluation ultimately rests on empirical considerations. There is now a wealth of information from a wide variety of languages available in the literature, and this continues to motivate and regulate theoretical developments. While it cannot be said that the phenomenon of scope and quantification has been nailed down, it is clear that considerable strides have been made in our attempt to do so.

23

Syntax, information structure, and prosody

Daniel Büring

23.1 Introduction

23.1.1 Syntax and prosody

This chapter surveys the relation between syntactic structure, information structure, and prosodic structure. It will explicate what prosodic structures look like in general, and which prosodic structures go with which syntactic structures. As suggested by this formulation, the perspective here is that syntax and prosody are each generative systems, which independently define two sets of well-formed structures, one of syntactic phrase markers, one of prosodic structures; in addition, MAPPING CONSTRAINTS define the set of possible pairs ⟨s,p⟩ of syntactic and prosodic structures, which correspond to the well-formed sentences of the language. This is illustrated in Figure 23.1.

An overall architecture like this has been proposed, e.g., in Jackendoff (1997). It is worth noting that it imposes no specific conditions on the nature of syntactic rules and representations itself, i.e., whether a syntactic representation is built by rules or constraints, and whether it consists of one or more (PF, LF) sub-representations.

23.1.2 Narrow syntactic mapping vs. extraneous feature mapping

It seems useful to distinguish two aspects in which non-prosodic information is reflected in prosody, and hence two classes of mapping constraints. The first I will call NARROW SYNTACTIC MAPPING (NSM); by that I mean the way prosodic structure reflects aspects of syntactic structure proper, such as constituency, embedding, perhaps syntactic category, etc. The second I will call EXTRANEOUS FEATURE MAPPING (EFM), by which I mean the way things like focus, topic, givenness, etc. are reflected in prosody. Unlike NSM, EFM relates to features and properties that probably would not have a life in syntax, were it not for their prosodic effects. More

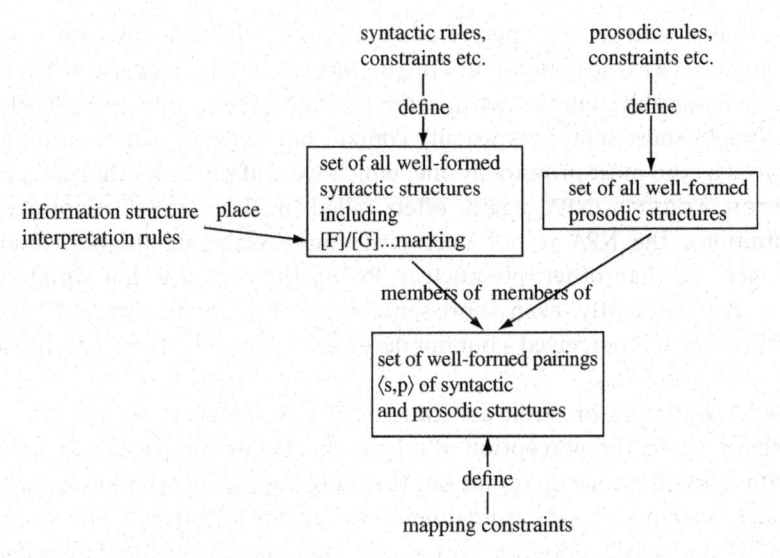

Figure 23.1. Architecture of grammar

concretely, these are commonly thought to be encoded in the form of privative features like [F], [G], etc. which are present on syntactic nodes *in addition* to their narrow syntactic features (such as syntactic category, case, etc.), see the leftmost column in Figure 23.1.

23.2 Syntax–prosody interface

The two aspects of (English) prosody most easily detected by naive listeners are (RELATIVE) PROMINENCE and PAUSES or BREAKS. A third may be TUNE or MELODY, e.g., whether the voice at a certain point in a sentence goes 'up' or 'down.' I will elaborate on these notions in turn, using English as the language of illustration.

23.2.1 Elements of prosodic structure

23.2.1.1 Prominence and pitch accents

The primary acoustic cue for perceived prominence in English (and many other languages) is fundamental frequency, or pitch: very roughly, a syllable (and derivatively the word or phrase containing it) that is the location of a local maximum ('peak') or minimum ('valley') in the fundamental frequency curve is perceived as prominent, or more prominent than those that do not. (Other factors like length, amplitude, and formant structure of vowels correlate with perceived prominence as well, but in cases of doubt, pitch overrides them all; see Fry, 1955, 1958, Terken and Hermes, 2000, and the references in the last.[1])

The direct theoretical correlates of these frequency peaks and valleys are PITCH ACCENTS (PAs): tonal targets like high (H*) or low (L*) tones that are associated with syllables perceived as prominent. Pitch accents are not the same as STRESS (though parts of the literature appear to use the terms interchangeably), but the two are closely related, see Section 23.2.2.2 below.

Simple short sentences usually contain one syllable that is easily perceived as the most prominent one, which we will say bears the NUCLEAR PITCH ACCENT (NPA; again, often called 'nuclear stress'). Contrary to intuitions, the NPA is not necessarily more elaborate (higher, louder, longer, ...) than other, pre-nuclear, PAs in the sentence, but simply the last. Put differently, even short sentences often contain several PAs, the last of which is perceived – but not necessarily realized – as the 'strongest.'[2]

23.2.1.2 Pauses, prosodic constituents, and boundary tones

What triggers the perception of a pause/break? Actual periods of silence within an utterance do occur, but the more common correlates are again tonal movements – the fundamental frequency falls or rises toward the end of the word before the 'pause' – and lengthening of the final syllable before the 'pause.' Correlates in the prosodic theory are BOUNDARIES of prosodic constituents (prosodic words, phonological phrases, etc.; see next section); in particular, syllables before a right boundary are lengthened, and in the case of larger constituents, associated with so-called BOUNDARY TONES, written as H% (high) or L% (low).

A more subtle cue is the SCALING of PAs: within a prosodic constituent, subsequent high tones often follow a pattern of relative lowering from one to the next, the so-called DOWNSTEP. This pattern is reset after a prosodic constituent boundary, i.e., the absolute height of pitch accents after a boundary may be 'reset' to a higher frequency than the previous PAs.

Where a sentence contains a prosodic break, the last PA before it, i.e., the final one in the prosodic constituent ending at the break, is again usually perceived as more prominent than PAs preceding it within that constituent; it is nuclear within that constituent. As a consequence, among the non-final (pre-nuclear) pitch accents in a sentences with complex prosodic structure, some may be perceived as more prominent than others, namely those that are final/nuclear within smaller prosodic constituents. It is in fact conceivable that whenever one accent is perceived as more prominent than another, it is because it is final in some prosodic constituent.

23.2.2 Assumptions about prosodic structure

There are two kinds of prosodic representations regularly employed in the literature: METRICAL STRUCTURE, which represents prosodic units of various sizes (syllable, foot, prosodic word, phonological phrase, etc.) and their stress patterns (more about which momentarily);[3] and INTONATIONAL STRUCTURE, which also represents certain prosodic units like the intonational and intermediate phrases, but focused on *tonal* events such as pitch accents and boundary tones mentioned above.[4]

23.2.2.1 Prosodic constituents, heads, and stress

In this chapter, I will employ a single prosodic representation, which consists of hierarchically ordered prosodic constituents of various sizes (as in metrical structures). These are indicated by parentheses above the examples, as in (1a). The higher/bigger phrasal ones of these are the same as the phrases of intonational structure (called INTERMEDIATE and INTONATIONAL PHRASE in English); their boundaries are the anchoring points for boundary tones in intonational structure.

Each prosodic constituent has one metrically strongest element, its HEAD, indicated by an asterisk. Thus being stressed is by assumption the same as being the head of some prosodic constituent. Prosodic element A has more/higher stress than prosodic element B if A is the head of some constituent containing B.[5]

As I said in the introduction, it is instructive to think of prosodic structure as a generative system in its own right. That is to say, there is a set of PROSODIC WELL-FORMEDNESS CONSTRAINTS (the top right corner in Figure 23.1) which, in purely prosodic terms, define the set of well-formed prosodic structures: strings of segments and syllables, organized into higher prosodic units, their boundaries and heads marked by accents, boundary tones, particular timing, etc. Take (1) as an illustration at the word level:[6]

```
        (     *     ) prosodic word
        (*   )(*    ) foot
        (*)( *)( *)( * ) syllable
(1) a. in-tro-duc-tion
    b. is-tor-ga-tid
    c. in-stru-ment-ion
```

Introduction is a well-formed word of English: its prosodic structure (1a) is well-formed, it has a well-formed morphological analysis, and the two can be mapped onto one another by the rules of morphology-to-prosody mapping; *istorgatid* and *instrumention*, with the same prosodic structure, are prosodically well-formed, too. But (1b) cannot be mapped onto English morphemes at all, and (1c) cannot be mapped onto a well-formed morphological structure (because the suffix *-tion* cannot attach to a nominal stem like *instrument*); hence they are not words of English.

(1a) also illustrates a perhaps trivial point: that morphological structure – here [[*introduc*][*tion*]] (or perhaps [[[*intro*][*duc*]][*ion*]]) – and prosodic structure (here: at the foot level) are not always isomorphic. The same is true, as we will see, for syntactic and prosodic structure.

23.2.2.2 Stress and accent

The columns of asterisks in (1a) correspond to metrical strength or STRESS. I remarked above that stress is related to, but not the same as, accent. For example, *introduction* can be produced with one, two, even three, or no pitch accent (!H here marks a DOWNSTEPPED high tone, i.e., one that is high, but lower than the preceding one; this is a common realization for citation forms, though of course not the only one):

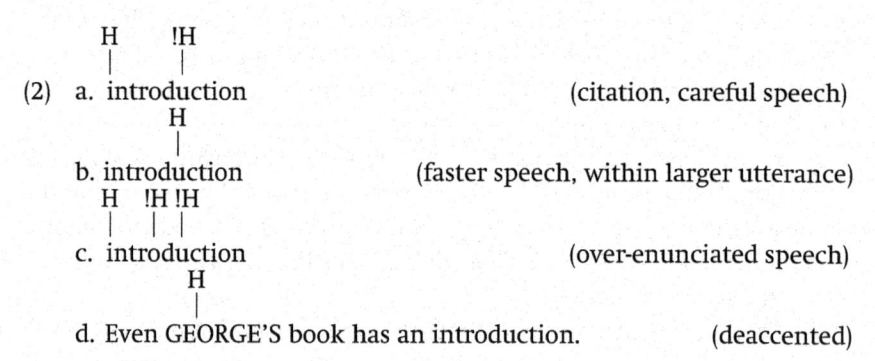

(2)   H   !H
         | |
a. introduction   (citation, careful speech)

          H
          |
b. introduction   (faster speech, within larger utterance)

         H !H !H
         | | |
c. introduction   (over-enunciated speech)

               H
               |
d. Even GEORGE'S book has an introduction.   (deaccented)

I assume here that in all of these realizations, *introduction* has the same metrical structure, (1a). While this means that the number of pitch accents is not determined by the stress pattern, there are strict rules on the association of the two. If a constituent contains a pitch accent, its head is pitch accented. Put differently, PA are assigned 'from top to bottom': the accent on *tro* is only possible if *in* is accented, which in turn is possible only if *duc* is. In addition, there cannot be pitch accents after the metrically strongest syllable, so no PA on *tion*, which follows the strongest syllable *duc*; this will be of importance later on. Both these properties are encoded in (3):[7]

(3)   STRESS-TO-ACCENT PRINCIPLE (a prosodic well-formedness constraint)
The last pitch accent within a prosodic constituent (if there is one) is on the head of that constituent.

I noted above that the last pitch accent before a break is perceived as most prominent; by (3), this has now a theoretical counterpart: the last pitch accent within a metrical constituent C will always be on the metrically strongest syllable of C, i.e., the one with the strongest stress.

    Experimental evidence suggests that stressed syllables are phonetically distinguished from less stressed ones even apart from accenting, e.g., by length, intensity, or more careful articulation (Baumann et al. 2010, Beaver et al. 2007, Cooper et al. 1985, Eady and Cooper 1986, Eady et al. 1986, Xu and Xu 2005, among others). These effects are very subtle though and will not play much of a role in what follows.

23.2.3 The syntax–prosody mapping

In this section and the following I will use the terms 'prosodic phrase/unit,' ϕ for short, to refer to any prosodic constituent above the prosodic word level. I will refer to the heads of φ as phrasal stresses, and, where we deal with entire sentences, to the head of the highest φ as SENTENTIAL STRESS. To ease the exposition, English is the sole language of illustration, although the framework sketched here has been developed primarily in the analysis of a wide variety of other languages.[8]

It can be observed that major prosodic constituent breaks – usually called intonational phrase boundaries – often mark the end of embedded clauses; thus (4) can be disambiguated by prosodic boundary placement:

(4) when Roger left the house became irrelevant
    (i) when Roger left [PAUSE] the house became irrelevant
    (ii) when Roger left the house [PAUSE] became irrelevant

Similarly, a complex DP like *fancy books* is regularly separated off as a (smaller) prosodic phrase with *books* being the head (and thus stronger), as in (5a); compare to (5b), where *Nancy* and *books* are equally strong (in both (5a–b), *bebop* is stronger than the rest because it is the final phrasal stress and thus the head of the topmost φ, as indicated):

(5) a. (I like) fancy books and bebop
    b. (I like) Nancy, books, and bebop

```
    ...                *    )
          (     *  ) (      *    )
          (*   ) ( *  ) (   *    )
(6) a.  fancy books and bebop
    ...                *    )
          (*   ) ( *  ) (   *    )
    b.  Nancy books and bebop
```

(Note that the absolute height of columns is not relevant here; what is important is their relative height and phrasing.) Data like these lend credence to the idea that prosodic phrasing corresponds closely to syntactic phrases. On the other hand, especially right-branching structures 'flatten out' in the prosody, which is to say that there is no evidence for prosodic phrases that contain just *met the girl at the teach-in* in (7a) and *the girl and the teacher* in (7b), even though these are syntactic constituents:[9]

```
          (                 *    )
          (   *) (     *) (   *    )
(7) a.  the boy met the girl at the teach-in
          (                 *    )
          (   *) (   *) (       *    )
    b.  the boy, the girl, and the teacher
```

What is also evident is that in (7) function words like *the* and *at* are grouped with their closest lexical elements, and the verb with its complement (more on which momentarily).

One possibility to derive such 'flattened' prosodic phrasing is the EDGE BASED approach (Selkirk 1986). For example, the desired phrasing in the above examples can be achieved if every *right* boundary of every NP and VP is aligned with a right prosodic phrase boundary; left boundaries are then inserted mechanically, as (8) illustrates for (7a) (ϕ-heads as indicated have to be located by additional principles, see right below):

(8)   )   )   )
     a. [$_{DP}$the [$_{NP}$boy]][[$_{VP}$met [$_{DP}$the [$_{NP}$girl]]][$_{PP}$at[$_{DP}$the[$_{NP}$teach-in]]]]
          (*   ) (*   ) (*   )
     b. [$_{DP}$the [$_{NP}$boy]][[$_{VP}$met [$_{DP}$the [$_{NP}$girl]]][$_{PP}$at[$_{DP}$the[$_{NP}$teach-in]]]]

Note in particular that the ϕ-boundaries both after *girl* and after *teach-in* correspond to the right boundaries of an NP, a PP, and a VP segment at the same time; this way, branching to the right is systematically flattened out.

Truckenbrodt (1995b, 2006) instead argues for a STRESS/CONTAINMENT BASED mapping, using (9):

(9)   STRESSXP (a mapping constraint)
        Every lexical XP contains a ϕ-level stress

The stress pattern in (8b) follows from STRESSXP; in particular, the stress on *girl* is contained in NP, but also in VP. Therefore, VP meets STRESSXP, even though V itself does not have phrasal stress.

To account for the location of the phrase boundaries in (8b), we modify STRESSXP as in (10):[10]

(10)   XP↔ϕ (a mapping constraint)
        Every lexical XP contains a ϕ-level stress *, where * is the head of a ϕ containing XP.

(8b) meets XP↔ϕ: the first ϕ contains the subject DP/NP, the second the inner VP and the object, the third the PP/DP/NP. The head of each is located within the phrases it contains. As far as higher constituents like the outer VP or TP are concerned, these meet XP↔ϕ once we consider the ϕ that contains the entire sentence:

            (*   )
            (*   ) (*   ) (*   )
(11)   [$_{DP}$the [$_{NP}$boy]][[$_{VP}$met [$_{DP}$the [$_{NP}$girl]]][$_{PP}$at[$_{DP}$the[$_{NP}$teach-in]]]]

The highest ϕ meets XP↔ϕ for the higher VP and the entire sentence (and, incidentally, for the final PP/DP/NP). Note that, according to XP↔ϕ, the head of that ϕ could also be on *girl*, since that, too, is contained in VP and all higher syntactic constituents. To derive the correct placement (as in (11)), we therefore add the following constraint:

(12) HEADRIGHT (a prosodic well-formedness constraint)
Among sister ϕs, the rightmost one is the head of its mother.

23.2.4 Phrasal stress, pitch accents, integration

One interesting and important consequence of XP↔ϕ (or STRESSXP) is that syntactic heads will not bear phrasal stress if they have a syntactic complement (syntactic XPs, on the other hand, will always bear phrasal stress). The default phrasing/stress for a V plus (prosodically simple) object will thus be as in (13):

```
            (       x  )ϕ              (       x        )ϕ
            (  x ) ( x  )PWd           (   x  )( x  )PWd
(13) a. [ᵥₚ verb object]      b. [ᵥₚ object verb]
```

These phrasal stress patterns determine not just metrical prominence, but also possible pitch accent patterns, using the STRESS-TO-ACCENT Principle (3), repeated here:

(14) STRESS-TO-ACCENT PRINCIPLE (a prosodic well-formedness constraint)
The last pitch accent within a prosodic constituent (if there is one) is on the head of that constituent.

Due to (14), the verb may (but need not) bear a PA in (13a), where its stress is pre-nuclear, but not in (13b), where its stress is post-nuclear. This effect is known as INTEGRATION in the literature: verbs, or generally heads, bear less stress than their complements, and in head-final structures, cannot bear a PA.[11] It is most striking in OV languages like German and Dutch, where it leads to an apparent shift of the NPA to the left:

(15) Peter will   ein BUCH lesen. (not: ein Buch LESen)   (German)
     P.   wants a book   read
     'Peter wants to read a book'

The integration effect follows from the syntax–prosody mapping rule XP↔ϕ (following the lead of Truckenbrodt 2006). It is worth emphasizing that the integration effect does not follow from anything about the assignment of sentential stress. It follows from the assignment of phrasal stresses, the last of which becomes, by (12), HEADRIGHT, the sentential stress. It is thus a very local phenomenon.

To predict default accent patterns, we assume, besides (14), that pitch accents in complex prosodic structures do not align with stresses below the word level (i.e., that prosodic words usually bear at most one accent), and that phrase level stresses align with pitch accents where allowed by (15) (i.e., ϕs contain at least one pitch accent).

Taken together, our rules then predict the following sentential DEFAULT ACCENTING:

- every lexical head bears a pitch accent, except ...
- heads with a complement
    - need not when preceding the complement
    - must not when following the complement (integration)
- the rightmost accent within a complex ϕ will be strongest

This concludes our survey of the basic mapping from narrow syntax to prosody. I will refer to the prosodic structures defined jointly by mapping constraints like XP↔ϕ and prosodic well-formedness constraints like HEADRIGHT, STRESS-TO-ACCENT, etc. as the DEFAULT PROSODY – as opposed to prosody co-determined by mapping extraneous features like focus, to be discussed in Section 23.4 below.

23.2.5 Mismatches

Especially at higher levels of prosodic organization such as the intonational phrases, phrase boundaries are relatively easy to determine, using mainly boundary cues such as pausing, lengthening, and boundary tones. Therefore it is rather easy to spot cases in which – as Steedman (2000a:649) aptly puts it – "phrasal intonation in English is ... orthogonal to traditional notions of surface syntactic structure":

(16) a. [$_{DP}$ the [$_{NP}$ [$_{AP}$[older] and [more experienced]] divers]]
(   )(   )(   )

b. [the [cat [that chased [the [rat [that ate the cheese]]]]]]
(   )(   )(   )

c. [everyone [knows [that this is not true]]]
(   )(   )

Taglicht (1998) provides discussion of such cases and gives a number of constraints that limit the choice of prosodic phrasing based on syntactic structure. Generally, however, little is known about the rules that govern the construction of higher prosodic phrases in English and how they relate to syntactic structure.

Unlike Taglicht, and most others, Steedman (1991, 1994, 2000a, 2000b, 2006), assumes that prosodic and syntactic structure are always isomorphic: there are no mismatches (similarly Wagner 2005b, 2010). On this account, any prosodic constituent corresponds to a syntactic constituent, which in turn has to receive an independent interpretation. Thus, in the following examples from Selkirk (1981, 1984) via Steedman (2000a), the parentheses not only indicate prosodic phrasing, but also syntactic constituents (the same would probably be claimed for Taglicht's 1998 examples in (16)):

(17) a. (the absent-minded professor) (was avidly reading) (about the latest biography) (of Marcel Proust)
b. (Marcel proved) (completeness)

According to Steedman, grammar has to specify the full range of possible syntactic constituents, including 'non-standard' constituents as in (17) (which, for example, also occur in 'non-standard' coordinations like *John suspected, and Marcel proved, completeness*). The syntax–prosody relation, in turn, is rather simple, since each prosodic constituent corresponds to a syntactic one.[12]

23.3 How prosody influences syntax

An empirically plausible, and theoretically interesting hypothesis is that syntax should be 'phonology free' (Pullum and Zwicky 1986, Zwicky 1985); for example, syntactic rules/constraints do not appear to make reference to the segmental features of the elements they manipulate, nor could they, if one assumes that syntactic computations do not even have access to non-syntactic elements (such as Distributed Morphology; see Halle and Marantz 1993, 1994). But there appear to be many cases of prosodically motivated variations in word and constituent order. I will review some of these in this section and then ask what they imply for the architecture of grammar.

A terminological note first: I will use transformationalist terminology such as 'base position,' 'movement,' etc. in the following discussion; all that is really necessary to assume, though, is that two (or more) syntactic structures can be identified as alternative realizations of 'the same sentence,' and – crucially, as we will see in Section 23.5.4 below – one of them as the 'unmarked' or 'basic' one. Generally, prosodically driven movement (and below: focus driven movement) should more neutrally be understood as 'prosodically/focus driven deviation from canonical constituent order.'

23.3.1 Heavy NP shift

Can prosody influence syntax? A case in point may be various so-called stylistic rules such as heavy NP shift (HNPS; Ross 1967a). While the exact line between merely marked and categorically impossible may be hard to draw, it seems clear that structural and/or prosodic complexity facilitates rightward positioning of complement DPs:

(18) a. I explained to Bill the reasons why he shouldn't attend
b. I explained to Bill the reinforcement resistance test
c. ??I explained to Bill the test/the reasons
d. *I explained to Bill them

There are two issues that it is advantageous to keep apart: first, the less than categorical nature of the judgments themselves; second, the dependency between syntax and prosody that they seem to reveal. My sole point of interest here is the second. That is, I do not believe that prosody–syntax interactions like this one are generally limited to weak 'stylistic,' rather than stronger categorical acceptability judgments, nor that these kinds of graded judgments are essentially different from many found in arguably core morphosyntactic domains such as agreement, extraction, or Binding Theory. Whatever rule or constraint format one finds adequate to deal with the one can plausibly be expected in the other.

Returning to HNPS, then, it appears that syntax needs to look at the internal, perhaps prosodic, complexity of a constituent before deciding whether it must, may, or cannot occur in shifted position (Hawkins 1994, Kimball 1973, Wasow 1997, Zec and Inkelas 1990). If a constituent is 'too light,' HNPS is impossible.

Zec and Inkelas (1990: 377) assume that, as a matter of syntax-to-prosody mapping, rightward shifted constituents need to be mapped onto prosodic constituents of a certain size. Such phrases in turn, as a matter of prosodic well-formedness requirements, need to contain a certain number of phonological phrases. (Zec and Inkelas 1990 speculate that the pertinent phrase is the intonational phrase, which in turn needs to contain at least two ϕs.) According to such a view, prosodic well-formedness constraints restrict syntactic (re)ordering possibilities.[13]

23.3.2 Prosodic extraposition

Relative clauses (RCs), and embedded clauses in general, often occur in extraposed positions, like the subject relatives in (19):

(19) Suddenly some people started laughing who had been silent before.

Extraposition is ubiquitous in German (and Dutch), where embedded clauses overwhelmingly, in many constructions obligatorily, appear *after* the sentence-final verb, even though they originate to the left of it:

(20) a. wir haben niemanden gesehen, den du kennst
we have no one seen who you know
'we saw no one you know'
b. er hat gesagt, dass er hungrig ist
he has said that he hungry is
'he said that he was hungry'

Arguably, extraposition structures elegantly resolve a problem in the syntax–prosody mapping. Suppose that subordinate clause and matrix clause, both being clausal, should be mapped onto intonational phrases (IntPs). But, by assumption, an intonational phrase cannot contain another intonational phrase[14]; consequently, as long as one clause is contained in the other, they cannot each be mapped to an independent intonational phrase[15]:

(21) a. *(( )IntP)IntP
[some people [who had been silent before] started laughing]
     (   )IntP(   )IntP
b. [some people t_{CP} started laughing]   [who had been silent before]

In the extraposed structure, the RC, but crucially also the matrix clause to the exclusion of the RC, corresponds to contiguous strings and can thus each be mapped onto an intonational phrase. A prosodically based analysis would thus claim that extraposition is *triggered* by a conflict between the mapping constraints and prosodic well-formedness constraints.

Perhaps even more clearly than in the case of HNPS above, such an analysis would argue that the *in situ* structures in many of these cases are prosodically less than perfectly well-formed. (22), for example, shows an attested phrasing, where the center-embedded relative clause *is* mapped onto its own IntP, at the price of breaking up the matrix clause into three phrases, the last of which is also prosodically very light, consisting of the prosodic word *gesehen* only:

(22) (   ) (   ) (   )
      wir haben niemanden, den du kennst, gesehen
      we have no one   who you know   seen
      'we saw no one you know'

This rendering, though possible, sounds much less natural than the extraposed version, which has one intermediate or intonational phrase for each clause:[16]

(23) (   ) (   )
      wir haben niemanden gesehen, den du kennst

So as in HNPS and the English cases discussed above, extraposition would serve to create a structure in which both clauses are mapped to IntPs, and undersized IntPs are avoided (prosody-internal constraint). In addition, as first pointed out in Truckenbrodt (1995a:Section 2.2), the class of landing-sites for extraposition in German is most easily defined in prosodic terms: descriptively, the extraposed clause has to follow the last verb in the sentence-final verb cluster (i.e., the edge of the matrix clause), (24a), and cannot occur between a selecting verb and its VP complement, (24b). On the other hand, when a lower VP is topicalized as in (24c), a relative clause can extrapose to the embedded VP's edge (relative clause and head noun in bold):

(24) a. er wird nicht [$_{VP1}$[$_{VP2}$ **alles** tun] können] **was du willst** (German)
        he will not   all   do   can   what you want
        'he won't be able to do everything you want'
     b. *er wird nicht [$_{VP1}$ [$_{VP2}$ **alles** tun] **was du willst** können]
     c. [$_{VP2}$ **alles** tun] **was du willst** wird er nicht [$_{VP1}$ t_{VP2} können]

This otherwise puzzling distribution – the extraposed clause would seem to attach to VP$_2$ in (24b) as well as (24c) – makes sense from a prosodic point of view, since topicalized VPs are generally set off into their own prosodic phrase (whereas clause-medial ones never are). It appears, then, that extraposition generally targets a prosodic phrase boundary (maybe IntP) to the right (see Truckenbrodt 1995a, Göbbel 2007, Bobaljik and Wurmbrand 2005b, Inaba 2007, for more and a similar analysis for English).

23.3.3 Prosodic movement?

What are we to make of cases of prosodically triggered movement, henceforth P-MOVEMENT, as those in the last two sections? Do we have to assume that prosodic factors can trigger syntactic movement (license non-canonical syntactic structures) the same way that, e.g., a *wh*-feature can? How can syntax even know what is of the proper size to shift or extrapose, if prosodic structure is to be construed only on its output?

A palatable account may have the following general format: both canonical and shifted structures are *syntactically* well-formed. In order for them to correspond to acceptable sentences, however, there must also be *prosodically* well-formed structures that correspond to them. In certain cases, the canonical structures may not correspond to a well-formed prosodic structure, in others the shifted structures may not. Whenever the shifted structure's prosodic correspondents are well-formed, but the canonical one's are not (or less so), we get the effect of p-movement.

What this perspective requires, though, is that several syntactic variants, e.g., canonical and shifted, can exist side-by-side, i.e., be equally syntactically well-formed. Narrow syntax, in short, must allow for a certain amount of optionality (even more than it must anyway, because now some syntactically well-formed options may still not occur in well-formed sentences since they fail on prosodic grounds). In a framework in which all syntactic variation must be triggered by corresponding syntactic features ('movement must be feature driven,' see e.g. Section 4 2.2), the features in question will not be [+heavy] or [+intonational phrase worthy] (even if those may be what ultimately characterizes the class of moveable elements), but narrow syntactic features ('word order features,' EPP-type features, etc.) which have no particular prosodic (or otherwise) interpretation, but which can be, randomly as it were, added to the input of syntactic computation for the sake of modeling optionality. The movements are not strictly speaking triggered by prosody (they are triggered by random features), but exploited (to use Fanselow's 2007 apt term) by prosody. In an evolutionary metaphor, syntactic constituent order variation is a random mutation, and prosodic well-formedness conditions are the natural selection that will let some mutations thrive, and others die. More prosaically, I will refer to this as the TRY-AND-FILTER APPROACH.

The Try-and-Filter approach analyzes p-movement as run-of-the-mill syntactic movement. It has been suggested in some transformational analyses, though, that p-movement (or at any rate certain cases of it) constitutes a genuinely different kind of movement operation, sometimes labelled PF-movement, from those driven by core syntactic features such as *wh-* or argument movement. PF-movement would still move syntactic constituents and merge them with other constituents, but it would do so in a different 'branch' of the syntactic derivation, namely after spell-out ('on the PF-branch'), presumably because it serves no syntax-internal purpose and hence need not be visible at Logical Form, the syntactic level at which syntactic feature checking needs to be completed.[17]

Consequently, PF-movement may be set apart from, say, *wh-*movement not only by its 'motivation,' but also by syntax-internal properties such as its locality restrictions (cf. Chapter 18), or the choice of possible target positions (or even the directionality of movement); most crucially, PF-movement would, by definition, not have any interpretive effect, since it takes place after spell-out, i.e., after LF relevant information has been sent off.[18] This hypothesis goes farther than the one we have contemplated so far, namely that the output of syntactic movement (or the lack thereof) may be filtered by prosodic well-formedness constraints, giving the appearance of prosodically motivated movement. Since I cannot review the empirical arguments in favor of the PF-movement hypothesis in the space of this chapter, I will merely conclude at this point that various movements, among them HNPS and extraposition, appear to satisfy prosodic requirements or, put differently, that the question of whether or not a particular syntactic structure yields an acceptable sentence (or how acceptable a sentence) may depend on the prosodic properties of the resulting structure.

23.4 Extraneous feature mapping

In this section we will turn to those aspects of prosody that are clearly related to meaning. These include the marking of focus, givenness, contrastive topic, and possibly other categories, subsumed under the label INFORMATION STRUCTURE, but also features like [comma] in Potts (2003). For reasons of space, though, I will limit the discussion to focus and its complements, background or given.[19] Likewise we restrict attention to stress/accent as their prosodic correlate (though phrasing and tune-choice are presumably relevant, too).

23.4.1 Basics of information structure realization: marked and unmarked intonation

The default prosody for (25) – intuitively and as defined by the rules in Section 23.2 above – has the NPA on *friends*; *John* bears a secondary accent, another accent on *brought* is possible, too; this is indicated in (25a):

(25) John brought two friends along.
   a. JOHN brought/BROUGHT two FRIENDS along
   b. JOHN brought two friends along
   c. John brought two friends ALONG
   d. John brought TWO friends along

(25b–d), by contrast, are marked realizations. In each of them, the NPA is on a different element, *John*, *along*, and *two*, respectively (secondary accents are not indicated in (25b)–(25d), but will likely be on the same elements that are accented in (25a)). In relation to (25a), we can think of these marked patters as omission of PAs on *friends* (and *brought*) in (25b), addition of a PA on *along* in (25c), and omission of the accent on *friends* plus addition of a PA on *two* in (25d).

Each of these marked patterns seems to signal a different emphasis relating to interpretation. In trying to make this more precise, we start with the two prevalent intuitions found in the literature regarding the meaning of such accent patterns, which I will illustrate using (25b): On the first, the marked accent pattern does not really emphasize *John*, but de-emphasizes the rest: *brought two friends along*. This could happen because 'bringing two friends along' is already salient at the time of utterance, or given in a previous conversational move. This jibes well with the intuition that the pronunciation in (25b) seems very odd out of the blue; we immediately interpret it as part of an ongoing conversation (e.g., one that started by someone saying *Bill brought two friends along*, or asking *who brought two friends along?*).

The second kind of intuition is that in (25b), *John* is emphasized, possibly to contrast John with other people who might have brought two friends along (but did not). Omission of other accents is a side-effect of emphasizing *John*. I will now flesh out these intuitions some more.

23.4.2 Background: interpreting information structure

23.4.2.1 Givenness

In its simplest form, a givenness theory would hold that there is a one-to-one correspondence between being discourse-new and being accented. Often, for example, leaving a lexical expression unaccented signals that that constituent is, in a sense to be elaborated momentarily, given; the unaccented object NP in (26a) is interpreted anaphorically, while accenting it blocks that interpretation, as in A′, rendering the reply somewhat incoherent:

(26) Q: (Did you see Dr Cremer to get your root canal?)
     A: (Don't remind me.) I'd like to STRANGLE the butcher.
     A′: #(Don't remind me.) I'd like to STRANGLE the BUTCHER.

In (26), the given constituents are anaphoric, but anaphoricity does not suffice as a general characterization of givenness: The N *Italian* may be unaccented in (27a), because it is given; but the DP it heads is not anaphoric. Even verbs, like *jump* in (27b), for which the notion of anaphoricity is not generally assumed to be relevant, can be given and hence deaccented:

(27) a. (Why do you study Italian?) I'm MARRIED to an Italian
b. (Don't jump! –) But I WANT to jump.

We may characterize givenness as in (28):

(28) An expression E is given in a context C if there is a synonym or hyponym A to E such that the meaning of A is salient in C.

On its anaphoric reading, *the butcher* is synonymous with *Dr Cremer* in (26), as is of course *jump* to *jump* in (27b). By assumption, using an expression makes its meaning salient, so (28) is met. While *Italian*, the language, is not synonymous with *Italian*, the nationality, we may assume that mentioning of the one can make salient the meaning of the other. Finally, the reference to hyponymy allows us to subsume cases like (29) (adapted from van Deemter 1999), in which mentioning of *violin* makes *string instruments* given:

(29) (I want to learn to play the violin,) because I LIKE string instruments.

It is inappropriate to speak of given constituents (or their meanings) as 'presupposed,' for at least two reasons: First, one can only presuppose entire propositions or statements, but not properties, individuals, relations, etc. (the same caveat applies to the notion 'old information' to characterize givenness). Second, even if a given constituent is propositional, its content need not be accepted by the interlocutors:

(30) A: Do you think we'll see Kim at the party?
B: I DOUBT she'll be there.

The underlined part in B's reply is unaccented because it is given. But neither A nor B actually holds the belief that Kim will be at the party; the proposition that she will is salient (and hence makes the embedded clause given), but not presupposed.

Is it empirically correct that given elements are never accented? No. First, given elements, especially content words, frequently bear secondary accents. Second, if a given element appears in narrow focus, it will bear the main accent. We will return to these cases below. Nevertheless, the relevance of givenness (or something like it) for deriving prosody is hard to deny (see Ladd 1983; and Section 23.4.2.3 below).

23.4.2.2 Focus

The intuition behind the notion focus is virtually the opposite of givenness: a constituent is highlighted by accent in order to emphasize its novelty or importance to what is expressed. Two representative examples are ANSWER FOCUS and CONTRASTIVE FOCUS:

(31) Answer focus: Focus marks the constituent in the answer that corresponds to the *wh*-phrase in the question
Q: Who did Jones's father vote for?
A: He voted for JONES.

(32) Contrastive focus: Focus marks the constituent that distinguishes a larger constituent from a previously uttered one
a. Last year Jones's father voted for Smith.
b. This year he voted for JONES.

It bears mentioning that the example in (32) is contrastive, but not corrective (as it would be if you replaced *This year* by *No!*); we assume here that corrections are one use of contrastive foci.

Since von Stechow (1981, 1989) and especially Rooth (1985), the notion of ALTERNATIVES has been successfully applied in analyzing foci. For example, in (32b), we can pick a FOCUS DOMAIN, here the clause *he voted for Jones*, replace the focus in it with a cleverly chosen alternative, here 'Smith', and thus get to the (meaning) of the TARGET, the clause *he/Jones's father voted for Smith*. Roughly, any sentence for which this procedure is successful qualifies as a contrastive focus sentence.

In the same vein, we can analyze answer focus. Either assume that a *wh*-expression like *who* can be an alternative to *Jones* in A in (31). Or stipulate that the sum total of alternative instantiations (that he voted for Jones, that he voted for Smith, that he voted for ...) equals the set of answers to the question under discussion, Q in (31); such a stipulation is called QUESTION-ANSWER CONGRUENCE (e.g., Kadmon 2001:253, Rooth 1996:271f.; presumably based on the use of the term 'congruence' in Halliday 1967) and underlies all uses of questions, or question-answer tests as indicators of focus (e.g., Comrie 1981b:62ff., Hajičová et al. 1998:207f., Lambrecht 1994:121).

In either case we can say that focus marks the (minimal) element in a focus domain which makes that domain different from a previous utterance. As in the case of givenness, we cannot say that the non-focus part is presupposed, nor that the focus part is '(new) information,' since neither of them is propositional.

23.4.2.3 The relation between givenness and focus

Comparing givenness and focus, it seems tempting to reduce one to the (inverse of the) other: Couldn't focus simply be the non-given part? Or, inversely, couldn't givenness be the same as background of a focus within a focus domain? The arguments are complex and impossible to do justice to within the scope of this chapter, so a few short notes must suffice, starting with three arguments suggesting the need for givenness.

First, the majority of sentences are neither answers nor explicitly contrastive, yet many of these show marked accent patterns. These are open to explanations in terms of givenness, but require invocation of implicit questions or contrast targets to be subsumed under focus.

Second, if a sentence contains, in addition to an answer focus or a corrective focus, new material, that material is accented just like a focus:[20]

(33) Q: What did you buy?
A: I bought [a BOOK]_F at the FLEA market.

Third, within larger foci, the actual accent placement may depend on givenness:

(34) Q: Who did Jones's father vote for?
A1: He voted for [a friend of his WIFE]_F.
A2: He voted for [a FRIEND of Jones]_F.

On the other hand, given elements may end up accented, in case they are narrowly focused, as in our original examples in (31A) and (32b); so plausibly, focus is needed in addition to givenness.

All these distributional arguments suggest that a unification is impossible. Nevertheless, Schwarzschild (1999) develops an intriguing proposal to subsume the two under what he calls GIVENNESS (with a capital G). In a nutshell, a constituent counts as Given if, after replacing the focus, it finds a salient antecedent; this is virtually identical to the concept of focus discussed in Section 23.4.2.2 above and in particular allows for given elements to be accented if they happen to be the smallest locus of novelty within a focus domain. On the other hand, if a constituent does not contain focus, it is Given if it is given (since there is nothing to be replaced in it, it has to find a literal antecedent). So even though Schwarzschild's Givenness theory is often contrasted with 'focus theories' such as Rooth (1992a), it is actually simply a generalization thereof (indeed Rooth 2010 subsumes both under 'anaphoric theories of focus').

An entirely different argument for distinguishing givenness and focusing invokes interpretation. Indeed, early discussions of givenness emphasize the absence of what we may call 'semantic contrast' in typical givenness examples such as (35) ((7b) from Ladd 1980:55):

(35) A: Why don't you have some French toast.
B: I've forgotten how to MAKE French toast.

Here, the argument goes, *make* is not understood as contrasting with any other relation ('... but not how to sell French toast'). Similarly for our examples in Section 23.4.2.1 above. Granting this point (though see Büring 2008b, Wagner, 2006 for a different view), it is interesting to note though that formal theories of focus such as Rooth (1992a) do not incorporate any notion of contrast other than the very weak one of finding an alternative that will match the focus domain to the target (which of course you can do in (35) by using 'have' as an alternative to *make* in VP). In other words, there is no 'true contrast' requirement on a focus domain and its target in discourse in such theories – this is of course the reason why Schwarzschild (1999) succeeds in subsuming focus under Givenness. Indeed, meaningful definitions of 'contrast' in a stronger sense prove difficult to formalize and often remain imprecise or circular (see, e.g., É. Kiss 1998, López 2009, Vallduví and Vilkuna 1998). It remains an open challenge to distinguish (non-)Givenness and focus on a semantic/pragmatic basis (see Krifka 2008, Repp 2010, for useful overviews, and Repp and Cook 2010 for a recent monograph).

Summarizing, the question whether givenness and focusing can be unified in their interpretation, and hence reduced to a single marking in the syntax is controversial. I will err on the side of caution here and assume that they are distinct.

23.4.3 The influence of focus/givenness on prosody

Building on our earlier assumptions about NSM, I will assume that extraneous features like focus and givenness will (sometimes) yield *amendments* to the prosodic structure(s) based on narrow syntactic information and prosody-internal factors alone (an idea that goes back at least to Selkirk 1984, where NSM builds a metrical structure, which is then amended to accommodate focus-driven PAs). Assume that focus and givenness are marked in the syntax by privative features [F] and [G]; then (36) provides a minimal version of a constraint set that achieves this:

(36) a. FOCUS PROMINENCE (a mapping constraint)
An [F]-marked constituent contains the nuclear stress (in its focus domain).[21,22]
b. GIVEN NON-NUCLEAR (a mapping constraint)
A [G]-marked element does not contain the nuclear stress (unless it is [F]-marked).[23]

In addition, the constraints of narrow syntactic mapping, as well as prosody-internal well-formedness constraints as discussed in Section 23.2, remain active, giving rise to what we may call:

(37) Prosodic Inertia: Default Prosody is retained as much as possible while respecting FOCUS PROMINENCE and GIVEN NON-NUCLEAR.

The two most important ingredients of Default Prosody regarding stress/accents are that regular phrasal stresses are assigned to the heads of lexical XPs, *modulo* integration (STRESSXP/xp↔φ, (10)), and no accents can follow the nuclear stress (STRESS-TO-ACCENT, (3)). Crucially, the latter principle, but not the former, is inviolable, so that both FOCUS PROMINENCE in (36a) and GIVEN NON-NUCLEAR in (36b) will result in the avoidance of pitch accents ('deaccenting') on given or non-focal elements if these would otherwise bear the last pitch accent (in the domain). The effects of (36) can be summarized as follows:

- The nuclear (strongest) stress/pitch accent of the sentence will be within a focus, if there is one (due to FOCUS PROMINENCE).

- Within a focus or in a sentence without focus (if there are such), the NPA will fall on a non-given element if there is one (due to GIVEN NON-NUCLEAR).
- Given a choice between several F-marked, G-less constituents, the nuclear pitch accent goes to the rightmost one (by Prosodic Inertia, particularly HEADRIGHT), *modulo* integration (see Section 23.2.4 above); same if nothing is F/G-marked.
- There will be regular phrasal stresses, and thus (non-nuclear) pitch accents on eligible elements before the nuclear PA, regardless of their F/G-marking (Prosodic Inertia, in particular STRESSXP/xp↔φ).
- There will be no pitch accents after the final focus or non-given element, because there cannot be PAs after the nuclear stress (Prosodic Inertia, particularly STRESS-TO-ACCENT), which by FOCUS PROMINENCE must be on an F-marked (and otherwise by GIVEN NON-NUCLEAR, on a non-given) element.
- All the above generalizations will apply to subconstituents of sentences if these contain F/G-markings.

23.4.4 Prosodic inertia and focus projection

By coining the term 'Prosodic Inertia,' I have emphasized that principles of default prosody are integral, too, to understanding the realization of focus and givenness. Apart from the bullet points above, this is particularly evident in examples with multi-element foci: if the focus does not contain the rightmost phrase accent and hence the NPA by default, prosodic structure will be changed so as to achieve this. *Within* the focus, accents will fall as usual (i.e., on all lexical elements *modulo* integration), and the last of those will become nuclear. This has essentially been noted in Jackendoff (1972:237): "the highest stress in S will be on the syllable of P [the focus of S – DB] that is assigned the highest stress by the regular stress rules." The same follows from the transderivational system in Reinhart (1995: Chapter. 3): The NS on word W can realize focus on a higher constituent P only if nuclear stress on W presents the *minimal change* to the default prosody that results in P containing the NS.

Prosodic Inertia derives the very same effect. There are thus no specific rules to determine possible foci from accent positions, or accent positions within foci, so-called FOCUS PROJECTION RULES,[24] other than the general rule *not* to change anything unless required by FOCUS PROMINENCE/ GIVEN NON-NUCLEAR.

23.5 How information structure influences syntax

So far I have concentrated on the effect of focus on prosody (and, to some extent, interpretation). Indeed, I have characterized [F]-features as 'extraneous,' suggesting that they do not have syntax-internal relevance at all. But is this correct? Are there really no narrow syntactic effects of focus – and more generally, information structure features – at all?

23.5.1 Focus effects on constituent order: three types of approaches

That focus/givenness structure (in one of its nominal incarnations) can influence constituent order has been noted for a long time, in at least two ways. First, as a general ordering principle, usually 'old-before-new,' e.g., in Czech and other Slavic languages (see among others the work of the so-called Prague School, revisited, e.g., in Hajičová *et al.* 1998), or earlier studies of German scrambling (Lenerz 1977, Lötscher, 1972). Second, in the form of reference to, usually peripheral, focus positions, especially in non-European languages.

Independent of that, Chomsky (1976a) contained an argument that focus in English had to undergo Quantifier Raising at Logical Form (Chomsky's argument has since been convincingly criticized and will not be repeated here).[25] For simplicity I will use the term 'IS-movement' to refer to all of these; a more apt, but discouragingly cumbersome term would be 'information structure related constituent order variation.'

Horvath (1986) presents an early formal analysis of Hungarian focus in which a feature [F] is assigned in a particular syntactic position (preverbally); this is refined in Brody (1990), according to which focus needs to move to the specifier of a functional projection whose head itself bears the feature [F]. Subsequently, Rizzi (1997) proposed that that head is a designated Focus head, located in the left, CP region of the clause, and that hence, focus is moved to SpecFocusP. Movement of the focus to SpecFocusP is triggered by the necessity to check the focus's [F] feature against that of the Focus^0 head.

What is common to such approaches is that they assume the focus position to be located in absolute syntactic terms, i.e., in a particular position relative to other clausal heads and the elements occupying them. Because of that property approaches of this ilk are often called CARTOGRAPHIC APPROACHES (see Chapter 12). Cartographic approaches also typically assume that focus movement is triggered syntax internally by the feature [F].[26]

As opposed to that, the analysis of Catalan in Vallduví (1990) is an early example of what I will call a MAPPING APPROACH to IS-movement. According to Vallduví, all and only material within the core IP at s-structure is interpreted as focus (by an operator called Φ); non-focal material is left-or right-adjoined to IP, where it gets interpreted as background ('ground' in Vallduví's terms, split into 'links' to the left, and 'tail' to the right). It appears from Vallduví's discussion that movements to dislocated positions are in principle optional, but will result in a particular interpretation in the pragmatic component (his 'informatics'), due to the nature of the syntax-to-pragmatics mapping.[27]

A recent version of a mapping approach is the analysis of Czech in Kučerová (2007), which, like Vallduví's, assumes that all non-given (focal) material has to form a core sentential constituent, c-commanded (and in the case of Czech, preceded) by all given material (within a certain syntactic domain).

Mapping approaches like Vallduví's and Kučerová's do not assume that there are designated, labeled focus positions in the syntax, nor do they rely on the existence of features like [F] in the syntax. In the case of Kćerová (2007), there is not even a designated syntactic boundary between background and focus (what the innermost IP is in Vallduví 1990), since *any* constituent can mark the boundary between given and focal material (marked by an operator G in Kučerová (2007).

Finally, Zubizarreta's (1998) analysis of Spanish initiates the line of PROSODY-DRIVEN APPROACHES to IS-movement. Like mapping approaches, these do not assume syntactically defined focus positions or heads (nor necessarily focus features), but unlike mapping approaches, they assume that the domains in which elements are interpreted as focus and background, respectively, are defined by the syntax-to-prosody interface, not the interface to interpretation. The core principle of all these approaches is the requirement that focus needs to bear the main stress of the sentence (FOCUS PROMINENCE). IS-movement emerges in cases where this is achieved by bringing the focus constituent into the default main stress position, rather than shifting the main stress onto the focus constituent(s).

Prosody-based approaches provide an intriguing link between IS-movement and focus realization by prosody *in situ:* in both cases, the same underlying principle is operative: to align pragmatic focus and prosodic prominence. The difference is whether this is done by changing constituent order, or prosodic patterns.

Because of this interesting property, because of the number of thorough prosodically based analyses available, and because these are most pertinent to the topic of the present chapter, I will focus on prosody-based approaches to IS-movement in what follows.

23.5.2 Prosodically driven movement

In a number of unpublished manuscripts, and eventually her 1998 book, Maria-Luisa Zubizarreta has pioneered a prosody-based approach to focus placement in Spanish (and other languages). Spanish answer focus has to occur in the rightmost position of the core clause, followed at most by right-dislocated, prosodically separated material. Hence, narrow subject focus can only be realized in V(O)S order, and likewise, focus on an initial object requires dislocation of any following objects (based on examples (57–58) in Zubizarreta 1998:22):

(38) (Context: Who ate an apple?)
    a. comio una manzana JUAN
       ate   an apple   Juan
       'Juan ate an apple'
    b. #JUAN comio una manzana.

(39) (Context: What did María put on the table?)
    a. María puso sobre la mesa el   LIBRO
       M.   put on   the table the book
       'María put the BOOK on the table'
    b. #María puso el libro sobre la mesa

Zubizarreta (1998) connects this to the fact that main sentential stress in Spanish is likewise strictly right-peripheral, and – unlike in English – cannot shift leftward in cases of narrow answer focus. Assuming that sentence stress is invariably assigned to the rightmost phrase in a Spanish clause, Zubizarreta then proposes that any non-canonical orderings such as VS, VOS, ..., etc. result from a last resort operation called P-MOVEMENT, which moves non-focal material leftward across focused material, until the latter is ultimately in a right-peripheral, main stress position – in accordance with a principle like FOCUS PROMINENCE in (36) above, which requires focus to bear the main stress (called the 'Focus Prosody Correspondence Principle' in Zubizarreta 1998:38).[28]

As emphasized in Zubizarreta (1998), this analysis connects focus realization by peripheral placement in Romance languages like Spanish to focus marking by intonation in English and German, and even allows for incorporating optional focus movement (in French) and non-focus related prosodic movements such as HNPS in English, discussed in Section 23.3.1 above (cf. especially Zubizarreta 1998: Section 3.6).

As also discussed at length in that book (see especially, pp. 30–33), P-MOVEMENT poses a bit of a conundrum in terms of standard transformational assumptions: the need for p-movement can only be assessed *after* main stress has been assigned, and hence after the syntactic derivation is complete (i.e., all 'normal' merges and moves have been completed); after all, it is not the [F] feature that triggers p-movement, but a configuration in which the 'normal' position of the [F]-marked element does not include the structurally assigned main stress. The resulting picture can thus be depicted as in points 1–4 below.

Note that in this picture, stress assignment must happen in the syntax proper (albeit at the very end), because it triggers syntactic movement (p-movement) and because the output of that movement can, at least in principle, influence interpretation, hence 'feed LF' (Zubizarreta 1998:146). Consequently, Zubizarreta assumes that stress is assigned to syntactic, not prosodic, constituents.

1. Main syntactic derivation (all merges and movements driven by feature checking)
2. Main Stress Assignment by Nuclear Stress Rule and Focus Prosody Correspondence Principle
3. If stress assignment is contradictory:
   (a) p-movement of right sister across left sister
   (b) back to step 2
   else on to next step
4. Proceed to LF and PF

Büring and Gutiérrez-Bravo (2001) transpose Zubizarreta's analysis into a prosody-based framework like the one discussed in Section 23.2, i.e., in particular one that assumes that stress is a property of prosodic structure, as built off of syntax, but not present in the syntax itself (that paper also extends the analysis to focus-related scrambling in German, as do Büring 2001a, 2001b). In that setting, the question of the role of p-movement in grammar presents itself with new urgency: If stress is only present in prosodic structure, i.e., after the PF-interface, what triggers p-movement in the syntax? Büring and Gutiérrez-Bravo's (2001) answer is the same we adopted in Section 23.3: 'Try-and-Filter.' P-movement is a run-of-the-mill syntactic movement; whether it is legitimate or not can only be assessed by looking at the resulting syntactic *and* prosodic structure. A sentence is well-formed if it is prosodically well-formed – which in the case of Spanish means it has right-peripheral main stress – and meets FOCUS PROMINENCE, i.e., has the [F]-marked element correspond to a prosodic constituent that bears main sentential stress. In a standard object focus case, the basic constituent order meets these constraints, while a subject-final order does not; in the case of narrow subject focus, the subject-final order (ostensibly derived by movement) does, whereas the basic SVO or VSO orders do not.

Analyses in exactly the same spirit, but much more detail, are presented for Italian and a number of other languages in Samek-Lodovici (2005), and for Hungarian in Szendrői (2001). Abstracting away from the details of particular analyses, the blueprint for these kinds of analyses based on prosodic structure[29] is thus as follows: movement of focus, as well as backgrounded, constituents is not technically triggered by any focus (background) feature (in agreement with Zubizarreta 1998), in fact it is syntactically optional (*pace* Zubizarreta 1998); however, a derivation that fails to move and thereby ultimately violates FOCUS PROMINENCE, as well as a derivation that does involve movement but ultimately violates FOCUS PROMINENCE (e.g., 'wrongly' creates VSO order in a object focus sentence), will 'crash' (in Minimalist terminology), or be blocked by a competitor that does not involve these violations (in the terminology of ranked violable constraints as used in most of the works cited), thus yielding the effect of focus-prosody-driven movement.

As the reader may have noted, it is indeed irrelevant for this kind of analysis by which means competing word orders are generated, since all relevant structures must be syntactically freely available, only to be filtered out once syntactic, prosodic and F-structure are, simultaneously, assessed by grammatical constraints. (There is, however, an additional complication having to do with the least effort nature of IS-movement, which I will discuss in Section 23.5.4.)

23.5.3 Properties and predictions of prosody-based approaches

23.5.3.1 Multiplicity of 'focus positions'

If focus configurations are defined prosodically, there is no expectation that focused elements will occupy syntactically identical positions across sentences. For example, a clause-final element in Spanish may be an object (hence VP internal) or an adjunct (hence VP external), or an intransitive verb:[30]

(40) a. (Context: What did Juan buy?)
Juan compro el peRIÓdico (Spanish)
J. bought the newspaper
b. (Context: Where did Juan plant a rose bush?)
Juan planté un rosal en el jarDÍN
J. planted a rose bush in the garden
c. (Context: What did María do?)
Maria BAIla
M. danced

Syntactic evidence shows that indeed all of these elements occupy the same position they do in 'normal' (broad focus) sentences. They uniformly end up receiving sentential stress because they happen to end up being the last content word in the clause.

Similarly, according to Szendrői (2001, 2003) Hungarian assigns main stress clause initially, making that position, following topicalized (ostensibly TP adjoined) elements, the focus position. This position is often filled by movement (of the element to be focused) to a functional specifier, accompanied by raising of the verb (but not the verbal particle; accordingly, the order *mutattam be* – as opposed to the unmarked *bemutattam* – diagnoses focus movement):

(41) (Context: Who did you introduce Peter to last night?)
tegnap este MARinak mutattam be Pétert (Hungarian)
last night Mary.DAT introduced.I PERF Peter.ACC
'it was to Mary that I introduced Peter last night'

If that position remains empty, however, the finite verb itself – now leftmost in the core clause – receives main stress. This is the pattern found in narrow V focus, as well as verum focus sentences:[31]

(42) de, én ODA VITTEM a levelet (Hungarian)
but I PRT took the letter.acc
'but I TOOK the letter there / DID take the letter there'

As in Spanish, one can show that the verb here remains *in situ* and does not occupy a higher functional position (e.g., a hypothetical syntactic focus head): the verb *vittem* in (42) *follows* the preverbal particle *oda*.

In sum, prosody-based accounts define focus configurations in terms of alignment with a prosodically defined position, not structurally. Accordingly, focused elements can occupy different syntactic positions. Likewise, IS-movement will occur where an element to be focused does not occupy that position in the unmarked order, but there will not be string-vacuous movements of foci for the sake of checking a focus feature; being in the focus configuration is obligatory, moving focus is not.[32]

23.5.3.2 Multiplicity of 'focus movements'

As discussed in the previous section, prosodic approaches predict that the focus configuration can be obtained by moving the to-be focus into the main stress position, or, where applicable, leaving it in its base position. In addition, an element to be focused can get into the main stress position through 'evacuation' of other elements (which would otherwise receive main stress). Common strategies of evacuation include pronominalization, right (or, especially in case the element to be evacuated is a contrastive topic, left) dislocation, and VP internal swapping of positions (Romance p-movement, Dutch/German scrambling), as well as possibly object shift in Scandinavian:[33]

(43) Right dislocation
(Context: What has John given to Mary?)
ha regalato un LIBro, Gianni, a Maria   (Italian)
has donated a book, John, to Mary
'John has given a BOOK to Mary'
(from unmarked *Gianni ha regalato un libro a Maria*)

(44) Scrambling
(Context: When did Jan kiss Marie?)
Jan heeft Marie GISTeren gekust   (Dutch)
J. has M. yesterday kissed
'Jan kissed Marie yesterday'
(from unmarked *Jan heeft gisteren Marie gekust*)

(45) VP internal p-movement
(Context: What did Juan plant in the garden?)
Juan planto en el jardin un ROSAL   (Spanish)
J. planted in the garden a rose bush
'Juan planted a rose bush in the garden'
(from unmarked *Juan plantó un rosal en el jardín* (=(40b)))

(46) DP internal p-movement
(Context: Which place did the people denounce the invasion of by the Americans?)

el pueblo denunció   la invasión por los americanos del
the people denounced the invasion by the Americans of
Canal de PANAMÁ   (Spanish)
canal of Panama

(from unmarked [_DP_ *la invasion del Canal de Panamá por los americanos*])

In other words, such approaches are compatible with focus movement as well as 'givenness movement.'[34]

23.5.3.3 Mixing of strategies

As pointed out above, prosody-based accounts draw a direct connection between focus realization by position and focus realization by accent. They are thus also well suited to the analysis of languages in which both of these focus realization strategies occur. Thus in German, focus on an initial (indirect) object can be realized by shifting the main stress leftward, or by evacuating (via scrambling) the final (direct) object to the left, making the focus right-peripheral. The analogous situation is found in French, though there the direct object is initial in the unmarked order (French from Zubizarreta 1998:147, examples (139a/140a)):

(47) (Context: Who does she bequeath her poodle to?)
 a. sie vermacht ihrer SCHWESter ihren   Pudel   (German)
    she bequeaths her.DAT sister   her.ACC poodle
 b. sie vermacht ihren   Pudel ihrer   SCHWESter
    she bequeaths her.ACC poodle her.DAT sister
    'she bequeaths her poodle to her sister'

(48) (Context: What did you return to Marie?)
 a. nous avons rendu   son LIVRE à Marie   (French)
    we   have returned his book to Marie
 b. nous avons rendu à Marie son LIVRE
    'we returned his book to Marie'

As proposed, e.g., in Zubizarreta (1998:146) and Büring (2001a), such a pattern can be analyzed as the coexistence of two grammars (formalizable, e.g., as a constraint tie[35]), one of which favors preserving unmarked constituent order (as in (48a)), the other standard prosody (as in (48b)). A similar analysis could be devised for 'stylistic' movements such as particle shift in English:

(49) (Context: What did she do when her neighbors complained about the loud music?)
 a. she turned DOWN the music
 b. she turned the music DOWN

Crucially, under the prosodic account, these two strategies are closely related: both serve to satisfy FOCUS PROMINENCE, differing only in whether principles preserving standard prosody (i.e., principles of NSM) or preserving standard constituent order (e.g., principles penalizing movement) are ranked below it.

23.5.4 Syntactic inertia

I have described prosody-based approaches above as ones that 'blindly' generate different constituent orders, then pair these with appropriate prosodic structures, and finally evaluate these pairs with regard to mapping constraints. This, however, cannot be the entire story. Characteristically, variation in constituent order for focus reasons is subject to SYNTACTIC INERTIA: unmarked constituent order is preserved as much as possible while achieving the focus configuration. I briefly illustrate with two sets of phenomena. First, marked constituent orders are generally narrow focus. For example, in subject-final structures in Romance, only the subject (or a part thereof) can be interpreted as focus; in an object-final structure, on the other hand, (parts of) the object, the VP, or the entire sentence, can be interpreted as focus (note that in all of these cases, the (would-be) focus contains the final constituent and hence the main stress):

(50) a. (Context: # What happened?
         Who ate an apple?)
      comió una manzana Juan   VOS   (Spanish)
      ate   an apple   Juan
      'Juan ate an apple'
    b. (Context: What happened?
         What did Juan do?
         What did Juan eat?)
      Juan comió una manzana   SVO

One may suspect that this is because subjects in general cannot project focus. (51) shows that that cannot be the reason:

(51) a. (Context: What happened?/What did Juan do?)
      Juan plantó un rosal   (Spanish)
      Juan planted a rose bush
    b. Juan plantó un rosal   en el jardín
      Juan planted a rose bush in the garden
    c. #Juan plantó en el jardín un rosal

In the marked order *V PP O* in (51c), only the final object *un rosal* can be interpreted as focus. The sentence is thus odd in the contexts given; instead, the unmarked order *V O PP* as in (51b) must be used. But, as (51a) shows, the object can in principle project VP and sentence-wide focus, when in unmarked sentence-final position. Thus the impossibility of wide focus in (51c) must be blamed on the marked constituent order, not a general inability of objects to project focus.

The second set of data comes from languages that allow both order variation and accent shift (cf. Section 23.5.3.3 above): While each is possible in isolation, a constituent in non-canonical position cannot bear non-canonical main stress; this is illustrated for German in (52):

(52) a. (Context: What does she bequeath to her sister?)
sie vermacht ihrer Schwester ihren PUdel (German)
she bequeaths her.DAT sister her.ACC poodle
b. #?sie vermacht ihren PUdel ihrer Schwester
she bequeaths her.ACC poodle her.DAT sister
'she bequeaths her poodle to her sister'

Although accusative-before-dative order is in principle possible – see (47b) above – it is not if the accusative is to be narrowly focused. Generally, moving a narrow focus to the left is highly marked in Dutch and German, even though both languages allow non-final sentential stress and foci.

Both these patterns can be conceptualized in terms of Syntactic Inertia: do not change constituent order unless the resulting structure allows you to realize the focus pattern with a less marked intonation. In wide-focus cases like those in (50) and (51), constituent order changes within the focus do not improve prosodic structure, and in the narrow-focus cases like (52b), scrambling make the prosody even worse.

In the account of Zubizarreta (1998), this is implemented straightforwardly: p-movement is *triggered* by a mismatch between focus realization and structural stress, and accordingly would not take place if the pre-movement structure did not have a mismatch to begin with.

On a Try-and-Filter approach, Syntactic Inertia has to be implemented by a constraint that penalizes non-canonical order relative to <s,p> pairs. In particular, even where both s and p are independently well-formed – as they are in (51c) and (52b) – and meet FOCUS PROMINENCE on the intended focusing – as they do for wide focus in (51c), and focus on the accusative object in (52b)) – <s,p> will only be admitted by the grammar if there is no competitor <s',p'> that meets these criteria and involves less deviance from the canonical constituent order.

In other words, deciding whether a given syntax–prosody pair of representations is well-formed involves comparing it to a set of other syntax–prosody pairs, its comparison class, in terms of some metric of 'canonicity,' e.g., the number (and possibly distance) of movements, or more generally, a measure of deviance from the canonical order for the same sentence (where again 'same sentence' is in need of a formal definition).[36] The comparison class itself should comprise different prosodic structures paired with the same syntactic structure (as already seen in Section 23.4.4 above), but also, and crucially, different syntactic permutations of the same sentence (where, again, 'same sentence' should be defined in terms of identity of numeration, or some other measure that relates to sameness of lexical material and structural relations).

23.5.5 Problems

Though prosody-based approaches have been applied successfully across a wide range of languages, there are also known problems, some of which will be mentioned in this section. First, an obvious prediction of these approaches is that the position of main stress and the position of focus should coincide. While this is the case in most languages studied, there is at least one glaring exception, Nɬe?kepmxcin (Thompson River Salish), as analyzed in Koch (2008). In Nɬe?kepmxcin, focus has to align on the left of the clause, but prosodic prominence is clearly on the right.

Second, as per the discussion in Section 23.5.3.1, the prosody-based account predicts that the will be no string vacuous IS-movement,[37] or generally no IS-movement which does not bring the focus closer to a prosodically defined edge. However, in Hausa, which otherwise has optional movement to a left-peripheral focus position, subjects obligatorily have to move to that position, even though their base position is sentence-initial (examples from Hartmann and Zimmermann 2007, and p.c.):

(53) Q: Wàa ya-kèe   kirà-ntà?   (Hausa)
         who 3sg-rel.cont call-her
         'Who is calling her?'
    A1: Daudàa (nee) ya-kèe   kirà-ntà
         D.   PRT 3sg-rel.cont call-her
         'Dauda$_F$ is calling her'
    A2: #Daudàa ya-nàa   kirà-ntà
         D.$_F$ 3sg-cont call-her

That movement has taken place is indicated by the so-called relative form of the verb (*ya-kèe* instead of *ya-nàa*) and the possibility of the particle *nee*. A regular SV structure with a non-relativized verb as in A2 is impossible with subject focus.

Finally, it appears there are cases in which given elements are moved leftward even if they are not, prior to movement, in nuclear stress position. According to López (2009:181), *dos pimientos* moves across *a mi hermana* in (54b) because it is part of the background – unlike in (54a). In both cases, the nuclear accent is on *madre*, which is part of the focus: *para mi madre* in (54a), and *di ... a mi hermana para mi madre* in (54b). It is thus unclear what motivates the movement in (54b) (example (5.25) in López 2009):

(54) a. (Context: For whom did you give your sister two peppers?)
    le   di   a   mi hermana dos pimientos para mi
    Cl.DAT gave. 1st.sg DAT my sister   two peppers for my
    madre
    mother
    'I gave my sister two peppers for my mother'
  b. (Context: What did you do with two peppers?)
    le di **dos pimientos** a mi hermana t para mi madre

At the very least, then, something other than nuclear stress must motivate the movement of *dos pimientos* in (54b).

23.5.6 The three types of approaches compared

As should have become clear from the forgoing discussion, there are many phenomena that jibe well with prosody-based approaches as well as mapping approaches, but not cartographic approaches: the multiplicity of focus positions, the coexistence of movement into focus positions (of constituents to be focused) and away from focus positions (for constituents not to be focused), and the coexistence of positional and prosodic marking strategies in the same language. Generally, cartographic approaches do well with defined narrow-focus positions, but have problems dealing with broader foci, including all-new sentences. Perhaps because of that, virtually no in-depth analyses of focus marking within the cartographic approach exist; despite its wide adoption (perhaps due to its simplicity and compatibility with syntactic ideas of a certain period – in particular that all movement needs to be feature-driven) its empirical success in this realm has yet to be demonstrated.

As pointed out before, too, prosodic and mapping approaches are much harder to tease apart in their predictions. I have listed some problems for prosodic approaches in Section 23.5.5 above, some of which may be amenable to solutions within mapping approaches. The reason for that is, of course, that mapping approaches are not committed to the existence of any independent correlates of their focus configurations; that affords them more analytical liberties. That, however, may also be considered their biggest shortcoming: they fail to make a connection to prosody, and thereby to languages in which accent shift or other prosodic manoeuvres are the primary means of focus realization.

23.6 Summary

Prosodic structure is a structure in its own right, not just syntactic structure garnished with segments, stresses, and accents. While narrow syntactic mapping constraints (like XP↔φ) co-determine what prosodic structures occur, many aspects of prosodic structure follow from prosody-internal restrictions on prosodic well-formedness, including, I argued, main stress placement and accent assignment (HEADRIGHT, STRESS-TO-ACCENT). Extraneous features like [F], too, influence the shape of prosodic structure, but the ultimate realization of focus and other information structural features is best understood as an interplay between narrow syntactic mapping constraints, prosody-internal well-formedness constraints (jointly defining default prosody) and constraints of extraneous feature mapping like FOCUS PROMINENCE. Finally, prosodically motivated movements (heavy NP shift, extraposition), including arguably information structure related movements (focus/givenness movement), can be reconciled with a 'prosody-free' syntax, at the price of adopting a Try-and-Filter approach, i.e., syntactic optionality which in some cases leads to structures that cannot be paired with well-formed prosodic structures.

Notes

Thanks to Stefan Baumann, Kay González, Hubert Truckenbrodt and Michael Wagner for help and suggestions, and Marcel den Dikken for extensive comments on the draft version.

1. Interestingly, pitch might be less of a central cue for the automatic recognition of prominence, see the results in Howell (2011).
2. Currie (1980, 1981), Liberman and Pierrehumbert (1984:182ff.), Ladd (1996: esp. Chapter 6). Katz and Selkirk (2011) argue that there are instances in which a non-final pitch accent is in a grammatical sense stronger than the final one. If so, the picture is more complicated than outlined here.
3. Other representation formats proposed in the literature include metrical grids, bracketed metrical grids, and metrical trees (see, e.g., Halle and Vergnaud 1987, Hayes 1995, Liberman and Prince 1977, Prince, 1983). The prosodic structures employed here are special instances of bracketed metrical grids and as such represent the same information as those.
4. Structures of the former kind are the primary object of investigation in PROSODIC PHONOLOGY, which often diagnoses prosodic units as the domains for segmentai phenomena, and METRICAL PHONOLOGY, which is interested primarily in stress patterns. Structures of the latter kind (intonational structures) are the representation of choice in INTONATIONAL PHONOLOGY.
5. Formally: A has more stress than B iff (i) A is the head of some constituent containing B, or (ii) A is the head of some constituent that has more stress than B. By this definition, the syllables *in* and *duc* in (1a) are stronger than *tro* and *tion*, and the foot *duction* is stronger than the foot *intro* and the syllables *in* and *tro*, all according to clause (i). Clause (ii) furthermore makes *duc* stronger than the syllables *in*, *tro* and the foot

intro, which accords with the intuitive use of the terms 'stronger' or 'more stressed.'
6. Cf. Giegerich (1992:203).
7. The same logic for accent assignment is argued for e.g., in Pierrehumbert (1980: 37ff.)
8. See, e.g., Elordieta and Vigário (2005), Frascarelli (2000), Frota (1998), Hayes and Lahiri (1991), Nespor and Vogel (1986), Selkirk (1986); Sugahara (2002), Truckenbrodt (1999), or the papers collected in Inkelas and Zec (1990).
9. Cf. also the difference between (ia) – flat – and (ib) – grouped as (A and B) or C – on their culinarily natural readings:

   (i) a. steak and rice or noodles
       b. steak and rice or pizza

   For a recent thorough discussion of facts like these see Wagner (2005b, 2010).
10. XP↔ϕ combines Truckenbrodt's (1995b) STRESSXP and WRAPXP, following Truckenbrodt and Büring (in preparation).
11. See Fuchs (1976, 1984), Gussenhoven (1983), Jacobs (1992, 1999), Schmerling (1976), Uhmann (1991), among many others.
12. Additionally, Steedman assumes that the syntactic constituency – at least in the non-standard cases – reflects information structure, i.e., syntactic constituents correspond to information structural categories like topic and comment. This aspect of the proposal is orthogonal to the more general claim that prosodic constituents always correspond to syntactic ones. We will return to issue of information structure, syntax and prosody in Sections 23.4.3ff. below.
13. Since it is much less clear that HNPS is ever obligatory, I will not speculate about factors that may disfavor non-shifted structures. As is well known, however, there are parsing advantages to reaching the beginning of complements earlier rather than later, which generally favors ordering shorter complements before longer ones, see, e.g., Hawkins (1988, 1994).
14. An assumption based on Selkirk (1984) – where it is part of the 'Strict Layer Hypothesis' – and since widely adopted, though see, e.g., Ladd (1996:238ff.) and the references there for critical discussion.
15. To be sure, there are other ways of phrasing the non-extraposed (21a), most notably (D N)(RC)(VP) and (D N RC)(VP). But none of them succeeds in mapping both the matrix clause and the RC onto a single ϕ.
16. Very arguably, (22) is not just stylistically marked, but also restricted to certain information structural configurations, in particular one in which VP is not a broad focus.
17. There is, of course, the possibility that the movement itself is not syntactic at all, but done 'in the phonology,' as it were. This would lead us to expect, among other things, movements that affect non-

constituents. This does not seem to be the case for the instances of p-movement discussed here; it has been argued for in cases of clitic movement in Serbo-Croatian, where clausal clitics sometimes seems to appear *inside* clause mates (i.e., between non-constituents). It is, however, controversial whether these really involve non-constituents, so we will not discuss them further here. See, e.g., Bošković (2001), Halpern (1992), Wilder and Ćavar (1994), Zec and Inkelas (1990), Zec (2005), Yu (2008) for a recent survey.

18. Büring and Hartmann (1997), for example, claim that all extraposition is obligatorily reconstructed for the purposes of binding theory. This would of course follow if extraposition, being PF-movement, were 'invisible' to interpretation in the first place.

19. Apart from focus/givenness, other information-structural categories have been proposed, sometimes in addition, sometimes as alternatives. Most notably among them are probably various notions of topic, both contrastive and plain (i.e., non-contrastive). There seems to be a consensus that the treatment of topics, in particular contrastive ones, requires additional categories, such as T(opic) or C(ontrastive) T(opic). These are either paradigmatic with categories like F(ocus) (i.e., a constituent is either F- or T-marked (or neither)), or cross-classify with them (e.g., F can be within a topic constituent or a non-topic constituent). For more on this see, e.g., Lambrecht (1994), and, on contrastive topics, Büring (1999, 2003), Kadmon (2001:Chapter 20) and references therein, and Steedman (2000b).

20. Recent experimental results by Katz and Selkirk (2011) suggest, however, that there are subtle differences between the realization of new material vis-à-vis the accenting of (associated) foci. If these are systematic, they would constitute another, strong argument in favor of separating the given/new dimension from the focus/background dimension.

21. See the Focus constraint in Truckenbrodt (1995b et seq.), from which I also adopt the assumption that FOCUS PROMINENCE is the *only* way in which focusing influences prosody (see also Section 23.4.4 below). An alternative formulation would be '...contains a phrasal stress.' Assuming that material outside of the focus is always given, it follows from (36b) that the main stress falls on a focus; assuming, on the other hand, that there can be new material outside of the focus, it would allow for non-nuclear foci, which may or may not be empirically correct, cf. (33) above – see again Katz and Selkirk (2011).

22. In relating [F]/[G] to stress, rather than directly to accents, I follow among others Ladd (1996) and Truckenbrodt (1995b). This is advantageous in particular to account for SECOND OCCURRENCE FOCUS phenomena (see the proposal in Büring 2008a), but also focus realization in other types of language (Truckenbrodt 1995b; also Büring 2009).

23. Cf. DEACCENTGIVEN in Féry and Samek-Lodovici (2006) among others. The principle given here is weaker in that it allows for

'ornamental accents' (Büring 2001a), i.e., pre-nuclear accents on given elements, which are widely attested.

24. See Rochemont (1986), Selkirk (1984, 1995), and Büring (2006) for a recent reassessment.

25. See Krifka (2006) for a recent overview of arguments for and against LF focus movement, Wagner (2005a) for a rather compelling, if complex, novel argument, and Wold (1996) for more critical remarks. Historically, the need to isolate focus and background for the purposes of interpretation may have added to the attractiveness of focus movement, since its output would provide a sentence neatly separated into focus and background. However both Structured Meaning approaches (e.g., Jacobs 1988, 1991/1992b, Krifka 1991/1992, 1992a, von Stechow 1981, 1982, 1989) and Alternative Semantics (Rooth 1985) have since provided frameworks for interpreting focus *in situ*. Indeed, all current theories that assume focus movement still assume one of these (usually Alternative Semantics) as part of focus interpretation, since in many cases the moved constituent must be bigger than the semantically interpreted focus (see Drubig 1994, Krifka 2006, for arguments). From a semantic point of view, then, focus movement does not simplify the theory.

26. The latter is not a logical necessity, though. In López's (2009) analysis of Catalan and other Romance languages, information structural interpretations are assigned in specific syntactic positions to whatever elements happen to move into or through those positions for whatever reasons. Thus, López's analysis resembles the cartographic ones in that it assumes fixed syntactic positions for particular information structural features (which in his case are not [F] but [anaphoric] and [contrast]), but unlike the cartographic approaches, it does not assume that information-structure features themselves trigger movement.

27. Since Vallduví (1990) builds upon the Government and Binding model of syntax, movements are generally assumed to be optional, with apparent 'purposes' achieved solely *ex post facto*.

28. Technically, the Focus Prosody Correspondence Principle assigns metrical strength to the [F]-marked constituent, while the Nuclear Stress Rule assigns metrical strength to the rightmost one. Where this results in two metrically strong sisters – something which is not allowed by grammar – p-movement of the right sister across the left sister results; see Zubizarreta (1998: Section 3.5).

29. And not just prosody, or rather, stress, as an aspect of syntax, as is the case in Zubizarreta's seminal work.

30. Example (40b) is (105) in Zubizarreta (1998:134), (a) and (c) courtesy of Kay González, p.c.

31. Example (42) from Szendrői (2001:54).

32. Mapping approaches share these general features with prosody-based approaches. In particular, since prosodic structure is aligned with

syntactic structure, as discussed in Section 23.2, it is often difficult to tease apart alignment with, say, a main stress position at the right edge of the intonational phrase (as in prosody-based approaches), and alignment with a syntactic domain, say the right edge of TP (as in a mapping approach).

33. Italian from Samek-Lodovici (2005:720, example (50)), Dutch from Costa (1998b:161, example (110a)), Spanish from Zubizarreta (1998:134, examples (104), (105b)). On object shift and its relation to information structure see among others Erteschik-Shir (2005), Hosono (2006), Mikkelsen (2011), and Vikner (2006); see also Section 5 3.1.

34. Note incidentally that (46) shows that G-movement, too, is not 'position bound' in Spanish; here, it moves one DP-internal argument across another.

35. A similar technique is employed in Kroch's work on synchronic intra-speaker variation, see Section 24.3.2 for discussion and references.

36. Examples of the former are the anti-movement constraints Stay in Samek-Lodovici (1996:698) and Büring (2001b:73) and *Structure in Szendrői (2001:154), as well as the canonical order constraints SO (for 'subject structurally above object') in Büring and Gutiérrez-Bravo (2001:44), Dative (precedes accusative) in Büring (2001b:93), and Animacy (animate precedes inanimates), Dative and Definiteness (definites precede indefinites) in Büring (2001b:78) (based on Grimshaw 1997, Müller 1999, Prince and Smolensky 1993, respectively).

37. Assuming there is string vacuous movement; see the discussion of Chomsky's (1986a) Vacuous Movement Hypothesis in Section 18.11.

Part VI

Syntax and the external interfaces

24
Microsyntactic variation

Sjef Barbiers

24.1 Introduction: the role of variation in generative grammar

Until the late 1980s dialects played a rather marginal role in generative syntactic research. A first sign that this was changing was the publication of a collection of articles in Benincà (1989), soon to be followed by more generative work on dialects, e.g., Haegeman (1992), Zwart (1993), Henry (1995), Holmberg and Platzack (1995), and Poletto (2000). The past ten years have seen an enormous increase in work and publications on dialect syntax within the generative framework, in particular in Europe, some of which even combine the generative and the dialectological traditions, such as the *Syntactic Atlas of the Dutch Dialects* (*SAND*; Barbiers et al. 2005, 2008).[1]

If we want to understand and appreciate this changing role of dialects in generative grammar (henceforth: GG) we have to consider the role of syntactic variation within GG more generally. Despite claims to the contrary (e.g., Evans and Levinson 2009), the inherent variability of language at all levels of linguistic analysis has been recognized from the outset of the generative enterprise, and developing an explicit theory of syntactic variation has always been one of the major goals of GG.

The central hypothesis of GG is that underlying the wealth of cross-linguistic syntactic variation there is a core of syntactic principles that are universal and innate, so-called Universal Grammar (UG). Language-specific grammars are the result of the interaction between these UG principles and the linguistic environment, i.e., the linguistic input during the process of language acquisition (see Chapters 3, 4, and 25). The task of GG is then to discover the set of universal principles that correctly describe the possible grammars and rule out impossible ones, and to explain the process of language acquisition on the basis of this. Thus, according to this hypothesis UG principles determine the variation space, and the child has to establish which language-specific grammar allowed by UG is his.

In this way, the UG hypothesis defines a clear program for research into syntactic variation. The goal is not so much to describe surface language variation, but to find the shared building principles underlying this variation. GG therefore abstracts away from more peripheral language variation that is the result from borrowings, historical residues, and inventions (Chomsky 1981:8). Being a theory of competence (knowledge of language), GG also abstracts away from actual language use (performance) (Chomsky 1965:10ff.). Finally, GG abstracts away from language-external factors that may determine language variation, such as social class, geographical origin, age, gender, style, register, and language contact. There is no such thing as English, or a Scottish dialect of English, since each individual language variety is variable within time, space, community, and even speaker. It is therefore not the goal of GG to provide a grammar of English or to describe and explain the geographic distribution of different dialectal properties. Rather, GG investigates idealized idiolects in the search for universal building principles, while fully acknowledging that these idealized idiolects do not surface in actual language use.[2]

Obviously, the precise demarcation of core grammar, periphery, competence, performance, and language-external factors is not pregiven. It involves complex systems that interact with each other and potentially determine (part of) each other's properties. Whenever a certain language phenomenon is put aside as irrelevant for the study of competence, we should be aware that this is a hypothesis and we should try to find arguments in support of or against this hypothesis.

Given the main goal of GG and the abstractions used to reach it, any idiolect can serve as its research object. There is no privileged position for any language variety. Consequently, generative linguists started by studying their own idiolects and those of the people surrounding them. As the GG enterprise originates in the US, in the beginning this mainly involved American English idiolects. Soon, other language varieties were added to the research domain, both Indo-European and non-Indo-European. As the in-depth description and analysis of each idiolect is a tremendous task, there was no reason to include dialects in the task, but also no reason to exclude them.[3] To understand why they nevertheless have become so relevant and prominent in recent years, we have to look at the locus of variation within the GG model.

24.2 The locus of variation in GG models

The abstract principles of UG define the variation space for possible languages. The locus of syntactic variation in GG models has changed over the years. We limit ourselves to three GG versions: (i) Transformational

Generative Grammar (TGG; Chomsky 1957, 1965); (ii) Principles and Parameters (P&P; Chomsky 1981); and (iii) The Minimalist Program (MP; Chomsky 1995c).

24.2.1 Transformational Generative Grammar (TGG)

TGG (see Chapter 2) had a lexicon, a set of universal categories (Noun, Verb, etc.), a set of rewrite rules to generate structural descriptions (modeling the constituent structure of a sentence), and a set of transformations operating on these structural descriptions. This is exemplified by the simplified grammar fragment in (1c) for the English sentences in (1a–b). The sentence *John has eaten the apple* is generated by applying the three rewrite rules in (1c) and associating each category with a matching element from the lexicon, giving rise to the structural description in (1d). The sentence in (1b) is then derived from this structural description by a transformational rule that preposes the object (1e).

(1) a. John has eaten the apple
    b. the apple John has eaten
    c. Grammar fragment
       Rewrite rules
       S → NP Aux VP
       VP → V NP
       NP → (Det) N
       Lexicon
       N = John
       N = apple
       V = eaten
       Aux = has
       Det = the
    d. Structure: [$_S$ [$_{NP}$ John] [$_{Aux}$ has] [$_{VP}$ [$_V$ eaten] [$_{NP}$ [$_{Det}$ the] [$_N$ apple]]]]
    e. **Transformation**
       NP1 Aux V NP2 → NP2 NP1 Aux V

Let us now compare the two English sentences in (1) with their Dutch equivalents in (2) to see where syntactic variation enters the formalism.

(2) a. Jan   heeft de   appel gegeten
       John has   the   apple eaten
    b. de   appel heeft Jan   gegeten
       the   apple has   John eaten

The fact that Dutch has OV (Object–Verb)order while English has VO (Verb–Object) can be captured if the rewrite rule for VP in Dutch is VP => NP V rather than VP => V NP. The fact that in Dutch subject–verb inversion has to take place when a constituent different from the subject is preposed can be captured by writing a different transformational rule: NP1 Aux

V NP2 => NP2 Aux NP1 V. The lexicon (including morphology) is also a source of variation with potentially syntactic consequences, e.g., the morphological difference between *eaten* and *ge-geten*.

24.2.2 Principles and Parameters (P&P)

In TGG, syntactic variation arises at every level and is rather unconstrained and, consequently, the model may be too powerful (cf. Chomsky 1981: Chapter 1, for some discussion). Perhaps more importantly, the TGG model did not capture two important generalizations: (i) the fact that phrase structure as generated by rewrite rules is highly similar across categories, as shown in work by Chomsky (1970a), Jackendoff (1977) and Stowell (1981 esp. Chapter 11); (ii) the fact that reordering transformations are highly similar across constructions and languages. This led to a more general phrase structure Theory called X-bar Theory (see Chapter 11), and a general reordering operation, Move α, and a model known as Principles and Parameters theory (Chomsky 1981).

X-bar Theory involves three general rewrite rules:

(3)   (i) XP $\rightarrow$ (Specifier) X'   or XP $\rightarrow$ X' (Specifier)
     (ii) X' $\rightarrow$ (Adjunct) X'   or X' $\rightarrow$ X' (Adjunct)
     (iii) X' $\rightarrow$ X (Complement) or X' $\rightarrow$ (Complement) X

Specifiers, adjuncts, and complements are XPs themselves. In each rule in (3), zero or one specifier, adjunct, or complement can be introduced and since (3ii) is recursive, the number of adjuncts is unrestricted. The rewrite rules in (3) would be able, e.g., to generate a phrase like *John's beautiful book about bats*, with *John* a specifier, *beautiful* an adjunct, and *about bats* a complement of the head *book*, and the XP as a whole a projection of the head *book*.

In this model, a certain amount of cross-linguistic variation can still be captured by the rewrite component. Linguistic categories and languages do not differ in the phrase structures they can project. Every projection has a head and a number of specifiers, adjuncts, and complements, in this hierarchical order. But the rules in (3) in fact say that identical hierarchical structures can be linearized in two ways. Thus (3iii) captures the VO-OV difference. We can say that X-Bar Theory is a principle that contains a linearization parameter, the value of which has to be set on the basis of language input. Notice that the P&P theory of phrase structure is still powerful, as the number of adjuncts is variable, the presence of specifiers and complements is optional, and the linearization can be different for each level. Thus, the model predicts for VPs all logically possible orders for S, V, and O (where S = subject = specifier; O = object = complement; V = verb): SVO, SOV, VSO, VOS, OSV, and OVS, which may be incorrect because OSV and OVS are typologically very rare.

Since the individual reordering transformations were replaced by one general reordering operation Move α, the model no longer allowed construction- or language-specific movement operations. Move α was in principle allowed everywhere. In cases where it was not, this was due to universal and language-specific constraints, many of which were still to be discovered. Questions of the type 'Why do some languages (e.g., English) have *wh*-movement, while others do not (e.g., Chinese)?' now become more urgent. There had to be some property in the grammar of Chinese such that the general rule Move α could not apply to *wh*-constituents. One answer proposed was that all languages have *wh*-movement, but languages differ with respect to the level at which this movement applies: in overt or in covert syntax, where covert syntax means LF, Logical Form, the level at which the semantic interpretation of a syntactic structure is determined (Huang 1982a; see Chapter 22, this volume). Thus, in addition to the linearization parameter in the phrase-structure rules, we have a second parameter taking care of word-order variation: parameterization of the level at which Move α applies.

The parameters in the P&P model have two important properties: (i) they are part of the syntactic module of the mental grammar. The syntactic module can thus be a source of syntactic variation, in addition to the lexicon and PF (the level of phonological form). (ii) Parameters in the P&P model can be global ('macroparameters'), applying to entire languages, not to individual construction types. Parameters were thought to capture clusters of syntactic differences. The best-known example of this is the null Subject Parameter (Rizzi 1982a; see Chapter 25, this volume), which was supposed to capture the clustering of null subjects, free inversion, the lack of *that*-trace effects, and the distribution of expletives.

24.2.3 The Minimalist Program (MP)
As has been shown many times (cf. Newmeyer 2004, 2005, Biberauer 2008b for recent discussion), the Null Subject Parameter cannot be maintained in view of the many counterexamples showing that these properties do not cluster cross-linguistically. Also, it is clear that the Null-Subject Parameter cannot be a global 'macroparameter' applying to an entire language, as there are language varieties in which null subjects are only possible with one member of the verbal paradigm. For example, in Frisian and Groningen dialects (North-Eastern Dutch) only the second person singular subject can be silent (cf. *SAND* Volume I, map 41a). Thus, parameterization must apply at the level of the lexical specification of individual functional items. Other parameters underwent the same fate (cf. Haspelmath 2008), with the possible exception of the polysynthesis parameter proposed by Baker (1996).[4]

In the next stage of GG, the Minimalist Program (Chomsky 1995c, 2005), the idea of global parameters is therefore abandoned. Also, it is hypothesized that there is no parameterization in the syntactic module of the mental grammar. This module consists of a set of universal building principles and is not a source of cross-linguistic variation or intra-linguistic optionality. X-bar Theory is further reduced to the operation of Merge (essentially: combine two phrase markers). Derivations are from bottom to top, and binary branching, following Kayne (1984). Move α is an instance of Merge, namely a case in which a subpart of a phrase marker is remerged with that phrase marker. In the antisymmetric variant of MP (Kayne 1994), all movement, and, more generally, all instances of Merge, are leftward and upward and the Universal Base Hypothesis is adopted, according to which all languages have the same underlying structure.

The consequence of this set of very restrictive building principles is that all word-order variation must be the result of movement, because there is no freedom in the phrase-structure building component. Also, cross-linguistic differences in word order cannot be explained in terms of movement parameters (e.g., [± move]), because this would involve a parameter in the syntactic component, and, by hypothesis, such parameters do not exist. Similarly, intra-linguistic optionality in word order cannot be attributed to such movement parameters. The task of MP is therefore to reduce apparent differences in movement to either the lexicon (the 'Borer-Chomsky conjecture'; see also Chapters 2, 4, and 25) or to the level of phonological Spell-out (PF).

In this way, MP considerably reduces the learning task, as all syntactic principles are universal and nothing about syntax has to be learnt. The lexicon has to be learnt anyway and is therefore a source of variation. Variation at PF has to be admitted as well. For example, it is well known that certain parts of a syntactic structure can remain silent under syntactic and semantic equivalence (see Chapter 19).

An example of this is the Dutch pair in (4a–b):

(4) Context: Do you want that book?
    a. nee, dat   heb ik gisteren   al   uitgelezen
        no   that   have I yesterday already read
    b. nee, Ø   heb ik gisteren   al   uitgelezen
    c. nee, gisteren heb ik dat   al   uitgelezen
        no   yesterday have I that   already read
    d. *nee, gisteren heb ik Ø   al   uitgelezen

The sentences in (4a–b) mean the same, and it can be shown that their syntactic properties are the same. In particular, although there is no audible constituent in the position preceding the finite verb in (4b), it is impossible to prepose another constituent (e.g. *gisteren* 'yesterday') in this sentence, just like in (4a), while preposing is normally possible in Dutch when the position before the finite verb is empty, as (4c) illustrates. Thus, in (4b) *dat* 'that' is syntactically present but phonetically empty. The task defined by MP is then to find out under which conditions a constituent can remain silent. In the example in (4) one condition seems to be that the silent constituent has to be in the position preceding the finite verb. In other positions, *dat* 'that' cannot be silent (4d).

In sum, word-order variation in MP is thought to be reducible to the lexicon and PF. To support this hypothesis, we have to look for lexical properties that play a role in word-order variation, reveal the mechanisms by which they do this, and show how this explains cross-linguistic and intra-linguistic variation.[5] For the level of PF, we need to develop a theory of silence that captures the distribution of silent constituents and also explains linguistic variation. Alternatively, we can try to falsify the Minimalist hypothesis by showing that there are cases of variation in the syntactic module that cannot be reduced to the lexicon or PF.

Under a slightly looser interpretation, the Minimalist hypothesis leaves some space for variation in the syntactic module even given the hypothesis that there is one and the same set of invariant syntactic principles for all language varieties. If these principles are not parameterized, then variation in the syntactic component can arise if we assume that a particular language variety need not exploit all the building principles given by UG. This is very close to the approach advocated in Bouchard (2003). Bouchard observes that cross-linguistically there are four ways to express a relation between two constituents: (i) head marking: a property of the dependent is marked on the head, e.g., subject agreement on a verb; (ii) dependent marking: a property of the head is marked on the dependent argument, e.g., case marking of an argument by a verb; (iii) juxtaposition: two constituents are placed next to each other to express their relation (in which case the order has to be kept constant to keep the relation constant), e.g., VO order in English; (iv) superimposition, e.g. intonation on a word to express grammatical function in a tone language. A particular language can pick one or more of these solutions but it does not have to choose all of them.

Crucially, in Bouchard's view the four available building principles are not part of UG, they are the only four logically possible ways to meet the interface requirements of expressing linearly the hierarchical relations between constituents. It is an open question, also in MP (see in particular Chomsky 2005), whether the invariant syntactic principles should be identified with the set of innate UG principles specific to the language faculty, as hypothesized in the TGG and P&P models, or whether they are not specific to language but follow from interface conditions.

Either way, these approaches are still very close to the P&P model and MP is usually taken to be a natural continuation of P&P. There is an important consequence, however. In P&P, dialectal variation was often implicitly considered to be superficial and hence non-parametric (cf. Newmeyer 2004 for discussion). The dialects of one family would have largely the same grammar but differ in the details of some language-specific rules and constraints, their lexicons, and surface realizations. The differences between two genetically more remote language varieties would be the result of different settings of global parameters, i.e., the two languages would have the same UG but different grammars due to these different parameter settings. For the most elaborated version of this view, see Baker (1996, 2001, 2008a).

In MP, on the other hand, both variation between closely related dialects and between genetically more remote languages is the result of differences in the lexicon and PF. In this view, there is no principled difference between microvariation (the differences within one dialect family, say the dialects of English), mesovariation (the systematic differences between, say, the English dialect family and the Dutch dialect family), and macrovariation (the differences between genetically remote languages, say English and Japanese). Meso- and macrovariation are taken to be a cumulation of micro-differences at the lexical level and PF (cf. Kayne 2005). Huge and global effects, such as the differences between uniformly head-first languages (English) and head-final languages (Japanese) should then be the result of the (abstract) features of elements that can affect the entire grammar.[6] The features of functional elements, such as Tense, Determiner, and Complementizer are good candidates for this. Commonly, in MP the morphosyntactic feature specifications of functional elements (as opposed to lexical elements) is taken to be the main source of syntactic variation and they are therefore the central research topic in MP.

24.2.4 The relation between morphosyntactic features and word order

The idea that there is a relation between the morphosyntactic feature specification of functional elements in the lexicon and word-order differences goes back to at least Pollock (1989). Pollock starts out with Emonds's (1976) observation that English and French differ with respect to verb movement (see Chapters 12 and 14). Both languages have three positions for verbs in the clause, but in English only auxiliaries can move from their base position (position 3 in (5)) to the two higher positions. This is illustrated in (5).

(5) V:

		1		2		3	
a.		il		<mange>	souvent	<*mange>	une pomme
b.		he		<*eats>	often	<eats>	an apple
c.		he		do-es	not	eat	an apple
d.		il		a	souvent	mangé	une pomme
e.		he		has	often	eaten	an apple
f.				to	often	have eaten	an apple
g.	Mange-t-il				souvent		une pomme?
h.	A-t-	il			souvent	mangé	une pomme?
i.	*Eats	he			often		an apple?
j.	Has	he			often	eaten	an apple?

The position of the main verb in French depends on its morphology (5a–d). A finite main verb precedes OFTEN (position 2), while a participial main verb follows it (position 3). In English, position 2 is also only accessible for finite verbs (5c,e,f), but there is an additional restriction: only auxiliaries can go there (5b,c,e). Only verb forms that can occur in position 2 can also occur in position 1 (assuming that the subject stays put): French (5g–h) are both possible, but in English again only finite auxiliaries can occur in position 1 (5i–j).

Position 2 has been identified as the position where finiteness features, i.e., tense and agreement, are generated. Let us say that there is a functional element I (= T + Agr) in that position. Some evidence for this is (5c) if we analyze it as follows: the finiteness features in position 2 cannot be associated with the main verb in position 3 when negation intervenes. To get a grammatical sentence, a dummy element DO is inserted that can host the morphosyntactic features of I.

The difference between French and English is then, according to Pollock, that finite I is strong in French and weak in English, where [strong] correlates with a rich agreement paradigm (French -*e(s)*, -*ons*, -*ez*) and [weak] with a poor agreement paradigm (English -*s*). If finite agreement is strong, both lexical and auxiliary verbs move to I. If finite agreement is weak, only auxiliaries move to I. This difference between lexical and auxiliary verbs follows from a difference in the theta-role assigning properties of these verbs.[7]

24.2.5 The Minimalist Program for dialect research

The above comparison of verb positions in English and French keeps the number and hierarchy of positions for the verb constant and attributes intra- and cross-linguistic variation in the positioning of the verb to the application of movement: from V(erb) (position 3), to I(nflection) (position 2), to C(omplementizer) (position 1). The hypothesis is that V-movement can apply if a language has rich inflection. This raises a number of general and specific questions:

(i) Why would there be a relation between rich inflection and verb displacement?
(ii) What is the relevant definition of rich inflection (what kind of and how many distinctions in the verbal paradigm)?
(iii) What is the role of paradigms?
(iv) Does the implication only work in one direction (if V-movement, then rich agreement) or also in the other (if rich agreement, then V-movement)?
(v) Which morphosyntactic features play a role in agreement phenomena?
(vi) If function words are feature bundles, how are these feature bundles organized and specified (binary or unary features, linear array of features or hierarchy)?
(vii) What is the relation between a feature specification and phonological spell-out?

(viii) Is it possible that languages vary with respect to which positions are available, e.g., is it possible that C and/or I is missing in a particular language? If so, this would be another case of variation under a looser interpretation of the Minimalist Hypothesis: all languages draw from the same set of categories and syntactic building principles, but not all languages use the full set. Conceivably, a language could dispense with I while all other syntactic properties would be universal.

(ix) A variant of (viii): Are there languages that fuse two positions into one, e.g., C and I are one position or I and V are one position?

Dialects provide an interesting testing ground for all of these questions. As dialects show minimal differences in morphosyntactic feature specification and spell-out, while most other grammatical properties are identical, the effect of such minimal differences on, e.g., word order, doubling, and unpronounced constituents can be more directly investigated. As before, there is no principled difference between comparing French and English and comparing a number of closely related dialects. The only difference is that in the latter case the number of differences between the dialects is smaller than the number of differences between English and French, such that it becomes easier to detect which properties of a language variety depend on each other.

Verb placement is a domain that is understood well enough to make more precise and detailed investigation of microdifferences possible and necessary. Variation in verb placement will be taken up in the cases studies discussed in Section 24.3. The relevance of morphosyntactic agreement for displacement is, however, not restricted to the domain of verb placement. The general hypothesis is that movement is only possible if there is agreement between the moving element and the functional element triggering the movement. This agreement relation can be abstract, such that richness of the phonological exponent of an Agree relationship is not required for movement to be possible. Some examples outside the domain of verb movement include subjects that move under the condition that there is agreement between the subject DP and I, *wh*-elements that move if there is agreement between C and wh, etc.[8] For such domains as well, dialects provide an ideal testing ground, as we would like to know which morphosyntactic features play a role in agreement phenomena, whether agreement must be full agreement or can also be partial, and what the consequences are of minimal differences in feature specification/agreement for movement possibilities.

24.3 Microsyntactic variation: two case studies

A general theory of syntactic variation should at least account for the phenomena in (6); the list is by no means exhaustive. These types of variation occur both at the micro-, the meso- and the macrolevel. In view of the goal of this chapter we will discuss a number of microvariational cases.

(6) Types of syntactic variation
- A. Variation in word order
   Examples: (i) In Icelandic, the finite verb in embedded clauses precedes negation, while in Mainland Scandinavian it follows it (Holmberg and Platzack 1995). (ii) In German and Dutch dialects, the finite verb is in second position (V2) in root clauses (i.e., C or I, see below for discussion), but in clause-final position (i.e., V) in embedded clauses (Paardekooper 1961, den Besten 1989b). (iii) In German and Dutch dialects, verbs clustering at the end of the clause show various positional options, from two for two verbs to four for three verbs (Wurmbrand 2006, Barbiers 2005b).
   Analyses
   (a) [± movement]; (b) movement in overt syntax vs. (invisible) movement at LF; (c) copying in Syntax and spell-out options at PF, i.e., in base position or landing-site (Bobaljik 2002a).
- B. Variation in agreement
   Examples: (i) The agreement on finite verbs in embedded clauses in some eastern varieties of Dutch is identical to the agreement on the finite verb in subject-initial V2 clauses but distinct from finite agreement in non-subject-initial V2 clauses, which in turn is identical to agreement on the finite complementizer (Zwart 1993). (ii) The agreement paradigm of a dialect shows syncretisms different from the ones in the standard language.
   Analyses
   (a) Cross-linguistic differences in morphosyntactic feature specification (Adger 2006). (b) Cross-linguistic differences in the spell-out of morphosyntactic features (strong version of Distributed Morphology; Halle and Marantz 1993).
- C. Variation in spell-out I: morphosyntactic doubling
   Some examples include *wh*-word doubling, subject pronoun doubling, comparative doubling, focus particle doubling (cf. Barbiers et al. 2008 for an overview).
   Analyses
   (a) Multiple spell-out of chain positions (Nunes 2004, Barbiers et al. 2009); (b) Partial movement from big XPs (Kayne 1994, Poletto and Pollock (2004); (c) Doubling as agreement (cf. Barbiers 2008a).
- D. Variation in spell-out II: silent constituents
   Example: In many languages (e.g., Italian) subject pronouns can be silent. It has been suggested that, at least for the Italian-like subset of pro-drop languages, there is a relation with rich agreement (cf. the papers in Biberauer 2008b).
   Analyses
   (a) pro (in subject position) locally identified by rich agreement (Rizzi 1982a); (b) Agreement morpheme fulfills the subject role and makes a subject pronoun superfluous (Barbosa 1997); (c)

Morphosyntactic features of the silent category are underlyingly present but can be left unpronounced under local recoverability, e.g., spec–head agreement, head–head government, or chain government, (Rizzi 1986a).

E. Variation in pied-piping
Example: When a constituent needs to undergo movement it may or may not pied-pipe the constituent that it is part of. An example is the WHAT FOR split construction found in German and Dutch in which either WHAT alone or the entire constituent containing WHAT (e.g., WHAT FOR BOOK) is fronted (cf. Leu 2008, Chapter 5 and references cited there).

Analyses
(a) Pied-piping: the movement is triggered by the features of the subconstituent, and this subconstituent drags along the containing constituent (e.g., Koopman and Szabolcsi 2000); (b) Partial copying vs. full copying. In partial copying only the subconstituent is copied and spelled out in a higher position, not giving rise to pied-piping. In full copying, the entire constituent is copied, giving rise to pied-piping.

In the remainder of this chapter we will discuss two case studies to demonstrate the kind of questions that the various types of syntactic variation raise, the kind of analyses that have been proposed to capture these types of variation, and the analysis we arrive at if we try to reduce the variation to the Lexicon and PF.

24.3.1 Finite verb placement and complementizer agreement in dialects of Dutch

The Minimalist analysis of the verb placement contrasts in French and English discussed above contained the following ingredients:[9]

(7) (i) All languages are right-branching, i.e., uniformly head-first.
  (ii) All movement is upward (and leftward).
  (iii) All languages have the same base structure (set and hierarchy of functional projections).
  (iv) This structure contains (at least) three verbal positions; V(erb) is the base position; I(nflection) is a position in the middle field containing inflectional features; C(omplementizer) is a position in the left periphery. The hierarchy is $[_{CP}\, C\, [_{IP}\, I\, [_{VP}\, V]]]$
  (v) Whether a verb occurs in V, I, or C depends on its morphology: only finite verbs can go to I and C (and English has the further restriction that these finite verbs must be auxiliaries).
  (vi) English main verbs cannot go to I and C because of a link between weak agreement and thematic opacity.

(vii) Arguments (subject, object, indirect object) originate in VP. The subject moves to SpecIP to check its case and phi-features.
(viii) A fronted constituent can move to SpecCP.

The tense/agreement suffix in I seems to attract V-to-I. How exactly this works is a central issue in MP. Very interesting microcomparative work on this has been done in the Scandinavian area.[10] On the basis of contrasts such as between Icelandic (rich agreement and V-to-I) and Danish (poor agreement and no V-to-I), it was hypothesized that rich agreement was the cause of V-to-I movement (Rohrbacher 1999). Fine-grained comparison of closely related varieties of Scandinavian showed that this hypothesis was incorrect. In the absence of consensus on what counts as rich agreement, the most convincing arguments against the rich agreement hypothesis come from language varieties that have V-to-I but no agreement at all, as is the case in the Kronoby dialect of Swedish.[11]

Bobaljik (2002b) proposes that the following one-way implication holds. If a language has rich inflection then it has verb movement to Infl.[12] This implication allows for languages that have V-to-I but no rich inflection. Verbal inflection is rich only if finite verbs may bear multiple distinct inflectional morphemes, e.g., tense and person/number agreement, and this morphological richness is a sign that the language has a split IP (AgrP dominating TP). Morphologically poor languages have either IP or split IP.[13] The property of having a split IP correlates, according to Bobaljik and Thráinsson (1998), with various other syntactic properties, such as multiple subject positions and transitive expletive constructions. Clearly, parameterization is taken here to apply to the syntactic module, as language varieties can differ with respect to the functional projections they have in the clause.

Let us now see if this analysis can be applied to Dutch. Since finite verbs in Standard Dutch show multiple distinct inflections (e.g., *wandel-de-n* walk.PAST.PL), we expect them to have V-to-I as well. As is well known, Standard Dutch is an asymmetric V2 language. Suppose this would mean that the finite verb is in C in main clauses, in complementary distribution with the complementizer (den Besten 1989b) and that the finite verb is in final position (V) in embedded clauses, just like all non-finite verbs.

(8)   C   V

		C		V
a.	Jan	heeft	een appel	gegeten
	John	has	an apple	eaten
b.	Jan	eet	een appel	
	John	eats	an apple	
c.		dat Jan	een appel	eet
		that John	an apple	eats
d.		dat Jan	een appel	heeft gegeten
		that John	an apple	has eaten

These sentences do not provide any evidence for the availability of an I-position in the middle field of Standard Dutch. It is also impossible to deduce the existence of I by using the diagnostic of adverbs with a designated and rigid position, like OFTEN and negation in English and French, as these adverbs all occur between C and V and do not tell us anything about I.

This state of affairs has led some researchers to conclude either that Standard Dutch does not have an I position or that I and V are fused, or that I is to the right of VP in Dutch, selecting VP as its lefthand sister, as in [$_{CP}$ C [$_{IP}$ [$_{VP}$ V] I]] (Weerman 1989, Koster 2008). Both proposals give up the Universal Base Hypothesis (UBH) in its strongest form, as the first claims that there is no I position in Standard Dutch, while the second claims that there is no uniform branching direction. The first is still compatible with the looser interpretation of the UBH and Minimalism, because it draws from the same set of invariable syntactic building blocks but does not exploit the full set. The second proposal retains the idea of a universal hierarchy, but has to allow parameterization in the syntactic module of the grammar by allowing mixed right- and left-branching structures.

It is possible to find evidence for I in the middle field if we use different diagnostics and also take Dutch dialects into account. As Travis (1984) and Zwart (1993) have shown, there is a remarkable contrast between the distribution of weak subject pronouns and other weak pronouns in all varieties of Dutch. Whereas weak subject pronouns can occur in claus-initial position, weak object, indirect object pronouns, etc. cannot.

(9)

		C	I	V	
a.			je/jij you.W/you.S	hebt have	een appel gegeten an apple eaten
b.	jou/*je you.S/you.W	hebben have	ze/zij they.W/they.S		een appel gegeven an apple given
c.			't/Dat it.W/that.S	bevalt ons pleases us	goed well
d.	dat/*'t that.S/it.W	heb have	ik I		niet gezien not seen

This contrast can be captured if we assume that fronted constituents go to SpecCP, that this position in declarative clauses is associated with stress and that weak pronouns cannot bear stress. Weak subject pronouns cannot be in SpecCP, so they must be in SpecIP. It then follows that the finite verb in clauses like (9a) and (9c) must be in I, and that subject initial clauses are IPs, not CPs. Only in sentences in which some constituent other than the subject has been fronted, as in (9b,d), is the finite verb in C, contrary to the analysis in (8).

The Dutch dialects provide us with a second argument in favor of an I position in the middle field (Zwart 1993). Some eastern Dutch dialects have a double agreement paradigm. In subject-initial clauses, first person plural agreement on the verb is -*t* and cannot be -*e* (10a-b). In the inverted order, it is the other way around: first person plural agreement on the verb is -*e* and cannot be -*t* (10c-10d). Strikingly, the same -*e* ending is found on the complementizer (10e). The relevant eastern Dutch dialects are complementizer agreement dialects, in which the complementizer agrees with the subject for first person plural. These facts follow immediately if we associate the -*e* ending with the C-position, such that complementizers and inverted verbs have it but verbs in subject-initial clauses do not. In positions other than C, the 1PL finite verb has a -*t* ending (10a,10e).[14]

(10)   C   SpecIP   I   V

a.   wij   speul-t
                     we   play.1PL
b.   *wij   speul-e
                     we   play.1PL
c.   *speul-t   wij
         play.1PL   we
d.   speul-e   wij
         play.1PL   we
e.   dat-e   wij   speul-t
         that.1PL   we   play.1PL

The assumption that there is a relation between a particular suffix and a particular position is crucial here. It implies that the feature specifications underlying these two suffixes must be distinct. PF has to know that 1PL in I is spelled out as -*t* whereas it is spelled out as -*e* in C. Strictly speaking then, the glossing in (10) is not correct. A possibly better feature specification is PL for -*t* and 1PL for C. An important conclusion is that variation in agreement depending on position (i.e., variation of type B) is reduced here to variation in underlying feature specification.

The third argument in favor of an I position in the middle field also comes from the dialects and from child language (Barbiers and van Koppen 2006). In a number of western dialects of Dutch we find the phenomenon of subject pronoun metathesis. The subject pronoun occurs between the stem of the verb and past-tense inflection (11a; *SAND* Volume II, map 45b). This also happens with number agreement (11b; de Schutter 1994). The same phenomenon has been observed in Standard Dutch child language (11c; cf. also Flikweert 1994).[15]

(11) a. gisteren   wandel-**die**-de   door   het   park
        yesterday   walked-he-PAST   through   the   park
        'yesterday he walked through the park'
     b. nu   ga-**me**-n   naar   huis
        now   go-we.PL   to   house
        'now we go home'

c. dan   noem-**ik**-te jou Sinterklaas
   then   call-I-PAST   you St-Nicholas
   'then I would call you Sinterklaas'

If we want to apply the analysis for verb positions sketched above, we only need one additional assumption, namely that in certain language varieties a suffix can be stranded under movement of its host.[16] In (12), all other constituents are in their usual, cross-linguistically well-motivated positions, such that the Universal Base Hypothesis in its strongest form can be maintained. The past-tense and plural suffixes remain in their base positions. The word-order difference between Standard Dutch and child and western Dutch is not the result of differences in the number of movement steps or movement targets, but of the amount of material that is carried along in a movement operation, i.e., pied-piping.

(12)   **SpecCP**   C   SpecIP   I   V

   a. gisteren   wandel   die   -de   door het park
       yesterday   walk   he   PAST   through the park
   b. nu   ga   me   -n   naar huis
       now   go   we   PL   to house
   c. dan   noem   ik   -te   jou   Sinterklaas
       then   call   I   PAST   you   St-Nicholas

We know independently that languages differ with respect to how much structure they keep together under movement. For example, degree *wh*-constituents in Standard Dutch cannot be split under movement, although this is possible in Dutch child language and in languages like Italian (13a–c; van Kampen 1997, see also Chapter 11, note 69). We also find other cases of suffix stranding in Dutch child language (13d; Barbiers and van Koppen 2006).

(13) a. Hoe lang denk je dat ik   ben?   (Standard Dutch)
      b. Hoe   denk je dat ik lang ben? (Child/*Standard Dutch)
          how tall think you that I   tall am
          'How tall do you think I am?'
      c. Quanto   è   alto?   (Italian)
          how   is (he) tall
          'How tall is he?'
      d. Hoeveel   is   het -ste?   (Child /*Standard Dutch)
          how-many is   it SUPERL
          'What day is it?'

The question now arises if pied-piping differences are an instance of parameterization at the level of syntax. As was noted above, the strongest version of the Minimalist hypothesis does not allow any parameterization in that module and we need to establish if subject pronoun metathesis is a counterexample to this hypothesis. It is only a counterexample if pied-piping differences are technically modeled as cases of subextraction (or partial copying, in which case the trace is a copy), as was common in the Principles and Parameters approach. This is illustrated in (14a) for *wh*-subextraction. Under a Copy and Delete approach, pied-piping differences can be handled at PF if the Delete operation takes place at PF (Bobaljik 2002a). This is shown in (14b–c). The deletion operation would be obligatory to make sure that two copies are not identical at PF, as this would prevent them from linearization (Nunes 2004).

(14) a. wat$_i$ heb   je   [$_{DP}$ t$_i$ [voor boek]]
      what   have   you   for   book
      'What kind of book do you have?'
   b. [wat   [voor   boek]]   heb   je   [wat   [voor boek]]
      what   for   book   have   you   what   for   book
                                                                   (Copying in Syntax)
   c. [wat   [~~voor~~   ~~boek~~]]   heb   je   [~~wat~~   [voor boek]]
      what   for   book   have   you   what   for   book
                                                                     (Deletion at PF)

This analysis does not directly carry over to subject pronoun metathesis in varieties of Dutch. If the fully inflected verb is generated in V, following the lexicalist hypothesis of Chomsky (1970a), and subsequently copied to I and C, the representation in (15) is the input for PF.

(15) [$_{CP}$ nu [$_{C'}$ wandel-de [$_{IP}$ die [$_{I'}$ wandel-de [$_{VP}$ door het park [$_V$ wandel-de]]]]]]
      now   walk-ed   he   walk-ed   through the park   walk-ed

PF-deletion derives various orders, among others (16a–c), only one of which is attested (16c).

(16) a. *[$_{CP}$ nu [$_{C'}$ wandel-de [$_{IP}$ die [$_{I'}$ ~~wandel-de~~ [$_{VP}$ door het park [$_V$ ~~wandel-de~~]]]]]]
   b. *[$_{CP}$ nu [$_{C'}$ ~~wandel-de~~ [$_{IP}$ die [$_{I'}$ ~~wandel-de~~ [$_{VP}$ door het park [$_V$ wandel-de]]]]]]
   c. [$_{CP}$ nu [$_{C'}$ wandel-de [$_{IP}$ die [$_{I'}$ ~~wandel-de~~ [$_{VP}$ door het park [$_V$ ~~wandel-de~~]]]]]]

Clearly, it is possible to make additional stipulations to rule out the ungrammatical (16a–b). The point is, however, that no such stipulations are necessary for the derivation in (12), which is presented in more detail in (17). The situation where the past-tense suffix is stranded in V simply does not arise because this suffix is generated in I, not in V.

(17)   (i) **Base order**   **(all Dutch varieties)**
                                          [$_{IP}$ die [$_{I'}$ -de   [$_{VP}$ ... [$_{V'}$ wandel]]]]
                                                  he   PAST   walk
   (ii) **V-to-I**   **(all Dutch varieties)**
                                         [$_{IP}$ die [$_{I'}$ wandel-de   [$_{VP}$ ... [$_{V'}$ ~~wandel~~]]]]
   (iii) **I-to-C**   **(Standard Dutch)**
                      [$_{CP}$ nu [$_{C'}$ wandel-de   [$_{IP}$ die [$_{I'}$ ~~wandel-de~~ [$_{VP}$ ... [$_{V'}$ wandel-]]]]]]
   (iv) **I-to-C**   **(western Dutch dialects and child Dutch)**
                      [$_{CP}$ nu [$_{C'}$ wandel   [$_{IP}$ die [$_{I'}$ ~~wandel-de~~ [$_{VP}$ ... [$_{V'}$ ~~wandel-~~]]]]]]

Thus we see that the dialectal phenomenon of subject pronoun metathesis provides an interesting argument against the lexicalist hypothesis according to which inflected words are inserted in the structure as a whole and in favor of the hypothesis that inflected words are derived by movement in the syntactic module where the lexical host moves and attaches to the left of the suffix that is generated higher up in the structure (cf. Baker 1985).

As was noted in Section 24.3 under (6), Distributive Morphology (DM; Halle and Marantz 1993) offers an alternative way of handling variation such as subject pronoun metathesis at PF. In DM, it is not fully inflected words or even separate functional and lexical morphemes that are merged in syntax, but rather morphosyntactic feature bundles. These morphosyntactic feature bundles are combined into hierarchical structures in syntax and then delivered to the morphological module. That module, applying before PF spell-out, allows several operations, including Local Dislocation (or Lowering) and Reduplication and Deletion. Harris and Halle (2005) show that certain metathesis phenomena in Spanish can be captured in such a model. Let me briefly illustrate this analysis and then ask if this also works for subject pronoun metathesis in Dutch dialects.

Harris and Halle discuss the data in (18), where 'normative' means normative European Spanish and 'alternative' means colloquial Latin-American Spanish varieties.

(18) Normative   Alternative
   a. vénda-n lo   b. vénda-n lo-n
      sell.PL   it   c. vénda-∅ lo-n

In Harris and Halle's account, (18b–c) are the result of partial reduplication, i.e., reduplication + deletion, as illustrated in (19).

(19) Syntax →   Reduplication in Morphology → Deletion in Morphology
     vénda n lo   vénda n lo n lo   (i) vénda n lo n l̶o̶
                                               (ii) vénda n lo n l̶o̶

This analysis elegantly derives the two alternatives and would be able to derive Dutch subject pronoun metathesis. After reduplication, *wandel-de-die* 'walk-ed-he' would be *wandel-de-die-de-die* 'walk-ed-he-ed-he'. After deletion of the first *-de* and the second *-die* we would have *wandel-die-de* 'walk-he-ed', which is fully parallel to the derivation of (19ii). However, this Distributed Morphology analysis predicts the order *wandel-de-die-de* 'walk-ed-he-ed' to be possible in the relevant Dutch varieties (parallel to (19i) and if deletion is optional, the order *wandel-de-die-de-die* 'walk-ed-he-ed-he' as well. Neither of these two orders are attested in the Dutch language area. It seems that the operations allowed in the Morphological Structure module in Distributed Morphology need to be restricted in a principled way to prevent them from overgenerating.

In conclusion, the analysis of subject pronoun metathesis in Dutch proposed above in terms of variation in pied-piping is, for the time being, empirically the most adequate and theoretically the most economical. At first sight, this account has two disadvantages. First, we seem to have to allow parameterization for pied-piping in the syntactic module, i.e., certain varieties allow for suffixes that can optionally be stranded when their host moves. This is a complex, not very elegant type of parameterization. Since it involves excorporation from a morphological word it violates lexical integrity (Lapointe 1980) and it is hard to distinguish from a violation of the Head Movement Constraint (see note 9). Reduction of this variation to the lexicon is possible if we assume that in the relevant varieties of Dutch the past-tense morpheme is lexically specified as a word, not as a suffix.[17]

Second, the proposed analysis crucially assumes that the past-tense morpheme and agreement morphemes are generated in I and thus abandons strict lexicalism.[18] This must then be the case in embedded clauses as well, which is consistent with the fact that in the double agreement varieties of eastern Dutch the plural inflection on the finite verb in embedded clauses is identical to the plural inflection on the verb in subject-initial main clauses but distinct from the plural inflection on the finite verb in inversion contexts and on the finite complementizer. This forces the conclusion that after V has moved from V to I, remnant movement of the complement of I to the left of I takes place, as was proposed first in Hallmann (2000).[19]

We have seen in this section that all types of syntactic variation listed in (6) are relevant for the analysis of finite verb placement in varieties of Dutch. Variation in agreement plays a role in eastern varieties of Dutch that have a double agreement paradigm. One paradigm was shown to be associated with the C-position, while the other was associated with the I-position. If we assume that the relevant morphemes are specified in the lexicon for C and I relatedness this difference can be reduced to the lexicon. The variation in word order found in subject pronoun metathesis constructions was shown to not be the result of parameterization of movement operations, but rather to variation in pied-piping options. This variation was in turn reduced to the lexicon by the assumption that in some varieties of Dutch the past-tense suffix is specified as a word, not as a suffix. Variation in morphosyntactic doubling was shown to arise by copying in the syntactic module or by reduplication in the morphological module. Such configurations also give rise to variation in silent categories, as copies can or must be (partially) deleted. How doubling and deletion are restricted could not be addressed here, but it seems to be clear that local recoverability of morphosyntactic features plays an important role, where 'local' means under spec–head agreement or in a chain.

The case study in this section also clearly shows why it is important to take dialectal variation into account. While the contrast in the distribution of weak subject pronouns in Standard Dutch provides us with only one piece of evidence supporting the hypothesis that Dutch has an I position in the middle field just like English and French, the study of double agreement paradigms and subject pronoun metathesis in certain Dutch dialects provides us with two more converging arguments.

24.3.2 Word order variation in three-verb clusters in dialects of Dutch

The second case study involves constructions of the type given in (20), where three verbs line up at the end of the clause.

(20) ik vind dat iedereen goed moet kunnen zwemmen
      I find that everyone well must can.INF swim.INF
      'in my opinion everyone should be able to swim well'

The 267 dialects of Dutch investigated between 2000 and 2005 (cf. Barbiers and Bennis 2007) show word-order variation in these three-verb clusters, which depends on the type of auxiliaries in the cluster and the geographic area. The goals of this case study are: (i) to show that the theoretical questions listed in Section 24.2.5, including the source of word-order variation, the trigger and grammar level of movement, and the relation with universal syntactic principles, arise in this domain as well, but in a different way. (ii) To discuss the interaction between language-internal and language-external factors determining syntactic variation and the division of labor between GG on the one hand and sociolinguistics and dialect geography on the other. (iii) To demonstrate the added value of large-scale microcomparative research involving large numbers of closely related dialects.[20]

The descriptive generalizations on Dutch three-verb clusters are given in (21), where the left-hand column gives the hierarchy of three different types of verb clusters and the other six columns give the possible linear orders.

(21)

	1-2-3	1-3-2	3-1-2	2-1-3	2-3-1	3-2-1
Type A: 1.MUST 2.CAN 3.SWIM	yes	yes	yes	no	no	yes
Type B: 1.MUST-2.HAVE-3.MADE	yes	yes	yes	no	no	yes
Type C: 1.IS-2.GONE-3.SWIM[21]	yes	yes	no	no	yes	yes

The geographic distribution of these linear orders is given in *SAND* Volume II (maps 17a,b, 18a). Some rough generalizations are that the 3-2-1 order for all three cluster types is typical for northern Dutch dialects (including Frisian dialects), the 2-3-1 order, only possible for cluster type C, is typical for southern Dutch, in particular the Dutch dialects in Belgium. The 1-3-2 order with cluster type A is typical for a narrow zone along the eastern border of the language area, while the same order for clusters of type B is typical for the Dutch dialects spoken in Belgium. The maps in *SAND* Volume II also show that many speakers across the entire language area allow two, three, or even four linear orders for each cluster type, raising the question whether their mental grammar allows optionality, in violation of the Minimalist hypothesis.

Assuming again uniform right-branching (head-initial) structure, the base order of all of these clusters is as in (22), which is also the order we find in many SVO languages such as English.

(22)   [$_{VP1}$ V1 [$_{VP2}$ V2 [$_{VP3}$ V3]]]

The alternative linear orders can be derived by assuming roll-up movement, where VP3 first moves to a position preceding V2 and then VP2 (including VP3) moves to a position preceding V1.[22] If these movement operations are optional, we can derive the 1-2-3 order (no movement), the 1-3-2 order (movement of VP3), the 3-2-1 order (movement of VP3 and VP2), and the 2-3-1 order (movement of VP2).

(23) a. **1-2-3 order: no movement**
       [$_{VP1}$ V1   [$_{VP2}$ V2   [$_{VP3}$ V3   ]]]
    b. **1-3-2 order: movement of VP3**
       [$_{VP1}$ V1   [$_{VP2}$ [$_{VP3}$ V3]   V2   [$_{VP3}$ V3   ]]]
    c. **3-2-1 order: movement of VP3 and VP2**
       [$_{VP1}$ [$_{VP2}$ [$_{VP3}$ V3] V2 [$_{VP3}$ V3]]]   V1 [$_{VP2}$ [$_{VP3}$ V3] V2 [$_{VP3}$ V3]]]
    d. **2-3-1 order: movement of VP2**
       [$_{VP1}$ [$_{VP2}$ V2 [$_{VP3}$ V3]]   V1 [$_{VP2}$ V2 [$_{VP3}$ V3   ]]]

The order 2-1-3 cannot be derived in this way. Since VP3 is contained in VP2 and V2 can only precede V1 if VP2 moves, VP3 will always precede V1 when V2 precedes V1. Thus, the categorical ungrammaticality of 2-1-3 follows automatically. The 3-1-2 order can only be derived if VP3 first moves across VP2 and then across VP1. There are reasons to believe that this word order, only possible with cluster types A and B, involves nominalizations (cf. Broekhuis 2008), so we will not discuss this order any further.

There are four interconnected problems with the analysis so far:

(i) The movement operations seem to be optional, as many speakers allow more than one of the linear orders for each cluster. This is the problem of intra-speaker variation.

(ii) The trigger of these movements is unclear.

(iii) The analysis does not explain the differences between the three cluster types.
(iv) The analysis does not explain the geographic distribution of the different word orders.

A possible solution to problem (i) is that speakers who allow more than one order for each cluster in fact have multiple competing grammars (cf. Kroch 2001). This would, however, lead to an explosion of the number of grammars that one speaker can have, as, e.g., the same optionality in word order can be observed in multiple PP-Extraposition constructions and there does not seem to be a correlation between the orders that a speaker allows in verb clusters and the ones he allows in multiple PP Extraposition.[23]

An alternative solution to the problem of intra-speaker variation would be to assume that all speakers in the Dutch language area have one and the same grammar (for the phenomena under discussion) and that speakers (hence dialects) differ with respect to the linear orders they actually use and accept, depending on the language environment they grew up in.[24] Put differently, this one grammar of Dutch dialects generates all the grammatical options in the table in (21) as possible orders and thus determines the variation space, while sociolinguistic factors determine which of these options are actually realized.[25] We make a distinction, then, between impossible and possible structures, and within the class of possible structures, between actual and unrealized structures. Impossible structures are ruled out by universal and language-specific building principles, unrealized structures are grammatically possible but happen to be absent in some varieties, as not all varieties exploit the full variation space determined by the grammar. In this respect, syntax is taken to be similar to phonotaxis and morphology, where the distinction within the class of possible forms between actual and unrealized forms is common.[26]

If this analysis of intra-speaker variation is on the right track, this has two important consequences. A methodological consequence is that when a particular structure is absent in a corpus and/or a speaker reports that he does not use or accept it, this can either mean that the structure is ungrammatical or unrealized. Sophisticated methodology will be needed to distinguish these two possibilities. A consequence for the grammar model is that we have to assume that syntactic structures can be conventionalized, hence stored, similar to lexical items.[27] This seems to be necessary anyway in view of idioms and collocations but also, e.g., the phrasal analysis of verbs (e.g., Hale and Keyser 1993) and pronouns (e.g., Déchaine and Wiltschko 2002).

Optionality in the grammar can be modeled in various ways. A common way in MP is to assume that the movement and non-movement variants differ with respect to the features involved. In the movement variant there would be a strong (as opposed to weak) feature or an EPP feature that is triggering the movement. However, these features are abstract, there is no independent empirical support for them (at least not for the phenomena under discussion), and if they are optionally present they massively overgenerate if not properly restricted.

A better alternative is to assume that optionality arises when two syntactic structures are syntactically and semantically completely equivalent, i.e., the number of movement operations is equal and the semantic interpretation is equal. This leads to an analysis of word-order variation in verb clusters where all movement operations are obligatory and variation arises at PF, as a result of the choice to delete a copy in its base position or in its landing-site. The structure that is the output of the syntactic module after all the movement (copying) operations have taken place is given in (24). The different variants arise from the various deletion options. Constituents in their base positions are marked with B (Base), constituents in their positions after copying are marked with A (After).

(24) [$_{VP1}$ [$_{VP2-A}$ [$_{VP3-A}$ V3] V2 [$_{VP3-B}$ V3]] V1 [$_{VP2-B}$ [$_{VP3-A}$ V3] V2 [$_{VP3-B}$ V3]]]

(25) **PF deletion options**
    (i) Delete VP2-A. Delete VP3-A. Resulting order 1–2–3
        [$_{VP1}$ [$_{VP2-A}$ [$_{VP3-A}$ V3] V2 [$_{VP3-B}$ V3]] V1 [$_{VP2-B}$ [$_{VP3-A}$ V3] V2 [$_{VP3-B}$ V3]]]
    (ii) Delete VP2-A. Delete VP3-B. Resulting order 1–3–2
        [$_{VP1}$ [$_{VP2-A}$ [$_{VP3-A}$ V3] V2 [$_{VP3-B}$ V3]] V1 [$_{VP2-B}$ [$_{VP3-A}$ V3] V2 [$_{VP3-B}$ V3]]]
    (iii) Delete VP2-B. Delete VP3-A. Resulting order 2–3–1
        [$_{VP1}$ [$_{VP2-A}$ [$_{VP3-A}$ V3] V2 [$_{VP3-B}$ V3]] V1 [$_{VP2-B}$ [$_{VP3-A}$ V3] V2 [$_{VP3-B}$ V3]]]
    (iv) Delete VP2-B. Delete VP3-B. Resulting order 3–2–1
        [$_{VP1}$ [$_{VP2-A}$ [$_{VP3-A}$ V3] V2 [$_{VP3-B}$ V3]] V1 [$_{VP2-B}$ [$_{VP3-A}$ V3] V2 [$_{VP3-B}$ V3]]]

This correctly derives the four possible orders and rules out the categorically ungrammatical order 2-1-3. The presence of 2 before 1 indicates that VP2-B has been deleted, together with all occurrences of VP3 inside VP2-B.

Question (ii), the trigger of these movements, is now slightly simplified because all Dutch dialect varieties and word-order variants have the same set of movements. They differ only in the locus of deletion. It would be sufficient to assume that there is an abstract movement triggering feature that all auxiliaries have in common. Since there is no obvious morphosyntactic counterpart to this feature (the triggering auxiliaries can be finite, infinitival, and participial), an alternative would be that these VP-movements are necessary to establish a predication relation between the auxiliary and the moving VP.[28]

Still, we have to model the relation between type of auxiliary and order in the cluster (question (iii)), in particular the fact that only clusters of the type Aux–Mod/Asp–V (e.g., 1.IS 2.GO3.SWIM) allow the 2-3-1 (GO-SWIM-IS) order, as opposed to clusters of the type Mod–Mod/Asp–V. There is some evidence that this correlates with the selectional relations between the highest auxiliary (BE/HAVE or Modal) and the other verbs inside the cluster, but we will not go into this here.[29]

This case study thus shows that microcomparison of large numbers of closely related dialects may provide insight into the limits of variation, the variation space determined by the grammar, the role of intra-speaker variation, and the way this variation can be captured theoretically. The way geographic (and other sociolinguistic) factors determine the distribution of the different variants was not addressed here, as the primary goal of GG is to characterize the mental grammar, not the external distribution of language variants. On the more technical side, it was argued that the word-order variation found in verb clusters is best analyzed as the result of cross-dialectally uniform VP copying followed by obligatory deletion of one copy, where there is a choice to delete the copy in its base position or in its landing-site. The analysis adopts the Universal Base Hypothesis, uniform rightward branching and leftward movement, and derives all and only the possible verb cluster orders.

24.4 Concluding remarks

The model of language variation discussed in Section 24.3 of this chapter is a strong version of the Minimalist Program, according to which all language varieties have the same syntactic building principles, including the same types, number, and hierarchy of functional projections (Universal Base), uniform right branching, only upward (lefward) movement, and the same movement options. In principle, in this model the syntactic module of the grammar cannot be a source of variation or optionality, and all language varieties have the same movement options. Observable syntactic variation must then be due to other factors. In the domain of V-to-I and I-to-C, we have seen that some word-order variation can be reduced to the lexicon (variation in morphosyntactic feature specification). In the domain of verb clusters, word-order variation can be reduced to deletion options at PF.

It may be necessary to loosen the Minimalist hypothesis slightly. First, it may be that language varieties do not have to project the full range of functional categories but can select a subset. This assumption seems necessary for the Split-IP hypothesis to work. Second, it may be necessary to allow partial copying in the syntactic component to explain differences in pied-piping that cannot be explained under a PF-deletion account. The Minimalist idea that optionality (intra-speaker variation) cannot arise in the syntactic module can be maintained. It was suggested that syntactic optionality arises when two or more syntactic structures are syntactically and semantically equivalent but differ in the positions in which copies are spelled-out.

All of these issues were illustrated with data from dialect syntactic research, as the main goal of this chapter was to describe the relation between dialect syntax and GG. It was argued that in the current version of MP there is no principled distinction between micro-, meso-, and macrosyntactic variation. There are no global parameters ('macroparameters'). Parameterization involves different feature specifications of functional elements, i.e., all parameterization is microparameterization (on whether macroparameters exist, see also Chapter 25). According to this view, meso-, and macrovariation is an accumulation of microparametric differences. The study of dialects gives direct access to these microparametric fundaments of all syntactic variation, as it makes it possible to establish correlations between certain grammatical properties while keeping (almost) all other grammatical properties constant.

The study of the syntax of dialects in GG has the same goal as GG in general, to describe and analyze possible human grammars as a mental reality. At the same time, it raises a number of research issues that have not been sufficiently addressed in the GG literature so far. The first issue involves intra-speaker variation. We have handled this by arguing that the grammar determines the variation space and sociolinguistic factors determine how many and which of the variants a speaker uses and in which situation. The latter is traditionally not taken to be part of linguistic competence, but the literature has called into question whether this is the right decision. A speaker has clear intuitions about the sociolinguistic circumstances in which a particular variant is used, including the relative frequency of each variant. This view was already present in Labov (1969), who incorporates sociolinguistic factors and frequency in so-called variable rules. In fact we are dealing with a demarcation problem here, namely the question whether sociolinguistic factors and frequency belong to linguistic competence or to performance. Since in recent versions of MP linguistic competence is reduced to a minimum and the possibility is left open that some of the universal building principles are not specific to the domain of linguistics and/or determined by interface requirements, the demarcation between competence and performance seems to be less clear today than it was in older versions of GG.

A related point arising from the study of dialectal and intra-speaker variation is the criticism that GG treats grammar as categorical. According to Keller (2000), Bod et al. (2003:1), language is variable and gradient, involving probability distributions. Generative linguistics studies the endpoints of such distributions, where the probability is one or zero, i.e., categorical properties of language. Concentrating on the extremes of the continua leaves half the phenomena unexplored and unexplained. Manning (2003) states that categorical linguistic theories such as GG place a hard categorical boundary of grammaticality where really there is a fuzzy edge, determined by many conflicting constraints and issues of conventionality versus human creativity. Both Bod et al. and Manning argue that probabilistic models (e.g., Stochastic Optimality Theory) are required to capture gradience in language. It is true that GG is not able to handle gradience, but since probabilistic models mix in performance factors (including world knowledge), the most important open question seems to be whether it is a good idea methodologically and theoretically to give up the distinction between competence and performance.

Notes

1. In Europe, in the past fifteen years a number of large-scale dialect syntax projects have been carried out or started that intend to systematically describe and analyze syntactic variation in a large number of closely related dialects, using both generative, dialectological, and sociolinguistic methods and perspectives. Some examples include Northern Italian dialects, Portuguese dialects, Dutch dialects, and Scandinavian dialects. See www.dialectsyntax.org, Barbiers *et al.* (2007), Barbiers and Bennis (2007) and Barbiers (2009).
2. To be able to talk about different language varieties, however, one cannot avoid using terms such as English, Dutch, or a Scottish dialect in a loose sense, which is what I do in this chapter. Similarly, the term 'language' cannot be avoided. In general, I will use this term as a shorthand for 'grammar used consistently by one or more speakers,' so the term 'language' covers both languages, dialects, and idiolects (except in parts where these terms are used in direct opposition).
3. A reason why comparative GG research into dialects used to be relatively rare is that it is methodologically more complex than investigating one's own idiolect. Complications such as code-switching between dialect, regiolect, and standard language and accommodation toward the language variety of the interviewer need to be dealt with. For discussion of methodological problems and solutions, see Barbiers *et al.* (2007), Barbiers and Bennis (2007).
4. But see Newmeyer (2004) for extensive criticism.
5. The term 'cross-linguistic variation' in this chapter refers to variation among different language varieties, where language varieties include all idiolects, dialects, and sociolects, and standard languages. The term 'intralinguistic variation' refers to variation within one idiolect, i.e., optionality.
6. As opposed to elements where varying feature specification only has a very local effect on the grammar. For instance, the feature specification for concord on attributive adjectives presumably will only have an effect on the structure of DPs, not on clausal grammar.
7. See Pollock (1989:386–89). Pollock's account of the data in (5) is much more complex than is indicated in the text. Among other things, he assumes that IP in fact splits into TP and AgrP (see Chapters 12 and 14). These properties of his account are not relevant for the discussion here, as the goal is to show that there is a relation between position and verbal morphology. For other versions of the split-IP hypothesis, see Section 24.3.1, below.
8. In more recent versions of MP (e.g., Chomsky 2001), agreement is still a precondition for movement, but agreement itself is no longer the trigger of movement. It is the (optional) presence of EPP that triggers (optional) movement. I will not consider the consequences of this change in this chapter.

9. The discussion here is restricted to three verbal positions C, I, and V for ease of explanation. This is a considerable simplification, given proposals in the literature that all three domains have to be split up in a number of projections. Cf., e.g., Poletto (2000) and references cited there for the fine structure of the CP-domain, Cinque (1999) for the fine structure of the middle-field, and Ramchand (2008) for the fine structure of VP.
10. Cf. Garbacz (2010) for a recent overview.
11. Cf. Bobaljik (2002b) for more counterexamples.
12. Cf. Garbacz (2010) for potential counterexamples, such as the Swedish dialect Övdalian that has rich agreement in the sense of Bobaljik (2008) but optional V-to-I.
13. Thus, this approach does not accept the hypothesis that all languages have the same number and order of functional projections (7iii).
14. As, e.g., (9a) shows, (10a–b) cannot be taken to provide evidence for the alternative idea that the head I follows VP in Dutch. In (9a), the participle is in VP and the internal argument intervenes between the auxiliary and V, so I must be to the left of VP. In general, DP arguments and predicative complements of verbs cannot follow the clause-final verb position, so whenever they seem to do, the finite verb has moved to the I or C position. Thus, in (11b–c) the fact that the predicative complements *naar huis* 'to house' and *Sinterklaas* follow the finite verbs shows that the finite verbs are not in a position I that follows VP.
15. For reasons that I do not understand, not all members of the subject pronoun paradigm seem to occur in this construction, e.g., second person singular cannot occur in between the verb and the suffix.
16. If it is possible to strand a suffix under movement and if head movement involves more than one step, the result looks like a violation of the Head Movement Constraint (Travis 1984). For example, in (11), it looks as if the verb has skipped the tense or agreement head on its way from V up to C. It is not entirely clear how to rule out violations of the Head Movement Constraint if excorporation as proposed here is generally allowed.
17. It would then be similar to the infinitival marker *te* 'to' that has word status too. Cf. the minimal pairs in (i–ii), which show that infinitival marker *te* 'to' is a word and the applicative morpheme *be* is a prefix.

    (i) Jan   probeert de   hond   te vinden en (te) redden
        John tries   the dog   to find   and to save
        'John tries to find the dog and to save it'
    (ii) Jan wil   het artikel   be- studeren en *(be-) werken
         John wants the paper   APPL study   and APPL work
         'John wants to study the paper and adapt it'

18. This does not necessarily mean that it is impossible to have an agreement relation between I and V. E.g., the lexical representation of the past tense morpheme can be such that it needs (the features of) a verb stem to

be fully interpretable and the lexical representation of the verb can be such that it needs (the features of) an affix to be fully interpretable.
19. Cf. also Barbiers and van Koppen (2006).
20. Data and analysis in this section are from Barbiers (2005b, 2008b). The latter is based on the theory proposed in Barbiers (1995).
21. The hierarchically second verb in this cluster can be an infinitive or a participle, depending on the dialect. I will not discuss this variation here. See Wurmbrand (2006), who also gives the state of the art in the research into V-clusters.
22. Head movement is not an alternative, as this would lead to the expectation that particles such as *op* 'up,' *in* 'in,' etc. can be stranded to the right of the verbal clusters when the main verb moves across an auxiliary. Such stranding is strongly ungrammatical, while stranding of a particle under verb second of the main verb, a classical type of head movement, is possible.
23. Cf. Barbiers (1995, 2008b). Cf. Bresnan and Deo (2000) for a similar point.
24. Cf. Barbiers (2005b).
25. Cf. Biberauer and Richards (2006) for similar ideas.
26. Cf. Aronoff (1976).
27. The idea that syntactic structures can be conventionalized is at the heart of Construction Grammar (CG; e.g., Goldberg 1995 – see also Section 3.4). A crucial difference between the generative approach and Construction Grammar (in fact, Cognitive Grammar more generally, cf. Langacker 1987) is that CG takes the grammar of a particular language to be entirely the result of conventionalization, i.e., CG does not accept the GG assumption that there is a set of building principles that all languages share and that cannot be explained from conventionalization but rather must be innate and possibly specific to the linguistic module of cognition. In the analysis in the main text, generative grammar and conventionalization go hand in hand. Generative principles determine the limits of syntactic variation, while conventionalization captures the fact that a language need not exploit the full variation space defined by these principles.
28. As proposed and technically developed in Barbiers (1995, 2008b).
29. See Barbiers (2005b, 2008b) for a proposal.

25

Parameters: the pluses and the minuses

Rosalind Thornton and Stephen Crain

25.1 Introduction

From the inception of generative linguistics, both theoretical linguists and researchers in language acquisition have been concerned with how knowledge of language develops in children. The central research strategy has been to uncover which aspects of children's linguistic knowledge are best accounted for as the products of human biology ('nature') and which are best accounted for as the products of experience ('nurture'). By hypothesis, the first factor, the human genetic blueprint for language (Universal Grammar) is essentially uniform for the species (Chomsky 1981, 1995c). This enables children to reflexively execute several non-trivial tasks, including tasks that are prerequisite for successful navigation through the considerable latitude of experience they may encounter as they advance toward the final state. By age three or four, children around the globe have mastered a rich grammatical system that is equivalent to that of adult speakers of the local linguistic community.

The second factor in the development of language is experience. Not even the staunchest nativist denies that experience matters for language development. After all, children raised in Beijing acquire Mandarin, and children raised in Sydney acquire English. It is important, however, not to overestimate the extent to which experience leaves its mark on the linguistic systems that children develop. Despite the considerable latitude in the experiences of different children, even children exposed to vastly different sets of data within a linguistic community settle on grammatical systems that are remarkably similar. This naturalistic observation is constantly being repeated, with the same outcome, by children learning all varieties of human languages. Advocates of the theory of Universal Grammar contend that this observation follows from the fact that all human languages share a set of core linguistic principles, and that children adhere to these principles by virtue of their genetic endowment.

These core principles are linguistic universals that establish boundary conditions on language learning and on the extent to which human languages can differ (Chomsky 1981).

There is a further observation about universal linguistic principles. The observation is that the effects of these principles are far-reaching. Core principles tie together a range of linguistic facts that often have seemingly unrelated surface properties. A familiar example from syntax is Principle C (Chomsky 1981, 1986b, Lasnik 1976). This principle applies to referring expressions in declarative sentences, to quantificational structures involving variable binding, to *wh*-questions (e.g., strong crossover questions), and even to fragment answers to *wh*-questions in discourse (see Chapter 15 on binding, and Chapter 14 on fragment answers). Another example of a core linguistic principle is the semantic property of downward entailment (see Chapter 21). Downward entailment also unifies several phenomena which appear, on the surface, to be unrelated. Downward entailing expressions license the appearance of negative polarity items, they suspend scalar implicatures, and they generate conjunctive truth conditions for disjunctive words (e.g., English *or*, Chinese *huozhe*), as in de Morgan's laws (e.g., Crain 2008, Crain et al. 2007).

Principle C and downward entailment are expected to be operative in all human languages, even ones that are historically unrelated. This diminishes the differences across languages. Moreover, the fact that such principles govern a range of phenomena further diminishes the differences across languages, at least to a degree. In addition, the fact that core principles provide a unified explanation of disparate-looking linguistic phenomena often requires such principles to be described in abstract terms. The abstract nature of core linguistic principles seemingly drives a wedge between Universal Grammar and experience-based approaches to language acquisition. According to experience-based approaches, linguistic phenomena receive only shallow descriptions, and the processes for unification are based on information structure and discourse function (e.g., Goldberg 2003, 2006, Lieven and Tomasello 2008, Tomasello 2000a, 2000b, 2003). These theoretical differences have empirical consequences for the course children take during language development. According to the generative approach, the linguistic phenomena which are unified by core linguistic principles are, ceteris paribus, expected to be acquired en masse by children, regardless of particular features of the ambient input. In the absence of universal linguistic principles like Principle C and downward entailment, experience-based approaches to language acquisition anticipate that linguistic phenomena are acquired piecemeal, according to the respective frequency of the distinct phenomena in the input.

Still, languages differ, and experience is certainly involved in children's decisions about those properties that distinguish the local language from languages spoken elsewhere around the globe. But just how extensive are the differences or, to put it the other way around, how extensive are the commonalities? To the degree that languages share properties, based on the first factor, the role of experience is diminished. This may be true even for properties that are not universal. Languages could share a fixed set of options, in additional to the core linguistic universals. This is where 'parameters' enter the picture. According to the theory of Universal Grammar, important aspects of language variation are biologically given, as part of Universal Grammar. As part of the human genetic blueprint for language, these parameters further circumscribe the hypothesis space available to language learners and, thereby, further diminish the role of experience in language acquisition (Chomsky 1981, 1986b, 1995c).

Parameters may reduce the role of experience in another way. The contribution of experience to the final state of language acquisition is further diminished if parameters, like core principles, afford a unification of linguistic phenomena. This was one of the main selling points in the introduction of parameters into the theory of Universal Grammar. We will discuss the extent to which this property of 'unification' remains an attribute of parameters in current models. Parameters and core linguistic principles share another property. The introduction of parameters into the theory of Universal Grammar was designed to explain why the particular primary linguistic data different children experience do not leave any indelible marks on the final state children attain. As already noted, different experiences by children in the same linguistic community do not yield grammars that are sufficiently different to impede communication. This, in turn, explains why linguists are able to construct grammars for (adult) human languages, as well as to discover universal principles and parameters. Linguistic research proceeds by making an 'idealization to instantaneous acquisition,' as discussed in Chomsky (1965) and in Lasnik and Crain (1985). To the extent that the research enterprise succeeds, the idealization is justified.

However parameters are conceived, experience plays a significant role in parameter setting. Ceteris paribus, experience is needed to 'set' parameters to the values featured in the local language. But to the extent that language variation is explained by innate parameters, the role of experience is minimized, as compared to the role that experience would play if language variation were unrestrained, as it is on experience-based models of language development (e.g., Goldberg 2003, 2006, Tomasello 2000a, 2000b, 2003, Evans and Levinson 2009). By reducing the imprint of experience on language learning, parameters are vehicles for guaranteeing that children converge on grammars that are sufficiently similar to those of other children and adults to permit effortless and seamless communication.

Reducing the role of experience by invoking parameters raises new questions, however. Is parameter setting like a scavenger hunt, where items can be gathered in any order, or is it like a treasure hunt where clues must be followed in a specific order? (Lasnik and Crain 1985). As for individual parameters, do learners have all of the options on the table early in the course of language acquisition, to be weighed against experience, or do learners begin with an initial default value? If learners begin with an initial value, what determines that value? The answer presumably appeals to a third factor effect. If multiple options are initially available, how much experience is needed to set a parameter? If there is a default value, and this turns out to be incorrect for the local language, how much experience is needed to reset a parameter? What is the exact nature of the experience children require to set parameters?

The answers to these questions will not all fall within the purview of Universal Grammar. Moreover, the answers that do not receive an accounting within Universal Grammar will not necessarily be explained by appealing to the kinds of resources for culling data and for forming generalizations that are attributed to children on experience-based models. In short, the answers to some of the questions about parameter setting will invoke a third factor, or a number of third factors, in addition to genetic endowment and experience. Although third factor properties are "not specific to the faculty of language" (Chomsky 2005:6), these factors clearly contribute to the acquisition of linguistic knowledge. At the same time, these third factors apparently do not impede language development; they also do not leave their mark on the final states that learners achieve.

Recently, within the Minimalist linguistic research program, linguists have been seeking to identify the extent to which one or more of these third factors enter into the equation for language development (cf. Holmberg 2010, Lohndal and Uriagereka 2010, Roberts and Holmberg 2010, I. Roberts 2010). Four types of third factor properties are most often discussed. One concerns the cognitive tools used by children to analyze the data they encounter in the course of language acquisition. A second third factor is the human sentence processing system, or parser (see Chapter 26). The linear strings of sounds that speakers produce must be converted by children into words and phrasal structures for semantic interpretation and integration into the conversational context. The linguistic knowledge and performance routines that accomplish this feat are by no means trivial (see, e.g., Fodor 1998). To cite just one example, the parser is responsible for resolving so-called filler–gap dependencies. Whenever the parser encounters an expression that has been 'moved' from its original position (a filler), the parser assigns it a partial semantic interpretation at the landing-site, but the parser must also identify the position from which the expression originated (a gap), so that the meaning of the displaced constituent can be integrated with the meanings of its neighboring expressions at the site of extraction. Several features of the human parser are reasonably well understood. For example, filler–gap dependencies pose less difficulty for the parser if the filler precedes the gap, and if the gap can be readily identified (see Crain and Fodor 1985). The task of the parser is also easier if no expressions intervene between the filler and gap which are similar in features to the filler (e.g., object-gap relative clauses are more difficult that subject-gap relatives). A final example is ambiguity. Less ambiguity is better, as far as the parser is concerned.

A third third factor concerns the cognitive architecture that determines efficient computation in complex cognitive systems such as language (Chomsky 2005:6). Although there is no detailed theory of efficient computation, clear examples can be identified, such as computing the shortest possible movement of a constituent, or keeping to a minimum the number of copies of expressions that are pronounced. Interestingly, principles of computational efficiency apparently override parsing considerations. For example, providing a copy of a displaced constituent at the site of extraction would assist the parser in identifying gaps, thereby assisting the parser in resolving ambiguities involving filler–gap dependencies. Nevertheless, the need to minimize copies, for computational efficiency, apparently carries more weight than resolving filler–gap dependencies. This is evident from the architecture of the language faculty, which has evolved to limit copies, despite the parsing difficulties that ensue.

The fourth third factor is maturation. Although most of the prerequisite genetic elements for language acquisition are presumably fixed at the initial state, some may become operative according to a maturational timetable. According to the maturation hypothesis, children initially lack certain structural principles and/or computational resources, such that their early hypotheses may be compromised to a greater extent than they are for older children and adults. But as children reach the critical neurological benchmarks, the previously latent structural principles emerge or children's computational resources are extended (see Borer and Wexler 1992, Radford 1990, Rizzi 2005a, Wexler 1992, 1994, 1998).

It had been assumed until quite recently that the language apparatus used in setting parameters was specific to language (i.e., domain-specific). This assumption has been called into question as third factor considerations, such as computational efficiency, have entered into the equation for models of parameter setting. Empirical findings about children's abilities to mine data, as well as considerations of computational efficiency, have been instrumental in leading researchers to reexamine the nature of parameters (cf. Saffran et al. 1996, Saffran 2001, 2002, Yang 2002, 2004, 2010). Further scrutiny about the involvement of third factor properties, seen to be critical for parameter setting, have led to new models. According to some recent models of parameter setting, third factors effects such as computational efficiency have replaced the specific genetic inscriptions of parameter values that were assumed in earlier models (e.g., Rizzi 2005a, I. Roberts 2010, Roberts and Holmberg 2010). The main purpose of the next two sections is to compare these newly emergent models to the more classical conception of parameters.

This concludes our introductory remarks. The next section reviews the early conception of parameters. We describe how parameters were initially stated, and where they were thought to reside in the language faculty. Section 25.3 reviews the concerns, both theoretical and empirical, that were subsequently raised for the early model of parameters and parameter setting, and introduces recent conceptions of parameters. In Section 25.4 we discuss how parameters are set. Section 25.5 describes five recent models of parameters, which are compared with the 'classic' model of Chomsky (1981). Finally, Section 25.6 describes new directions that are being taken in the investigations of parameters in child language.

25.2 The early conception of parameters

The last thirty years have seen remarkable advances in linguistic theory and corresponding advances in our understanding of how children acquire language. Advances on both fronts have resulted in large part because of a shift from the rule-based theories of grammar advanced in the 1960s and early 1970s to the Principles and Parameters (P&P) theory of the 1980s and 1990s, and its descendant, the Minimalist Program (e.g., Chomsky 1981, 1995c; see Chapter 4). The P&P model enabled researchers in language development to formulate, and then evaluate, far-reaching predictions about the course of language acquisition. According to this approach, children were not expected to accrue individual rules of the local language, as had been supposed on earlier models. Instead, general principles common to all human languages were seen to establish boundary conditions for grammar formation, and children were seen to work within these boundaries, filling in the specific details that distinguished the local language from other languages. Filling in the details was accomplished, in part, by the mechanisms of parameter setting.

In broad outline, the story of parameter setting goes as follows. It was postulated first that parameter setting was largely a matter of genetic specification (first factor), along with a fairly minimal contribution from the experiential input (second factor) (Chomsky 1981, Lightfoot 1999, 2006, Baker 2001, 2005). In more recent models, by contrast, it is postulated that setting parameters often involves third factor properties (e.g., statistical learning, computational efficiency) (Chomsky 2005, Rizzi 2005a, Roberts and Holmberg 2010, Yang 2002, 2004). The contribution of third factor effects has the advantage of reducing the amount of genetic information that is encoded in the biological blueprint for language learning. This is one of the primary goals of the Minimalist Program. The involvement of computational efficiency in generating the values of parameters reduces the requisite genetic contribution to language development, without increasing the role of experience. That said, the involvement of certain third factor effects, such as statistical learning, could lead to an increase in the role of experience in language acquisition, again without adding to the genetic contribution of Universal Grammar. In the remainder of this section, we chart the history of how and why parameters were conceived, and how they have been reconceived since their inception. One of the main points of focus will be the degree to which parameters are taken to be part of the human faculty for language (first factor) or involve third factor effects.

When the P&P model emerged in the late 1970s and early 1980s, there was no associated change of perspective regarding universal linguistic principles. P&P models continued to maintain that the initial state of the language faculty included core principles. These principles were seen to demarcate the hypothesis space through which children navigate, so children were not expected to deviate from these principles in the course of language development (see, e.g., Atkinson 1992, Crain 1991, Guasti 2002). But another aspect of the child's developing linguistic competence took on a new look in the P&P model, namely how children uncovered aspects of grammar that distinguished the local language from other languages. With the advent of a parameter-setting model of language acquisition, many of the cross-linguistic differences that had previously been supposed to fall outside the language faculty were reconceived. Essentially, these cross-linguistic differences were hypothesized to be innately specified as part of the language faculty, alongside universal linguistic principles. The language faculty was then conceived to contain both core linguistic principles and a finite set of parameters that established choice points of language variation. These choice points, or parameters, partitioned human languages into broad classes.

At the broadest cut, the introduction of parameters into the theory of Universal Grammar was designed to make language learning easier than it would have been otherwise (Chomsky 2002). On the early version of the P&P model, the learner was viewed as navigating through an innately specified space, circumscribed by both core principles and parametric options of Universal Grammar. Since neither the principles nor the parametric options were learned, learning was replaced, at least to some extent, by parameter setting (cf. Clahsen 1990). This advanced the theory of Universal Grammar toward the goal of 'explanatory adequacy' (see Section 3.2.5), i.e., explaining children's rapid mastery of any human language (Chomsky 1965; 1981; 1986b). As Chomsky states it:

> The theory of UG must meet two obvious conditions. On the one hand, it must be compatible with the diversity of existing (indeed, possible) grammars. At the same time UG must be sufficiently constrained and restrictive in the options it permits so as to account for the fact that each of these grammars develops in the mind on the basis of quite limited evidence. (Chomsky 1981:3)

Parameter setting was initially conceived of as initiating radical changes in child languages. Setting the pro-drop parameter one way or the other would lead children to postulate a grammar with null subjects versus one with overt subjects, and setting the *wh*-parameter one way or the other could lead children to postulate a grammar without *wh*-movement or one with *wh*-movement. Moreover, parameters such as these could alter children's grammars quite dramatically. We noted earlier that core principles of Universal Grammar, such as Principle C and downward entailment, represent 'deep' properties of human language in the sense that they tie together a number of superficially unrelated linguistic phenomena. Such unifications of disparate phenomena reduced the role of experience in language development. Instead of piecemeal acquisition of specific constructions, as advocated by experience-dependent accounts of language development, acquisition was seen to involve the mastery of clusters of linguistic phenomena in one fell swoop. It was suggested, in early P&P models, that parameters might accomplish similar kinds of unification, limiting the role of experience still further. On this view, setting a single parameter might introduce a cluster of properties into children's emerging grammars. As Chomsky (1981) remarked:

> We will see that there are certain complexes of properties typical of particular types of language; such collections of properties should be explained in terms of the choice of parameters in one or another subsystem. In a tightly integrated theory with fairly rich internal structure, change in a single parameter may have complex effects, with proliferating consequences in various parts of the grammar. Ideally, we hope to find that complexes of properties differentiating otherwise similar languages are reducible to a single parameter, fixed in one or another way. (Chomsky 1981:6)

The metaphor that was often coupled with descriptions of parameter-setting was that of a switch, as in a circuit box. The learner flicked the switch one way or the other in response to the 'triggering' experience. If the switch was flicked one way, then the child's grammar took one format; if the switch was flicked the other way, the child's grammar took a completely different format. Here is how Chomsky put it:

> If these parameters are embedded in a theory of UG that is sufficiently rich in structure, then the languages that are determined by fixing their values one way or another will appear to be quite diverse, since the consequences of one set of choices may be very different from the consequences of another set; yet at the same time, limited evidence, just sufficient to fix the parameters of UG, will determine a grammar that may be very intricate and will in general lack grounding in experience in the sense of an inductive basis. (Chomsky 1981:4)

The switch metaphor suggested that during some circumscribed period in the course of development, parameters would be decisively triggered by positive input from the ambient language (Hyams 1986, Gibson and Wexler 1994, Fodor 1998, Roeper 2000). Although evidence was prerequisite to setting parameters, parameter setting did not have the character of 'learning.' Instead, parameters were assumed to be set 'reflexively.' Reflexive responses by a species to particular inputs are characteristic of genetically determined acquisition in any domain (Chomsky 2007). The expectation was that parameter values were similarly 'triggered' or 'fixed' by experience, as in one-trial learning. This assumption rendered third factor properties inconsequential for parameter-setting, at the time. In particular, the possibility that the parameter setting mechanism might involve general cognitive principles was not seriously entertained until recently (Yang 2002; 2004, Chomsky 2005, Rizzi 2005a, Roberts and Holmberg 2010). The exact mechanisms of parameter setting were not discussed in detail at the time, but the assumption was that they were internal to the language faculty. This accounted in part for the rapidity of children's acquisition of language as compared with other cognitive skills, such as the ability to count, or draw, or play a musical instrument.

As noted, parameters were seen to encompass sets of grammatical properties that varied across languages. In current practice, parameters with a cluster of grammatical consequences are called macroparameters (see also Chapter 24). Macroparameters often make broad typological cuts. Examples of macroparameters which cut across typological families include the polysynthesis parameter (Baker 1996, 2001), the *wh*-parameter (Huang 1982b), the pro-drop parameter (Rizzi 1982a), the head direction parameter (Travis 1984), and the NP/DP parameter (Bošković 2008b, Bošković and Gajewski 2011), though some proposed macroparameters gave rise to clusters of properties within typological families, such as the parameter proposed by Holmberg (2010) that explains the differing properties of subjects in Insular and Mainland Scandinavian, and Rizzi's (1982a) pro-drop parameter that explains differences across Romance languages. Putting differences of scale aside, it soon became apparent that some of the macroparameters that had been postulated, such as the pro-drop parameter and the head direction parameter, needed to be further articulated into several sub-parameters. Research into how the head direction parameter would work across languages raised difficulties in accounting for the fact that languages typically do not have a uniform setting for head direction (Travis 1984, Fodor and Crain 1990). Furthermore, pro-drop languages have been found to be more diverse than previously thought, invoking more fine-grained analyses (as recorded in the papers in Biberauer *et al.* 2010). Consequently, the existence of macroparameters has become controversial, as discussed in the next section. Less controversial are microparameters (see again Chapter 24), which target a single grammatical property (though as we will see, Roberts and Holmberg 2010 show that microparameters can be formulated to give rise to a cluster of effects).

The actual decisions about which parameter settings were correct for the local language were attributed to the learner's experience, and such decisions might well have involved a variety of factors that were, using current parlance, third factor properties. Among these properties are (a) the amount of evidence that the learner needs to set a given parameter and (b) the possibility of pre-established orderings of parameter values. One early and important proposal about the ordering of parameter values was the Subset Principle of Berwick (Berwick 1985) and others (see also Manzini and Wexler 1987, Wexler and Manzini 1987, Clark 1992, Fodor and Sakas 2005). The Subset Principle ordered parameter settings according to the number of linguistic structures (and corresponding interpretations) that could be assigned to a given linguistic expression across languages. The Subset Principle became operative when the class of languages that adopted one setting of parameter P (call these P1 languages) generated fewer structures for a given type of expression than the class of languages that adopted the alternative setting of P (call these P2 languages). In such cases, the Subset Principle compels children learning both P1 and P2 languages to initially hypothesize that the local language is a P1 language (i.e., one of the subset languages), rather than a P2 language (the superset languages). The Subset Principle was generally assumed to be part of a language-learning module (i.e., the Language Acquisition Device or LAD) which was, more likely than not, part of the language faculty. In recent work, Fodor (1998, 2001) and Fodor and Sakas (2005) have pointed out the significant computational and psychological (e.g., memory) difficulties that would be incurred by learners if their decisions were based on the formulation of parameters as involving comparisons of the linguistic structures that were generated by the different settings. For example, comparing the structures that are generated on one value of the parameter with those generated on the other value would seemingly require that learners store examples of linguistic structures in memory. As Fodor and Sakas (2005) argue, this seems unrealistic at best. The parameters we discuss in the final section seemingly avoid this problem, because the effects of the alternative values of the parameter are truth conditions, and these can be computed for any given sentence that has the requisite structure. Nevertheless, as Fodor and Sakas make clear, not all parameters are the same, and even if some parameters enable learners to circumvent learnability problems, others may not.

Although little attention was paid to this at the time, applications of the Subset Principle to the values of parameters relied on third factor effects, because the ordering of parametric options does not follow from the theory of Universal Grammar, or from experience. Specification of the initial settings of parameters needed to be 'written' into the mechanism for language learning (the LAD), most likely through evolution. Besides the Subset Principle, however, little else was seen to be involved in establishing defaults, or in resetting individual parameters.

The earliest proposals applying the Subset Principle in parameter setting involved principles of Universal Grammar. For example, Rizzi (1982a) proposed that languages could vary in the kinds of (bounding) nodes that were relevant for the application of one of the principles of extraction (Subjacency; see Chapter 18). The Subset Principle compelled learners to initially hypothesize the value that was associated with the lowest nodes in phrasal structure, since extraction involving higher nodes produced a superset of the sentences that corresponded to extraction involving the lower nodes. Manzini and Wexler (1987) made similar claims about the application of binding principles across languages (see Chapter 3, note 6, and Chapter 15). The binding principles were taken to initially apply in the most restricted syntactic domains, and these domains could be relaxed by learners, on the basis of positive evidence from the local language. In both cases, the initial options were viewed as 'default' settings, ones that generated fewer linguistic structures (and their associated meanings) than the alternative settings, as entreated by the Subset Principle.

As these examples of extraction and binding illustrate, parameters were initially assumed to be tied to the principles of Universal Grammar. Parameters filled out the detailed specifications of principles. This made sense, at least for the earliest parameters, such as Subjacency and Principle A of the Binding Theory. It soon became apparent, however, that this assumption was not tenable. For one thing, some principles did not readily allow for parameterization, such as Principle C of the Binding Theory. More importantly, it was discovered that some parameters were tied to the presence or absence of special lexical items. For example, certain kinds of lexical anaphors permit long-distance relationships with their antecedents, whereas other kinds do not (Manzini and Wexler 1987, Wexler and Manzini 1987). This soon led to the conjecture that all parameters were represented in the lexicon – the 'Borer–Chomsky conjecture' (Borer 1984a, Chomsky 1995c). As the nature of universal principles changed, in the Minimalist Program, the idea that parameters are associated with a specific class of lexical items, namely functional heads, gained traction. The allure of limiting parameters to properties of functional heads has been enhanced by two recent developments in the field. One is the fact that the number of principles of UG has been reduced, to include only a few basic operating principles (i.e., Merge, Move, Spell-Out, economy of derivation, economy of representation; see especially Chapter 14). Consequently, the number of parameters far outstripped the number of principles. The second development is the articulation of rich systems of functional heads in the left periphery of the clause, in major phrases, in DPs, and elsewhere. This is called the cartographic approach to grammar (see Chapter 12). By adopting the cartographic approach, the natural move was to tie parameters to properties of heads, i.e., the categories they select (Merge), the categories they attract (Move), and whether they are overt or null (Spell-out).

25.3 Current conceptions of parameters

One recent approach to parameters, by Baker (2001, 2005), contends that the classic view of parameters is essentially correct. Baker has championed a parameter hierarchy that attempts a unification of language typology and language acquisition. The hierarchy ensures that language learners consider parameters in a specific ordering, focusing first on the typologically most robust parameters in the hierarchy. These macroparameters reside at the top of the hierarchy and, hence, make the broadest typological cuts among language families. Children's selection of the values for the highest parameters in the hierarchy is presumably based on readily available positive evidence, so the top-most parameters are set early in the course of language development, perhaps even before children produce their first words. One example is the polysynthesis parameter (Baker 1996). For example, English-speaking children immediately set the polysynthesis parameter to the 'minus' value, based on the abundant evidence that English is not a polysynthetic language; children have evidence that English is a configurational isolating language and no evidence that it is non-configurational, and that it forms large 'words' through multiple affixation. From that point onwards, English-speaking children traverse that portion of the hierarchy that is associated with the minus value of the polysynthesis parameter. They never again consider any of the parameters associated with the 'plus' value on the hierarchy – i.e., those parameters that pertain to polysynthetic languages, such as the parameter that neutralizes adjectives into verbs or nouns, or the ergative case parameter. In short, the hierarchical nature of parameters, as proposed by Baker (2001, 2005), has the advantage of making the task of language learning easier, by eliminating entire collections of parameters from consideration. Although these collections of parameters are never engaged by children, these parameters are nevertheless fully specified within the syntactic component of the language faculty. Thus, Baker's approach to parameters can be considered to be an *overspecification* model, since the parameters and their potential values are all prewired in Universal Grammar.

Another proposal about parameters within the overspecification approach has been advanced by Lightfoot (2006), who opts for what he terms an 'I-language' model of language acquisition. According to Lightfoot, the 'triggering' learnability models espoused by Gibson and Wexler (1994) and by Clark (1992) are too reliant on 'E-language,' the language that the child encounters from experience. Lightfoot contends that, although these approaches endow children with innate parameters, they are mainly concerned with the mechanisms that children use to analyze the input data so as to converge on the target grammar. On these models, according to Lightfoot, children are required to perform excessive computations, such as comparing sentences that are derived from the grammars children hypothesize against the input they encounter (see also Fodor 1998). To alleviate such computational requirements, Lightfoot proposes a model of parameters that specifies considerably more of the content of the values of parameters as part of the child's innate linguistic knowledge. In addition to specifying the parameters and their values, Lightfoot (1999, 2006) proposes that children scan the local language for specific linguistic 'cues' about the structure of the corresponding I-language. On the Lightfoot model, UG fully specifies the cues that children attempt to instantiate. For example, children scour the input for the cue [$_{VP}$ V DP] in order to establish whether or not the local language is a verb–object language. In Lightfoot's words, "[t]he insight behind cue-based learning is that brains make certain structures, cues, available for interpreting what a person experiences. That is the role of the brain in learning, the contribution of the organism to the processing of experience" (Lightfoot 2006:86).

Although full specification of parameters and their cues in the syntax might be profitable from a learnability perspective, some researchers began to question the idea that parameters are fully specified in the syntactic component of Universal Grammar, even before the Minimalist Program was introduced (Chomsky 1995c). An alternative proposal, attributed to Borer (1984a), rapidly gained momentum. Borer proposed that 'interlanguage variation' is associated with individual lexical items, an area where we know learning is necessary. Here is how Borer put it.

> The inventory of inflectional rules and of grammatical formatives is idiosyncratic and learned on the basis of input data. If all interlanguage variation is attributable to that system, the burden of learning is placed exactly on that component of grammar for which there is strong evidence of learning: the vocabulary and its idiosyncratic properties. We no longer have to assume that the data to which the child is exposed bear directly on universal principles, nor do we have to assume that the child actively selects between competing grammatical systems. (Borer 1984a:29)

Borer's statement has been widely taken to express the view that parametric variation is limited to the lexicon.[1] At any rate, the proposal that parametric variation is limited to the lexicon was taken up by Chomsky (1995c) and termed the 'Borer–Chomsky conjecture' by Baker. Baker's version of the Borer–Chomsky conjecture is stated as follows (Baker 2008a:353, 2008b:155f.).

(1) All parameters of variation are attributable to differences in the features of particular items (e.g. the functional heads) in the Lexicon.

The Borer–Chomsky conjecture removed the parametric architecture from the syntax, and repositioned it in the repository of language learning, the lexicon. So the parameter-setting mechanism was moved out of the component associated with the first factor, genetic endowment, and into the component associated with the second factor, experience.

Of course, even the acquisition of lexical items may draw upon innate conceptual knowledge, as well as on third factor properties. The exact nature of word learning, and the extent to which it draws on both innate and extra-linguistic cognitive principles is a matter of continuing debate (cf. Markman 1990, Bloom and Markson 1998, 2000, Bloom 2002, Waxman and Booth 2000, 2001, for example). For present purposes, the important observation is that the Borer–Chomsky conjecture repositioned the architecture used for encoding parameters and fixing on the correct settings for the local language in the lexicon. Assuming that parameter-setting has the same character as word learning (as in Borer's original version), the parameter-setting model no longer anticipated that children would rapidly master even those aspects of grammar that vary cross-linguistically, but are associated with language families rather than with particular languages. Instead, the Borer–Chomsky conjecture suggested that children needed lexical learning to decide, for example, whether or not to ascribe a specific functional feature (usually considered to be from a universally specified pool) that was present in grammar of the local language.

As a consequence of these changes in the conception of parameters, many parameters were recast as lexical parameters. The reanalysis of parameters has not always been straightforward, however. Consider the *wh*-movement parameter proposed by Huang (1982b). This parameter concerned the level of representation at which *wh*-movement applied in classes of languages, i.e., whether *wh*-movement applied at S-structure, as in English, or at LF, in *wh-in-situ* languages like Chinese. Tsai (1994) recast the alternative manifestations of *wh*-movement as a lexical parameter. The new formulation of the *wh*-parameter by Tsai (1994) made no reference to the levels of representation of Huang's parameter. Instead, the parameter was stated in terms of features that *wh*-words may or may not bear (cf. Huang et al. 2009). In brief, setting the *wh*-parameter amounted to deciding whether to assign a plus feature [+wh] or a minus feature [–wh] to a lexical item (the head of a *wh*-phrase). The lexical parameter proposed by Tsai (1994) was designed to reflect the observation made by Aoun and Li (1993) and Cheng (1991; 1995) that *wh*-words in Chinese have a different semantic character than *wh*-words in English. In English, *wh*-words are [+wh]. This bestows upon them inherent quantificational force. By contrast, *wh*-words in Chinese are [–wh], lacking inherent quantificational force. They function more like variables that inherit the force from quantificational expressions that bind them, including quantificational expressions, such as the quantificational adverb *dou* 'all.' In many respects, *wh*-phrases in Chinese-type languages were seen to function in the same way as indefinite expressions in conditional statements (see Lewis 1975, Heim 1982).

Turning to language learning, it seems reasonable to suppose that the initial value of the *wh*-parameter is [−wh]. Alternatively, the parameter could be considered to be privative, with the initial option being that it has no value at all, versus [+wh]. On the privative approach, children initially assign no value, and add the feature [+wh] in response to positive evidence that *wh*-words require this feature in the local language. In either case, children acquiring English must figure out, based on lexical learning, that a [+wh] feature is assigned to *wh*-phrases. Once they figure this out, *wh*-movement is enforced in languages like English.[2] Children acquiring Chinese, on the other hand, encounter no evidence for the feature assignment [+wh]. Therefore, children exposed to Chinese take no action, and *wh*-words remain *in-situ*. The fact that *wh*-movement takes place at LF in languages like Chinese was no longer explicitly written into the parameter; this was handled by independent linguistic principles.

Despite any drawbacks that might be attributed to lexical parameters due to learnability considerations, from a theoretical standpoint the proposal that all parameters reside in the lexicon is more constrained than a model that takes parameters to be syntax-internal. Parameters are more constrained in the sense that variation is restricted to the formal features that can be associated with lexical items; formal features are finite in number, because lexical items are (Roberts and Holmberg 2010). In the previous model, there was no corresponding guarantee that parameters were finite, because there were no limitations on their formulation. However, Rizzi (2009a, 2009b) suggests that we can envisage quite a rich parametric system if we combine the view that parameters can be expressed as properties of functional heads together with the cartographic approach to linguistic structure. On the cartographic approach, it is assumed that languages have a rich functional structure that varies cross-linguistically, as Rizzi (1997, 2001a) demonstrates for the left periphery. A more fleshed-out version is offered in Rizzi (2009b). Rizzi provides a typology of three kinds of parameters that relate to the computational processes of Merge, Move (which is 'Internal Merge') and Spell-out, shown in (2).

(2) For H a functional head, H has F, where F is a feature determining H's properties with respect to the major computational processes of Merge, Move (Internal Merge) and Spell-out. For instance:

Merge parameters:	– what category does H select as a complement
	– to the left or the right?
Move parameters:	– does H attract a lower head?
	– does H attract a lower phrase to its Spec?
Spell-out parameters:	– is H overt or null?
	– does H license a null Spec or complement?

The statement offered in (2) takes parameters to be microparameters. For example, the Merge parameters require the complement direction to be set separately for each functional head. There is no macroparameter for head direction that separates languages into two types according to cross-categorial head direction. If there are tendencies for languages to adopt the same head direction across categories, this must presumably be explained by invoking a different mechanism. One such mechanism, proposed by Roberts and Holmberg (2010), invokes a markedness convention that establishes a harmonic ordering in the direction of heads across categories (see below).

These and other developments in the theory of parameters have not been received enthusiastically by all generative linguists. In particular, Newmeyer (2004, 2005) has questioned the enterprise of reducing typological variation to parameters (see also Chapter 3). Instead, Newmeyer advocates a UG with principles, and language-particular rules. On this account, typological variation is handled by principles of performance. That is, they are attributed to third factor effects (also see Boeckx 2010). Newmeyer (2004) argues that the "hopeful vision" of the classic model of parameters has not been fulfilled. For one thing, he contends that parameters have not turned out to be descriptively simpler than rules, they are not uniformly binary, and they are not few in number. Newmeyer also questions the hierarchy presented by Baker, and suggests that parametric clustering has not produced the typological divisions it was intended to. Finally, Newmeyer contends that studies of child language have provided little support for parameters. We take issue with the last point in Section 25.6, where we present empirical evidence from studies of language acquisition that weighs on the side of parameters. As we demonstrate with two scope parameters, there is ample evidence that children sometimes misset parameters, which supports the proposal that UG contains both principles and parameters. Newmeyer's negative critique has engendered considerable debate in the literature which the reader can follow, e.g., Boeckx (2010), Holmberg (2010), Roberts and Holmberg (2010), and Lohndal and Uriagereka (2010). Two critical issues of contention have emerged. The first issue is whether macroparameters exist, or whether all parameters are microparameters. The second issue is the degree to which the parametric system should be part of the innately specified language faculty or, instead, should be attributed to third factor effects.

Not all lexical parameters must be conceived of as microparameters, as argued by Baker (2008a) and Roberts and Holmberg (2010). Although microparameters typically encode small-scale differences in linguistic structures, such as occur among closely related languages, or even dialects of the same language, some lexical parameters could encode larger-scale language variation.[3] For example, Roberts and Holmberg (2010) observe that Rizzi's (1982a, 1986a) Null Subject Parameter can naturally be reconceived as a lexical parameter that governs a cluster of properties (the lack of expletives, the possibility of postverbal subjects, the absence of *that*-trace effects, etc.). In Rizzi's original proposal, the inflection node contained a pronominal Agr feature which licensed the subject as pro in languages with null subjects, such as Italian. Roberts and Holmberg (2010) observe that the parameter can be restated in Minimalist terms by invoking the presence or absence of a D-feature that is associated with the functional head T, yielding the same cluster of effects as in Rizzi's earlier formulation. This would be a welcome result as it would regain the powerful predictions from the 'classic model' of parameters that seemingly unrelated phenomena would be acquired at the same time. As we have noted, such predictions set UG models of language acquisition apart from usage-based models of language development. (See Snyder and Stromswold 1997 and Snyder 2001 for investigations of different properties emerging in the grammar during the same time period.)

Although the tide continues to flow in the direction of lexical parameters and microparameters, Baker (2008a) has offered cogent arguments against both of these conclusions. He has argued, first, that parameters cannot all be stated in terms of variation in the formal features of functional heads. In Baker's view, recalcitrant parameters include the polysynthesis parameter (Baker 1996), possibly the head parameter, and two agreement parameters he has proposed to explain cross-linguistic facts in Niger-Congo and Indo-European languages (Baker 2008a, 2008b). For example, Baker's statement of one of the agreement parameters crucially relies on the syntactic property of c-command and, therefore, cannot be relegated to the lexicon. For this reason, as well as for others, Baker also argues for a grammar that incorporates both microparameters and macroparameters. As we saw, Baker's (2001) model of parameter setting introduces a parameter hierarchy. The hierarchy serves double duty. It accounts for typological differences, and it has empirical consequences for language learning. On the Baker model, the macroparameters reside at the top of the hierarchy, and are set first, whereas microparameters are closer to the bottom, and are set later in the course of language acquisition as children work their way down one side or the other, following their decisions about the macroparameters. Thus, microparameters determine the fine-tuning of grammars, across languages, including properties of neighboring dialects.

Another cluster of linguistic properties that may be associated with a macroparameter has been the focus of research by Bošković (2008b) and Bošković and Gajewski (2011). In a series of papers, Bošković and Gajewski have offered a number of syntactic and semantic generalizations that appear to be consequences of one setting or the other of the NP/DP parameter (see also Chapter 11). For example, NP languages (lacking articles) permit left-branch extraction, scrambling, and NEG-raising, whereas DP languages do not. If these generalizations continue to be verified across languages, this will bolster the case for macroparameters, in addition to microparameters (but see Boeckx 2010). It is worth noting also that the NP/DP parameter concerns variation in syntactic structure, so this parameter does not fit within the Borer–Chomsky conjecture that all parameters are positioned in the lexicon.

A model advanced by Roberts and Holmberg (2010) also supposes that all parameters are microparameters, in order to adhere to the Borer–Chomsky conjecture that all parameters can be stated in the lexicon, for reasons alluded to earlier. Despite this supposition, Roberts and Holmberg concede that Baker (2001, 2008a) has offered valid arguments for the existence of macroparameters. They propose a compromise. On their view, macroparameters are epiphenomenal. They argue that the effects that Baker attributes to macroparameters are the result of "aggregates of microparameters acting in concert for markedness reasons" (Roberts and Holmberg 2010:41). Instead of a macroparameter that sets the head direction for all syntactic categories in a language, one way or the other, Roberts and Holmberg propose that each head could, in principle, be set separately, with a markedness convention prompting a harmonic ordering in the direction of heads across categories. Thus, an unmarked parameter system would comprise a harmonic cluster of microparameters, either all head-first or all head-last. Languages that mix the direction of headedness across categories would be more marked, so fewer of these mixed languages are anticipated. This is stated in the following generalization:

(3) Generalization of the Input
If acquirers assign a marked value to H, they will assign the same value to all comparable heads.

This markedness convention is seen to follow from the conservativity of the learner. Learners are conservative in the sense that they set parameters in the most efficient way possible. One consideration that must be confronted, however, is how well generalization (3) serves the cause of language learnability, since learners who adhere to the generalization would presumably produce non-adult structures whenever the target language is one of the mixed languages. If so, then the proposal confronts the question of how learners manage to detect and recover from errors in the absence of negative evidence. But let us set this question aside momentarily.

As noted earlier, there were two advantages to placing parametric variation in the lexicon. First, this constrained the mechanisms by which languages can vary. The nature of parameters becomes well-defined, such that cross-language variation is limited to differences in features. Second, by its very nature, parameter setting involves learning, and the lexicon is clearly a domain of language that involves learning. Roberts and Holmberg (2010) point out, however, that this does not solve the problem of overspecification. They point out that, even under the Borer–Chomsky conjecture, the potential formal features (and their values) that may be associated with functional heads must all be innately specified in the language faculty. Innate specification of parameter values runs counter to the basic goals of the Minimalist Program, according to many of its advocates. Under Minimalist assumptions, the language faculty should not impose more innate specification than necessary.

On Baker's hierarchical model, once learners set the polysynthesis parameter, say, they never need to consider the pro-drop parameter, because the pro-drop parameter resides on the other side of the hierarchy. Nevertheless, the pro-drop parameter is still specified in the parameter architecture, whether considered or not, so the system is still overspecified. Roberts and Holmberg (2010) attempt to resolve this issue by proposing a parametric system based on underspecification. The child is not presented with a menu of choices with potential values of parameters spelled out in advance, as in the earlier P&P framework. Instead, according to I. Roberts (2010), underspecification means that there is a default specification for a particular formal feature. Children begin with the [−F] value as the default (or no value in privative systems), and only adopt the [+F] value if positive data initiate this change. Adopting argumentation due to Gianollo et al. (2008) and Roberts and Roussou (2003), Roberts and Holmberg (2010) limit the innate specification of parameters to the pool of features that define cross-linguistic variation and a general 'schema' that defines the options to be considered for any formal feature. The schema walks learners bit by bit through a number of successive options, leading them to gradually create a parameter network. The proposal by Roberts and Roussou (2003) is illustrated as follows in Roberts and Holmberg (2010):

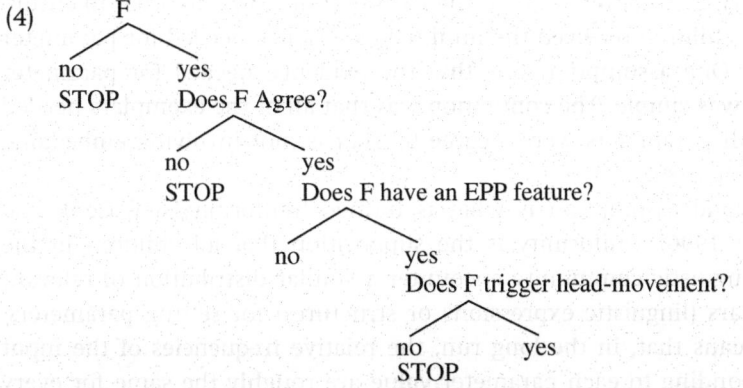

(4) F
　　 ╱╲
　 no　yes
　STOP　Does F Agree?
　　　　　╱╲
　　　　 no　yes
　　　STOP　Does F have an EPP feature?
　　　　　　　　╱╲
　　　　　　　no　yes
　　　　　　　　　Does F trigger head-movement?
　　　　　　　　　　╱╲
　　　　　　　　　no　yes
　　　　　　　　STOP

According to the innate schema, for any given formal feature, a learner first considers whether or not that feature enters an Agree relation. If the formal feature does not enter into an Agree relation, the 'network' develops no further, and the learner's system is left with the unmarked option of the feature. If the formal feature does enter into an Agree relation, then the learner considers the next decision, whether or not the formal feature has an EPP feature. If it does, the learner proceeds to consider whether or not the formal feature in question triggers head movement. As the network develops more and more detail, it becomes more marked, because expanding the network requires the learner to engage in more computations. Roberts and Holmberg speculate that such parameter networks could account for the major typological differences across languages, with the appearance of macroparameters consisting of decisions that are made at earliest steps along the learning path. In I. Roberts (2010), five networks drive typological distinctions. Roberts suggests that there exist both syntactic parameters and lexical parameters. The syntactic parameters mostly concern movement. Lexical parameters are reduced to those parameters that deal with the realization of functional heads at PF (as overt or not), i.e., 'PF parameters.' The Minimalist assumptions are clearly visible – the objective is to minimize the learners' genetic endowment, by attributing as much of the responsibility for parameter setting as possible to third factor properties.

25.4 Setting parameters

Although distinct from learning, parameter setting involves experience, at least to some degree, on all of the accounts that have been proposed. This invites us to ask about the nature of the experience that is prerequisite to parameter setting. Even if the role of experience for parameter setting is minimal, there must be some guarantee that all children will encounter the requisite experience, since all children converge on the final state in the first few years of life. In the 'classic' view of parameter setting, several assumptions were made about the nature of the input in order to ensure that all children received the minimal experience needed for parameter setting. One assumption was that the evidence needed for parameter setting was simple. The contention was that all of the exemplars needed to set all parameters were 'degree 0,' that is, not involving embedding (Lightfoot 1989).

A second assumption is what is termed 'uniformity' (cf. Cook and Newson 1996). Uniformity is the supposition that all children in the same linguistic community encounter a similar distribution of relevant exemplars (linguistic expressions or structures) for setting parameters. This means that, in the long run, the relative frequencies of the input corresponding to each parameter value are roughly the same for every child. The usual assumption was that the ambient input sufficed for 'early parameter setting' (see, e.g., Borer and Wexler 1987, Wexler 1998). Nothing in the theory itself prevented parameters from being set early, so if it turned out that they were not set early, then something outside the theory must be responsible for delayed setting of parameters. Therefore, it was the 'null hypothesis' that parameters were set early. We return to the idea that parameters are set 'very early' later when we introduce Wexler's (1998) proposal. Finally, researchers working within the parameter-setting framework assumed that children were initially free to pick one or the other setting, unless a subset problem would arise if one particular setting were adopted, rather than the other. The possibility of 'default' settings was available, in principle, but there was no reason to suppose that there were default settings a priori.

Another assumption was that the experience needed for parameter setting consisted solely of 'positive' data. If there was negative evidence, then all parameters could be set in any order. In the absence of negative evidence, however, the values of at least some parameters must be entertained in a prescribed order, to ensure that children can reset these parameters, if need be, using positive data. The parameters in question involve the Subset Principle discussed earlier (Berwick 1985). In the last section, we will discuss two parameters whose alternate values fall in a subset/superset relation (for other examples, see Berwick and Weinberg 1984; Wexler and Manzini 1987, Roeper and Williams 1987, Crain et al. 1994). Subset problems aside, the picture of language development that emerged in the early days of the Principles and Parameters approach was one in which children could freely choose any parameter value, and would quickly be confronted with relevant input if the value they had adopted was incorrect for the local language.

25.4.1 Can parameters be misset?

On the underspecification account proposed by Roberts and Holmberg (2010), children begin their parameter-setting journey with default values, these being values that are computationally unmarked in the parameter network under creation by the child. Children are also seen to assign defaults in setting parameters whose values are in a subset/superset relation. On a number of models of parameter setting, the null hypothesis has been that parameters are initially set to the subset value. One of the earliest proposals along these lines was Hyams's proposal about null subjects (Hyams 1986, 1987). Hyams proposed that children begin with the [+pro drop] setting, moving only to the [-pro drop] setting once they had encountered relevant data (such as expletives, for example) in the positive input. Another class of parameter-setting models supposes that both parameter values are active in children's grammars, and they compete with each other to see which provides a better fit with the input. This view was probably advanced first by Lebeaux (1988), who proposed that children began with both parameter values being operative, with one of them taking priority in response to input from the local language. This is the view taken by Yang (2002, 2004), which we present in more detail below.

More common, however, is the view that children are free to adopt either value of a number of parameters, and that readily available experience instructs children to jettison values that are incorrect for their local language. The idea that children could initially adopt a parameter value that differs from that used by adult speakers led to what is called the continuity hypothesis. The continuity hypothesis maintains that each value of a parameter corresponds to a possible human language (cf. Crain 1991, Pinker 1984, Crain and Pietroski 2001, 2002, Baker 2001, Smith and Law 2009). Cases in which children adopt parameter values that are inconsistent with the target language are termed 'parametric discontinuity' by Rizzi (2005a). To avoid confusion, let us simply refer to the continuity hypothesis. Not all parametric approaches anticipate non-target parameter settings, however. For example, Snyder (2007) argues that children cannot 'reset' parameters; for this reason children's grammatical hypotheses are inherently conservative according to Snyder (2007: Section 2.5.6).

The expectations generated by the continuity hypothesis also differ sharply from usage-based approaches, where learners are seen to be conservative learners, attempting to match the input, by accruing rules or constructions on the basis of positive examples. On such accounts, it would be very surprising if children were found to be producing utterances that featured a property of other languages but not the language spoken in the surrounding community (see also Snyder 2007).

According to the continuity hypothesis, even if the value children initially adopt is different from the value that is operative in the local language, children's grammars are nevertheless compatible with UG. At every stage of acquisition children are speaking well-formed structures from a possible human language, but perhaps not only structures exhibited in the local language, but also some 'foreign' language structures. In most cases, children's non-adult grammars will not be readily apparent, because mismatches between the current setting of the parameter would be easily detectable, and quickly set straight. Still, for one reason or another (e.g., maturation) it could take a child some amount of time to reset a parameter, and during the intervening period, the child would be observed to be speaking a fragment of a 'foreign' language. Therefore, the investigation of children's early productions promised, potentially, to offer empirical support for both the concept of parameters, and the theory of Universal Grammar (Crain 1991, Crain and Thornton 1998, Crain and Pietroski 2001, 2002, Rizzi 2005a). As a historical note, the earliest empirical support for the concept of parameters was a case of apparent parameter missetting, reported in Hyams (1986). This study investigated young English-speaking children, who were found to spontaneously produce sentences lacking overt subjects. The interpretation of this finding given by Hyams was that children's omissions of subjects were the product of the missetting of the pro-drop parameter. The pro-drop parameter distinguishes languages that require overt subjects, such as English, from languages that tolerate both overt and covert subjects, such as Italian.[4] Children acquiring English were seen to be speaking a 'foreign' language, at least in part, in line with the continuity hypothesis (cf. Hyams 1986, 1987).

25.4.2 Timing issues

Although nothing in the theory of Universal Grammar specifies precisely how parameter setting might unfold in real time, the expectation has been that parameter setting (and even parameter resetting) would transpire early in the course of language development, possibly triggering immediate and far-reaching changes from one kind of grammar to another. However, children have not always been found to make rapid transitions in acquiring the linguistic properties that vary across languages. There are a number of ways to deal with the mismatch between linguistic theory and data from empirical studies of child language.

One response has been to continue to suppose that parameters are set early in the course of acquisition, and to invoke maturation for late-developing grammatical properties (Borer and Wexler 1987, Wexler 1992, 1994, 1998). Recently, Wexler has argued that basic parameters are set by the time the child enters the two-word stage, at around eighteen months (Wexler 1998). In fact, Wexler speculates that these parameters are set 'perceptually,' so that children set parameters before they actually use the acquired values in production. If so, children will never be witnessed to have misset parameter values. In support of this claim, Wexler offers a number of parameters, including word-order parameters (VO or OV; V-to-I; V2) and the Null Subject Parameter, which he argues are set very early. Other syntactic structures that appear late or are prone to error in comprehension are proposed to incorporate properties that mature (e.g., Babyonyshev *et al.* 2001, Borer and Wexler 1987, 1992, Hirsch and Wexler 2007, Wexler 1994, 1998). Empirical investigations have offered further support for the claim that word-order parameters are set early. The Null Subject Parameter is more controversial. If we take children's omission of subjects to be aligned with the root subject drop parameter, as argued by Rizzi (2005a) (cf. note 4), however, then it can be assumed that the Null Subject Parameter is set very early, in line with Wexler's claim.

As Rizzi (2005a) also points out, however, there are properties of language that vary cross-linguistically, but do not fit the mold predicted by the early parameter-setting model. Rizzi (2005a) lists the following candidates as properties that appear to be set later in development:

(5) Root subject drop (Rizzi 1994, 2005a)
    Determiner drop (Chierchia *et al.* 2001)
    Ellipsis of copulas and auxiliaries (Becker 2000, Franchi 2004)
    Root infinitives (Avrutin 1998)
    Residual V2 (de Villiers 1991, Thornton 2004, Hamann 2003)
    Grammatical devices for A'-extraction (Thornton 1990, 1995, van Kampen 1997, Gutierrez 2004, see also Section 22.4, on *wh*-scope marking and *wh*-copying)

Rizzi (2005a) attributes the differences between the early- and late-set parameters to a learning principle of the LAD. This principle compels learners to adopt parameter values that reduce the computational load on the production system. According to the proposal, if one value of a parameter requires less articulatory effort at PF than the other, the value associated with least effort will be initially favored. As a consequence, learners could incur delays in the acquisition of the 'correct' parameter value, if that value requires additional computational resources over and above those required by the initial value. The proposal about early versus late parameter setting is not formulated to extend to word-order parameters, so those parameters are set early, whereas other parameters are initially set to the value that requires less phonologically overt structure, and may need to be changed in response to evidence that more phonological processing is required in the local language. As Rizzi points out, the fit between theory and data is not perfect. For example, the extra 'medial-wh' found in wh-copying structures such as *What do you think what Cookie Monster eats?* (see Section 22.4) is evidence of parameter missetting that involves commission, not omission (cf. Thornton 1990, 1995, Crain and Thornton 1998). However, since such long-distance questions are typically found in children older than three, he proposes that these cases may not fall under the performance umbrella.

A more challenging counterexample to the least-effort production principle proposed by Rizzi (2005a) comes from a longitudinal study of the emergence of VP ellipsis in two-year-old English-speaking children's speech (Thornton 2010). Languages differ in the syntactic categories that allow for ellipsis (see Chapter 19). In short, whether a language allows VP ellipsis or not is potentially due to a parameter. English allows VP ellipsis, French and German do not, Spanish and Irish do, and so on. According to Rizzi's proposal, children are expected to initially favor ellipsis for all syntactic categories. This remains to be fully examined, but at least for VP ellipsis, Thornton found that not all English-speaking children start out using ellipsis in their production. In a detailed study of two children's answers to *yes/no*-questions, Thornton found that one of the children gave only full sentence answers at first, adopting answers with elided VPs considerably later. Furthermore, Thornton provides data to suggest that the delay in VP ellipsis is not caused by the morphological licensing conditions governing VP ellipsis in English, which could potentially be argued to explain why children do not initially adopt the ellipsis option.

Another possible consequence of the LAD preference for phonological economy could be to encourage children to select the superset value of parameters whose values stand in a subset/superset relation, in violation of the Subset Principle. The root subject drop parameter is a case in point. A minus value would require overt subjects, whereas a positive value would optionally permit subjects in the root to be omitted. The positive optional root subject drop value is the value adopted by two-year-old children. This is not problematic, on Rizzi's view. The LAD strategy applies to children younger than three. By then, children's computational/articulatory system will have matured to the point that it can accommodate all parametric options. Once the LAD strategy is no longer in effect, the Subset Principle will be engaged. Unless there is positive evidence to the contrary, children will revert to the subset value, thus averting potential learnability problems.

It is interesting to note some points of similarity between Rizzi's (2005a) proposal and that of I. Roberts (2010), especially since Roberts's proposal is based solely on theoretical considerations. Both Rizzi and Roberts argue that children begin with the most computationally economical value of a parameter. For Roberts, this is the computationally unmarked value of the parameter, and the subset value. On the other hand, for Rizzi, the value that is computationally more economical is the one requiring less effort at PF. This value can, on occasion, be the superset value, if this generates less structure to be pronounced. The more striking point of similarity, however, is that Rizzi's early- and late-set parameters correspond closely to the syntactic and PF parameters proposed by I. Roberts (2010). Roberts proposes five syntactic macroparameters. Three of these are related to movement (word order/linearization, discourse configurationality, and alignment (ergative vs. accusative) and the other two regulate features that are implicated in the Agree relation; these control the possibility of null arguments and word structure properties. These parameters are set very early in acquisition. PF parameters, on the other hand, "merely involve the differing realization of otherwise invariant features; in the simplest case, the realization of heads" (I. Roberts 2010). Although the later set parameters in Rizzi's list may not all be dependent on whether or not heads are realized at PF, they are all concerned with the expression of structure as overt or covert.

Another way to explain the fact that children do not acquire some properties until later in the course of acquisition is to invoke a parameter hierarchy. Let us illustrate the point using the hierarchy proposed by Baker (2001). The broad typological parameters at the top of the hierarchy include the polysynthesis parameter, so this will be among those that are set early. The parameters much lower on the hierarchy include ones that distinguish closely related language families or dialects and, therefore, these are expected to be set later. The parameter networks proposed by Roberts and Holmberg (2010) also establish an ordering with temporal consequences, such that unmarked values will be acquired early, and more marked values later. Finally, it seems fair to say that the underspecification model proposed by Roberts and Holmberg (2010), although not yet fully developed, anticipates late acquisition of some parameter values, on the supposition that children must analyze considerable data before moving from the default (minus) value of a parameter to the positive value.

Another response to the observed delays in language acquisition invokes statistical learning, in addition to the principles and parameters of Universal

Grammar. A model of parameter setting that is augmented by statistical learning was advanced in Yang (2002, 2004). The conception of parameter setting as 'triggering' is simply wrong, according to Yang, who argues for what he calls the 'Variational' model of parameter setting. On this model, parameter values are binary, and stated in the language faculty. However, Yang departs from standard assumptions by arguing that parameters are set on the basis of statistical frequencies of input structures. Thus the parameter setting mechanism is recast as a third factor property, specifically an information processing mechanism (Chomsky 2005). On this model, different parameter values amount to different grammars, which are in competition with each other. The value/grammar that survives is the one that is better instantiated in the input. There is abundant input for some parameters, of course, and learners are expected to decide on the value of such parameters earlier in the course of language acquisition, as compared to cases where the input needed to push the learner one way or another is less abundant. In these cases, a gradual learning curve should be witnessed in the course of development. Yang points to evidence of late parameter setting as support for the Variational model.

This section has reviewed several models of parameter setting in order to indicate how these models might explain early versus late parameter setting. In addition, a new model, by Yang, was introduced. This model explicitly introduced a third factor, a statistical learning mechanism, as a way of dealing with the observation that some parameters are set earlier than others. Next we will compare these models of parameter setting once again, this time highlighting their differences, before turning to an assessment of their ability to cope with the empirical data in the literature on child language.

25.5 A comparison of parameter-setting models

We begin by comparing the classic triggering model of parameter setting to the five recent proposals of parameters, and parameter setting. The models are: (a) the Very Early Parameter Setting model (Wexler 1994, 1998) (henceforth the VEPS model); (b) the Hierarchical Acquisition model (Baker 2001, 2005); (c) the Underspecification model (Roberts and Holmberg 2010, Roberts 2010); (d) the PF-Constrained model (Rizzi 2005a); and (e) the Variational model (Yang 2002, 2004).

All five of these models derive from the P&P framework, but they diverge in their predictions concerning the following characteristics:

(a) the time course of parameter setting;
(b) the need for statistical learning mechanisms in parameter setting;
(c) how parameter values are engaged, i.e., whether children start with a single parameter value, or with both values operative;

(d) the behavioral patterns that should be observed in parameter setting, i.e., whether behavior should take the shape of a gradual curve or a steep climb;
(e) whether or not the behavior patterns in parameter setting should assume the same form for all children.

By comparing the five models against these features, we can then proceed to evaluate how well each of the models stands up against the empirical findings from the last thirty years.

25.5.1 Six characteristics of parameter setting models
This section identifies some key criteria about language development to be used in comparing the alternative models of parameter setting:

(A) Uniformity
All five of the generative P&P models share the assumption that children are exposed to a uniform set of data. More specifically, children in the same linguistic community are assumed to be exposed to roughly the same linguistic data, and any minor differences in the environmental input are not sufficient to leave an imprint on the language that is acquired. It is worth noting that this assumption is not shared by usage-based models, which attempt to correlate the observed differences in the input to children with individual differences in grammatical development, and even differences in adult grammars.

(B) Ordering
Parameter-setting models postulate either that (a) parameters are set in a particular order or partially ordered, or that (b) parameters can be set in any order. On the Hierarchical Acquisition model, parameters are organized hierarchically with typologically 'major' parameters set before minor ones (but see also early work on parameter ordering by Nishigauchi and Roeper 1987, Roeper and de Villiers 1991). An ordering of the parameter space could also be imposed in other ways, with certain parameters being biologically timed to become operative at a later point in development than others, or, as in Rizzi's (2005a) proposal, due to a learning principle that enforces the parameter setting invoking the least articulatory effort, until the production system matures.

Unordered parameters are said to be 'independent.' If parameters are independent, then acquisition is like a scavenger hunt, where items (values) may be acquired in any order. This can be contrasted with a treasure hunt, in which items must be acquired in a particular sequence (cf. Lasnik and Crain 1985). The Hierarchical Acquisition model views parameter setting as a treasure hunt; except for the Underspecification model, the other models view parameter setting as a scavenger hunt. The Underspecification model in I. Roberts (2010) seems to be a mix of treasure hunt and scavenger hunt. Ceteris paribus, scavenger hunt models anticipate more rapid acquisition (i.e., the completion of parameter setting) than treasure hunt models. Indeed, the Hierarchical Acquisition model advanced by Baker exploits the ordering of the parametric hierarchy to argue for later acquisition of certain grammatical properties (Baker 2005).

(C) The initial value

This refers to the number of values that are in play when the learner first engages in setting a parameter. The VEPS model, the Hierarchical Acquisition model, and the Underspecification model all assume that the learner initially adopts a single value. In cases where the values are nested in a subset/superset relation, children initially begin with the default subset value. Where subset issues don't arise, the VEPS and the Hierarchical Acquisition model assume that learners can, in principle, begin with either value. The Underspecification model assumes that the child always begins with the default 'minus' value of the parameter. This value is considered to be less marked and therefore computationally simpler than the positive value of the parameter, which is only considered if the data drive the child to look for an alternative. Likewise, the PF-Constrained model postulates that an initial value is selected for the later set parameters. The Variational model contrasts with the other models in assuming that learners entertain both competing values from the earliest stages (cf. Lebeaux 1988, Valian 1991).

(D) Input

The classic parameter-setting model assumed that the primary linguistic data is available in sufficient quantity to ensure 'easy' acquisition of parameters. This position is shared by all of the models, except for the Variational model. The Variational model assumes that learners need to have encountered a sufficient quantity of data as a prerequisite to setting any parameter, and the model contends that the requisite data are not uniformly available, in similar frequency counts, for all parameters. On this model, it is more difficult to establish the target value of parameters with sparse requisite input, as compared to parameters that have abundant corresponding input. Therefore the amount of relevant data in the input will decide how quickly children bring the competition between the alternative parameter values to a close.

(E) Trajectory

Trajectory refers to the pattern of development that learners are expected to exhibit in selecting the value of a parameter in response to input. If parameters are set using minimal input, or if input is abundant, then no special record-keeping is required for parameter setting. This is the view of VEPS, and the Hierarchical model. On these models, the ('idealized') expected developmental pattern is a step function. If both values are active, the expected pattern is a rapid incline in one value of the parameter, and a corresponding, and equally rapid decline in the alternative value. Alternatively, extensive record-keeping may be required for parameters for which there is not abundant input. This is the perspective of the Variational model. However, what constitutes rapid or gradual parameter setting has not been established in the literature. We will follow the criterion in Thornton and Tesan (2007) and assume that if a parameter setting transitions from one setting to the other in three months or less, then this is categorical, or rapid acquisition.

(F) Conformity

Conformity refers to individual differences or lack thereof. There are two possibilities, either (a) all learners navigate the same course through the parameter space, or (b) different children chart different courses. If parameters are ordered, then individual differences are expected to appear, even with uniform and abundant input, because children may adopt different initial values (starting points). Some children will immediately advance through the hierarchical parameter space, others will make just a few missteps, and some children will make many missteps; consequently, children will differ in the amount of time they take to complete the process of parameter setting. If children all start with both parameter values active, and parameters are not ordered hierarchically, and the input is abundant and uniform for all parameters, then individual differences are not expected. Similarly, if children all start with the default value, as in the Underspecification model, individual differences in the course of development are not anticipated. It should be noted that, if individual differences are observed in development, these differences do not extend to the final state. By the time children reach three or four years old they have reached a level of linguistic competence that is essentially equivalent to that of adults, with just a handful of exceptions.

25.5.2 The Very Early Parameter Setting model

The main feature that distinguishes the Very Early Parameter Setting model (VEPS) (Wexler 1994, 1998) from the classic parameter setting model is the timing of parameter-setting. As in the classic model, differences in the primary linguistic data have little impact on the observed course of parameter setting; the data is considered by both models to be abundant enough for parameter setting to take place. In fact, the data in the input must be plentiful for parameter setting to be achieved by the time children are producing multi-word utterances. The earliness of parameter setting is not a function of ordering of the parameters, however. Parameters are independent. Children initially begin with a single parameter value, but may adopt either value, unless this would lead to subset problems, as in the classic model. However, given the expectation that all 'basic' parameters will be set by the time the child is about eighteen months old, there will be no visible consequences of the earlier choice of a parameter value. Evidence of misset parameters or individual variation will fail to surface in children's productions. Thus, grammar formation is characterized by abrupt changes in grammars within a very short timeframe, with no 'third factor' learning mechanisms needed to assist in parameter setting.

The VEPS model has little room to maneuver in responding to empirical evidence of delayed acquisition of properties that vary across languages. Maturation is one possible explanation but, as far as we know, this has not been invoked for late setting of parameters. Instead, in Wexler's view, evidence of late emergence casts doubt on the assumption that the phenomenon in question is governed by a parameter (cf. Borer and Wexler 1987). This perspective is not shared by all models, however. As seen in Section 25.4, Rizzi (2005a) lists a number of phenomena that are likely candidates to be governed by parameters, but which are not set early in the course of acquisition.

25.5.3 The Hierarchical model

The Hierarchical model is largely based on the 'implicational universals' proposed in Baker (2001, 2005). On this model, parameters are ordered in a hierarchy, with large-scale typological parameters at the top of the hierarchy, including the polysynthesis parameter and the head directionality parameter. The parameters are interlocking and must be set in the top-down order specified by the hierarchy. As Baker says, "an efficient learner should learn in a structured way in which some parameters are entertained first and others later" (2005:95). It is quite possible that the broad typological parameters at the top of the hierarchy on this model could be set before the onset of production, just as Wexler (1998) contends. The smaller-scale parameters residing lower in the hierarchy are not necessarily set early because they must await decisions about parameters that are more dominant in the hierarchy.

As the learner traverses the parameter hierarchy, the parameters that are subsequently encountered differentiate fewer and fewer languages. The more minor parameters at the bottom of the hierarchy are seen to encode fine-grained features of the local dialect. Presumably these parameters are set well after children are talking (cf. Baker 2001:192–95). An interesting consequence of this model is that, although children can misset parameters, they are not expected to produce fragments of linguistic properties that are attested in typologically different languages, but not in the local language. Instead, children's non-target productions should be confined to properties of the same larger language family. It is conceivable that an English-speaking child could err by selecting a parameter value that is associated with a question form that is appropriate for a related

Germanic language. But, it is unlikely that an English-speaking child will posit that English has an ergative case system, for example.

In most respects, the model is like the classic parameter setting model. Children initially begin with a single parameter value. Initially, either value may be selected. Grammar formation is characterized by abrupt changes in grammars. Differences in the primary linguistic data have little impact on the observed course of parameter setting, so no special (e.g., statistical) learning mechanisms need to be invoked to explain parameter setting. Children may adopt different starting values and, given that different children may set the same parameters at different times, individual variation is expected on this model.

25.5.4 The Underspecification model

The Underspecification model is proposed by Roberts and Holmberg (2010) and I. Roberts (2010). This model bears some similarity to Baker's Hierarchical Acquisition model in that it attempts to address the finding, emphasized by Baker, that some parameters partition large classes of languages, and some manifest themselves in clusters of properties. These parameters tend to be syntactic parameters, according to Roberts (2010), in contrast to PF parameters which regulate whether or not heads are realized. As in the Hierarchical model, the syntactic parameters constitute a parameter network (hierarchy) on the Underspecification model. However, the network arises for markedness reasons, rather than being attributed to the architecture that has evolved to become part of the human genetic endowment for language, as on the Hierarchical Acquisition model. The consequences of the Underspecification model for language acquisition have not yet been fully developed, but for comparative purposes, we will attempt to flesh out some of its implications.

It is likely that the syntactic typological parameters are set early, since they contribute to the overall shape of the language being acquired. Some options that evolve from the parameter network are more marked than others, however, and the expectation is the more marked they are, the later acquired they are, as compared to less-marked options that reside at the top of the network. PF parameters reduce to questions about whether heads (at least) are pronounced or not. The PF parameters are, in principle, independent of the syntactic parameters. That being the case, the PF parameters could be set after the syntactic parameter values are settled on, or at the same time.

On the Underspecification model, children initially begin with a single parameter value. The default is the unmarked value, since this is computationally simpler. For some languages, this remains the correct value; for other languages, third factor effects will ensue. These effects will presumably draw upon resources for data analysis to initiate parameter resetting, such that the default value will drop to 0 percent over time. As noted earlier, the nature of the necessary third factor principle of learning is yet to be specified, but we can assume it is not a statistical learning mechanism of the sort that Yang (2002, 2004) proposes, because the values of parameters are not in competition on the Underspecification model. In any event, the model does not appear to predict early parameter resetting, as in the classic model. Given that all children begin with the default value and resetting is a response to input data, all children are expected to follow the same developmental path. Missetting of parameters can occur, but only if the local language does not conform to the markedness conventions of the theory.

25.5.5 The PF-Constrained model

Rizzi's (2005a) model harnesses aspects of the child's developing performance system, in particular production abilities, in addition to grammatical competence – hence we have dubbed this the 'PF-Constrained model.' The model is similar in many respects to the classic model, but augments the classical model with a learning principle. The learning principle is presumably part of the innate language faculty. Rizzi (2005a) is in agreement with Wexler (1998) that some parameters are set very early, but Rizzi wants to also explain why other parameters may be set late. The innovation of Rizzi's model is the proposal that late parameter setting is due to the fact that, before children are three years old, their production systems are not yet fully developed. To cope with an immature production system, an innate learning principle guides the child to initially adopt whichever parameter setting best serves to facilitate production. The parameter settings that are favored are ones that coincide with processes of ellipsis in Universal Grammar, according to which linguistic material is omitted in production. Though the learning principle is impinging on developing grammars, the child's productions are still within the boundaries of UG, so this model adheres to the continuity hypothesis. Although requisite data may be available for parameter resetting, if need be, this will be delayed until the production system matures enough to cope with the value that requires additional production of overt material corresponding to the syntactic structure. Thus, there are two sets of parameters, those parameters that are set before eighteen months and those that are set after. The parameters that are set very early can engage either parameter value, while the ones set later can initially engage only one value, the value that facilitates ellipsis. According to the facts about the local language, the initial setting may continue, or may change once the production system has matured.

Once parameter resetting takes place, the developmental trajectory is anticipated to be rapid, since the delay is not based on the relative abundance of input. Assuming that the production system of all young children is roughly equivalent, all children will assume the same learning strategy, and therefore no individual differences are expected on this model.

25.5.6 The Variational model

As in the classic model, the Variational model supposes that the alternative values of parameters are fully specified as part of the genetic endowment of the species (Legate and Yang 2007, Yang 2002, 2004, 2010). The distinguishing characteristic of this model is that children initially begin with both parameter values active, and in competition. That is, children initially attempt to parse the linguistic input using two 'grammars,' one grammar with one value of the parameter being active, and the other grammar with the other value active. If one of the competing grammars parses the input successfully, then that grammar is 'reinforced,' increasing the probability that it will be used in the future. Assuming that the opposing grammar, with the alternative parameter value, is unable to parse the same input, then that grammar is 'penalized,' and its probability of being selected in the future is correspondingly reduced. Gradually, probability weights are adjusted until the grammar with the non-target parameter value is no longer a contender and becomes obsolete. The model may be augmented by the addition of a 'learning parameter' that adjusts how much penalty or reward is awarded to the alternative grammars, according to their success or failure in parsing the input. Adjusting these weights has the effect of speeding up or slowing down the rate of learning, as the learner accumulates data such that confidence in one grammar increases.

This model uses quantitative input frequencies to estimate the learning trajectory to assess when parameter settings assume dominance, i.e., early or late in the course of development. Because parameters are set on the basis of statistical learning, there is no assumption that parameters are set early, as on the VEPS model. Based on his calculations, Yang proposes that if the 'signature' sentences relevant for parametric change constitute 7 percent or more of the data, a parameter will be set early. The earliest parameter is depicted to be set at around eighteen months. According to Yang, if the signature sentences comprise 1.2 percent or less of the data, there will be an extended struggle between the two values and the target setting will be consolidated later. The main point is that gradualness is expected in parameter setting. There will be a gradual rise and fall for many competing parameter values, rather than abrupt changes. This scenario contrasts with rapid ascent and descent of parameter values, as expected on the classic triggering model, when parameters are simply switched from one value to the other, in response to triggering data.

The amount of data available in the input for a particular property has no long-term imprint on the grammar. This is based on the assumption of uniformity. So, parameter setting on this model conforms to the idealization to instantaneous acquisition discussed earlier. Nevertheless, the frequency of input determines the course of parameter setting in the short term. In the short term children are all expected to follow the same path, so individual differences are not anticipated. The strength of the model is that it brings a solution to the problem of why children do not set parameters 'decisively,' as suggested by the switch metaphor. Moreover, the observation that children's linguistic output is often characterized by optionality further motivates the assumption that parameter values are initially in competition.

25.5.7 Summary: comparison of the five parameter-setting models

	'Classic'	VEPS	Hierarchical	Under specification	PF-Constrained	Variational
Uniformity of data	✓	✓	✓	✓	✓	✓
Ordering of parameters	✗	✗	✓	✗?	✓	✗
Initial value	A or B	A or B	A or B	Default A	Performance– preferred A or B	A and B
Requisite input available	✓	✓	✓	✓?	✓	✗
Rapid trajectory	✓	✓	✓	✓?	✓	✗
Conformity: individual differences expected	✓	✗	✓	✗	✗	✗

25.6 Alternatives to parameters and new directions

This section concludes our review of parameters and parameter setting in child language. To finish, we will survey some recent developments, beginning with two alternatives to parameter-setting models of language acquisition, and ending with two new models of parameter setting based on the findings from research on child language.

25.6.1 Optimality Theory

One alternative to parameter setting models is the Optimality-theoretic (OT) approach to language acquisition (on OT, see Chapter 5). The OT approach endows the child with a universal grammar that consists of linguistic constraints. However, cross-linguistic variation is not handled by a system of parameters. Instead, variation is expressed by different rankings of the constraints in a hierarchy. The constraints are 'soft' constraints that can be violated if they are outranked by other constraints with a more important part to play in the language under consideration. Constraint re-ranking is initiated by the input. The constraint hierarchy in the language faculty provides information about properties attested in human languages and, as such, this approach can be considered to be one in which linguistic knowledge is 'overspecified.' Viewing OT from the perspective of Chomsky's (2005) three factors of language design, this theory emphasizes the genetic endowment, and minimizes both experience and third factor properties, much like the 'classic' early P&P view. OT approaches also assume uniformity, as do all of the parameter proposals we have reviewed.

According to OT, the task facing learners is to attain the correct ranking of a series of innately specified constraints. There are two families of constraints, faithfulness constraints and markedness constraints. Faithfulness constraints assess the relationship between the input and the surface form, the output. Markedness constraints impose structural requirements on the input, basically favoring economical (minimal) structures. This family of constraints has a universal rank ordering that can be adjusted in response to experience. The child ultimately must figure out the correct rankings of these interacting constraints. At the initial state, the constraints are ordered such that markedness constraints outrank faithfulness constraints (Smolensky 1996). The net result is that 'small' structures, lacking functional categories, are favored over 'filled in' structures that are generated in the adult grammar. This bears some similarity to Rizzi's (2005a) PF-constrained model, although in the OT system, omissions in children's early productions are grammatically based, and not induced by the performance system interacting with the grammatical system. Legendre et al. (2004) conjecture, however, that it is possible for markedness constraints to be viewed as a formal encoding of processing limitations. At any rate, as the child develops linguistically, faithfulness constraints come to dominate markedness constraints. At present, however, it remains unclear what steers children as they progress through the process of re-ranking (Legendre 2006).

The fact that various options can surface in the child's productions means that the child is not inherently conservative on this model. In this way, the OT theory differs from the kind of grammatical conservatism postulated by Snyder (2007), to be discussed below. In principle, children can produce utterances that are not aligned with those of the local language; presumably the properties of these productions reflect the rankings that hold in other possible human languages. In this sense, the OT model is similar to the P&P model, in which parameters can be misset, in line with the continuity hypothesis.

Given that the assumption is that the requisite data for grammar formation is available and abundant for constraint re-ranking, a rapid trajectory to the adult grammar is anticipated. It will be important for future research to articulate the mechanisms for re-ranking that engender changes in child grammars. In particular, given recent developments in parameter theory, it will be important to establish whether third factor effects play a part in re-ranking or whether it is due to a mechanism of the innate language faculty.

25.6.2 The usage-based approach

In addition to models of language acquisition that attribute innate knowledge to children, an alternative approach has gained traction in many circles. This the usage-based approach (see also Sections 3.4 and 26.2.2.1, on Construction Grammar). By endowing the child with innate linguistic knowledge, generative approaches to language acquisition have aimed to explain children's rapid and relatively error-free acquisition of the language(s) spoken in the local linguistic community. Usage-based approaches to language development take issue with this view, claiming just the opposite – that acquiring a language is a slow and arduous task, especially when one considers the extent of a child's immersion in contexts of language use. Children use their linguistic experience to gradually build up an inventory of constructions (Goldberg 2003, 2006, Tomasello 2000a, 2000b, 2003, 2005, 2006a, 2006b, Lieven and Tomasello 2008).[5]

In stark contrast to generative models, the Lieven/Tomasello view is that children come to the task of acquiring their language with no advanced linguistic knowledge, except, perhaps the category NP, presumably because it is important for referring to concrete objects in the child's world (Tomasello 2000a, 2000b). Instead of innate linguistic knowledge, children draw on general cognitive resources to break into language. According to these researchers, children's attention to the referential intentions of others helps them focus on the presentation of language in context, which in turn facilitates learning, especially early word learning. As children develop, they observe 'usage events' and start to acquire basic constructions first, and then combine these to form more complex constructions. At first, children acquire constructions that are fully 'lexically specific,' but gradually they start to form limited 'schemas' with empty slots that can be replaced by a piece of language with a matching function. Gradually, the 'schemas' become more complex, with more open slots, until they assume the adult-like forms. Eventually children build up relations between constructions. At this later point, for example, children learn that active and passive constructions are related. On this view, then, the trajectory of language acquisition is piecemeal, at least initially, and gradual.

On parameter-setting models that assume triggering of parameter setting, certain stages of language acquisition are explained by supposing that there is an ordering of parameters. By contrast, usage-based models contend that the frequency of constructions in the parental input to children explains why certain constructions appear before others in children's productions; frequent constructions are incorporated into the grammar before less-frequent ones. Frequency may interact with other factors such as the consistency of the form–function mapping of the construction in the input (Lieven and Tomasello 2008), but frequency is the key predictor of the order of acquisition on such models.

The usage-based language acquisition literature makes little reference to the acquisition of properties that vary across language – properties considered to be in the purview of parameters in the theory of Universal Grammar. The focus of usage-based approaches is on constructions that are instantiated in the particular language being investigated. In view of the tight relationship between the child's developing linguistic knowledge and the input provided by their caretakers, children are not expected to produce constructions that are not present in the input. It would be mysterious, on this view, if a child produced a construction or property of language that was not attested in the local language, but attested in other languages of the world. In short, the evidence that is offered in support of the continuity hypothesis poses a challenge to usage-based approaches (Crain and Pietroski 2001, 2002). Recall that the continuity hypothesis anticipates that child and adult languages will differ within the limits imposed by Universal Grammar. On some of the principles and parameters models we have reviewed, such non-target utterances are expected, on the supposition that children can misset parameters. Children's non-adult linguistic behaviors that fall outside the scope of the continuity hypothesis have been labeled 'accidents' by Smith and Law (2009).

25.6.3 Grammatical conservatism

Two new models of parameters have been advanced within the generative framework. Both of these models have been developed in response to findings from the literature on child language. On the surface, the two proposals have much in common. Both maintain that the formulation of parameters must be based on findings from cross-linguistic research, adopting linguistic properties from typologically distinct languages, and both of them adopt a version of the subset principle. However, they reach quite different conclusions, in particular pertaining to the continuity hypothesis.

One recent model of parameters is the grammatical conservatism model, proposed by Snyder (2007). While Snyder contends that children are innately equipped with the principles and parameters of UG, he embraces grammatical conservatism. According to grammatical conservatism, "children do not begin making productive use of a new grammatical construction in their spontaneous speech until they have both determined that the construction is permitted in the adult language, and identified the adults' grammatical basis for it" (p. 8).

Because he embraces grammatical conservatism, Snyder is compelled to re-structure the parameters of UG, so that their (binary) values form a subset/superset relation (although Snyder readily concedes that this may prove problematic for some parameters). In the absence of negative evidence in the input to children, the subset value must be the initial setting for all parameters. This ensures that children's spontaneous speech will always match the target language, regardless of the value of the parameter assigned by adults. If children initially assign a different value than adults do, children will simply undergenerate, and will have readily available positive evidence to extend their grammars if the superset value of the parameter is operative in the adult language.

At first look, adherence to grammatical conservatism would seem to align Snyder's model with the usage-based approach. However, Synder appeals to two other features of his model to distinguish his theory of parameters from the experience-based ('input matching') approach to language development. First, the alternative values of the parameters postulated by Snyder incorporate linguistic properties that are taken from a survey of typologically different languages. Second, Snyder investigates the time course of acquisition of these properties, to see if the different linguistic properties associated with a particular parameter value emerge at the same time in children's spontaneous productions. Provided that alternative, third-factor effects such as computational complexity can be factored out, the finding that the relevant different linguistic properties emerge at the same time invites the inference that these properties are innately specified in children's grammars.

25.6.4 Scope parameters

Another model of parameters has been proposed by Goro (2004), and taken up by Crain and colleagues (see, e.g., Crain et al. 2006, Crain 2012). On this model, some parameters encode differences in scope relations between logical expressions (on the syntax and semantics of scope, see Chapter 22). Like the parameters advanced by Snyder, these scope parameters involve default settings and partition languages that are typologically distinct. However, this approach does not adhere to grammatical conservatism. In fact, scope parameters predict that children acquiring different languages will differ in systematic ways from adult speakers, albeit within the confines of the continuity hypothesis.

Scope ambiguities typically arise when two logical operators appear in the same clause. One example is sentences with negation (see Chapter 21) and disjunction. In negated disjunctions in English, negation takes scope over disjunction, so disjunction yields a conjunctive entailment. For example, (6) entails that Ted didn't order pasta and Ted didn't order sushi. This shows that English negative statements with disjunction correspond to one of de Morgan's Laws of propositional logic: $\neg(A \lor B) \Rightarrow \neg A \land \neg B$.

(6) Ted didn't order pasta or sushi.

Other languages, including Japanese and Mandarin Chinese, assign the opposite scope relations. In (7), the Mandarin disjunction word, *huozhe*, appears with negation, *meiyou*. Although the surface order of negation and disjunction are the same in Mandarin as in English, adult speakers of

Mandarin judge (7) to mean that Ted didn't order sushi *or* Ted didn't order pasta. Adult speakers of Mandarin accept (7) in three circumstances, where (i) Ted ordered pasta, but not sushi, (ii) Ted ordered sushi, but not pasta, and (iii) Ted ordered neither pasta nor sushi. In logic, the corresponding formula for the interpretation of (7) in Mandarin is ($\neg A \vee \neg B$), which does not entail ($\neg A \wedge \neg B$).

(7) (wo cai) Ted **meiyou** dian yidalimianshi huozhe shousi
 (I   guess) Ted not   order pasta   or   sushi
 'it's either pasta or sushi that Ted did not order'

The different interpretations across languages are attributed to a parameter, called the Disjunction Parameter. In one class of languages, disjunction takes scope over negation in simple negative sentences. Let us call this the (OR > NEG) value of the parameter. In the second class of languages, negation takes scope over disjunction, so this is the (NEG > OR) value.

Another difference across languages is the interpretation that is assigned to negated conjunctions, as in (8).

(8) Ted didn't order both sushi and pasta

Adult English-speakers take (8) to be true in three circumstances, where (i) Ted ordered just sushi, where (ii) Ted ordered just pasta, or where (iii) Ted ordered neither sushi nor pasta. Thus, English maintains the surface scope interpretation of negated conjunctions. Mandarin differs from English. Mandarin assigns the inverse scope interpretation of negated conjunctions. One way to translate the English example (8) into Mandarin mirrors the word order of English. The translation is given in (9), where *meiyou* is the Mandarin equivalent of English *not*, and *he* is the equivalent of *and*. In contrast to English, however, the conjoined clause in (9) is interpreted as having scope over negation at the level of logical form.

(9) Taide **meiyou** dian yidalimianshi **he** shousi
 Ted not order pasta and sushi
 'as for both pasta and sushi, Ted did not order them'

The variation illustrated by English versus Mandarin can be attributed to a second scope parameter. Although the meaning of conjunction is the same across languages (i.e., Boolean conjunction), human languages fall into one of two classes, according to which parameter value they adopt. In one class of languages, conjunction takes scope over negation in simple negative sentences (the (AND > NEG) value). In the other class, negation takes scope over conjunction, so this is the (NEG > AND) value. This second class of languages includes English. These are the two values of what we will call the Conjunction Parameter.

It has been proposed that children's initial settings of scope parameters are constrained by a learning principle called the Semantic Subset Principle (Crain *et al.* 1994).

Consider the Disjunction Parameter. It is easily verified that the circumstances in which sentences are true on the (OR > NEG) value comprise a superset of those circumstances that make sentences true on the (NEG > OR) value. In other words, the binary values are in a subset/superset relation. To see this, note that the NEG > OR value yields a 'neither' reading, whereas the OR > NEG value yields a 'not both' reading. Clearly, the statement *neither A nor B* is true in a subset of the circumstances corresponding to the statement *not both A and B*. When parameter values are in a subset/superset relation, a principle of learning dictates that children acquiring all languages must initially select the subset value.

Adopting the Semantic Subset Principle, Goro (2004) predicted that children learning languages like Mandarin and Japanese (which Goro studied) would initially interpret (7) in the same way as English-speaking children and adults interpret *Ted did not order pasta or sushi*. That is, children acquiring Mandarin were predicted to initially set the parameter to (NEG > OR), whereas adults assign the alternative value. If so, then children should generate a conjunctive entailment for (7), whereas adult speakers do not. In short, the commonality that is predicted is between Mandarin child language and English rather than between Mandarin child language and Mandarin adult language.

The prediction, then, is that children learning Mandarin would speak a fragment of a foreign language, selected from a class of languages that includes English. This prediction was first confirmed in an experimental study of Japanese-speaking children, reported by Goro and Akiba (2004b). We have replicated the Goro and Akiba findings with Mandarin-speaking children. Children acquiring both languages generate a conjunctive entailment for disjunction when it appears in the scope of negation, whereas adult speakers of both languages do not. The experience-based approach owes us an account of such findings.

Interestingly, the Conjunction Parameter has the opposite effects. It can easily be verified that the circumstances in which sentences are true on the (AND > NEG) value comprise a subset of those circumstances that make sentences true on the (NEG > AND) value. Simply note that the AND > NEG value yields a 'neither' reading, whereas the NEG > AND value yields a 'not both' reading. Clearly, the statement *neither A nor B* is true in a subset of the circumstances corresponding to the statement *not both A and B*. According to the Semantic Subset Principle, children acquiring all languages must initially select the subset value, i.e., the *neither* reading of the parameter, AND > NEG, which corresponds to Mandarin. Logical nativism is therefore compelled to predict that children learning English, a superset language, should initially behave like child and adult speakers of Mandarin, a subset language. In short, the commonality that is predicted is between English child language and Mandarin, rather than between English child language and English adult language.

This finding was also confirmed in a series of recent experiments conducted at our laboratory. We found that English-speaking children rejected negated conjunctions, such as (10) as a description of circumstances where Ted ordered just sushi, or just pasta, or neither dish.

(10) Ted didn't order both sushi and pasta

The only circumstance that makes (10) true for English-speaking children is one in which Ted failed to ordered either sushi or pasta. This is the same interpretation of negated conjunctions that is assigned to the corresponding Mandarin sentences by Mandarin-speaking children and adults, but it is not the interpretation favored by English-speaking adults. This finding is, once again, in keeping with the continuity hypothesis.

Child language differs from the language of adults, such that child and adult Mandarin differ, and child and adult English differ. However, the initial assignments of meanings by children do not differ across languages. In interpreting negated disjunctions, both children acquiring Mandarin and ones acquiring English initially favor the NOT > OR value of the parameter. And, in interpreting negated conjunctions, children acquiring both languages initially favor the AND > NOT value. The interpretations assigned by children are evidence that children acquiring both English and Mandarin favor the subset value of the relevant parameters. Positive evidence brings children back on track when they have taken a wrong path. This guarantees that children will converge on a grammar that is equivalent to those of adults in the same linguistic community. In contrast to Snyder's grammatical conservatism, the postulation of scope parameters predicts that child and adult languages will differ, when adults adopt the superset value of one of these parameters.

Because scope parameters are based on subset/superset relations in logical entailments, both children's productions and their interpretations may be different from adults, depending on the default parameter setting, and the setting that is operative for adullts. For example, it has been found that many English-speaking children produce the existential indefinite *some* in contexts where it is not licensed in the adult grammar. For adult English-speakers, *some* is a Positive Polarity Item (PPI; see Section 21.3.5) and must take scope over local negation. For children, however, *some* is not a PPI, and can be interpreted and even produced in the scope of local negation, as in the examples in (11).

(11) a. he didn't get something to eat (C.E-K. 4;6)
 b. well, they didn't get some food (E.E. 4;7)
 c. none people had some presents (E.P. 4;9)
 d. so he didn't get some money (E.G. 4;10)

As these example illustrate, children used *some* or *something* in contexts where adults would have used *any* or *anything* to express the same message. In a follow-up study, Musolino et al. (2000) found that English-speaking children also interpreted *some* as truth-conditionally equivalent to *any* in negative sentences. Assuming that the Semantic Subset Principle is the force behind children's non-adult productions and comprehension, these findings run counter to grammatical conservatism while being consistent with a variant of the subset principle.

Scope parameters can easily be formulated as a lexical parameters, in line with the Borer–Chomsky conjecture. Goro (2004) proposed that the lexical items in a language that denote conjunction and disjunction bear a feature [+PPI] in some languages which causes them to 'move' at LF, so as to be interpreted outside the scope of negation. These are also both binary parameters, since what is at stake are scope relations between two logical expressions. The syntactic nature of these parameters may not be obvious, but Goro (2004) proposes that a syntactic feature on conjunction and on disjunction drives these scope parameters, so his proposal is consistent with the widely held view that all parameters are syntactic in nature.

It is clear that scope parameters require close investigation of typologically distinct languages, a point emphasized by Baker (2008a) in his paper arguing for macroparameters. At this point, it is not easy to assess the 'scale' of the disjunction and conjunction parameters – this will take further study. These parameters may well be macroparameters. For one thing, the parameters that are operative here may not be specific to negation, but may extend to the entire class of downward entailing operators, which includes a host of verbs, adverbs, and prepositional phrases like *without* and expressions like *before* (Notley et al. 2012). It is worth noting, however, that macroparameters are generally viewed as 'large-scale' parameters that tend to be set early in the course of acquisition (e.g., Baker 2001). This does not seem to be the case for these scope parameters. The scope parameters we have introduced have a different, semantic character, in that their consequences are not witnessed in the syntactic component but, instead, in the truth conditions that children assign to sentences. Since these parameters have little impact on the child's productive syntax, it is possible that these are macroparameters, yet not set early in the course of acquisition.

Many of the parameter models we have reviewed have assumed that both settings of the parameter are specified in the innate language component. One or other value of the parameter, in the form of a feature assignment, is then assigned to a lexical item in the lexicon. In an attempt to avoid such overspecification, Roberts and Holmberg (2010) and I. Roberts (2010) propose that children always approach acquiring the target language with a default setting that is only overridden with positive evidence to the contrary. The positive evidence provides the alternative that needs to be adopted, but it is not specified in UG. In general, the default setting is the one that is computationally simpler, but presumably, it could also be the subset value, if this is required for learnability reasons. However, the conjunction and disjunction parameters require full specification of both values of the parameter, so this aspect of the underspecification model cannot work in this case. Full specification of both values of the parameter is needed so that learners compute the subset/superset truth conditions in order to determine the initial setting.

It is likely that that both values of scope parameters are available to the child from the outset of acquisition. In this respect, scope parameters are compatible with Yang's Variational model, in which the child entertains competing grammars, with one grammar (parameter value) achieving dominance in the long run. The current version of Yang's Variational model does not incorporate default settings (i.e., the subset value), so the observation that children and adults assign different interpretations to the same sentences is not anticipated. The model could easily be modified to accommodate default settings, rather than having alternative grammars start out on an equal footing. Finally, since children are slow to oust the default settings prescribed by the Semantic Subset Principle, the Variational model would presumably anticipate that the signature data are rare in the input to children. This is likely to be correct, for in the case of scope parameters, the required positive evidence would consist of sentence/meaning pairs. Other parameter-setting models on which little evidence is needed for parameter setting will have difficulty explaining why children take such a long time to reset the values of scope parameters. On these accounts, maturation, or some alternative to it, may be called upon.

Given that children begin with the value of the parameter as specified by the Semantic Subset Principle, all children, no matter what language they are acquiring, begin with the same value. Thus, the parameters discussed in this section do not offer any information on the issue of Conformity. As a final comment, it is worth pointing out that the Semantic Subset Principle avoids many of the noteworthy difficulties associated with the syntactic Subset Principle. One is memory and a second is computational efficiency. The subset/superset relations that hold among the truth conditions that are associated with the alternative scope assignments can be computed with minimal effort, and there is no need, in deciding which is the subset value and which is superset value, to recall the effects of these values on previous input. So children need not keep accurate records of preceding sentence/meaning pairs. That said, the fact that these parameters remain at the default setting until children are five or six years old is all the more mysterious. Perhaps some maturational story is needed. It should be kept in mind, as always, that other parameters will not work in the same way as these scope parameters, as Fodor and Sakas (2005) have been keen to point out. As a final comment, the fact that children initially adopt values of typologically different languages, and do not attempt to match the input from adult speakers of the local language, is compelling support for the continuity hypothesis. On the other hand, these facts are difficult to explain on usage-based accounts of language development.

Notes

1. An exception is Boeckx (2010), who interprets Borer's last sentence as denying the need for parameters at all.
2. It is an open question whether the child assigns plus values across the board, i.e., to every *wh*-phrase in the lexicon, or whether *wh*-phrases must be assigned values, one at a time. Empirical research with English-speaking children suggests that at least the adjunct *wh*-word *why* may be treated differently than argument *wh*-words. The *wh*-word *why* may not initially undergo movement in the grammars of English-speaking children, but may be 'base generated' or introduced by Merge, as Rizzi (2001a) has proposed for Italian (see Ko 2005a, Thornton 2008).
3. Research on microparameters is often associated with Kayne's research program (e.g., Kayne 2005); see also Chapter 24.
4. Subsequent research led to the proposal that children did not misset the pro-drop parameter; rather, children's null subjects in root clauses are sometimes phonologically null due to another parameter, i.e., the so-called 'root subject drop' parameter (Rizzi 2005a). The root subject drop parameter distinguishes those languages and registers of languages which permit null subjects in the specifier of the root of the clause (whatever that may be in the relevant grammar) from those languages that do not. Within this theory, English-speaking children are seen to permit IP, rather than CP, to be the root of the clause, and so they permit null subjects in SpecIP. Once the production system matures, children can entertain the alternative setting of the parameter.
5. Constructions can be of varying size and complexity; they can be entire sentences (which might be labeled as a 'transitive' construction, a 'passive' construction,' a 'causative' construction and so on); idioms; smaller pieces of structures such as phrases, and even word plus morpheme combinations such as the 'plural' construction. Constructions can be related to each other, but constructions are not related to each other by syntactic movement since construction grammars do not take movement to be a property of the grammar.

26

Syntax and the brain

Jon Sprouse and Ellen F. Lau

26.1 The role of syntactic theory in a cognitive neuroscience of syntax

Marr (1982:19–29) argued that a complete description of any information-processing device, including the human brain, will necessarily involve three levels of description: the computational level, the algorithmic level, and the implementational level. The computational level can best be described as an answer to the question "What problem is being solved by the device?" (and to some extent "Why does the problem have the form that it does?"). The algorithmic level is a description of the specific operations necessary to solve the problem. And the implementational level is a description of how those operations are implemented in the hardware of the device itself. Although this partitioning of the problem into three neat levels of analysis can be abused (see Phillips and Lewis 2012 for discussion), it also provides a good starting point for understanding the relationship between syntactic theory, the theory of sentence processing within psycholinguistics, and the neural implementation of sentence processing within neurolinguistics. Therefore we will begin our discussion with Marr's three levels and how they map to the cognitive neuroscience of sentences.

26.1.1 The computational level – syntactic theory

Marr famously used a cash register to illustrate the three levels, so it seems appropriate to continue the tradition. The computational theory of a cash register (i.e., the problem that a cash register must solve) is the tallying of the cost of purchasing multiple items from a store, or more abstractly, the theory of addition. The properties of addition are familiar from arithmetic: (i) the order of addition for two numbers has no effect on the final sum (commutativity); (ii) the grouping of three or more items into pairs prior to addition also has no effect on the final sum (associativity); (iii) the addition of zero to a number has no effect on the number (identity); and (iv) the addition of a number and its inverse results in zero. As Marr (1982: 22) stated, "these properties are part of the fundamental *theory* of addition," which means that "they are true no matter how the numbers are written ... and no matter how the addition is executed." In many ways, syntactic theory is the computational theory of the "human sentence processor," as syntactic theory seeks to describe the fundamental properties of the sentences that are the input to comprehension and the output of production – properties that are true of sentences no matter how they are actually constructed during processing. However, as we will see shortly, the three levels are highly interactive, and the difficulties inherent in studying the human brain mean that it is impossible to completely isolate the computational properties of sentences from the algorithmic and implementational properties the same way that one can with a cash register.

26.1.2 The algorithmic level – sentence processing

Once the computational theory is established, it is then possible to investigate how it is that the computational problem is solved. In the case of the cash register's need to solve the problem of addition, several possible algorithms are possible depending on the basic units that are used to compose the representation. For example, if the basic units of the representation are the base-10 Arabic numerals (0, 1, 2, 3 ...), then one possible algorithm is the 'carry-over' procedure familiar to all school children: add the digits farthest to the right (least significant), and if the sum exceeds 9, carry over the leftmost digit of the sum to the next column to the left. Crucially, other units could be chosen for the representation, such as base-2 or binary units (0,1), which will necessitate a different algorithm for executing the addition. In other words, representational assumptions constrain algorithmic choices. Furthermore, there may be several different algorithms available for any given choice of units of representation, in which case the choice of algorithm may depend upon issues of efficiency or the desire to make certain types of information more easily available than others. Just as syntactic theory is in many ways a computational theory of sentences, the theories of sentence processing developed by psycholinguists are in many ways algorithmic theories. As we will see shortly, theories of sentence processing begin with different representational assumptions drawn from the computational theory (some assume that the basic units are words and syntactic rules, others that the basic units are syntactic frames) that constrain the types of algorithms that are proposed (structure-generation versus retrieval and unification).

26.1.3 The implementational level – neurolinguistics

Obviously there are multiple ways to physically implement a device like a cash register. One could use multiple spinning cylinders like the analog cash registers of the twentieth century, or microchips as is common in computers today. However, the choice of implementation constrains both the units of the representation and the algorithms that are available for executing addition: analog cylinders tend to use base-10 numerals and an algorithm similar to the 'carry-over' procedure, whereas computers use a binary representation and a bit-wise calculation. When it comes to cognitive tasks such as vision or sentence processing, the physical implementation is obviously the human brain. And although we know relatively little about the types of representations and algorithms that the human brain can (and cannot) implement, it is clear that the areas of the brain that form the network for any given cognitive task must be capable of carrying out at least one algorithm that solves the computational problem of the task. The task of developing an implementational theory of sentences rests with neurolinguists, as they leverage neuropsychological patient studies and various neuroimaging technologies (e.g., fMRI, PET, EEG, MEG) to identify the neural circuits involved in sentence processing.

26.1.4 The interaction across levels

In principle, the three levels are only loosely related: for any given computational theory, there are any number of algorithms that can be adopted, and any number of physical devices that can be used to implement a given algorithm. In fact, the very definition of the computational level suggests that it can be investigated completely independently of the other two levels, as it is defined as the properties of the problem that are independent of how it is solved. However, in practice it is impossible to study human language at only one level. Any study of the implementational level must begin with an assumption about the set of algorithms (often called *processes* in the language literature) that one wants to localize. Any study of the algorithmic level must begin with an assumption about the syntactic structures (often called *representations*) that must be built, and the units that can be used in the construction (e.g., words and syntactic rules, or just syntactic frames). And any study of the computational level (i.e., syntactic theory) can only be constructed by observing human behavior. For example, the primary behavioral response used as evidence in generative syntax is the acceptability judgment, as it is assumed that one of the primary factors affecting acceptability judgments is the well-formedness of the syntactic structure. However, it is well known that acceptability judgments are also affected by factors that are more closely related to the algorithmic or implementational levels such as processing complexity (e.g., Chomsky and Miller 1963). The behaviors that form the empirical basis of the computational theory of language are rooted in algorithms implemented in the human brain.

The interaction of the three levels in language research makes the goal of a complete description of the cognitive neuroscience of language both challenging and exciting. The interaction of the three levels also suggests that progress toward that goal can only be achieved through a close interaction of syntacticians, psycholinguists, and neuroscientists. The field has made some strong advances in this respect over the past several decades, but the work is far from over. Our goal in this chapter is to illustrate the close, but often unstated, relationship between syntactic theory and brain-based studies of sentence processing (both electrophysiological and neuroimaging). Our hope is that by highlighting this relationship, we can draw attention to both the areas where there has been productive cross-fertilization, and the areas where the relationship could be closer. Along the way, we also intend to provide a primer for syntacticians on some of the driving questions underlying brain-based studies of sentence processing, as well as some of the primary results of those investigations[1].

26.2 The mentalistic commitments of syntactic theories

Syntactic theories are primarily concerned with properties of the full syntactic representation of a sentence, such as the structural configuration of the words in the sentence, and the various relationships that exist between those words (agreement, coreference, etc.). Decades of syntactic research have revealed that syntactic representations are complex cognitive objects containing a sophisticated set of relationships. Despite this complexity, there is generally broad agreement among the various syntactic theories about what the properties of the full syntactic representation are for any given sentence. However, syntactic theories disagree vehemently about the fundamental building blocks of syntactic representations, and the combinatorial mechanics necessary to combine those building blocks into all and only the syntactic representations that are licit in any given language. The different assumptions by the various syntactic theories necessarily entail different mentalistic commitments about the language units that must be stored in long-term memory in the brain, the cognitive processes necessary to retrieve those units from memory, and the cognitive processes that must be deployed to assemble those units into the relevant syntactic representations. And as we shall see in Section 26.4, those mentalistic commitments also affect how the results of neuroimaging studies are interpreted to reveal the neural circuitry involved in sentence processing.

To be sure, it is not always straightforward to discern the mentalistic commitments of any given syntactic theory. In fact, given the delimited goal of syntactic theory to describe syntactic representations, and Marr's proviso that there are likely to be any number of algorithms to execute a given computational theory, there is no reason to believe that the mentalistic commitments of a given syntactic theory will fully constrain the space of possible sentence processes (indeed, they do not). However, a discussion of the potential mentalistic commitments of syntactic theories is an important component of any discussion of syntax and the brain, as these commitments play defining roles in the interpretation of electrophysiological and neuroimaging evidence. We believe that if progress in generative syntax is to benefit the broader cognitive neuroscience community, and vice versa, the relationship between the mentalistic commitments of syntactic theories and the evidence gathered in cognitive neuroscience experiments must be a central part of the discussion.

26.2.1 The generative framework
The following three questions provide a helpful starting point for the discussion of the mentalistic commitments of generative syntactic theories, and indeed, any syntactic theories.

What are the basic units of the syntactic representation?
What types of operations are necessary to build the syntactic representation from the basic units?
How are the syntactic operations influenced by non-syntactic information that may be available during sentence comprehension (e.g., semantic information)?

As we shall see in the following sections, the answers to these questions are highly dependent on each other. And given the difficulties inherent in studying the human brain, it is not always possible to obtain empirical evidence that unambiguously supports one answer over another.

26.2.1.1 The units of the syntactic representation in the generative framework
Even within the generative framework there is healthy debate and active research on the basic units of the syntactic representation (Chomsky 1995c, Halle and Marantz 1993, Pollard and Sag 1994, Bresnan 2001). However, we believe it is fair to say that there is some degree of consensus that the basic units are bundles of features. These features can encode morphosyntactic properties of the bundle (e.g., phi-features: Person, Number, Gender), morphosyntactic requirements of the bundle (e.g., case features), discourse properties (e.g., focus), meaning (e.g., lexical semantic features), and even pronunciation (e.g., phonetic features). The bundles themselves can map to the canonical idea of a word, to a morpheme, or even to a silent element such as a functional head or covert pronoun. The overarching architectural

idea in the generative framework is that if certain features are present in a sentence (e.g., the uninterpretable features in the Minimalist Program), they must be arranged in very specific syntactic configurations in order for that sentence to be well formed. Although the rules for combining the features into well-formed configurations take various forms depending on the precise version of generative theory, it is generally true that the combinatory rules (e.g., phrase-structure rules, transformations) are stored separately from the basic units themselves (which are hypothesized to be stored in the mental lexicon).

26.2.1.2 The operations that build the syntactic representation in the generative framework

The generative commitment to (bundles of) features as the basic unit of the syntactic representation has direct consequences for the generative commitment to syntactic structure-building operations during sentence processing. For example, in order to combine bundles of features, the Minimalist Program posits a grammatical structure-building operation Merge, which concatenates two bundles of features into a single unit. Because sentence processing is necessarily incremental (word-by-word) and directional (the order of the words is 'left to right'), the parsing equivalent of Merge must (at least superficially) be subdivided into the options made available by the syntactic rules of the language. Presented with the following partial sentence, the parser can potentially concatenate the preceding word in any one of four structural positions:

(1) Bill spread the rumor that Mary left ...
    (i) the complement of the immediately preceding head (e.g., *the band*)
    (ii) the complement of a non-immediately previous head (e.g., *to John*)
    (iii) the adjunct of the most recent phrase (e.g., *suddenly*)
    (iv) the adjunct of a previous phrase (e.g., *maliciously*)

The choice of concatenation location is licensed by the syntactic rules governing feature combinatorics, and presumably mediated by the parsing strategies that the human parser utilizes to rapidly and efficiently assign structure to incoming sentences (e.g., minimal attachment and late closure: Frazier 1978, Frazier and Fodor 1978, Frazier 1987). Whether there are multiple concatenation operations (one for each location) or just a single operation is an open question, and a good example of how syntactic theories will not completely constrain the space of possible parsing processes.

In addition to Merge, many generative theories also include the operation Move, which displaces words or phrases from their canonical position to a position elsewhere in the sentence. There is quite a bit of research in the sentence-processing literature devoted to the cognitive operations necessary to parse displaced elements, a full review of which is well beyond the scope of this chapter (Crain and Fodor 1985, Stowe 1986, Traxler and Pickering 1996, Nicol and Swinney 1989, Nicol et al. 1994; but cf. McKoon et al. 1994, Garnsey et al. 1989, Kaan et al. 2000, Phillips et al. 2005, Felser et al. 2003, Sussman and Sedivy 2003, Wagers and Phillips 2009). One relatively popular view of the parsing of movement dependencies maps the grammatical operation movement to (at least) three parsing operations: (i) encoding of the displaced element (called the filler) in working memory (for interpretation later in the sentence); (ii) an active search for potential gap locations (verbs, prepositions, etc.); and (iii) integration of the filler with the appropriate gap location. From a parsing perspective, syntactic constraints on the grammatical operation Move are realized as constraints on the distribution of gap locations, and thus potentially surface as constraints on the gap-searching operation. Taken together with the discussion of Merge above, it is clear that generative theories appear to be committed to the assumption that (bundles of) features are the basic unit of syntactic structure, and to the assumption that the combinatory rules for combining those features are stored separately from the features themselves. This leads to the postulation of several (syntactic) parsing operations, and the idea that the constraints on grammatical operations that are familiar from generative syntax surface as constraints on the various (syntactic) parsing operations (e.g., Stowe 1986, Clifton and Frazier 1989, Neville et al. 1991, Phillips 2006, Wagers and Phillips 2009).

26.2.1.3 The interaction of syntactic and semantic information in the generative framework

In addition to the quantity and quality of parsing operations, syntactic theories have constrained theories of the architecture of the human sentence parser in other ways. One prominent example of this can be seen in the long-standing debate in the sentence-processing literature about the temporal dynamics of 'syntactic' and 'semantic' operations during sentence comprehension. A priori, there are at least three logical possibilities:

(i) Syntactic operations are computed independently of, and functionally prior to, semantic operations (often called syntax-first models).
(ii) Syntactic and semantic operations interact from the earliest stages of sentence processing (highly interactive models are often called constraint-based, as both syntactic and semantic constraints have equal importance and precedence).
(iii) Syntactic and semantic operations can operate independently of the other.

As we will see in Section 26.3.3 and again in Section 26.4, some care is necessary when interpreting macroscopic labels such as 'syntax' and 'semantics,' as different authors can have very different conceptions of what phenomena fit under each label, especially when it comes to the fuzzy boundaries between morphology and syntax, and between lexical and compositional semantics. It is also important to note the distinction between computing the syntactic structure for a string and choosing one from multiple licit syntactic structures; for syntactically ambiguous strings, all parsing theories are likely to agree that the parser may use semantic information at some point to arbitrate between the possibilities.

Classic generative syntax assumes that syntactic rules alone are sufficient to characterize the set of well-formed sentences in a given language, but this assumption does not, strictly speaking, constrain the temporal relationship between syntactic and semantic operations in parsing. For example, nothing about the representational commitments of the generative theory rules out a processing module that rapidly generates likely propositions from a non-syntactic 'bag-of-words' representation, which is then used by the parser to decide between alternative syntactic parses (see Townsend and Bever 2001 for another example). However, since the generative theory already posits syntactic representations that are sufficient to uniquely determine argument structure, it might seem more parsimonious to assume a parser that simply computes the syntactic representation first and then uses the syntactic representation to compute the interpretation, as in (i). This kind of consideration has led to a historical association between generative theories of syntax and syntax-first theories of parsing.

26.2.2 The unification framework

The parallel architecture proposed by Jackendoff (1999, 2002) may provide a good second case study in the role of syntactic theory in a broader cognitive neuroscience of sentences. The parallel architecture has been adopted by Hagoort and colleagues (e.g., Hagoort 2003a, 2005) to interpret a range of electrophysiological and neuroimaging findings. As we will describe in this section, the parallel architecture has led Hagoort to propose a radically different conception of parsing in which there is only one parsing process, unification, which acts on syntactic, semantic, and phonological representations simultaneously (i.e., in parallel).

26.2.2.1 The units of the representation in the unification framework

The basic units within the unification framework are similar to the basic units in generative syntax in that they contain three types of information: syntactic, semantic, and phonological. However, whereas generative syntax makes a distinction between the units and the rules that combine them, the unification framework collapses the syntactic rules into the units themselves by assuming that each unit (or word) is stored in the lexicon as part of a syntactic frame that specifies the structure(s) that the unit can appear in (as well as a semantic frame and a phonological frame). This is similar in some respects to other frame-based theories such as Construction Grammar within cognitive linguistics (e.g., Goldberg 1995, 2006, Croft and Cruse 2004; see Sections 3.4 and 25.6.2), and Tree Adjoining Grammar within computational linguistics (Joshi and Schabes 1997, Vosse and Kempen 2000; see Chapter 8). In other words, in the unification framework, the basic units are small chunks of syntactic structure that are stored in the mental lexicon.

26.2.2.2 The operations that build the representation in the unification framework

Because the basic units of the unification framework are lexicalized chunks of syntactic structure, the unification framework does not require several different parsing operations to compose the variety of syntactic structures made available by each language. Instead, there are just two operations: lexical retrieval, which we assume that all theories must posit since all theories must retrieve lexical material from the mental lexicon, and unification, which is the process of integrating two syntactic frames together. In cases of ambiguity, the assumption is that two (or more) frames will be accessed from the lexicon, and a winner-takes-all competitive process based on various factors (plausibility, frequency, temporal decay, etc.) will yield a single phrasal configuration.

26.2.2.3 The interaction of syntactic and semantic information in the unification framework

Unification is assumed to occur in parallel at all three levels (syntactic, semantic, and phonological). The unification framework is thus a type of constraint-based parsing architecture, in which syntactic and semantic information is assumed to be highly interactive from the earliest stages of the parsing process. In this way the mentalistic commitments of the unification framework (lexicalized syntactic frames, a single parsing process, highly interactive syntax and semantics) are very different from the mentalistic commitments of generative syntax (a distinction between lexical units and syntactic rules, which allows for the possibility of multiple parsing operations and/or a syntax-first parsing architecture), and begin to demonstrate the role that syntactic theory can play in a full cognitive neuroscience of sentences.

26.2.3 Other frameworks

Our focus on the generative framework and the unification framework in this chapter is not meant to suggest that these are the only two syntactic theories that are useful in interpreting electrophysiological and neuroimaging data. Our choices simply reflect the theme of this volume and our goal of concisely illustrating the important role that the mentalistic commitments of syntactic theories play. There are other frameworks that the interested reader may wish to investigate, such as the argument-dependency framework of Bornkessel and Scheslewsky (2006) based upon the theoretical framework of van Valin and la Polla (1997), in which syntactic representations are built using a frame/unification approach, but argument linking is computed according to various supra-syntactic precedence hierarchies familiar from typological research (animacy, referentiality, case marking). The argument–dependency framework will appear in the discussion of Broca's area in Section 26.4; however, many other interesting frameworks had to be left out due to space limitations.

26.3 Electrophysiological responses

When it comes to non-invasively studying brain responses to cognitive stimuli, there really are only two widely available options: electrophysiological responses or hemodynamic responses. We will begin our discussion with electrophysiological responses. The most common method for measuring electrophysiological responses is electroencephalography (EEG), which is the placement of electrodes on the scalp to measure the underlying brain-based electrical activity. The advantage of all electrophysiological measures is that electricity travels very quickly, even in biological substrates, such that changes in the underlying brain state can be detected with millisecond-level temporal accuracy. The advantage of EEG in particular is that the machines themselves are relatively affordable (on the order of tens of thousands of dollars), and have been around for decades (the first EEG recordings were done in the 1930s, the first language-related responses were recorded in the 1970s). The disadvantage of EEG is that it is very difficult to determine the spatial origin of electrical activity that is recorded on the scalp, because the distribution of electrical activity is distorted by passing through various layers of biological matter before being realized on the two-dimensional surface of the scalp. In other words, EEG sacrifices spatial resolution for temporal resolution and cost-efficiency (Nunez and Srinivasan 2006). More recently, magnetoencephalograms (MEG) have been developed that can measure the magnetic fields that are created by the electrical activity in the brain. MEG offers the same temporal resolution of EEG, and overcomes many of the spatial resolution problems of EEG as magnetic fields are not significantly affected by intervening biological matter. The two primary disadvantages of MEG are (i) that the machines themselves are relatively rare because they are extremely expensive compared to EEG (on the order of millions of dollars), and (ii) that MEG can only measure magnetic fields that leave the head, leaving some sources of neuronal activity undetectable. The majority of sentence-related electrophysiological studies have been conducted using EEG.

26.3.1 Event-related potentials

Because the brain simultaneously controls almost all human activity, from core bodily functions like breathing, to sensory functions like vision, to high-level cognitive functions like language, the electrical activity that can be measured on the scalp at any given moment is potentially composed of activity from hundreds of neuronal sources. This means that the mapping procedure from scalp-recorded activity to the cognitive process(es) of interest is extremely difficult. One highly successful technique for eliminating activity that is not related to the cognitive process(es) of interest is to look for activity that is both time-locked and phase-locked to a specific event, such as the onset of a critical word during sentence comprehension. The process for this is a simple averaging procedure: EEG activity is recorded for multiple trials of each condition, and then the multiple trials are averaged together using the event as the time reference point (time point 0). The use of the event as the reference point time-locks the resulting averaged activity, and the averaging procedure phase-locks the averaged activity according to the principles of constructive and destructive wave interference: for each frequency of activity present in the raw EEG recordings, waves that are in phase (peaks line up with peaks) survive, and waves that are out of phase (peaks line up with troughs) are eliminated. The idea behind this averaging procedure is that any non-event related electrical activity will be eliminated by destructive interference, leaving behind only the electrical activity that is related to the event of interest. The resulting averaged activity is called an event-related potential, or ERP (see Luck 2005 for an introduction to the ERP technique).

Although time-locking the EEG to a stimulus is what makes it possible to estimate the timing of some processes down to a few milliseconds, this temporal precision paradoxically carries its own limitations. Operations that are tied very closely to a particular word of input, such as early visual or auditory processing, orthographic processing, and lexical access, are easier to associate with a particular time window in the ERP following the stimulus presentation. In contrast, one cannot always assume that the sentence-level and discourse-level processes that support syntactic and semantic combination will happen at a neat fixed time interval from the presentation of a particular word, as their timing is likely to be dependent on many more factors (e.g., how much structure has been built already, how much structure could be predicted before the word was presented, how much time was required for basic lexical access and selection). For this reason, much of the ERP literature on sentence processing has focused on the ERP responses to syntactic and semantic violations of different types, which allows investigation of processing at a given representational level in a fixed time window by ensuring that the presentation of one particular word will disrupt processing at that representational level. Although this approach has proved very powerful, we must be careful to keep in mind that a syntactic violation does not only impact basic syntactic operations, but may also invoke reanalysis or rereading operations and other strategic mechanisms.

There is some terminological confusion in the ERP literature. This is because an ERP is a physiological response to a stimulus (e.g., the critical word in a sentence), but cognitive theories are generally interested in unobservable cognitive processes that can only be isolated by comparing *two* (or more) stimuli that are hypothesized to differ with respect to that process. Therefore there are times when the same label is given to both a component of the ERP for an individual stimulus and the relative difference between the ERPs of two experimentally matched stimuli. For example, we will shortly review one prominent ERP known as the N400 (Kutas and Hillyard 1980). The N400 is a negative-going wave peaking around 400 ms that is elicited by all meaningful stimuli. As such, every word is expected to have an N400 ERP. However, the label N400 is also used for the relative difference in the amplitude of the N400 between two experimentally matched words. Although such terminological ambiguity is potentially troublesome, context is usually sufficient to disambiguate the intended meaning. Nonetheless, it is important to be aware of these two senses, as well as the fact that the cognitive interpretation of ERPs depends entirely on the theoretical assumptions underlying the hypothetical difference between two stimuli. As we shall see, the mentalistic commitments of syntactic theories play a large role in those assumptions.

While many ERPs have been identified in the broader EEG literature, four ERPs have played a central role in the sentence processing literature: the early left anterior negativity (ELAN), the left anterior negativity (LAN), the N400, and the P600. Although a complete review of each of these ERPs would be beyond the scope of this article, in this section we will provide a basic review of each and discuss how these ERPs have been interpreted according to various syntactic theories.

26.3.1.1 The ELAN

As the name suggests, the ELAN (early left anterior negativity) is a negative-going deflection that peaks in a relatively early processing window (100–250 ms post-stimulus onset) and is greatest over left anterior electrode sites. The ELAN was first reported by Neville *et al.* (1991) to a specific phrase-structure violation in which a preposition appears in an ungrammatical position (note that the critical position must contain either a noun or an adjective):

(2) a. the boys heard Joe's stories *about* Africa
　　b. *the boys heard Joe's *about* stories Africa

A similar effect was reported by Friederici *et al.* (1993) in German, in this case when a participle appears in a position that must contain a noun or adjective (*Das Baby wurde im gefürttert* 'the baby was in-the fed'). The ELAN has since been elicited to very similar phrase structure violations in Spanish (Hinojosa *et al.* 2003), French (Isel *et al.* 2007), and further replicated in English (Lau et al. 2006, Dikker et al. 2009) and German (e.g., Hahne and Friederici 1999, Hahne and Friederici 2002, Rossi et al. 2005). The ELAN is not affected by task (Hahne and Friederici 2002), by the probability of the violation in the experiment (Hahne and Friederici 1999), or by the frequency of a disambiguated structure (Ainsworth-Darnell et al. 1998, Friederici et al. 1996). Taken as a whole, these results suggest that the ELAN is a very specific response to phrase-structure violations, and not simply a response to difficult or unlikely structures.

Recent research on the ELAN has focused on the extremely early latency of the response. The 100–250 ms post-stimulus window is remarkably early for syntactic analysis (and error diagnosis) given that estimates of lexical access often center around 200 ms post-stimulus (Allopenna et al. 1998, van Petten et al. 1999). Three approaches have been offered to explain the early latency of the ELAN. Friederici (1995) adopts a parsing model in which the earliest stage considers only word category information (e.g., Frazier 1978, 1987, 1990, Frazier and Rayner 1982), thus limiting the number of processes that need to be performed in the earliest time window. Lau et al. (2006) suggest that the early latency can be explained if the parser has predicted the properties of the critical word prior to encountering it, such that many of the syntactic features are in some sense 'pre-parsed.' Dikker et al. (2009) propose the 'sensory ELAN hypothesis,' in which the ELAN indexes a processing stage prior to lexical access that occurs in the sensory cortices (visual or auditory cortex). This pre-lexical processing is based purely on the form typicality of the words – i.e., the sensory cortices use the probability of certain phonetic forms to determine if the incoming string is most likely a noun, verb, etc. Though it is too early to declare a dominant view, it is clear that any interpretation of the ELAN must explain two facts: (i) that it only arises to very specific violations (phrase structure violations); and (ii) that it occurs in an extremely early time window.

26.3.1.2 The LAN

While the LAN (left anterior negativity) and the ELAN share many properties (i.e., they are both negative-going deflections that occur primarily over left anterior electrode sites), they differ along two critical dimensions. First, the LAN occurs in a slightly later time window, usually 300–500 ms post-stimulus onset, which eliminates many of the complex timing questions associated with the ELAN. Second, the LAN has been elicited by a broad array of (morpho-)syntactic violations, such as agreement violations (Coulson et al. 1998, Gunter et al. 1997, Münte et al. 1997, Kaan 2002, Osterhout and Mobley 1995), case violations (Münte and Heinze 1994), phrase-structure violations (Friederici et al. 1996, Hagoort et al. 2003), island constraint violations (Kluender and Kutas 1993b), and even garden-path sentences (Kaan and Swaab 2003). The LAN has also been elicited during the processing of long-distance dependencies such as *wh*-movement, at both the displaced *wh*-word and the unambiguous cue for the gap location (Kluender and Kutas 1993a, Phillips et al. 2005).

26.3.1.3 The N400

The N400 is a negative-going deflection that is generally largest over centro-parietal electrode sites, and tends to occur 300–500 ms post-stimulus onset (with a peak amplitude occurring at 400 ms). The N400 was first found by Kutas and Hillyard (1980) when they presented participants with sentences that ended with unexpected words. They compared baseline sentence with semantically congruent endings to (a) sentences with semantically incongruent endings and (b) to sentences with endings that were incongruent due to the physical properties of the stimulus, such as words written in all capital letters (c):

(3) a. I spread the warm bread with butter
    b. I spread the warm bread with socks
    c. I spread the warm bread with BUTTER

Kutas and Hillyard (1980) observed a larger N400 for (b) compared to (a), and a larger P300 (also known as a P3b) to (c) compared to (a). This qualitative difference in the responses to (b) versus (a) suggests that the N400 is specifically related to semantic processes rather than general error detection. In the decades since its discovery, the N400 has been elicited by a broad array of linguistic and non-linguistic stimuli, with the common pattern being that they are all meaningful in some way: spoken words, written words, signed words, pseudowords, acronyms, environmental sounds, faces, and gestures (Kutas et al. 2006).

Although the idea that the N400 is related to semantic processes is almost universally accepted, there has been quite a bit of debate about the exact nature of those processes in the literature due to the complex pattern of N400 results that have been reported. For example, although semantic incongruence often elicits a larger N400 than semantic congruence, this is not always the case. Congruent endings that are less predictable elicit a larger N400 than congruent endings that are more predictable: a sentence like *I like my coffee with cream and* **honey** produces a larger N400 than *I like my coffee with cream and* **sugar** because *honey* is less predictable than *sugar*, though both are semantically plausible endings. It is also the case that the N400 is affected by the degree of semantic relatedness between the realized ending and the unrealized predicted ending. For example, both *salt* and *socks* are incongruent endings to the 'coffee' sentence above. However, *salt* produces a smaller N400 than *socks*, presumably because *salt* shares more semantic features with the predicted ending *sugar* than *socks* does (Federmeier and Kutas 1999, Kutas and Federmeier 2000).

There are two popular theories of the N400 effect. The first is that the N400 indexes processes related to the semantic integration of the critical word with the preceding semantic context. Under this view, increases in N400 amplitude reflect the increased difficulty of integrating incongruent, unexpected, or semantically unrelated words into the preceding context (Hagoort 2008, Osterhout and Holcomb 1992, Brown and Hagoort 1993). The second view is that the N400 indexes processes related to the activation of semantic features in the mental lexicon (long-term or semantic memory). Under this view, decreases in N400 amplitude reflect the ease of activation (or pre-activation) for congruent, predicted, and semantically related words (Federmeier and Kutas 1999, Kutas and Federmeier 2000, Lau et al. 2009).

Though this chapter is primarily focused on brain responses to syntactic processing, it would be a mistake to overlook the role of the N400 in sentence-processing theories. The N400 is often interpreted as an index of 'semantic' processing, especially when it comes to the relative timing of syntactic and semantic processes. However, it is important to regard macroscopic labels such as 'semantics' and 'syntax' with healthy skepticism: though no one would argue that the N400 is related to aspects of the semantic processing of words in sentences, it is unlikely that the N400 is a direct reflection of the compositional semantic processes that occupy much of semantic theory, especially within generative grammar. For example, the N400 is not sensitive to classic sentence-level compositional semantic effects such as negation (Chapter 21) and quantification (Chapter 22). Sentences such as *A robin is a **tree*** elicit a larger N400 at the final word when compared to *A robin is a **bird***. However, adding negation to the sentence does not reverse the N400 pattern (*A robin is not a **tree/bird***); in fact, *tree* still elicits the larger N400, even though *tree* is the true continuation (Fischler et al. 1983). The same is true for other scope-taking elements (Kounios and Holcomb 1992). Furthermore, N400 effects are derived from non-sentential paradigms such as word–word priming paradigms just as often as they are derived from sentential paradigms. Although there is likely some form of composition between two words in a priming paradigm, it is unlikely to be identical to the compositional processes at the core of sentence-level compositional semantics. N400 effects have also been modulated by discourse-level manipulations (van Berkum et al. 2003, Nieuwland and van Berkum 2006), which, taken together with the lexical-level effects from priming and the lack of negation/quantification effects, suggests that the mapping between the N400 and sentence-level compositional semantics is anything but straightforward.

26.3.1.4 The P600

The P600 (alternatively the 'syntactic positive shift') is a positive-going deflection that is generally largest over centro-parietal electrode sites and tends to occur 500–800 ms post-stimulus onset (although there is a good deal of variability in the latency in the ERP literature). Like the LAN, the P600 has been reported for a broad array of syntactic violations, in many cases co-occurring with a preceding LAN. For example, P600s have been elicited to phrase-structure violations (Hagoort et al. 1993, Friederici et al. 1993, Hahne and Friederici 1999, Friederici and Frisch 2000, Osterhout and Holcomb 1992), agreement violations (Hagoort et al. 1993, Kaan 2002), syntactic garden-paths (Friederici et al. 1996, Kaan and Swaab 2003, Osterhout et al. 1994), and island violations (McKinnon and Osterhout 1996). The sheer number of violation types that elicit a P600 has led some researchers to suggest that the P600 may be a (slightly delayed) version of the P300 (or P3b), which is a general response to unexpected stimuli (Coulson et al. 1998; see Osterhout 1999 for a response). P600's have also been elicited by the processing of grammatical sentences with particularly complex syntactic properties, such as ambiguous structures (Frisch et al. 2002) and wh-movement (Fiebach et al. 2002, Kaan et al. 2000, Phillips et al. 2005). Current research on the P600 has focused on cases of unexpected theta-role assignment (Kim and Osterhout 2005, Kuperberg et al. 2003, van Herten et al. 2005, Kuperberg 2007, Bornkessel-Schlesewsky and Schlesewsky 2008, Stroud and Phillips 2011), which we will discuss in more detail in the next section as these P600s have been interpreted as evidence of an independent semantic processing stream.

26.3.2 The role of syntactic theory in the interpretation of ERPs

As the brief review above makes clear, ERPs do not map cleanly to single parsing operations, but rather seem to track macroscopic classes of violations or processing difficulties. Consequently, there is quite a bit of variation in the literature when it comes to the interpretation of ERPs. It is not our intention to review the entire ERP literature in this chapter, but rather to illustrate how the mentalistic (architectural) commitments of syntactic theory play a key role in the interpretation of electrophysiological responses. Before continuing it should be noted that for convenience throughout the chapter we are going to use terminology such as 'the generative framework' or 'the unification framework' to refer to the mentalistic commitments of the respective syntactic theories. The fact that we describe certain interpretations of electrophysiological (and later hemodynamic) responses as using the generative framework does not necessarily mean that the cited authors explicitly endorse generative syntactic theories. Instead, we simply mean that the architectural assumptions that they assume for human sentence processing system are consistent with the mentalistic commitments of generative syntactic theories. Because syntactic theories are not themselves theories of sentence processing, it is not the case that a set of architectural assumptions is uniquely specified by a single syntactic theory. Therefore it is possible that some of the authors have other syntactic theories in mind that also lead to the same mentalistic commitments as generative theories.

26.3.2.1 ERPs and the generative framework

Recall from Section 26.2 that generative syntax is likely committed to a mental architecture in which (bundles of) features are stored in the lexicon and composed by a number of structure-building operations that obey a set of complex syntactic rules. Generative syntax is also straightforwardly compatible with a parsing architecture in which the syntactic structure-building precedes (compositional) semantics, as generative syntactic theories tend to be committed to an interpretive (compositional) semantics (Frazier 1978, 1987). Friederici (1995, 2002) has argued that the ERPs identified in the sentence-processing literature are consistent with just such an architecture. Under this view, the ELAN reflects an initial stage in which syntactic structure is built according to syntactic rules using only the word category information of the incoming word (i.e. no semantic information is used to direct the structural parse at this stage). Friederici argues that three properties of the ELAN point to such a function: (i) it is extremely early in the parse, suggesting that only partial information could be available at that time; (ii) it is only elicited by phrase-structure violations, suggesting that it is specific to syntactic structure building; and (iii) it is not affected by any task-level factors (such as the likelihood of encountering a violation in the experiment), suggesting that it is a relatively automatic process. Because the LAN is elicited by many different kinds of morphosyntactic violations, this theory interprets the LAN as an index of the second half of the initial syntactic stage where other morphosyntactic properties are established or checked, such as agreement and case marking. The N400 reflects a second stage where lexical semantic information is processed and argument relations are established. Finally the P600 represents a third stage of processing in which the syntactic and semantic information is integrated into a single representation, and any mistakes are rectified by reanalysis (which explains the fact that the P600 is elicited by both syntactic violations and garden-path sentences, and can be affected by the likelihood of encountering a violation in the experiment).

One of the defining characteristics of the three-stage model proposed by Friederici (1995, 2002) is that it temporally orders syntactic processing (stage 1) and semantic processing (stage 2), before finally integrating both types of information in stage 3. This is often called a syntax-first parsing architecture (Frazier 1978, 1987, Frazier and Rayner 1982). The primary evidence for this temporal ordering comes from the relative ordering of the ERPs themselves: the ELAN occurs 150–250 ms post-stimulus, the N400 occurs 300–500 ms post-stimulus, and the P600 occurs 500–800 ms post-stimulus. However, some studies have been designed to directly test the syntax-first hypothesis. For example, Friederici et al. (2004) used a sentence that violates both syntactic and semantic constraints as a way to test the syntax-first view:

(4) das Buch wurde trotz   verpflanzt von einem Verleger, den
     The book was despite replanted by a publisher, who(m)
     wenige empfahlen
     few   recommended

The critical word *verpflanzt/replanted* violates both the phrase-structure rules of German, and the selectional requirements of the subject *Buch/book*. Friederici et al. (2004) argued that a syntax-first architecture predicts an (E)LAN-P600 response to the syntactic violation caused by the verb, but no N400 because the syntactic integration failure would mean that the verb cannot be (subsequently) semantically integrated into the structure. On the other hand, the elicitation of an N400 would suggest that semantic integration does not require successful syntactic integration. They found a LAN and a P600 but no N400.

The double violation paradigm was also used by Hagoort (2003b) to determine the type of interaction between syntactic violations and semantic violations during processing. In this case, Dutch NPs containing an agreement error (between the determiner and the NP) and a selection error (between an adjective and the NP) were compared to sentences containing only one of the errors:

(5) het / de zoute / bekwame *vaklieden* zien de kwaliteit van het produkt
     the$_{sg}$ / the$_{pl}$ salty / skilled craftsmen$_{pl}$ appreciate the quality of the product

On the one hand, Hagoort found that the N400 to the selection violation was larger for the double violation than for the selection violation in isolation. This suggests that syntax and semantics interact in a way that boosts the N400 effect. On the other hand, Hagoort also found that the P600 to the agreement violation did not change between the double violation and the agreement violation in isolation, suggesting that the semantic violation has no impact on the P600 response to the syntactic violation. This asymmetry in the interaction (syntax affects semantics, but semantics does not affect syntax) is consistent with a syntax-first view in which syntax functionally precedes syntax.

26.3.2.2 ERPs and the unification framework

Recall that under the unification framework, words are stored in the lexicon as part of a structural frame that contains the syntactic environment(s) for that word. Parsing then consists of a single combinatorial operation called unification that joins two structural frames together (Hagoort 2003a, 2005). In cases of ambiguity, the assumption is that two (or more) frames will be accessed from the lexicon, and a process of lateral inhibition based on various factors (plausibility, frequency, temporal decay, etc.) will yield a single phrasal configuration. This model also assumes that syntactic and semantic processing is highly interactive: unification takes place at the syntactic, semantic, and phonological levels simultaneously, and both syntactic and semantic information will interact to produce the correct phrasal unification.[2] Given these properties, the unification architecture requires very different interpretations of the major ERP components. For example, the interpretation of the ELAN as an index of a purely syntactic structure-building process, and the interpretation of the P600 as an index of structural reanalysis and syntactic–semantic integration, are both meaningless within a highly interactive architecture.

Within the unification framework, the three 'syntactic' ERP components are not interpreted as indexing distinct processes or stages of processing, but rather are interpreted as indexing different aspects of the unification process itself. Under this view, the ELAN is a response to impossible unification such as when there are no nodes that can be combined between two structural frames, as is the case with the assumed structure of the phrase-structure violations that have historically elicited an ELAN. The LAN is also an index of failed unification, but whereas the ELAN is a response to impossible structural unification, the LAN is a response to morphosyntactic mismatches (e.g., agreement) that occur after two syntactic frames have been combined. The other major syntactic component, the P600, is not viewed as a response to impossible or invalid unification, but rather an index of the difficulty of the unification, which explains the fact that the P600 is elicited by various types of grammatical sentences that are either structurally ambiguous or syntactically complex. Finally, the N400 is interpreted in this framework as an index of the (lexical-)semantic unification that is assumed to occur in parallel with syntactic unification (Hagoort 2003a).

As the interpretation of the ERPs above suggests, the interaction of syntactic and semantic processes plays a critical role in the architecture of the unification framework. Electrophysiological evidence for this type of interaction (and against a syntax-first architecture) was presented by van den Brink and Hagoort (2004) using the word-final morphology of Dutch verbs as a way to ensure that (lexical-)semantic information became available before word category information. For example, during auditory presentation of the Dutch word *kliederde* 'messed,' the information that this is the past tense verb 'to mess' as opposed to the noun *kliederboel* 'mess' is not available until the word-final past-tense morpheme -*de* is encountered (approximately 300 ms after the onset of the first phoneme). By embedding verbs with this property in a sentential context that creates both a syntactic and semantic violation, van den Brink and Hagoort were able to induce both an ELAN and an N400 to the two kinds of violations. However, in this case the ELAN actually occurred after the N400, as the syntactic violation could not be recognized until the word-final suffix *de* was encountered. Van den Brink and Hagoort argue that this demonstrates that syntactic integration does universally precede semantic integration, as the N400 (an index of difficult semantic integration) can precede the ELAN (an index of failed syntactic integration). Of course, this interpretation assumes that no word category was assigned to the incomplete string *klieder* prior to the final morpheme *-de*. If the category noun were assigned to the incomplete string prior to the final morpheme, perhaps due to the fact that the syntactic environment strongly predicts a noun, correct syntactic integration could occur prior to semantic integration.

26.3.2.3 Thematic P600s and the possibility of independent semantic processing

By focusing on the interpretation of ERPs within the generative and unification frameworks, we have seen both a syntax-first architecture in which syntactic processing is independent of semantic processing, and a highly interactive (or constraint-satisfaction) architecture in which syntactic and semantic processing are co-dependent. Recent work in the ERP literature has suggested that a third type of model may be possible in which semantic processing actually occurs independently of syntactic processing, leading to situations in which an ungrammatical structure associated with a plausible interpretation may be selected by the parser over a grammatical structure which is implausible. These models run contrary to the (likely) assumptions of many syntacticians, who assume that a syntactically licit structure will always be selected over an illicit structure, even if the licit structure leads to an implausible interpretation. These studies focus on 'thematic P600' effects in which it appears that the comprehender has constructed a semantic interpretation that is not licensed by the syntactic structure of the sentence, thus eliciting a P600 (an index of syntactic violation, or of conflict between the syntactic and semantic representations) when the mismatch between the independent semantic interpretation and the syntactic structure is encountered. For example, Kim and Osterhout (2005) presented the following sentences to participants and recorded ERPs to the italicized verbs:

(6)	sentence	prediction	result
		control	
a.	the hungry boy was *devouring* the cookies		
b.	the dusty tabletop was *devouring* the kids	N400	N400
c.	the hearty meal was *devouring* the kids	N400	P600

In the (a) sentence *the hungry boy* is an agentive subject of the active verb *devouring*. In the (b) sentence, *the dusty tabletop* is in subject position, but does not match the agent requirements of the active verb *devouring*. A familiar N400 effect results, apparently due to the mismatch between the lexical-semantic selectional requirements of the verb and the subject. A similar scenario appears to be unfolding in the (c) sentence: *the hearty meal* is in the subject position, but it does not match the agent requirements of the active verb *devouring*. However, instead of eliciting an N400, the (c) sentence elicits a P600.[3] Similar 'thematic P600s' have been found in English (Kim and Osterhout 2005, Kuperberg et al. 2003, Kuperberg et al.

2006, Kuperberg et al. 2007), Dutch (e.g., Kolk et al. 2003, van Herten et al. 2006, van Herten et al. 2005), German (e.g., Friederici and Frisch 2000), and Spanish (Stroud and Phillips 2011).

Kim and Osterhout (2005) argue that the asymmetry between the ERP responses to (b) and (c) suggests that the semantic relationship (what they call semantic attraction) between *the hearty meal* and the verb *devour* is processed independently of the syntactic structure of the sentence. Specifically, they argue that at some point prior to the processing of the verbal morphology of *devouring*, the parser recognizes, based on world knowledge, that the NP *the hearty meal* is likely to be the theme of *devour* (but not the agent), and assigns that thematic relationship. This sets up a syntactic prediction for passive verbal morphology on the verb *devour*. Therefore when the active verbal morphology is encountered, they argue that a syntactic violation occurs, eliciting a P600 (as opposed to a semantic violation which they assume would elicit an N400). Although data from languages with different word orders has led to several different accounts for these effects (see Bornkessel-Schlesewsky and Schlesewsky 2008, Kuperberg 2007, van Herten et al. 2005, 2006 for three other major approaches), they all appear to share the assumption that some form of semantic processing can occur independently of syntactic processing (but see Stroud and Phillips 2011 for a different view).

26.3.3 Synchronous neuronal oscillations

An underlying assumption of electrophysiological studies of neuronal oscillations is that when groups of neurons begin to work in concert, they will adopt a similar rate of oscillatory firing – something akin to a rhythm (Nunez and Srinivasan 2006). The various rates of oscillatory firing are conventionally divided into various frequency bands: activity between 0–4 Hz is called *delta* activity, 4–7 Hz is called *theta* activity, 8–12 Hz is called *alpha* activity, 13–30 Hz is called *beta* activity (and it sometimes subdivided into upper and lower), and 30 Hz and above is called *gamma* activity. When a group of neurons begin to act in concert, the synchrony of their activity means that the EEG will show an increase in amplitude in the frequency band that the group of neurons has adopted. In this way, an increase in the amplitude of activity in a specific frequency band over a single scalp region suggests that a single group of neurons was recruited to perform a task related to the experimental event. Similarly, an increase in the oscillatory coherence at a specific frequency band between two or more *distinct* scalp regions suggests that multiple groups of neurons have been recruited by the experimental task. These two oscillatory responses – an increase in amplitude or an increase in coherence – provide a method for studying the local and long-distance synchrony of populations of neurons (Nunez and Srinivasan 2006).

To date, the majority of EEG studies of sentence processing has focused on ERPs, so it may be useful to briefly discuss the difference between ERPs and neuronal oscillations. As mentioned previously, ERPs are calculated by averaging the EEG activity of several trials using the event as time point zero. This averaging procedure means that only time-locked and phase-locked activity remains (which is called evoked activity). Neuronal oscillations are similarly time-locked to an event, but do not need to be phase-locked (which is called induced activity): two neurons can both adopt a synchronous rate of firing without the peaks and troughs of the waves necessarily lining up, just as two musicians can play a piece together at the same rhythm without necessarily creating notes at the same time. This means that oscillation activity can reveal patterns of activations that are very different from the ERP activity.

Although the vast majority of EEG studies of sentence processing have focused on ERPs, some recent research has started to look at neuronal oscillations to sentence-processing events (Bastiaansen, van Berkum, and Hagoort 2002a, 2002b, Bastiaansen and Hagoort 2003, Bastiaansen et al. 2005, Hald et al. 2006). For example, Bastiaansen et al. (2002b) looked at two paradigms in Dutch that have been shown to elicit a P600 response: number agreement violations and gender agreement violations (van Berkum et al. 2000).

(7) number agreement violation
 ik zag enkele donkere wolk aan de horizon
 I saw several dark cloud on the horizon

(8) gender agreement violation
 ik zag een donker wolk aan de horizon
 I saw a dark$_{NEUT}$ cloud$_{NON\text{-}NEUT}$ on the horizon

They found local increases in amplitude in the theta band (4–7 Hz) between 300–500 ms post-stimulus onset for both violation types; however, the scalp distribution of the maximum amplitude increase was different for each violation type: number agreement violations elicited a theta power increase over left anterior electrode sites, whereas gender agreement violations elicited a theta power increase over right anterior electrode sites. This result is interesting in a number of ways. First, it demonstrates a possible electrophysiological difference between number and gender agreement violations (although the precise functional interpretation of this difference remains unclear). Second, it demonstrates a difference between the latency of the ERP effect (500–800 ms post-stimulus onset) and the latency of the theta band increase (300–500 ms). Third, it demonstrates a difference between the scalp distribution of the ERP (centro-parietal for both violation types) and the scalp distribution of the theta band increase (left and right anterior). And finally, it demonstrates an asymmetry in the types of differences between the two analyses: the

ERP analyses revealed a quantitative difference between the two violations (the P600 to number violations was larger than the P600 to gender violations), whereas the oscillation analysis revealed a qualitative difference in scalp distribution. These results suggest that the two analyses yield different types of information about EEG activity during sentence processing (see also Hald et al. 2006 for similar results for the N400 to semantic violations).

26.4 Hemodynamic responses

As the previous section demonstrates, electrophysiological studies provide information about the types of processes that occur during syntactic processing, and about the time course of information flow (e.g., the relative ordering of syntactic and semantic processes). However, a complete cognitive neuroscience of syntactic processing also requires a theory of how those processes are implemented in the neural circuitry of the brain. The first step to a complete implementational theory is to identify the neural circuits involved in these processes. To be clear, this first 'mapping' step is not itself an implementational theory; but it does constrain the search for how individual (or populations of) neurons implement individual processes. First, what we know about properties of particular brain regions may give us insight into how computations are implemented there. Although cellular organization is surprisingly similar throughout the brain (e.g. Mountcastle 1997), we know from many patient studies and neuroimaging studies that cognitive functions are often localized to particular regions, which may correspond to subtle cytoarchitectural differences (e.g., the Brodmann map; see Zilles and Amunts 2010 for a recent review). While our understanding is still very limited, future research may show that these differences at the cellular level indeed constrain the kinds of computations that can be done in a given region. Second, knowledge about the anatomical connections that exist between different brain regions may help us to understand the larger circuits involved in sentence comprehension. We have rudimentary knowledge about the strongest of these connections from histology studies of gross anatomy, and new methods from functional neuroimaging such as diffusion imaging are continually improving our estimates of both structural and functional connectivity. Third, many brain regions seem to implement similar computations across domains; therefore if one localizes a syntactic computation to a region known to also be involved in another domain, it may provide clues to how the syntactic computation is implemented. Finally, in a practical sense, localization of a computation to a specific brain area can provide perhaps one of the most unambiguous ways of querying properties of that computation for future research, as compared with behavioral or scalp-recorded electrophysiological data that may reflect a mix of syntactic and more general processes.

Currently the most popular methodology for localizing cognitive function is measuring changes in blood flow related to neural activity with functional magnetic resonance imaging (fMRI). Neural firing depletes local energy stores, so in response, fresh blood carrying more glucose is delivered. The magnetic properties of fresh, oxygenated blood are different from old, deoxygenated blood, which is the source of the BOLD (Blood Oxygen-Level Dependent) signal that can be measured with MRI. If neural firing suddenly increases in a given region in response to a stimulus, the amount of oxygenated blood sent to this region should also increase (often referred to as the hemodynamic response), allowing the backwards inference that a region is involved in a computation if it demonstrates an increase in the BOLD signal when this computation is performed.

BOLD fMRI has a number of advantages as a localization methodology. It has much better spatial resolution than equally non-invasive techniques such as MEG and EEG, usually localizing the signal within 3–5 mm. The model for recovering the spatial coordinates of the MR signal is straightforward and universally agreed upon, in contrast to MEG or EEG source localization models that require many controversial assumptions. And although MRI scanning is expensive, MRI scanners are available all over the world, because of their clinical applications. However, BOLD fMRI also has well-known weaknesses for measuring cognitive processing. The most significant problem is the very poor temporal resolution of the technique, which is constrained more by the signal itself than by the measurement technology. As one might imagine, blood flows much more slowly than neurons fire; while electrophysiology suggests that basic processing stages take place on the scale of tens or hundreds of milliseconds, blood oxygenation changes on the scale of seconds. Therefore, if multiple subcomputations are sequentially engaged in the process of interest, a BOLD contrast isolating this process will show effects in all of the underlying regions in one image, as if they were all occurring simultaneously. It is left to the investigator to be sufficiently clever and lucky to be able to map the multiple regions that almost inevitably show up in a whole-brain contrast to the multiple hypothesized subcomponents of the computation.

All mainstream localization techniques (fMRI, MEG, PET) face difficulties in generalizing results across individuals, due to the large individual variation in brain size and morphology. Although algorithms for converting individual brains to a common space are constantly improving, these algorithms cannot solve the problem of variation in cytoarchitecture or 'functional' anatomy, for instance, if characteristic neuron types are not in exactly the same place with respect to larger brain structures. Regions of inferior frontal cortex historically implicated in language comprehension have been shown to have a particularly large amount of this form of variability (Amunts *et al.* 1999, Fedorenko and Kanwisher 2009).

26.4.1 Broca's area

Our models of the cortical networks involved in the earliest stages of language processing such as speech or visual word-form recognition are still very crude. How can we even begin to approach questions about the cortical regions that process syntactic information? One simple approach is to manipulate the number or type of formal operations hypothesized by the syntactic theory in sentences presented to subjects during neuroimaging recordings. Even without committing to a specific parsing algorithm, we can start from the simple assumption that parsing representations that differ at the computational level will also differ in the operations required to parse them. Once we identify regions for which activity seems to correlate with our manipulation of structural properties of the sentence, we can then begin the more challenging task of determining what part of the parsing algorithm this region is implementing.

Broca's area is probably the most famous brain region to be correlated with structural properties of sentences. The term 'Broca's area' usually refers to a portion of the left inferior frontal gyrus (LIFG) composed of the more anterior *pars triangularis* (Brodmann area 45) and the more posterior *pars opercularis* (Brodmann area 44). Paul Broca originally identified this area as central to speech processing based on the post-mortem inspection of the brains of two patients that exhibited severe aphasia: one patient could only produce the word 'tan,' the other only a handful of basic words. With the advent of non-invasive neuroimaging techniques such as PET and fMRI, Broca's area has taken center stage in the investigation of the neural substrates of syntactic processing. At least two-thirds of the neuroimaging studies of the brain areas involved in sentence processing (in health) over the past fifteen years reveal an increased activation in (at least part of) Broca's area for at least one of the reported contrasts, suggesting that this area indeed plays a significant role in some aspect of sentence processing.

Although there has been great debate about the key property that modulates activity in Broca's area in sentence processing, perhaps the most theory-neutral description of the central data is that Broca's area tends to respond more to sentences with non-canonical word order than sentences with canonical word order. For example, relative to controls with canonical word order, Broca's area shows increased BOLD signal for relative clauses (e.g., Just et al. 1996, Ben-Shachar et al. 2003), wh-movement (e.g., Ben-Shachar et al. 2004, Santi and Grodzinsky 2007a, 2007b), topicalization (e.g., Ben-Shachar et al. 2004), clefting (e.g., Caplan et al. 1999), and scrambling (e.g., Friederici et al. 2006b, Bornkessel et al. 2005, Bornkessel-Schlesewsky et al. 2009). The question then is which cognitive processes these comparisons have in common – a question that is inextricably tied to assumptions about syntactic theory. As the ongoing debate over the role of Broca's area illustrates, the interpretation of neuroimaging results at the implementational and algorithmic level is fundamentally shaped by the syntactic theory assumed at the computational level. Three prominent hypotheses regarding what structural property of sentences might account for variation in Broca's area activity are based in three different syntactic frameworks: movement (based on generative syntactic theory), unification (based on unification theory), and linearization (based on argument–dependency theory).

26.4.2 Movement hypothesis

Grodzinsky and colleagues have argued that Broca's area seems to be more active for non-canonical word orders because Broca's area supports the syntactic mechanism of movement that is familiar from generative syntactic theory (Grodzinsky 1986; see Grodzinsky and Santi 2008 for a recent review). To demonstrate the specialization of Broca's area to the syntactic mechanism of movement, Grodzinsky and colleagues have conducted a series of experiments designed to tease apart movement from other possible functions of Broca's area. For example, Ben-Shachar et al. (2004) argue against the idea that Broca's area is sensitive to the syntactic complexity of non-canonical word orders in Hebrew by demonstrating increased activation for topicalization, which they assume is derived via A'-movement, compared to dative shift, which is a superficially similar displacement of an argument, but is either derived via A-movement, or simply base generated (see Chapter 9):

(9) Dative shift: John natan [la-professor   me-Oxford] ['et ha-sefer
John gave   [to-the-professor from-Oxford] [the-book
ha-'adom] __
the-red] __

Topicalization: [la-professor   me-Oxford] John natan ['et ha-sefer
[to-the-professor from-Oxford] John gave [the-book
ha-'adom] __
the-red] __

'John gave the red book to the professor from Oxford'

26.4.3 Unification hypothesis

Remember that the unification framework argues that the smallest unit of syntactic combination are words already associated with structural frames, and that syntactic combination proceeds by combining these small trees together, much as in Tree Adjoining Grammar (Chapter 8). Assuming this view, Hagoort and colleagues have suggested that Broca's area is responsible for syntactic unification (Hagoort, 2005), with the prediction that factors that increase the difficulty of syntactic unification will also increase activation in Broca's area. For example, Snijders et al. (2009) compared sentences containing a word-class ambiguous word (either noun or verb) to sentences containing no ambiguous words, with the prediction that the word-class ambiguity will force the parser to consider two syntactic frames simultaneously, thus increasing the unification difficulty in the ambiguous condition. They found increased activation for the ambiguous condition in the posterior portion of LIFG. On this view, the reason for effects of non-canonical word order must be that such sentences in some way increase syntactic unification difficulty.

(10) Ambiguous: zodra zij bewijzen$_{(N/V)}$ leveren kunnen we beginnen
                   as-soon-as they evidence/proof provide can we start
                   'as soon as they provide evidence we can start'
      Unambiguous: zodra zij kopij leveren kunnen we beginnen
                   as-soon-as they copy provide can we start
                   'as soon as they provide a copy we can start'

26.4.4 Linearization hypothesis

As mentioned briefly in Section 26.2, Bornkessel-Schlesewsky and colleagues have proposed the argument-dependency framework, which assumes a parsing stage in which the argument relations of the sentence are computed according to several prominence hierarchies that are familiar from typological research (e.g., the animacy hierarchy, the case hierarchy, the definiteness hierarchy) (Comrie 1989, Bornkessel and Schlesewsky 2006, Wolff et al. 2008). Based on this framework, several studies have argued that Broca's area in fact supports the linearization processes that map word order to argument structure according to these prominence hierarchies. For example, Chen et al. (2006) manipulated the animacy of the relevant arguments in center-embedded object relative clauses:

(11) a. the golfer [that the lightning struck __] survived the accident
      b. the wood [that the man chopped __] heated the cabin

They found increased activation in several areas of the LIFG (BA 47, 9, 6) for the (a) sentences in which the relativized object was more animate than the subject of the relative clause (see Grewe et al. 2006 for similar effects of animacy in German). Bornkessel-Schlesewsky et al. (2009) manipulated both the order of the NPs in German sentences (subject first (SO) or object first (OS)) and the referentiality of the NPs (proper names first (REF) versus common nouns first (NREF)) to assess whether Broca's area is sensitive to both word order manipulations and referentiality manipulations, and found a gradient activation response in BA 44 that seemed to follow the referentiality hierarchy: SO-REF > SO-NREF > OS-REF > OS-NREF (where '>' denotes 'higher on the hierarchy than'; see also Bornkessel et al. 2005 and Grewe et al. 2005).

26.4.5 The role of linking hypotheses

The movement, unification, and linearization hypotheses all demonstrate the role that syntactic theory can play in the interpretation of brain activation. However, it is important to note that this role is predicated upon an often unstated assumption about the linking hypothesis between a given syntactic theory (the computational level), a given parsing theory (the algorithmic level), and the correct level of description of brain activation (the implementational level). For example, the movement hypothesis of Grodzinsky and colleagues assumes a relatively direct linking hypothesis between syntactic theory and brain areas, such that parsing theories do not play much of a role in the interpretation of brain activation. Grodzinsky has called this assumption the syntactotopic conjecture (Grodzinsky and Friederici 2006): formal mechanisms of syntactic theory are themselves neurologically distinct elements of linguistic knowledge that can be localized to distinct brain areas. Superficially, the unification framework of Hagoort (2003a, 2005) also appears to assume a relatively direct linking between syntactic theory and brain areas. However, this direct linking between syntax and brain activation is in some ways an illusion created by the fact that there is a relatively direct linking between all three levels: the syntactic theory is based upon the grammatical operation of unification, the parsing theory is based upon the parsing process of unification, and brain activation is assumed to reflect aspects of the neural computation of unification. Of course, other linking hypotheses are logically possible. In this section, we would like to review one approach that has enjoyed widespread support in recent years, in which the syntactic configurations licensed by syntactic theory place demands on non-structure-building parsing processes such as working memory processes, and it is these working memory processes that are assumed to be driving the activation in Broca's area.

The idea that Broca's area may be involved in the working memory requirements of sentence processing is consistent with the pre-theoretical observation that non-canonical word order leads to activation in Broca's area. Much research in the sentence processing literature has focused on the role of working memory during the processing of non-canonical word orders (e.g., King and Just 1991, Just and Carpenter 1992, MacDonald et al. 1992, Gibson 1998, Caplan and Waters 1999, Vos et al. 2001, Fiebach et al. 2002, Roberts and Gibson 2002, Phillips et al. 2005, Fedorenko et al. 2006, 2007). However, to truly dissociate the working memory hypothesis from those that postulate a more direct link between structural properties and brain regions, it is necessary to find cases that share the same structural properties but differ in working memory demands and vice versa. A number of studies have done this over the last fifteen years, with mixed results. For example, Fiebach et al. (2005) used embedded object *wh*-questions in German to manipulate dependency distance (short versus long) without the confound of embedding type, and found increased activation in Broca's area (BA 44 and 45) for the longer dependencies, which would be predicted on a working memory view, but not on a view such as Grodzinsky's in which activity should only be modulated by differences in the presence or number of movements rather than their length.

In defense of the movement hypothesis, Santi and Grodzinsky (2007b) have presented opposing evidence in a study in which they manipulated the distance between a moved *wh*-word and its gap (0 intervening NPs, 1 intervening NP, 2 intervening NPs), and compared that to the distance between an anaphor and its antecedent (0, 1, and 2 intervening NPs). They argued that both *wh*-movement and anaphoric binding dependencies require working memory resources to resolve, therefore the working memory interpretation of Broca's area should predict that both manipulations will increase activation. In contrast, they find that Broca's area is selectively sensitive to the *wh*-movement manipulation but not the binding manipulation.

(12) Distance manipulation

Move0: the mailman and the mother of Jim love **the woman** who Kate burnt __

Move1: the mother of Jim loves **the woman** who the mailman and Kate burnt __

Move2: Kate loves **the woman** who the mailman and the mother of Jim burnt __

Bind0: the sister of Kim assumes that Anne loves **the mailman** who burnt **himself**

Bind1: the sister of Kim assumes that **the mailman** who loves Anne burnt **himself**

Bind2: Anne assumes that **the mailman** who loves the sister of Kim burnt **himself**

Of course, Santi and Grodzinsky (2007b, 2010) are careful to acknowledge that it is untenable to hold that Broca's area as classically defined is *only* involved in a very specific linguistic computation such as syntactic movement, because numerous neuroimaging studies have localized activity here for working memory tasks that do not involve sentences, such as the n-back task (Braver et al. 1997, Smith and Jonides 1998, 1999) and semantic priming tasks (Gold et al. 2006). They argue instead that Broca's area may serve multiple functions across the various domains of cognition, but that its role in sentence processing is specifically related to movement, and crucially not other non-movement constructions (see also Makuuchi et al. 2009 for a different approach to the tension between generality and specificity in Broca's area).

Another approach to dissociating the working memory hypothesis from the others that has been proposed recently is to tax processes involved in working memory with an external manipulation to see if this affects the contrasts observed during sentence processing of non-canonical word orders. The logic of this approach is straightforward: if the difference observed between two sentences is due to different working memory requirements, then increasing the working memory requirements for both sentences with a non-linguistic working memory task should eliminate the activation difference between the two sentences (as both will show maximum activation). Rogalsky et al. (2008) asked participants to listen to sentences containing center-embedded subject relatives (a) and center-embedded object relatives (b) – a contrast that reliably activates Broca's area – while performing one of three concurrent tasks: (i) no concurrent task, (ii) whispering 'ba da ga da' repeatedly, (iii) tapping their fingers in sequence from thumb to pinky repeatedly. They found that object relatives led to an increased activation in both BA 44 and 45 when there was no concurrent task as reported by previous studies. However, the concurrent articulatory task ('ba da ga da') eliminated the activation in BA 44, leaving only activation in BA 45. Interestingly, they found a complementary pattern for the finger-tapping task: object relatives led to increased activation in BA 44 but not in BA 45. Rogalsky et al. interpret these results as evidence that BA 44 supports the articulatory rehearsal component of working memory, and that non-canonical word orders like object relative clauses generate activation in Broca's area because they recruit articulatory rehearsal based working memory (such as silently repeating sentences). They also suggest that BA 45 may support domain-general sequencing operations that are deployed during both sentence comprehension and sequential tasks like finger tapping. Clearly, the evidence gathered to date is consistent with multiple theories of the role of Broca's area in syntactic processing.

26.4.6 The temporal lobe

Although Broca's area has been the focus of many neuroimaging studies of syntax, there is a growing literature implicating portions of the temporal lobe in syntactic processing. Notably, different formal syntactic theories make different predictions about which part of temporal cortex is likely to play the central role in basic syntactic combination. Theories like unification theory and Tree Adjoining Grammar argue that much of syntactic structure is stored with lexical entries, and therefore that most of the important syntactic work is done by lexical retrieval. As we will see, it has been suggested that lexical retrieval can be localized to areas of the posterior temporal cortex. In contrast, generative syntactic theory assumes that syntactic structure is built up by Merge-type operations that combine simple lexical terminals, and therefore predict that the areas involved in syntactic combination will show more activity than areas involved in simple lexical retrieval. As we will see, several researchers have suggested that parts of the anterior temporal cortex are involved in syntactic combination.

26.4.7 Anterior temporal cortex

One of the most robust neuroimaging findings about sentence-level processing is that lateral anterior portions of the superior and middle temporal cortex show greater activation bilaterally for reading or listening to sentences than word lists (Mazoyer et al. 1993, Stowe et al. 1998, Friederici et al. 2000, Vandenberghe et al. 2002, Humphries et al. 2005, 2006, Brennan and Pylkkänen 2012). This pattern holds in at least some regions of the anterior temporal lobe (ATL) even with Jabberwocky sentences in which the content words are replaced with nonsense words (Humphries et al. 2006). Furthermore, voxel-based lesion mapping has associated damage to left lateral ATL with comprehension impairment for most sentences more complex than simple declaratives (Dronkers et al. 2004, although cf. Kho et al. 2008). These findings suggest that ATL supports sentence-level computations that do not rely on lexical semantics, but this leaves open a number of possible candidate processes: syntactic processes, argument structure processes, discourse processes, and even prosodic processes (although Humphries et al. 2005 show that the sentence > word list effect holds in some areas of ATL even when sentences are pronounced with list prosody instead of normal prosody).

If there were a brain region dedicated to basic syntactic phrase structure computation in comprehension (as opposed to the dependency structure building suggested for Broca's area), one would expect it to show a profile exactly like ATL, showing more activity for processing word strings with syntactic structure than those without. However, demonstrating that this area is specifically involved in syntax as opposed to other phrase-level computations has proved challenging. An interesting recent attempt comes from a study by Brennan et al. (2010), who used a naturalistic comprehension paradigm in which they asked participants to listen to a portion of *Alice in Wonderland* while recording fMRI. Brennan et al. counted the number of syntactic nodes being constructed at each time point in the story and found that this syntactic node count significantly correlated with the BOLD signal in left anterior temporal cortex (notably, this was not the case for Broca's area). This finding is thus consistent with a syntactic interpretation of ATL function; however, as the authors themselves point out, syntactic node count is likely to be correlated with other factors such as the number of compositional semantic operations required and therefore this evidence is not decisive.

A few studies have shown increased activity in ATL for phrase-structure violations (Meyer et al. 2000, Friederici et al. 2003). For example, Friederici et al. (2003) have demonstrated that ATL is sensitive to the phrase-structure violations that give rise to the ELAN in ERP research:

(13) correct: das Hemd wurde gebügelt   (German)
                 the shirt was ironed
     syntactic violation: *die Bluse wurde am gebügelt
                 the blouse was on-the ironed

Similarly, Meyer et al. (2000) demonstrated that ATL is sensitive to other basic syntactic violations such as gender disagreement, number disagreement, and case-marking violations. However, the interpretation of these results really depends on our hypothesis about the processes invoked when the parser encounters a syntactic violation. If syntactic violations induce the parser to try additional phrase-structure combinations, one might indeed expect more activity in the region involved in building phrase structure. Yet syntactic violations might also lead the parser to initiate non-structure-building processes with the goal of reanalysis/repair, for example working memory processes to recall the previous material, or semantic interpretation processes to get clues toward how the structure is repaired. Under this latter view, activation to syntactic violations in ATL may not index syntactic structure-building at all. Until we have a good theory of the algorithm used to deal with syntactic violations in comprehension, these data do not provide unambiguous evidence about the neural implementation.

Finally, in a novel attempt to get around the syntax/semantics confound in sentence-level processing, Rogalsky and Hickok (2008) used a selective attention paradigm to attempt to tease apart syntactic and semantic activation in ATL by telling subjects that their task was to either identify syntactic violations (syntactic attention) or identify semantic violations (semantic attention). The analysis was then performed only on correct sentences to avoid contamination from the error detection. They found that large portions of ATL were activated equally for both syntactic and semantic attention, with a small region activated more by semantic attention. The authors interpret these results as evidence that ATL supports both syntactic and semantic processing. However, although no violations were included in the analysis, this study shares some of the problems of interpretation of the violation studies: there is not yet a well-worked out theory of how processing changes when subjects are told to direct their attention to syntactic or semantic violations. If typical sentence comprehension processes are not under attentional control, then it would not be surprising that ATL is similarly activated (relative to word lists) in both cases, nor would it be informative about whether ATL is involved in syntactic or semantic computations.

Although the majority of neuroimaging studies of syntactic processing have focused on Broca's area, it is becoming increasingly obvious that ATL plays an important role in some aspect(s) of sentence-level processing. However, progress in this area is going to require specific theories about the types of syntactic and semantic processes that are incrementally deployed during sentence processing, which we have already seen are highly dependent upon the assumptions of syntactic theory.

26.4.8 Posterior temporal cortex

Within the unification framework there are two primary parsing operations: lexical retrieval of lexically bound syntactic frames, and unification of these frames into sentence structures (Hagoort 2005). Unification is argued to occur in left IFG, which is thought to account for the effects of syntactic structure observed in Broca's area, as we discuss above. However, unlike in traditional generative theories, much of syntactic structure is thought to be retrieved with the lexical entry rather than compiled online, and therefore, the other critical operation for syntactic processing in the unification framework is memory retrieval of stored lexical representations. A large body of functional neuroimaging evidence suggests that retrieval of lexical representations across both comprehension and production is supported by posterior temporal cortex, in particular the region encompassing mid-posterior middle temporal gyrus (MTG) and parts of the neighboring superior temporal sulcus (STS) and inferior temporal cortex (IT) (see Indefrey and Levelt 2004, Hickok and Poeppel 2004, Martin 2007, Lau et al. 2008 for review). In addition, neuropsychological studies show that lesions to posterior temporal cortex are associated with difficulty in comprehension of single words (Hart and Gordon 1990) and even the simplest sentences (Dronkers et al. 2004).[4]

Since the unification framework posits that parsing involves retrieving the syntactic frame stored with each lexical representation, it predicts that manipulations that affect this syntactic frame retrieval should change activity in posterior temporal cortex. In one recent study, Snijders et al. (2009) used syntactic category-ambiguous words presented in word lists and sentences (e.g., *duck*, which has both a noun and a verb meaning) to operationalize lexical retrieval, as category-ambiguous words require (at least) two frames to be retrieved from the lexicon, whereas unambiguous words only require one. They predicted that lexical retrieval would be more taxed for ambiguous than unambiguous words in both word lists and sentences (because two syntactic frames must be retrieved instead of one) but that because word lists do not require syntactic unification, only ambiguous words in sentences would be associated with increased syntactic unification difficulty. Consistent with this prediction, Snijders et al. found a main effect of ambiguity for left posterior middle temporal gyrus (LpMTG) in both word lists and sentence contexts, while a left inferior frontal gyrus (LIFG) region of interest only showed an ambiguity effect for sentence contexts. However, alternative interpretations of this pattern are possible; for example the increase in LpMTG may reflect the cost of retrieving multiple conceptual representations rather than multiple syntactic frames, and the increase in LIFG for sentences may reflect the resolution of lexical competition made possible by the sentence context (e.g., Bedny et al. 2008, Grindrod et al. 2008) rather than syntactic unification. To more conclusively show that posterior temporal cortex is involved in the retrieval of syntactic frames, more work will be needed; one possibility might be to contrast the processing of category-ambiguous words such as *duck* with words whose two meanings share the same syntactic frame such as *bank*, or with category-ambiguous words whose meanings are semantically similar such as *vote* (Lee and Federmeier 2006).

26.5 Conclusion: toward a cognitive neuroscience of syntax

The preceding discussion is far from exhaustive, but we hope that it provides a coherent introduction to the major strands of research on syntactic processing in the human brain. We also hope that this chapter has also made it clear that syntactic theory, and the linking hypotheses between syntactic theory and sentence processing, plays a pivotal (but often unstated) role in the interpretation of electrophysiological and hemodynamic neuroimaging studies. This suggests that syntacticians may be well positioned to become central players in the progress toward a cognitive neuroscience of syntax, and help resolve some of the long-standing puzzles discussed in this chapter.

Notes

1. It should be noted from the outset that this is not intended to be, and indeed could not be, a complete review of the psycho- or neurolinguistics literature on sentence processing. It is unfortunate that many interesting areas (and results) of psycho/neurolinguistics research on sentence processing had to be left out of this chapter in the interest of presenting a coherent narrative in the space available. We hope that readers with psycho/neurolinguistics backgrounds will interpret these omissions as nothing more than the consequence of these limitations, and that readers who are new to psycho/neurolinguistics studies can use the (copious) references that we have supplied to find the many interesting studies that we could not cover here.
2. Highly interactive architectures are sometimes also known as constraint-satisfaction architectures to make reference to the fact that both syntactic constraints and semantic constraints are just constraints that need to be satisfied in whatever order possible (Altmann and Steedman 1988, Levy 2008, MacDonald et al. 1994, Tanenhaus et al. 1995).
3. As discussed above, previous evidence suggests that the N400 may not be a reliable index of compositional semantic processes. Therefore, the N400 contrast between (a) and (b) may simply reflect the degree to which the theme primes/predicts the verb root (*tabletop – devour* vs. *meal – devour*), and thus may not be informative about whether or not the thematic mismatch is perceived in both cases. Therefore, it is not the absence of the N400 effect but the presence of the P600 effect that is hardest to account for under previous assumptions.

4. Note that an alternative view has suggested that lexical-semantic information is localized in an anterior temporal 'semantic hub' region, because semantic dementia is characterized by severe anterior temporal atrophy (Patterson et al. 2007). However, there is evidence that the atrophy extends to posterior parts of the temporal lobe as well (e.g. Mummery et al. 1999), and recent studies support the idea that this posterior temporal damage is the cause of the general lexical-semantic deficits, while the anterior 'semantic hub' region may have a more specific function in representing living things or people (Noppeney et al. 2007, Simmons et al. 2010). Also see Tyler and Marslen-Wilson (2008) for arguments that posterior temporal cortex contains distinct syntactic and semantic subregions.

References

Abeillé, Anne (1991). Une grammaire lexicalisée d'Arbes Adjoints pour le français. PhD dissertation, Université Paris 7.

Abeillé, Anne and Owen Rambow (eds.) (2000). *Tree adjoining grammars: Formalisms, linguistic analysis and processing*. Stanford, CA: CSLI Publications.

Abeillé, Anne and Yves Schabes (1989). Parsing idioms with a lexicalized tree adjoining grammar. In *Proceedings of the European Conference of the Association for Computational Linguistics*, 161–165. Manchester.

Abels, Klaus (2003). Successive cyclicity, anti-locality, and adposition stranding. PhD dissertation, University of Connecticut.

Abels, Klaus, and Kristine Bentzen (to appear). Are movement paths punctuated or uniform? In A. Alexiadou, T. Kiss, and G. Müller (eds.), *Local modelling of non-local dependencies in syntax*. Tübingen: Linguistische Arbeiten, Niemeyer.

Abney, Steven (1986). The noun phrase. Unpublished ms. MIT.

(1987). The English noun phrase in its sentential aspect. PhD dissertation, MIT.

Aboh, Enoch Oladé (2004a). *The morphosyntax of complement-head sequences*. Oxford University Press.

(2004b). Topic and Focus within D. *Linguistics in the Netherlands* 21, 1–12.

(2010). The P route. In Cinque and Rizzi (2010b), 225–260.

Abusch, Dorit (1985). On verbs and time. PhD dissertation, University of Massachusetts.

(2004). On the temporal composition of infinitives. In Guéron and Lecarme (2004), 27–53.

Ackema, Peter (2001). On the relation between V-to-I and the structure of the inflectional paradigm. *The Linguistic Review* 18, 233–263.

Ackema, Peter and Maaike Schoorlemmer (1995). Middles and nonmovement. *Linguistic Inquiry* 26, 173–197.
Ackema, Peter and Kriszta Szendrői (2002). Determiner sharing as an instance of dependent ellipsis. *Journal of Comparative Germanic Linguistics* 5, 3–34.
Acquaviva, Paolo (1997). *The logical form of negation: A study of operator-variable structures in syntax.* Garland outstanding dissertations in linguistics. New York: Garland.
Adésolá, Olúsèye (2004). Null operators and pronouns – A-bar dependencies and relations in Yoruba. PhD dissertation, Rutgers University.
Adger, David (2006). Combinatorial variability. *Journal of Linguistics* 42, 503–530.
Adger, David and Daniel Harbour (2007). Syntax and syncretisms of the Person Case Constraint. *Syntax* 10, 2–37.
Adger, David, Daniel Harbour, and Laurel Watkins (2009). *Mirrors and microparameters: Phrase structure beyond free word order.* Cambridge University Press.
Adger, David and Gillian Ramchand (2003). Predication and equation. *Linguistic Inquiry* 34, 325–359.
Aelbrecht, Lobke (2007). A movement account of Dutch gapping. Unpublished ms, Catholic University of Brussels.
(2010). *The syntactic licensing of ellipsis.* Amsterdam: John Benjamins.
Åfarli, Tor A. (1992). *The syntax of Norwegian passive constructions.* Amsterdam: John Benjamins.
Åfarli, Tor A. and Katrin Eide (2000). Subject requirement and predication. *Nordic Journal of Linguistics* 23, 27–48.
Afranaph Project (Ongoing). Edited by Ken Safir, Rutgers University and University of Utrecht: available at www.africananaphora.rutgers.edu.
Agbayani, Brian (1998). Feature attraction and category movement. PhD dissertation, University of California, Irvine.
Agüero-Bautista, Calixto (2007). Diagnosing cyclicity in sluicing. *Linguistic Inquiry* 38, 413–443.
Ainsworth-Darnell, Kim, Harvey Shulman, and Julie Boland (1998). Dissociating brain responses to syntactic and semantic anomalies: Evidence from event-related potentials. *Journal of Memory and Language* 38, 112–130.
Aissen, Judith (1997). On the syntax of obviation. *Language* 73, 705–750.
(2003). Differential object marking: Iconicity vs. economy. *Natural Language and Linguistic Theory* 21, 435–483.
Akmajian, Adrian and Thomas Wasow (1975). The constituent structure of VP and AUX and the position of the verb BE. *Linguistic Analysis* 1, 205–246.
Alexiadou, Artemis (1997). *Adverb placement: A case study in antisymmetric syntax.* Amsterdam: John Benjamins.
(2001a). Adjective syntax and noun raising: Word order asymmetries in the DP as the result of adjective distribution. *Studia Linguistica* 55, 217–248.

(2001b). *Functional structure in nominals: Nominalization and ergativity.* Amsterdam: John Benjamins.

(2002a). State of the article on the syntax of adverbs. *GLOT International*, 6, 33–54.

(2002b). On the status of adverb in a grammar without a lexicon. In F. Schmöe (ed.) *Das Adverb: Zentrum und Peripherie einer Wortklasse*, 25–42. Wien: Präsens edition.

(ed.) (2004). Adverbs across frameworks. *Lingua* 114.

(2009). Tense marking in the nominal domain: Implications for grammar architecture. *Linguistic Variation Yearbook* 8, 33–59.

(2010). On the morphosyntax of (anti)-causative verbs. In M. Rappaport Hovav, E. Doron, and I. Sichel (eds.), *Syntax, lexical semantics and event structure*, 177–203. Oxford University Press.

Alexiadou, Artemis and Elena Anagnostopoulou (2004). Voice morphology in the causative–inchoative alternation: Evidence for a non-unified structural analysis of unaccusatives. In Alexiadou, Anagnostopoulou, and Everaert (2004), 114–136.

Alexiadou, Artemis, Elena Anagnostopoulou, and Martin Everaert (eds.) (2004). *The unaccusativity puzzle: Explorations of the syntax–lexicon interface.* Oxford University Press.

Alexiadou, Artemis, Elena Anagnostopoulou, Gianina Iordachioaia and Mihaela Marchis (2010). No objections to backward control. In Hornstein and Polinsky (2010), 89–117.

Alexiadou, Artemis and Edit Doron (2007). The syntactic construction of two non-active voices: Passive and middle. Handout, GLOW XXX, University of Tromsø.

Alexiadou, Artemis and Kirsten Gengel (2008). Classifiers as morphosyntactic licensors of NP ellipsis: English vs. Romance. In *Proceedings of NELS 39*, 15–28. Amherst, MA: GSLA.

Alexiadou, Artemis, Liliane Haegeman, and Melita Stavrou (2007). *Noun phrase in the generative perspective.* Berlin: Walter de Gruyter.

Alexiadou, Artemis and Melita Stavrou (2011). Ethnic adjectives as pseudo-adjectives. *Studia Linguistica* 65, 1–30.

Alexiadou, Artemis and Chris Wilder (1998a). Adjectival modification and multiple determiners. In Alexiadou and Wilder (1998b), 303–332.

(1998b). *Possessors, predicates and movement in the determiner phrase.* Amsterdam/Philadelphia: John Benjamins.

Allopenna, Paul, James Magnuson, and Michael Tanenhaus (1998). Tracking the time course of spoken word recognition using eye movements: Evidence for continuous mapping models. *Journal of memory and language* 38, 419–439.

Almeida, Diogo de A. and Masaya Yoshida (2007). A problem for the preposition stranding generalization. *Linguistic Inquiry* 38, 349–362.

Aloni, Maria (2006). Free choice and exhaustification: An account of sub-triggering effects. In E. P. Waldmüller (ed.), *Proceedings of Sinn und Bedeutung 11*, 16–30. Barcelona: Universitat Pompeu Fabra.

Aloni, Maria and Robert van Rooij (2007). Free-choice items and alternatives. In G. Bouma, I. Krämer, and J. Zwarts (eds.), *Proceedings of KNAW Colloquium: Cognitive Foundations of Interpretation in 2004*, VLN 190. 5–26. Amsterdam: Royal Netherlands Academy of Arts and Sciences.

Alsina, Alex (1992). On the argument structure of causatives. *Linguistic Inquiry* 23, 517–555.

— (1993). Predicate composition: A theory of syntactic function alternations. PhD dissertation, Stanford University.

Alsina, Alex and Smita Joshi (1993). Parameters in causative constructions. In L. Dobrin, L. Nichols, and R. Rodriguez (eds.), *Papers from CLS 27*, 1–15. Chicago, IL: Chicago Linguistic Society.

Altmann, Gerry and Mark Steedman (1988). Interaction with context during human sentence processing. *Cognition* 30, 191–238.

Altmann, Hans (1988). *Intonationsforschungen*. Tübingen: Niemeyer.

Amunts, K., A. Schleicher, U. Burgel, H. Mohlberg, H. B. M. Uylings, and K. Zilles (1999). Broca's region revisited: Cytoarchitecture and intersubject variability. *Journal of Computational Neurology* 412, 319–341.

Anagnostopoulou, Elena and Martin Everaert (1999). Towards a more complete typology of anaphoric expressions. *Linguistic Inquiry* 30, 97–114.

Anand, Pranav (2006). De de se. PhD dissertation, MIT.

Anderson, Stephen (1976). On the notion of subject in ergative languages. In C. N. Li (ed.), *Subject and topic*, 1–23. New York: Academic Press.

Andrews, Avery D. (1982). The representation of case in modern Icelandic. In Bresnan (1982a), 427–503.

— (1983). A note on the constituent structure of modifiers. *Linguistic Inquiry* 14, 695–697.

— (1990). Case structures and control in modern Icelandic. In Maling and Zaenen (1990), 187–234.

Aoun, Joseph (1981). Parts of speech: A case of redistribution. In Belletti, Brandi, and Rizzi (1981), 3–24.

— (1986). *Generalized binding: The syntax and logical form of wh-interrogatives*. Dordrecht: Foris.

Aoun, Joseph, Lina Choueiri, and Norbert Hornstein (2001). Resumption, movement and derivational economy. *Linguistic Inquiry* 32, 371–404.

Aoun, Joseph, Norbert Hornstein, David Lightfoot, and Amy Weinberg (1987). Two types of locality. *Linguistic Inquiry* 18, 537–578.

Aoun, Joseph and Yen-Hui Audrey Li (1989). Scope and constituency. *Linguistic Inquiry* 24, 365–372.

— (1993). *Syntax of scope*. Cambridge, MA: MIT Press.

Aoun, Joseph and Dominique Sportiche (1983). On the formal theory of government. *The Linguistic Review* 2, 211–236.

Archangeli, Diana (1997). Optimality Theory. An introduction to linguistics in the 1990s. In Archangeli and Langendoen (1997), 134–170.

Archangeli, Diana and Terence Langendoen (eds.) (1997), *Optimality Theory: An overview.* Malden/Oxford: Blackwell.

Ariel, Mira (1990). *Assessing noun-phrase antecedents.* London: Routledge.

Arka, I. Wayan (2003). *Balinese morphosytax: A Lexical-Functional approach* (Pacific Linguistics 547). Canberra: Australian National University, Research School of Pacific and Asian Studies.

Arnold, Jennifer, Anthony Losongco, Thomas Wasow, and Ryan Ginstrom (2000). Heaviness vs. newness: The effects of structural complexity and discourse status on constituent ordering. *Language* 76, 28–55.

Aronoff, Mark (1976). *Word formation in generative grammar.* Cambridge, MA: MIT Press.

Arregui, Ana, Charles Clifton Jr., Lyn Frazier, and Keir Moulton (2006). Processing elided verb phrases with flawed antecedents: The recycling hypothesis. *Journal of Memory and Language* 55, 232–246.

Asbury, Anna (2008). The morphosyntax of case and adpositions. PhD dissertation, Utrecht University.

Asbury, Anna, Jakub Dotlacil, Berit Gehrke, and Rick Nouwen (2008). *Syntax and semantics of spatial P.* Amsterdam/Philadelphia: John Benjamins.

Asher, Nicholas, Daniel Hardt, and Joan Busquets (1997). Discourse parallelism, scope, and ellipsis. In A. Lawson (ed.), *Proceedings of the Seventh Conference on Semantics and Linguistic Theory,* 19–36.

— (2001). Discourse parallelism, ellipsis, and ambiguity. *Journal of Semantics* 18, 1–25.

Ashton, Eric Ormerod (1947). *Swahili Grammar.* London: Longmans, Green and Co.

Asudeh, Ash (2006). Direct compositionality and the architecture of LFG. In M. Butt, M. Dalrymple, and T. H. King (eds.), *Intelligent linguistic architectures: Variations on themes by Ronald M. Kaplan,* 363–387. Stanford, CA: CSLI Publications.

Asudeh, Ash and Ida Toivonen (2010). Lexical-Functional Grammar. In Heine and Narrog (2010), 425–458.

— (2012). Copy raising and perception. *Natural Language and Linguistic Theory* 30, 321–380.

Atkinson, Martin (1992). *Children's syntax: An introduction to principles and parameters theory.* Cambridge, MA: Blackwell.

Atlas, Jay David (1996). *Only* noun phrases, pseudo-negative quantifiers, negative polarity items, and monotonicity. *Journal of Semantics* 13, 265–328.

Austin, Peter and Joan Bresnan (1996). Nonconfigurationality in Australian aboriginal languages. *Natural Language and Linguistic Theory* 14, 215–268.

Authier, J.-Marc (1991). V-governed expletives, case theory, and the Projection Principle. *Linguistic Inquiry* 22, 721–740.

Avrutin, Sergei (1994). Psycholinguistic investigations in the theory of reference. PhD dissertation, MIT.

(1998). EVENTS as units of discourse representation in root infinitives. In J. Schaeffer (ed.), *The interpretation of root infinitives and bare nouns in child language* (MIT Occasional Papers 12), 65-91.

Babyonyshev, Maria, Jennifer Ganger, David Pesetsky, and Kenneth Wexler (2001). The maturation of grammatical principles: Evidence from Russian unaccusatives. *Linguistic Inquiry* 32, 1-44.

Bach, Emmon W. (1964). *An introduction to transformational grammars.* New York: Holt, Rinehart and Winston.

(1979). Control in Montague Grammar. *Linguistic Inquiry* 10, 515-531.

(1980). In defense of passive. *Linguistics and Philosophy* 3, 297-341.

(1982). Purpose clauses and control. In Jacobson and Pullum (1982), 35-57.

Bailyn, John (1995). Configurational case assignment in Russian syntax. *The Linguistic Review* 12, 315-360.

(2002). Overt predicators. *Journal of Slavic Linguistics* 10, 23-52.

Bailyn, John and Edward Rubin (1991). The unification of instrumental case assignment in Russian. In J.A. Toribio and W. Harbert (eds.), *Cornell Working Papers in Linguistics* 9, 99-126. Ithaca, NY.

Baker, Carl Lee (1970a). Notes on the description of English questions: The role of an abstract question morpheme. *Foundations of Language* 6, 197-219.

(1970b). Double negatives. *Linguistic Inquiry* 1, 169-186.

(1991). The syntax of English *not*: The limits of core grammar. *Linguistic Inquiry* 22, 387-429.

(1994). Contrast, discourse prominence and intensification, with special reference to locally-free reflexives in British English. *Language* 71, 63-101.

Baker, Mark C. (1985a) The Mirror Principle and morphosyntactic explanation. *Linguistic Inquiry* 16, 373-416.

(1985b). Syntactic affixation and English gerunds. In S. MacKaye, M. Cobler, and M.T. Wescoat (eds.), *Proceedings of the West Coast Conference of Formal Linguistics* 4, 1-11. Palo Alto: Stanford University.

(1988). *Incorporation. A theory of grammatical function changing.* University of Chicago Press.

(1993). Noun incorporation and the nature of linguistic representation. In W. A. Foley (ed.), *The role of theory in language description*, 13-44. Berlin: Mouton de Gruyter.

(1996). *The polysynthesis parameter.* Oxford University Press.

(1997). Thematic roles and syntactic structure. In Haegeman (1997b), 73-137.

(1998). On logophoricity and focus. Unpublished incomplete ms, McGill University.

(2001). *The atoms of language: The mind's hidden rules of grammar.* New York: Basic Books.

(2003). *Lexical categories: Verbs, nouns, and adjectives.* Cambridge University Press.

(2005). Mapping the terrain of language acquisition. *Language Learning and Development* 1, 93–129.

(2008a). The macroparameter in a microparametric world. In Biberauer (2008b), 351–374.

(2008b). *The syntax of agreement and concord.* Cambridge University Press.

(2012). On the relationship of object agreement and accusative case: Evidence from Amharic. *Linguistic Inquiry* 43, 255–274.

(to appear). Types of crosslinguistic variation in case assignment. In J. Brucart and C. Picallo (eds.), *Linguistic variation in the Minimalist Program.* Oxford University Press.

Baker, Mark C., Kyle Johnson, and Ian Roberts (1989). Passive arguments raised. *Linguistic Inquiry* 20, 219–251.

Baker, Mark C. and Nadezhda Vinokurova (2010). Two modalities of case assignment in Sakha. *Natural Language and Linguistic Theory* 28, 593–642.

Baltin, Mark (1982). A landing-site theory of movement rules. *Linguistic Inquiry* 13, 1–38.

(1987a). Degree complements. In Huck and Ojeda (1987), 11–26.

(1987b). Do antecedent-contained deletions exist? *Linguistic Inquiry* 18, 279–295.

(1995). Floating quantifiers, PRO, and predication. *Linguistic Inquiry* 26, 199–248.

(2002). Movement to the higher V is remnant movement. *Linguistic Inquiry* 33, 653–659.

(2010). Deletion versus pro-forms: An overly simple dichotomy? *Natural Language and Linguistic Theory* 30, 381–423.

Baltin, Mark and Chris Collins (eds.) (2001). *The handbook of contemporary syntactic theory.* Malden, MA: Blackwell Publishing.

Baltin, Mark and Anthony Kroch (eds.) (1989). *Alternative conceptions of phrase structure.* University of Chicago Press.

Barbiers, Sjef (1995). The syntax of interpretation. PhD dissertation, Leiden University.

(2005a). Variation in the morphosyntax of one. *Journal of Comparative Germanic Linguistics* 8, 159–183.

(2005b). Word order variation in three-verb clusters and the division of labour between generative linguistics and sociolinguistics. In L. Cornips and K. Corrigan (eds.), *Syntax and variation. Reconciling the biological and the social,* 233–264. Amsterdam/Philadelphia: John Benjamins.

(2008a). Microvariation in syntactic doubling – An introduction. In Barbiers, Koeneman, Lekakou, and van der Ham (2008), 1–36.

(2008b). Werkwoordclusters en de Grammatica van de Rechterperiferie. *Nederlandse Taalkunde* 13, 160–187.

(2009). Locus and limits of syntactic variation. *Lingua* 119, 1607–1623.

Barbiers, Sjef, Johan van der Auwera, Hans Bennis, Eefje Boef, Gunther de Vogelaer, and Margreet van der Ham (2008). *Syntactic atlas of the Dutch dialects (SAND) Vol. II.* Amsterdam University Press.

Barbiers, Sjef and Hans Bennis (2007). The syntactic atlas of the Dutch dialects. A discussion of choices in the SAND-project. *Nordlyd* 34, 53-72. Available at: www.ub.uit.no/baser/nordlyd/

Barbiers, Sjef, Hans Bennis, Gunther de Vogelaer, Magda Devos, and Margreet van der Ham (2005). *Syntactic atlas of the Dutch dialects (SAND) Vol. I.* Amsterdam University Press.

Barbiers, Sjef, Leonie Cornips, and Jan-Pieter Kunst (2007). The syntactic atlas of the Dutch dialects: A corpus of elicited speech and text as an on-line dynamic atlas. In J. C. Beal, K. C. Corrigan, and H. Moisl (eds.), *Creating and digitizing language corpora. Volume 1: Synchronic databases*, pp. 54-90. Basingstoke: Palgrave Macmillan.

Barbiers, Sjef, Olaf Koeneman, and Marika Lekakou (2009). Syntactic doubling and the structure of wh-chains. *Journal of Linguistics* 46, 1-46.

Barbiers, Sjef, Olaf Koeneman, Marika Lekakou, and Margreet van der Ham (eds.) (2008). *Microvariation in syntactic doubling* (Syntax and Semantics 36). Bingley: Emerald.

Barbiers, Sjef and Marjo van Koppen (2006). Een Plaats voor Tijd in het Middenveld van het Nederlands. *Taal & Tongval Themanummer* 19, 24-39.

Barbosa, Pilar (1997). Subject positions in the null subject languages. *Seminarios de Linguistica* 1, 39-63.

Barker, Chris (2012). Quantificational binding does not require c-command. *Linguistic Inquiry* 43, 614-643.

Barss, Andrew (1986). Chains and anaphoric dependence. On reconstruction and its implications. PhD dissertation, MIT.

(2001). Syntactic reconstruction effects. In Baltin and Collins (2001), 670-696.

Barss, Andrew and Howard Lasnik (1986). A note on anaphora and double objects. *Linguistic Inquiry* 17, 347-354.

Bartning, Inge (1976). Remarques sur la Syntaxe et la Semantique des Pseudo-Adjectifs denominaux en français. Thèse de doctorat. Université de Stockholm.

Barton, Ellen (1990), *Nonsentential constituents*. Amsterdam: John Benjamins.

Bartos, Huba (2000). Topics, quantifiers, subjects. Paper presented at the International Symposium on Topic and Focus in Chinese, Hong Kong, 21-22 June.

Bartsch, Renate (1976). *The grammar of adverbials: A study in the semantics and syntax of adverbial constructions*. Amsterdam: North-Holland.

Barwise, John and Robin Cooper (1981). Generalized quantifiers and natural language. *Linguistics and Philosophy* 4, 159-219.

Bastiaansen, Marcel and Peter Hagoort (2003). Special issue event-induced theta responses as a window on the dynamics of memory. *Cortex* 39, 967-992.

Bastiaansen, Marcel, Jos van Berkum, and Peter Hagoort (2002a). Event-related theta power increases in the human EEG during online sentence processing. *Neuroscience Letters* 323, 13-16.

(2002b). Syntactic processing modulates the [theta] rhythm of the human EEG. *NeuroImage* 17, 1479-1492.

Bastiaansen, Marcel, Marieke van der Linden, Mariken ter Keurs, Ton Dijkstra, and Peter Hagoort (2005). Theta responses are involved in lexical-semantic retrieval during language processing. *Journal of Cognitive Neuroscience* 17, 530-541.

Battistella, Edwin (1989). Chinese reflexivization: A movement to INFL approach. *Linguistics* 27, 987-1012.

Baumann, Stefan, Doris Mücke, and Johannes Becker (2010). Expression of second occurrence focus in German. *Linguistische Berichte* 221, 61-78.

Bayer, Josef (1984). Comp in Bavarian. *The Linguistic Review* 3, 209-274.

Bayer, Josef, Jana Häussler, and Martin Salzmann (2011). *That*-trace effects without traces: An experimental investigation. Unpublished ms., Universities of Konstanz, Potsdam, and Zürich.

Bayer, Josef and Jaklin Kornfilt (1994). Against scrambling as an instance of Move-alpha. In Corver and van Riemsdijk (1994), 17-60.

Bayer, Samuel (1996). The coordination of unlike categories. *Language* 72, 579-616.

Bear, John (1982). Gaps as syntactic features. Technical note, Indiana University Linguistics Club.

Beaver, David, Brady Clark, Edward Flemming, Florian Jaeger, and Maria Wolters (2007). When semantics meets phonetics: Acoustical studies of second occurrence focus. *Language* 83, 251-282.

Beck, David (1999). The typology of parts of speech: The markedness of adjectives. PhD dissertation, University of Toronto.

Beck, Sigrid and Stephen Berman (2000). *Wh*-scope marking: Direct vs. indirect dependency. In Lutz, Müller, and von Stechow (2000), 17-44.

Becker, Misha (2000). The development of the copula in child English: The lightness of *be*. PhD dissertation, UCLA.

Becker, Tilman, Owen Rambow, and Michael Niv (1992). The derivational generative power of scrambling is beyond LCFRS. Technical Report IRCS 92-38, Institute for Research in Cognitive Science, University of Pennsylvania.

Bedny, Marina, Megan McGill, and Sharon Thompson-Schill (2008). Semantic adaptation and competition during word comprehension. *Cerebral Cortex* 18, 2574-2585.

Beghelli, Filippo (1997). The syntax of distributivity and pair-list readings. In Szabolcsi (1997c), 349-408.

Beghelli, Filippo and Tim Stowell (1997). Distributivity and negation: The syntax of *each* and *every*. In Szabolcsi (1997c), 71-109.

Bellert, Irena (1977). On semantic and distributional properties of sentential adverbs. *Linguistic Inquiry* 13, 1-38.

Belletti, Adriana (1988). The Case of unaccusatives. *Linguistic Inquiry* 19, 1-34.

(1990). *Generalized verb movement*. Turin: Rosenberg & Sellier.

(2001a) Agreement projections. In Baltin and Collins (2001), 483-510.

(2001b). Inversion as focalization. In A. Hulk and J.-Y. Pollock (eds.), *Inversion in romance*, 60–90. Oxford University Press.

(2004a). Aspects of the low IP area. In Rizzi (2004c), 16–51.

(ed.) (2004b). *Structures and beyond: The cartography of syntactic structures, vol. 3*. Oxford University Press.

(2009) *Structures and strategies*. London: Routledge.

Belletti, Adriana, Luciana Brandi, and Luigi Rizzi (eds.) (1981). *Theory of markedness in generative grammar: Proceedings of the 1979 GLOW Conference* Pisa: Scuola Normale Superiore.

Belletti, Adriana and Luigi Rizzi (1988). Psych-verbs and θ-theory. *Natural Language and Linguistic Theory* 6, 291–352.

Benincà, Paola (ed.) (1989). *Dialect variations and the theory of grammar: Proceedings of the GLOW workshop in Venice 1987*. Dordrecht: Foris.

(2006). A detailed map of the Left Periphery in Medieval Romance. In R. Zanuttini, H. Campos, E. Herburger, and P. Portner (eds.), *Negation, tense, and clausal architecture: Crosslinguistic investigations*, 53–86. Washington, DC: Georgetown University Press.

Benincà, Paola and Cecilia Poletto (2004). Topic, Focus and V2: Defining the CP sublayers. In Rizzi (2004a), 52–75.

Benincà, Paola and Laura Vanelli (1982). Appunti di sinatassi veneta. In M. Cortelazzo (ed.), *Guida ai dialetti veneti, vol. 4*, 7–38. Padua: CLEUP.

Bennis, Hans (1986). *Gaps and dummies*. Dordrecht: Foris.

Bennis, Hans, Norbert Corver, and Marcel den Dikken (1998). Predication in nominal phrases. *Journal of Comparative Germanic Linguistics* 1, 85–117.

Ben-Shachar, Michal, Talma Hendler, Itamar Kahn, Dafna Ben-Bashat, and Yosef Grodzinsky (2003). The neural reality of syntactic transformations: Evidence from functional magnetic resonance imaging. *Psychological Science* 14, 433–440.

Ben-Shachar, Michal, Dafna Palti, and Yosef Grodzinsky (2004). Neural correlates of syntactic movement: Converging evidence from two fMRI experiments. *NeuroImage* 21, 1320–1336.

Benthem, Johan van (1989). Polyadic quantifiers. *Linguistics and Philosophy* 12, 437–464.

Bentley, Delia (2004). 'ne'-cliticization and split intransitivity. *Journal of Linguistics* 40, 219–262.

(2006). *Split intransitivity in Italian*. Berlin: Mouton de Gruyter.

Bentzen, Kristine (2007). Order and structure in embedded clauses in Northern Norwegian. PhD dissertation, CASTL, University of Tromsø.

Berkum, Jos van, Pienie Zwitserlood, Colin Brown, and Peter Hagoort (2000). Processing gender and number agreement in parsing: An ERP-based comparison. Paper presented at the *6th Conference on Architectures and Mechanisms of Language Processing*, Leiden.

Berkum, Jos van, Pienie Zwitserlood, Peter Hagoort, and Colin Brown (2003). When and how do listeners relate a sentence to the wider discourse? Evidence from the n400 effect. *Cognitive Brain Research* 17, 701–718.

Bernstein, Judy (1993a). Topics in the syntax of nominal structure across Romance. PhD dissertation, City University of New York.
  (1993b). The syntactic role of word markers in null nominal constructions. *Probus* 5, 5–38.
  (2001). The DP hypothesis: Identifying clausal properties in the nominal domain. In Baltin and Collins (2001), 536–561.
Bernstein, Judy and Christina Tortora (2005). Two types of possessive forms in English. *Lingua* 115, 1221–1242.
Berwick, Robert C. (1985). *The acquisition of syntactic knowledge*. Cambridge, MA: MIT Press.
Berwick, Robert C. and Noam Chomsky (2011). The biolinguistic program: The current state of its evolution and development. In A. M. di Sciullo and C. Aguero (eds.), *Biolinguistic investigations*. Cambridge, MA: MIT Press.
Berwick, Robert C. and Amy Weinberg (1984). *The grammatical basis of linguistic performance*. Cambridge, MA: MIT Press.
Besten, Hans den (1983). On the interaction of root transformations and lexical deletive rules. In W. Abraham (ed.), *On the formal syntax of the Westgermania. Papers from the 3rd Groningen Grammar Talks, January 1981*, 47–131. Amsterdam/Philadelphia: John Benjamins.
  (1989a). Double negation and the genesis of Afrikaans. In Pieter Muysken and Norval Smith (eds.), *Substrata versus universals in Creole genesis*, 185–230. Amsterdam: John Benjamins.
  (1989b). Studies in West-Germanic syntax. PhD dissertation, Catholic University Brabant.
Bever, Thomas G. (1970). The cognitive basis for linguistic structures. In J. R. Hayes (ed.), *Cognition and the development of language*, 227–360. New York: Wiley.
Bever, Thomas G. and D. Terence Langendoen (1972). The interaction of perception and grammar in linguistic change. In R. Stockwell and R. K. S. Macaulay (eds.), *Historical linguistics in the perspective of transformational theory*, 32–95. Bloomington: Indiana University Press.
Bhat, D. N. Shankara (1994). *The adjectival category: Criteria for differentiation and identification*. Amsterdam: John Benjamins.
Bhatt, Rajesh (2003). Causativization in Hindi. Unpublished class handout, March 2003.
  (2005). Long distance agreement in Hindi-Urdu. *Natural Language and Linguistic Theory* 23, 757–807.
Bhatt, Rajesh and Aravind K. Joshi (2004). Semilinearity is a syntactic invariant: A reply to Michaelis and Kracht 1997. *Linguistic Inquiry* 35, 683–692.
Bhatt, Rajesh and Roumyana Pancheva (2004). Late merger and degree clauses. *Linguistic Inquiry* 35, 1–46.
Bianchi, Valentina (2003). On finiteness and logoforic anchoring. Unpublished ms., University of Siena.

Bianchi, Valentina and Mara Frascarelli (2009). Is topic a root phenomenon? Unpublished ms., University of Siena, University of Roma 3.
Biber, Douglas (1988). *Variation across speech and writing.* Cambridge University Press.
Biberauer, Theresa (2008a). Doubling vs. omission: Insights from Afrikaans negation. In Barbiers, Koeneman, Lekakou, and van der Ham (2008), 103–140.
— (ed.) (2008b). *The limits of syntactic variation* (Linguistics Today 132). Amsterdam/Philadelphia: John Benjamins.
Biberauer, Theresa, Anders Holmberg and Ian Roberts (2008). Disharmonic word orders and the final-over-final constraint (FOFC). In A. Bisetto and F. Barbieri (eds), *Proceedings of the XXXIII Incontro di Grammatica Generativa.* Available at: http://amsacta.unibo.it/2397/1/PROCEEDINGS_IGG33.pdf.
Biberauer, Theresa, Anders Holmberg, Ian Roberts and Michelle Sheehan (2010). *Parametric variation.* Cambridge University Press.
Biberauer, Theresa and M. Richards (2006). True optionality: When the grammar does not mind. In C. Boeckx (ed.), *Minimalist essays*, 35–67. Amsterdam/Philadelphia: John Benjamins.
Biberauer, Theresa and Ian Roberts (2005). Changing EPP parameters in the history of English; Accounting for variation and change. In W. van der Wurff (ed.), Special Issue of *Journal of English Language and Linguistics* on Word Order Change, 5–46.
Biloa, Edmond (2008). The cartography of the left periphery in Tuki. Unpublished ms., University of Yaounde I, Cameroon.
Birner, Betty (1992). The discourse function of inversion in English. PhD thesis, Northwestern University.
Bittner, Maria (1991). *Case, scope, and binding.* Dordrecht: Kluwer.
Bittner, Maria and Kenneth Hale (1996a). The structural determination of case and agreement. *Linguistic Inquiry* 27, 1–68.
— (1996b). Ergativity: Toward a theory of a heterogeneous class. *Linguistic Inquiry* 27, 531–604.
Blake, Barry J. (2001). *Case,* 2nd edn. Cambridge University Press.
Blevins, James P. (1990). Syntactic complexity: Evidence for discontinuity and multidomination. PhD dissertation, University of Massachusetts, Amherst.
— (2007). Periphrasis as syntactic exponence. In F. Ackerman, J. P. Blevins, and G. S. Stump (eds.), *Patterns in paradigms.* Stanford, CA: CSLI Publications.
— (2011). Feature-based grammar. In Borsley and Börjars (2011), 297–324.
Bloch, Bernard (1941). Phonemic overlapping. *American Speech* XVI, 278–284. Reprinted in Joos (1957), 93–96.
— (1946). Studies in colloquial Japanese II: Syntax. *Language* 12, 200–248. Reprinted in Joos (1957), 154–185.

Blom, Alied and Saskia Daalder (1977). *Syntaktische theorie en taalbeschrijving*. Muiderberg: Coutinho.

Bloom, Paul (2002). *How children learn the meanings of words*. Cambridge, MA: MIT Press.

Bloom, Paul and Lori Markson (1998). Capacities underlying word learning. *Trends in Cognitive Sciences* 2, 67–73.

(2000). Are there principles that apply only to the acquisition of words? A reply to Waxman and Booth. *Cognition* 78, 89–90.

Bloomfield, Leonard (1926/1957). A set of postulates for the science of language. *Language* 2, 153–164. [Reprinted in Joos (1957), 26–31.]

(1933). *Language*. New York: Henry Holt.

Blutner, Reinhard (2000). Some aspects of optimality in natural language interpretation. *Journal of Semantics* 17, 189–216.

Bobaljik, Jonathan David (1993). Nominally absolutive is not absolutely nominative. In Jonathan Mead (ed.), *Proceedings of the Eleventh West Coast Conference on Formal Linguistics*, 44–60. Stanford, CA: CSLI Publications.

(1995). Morphosyntax: The syntax of verbal inflection. PhD dissertation, MIT.

(2001). The implications of rich Agreement: Why morphology doesn't drive syntax. In *Proceedings of WCCFL* 6, 129–167.

(2002a). A-chains at the PF interface: Copies and covert movement. *Natural Language and Linguistic Theory* 20, 197–267.

(2002b). Realizing Germanic inflection: Why morphology does not drive syntax. *Journal of Comparative Germanic Linguistics* 6, 129–167.

(2008). Where's phi? Agreement as a post-syntactic operation. In D. Harbour, D. Adger, and S. Béjar (eds.), *Phi-theory: Phi features across interfaces and modules*, 295–328. Oxford University Press.

Bobaljik, Jonathan David and Samuel Brown (1997). Interarboreal operations: Head movement and the extension requirement. *Linguistic Inquiry* 28, 345–356.

Bobaljik, Jonathan David and Idan Landau (2009). Icelandic control is not A-movement: The case from Case. *Linguistic Inquiry* 40, 113–132.

Bobaljik, Jonathan David and Höskuldur Thráinsson (1998). Two heads aren't always better than one. *Syntax* 1, 37–71.

Bobaljik, Jonathan David and Susi Wurmbrand (2005a). The domain of agreement. *Natural Language & Linguistic Theory* 23, 809–865.

(2005b). Adjacency, PF, and extraposition. In H. Broekhuis, N. Corver, R. Huybregts, U. Kleinhenz, and J. Koster (eds.), *Organizing grammar: Linguistic studies in honor of Henk van Riemsdijk*, 679–688. New York: Mouton de Gruyter.

Bobaljik, Jonathan David and Cynthia Levart Zocca (2011). Gender markedness: The anatomy of a counter-example. *Morphology* 21, 141–166.

Bocci, Giuliano (2009). On syntax and prosody in Italian. PhD dissertation, University of Siena.

Bod, Rens, Jennifer Hay, and Stefanie Jannedy (2003). *Probabilistic linguistics.* Cambridge, MA: MIT Press.

Boeckx, Cedric (2000). A note on contraction. *Linguistic Inquiry* 31, 357–366.

(2003). *Islands and chains: Resumption as stranding.* Amsterdam/Philadelphia: Benjamins.

(2004). Long-distance agreement in Hindi: Some theoretical implications. *Studia Linguistica* 58, 23–36.

(2006). *Linguistic Minimalism: Origins, concepts, methods, and aims.* Oxford University Press.

(2007a). *Understanding Minimalist syntax.* Oxford: Blackwell.

(2007b). Isolating Agree. Paper presented at Workshop on Morphology and Argument Encoding, Harvard University, September 2007.

(2008). Approaching parameters from below. Unpublished ms., Harvard University.

(2010). What principles and parameters got wrong. Available at: http://ling.auf.net/lingBuzz/001118

Boeckx, Cedric and Kleanthes K. Grohmann (2006). Putting phases into perspective. *Syntax* 10, 204–222.

(2010). Focus and scope of the on-line journal Biolinguistics. Available at: www.biolinguistics.eu/index.php/biolinguistics/about/editorialPolicies#focusAndScope.

Boeckx, Cedric and Norbert Hornstein (2003). Reply to 'Control is not movement'. *Linguistic Inquiry* 34, 269–280.

(2004). Movement under control. *Linguistic Inquiry* 35, 431–452.

(2006a). Control in Icelandic and theories of control. *Linguistic Inquiry* 37, 591–606.

(2006b). The virtues of control as movement. *Syntax* 9, 118–130.

(2010). Icelandic control really is A-movement: A reply to Bobaljik and Landau. *Linguistic Inquiry* 41, 111–130.

Boeckx, Cedric and Fumikazu Niinuma (2004). Conditions on agreement in Japanese. *Natural Language and Linguistic Theory* 22, 453–480.

Boeckx, Cedric and Sandra Stjepanović (2001). Head-ing toward PF. *Linguistic Inquiry* 32, 345–355.

Boersma, Paul (1998). Functional phonology. Formalizing the interactions between articulatory and perceptual drives. PhD thesis, IfOTT/University of Amsterdam.

Bok-Bennema, Reineke (1991). *Case and agreement in Inuit.* Dordrecht: Foris.

Bolinger, Dwight (1967). Adjectives in English: Attribution and predication. *Lingua* 18, 1–34.

(1973). Ambient *it* is meaningful too. *Journal of Linguistics* 9, 261–270.

Boogaart, Ronny (2004). Temporal relations in modal constructions. Paper presented at Chronos VI, Geneva, 22–24 September, 2004.

Borer, Hagit (1984a). *Parametric syntax: Case studies in Semitic and Romance languages* (Studies in Generative Grammar, vol. 13). Dordrecht: Foris.

(1984b). The Projection Principle and rules of morphology. In C. Jones and P. Sells (eds.), *Proceedings of the XIV Annual Meeting of the North-Eastern Linguistic Society*, 16–33. Amherst, MA: GLSA.

(1986). I-subjects. *Linguistic Inquiry* 17, 375–416.

(1989). Anaphoric AGR. In O. Jaeggli and K. Safir (eds.), *The Null Subject Parameter*, 69–109. Dordrecht: Kluwer Academic Publishers.

(1998). Deriving passive without theta roles. In S. G. Lapointe, D. K. Brentari, and P. M. Farrell (eds.), *Morphology and its relation to phonology and syntax*, 60–99. Stanford, CA: CSLI Publications.

(2003). Exo-skeletal vs. endo-skeletal explanations: Syntactic projections and the lexicon. In J. Moore and M. Polinsky (eds.), *The nature of explanation in linguistic theory*, 31–67. Stanford, CA: CSLI Publications.

(2005a). *In name only* (Structuring Sense, vol. I). Oxford University Press.

(2005b). *Structuring sense: An exo-skeletal trilogy*. Oxford University Press.

Borer, Hagit and Kenneth Wexler (1987). The maturation of syntax. In T. Roeper and E. Williams (eds), *Parameter setting*, 123–172. Dordrecht: D. Reidel Publishing Company.

(1992). Bi-unique relations and the maturation of grammatical principles. *Natural Language and Linguistic Theory* 10, 147–190.

Borgonovo, Claudia and Sarah Cummins (2007). Past tense modals in Spanish and French. In L. Eguren and O. Fernandez Soriano (eds.), *Proceedings of the 16th Colloquium on Generative Grammar*, 1–18. Amsterdam: John Benjamins.

Bornkessel, Ina and Matthias Schlesewsky (2006). The extended argument dependency model: A neurocognitive approach to sentence comprehension across languages. *Psychological Review* 113, 787–821.

Bornkessel, Ina, Stefan Zysset, Angela Friederici, D. Yves von Cramon, and Matthias Schlesewsky (2005). Who did what to whom? The neural basis of argument hierarchies during language comprehension. *NeuroImage* 26, 221–233.

Bornkessel-Schlesewsky, Ina and Matthias Schlesewsky (2008). An alternative perspective on 'semantic p600' effects in language comprehension. *Brain Research Reviews* 59, 55–73.

Bornkessel-Schlesewsky, Ina, Matthias Schlesewsky, and D. Yves von Cramon (2009). Word order and Broca's region: Evidence for a supra-syntactic perspective. *Brain and Language* 111, 125–139.

Borsley, Robert D. and Kersti Börjars (eds.) (2011). *Non-transformational syntax: Formal and explicit models of grammar*. Oxford: Wiley-Blackwell.

Borsley, Robert D., Maria-Luisa Rivero, and Janig Stephens (1996). Long head movement in Breton. In Robert D. Borsley and Ian Roberts (eds.), *The syntax of the Celtic languages: A comparative perspective*, 53–74. Cambridge University Press.

Bosch, Peter and Rob van der Sandt (1994). *Proceedings of the Conference on Focus and Natural Language Processing* (Working Papers of the Institute for Logic and Linguistics). Heidelberg: IBM Scientific Centre.

(1999). *Focus – Linguistic, cognitive, and computational perspectives.* Cambridge University Press.

Bošković, Željko (1994). D-structure, Theta-Criterion, and movement into Theta-positions. *Linguistic Analysis* 24, 247–286.

(1997). The syntax of nonfinite complementation: An economy approach. *Linguistic Inquiry Monographs* 32. Cambridge, MA: MIT Press.

(1998). LF movement and the Minimalist Program. In P. N. Tamanji and K. Kusumoto (eds.), *NELS 28*, 43–57. GLSA, University of Massachusetts, Amherst.

(1999). On multiple feature-checking: Multiple *wh*-fronting and multiple head-movement. In S. Epstein and N. Hornstein (eds.), *Working Minimalism*, 159–187. Cambridge, MA: MIT Press.

(2001). *On the nature of the syntax–phonology interface: Cliticization and related phenomena.* Amsterdam: Elsevier.

(2002a). On multiple *wh*-fronting. *Linguistic Inquiry* 33, 351–383.

(2002b). Clitics as non-branching elements and the Linear Correspondence Axiom. *Linguistic Inquiry* 33, 329–340.

(2002c). A-Movement and the EPP. *Syntax* 5, 167–218.

(2005a). On the locality of left branch extraction and the structure of NP. *Studia Linguistica* 59, 1–45.

(2005b). On the Operator Freezing Effect. Unpublished ms., University of Connecticut.

(2007a). Agree, phases and intervention effects. *Linguistic Analysis* 33, 54–96.

(2007b). On the locality and motivation of Move and Agree: An even more minimal theory. *Linguistic Inquiry* 38, 589–644.

(2008a). On successive-cyclic movement and the freezing effect of feature checking. In J. Hartmann, V. Hegedűs, and H. C. van Riemsdijk (eds.), *Sounds of silence: Empty elements in syntax and phonology*, 195–205. Oxford/Amsterdam: Elsevier.

(2008b). What will you have, DP or NP? In E. Elfner and M. Walkow (eds.), *Proceedings of NELS 37*, 101–114. Amherst, MA: GLSA.

(2011a). Last resort with Move and Agree in derivations and representations. In C. Boeckx (ed.), *The handbook of linguistic Minimalism*, 327–353. Oxford University Press.

(2011b). On valued uninterpretable features. In *Proceedings of NELS 39*. Amherst, MA: GLSA.

Bošković, Željko and Jon Gajewski (2011). Semantic correlates of the NP/DP parameter. In S. Lima, K. Mullin, and B. Smith (eds.), *Proceedings of NELS 39*. Amherst, MA: GLSA.

Bošković, Željko and Howard Lasnik (2003). On the distribution of null complementizers. *Linguistic Inquiry* 34, 527–546.

Bošković, Željko and Jairo Nunes (2007). The copy theory of movement: A view from PF. In N. Corver and J. Nunes (eds.), *The copy theory of movement*, 13–74. Amsterdam/Philadelphia: John Benjamins.

Bosque, Ignacio and M. Carme Picallo (1996). Postnominal adjectives in Spanish indefinites DPs. *Journal of Linguistics* 32, 349–385.

Botwinik-Rotem, Irena (2004). The category P: Features, projections, interpretation. PhD dissertation, Tel Aviv University.

Bouchard, Denis (1984). *On the content of empty categories*. Dordrecht: Foris.

(1995). *The semantics of syntax*. University of Chicago Press.

(2002). *Adjectives, number and interfaces: Why languages vary*. Amsterdam: North-Holland Linguistic Series.

(2003). The origins of language variation. In P. Pica and J. Rooryck (eds.), *Linguistic variation yearbook*, Vol. 3, 1–41. Amsterdam/Philadelphia: John Benjamins.

Bouma, Gosse, Rob Malouf, and Ivan A. Sag (2001). Satisfying constraints on extraction and adjunction. *Natural Language and Linguistic Theory* 19, 1–65.

Bouton, Lawrence (1970). Antecedent-contained proforms. In M. A. Campbell et al. (eds.), *Proceedings of CLS 6*, 154–167. University of Chicago.

Bowers, John (1975). Adjectives and adverbs in English. *Foundations of Language* 13, 529–562.

(1991). The syntax and semantics of nominals. In Steven Moore and Adam Wyner (eds.), *Proceedings of the First Semantics and Linguistic Theory Conference* (Cornell Working Papers in Linguistics 10), 1–30, Ithaca, NY: Cornell University.

(1993). The syntax of predication. *Linguistic Inquiry* 24, 591–656.

(2001). Predication. In Baltin and Collins (2001), 299–333.

Brame, Michael K. (1976). *Conjectures and refutations in syntax and semantics*. New York: Elsevier.

(1982). The head-selector theory of lexical specifications and the non-existence of coarse categories. *Linguistic Analysis* 10, 321–325.

Brandi, Luciana and Patrizia Cordin (1989). Two Italian dialects and the Null Subject Parameter. In O. Jaeggli and K. Safir (eds.), *The Null Subject Parameter*, 111–142. Dordrecht: Kluwer Academic Publishers.

Branigan, Phil and Marguerite MacKenzie (2002). Altruism, A-bar movement, and object agreement in Innu-aimun. *Linguistic Inquiry* 33, 385–408.

Braver, Todd, Jonathan Cohen, Leigh Nystrom, John Jonides, Edward Smith, and Douglas Noll (1997). A parametric study of prefrontal cortex involvement in human working memory. *NeuroImage* 5, 49–62.

Breitbarth, Anne (2009). A hybrid approach to Jespersen's Cycle in West Germanic. *Journal of Comparative Germanic Linguistics* 12, 81–114.

Brennan, Jonathan, Yuval Nir, Uri Hasson, Rafael Malach, David J. Heeger, and Liina Pylkkänen (2010). Syntactic structure building in the anterior temporal lobe during natural story listening. *Brain and Language* 120, 1–11.

Brennan, Jonathan and Liina Pylkkanen (2012). The time-course and spatial distribution of brain activity associated with sentence processing. *NeuroImage* 60, 1139–1148.

Bresnan, Joan (1970). On complementizers: Toward a syntactic theory of complement types. *Foundations of Language* 6, 297–321.

(1971a). A note on the notion 'Identity of Sense Anaphora'. *Linguistic Inquiry* 2, 589–597.

(1971b). Sentence stress and syntactic transformations. *Language* 47, 257–281.

(1971c). Contraction and the transformational cycle. Unpublished ms., MIT.

(1972). Theory of complementation in English syntax. PhD dissertation, MIT (Published by Garland 1979).

(1973). Syntax of the comparative clause construction in English. *Linguistic Inquiry* 4, 275–343.

(1974). The position of certain clause-particles in phrase structure. *Linguistic Inquiry* 5, 614–619.

(1976). On the form and functioning of transformations. *Linguistic Inquiry* 7, 3–40.

(1977). Variables in the theory of transformation. In P. Culicover, T. Wasow, and A. Akmajian (eds.), *Formal syntax*, 157–196. New York: Academic Press.

(ed.) (1982a). *The mental representation of grammatical relations*. Cambridge, MA: MIT Press.

(1982b). The passive in lexical theory. In Bresnan (1982a), 3–86.

(1982c). Control and complementation. *Linguistic Inquiry* 13, 343–434. Also in Bresnan (1982a), 282–390.

(2000). Optimal syntax. In J. Dekkers, F. van der Leeuw, and J. van de Weijer (eds.), *Optimality Theory: Phonology, syntax and acquisition*, 334–385. Oxford University Press.

(2001). *Lexical-Functional Syntax* (Blackwell Textbooks in Linguistics, vol. 16). Oxford: Blackwell.

Bresnan, Joan and Judith Aissen (2002). Optimality and functionality: Objections and refutations. *Natural Language and Linguistic Theory* 21, 81–95.

Bresnan, Joan, Anna Cueni, Tatiana Nikitina, and Harald Baayen (2007). Predicting the dative alternation. In I. K. G. Bouma, I. Kraemer, and J. Zwarts (eds.), *Cognitive foundations of interpretation*, 69–94. Amsterdam: Royal Netherlands Academy of Science.

Bresnan, Joan and Ashwini Deo (2000). 'Be' in the Survey of English Dialects: A Stochastic OT account. Paper presented at the Symposium on Optimality Theory, English Linguistic Society of Japan, 18 November 2000, Kobe, Japan.

Bresnan, Joan and Jonni Kanerva (1989). Locative inversion in Chicheŵa: A case study of factorization in grammar. *Linguistic Inquiry* 20, 1–50.

Bresnan, Joan and Sam Mchombo (1987). Topic, pronoun, and agreement in Chicheŵa. *Language* 63, 741-782.

Bresnan, Joan and Lioba Moshi (1990). Object asymmetries in comparative Bantu syntax. *Linguistic Inquiry* 21, 147-185.

Bresnan, Joan and Annie Zaenen (1990). Deep unaccusativity in LFG. In K. Dziwirek, P. Farrell, and E. Mejías-Bikandi (eds.), *Grammatical relations: A cross-theoretical perspective*, 45-58. Stanford, CA, CSLI Publications.

Brink, Daniëlle van den and Peter Hagoort (2004). The influence of semantic and syntactic context constraints on lexical selection and integration in spoken-word comprehension as revealed by ERPS. *Journal of Cognitive Neuroscience* 16, 1068-1084.

Brisson, Christine (1998). Distributivity, maximality, and floating quantifiers. PhD thesis, Rutgers University.

Brody, Michael (1990). Some remarks on the focus field in Hungarian. In *UCL Working Papers in Linguistics* 2, 201-225. University College London.

(1993). θ-theory and arguments. *Linguistic Inquiry* 24, 1-23.

(1995). *Lexico-logical form: A radically minimalist theory*. Cambridge, MA: MIT Press.

(2001). Mirror Theory: Syntactic representation in perfect syntax. *Linguistic Inquiry* 31, 29-56.

(2002). On the status of representations and derivations. In S. D. Epstein and T. D. Seely (eds.), *Derivation and explanation in the Minimalist Program*, 19-41. Malden: Blackwell.

(2003). *Towards an elegant syntax*. London: Routledge.

Broekhuis, Hans (2000). Against feature strength: The case of Scandinavian object shift. *Natural Language and Linguistic Theory* 18, 673-721.

(2005). Extraction from subjects: Some remarks on Chomsky's *On Phases*. In H. Broekhuis, N. Corver, R. Huybregts, U. Kleinhenz, and J. Koster (eds.), *Organizing grammar. Linguistic studies in honor of Henk van Riemsdijk*, 59-68. Berlin/New York: Mouton de Gruyter.

(2008). *Derivations and evaluations: Object shift in the Germanic languages* (Studies in Generative Grammar). Berlin/New York: Mouton de Gruyter.

Broekhuis, Hans and Joost Dekkers (2000). The Minimalist Program and Optimality Theory: Derivations and evaluations. In J. Dekkers, F. van der Leeuw, and J. van de Weijer (eds.), *Optimality Theory: Phonology, syntax and acquisition*, 386-422. Oxford University Press.

Brown, Colin and Peter Hagoort (1993). The processing nature of the n400: Evidence from masked priming. *Journal of Cognitive Neuroscience* 5, 34-44.

Brown, Roger (1973). *A first language: The early stages*. Cambridge, MA: Harvard University Press.

Browning, Marguerite (1987). Null operator constructions. PhD thesis, MIT.

(1996). CP Recursion and that-t Effects. *Linguistic Inquiry* 27, 237-256.

Brucart, José M. (1987). *La elision sintactica en español*. Bellaterra: Publicacions de la Universitat Autonoma de Barcelona.

(1999). La elipsis. In I. Bosque and V. Demonte (eds.), *Gramática descriptiva de la lengua española*, 787-863. Madrid: Espasa Calpe.

Bruening, Benjamin (2001). Syntax at the edge: Cross-clausal phenomena and the syntax of Passamaquoddy. PhD dissertation, MIT.

(2004). Two types of wh-scope marking in Passamaquoddy. *Natural Language & Linguistic Theory* 22, 229-305.

(2006). Differences between the wh-scope-marking and wh-copy constructions in Passamaquoddy. *Linguistic Inquiry* 37, 25-49.

Brunetti, Lisa (2003a). A unification of focus. PhD thesis, University of Florence.

(2003b). 'Information' focus movement in Italian and contextual constraints on ellipsis. In G. Garding and M. Tsujimura (eds.), *Proceedings of the 22nd West Conference on Formal Linguistics*, 95-108. Somerville, MA: Cascadilla Press.

Büring, Daniel (1998). Identity, modality, and the candidate behind the wall. In D. Strolovich and A. Lawson (eds.), *Proceedings of SALT 8*, 36-54. Ithaca, NY: CLC Publications.

(1999). Topic. In Bosch and van der Sandt (1999), 142-165.

(2001a). Let's phrase it! - Focus, word order, and prosodic phrasing in German double object constructions. In Müller and Sternefeld (2001), 101-137.

(2001b). What do definites do that indefinites definitely don't? In Féry and Sternefeld (2001), 70-100.

(2003). On D-trees, beans, and B-accents. *Linguistics & Philosophy* 26, 511-545.

(2005). *Binding Theory*. Cambridge University Press.

(2006). Focus projection and default prominence. In Valéria Molnár and Susanne Winkler (eds.), *The architecture of focus*, 321-346. Berlin/New York: Mouton de Gruyter.

(2008a). Been there, marked that - A theory of second occurrence focus. Unpublished ms., UCLA.

(2008b). What's new (and what's given) in the theory of focus? In *Proceedings of the 4th Berkeley Linguistics Society Meeting, Parasession on Information Structure*. Berkeley, CA.

(2009). Towards a typology of focus realization. In Malte Zimmermann and Caroline Féry (eds.), *Information structure*, 177-205. Oxford University Press.

Büring, Daniel and Rodrigo Gutiérrez-Bravo (2001). Focus-related word order variation without the NSR: A prosody-based crosslinguistic analysis. In S. Mac Bhloscaidh (ed.), *Syntax at Santa Cruz 3*, 41-58.

Büring, Daniel and Katharina Hartmann (1997). Doing the right thing. *The Linguistic Review* 14, 1-42.

Burkhardt, Petra (2005). *The syntax-discourse interface.* Amsterdam/Philadelphia. Benjamins.

Burzio, Luigi (1986). *Italian syntax: A Government-Binding approach.* Dordrecht/Boston/Lancaster/Tokyo: Reidel.

(1989). On the non-existence of disjoint reference principles. *Rivista di Grammatica Generativa* 14, 3-27.

(1991). The morphological basis of anaphora. *Journal of Linguistics* 27, 81-105.

(1996). The role of the antecedent in anaphoric relations. In R. Freidin (ed.), *Current issues in comparative grammar*, 1-45. Dordrecht: Kluwer.

(1998). Anaphora and soft constraints. In P. Barbosa, D. Fox, P. Hagstrom, M. McGinnis, and D. Pesetsky (eds.), *Is the best good enough?*, 93-113. Cambridge, MA: MIT Press.

(2000). Anatomy of a generalization. In Reuland (2000), 195-240.

Butt, Miriam (1995). *The structure of complex predicates in Urdu* (Dissertations in Linguistics). Stanford, CA: CSLI Publications.

(2003). The morpheme that wouldn't go away. Unpublished ms. on Urdu causatives, Universität Konstanz. Available at: http://ling.uni-konstanz.de/pages/home/butt.

(2006). *Theories of Case.* Cambridge University Press.

Caha, Pavel (2009). The nanosyntax of case. PhD dissertation, University of Tromsoe.

Calabrese, Andrea (1986). Some properties of the Italian pronominal system: An analysis based on the notion of thema as subject of predication. In H. Stammerjohann (ed.), *Tema-Rema in Italiano*, 25-36. Tuebingen: Gunter Narr Verlag.

Campana, Mark (1992). A movement theory of ergativity. PhD dissertation, McGill University.

Cann, Ronnie, Ruth Kempson, and Lutz Marten (2005). *The dynamics of language.* Oxford: Elsevier.

Caplan, David, Nathaniel Alpert, and Gloria Waters (1998). Effects of syntactic structure and propositional number on patterns of regional cerebral blood flow. *Journal of Cognitive Neuroscience* 10, 541-552.

(1999). Pet studies of syntactic processing with auditory sentence presentation. *NeuroImage* 9, 343-351.

Caplan, David, Nathaniel Alpert, Gloria Waters, and Anthony Olivieri (2000). Activation of Broca's area by syntactic processing under conditions of concurrent articulation. *Human Brain Mapping* 9, 65-71.

Caplan, David, Evan Chen, and Gloria Waters (2008). Task-dependent and task-independent neurovascular responses to syntactic processing. *Cortex* 44, 257-275.

Caplan, David, Louise Stanczak, and Gloria Waters (2008). Syntactic and thematic constraint effects on blood oxygenation level dependent signal correlates of comprehension of relative clauses. *Journal of Cognitive Neuroscience* 20, 643–656.

Caplan, David, Sujith Vijayan, Gina Kuperberg, Caroline West, Gloria Waters, Doug Greve, and A. M. Dale (2002). Vascular responses to syntactic processing: Event-related fMRI study of relative clauses. *Human Brain Mapping* 15, 26–38.

Carden, Guy and Thomas Dietrich (1981). Introspection, observation, and experiment: An example where experiment pays off. In P. D. Asquith and R. N. Giere (eds.), *Proceedings of the 1980 Biennial Meeting of the Philosophy of Science Association*, 583–597. East Lansing, MI: Philosophy of Science Association.

Cardinaletti, Anna (2004). Towards a cartography of subject positions. In L. Rizzi (ed.), *The structure of CP and IP*, 115–165. Oxford University Press.

Cardinaletti, Anna and Giuliana Giusti (1992). Partitive *ne* and the QP-Hypothesis. A case study. In E. Fava (ed.), *Proceedings of the XVII Meeting of Generative Grammar*, Trieste, 22–24 February 1991 (Volume presented to G. Francescato on the occasion of his seventieth birthday), 121–142. Torino: Rosemberg & Sellier.

Cardinaletti, Anna and Michal Starke (1999). The typology of structural deficiency. In H. van Riemsdijk (ed.), *Clitics in the languages of Europe*, 145–234. Berlin: Mouton de Gruyter.

Carlson, Gregory (1977). A unified analysis of the English bare plural. *Linguistics and Philosophy* 1, 413–457.

Carnie, Andrew (1997). Two types of non-verbal predication in Modern Irish. *Canadian Journal of Linguistics* 42, 57–73.

(2008). *Constituent structure*. Oxford University Press.

Carpenter, Bob (1992). *The logic of typed feature structures*. Cambridge University Press.

Carrier, Jill and Janet Randall (1992). The argument structure and syntactic structure of resultatives. *Linguistic Inquiry* 23, 173–234.

Carstens, Vicki (2001). Multiple agreement and case deletion: Against phi-(in)completeness. *Syntax* 4, 147–163.

(2003). Rethinking complementizer agreement: Agree with a case-checked goal. *Linguistic Inquiry* 34, 393–412.

(2005). Agree and EPP in Bantu. *Natural Language and Linguistic Theory* 23, 219–279.

(2011). Hyperactivity and hyperagreement in Bantu. *Lingua* 121, 721–741.

Carston, Robyn (2002). Linguistic meaning, communicated meaning and cognitive pragmatics. *Mind and Language* 17, 127–148.

Chalcraft, Faye (2006). *Do*-doubling in West Yorkshire English. Paper presented at workshop Syntactic doubling in European dialects, Meertens Institute, Amsterdam. Available at: http://www.dialectsyntax.org/wiki/European_Dialect_Syntax_II.

Chametzky, Robert A. (2000). *Phrase Structure: From GB to Minimalism*. Malden: Blackwell.

Chao, Wynn (1987). On ellipsis. PhD dissertation, University of Massachusetts at Amherst.

Chaves, Rui (2012). On the grammar of extraction and coordination. *Natural Language & Linguistic Theory* 30, 465–512.

Chen, Evan, Caroline West, Gloria Waters, and David Caplan (2006). Determinants of bold signal correlates of processing object-extracted relative clauses. *Cortex* 42, 591–604.

Cheng, Lisa Lai-Shen (1991). On the typology of *wh*-questions. PhD dissertation, MIT.

(1995). On dou-quantification. *Journal of East Asian Linguistics* 4, 197–234.

(2000). Moving just the feature. In Lutz, Müller, and von Stechow (2000), 77–99.

Cheng, Lisa Lai-Shen and Hamida Demirdache (1993). External arguments in Basque. In J. I. Hualde and J. O. de Urbina (eds.), *Generative studies in Basque linguistics*, 71–87. Amsterdam: John Benjamins.

Cheng, Lisa Lai-Shen and Rint Sybesma (1999). Bare and not-so-bare nouns and the structure of NP. *Linguistic Inquiry* 30, 509–542.

Chierchia, Gennaro (1984). Topics in the syntax and semantics of infinitives and gerunds. PhD thesis, University of Massachusetts at Amherst.

(1985). Formal semantics and the grammar of predication. *Linguistic Inquiry* 16, 417–443.

(1989). Anaphora and attitudes *de se*. In R. Bartsch, J. van Benthem, and P. van Emde Boas (eds.), *Semantics and contextual expression*, 1–31. Dordrecht: Foris.

(1993). Questions with quantifiers. *Natural Language Semantics* 1, 181–234.

(2004a). Scalar implicatures, polarity phenomena and the syntax/pragmatics interface. In Belletti (2004b), 39–103.

(2004b). A semantics for unaccusatives and its syntactic consequences. In Alexiadou, Anagnostopoulou, and Everaert (2004), 22–59. [First circulated in 1989.]

(2006). Broaden your views. Implicatures of domain widening and the 'Logicality' of language. *Linguistic Inquiry* 37, 535–590.

Chierchia, Gennaro, Maria Teresa Guasti, and Andrea Gualmini (2001). Nouns and articles in child grammar: A syntax/semantics map. Unpublished ms., University of Milano-Bicocca.

Chierchia, Gennaro and Sally McConnell-Ginet (1990). *Meaning and grammar*. Cambridge, MA: MIT Press.

Chierchia, Gennaro and Raymond Turner (1988). Semantics and property theory. *Linguistics and Philosophy* 11, 261–302.

Choe, Jae-Woong (1984). LF *wh*-movement: A case of pied piping? Unpublished ms., University of Massachusetts, Amherst.

Chomsky, Noam (1955/1975). *The logical structure of linguistic theory*. New York: MIT Humanities Library and London: Plenum Press.

(1956). Three models for the description of language. *Institute of Radio Engineers Transactions on Information Theory* II, 113-124 [Reprinted in Luce et al. (1965), 105-124].

(1957). *Syntactic structures* (Janua Linguarum Series Minor, vol. 4). The Hague: Mouton.

(1958/1962). A transformational approach to syntax. In Archibald A. Hill (ed.), *Proceedings of the Third Texas Conference on Problems of Linguistic Analysis in English*, 124-158. Austin: University of Texas Press.

(1961). Some methodological remarks on generative grammar. *Word* 17, 219-239.

(1962). Explanatory models in linguistics. In E. Nagel, P. Suppes, and A. Tarski (eds.), *Logic, methodology, and philosophy of science*, 528-550. Stanford University Press.

(1964a). *Current issues in linguistic theory*. The Hague: Mouton. [This is a revised and expanded version of Chomsky (1964c).]

(1964b). Current issues in linguistic theory. In J. A. Fodor and J. Katz (eds.), *The structure of language: Readings in the philosophy of language*, 50-118. Englewood Cliffs, NJ: Prentice Hall.

(1964c). The logical basis of linguistic theory. In H. G. Lunt (ed.), *Proceedings of the Ninth International Congress of Linguists*, 914-977. The Hague: Mouton. [Reprinted as Chomsky (1964b).]

(1965). *Aspects of the theory of syntax*. Cambridge, MA: MIT Press.

(1966). *Cartesian linguistics: A chapter in the history of rationalist thought*. New York: Harper & Row.

(1968). *Language and mind*. New York: Harcourt Brace & World.

(1969). Quine's empirical assumptions. In D. Davidson and J. Hintikka (eds.), *Words and objections: Essays on the work of W. V. Quine*, 53-68. Dordrecht: Reidel.

(1970a). Remarks on nominalization. In R. A. Jacobs and P. S. Rosenbaum (eds.), *Readings in English transformational grammar*, 184-221. Waltham: Ginn and Company [Reprinted in Chomsky (1976b), 1-61].

(1970b). Deep structure, surface structure, and semantic interpretation. In R. Jakobson and S. Kawamoto (eds.), *Studies in general and oriental linguistics presented to Shirô Hattori on the occasion of his sixtieth birthday*, 52-91. Tokyo: TEX Company, Ltd.

(1973). Conditions on transformations. In S. Anderson and P. Kiparsky (eds.), *A festschrift for Morris Halle*, 232-286. New York: Holt, Rinehart and Winston.

(1975a). *The logical structure of linguistic theory*. University of Chicago Press.

(1975b). *Reflections on language*. New York: Pantheon.

(1976a). Conditions on rules of grammar. *Linguistic Analysis* 2, 303-351.

(1976b). *Studies on semantics in generative grammar*. The Hague: Mouton.

(1977). On *wh*-movement. In P. Culicover, T. Wasow, and A. Akmajian (eds.), *Formal syntax*, 71–132. New York: Academic Press.

(1980a). On binding. *Linguistic Inquiry* 11, 1–46.

(1980b). On cognitive structures and their development: A reply to Piaget. In M. Piattelli-Palmarini (ed.), *Language and learning: The debate between Jean Piaget and Noam Chomsky*, 35–54. Cambridge, MA: Harvard University Press.

(1981). *Lectures on government and binding* (Studies in Generative Grammar, vol. 9). Dordrecht: Foris.

(1982). *Some concepts and consequences of the theory of Government and Binding* (Linguistic Inquiry Monographs vol. 6). Cambridge, MA: MIT Press.

(1986a). *Barriers*. Cambridge, MA: MIT Press.

(1986b). *Knowledge of language: Its nature, origin and use*. New York: Praeger.

(1991a). Linguistics and cognitive science: Problems and mysteries. In A. Kasher (ed.), *The Chomskyan turn: Generative linguistics, philosophy, mathematics, and psychology*, 26–55. Oxford: Blackwell.

(1991b). *Some notes on economy of derivation and representation: Principles and parameters in comparative grammar*. Cambridge, MA: MIT Press.

(1993). A Minimalist Program for linguistic theory. In K. Hale and S. J. Keyser (eds.), *The view from Building 20: Essays in honor of Sylvain Bromberger*, 1–52. Cambridge, MA: MIT Press [Reprinted as Chapter 3 of Chomsky (1995c), 167–217].

(1994). Bare phrase structure. In *MIT Occasional Papers in Linguistics* 5 (MITWPL). Cambridge, MA: Department of Linguistics and Philosophy, MIT.

(1995a). Bare phrase structure. In H. Campos and P. Kempchinsky (eds.), *Evolution and revolution in linguistic theory: A festschrift in honor of Carlos Otero*, 51–109. Washington, DC: Georgetown University Press.

(1995b). Bare phrase structure. In G. Webelhuth (ed.), *Government and Binding Theory and the Minimalist Program*, 385–439. Oxford/Cambridge, MA: Blackwell Publishers.

(1995c). *The Minimalist Program*. Cambridge, MA: MIT Press.

(1998). Some observations on economy in generative grammar. In P. Barbosa, D. Fox, P. Hagstrom, M. McGinnis, and D. Pesetsky (eds.), *Is the best good enough?*, 115–127. Cambridge, MA: MIT Press.

(2000a). *New horizons in the study of language and mind*. Cambridge University Press.

(2000b). Minimalist inquiries: The framework. In R. Martin, D. Michaels, and J. Uriagereka (eds.), *Step by step: Essays on Minimalist syntax in honor of Howard Lasnik*, 89–155. Cambridge, MA: MIT Press.

(2001). Derivation by phase. In M. Kenstowicz (ed.), *Ken Hale. A life in language*, 1–52. Cambridge, MA: MIT Press.

(2002). *On nature and language*. Cambridge University Press.

(2004). Beyond explanatory adequacy. In Belletti (2004b), 104–131.

(2005). Three factors in language design. *Linguistic Inquiry* 36, 1–22.

(2007). Approaching UG from below. In U. Sauerland and H.-M. Gärtner (eds.), *Interfaces + Recursion = Language?*, 1-29. Berlin/New York: Mouton de Gruyter.

(2008). On phases. In R. Freidin, C. Otero, and M.-L. Zubizarreta (eds.), *Foundational issues in linguistic theory: Essays in honor of Jean-Roger Vergnaud*, 133-166. Cambridge, MA: MIT Press.

Chomsky, Noam and Howard Lasnik (1977). Filters and control. *Linguistic Inquiry* 11, 425-504.

(1993). The theory of principles and parameters. In J. Jacobs *et al.* (eds.), *An international handbook of contemporary research. Syntax: vol. 1*, 506-569. Walter de Gruyter [Reprinted as Chapter 1 of Chomsky (1995c), 13-127].

Chomsky, Noam and George Miller (1963). Introduction to the formal analysis of natural languages. In Luce, Bush, and Galanter (1965), 269-322.

Chung, Sandra (1998). *The design of agreement: Evidence from Chamorro*. Chicago University Press.

(2006). Sluicing and the lexicon: The point of no return. In R. T. Cover and Y. Kim (eds,), *Proceedings of the Annual Meeting of the Berkeley Linguistics Society 31*, 73-91. Berkeley, CA: Berkeley Linguistics Society.

Chung, Sandra, William Ladusaw and James McCloskey (1995). Sluicing and Logical Form. *Natural Language Semantics* 3, 239-282.

Churchward, C. Maxwell (1953). *Tongan grammar*. Oxford University Press.

Cinque, Guglielmo (1990a). Ergative adjectives and the lexicalist hypothesis. *Natural Language and Linguistic Theory* 8, 1-39.

(1990b). *Types of A'-dependencies*. Cambridge, MA: MIT Press.

(1994). On the evidence for partial N-movement in the Romance DP. In G. Cinque, J. Koster, J.-Y. Pollock, L. Rizzi, and R. Zanuttini, (eds.), *Paths towards Universal Grammar*, 85-110. Washington, DC: Georgetown University Press.

(1999). *Adverbs and functional heads. A cross-linguistic perspective*. Oxford University Press.

(ed.) (2002). *Functional structure in DP and IP. The cartography of syntactic structures, vol. 1*. Oxford University Press.

(2004). Issues in adverbial syntax. *Lingua* 114, 683-710.

(2005). Deriving Greenberg's Universal 20 and its exceptions. *Linguistic Inquiry* 36, 315-332.

(2006). *Restructuring and functional heads – The cartography of syntactic structures*, Vol. IV. Oxford University Press.

(2010). *The syntax of adjectives: A comparative study*. Cambridge, MA: MIT Press.

Cinque, Guglielmo and Luigi Rizzi (2010a). The cartography of syntactic structures. In Heine and Narrog (2010), 51-65.

(eds.) (2010b). *Mapping spatial PPs: The cartography of syntactic structures, vol. 6*. Oxford University Press.

Cirillo, Robert (2009). The syntax of floating quantifiers: Stranding revisited. PhD dissertation, University of Amsterdam.

Citko, Barbara (2008). Small clauses reconsidered: Not so small, and not all alike. *Lingua* 118, 251–295.

Clahsen, Harald (1990). Constraints on parameter setting: A grammatical analysis of some acquisition stages in German child language. *Language Acquisition* 1, 361–391.

Clark, Robin (1992). The selection of syntactic knowledge. *Language Acquisition* 2, 83–149.

Clements, George N. (1975). The logopohoric pronoun in Ewe: Its role in discourse. *Journal of West African Languages* 10, 141–177.

(1984). Principles of tone assignment in Kikuyu. In G. Clements and J. Goldsmith (eds.), *Autosegmental studies in Bantu tone*, 281–339. Dordrecht: Foris.

Clifton, Charles Jr. and Lyn Frazier (1989). Comprehending sentences with long-distance dependencies. In M. Tanenhaus and G. Carlson (eds.), *Linguistic structure in language processing*, 273–317. Dordrecht: Reidel.

Coene, Martine and Yves d'Hulst (2003). *From NP to DP. Vol. 1: The syntax and semantics of noun phrases*. Amsterdam/Philadelphia: John Benjamins.

Cole, Peter (1982). Subjacency and successive cyclicity: Evidence from Ancash Quechua. *Journal of Linguistic Research* 2, 35–58.

Cole, Peter, Gabriella Hermon, and Cher Leng Lee (2001). Grammatical discourse conditions on long distance reflexives in two Chinese dialects. In P. Cole, G. Hermon, and C.-T. J. Huang (eds.), *Syntax and semantics 33: Long distance reflexives*, 1–46. New York: Academic Press.

Cole, Peter and Li-May Sung (1994). Head movement and long distance reflexives. *Linguistic Inquiry* 25, 355–406.

Collins, Chris (1997). *Local economy*. Cambridge, MA: MIT Press.

(2002). Eliminating labels. In S. D. Epstein and T. D. Seely (eds.), *Derivation and explanation in the Minimalist Program*, 42–64. Oxford: Blackwell.

(2005a). A smuggling approach to English raising. *Linguistic Inquiry* 36, 289–298.

(2005b). A smuggling approach to the passive in English. *Syntax* 8, 81–120.

Comorovski, Ileana (1996). *Interrogative phrases and the syntax–semantics interface*. Dordrecht: Kluwer.

Comrie, Bernard (1976). *Aspect*. Cambridge University Press.

(1981a). *The languages of the Soviet Union* (Cambridge Language Surveys). Cambridge University Press.

(1981b). *Language universals and linguistic typology*. University of Chicago Press.

(1984). Subject and object control: Syntax, semantics, pragmatics. *Proceedings of the Berkeley Linguistic Society* 10, 450–464.

(1985a). Reflections on subject and object control. *Journal of Semantics* 4, 47–65.

(1985b). *Tense*. (Cambridge Textbooks in Linguistics). Cambridge University Press.

(1989). *Language universals and linguistic typology*. Oxford: Blackwell; University of Chicago Press.

(2005). Alignment of case marking of full noun phrases. In M. Haspelmath, M. Dryer, D. Gil, and B. Comrie (eds.), *The world atlas of language structures*, 398–403. Oxford University Press.

Condoravdi, Cleo (1989). The middle: Where semantics and morphology meet. In P. Branigan, J. Gaulding, M. Kubo, and K. Murasugi (eds.), *Proceedings of the Student Conference in Linguistics* (MIT Working Papers in Linguistics 11), 16–30. Cambridge, MA: MITWPL.

(2001). Temporal interpretation of modals: Modals for the present and for the past. In D. Beaver, S. Kaufmann, B. Clark, and L. Casillas (eds.), *Stanford papers on semantics*, 59–88. Stanford, CA: CSLI Publications.

Cook, Vivian and Mark Newson (1996). *Chomsky's Universal Grammar*, 2nd edn. Oxford: Blackwell.

Cooke, Ayanna, Edgar Zurif, Christian DeVita, David Alsop, Phyllis Koenig, John Detre, James Gee, Maria Pinango, Jennifer Balogh, and Murray Grossman (2002). Neural basis for sentence comprehension: Grammatical and short-term memory components. *Human Brain Mapping* 15, 80–94.

Cooper, Robin (1983). *Quantification and syntactic theory*, Dordrecht: D. Reidel.

Cooper, William J., Stephen J. Eady, and Pamela R. Mueller (1985). Acoustical aspects of contrastive stress in question–answer contexts. *Journal of the Acoustical Society of America* 77, 2142–2155.

Copley, Bridget (2002). The semantics of the future. PhD dissertation, MIT.

Coppock, Elizabeth (2001). Gapping: In defense of deletion. In M. Andronis, C. Ball, H. Elston, and S. Neuvel (eds.), *Proceedings of the 37th Annual Chicago Linguistic Society Conference*, 252–286. Chicago: Chicago Linguistic Society.

Corbett, Greville (1991). *Gender*. Cambridge University Press.

Corblin, Francis, Viviane Déprez, Henriette de Swart, and Lucia Tovena (2004). Negative concord. In F. Corblin and H. de Swart (eds.), *Handbook of French semantics*, 417–452. Stanford, CA: CSLI Publications.

Cormack, Annabel (1999). Without specifiers. In D. Adger, S. Pintzuk, B. Plunkett, and G. Tsoulas (eds.), *Specifiers: Minimalist approaches*, 46–68. Oxford University Press.

Cormack, Annabel and Neil Smith (2004). Backward control in Korean and Japanese. *University College London Working Papers in Linguistics* 16, 57–83.

Cornilescu, Alexandra (1995). Rumanian genitive constructions. In G. Cinque and G. Giusti (eds.), *Advances in Rumanian linguistics*, 1–54, Amsterdam/Philadelphia: John Benjamins.

Corver, Norbert (1990). The syntax of left branch extractions. PhD dissertation, Tilburg University.

(1991). Evidence for DegP. In T. Sherer (ed.), *Proceedings of the North Eastern Linguistic Society* 21, 33–47. Amherst, MA: GLSA.

(1992). On deriving certain left branch extraction asymmetries: A case study in parametric syntax. *Proceedings of the Northeast Linguistic Society* 22, 67–84. Amherst, MA: GLSA.

(1997a). The internal syntax of the Dutch extended adjectival projection. *Natural Language and Linguistic Theory* 15, 289–368.

(1997b). *Much*-support as a last resort. *Linguistic Inquiry* 28, 119–164.

(1998). Predicate movement in pseudopartitive constructions. In Alexiadou and Wilder (1998b), 215–257.

(2000). Degree adverbs as displaced predicates. *Italian Journal of Linguistics* 12, 155–191.

(2003). On three types of movement within the Dutch nominal domain. In Coene and D'Hulst (2003), 297–328.

(2005). Double comparatives and the Comparative Criterion. *Revue Linguistique de Vincennes* 34, 165–190.

(2006a). Comparative deletion and subdeletion. In Everaert, van Riemsdijk, Goedemans, and Hollebrandse (2006), Vol. I, 582–637.

(2006b). Subextraction. In Everaert, van Riemsdijk, Goedemans, and Hollebrandse (2006), Vol. IV, 566–600.

(2009). Getting the (syntactic) measure of measure phrases. *The Linguistic Review* 26, 67–134.

Corver, Norbert and Denis Delfitto (1999). On the nature of pronoun movement. In H. van Riemsdijk (ed.), *Clitics in the languages of Europe*, 799–861. Berlin: Mouton de Gruyter.

Corver, Norbert and Marjo van Koppen (2007). Ellipsis in possessive noun phrases: A comparative approach. Unpublished ms., University of Utrecht, UiL-OTS.

(2009). Let's focus on NP-ellipsis. *GAGL (Groninger Arbeiten zur Germanistischen Linguistik)* 48, 3–26. Available at: http://Gagl.eldoc.ub.rug.nl

Corver, Norbert and Henk van Riemsdijk (eds.) (1994), *Studies on scrambling: Movement and non-movement approaches to free word-order phenomena*. Berlin: Mouton de Gruyter.

(2001). *Semi-lexical categories. The function of content words and the content of function words*. Berlin: Mouton de Gruyter.

Costa, João (1998). *Word order variation*. The Hague: Holland Academic Graphics.

Coulson, Seana, Jonathan King, and Marta Kutas (1998). Expect the unexpected: Event-related brain response to morphosyntactic violations. *Language and Cognitive Processes* 13, 21–58.

Cowart, Wayne (1997). *Experimental syntax: Applying objective methods to sentence judgments*. Newbury Park, CA: SAGE Publications.

Craenenbroeck, Jeroen van (2009). Ellipsis and accommodation. The (morphological) case of sluicing. Colloquium talk presented at MIT.

(2010a). *The syntax of ellipsis. Evidence from Dutch dialects.* Oxford University Press.

(2010b). Invisible last resort. A note on clefts as the underlying source for sluicing. *Lingua* 120, 1714–1726.

Craenenbroeck, Jeroen van and Marcel den Dikken (2006). Ellipsis and EPP repair. *Linguistic Inquiry* 37, 653–664.

Craenenbroeck, Jeroen van and Anikó Lipták (2005). Ellipsis in Hungarian and the typology of sluicing. In K. Choi and C. Yim (eds.), *Ellipsis in Minimalism. Proceedings of the 7th Seoul International Conference on Generative Grammar*, 103–133. Seoul: Hankook.

(2006). The cross-linguistic syntax of sluicing: Evidence from Hungarian relatives. *Syntax* 9, 248–274.

(2008). On the interaction between verb movement and ellipsis: New evidence from Hungarian. In C. B. Chang, and H. J. Haynie (eds.), *Proceedings of the 26th West Coast Conference on Formal Linguistics*, 138–146. Somerville, MA: Cascadilla.

(2009). What sluicing can do, what it can't and in which language. On the cross-linguistic syntax of ellipsis. To appear in: L. Cheng and N. Corver (eds.), *Diagnosing syntax*. Oxford University Press.

Craig, Colette G. (1974). A wrong-cyclical rule in Jacaltec? In *Proceedings of the 10th Regional Meeting of the Chicago Linguistic Society*, 103–116. Chicago Linguistic Society, University of Chicago.

(1977). *The structure of Jacaltec*. Austin: University of Texas Press.

Crain, Stephen (1991). Language acquisition in the absence of experience. *Behavioral and Brain Sciences* 14, 597–650.

(2008). The interpretation of disjunction in Universal Grammar. *Language and Speech* 51, 151–169.

(2012). *The emergence of meaning*. Cambridge University Press.

Crain, Stephen and Janet Dean Fodor (1985). How can grammars help parsers? In D. R. Dowty, L. Karttunen, and A. Zwicky (eds.), *Natural language parsing: Psychological, computational, and theoretical perspectives*, 94–128. Cambridge University Press.

Crain, Stephen, Takuya Goro, and Utako Minai (2007). Hidden units in child language. In A. Schalley and D. Khlentzos (eds.), *Mental states: Nature, function and evolution*, 275–294. Amsterdam: John Benjamins.

Crain, Stephen, Takuya Goro, and Rosalind Thornton (2006). Language acquisition is language change. *Journal of Psycholinguistic Research* 35, 31–49.

Crain, Stephen and Drew Khlentzos (2008). Is logic innate? *Biolinguistics* 2, 24–56.

Crain, Stephen, Weijia Ni, and Laura Conway (1994). Learning, parsing and modularity. In C. Clifton, L. Frazier, and K. Rayner (eds.), *Perspectives on sentence processing*, 443–468. Hillsdale, NJ: Lawrence Erlbaum.

Crain, Stephen and Paul Pietroski (2001). Nature, nurture and Universal Grammar. *Linguistics and Philosophy* 24, 139–185.

(2002). Why language acquisition is a snap. *The Linguistic Review* 19, 163-183.

Crain, Stephen and Rosalind Thornton (1998). *Investigations in Universal Grammar: A guide to experiments on the acquisition of syntax and semantics.* Cambridge, MA: MIT Press.

Cresti, Diana (1995). Extraction and reconstruction. *Natural Language Semantics* 3, 79-122.

Croft, William (1984). *The representation of adverbs, adjectives and events in logical form* (Technical Report 344). Menlo Park, CA: SRI International.

(1990). *Typology and universals.* Cambridge University Press.

(1991). *Syntactic categories and grammatical relations.* University of Chicago Press.

(1998). Event structure in argument linking. In M. Butt and W. Geuder (eds.), *The projection of arguments,* 1-43. Stanford, CA: CSLI Publications.

(2001). *Radical construction grammar: Syntactic theory in typological perspective.* Oxford University Press.

Croft, William and D. Alan Cruse (2004). *Cognitive linguistics.* Cambridge University Press.

Cruschina, Silvio (2008). Discourse-related features and the syntax of peripheral positions – A comparative study of Sicilian and other Romance languages. PhD dissertation, University of Cambridge.

Culbertson, Jennifer (2010). Convergent evidence for categorial change in French: From subject clitic to agreement marker. *Language* 86, 85-132.

Culicover, Peter (1991). Topicalisation, inversion and complementizers in English. In D. Delfitto, M. Everaert, A. Evans, and F. Stuurman (eds.), *Going Romance and beyond,* 1-43. University of Utrecht.

(1999). *Syntactic nuts: Hard cases, syntactic theory, and language acquisition.* Oxford University Press.

Culicover, Peter and Ray Jackendoff (2001). Control is not movement. *Linguistic Inquiry* 32, 493-511.

(2005). *Simpler syntax.* Oxford University Press.

Culicover, Peter and Louise McNally (eds.) (1998). *The limits of syntax* (Syntax and Semantics vol. 29). New York: Academic Press.

Culicover, Peter and Michael Rochemont (1992). Adjunct extraposition from NP and the ECP. *Linguistic Inquiry* 23, 496-501.

Culy, Christopher (1985). The complexity of the vocabulary of Bambara. *Linguistics and Philosophy* 8, 345-351.

(1994). Aspects of logophoric marking. *Linguistics* 32, 1055-1094.

(1997). Logophoric pronouns and point of view. *Linguistics* 35, 845-859.

Currie, Karen L. (1980). An initial 'search for tonics'. *Language and Speech* 23, 329-350.

(1981). Further experiments in the 'search for tonics'. *Language and Speech* 24, 1-28.

Czepluch, Hartmut (1988). Case patterns in German: Some implications for the theory of abstract case. *McGill Working Papers in Linguistics. Special*

Issue on Comparative Germanic Syntax, 79–122. Montreal: Department of Linguistics, McGill University.

Dagnac, Anne (2010). Modal ellipsis in French, Spanish and Italian: Evidence for a TP-deletion analysis. In K. Arregi, Z. Fagyal, S. A. Montrul, and A. Tremblay (eds.), *Romance Linguistics 2008* (Interactions in Romance), 157–170. Amsterdam: Benjamins.

Dahl, Östen (1979). Typology of sentence negation. *Linguistics* 17, 79–106.

Dalrymple, Mary (1993). *The syntax of anaphoric binding*. Stanford, CA: CSLI Publications.

—— (2001). *Lexical-Functional Grammar* (Syntax and Semantics 34). New York: Academic Press.

—— (2006). Lexical-Functional Grammar. In K. Brown (ed.), *Encyclopedia of language and linguistics*, 2nd edn, 82–94. Oxford: Elsevier.

Dalrymple, Mary, Ronald M. Kaplan, John T. Maxwell, III, and Annie Zaenen (eds.) (1995). *Formal issues in Lexical-Functional Grammar*. Stanford, CA: CSLI Publications.

Dalrymple, Mary, Stuart M. Sheiber, and Fernando C. N. Pereira (1991). Ellipsis and higher-order unification. *Linguistics and Philosophy* 14, 399–452.

Dapretto, Mirella and Susan Bookheimer (1999). Form and content: Dissociating syntax and semantics in sentence comprehension. *Neuron* 24, 427–432.

Davidson, Donald (1967). The logical form of action sentences. In N. Resher (ed.), *The logic of decision and action*, 81–95. University of Pittsburg Press.

Davies, William and Stanley Dubinsky (2003). On extraction from NPs. *Natural Language and Linguistic Theory* 21, 1–37.

—— (2004). *The grammar of raising and control*. Malden, MA: Blackwell.

Davis, Henry and Hamida Demirdache (2000). On lexical verb meanings: Evidence from Salish. In C. Tenny and J. Pustejovsky (eds.), *Events as grammatical objects: The converging perspectives of lexical semantics and syntax*, 97–142. Stanford, CA: CSLI Publications.

Davis, Martin (1958). *Computability and unsolvability*. New York: McGraw-Hill Book Company.

Davison, Alice (2000). Lexical anaphora in Hindi/Urdu. In K. Wali, K. V. Subbarao, B. Lust, and J. Gair (eds.), *Lexical pronouns and anaphors in some South Asian languages: A principled typlogy*, 397–470. Berlin: Mouton de Gruyter.

—— (2001). Long distance anaphors in Hindi/Urdu. In P. Cole, G. Hermon, and C.-T. J. Huang (eds.), *Long distance reflexives* (Syntax and Semantics 33), 47–82. New York: Academic Press.

Dayal, Veneeta (1994). Scope marking as indirect *wh*-dependency. *Natural Language Semantics* 2, 137–170.

—— (1996). *Locality in* wh-*quantification, questions and relative clauses in Hindi* (SLAP 62). Dordrecht: Kluwer.

—— (1998). ANY as inherently modal. *Linguistics and Philosophy* 21, 433–476.

(2000). Scope marking: Cross-linguistic variation in indirect dependency. In Lutz, Müller, and von Stechow (2000), 157–193.

(2002). Single-pair vs. multiple-pair answers: *wh* in-situ and scope. *Linguistic Inquiry* 33, 512–520.

(2004). The universal force of free choice *any*. *Linguistic Variation Yearbook* 4, 5–40.

(2005). Multiple *wh* questions. In Everaert, van Riemsdijk, Goedemans, and Hollebrandse (2006), Vol. III, 275–326.

de Cuba, Carlos (2007). On factivity, clausal complementation and the CP-field. PhD dissertation, Stony Brook University.

de Vaugelas, Claude (1647). *Remarques sur la langue française*. Paris: Librairie E. Droz [1934 facsimile edition].

de Villiers, Jill (1991). Why questions? In T. Maxfield, and B. Plunkett (eds), *UMOP special edition: Papers in the acquisition of* wh, 155–175. Amherst, MA: GLSA.

Deal, Amy Rose (2010). Ergative case and the transitive subject: A view from Nez Perce. *Natural Language and Linguistic Theory* 28, 73–120.

Dean, Janet (1967). Noun phrase complementation in English and German. Unpublished ms., MIT.

Déchaine, Rose-Marie (1993). Predicates across categories: Towards a category-neutral syntax. PhD thesis, University of Massachusetts at Amherst.

Déchaine, Rose-Marie and Martina Wiltschko (2002). Decomposing pronouns. *Linguistic Inquiry* 33, 409–442.

Deemter, Kees van (1999). Contrastive stress, contrariety, and focus. In Bosch and van der Sandt (1999), 3–17.

Dekkers, Joost (1999). Derivations & evaluations. On the syntax of subjects and complementizers. PhD thesis, University of Amsterdam/HIL.

Delfitto, Denis (2006). Adverb classes and adverb placement. In Everaert, van Riemsdijk, Goedemans, and Hollebrandse (2006), Vol. I, 83–120.

Delfitto, Denis and Gaetano Fiorin (2011). Person features and pronominal anaphora. *Linguistic Inquiry* 42, 193–224.

Delsing, Lars-Olof (1988). The Scandinavian noun phrase. *Working Papers in Scandinavian Syntax* 42, 57–79.

(1993). The internal structure of noun phrases in Scandinavian languages: A comparative study. PhD dissertation, University of Lund.

(1998). Possession in Germanic. In Alexiadou and Wilder (1998b), 87–108.

Demirdache, Hamida and Myriam Uribe-Etxebarria (2000). The primitives of temporal relations. In R. Martin, D. Michaels, and J. Uriagereka (eds.), *Step by step: Essays on Minimalist syntax in honor of Howard Lasnik*, 157–186. Cambridge, MA: MIT Press.

(2007). The syntax of time arguments. *Lingua* 117, 330–366.

Demonte, Violeta (1999). A minimal account of Spanish adjective position and interpretation. In J. Franco, A. Landa, and J. Martin (eds.),

Grammatical analyses in Basque and Romance linguistics. Papers in honor of Mario Saltarelli, 45–75. Amsterdam: John Benjamins.

Depiante, Marcela A. (2000). The syntax of deep and surface anaphora: A study of null complement anaphora and stripping/bare argument ellipsis. PhD thesis, University of Connecticut.

—— (2001). Ellipsis in Spanish and the stranded affix filter. In Minjoo Kim, and Uri Strauss (eds.), *North East Linguistic Society*, 215–224. Georgetown University: GLSA.

Depiante, Marcela A. and Jorge Hankamer (2008). La condición de identidad en la elipsis: El caso del truncamiento. Unpublished ms., Universidad Nacional del Comahue and UCSC.

Depiante, Marcela A. and Pascual José Masullo (2001). Género y número en la elipsis nominal: Consecuencias para la hipótesis lexicalista. Paper presented at the 1st Encuentro de Gramática Generativa.

Déprez, Viviane (1989). On the typology of syntactic positions and the nature of chains: Move alpha to the specifier of functional projections. PhD thesis, MIT.

Derwing, Bruce L. (1973). *Transformational grammar as a theory of language acquisition: A study in the empirical, conceptual, and methodological foundations of contemporary linguistic theory* (Cambridge Studies in Linguistics, vol. 10). Cambridge University Press.

Dewey, Tonya Kim (2006). The origins and development of Germanic V2. PhD thesis, University of California, Berkeley.

Diercks, Michael (2010). Agreement with subjects in Lubukusu. PhD dissertation, Georgetown University.

Diesing, Molly (1989). Bare plural subjects, inflection, and the mapping to LF. In E. Bach, A. Kratzer, and B. H. Partee (eds.), *Papers on quantification*. Amherst: Department of Linguistics, University of Massachusetts, Amherst.

—— (1990). Verb movement and subject position in Yiddish. *Natural Language and Linguistic Theory* 8, 41–79.

—— (1992). *Indefinites*. Cambridge, MA: MIT Press.

—— (1996). Semantic variables and object shift. In H. Thráinsson and S. Epstein (eds.), *Studies in comparative Germanic syntax*, Vol. 2, 66–84. Dordrecht: Kluwer.

—— (1997). Yiddish VP order and the typology of object movement in Germanic. *Natural Language and Linguistic Theory* 17, 369–427.

Dikken, Marcel den (1992). *Particles*. Leiden: Holland Institute of Generative Linguistics.

—— (1995). *Particles: On the syntax of verb-particle, triadic, and causative constructions*. Oxford University Press.

—— (1998). Predicate inversion in DP. In Alexiadou and Wilder (1998b), 177–214.

—— (2001). 'Pluringulars', pronouns and quirky agreement. *The Linguistic Review* 18, 19–41.

(2002). Direct and indirect polarity item licensing. *Journal of Comparative Germanic Linguistics* 5, 35–66.

(2003). On the morphosyntax of *wh*-movement. In C. Boeckx and K. Grohmann (eds), *Multiple wh-fronting*, 77–98. Amsterdam: John Benjamins.

(2005). Comparative correlatives comparatively. *Linguistic Inquiry* 36, 497–532.

(2006a). Parasitism, secondary triggering and depth of embedding. In R. Zanuttini, H. Campos, E. Herburger, and P. Portner (eds.), *Crosslinguistic research in syntax and semantics: Negation, tense, and clausal architecture*, 151–174. Washington, DC: Georgetown University Press.

(2006b). *Relators and linkers: The syntax of predication, predication inversion, and copulas*. Cambridge, MA: MIT Press.

(2006c). A reappraisal of vP being phasal – A reply to Legate. Unpublished ms., CUNY Graduate Center.

(2006d). Specificational copular sentences and pseudoclefts. In Everaert, van Riemsdijk, Goedemans, and Hollebrandse (2006), Vol. IV, 292–409.

(2007). Phase extension. Contours of a theory of the role of head movement in phrasal extraction. *Theoretical Linguistics* 33, 1–42.

(2010a). On the functional structure of locative and directional PPs. In Cinque and Rizzi (2010), 74–126.

(2010b). Arguments for successive-cyclic movement through SpecCP: A critical review. *Linguistic Variation Yearbook* 9, 89–126.

(to appear). On the strategies for forming long A′-dependencies: Evidence from Hungarian. In B. Surányi (ed.), (Volume of papers from the conference on Minimalist Approaches to Syntactic Locality). Cambridge University Press.

Dikken, Marcel den and Anastasia Giannakidou (2002). From *Hell* to polarity: 'aggressively non-D-linked' *wh*-phrases as polarity items. *Linguistic Inquiry* 33, 31–61.

Dikken, Marcel den, André Meinunger, and Chris Wilder (2000). Pseudoclefts and ellipsis. *Studia Linguistica* 54, 41–89.

Dikker, Suzanne, Hugh Rabagliati, and Liina Pylkkänen (2009). Sensitivity to syntax in visual cortex. *Cognition* 110, 293–321.

Dimitriadis, Alexis (2008a). The event structure of irreducibly symmetric reciprocals. In J. Dölling, T. Heyde-Zybatow and M. Schäfer (eds.), *Event structures in linguistic form and interpretation*, 327–354. Berlin: Mouton de Gruyter.

(2008b). Irreducible symmetry and reciprocal constructions. In E. König and V. Gast (eds.), *Reciprocals and reflexives: Theoretical and typological explorations*, 375–410. Berlin: Mouton de Gruyter.

Dixon, Robert (1972). *The Dyirbal language of North Queensland*. Cambridge University Press.

(1982). *Where have all the adjectives gone?* Berlin: Mouton.

(1994). *Ergativity.* Cambridge University Press.

(2004). *Adjective classes: A cross-linguistic typology.* Oxford University Press.

Dobashi, Yoshihito (2003). Phonological phrasing and syntactic derivation. PhD thesis, Cornell University.

Dobrovie-Sorin, Carmen (1988). A propos de la structure du groupe nominal en Roumain. *Rivista di Grammatica Generativa* 12, 126–151.

(1994). *The syntax of Romanian: Comparative studies in Romance.* Berlin/New York: Mouton de Gruyter.

Doetjes, Jenny (1997). *Quantifiers and selection: On the distribution of quantifying expressions in French, Dutch, and English* (volume 32 of HIL Dissertations). The Hague: Holland Academic Graphics.

(2008). Adjectives and degree modification. In L. McNally and C. Kennedy (2008), 123–155.

Doetjes, Jenny and Johan Rooryck (2003). Generalizing over quantitative and qualitative constructions. In Coene and d'Hulst (2003), 277–295.

Doke, Clement (1963). *Textbook of Zulu grammar.* London: Longmans.

Dormer, Anya (2009). Feature valuation without deletion: Evidence from aspect and tense system of Russian. PhD dissertation, University of Washington, Seattle.

Doron, Edit (1983). Verbless predicates in Hebrew. PhD thesis, University of Texas at Austin.

(1999). V-movement and VP-ellipsis. In S. Lappin, and E. Benmamoun (eds.), *Fragments: Studies in ellipsis and gapping*, 124–140. Oxford University Press.

Dougherty, Ray C. (1973). A survey of linguistic methods and arguments. *Foundations of Language* 10, 432–490.

Dowty, David (1979). *Word meaning and Montague Grammar: The semantics of verbs and times in generative semantics and in Montague's PTQ.* Dordrecht: D. Reidel.

(1982). Grammatical relations and Montague Grammar. In Jacobson and Pullum (1982), 79–130.

(1985). On recent analyses of the semantics of control. *Linguistics and Philosophy* 8, 291–331.

(1989). On the semantic content of the notion 'thematic role'. In B. P. G. Chierchia and R. Turner (eds.), *Properties, types and meaning*, 69–129. Dordrecht: Reidel.

(1991). Thematic proto-roles and argument selection. *Language* 67, 547–619.

Dowty, David and Belinda Brodie (1984). The semantics of 'floated' quantifiers in a transformationless grammar. In M. Cobler, S. MacKaye, and M. Wescoat (eds.), *Proceedings of the West Coast Conference on Formal Linguistics* 3, 75–90. Stanford, CA: Stanford Linguistics Association.

Dowty, David, R. Wall and S. Peters (1981). *Introduction to Montague semantics.* Dordrecht: Reidel Publishing Company.

Dronkers, Nina F., David P. Wilkins, Robert D. van Valin, Brenda B. Redfern, and Jeri J. Jaeger (2004). Lesion analysis of the brain areas involved in language comprehension. *Cognition* 92, 145–77.

Drubig, Hans Bernhard (1994). *Island constraints and the syntactic nature of focus and association with focus* (Arbeitspapiere des Sonderforschungbereichs 340). Tübingen.

Drummond, Alex, Norbert Hornstein, and Howard Lasnik (2010). A puzzle about P-stranding, and a possible solution. *Linguistic Inquiry* 41, 689–692.

Dryer, Matthew S. (1987). On primary objects, secondary objects, and antidative. *Language* 62, 808–845.

(1991). SVO languages and the OV:VO typology. *Journal of Linguistics* 27, 443–482.

(1992). The Greenbergian word order correlations. *Language* 68, 81–138.

(1996). Grammatical relations in Ktunaxa (Kutenai): The Belcourt Lecture delivered before the University of Manitoba on 24 February 1995. Winnipeg: Voices of Rupert's Land.

(1997). Are grammatical relations universal? In J. Bybee, J. Haiman, and S. A. Thompson (eds.), *Essays on language function and language type, dedicated to T. Givón*, 115–143. Amsterdam: John Benjamins.

Dubinsky, Stanley and Robert Hamilton (1998). Epithets as anti-logophoric pronouns. *Linguistic Inquiry* 29, 685–693.

Duffley, Patrick and Pierre Larrivée (2010). Anyone for non-scalarity? *English Language and Linguistics* 14, 1–17.

Durrleman, Stephanie (2008) *The syntax of Jamaican Creole – A cartographic perspective* (Linguistics Today). Amsterdam/Philadelphia: John Benjamins Publishing Company.

É. Kiss, Katalin (1987). *Configurationality in Hungarian*. Dordrecht: Reidel.

(1991). Logical structure in syntactic structure: The case of Hungarian. In C.-T. J. Huang and R. May (eds.), *Logical structure and linguistic structure: Cross-linguistic perspectives*, 123–148. Dordrecht: Reidel.

(1993). Wh-movement and specificity. *Natural Language and Linguistic Theory* 11, 85–120.

(ed.) (1995). *Discourse configurational languages*. Oxford University Press.

(1998). Identificational focus and information focus. *Language* 74, 245–273.

(2006). Quantifier scope ambiguities. In Everaert, van Riemsdijk, Goedemans, and Hollebrandse (2006), Vol. IV, 1–34.

Eady, Stephen J. and William J. Cooper (1986). Speech intonation and focus location in matched statements and questions. *Journal of the Acoustical Society of America* 80, 402–415.

Eady, Stephen J., William J. Cooper, Gayle V. Klouda, Pamela R. Mueller, and Dan W. Lotts (1986). Acoustic characteristics of sentential focus: Narrow vs. broad focus and single vs. dual focus environments. *Language and Speech* 29, 233–251.

Eguren, Luis (2010). Contrastive focus and nominal ellipsis in Spanish. *Lingua* 120, 435–457.

Eide, Katrin and Tor Åfarli (1999). The syntactic disguises of the predication operator. *Studia Linguistica* 53, 155–181.
Einstein, Albert (1934). On the method of theoretical physics. In Einstein (1954), 270–276.
(1954). *Ideas and opinions*. New York. Bonanza Books.
Elbourne, Paul (2005). On the acquisition of Principle B. *Linguistic Inquiry* 36, 333–366.
(2008). Ellipsis sites as definite descriptions. *Linguistic Inquiry* 39, 191–220.
Elordieta, Gorka, Sóniá Frota, and Marina Vigârio (2005). Subjects, objects and intonational phrasing in Spanish and Portuguese. In M. Horne and M. van Oostendorp (eds.), *Studia Linguistica* (Special issue: Boundaries in intonational phonology) 59, 110–143.
Embick, David (2010). *Localism versus globalism in morphology and phonology*. Cambridge, MA: MIT Press.
Embick, David and Rolf Noyer (2001). Movement operations after syntax. *Linguistic Inquiry* 32, 555–595.
(2006). Distributed morphology and the syntax/morphology interface. In G. Ramchand and C. Reiss (eds.), *The Oxford handbook of linguistic interfaces*, 289–324. Oxford University Press.
Emonds, Joseph E. (1970). Root and structure preserving transformations. PhD dissertation, MIT.
(1976). *A transformational approach to English syntax: Root, structure preserving and local transformations*. New York: Academic Press.
(1978). The verbal complex V'-V in French. *Linguistic Inquiry* 9, 151–175.
(1985). *A unified theory of syntactic categories*. Dordrecht: Foris.
(2000). *Lexicon and grammar: The English syntacticon* (Studies in Generative Grammar 50). Berlin: Mouton de Gruyter.
Enç, Mürvet (1981). Tense without scope: An analysis of nouns as indexicals. PhD dissertation, University of Wisconsin, Madison.
(1987). Anchoring conditions for tense. *Linguistic Inquiry* 18, 633–657.
(1996). Tense and modality. In S. Lappin (ed.) *The handbook of contemporary semantic theory*, 345–358. Oxford: Blackwell.
Endo, Yoshio (2007). *Locality and information structure – A cartographic approach to Japanese* (Linguistics Today). Amsterdam/Philadelphia: John Benjamins Publishing Company.
Engdahl, Elisabet (1986). *Constituent questions*. Dordrecht: Reidel.
England, Nora (1991). Changes in basic word order in Mayan languages. *International Journal of American Linguistics* 57, 446–486.
Epstein, Samuel David (1999). Un-principled syntax: The derivation of syntactic relations. In S. D. Epstein and N. Hornstein (eds.), *Working Minimalism*, 317–345. Cambridge, MA: MIT Press. [Reprinted in *Essays in syntactic theory*, 183–210. New York: Routledge, 2000.]
(2003/2007). On I(nternalist) functional explanation in Minimalism. *Linguistic Analysis* 33, 20–53 [published in 2007].

Epstein, Samuel David, Erich Groat, Ruriko Kawashima, and Hisatsugu Kitahara (1998). *A derivational approach to syntactic relations*. Oxford University Press.

Epstein, Samuel David, Hisatsugu Kitahara, and T. Daniel Seely (2010). Uninterpretable features: What are they and what do they do? In M. Putnam (ed.), *Exploring crash-proof grammars* (Language Faculty and Beyond), 125-142. Amsterdam: John Benjamins Publishing Co.

(to appear a). Structure building that can't be. In V. Valmala and M. Uribe-Etxebarria (eds.), *Ways of structure building*.

(to appear b). Derivations. In C. Boeckx (ed.), *Handbook of Minimalism*. Oxford University Press.

Epstein, Samuel and T. Daniel Seely (2002a). Introduction. In S. D. Epstein and T. D. Seely (eds.), *Derivation and explanation in the Minimalist Program*, 1-18. Oxford/New York: Blackwell.

(2002b). Rule application as cycles in a level-free syntax. In S. D. Epstein and T. D. Seely (eds.), *Derivation and explanation in the Minimalist Program*, 65-89. Oxford/New York: Blackwell.

(2006). *Derivations in Minimalism*. Cambridge University Press.

Ernst, Thomas (1992). The phrase structure of English negation. *The Linguistic Review* 9, 109-144.

(1998). Scope based adjunct licensing. In P. Tamanji and K. Kusomoto (eds.), *Proceedings of NELS 28*, 127-142. Amherst, MA: GLSA.

(2002). *The syntax of adjuncts*. Cambridge University Press.

(2007). On the role of semantics in a theory of adverb syntax. *Lingua* 117, 1008-1033.

(2009). Speaker oriented adverbs. *Natural Language and Linguistic Theory* 27, 497-544.

Erteschik-Shir, Nomi (1973). On the nature of island constraints. PhD dissertation, MIT.

(2005). The sound patterns of syntax: The case of object shift. *Theoretical Linguistics* 31, 47-94.

(2007). *Information structure: The syntax-discourse interface*. Oxford University Press.

Etxepare, Ricardo (2006). Number long distance agreement in (substandard) Basque. Unpublished ms., CNRS-IKER.

Evans, F. (1988). Binding into anaphoric verb phrases. In J. Powers and K. de Jong (eds.), *5th ESCOL Proceedings*, 122-129. Columbus: Ohio State University.

Evans, Gareth (1980). Pronouns. *Linguistic Inquiry* 11, 337-362.

Evans, Nicholas (1995). *A grammar of Kayardild*. Berlin: Mouton de Gruyter.

Evans, Nicholas and Stephen C. Levinson (2009). The myth of language universals: Language diversity and its importance for cognitive science. *Behavioral and Brain Sciences* 32, 429-492.

Everaert, Martin (1986). *The syntax of reflexivization*. Dordrecht: Foris.

(1991). Contextual determination of the anaphor/pronominal distinction. In J. Koster and E. Reuland (eds.), *Long distance anaphora*, 77–118. Cambridge University Press.

(2000). Types of anaphoric expressions: Reflexives and reciprocals. In Z. Frajzyngier and T. S. Curl (eds.), *Reciprocals: Forms and functions*, 63–84. Amsterdam/Philadelphia: John Benjamins.

Everaert, Martin, Henk van Riemsdijk, Rob Goedemans, and Bart Hollebrandse (eds.) (2006). *The Blackwell companion to syntax*, vols. I–V. Oxford: Wiley-Blackwell.

Fabb, Nigel (1984). Syntactic affixation. PhD dissertation, MIT.

Fábregas, Antonio (2007). The internal structure of relational adjectives. *Probus* 19, 135–170.

Falaus, Anamaria (2009). Polarity items and dependent indefinites in Romanian. PhD dissertation, University of Nantes.

Falk, Yehuda (2001). *Lexical-Functional Grammar: An introduction to parallel constraint-based syntax*. Stanford, CA: CSLI Publications.

Faltz, Leonard (1985). *Reflexivization: A study in universal syntax*. New York: Garland Publishing.

Fang, Ji and Peter Sells (2007). A formal analysis of the verb copy construction in Chinese. In M. Butt and T. H. King (eds.), *Proceedings of the LFG07 Conference*, 198–213. Stanford, CA: CSLI Publications.

Fanselow, Gisbert (2006). Partial wh movement. In Everaert, van Riemsdijk, Goedemans, and Hollebrandse (2006), Vol. III, 437–492.

(2007). The restricted access of information structure to syntax: A minority report. In C. Féry, G. Fanselow, and M. Krifka (eds.), *The notions of information structure* (Working Papers of the SFB632 no. 6: Interdisciplinary Studies on Information Structure (ISIS)), 205–220. Universitätsverlag Potsdam.

Fanselow, Gisbert and Anoop Mahajan (2000). Towards a Minimalist theory of wh-expletives, wh-copying, and successive cyclicity. In Lutz, Müller, and von Stechow (2000), 195–230.

Faraci, Robert (1970). On the deep question of pseudo-clefts. Unpublished ms., MIT.

Farkas, Donka F. (1981). Quantifier scope and syntactic islands. In Roberta Hendrick, Carrie Masek, and Mary F. Miller (eds.), *Papers from the Seventeenth Regional Meeting of the Chicago Linguistic Society*, 59–66. Chicago: Chicago Linguistic Society.

(1988). On obligatory control. *Linguistics and Philosophy* 11, 27–58.

Farmer, Ann (1984). *Modularity in syntax*. Cambridge, MA: MIT Press.

Farmer, Ann and Robert Harnish (1987). Communicative reference with pronouns. In J. Verschueren and M. Berucelli-Papi (eds.), *The pragmatic perspective*, 547–565. Amsterdam: Benjamins.

Faroqi-Shah, Yasmeen and Michael Walsh Dickey (2009). On-line processing of tense and temporality in agrammatic aphasia. *Brain and Language* 108, 97–111.

Fassi Fehri, Abdelkader (1993). *Issues in the structure of Arabic clauses and words*. Dordrecht: Kluwer.

Fauconnier, Gilles (1979). Implication reversal in a natural language. In F. Guenther and S. J. Schmidt (eds.), *Formal semantics and pragmatics for natural languages*, 289–301. Dordrecht: Reidel.

Federmeier, Kara and Marta Kutas (1999). A rose by any other name: Long-term memory structure and sentence processing. *Journal of Memory and Language* 41, 469–495.

Fedorenko, Evelina, Edward Gibson, and Douglas Rohde (2006). The nature of working memory capacity in sentence comprehension: Evidence against domain-specific resources. *Journal of Memory and Language* 54, 541–53. Available at: <http://web.mit.edu/evelina9/www/Downloads/Journal%20pubs/Fedorenko_et_al_2006_JML.pdf>.

(2007). The nature of working memory in linguistic, arithmetic and spatial integration processes. *Journal of Memory and Language* 56, 246–269. Available at: <http://web.mit.edu/evelina9/www/Downloads/Journal%20pubs/Fedorenko_et_al_2007_JML.pdf>.

Fedorenko, Evelina and Nancy Kanwisher (2009). Neuroimaging of language: Why hasn't a clearer picture emerged? *Language and Linguistics Compass* 3, 839–865.

Feldhausen, Ingo (2008). The prosody–syntax interface in Catalan. PhD dissertation, University of Potsdam.

Felser, Claudia (1998). Perception and control: A Minimalist analysis of English direct perception complements. *Journal of Linguistics* 34, 351–385.

(2004). Wh-copying, phases and successive cyclicity. *Lingua* 114, 543–574.

Felser, Claudia, Harald Clahsen, and Thomas Münte (2003). Storage and integration in the processing of filler–gap dependencies: An ERP study of topicalization and *wh*-movement in German. *Brain and Language* 87, 345–354.

Fernald, Theodore and Ellavina Perkins (2007). Negative polarity Items in Navajo. In S. Tuttle (ed.), *Athabaskan languages conference papers* (Alaska Native Language Center Working Papers 7), 19–48.

Féry, Caroline and Vieri Samek-Lodovici (2006). Focus projection and prosodic prominence in nested foci. *Language* 82(1): 131–150.

Féry, Caroline and Wolfgang Sternefeld (eds.) (2001). *Audiatur vox sapientiae: A festschrift for Arnim von Stechow* (Studia Grammatica no. 52). Berlin: Akademie Verlag.

Fiebach, Christian, Matthias Schlesewsky, and Angela Friederici (2002). Separating syntactic memory costs and syntactic integration costs during parsing: The processing of German *wh*-questions. *Journal of Memory and Language* 47, 250–272.

Fiebach, Christian, Matthias Schlesewsky, Gabriele Lohmann, D. Yves von Cramon, and Angela Friederici (2005). Revisiting the role of Broca's area in sentence processing: Syntactic integration versus syntactic working memory. *Human Brain Mapping* 24, 79-91.

Fiengo, Robert (1974). Semantic conditions on surface structure. PhD dissertation, MIT.

(1977). On trace theory. *Linguistic Inquiry* 8, 35-62.

Fiengo, Robert and Robert May (1994). *Indices and identity*. Cambridge, MA: MIT Press.

Fillmore, Charles J. (1963). The position of embedding transformations in a grammar. *Word* 19, 208-231.

(1968). The case for case. In E. Bach and R. T. Harms (eds.), *Universals in linguistic theory*, 1-88. New York: Holt, Rinehart.

Fillmore, Charles J., Paul Kay, and Mary Catherine O'Connor (1988). Regularity and idiomaticity in grammatical constructions: The case of 'let alone'. *Language* 64, 501-538.

Fintel, Kai von (1999). NPI-licensing, Strawson-entailment, and context-dependency. *Journal of Semantics* 16, 97-148.

Fintel, Kai von and Sabine Iatridou (2003). Epistemic containment. *Linguistic Inquiry* 34, 173-198.

(2007). Anatomy of a modal construction. *Linguistic Inquiry* 38, 445-483.

Fischer, Silke (2004). Optimal binding. *Natural Language & Linguistic Theory* 22, 481-526.

Fischler, Ira, Paul Bloom, Donald Childers, Salim Roucos, and Nathan Perry Jr (1983). Brain potentials related to stages of sentence verification. *Psychophysiology* 20, 400-409.

Fitzpatrick, Justin (2002). On Minimalist approaches to the locality of movement. *Linguistic Inquiry* 33, 443-466.

(2006). The syntactic and semantic roots of floating quantifiers. PhD thesis, MIT.

Fleischman, Suzanne (1982). *The future in thought and language: Diachronic evidence from Romance*. Cambridge University Press.

Flikweert, Margriet (1994). Wat hoor-ik-te jou zeggen? Over het verschijnen van een pronomen tussen werkwoordstam en flexie-morfeem, in kindertaal en enkele Nederlandse dialecten. MA thesis, Utrecht University.

Fodor, Janet Dean (1998). Unambiguous triggers. *Linguistic Inquiry* 29, 1-36.

(2001). Setting syntactic parameters. In Baltin and Collins (2001), 730-767.

Fodor, Janet Dean and Stephen Crain (1990). Phrase structure parameters. *Linguistics and Philosophy* 13, 619-659.

Fodor, Janet Dean and Lyn Frazier (1980). Is the human sentence parsing mechanism in ATN? *Cognition* 8, 417-459.

Fodor, Janet Dean and Ivan Sag (1982). Referential and quantificational indefinites. *Linguistics and Philosophy* 5, 355-398.

Fodor, Janet Dean and William G. Sakas (2005). The subset principle in syntax: Costs of compliance. *Journal of Linguistics* 41, 513-569.

Foley, William and Robert van Valin (1984). *Functional syntax and Universal Grammar*. Cambridge University Press.

Folli, Raffaella (2001). On the relation of priority between causative and inchoative constructions. In Y. d'Hulst, J. Rooryck, and J. Schroten (eds.), *Romance languages and modern linguistic theory 1999*, 143–166. Amsterdam: John Benjamins.

(2003). Deriving telicity in English and Italian. PhD thesis, Oxford University.

Folli, Raffaella and Heidi Harley (2004). Flavors of v: Consuming results in Italian and English. In R. Slabakova and P. Kempchinsky (eds.), *Aspectual inquiries*, 95–120. Dordrecht: Kluwer.

Fortson, Benjamin W., IV (2004). *Indo-European language and culture: An introduction*. Oxford: Blackwell.

Fox, Danny (1995). Economy and scope. *Natural Language Semantics* 3, 283–341.

(2000). *Economy and semantic interpretation*. Cambridge, MA: MIT Press.

(2002). Antecedent contained deletion and the copy theory of movement. *Linguistic Inquiry* 33, 63–96.

(2003). On logical form. In R. Hendrick (ed.), *Minimalist syntax*, 82–123. Oxford: Blackwell.

Fox, Danny and Howard Lasnik (2003). Successive-cyclic movement and island repair: The difference between sluicing and VP-ellipsis. *Linguistic Inquiry* 34, 143–154.

Fox, Danny and David Pesetsky (2005). Cyclic linearization of syntactic structure. *Theoretical Linguistics* 31, 1–46.

Frajzyngier, Zygmunt (2000a). Domains of point of view and coreferentiality. In Frajzyngier and Curl (2000a), 125–152.

(2000b). Coding the reciprocal function. In Frajzyngier and Curl (2000b), 179–194.

Frajzyngier, Zygmunt and Tracy S. Curl (eds.) (2000a). *Reflexives: Forms and functions* (Typological Studies in Language 40). Amsterdam/Philadelphia: Benjamins.

(eds.) (2000b). *Reciprocals: Forms and functions* (Typological Studies in Language 41). Amsterdam/Philadelphia: Benjamins.

Franchi, Elisa (2004). L'acquisizione dei verbi funzionali in italiano infantile. *Rivista di Grammatical Generativa* 29, 85–124.

Franck, Julie, Glenda Lassi, Ulrich Frauenfelder, and Luigi Rizzi (2006). Agreement and movement: A syntactic analysis of attraction. *Cognition* 101, 173–216.

Frank, Robert (2002). *Phrase structure composition and syntactic dependencies*. Cambridge, MA: MIT Press.

(2004). Restricting grammatical complexity. *Cognitive Science* 28, 669–697.

(2006). Phase theory and tree adjoining grammar. *Lingua* 116, 145–202.

(2010). Lexicalized syntax and phonological merge. In S. Bangalore and A. K. Joshi (eds.), *Supertagging: Using complex lexical descriptions in natural language processing*, 373–405. Cambridge, MA: MIT Press.

Franks, Steven (1998). Clitics in Slavic. Paper presented at the Comparative Slavic Morphosyntax Workshop, Spencer Creek, Indiana, June 1998.

Franks, Steven and Željko Bošković (2001). An argument for multiple spell-out. *Linguistic Inquiry* 32, 174–183.

Frascarelli, Mara (2000). *The syntax–phonology interface in focus and topic constructions in Italian.* (Studies in Natural Language and Linguistic Theory 50). Dordrecht/Boston/London: Kluwer.

Frascarelli, Mara and Roland Hinterhölzl (2007). Types of topics in German and Italian. In S. Winkler and K. Schwabe (eds.), *On information structure, meaning and form*, 87–116. Amsterdam: Benjamins.

Fraser, Norman (1994). Dependency grammar. In R. E. Asher (ed.), *The Encyclopedia of language and linguistics*, 860–864. Oxford: Pergamon Press.

Frazier, Lyn (1978). On comprehending sentences: Syntactic parsing strategies. PhD dissertation, University of Connecticut.

(1987). Sentence processing: A tutorial review. In M. Coltheart (ed.), *Attention and performance XII: The psychology of reading*, 559–586. Hillsdale, NJ: Lawrence Erlbaum.

(1990). Exploring the architecture of the language processing system. In G. T. M. Altmann (ed.), *Cognitive models of speech processing*, 409–433. Cambridge, MA: MIT Press.

(2008). Processing ellipsis: A processing solution to the undergeneration problem? In C. B. Chang and H. J. Haynie (eds.), *Proceedings of the 26th West Coast Conference on Formal Linguistics*, 21–32. Somerville, MA: Cascadilla Proceedings Project.

Frazier, Lyn and Janet Dean Fodor (1978). The sausage machine: A new two-stage parsing model. *Cognition* 6, 291–325.

Frazier, Lyn and Keith Rayner (1982). Making and correcting errors during sentence comprehension: Eye movements in the analysis of structurally ambiguous sentences. *Cognitive Psychology* 14, 178–210.

Freidin, Robert (1978). Cyclicity and the theory of grammar. *Linguistic Inquiry* 9, 519–549.

(1999). Cyclicity and Minimalism. In S. D. Epstein and N. Hornstein (eds.), *Working Minimalism*, 95–126. Cambridge, MA: MIT Press.

Freidin, Robert and Howard Lasnik (1981). Disjoint reference and *wh*-trace. *Linguistic Inquiry* 12, 39–53.

Friederici, Angela (1995). The time course of syntactic activation during language processing: A model based on neuropsychological and neurophysiological data. *Brain and Language* 50, 259–281.

(2002). Towards a neural basis of auditory sentence processing. *Trends in Cognitive Sciences* 6, 78–84.

(2009). Pathways to language: Fiber tracts in the human brain. *Trends in Cognitive Sciences* 13, 175–181.

Friederici, Angela, Jörg Bahlmann, Stefan Heim, Ricarda Schubotz, and Alfred Anwander (2006a). The brain differentiates human and non-human grammars: Functional localization and structural connectivity.

Proceedings of the National Academy of Sciences of the United States of America 103, 2458-2463.

Friederici, Angela, Christian Fiebach, Martin Schlesewsky, Ina Bornkessel, and D. Yves von Cramon (2006b). Processing linguistic complexity and grammaticality in the left frontal cortex. *Cerebral Cortex* 16, 1709-1717.

Friederici, Angela and Stefan Frisch (2000). Verb argument structure processing: The role of verb-specific and argument-specific information. *Journal of Memory and Language* 43, 476-507.

Friederici, Angela, Thomas Gunter, Anja Hahne, and K. Mauth (2004). The relative timing of syntactic and semantic processes in sentence comprehension. *NeuroReport* 15, 165-169.

Friederici, Angela, Anja Hahne, and Axel Mecklinger (1996). Temporal structure of syntactic parsing: Early and late event-related brain potential effects. *Journal of Experimental Psychology: Learning, Memory, and Cognition* 22, 1219-1248.

Friederici, Angela and Sonja Kotz (2003). The brain basis of syntactic processes: Functional imaging and lesion studies. *NeuroImage* 20, S8-S17.

Friederici, Angela, Martin Meyer, and D. Yves von Cramon (2000). Auditory language comprehension: An event-related fMRI study on the processing of syntactic and lexical information. *Brain and Language* 74, 289-300.

Friederici, Angela, Erdmut Pfeifer, and Anja Hahne (1993). Event-related brain potentials during natural speech processing: Effects of semantic, morphological and syntactic violations. *Cognitive Brain Research* 1, 183-192.

Friederici, Angela, Shirley-Ann Rüschemeyer, Anja Hahne, and Christian Fiebach (2003). The role of left inferior frontal and superior temporal cortex in sentence comprehension: Localizing syntactic and semantic processes. *Cerebral Cortex* 13, 170-177.

Fries, Charles C. (1952). *The structure of English: An introduction to the construction of English sentences*. New York: Harcourt, Brace, and World.

Frisch, Stefan, Martin Schlesewsky, Douglas Saddy, and Annegret Alpermann (2002). The p600 as an indicator of syntactic ambiguity. *Cognition* 85, B83-B92.

Frishberg, Nancy (1972). Navajo object markers and the great chain of being. In J. P. Kimball (ed.), *Syntax and semantics*, Vol. 1, 259-266. New York: Academic Press.

Fromkin, Victoria A. et al. (2000). *Linguistics: An introduction to linguistic theory*. Malden, MA: Blackwell.

Frota, Sónia (1998). *Prosody and focus in European Portuguese*. PhD thesis, University of Lisbon. Published by Garland, New York, 2000.

Fry, D. B. (1955). Duration and intensity as physical correlates of linguistic stress. *Journal of the American Acoustic Association* 27, 765-769.

(1958). Experiments in the perception of stress. *Language and Speech* 1, 205-213.

Fuchs, Anna (1976). Normaler und kontrastiver Akzent. *Lingua* 38, 293-312.

(1984). 'Deaccenting' and 'default' accent. In Gibbon and Richter (1984), 134-164.

Fukaya, Teruhiko (2002). Sluicing and stripping in Japanese. Unpublished ms., University of Southern California.

(2007). Sluicing and stripping in Japanese and some implications. PhD dissertation, USC.

Fukaya, Teruhiko and Hajime Hoji (1999). Stripping and sluicing in Japanese and some implications. In S. Bird, A. Carnie, J. Haugen, and P. Norquest (eds.), *Proceedings of the 18th West Coast Conference on Formal Linguistics*, 145-158. Somerville, MA: Cascadilla Press.

Fukuda, Minoru (1991). A movement approach to multiple subject constructions in Japanese. *Journal of Japanese Linguistics* 13, 21-51.

Fukuda, Shin (2008). Backward control. *Language and Linguistic Compass* 2, 168-195.

Fukui, Naoki (1986). A theory of category projection and its applications. PhD dissertation, MIT.

(1988). Deriving the differences between English and Japanese. *English Linguistics* 5, 249-270.

(1993). Parameters and optionality. *Linguistic Inquiry* 24, 399-420.

(1995). *Theory of projection in syntax*. Stanford: Center for the Study of Language and Information.

(2001). Phrase structure. In Baltin and Collins (2001), 374-406.

Fukui, Naoki and Margaret Speas (1986). Specifiers and projection. In N. Fukui, T. Rappaport, and E. Sagey (eds.), *MIT Working Papers in Linguistics: Papers in Theoretical Linguistics* 8, 128-172.

Furuya, Kaori (2008). The DP hypothesis through the lens of Japanese nominal collocation constructions. PhD dissertation, CUNY.

Gallego, Ángel (2005). Phase sliding. Unpublishing ms., Universitat Autónoma de Barcelona.

Gallego, Ángel and Juan Uriagereka (2006). Sub-extraction from subjects: A phase theory account. Unpublished ms., Universitat Autónoma de Barcelona and University of Maryland.

Garbacz, Piotr (2010). Word order in Övdalian. A study in variation and change. PhD dissertation, Lund University.

Garnsey, Susan, Michael Tanenhaus, and Robert Chapman (1989). Evoked potentials and the study of sentence comprehension. *Journal of Psycholinguistic Research* 18, 51-60.

Gast, Volker (2006). *The grammar of identity*. London: Routledge.

Gazdar, Gerald (1981). Unbounded dependencies and coordinate structure. *Linguistic Inquiry* 12, 155-184.

Gazdar, Gerald, Ewan Klein, Geoffrey K. Pullum, and Ivan A. Sag (1985). *Generalized Phrase Structure Grammar*. Oxford: Basil Blackwell; Cambridge, MA: Harvard University Press.

Gazdar, Gerald and Geoffrey K. Pullum (1981). Subcategorization, constituent order, and the notion 'Head'. In M. Moortgat, H. van der Hulst, and T. Hoekstra (eds.), *The scope of lexical rules*, 107-123. Dordrecht: Foris.

Gazdar, Gerald, Geoffrey K. Pullum, and Ivan A. Sag (1982a). Auxiliaries and related phenomena in a restrictive theory of grammar. *Language* 58, 591-638.

Gazdar, Gerald, Geoffrey K. Pullum, Ivan A. Sag, and Thomas Wasow (1982b). Coordination and transformational grammar. *Linguistic Inquiry* 13, 663-676.

Gee, James Paul (1977). Comments on the paper by Akmajian. In P. Culicover, T. Wasow, and A. Akmajian (eds.), *Formal syntax*, 461-482. New York: Academic Press.

Gelderen, Elly van (2000a). *A history of English reflexive pronouns* (Linguistik Aktuell 39). Amsterdam/Philadelphia: Benjamins.

(2000b). Bound pronouns and non-local anaphors. In Frajzyngier and Curl (2000a), 187-225.

(2009). *Cyclical change*. Amsterdam: Benjamins.

Gengel, Kirsten (2007). Focus and ellipsis: A generative analysis of pseudogapping and other elliptical structures. PhD dissertation, University of Stuttgart.

Geniušiene, Emma (1987). *The typology of reflexives*. Berlin: Mouton de Gruyter.

George, Leland Maurice (1980). Analogical generalization in natural language syntax. PhD dissertation, MIT.

George, Leland Maurice and Jaklin Kornfilt (1981). Finiteness and boundedness in Turkish. In F. Heny (ed.), *Binding and filtering*, 105-129. Cambridge, MA: MIT Press.

Gerassimova, Veronica (2005). Unbounded dependency constructions in Western Austronesian. PhD dissertation, Stanford University.

Gergel, Remus (2009). *Modality and ellipsis. Diachronic and synchronic evidence*. Berlin: Mouton.

Gerken, LouAnn and Thomas G. Bever (1986). Linguistic intuitions are the result of interactions between perceptual processes and linguistic universals. *Cognitive Science* 10, 457-476.

Ghomeshi, Jila (1997). Non-projecting nouns and the EZAFE: construction in Persian. *Natural Language and Linguistic Theory* 15, 729-788.

(2001). Control and thematic agreement. *Canadian Journal of Linguistics* 46, 9-40.

Giannakidou, Anastasia (1997). The landscape of polarity items. PhD dissertation, University of Groningen.

(1999). Affective dependencies. *Linguistics and Philosophy* 22, 367-421.

(2000). Negative ... concord? *Natural Language and Linguistic Theory* 18, 457-523.

(2001). The meaning of free choice. *Linguistics and Philosophy* 24, 659-735.

(2006a). *Only*, emotive factive verbs, and the dual nature of polarity dependency. *Language* 82, 575-603.

(2006b). N-words and negative concord. In M. Everaert, H. van Riemsdijk, and R. Goedemans (eds.), *The linguistics companion*, Vol. 3, 327-391. Oxford: Blackwell Publishing.

(2007). The landscape of EVEN. *Natural Language and Linguistic Theory* 25, 39-81.

(2010). The dynamics of change in Dutch: From non-veridicality to strong negative polarity. *Natural Language and Linguistic Theory* 28, 561-875.

(2011). Negative and positive polarity items. In K. von Heusinger, C. Maienborn, and P. Portner (eds.), *Semantics: An international handbook of natural language meaning*, vol. 2, 1660-1712. Berlin: Mouton de Gruyter.

Giannakidou, Anastasia and Lisa Lai-Shen Cheng (2006). (In)definiteness, polarity, and the role of *wh* morphology in free choice. *Journal of Semantics* 23, 135-183.

Giannakidou, Anastasia and Josep Quer (1997). Long distance licensing of negative indefinites. In D. Forget, P. Hirschbühler, F. Martineau, and M.-L. Rivero (eds). *Negation and polarity, syntax and semantics*, 95-113. Amsterdam: John Benjamins.

Giannakidou, Anastasia and Melita Stavrou (1999). Nominalization and ellipsis in the Greek DP. *The Linguistic Review* 16, 295-331.

Giannakidou, Anastasia and Suwon Yoon (2010). No NPI-licensing in comparatives. *Proceedings of CLS 2010*.

Gianollo, Chiara, Cristina Guardiano, and Giuseppe Longobardi (2008). Three fundamental issues in parametric linguistics. In Biberauer (2008b), 109-142.

Gibbon, Dafydd and Helmut Richter (1984). *Intonation, accent and rhythm: Studies in discourse phonology*. Berlin: Walter de Gruyter.

Gibson, Edward (1998). Linguistic complexity: Locality of syntactic dependencies. *Cognition* 68, 1-76.

Gibson, Edward and Evelina Fedorenko (2010a). Weak quantitative standards in linguistic research. *Trends in Cognitive Science* 14, 233-234.

(2010b). The need for quantitative methods in syntax and semantics research. *Language and Cognitive Processes* 1-37.

Gibson, Edward and Kenneth Wexler (1994). Triggers. *Linguistic Inquiry* 25, 355-407.

Giegerich, Heinz J. (1992). *English phonology*. Cambridge University Press.

Gilligan, Gary M. (1987). A cross-linguistic approach to the pro-drop parameter. PhD dissertation, University of Southern California.

Ginzburg, Jonathan and Ivan A. Sag (2000). *Interrogative investigations: The form, meaning, and use of English interrogatives*. Stanford, CA: CSLI Publications.

Giorgi, Alessandra (2007). On the nature of long distance anaphors. *Linguistic Inquiry* 38, 321–342.

(2010). *About the speaker: Towards a syntax of indexicality.* Oxford University Press.

Giorgi, Allesandra and Giuseppe Longobardi (1991). *The syntax of noun phrases: Configuration, parameters and empty categories.* Cambridge University Press.

Giorgi, Alessandra and Fabio Pianesi (1991). Toward a syntax of temporal representations. *Probus* 3, 1–27.

(1997). *Tense and aspect: From semantics to morphosyntax.* Oxford University Press.

(2000). Sequence of tense phenomena in Italian: A morphosyntactic analysis. *Probus* 12, 1–32.

Giusti, Giuliana (1991). The categorial status of quantified nominals. *Linguistische Berichte* 136, 438–452.

(1994). Enclitic article and double definiteness: A comparative analysis of nominal structure in Romance and Germanic. *The Linguistic Review* 11, 241–255.

(1996). Is there a FocusP and a TopicP in the noun phrase structure? *University of Venice Working Papers in Linguistics* 6, 105–128.

(1997). The categorial status of determiners. In L. Haegeman (ed.), *The new comparative syntax*, 95–123. London: Longman.

(2002). The functional structure of Noun Phrases: A bare phrase structure approach. In Cinque (2002), 54–90.

(2006). Parallels in clausal and nominal periphery. In M. Frascarelli (ed.), *Phases of interpretation* (Studies in Generative Grammar 91), 163–184. Berlin: Mouton de Gruyter.

Gleason, Henry Allan (1955). *An introduction to descriptive linguistics.* New York: Holt, Rinehart and Winston. [Second revised edition (1961).]

(1965). *Linguistics and English grammar.* New York: Holt, Rinehart and Winston.

Göbbel, Edward (2007). Extraposition as PF movement. In E. Bainbridge and B. Agbayani (eds.), *Proceedings of the Thirty-fourth Western Conference on Linguistics*, 132–145.

Godard, Danièle (1992). Extraction out of NP in French. *Natural Language and Linguistic Theory* 10, 233–277.

Goh, Gwang-Yoon (2000a). Is the *tough* subject thematic? Paper presented at the annual meeting of the LSA, Chicago, IL.

(2000b). Pragmatics of the English *tough* construction. In M. Hirotani, A. Coetzee, N. Hall, and J.-Y. Kim (eds.), *Proceedings of NELS 30*, 219–230. Amherst, MA: University of Massachusetts, Graduate Linguistic Student Association.

Gold, Brian T., David A. Balota, Sara J. Jones, David K. Powell, Charles D. Smith, and Anders H. Andersen (2006). Dissociation of automatic and strategic lexical-semantics: Functional magnetic resonance imaging evidence for differing roles of multiple frontotemporal regions. *Journal of Neuroscience* 26, 6523–6532.

Goldberg, Adele (1995). *Constructions. A Construction Grammar approach to argument structure* (Cognitive Theory of Language and Culture Series). University of Chicago Press.

(2003). Constructions: A new theoretical approach to language. *Trends in Cognitive Science* 7, 219–224.

(2006). *Constructions at work: The nature of generalization in language.* Oxford University Press.

Goldberg, Adele and Ray Jackendoff (2004). The English resultative as a family of constructions. *Language* 80, 532–568.

Goldberg, Lotus (2005). Verb-stranding VP ellipsis: A cross-linguistic study. PhD dissertation, McGill University.

Goldsmith, John A. (1985). A principled exception to the coordinate structure constraint. *Papers from the Twenty-first Annual Regional Meeting of the Chicago Linguistic Society* 21, 133–143.

Gonzalez, Nora (1988). *Object raising in Spanish.* New York: Garland.

Goro, Takuya (2004). The emergence of Universal Grammar in the emergence of language: The acquisition of Japanese logical connectives and positive polarity. Unpublished ms, University of Maryland at College Park.

Goro, Takuya and Sachie Akiba (2004a). The acquisition of disjunction and positive polarity in Japanese. In V. Chand, A. Kelleher, A. Rodríguez and B. Schmeiser (eds.), *WCCFL 23*, 251–264. Somerville, MA: Cascadilla Press.

(2004b). Japanese disjunction and the acquisition of positive polarity. In Y. Otsu (ed.), *Proceedings of the 5th Tokyo Conference on Psycholinguistics (TCP)*, 243–254. Tokyo: Hituzi Syobo.

Gouskova, Maria (2003). Deriving economy: Syncope in Optimality Theory. PhD dissertation, Graduate Linguistics Student Association, University of Massachusetts, Amherst. [Rutgers Optimality Archive #610.]

Green, Georgia (1974). *Semantics and syntactic regularity.* Bloomington, IN: Indiana University Press.

Greenberg, Joseph H. (1963). Some universals of grammar with special reference to the order of meaningful elements. In J. H. Greenberg (ed.), *Universals of language*, 73–113. Cambridge, MA: MIT Press.

Grewe, Tanya, Ina Bornkessel, Stefan Zysset, Richard Wiese, D. Yves von Cramon, and Matthias Schlesewsky (2005). The emergence of the unmarked: A new perspective on the language-specific function of Broca's area. *Human Brain Mapping* 26, 178–190.

(2006). Linguistic prominence and Broca's area: The influence of animacy as a linearization principle. *NeuroImage* 32, 1395–1402.

Grewendorf, Günther (2002). Left dislocation as movement. In S. Manck and J. Mittelstaedt (eds.), *Georgetown University Working Papers in Theoretical Linguistics*, 31–81. Washington, DC.

Gribanova, Vera (2009). Prefixation, verb phrase ellipsis and the structure of the Russian verbal complex. Unpublished ms., UCSC.

Grice, Paul (1989). *Studies in the way of words*. Cambridge, MA: Harvard University Press.

Grimshaw, Jane (1979). Complement selection and the lexicon. *Linguistic Inquiry* 10, 270-326.

(1981). Form, function and the language acquisition device. In C. L. Baker and J. J. McCarthy (eds.), *The logical problem of language acquisition*, 165-182. Cambridge, MA: MIT Press.

(1990). *Argument structure*. Cambridge, MA: MIT Press.

(1991). Extended projection. Unpublished manuscript, Brandeis University, Waltham, MA. [Published in Grimshaw (2005), 1-73.]

(1997). Projection, heads, and optimality. *Linguistic Inquiry* 28, 373-422.

(2000). Locality and extended projection. In P. Coopmans, M. Everaert, and J. Grimshaw (eds.), *Lexical specification and insertion*, 115-133. Amsterdam/Philadelphia: John Benjamins.

(2005). *Words and structure*. Stanford, CA: CSLI Publications.

Grimshaw, Jane and Sara T. Rosen (1990). Knowledge and obedience: The developmental status of the binding theory. *Linguistic Inquiry* 21, 187-222.

Grimshaw, Jane and Sten Vikner (1992). Obligatory adjuncts and the structure of events. In E. Reuland and W. Abraham (eds.), *Knowledge and language, Vol. 2 Lexical and conceptual structure*, 145-159. Dordrecht: Kluwer.

Grindrod, C. M., N. Y. Bilenko, E. B. Myers, and S. E. Blumstein (2008). The role of the left inferior frontal gyrus in implicit semantic competition and selection: An event-related fMRI study. *Brain Research* 1229, 167-178.

Groat, Erich and John O'Neil (1996). Spell-out at the LF interface. In W. Abraham, S. D. Epstein, and H. Thráinsson (eds.), *Minimal ideas. Syntactic studies in the Minimalist framework*, 113-139. Amsterdam/Philadelphia: John Benjamins.

Grodzinsky, Yosef (1986). Language deficits and the theory of syntax. *Brain and Language* 27, 135-159.

(2010). The picture of the linguistic brain: How sharp can it be? Reply to Fedorenko & Kanwisher. *Language and Linguistics Compass* 4, 605-622.

Grodzinsky, Yosef and Angela Friederici (2006). Neuroimaging of syntax and syntactic processing. *Current Opinion in Neurobiology* 16, 240-246.

Grodzinsky, Yosef and Tanya Reinhart (1993). The innateness of binding and coreference. *Linguistic Inquiry* 24, 69-102.

Grodzinsky, Yosef and Andrea Santi (2008). The battle for Broca's region. *Trends in Cognitive Sciences* 12, 474-480.

Groenendijk, Jeroen and Martin Stokhof (1984). *Studies on the semantics of questions and the pragmatics of answers*. Amsterdam: Juriaans.

Grohmann, Kleanthes (2003). *Prolific domains. On the anti-locality of movement dependencies*. Amsterdam: John Benjamins.
Grosu, Alex (1988). On the distribution of genitive phrases in Roumanian. *Linguistics* 26, 931–949.
Grosz, Patrick and Pritty Patel (2006). Long distance agreement and restructuring predicates in Kutchi Gujarati. Unpublished ms., MIT.
Gruber, Jeffrey (1965). Studies in lexical relations. PhD thesis, MIT, Department of Modern Languages.
Guasti, Maria Teresa (1993). *Causative and perception verbs: A comparative study*. Turin: Rosenberg & Sellier.
 (2002). *Language acquisition: The growth of grammar*. Cambridge, MA: MIT Press.
Guasti, Maria Teresa and Luigi Rizzi (2002). On the distinction between T and Agr : Evidence from acquisition. In Cinque (2002).
Guéron, Jacqueline (1992). Types syntaxiques et types sémantiques: la phrase copulative comme palimpseste. *Revue québécoise de linguistique* 22, 77–115.
 (1993). Beyond predication: The inverse copula construction in English. Unpublished ms., Université Paris X – Nanterre.
 (2004). Tense construal and auxiliaries. In Guéron and Lecarme (2004), 299–328.
 (2008). On the difference between telicity and perfectivity. *Lingua* 18, 1816–1840.
Guéron, Jacqueline and Teun Hoekstra (1988). T-Chains and the constituent structure of auxiliaries. In A. Cardinaletti, G. Cinque, and G. Guisti (eds.), *Proceedings of the GLOW Conference 1987*, 35–100. Dordrecht: Foris.
Guéron, Jacqueline and Jacqueline Lecarme (eds.) (2004). *The syntax of time*. Cambridge, MA: MIT Press.
 (eds.) (2008). *Time and modality*. Dordrecht: Springer.
Gundel, Jeanette (1974/1989). *The role of topic and comment in linguistic theory*. PhD dissertation, University of Texas at Austin [published by Garland in 1989].
Gunter, Thomas, Laurie Stowe, and Gusbertus Mulder (1997). When syntax meets semantics. *Psychophysiology* 34, 660–676.
Gussenhoven, Carlos (1983). Focus, mode, and the nucleus. *Journal of Linguistics* 19: 377–417. [Reprinted as Chapter 1 in Gussenhoven (1984).]
 (1984). *On the grammar and semantics of sentence accents*. Dordrecht: Foris.
Gutierrez, J. (2004). Non-adult questions in the acquisition of L1 Spanish long-distance *wh*-questions. A longitudinal investigation. Paper presented at The Romance Turn, Workshop on the Acquisition of Romance Languages, Madrid, September 2004.
Haddad, Youssef A. (2009a). Copy control in Telugu. *Journal of Linguistics* 45, 69–109.
 (2009b). Adjunct control in Telugu: Exceptions as non-exceptions. *Journal of South Asian Linguistics* 2, 35–51.

(2010). Raising in Standard Arabic: Forward, backward, and none. Unpublished ms., University of Florida.

(2011). *Control into conjunctive participle clauses: The case of Assamese.* Berlin: Mouton de Gruyter.

Haddican, William (2007). The structural deficiency of verbal pro-forms. *Linguistic Inquiry* 38, 539–547.

Haegeman, Liliane (1992). *Theory and description in generative grammar: A case study in West-Flemish.* Cambridge University Press.

(1994). *An introduction to Government-Binding Theory.* Oxford: Blackwell.

(1995). *The syntax of negation* (Cambridge Studies in Linguistics 75). Cambridge University Press.

(1997a). The syntax of N-words and the Neg Criterion. In D. Forget, P. Hirschbühler, F. Martineau, and M.-L. Rivero (eds.), *Negation and polarity: Syntax and semantics,* 115–137. Amsterdam: John Benjamins.

(ed.) (1997b). *Elements of grammar: Handbook in generative syntax.* Dordrecht: Kluwer.

(2006). Conditionals, factives and the left periphery. *Lingua* 116, 1651–1669.

(2010). Adverbial clauses, main clause phenomena, and the composition of the left periphery. Unpublished ms., University of Gent.

Haegeman, Liliane and Terje Lohndal (2010). Negative concord and (multiple) agree: A case study of West Flemish. *Linguistic Inquiry* 41, 181–212.

Haegeman, Liliane and Henk van Riemsdijk (1986). Verb projection raising, scope and the typology of rules affecting verbs. *Linguistic Inquiry* 17, 417–466.

Haegeman, Liliane and Raffaella Zanuttini (1991). Negative heads and the neg criterion. *The Linguistic Review* 8, 233–251.

(1996). Negative concord in West Flemish. In A. Belletti and L. Rizzi (eds), *Parameters and functional heads. Essays in comparative syntax,* 117–179. Oxford University Press.

Hagège, Claude (1974). Les pronoms logophorique. *Bulletin de la société de linguistique de Paris* 69, 287–310.

Hagoort, Peter (2003a). How the brain solves the binding problem for language: A neurocomputational model of syntactic processing. *NeuroImage* 20, S18–S29.

(2003b). Interplay between syntax and semantics during sentence comprehension: ERP effects of combining syntactic and semantic violations. *Journal of Cognitive Neuroscience* 15, 883–899.

(2005). On Broca, brain, and binding: A new framework. *Trends in Cognitive Sciences* 9, 416–423.

(2008). The fractionation of spoken language understanding by measuring electrical and magnetic brain signals. *Philosophical Transactions of the Royal Society B: Biological Sciences* 363, 1055–1069.

Hagoort, Peter, Colin Brown, and Jolanda Groothusen (1993). The syntactic positive shift (SPS) as an ERP measure of syntactic processing. *Language and Cognitive Processes* 8, 439–483.

Hagoort, Peter, Marlies Wassenaar, and Colin Brown (2003). Syntax-related ERP-effects in Dutch. *Cognitive Brain Research* 16, 38–50.

Hahne, Anja and Angela Friederici (1999). Electrophysiological evidence for two steps in syntactic analysis: Early automatic and late controlled processes. *Journal of Cognitive Neuroscience* 11, 194–205.

(2002). Differential task effects on semantic and syntactic processes as revealed by ERPs. *Cognitive Brain Research* 13, 339–356.

Haider, Hubert (1988). Matching projections. In A. Cardinaletti, G. Cinque, and G. Giusti (eds.), *Constituent structure: Papers from the 1987 Glow Conference*, 101–121. Dordrecht: Foris.

(2000). Adverb placement: Convergence of structure and licensing. *Theoretical Linguistics* 26, 95–134.

Haïk, Isabelle (1987). Bound VPs that need to be. *Linguistics and Philosophy* 10, 503–530.

Hajičová, Eva, Barbara Partee, and Petr Sgall (1998). *Topic–Focus articulation, tripartite structures, and semantic content*. Dordrecht: Kluwer.

Hald, Lea, Marcel Bastiaansen, and Peter Hagoort (2006). EEG theta and gamma responses to semantic violations in online sentence processing. *Brain and Language* 96, 90–105.

Hale, Kenneth L. (1972). A note on subject–object inversion in Navajo. In B. Kachru, R. Lees, Y. Malkiel, A. Pietrangeli, and S. Saporta (eds.), *Issues in linguistics: Papers in honor of Henry and Renée Kahane*, 300–309. Urbana: University of Illinois Press.

(1979). *On the position of Walbiri in a typology of the base*. Bloomington: Indiana University Linguistics Club.

(1981). *On the position of Warlpiri in a typology of the base*. Bloomington: Indiana University Linguistics Club.

(1982). Some essential features of Warlpiri verbal clauses. In S. Swartz (ed.), *Papers in Warlpiri grammar: In memory of Lothar Jagst* (Working Papers of SIL-ABB Series A Volume 6), 217–315. Darwin: Summer Institute of Linguistics.

(1983). Warlpiri and the grammar of non-configurational languages. *Natural Language and Linguistic Theory* 1, 5–47.

Hale, Kenneth L. and Samuel Jay Keyser (1987). *A view from the middle* (Lexicon Project Working Papers 10) Cambridge, MA: Center for Cognitive Science, MIT.

(1993). On argument structure and the lexical expression of syntactic relations. In K. Hale and S.J. Keyser (eds.), *The view from Building 20: Essays in linguistics in honor of Sylvain Bromberger* (Current Studies in Linguistics 24), 53–109. Cambridge, MA: MIT Press.

(1997). On the complex nature of simple predicates. In A. Alsina, J.W. Bresnan, and P. Sells (eds.), *Complex predicates*, 29–65. Stanford CA: CSLI Publications.

(2000). On the time of Merge. Unpublished ms, MIT.

(2002). *Prolegomenon to a theory of argument structure* (Linguistic Inquiry Monograph 39). Cambridge, MA: MIT Press.

Halle, Morris (1959). *The sound pattern of Russian: A linguistic and acoustical investigation*. The Hague: Mouton.

Halle, Morris and Alec Marantz (1993). Distributed morphology and the pieces of inflection. In K. Hale and S. J. Keyser (eds.), *The view from Building 20: Essays in linguistics in honor of Sylvain Bromberger*, 111–176. Cambridge, MA: MIT Press.

(1994). Some key features of distributed morphology. In A. Carnie and H. Harley (eds.), *MITWPL 21: Papers on phonology and morphology*, 275–288. Cambridge, MA: MIT Linguistics Department.

Halle, Morris and Jean-Roger Vergnaud (1987). *An essay on stress*. Cambridge University Press.

Halliday, M. A. K. (1967). Notes on transitivity and theme in English, Part II. *Journal of Linguistics* 3, 199–244.

Hallmann, Peter (2000). Verb-final as a subcase of Verb-second. M. Hirotani, A. Coetzee, N. Hall, and J.-Y. Kim (eds.), *Proceedings of NELS 30*, 287–298. Amherst, MA: GLSA.

Halpern, Aaron (1992). *Topics in the placement and morphology of clitics*. PhD dissertation, Stanford (published by CSLI, Stanford, 1995).

Halvorsen, Per-Kristian (1983). Semantics for Lexical-Functional Grammar. *Linguistic Inquiry* 14, 567–615.

Hamann, Cornelia (2003). Phenomena in French impaired and normal language acquisition and their implications for hypotheses on language development. *Probus* 15, 91–122.

Hammond, Michael, Edith Moravcsik, and Jessica Wirth (1988). Language typology and linguistic explanation. In M. Hammond, E. Moravcsik, and J. Wirth (eds.), *Studies in syntactic typology*, 1–24. Amsterdam: John Benjamins.

Han, Chung-Hye (2001). Force, negation and imperatives. *The Linguistic Review* 18, 289–325.

(2007). Pied-piping in relative clauses: Syntax and compositional semantics using synchronous tree adjoining grammar. *Research on Language and Computation* 5, 457–479.

Hankamer, Jorge (1973). Unacceptable ambiguity. *Linguistic Inquiry* 4, 17–68.

(1979). *Deletion in coordinate structures*. New York: Garland Publishing.

Hankamer, Jorge and Line Mikkelsen (2005). When movement must be blocked: A reply to Embick and Noyer. *Linguistic Inquiry* 36, 85–125.

Hankamer, Jorge and Ivan A. Sag (1976). Deep and surface anaphora. *Linguistic Inquiry* 7, 391–428.

Hardt, Daniel (1993). Verb phrase ellipsis: Form, meaning and processing. PhD dissertation, University of Pennsylvania.

(1999). Dynamic interpretation of verb phrase ellipsis. *Linguistics and Philosophy* 22, 185–219.

Harley, Heidi (1995). Subjects, events, and licensing. PhD thesis, MIT.

(2000). Possession and the double object construction. Unpublished ms., University of Arizona.

(2001). Irish, the EPP and PRO. Unpublished ms., University of Arizona.

(2005). Bare phrase structure, acategorial roots, one-replacement and unaccusativity. In S. Gorbachov and A. Nevins (eds.), *Harvard working papers on linguistics*, Vol. 9, 45–63. Cambridge, MA: Harvard University Press.

Harley, Heidi and Rolf Noyer (1999). State of the article: Distributed morphology. *GLOT International* 4, 3–9.

(2000). Licensing in the non-lexicalist lexicon. In B. Peeters (ed.) *The lexicon/encyclopaedia interface*, 349–374. Amsterdam: Elsevier.

(2003). Distributed morphology. In L. Cheng and R. Sybesma (eds.), *The second GLOT international state-of-the-article book*, 463–496. Berlin: Mouton de Gruyter.

Harlow, Stephen (1981). Government and relativization in Celtic. In F. Heny (ed.), *Binding and filtering*, 213–254. Cambridge, MA: MIT Press.

Harman, Gilbert H. (1963). Generative grammars without transformation rules: A defense of phrase structure. *Language* 39, 597–616.

Harris, John and Morris Halle (2005). Unexpected plural inflections in Spanish: Reduplication and metathesis. *Linguistic Inquiry* 36, 195–222.

Harris, Zellig S. (1951). *Methods in structural linguistics*. University of Chicago Press (Reissued as *Structural linguistics*).

(1957). Co-occurrence and transformation in linguistic structure. *Language* 33, 283–340. [Published version of 1955 LSA Presidential Address; reprinted in Harris (1981), 143–210.]

(1968). *Mathematical structures of language*. New York: John Wiley and Sons.

(1981). *Papers in syntax*. Dordrecht: Reidel.

Hart, John Jr. and Barry Gordon (1990). Delineation of single-word semantic comprehension deficits in aphasia, with anatomical correlation. *Annals of Neurology* 27, 226–231.

Hartman, Jeremy (2007). Focus, deletion, and identity: Investigations of ellipsis in English. BA thesis, Harvard University.

(2009). Intervention in *tough*-constructions. In S. Lima, K. Mullin, and B. Smith (eds.), *Proceedings of Northeastern Linguistic Society* 39. Amherst, MA: GLSA.

(2010). The semantic uniformity of traces: Evidence from ellipsis parallelism. Unpublished ms., MIT.

Hartman, Jeremy and Ruixi Ressy Ai (2007). A focus account of swiping. Unpublished ms., Harvard University.

Hartmann, Katharina (2000). *Right node raising and gapping: Interface conditions on prosodic deletion*. Amsterdam: John Benjamins.

Hartmann, Katharina and Malte Zimmermann (2007). Place – Out of place: Focus in Hausa. In K. Schwabe and S. Winkler (eds.), *Information structure* and the architecture of grammar: A typological perspective, 365–403. Amsterdam: John Benjamins.

Hasegawa, Hiroshi (2007). Swiping involves preposition stranding, not pied-piping. Hand-out of a talk delivered at GLOW 30, 13 April 2007, University of Tromsoe.

Hashemipour, Margaret (1988). Finite control in Modern Persian. In Hagi Borer (ed.), *WCCFL 7: Proceedings of the Seventh West Coast Conference on Formal Linguistics*, 43–54. Stanford, CA: CSLI Publications.

—— (1989). Pronominalization and control in Modern Persian. PhD dissertation, University of California, San Diego.

Haspelmath, Martin (1993a). *A grammar of Lezgian* (Mouton Grammar Library 9). Berlin: Mouton de Gruyter.

—— (1993b). More on the typology of inchoative/causative verb alternations. In B. Comrie and M. Polinsky (eds.), *Causatives and transitivity*, 87–120. Amsterdam/Philadelphia: John Benjamins.

—— (1997). *Indefinite pronouns* (Oxford Studies in Typology and Linguistic Theory). Oxford University Press.

—— (2007). Pre-established categories don't exist: Consequences for language description and typology. *Linguistic Typology* 11, 119–132.

—— (2008). Parametric versus functional explanations of syntactic universals. In Biberauer (2008b), 75–108.

Haspelmath, Martin, Matthew Dryer, David Gil, and Bernard Comrie (eds.) (2005). *The world atlas of language structures*. Oxford University Press.

Haumann, Dagmar (2007). *Adverb licensing and clause structure in English*. Amsterdam: John Benjamins.

Hauser, Marc D., Noam Chomsky, and W. Tecumseh Fitch (2002). The faculty of language: What is it, who has it and how did it evolve? *Science* 298, 1569–1579.

Hausser, Roland and Dietmer Zaefferer (1978). Questions and answers in a context-dependent Montague Grammar. In F. Guenther and S. J. Schmidt (eds.), *Formal semantics and pragmatics for natural language*, 339–358, Dordrecht: Reidel.

Hawkins, John A. (ed.) (1988). *Explaining language universals*. Oxford: Basil Blackwell.

—— (1994). *A performance theory of order and constituency* (Cambridge Studies in Linguistics 73). Cambridge University Press.

Hay, Jemifer, Christopher Kennedy, and Beth Levin (1999). Scalar structure underlies telicity in 'Degree Achievements'. In T. Matthews and D. Strolovitch (eds.) *Proceedings of SALT IX*, 127–144. Ithaca, NY: CLC Publications.

Hayes, Bruce (1995). *Metrical theory*. Chicago University Press.

Hayes, Bruce and Aditi Lahiri (1991). Bengali intonational phonology. *Natural Language & Linguistic Theory* 9, 47–96.

Heck, Fabian (2008). *On pied-piping. Wh-movement and beyond*. Berlin: Mouton de Gruyter.

Heck, Fabian and Gereon Müller (2000). Successive cyclicity, long-distance superiority, and local optimization. In R. Billerey and B. D. Lillehaugen (eds.), *WCCFL 19*, 218–231. Somerville, MA: Cascadilla Press.

Heck, Fabian and Malte Zimmermann (2004). Argumente für die DP als Phase. Unpublished ms., University of Leipzig and Humboldt University, Berlin.

Hegarty, Michael (1993). Deriving clausal structure in tree adjoining grammar. Unpublished ms., University of Pennsylvania.

Heggie, Lorie (1988a). The syntax of copular structures. PhD thesis, University of Southern California.

—— (1988b). A unified approach to copular sentences. In H. Borer (ed.), *Proceedings of WCCFL 7*, 129–142. Stanford, CA: CSLI Publications.

Heim, Irene (1979). Concealed questions. In R. Bäuerle, U. Egli, and A von Stechow (eds.), *Semantics from different points of view* (Springer Series in Language and Communication), 51–74. Berlin: Springer-Verlag.

—— (1982). The semantics of definite and indefinite noun phrases. PhD dissertation, University of Massachusetts, Amherst.

—— (1984). A note on negative polarity and downward entailingness. In C. Jones and P. Sells (eds.), *NELS 14*, 98–107. Amherst, MA: GLSA.

—— (1993). *Anaphora and semantic interpretation: A reinterpretation of Reinhart's approach*. S-f-S report-07-93. University of Tübingen. [Reprinted in U. Sauerland and O. Percus (eds.) (1998), *The interpretive tract* (MIT Working Papers in Linguistics 25), 205–246. Cambridge, MA: MIT Press.

—— (2000). Degree operators and scope. In B. Jackson and T. Matthews (eds.), *SALT X*, 40–64. Ithaca, NY: Cornell University, CLC Publications.

Heim, Irene and Angelika Kratzer (1998). *Semantics in generative grammar*. Oxford: Blackwell.

Heim, Irene, Howard Lasnik, and Robert May (1991). Reciprocity and plurality. *Linguistic Inquiry* 22, 63–101.

Heim, Stefan, Simon Eickhoff, and Katrin Amunts (2008). Specialisation in Broca's region for semantic, phonological, and syntactic fluency? *NeuroImage* 40, 1362–1368.

Heinat, Fredrik (2006). Probes, pronouns and binding in the Minimalist Program. PhD dissertation, Lund University.

Heine, Berndt (2000). Polysemy involving reflexive and reciprocal markers in African languages. In Z. Frajzyngier and T. S. Curl (eds.), *Reciprocals: Forms and functions*, 1–31. Amsterdam/Philadelphia: John Benjamins.

Heine, Berndt and Heiko Narrog (eds.) (2010), *The Oxford handbook of linguistic analysis*. Oxford University Press.

Helke, Michael (1971). The grammar of English reflexives. PhD dissertation, MIT.

Hellan, Lars (1986). The headedness of NPs in Norwegian. In P. Muysken and H. van Riemsdijk (eds.), *Features and projections*, 89–122. Dordrecht: Foris.

—— (1988). *Anaphora in Norwegian and the theory of grammar*. Dordrecht: Foris.

Heller, Daphna (2005). Identity and information: Semantics and pragmatic aspects of specificational sentences. PhD thesis, Rutgers University.

Helmantel, Marjon (2002). Interactions in the Dutch adpositional domain. PhD dissertation, Leiden University.

Hendrick, Randall (1976). Prepositions and the X'-theory. In J. Emonds (ed.), *UCLA papers in syntax*, Vol. 7, 95–122. University of California, Los Angeles.

(1978). The phrase structure of adjectives and comparatives. *Linguistic Analysis* 4, 255–297.

Hendriks, Petra (1995). Comparatives in categorial grammar. PhD thesis, University of Groningen.

(2004). Coherence relations, ellipsis and contrastive topics. *Journal of Semantics* 21, 375–414.

Hendriks, Petra and Jennifer Spenader (2005). Why be silent? Some functions of ellipsis in natural language. In J. Spenader and P. Hendriks (eds.), *Proceedings of the ESSLLI '05 workshop on cross-modular approaches to ellipsis*, Heriot-Watt University, Edinburgh, 29–36.

Henry, Alison (1995). *Belfast English and Standard English. Dialect variation and parameter setting* (Oxford Studies in Comparative Syntax). Oxford University Press.

Herburger, Elena (2001). The negative concord puzzle revisited. *Natural Language Semantics* 9, 289–333.

Herburger, Elena and Simon Mauck (2007). A new look at Ladusaw's puzzle. In H. Zeijlstra and J.-Ph. Sohn (eds.), *Proceedings of the workshop on negation and polarity*. Tübingen: SFB 441.

Herten, Marieke van, Dorothee Chwilla, and Herman Kolk (2006). When heuristics clash with parsing routines: ERP evidence for conflict monitoring in sentence perception. *Journal of Cognitive Neuroscience* 18, 1181–1197.

Herten, Marieke van, Herman Kolk, and Dorothee Chwilla (2005). An ERP study of p600 effects elicited by semantic anomalies. *Cognitive Brain Research* 22, 241–255.

Hestvik, Arild (1991). Subjectless binding domains. *Natural Language and Linguistic Theory* 9, 455–496.

(1992). LF-movement of pronouns and anti-subject orientation. *Linguistic Inquiry* 23, 557–594.

(1995). Reflexives and ellipsis. *Natural Language Semantics* 2, 1–27.

Heycock, Caroline (1993). Syntactic predication in Japanese. *Journal of East Asian Linguistics* 2, 167–211.

(1994a). The internal structure of small clauses. In J. Beckman (ed.), *Proceedings of NELS 25*, vol. one, 223–238. Amherst, MA: GLSA.

(1994b). *Layers of predication: The non-lexical syntax of clauses*. New York: Garland.

(1995a). Asymmetries in reconstruction. *Linguistic Inquiry* 26, 547–570.

(1995b). The internal structure of small clauses: New evidence from inversion. In J. N. Beckman (ed.), *Proceedings of the 25th Annual Meeting of the North East Linguistics Society*, 223–238. Amherst, MA: GLSA.

Heycock, Caroline and Anthony Kroch (1998). Inversion and equation in copular sentences. In A. Alexiadou, N. Fuhrhop, U. Kleinhenz, and P. Law (eds.), *Papers in linguistics*, vol. 10, 71–87. Berlin: Zentrum für Allgemeine Sprachwissenschaft, Sprachtypologie und Universalienforschung (ZAS).

(1999). Pseudocleft connectedness: Implications for the LF interface level. *Linguistic Inquiry* 30(3). 365–397.

(2002). Topic, focus, and syntactic representations. In L. Mikkelsen and C. Potts (eds.), *Proceedings of WCCFL 21*, 101–125. Somerville, MA: Cascadilla Press.

Heycock, Caroline, Antonella Sorace, and Zakaris Svabo Hansen (2010). V-to-I and V2 in subordinate clauses: An investigation of Faroese in relation to Icelandic and Danish. *Journal of Comparative Germanic Linguistics* 13, 61–97.

Hickok, Gregory and David Poeppel (2004). Dorsal and ventral streams: A framework for understanding aspects of the functional anatomy of language. *Cognition* 92, 67–99.

Hicks, Glyn (2009a). *The derivation of anaphoric relations*. Amsterdam/New York. Benjamins.

(2009b). *Tough*-constructions and their derivation. *Linguistic Inquiry* 40, 535–566.

Hiemstra, Inge (1986). Some aspects of *wh*-questions in Frisian. *Nowele* 8, 97–110.

Higginbotham, James (1983a). Logical form, binding and nominals. *Linguistic Inquiry* 14, 395–420.

(1983b). The logic of perceptual reports: An extensional alternative to Situational Semantics. *Journal of Philosophy* 80, 100–127.

(1985). On semantics. *Linguistic Inquiry* 16, 547–594.

(2008). The English perfect and the metaphysics of events. In J. Guéron and J. Lecarme (2008), 173–193.

(2009). Remembering, imagining, and the first person. Unpublished ms., USC.

Higginbotham, James and Robert May (1981). Questions, quantifiers and crossing. *The Linguistic Review* 1, 41–79.

Higgins, Francis Roger (1973). The pseudo-cleft construction in English. PhD thesis, MIT.

Hinojosa, José, Manuel Martin-Loeches, Pilar Casado, Francisco Munoz, and Francisco Rubia (2003). Similarities and differences between phrase structure and morphosyntactic violations in Spanish: An event-related potentials study. *Language and Cognitive Processes* 18, 113–142.

Hintikka, Jaakko (1986). The semantics of *a certain*. *Linguistic Inquiry* 17, 331–336.

Hinton, Geoffrey and Steven Nowlan (1987). How learning can guide evolution. *Complex Systems* 1, 495–502.

Hiraiwa, Ken (2001). Multiple agreement and the defective intervention effect. In O. Matsushansky *et al.* (eds.), *The Proceedings of the MIT-Harvard Joint Conference (HUMIT 2000)*, 67–80. Cambridge, MA: MITWPL.

(2005). Dimensions in syntax. Unpublished ms., University of Tokyo.

Hirsch, Christopher and Kenneth Wexler (2007). The late development of raising: What children seem to think about *seem*. In S. Dubinsky and W. Davies (eds.), *New horizons in the analysis of control and raising*, 35–70. New York/Dordrecht: Springer.

Hirschbühler, Paul (1982). VP-deletion and across-the-board quantifier scope. In J. Pustejovsky and P. Sells (eds.), *Proceedings of NELS 12*, 132–139. Amherst, MA: GLSA.

Hobbs, Jerry and Andrew Kehler (1997). A theory of parallelism and the case of VP ellipsis. In P. R. Cohen, and W. Wahlster (eds.), *Proceedings of the 35th Conference of the Association for Computational Linguistics*, 394–401. East Stroudsburg, PA: Association for Computational Linguistics.

Hockett, Charles F. (1958). *A Course in modern linguistics*. New York: MacMillan.

Hoeksema, Jack (1986). Monotonie en superlatieven. In C. Hoppenbrouwers, J. Houtman, I. Schuurman, and F. Zwarts (eds), *Proeven van taalwetenschap*, 38–49. Groningen: Nederlands Instituut RUG.

(1999). Aantekeningen bij *ooit*, deel 2: de opkomst van niet polair 'ooit'. *Tabu* 29, 147–172.

(2007). Parasitic licensing of negative polarity items. *Journal of Comparative Germanic Linguistics* 10, 163–182.

Hoekstra, Eric (1991). Licensing conditions on phrase structure. PhD dissertation, University of Groningen.

(1994). Agreement and the nature of specifiers. In C. J.-W. Zwart (ed.), *Minimalism and Kayne's Antisymmetry Hypothesis* (Groninger Arbeiten zur Germanistischen Linguistic 37), 159–168. Groningen.

Hoekstra, Jarich (1993). The split CP hypothesis and the Frisian complementizer system. Unpublished ms., Frisian Academy.

Hoekstra, Teun. (1983). The distribution of sentential complements. In H. Bennis and W. U. S. van Lessen Kloeke (eds.), *Linguistics in the Netherlands 1983*, 93–103. Dordrecht: Foris.

(1984). *Transitivity. Grammatical relations in Government-Binding Theory*. Dordrecht: Foris.

(1988). Small clause results. *Lingua* 74, 101–139.

Hoekstra, Teun and Peter Jordens (1994). From adjunct to head. In T. Hoekstra and B. D. Schwartz (eds.), *Language acquisition studies in generative grammar*, 119–149. Amsterdam/Philadelphia: Benjamins.

Hoekstra, Teun and Jan G. Kooij (1988). The innateness hypothesis. In Hawkins (1988), 31–55.

Hoekstra, Teun and René Mulder (1990). Unergatives as copular verbs: Locational and existential predication. *The Linguistic Review* 7, 1–79.

Hoekstra, Teun and Ian Roberts (1993). Middle constructions in Dutch and English. In E. Reuland and W. Abraham (eds.), *Knowledge and* language Vol 2: Lexical and conceptual structure, 183–220. Dordrecht: Kluwer.

Höhle, Tilman (2000). The w-...w-construction: Appositive or scope indicating? In Lutz, Müller, and von Stechow (2000), 317–332.

Hoji, Hajime (1986). Logical form constraints and configurational structures. PhD dissertation, University of Washington.

(1987). Japanese clefts and reconstruction/chain binding effects. Handout of Talk Presented at WCCFL 6, University of Arizona.

(1990). Theories of anaphora and aspects of Japanese syntax. Unpublished ms., University of Southern California.

Hoji, Hajime and Teruhiko Fukaya (2001). On island repair and CM vs. non-CM constructions in English and Japanese. Handout of presentation at Kaken Workshop on Ellipsis, Kyoto.

Holmberg, Anders (1986). Word order and syntactic features in the Scandinavian languages and English. PhD thesis, University of Stockholm.

(1999). Remarks on Holmberg's Generalization. *Studia Linguistica* 53, 1–39.

(2010). Parameters in Minimalist theory: The case of Scandinavian. *Theoretical Linguistics* 36, 1–48.

Holmberg, Anders and Christer Platzack (1995). *The role of inflection in Scandinavian syntax* (Oxford Studies in Comparative Syntax). Oxford University Press.

Homer, Vincent (2010). Epistemic modals: High ma non troppo. To appear in The proceedings of NELS 40.

Hook, Peter (1979). *Hindi structures: Intermediate level* (Michigan Papers on South and South East Asia 16) Ann Arbor: University of Michigan.

Hopper, Paul and Elizabeth Closs Traugott (1993). *Grammaticalization*. Cambridge University Press.

Horn, Laurence (1989). *A natural history of negation*. University of Chicago Press.

(2001). Flaubert triggers, squatitive negation, and other quirks of grammar. In J. Hoeksema, H. Rullmann, V. Sánchez-Valencia, and T. van der Wouden (eds.), *Perspectives on negation and polarity items*, 173–200. Amsterdam/Philadelphia: John Benjamins.

Hornstein, Norbert (1977). S and X-bar convention. *Linguistic Analysis* 3, 137–176.

(1981). The study of meaning in natural language: Three approaches to tense. In N. Hornstein and D. Lightfoot (eds.), *Explanation in linguistics*, 116–151. London and New York: Longman.

(1990). *As time goes by: Tense and universal grammar*. Cambridge, MA: MIT Press.

(1995). *Logical Form: From GB to Minimalism*. Cambridge, MA/Oxford: Blackwell.

(1999). Movement and control. *Linguistic Inquiry* 30, 69–96.

(2001). *Move! A Minimalist theory of construal*. Malden, MA/Oxford: Blackwell.

(2003). On control. In R. Hendrick (ed.), *Minimalist syntax*, 6–81. Oxford: Blackwell.

(2007). Pronouns in a Minimalist setting. In N. Corver and J. Nunes (eds.), *The copy theory of movement*, 351–384. Amsterdam/Philadelphia: Benjamins.

(2009). *A theory of syntax. Minimalist operations and Universal Grammar*. Cambridge University Press.

Hornstein, Norbert and Maria Polinsky (eds.) (2010). *Movement theory of control*. Amsterdam: John Benjamins.

Horvath, Julia (1986). *Focus in the theory of grammar and the syntax of Hungarian*. Dordrecht: Foris.

(1997). The status of wh-expletives and the partial wh-movement construction of Hungarian. *Natural Language & Linguistic Theory* 15, 509–572.

Horvath, Julia and Tali Siloni (2002). Against the little-v hypothesis. *Revista di Grammatica Generativa* 27, 107–122.

Hosono, Mayumi (2006). An investigation of object shift based on information structure. In C. Davis, A. R. Deal, and Y. Zabbal (eds.), *Proceedings of NELS 36*, Vol. 1, 343–356. Amherst, MA: GLSA.

Hout, Angeliek van (2000). Event semantics in the lexicon–syntax interface. In C. Tenny and J. Pustejovsky (eds.), *Events as grammatical objects*, 239–282. Stanford, CA: CSLI Publications.

Hout, Angeliek van and Thomas Roeper (1998). Events and aspectual structure in derivational morphology. in H. Harley (ed.), *Papers from the University of Pennsylvania/MIT Roundtable on Argument Structure and Aspect* (MIT Working Papers in Linguistics 32), 175–200. Cambridge, MA: MIT Press.

Howell, Jonathan (2011). Meaning and prosody: On the Web, in the lab and from the theorist's armchair. PhD thesis, Cornell University.

Huang, C.-T. James (1982a). Logical relations in Chinese and the theory of grammar. PhD dissertation, MIT.

(1982b). Move WH in a language without WH movement. *The Linguistic Review* 1, 369–416.

(1983). A note on the binding theory. *Linguistic Inquiry* 14, 554–561.

(1984). On the distribution and reference of empty pronouns. *Linguistic Inquiry* 15, 531–574.

(1989). Pro-drop in Chinese: A generalized Control theory. In O. Jaeggli and K. Safir (eds.), *The null subject parameter*, 185–214. Dordrecht: Kluwer.

(1993). Reconstruction and the structure of VP: Some theoretical consequences. *Linguistic Inquiry* 24, 103–138.

Huang, C-T. James, Yen-Hui Audrey Li and Yafei Li (2009). *The syntax of Chinese*. Cambridge University Press.

Huang, C.-T. James and C.-S. Luther Liu (2001). Logophoricity, attitudes and *ziji* at the interface. In P. Cole, G. Hermon. and C.-T. J. Huang (eds.), *Syntax and semantics 33: Long-distance reflexives*, 141–195. New York: Academic Press.

Huang, C.-T. James and C.-C. Jane Tang (1991). The local nature of long distance reflexives in Chinese. In J. Koster and E. Reuland (eds.), *Long-distance anaphora*, 263–282. Cambridge University Press.

Huang, Yan (2000). *Anaphora: A crosslinguistic study*. Oxford University Press.

Huck, Geoffrey J. and Almerindo E. Ojeda (eds.) (1987), *Discontinuous constituency* (Syntax and Semantics 20). New York: Academic Press.

Huddleston, Rodney and Geoffrey K. Pullum (2002). *The Cambridge grammar of the English language*. Cambridge University Press.

Hudson, Richard (1976). Conjunction reduction, gapping and right-node raising. *Language* 52, 535–562.

(1984). *Word grammar*. Oxford: Blackwell.

Humphries, Colin, Jeffrey Binder, David Medler, and Einat Liebenthal (2006). Syntactic and semantic modulation of neural activity during auditory sentence comprehension. *Journal of Cognitive Neuroscience* 18, 665–679.

Humphries, Colin, Tracy Love, David Swinney, and Gregory Hickok (2005). Response of anterior temporal cortex to syntactic and prosodic manipulations during sentence processing. *Human Brain Mapping* 26, 128–138.

Humphries, Colin, Kimberley Willard, Bradley Buchsbaum, and Gregory Hickok (2001). Role of anterior temporal cortex in auditory sentence comprehension: An fMRI study. *NeuroReport* 12, 1749–1752.

Hyams, Nina (1986). *Language acquisition and the theory of parameters*. Dordrecht: D. Reidel.

(1987). The theory of parameters and syntactic development. In T. Roeper and E. Williams (eds.), *Parameter setting*, 1–22. Dordrecht: D. Reidel Publishing Company.

Hyman, Larry and Bernard Comrie (1981). Coreference and logophoricity in Gokana. *Journal of African Linguistics* 3, 19–37.

Iatridou, Sabine (1990) About Agr(P). *Linguistic Inquiry* 21, 551–577.

(2000). The grammatical ingredients of counterfactuality. *Linguistic Inquiry* 31, 231–270.

Iatridou, Sabine, Elena Anagostopoulou and Roumyana Izvorski (2001). Observations about the form and meaning of the perfect. In M. Kenstowicz (ed.), *Ken Hale: A life in language*, 189–238. Cambridge, MA: MIT Press.

Iatridou, Sabine and Hedde Zeijlstra (2009). On the scopal interaction of negation and deontic modals. In K. Schulz and M. Aloni (eds), *Preproceedings of the Amsterdam Colloquium*, 315–324. Amsterdam: ILLC.

Inaba, Jiro (2007). *Die Syntax der Satzkomplementierung* (Studia Grammatica 66). Berlin: Akademie Verlag.

Indefrey, Peter and Willem Levelt (2004). The spatial and temporal signatures of word production components. *Cognition* 92, 101–144.

Ingria, Robert J. (1990). The limits of unification. In R. Berwick (ed.), *Proceedings of the 28th Annual Meeting of the Association for Computational Linguistics*, 194–204. University of Pittsburgh, Association for Computational Linguistics.

Inkelas, Sharon and Draga Zec (1990). *The phonology-syntax connection*. University of Chicago Press.

Isel, Frédéric, Anja Hahne, Burkhard Maess, and Angela Friederici (2007). Neurodynamics of sentence interpretation: ERP evidence from French. *Biological Psychology* 74, 337–346.

Ishihara, Shinichiro (2004). Prosody by phase: Evidence from focus intonation-*wh*-scope correspondence in Japanese. In S. Ishihara, M. Schmitz, and A. Schwarz (eds.), *Interdisciplinary studies on information Structure 1: Working papers of SFB632*, 77–119. University of Potsdam.

(2007). Major phrase, focus intonation, multiple spell-out. *The Linguistic Review* 24, 137–167.

Israel, Michael (1996). Polarity sensitivity as lexical semantics. *Linguistics & Philosophy* 19, 619–666.

(2007). *The least bits of grammar: Pragmatics, polarity, and the logic of scales*. Cambridge Universtity Press.

Itkonen, Esa (1992). Remarks on the language universals research II. In M. Vilkuna (ed.), *SKY 1992* (Suomen Kielitieteellisen Yhdistyksen Vuosikirja 1992), 53–82. Helsinki: Suomen Kielitieteellisen Yhdistyks.

Jackendoff, Ray S. (1969). Some rules of semantic interpretation for English. PhD dissertation, MIT.

(1971). Gapping and related rules. *Linguistic Inquiry* 2, 21–35.

(1972). *Semantic interpretation in generative grammar*. Cambridge, MA: MIT Press.

(1973). The base rules for prepositional phrases. In S. Anderson and P. Kiparsky (eds.), *A festschrift for Morris Halle*, 345–356. New York: Holt, Rinehart and Winston.

(1975). Morphological and semantic regularities in the lexicon. *Language* 51, 639–671.

(1977). *X-bar syntax: A study of phrase structure*. Cambridge, MA: MIT Press.

(1983). *Semantics and cognition*. Cambridge, MA: MIT Press.

(1990a). *Semantic structures* (Current Studies in Linguistics 18). Cambridge, MA: MIT Press.

(1990b). On Larson's account of the double object construction. *Linguistic Inquiry* 21, 427–454.

(1992). Mme Tussaud meets the binding theory. *Natural Language and Linguistic Theory* 10, 1–31.

(1996a). The proper treatment of measuring out, telicity and perhaps even quantification in English. *Natural Language and Linguistic Theory* 14, 305–354.

(1996b). The architecture of the linguistic–spatial interface. In P. Bloom, M. A. Peterson, L. Nadel, and M. F. Garrett (eds.), *Language and space*, 1–30. Cambridge, MA: MIT Press.

(1997). *The architecture of the Language Faculty*. Cambridge, MA: MIT Press.

(1999). The representational structures of the language faculty and their interactions. In C. N. Brown and P. Hagoort (eds.), *The neurocognition of language*, 37–79. Oxford University Press.

(2002). *Foundations of language: Brain, meaning, grammar, evolution*. Oxford University Press.

Jackendoff, Ray and Peter Culicover (2003). The semantic basis of control in English. *Language* 79, 517–556.

Jacobs, Joachim (1980). Lexical decomposition in Montague Grammar. *Theoretical Linguistics* 7, 121–136.

(1988). Fokus-Hintergrund-Gliederung und Grammatik. In Altmann (1988), 89–134.

(1991/1992a). *Informationsstruktur und Grammatik (Linguistische Berichte Sonderheft 4)*. Opladen: Westdeutscher Verlag.

(1991/1992b). Neutral stress and the position of heads. In Jacobs (1991/2a), 220–244.

(1992). *Integration* (Tech. Rep. 14, SFB 282). Düsseldorf: Köln & Wuppertal.

(1999). Informational autonomy. In Bosch and van der Sandt (1999), 56–81.

Jacobs, Roderick and Peter Rosenbaum (eds.) (1968). *Readings in English transformational grammar*. Waltham, MA: Blaisdell.

Jacobson, Pauline (1987). Review of *Generalized Phrase Structure Grammar*. *Linguistics and Philosophy* 10, 389–426.

(1992). Antecedent contained deletion in a variable-free semantics. *SALT 2*, 193–213.

(1999) Towards a variable-free semantics. *Linguistics and Philosophy* 22, 117–184.

(2000) Paycheck pronouns, Bach–Peters sentences, and variable-free semantics. *Natural Language Semantics* 8, 77–155.

Jacobson, Pauline and Geoffrey Pullum (eds.) (1982). *The nature of syntactic representation*. Dordrecht: Reidel.

Jaeggli, Osvaldo (1980). On some phonologically null elements in syntax. PhD dissertation, MIT.

(1986). Passive. *Linguistic Inquiry* 17, 587–622.

Jakobson, Roman (1941/1968). *Child language, aphasia, and phonological universals* (Janua Linguarum Series Minor 72). The Hague: Mouton.

Jayaseelan, K. A. (1990). Incomplete VP deletion and gapping. *Linguistic Analysis* 20, 64–81.

(1997). Anaphors as pronouns. *Studia Linguistica* 51, 186–234.

(2008). Bare phrase structure and specifier-less syntax. *Biolinguistics* 2, 87–106.

(2010). Stacking, stranding and pied piping: A proposal about word order. *Syntax* 13, 298–330.

Jayez, Jacques and Lucia Tovena (2005). When 'widening' is too narrow. In P. Dekker and M. Franke (eds.), *Proceedings of the 15th Amsterdam Colloquium*, 131–136. Amsterdam: ILLC.

Jeanne, LaVerne Masayesva (1978). Aspects of Hopi grammar. PhD dissertation, MIT.

Jelinek, Eloise and Richard Demers (1994). Predicates and pronominal arguments in Straits Salish. *Language* 70, 697–736.

Jespersen, Otto (1917). *Negation in English and other languages* (Historisk-filologiske Meddelelser 1). Copenhagen: A. F. Høst.

Jing, C., Stephen Crain and Jean C.-F. Hsu (2005). Interpretation of focus in Chinese: Child and adult language. In Y. Otsu (ed.), *Proceedings of the Sixth Tokyo Conference on Psycholinguistics*, 165–190. Tokyo: Hituzi Syobo Publishing Company.

Johannessen, Janne Bondi (1998). *Coordination*. Oxford University Press.

Johnson, David E. and Shalom Lappin (1999). *Local constraints vs economy*. Stanford, CA: CSLI Publications.

Johnson, David E. and Paul M. Postal (1980). *Arc pair grammar*. Princeton University Press.

Johnson, Kyle (1991). Object positions. *Natural Language and Linguistic Theory* 9, 577–636.

(1996). When verb phrases go missing. *Glot International* 2, 3–9.

(2001). What VP-ellipsis can do, and what it can't, but not why. In Baltin and Collins (2001), 439–479.

(2008). Introduction. In K. Johnson, (ed.), *Topics in ellipsis*, 1–14. Cambridge University Press.

(2009). Gapping is not (VP) ellipsis. *Linguistic Inquiry* 40, 289–328.

Jonas, Diane (1996) Clause structure and verb syntax in Scandinavian and English. PhD dissertation, Harvard University.

Jónsson, Jóhannes G. (1996). Clausal architecture and Case in Icelandic. PhD. thesis, GLSA, University of Massachusetts.

Joos, Martin (ed.) (1957). *Readings in linguistics: The development of descriptive linguistics in America since 1925*. Chicago: University of Chicago Press.

Joshi, Aravind K. (1985). Tree adjoining grammars: How much context-sensitivity is required to provide reasonable structural descriptions? In D. Dowty, L. Karttunen, and A. Zwicky (eds.), *Natural language parsing: Psychological, computational and theoretical perspectives*, 206–250. Cambridge University Press.

Joshi, Aravind K., Tilman Becker, and Owen Rambow (2000). Complexity of scrambling: A new twist on the competence-performance distinction. In Abeillé and Rambow (2000), 167–181.

Joshi, Aravind K. and Seth Kulick (1997). Partial proof trees as building blocks for a categorial grammar. *Linguistics and Philosophy* 20, 637–667.

Joshi, Aravind K., Leon Levy, and Masako Takahashi (1975). Tree adjunct grammars. *Journal of the Computer and System Sciences* 10, 136–163.

Joshi, Aravind K. and Yves Schabes (1997). Tree-adjoining grammars. In G. Rozenberg, and A. Salomaa (eds.), *Handbook of formal languages, vol. 3: Beyond words*, 69–124. New York: Springer.

Joshi, Aravind K. and K. Vijay-Shanker (1989). Treatment of long distance dependencies in LFG and TAG: Functional uncertainty in LFG is a corollary in TAG. In *Proceedings of the 27th Annual Meeting of the Association for Computational Linguistics*, 220–227. Vancouver.

Joshi, Aravind K., K. Vijay-Shanker, and David Weir (1991). The convergence of mildly context-sensitive grammatical formalisms. In P. Sells, S. Shieber, and T. Wasow (eds.), *Foundational issues in natural language processing*, 31–81. Cambridge, MA: MIT Press.

Julien, Marit (2002). Determiners and word order in Scandinavian DPs. *Studia Linguistica* 56, 265–315.

—— (2005). *Nominal phrases from a Scandinavian perspective*. Amsterdam/Philadelphia: John Benjamins.

Just, Marcel and Patricia Carpenter (1992). A capacity theory of comprehension: Individual differences in working memory. *Psychological Review* 99, 122–149.

Just, Marcel, Patricia Carpenter, Timothy Keller, William Eddy, and Keith Thulborn (1996). Brain activation modulated by sentence comprehension. *Science* 274, 114–116.

Kaan, Edith (2002). Investigating the effects of distance and number interference in processing subject–verb dependencies: An ERP study. *Journal of Psycholinguistic Research* 31, 165–193.

Kaan, Edith, Anthony Harris, Edward Gibson, and Philip Holcomb (2000). The p600 as an index of syntactic integration difficulty. *Language and Cognitive Processes* 15, 159–201.

Kaan, Edith and Tamara Swaab (2002). The brain circuitry of syntactic comprehension. *Trends in Cognitive Sciences* 6, 350–356.

—— (2003). Electrophysiological evidence for serial sentence processing: A comparison between non-preferred and ungrammatical continuations. *Cognitive Brain Research* 17, 621–635.

Kadmon, Nirit (2001). *Formal Pragmatics*. Oxford: Blackwell.

Kadmon, Nirit and Fred Landman (1993). Any. *Linguistics and Philosophy* 16, 353–422.

Kahnemuyipour, Arsalan (2009). *The syntax of sentential stress*. Oxford University Press.

Kallmeyer, Laura and Maribel Romero (2008). Scope and situation binding in LTAG using semantic unification. *Research on Language and Computation* 6, 3–52.

Kam, Xuan-Nga Cao, Iglika Stoyneshka, Lidiya Tornyova, Janet D. Fodor, and William G. Sakas (2008). Bigrams and the richness of the stimulus. *Cognitive Science* 32, 771–787.

Kameyama, Megumi (1985). Zero anaphora: The case of Japanese. PhD dissertation, Stanford University.

Kamp, Hans (1975). Two theories about adjectives. In E. Keenan (ed.), *Formal semantics of natural language*, 123–155. Cambridge University Press.

(1981). A theory of truth and discourse representation. In J. Groenendijk, Th. Janssen, and M. Stockhoff (eds.), *Formal methods in the study of language*, 277–322. Amsterdam: Institute Mathematical Center.

Kamp, Hans and Barbara H. Partee (1995). Prototype theory and compositionality. *Cognition* 57, 121–191.

Kampen, Jacqueline van (1997). First steps in *wh*-movement. PhD dissertation, Utrecht University.

(2009). The 'phased' learnability of long *wh*-questions. In J. Crawford, K. Otaki, and M. Takahashi (eds.), *Proceedings of the 3rd Conference on Generative Approaches to Language Acquisition North America (Galana 2008)*, 127–138. Somerville, MA: Cascadilla Press.

Kandybowicz, Jason and Harold Torrence (2011). Are syntax and prosody entangled? Insights from Krachi *in-situ* interrogatives. Unpublished ms., Swarthmore College and University of Kansas.

Kaplan, Ronald M. and Joan Bresnan (1982). Lexical-functional grammar: A formal system for grammatical representation. In Bresnan (1982a), 173–281.

Kaplan, Ronald M. and Annie Zaenen (1989). Long-distance dependencies, constituent structure, and functional uncertainty. In Baltin and Kroch (1989), 17–42.

Kariaeva, Natalia (2009). Radical discontinuity syntax at the interface. PhD dissertation, Rutgers University.

Karimi, Simin (2008). Raising and control in Persian. In Simin Karimi, Donald Stilo, and Vida Samiian (eds.). *Aspects of Iranian linguistics*, 177–208. Newcastle upon Tyne: Cambridge Scholars.

Kas, Mark (1993). Essays on Boolean functions and negative polarity. PhD thesis, University of Groningen.

Kasper, Robert, Bernd Kiefer, Klaus Netter, and K. Vijay-Shanker (1995). Compilation of HPSG to TAG. In *Proceedings of the 33rd Annual Meeting of the Association for Computational Linguistics*, 92–99. Cambridge, MA.

Kathol, Andreas (2000). *Linear syntax*. Oxford University Press.

Katz, Jerrold J. and Paul M. Postal (1964). *An integrated theory of linguistic descriptions*. Cambridge, MA: MIT Press.

Katz, Jonah and Elisabeth Selkirk (2011). Contrastive focus vs. discourse-new: Evidence from prosodic prominence in English. *Language* 87, 771–816.

Kawasaki, Noriko (1993). Control and arbitrary interpretation in English. PhD dissertation, University of Massachussetts at Amherst.

Kay, Paul and Filmore, Charles J. (1999). Grammatical constructions and linguistic generalizations: The *What's X doing Y?* construction. *Language* 75, 1–33.

Kayne, Richard S. (1969). The transformational cycle in French syntax. PhD dissertation, MIT.

(1975). *French syntax: The transformational cycle*. Cambridge, MA: MIT Press.
(1981). Unambiguous paths. In R. May and J. Koster (eds.), *Levels of syntactic representation*, 143–185. New York: Mouton de Gruyter.
(1984). *Connectedness and binary branching*. Dordrecht: Foris.
(1985). Principles of particle constructions. In J. Guéron, H.-G. Obenauer, and J.-Y. Pollock (eds.), *Grammatical representation*, 101–140. Dordrecht: Foris.
(1989a) Facets of Romance past participle agreement. In Benincà (1989), 85–103.
(1989b). Null subjects and clitic climbing. In O. Jaeggli and K. J. Safir, (eds.), *The null subject parameter*, 239–261. Dordrecht: Reidel.
(1994). *The antisymmetry of syntax*. Cambridge, MA: MIT Press.
(2000a). Person morphemes and reflexives in Italian, French, and related languages. In *Parameters and universals*, 131–162. Oxford University Press.
(2000b). *Parameters and universals*. Oxford University Press.
(2002a). Pronouns and their antecedents. In S. D. Epstein and T. D. Seely (eds.), *Derivation and explanation in the Minimalist Program*, 133–166. Oxford: Blackwell.
(2002b). On some prepositions that look DP-internal: English *of* and French *de*. *Catalan Journal of Linguistics* 1, 71–115.
(2005). Some notes on comparative syntax, with special reference to English and French. In G. Cinque and R. Kayne (eds.), *The Oxford handbook of comparative syntax*, 3–69. Oxford University Press.
Kayne, Richard S. and Jean-Yves Pollock (1978). Stylistic inversion, successive cyclicity, and move NP in French. *Linguistic Inquiry* 9, 595–621.
Keenan, Edward L. (1976). Towards a universal definition of 'subject'. In C. Li (ed.), *Subject and Topic*, 303–333. New York: Academic Press.
(2002). Explaining the creation of reflexive pronouns in English. In D. Minkova and R. Stockwell, *Studies in the history of English: A millennial perspective*, 325–355. Berlin: Mouton de Gruyter.
(2007). On denotations of anaphors. *Research on language and computation* 5, 1–16.
Keenan, Edward L. and Bernard Comrie (1977). Noun phrase accessibility and Universal Grammar. *Linguistic Inquiry* 8, 63–99.
Keenan, Edward L. and Dag Westerståhl (1997). Generalized quantifiers in linguistics and logic. In J. van Benthem and A. ter Meulen (eds.), *Handbook of logic and language*, 837–893. Amsterdam: Elsevier.
Kehler, Andrew (2002). *Coherence, reference, and the theory of grammar*. Stanford, CA: CSLI Publications.
Keine, Stefan (2008). LDA und Zyklisches Agree. Unpublished ms., University of Leipzig.
Keller, Frank (2000). Gradience in grammar: Experimental and computational aspects of grammaticality. PhD thesis, University of Edinburgh.

Kemmer, Suzanne (1993). *The middle voice: A typological and diachronic study.* Amsterdam/Philadelphia: Benjamins.

Kempson, Ruth, Wilfried Meyer-Viol, and Dov Gabbay (1999). VP ellipsis: Toward a dynamic, structural account. In S. Lappin and E. Benmamoun (eds.), *Fragments: Studies in ellipsis and gapping,* 227–289. Oxford University Press.

(2001). *Dynamic syntax: The flow of language understanding.* Oxford: Blackwell.

Kennedy, Christopher (1994). Argument-contained ellipsis. LRC-report, University of California, Santa Cruz.

(1997a). Antecedent-contained deletion and the syntax of quantification. *Linguistic Inquiry* 28, 662–688.

(1997b). Projecting the adjective: The syntax and semantics of gradability and comparison. PhD dissertation, University of California, Santa Cruz.

(1999a). Gradable adjectives denote measure functions, not partial functions. *Studies in the Linguistic Sciences* 29, 65–80.

(1999b). *Projecting the adjective: The syntax and semantics of gradability and comparison.* New York: Garland.

(2002). Comparative deletion and optimality in syntax. *Natural Language and Linguistic Theory* 20, 553–621.

(2003). Ellipsis and syntactic representation. In S. Winkler and K. Schwabe (eds.), *The syntax–semantics interface: Interpreting (omitted) structure,* 29–54. Amsterdam: John Benjamins.

Kennedy, Christopher and Jeffrey Lidz (2001). A (covert) long distance anaphor in English. In K. Megerdoomian and L. A. Bar-El (eds.), *Proceedings of WCCFL 20,* 318–331. Somerville, MA: Cascadilla Press, 2002.

Kennedy, Christopher and Jason Merchant (2000). Attributive comparative deletion. *Natural Language and Linguistic Theory* 18, 89–146.

Kester, Ellen-Petra (1992). Adjectival inflection and dummy affixation in Germanic and Romance languages. In A. Holmberg (ed.), *Papers from the workshop on the Scandinavian noun phrase,* 72–87. University of Umeå.

(1996). *The nature of adjectival inflection.* Utrecht: LEd.

Khalaily, Samir (1995). QR and the Minimalist Theory of syntax: The case of universally and negative quantified expressions in Palestinian Arabic. Unpublished ms., University of Leiden.

Khalilova, Zaira (2007). Clause linkage: Coordination, subordination and cosubordination in Khwarshi. Unpublished ms., Max-Planck Institute for Evolutionary Anthropology, Leipzig.

Kho, Kuan, Peter Indefrey, Peter Hagoort, C. W. M. van Veelen, Peter van Rijen, and Nick Ramsey (2008). Unimpaired sentence comprehension after anterior temporal cortex resection. *Neuropsychologia* 46, 1170–1178.

Kim, Albert and Lee Osterhout (2005). The independence of combinatory semantic processing: Evidence from event-related potentials. *Journal of Memory and Language* 52, 205–225.

Kim, Christina S., Gregory M. Kobele, Jeffrey T. Runner, and John T. Hale (2011). The acceptability cline in VP ellipsis. *Syntax* 14, 318-354.

Kim, Jeong-Seok (1997). Syntactic focus movement and ellipsis: A Minimalist approach. PhD dissertation, University of Connecticut.

(1998). A Minimalist account of gapping in Korean/Japanese. *Studies in Generative Grammar* 8, 105-137.

Kim, Jong-Bok (2000). *The grammar of negation: A constraint-based approach.* Stanford, CA: CSLI Publications.

Kim, Soowon (1999). Sloppy/strict identity, empty objects, and NP ellipsis. *Journal of East Asian Linguistics* 8, 255-284.

Kimball, John (1973). The grammar of existence. In Claudia Corum, C. T. Smith-Stark, and A. Weiser (eds.), *Proceedings of CLS 9*, 262-270. Chicago.

King, Harold (1970). On blocking the rules for contraction in English. *Linguistic Inquiry* 1, 134-136.

King, Jeffrey (1988). Are indefinite descriptions ambiguous? *Philosophical Studies* 53, 417-440.

King, Jonathan and Marcel Just (1991). Individual differences in syntactic processing: The role of working memory. *Journal of Memory and Language* 30, 580-602.

King, Tracy Holloway (1995). *Configuring topic and focus in Russian* (Stanford Dissertations in Linguistics). Stanford, CA: CSLI Publications.

Kinyalolo, Kasangati (1991). Syntactic dependencies and the SPEC-head agreement hypothesis in KiLega. PhD dissertation, UCLA.

Kiparsky, Paul (1988). Agreement and linking theory. Unpublished ms., Stanford University.

(1997). Remarks on denominal verbs. In A. Alsina, J. Bresnan, and P. Sells (eds.), *Complex predicates*, 473-499. Stanford, CA: CSLI Publications.

(2001). Structural case in Finnish. *Lingua* 111, 315-376.

Kirby, Simon (1998). *Function, selection and innateness: The emergence of language universals.* Oxford University Press.

Kirby, Simon and James Hurford (1997). Learning, culture, and evolution in the origin of linguistic constraints. In P. Husbands and H. Inman (eds.), *Proceedings of the Fourth European Conference on Artificial Life*, 493-502. Cambridge, MA: MIT Press.

Kiss, Tibor (2006). On the empirical viability of the movement theory of control. Unpublished ms., Bochum University.

Kitagawa, Yoshi (1986). Subjects in Japanese and English. PhD dissertation, University of Massachusetts, Amherst.

Kitahara, H. (1995). Target α: Deducing strict cyclicity from derivational economy. *Linguistic Inquiry* 26, 47-77.

(1997). *Elementary operation and optimal derivations.* Cambridge, MA: MIT Press.

Klein, Wolfgang (1995). A time-relational analysis of Russian aspect. *Language* 71, 669-695.

Klepp, M. (2001). Partial *wh*-movement in German. PhD dissertation, University College Dublin.

Klima, Edward (1964). Negation in English. In J. Fodor and J. Katz (eds.), *The structure of language*, 246–323. Englewood Cliffs, NJ: Prentice-Hall.

Kluender, Robert (1992). Deriving island constraints from principles of predication. In H. Goodluck and M. Rochemont (eds.), *Island constraints: Theory, acquisition and processing*, 223–258. Dordrecht: Kluwer.

(1998). On the distinction between strong and weak islands: A processing perspective. In Culicover and McNally (1998), 241–279.

Kluender, Robert and Marta Kutas (1993a). Bridging the gap: Evidence from ERPs on the processing of unbounded dependencies. *Journal of Cognitive Neuroscience* 5, 196–214.

(1993b). Subjacency as a processing phenomenon. *Language and Cognitive Processes* 8, 573–633.

Ko, Heejeong (2005a). Syntax of why-in-situ: Merge into [Spec, CP] in the overt syntax. *Natural Language & Linguistic Theory* 23(4): 867–916.

(2005b). Syntactic edges and linearization. PhD dissertation, MIT.

Koch, Karsten (2008). Intonation and focus in Nte?kepmxcin (Thompson River Salish). PhD thesis, University of British Columbia.

Koeneman, Olaf and Hedde Zeijlstra (2010). Resurrecting the Rich Agreement Hypothesis: Weak isn't strong enough. In D.-H. An and S.-Y. Kim (eds.), *Movement in Minimalism. Proceedings of the 12th Seoul Conference on Generative Grammar*.

Koizumi, Masatoshi (1994). Layered specifiers. In M. González (ed.), *Proceedings of the North East Linguistic Society 24*, 255–269. Amherst: GLSA, University of Massachusetts.

(1995). Phrase structure in Minimalist syntax. PhD dissertation, MIT.

Kolk, Herman, Dorothee Chwilla, Marieke van Herten, and Patrick Oor (2003). Structure and limited capacity in verbal working memory: A study with event-related potentials. *Brain and Language* 85, 1–36.

Kolliakou, Dimitra (2004). Monadic definites and polydefinites: Their form, meaning and use. *Journal of Linguistics* 40, 263–333.

König, Ekkehard and Peter Siemund (2000). Intensifiers and reflexives: A typological perspective. In Frajzyngier and Curl (2000a), 41–74.

Koopman, Hilda (1984). *The syntax of verbs: From verb movement rules in the Kru languages to Universal Grammar* (Studies in Generative Grammar 15). Dordrecht: Foris.

(1992). On the absence of Case chains in Bambara. *Natural Language and Linguistic Theory* 10, 555–594.

(1993). The structure of Dutch PPs. Unpublished ms., University of California, Los Angeles.

(2000). Prepositions, postpositions, circumpositions, and particles. In H. Koopman (ed.), *The syntax of specifiers and heads*, 204–260. Routledge: London.

(2005). Agreement configurations: In defense of Spec head. Unpublished ms., UCLA.

Koopman, Hilda and Dominique Sportiche (1989). Pronouns, logical variables and logophoricity in Abe. *Linguistic Inquiry* 20, 555–588.

(1991). The position of subjects. *Lingua* 85, 211–258.

Koopman, Hilda and Anna Szabolcsi (2000). *Verbal complexes*. Cambridge, MA: MIT Press.

Koppen, Marjo van (2005). One probe – two goals: Aspects of agreement in Dutch dialects. PhD dissertation, University of Leiden.

Kornfeld, Laura M. and Andrés L. Saab (2002). Nominal ellipsis and morphological structure in Spanish. In R. Bok-Bennema (ed.), *Romance languages and linguistic theory 2002: Selected papers from Going Romance*, 183–199. Amsterdam: John Benjamins.

Kornfilt, Jaklin (1984). Case marking, agreement, and empty categories in Turkish. PhD dissertation, Harvard University.

(1997). *Turkish*. New York: Routledge.

Koster, Jan (1975). Dutch as an SOV language. *Linguistic Analysis* 1, 111–136.

(1978a). *Locality principles in syntax*. Dordrecht: Foris.

(1978b). Why subject sentences don't exist. In S.J. Keyser (ed.), *Recent transformational studies in European languages*, 53–64. Cambridge, MA: MIT Press.

(1984). On binding and control. *Linguistic Inquiry* 15, 417–459.

(1987). *Domains and dynasties: The radical autonomy of syntax*. Dordrecht: Foris.

(1997). Anaphora and uniformity of grammar. In H. Bennis, P. Pica, and J. Rooryck (eds.), *Atomism and binding*. 235–250. Dordrecht: Foris.

(2003) All languages are tense second. In J. Koster and H. van Riemsdijk (eds.), *Germania et Alia: A Linguistic Webschrift for Hans den Besten* University of Groningen. Available at: http://www.let.rug.nl/~koster/DenBesten/contents.htm.

(2008). A reappraisal of classical V2 and scrambling in Dutch. *Groninger Arbeiten zur germanistischen Linguistik* 46, 27–54.

Kounios, J. and P.J. Holcomb (1992). Structure and process in semantic memory: Evidence from event-related brain potentials and reaction times. *Journal of Experimental Psychology: General* 121, 459–479.

Kratzer, Angelika (1995). Stage-level and individual-level predicates. In G. Carlson and F. Pelletier (eds.), *The generic book*, 125–175. Chicago University Press.

(1996). Severing the external argument from its verb. In J. Rooryck, and L. Zaring (eds.), *Phrase structure and the lexicon*, 109–138. Dordrecht: Kluwer.

(2004). Telicity and the meaning of objective case. In Guéron and Lecarme (2004), 398–425.

(2009). Making a pronoun: Fake indexicals as windows into the properties of pronouns. *Linguistic Inquiry* 40, 187–237.

Kratzer, Angelika and Elisabeth Selkirk (2007). Phase theory and prosodic spellout: The case of verbs. *The Linguistic Review* 24, 93–135.

Kratzer, Angelika and Junko Shimoyama (2002). Indeterminate phrases: The view from Japanese. In Y. Otsu (ed.), *Proceedings of the Third Tokyo Conference on Psycholinguistics*, 1–25. Tokyo: Hituzi Syobo.

Krifka, Manfred (1987). Nominal reference and temporal constitution: Towards a semantics of quantity. In J.J. Groenendijk, M. Stokhof, and F. Veltman (eds.), *Proceedings of the 6th Amsterdam Colloquium*, 153–173. Institute of Linguistics, Logic and Information, University of Amsterdam.

(1989). Nominal reference and temporal constitution and quantification in event semantics. In P. van Emde Boos, R. Bartsch and J. van Benthem (eds.), *Semantics and contextual expression*, 75–115. Dordrecht: Foris.

(1991/1992). A compositional semantics for multiple focus constructions. In Jacobs (1991/2a), 17–53.

(1992a). Focus, quantification and dynamic interpretation. Unpublished ms., University of Texas at Austin.

(1992b). Thematic relations and links between nominal reference and temporal constitution. In I.A. Sag and A. Szabolcsi (eds.), *Lexical matters*, 29–53. Stanford, CA: CSLI Publications.

(1995). The semantics and pragmatics of polarity items in assertion. *Linguistic Analysis* 15, 209–257.

(2001). Quantifying into question acts. *Natural Language Semantics* 9, 1–40.

(2006). Association with focus phrases. In V. Molnár and S. Winkler (eds.), *The architecture of focus*, 105–136. Berlin/New York: Mouton de Gruyter.

(2008). Basic notions of information structure. *Acta Linguistica Hungarica* 55, 243–276.

Kroch, Anthony (1987). Unbounded dependencies and subjacency in a tree adjoining grammar. In A. Manaster-Ramer (ed.), *The mathematics of language*, 143–172. Amsterdam: John Benjamins.

(1989a). Amount quantification, referentiality and long *wh*-movement. Unpublished ms., University of Pennsylvania.

(1989b). Asymmetries in long distance extraction in a tree adjoining grammar. In Baltin and Kroch (1989), 66–98.

(2001). Syntactic change. In Baltin and Collins (2001), 699–729.

Kroch, Anthony and Aravind K. Joshi (1985). The linguistic relevance of tree adjoining grammar (Technical Report MS-CS-85-16). Department of Computer and Information Sciences, University of Pennsylvania.

(1987). Analyzing extraposition in a tree adjoining grammar. In Huck and Ojeda (1987), 107–149.

Kroch, Anthony and Beatrice Santorini (1991). The derived constituent structure of the West Germanic verb raising construction. In R. Freidin (ed.), *Principles and parameters in comparative grammar*, 269–338. Cambridge, MA: MIT Press.

Kroeger, Paul (1993). *Phrase structure and grammatical relations in Tagalog* (Dissertations in Linguistics). Stanford, CA: CSLI Publications.

(2004). *Analyzing syntax: A Lexical-functional approach*. Cambridge University Press.

Kučerová, Ivona (2007). The syntax of givenness. PhD dissertation, MIT.

Kuno, Susumu (1972). Functional sentence perspective: A case study from Japanese and English. *Linguistic Inquiry* 3, 269–320.

(1973a). Constraints on internal clauses and sentential subjects. *Linguistic Inquiry* 4, 363–385.

(1973b). *The structure of the Japanese language*. Cambridge, MA: MIT Press.

(1987). *Functional syntax*. University of Chicago Press.

Kuno, Susumu and Jane Robinson (1972). Multiple *wh*-questions. *Linguistic Inquiry* 3, 463–487.

Kuperberg, Gina (2007). Neural mechanisms of language comprehension: Challenges to syntax. *Brain Research* 1146, 23–49.

Kuperberg, Gina, David Caplan, Tatiana Sitnikova, Marianna Eddy, and Phillip Holcomb (2006). Neural correlates of processing syntactic, semantic, and thematic relationships in sentences. *Language and Cognitive Processes* 21, 489–530.

Kuperberg, Gina, Donna Kreher, Tatiana Sitnikova, David Caplan, and Phillip Holcomb (2007). The role of animacy and thematic relationships in processing active English sentences: Evidence from event-related potentials. *Brain and Language* 100, 223–237.

Kuperberg, Gina, Tatiana Sitnikova, David Caplan, and Phillip Holcomb (2003). Electrophysiological distinctions in processing conceptual relationships within simple sentences. *Cognitive Brain Research* 17, 117–129.

Kuroda, Sige-Yuki (1965). Generative grammatical studies in the Japanese language. PhD dissertation, MIT.

(1988). Whether we agree or not. Paper presented at *The Second International Workshop on Japanese syntax*. Stanford.

Kutas, Marta and Kara D. Federmeier (2000). Electrophysiology reveals semantic memory use in language comprehension. *Trends in Cognitive Sciences* 4, 463–470.

Kutas, Marta and S. Hillyard (1980). Event-related brain potentials to semantically inappropriate and surprisingly large words. *Biological Psychology* 11, 99–116.

Kutas, Marta, Cyma van Petten, and Robert Kluender (2006). Psycholinguistics electrified ii: 1994–2005. In M. Traxler and M.A. Gernsbacher (eds.), *Handbook of psycholinguistics*, 2nd edn, 659–724. New York: Elsevier.

Labov, William (1969). Contraction, deletion, and inherent variability of the English copula. *Language* 45, 715–762.

(1972). *Sociolinguistic patterns*. Philadelphia: University of Pennsylvania Press.

Laca, Brenda (2005). Périphrases aspectuelles et temps grammatical dans les langues romanes. In H. Bat-Zeev Shyldkrot and N. Le Querler (eds.), *Les periphrases verbales* (Lingvisticae Investigationes Supplementa 25), 47–66. Amsterdam/Philadelphia: John Benjamins.

Ladd, Robert D. (1980). *The structure of intonational meaning.* Bloomington: Indiana University Press.

(1983). 'Even', focus and normal stress. *Journal of Semantics* 2, 157–170.

(1996). *Intonational phonology.* Cambridge University Press.

Ladusaw, William A. (1979). *Polarity sensitivity as inherent scope relations.* New York: Garland Publishing.

(1988). A proposed distinction between levels and strata. In S.-D. Kim (ed.), *Linguistics in the morning calm* 2, 37–51. Seoul: Hanshin.

(1992). Expressing negation. In C. Barker and D. Dowty (eds.), *SALT II*, 237–259. Ithaca, NY: Cornell Linguistic Circle.

(1996). Negation and Polarity Items. In S. Lappin (ed.), *The handbook of contemporary semantic theory*, 321–341. Oxford: Blackwell.

Laenzlinger, Christopher (1998). *Comparative studies in word order variation: Adverbs, pronouns and clause structure in Romance and Germanic.* Amsterdam: John Benjamins.

(2005). French adjective ordering: Perspectives on DP-internal movement types. *Lingua* 15, 645–689.

Lahiri, Utpal (1998). Focus and negative polarity in Hindi. *Natural Language Semantics* 6, 57–23.

Lahne, Antje (2008). Where there is fire there is smoke. Local modelling of successive-cyclic movement. PhD dissertation, University of Leipzig.

Laka, Itziar (1990). Negation in syntax: On the nature of functional categories and projections. PhD dissertation, MIT.

Lakoff, George (1970). Global rules. *Language* 46, 627–639.

(1971). On generative semantics. In D. D. Steinberg and L. A. Jakobovits (eds.), *Semantics: An interdisciplinary reader in philosophy, linguistics and psychology*, 232–296. Cambridge University Press.

(1986). Frame semantic control of the coordinate structure constraint. *Chicago Linguistic Society*, 22, 152–167.

Lamarche, Jacques (1991). Problems for N^0-movement to Num-P. *Probus* 3, 215–236.

Lambrecht, Knud (1994). *Information structure.* Cambridge University Press.

Lamers, Monique (2005). Resolving subject–object ambiguities with and without case: Evidence from ERPs. In M. Amberber and H. de Hoop (eds.), *Competition and variation in natural languages: The case for case* 251–293. Amsterdam: Elsevier.

Landau, Idan (2001). *Elements of control: Structure and meaning in infinitival constructions.* Dordrecht: Kluwer.

(2003). Movement out of control. *Linguistic Inquiry* 34, 471–498.

(2004). The scale of finiteness and the calculus of control. *Natural Language and Linguistic Theory* 22, 811–877.

(2006). Severing the distribution of PRO from Case. *Syntax* 9, 153–170.

(2007a). EPP extensions. *Linguistic Inquiry* 38, 485–523.

(2007b). Movement-resistant aspects of control. In W. D. Davies and S. Dubinsky (eds.), *New horizons in the analysis of control and raising*, 293–325. Dordrecht: Springer.

(2008). Two routes of control: Evidence from case transmission in Russian. *Natural Language and Linguistic Theory* 26, 877–924.

(2009). Predication vs. aboutness in copy raising. Unpublished ms., lingBuzz/000835.

(2011). Predication vs. aboutness in copy raising. *Natural Language and Linguistic Theory* 29, 779–813.

Landman, Fred (2004). *Indefinites and the type of sets*. Oxford: Wiley-Blackwell.

Lang, Ewald, Claudia Maienborn, and Cathrine Fabricius-Hansen (eds.) 2003. *Modifying adjuncts*. Berlin: Mouton de Gruyter.

Langacker, Ronald W. (1987). *Foundations of Cognitive Grammar. Vol. 1: Theoretical prerequisites*. Stanford University Press.

(1995). Raising and transparency. *Language* 71, 1–62.

Lapointe, Stephen (1980). A theory of grammatical agreement. PhD dissertation. University of Massachusetts at Amherst.

Lappin, Shalom (1984). Predication and raising. In C. Jones and P. Sells (eds.), *Proceedings of NELS 14*, 236–252. Amherst, MA: GLSA.

(1992). The syntactic basis of ellipsis resolution. In S. Berman and A. Hestvik (eds.), *Proceedings of the Stuttgart Ellipsis Workshop* (Arbeitspapiere des Sonderforschungsbereichs 340, Bericht No. 29-1992). Universitaet Stuttgart.

(1996). The interpretation of ellipsis. In S. Lappin (ed.), *The handbook of contemporary semantic theory*, 145–175. Oxford: Blackwell.

Larson, Richard K. (1985). Bare NP-adverbs. *Linguistic Inquiry* 16, 595–621.

(1987). Missing prepositions and the analysis of English free relatives. *Linguistic Inquiry* 18, 239–266.

(1988a). On the double object construction. *Linguistic Inquiry* 19, 335–391.

(1988b). Scope and comparatives. *Linguistics and Philosophy* 11, 1–26.

(1990). Extraction and multiple selection in PP. *The Linguistic Review* 7, 169–182.

(1991a). *The projection of DP (and DegP)*. SUNY–Stony Brook. [Published as *The Projection of DP (and DegP)*. In Larson (2013)].

(1991b). Promise and the theory of control. *Linguistic Inquiry* 21, 103–139.

(1998). Events and modification in nominals. In D. Strolovitch and A. Lawson (eds.), *Proceedings from Semantics and Linguistic Theory (SALT) VIII*, 145–168. Ithaca, NY: Cornell University.

(2003). Time and event measure. In J. Hawthorne, and D. Zimmerman (eds.), *Philosophical perspectives 17: Language and philosophical linguistics*, 247–258. Oxford University Press.

(2013). *On shell structure*. Oxford: Routledge.

Larson, Richard K. and Franc Marušič (2004). On indefinite pronoun structures with APs: Reply to Kishimoto. *Linguistic Inquiry* 35, 268-287.

Larson, Richard K. and Gabriel Segal (1995). *Knowledge of meaning*. Cambridge, MA: Bradford Books, MIT Press.

Lasnik, Howard (1975). On the semantics of negation. In D. J. Hockney (ed.), *Contemporary research in philosophical logic and linguistic semantics*, 279-311. Dordrecht: Reidel.

(1976). Remarks on coreference. *Linguistic Analysis* 2, 1-22.

(1981a). On two recent treatments of disjoint reference. *Journal of Linguistic Research* 1, 39-53. [Reprinted in Lasnik (1989), 125-133.]

(1981b). Restricting the theory of transformations. In N. Hornstein and D. Lightfoot (eds.), *Explanation in linguistics*, 152-173. London: Longmans.

(1989). *Essays on anaphora*. Dordrecht: Kluwer.

(1995). Case and expletives revisited: On greed and other human failings. *Linguistic Inquiry* 26, 615-634.

(1999a). *Minimalist analysis*. Oxford: Blackwell.

(1999b). Pseudogapping puzzles. In S. Lappin and E. Benmamoun (eds.), *Fragments: Studies in ellipsis and gapping*, 141-174. Oxford University Press.

(1999c). On feature strength: Three Minimalist approaches to overt movement. *Linguistic Inquiry* 30, 197-217.

(1999d). Chains of arguments. In S. D. Epstein and N. Hornstein (eds), *Working Minimalism*, 189-215. Cambridge, MA: MIT Press.

(2000). *Syntactic Structures revisited: Contemporary lectures on classic transformational theory*. Cambridge, MA: MIT Press.

(2001a). When can you save a structure by destroying it? In M. Kim and U. Strauss (eds.), *Proceedings of the North East Linguistic Society 31*, 301-320. Amherst, MA: GLSA.

(2001b). Derivation and representation in modern transformational syntax. In Baltin and Collins (2001), 62-88.

(2002). The Minimalist Program in syntax. *Trends in Cognitive Sciences* 6, 432-437.

(2006). Conceptions of the cycle. In L. Cheng and N. Corver (eds.), *Wh-movement moving on* 197-216. Cambridge, MA: MIT Press.

(to appear). Multiple sluicing in English? *Syntax*, 7-24.

Lasnik, Howard and Stephen Crain (1985). On the acquisition of pronominal reference. *Lingua* 65, 135-154.

Lasnik, Howard and Robert Fiengo (1974). Complement object deletion. *Linguistic Inquiry* 5, 535-572.

Lasnik, Howard and Joseph J. Kupin (1977). A restrictive theory of transformational grammar. *Theoretical Linguistics* 4, 173-196.

Lasnik, Howard and Terje Lohndal (2010). Government-Binding/Principles & Parameters Theory. *Wiley Interdisciplinary Reviews: Cognitive Science* 1, 40-50.

Lasnik, Howard and Mamoru Saito (1984). On the nature of proper government. *Linguistic Inquiry* 15, 235-290.

(1991). On the subject of infinitives. In L. M. Dobrin, L. Nichols, and R. M. Rodriguez (eds.), *Papers from the 27th Regional Meeting of the Chicago Linguistic Society Part One: The General Session*, 324–343. Chicago Linguistic Society, University of Chicago.

(1992). *Move α: Conditions on its application and output.* Cambridge, MA: MIT Press.

(1999). On the subject of infinitives. In Lasnik (1999a), 7–24.

Lau, Ellen F., Diogo Almeida, Paul C. Hines, and David Poeppel (2009). A lexical basis for n400 context effects: Evidence from Meg. *Brain and Language* 111, 161–172.

Lau, Ellen F., Colin Phillips, and David Poeppel (2008). A cortical network for semantics: (De)constructing the n400. *Nature Reviews Neuroscience* 9, 920–933.

Lau, Ellen F., Clare Stroud, Silke Plesch, and Colin Phillips (2006). The role of structural prediction in rapid syntactic analysis. *Brain and Language* 98, 74–88.

Launey, Michel (1981). *Introduction á la langue et á la litterature azteques*, vol. 1. Paris: L'Harmattan.

Lebeaux, David (1984a). Anaphoric binding and the definition of PRO. *Northeastern Linguistic Society* 14, 253–274.

(1984b). Locality and anaphoric binding. *The Linguistic Review* 4, 343–363.

(1988). Language acquisition and the form of grammar. PhD dissertation, University of Massachusetts at Amherst.

(1998). Where does Binding Theory apply? Princeton: Technical Report of the NEC Research Institute.

(2009). *Where does Binding Theory apply?* Cambridge, MA: MIT Press.

Lecarme, Jacqueline (1996). Tense in the nominal system: The Somali DP. In J. Lecarme, J. Lowenstamm, and U. Shlonsky (eds.), *Studies in Afroasiatic grammar: Papers from the 2nd Conference on Afroasiatic Languages, Sophia Antipolis 1994.* The Hague: Holland Academic Graphics. [Available at: www.llf.cnrs.fr/fr/Lecarme/]

(1999). Nominal tense and tense theory. In F. Corblin, C. Dobrovie-Sorin, and J.-M. Marandin, (eds.), *Empirical issues in formal syntax and semantics 2: Selected papers from the Colloque de Syntaxe et Sémantique à Paris (CSSP).* The Hague: Holland Academic Graphics. [Available at: http://www.llf.cnrs.fr/fr/Lecarme/]

(2004). Tense in nominals. In J. Guéron and J. Lecarme (eds.), *The syntax of time*, 440–475. Cambridge, MA: MIT Press.

(2008). Tense and modality in nominals. In Guéron and Lecarme (2008), 195–225.

Lechner, Winfried (1999). Comparatives and DP-structure. PhD dissertation, University of Massachusetts, Amherst.

(2001). Reduced and phrasal comparatives. *Natural Language and Linguistic Theory* 19, 683–735.

(2004). *Ellipsis in comparatives.* Berlin: Mouton de Gruyter.

Lee, Chia-lin and Kara Federmeier (2006). To mind the mind: An event-related potential study of word class and semantic ambiguity. *Brain Research* 1081, 191–202.

Lee, Felicia (2003). Anaphoric R-expressions as bound variables. *Syntax* 6, 84–114.

Lees, Robert B. (1961). Grammatical analysis of the English comparative construction. *Word* 17, 171–185.

(1963). *The grammar of English nominalizations*. The Hague: Mouton.

Lees, Robert B. and Edward S. Klima (1963). Rules for English pronominalization. *Language* 39, 17–28.

Lee-Schoenfeld, Vera (2004). Binding by phase: (Non)complementarity in German. *Journal of Germanic Linguistics* 16, 111–173.

Legate, Julie Anne (2002). The hows of *wh*-scope marking in Warlpiri. In M. Kadowaki and S. Kawahara (eds.), *Proceedings of the North Eastern Linguistic Society 33*. Boston: MIT.

(2003). Some interface properties of the phase. *Linguistic Inquiry* 34, 506–516.

(2005). Phases and cyclic agreement. *MIT Working Papers in Linguistics* 49, 147–156.

(2006). Split absolutive. In A. Johns, D. Massam, and J. Ndayiragije (eds.), *Ergativity: Emerging issues*, 143–171. Dordrecht: Kluwer.

(2008). Morphological and abstract case. *Linguisitic Inquiry* 39, 55–102.

Legate, Julie Anne and Charles Yang (2007). Morphosyntactic learning and the development of tense. *Language Acquisition* 14, 315–344.

Legendre, Geraldine (2006). Early child grammars: Qualitative and quantitative analysis of morphosyntactic production. *Cognitive Science* 30, 803–835.

Legendre, Geraldine, Paul Hagstrom, Joan Chen-Main, Liang Tao, and Paul Smolensky (2004). Deriving output probabilities in child Mandarin from a dual-optimization grammar. *Lingua* 114, 1147–1185.

Legendre, Geraldine, Yoshiro Miyata, and Pual Smolensky (1990). Can connectionism contribute to syntax? Harmonic Grammar, with an application. In M. Ziolkowski, M. Noske, and K. Deaton (eds.), *Proceedings of the 26th Meeting of the Chicago Linguistic Society*, 237–252. Chicago: Chicago Linguistic Society.

Lekakou, Marika (2005). In the middle, somewhat elevated: The semantics of middles and its crosslinguistic realization. PhD thesis, University of London.

Lenerz, Jürgen (1977). *Zur Abfolge nominaler Satzglieder im Deutschen*. Tübingen: Narr.

Leu, Thomas (2008). The internal syntax of determiners. PhD thesis, New York University. [*Groninger Arbeiten zur Germanistischen Linguistik* 47, Center for Language and Cognition Groningen. Available at: Ghttp://gagl.eldoc.ub.rug.nl.]

Levi, Judith (1978). *The syntax and semantics of complex nominals*. New York: Academic Press.

Levin, Beth (1993). *Verb classes in English*. Cambridge, MA: MIT Press.
Levin, Beth and Malka Rappaport (1998). Building verb meanings. In M. Butt and W. Geuder (eds.), *The projection of arguments: Lexical and compositional factors*, 97–134. Stanford, CA: CSLI publications.
Levin, Beth and Malka Rappaport Hovav (1995). *Unaccusativity: At the syntax–lexical semantics interface*. Cambridge, MA: MIT Press.
(2005). *Argument realization* (Research Surveys in Linguistics). Cambridge University Press.
Levin, Nancy (1978). Some identity-of-sense deletions puzzle me. Do they you? In D. Farkas, W. M. Jacobsen, and K. W. Todrys (eds.), *Proceedings of the Fourteenth Annual Meeting of the Chicago Linguistic Society*, 229–240. Chicago: Chicago Linguistic Society.
(1979). Main verb ellipsis in spoken English. PhD dissertation, Ohio State University.
Levine, Robert D. and Thomas Hukari (2006). *The unity of unbounded dependency constructions* (CSLI Lecture Notes 166). Stanford, CA: CSLI Publications.
Levinson, Stephen (1987). Pragmatics and the grammar of anaphora: A partial pragmatic reduction of binding and control phenomena. *Journal of Linguistics* 23, 379–434.
(1991). Pragmatic reduction of the binding conditions revisited. *Journal of Linguistics* 27, 107–162.
Levy, Roger (2008). Expectation-based syntactic comprehension. *Cognition* 106, 1126–1177.
Lewis, David (1975). Adverbs of quantification. In E. Keenan (ed.), *Formal semantics of natural language*, 3–15. Cambridge University Press.
(1979). Attitudes *de dicto* and *de se*. *Philosophical Review* 88, 513–554.
Li, Charles and Sandra Thompson (1976). Subject and topic: A new typology of language. In C. N. Li (ed.), *Subject and topic*, 457–489. New York: Academic Press.
Li, Hui-Ju Grace (1998). Null object and VP ellipsis in Chinese. I Hua Lin (ed.), *Proceedings of the 9th North American Conference on Chinese Linguistics, Vol. 1: Syntax, Semantics and Discourse*, 155–172. Los Angeles: GSIL Publications, University of Southern California.
(2002) Ellipsis constructions in Chinese. PhD dissertation, University of Southern California.
Li, Yen-Hui Audrey (1990). *Order and constituency in Mandarin Chinese*. Dordrecht: Kluwer Academic Publishers.
Liberman, Mark Y. and Janet Pierrehumbert (1984). Intonational invariance under changes in pitch range and length. In M. Aronoff and R. T. Oehrle (eds.), *Language sound structure*, 157–233. Cambridge, MA: MIT Press.
Liberman, Mark Y. and Alan Prince (1977). On stress and linguistic rhythm. *Linguistic Inquiry* 8, 249–336.
Lichtenberk, Frantisek (2000). Reciprocals without reflexives. In Z. Frajzyngier and T. S. Curl (eds.), *Reciprocals: Forms and functions*, 31–62. Amsterdam/Philadelphia: John Benjamins.

Lidz, Jeffrey (1995). Morphological reflexive-marking: Evidence from Kannada. *Linguistic Inquiry* 26, 705–710.
  (2001a). The argument structure of verbal reflexives. *Natural Language and Linguistic Theory* 19, 311–353.
  (2001b). Condition R. *Linguistic Inquiry* 32, 123–140.
  (2001c). Anti-antilocality. In Cole, Hermon, and Huang (2001), 226–254.
Lieven, Elena (2009). Developing constructions. *Cognitive Linguistics* 20, 191–199.
Lieven Elena and Michael Tomasello (2008). Children's first language acquisition from a usage-based perspective. In P. Robinson and N. Ellis (eds.), *Handbook of cognitive linguistics and second language acquisition*, 168–196. New York: Routledge.
Lightfoot, David (1989). The child's trigger experience: Degree-0 learnability. *Behavioral and Brain Sciences* 12, 321–334.
  (1991). *How to set parameters: Arguments from language change*. Cambridge, MA: MIT Press.
  (1999). *The development of language: Acquisition, change and evolution*. Oxford: Blackwell.
  (2006). *How new languages emerge*. Cambridge University Press.
Lin, Jo-Wang (1996). Polarity licensing and *wh*-phrase quantification in Chinese. PhD dissertation, University of Massachusetts, Amherst.
Lin, Vivian (2002). Coordination and sharing at the interfaces. PhD dissertation, MIT.
Linebarger, Marcia (1980). *The grammar of negative polarity*. PhD thesis. MIT.
  (1987). Negative polarity and grammatical representation. *Linguistics and Philosophy* 10, 325–387.
Liu, Feng-Hsi (1990). Scope and dependency in English and in Chinese. PhD thesis, UCLA.
Lobeck, Anne (1991). The phrase structure of ellipsis. In S. Rothstein (ed.), *Perspectives on phrase structure*, 81–103. San Diego: Academic Press.
  (1995). *Ellipsis: Functional heads, licensing and ellipsis*. Oxford University Press.
Löbel, Elisabeth (2001). Classifiers and semi-lexicality: Functional and semantic selection. In Corver and van Riemsdijk (2001), 223–272.
Lohndal, Terje (2012). Towards the end of argument structure. In M. C. Cuervo and Y. Roberge (eds.), *The end of argument structure?*, 156–184. Bingley: Emerald.
Lohndal, Terje and Juan Uriagereka (2010). The logic of parametric theories. *Theoretical Linguistics* 36, 69–76.
Longobardi, Giuseppe (1984). Connectedness and island constraints. In J. Guéron, H.-G. Obenauer, and J.-Y. Pollock (eds), *Grammatical representation*, 161–85. Dordrecht: Foris.
  (1994). Reference and proper names: A theory of N-movement in syntax and Logical Form. *Linguistic Inquiry* 25, 609–665.
  (2001). The structure of DPs: Some principles, parameters and problems. In Baltin and Collins (2001), 562–601.

(2003). Methods in parametric linguistics and cognitive history. *Linguistic Variation Yearbook* 3, 101–38.

(2005). Toward a unified grammar of reference. *Zeitschrift für Sprachwissenschaft* 24, 5–44.

López, Luis (1995). Polarity and predicate anaphora. PhD dissertation, Cornell University.

(2009). *A derivational syntax for information structure* (Oxford Studies in Theoretical Linguistics 23). Oxford University Press.

Lorimer, David L. R. (1935). *The Burushaski language 1: Introduction and grammar*, vol. 1. Cambridge, MA: Harvard University Press.

Lötscher, Andreas (1972). Some problems concerning Standard German relative clauses. In P. M. Peranteau, J. N. Levi, and G. C. Phares (eds.), *The Chicago which hunt. Papers From the Relative Clause Festival*, 47–58. Chicago, IL: Chicago Linguistics Society.

Luce, Duncan, Robert Bush, and Eugene Galanter (eds.) (1965). *Readings in mathematical psychology 2*. New York: Wiley and Sons.

Luck, Steven J. (2005). *An introduction to the event-related potential technique*. Cambridge, MA: MIT Press.

Ludlow, Peter (2005). A note on alleged cases of nonsentential assertion. In R. Elugardo and R. Stainton (eds.), *Ellipsis and non-sentential speech*, 95–108. Dordrecht: Springer.

Lutz, Uli, Gereon Müller, and Arnim von Stechow (eds.) (2000). *Wh-scope marking*. Amsterdam: John Benjamins.

Lyons, Christopher (1995). Voice, aspect and arbitrary arguments. In J. Smith and M. Maiden (eds.), *Linguistic theory and the Romance languages*, 77–114. Amsterdam: John Benjamins.

Lyons, John (1968). *Introduction to theoretical linguistics*. Cambridge University Press.

MacDonald, Jonathan (2008). *The syntactic nature of inner aspect: A Minimalist perspective*. Amsterdam: John Benjamins.

MacDonald, Maryellen, Marcel Just, and Patricia Carpenter (1992). Working memory constraints on the processing of syntactic ambiguity. *Cognitive Psychology* 24, 56–98.

MacDonald, Maryellen, Neal Pearlmutter, and Mark Seidenberg (1994). Lexical nature of syntactic ambiguity resolution. *Psychological Review* 191, 676–703.

Madigan, Sean (2009). Control constructions in Korean. PhD dissertation, University of Delaware.

Mahajan, Anoop (1990). The A/A-bar distinction and movement theory. PhD thesis, MIT.

(1991). Clitic doubling, object agreement and specificity. *NELS* 21, 263–277.

(1994). The ergativity parameter: *have-be* alternation, word order and split ergativity. In M. Gonzalez (ed.), *Proceedings of North Eastern Linguistic Society* 24, 317–331. Amherst, MA: GSLA.

(2000). Towards a unified treatment of *wh*-expletives in Hindi and German. In Lutz, Müller, and von Stechow (2000), 317–332.

Maienborn, Claudia and Martin Schäfer (2011). Adverbs and adverbials. In C. Maienborn, K. von Heusinger, and P. Portner (eds.), *Semantics. An international handbook of natural language meaning: Vol. 1* (Handbook of Linguistics and Communication Science), 1390–1420. Berlin/New York: Mouton de Gruyter.

Makihara, Hideo (2005). On the past tense in Japanese relative clauses. PhD dissertation, University of Washington, Seattle.

Makuuchi, Michiru, Jörg Bahlmann, Alfred Anwander, and Angela Friederici (2009). Segregating the core computational faculty of human language from working memory. *Proceedings of the National Academy of Sciences* 106, 8362–8367.

Maling, Joan (1983). Transitive adjectives: A case of categorial reanalysis. In F. Heny and B. Richards (eds.), *Linguistic categories: Auxiliaries and related puzzles, Vol. 1*, 253–289. Dordrecht: Reidel.

(2001). Dative: The heterogeneity of mapping among morphological case, grammatical functions, and thematic roles. *Lingua* 111, 419–464.

(2002). Verbs with dative objects in Icelandic. *Íslenskt m'al* 24: 31–105.

Maling, Joan and Annie Zaenen (eds.) (1990). *Syntax and semantics 24: Modern Icelandic syntax*. San Diego: Academic Press.

Manaster-Ramer, Alexis and Michael B. Kac (1990). The concept of phrase structure. *Linguistics and Philosophy* 13, 325–362.

Manning, Christopher D. (1996). *Ergativity: Argument structure and grammatical relations* (Dissertations in Linguistics). Stanford, CA: CSLI Publications.

(2003). Probabilistic syntax. In Bod, Hay, and Jannedy (2003), 289–342.

Manning, Christopher D. and Ivan A. Sag (1999). Dissociations between argument structure and grammatical relations. In G. Webelhuth, J.-P. Koenig, and A. Kathol (eds.), *Lexical and constructional aspects of linguistic explanation*, 63–78. Stanford, CA: CSLI, Publications.

Manzini, Maria Rita (1983). On control and control theory. *Linguistic Inquiry* 14, 421–446.

(1986). On control and binding theory. *Northeastern Linguistic Society* 16, 322–337.

(1992). *Locality: A theory and some of its empirical consequences*. Cambridge, MA: MIT Press.

(1994). Locality, Minimalism, and parasitic gaps. *Linguistic Inquiry* 25, 481–508.

Manzini, Maria Rita and Anna Roussou (2000). A Minimalist theory of A-movement and control. *Lingua* 110, 409–447.

Manzini, Maria Rita and Leonardo Savoia (2005). *I dialetti italiani e romanci*. Alessandria: Edizioni dell'Orso.

Manzini, Maria Rita and Kenneth Wexler (1987). Parameters, binding, and learning theory. *Linguistic Inquiry* 18, 413–444.

Marácz, László (1989). Asymmetries in Hungarian. PhD dissertation, University of Groningen.
Marantz, Alec (1984). *On the nature of grammatical relations*, (Linguistic Inquiry Monographs 10). Cambridge, MA: MIT Press.
(1991). Case and licensing. Paper presented at *The 8th Eastern States Conference on Linguistics*, University of Maryland, Baltimore.
(1993). Implications of asymmetries in double object constructions. In S. Mchombo (ed.), *Aspects of Bantu grammar 1*, 113–150. Stanford, CA: CSLI, Publications.
(1997). No escape from syntax: Don't try morphological analysis in the privacy of your own lexicon. In A. Dimitriadis and L. Siegel (eds.), *Proceedings of the 21st Annual Penn Linguistics Colloquium* (University of Pennsylvania Working Papers in Linguistics), 201–225. Philadelphia: University of Pennsylvania.
Marchis, Mihaela and Artemis Alexiadou (2008). On the distribution of adjectives in Romanian: The *cel* construction. In E. Aboh, E. van der Linden, J. Quer, and P. Sleeman (eds.), *Romance languages and linguistic theory: Selected papers from 'Going Romance' Amsterdam 2007*, 161–178. Amsterdam: John Benjamins.
Markman, Ellen (1990). Constraints children place on word meanings. *Cognitive Science* 14, 57–77.
Markman, Vita (2009). On the parametric variation of case and agreement. *Natural Language and Linguistic Theory* 27, 379–426.
Marr, David (1982). *Vision: A computational investigation into the human representation and processing of visual information*. Cambridge, MA: MIT Press.
Martí-Girbau, Núria (2010). The syntax of partitives. PhD dissertation, Universitat Autònoma de Barcelona.
Martin, Alex (2007). The representation of object concepts in the brain. *Annual Review of Psychology* 58, 25–45.
Martin, Roger (1992). On the distribution and case features of PRO. Unpublished ms., University of Connecticut.
(1996). A Minimalist theory of PRO and control. PhD dissertation, University of Connecticut.
(2001). Null Case and the distribution of PRO. *Linguistic Inquiry* 32, 141–166.
Martins, Anna-Maria (1994). Enclisis, VP-deletion and the nature of Sigma. *Probus* 6, 173–205.
Marušič, Franc (2005). On non-simultaneous phases. PhD dissertation, SUNY, Stony Brook.
Massam, Diane (2009). The morpho-syntax of tense particles in Niuean. In F. Mailhot (ed.), *Proceedings of the 2009 Annual Conference of the Canadian Linguistics Association*.
Masullo, Pascual José and Marcela A. Depiante (2004). Variable vs. intrinsic features in Spanish nominal ellipsis. Unublished ms., University of Pittsburgh and Universidad de Comahue.
Matthews, George Hubert (1965). *Hidatsa syntax*. The Hague: Mouton.

Matthewson, Lisa (1998). *Determiner systems and quantificational strategies. Evidence from Salish* (Worlds' theses 1). The Hague: Holland Academic Graphics.

Matushansky, Ora (2003). DPs and Phase theory. Handout UiL OTS, 30 January 2003.

Matushansky, Ora and Benjamin Spector (2005). Tinker, tailor, soldier, spy. In E. Maier, C. Bary, and J. Huitink (eds.), *Proceedings of Sinn und Bedeutung 9* (9th Sinn und Bedeutung conference of the Gesellschaft für Semantik, NCS), 241-255. Nijmegen.: Radboud University. Available at: http://www.ru.nl/ncs/sub9.

May, Robert (1977). The grammar of quantification. PhD thesis, MIT.

—— (1985). *Logical Form: Its structure and derivation*. Cambridge, MA: MIT Press.

Mazoyer, B. M., N. Tzourio, V. Frak, A. Syrota, N. Murayama, O. Levrier, G. Salamon, S. Dehaene, L. Cohen, and J. Mehler (1993). The cortical representation of speech. *Journal of Cognitive Neuroscience* 5, 467-479.

McCarthy, John (2007). *Hidden generalizations: Phonological opacity in Optimality Theory*. London: Equinox Publications.

—— (2008). The serial interaction of stress and syncope. *Natural Language and Linguistic Theory* 26, 499-546.

McCarthy, John and Alan Prince (1993). Prosodic morphology: Constraint interaction and satisfaction. Unpublished ms., University of Massachusetts and Amherst/Rutgers University. Available at: http://roa.rutgers.edu/files/482-1201/482-1201-MCCARTHY-0-1.PDF.

McCawley, James D. (1968a). Concerning the base component of a transformational grammar. *Foundations of Language* 4, 243-269.

—— (1968b). The role of semantics in a grammar. I E. Bach and R. T. Harms (eds.), *Universals in linguistic theory*, 124-169. New York: Holt, Rinehart and Winston.

—— (1981). The syntax and semantics of English relative clauses. *Lingua* 53, 99-149.

—— (1982). Parentheticals and discontinuous constituent structure. *Linguistic Inquiry* 13, 91-106.

—— (1988). Adverbial NPs: Bare or clad in see-through garb. *Language* 64, 583-590.

—— (1989). Individuation in and of syntactic structures. In Baltin and Kroch (1989), 117-138.

—— (1991). Contrastive negation and metalinguistic negation. In L. Dobrin, L. Nichols, and R. Rodriguez (eds.), *The parasession on negation* (CLS 27), 189-206. Chicago, IL: Chicago Linguistic Society.

McCloskey, James (1979). *Transformational syntax and model theoretic semantics: A case-study in Modern Irish*. Dordrecht/Boston: D. Reidel.

—— (1991). Clause structure, ellipsis and proper government in Irish. *Lingua* 85, 259-302.

(1992). Adjunction, selection and embedded verb second (Working Paper LRC-92-07). Santa Cruz: Linguistics Research Center, University of California.

(1996). On the scope of verb movement in Irish. *Natural Language and Linguistic Theory* 14, 47–104.

(2000). Quantifier float and *wh*-movement in an Irish English. *Linguistic Inquiry* 31, 57–84.

(2001). The morphosyntax of *wh*-extraction in Irish. *Journal of Linguistics* 37, 67–100.

(2002). Resumption, successive cyclicity, and the locality of operations. In S. D. Epstein and T. D. Seely (eds.), *Derivation and explanation in the Minimalist Program*, 184–226. Oxford: Blackwell.

(2004). A note on predicates and heads in Irish clausal syntax. In A. Carnie, H. Harley, and S. A. Dooley (eds.), *Verb first. On the syntax of verb-initial languages*, 155–174. Amsterdam/Philadelphia: John Benjamins Publishing Company.

McClure, William (1994). Syntactic projections of the semantics of aspect. PhD thesis, Cornell University.

McConnell-Ginet, Sally (1982). Adverbs and logical form: A linguistically realistic theory. *Language* 58, 144–184.

McDaniel, Dana (1989). Partial and multiple *wh*-movement. *Natural Language and Linguistic Theory* 7, 565–604.

McFadden, Thomas (2004). The position of morphological case in the derivation. PhD dissertation, University of Pennsylvania.

Mchombo, Sam (2004). *The syntax of Chichewa*. Cambridge University Press.

McKinnon, Richard and Lee Osterhout (1996). Constraints on movement phenomena in sentence processing: Evidence from event-related brain potentials. *Language and Cognitive Processes* 11, 495–524.

McKoon, Gail, Roger Ratcliff, and Gregory Ward (1994). Testing theories of language processing: An empirical investigation of the on-line lexical decision task. *Journal of Experimental Psychology: Learning, Memory, and Cognition* 20, 1219–1228.

McNally, Louise and Christopher Kennedy (eds.) (2008). *Adjectives and adverbs: Syntax, semantics, and discourse*. Oxford University Press.

Mehl, Matthias R., Simine Vazire, Nairán Ramirez-Esparza, Richard B. Slatcher, and James W. Pennebaker (2007). Are women really more talkative than men? *Science* 317, 82.

Menendez-Benito, Paula (2005). *The grammar of choice*. PhD dissertation, University of Massachusetts, Amherst.

Merchant, Jason (1998). 'Pseudosluicing': Elliptical clefts in Japanese and English. In A. Alexiadou, N. Fuhrhop, P. Law, and U. Kleinhenz (eds.), *ZAS Working Papers in Linguistics* 10, 88–112. Berlin: Zentrum für Allgemeine Sprachwissenschaft.

(2000a). Economy, the copy theory, and antecedent-contained deletion. *Linguistic Inquiry* 31, 566–575.

(2000b). Antecedent-contained deletion in negative polarity items. *Syntax* 3, 144–150.

(2001). *The syntax of silence. Sluicing, islands and the theory of ellipsis*. Oxford University Press.

(2002). Swiping in Germanic. In C. J.-W. Zwart and W. Abraham (eds.), *Studies in comparative Germanic syntax*, 289–315. Amsterdam: John Benjamins.

(2004). Fragments and ellipsis. *Linguistics and Philosophy* 27, 661–738.

(2006). Why no(t)? *Style* 20, 20–23.

(2007). *Voice and ellipsis*. Unpublished ms., University of Chicago.

(2008a). An asymmetry in voice mismatches in VP-ellipsis and pseudo-gapping. *Linguistic Inquiry* 39, 169–179.

(2008b). Variable island repair under ellipsis. In K. Johnson (ed.), *Topics in ellipsis*, 132–153. Cambridge University Press.

(2009a). Ellipsis. In A. Alexiadou, T. Kiss, and M. Butt (eds.), *Handbook of contemporary syntax*, 2nd edn. Berlin: Walter de Gruyter.

(2009b). Phrasal and clausal comparatives in Greek and the abstractness of syntax. *Journal of Greek Linguistics* 9, 134–164.

(2011). Not all (elided) genders are equal: Evidence from nominal ellipsis in greek. Unpublished ms., University of Chicago.

(to appear a). Diagnosing ellipsis. In L. Cheng and N. Corver (eds.), *Diagnosing syntax*. Oxford University Press.

(to appear b). Polarity items under ellipsis. In L. Cheng and N. Corver (eds.), *Diagnosing syntax*. Oxford University Press.

Meyer, Martin, Angela Friederici, and D. Yves von Cramon (2000). Neurocognition of auditory sentence comprehension: Event related fMRI reveals sensitivity to syntactic violations and task demands. *Cognitive Brain Research* 9, 19–33.

Michaelis, Jens and Marcus Kracht (1997). Semilinearity as a syntactic invariant. In C. Retoré (ed.), *Logical aspects of computational linguistics* (Lecture Notes in Computer Science 1328), 329–345. New York: Springer.

Miestamo, M. (2005). *Standard negation. The negation of declarative verbal main clauses in a typological perspective* (Empirical Approaches to Language Typology 31). Berlin: Mouton de Gruyter.

Mikkelsen, Line (2002). Specification is not inverted predication. In M. Hirotani (ed.), *Proceedings of NELS 32*, 403–422. Amherst, MA: GLSA.

(2004). Specifying who: On the structure, meaning, and use of specificational copular clauses. PhD thesis, University of California at Santa Cruz.

(2005). *Copular clauses: Specification, predication and equation* (Linguistik Aktuell 85). Amsterdam: John Benjamins.

(2011). On prosody and focus in object shift. *Syntax* 14, 230–264.

Miller, George A. (1956). The magical number seven, plus or minus two: Some limits on our capacity for processing information. *The Psychological Review* 63, 81–97.

Miller, Jim and Regina Weinert (1998). *Spontaneous spoken language: Syntax and discourse*. Oxford: Clarendon.
Miyagawa, Shigeru (1989). *Structure and case marking in Japanese*. San Diego: Academic Press, Inc.
Mohanan, K. P. (1983). Functional and anaphoric control. *Linguistic Inquiry* 14, 641-674.
Mohanan, Tara (1994). *Argument structure in Hindi* (Dissertations in Linguistics). Stanford, CA: CSLI Publications.
  (1995). Wordhood and lexicality: Noun incorporation in Hindi. *Natural Language and Linguistic Theory* 13, 75-134.
Monachesi, Paola (1999). *A lexical approach to Italian cliticization*. Stanford, CA: CSLI Publications.
Montague, Richard (1970). Universal grammar. *Theoria* 36, 373-398.
  (1973). The proper treatment of quantification in ordinary English. In K. Hintikka, J. Moravcsik, and P. Suppes (eds.), *Approaches to natural language*, 221-242. Dordrecht: Reidel.
  (1974). *Formal philosophy: Selected papers of Richard Montague*, R. H. Thomason (ed). New Haven: Yale University Press.
Morgan, Jerry (1973). Sentence fragments and the notion 'sentence'. In B. Kachru, R. B. Lees, Y. Malkiel, A. Pietrangeli, and S. Saporta (eds.), *Issues in linguistics*, 719-751. Urbana: University of Illinois Press.
  (1989). Sentence fragments revisited. In B. Music, R. Graczyk, and C. Wiltshire (eds.), *CLS 25, parasession on language in context*, 228-241. , Chicago: Chicago Linguistic Society.
Moro, Andrea (1988). Per una teoria unificata delle frasi copulari. *Rivista di Grammatica Generativa* 13, 81-110.
  (1990). *There*-raising: Principles across levels. Paper presented at the 13th GLOW Colloquium, Cambridge, England.
  (1991). The raising of predicates: Copula, expletives and existence. In L. L. S. Cheng and H. Demirdash (eds.), *MIT working papers in linguistics* 15, 183-218. Cambridge, MA: MIT.
  (1997). *The raising of predicates: Predicative noun phrases and the theory of clause structure*. Cambridge University Press.
  (2000). *Dynamic antisymmetry*. Cambridge, MA: MIT Press.
  (2009). Rethinking symmetry: A note on labelling and the EPP. *Snippets* 19, 17-18. Available at: http://ling.auf.net/lingBuzz/000635.
Mortensen, David (2003). Two kinds of variable elements in Hmong anaphora. Unpublished ms., UC Berkeley.
Moscati, Vincenzo (2010). *The scope of negation*. Cambridge: Cambridge Scholars Press.
Mountcastle, Vernon B. (1997). The columnar organization of the neocortex. *Brain* 120, 701-722.
Müller, Gereon (2000). Shape conservation and remnant movement. In A. Hirotani, N. Hall Coetzee, and J.-Y. Kim (eds.), *Proceedings of NELS 30*, 525-539. Amherst, MA: GLSA.

(2001). Order preservation, parallel movement, and the emergence of the unmarked. In G. Legendre, J. Grimshaw, and S. Vikner (eds.), *Optimality-theoretic syntax* (MITWPL), 113–142. Cambridge, MA/London: MIT Press.

(2004a). Phrase impenetrability and *wh*-intervention. In A. Stepanov, G. Fanselow, and R. Vogel (eds.), *Minimality effects in syntax*, 289–325. Berlin: de Gruyter.

(2004b). Verb-second as vP-first. *Journal of Comparative Germanic Linguistics* 7, 197–234.

(2006). *Deriving MLC effects*. Unpublished ms., University of Leipzig.

(2010). On deriving CED effects from the PIC. *Linguistic Inquiry* 41, 35–82.

Müller, Gereon and Wolfgang Sternefeld (1993). Improper movement and unambiguous binding. *Linguistic Inquiry* 24, 461–507.

(eds.) (2001). *Competition in Syntax* (Studies in Generative Grammar 49). Berlin/New York: de Gruyter.

Müller, Oliver and Peter Hagoort (2006). Access to lexical information in language comprehension: Semantics before syntax. *Journal of Cognitive Neuroscience* 18, 84–96.

Müller, Stefan (1999). *Deutsche Syntax deklarativ. Head-Driven Phrase Structure Grammar für das Deutsche* (Volume Linguistische Arbeiten). Tübingen: Niemeyer.

(2002). *Complex predicates: Verbal complexes, resultative constructions, and particle verbs in German* (Studies in Constraint-Based Lexicalism 13). Stanford, CA: CSLI Publications

(2004). Continuous or discontinuous constituents? A comparison between syntactic analyses for constituent order and their processing systems. *Research on Language and Computation* 2, 209–257.

(2010). *Grammatiktheorie* (in Stauffenburg Einführungen 20). Tübingen: Stauffenburg Verlag.

Mummery, C. J., K. Patterson, R. J. S. Wise, R. Vandenbergh, C. J. Price, and J. R. Hodges (1999). Disrupted temporal lobe connections in semantic dementia. *Brain* 122, 61–73.

Munn, Alan (1993). *Topics in the syntax and semantics of coordinate structures*. PhD dissertation, University of Maryland, College Park.

Münte, Thomas and Hans-Jochen Heinze (1994). ERP negativities during syntactic processing of written words. In H. J. Heinze, T. F. Münte, and H. R. Mangun (eds.), *Cognitive electrophysiology*, 211–238. La Jolla, CA: Birkhauser.

Münte, Thomas, Mike Matzke, and Sönke Johannes (1997). Brain activity associated with syntactic incongruencies in words and pseudo-words. *Journal of Cognitive Neuroscience* 9, 318–329.

Murasugi, Keiko (1992). *NP-movement and the ergative parameter*. PhD dissertation, MIT.

Musan, Renate (1999). Temporal interpretation and information-status of noun phrases. *Linguistics and Philosophy* 22, 621–661.

Musolino, Julien, Stephen Crain, and Rosalind Thornton (2000). Navigating negative semantic space. *Linguistics* 38, 1–32.

Mutaka, Ngessimo and Ken Safir (2007). Kinande anaphora sketch. In *Afranaph Project Website*, edited by Ken Safir, at http://www.africananaphora.rutgers.edu/.

Muysken, Pieter (1983). Parametrizing the notion 'head'. *Journal of Linguistic Research* 2, 57–75.

—— (2008). *Functional categories*. Cambridge University Press.

Muysken, Pieter and Henk van Riemsdijk (1986). Projecting features and featuring projections. In. P. Muysken and H. van Riemsdijk (eds.), *Features and projections*, 1–30. Dordrecht: Foris.

Namai, Kenichi (1997). The multiple subject construction in Japanese. PhD thesis, Georgetown University.

Napoli, Donna Jo (1988). Subjects and external arguments: Clauses and non-clauses. *Linguistics and Philosophy* 11, 323–354.

—— (1989). *Predication: A case study for indexing theory* (Cambridge Studies in Linguistics 59). Cambridge University Press.

Nedjalkov, Vladimir (2007). *Reciprocal constructions* (Typological Studies in Language 71). Amsterdam: Benjamins.

Neeleman, Ad (1994a). Complex predicates. PhD thesis, Utrecht University.

—— (1994b). Scrambling as a D-structure phenomenon. In Corver and van Riemsdijk (1994), 387–430.

Neeleman, Ad and Hans van de Koot (2002). The configurational matrix. *Linguistic Inquiry* 33, 529–574.

Neeleman, Ad, Hans van de Koot, and Jenny Doetjes (2004). Degree expressions. *The Linguistic Review* 21, 1–66.

Neeleman, Ad and Tanya Reinhart (1998). Scrambling and the PF interface. In M. Butt and W. Geuder (eds.), *The projection of arguments*, 309–353. Stanford, CA: CSLI Publications.

Neijt, Anneke (1979). *Gapping: A contribution to sentence grammar*. Dordrecht: Foris.

Nespor, Marina and Irene B. Vogel (1986). *Prosodic phonology*. Dordrecht: Foris.

Neville, Helen, Janet Nicol, Andrew Barss, Kenneth Forster, and Merrill Garrett (1991). Syntactically based sentence processing classes: Evidence from event-related brain potentials. *Journal of Cognitive Neuroscience* 3, 151–165.

Nevins, Andrew (2010). Multiple Agree with clitics: Person complementarity vs. omnivorous number. Unpublished ms., University College London.

Newmeyer, Frederick J. (1983). *Grammatical theory: Its limits and its possibilities*. University of Chicago Press.

—— (1991). Functional explanation in linguistics and the origins of language. *Language and Communication* 11, 3–28.

(2004). Against a parameter-setting approach to typological variation. In P. Pica, J. Rooryck, and J. van Craenenbroek (eds.), *Language variation yearbook, Vol. 4*, 181–234. Amsterdam: John Benjamins.

(2005). *Possible and probable languages. A generative perspective on linguistic typology.* Oxford University Press.

(2006). Negation and modularity. In B. Birner and G. Ward, *Drawing the boundaries of meaning: Neo-Gricean studies in pragmatics and semantics in honor of Laurence R. Horn*, 247–268. Amsterdam: Benjamins.

(2010a). What conversational English tells us about the nature of grammar: A critique of Thompson's analysis of object complements. In K. Boye and E. Engberg-Pedersen (eds.), *Usage and structure: A festschrift for Peter Harder*, 3–43. Berlin: Mouton de Gruyter.

(2010b). Accounting for rare typological features in formal syntax: Three strategies and some general remarks. In M. Cysouw and J. Wolgemuth (eds.), *Rethinking universals: How rarities affect linguistic theory*, 195–222. Berlin: Mouton de Gruyter.

Ngonyani, Deo (1996). VP ellipsis in Ndendeule and Swahili applicatives. In E. Garrett and F. Lee (eds.), *Syntax at sunset: UCLA working papers in syntax and semantics*, 1, 109–128.

Nichols, Johanna (1986). Head-marking and dependent-marking grammar. *Language* 62, 56–119.

Nicol, Janet, Janet Dean Fodor, and David Swinney (1994). Using cross-modal lexical decision tasks to investigate sentence processing. *Journal of Experimental Psychology: Learning, Memory, and Cognition* 20, 1–10.

Nicol, Janet and David Swinney (1989). The role of structure in coreference assignment during sentence comprehension. *Journal of Psycholinguistic Research* 18, 5–19.

Nida, Eugene A. (1966). *A synopsis of English grammar.* The Hague: Mouton.

Nieuwland, Mante, and Jos van Berkum (2006). When peanuts fall in love: N400 evidence for the power of discourse. *Journal of Cognitive Neuroscience* 18, 1098–1111.

Nilsen, Øystein (1998). The syntax of circumstantial adverbials. MA thesis, University of Tromsø.

(2003). Eliminating positions: Syntax and semantics of sentential modification. PhD disseration, Universiteit Utrecht.

(2004). Domains for adverbs. *Lingua* 114, 809–847.

Nishigauchi, Taisuke (1986). Quantification in syntax. PhD dissertation, University of Massachusetts, Amherst.

Nishigauchi, Taisuke and Thomas Roeper (1987). Deductive parameters and the growth of empty categories. In Roeper and Williams (1987), 91–122.

Nishiyama, Kunio (1999). Adjectives and the copula in Japanese. *Journal of East Asian Linguistics* 8, 183–222.

Nissenbaum, Jon (1998). Movement and derived predicates: Evidence from parasitic gaps. In U. Sauerland and O. Percus (eds.), *The interpretive tract*

(MIT Working Papers in Linguistics 25), 247-295. Cambridge, MA: MIT Press.

(2000). Investigations of covert phrase movement. PhD dissertation, MIT.

Noonan, Máire (2010). À to ZU. In Cinque and Rizzi (2010b), 161-195.

Noppeney, U., K. Patterson, L. K. Tyler, H. E. Moss, E. A. Stamatakis, P. Bright, C. Mummery, and C. J. Price (2007). Temporal lobe lesions and semantic impairment: A comparison of herpes simplex virus encephalitis and semantic dementia. *Brain* 130, 1138-1147.

Nordlinger, Rachel (1998). *Constructive case: Evidence from Australian languages* (Stanford Dissertations in Linguistics). Stanford, CA: CSLI Publications.

Nordlinger, Rachel and Louisa Sadler (2004). Nominal tense in cross-linguistic perspective. *Language* 80, 776-806.

(2008). When is a temporal marker not a tense? Reply to Tonhauser 2007. *Language* 84, 325-331.

Notley, Anna, Peng Zhou, Britta Jensen and Stephen Crain (in press). Children's interpretation of disjunction in the scope of 'before': A comparison of English and Mandarin. *Journal of Child Language*.

Nunes, Jairo (1995). The copy theory of movement and linearization of chains in the Minimalist Program. PhD dissertation, University of Maryland.

(2004). *Linearization of chains and sideward movement*. Cambridge, MA: MIT Press.

Nunes, Jairo and Juan Uriagereka (2000). Cyclicity and extraction domains. *Syntax* 3, 20-43.

Nunes, Jairo and Cynthia Zocca (2005). Morphological identity in ellipsis. In *Leiden working papers in linguistics 2.2*, 29-42. Leiden University.

(2010). Lack of morphological identity and ellipsis resolution in Brazilian Portuguese. In Jairo Nunes (ed.), *Minimalist essays on Brazilian Portuguese syntax*, 215-236. Amsterdam: John Benjamins.

Nunez, Paul and Ramesh Srinivasan (2006). *Electric fields of the brain: The neurophysics of EEG*. Oxford University Press.

O'Grady, William (1998). The syntax of idioms. *Natural Language and Linguistic Theory* 16, 279-312.

O'Neill, James (1995). Out of control. In J. N. Beckman (ed.), *Proceedings of the 25th Annual Meeting of the North East Linguistic Society*, 361-371. Amherst, MA: GLSA.

Obata, Miki (2010). Root, successive-cyclic and feature-splitting internal merge: Implications for feature-inheritance and transfer. PhD dissertation, University of Michigan.

Obenauer, Hans-Georg (1984). On the identification of empty categories. *The Linguistic Review* 4, 153-202.

(1994). Aspects de la Syntaxe A'. PhD thesis, University of Paris 8.

Oehrle, Richard (1976). The grammatical status of the English dative alternation. PhD thesis, MIT.

Ogihara, Toshiyuki (1995). The semantics of tense in embedded clauses. *Linguistic Inquiry* 26, 663–679.

(1996). *Tense, attitudes and scope*. Dordrecht: Kluwer.

(2007). Tense and aspect in truth-conditional semantics. *Lingua* 117, 392–418.

Oosthuizen, Johan (1998). The final nie in Afrikaans negative sentences. *Stellenbosch Papers in Linguistics* 31, 61–93.

Orgun, C. Orhan (1996). Sign-based morphology and phonology: With special attention to Optimality Theory. PhD thesis, University of California, Berkeley.

Ortiz de Urbina, Jon (1989). *Parameters in the grammar of Basque*. Dordrecht: Foris.

Osterhout, Lee (1999). A superficial resemblance does not necessarily mean you are part of the family: Counterarguments to Coulson, King and Kutas (1998) in the p600/sps-p300 debate. *Language and Cognitive Processes* 14, 1–14.

Osterhout, Lee and Phillip Holcomb (1992). Event-related brain potentials elicited by syntactic anomaly. *Journal of Memory and Language* 31, 785–806.

Osterhout, Lee, Phillip Holcomb, and David Swinney (1994). Brain potentials elicited by garden-path sentences: Evidence of the application of verb information during parsing. *Journal of Experimental Psychology: Learning, Memory, and Cognition* 20, 786–803.

Osterhout, Lee and Linda Mobley (1995). Event-related brain potentials elicited by failure to agree. *Journal of Memory and Language* 34, 739–773.

Osterhout, Lee and Janet Nicol (1999). On the distinctiveness, independence, and time course of the brain responses to syntactic and semantic anomalies. *Language and Cognitive Processes* 14, 283–317.

Otani, Kazuyo and John Whitman (1991). V-raising and VP-ellipsis. *Linguistic Inquiry* 22, 345–358.

Ouali, H. (2005). Negation and negative polarity items in Berber. In M. Ettlinger, N. Fleisher, and M. Park-Doob (eds.), *Proceedings of the Thirtieth Annual Meeting of the Berkeley Linguistics Society*, 330–340. Berkeley Linguistics Society.

Ouhalla, Jamal (1991a). *Functional categories and parametric variation*. London/New York: Routledge.

(1991b). Functional categories and the head parameter. Paper presented at the 14th GLOW Colloquium, Leiden.

Øvrelid, Lilja (2004). Disambiguation of syntactic functions in Norwegian: Modeling variation in word order interpretations conditioned by animacy and definiteness. In F. Karlsson (ed.), *Proceedings of the 20th Scandinavian Conference of Linguistics*, xx–xxx. University of Helsinki.

Paardekooper, Piet Cornelis (1961). Persoonsvorm en Voegwoord. *Nieuwe Taalgids* 54, 296–301.

Pak, Marjorie (2008). The postsyntactic derivation and its phonological reflexes. PhD dissertation, University of Pennsylvania.

Palmer, Frank (2001). *Mood and modality*, 2nd edn. Cambridge University Press.

Panagiotidis, Phoevos (2003a). *One*, empty nouns and θ-assignment. *Linguistic Inquiry* 34, 281–292.

(2003b). Empty nouns. *Natural Language and Linguistic Theory* 12, 381–432.

Pantcheva, Marina (2006). Persian preposition classes. In P. Svenonius (ed.), *Nord lyd: Tromsø Working Papers in Linguistics* 33, 1–25. Tromsø: CASTL.

Panther, Klaus-Uwe (1993). *Kontrollphänomene im Englischen und Deutschen aus Semantisch-pragmatisher Perspektive*. Tübingen: Narr.

Park, So-Young (2008). Functional categories: The syntax of DP and DegP. PhD dissertation, USC.

Parsons, Terence (1990). *Events in the semantics of English: A study in subatomic semantics*. Cambridge, MA: MIT Press.

Partee, Barbara H. (1973). Some structural analogies between tenses and pronouns in English. *Journal of Philosophy* 70, 601–609.

(1986). Ambiguous pseudoclefts with unambiguous *be*. In S. Berman, J.-W. Choe, and J. McDonough (eds.), *Proceedings of NELS 16*, 354–366. Amherst, MA: GLSA.

(1987). Noun phrase interpretation and type-shifting principles. In J. Groenendijk, D. de Jongh, and M. Stokhof (eds.), *Studies in discourse representation theory and the theory of generalized quantifiers* (Groningen-Amsterdam Studies in Semantics 5), 115–143. Dordrecht: Foris.

(1999). Copula inversion puzzles in English and Russian. In K. Dziwirek, H. Coats, and C. M. Vakareliyska (eds.), *Annual Workshop on Formal Approaches to Slavic Linguistics: The Seattle Meeting, 1998*, 361–395. Ann Arbor: Michigan Slavic Publications.

Partee, Barbara H. and Mats Rooth (1983). Generalized conjunction and type ambiguity. In R. Bauerle, C. Schwarze, and A. von Stechow (eds.), *Meaning, use and interpretation of language*, 361–383. Berlin: de Gruyter.

Patterson, Karalyn, Peter Nestor, and Timothy Rogers (2007). Where do you know what you know? The representation of semantic knowledge in the human brain. *Nature Reviews Neuroscience* 8, 976–987.

Paul, Ileana (2005). Or, *wh*- and not: Free choice and polarity in Malagasy. *French Studies Publications* 78. Available at http://ir.lib.uwo.ca/frenchpub/78

Payne, John (1985). Negation. In T. Shopen (ed.), *Language typology and syntactic description. Vol. I: Clause structure*, 197–242. Cambridge University Press.

Pearce, Elizabeth (1999). Topic and Focus in a head-initial language: Maori. In C. Smallwood and C. Kitto, *Proceedings of AFLA vi. The Sixth Meeting of the Austronesian Formal Linguistics Association, held at the University of Toronto April 16–18, 1999*, pp. 249–263. University of Toronto Working Papers in Linguistics.

Penka, Doris (2007). Negative indefintes. PhD dissertation, Tübingen University.
Penka, Doris and Hedde Zeijlstra (2010). Negation and polarity: An introduction. *Natural Language and Linguistic Theory* 28, 771–786.
Pereltsvaig, Asya (2007). *Copular sentences in Russian: A theory of intra-clausal relations.* (Studies in Natural Language and Linguistic Theory 70). Dordrecht: Springer.
Perlmutter, David M. (1968). Deep and surface constraints in syntax. PhD dissertation, MIT.
 (1970). The two verbs *begin*. In R. Jacobs, and P. Rosenbaum (eds.). *Readings in English transformational grammar*, 107–119. Waltham, MA: Blaisdell.
 (1972). Evidence for shadow pronouns in French relativization. In P. M. Peranteau, J. N. Levi, and G. C. Phares (eds.), *The Chicago which hunt: Papers from the relative clause festival*, 73–105. Chicago Linguistic Society.
 (1978). Impersonal passives and the unaccusative hypothesis. In J. J. Jaeger, A. C. Woodbury, F. Ackerman, C. Chiarello, O. D. Gensler, J. Kingston, E. E. Sweetser, H. Thompson, and K. W. Whitler (eds.), *Proceedings of the Fourth Annual Meeting of the Berkeley Linguistics Society*, 157–189. Berkeley: Berkeley Linguistics Society.
 (1980). Relational grammar. In E. A. Moravcsik and J. R. Wirth (eds.), *Syntax and semantics Vol. 13: Current approaches to syntax*, 195–229. New York: Academic Press.
Perlmutter, David M. and Paul M. Postal (1984). The 1-advancement exclusiveness law. In D. M. Perlmutter and C. A. Rosen (eds.), *Studies in relational grammar 2*, 81–128. Chicago University Press.
Perlmutter, David and Scott Soames (1979). *Syntactic argumentation and the structure of English*. Berkeley, CA: University of California Press.
Pesetsky, David (1982a) Complementizer-trace phenomena and the nominative island condition. *The Linguistic Review* 1, 297–343.
 (1982b). Paths and categories. PhD dissertation, MIT.
 (1985). Morphology and lexical form. *The Linguistic Inquiry* 16, 193–246.
 (1987). Wh-in-situ: Movement and unselective binding. In E. Reuland and A. ter Meulen (eds.), *The representation of (in)definiteness*, 98–129. Cambridge, MA: MIT Press.
 (1991). Zero syntax: vol. 2: Infinitives. Unpublished ms., MIT.
 (1995). *Zero syntax: Experiencers and cascades*. Cambridge, MA: MIT Press.
 (1997). Optimality Theory and syntax: Movement and pronunciation. In Archangeli and Langendoen (1997), 134–170.
 (1998). Some optimality principles of sentence pronunciation. In P. Barbosa, D. Fox, P. Hagstrom, M. McGinnis, and D. Pesetsky (eds.), *Is the best good enough?*, 337–383. Cambridge, MA/London: MIT Press/ MITWPL.
 (2000). *Phrasal movement and its kin*. Cambridge, MA: MIT Press.

Pesetsky, David and Esther Torrego (2001). T-to-C movement: Causes and consequences. In M. Kenstowicz (ed.), *Ken Hale: A life in language*, 355–426. Cambridge, MA: MIT Press.

(2004). Tense, case, and the nature of syntactic categories. In Guéron and Lecarme (2004), 495–537.

(2007). The syntax of valuation and the interpretability of features. In S. Karimi, V. Samiian, and W. Wilkins (eds.), *Phrasal and clausal architecture: Syntactic derivation and interpretation. In honor of Joseph E. Emonds*, 262–294. Amsterdam: John Benjamins.

Peters, P. Stanley and Robert W. Ritchie (1973). On the generative power of transformational grammars. *Information Sciences* 6, 49–83.

Petten, Cyma van, Seana Coulson, Susan Rubin, Elena Plante, and Marjorie Parks (1999). Time course of word identification and semantic integration in spoken language. *Journal of Experimental Psychology: Learning, Memory, and Cognition* 25, 394–417.

Petter, Marga (1998). *Getting PRO under control*. The Hague: Holland Academics Graphics.

Phillips, Colin (2006). The real-time status of island phenomena. *Language* 82, 795–823.

Phillips, Colin, Nina Kazanina, and Shani Abada (2005). ERP effects of the processing of syntactic long-distance dependencies. *Cognitive Brain Research* 22, 407–428.

Phillips, Colin and Shevaun Lewis (2012). Derivational order in syntax: Evidence and architectural consequences. In C. Chesi (ed.), *Directions in derivations*. Amsterdam: Elsevier.

Pica, Pierre (1984). Liage et contiguïté. In J. C. Milner (ed.), *Actes de la table ronde sur l'anaphore* (Cahiers de l'ERA 642). Paris: Université de Paris VII.

(1986). De quelques implications théoriques de l'étude des relations à longue distance. In M. Ronat and D. Couquaux, *La grammaire modulaire*, 187–209. Paris: Minuit.

(1987). On the nature of the reflexivization cycle. In *The Proceedings of NELS 17*, 483–499. Amherst: GLSA.

(1991). Antecedent government and binding: The case of long distance reflexivization. In J. Koster and E. Reuland *Long-distance anaphora*, 119–135. Cambridge University Press.

Picallo, Carme (1991). Nominals and nominalization in Catalan. *Probus* 3, 279–316.

Pierrehumbert, Janet (1980). The phonology and phonetics of English intonation. PhD thesis, MIT.

Pike, Kenneth L. (1943). Taxemes and immediate constituents. *Language* 19, 65–82.

Pinker, Steven (1984). *Language learnability and language development*. Cambridge, MA: Harvard University Press.

(1989). *Learnability and cognition: The acquisition of argument structure*. Cambridge, MA: MIT Press.

Pinker, Steven and Paul Bloom (1990). Natural language and natural selection. *Behavioral and Brain Sciences* 13, 707–784.
Plann, Susan (1982). Indirect questions in Spanish. *Linguistic Inquiry* 13, 297–312.
Platzack, Christer (1987). The Scandinavian languages and the null subject parameter. *Natural Language and Linguistic Theory* 5, 377–401.
Plessis, Hans du (1977). Wh-movement in Afrikaans. *Linguistic Inquiry* 8, 723–726.
Poletto, Cecilia (2000). *The higher functional field in the Northern Italian dialects.* Oxford University Press.
 (2008). *On negation splitting and doubling.* University of Venice – CNR Padua.
Poletto, Cecilia and Jean-Yves, Pollock (2001). On the left periphery of Romance interrogatives. Unpublished ms., Universities of Amiens and Padua.
 (2004). On *wh*-clitics, *wh*-doubling in French and some North-Eastern Italian dialects. *Probus* 16, 241–272.
Polinsky, Maria (2003). Non-canonical agreement is canonical. *Transactions of the Philological Society* 101, 279–312.
Polinsky, Maria and Eric Potsdam (2001). Long-distance agreement and topic in Tsez. *Natural Language and Linguistic Theory* 19, 583–646.
 (2002). Backward control. *Linguistic Inquiry* 33, 245–282.
 (2006). Expanding the scope of control and raising. *Syntax* 9, 171–192.
Pollard, Carl (1984). Generalized Phrase Structure Grammars, Head Grammars and natural language. PhD thesis, Stanford.
 (2005). Remarks on binding theory. In S. Müller (ed.). *Proceedings of the 12th International Conference on Head-Driven Phrase Structure Grammar (HPSG-2005)*, 561–577. Stanford, CA: CSLI Publications.
Pollard, Carl and Ivan A. Sag (1987). *Information-based syntax and semantics.* Stanford, CA: CSLI Publications.
 (1992). Anaphors in English and the scope of Binding Theory. *Linguistic Inquiry* 23, 261–303.
 (1994). *Head-driven Phrase Structure Grammar.* University of Chicago Press.
Pollock, Jean-Yves (1989). Verb movement, Universal Grammar and the structure of IP. *Linguistic Inquiry* 20, 365–424.
 (1993). *Notes on clause structure.* Unpublished ms., Université de Picardie, Amiens.
Poser, William J. (1996). Noun classification in Carrier. Paper presented at the winter meeting of the Society for the Study of the Indigenous Languages of the Americas, San Diego, California.
Post, Emil L. (1943). Formal reductions of the general combinatorial decision problem. *American Journal of Mathematics* 65, 197–215.
 (1944). Recursively enumerable sets of positive integers and their decision problems. *Bulletin AMS* 50, 284–316.

(1947). Recursive unsolvability of a problem of Thue. *Journal of Symbolic Logic* 12, 1–11.
Postal, Paul M. (1969). On so-called 'pronouns' in English. In D. Reibel and S. Schane (eds.), *Modern studies in English*, 201–244. Englewood Cliffs, NJ: Prentice-Hall.
(1970). On coreferential complement subject deletion. *Linguistic Inquiry* 1, 439–500.
(1971). *Cross-over phenomena*. New York: Holt, Rinehart and Winston.
(1972). The best theory. S. Peters (ed.), *Goals of linguistic theory*, 131–170. Englewood Cliffs, NJ: Prentice-Hall.
(1974). *On raising: One rule of English grammar and its theoretical implications.* Cambridge, MA: MIT Press.
(1998). *Three investigations of extraction*. Cambridge, MA: MIT Press.
(2000). *An introduction to the grammar of* squat. Unpublished ms., NYU.
(2001). Parasitic and pseudoparasitic gaps. In P. Culicover and P. Postal (eds.), *Parasitic gaps*, 253–313. Cambridge, MA: MIT Press.
Postal, Paul M. and Geoffrey Pullum (1988). Expletive noun phrases in subcategorized positions. *Linguistic Inquiry* 19, 635–670.
Potsdam, Eric (1997). English verbal morphology and VP ellipsis. In K. Kusumoto (ed.), *Proceedings of the NELS 27*, 353–368. Amherst, MA: GLSA.
(2009). Malagasy backward object control. *Language* 85, 754–784.
Potsdam, Eric and Maria Polinsky (2007). Missing complement subjects in Malagasy. *Oceanic Linguistics* 46, 277–303.
(2012). Backward raising. *Syntax* 15, 75–108.
Potsdam, Eric and Jeffrey Runner (2001). Richard returns: Copy raising and its implications. In M. Andronis, C. Ball, H. Elston, and S. Neuvel (eds.), *Proceedings of the 37th Regional Meeting of the Chicago Linguistic Society*, 453–468. Chicago Linguistic Society, University of Chicago.
Potts, Christopher (2000). When even no's Neg is splitsville. In N. Sanders (ed.), *Jorge Hankamer WebFest*. Available at: http://ling.ucsc.edu/Jorge/potts.html.
(2003). The logic of conventional implicatures. PhD thesis, UC Santa Cruz.
Preminger, Omer (2009). Breaking agreements: Distinguishing agreement and clitic doubling by their failures. *Linguisitic Inquiry* 40, 619–666.
Prince, Alan (1983). Relating to the grid. *Journal of Linguistics* 14, 19–100.
Prince, Alan and Paul Smolensky (1993). Optimality Theory: Constraint interaction in generative grammar. Technical Report 2, Rutgers University Center for Cognitive Science Technical Report.
(2004). *Optimality Theory: Constraint interaction in generative grammar.* Malden MA/Oxford: Blackwell.
Prince, Alan and Bruce Tesar (2010). OT Workplace 0.9.9.8beta. Available at: http://ruccs.rutgers.edu/~prince/papers/otwpl_0.9.9.8beta.xls.
Prior, Arthur N. (1967). *Past, present and future*. Oxford University Press.

Progovac, Ljiljana (1992). Negative polarity: A semantico-syntactic approach. *Lingua* 86, 271–299.
  (1993). Negative polarity: Downward entailment and binding. *Linguistics and Philosophy* 16, 149–180.
  (1994). *Negative and positive polarity: A binding approach* (Cambridge Studies in Linguistics 68). Cambridge University Press.
  (1998). Determiner phrase in a language without determiners. *Journal of Linguistics* 34, 165–179.
Progovac, Ljiljana, Kate Paesani, Eugenia Casielles, and Ellen Barton (2006). *The syntax of nonsententials. Multidisciplinary perspectives*. Amsterdam: John Benjamins.
Pullum, Geoffrey K. (2011). On the mathematics of *Syntactic Structures*. *Journal of Logic, Language and Information* 20, 277–296.
Pullum, Geoffrey K. and Barbara C. Scholz (2002). Empirical assessment of stimulus poverty arguments. *The Linguistic Review* 19, 9–50.
Pullum, Geoffrey K. and Arnold M. Zwicky (1986). Phonological resolution of syntactic feature conflict. *Language* 62, 751–773.
Puskás, Genoveva (2000) *Word order in Hungarian* (Linguistics Today). Amsterdam/Philadelphia: John Benjamins Publishing Company.
Pustejovsky, James (1995). *The generative lexicon*. Cambridge, MA: MIT Press.
Pylkkänen, Liina (1999). Causation and external arguments. In L. Pylkkänen, A. van Hout, and H. Harley (eds.), *Papers from the UPenn/MIT Roundtable on the Lexicon* (MITWPL 35), 161–183. Cambridge, MA: MIT Press.
Quer, Josep (1998). *Mood at the interface*. Utrecht: Utrecht Institute of Linguistics OTS.
Quirk, Randolph, Sidney Greenbaum, Geoffrey Leech, and Jan Svartvik (1985). *A comprehensive grammar of the English language*. London: Longman.
Rackowski, Andrea (2002). The structure of Tagalog: Specificity, voice and the distribution of arguments. PhD thesis, MIT.
Rackowski, Andrea and Norvin Richards (2005). Phase edge and extraction: A Tagalog case study. *Linguistic Inquiry* 36, 565–99.
Radford, Andrew (1990). *Syntactic theory and the acquisition of English syntax*. Oxford: Blackwell.
Radzinski, Daniel (1991). Chinese number-names, tree-adjoining languages, and mild context-sensitivity. *Computational Linguistics* 17, 277–299.
Rambow, Owen (1993). Mobile heads and strict lexicalization. Master's thesis, University of Pennsylvania.
Ramchand, Gillian (1997). *Aspect and predication: The semantics of argument structure*. Oxford University Press.
  (2005). Perfectivity as aspectual definiteness: Time and the event in Russian. *Lingua* 118, 1690–1715.
  (2008). *Verb meaning and the lexicon. A first phase syntax* (Cambridge Studies in Linguistics 116). Cambridge University Press.

Randriamasimanana, Charles (1999). Clausal architecture and movement verbs in Malagasy. In E. Zeitoun and P. Jen-kuei Li (eds.), *Selected Papers from the Eighth International Conference on Austronesian Linguistics*, 509-527. Symposium Series of the Institute of Linguistics, Academia Sinica, Number 1. Taipei: Institute of Linguistics (Preparatory Office), Academia Sinica.

Rapoport, Tova (1987). Copular, nominal, and small clauses: A study of Israeli Hebrew. PhD thesis, MIT.

Rappaport, Gilbert (2001). Extraction from nominal phrases in Polish and the theory of determiners. *Journal of Slavic Linguistics* 8, 159-198.

Rappaport-Hovav, Malka and Beth Levin (2000). Classifying single argument verbs. In P. Coopmans, M. Everaert, and J. Grimshaw (eds.), *Lexical specification and insertion*, 269-304. Amsterdam: John Benjamins.

Reali, Florencia and Morten Christiansen (2005). Uncovering the richness of the stimulus: Structure dependence and indirect statistical evidence. *Cognitive Science* 29, 1007-1028.

Reape, Mike (1996). Getting things in order. In H. Bunt and A. van Horck (eds.), *Discontinuous constituency*, 209-254. Berlin: Mouton de Gruyter.

Reeve, Matthew (2009). Clefts. PhD thesis, UCL.

Reich, Ingo (2002). Question/answer congruence and the semantics of *wh*-phrases. *Theoretical Linguistics* 28, 73-94.

— (2003). *Frage, Antwort und Fokus*. Berlin: Akademie Verlag.

Reichenbach, Hans (1947). *Elements of symbolic logic*. New York: The Macmillan Company.

Reinhart, Tanya (1975). 'Whose main clause': Point of view in sentences with parentheticals. In S. Kuno (ed.), *Harvard studies in syntax and semantics*, Vol. 1, 127-172. Cambridge, MA: Harvard University Press.

— (1976). The syntactic domain of anaphora. PhD dissertation, MIT.

— (1979). Syntactic domains for semantic rules. In F. Guenthner and S. J. Schmidt (eds.), *Formal semantics and pragmatics for natural language*, 107-130. Dordrecht: D. Reidel.

— (1981a). A second Comp position. In Belletti, Brandi, and Rizzi (1981), 517-557.

— (1981b). Pragmatics and linguistics - An analysis of sentence topics. *Philosophica* 27, 53-94.

— (1982). *Pragmatics and linguistics: An analysis of sentence topics*. Bloomington: Indiana University Linguistics Club.

— (1983). *Anaphora and semantic interpretation*. University of Chicago Press / London: Croon Helm.

— (1991). Ellipsis conjunctions - Non quantificational LF. In A. Kasher (ed.), *The Chomskyan turn*, 360-384. Oxford: Blackwell.

— (1995). Interface strategies. *OTS Working Papers in Theoretical Linguistics*, 95-002. Utrecht: OTS, Utrecht University.

— (1997). Quantifier scope: How labor is divided between QR and choice functions. *Linguistics and Philosophy* 20, 335-397.

(1998). Wh-in-situ in the framework of the Minimalist Program. *Natural Language Semantics* 6, 29–56.

(2002). The theta system – An overview. *Theoretical Linguistics* 28, 229–290.

(2006). *Interface strategies: Optimal and costly computations*. Cambridge, MA: MIT Press.

Reinhart, Tanya and Eric Reuland (1991). Anaphors and logophors: An argument structure perspective. In J. Koster and E. Reuland (eds.), *Long-distance anaphora*, 283–321. Cambridge University Press.

(1993). Reflexivity. *Linguistic Inquiry* 24, 657–720.

Reinhart, Tanya and Tal Siloni (2004). Against an unaccusative analysis of reflexives. In Alexiadou, Anagnostopoulou, and Everaert (2004), 159–180.

(2005). The lexicon–syntax parameter: Reflexivization and other arity operations. *Linguistic Inquiry* 36, 389–436.

Reis, Marga (2000). On the parenthetical features of German was... w-constructions and how to account for them. In Lutz, Müller, and von Stechow (2000), 317–332.

Repp, Sophie (2010). Defining 'contrast' as an information-structural notion in grammar. *Lingua* 120, 1333–1345.

Repp, Sophie and Philippa Cook (eds.) (2010). *Contrast as an information-structural notion in grammar*. Special Issue of *Lingua* (120(6)).

Rett, Jessica (2006). Pronominal vs. determiner *wh*-words: Evidence from the copy construction. In O. Bonami and P. Cabredo Hofherr (eds.), *Empirical issues in syntax and semantics*, 6, 355–374. Pais. Available at: http://www.cssp.cnrs.fr/eiss6/.

Reuland, Eric (1986). A feature system for the set of categorial heads. In P. Muysken and H. van Riemsdijk (eds.), *Features and projections*, 41–88. Dordrecht: Foris.

(ed.) (2000). *Argument and Case: Explaining Burzio's Generalization*. Amsterdam: John Benjamins.

(2001a). Primitives of binding. *Linguistic Inquiry* 32, 439–492.

(2001b). Anaphors, logophors and binding. In P. Cole, G. Hermon, and C.-T. J. Huang (eds.), *Syntax and semantics 33: Long distance reflexives*, 343–370. New York: Academic Press.

(2005a). Agreeing to bind. In H. Broekhuis, N. Corver, R. Huybregts, U. Kleinhenz, and J. Koster (eds), *Organizing grammar. Studies in honor of Henk van Riemsdijk*, 505–513. Berlin: Mouton de Gruyter.

(2005b). Binding conditions: How are they derived? In S. Müller (eds.), *Proceedings of the HPSG05 Conference*, 578–593. Stanford, CA: CSLI Publications.

(2011). *Anaphora and language design*. Cambridge, MA: MIT Press.

Reuland, Eric and Jan Koster (1991). Long distance anaphora: An overview. In J. Koster and E. Reuland (eds.), *Long-distance anaphora*, 1–25. Cambridge University Press.

Reuland, Eric and Tanya Reinhart (1995). Pronouns, anaphors and case. In H. Haider, S. Olsen, and S. Vikner (eds.), *Studies in comparative Germanic syntax*, 241–268. Dordrecht: Kluwer.

Reuland, Eric and Sigriður Sigurjónsdóttir (1997). In H. Bennis, P. Pica, and J. Rooryck (eds.), *Atomism and binding*, 323–340. Dordrecht: Foris.

Reuland, Eric and Yoad Winter (2009). Binding without identity: Towards a unified semantics for bound and exempt anaphors. In D. Sobha, A. Branco, and R. Mitkov (eds.), *Anaphora processing and applications*, 69–79. Berlin: Springer.

Rezac, Milan (2004). Elements of cyclic syntax: Agree and merge. PhD thesis, University of Toronto.

— (2006). On tough-movement. In Cedric Boeckx (ed.), *Minimalist essays*, 288–325. Amsterdam: John Benjamins.

Rice, Keren (2000). *Morpheme order and semantic scope*. Cambridge University Press.

Richards, Marc (2004). Object shift and scrambling in North and West Germanic. A case study in symmetrical syntax. PhD dissertation, University of Cambridge.

— (2007). On feature inheritance: An argument from the phase impenetrability condition. *Linguistic Inquiry* 38, 563–572.

— (2008). Probing the past: On reconciling LDA with PIC. Unpublished ms., University of Leipzig.

Richards, Norvin (1997a). Competition and disjoint reference. *Linguistic Inquiry* 28, 178–186.

— (1997b). What moves where in which language. PhD thesis, MIT.

— (2001). *Movement in languages. Interactions and architectures*. Oxford University Press.

— (2010). *Uttering trees*. Cambridge, MA: MIT Press.

Riedel, Kristina (2009). The syntax of object marking in Sambaa: A comparative Bantu perspective. PhD dissertation, University of Leiden.

Riemsdijk, Henk C. van (1978). *A case study in syntactic markedness: The binding nature of prepositional phrases*. Dordrecht: Foris Publications.

— (1982). Correspondence effects and the Empty Category Principle. Tilburg: Tilburg Papers in Language and Literature.

— (1983). The case of German adjectives. In F. Heny and B. Richards (eds.), *Linguistic categories: Auxiliaries and related puzzles*, vol. 1, 5–16. Dordrecht: Reidel.

— (1990). Functional prepositions. In H. Pinkster and I. Genee (eds.), *Unity and diversity. Papers presented to Simon C. Dik on his 50th birthday*, 229–242. Dordrecht: Foris.

— (1998). Categorial feature magnetism: The endocentricity and distribution of projections. *Journal of Comparative Germanic Linguistics* 2, 1–48.

Riemsdijk, Henk C. van and Riny Huybregts (2007). Location and locality. In S. Karimi, V. Samiian, and W. K. Wilkins (eds.), *Phrasal and clausal* architecture. Syntactic derivation and interpretation, 339-364. Amsterdam/Philadelphia: John Benjamins.

Riemsdijk, Henk C. van and Edwin Williams (1986). Introduction to the theory of grammar. Cambridge, MA: MIT Press.

Rijkhoek, Paulien (1998). On degree phrases & result clauses. PhD dissertation, University of Groningen.

Ritter, Elizabeth (1988). A head-movement approach to construct state Noun Phrases. *Linguistics* 26, 909-929.

(1991). Two functional categories in noun phrases: Evidence from Hebrew. In S. Rothstein (ed.), *Perspectives on phrase structure: Heads and licensing* (Syntax and Semantics 26), 37-62. San Diego: Academic Press.

Ritter, Elizabeth and Martina Wiltschko (2009). Varieties of INFL: TENSE, LOCATION and PERSON. In J. van Craenenbroeck, H. Broekhuis, and H. van Riemsdijk (eds.), *Alternatives to cartography*, 153-202. New York: Mouton de Gruyter.

Rivero, María Luisa (1992). Adverb incorporation and the syntax of adverbs in Modern Greek. *Linguistics and Philosophy* 15, 289-331.

(1993). Long head movement vs. V2 and null subjects in Old Romance. *Lingua* 89, 217-245.

Rivero, María Luisa and José Lema (1989). Long head movement: ECP vs. HMC. In J. Carter, R.-M. Dechaine, B. Philip, and T. Sherer (eds.), *Proceedings of the 20th Annual Meeting of the North Eastern Linguistic Society*, 333-347. Amherst, MA: GLSA. [Also in *Cahiers Linguistiques d'Ottawa* (1990) 18, 61-78.]

Rizzi, Luigi (1978a). A restructuring rule in Italian syntax. In S.J. Keyser (ed.), *Recent transformational studies in European languages*, 113-158. Cambridge, MA: MIT Press.

(1978b). Violations of the wh-island constraint in Italian and the subjacency condition. *Montreal Working Papers in Linguistics* no. 11. [Reprinted in Rizzi (1982a), 49-76.]

(1982a). *Issues in Italian syntax* (Studies in Generative Grammar 11). Dordrecht: Foris.

(1982b). Comments on Chomsky's chapter 'On the Representation of Form and Function'. In J. Mehler, E. Walker, and M.F. Garrett (eds.), *Perspectives on mental representation. Experimental and theoretical studies of cognitive processes and capacities*, 441-451. Hillsdale: Erlbaum.

(1986a). Null objects in Italian and the theory of *pro*. *Linguistic Inquiry* 17, 501-557.

(1986b). On chain formation. In H. Borer (ed.), *The grammar of pronominal clitics* (Syntax and Semantics 19), 65-95. New York: Academic Press.

(1990a). *Relativized Minimality*. Cambridge, MA/London: MIT Press.

(1990b). On the anaphor agreement effect. *Rivista di Grammatica* 2, 27-42.

(1990c). Speculations on verb-second. In J. Mascaró and M. Nespor (eds.), *Grammar in progress: a festschrift for Henk van Riemsdijk*, 375-385. Dordrecht: Foris.

(1991/1996). Residual verb second and the wh criterion. Geneva Working Papers on Formal and Computational Linguistics. [Published in A. Belletti and L. Rizzi (eds.) (1996), *Parameters and functional heads*, 63–90. Oxford University Press.]

(1994). Early null subjects and root null subjects. In T. Hoekstra and B. Schwartz (eds.), *Language acquisition studies in generative grammar*, 151–176. Amsterdam: John Benjamins.

(1997). The fine structure of the left periphery. In Haegeman (1997b), 281–337.

(2000). *Comparative syntax and language acquisition*. London: Routledge.

(2001a). On the position int(errogative) in the left periphery of the clause. In G. Cinque and G. Salvi (eds.), *Current studies in Italian syntax*, 287–296. Amsterdam: Elsevier.

(2001b). Reconstruction, weak island sensitivity and agreement. In C. Cecchetto, G. Chierchia, and M.T. Guasti (eds.), *Semantic interfaces: Reference, anaphora and aspect*, 145–176. Chicago: CSLI Publications.

(2001c). Relativized minimality effects. In Baltin and Collins (2001), 89–110.

(2004a). Locality and left periphery. In Belletti (2004b), 223–251.

(2004b). On the study of the language faculty: Results, developments, and perspectives. *The Linguistic Review* 21, 323–344.

(ed.) (2004c). *The structure of CP and IP – The cartography of syntactic structures*, vol. 3. Oxford University Press.

(2005a). On the grammatical basis of language development. In G. Cinque and R. Kayne (eds), *The Oxford handbook of comparative syntax*, 70–109. Oxford University Press.

(2005b). On some properties of subjects and topics. In L. Brugé, G. Giusti, N. Munaro, W. Schweikert, and G. Turano (eds.), *Proceedings of the XXX Incontro di Grammatica Generetiva*, 203–224. Venezia: Cafoscarina.

(2006a). Concepts of locality/On intermediate positions: Intervention and impenetrability. Lectures delivered at the XXV Curso de Verano, San Sebastián, June 2006, and the EALING Fall School, Paris, September 2006.

(2006b). On the form of chains: Criterial positions and ECP effects. In L.L.-S. Cheng and N. Corver (eds.), *WH-movement: Moving on*, 97–133. Cambridge, MA: MIT Press.

(2006c). Selective residual V-2 in Italian interrogatives. In P. Brandt and E. Fuss (eds.), *Form, structure and grammar* (Studia Grammatica 63), 229–242. Berlin: Akademie Verlag.

(2006d). Grammatically-based target-inconsistencies in child language. In K.U. Deen, J. Nomura, B. Schulz, and B.D. Schwartz (eds), *Proceedings of the Inaugural Conference on Generative Approaches to Language Acquisition–North America, Honolulu, HI* (University of Connecticut Occasional Papers in Linguistics 4), 19–49.

(2007). On some properties of criterial freezing. In V. Moscati (ed.), *CISCL working papers on language and cognition* (STiL Studies in Linguistics 1),145-158. Centro Interdipartimentale di Studi Cognitivi sul Linguaggio, Siena.

(2009a). Contribution to: Round table: Language universals: Yesterday, today, and tomorrow. In M. Piatelli Palmarini, J. Uriagereka, and P. Salaburu (eds.), *Of minds and language: The Basque Country encounter with Noam Chomsky*, 195-220. Oxford University Press.

(2009b). Some elements of syntactic computations. In D. Bickerton and E. Szathmáry (eds.), *Biological foundations and origin of syntax*, 63-88. Cambridge, MA: MIT Press and Frankfurt Institute for Advanced Studies.

(2009c). On some consequences of criterial freezing. Unpublished ms., University of Siena.

(2010). Delimitation effects and the cartography of the left periphery. Unpublished ms., University of Siena.

Rizzi, Luigi and Ur Shlonsky (2007). Strategies of subject extraction. In H.-M. Gärtner and U. Sauerland (eds.). *Interfaces + recursion = language? Chomsky's Minimalism and the view from syntax-semantics*, 115-116. Berlin: Mouton de Gruyter.

Roberts, C. (2010). Topics. Unpublished ms., University of Iowa.

Roberts, Ian (1987). *The representation of implicit and dethematized subjects.* Dordrecht: Foris.

(1993). *Verbs and diachronic syntax.* Dordrecht: Kluwer.

(2004). The C-system in Brythonic Celtic Languages, V2 and the EPP. In L. Rizzi (ed.), *The structure of CP and IP*, 297-328. Oxford University Press.

(2010). On the nature of syntactic parameters: A programme for Research. Talk presented at the University of Maryland Mayfest, May, 2010.

Roberts, Ian and Anders Holmberg (2005). On the role of parameters in Universal Grammar: A reply to Newmeyer. In H. Broekhuis, N. Corver, M. Everaert, and J. Koster (eds.), *Organising grammar: A festschrift for Henk van Riemsdijk*, 538-553. Berlin: Mouton de Gruyter.

(2010). Introduction: Parameters in Minimalist theory. In Biberauer, Holmberg, Roberts, and Sheehan (2010), 1-57.

Roberts, Ian and Anna Roussou (2003). *Syntactic change. A Minimalist approach to grammaticalisation.* Cambridge University Press.

Roberts, Rose and Edward Gibson (2002). Individual differences in sentence memory. *Journal of Psycholinguistic Research* 31, 573-598.

Rochemont, Michael (1986). *Focus in generative grammar.* Amsterdam/Philadelphia: John Benjamins.

Röder, Brigitte, Oliver Stock, Helen Neville, Siegfried Bien, and Frank Rösler (2002). Brain activation modulated by the comprehension of normal and pseudo-word sentences of different processing demands: A functional magnetic resonance imaging study. *NeuroImage* 15, 1003-1014.

Rodman, Robert (1976). Scope phenomena, 'movement transformations' and relative clauses. In B. Partee (ed.), *Montague Grammar*, 165–176. New York: Academic Press.

Rodrigues, Cilene, Andrew Nevins, and Luis Vicente (2009). Cleaving the interactions between sluicing and preposition stranding. In L. Wetzels and J. van der Weijer (eds.), *Romance languages and linguistic theory*, 175–198. Amsterdam: John Benjamins.

Roehrs, Dorian (2006). The morpho-syntax of the Germanic noun phrase: Determiners MOVE into the determiner phrase. PhD dissertation, Indiana University.

Roeper, Thomas (2000). Universal bilingualism. *Bilingualism: Language and Cognition* 2, 169–186.

Roeper, Thomas and Jill de Villiers (1991). Ordered decisions in the acquisition of *wh*-questions. In H. Goodluck, J. Weissenborn, and T. Roeper (eds.), *Theoretical issues in language development*, 191–236. Hillsdale, NJ: Erlbaum.

Roeper, Thomas and Edwin Williams (1987). *Parameter setting*. Dordrecht: D. Reidel.

Rogalsky, Corianne and Gregory Hickok (2008). Selective attention to semantic and syntactic features modulates sentence processing networks in anterior temporal cortex. *Cerebral Cortex* 19, 786–796.

Rogalsky, Corianne, William Matchin, and Gregory Hickok (2008). Broca's area, sentence comprehension, and working memory: An fMRI study. *Frontiers in Human Neuroscience* 2, 1–13.

Rogers, Andy (1974). Physical perception verbs in English: A study in lexical relatedness. PhD dissertation, UCLA.

Rohrbacher, Bernhard (1999). *Morphology driven syntax: A theory of V-to-I raising and pro-drop*. Amsterdam: John Benjamins.

Romero, Maribel (1998). Focus and reconstruction effects in *wh*-phrases. PhD dissertation, University of Massachusetts, Amherst.

(2005). Concealed questions and specificational subjects. *Linguistics and Philosophy* 28, 687–737.

(2007). Connectivity in a unified analysis of specificational subjects and concealed questions. In C. Barker and P. Jacobson (eds.), *Direct compositionality*, 264–305. Oxford University Press.

Rooij, Robert van (2003). Negative polarity items in questions: Strength as relevance. *Journal of Semantics* 20, 239–273.

(2008). Towards a uniform analysis of *any*. *Natural Language Semantics* 4, 297–315.

Rooryck, Johan and Guido vanden Wyngaerd (2011). *Dissolving binding theory*. Oxford University Press.

Rooth, Mats (1985). Association with focus. PhD thesis, University of Massachusetts, Amherst.

(1992a). A theory of focus interpretation. *Natural Language Semantics* 1, 75–121.

(1992b). Reduction redundancy and ellipsis redundancy. In S. Berman and A. Hestvik (eds.), *Proceedings of the Stuttgart Workshop on Ellipsis*, No. 29. Arbeitspapiere des SFB 340. University of Stuttgart.

(1996). Focus. In S. Lappin (ed.), *The handbook of contemporary semantic theory*, 271-297. London: Blackwell.

(2010). Second occurrence focus and relativized stress F. In C. Féry and M. Zimmermann (eds.), *Information structure*, 15-35. Oxford University Press.

Rosen, Carol (1976). Guess what about? In A. Ford, J. Reighard, and R. Singh (eds.), *Papers from the Sixth Meeting of the North Eastern Linguistic Society* (Montréal Working Papers in Linguistics), 205-211. Montréal.

(1984). The interface between semantic roles and initial grammatical relations. In D. M. Perlmutter and C. A. Rosen (eds.), *Studies in relational grammar 2*, 38-77. University of Chicago Press.

Rosenbaum, Peter S. (1967). *The grammar of English predicated complement constructions.* Cambridge, MA: MIT Press.

Ross, John Robert (1967a). Constraints on variables in syntax. PhD thesis, MIT. [Published as *Infinite syntax!* (1986). Norwood, NJ: Ablex.]

(1967b). On the cyclic nature of English pronominalization. In D. A. Reibel and S. A. Schane (eds.), *To honor Roman Jakobson III*, 1669-1682. The Hague: Mouton and Co.

(1969). Guess who? In R. Binnick, A. Davidson, G. Green, and J. Morgan (eds.), *Papers from the Fifth Regional Meeting of the Chicago Linguistic Society*, 252-286. Chicago Linguistic Society.

(1970). Gapping and the order of constituents. In M. Bierwisch and K. E. Heidolph (eds.), *Progress in linguistics*, 249-259. The Hague: Mouton.

(1972a). The category squish: Endstation Haputwort. *Papers from the Annual Regional Meeting of the Chicago Linguistic Society* 8, 316-328.

(1972b). Act. In D. Davidson and G. Harman (eds.), *Semantics of natural language*, 70-126. Dordrecht: Reidel.

(1973). Nouniness. In O. Fujimura (ed.), *Three dimensions of linguistic theory*, 137-257. Tokyo: TEC.

(1984). Inner islands. In C. Brugman and M. Macaulay (eds.), *Proceedings of the Tenth Annual Meeting of the Berkeley Linguistics Society*, 258-65. University of California, Berkeley.

(1985). The source of pseudoclefts sentences. Handout of a talk given at New York University, November 1985.

(1997). That is the question. Paper presented at the University of Pennsylvania, November 1997.

(2000). The frozenness of pseudoclefts – Towards an inequality-based syntax. In J. P. Boyle and A. Okrent (eds.), *Proceedings of the 36th Regional Meeting of the Chicago Linguistic Society*, 385-426. Chicago Linguistic Society.

Rossi, Sonja, Manfred Gugler, Anja Hahne, and Angela Friederici (2005). When word category information encounters morphosyntax: An ERP study. *Neuroscience Letters* 384, 228–233.

Rothstein, Susan (1983). The syntactic forms of predication. PhD dissertation, MIT. [Circulated by the Indiana University Linguistics Club, Bloomington, 1985.]

(1991a). Heads, projections, and category determination. In K. Leffel and D. Bouchard (eds.), *Views on phrase structure*, 97–112. Dordrecht: Kluwer Academic Publishers / San Diego: Academic Press.

(1991b). Syntactic licensing and subcategorization. In S. Rothstein (ed.), *Perspectives on phrase structure: Heads and licensing* (Syntax and Semantics 25), 139–157. San Diego: Academic Press.

(1995). Small clauses and copular constructions. In A. Cardinaletti and M. T. Guasti (eds.), *Small clauses*, 27–48. New York: Academic Press.

(2001). *Predicates and their subjects* (Studies in Linguistics and Philosophy 74). Dordrecht/Boston: Kluwer.

(2006). Secondary predication. In Everaert, van Riemsdijk, Goedemans, and Hollebrandse (2006), Vol. IV, 209–233.

Rouveret, Alain (1994). *Syntaxe du gallois*. Paris: CNRS Éditions.

Rudanko, Juhani (1989). *Complementation and case grammar: A syntactic and semantic study of selected patterns of complementation in present-day English*. New York: SUNY Press.

Rude, Noel (1986). Topicality, transitivity, and the direct object in Nez Perce. *International Journal of American Linguistics* 52, 124–153.

(1988). Ergative, passive, and antipassive in Nez Perce. In M. Shibatani (ed.), *Passive and voice*, 547–560. Amsterdam: John Benjamins.

Rudin, Catherine (1988). On multiple questions and multiple wh-fronting. *Natural Language and Linguistic Theory* 6, 445–501.

Rullmann, Hotze (2004). First and second person pronouns as bound variables. *Linguistic Inquiry* 35, 159–168.

Runner, Jeffrey T. (1998). *Noun phrase licensing*. New York: Garland.

(2006). Lingering challenges to the Raising-to-Object and Object-Control constructions. *Syntax* 9, 193–213.

Russell, Bertrand (1919). *Introduction to mathematical philosophy*. London: Muirhead Library of Philosophy.

Ruwet, Nicolas (1982). *Grammaire des insultes et autres études*. Paris: Seuil.

Ruys, Eddy G. (1992). The scope of indefinites. PhD dissertation, Utrecht University.

(2006). Unexpected wide-scope phenomena. In Everaert, van Riemsdijk, Goedemans, and Hollebrandse (2006), Vol. V, 175–228.

Růžička, Rudolf (1983). Remarks on control. *Linguistic Inquiry* 18, 309–324.

(1999). *Control in grammar and pragmatics. A cross-linguistic study*. Amsterdam: John Benjamins.

Sadler, Louisa (1997). Clitics and the structure-function mapping. In M. Butt and T. H. King (eds.), *Online Proceedings of the LFG97 Conference*. Stanford, CA: CSLI Publications.

Sadock, Jerry (1980). Noun incorporation in Greenlandic. *Language* 56, 300-319.

Sæbø, Kjell Johan (1996). Anaphoric presuppositions and zero anaphora. *Linguistics and philosophy* 19, 187-209.

Saffran, Jenny (2001). The use of predictive dependencies in language learning. *Journal of Memory and Language* 44, 493-515.

——— (2002). Constraints on statistical language learning. *Journal of Memory and Language* 47, 172-196.

Saffran, Jenny, Richard Aslin, and Elissa Newport (1996). Statistical learning by 8-month-old infants. *Science* 274, 1926-1928.

Safir, Kenneth J. (1985). *Syntactic chains*. Cambridge University Press.

——— (1987). Comments on Wexler and Manzini. In Roeper and Williams (1987), 77-89.

——— (1992). Implied non-coreference and the pattern of anaphora. *Linguistics and Philosophy* 15, 1-52.

——— (1993). Perception, selection, and structural economy. *Natural Language Semantics* 2, 47-70.

——— (1996). Semantic atoms of anaphora. *Natural Language and Linguistic Theory* 14, 545-589.

——— (1997). Symmetry and unity in the theory of anaphora. In H. Bennis, P. Pica, and J. Rooryck (eds.), *Atomism and binding*, 340-377. Dordrecht: Foris.

——— (2003). Anaphors, movement and coconstrual. In L.-O. Delsing, C. Falk, G. Josefsson, and H. Sigurðsson (eds.). *Festschrift for Christer Platzack*, 283-294. Lund: Institutionen för nordiska språk.

——— (2004a). *The syntax of anaphora*. Oxford University Press

——— (2004b). *The syntax of (in)dependence*. Cambridge, MA: MIT Press.

——— (2004c). Person, context and perspective. *Rivista di Linguistica* 16, 107-154.

——— (2005). Abandoning coreference. In J. L. Bermúdez (eds.), *Thought, reference and experience: Themes from the philosophy of Gareth Evans*, 124-163. Oxford University Press.

——— (2008). Coconstrual and narrow syntax. *Syntax* 11, 330-355.

——— (2010). Viable syntax: Rethinking Minimalist architecture. *Biolinguistics* 4, 35-107.

Safir, Kenneth J. and Justine Sikuku (forthcoming). Lubukusu anaphora sketch. Available at: http://www.africananaphora.rutgers.edu/images/stories/downloads/casefiles/lubukusu-as-3.1.pdf.

Sag, Ivan A. (1976). Deletion and Logical Form. PhD dissertation, MIT.

——— (1982). NP-movement dependencies. In Jacobson and Pullum (1982), 427-466.

——— (1997). English relative clause constructions. *Journal of Linguistics* 30, 431-483.

(2010a). English filler gap constructions. *Language* 86, 486–545.

(2010b). Feature geometry and predictions of locality. In A. Kibort and G. G. Corbett, (eds.) *Features: Perspectives on a key notion in linguistics*, 236–271. Oxford University Press.

(2012). Sign-based Construction Grammar: An informal synopsis. In H. Boas and I. A. Sag (eds.) *Sign-based Construction Grammar*, 69–202. Stanford, CA: CSLI Publications.

Sag, Ivan A. and Janet Dean Fodor (1994). Extraction without traces. In R. Aranovich, W. Byrne, S. Preuss, and M. Senturia (eds.), *Proceedings of the Thirteenth West Coast Conference on Formal Linguistics*, 365–384. Stanford, CA: CSLI, Publications.

Sag, Ivan A., Gerald Gazdar, Thomas Wasow, and Steven Weisler (1985). Coordination and how to distinguish categories. *Natural Language and Linguistic Theory* 3, 117–171.

Sag, Ivan A. and Joanna Nykiel (2008). Sluicing and stranding. Paper presented at the 83rd Annual Meeting of the Linguistic Society of America, January 8–11. San Francisco, CA, USA.

Sag, Ivan A. and Carl Pollard (1991). An integrated theory of complement control. *Language* 67, 63–113.

Sag, Ivan A., Thomas Wasow, and Emily M. Bender (2003). *Syntactic theory: A formal introduction*, 2nd edn. (CSLI Lecture Notes 152). Stanford, CA: CSLI Publications.

Saito, Mamuro (1985). Subject-object asymmetries in Japanese and their theoretical implications. PhD dissertation, MIT.

(2010). Sentence types and the Japanese right periphery. Unpublished ms., Nanzan University, Nagoya.

Saito, Mamoru and Keiko Murasugi (1999). Subject predication within IP and DP. In K. Johnson and I. Roberts (eds.), *Beyond principles and parameters: Essays in memory of Osvaldo Jaeggli*, 159–182. Dordrecht: Kluwer.

Salvi, Giampaolo (2005). Some firm points on Latin word order: The left periphery. In K. É. Kiss (ed.), *Universal Grammar and the reconstruction of ancient languages*, 429–456. Berlin: Mouton de Gruyter.

Samek-Lodovici, Vieri (1996). Constraints on subjects: An Optimality Theoretic analysis. PhD thesis, Rutgers University.

(2005). Prosody–syntax interaction in the expression of focus. *Natural Language and Linguistic Theory* 23, 687–755.

Sampson, Geoffrey R. (1975). The single mother condition. *Journal of Linguistics* 11, 1–11.

(1979). What was transformational grammar? *Lingua* 48, 355–378.

Sánchez, Liliana (2006). Kechwa and Spanish bilingual grammars: Testing hypotheses on functional interference and convergence. *International Journal of Bilingual Education and Bilingualism* 9, 535–556.

Santelmann, Lynn (1992). *Den*-support: An analysis of double determiners in Swedish. In A. Holmberg (ed.), *Papers from the Workshop on the Scandinavian Noun Phrase*, 100–118. University of Umeå.

Santi, Andrea and Yosef Grodzinsky (2007a). Taxing working memory with syntax: Bihemispheric modulations. *Human Brain Mapping* 28, 1089-1097.
  (2007b). Working memory and syntax interact in Broca's area. *NeuroImage* 37, 8-17.
  (2010). fMRI adaptation dissociates syntactic complexity dimensions. *NeuroImage* 51, 1285-1293.
Santos, Ana Lúcia (2009). *Minimal answers: Ellipsis, syntax, and discourse in the acquisition of European Portuguese.* Amsterdam: John Benjamins.
Sauerland, Uli (2003). Intermediate adjunction with A-movement. *Linguistic Inquiry* 34, 308-314.
Saussure, Ferdinand de (1916/1966). *Course in general linguistics.* New York: McGraw-Hill. [Translation of *Cours de linguistique générale*. Paris: Payot, 1916].
Schachter, Paul (1976). The subject in Philippine languages: Topic, actor, actor-topic, or none of the above. In C. Li (ed.), *Subject and topic*, 491-518. New York: Academic Press.
  (1981). Lovely to look at. *Linguistic Analysis* 8, 431-449.
Schaeffer, Florian (2008). The oblique causer construction across languages. In A. Schardl, M. Walkow, and M. Abdurrahman (eds.), *Proceedings of NELS 38*, 297-308. Amherst, MA: GLSA.
Scheer, Tobias (2008). Spell out your sister! In N. Abner and J. Bishop (eds.), *Proceedings of the 27th West Coast Conference on Formal Linguistics*, 379-387. Somerville: Cascadilla.
  (2009a). External sandhi: What the initial CV is initial of. *Studi e Saggi Linguistici* 57, 43-82.
  (2009b). Representational and procedural sandhi killers: Diagnostics, distribution, behaviour. In M. Docekal and M. Ziková (eds.), *Czech in formal grammar*, 155-174. München: Lincom Europa.
Schein, Barry (1993). *Plurals and events* (Current Studies in Linguistics 23). Cambridge, MA: MIT Press.
  (2003). Adverbial, descriptive reciprocals. *Philosophical Perspectives* 17, 333-367.
Schladt, Mathius (2000). The typology and grammaticalization of reflexives. In Z. Frajzyngier and T. S. Curl (eds.), *Reflexives: Forms and functions*, 103-124. Amsterdam/Philadelphia: John Benjamins.
Schlenker, Philippe (2003a). A plea for monsters. *Linguistics and Philosophy* 26, 29-120.
  (2003b). Clausal equations (a note on the connectivity problem). *Natural Language and Linguistic Theory* 21, 157-214.
Schmerling, Susan F. (1976). Aspects of English sentence stress. PhD thesis, Austin.
Scholz, Barbara C. and Geoffrey K. Pullum (2007). Tracking the origins of transformational generative grammar. *Journal of Linguistics* 43, 701-723.

Schoorlemmer, Erik and Tanja Temmerman (2010). On the interaction between verb movement and ellipsis in the PF component. Talk presented at GLOW 33, Wroclaw.

Schoorlemmer, Maaike (1998). Possessors, articles and definiteness. In Alexiadou and Wilder (1998b), 55–86.

Schutter, Georges de (1994). Voegwoordflectie en pronominale clitisering waarbij Vlaams en Brabants bijna elkaars tegengestelden zijn. *Taal & Tongval* 46, 108–131.

Schütze, Carson (1996). *The empirical basis of linguistics: Grammaticality judgments and linguistic methodology.* University of Chicago Press.

(1997). INFL in child and adult language: Agreement, case and licensing. PhD thesis, MIT.

(1999). English expletive constructions are not infected. *Linguistic Inquiry* 30, 467–484.

Schuyler, Tamara (2002). *Wh*-movement out of the site of VP ellipsis. MA thesis, UCSC.

Schwarzschild, Roger (1999). GIVENness, AvoidF and other constraints on the placement of accent. *Natural Language Semantics* 7, 141–177.

(2002a). Singleton Indefinites. *Journal of Semantics* 19, 289–314.

(2002b). The grammar of measurement. In B. Jackson (ed.), *Proceedings of SALT 12*, 225–245. Ithaca, NY: CLC Publications.

(2005). Measure phrases as modifiers of adjectives. *Recherches Linguistiques de Vincennes* 34, 207–228.

Schwarzschild, Roger and Karina Wilkinson (2002). Quantifiers in comparatives: A semantics of degree based on intervals. *Natural Language Semantics* 10, 1–41.

Scott, Gary-John (1998). Stacked adjectival modification and the structure of nominal phrases. *SOAS Working Papers in Linguistics and Phonetics* 8, 59–89.

(2002). Stacked adjectival modification and the structure of nominal phrases. In Cinque (2002), 91–120.

Selkirk, Elisabeth O. (1970). On the determiner systems of noun phrases and adjective phrases. Unpublished ms., MIT.

(1977). Some remarks on noun phrase structure. In P. Culicover, T. Wasow, and A. Akmajian (eds.), *Formal syntax*, 285–316. New York: Academic Press.

(1981). On prosodic structure and its relation to syntactic structure. In T. E. Fretheim (ed.), *Nordic prosody II*, 111–140. Trondheim: TAPIR.

(1984). *Phonology and syntax: The relation between sound and structure.* Cambridge, MA: MIT Press.

(1986). On derived domains in sentence phonology. *Phonology Yearbook* 3, 371–405.

(1995). Sentence prosody: Intonation, stress, and phrasing. In J. A. Goldsmith (ed.), *The handbook of phonological theory*, 550–569. London: Blackwell.

Sells, Peter (1987). Aspects of logophoricity. *Linguistic Inquiry* 18, 445–479.
   (1995). Korean and Japanese morphology from a lexical perspective. *Linguistic Inquiry* 26, 277–325.
   (2001a). Form and function in the typology of grammatical voice systems. In J. Grimshaw, G. Legendre and S. Vikner (eds.), *Optimality-Theoretic syntax*, 355–391. Cambridge, MA: MIT Press.
   (2001b). *Structure alignment and optimality in Swedish*. Stanford, CA: CSLI Publications.
   (2006). Using subsumption rather than equality in functional control. In M. Butt and T. H. King (eds.), *Proceedings of LFG06*, University of Konstanz. Stanford, CA: CSLI Publications.
   (2010). Symmetries and asymmetries in voice systems. Handout, Vienna Conference on Voice, June 2010.
Sharvit, Yael (1999). Connectivity in specificational sentences. *Natural Language Semantics* 7, 299–339.
   (2003). Tense and identity in copular sentences. *Natural Language Semantics* 11, 363–393.
Sherman (Ussishkin), Adam (1998). VP ellipsis and subject positions in Modern Hebrew. In A. Z. Wyne (ed.), *Proceedings of the 13th Annual Meeting of the Israel Association of Theoretical Linguistics, Bar-Ilan University, Tel-Aviv, Israel*, 211–229. Jerusalem: Akademon.
Shetreet, Einat, Naama Friedmann, and Uri Hadar (2009). An fMRI study of syntactic layers: Sentential and lexical aspects of embedding. *NeuroImage* 48, 707–716.
Shibatani, Masayoshi and Theodora Bynon (1995). Approaches to language typology: A conspectus. In M. Shibatani and T. Bynon (eds.), *Approaches to language typology*, 1–25. Oxford: Clarendon Press.
Shieber, Stuart M. (1985). Evidence against the context-freeness of natural language. *Linguistics and Philosophy* 8, 333–343.
   (1986). *An introduction to unification-based approaches to grammar*. Stanford, CA: CSLI, Publications.
Shimoyama, Junko (2001). *Wh*-constructions in Japanese. PhD thesis, University of Massachusetts, Amherst.
Shlonsky, Ur (1991). Quantifiers as functional heads: A study of quantifier float in Hebrew. *Lingua* 84, 159–180.
   (1997) *Clause structure and word order in Hebrew: An essay in comparative Semitic syntax*. Oxford University Press.
   (2004). The form of the Semitic noun phrase. *Lingua* 114, 1456–1526.
Shopen, Tim (1972). A generative theory of ellipsis: A consideration of the linguistic use of silence. Unpublished ms., Indiana University Linguistics Club.
   (1973). Ellipsis as grammatical indeterminacy. *Foundations of Language* 10, 65–77.
Sichel, Ivy (1997). Two pronominal copulas and the syntax of Hebrew non-verbal sentences. In R. C. Blight and M. Y. Moosally, (eds.) *Texas*

Linguistics Forum 38: Proceedings of the Texas Linguistic Society Conference, 295–306. University of Texas at Austin.

(2007). Raising in DP revisited. In W. D. Davies and S. Dubinsky (eds.), *New horizons in the analysis of control and raising*, 15–34. Dordrecht: Springer.

(2010). Towards a typology of control in DP. In Hornstein and Polinsky (2010), 245–267.

Siegel, Muffy (1976). Capturing the adjective. PhD thesis, University of Massachusetts.

Siewierska, Anna (1991). *Functional grammar*. London: Routledge.

(2005). Verbal person marking. In M. Haspelmath, M. Dryer, D. Gil, and B. Comrie (eds.), *The world atlas of language structures*, 414–417. Oxford University Press.

(2008). Passive constructions. In D. G. M. Haspelmath, M. Dryer, and B. Comrie (eds.), *The world atlas of language structure online*, Chapter 107. Available at: http://wals.info/static/descriptions/107/wals_feature_107.pdf.

Sigurðsson, Halldór (2002). To be an oblique subject: Russian vs. Icelandic. *Natural Language and Linguistic Theory* 20, 691–724.

(2004). Icelandic non-nominative subjects. In K. V. Subbarao and P. Bhaskararao (eds.), *Non-nominative subjects: Vol. 2*, 137–160. Amsterdam: John Benjamins.

Sigurðsson, Halldór and Anders Holmberg (2008). Icelandic dative intervention: Person and number are separate probes. In R. D'Alessandro, S. Fischer, and G. Hrafnbjargarson (eds.), *Agreement restrictions*, 251–280. Berlin: Mouton de Gruyter.

Siloni, Tal (1996). Hebrew noun phrases: Generalized noun raising: In A. Belletti and L. Rizzi (eds.), *Parameters and functional heads*, 239–267. Oxford University Press.

(1997). *Noun phrases and nominalizations*. Dordrecht: Kluwer.

(2002). Adjectival constructs and inalienable constructions. In J. Ouhalla and U. Shlonsky (eds.), *Themes in Arabic and Hebrew syntax*, 161–187. Dordrecht: Kluwer Academic Publishers.

Simmons, Kyle, Mark Reddish, Patrick Bellgowan, and Alex Martin (2010). The selectivity and functional connectivity of the anterior temporal lobes. *Cerebral Cortex* 20, 813–825.

Simpson, Andrew (2002). IP-raising, tone sandhi and the creation of S-final particles: Evidence for cyclic spell-out. *Journal of East Asian Linguistics* 11, 67–99.

Simpson, Jane (1991). *Warlpiri morpho-syntax: A lexicalist approach*. Dordrecht: Kluwer.

Sleeman, Petra (1996). Licensing empty nouns in French. PhD dissertation, Holland Institute of Generative Linguistics.

Smirniotopoulos, Jane and Brian Joseph (1998). Syntax vs. the lexicon: Incorporation and compounding in Modern Greek. *Journal of Linguistics* 34, 447–488.

Smith, Carlota S. (1961). A class of complex modifiers in English. *Language* 37, 342–365.

(1992/1997). *The parameter of aspect.* Dordrecht: Kluwer.

(2008). Time with and without tense. In Guéron and Lecarme (2008), 227–249.

Smith, Edward and John Jonides (1998). Neuroimaging analyses of human working memory. *Proceedings of the National Academy of Science* 95, 12061–12068.

(1999). Storage and executive processes in the frontal lobes. *Science* 283, 1657–1661.

Smith, Neil and Ann Law (2009). On parametric (and non-parametric) variation. *Biolinguistics* 3, 332–343.

Smolensky, Paul (1996). On the comprehension/production dilemma in child language. *Linguistic Inquiry* 27, 720–731.

Snarska, Anna (2009). On certain troublemakers to partial control as agree. *University of Pennsylvania Working Papers in Linguistics* 15, 203–212.

Snijders, Tineke, Theo Vosse, Gerard Kempen, Jos van Berkum, Karl Magnus Petersson, and Peter Hagoort (2009). Retrieval and unification of syntactic structure in sentence comprehension: An fMRI study using word-category ambiguity. *Cerebral Cortex* 19, 1493–1503.

Snyder, William (2001). On the nature of syntactic variation: Evidence from complex predicates and complex word-formation. *Language* 77, 324–342.

(2007). *Child language: The parametric approach.* Oxford University Press.

Snyder, William and Karen Stromswold (1997). The structure and acquisition of English dative constructions. *Linguistic Inquiry* 28, 281–317.

Sobin, Nicholas (1985). Case assignment in Ukrainian morphological passive constructions. *Linguistic Inquiry* 16, 649–662.

(1997). Agreement, default rules, and grammatical viruses. *Linguistic Inquiry* 28, 318–342.

Sorace, Antonella (2000). Gradients in auxiliary selection with intransitive verbs. *Language* 76, 859–890.

Speas, Margaret (1985). Saturation and phrase structure. *MIT Working Papers in Linguistics* 6, 174–198.

(1990). *Phrase structure in natural language.* Dodrecht: Kluwer Academic Publishers.

(2004). Evidentiality, logophoricity, and the syntactic representation of pragmatic features. *Lingua* 14, 255–276.

Sportiche, Dominique (1983). Structural invariance and symmetry in syntax. PhD dissertation, MIT.

(1988). A theory of floating quantifiers and its corollaries for constituent structure. *Linguistic Inquiry* 19, 425–449.

(1997). Clitic constructions. In J. Rooryck and L. Zaring (eds.), *Phrase structure and the lexicon*, 213–276. Dordrecht: Kluwer.

(1998). *Partitions and atoms of clause structure: Subjects, agreement, case and clitics*. London: Routledge.

(2006). Reconstruction, binding and scope. In Everaert, van Riemsdijk, Goedemans, and Hollebrandse (2006), Vol. IV, 35–93.

Sproat, Richard and Chilin Shih (1987). Prenominal adjectival ordering in English and Chinese. In J. Blevins and J. Carter (eds.), *Proceedings of NELS 18*, 465–489. Amherst, MA: GLSA.

(1991). The cross-linguistic distribution of adjective ordering restrictions. In C. P. Georgopoulos and R. L. Ishihara (eds.), *Interdisciplinary approaches to language. Essays in honor of S.-Y. Kuroda*, 565–593. Dordrecht. Academic Press.

Stainton, Robert (1995). Non-sentential assertions and semantic ellipsis. *Linguistics and Philosophy* 18, 281–296.

(1997). Utterance meaning and syntactic ellipsis. *Pragmatics and Cognition* 5, 51–78.

(1998). Quantifier phrases, meaningfulness 'in isolation', and ellipsis. *Linguistics and Philosophy* 21, 311–340.

(2005). In defense of non-sentential assertion. In Z. Szabo (ed.), *Semantics vs. Pragmatics*, 383–457. Oxford University Press.

(2006a). *Words and thoughts: Subsentences, ellipsis, and the philosophy of language*. Oxford University Press.

(2006b). Neither fragments nor ellipsis. In L. Progovac, K. Paesani, E. Casielles, and E. Barton (eds.), *The syntax of nonsententials*, 93–116. Amsterdam: John Benjamins.

Stanley, Jason (2000). Context and Logical Form. *Linguistics and Philosophy* 23, 391–434.

Starke, Michal (2001). Move dissolves into Merge: A theory of locality. PhD dissertation, University of Geneva.

(2004). On the inexistence of specifiers and the nature of heads. In Belletti (2004b), 252–268.

Stavrou, Melita (2003). Semi-lexical nouns, classifiers, and the interpretation(s) of the pseudopartitive construction. In Coene and D'Hulst (2003), 329–353.

Stechow, Arnim von (1981). Topic, focus, and local relevance. In W. Klein and W. Levelt (eds.), *Crossing the boundaries in linguistics*, 95–130. Dordrecht: Reidel.

(1982). *Structured propositions*. Arbeitspapiere des SFB 99, Konstanz.

(1989). *Focusing and backgrounding operators*. Technical Report 6, Fachgruppe Sprachwissenschaft, Universität Konstanz.

(2000). Partial *wh*-movement, scope marking, and transparent logical form. In Lutz, Müller, and von Stechow (2000), 317–332.

Steedman, Mark (1990). Gapping as constituent coordination. *Linguistics and Philosophy* 13, 207–264.

(1991). Structure and intonation. *Language* 67, 260–296.

(1994). Remarks on intonation and 'Focus'. In Bosch and van der Sandt (1994), vol. 1, 185–204.

(1996). *Surface structure and interpretation*. Cambridge, MA: MIT Press.

(2000a). Information structure and the syntax–phonology interface. *Linguistic Inquiry* 31, 649–689.

(2000b). *The syntactic process*. Cambridge, MA: MIT Press.

(2006). Information-structural semantics for English intonation. In C. Lee, M. Gordon, and D. Büring (eds.), *Topic and focus: Cross-linguistic perspectives on meaning and intonation* (Studies in Linguistics and Philosophy 82), 245–264. Dordrecht: Kluwer.

Steedman, Mark and Jason Baldridge (2011). Combinatory categorial grammar. In Borsley and Börjars (2011), 181–224.

Steinbach, Markus (2002). *Middle voice*. Amsterdam/Philadelphia: Benjamins.

Stenson, Nancy (1989). Irish autonomous impersonals. *Natural Language and Linguistic Theory* 13, 561–570.

Stepanov, Arthur (2001). Cyclic domains in syntactic theory. PhD dissertation, University of Connecticut.

(2007). The end of CED? Minimalism and extraction domains. *Syntax* 10, 80–126.

Stiebels, Barbara (2007). Towards a typology of complement control. In B. Stiebels (ed.), *Studies in complement control* (ZAS Papers in Linguistics 47), 1–80. Berlin.

(2010). Control. Unpublished ms., Zentrum für allgemeine Sprachwissenschaft, Berlin.

Stjepanović, Sandra and Shoichi Takahashi (2001). Eliminating the Phase Impenetrability Condition. Unpublished ms., Kanda University of International Studies.

Stockwell, Robert P. (1962). Discussion of 'A transformational approach to syntax'. In A. A. Hill (ed.), *Proceedings of the Third Texas Conference on Problems of Linguistic Analysis in English*, 158–169. Austin: University of Texas Press.

Stowe, Laurie (1986). Parsing *wh*-constructions: Evidence for on-line gap location. *Language and Cognitive Processes* 1, 227–245.

(1989). Thematic structures and sentence comprehension. In G. N. Carlson and M. K. Tanenhaus (eds.), *Linguistic structure in language processing*, 319–357. Dordrecht: Kluwer.

Stowe, Laurie, Cees Broere, Anne Paans, Albertus Wijers, Gijsbertus Mulder, Wim Vaalburg, and Frans Zwarts (1998). Localizing components of a complex task: Sentence processing and working memory. *NeuroReport* 9, 2995–2999.

Stowell, Timothy A. (1981). Origins of phrase structure. PhD dissertation, MIT.

(1983). Subjects across categories. *The Linguistic Review* 2, 285–312.

(1989). Subjects, specifiers and X-bar theory. In Baltin and Kroch (1989), 232–262.

(1996). The phrase structure of tense. In J. Rooryck and L. Zaring (eds.), *Phrase structure and the lexicon*, 277–291. Dordrecht: Klewer.

(2004). Tense and modals. In Guéron and Lecarme (2004), 621–35.

(2008). Where the past is in the perfect. In Á. Carrasco Gutiérrez (ed.), *Tiempos compuestos y formas verbales complejas*, 103–118. Madrid: Vervuert.

Stroik, Thomas (1992). Middles and movement. *Linguistic Inquiry* 23, 127–137.

Stromswold, Karen, David Caplan, Nathaniel Alpert, and Scott Rauch (1996). Localization of syntactic comprehension by positron emission tomography. *Brain and Language* 52, 452–473.

Stroud, Clare and Colin Phillips (2011). Examining the evidence for an independent semantic analyzer: An ERP study in Spanish. *Brain and Language* 118, 108–126.

Stump, Gregory (1977). Pseudogapping. Unpublished ms., Ohio State University.

Stuurman, Frits (1985). *Phrase structure theory in generative grammar*. Dordrecht: Foris.

Sugahara, Mariko (2002). Conditions on post-FOCUS dephrasing in Tokyo Japanese. In B. Bell and I. Marlien (eds.), *Proceedings of the First International Conference on Speech Prosody*, 655–658. Aix-En-Provence, France.

Sugayama, Kensei and Richard Hudson (2005). *Word grammar: New perspectives on a theory of language structure*. London: Continuum.

Sussman, Rachel and Julie Sedivy (2003). The time-course of processing syntactic dependencies: Evidence from eye movements. *Language and Cognitive Processes* 18, 143–163.

Svenonius, Peter (1992). Movement of P^0 in the English verb–particle construction. In H. A. Black and J. McCloskey (eds.), *Syntax at Santa Cruz 1*, 93–113. Santa Cruz, CA: Syntax Research Center, UCSC.

(1994a). Dependent nexus. PhD thesis, University of California at Santa Cruz.

(1994b). On the structural location of the attributive adjective. In E. Duncan, D. Farkas, and P. Spaelti (eds.), *Proccedings of the West Coast Conference on Formal Linguistics 12*, 439–454. Stanford, CA: CSLI Publications.

(2001a). On object shift, scrambling, and the PIC. In E. Guerzoni and O. Matushansky (eds.), *A few from Building E39: Working papers in syntax, semantics, and their interface* (MIT Working Papers in Linguistics), 267–289. Cambridge, MA: MIT Press.

(2001b). Impersonal passives and the EPP: A phase-based analysis. In A. Holmer, J.-O. Svantesson, and Å. Viberg (eds.), *Proceedings of the 18th*

Scandinavian Conference of Linguistics, 109–125. Lund: Travaux de l'Institut de Linguistique de Lund.

(2001c). Subject positions and the placement of adverbials. In P. Svenonius (ed.), *Subjects, expletives, and the EPP*, 199–240. Oxford University Press.

(2002a). Icelandic case and the structure of events. *Journal of Comparative Germanic Linguistics* 5, 197–225.

(2002b). Introduction. In P. Svenonius (ed.), *Subjects, expletives, and the Extended Projection Principle*, 3–28. Oxford University Press.

(2003). Limits on P: *filling in holes vs. falling in holes. Nordlyd: Proceedings of the 19th Scandinavian Conference of Linguistics* 31, 431–445.

(2004). On the edge. In D. Adger, C. de Cat, and G. Tsoulas (eds.), *Peripheries: Syntactic edges and their effects*, 259–287. Dordrecht: Kluwer.

(2006). The emergence of axial parts. *Nordlyd: Tromsø Working Papers in Language and Linguistics* 33, 49–77.

(2007). Adpositions, particles, and the arguments they introduce. In E. Reuland, T. Bhattacharya, and G. Spathas (eds.), *Argument structure*, 71–110. Amsterdam/Philadelphia: John Benjamins.

(2008). The position of adjectives and other phrasal modifiers in the decomposition of the DP. In McNally and Kennedy (2008), 16–42.

(2010). Spatial P in English. In Cinque and Rizzi (2010b), 127–160.

Swart, Henriëtte de (1998a). Licensing of negative polarity items under inverse scope. *Lingua* 105, 175–200.

(1998b). Introduction to Natural Language Semantics. Stanford, CA: CSLI Publications.

(2006). Marking and interpretation of negation: A bi-directional OT approach. In R. Zanuttini, H. Campos, E. Herburger, and P. Portner (eds.), *Comparative and cross-linguistic research in syntax, semantics and computational linguistics, GURT 2004*, 199–218. Washington, DC: Georgetown University Press.

(2010). *Expression and interpretation of negation*. Dordrecht: Springer.

Swart, Henriëtte de and Ivan Sag (2002). Negative concord in Romance. *Linguistics and Philosophy* 25, 373–417.

Sybesma, Rint (2007). Whether we tense-agree overtly or not. *Linguistic Inquiry* 38, 580–587.

Szabolcsi, Anna (1981). The semantics of topic/focus articulation. in J. Groenendijk, Th. Janssen, and M. Stokhof (eds.), *Formal methods in the study of language*, 513–540. Amsterdam: Mathematical Center.

(1983). The possessor that ran away from home. *The Linguistic Review* 3, 89–102.

(1987). Functional categories in the noun phrase. In I. Kenesei (ed.), *Approaches to Hungarian. Theories and analyses*, 167–190. Szeged: Jate.

(1994). The noun phrase. In F. Kiefer and K. É. Kiss (eds.), *The syntax of Hungarian* (Syntax and Semantics 27), 179–274. San Diego: Academic Press.

(1997a). Strategies for scope taking. In Szabolcsi (1997c), 109–155.
(1997b). Quantifiers in pair-list readings. In Szabolcsi (1997c), 311–347.
(ed.) (1997c). *Ways of scope taking*. Dordrecht: Kluwer.
(1999). Is DP analogous to IP or CP? In J. Payne (ed.), *Proceedings of the Manchester Colloquium on Noun Phrases*. The Hague: Mouton.
(2001). The syntax of scope. In Baltin and Collins (2001), 607–634.
(2002). Hungarian disjunction and positive polarity. In I. Kenesei and P. Siptár (eds.), *Approaches to Hungarian, Vol. 8*, 217–241. Budapest: Akadémiai Kiadó.
(2004). Positive polarity–negative polarity. *Natural Language and Linguistic Theory* 22, 409–452.
Szabolcsi, Anna and Marcel den Dikken (2003). Islands. In L. Cheng and R. Sybesma (eds.), *The second state-of-the-article book*, 213–240. Berlin: Mouton de Gruyter.
Szczegelniak, Adam (2005). All sluiced up, but no alleviation in sight . . . . Unpublished ms., Boston College.
(2008). Islands in sluicing in Polish. In N. Abner and J. Bishop (eds.), *Proceedings of the 27th West Coast Conference on Formal Linguistics*, 404–412. Somerville, MA: Cascadilla Proceedings Project.
Szendrői, Kriszta (2001). Focus and the syntax–phonology interface. PhD thesis, University College London.
(2003). A stress-based approach to the syntax of Hungarian focus. *The Linguistic Review* 20, 37–78.
Taglicht, Josef (1998). Constraints on intonational phrasing in English. *Linguistics* 34, 181–211.
Takahashi, Daiko (1994). Minimality of movement. PhD dissertation, University of Connecticut.
(2008a). Noun phrase ellipsis. In S. Miyagawa and M. Saito, *Oxford handbook of Japanese linguistics*, 394–422. Oxford University Press.
(2008b). Quantificational null objects and argument ellipsis. *Linguistic Inquiry* 39, 307–326.
Takahashi, Shoichi (2003). Pseudogapping: The view from Scandinavian languages. Paper presented at the *Comparative Germanic Syntax Workshop 18*. University of Durham, 18–20 September.
(2004). Pseudogapping and cyclic linearization. In K. Moulton and M. Wolf (eds.), *Proceedings of NELS 34*, 571–585. Amherst, MA: GLSA.
Takahashi, Shoichi and Danny Fox (2005). MaxElide and the re-binding problem. In E. Georgala and J. Howell (eds.), *Proceedings of SALT 15*, 223–240. Ithaca, NY: CLC Publications.
Tallerman, Maggie (1998). Word order in Celtic. In A. Siewierska (ed.), *Constituent order in the languages of Europe*, 21–45. Berlin/New York: Walter de Gruyter.
(2005). The Celtic languages. In G. Cinque and R. Kayne (eds.), *The Oxford handbook of comparative syntax*, 839–879. Oxford University Press.

Talmy, Leonard (1978). Figure and ground in complex sentences. In J. H. Greenberg (ed.), *Universals of human language*, Vol. 4, 625–649. Stanford University Press.

(2000). *Toward a cognitive semantics*. Cambridge, MA: MIT Press.

Tancredi, Christopher (1992). Deletion, deaccenting and presupposition. PhD dissertation, MIT.

Tanenhaus, Michael, Michael Spivey-Knowlton, Kathleen Eberhard, and Julie Sedivy (1995). Integration of visual and linguistic information in spoken language comprehension. *Science* 268, 1632–1634.

Taraldsen, Knut Tarald (1978). On the NIC, vacuous application and the *that*-trace filter. Unpublished ms., Bloomington, Indiana University Linguistics Club.

(1990). D-projections and N-projections in Norwegian. In J. Mascaró and M. Nespor (eds.), *Grammar in progress: Essays in honor of Henk van Riemsdijk*, 419–432. Dordrecht: Foris.

(1995). On agreement and nominative subjects in Icelandic. In H. Haider, S. Olsen, and S. Vikner (eds.), *Studies in comparative Germanic syntax*, 307–327. Dordrecht/Boston/London: Kluwer Academic Publishers.

Temmerman, Tanja (2010). Revisiting the syntax of Dutch and English fragment answers. Unpubished ms., University of Leiden.

Tenny, Carol (1987). Grammaticalizing aspect and affectedness. PhD thesis, MIT.

(1994). *Aspectual roles and the syntax–semantics interface*. Dordrecht: Kluwer.

Terken, Jacques M. B. and Dik J. Hermes (2000). The perception of prosodic prominence. In M. Horne (ed.), *Prosody: Theory and experiment – Studies presented to Gösta Bruce*, 89–127. Dordrecht: Kluwer Academic Publishers.

Terzi, Arhonto (1991). Governed PRO and finiteness. *Proceedings of Eastern States Conference on Linguistics (ESCOL)* 8, 359–370.

(1993). PRO in finite clauses: A study of the inflectional heads of the Balkan languages. PhD dissertation, City University of New York.

(2010). On locative prepositions. In Cinque and Rizzi (2010b), 196–224.

Thomason, Richmond and Robert Stalnaker (1973). A semantic theory of adverbs. *Linguistic Inquiry* 4, 195–220.

Thompson, Ellen (2005). *Time in natural language: Syntactic interfaces with semantics and discourse*. Berlin/New York: Mouton de Gruyter.

Thompson, Sandra A. (1983). Grammar and discourse: The English detached participial clause. In F. Klein-Andreu (ed.), *Discourse perspectives on syntax*, 43–65. New York: Academic Press.

Thoms, Gary (2010). 'Verb floating' and VP-ellipsis: Towards a movement account of ellipsis licensing. Unpublished ms., University of Strathclyde.

Thornton, Rosalind (1990). Adventures in long-distance moving: The acquisition of complex *wh*-questions. PhD dissertation, University of Connecticut.

(1995). Referentiality and *wh*-movement in child English: Juvenile D-linkuency. *Language Acquisition* 4, 139-175.

(2004). Why continuity. In A. Brugos, L. Micciula, and C. E. Smith (eds.), *Proceedings of the 28th Boston University Conference on Language Development (BUCLD 28)*, 620-632. Somerville, MA: Cascadilla Press.

(2008). Why continuity. *Natural Language and Linguistic Theory* 26, 107-146.

(2010). Verb phrase ellipsis in children's answers to questions. *Language Learning and Development* 6, 1-31.

Thornton, Rosalind and Stephen Crain (1994). Successful cyclic movement. In T. Hoekstra and B. Schwartz (eds.), *Language acquisition studies in generative grammar*, 215-253. Amsterdam/Philadelphia: John Benjamins Publishing Co.

Thornton, Rosalind and Graciela Tesan (2007). Categorical acquisition: Parameter setting in Universal Grammar. *Biolinguistics* 1, 49-98.

Thornton, Rosalind and Kenneth Wexler (1999). *Principle B, VP ellipsis, and interpretation*. Cambridge, MA: MIT Press.

Thráinsson, Höskuldur (1979). *On complementation in Icelandic*. New York: Garland.

Thráinsson, Höskuldur, Hjalmar P. Petersen, Jógvan í Lon Jacobsen, and Zakaris Svabo Hansen (2004). *Faroese: An overview and reference grammar*. Tórshavn: Føroya Fróðskaparfelag.

Tomasello, Michael (ed.) (1998). *The new psychology of language: Cognitive and functional approaches to language structure*. Mahwah, NJ: Lawrence Erlbaum.

(2000a). Do young children have adult syntactic competence? *Cognition* 74, 209-253.

(2000b). The item based nature of children's early syntactic development. *Trends in Cognitive Sciences* 4, 156-163.

(2003). *Constructing a language: A usage-based theory of language acquisition*. Cambridge, MA/London: Harvard University Press.

(2005). Beyond formalites: The case of language acquisition. *The Linguistic Review* 22, 167-181.

(2006a). Acquiring linguistic constructions. In D. Kuhn and R. Siegler (eds.), *Handbook of child psychology, Vol. 2: Cognition, perception and language*, 255-299. New York: Wiley.

(2006b). Construction Grammar for kids. *Constructions* 1, 1-11.

Tomioka, Satoshi (1999). A sloppy identity puzzle. *Natural Language Semantics* 7, 217-248.

Tomlin, Russell S. (1986). *Basic word order: Functional principles*. London: Croom Helm.

Tonhauser, Judith (2007). Nominal tense? The meaning of Guaraní nominal temporal markers. *Language* 83, 831-869.

Torrego, Esther (1984). On inversion in Spanish and some of its effects. *Linguistic Inquiry* 15, 103-129.

Tortora, Christina (2008). Aspect inside PLACE PPs. In A. Asbury, J. Dotlačil, B. Gehrke, Ø. Nilsen, and R. Nouwen (eds.), *Syntax and semantics of spatial P*, 273–301. Amsterdam/Philadelphia: John Benjamins.

Townsend, David and Thomas Bever (2001). *Sentence comprehension: The integration of habits and rules*. Cambridge, MA: MIT Press.

Travis, Lisa deMena (1984). Parameters and effects of word order variation. PhD dissertation, MIT.

(1988). The syntax of adverbs. *McGill Working Papers in Linguistics* (Special Issue on Comparative Germanic Syntax 32), 280–310.

(1989). Parameters of phrase structure. In Baltin and Kroch (1989), 263–279.

(1991). Inner aspect and the structure of VP. Paper presented at NELS 22, Newark, Delaware.

(2004). Agents and causes in Malagasy and Tagalog. In N. Erteschik-Shir and T. Rapoport (eds.), *The syntax of aspect*, 174–189. Oxford University Press.

Traxler, Matthew and Martin Pickering (1996). Plausibility and the processing of unbounded dependencies: An eye-tracking study. *Journal of Memory and Language* 35, 454–475.

Truckenbrodt, Hubert (1995a). Extraposition from NP and prosodic structure. In *Proceedings of NELS* 25, 503–517.

(1995b). *Phonological phrases: Their relation to syntax, focus, and prominence*. PhD thesis, MIT. [Published 1999 by MITWPL.]

(1999). On the relation between syntactic phrases and phonological phrases. *Linguistic Inquiry* 30, 219–255.

(2006). Phrasal stress. In K. Brown (ed.), *The encyclopedia of languages and linguistics*, vol. 9, 572–579. Oxford: Elsevier.

Truckenbrodt, Hubert and Daniel Büring (in preparation). Correspondence at the syntax–phonology interface.

Trueswell, John, Michael Tanenhaus, and Susan Garnsey (1994). Semantic influences on parsing: Use of thematic role information in syntactic ambiguity resolution. *Journal of Memory and Language* 33, 285–318.

Truswell, Robert (2011). *Events, phrases and questions*. Oxford University Press.

Tsai, W.-T. Dylan (1994). On nominal islands and LF extraction in Chinese. *Natural Language and Linguistic Theory* 12, 121–175.

(2007). Left periphery and why-how alternations. Unpublished ms., National Tsing-Hua University, Taiwan.

Tubau, Susagna (2008). Negative concord in English and Romance: Syntax-morphology interface conditions on the expression of negation. PhD dissertation, University of Amsterdam and UA Barcelona.

Tyler, Lorraine and William Marslen-Wilson (2008). Frontotemporal brain systems supporting spoken language comprehension. *Philosophical Transactions of the Royal Society of London B* 363, 1037–1054.

Uhmann, Susanne (1991). *Fokusphonologie*. Tübingen: Niemeyer.

Umbach, Carla (2006). Non-restrictive modification and backgrounding. In B. Gyuris, L. Kálmán, C. Piñón, and K. Varasdi (eds.), *Proceedings of the Ninth Symposium on Logic and Language*, 152–159. Budapest: Hungarian Academy of Sciences.

Ura, Hiroyuki (1996). Multiple feature-checking: A theory of grammatical function splitting. PhD dissertation, MIT.

Uriagereka, Juan (1995). Aspects of the syntax of clitic placement in Western Romance. *Linguisitic Inquiry* 26, 79–123.

(1999). Multiple spell-out. In S. D. Epstein and N. Hornstein (eds.), *Working Minimalism*, 251–282. Cambridge, MA: MIT Press.

(2002). *Derivations*. London: Routledge.

(2008). *Syntactic anchors: On semantic structuring*. Cambridge University Press.

Uribe-Etxebarria, Myriam (1996). Levels of representation and negative polarity item licensing. In J. Camacho, L. Choueiri, and M. Watanabe (eds.), *Proceedings of WCCFL 14*, 571–586. Stanford, CA: CSLI Publications.

Urk, Coppe van (2010). Deriving Visser's Generalization: A window into the syntax of control. Unpublished ms., MIT.

Ussery, Cherlon (2009). Optionality and variability: Syntactic licensing meets morphological spell-out. PhD thesis, University of Amherst.

Valian, Virginia (1991). Syntactic subjects in the early speech of American and Italian children. *Cognition* 40, 21–82.

Vallduví, Enric (1990). *The informational component*. PhD thesis, University of Pennsylvania. [published 1992 by Garland.]

(1992) *The informational component* (Outstanding Dissertations in Linguistics Series). New York: Garland.

Vallduví, Enric and Maria Vilkuna (1998). On rheme and contrast. In Culicover and McNally (1998), 79–180.

Valmala, Vidal (2007). The syntax of little things. In Y. Falk (ed.), *Proceedings of the 23rd Israel Association for Theoretical Linguistics Conference*. Available at http://linguistics.huji.ac.il/IATL/23/.

Valois, Daniel (1991). The internal syntax of DP. PhD dissertation, University of California at Los Angeles.

Van Valin, Robert (1990). Semantic parameters of split intransitivity. *Language* 66, 221–260.

Van Valin, Robert and Randy La Polla (1997). *Syntax: Structure, meaning and function*. Cambridge University Press.

Vandenberghe, Rik, Anna Nobre, and C. J. Price (2002). The response of left temporal cortex to sentences. *Journal of Cognitive Neuroscience* 14, 550–560.

Vangsnes, Øystein A. (1999). The identification of functional architecture. PhD dissertation, University of Bergen.

(2001). On noun phrase architecture, referentiality, and article systems. *Studia Linguistica* 55, 249–299.

Varlokosta, Spyridoula, Natalia Valeonti, Maria Kakavoulia, Mirto Lazaridou, Alexandra Economou, and Athanassios Protopapas (2006). The breakdown of functional categories in Greek aphasia: Evidence from agreement, tense and aspect. *Aphasiology* 20, 723–743.

Vasishth, Shravan (1999). Surface structure constraints on negative polarity and word order in Hindi and English. Paper presented at the 11th European Summerschool in Logic, Language and Information (ESSLI'99), August 1999, Utrecht, at the Workshop on Research Logics and Minimal Grammars.

Veenstra, Tonjes (1996). Serial verbs in Saramaccan. PhD dissertation, University of Amsterdam.

Vendler, Zeno (1967). Verbs and times. In *Linguistics and Philosophy*, 97–121. Ithaca, NY: Cornell University Press.

Vergnaud, Jean-Roger (1977). Letter to Noam Chomsky and Howard Lasnik. In R. Freidin, C. P. Otero, and M. Vernaud (eds.) (2008), *Foundational issues in linguistic theory*, 3–15. Cambridge, MA: MIT Press.

Verheugd, Els (1990). *Subject arguments and predicate nominals: A study of French copular sentences with two NPs*. Amsterdam: Rodopi.

Verkuyl, Henk J. (1972). *On the compositional nature of the aspects*. Dordrecht: Reidel.

 (1993). *A theory of aspectuality. The interaction between temporal and atemporal structure*. Cambridge University Press.

 (2008). *Binary tense*. Stanford, CA: CSLI Publications.

Vermeulen, Reiko (2005). Possessive and adjunct multiple nominative constructions in Japanese. *Lingua* 115, 1329–1363.

Vicente, Luis (2008). Syntactic isomorphism and non-isomorphism under ellipsis. Unpublished ms., University of California, Santa Cruz.

Vigneau, M., V. Beaucousin, P. Y. Herve, H. Duffau, F. Crivello, O. Houde, B. Mazoyer, and N. Tzourio-Mazoyer (2006). Meta-analyzing left hemisphere language areas: Phonology, semantics, and sentence processing. *NeuroImage* 30, 1414–1432.

Vijay-Shanker, K. (1987). A study of tree adjoining grammars. PhD dissertation, University of Pennsylvania.

Vikner, Sten (1994). Scandinavian object shift and West Germanic scrambling. In Corver and van Riemsdijk (1994), 487–517.

 (1995) *Verb movement and expletive subjects in the Germanic languages*. Oxford University Press.

 (2006). Object shift. In Everaert, van Riemsdijk, Goedemans, and Hollebrandse (2006), Vol. III, 392–436.

Visser, F. Th. (1973). *An historical syntax of the English language*. Leiden: Brill.

Vitale, Anthony (1981). *Swahili syntax*. Dordrecht: Foris.

Vogel, Ralf (2006a). The simple generator. In H. Broekhuis and R. Vogel *Optimality Theory and Minimalism: A possible convergence?* (Linguistics in Potsdam 25), 99–136. University of Potsdam. Available at: http://www.ling.uni-potsdam.de/lip.

(2006b). Weak function word shift. *Linguistics* 44, 1059-1093.
Vos, Riet (1999). A grammar of partitive constructions. PhD dissertation, Tilburg University.
Vos, Sandra, Thomas Gunter, Herbert Schriefers, and Angela Friederici (2001). Syntactic parsing and working memory: The effects of syntactic complexity, reading span, and concurrent load. *Language and Cognitive Processes* 16, 65-103.
Vosse, Theo and Gerard Kempen (2000). Syntactic structure assembly in human parsing: A computational model based on competitive inhibition and a lexicalist grammar. *Cognition* 75, 105-143.
Vries, Mark de (2009). On multidominance and linearization. *Biolinguistics* 3, 344-403.
Wachowicz, Kristina (1974). On the syntax and semantics of multiple questions. PhD dissertation, University of Texas at Austin.
Wagers, Matthew and Colin Phillips (2009). Multiple dependencies and the role of the grammar in real-time comprehension. *Journal of Linguistics* 45, 395-433.
Wagner, Michael (2005a). NPI-licensing and focus movement. In E. Georgala and J. Howell (eds.), *Proceedings of SALT XV*. Cornell University.
(2005b). Prosody and recursion. PhD thesis, MIT.
(2006). Givenness and locality. In J. Howell and M. Gibson (eds.), *Proceedings of SALT 16*, 295-312. Ithaca: CLC Publications.
(2010). Prosody and recursion in coordinate structures and beyond. *Natural Language and Linguistic Theory* 28, 183-237.
Wahba, Wafaa Abdel-Faheem Batran (1992). LF movement in Iraqi Arabic. In C. T. J. Huang and R. May (eds.), *Logical structure and linguistic structure*, 253-276. Dordrecht: Kluwer.
Warner, Anthony R. (1985). *The structure of English auxiliaries: A phrase structure grammar*. Bloomington, IN: Indiana University Linguistics Club.
Wasow, Thomas A. (1972). Anaphoric relations in English. PhD dissertation, MIT.
(1979). *Anaphora in generative grammar*. Ghent: E. Story Scientia.
(1997). Remarks on grammatical weight. *Language Variation and Change* 9, 81-105.
Watanabe, Akira (1992). Subjacency and S-structure movement of *wh*-in-situ. *Journal of East Asian Linguistics* 1, 255-291.
(1993). Agr-based case theory and its interaction with the A-bar system. PhD thesis, MIT.
(2004). The genesis of negative concord. *Linguistic Inquiry* 35, 559-612.
Waxman, Sandra and Amy Booth (2000). Principles that are invoked in the acquisition of words, but not facts. *Cognition* 77, B33-B43.
(2001). On the insufficiency of evidence for a domain-general account of word learning. *Cognition* 78, 277-279.

Webber, Bonnie (1978). A formal approach to discourse anaphora. PhD dissertation, Harvard.

Wechsler, Stephen M. (2001). An analysis of English resultatives under the event-argument homomorphism model of telicity. In *Proceedings of the 3rd Workshop on Text Structure*, 1–17. Austin, TX.

Wechsler, Stephen M. and Bokyung Noh (2001). On resultative predicates and clauses: Parallels between Korean and English. *Language Sciences* 23, 391–423.

Wechsler, Stephen M. and Larisa Zlatić (2003). *The many faces of agreement*. Stanford, CA: CLSI.

Weerman, Fred (1989). *The V2 conspiracy. A synchronic and a diachronic analysis of verbal positions in Germanic languages*. Dordrecht: Foris.

Wegener, Heide (1989). Kontrolle-semantish gesehen. *Deutshe Sprache* 3, 206–228.

Wells, Rulon S. (1947). Immediate constituents. *Language* 23, 81–117.

Wexler, Kenneth (1992). Some issues in the growth of control. In R. Larson, S. Iatridou, I. Lahiri, and J. Higginbotham (eds.), *Control and grammar*, 253–295. Dordrecht: Kluwer.

(1994). Optional infinitives, head movement, and the economy of derivation in child language. In D. Lightfoot and N. Hornstein (eds.), *Verb movement*, 288–315. Cambridge University Press.

(1998). Very early parameter setting and the unique checking constraint: A new explanation of the optional infinitive stage. *Lingua* 106, 23–79.

Wexler, Kenneth and Peter Culicover (1980). *Formal principles of language acquisition*. Cambridge, MA: MIT Press.

Wexler, Kenneth and Rita Manzini (1987). Parameters and learnability in binding theory. In Roeper and Williams (1987), 41–76.

White, Jonathan R. (1997). Result clauses and the structure of degree phrases. *UCL Working Papers in Linguistics* 9, 315–333.

Wilder, Christopher (1991). Tough movement constructions. *Linguistische Berichte* 132, 115–132.

(1995). Some properties of ellipsis in coordination. *Geneva Generative Papers* 2, 23–61.

Wilder, Christopher and Damir Ćavar (1994). Long head movement? Verb movement and cliticization in Croatian. *Lingua* 93, 1–58.

Willems, Roel and Peter Hagoort (2009). Broca's region: Battles are not won by ignoring half of the facts. *Trends in Cognitive Sciences* 13, 101.

Williams, Edwin (1977). Discourse and Logical Form. *Linguistic Inquiry* 8, 101–139.

(1978). Across-the-board rule application. *Linguistic Inquiry* 9, 32–43.

(1980). Predication. *Linguistic Inquiry* 11, 208–238.

(1981a). On the notions 'lexically related' and 'head of a word'. *Linguistic Inquiry* 12, 245–274.

(1981). Argument structure and morphology. *The Linguistic Review* 1, 81–114.

(1982). The NP cycle. *Linguistic Inquiry* 13, 277–295.
(1983a). Against small clauses. *Linguistic Inquiry* 14, 287–308.
(1983b). Semantic vs. syntactic categories. *Linguistics and Philosophy* 6, 423–446.
(1984). There-insertion. *Linguistic Inquiry* 15, 131–153.
(1985). PRO and subject NP. *Natural Language and Linguistic Theory* 3, 297–315.
(1987). NP trace in Theta Theory. *Linguistics and Philosophy* 10, 433–447.
(1990). Pseudoclefts and the order of the logic of English. *Linguistic Inquiry* 21, 485–489.
(1991). Reciprocal scope. *Linguistic Inquiry* 22, 159–172.
(1992). Adjunct control. In R. Larson, S. Iatridou, U. Lahiri, and J. Higginbotham (eds.), *Control and grammar*, 297–322. Dordrecht: Kluwer.
(1994). *Thematic structure in syntax* (Linguistic Inquiry Monograph 23). Cambridge, MA: MIT Press.
(1995) Theta theory. In G. Webelhuth (ed.), *Government and Binding Theory and the Minimalist Program*, 99–124. Blackwell: Oxford.
(2003). *Representation theory*. Cambridge, MA: MIT Press.
Willson, Stephen (1996). Verb agreement and case marking in Burushaski. *Work Papers of the Summer Institute of Linguistics North Dakota* 40, 1–71.
Wilson, Colin (2001). Bidirectional optimization and the theory of anaphora. In G. Legendre, J. Grimshaw, and S. Vikner (eds.), *Optimality-theoretic syntax*, 465–507. Cambridge: MIT Press.
Wiltschko, Martina (2003). On the interpretability of tense on D and its consequences for case theory. *Lingua* 113, 659–696.
Winkler, Susanne (2005). *Ellipsis and focus in generative grammar*. Berlin: Mouton de Gruyter.
Winter, Yoad (1997). Choice functions and the scopal semantics of indefinites. *Linguistics and Philosophy* 20, 399–467.
Wold, Dag (1996). Long distance selective binding: The case of focus. In T. Galloway and J. Spence (eds.), *Proceedings of Semantics and Linguistic Theory (SALT) VI*, 311–328. Ithaca, NY: Cornell University.
Wolff, Susann, Masako Hirotani and Ina Bornkessel-Schlesewsky (2008). The neural mechanisms of word order processing revisited: Electrophysiological evidence from Japanese. *Brain and Language* 107, 133–157.
Wood, Mary McGee (1993). *Categorial grammar*. London: Routledge.
Woolford, Ellen (1997). Four-way case systems: Ergative, nominative, objective and accusative. *Natural Language and Linguistic Theory* 15, 181–227.
(1999). More on the anaphor agreement effect. *Linguistic Inquiry* 30, 257–287.
(2001). Case patterns. In G. Legendre, S. Vikner and J. Grimshaw (eds.). *Optimality Theoretic syntax*, 509–543. Cambridge, MA: MIT Press.

(2003a). Burzio's Generalization, markedness, and constraints on nominative objects. In E. Brandner and H. Zinsmeister (eds.), *New perspectives on case theory*, 301–329. Stanford, CA: CSLI Publications.

(2003b). Nominative objects and Case locality. In W. Browne, J.-Y. Kim, B. H. Partee, and R. A. Rothstein (eds.), *Formal approaches to Slavic linguistics 11*, 539–568. Ann Arbor: Michigan Slavic Publications.

(2006). Lexical case, inherent case and argument structure. *Linguistic Inquiry* 37, 111–130.

(2007). Case locality: Pure domains and object shift. *Lingua* 117, 1591–1616.

Wouden, Ton van der (1994). Negative contexts. PhD dissertation, university of Groningen.

Wunderlich, Dieter (1997). Cause and the structure of verbs. *Linguistic Inquiry* 28, 27–68.

Wurmbrand, Susanne (1999). Modal verbs must be raising verbs. In S. Bird, A. Carnie, J. D. Haugen, and P. Norquest (eds.), *Proceedings of the 18th West Coast Conference on Formal Linguistics* (WCCFL 18), 599–612. Somerville, MA: Cascadilla Press.

(2001). *Infinitives. Restructuring and clause structure*. Berlin: Mouton de Gruyter.

(2006). Verb clusters, verb raising, and restructuring. In Everaert, van Riemsdijk, Goedemans, and Hollebrandse (2006), Vol. V, 229–343.

(2007). Infinitives are tenseless. *Penn Working Papers in Linguistics* 13, 407–420.

XTAG Research Group (2001). A lexicalized tree adjoining grammar for English. Technical Report IRCS-01-03, Institute for Research in Cognitive Science, University of Pennsylvania.

Xu, Yi and Xu Ching (2005). Phonetic realization of focus in English declarative intonation. *Journal of Phonetics* 33, 159–197.

Yang, Charles (2002). *Knowledge and learning in natural language*. Oxford University Press.

(2004). Universal grammar, statistics, or both? *Trends in Cognitive Science* 8, 451–456.

(2010). Three factors in language variation. *Lingua* 120, 1160–1177.

Yang, Dong-Whee (1983). The extended binding theory of anaphors. *Language Research* 19, 169–192.

Yanofsky, Nancy (1978). NP utterances. In D. Farkas, W. Jacobsen, and K. Todrys (eds.), *CLS 14*, 491–502. Chicago, IL: Chicago Linguistic Society.

Yip, Moira, Joan Maling, and Ray Jackendoff (1987). Case in tiers. *Language* 63, 217–250.

Yu, Christine M. (2008). The prosody of second position clitics and focus in Zagreb Croatian. Master's thesis, University of California, Los Angeles.

Zaenen, Annie (1993). Unaccusativity in Dutch: An integrated approach. In J. Pustejovsky (ed.), *Semantics and the lexicon*, 129-161. Dordrecht: Kluwer.

Zaenen, Annie and Elisabet Engdahl (1994). Descriptive and theoretical syntax in the lexicon. In B. T. S. Atkins and A. Zampolli (eds.), *Computational approaches to the lexicon: Automating the lexicon* II, 181-212. Oxford University Press.

Zaenen, Annie, Joan Maling, and Höskuldur Thráinsson (1990 [1985]). Case and grammatical relations: The Icelandic passive. In Maling and Zaenen (1990), 95-136. [Reprinted from *Natural Language and Linguistic Theory* 3 (1985), 441-483.]

Zagona, Karen (1982). Government and proper government of verbal projections. PhD dissertation, University of Washington, Seattle.

(1988a). Proper government of antecedentless VPs in English and Spanish. *Natural Language and Linguistic Theory* 6, 95-128.

(1988b). *Verb phrase syntax*. Dordrecht: Kluwer.

(1990). Temporal argument structure. Paper presented at the TIME Conference, MIT, Cambridge, MA.

(2002). Tenses and anaphora: Is there a tense-specific theory of coreference? In A. Barss (ed.), *Anaphora: An overview*, 140-171. Cambridge, MA/ Oxford: Blackwell.

(2007). On the syntactic features of epistemic and root modals. In L. Eguren and O. Fernández Soriano (eds.), *Coreference, modality and focus*, 221-236. Amsterdam: John Benjamins.

(2008). Phasing in modals: Phasing and the epistemic/root distinction. In Guéron and Lecarme (2008), 273-291.

Zamparelli, Roberto (1993). Pre-nominal modifiers, degree phrases and the structure of AP. *WPL*, University of Venice.

(1995). Layers in the determiner phrase. PhD dissertation, University of Rochester.

(2008). Bare prediate nominals in Romance languages. In H. H. Müller and A. Klinge (eds.), *Essays on nominal determination*, 101-130. Amsterdam: John Benjamins.

Zanuttini, Raffaella (1991). Syntactic properties of sentential negation. PhD dissertation, University of Pennsylvania.

(1997). *Negation and clausal structure. A comparative study of Romance languages* (Oxford Studies in Comparative Sntax). Oxford University Press.

(2001). Sentential negation. In Baltin and Collins (2001), 511-535.

Zaring, Laurie (1996). 'Two *be* or not two *be*': Identity, predication and the Welsh copula. *Linguistics and Philosophy* 19, 103-142.

Zec, Draga (2005). Prosodic differences among function words. *Phonology* 22, 77-112.

Zec, Draga and Sharon Inkelas (1990). Prosodically constrained syntax. In Inkelas and Zec (1990), 365-378.

Zeijlstra, Hedde (2004) Sentential negation and negative concord. PhD dissertation, University of Amsterdam.
- (2006). The ban on true negative imperatives. *Empirical Issues in Formal Syntax and Semantics* 6, 405-424.
- (2007). Negation in natural language: On the form and meaning of negative elements. *Language and Linguistics Compass* 1, 498-518.
- (2008). *Negative concord is syntactic agreement.* LingBuzz/000645.
- (2009). Functional structure, formal features and parametric variation: Consequences of conflicting interface conditions. In K. Grohmann (ed.), *InterPhases*, 82-113. Oxford University Press.
- (2010). On French negation. In I. Kwon, H. Pritchett, and J. Spence (eds.), *Proceedings of the Thirty-fifth Annual Meeting of the Berkeley Linguistics Society, 14-16 February 2009: General session and parasession on negation*, 447-458. Berkeley, CA: Berkeley Linguistics Society.

Zeller, Jochen (2001). *Particle verbs and local domains.* Amsterdam: John Benjamins.

Zilles, Karl and Katrin Amunts (2010). Centenary of Brodmann's map: Conception and fate. *Nature Reviews Neuroscience* 11, 139-145.

Zlatić, Larisa (1997). *The structure of the Serbian noun phrase.* PhD dissertation, University of Texas, Austin.

Zribi-Hertz, Anne (1989). Anaphor binding and narrative point of view. *Language* 65, 695-727.
- (1995). Emphatic or reflexive? On the endophoric character of French *lui-même* and similar complex pronouns. *Journal of Linguistics* 31/32, 333-374.

Zubizarreta, Maria Luisa (1987). *Levels of representation in the lexicon and in the syntax.* Dordrecht: Foris.
- (1998). *Prosody, focus and word order.* Cambridge, MA: MIT Press.

Zwart, C. Jan-Wouter (1993). *Dutch syntax. A Minimalist approach.* Groningen: Groningen Dissertations in Linguistics.
- (1996). 'Shortest move' versus 'Fewest steps'. In W. Abraham, S. D. Epstein, H. Thráinsson, and C. J.-W. Zwart (eds.), *Minimal ideas*, 305-327. Amsterdam: John Benjamins Publishing Co.
- (2001). Syntactic and phonological verb movement. *Syntax* 4, 34-62.
- (2002). Issues related to a derivational theory of binding. In S. D. Epstein and T. D. Seely (eds.), *Derivation and explanation in the Minimalist Program*, 269-304. Oxford: Blackwell.

Zwarts, Frans (1981). Negatief polaire uitdrukkingen I. *GLOT - Tijdschrift voor Taalwetenschap* 4, 35-132.
- (1986). Categoriale Grammatica en Algebraische Semantiek. Een studie naar negatie en polariteit in het Nederlands. PhD thesis, University of Groningen.
- (1995). Three types of polarity. In F. Hamm and E. Hinrichs (eds.), *Plural quantification*, 177-238. Dordrecht: Kluwer.

Zwarts, Joost (1992). X′-syntax–X′-semantics. PhD dissertation, Utrecht University.
  (2005). Prepositional aspect and the algebra of paths. *Linguistics and Philosophy* 28, 739–779.
Zwicky, Arnold (1985). How to describe inflection. *Berkeley Linguistic Society* 11, 372–386.

Index of language names

Acehnese, 88
Afrikaans, 805, 819
Albanian, 819
Algonquian, 589, 617
Altaic, 424
American English, 715
Amharic, 538, 563, 572, 622, 624, 643, 651
Arabic, 399, 592, 603, 613, 649
Assamese, 595
Athabaskan, 735, 736
Austronesian, 167, 317, 436, 589, 591

Balinese, 200
Balkan languages, 603
Bambara, 214
Bantu, 298, 300, 433, 436, 533, 536, 559, 563, 564, 607, 613, 624, 625, 626, 627, 628, 630, 636, 643, 649, 650, 652
Basque, 292, 305, 639, 641, 642, 651, 823
Bavarian, 820
Berber, 803
Brazilian, 728
Brazilian Portuguese, 450, 734
Breton, 780
British English, 702, 703, 709, 715, 717
Bulgarian, 114, 177, 181, 730, 834, 853
Burushaski, 321, 636, 642, 643

Carrier, 735
Catalan, 798
Caucasian, 640
Cebuano, 88
Celtic, 381
Central Pomo, 781
Chamorro, 299, 682
Chichewa, 298, 299, 433, 564
Chilean Spanish, 99
Chinese, 97, 370, 475, 535, 537, 557, 790, 824, 832, 835, 840, 853, 903, 928, 940, 941
Chukchi, 641
Classical languages, 436
Cree, 88
Creole, 436
Czech, 719, 797, 801, 819, 880, 881

Danish, 135, 136, 138, 139, 140, 141, 142, 143, 144, 330, 346, 431, 472, 546, 547, 574, 911
Dravidian, 595
Dutch, 15, 140, 142, 145, 292, 319, 329, 330, 376, 383, 401, 402, 403, 404, 421, 422, 446, 541, 542, 543, 547, 558, 559, 564, 566, 567, 573, 621, 625, 703, 708, 717, 719, 730, 738, 743, 757, 790, 798, 801, 804, 808, 819, 824, 867, 870, 885, 888, 895, 901, 903, 904, 906, 909, 911, 912, 913, 914, 915, 916, 917, 918, 919, 920, 921, 924, 925, 988, 989, 991, 992
Dyirbal, 88, 168, 305

East Asian languages, 195
Eastern Ostyak, 646
English, 21, 22, 66, 68, 79, 83, 85, 95, 96, 104, 126, 128, 129, 135, 142, 143, 151, 168, 169, 171, 176, 181, 185, 186, 197, 200, 216, 223, 246, 261, 266, 277, 282, 283, 284, 285, 286, 287, 291, 292, 295, 296, 297, 300, 301, 302, 310, 319, 321, 330, 333, 338, 340, 343, 346, 349, 350, 351, 359, 360, 362, 363, 369, 370, 390, 401, 403, 411, 412, 426, 427, 428, 429, 430, 431, 436, 437, 443, 451, 453, 457, 469, 470, 473, 474, 475, 476, 478, 480, 494, 495, 502, 503, 509, 512, 532, 533, 534, 535, 536, 537, 539, 542, 543, 545, 548, 551, 557, 558, 559, 560, 563, 564, 565, 573, 576, 583, 591, 607, 608, 609, 611, 614, 625, 629, 634, 636, 637, 638, 640, 642, 647, 648, 650, 653, 675, 683, 686, 692, 728, 729, 730, 731, 756, 757, 764, 767, 778, 781, 782, 783, 785, 787, 789, 790, 791, 792, 796, 798, 800, 801, 805, 806, 807, 808, 813, 815, 816, 817, 821, 823, 824, 825, 826, 827, 828, 835, 836, 843, 845, 848, 853, 854, 855, 856, 858, 861, 863, 865, 868, 871, 872, 880, 882, 886, 900, 901, 903, 906, 907, 908, 910, 912, 918, 924, 928, 938, 940, 941, 948, 950, 956, 957, 964, 965, 966, 967, 970, 983, 990
Eskimo, 385
Estonian, 85, 636, 638
Evenki, 796
Ewe, 538

Index of language names

Faroese, 146, 148, 149, 150, 151, 152, 153, 431
Finnish, 136, 139, 423, 638
Finnish-Swedish, 136, 139
Finno-Ugric, 436
French, 49, 112, 113, 126, 128, 129, 181, 282, 343, 350, 383, 388, 418, 419, 427, 428, 430, 432, 438, 439, 440, 441, 451, 473, 475, 476, 494, 495, 502, 503, 512, 541, 543, 545, 558, 559, 563, 564, 566, 567, 612, 623, 627, 703, 717, 719, 728, 730, 778, 779, 780, 782, 783, 785, 787, 791, 798, 799, 804, 805, 820, 823, 826, 846, 849, 882, 886, 906, 907, 908, 910, 912, 918, 950, 982
Frisian, 719, 855, 903, 919

Galician, 704
German, 15, 21, 140, 142, 145, 300, 304, 339, 343, 410, 478, 536, 557, 558, 564, 566, 574, 575, 583, 586, 621, 622, 631, 637, 638, 644, 651, 692, 703, 717, 719, 730, 797, 801, 804, 819, 854, 855, 856, 867, 870, 871, 880, 882, 883, 885, 886, 888, 909, 950, 982, 988, 991, 997, 998, 1001
Germanic, 133, 142, 143, 287, 299, 300, 308, 320, 330, 346, 376, 388, 390, 432, 436, 443, 456, 469, 475, 476, 477, 559, 652, 803, 819, 957
Gokana, 538
Greek, 287, 288, 419, 479, 603, 605, 631, 647, 651, 722, 734, 736, 800, 809, 810, 812, 819, 824
Greenlandic, 638, 641
Greenlandic Eskimo, 302, 303
Groningen, 903
Gungbe, 446, 448, 449, 564

Hausa, 889
Hebrew, 287, 340, 389, 399, 450, 704, 996
Hibernian English, 557
Hindi, 145, 146, 147, 196, 277, 282, 283, 284, 285, 286, 304, 305, 321, 536, 547, 554, 558, 575, 609, 615, 617, 639, 641, 642, 643, 811, 824, 834, 853, 854, 855, 856
Hungarian, 21, 22, 259, 385, 387, 388, 406, 419, 423, 449, 586, 624, 638, 682, 720, 730, 731, 733, 840, 853, 855, 880, 883, 884

Icelandic, 124, 133, 135, 136, 139, 140, 141, 142, 143, 144, 145, 146, 147, 148, 149, 150, 152, 153, 154, 155, 156, 217, 220, 225, 304, 431, 534, 538, 539, 547, 554, 586, 605, 615, 629, 639, 648, 650, 675, 909, 911
Ika, 646
Indo-Aryan, 286
Indo-European, 26, 142, 143, 607, 609, 610, 621, 625, 626, 627, 630, 643, 650, 652, 653, 819, 823, 900, 943
Indonesian, 277, 282
Innu-Aimûn, 617
Inuit, 146
Irish, 381, 443, 452, 605, 682, 704, 705, 950
Italian, 66, 119, 148, 282, 283, 284, 289, 292, 319, 330, 343, 388, 390, 391, 392, 393, 394, 399, 421, 427, 438, 440, 441, 444, 445, 449, 450, 451, 453, 457, 463, 477, 533, 534, 558, 612, 703, 717, 728, 789, 797, 800, 803, 804, 819, 820, 821, 822, 823, 883, 885, 895, 909, 914, 924, 943, 970
Itel'men, 617

Jacaltec, 308
Jamaican Creole, 426
Japanese, 15, 95, 102, 116, 142, 180, 181, 187, 194, 282, 333, 339, 369, 370, 411, 424, 426, 452, 454, 537, 557, 608, 625, 641, 651, 675, 745, 792, 833, 834, 851, 852, 906, 964, 966
Jiwarli, 198

Kanuri, 646
Kayardild, 608
Kilega, 613, 614, 625, 626, 650, 840
Kinande, 541, 564, 607, 625, 626, 627
Korean, 187, 424, 452, 592
Kronoby, 911

Lamas Kechwa, 757
Latin, 647
Lezgian, 636, 638, 640, 641, 653
Logudorese Sardinian, 438
Lubukusu, 533, 536, 559, 563

Malagasy, 423, 591, 592, 603, 815
Malayalam, 194, 195, 537
Mandarin Chinese, 198, 964

Nahuatl, 625, 651
Navajo, 307, 406, 824
Ndenduele, 704
Nez Perce, 643, 644, 646, 654
Niger-Congo, 943
Nłe?kepmxcin, 889
Northwest Caucasian, 592
Norwegian, 286, 308, 330, 334, 339, 431, 534, 536, 546, 549, 556, 560, 562, 567, 575, 719

Paduan, 800
Palestinian Arabic, 840
Passamaquoddy, 617, 856
Persian, 407, 602, 603
Polish, 421, 728, 730
Portuguese, 704, 728, 736

Quechua, 757

Rapanui, 436, 437
Romance, 49, 191, 211, 277, 283, 284, 287, 300, 308, 376, 388, 390, 418, 427, 432, 436, 443, 444, 455, 456, 469, 470, 475, 476, 477, 479, 480, 536, 559, 624, 692, 732, 782, 789, 791, 803, 819, 822, 823, 824, 882, 885, 894, 935
Romani, 855
Romanian, 21, 103, 107, 108, 110, 254, 391, 392, 411, 605, 730, 820, 824, 826
Russian, 96, 177, 183, 282, 300, 338, 536, 547, 557, 586, 637, 651, 652, 704, 730, 764, 766, 767, 789, 791

Sakha, 643, 644, 649, 653
Salish, 282, 284, 824, 889
Scandinavian, 133, 140, 141, 144, 183, 391, 419, 430, 431, 455, 533, 534, 536, 543, 548, 559, 561, 573, 696, 885, 909, 911, 924, 935
Scottish Gaelic, 339
Semitic, 436
Serbo-Croatian, 117, 121, 719, 730, 815, 893
Shakespearian English, 428
Shipibo, 641

Sicilian, 445
Slavic, 277, 284, 287, 300, 412, 819, 880
Spanish, 184, 185, 191, 192, 200, 453, 607, 627, 630, 703, 717, 727, 728, 731, 732, 733, 736, 763, 782, 783, 785, 787, 788, 789, 791, 801, 821, 881, 882, 883, 884, 885, 886, 887, 895, 916, 950, 982, 991
Swahili, 285, 613, 618, 620, 625, 651, 704
Swedish, 142, 143, 431, 801, 911
Swiss German, 214, 256, 257

Tagalog, 167, 198, 200, 317, 682
Tongan, 85, 796
Tsez, 605, 617, 649
Turkish, 85, 385, 537, 637, 797, 802, 803
Tuscarora, 299
Tzotzil, 299

Ukrainian, 285, 653, 686
Urdu, 282, 283, 284, 304, 305

Wambaya, 188
Warlpiri, 146, 180, 187, 188, 189, 192, 198, 411, 416
Welsh, 180, 183, 398, 421, 443, 476, 621, 625, 626, 651
West African, 436
West Flemish, 21, 621, 625, 626, 798, 805, 819, 820, 824

Yareba, 436, 437
Yiddish, 200, 819
Yoruba, 538, 539, 557, 559, 563, 572
Yup'ik, 385

Zulu, 622, 623, 625, 645, 651

Index

Entries in **bold** denote definitions; entries in *italic* denote Figures.

A-over-A Principle, 656, 657, **658**, 659, **673**, 687, 689
abstractness, 11, 14, 306, 339, 488, 704, 710, 713, 724, 846
  of parameters, 66
  of structure, 29, 32, 708, 710, 720, 722, 723, 724
acategorial root: *see* root
acceptability judgments: *see* introspective data, judgments
Accessibility Hierarchy, 162, 654
accusativus-cum-infinitivo: *see* Exceptional Case-Marking (ECM)
acquisition: *see* language acquisition
across-the-board (ATB) dependencies, extraction, movement, *210*, 719, 743
activity condition, 615, 616, 620, 621, 629, 630, 631, 636, 650, 651
adequacy, levels of, 71
  descriptive, 43, 52, 71, 140, 487
  explanatory, 11, 27, 28, 43, 52, 71, 73, 359, 487, 933
  observational, 71
adjacency, 45, 200, 433, 453, 468, 644, 678, 691, 716, 742
adjective, 22, 180, 181, 296, 346, 396, 397, 410, 458, 459, 460, 608, 627, 628, 731, 732, 733, 738, 739, 745, 938
  attributive, 390, 419
  predicative, 464, 465, 475
adjoining (TAG), 15, 230, 231, 232, 241, 243, 245, 246, 250
  null, 233, 235, 244
  obligatory, 233, 235, 244
  selective, 233
adjunct(ion), 21, 47, 110, 111, 120, 180, 198, 199, 248, 249, 258, 260, 303, 331, 414, 435, 462, 466, 467, 472, 473, 497, 538, 613, 664, 666, 668, 669, 676, 678, 683, 694, 755, 758, 765, 767, 768, 772, 776, 781, 788, 800, 803, 831, 836, 859, 902

Chomsky-adjunction, 231, 249, 414
Adjunct Condition, 111, 664, 665, 672; *see also* Condition on Extraction Domain (CED)
adposition, 22, 181, 384, 403, 406, 608, 620, 637
  circumposition(al), 404, 405
  directional, 401, 404, 405, 410, 422
  locative, 401, 404, 409, 410, 422
  postposition(al), 402, 404, 405, 406, 459
  preposition(al), 404, 405, 406, 422
adverb, 22, 85, 140, 337, 376, 397, 425, 426, 427, 428, 429, 433, 435, 436, 439, 443, 450, 453, 458, 459, 461, 470, 473, 480, 565, 580, 751, 776, 780, 797, 801, 804, 817, 846, 849, 850, 851, 912, 940
Affect Alpha/α, 17, 50, 488, 492, 497
affectedness, affected argument, 288, 293, 294, 295, 297, 298, 309, 316
Affix Hopping, 31, 211, 429
Agree, 7, 56, 116, 118, 123, 131, 132, 137, 145, 147, 148, 149, 151, 157, 233, 429, 430, 505, 506, 509, 549, 552, 554, 555, 559, 560, 567, 568, 573, 600, 610, 612, 614, 615, 617, 631, 633, 684, 685, 686, 687, 696, 697, 704, 714, 754, 761, 771, 773, 782, 802, 908, 945, 951; *see also* agreement
agreement, 9, 19, 20, 47, 110, 118, 155, 164, 168, 170, 180, 185, 191, 195, 259, 286, 299, 303, 316, 320, 321, 334, 343, 385, 386, 405, 406, 423, 425, 428, 429, 431, 433, 434, 435, 438, 455, 499, 500, 501, 538, 547, 550, 552, 553, 554, 558, 559, 560, 587, 607, 610, 618, 620, 621, 625, 649, 697, 704, 731, 735, 736, 737, 738, 746, 750, 761, 765, 769, 771, 772, 773, 774, 778, 779, 787, 822, 849, 850, 870, 907, 908, 909, 910, 913, 917, 918, 943, 983, 988, 989, 992, 1001; *see also* concord
alternation, 276, 280, 302, 307, 309, 317
  causative/inchoative, 277, 282, 286, 287, 291, 317
  conative, 276, 294, 315, 320
  contactive, 276

Index

alternation (cont.)
   dative, 299, 309, 996; *see also* ditransitive constructions
   locative, 276
   'spray/load', 278, 294
anaphora, anaphoric relations, 37, 39, 77, 515, 619, 772, 999
   deep *vs* surface, 719, 743
anaphor movement (at LF), 106
Antecedent Contained Deletion (ACD), 740, 837, 845
anti-adjacency, 453
anti-causative, 287, 565, 566; *see also* decausative
anti-locality, 72, 119, 549, 682, 683, 696
antipassive, 302, 320
antisymmetry, 47, 59, 370, 406, 415, 416, 454, 483, 904
   dynamic, **8**
aphasia, 74, 747, 995
applicatives, 298; *see also* ditransitive constructions
Arc Pair Grammar, 6
argument structure, 16, 218, 265, 355, 377, 564, 565, 566, 596, 598, 997, 1001
aspect, 141, 211, 294, 324, 334, 409, 410, 423, 429, 434, 436, 437, 438, 439, 447, 460, 462, 463, 474, 566, 578, 609, 620, 746, 761, 763, 764, 766, 767, 769, 772, 774, 797, 799, 859
   delimited(ness): *see* telic(ity)
Aspectual Interface Hypothesis (AIH), 274
Attract, **102**
attribute-value matrices (AVM), 215
autonomy of syntax, 20, 23, 81, 82, 85
auxiliary (verb), 31, 43, 63, 66, 78, 79, 83, 85, 142, 143, 181, 188, 189, 190, 207, 210, *211*, 212, 224, 285, 289, 291, 374, 380, 425, 426, 430, 512, 610, 642, 643, 670, 694, 711, 712, 716, 717, 786, 787, 799, 850, 906, 907, 918, 921, 925, 926, 949
   selection, 292
axial part, 407, 423

Bare Phrase Structure: *see* phrase structure
barrier, 392, 419, 656, 665, 675, 679, 687
   absolute, 656, 684, 685, 686, 687, 688
   inherent, 392, 665, 695
   inheritance, 392, 665
   relative, 656, 686, 687, 688, 696
behaviorism, 27
binarity, 46, 66, 136, 203, 204, 490, 510, 942, 968
   of parameters: *see* parameters
   of structure, 198
binary branching, 198, 203, 371, 408, 435, 904; *see also* antisymmetry
binding, 28, 91, 100, 194, 195, 197, 198, 200, 224, 346, 347, 380, 382, 417, 490, 578, 579, 584, 589, 598, 600, 601, 619, 667, 722, 723, 777, 813, 837, 850, 856, 870, 928, 937, 999
   unselective, 833, 840, 844, 852
Binding Theory, 18, **103**, 318, 518, 529, 600, 672, 714, 937
binominal construction, 395
Borer–Chomsky conjecture, **7**, 24, **66**, 824, 904, 937, 939, 940, 944, 968
bound variable anaphora, 516, 517, 519, 520, 558
boundary tone, **862**, 863
bounding node, 66, 392, 491, 656, 662, 663, 665, 937; *see also* barrier; cyclic; node; phase

bridge verbs, 662, 690
Burzio's Generalization, 122, 147, **150**, 151, 157, 305, 321, 635, 636

cartographic approach, cartography, 22, 23, **48**, 82, 429, 434, 435, 436, 447, 803, 880, 890, 894, 937, 941
case, 7, 9, 19, 20, 24, 96, 102, 110, 118, 131, 137, 145, 147, 148, 151, 157, 168, 185, 186, 187, 189, 196, 198, 200, 220, 266, 267, 270, 275, 285, 286, 298, 303, 304, 307, 315, 318, 320, 321, 327, 328, 334, 348, 434, 435, 489, 492, 499, 501, 551, 557, 584, 589, 591, 603, 607, 618, 628, 630, 631, 632, 635, 649, 685, 686, 694, 722, 723, 769, 905, 911, 938, 957, 975, 980, 983, 1002
   abstract, 530
   concord, 586, 631, 654
   default, 160, 423, 643, 648
   dependent, 643, 646
   inherent, 99, 145, 146, 147, 148, 149, 152, 304, 306, 638, 639, 641
   lexical/idiosyncratic, 304, 423, 586, 616, 639, 641
   morphological, 723
   null, 104, 586, 587, 590, 591
   quirky, 217, *218*, 225, 304, 586, 639, 648
   semantic: *see* case, inherent
   structural, 150, 152, 157, 304, 306, 320, 363, 500, 502, 508, 586, 636, 639, 641, 644, 652
Case Filter: *see* filter
Case Theory, 45, 103, 104, 363, 370, 461, 489, 499, 530, 531, 586
Categorial Grammar, 6, 14, 209, 222, 224, 238, 258, 259
category, 88, 218, 259
   functional, 23, 66, 181, 185, 302, 310, 313, 314, 320, 355, 356, 375, 382, 383, 407, 412, 425, 432, 434, 500, 513, 623, 746, 753, 761, 774, 824, 906, 922
   label(ing), 183
   lexical, 141, 355, 356, 360, 383, 407, 412, 425, 432, 434
   semi-lexical, 395, 413
causative
   lexical, 163
   syntactic, 163
CED: *see* Condition on Extraction Domain (CED)
center-embedding, 255, 871, 997, 1000
chain, 491, 497, 553, 554, 838, 845, 857, 858, 918
   uniformity, 497
Chain Condition, 542, 543
Chain Reduction, 595
checking theory, 406, 429, 499, 502, 714, 838; *see also* features
child language: *see* language acquisition
circumposition: *see* adposition
classifier, 396, 733, 735, 736
clause typing: *see* illocution(ary force)
cleft, 22, 351, 626, 677, 724, 726, 727, 728, 995
clitic, 110, 146, 167, 185, 186, 191, 192, 193, 194, 200, 211, 283, 287, 289, 291, 319, 365, 391, 393, 419, 441, 443, 455, 474, 536, 543, 557, 558, 559, 563, 564, 565, 612, 620, 623, 624, 625, 649, 651, 652, 678, 737, 744, 798, 799, 823, 893
Clitic Left Dislocation, 441, 443, 678
Clitic Right Dislocation, 678
clustering, 68; *see also* parameter

coconstrual, 516; *see also* binding
    as movement, 526, 550
Cognitive(-Functional) Linguistics/Grammar, 36, 87, 88, 89, 90, 598, 599
comment, 89, 443, 444, 446, 456; *see also* discourse; pragmatic (function); topic
comparative, 396, 398, 410, 424, 732, 737, 743, 809
competence, 64, 79, 128, 900, 923, 958; *see also* I(nternalized)-language; performance
complement, complementation, 7, 42, 45, 59, 109, 180, 182, 183, 184, 267, 339, 366, 373, 375, 382, 384, 385, 390, 406, 414, 418, 435, 466, 472, 513, 531, 554, 571, 604, 605, 621, 623, 654, 673, 676, 792, 868, 902; *see also* subcategorization
complementarity: *see* complementary distribution
complementary distribution, 532, 537, 539, 540, 544, 545, 549
Complex NP Constraint (CNPC), **660**, 662
computational, 6, 227, 228, 257
complexity, efficiency, 256, 492, 931, 932, 969
concord, 607, **627**, 628, 630, 686, 697, 858; *see also* agreement
Condition on Domain Exclusivity, 684
Condition on Extraction Domain (CED), 656, 664
conditional clause, 755, 844, 940
configurationality, 183, 185, 188, 197, 200, 411, 424, 938
    discourse, 177
conflation, 311
conjunction, 203, 224, 464, 538, 742, 965, 966, 967, 968
    reduction, 37, 743
connectedness, 693, 694
connectivity effects, 584, 681, 695, 722, 723, 724; *see also* reconstruction
constituency, 179, 226, 353, 892
constraint, 23, 24, 86, 123, **125**, 132, 138, 157, 181, 201, 214, 215, 217, 223, 228, 233, 240, 244, 257, 488, 598, 706, 960, 977, 979, 1004
    derivational, 52
    tie, **126**, 127, 128, 129, 155, 574, 846, 886, 928, 934
    transderivational, 49, 50
construct state construction, 389, 399, 418
Construction Grammar, 6, 36, 87, 222, 321, 962, 978
    Sign-Based (SBCG), 222
constructivist approaches (to linking), 274, 276, 310, 311, 315, 316, 318, 320, 321
contactive alternation: *see* alternation
context-free (phrase structure) grammar, 258
context-free/sensitive rules: *see* rules
continuity hypothesis, 947, 948, 967; *see also* language acquisition
contrastive topic: *see* topic
control, 16, 100, 172, 174, 175, 179, 198, 200, 217, 219, 220, 224, 225, 280, 317, 318, 329, 442, 535, 551, 577, 640, 648, 787, 831, 837
    as movement, 16, 590, 606
    backward/inverse, 591, 592, 597
    into adjunct clauses (adjunct control), 592, 593, 594, 595, 601
    into nominals, 592
    object, 189, 581
    obligatory vs. non-obligatory, 527, 551, 582, 591, 592, 593, 594, 595, 597, 601

shift, 583
    subject, 581
    unique vs. non-unique/partial, 582, 586, 593
conversation, conversational data, 74, 76, 77, 79, 80, 90
Coordinate Structure Constraint (CSC), 71, 210, **660**, 663
coordinate structure, coordination, 203, 209, 210, 217, 223, 224, 227, 255, 869
coordinating conjunction, 224
copula, 246, 247, 350, 394, 419, 425, 430, 628, 631, 726, 728, 745, 949; *see also* linker
copular constructions, 247, 340, 347, 468, 520
    equative, 341
    inverse: *see* inversion, predicate
    predicational, 341
    specificational, 342
copy (theory of movement), 17, 105, 106, 107, 108, 109, 198, 510, 526, 527, 532, 543, 551, 585, 590, 592, 696, 716, 725, 729, 909, 910, 915, 917, 921, 922, 931; *see also* trace, trace theory
copy raising, 332, 348, 602; *see also* NP-raising
copy control, 592, 595, 602; *see also* control
coreference, 516, 519
    accidental, 516
covert movement, 104, 115, 116, 535, 536, 832, 843; *see also* feature movement
criterial position, 335, 446, 448, 450
crossover, 521, 522, 523
    strong (SCO), 522, 928
    weak (WCO), 196, 197, 522, 569, 830, 832, 842
cross-serial dependencies, 255, 257, 261
cycle, cyclicity, 15, 39, 57, 99, 100, 110, 111, 112, 116, 132, 491, 507, 508, 614
cyclic
    linearization, 8; *see also* linear order, linear precedence, linearity, linearization
    node, 8, 16, 656, 659, 662, 663, 665, 689; *see also* barrier; bounding node; phase

dative alternation, dative shift: *see* alternation
de se readings, 560
decausative, 566
decomposition, 82, 207, 239, 270, 274, 310, 313, 407, 563, 638, 653, 713
definiteness, 355; *see also* double definiteness phenomenon
degree, 355, 373, 374, 397, 398, 407, 410, 420, 421, 422, 424, 914
deictic, deixis, 407, 409, 410, 557, 558, 758, 759, 760, 761, 770, 771, 774, 784, 786
delimited(ness): *see* aspect
demonstrative, 410, 628, 630, 719
Dependency Grammar, 6
dependent identity readings, 523, 524, 525
derivational vs. representational, 52, 100, 147, 212, 223
determiner, 384, 397, 418, 420, 459, 468, 479, 731, 732, 733; *see also* DP-hypothesis
diachronic, diachrony, 798
differential argument/case/object marking, 308, 644
directional: *see* adposition
directionality, 338; *see also* parameter
discontinuity, discontinuous constituents, discontinuous dependencies, 203, 204, 205, 207, 208, 223

discourse, 10, 22, 37, 75, 80, 171, 172, 182, 183, 224, 266, 316, 319, 345, 376, 442, 443, 444, 445, 447, 453, 456, 457, 537, 690, 859, 874, 928, 975, 1001; *see also* information structure; pragmatic (function)
configurationality: *see* configurationality, discourse
disjunction, 964, 965, 966, 968
dislocation, 881, 885
  right, 885
Distributed Morphology, 9, 268, 314, 315, 320, 461, 483, 573, 802, 869, 909, 916, 917
ditransitive constructions, 169, 223, 277, 300, 310, 381, 455, 619, 620, 680; *see also* alternation, dative
D-linking, 847; *see also* reference; specificity; topic
donkey pronoun anaphora, 523, 845
do-support, 429, 455, 495, 611
double definiteness phenomenon, 391, 419, 479
double object constructions: *see* ditransitive constructions
doubling, 909
  comparative, 909
  focus particle, 909
  subject pronoun, 909
  wh-word, 909
Doubly-filled Comp Filter, 125, 442
downward entailment (DE), downward-entailing (DE) contexts, 807, 811, 812, 813, 814, 817, 818, 821, 928, 934, 968
DP-hypothesis, 385, 386, 388, 392; *see also* determiner
dummy (elements), 100, 112, 389, 394, 395, 907; *see also* expletive
Dynamic Syntax, **6**

E(xternalized)-language, 64, **938**; *see also* I(nternalized)-langauge
Earliness Principle, 25
economy, 17, 21, 56, 57, 105, 113, 114, 115, 137, 142, 150, 157, 250, 457, 492, 499, 546, 547, 548, 550, 553, 555, 568, 683, 950
  global vs. local, 114, 124, 132, 504, 505
  of derivation, 17, 57, 114, 493, 502, 937
  of representation, 17, 496, 502, 937
effect-on-output condition, 124, 132, 136
edge (of phase), 16, 20, 25, 237, 258, 508, 510, 553, 676, 678, 680, 682, 683, 686, 780; *see also* locality; phase; successive-cyclic movement
ellipsis, 24, 343, 353, 521, 524, 527, 701, 732, 831, 838, 949, 950, 958
  clausal, 706, 712, 713, 718, 730, 731, 743, 745
  modal complement (MCE), 702, 703, 709, 717, 741
  predicate, 702, 714, 717, 731
  VP/Verb Phrase (VPE), 68, 525, 551, 702, 703, 704, 705, 706, 707, 708, 711, 713, 714, 715, 716, 717, 721, 740, 742, 743, 950
empty category, 196, 197, 519, 585, 594, 650, 672; *see also* copy (theory of movement); pro; PRO; trace, trace theory
Empty Category Principle (ECP), 196, 197, 490, 585, 594, 599, 650, 669, 671, 692, 696, 715, 831, 833
endocentric(ity), 45, 207, 354, 360, 361, 375
EPP constraint, 137, 141, 144, 145

EPP feature, property, 20, 25, **102**, 122, 123, 124, 130, 132, 133, 134, 135, 136, 137, 144, 145, 158, 408, 508, 945; *see also* Extended Projection Principle (EPP)
Equi (NP deletion): *see* control
equidistance, 220, 672, 673, 674, 695
ergative, 146, 147, 151, 152, 157, 168, 170, 186, 189, 302, 304, 305, 318, 320, 321, 385, 566, 609, 641, 643, 644, 649, 654, 938, 951, 957
ergativity, 639, 640
escape hatch, 387, 402, 410, 419, 422, 662, 663, 664, 666, 696; *see also* successive-cyclic movement
evaluation metric: *see* markedness
evaluator, 23, **125**, 130, 132, 136, 157; *see also* Optimality Theory (OT)
event, event structure, 260, 275, 279, 281, 282, 283, 288, 293, 294, 305, 306, 309, 313, 314, 315, 319, 348, 376, 409, 412, 423, 462, 465, 481, 599, 668, 746, 747, 748, 750, 752, 753, 756, 758, 761, 762, 763, 767, 769, 771, 772, 774, 775, 776, 779, 780, 781, 784, 795, 840
evidential, 747, 781
Exceptional Case-Marking (ECM), 19, 103, 499, 530, 535, 542, 547, 563, 588, 589, 590, 634, 636, 652
exclamative constructions, 21
excorporation, 674, 917; *see also* excorporation
existential closure, 159, 622, 623, 645, 795, 843
exocentric: *see* endocentric(ity)
expletive, 52, 96, 156, 161, 191, 260, 286, 324, 327, 334, 335, 340, 348, 378, 379, 505, 507, 578, 581, 614, 647, 648, 671, 682, 686, 696, 787, 903, 947; *see also* dummy (elements)
Extended Projection Principle (EPP), 20, 96, 334, 379, 584, 648, 746, 872, 920; *see also* Projection Principle; EPP feature, property
Extended Standard Theory, **37**, 39, 75
Extension Condition, 56, 57, 99; *see also* cycle, cyclicity
extraposition, 73, 329, 330, 396, 414, 663, 677, 681, 871, 873, 920
  prosodic, 870
ezafe-constructions, 423

features, 151, 500, 813
  categorial, 363, 364, 459
  checking, 20, 56, 116, 117, 429, 430, 500, 685, 839
  interpretable vs. uninterpretable, 19, 20, 102, 117, 147, 151, 501, 502, 508, 682, 704, 755, 774, 784, 786, 813, 976
  strong, 20, 54, 55, 137, 502
  valued vs. unvalued, 117, 118, 123, 137, 147, 148, 149, 151, 555, 615, 618, 633, 754, 771
  weak, 137, 502
feature inheritance, 509, 513
feature movement, 116; *see also* covert movement
figure-ground asymmetry, 281, 297
filter, 44, 45, 49, 51, 96, 124, 125, 131, 132, 133, 134, 135, 136, 137, 141, 145, 157, 488, 490, 872, 873, 888
  Case Filter, 56, 96, 267, 488, 490, 499, 501, 502, 632, 647, 648, 649, 692
  Stranded/Stray Affix filter, 51

finite control, 602, 603; *see also* control
floating quantifier: *see* quantifier, quantification
focus, 23, 37, 115, 134, 135, 138, 139, 171, 172, 176, 178, 182, 259, 335, 336, 337, 344, 351, 396, 442, 443, 444, 445, 446, 450, 451, 452, 453, 457, 478, 538, 599, 672, 690, 706, 720, 730, 738, **739**, 741, 860, 873, 876, 878, 879, 880, 884, 887, 889, 975; *see also* discourse
  answer, 876, 881
  contrastive, 876
  narrow, 887, 888, 890
  projection, 879, 887, 888
  verum, 884
  wide, 888
force: *see* illocution(ary force)
Form Chain, 503, 504, 595
fragments, fragment answers, 718, 719, 721, 723, 730, 928; *see also* ellipsis, clausal
free word-order languages: *see* configurationality; linear order, linear precedence, linearity, linearization
free-choice (FC) items/readings, 807, 815
freezing, 335, 589
  scope, 680
Full Interpretation, Principle of, 17, 95, 112, 117, 123, 334, 492, **493**, 496, 502, 506, 508, 509, 590
functional categories, projections: *see* category; projection
Functional Head Hypothesis, 238, 301, 357, 373, 376, 397, 420
Functional Linguistics: *see* Cognitive (-Functional) Linguistics/Grammar

g-projection, 693
gapping, 50, 78, 718, 719, 743, 744; *see also* ellipsis, clausal
garden-path sentences, 983, 986, 987; *see also* sentence processing
gender, 19, 117, 216, 344, 396, 435, 557, 560, 612, 615, 628, 629, 630, 631, 633, 733, 734, 735, 736, 737, 738, 857, 975, 992, 1001; *see also* phi/φ-features
generalized binding, 656
Generalized Phrase Structure Grammar (GPSG), 188, 207, 213, 214, 215, 217, 221, 222, 237, 255, 256
generalized quantifiers: *see* quantifier, quantification
Generative Semantics, 14, 28, **36**, 82, 86
generator, 23, **125**, 130, 131, 132, 137; *see also* Optimality Theory (OT)
gerund, 79, 186, 348, 386
given(ness), 873, **874**, 875, 876, 878, 880, 886; *see also* information structure; presupposed, presupposition; topic
global comparison, 549, 550, 568
global rules: *see* rules
goals (of generative grammar), **61**, 86, 89
government, 7, 28, 103, 311, 488, 489, 490, 499, 500, 530, 531, 633, 910
  proper, 669
Government and Binding theory, 8, 28, 38, 39, 45, 72, 73, 95, 119, 183, 200, 238, 273, 290, 305, 318, 334, 354, 378, 425, 487, 489, 510, 585, 633, 691, 829
grammatical functions, relations, 88, 162, 167, 168, 689

grammaticalization, 66, 307, 320, 565
Greed, **102**, 498
Greenbergian correlations, 69; *see also* parameter; directionality

Harmonic Grammar, 158; *see also* Optimality Theory (OT)
Harmonic Serialism, 156; *see also* Optimality Theory (OT)
Head Feature Convention/Principle, 225
Head Grammar, 206
head marking, 190, 200, 437, 609, 905
head movement, 73, 381, 383, 390, 391, 392, 394, 398, 405, 435, 455, 468, 469, 473, 475, 476, 501, 505, 535, 716, 721, 724, 802, 945
Head Movement Constraint (HMC), 472, 503, 670, 692, 800, 917, 925
head(edness) parameter: *see* parameters
Head-Driven Phrase Structure Grammar (HPSG), 13, 87, 203, 206, 214, **215**, 217, 222, 223, 238, 598, 606, 652, 693
Heavy NP Shift (HNPS), **869**, 871, 873, 882; *see also* extraposition
Holmberg's Generalization, 122, 134, 138, 139, 140, 141, 680, 695; *see also* object shift
honorific (marking), 187, 651

I(nternalized)-language, 64, **371**; *see also* E(xternalized)-language
idiom, 18, 19, 87, 168, 169, 242, 260, 312, 381, 417, 575, 578, 579, 581, 604, 824, 920, 970
illocution(ary force), 376, 409, 410, 442, 443, 454, 507, 677, 746, 758, 759, 761, 769, 770, 774, 781, 788, 804
Immediate Constituent (IC) analysis, 202, 203, 204, 205, 206, 207, 209, 213
Immediate Scope Constraint, 688, 814, 815
imperative, 167, 168, 200, 280, 455
inalienable possession, possessor: *see* possession, possessor
Inclusiveness Condition, **48**, **105**, 109, 355, 415, 510, 511, 525, 568, 754
incorporation, 299, 300, 302, 303, 311, 404, 413, 422, 473, 474, 566, 623, 624
index, indices, 195, 491, 510, 524, 525, 568, 598, 667, 752, 753, 754, 777, 841, 842
indexicals, indexicality, 572
individual-level vs. stage-level, 324, 477
inflection(al): *see* morphology
information structure, 22, 23, 133, 176, 309, 325, 344, 590, 599, 690, 860, 873, 874, 879, 892, 894, 895, 928; *see also* discourse; pragmatic (function)
innateness, innatism, 62, 63, 66, 70, 73, 88, 91, 899, 926, 929, 933, 938, 939, 940, 942, 945, 958, 961, 962, 963, 964, 968
interface, 6, 9, 18, 19, 23, 98, 100, 306, 354, 370, 447, 456, 481, 491, 492, 496, 498, 499, 501, 502, 507, 509, 516, 567, 590, 761, 905, 923
  conditions, 124, 132, 137, 138, 498, 499, 507
  syntax/phonology interface, 108
  syntax/semantics interface, 35, 293
intersective, intersectivity, 463, 464, 465, 466, 471, 475, 483, 484
intervention (effects), 56, 430, 452, 615, 616, 618, 620, 621, 629, 635, 671, 672, 687, 695, 696
intonation: *see* prosody

introspective data, judgments, 73, 74, 76, 80, 87, 89
inversion, 212, 224, 246, 260, 450, 451, 452, 457, 625, 854, 903
   locative, 613, 614, 650, 790
   negative, 443
   predicate, 343, 344, 346, 680
   stylistic, 68, 451
   subject–aux(iliary), 212, 345, 670
islands, 43, 49, 200, 210, 248, 250, 258, 260, 392, 400, 528, 537, 589, 590, 656, 660, 667, 668, 687, 693, 721, 722, 724, 741, 744, 832, 833, 834, 843, 847, 983, 986; *see also* barrier
   inner/negative, 671, 672, 847
   locked vs. unlocked, 693
   selective, 657
   strong, 667, 672, 693
   weak, 261, 672, 690, 693

Jespersen's Cycle, 798

kernel sentences/structures, 10, 53, 228, 229

L-marking, 392
label(ing): *see* category
lambda abstract(ion), 517, 601
language acquisition, 11, 24, 25, 62, 74, 452, 453, 858, 899, 928, 929, 930, 931, 932, 933, 934, 949, 952, 960, 969
language change: *see* diachronic, diachrony
language development: *see* language acquisition
Last Resort, 17, 21, 72, **102**, 113, 124, 136, 455, 495, 497, 498, 499, 504, 505, 506, 614, 673, 716
late closure, 976
late insertion, 111
learnability: *see* language acquisition
least effort: *see* economy, of derivation
Left Branch Condition, 393, 400, 412, 659, **661**, 663, 689, 692
left periphery, 20, 22, 441, 747, 753, 761, 937
levels of representation, 18, 33, 39, 96, 98, 100, 488, 491, 498
   deep structure/D-structure, 18, 34, 36, 37, 38, 50, 86, 96, 273, 318, 332, 347, 378, 379, 417, 468, 498
   Logical Form (LF), 18, **38**, 96, **98**, 378, 418, 513, 532, 570, 571, 650, 688, 825, 894
   Phonological Form (PF), **38**, 73, **96**
   surface structure/S-structure, 18, 96, 378, 498, 532
lexical (sub)array: *see* numeration
lexical categories, projections: *see* category; projection
lexical conceptual structure, 283
Lexical Functional Grammar (LFG), 13, 14, 28, **53**, 130, 162, 185, 196, 203, 214, 215, 216, 221, 224, 225, 260, 272, 273, 277, 280, 316, 571, 596, 598, 606
Lexical Head Hypothesis, 357, 363
lexical insertion, 98, 111, 112
lexical integrity, 163, 179, 917
Lexical Mapping Theory, 169, 221
lexicalist (hypothesis), 86, 802, 915, 916
Linear Correspondence Axiom (LCA), **8**, 47, 71, 130, 169, 595, 904, 912, 914, 922
linear order, linear precedence, linearity, linearization, 6, 7, 8, 23, 47, 101, 130, 131, 179, 194, 201, 206, 213, 214, 367, 369, 370, 372, 417, 460, 467, 469, 470, 474, 475, 476, 477, 478, 479, 480, 481, 482, 510, 663, 683, 685, 686, 695, 696, 716, 902, 904, 905, 906, 915, 918, 919, 920, 921, 922, 930, 949, 991, 995, 996, 997, 998, 999
linker, 395; *see also* copula
linking, linking rules, 272, 321
locality, 28, 43, 97, 103, 104, 113, 145, 147, 218, 233, 237, 247, 248, 252, 260, 392, 404, 429, 430, 518, 529, 533, 535, 538, 540, 543, 544, 550, 552, 556, 560, 561, 564, 581, 600, 601, 655, 687, 688, 706, 707, 722, 724, 744, 830, 835, 837, 846, 873; *see also* islands
locative: *see* adposition
locative alternation: *see* adposition
locative inversion: *see* inversion
Logical Form (LF): *see* levels of representation
logophor, 534, 537, 538, 539, 540, 594, 627
long-distance, 937
   agreement, 616, 617, 685, 686, 696
   binding, 536, 545, 559, 561
   concord, 686
   dependencies, 15, 16, 178, 200, 224, 228, 655, 680, 681, 852, 858, 950, 983
   movement, 237, 246, 248, 250, 496, 561, 855
   reciprocals, 563
look-ahead, 108, 113, 114, 350, 505, 506, 513

macroparameter: *see* parameter
Mapping Hypothesis, 624, 836, 837; *see also* existential closure; object shift; scrambling; specificity
mapping principles (for theta-roles): *see* linking, linking rules
markedness, 50, 67, 149, 160, 735, 942, 944, 957, 958, 961
mass/count distinction, 409
maturation, 931, 948, 949, 956, 969; *see also* language acquisition
measure phrase, 396, 401, 403, 410
Merge, 72, 84, 108, 137, 226, 227, 228, 233, 240, 241, 242, 246, 436, 492, 505, 509, 510, 550, 567, 589, 595, 610, 614, 904, 937, 941, 976, 1000
   External, 109, 123, 226, 408, 510
   Internal, 109, 123, 226, 233, 240, 242, 246, 248, 379, 408, 436, 492, 505, 509, 510, 550, 585, 610, 614, 685, 697, 937, 941, 976
metathesis, 916
   subject pronoun, 913, 914, 915, 916, 917, 918
methods, methodology, 11, 25, 73, 74, 82, 83, 85, 86, 89, 90, 91, 924
microparameter, microparametric variation: *see* parameter
middle, 287, 288, 318, 565, 566
minimal attachment, 976
Minimal Distance Principle (MDP), 586, 591, 594
Minimal Link Condition, 17, 104, 145, 147, 149, 157, 656, 661, 672, 673, 687; *see also* minimality
   as violable constraint, 147
Minimal Link Constraint, 147, 149, 156, 157
Minimalism, the Minimalist Program (MP), 7, 8, 9, 13, 15, 18, 20, 25, 28, 31, 39, 73, **85**, 98, 104, 113, 116, 117, 119, 122, 123, 130, 131, 158, 163, 212, 226, 238, 240, 242, 258, 286, 321, 332, 334, 335, 347, 354, 379, 489, 492, 498, 505, 507, 508, 525, 550, 554, 555, 564, 567, 571, 584, 585, 586, 588, 590, 600, 606,

614, 625, 633, 653, 656, 667, 687, 695, 704, 729, 752, 753, 754, 813, 823, 836, 837, 843, 901, 903, 905, 907, 912, 922, 930, 932, 937, 939, 943, 944, 976
minimality, 57, 72, 97, 104, 120, 150, 160, 239, 248, 252, 430, 452, 503, 505, 600, 656, 657, 660, 665, 669, 670, 671, 672, 674, 675, 687, 688, 694, 847
Minimize Chain Links: *see* Minimal Link Condition
minimizers, 741
Mirror Principle, 9, 434, 436, 437
Mirror Theory, **7**
modal, modality, 83, 84, 142, 143, 210, 212, 425, 436, 437, 443, 462, 463, 466, 578, 703, 716, 717, 746, 756, 763, 764, 769, 773, 774, 781, 812, 817, 859
model-theoretic grammar, 214
modifier, 22, 23, 227, 231, 240, 249, 259, 260, 364, 396, 397, 400, 402, 404, 418, 420, 421, 422, 458, 459, 461, 466, 473, 607, 627, 727, 728, 763, 765, 772, 851
   direct vs. indirect, 469, 470, 474, 475
   restrictive vs. non-restrictive, 478, 479
Montague grammar, 206
mood, 425, 428, 437, 439, 447, 747, 753, 755, 756, 757, 761, 762, 766, 767, 769, 770, 772, 773, 774, 778, 781, 786, 799, 802, 803, 804
   subjunctive, 755, 782, 788, 809
morphology, 19, 24, 187, 189, 190, 200, 225, 277, 280, 282, 283, 285, 286, 287, 288, 298, 299, 300, 301, 302, 303, 314, 315, 317, 320, 321, 427, 428, 430, 431, 435, 439, 455, 460, 475, 533, 538, 540, 546, 547, 550, 551, 552, 554, 555, 556, 558, 559, 560, 561, 562, 567, 632, 638, 681, 682, 705, 710, 711, 712, 732, 738, 747, 764, 766, 772, 778, 780, 783, 788, 789, 797, 802, 834, 902, 906, 910, 916, 920, 950, 977, 989, 991
   inflectional, 428, 429, 430, 435, 455
Move
   Internal, 366, 371
Move Alpha/α, 50, 96, 97, 366, 488, 492, 902, 903; *see also* Merge, Internal
multi-dominance, 371, 372, 416
multiple spell-out: *see* spell-out
multiple subject construction, 333

N *of (a)* N construction: *see* binominal construction
negation, 21, 85, 428, 429, 431, 433, 439, 455, 671, 672, 715, 716, 727, 742, 746, 761, 789, 793, 840, 859, 964, 965, 966, 967, 968, 985
   constituent, 589, **794**
   sentential, **794**
negative concord, 68, 439, 440, **794**, 818, 819
negative islands: *see* islands
negative polarity items (NPI): *see* polarity items
No Tampering Condition (NTC), 57, 510, 511
node admissibility, 212
nominalization, 10, 14, 330, 348, 582, 596, 604, 732, **919**
non-configurational(ity): *see* configurationality
nonlocal dependencies: *see* long-distance
non-veridicality, 809, 812, 815, 816, 817
NP-raising, 12, 16, 155, 219, 225, 252, 379, 380, 577, 602, 629, 787, 831, 837
   backward/inverse, 592

NPI: *see* polarity items
null complement anaphora (NCA), 708, 709, 710, 718, 719, 721
null operator, 331, 332, 333, 627, 833, 834
null-subject languages: *see* pro-drop languages
Null Subject Parameter: *see* parameter
number, 19, 216, 344, 389, 406, 435, 557, 612, 615, 628, 629, 630, 631, 633, 736, 855, 857, 975, 992, 1001; *see also* phi/ϕ-features
numeration, 105, 123, 366, 429, 504, 513, 525, 550, 570, 889
n-words, 793, 819, 820, 821, 822; *see also* negation

object control: *see* control
object shift, 54, 73, 104, 122, 124, 133, 134, 137, 140, 143, 144, 145, 157, 276, 590, 622, 623, 624, 644, 646, 674, 695, 696, 885, 895
obviation, 518, 520, 547, 549, 550, 555, 568
Old English, 545
Optimality Theory (OT), 23, 122, **124**, 131, 573, 960
   Bidirectional, 158
   Stochastic, 128, 158
optional(ity), 9, 32, 35, 46, 85, 113, 134, 144, 185, 192, 200, 507, 592, 872, 883, 904, 919, 920, **921**, 922, 960
order, 186, 440; *see also* linear order, linear precedence, linearity, linearization
ordering: *see* rules, ordering; linear order, linear precedence, linearity, linearization
OV/VO: *see* parameter, directionality

P-marker, 31, **32**, 34, 35
p-movement: *see* prosodic(ally driven) movement (p-movement)
pair-list answers/readings, 830, 831, 834, 835, 836, 840, 842, 844, 853, 854
parameter, 7, 11, 24, 50, 51, 65, 66, 67, 70, 73, 95, 119, 136, 137, 145, 153, 153, 157, 170, 338, 370, 416, 431, 445, 446, 449, 491, 492, 493, 512, 513, 533, 539, 564, 625, 626, 627, 630, 639, 678, 803, 844, 845, 899, 902, 903, 904, 905, 911, 912, 914, 917, 922, 927, 929
   binar(it)y, 952
   directionality, 8, 130, 370, 626, 941, 956
   head(edness), 69, 70, 95, 369, 935, 943
   hierarchy, 938, 943, 951, 956
   macroparameter, 67, 133, 627, 903, 922, 923, 935, 938, 942, 943, 944, 946, 951, 968
   microparameter, microparametric variation, 67, 627, 935, 941, 942, 943, 944
   network, 945, 946
   null subject: *see* pro-drop
   polysynthesis, 903, 935, 938, 943, 945, 956
parasitic gap, 11, 117, 570
parentheticals, 223
parser, parsing, 256, 930, 976, 977, 978, 979, 986, 988, 995, 996, 998, 1002; *see also* sentence processing
partial *wh*-movement, 8, 681, 854, 909; *see also* *wh*-scope marking
particle, 10, 204, 300, 302, 426, 436, 437, 443, 446, 475, 580, 630, 747, 885, 886
   discourse, 804
   negative, 797, 798, 799, 800, 801, 802, 823
partitive (construction), 395, 420

passive, 14, 15, 53, 75, 81, 96, 101, 151, 169, 198, 211, 215, 221, 224, 247, 276, 284, 287, 299, 303, 316, 320, 372, 488, 530, 531, 541, 565, 566, 580, 581, 603, 612, 620, 626, 640, 646, 648, 649, 651, 653, 654, 658, 670, 674, 682, 692, 695, 712, 713, 724, 741, 850, 962, 970
pause, 862
percolation, 208
performance, 26, 64, 128, 900, 923, 930, 950, 958, 961; *see also* E(xternalized)-language
person, 19, 216, 406, 428, 545, 547, 557, 572, 615, 628, 633, 636, 642, 754, 758, 759, 760, 770, 784, 802, 855, 857, 975; *see also* phi/--features
PF-movement, 873, 903; *see also* prosodic(ally driven) movement (p-movement)
phase, 72; *see also* barrier; bounding node; cyclic, node
  extension, 680
  sliding, 680
Phase Impenetrability Condition (PIC), 8, 16, 39, 56, 72, 73, 104, 123, 135, 155, 156, 241, 457, 491, 507, 508, 509, 511, 552, 553, 555, 615, 616, 623, 629, 645, 656, 675, 676, 685, 686, 687, 695, 696, 697, 754, 770, 777, 780
phi/φ features, 19, 24, 118, 137, 144, 500, 501, 508, 509, 549, 555, 557, 594, 631, 634, 682, 685, 704, 761, 911, 975
phrasal verbs, 204, 223
phrase structure, 40, 109, 164, 195, 198, 199, 200, 242, 353, 358, 366, 408, 414, 415, 481, 983, 986, 987, 1001, 1002
  bare, 109, 110, 120, 366, 415, 823
  grammar, 14, 28, 40, 53, 202, 208, 242, 255, 413, 416, 693; *see also* Generalized Phrase Structure Grammar (GPSG); Head-Driven Phrase Structure Grammar (HSPG)
  marker, 205, 210, 213, 224
  rules, 7, 10, 12, 13, 31, 32, 181, 199, 213, 226, 228, 237, 238, 360, 363, 374, 375, 488, 976, 988; *see also* rules, rewrite
Phonetic/Phonological Form (PF): *see* levels of representation
pied-piping, 68, 393, 400, 401, 665, 667, 668, 675, 693, 833, 910, 914, 917
pitch (accent), 861, **862**, 864, 867, 878, 879
Plato's problem, **10**, 51, **62**, 95, 359, 515
polar questions: *see* yes/no-questions
polarity, 714, 719, 761, 763, 793, 795, 805
polarity items, 714, 725, 741
  negative (NPI), 741, **793**, 822, 928
  positive (PPI), 807, 817, 967
polysemy, 564, 567
polysynthesis parameter: *see* parameter
positive polarity items (PPI): *see* polarity items
possession, possessor, 301, 333, 385, 386, 387, 419, 522, 545, 546, 560, 563, 607, 630, 637
  inalienable, 566
postposition: *see* adposition
poverty of the stimulus, 63
pragmatic (function), 76, 177, 307, 345, 350, 444, 447, 456, 462, 520, 521, 528, 537, 546, 547, 556, 558, 599, 785, 806, 810, 811, 812, 813, 818, 878, 880, 881; *see also* comment; discourse; focus; topic
Prague School, 880
precedence: *see* linear order, linear precedence, linearity, linearization

predication, 16, 246, 260, 298, 300, 301, 322, 394, 395, 418, 420, 426, 465, 468, 470, 471, 472, 540, 543, 549, 550, 594, 600, 601, 627, 628, 629, 631, 679, 735, 851
  inverse: *see* inversion, predicate
  operator, 323, 462
  reverse, 339, 349
  secondary, 279, 322, 347, 349
preposition: *see* adposition
preposition stranding, 68, 708, 722, 723, 725, 726, 727, 728
preservation
  of meaning, 75, 81
  of structure, 376, 455
presupposed, presupposition, 37, 74, 133, 134, 135, 136, 139, 349, 443, 444, 446, 447, 449, 456, 622, 836, 875; *see also* discourse; given (ness); topic
Principle of Full Interpretation: *see* Full Interpretation, Principle of
principles, 51, 95, 119
Principles and Parameters theory, 6, 16, 18, 28, 51, 61, 67, 95, 119, 130, 334, 369, 466, 487, 584, 590, 591, 600, 603, 606, 671, 685, 901, 902, 905, 915, 932, 933, 934, 947, 961
pro, 594, 599, 674, 694, 739, 850, 943
processing: *see* sentence processing
pro-drop, 16, 191, 195, 592, 740, 745, 909, 933, 935, 947, 948, 949, 970; *see also* parameter, null subject
PRO Theorem, 103, 531, 600, 603
processing: *see* sentence processing
Procrastinate, 25, 54, 119, 498, 503
Project Alpha, 365
projection, 182, 239, 407
  extended, 141, 142, 180, 183, 239, 240, 260, 357, 382, 384, 394, 395, 397, 403, 407, 408, 409, 410, 412, 420, 474
  functional, 46, 363, 383, 385, 414, 474, 799, 802
  lexical, 356, 357, 363, 373, 375, 380, 383, 385, 386, 387, 389, 392, 397, 399, 400, 403, 412, 413
Projection Principle, 16, 18, 46, 99, 272, 274, 334, 354, 359, 378, 408, 586, 591, 647; *see also* Extended Projection Principle (EPP)
prolepsis, 686
prolific domains, 684
proper government: *see* government
Propositional Island Condition (PIC), 661, **662**, 695
prosodic(ally driven) movement (p-movement), 872, 873, 881, 883, 885, 886; *see also* PF-movement
prosody, 23, 444, 453, 677, 678, 854, 859, 860, 861, 878, 879, 881, 892, 893, 894, 1001
proto-roles, 271; *see also* theta-roles
Proto-Germanic, 143
proxy readings, 561, 562
pseudocleft: *see* cleft
pseudogapping, 702, 703, 704, 707, 708, 717, 741
pseudopassive, 372
pseudosluicing, 726, 745; *see also* sluicing

quantifier, quantification, 21, 22, 36, 82, 295, 313, 348, 380, 396, 397, 398, 418, 439, 452, 471, 522, 523, 524, 525, 563, 619, 630, 672, 680, 730, 748, 749, 795, 808, 809, 816, 820, 821, 827, 928, 940, 985; *see also* scope

float(ing), 167, 317, 380, 591, 829, 846, 849, 850, 851
  generalized, 827, 828, 832, 840, 857, 859
  split, 829
quantification at a distance (QAD), 852
Quantifier Lowering, 75, 831
Quantifier Raising (QR), 21, 103, 522, 563, 688, 706, 829, 830, 831, 836, 837, 840, 842, 845, 880
quantization, quantized(ness), 306
quasi-argument, 329; *see also* expletive
quirky case: *see* case
quiz questions, 132

R-pronoun, 402, 403, 422
raising: *see* NP-raising; verb movement/raising
reciprocal, 529, 548, 550, 552, 558, 560, 561, 562, 563, 564, 567, 578
reconstruction, 15, 346; *see also* connectivity effects
recoverability (condition), 15, 106, 125, **126**, 128, 132, 186, 259, 346, 532, 579, 582, 584, 589, 596, 682, 695, 702, 710, 712, 714, 724, 725, 727, 728, 729, 744, 760, 831, 838, 839, 840, 847, 848, 849, 910, 917
recursion, recursive, 26, 30, 33, 72, 73, 227, 228, 230, 231, 237, 241, 245, 251, 255, 259, 260, 333, 364, 415, 449, 492, 655, 751, 780, 902
redundancy, 72, 651
reference, referential, 201, 261, 341, 342, 392, 394, 582, 587, 596, 598, 599, 600, 667, 749, 750, 751, 752, 753, 772, 810, 812, 844, 847, 997
referential index, 459
referentiality: *see* reference, referential
Relational Grammar (RG), 6, 59, 162, 273, 290, 417
relative clause, 21, 223, 418, 468, 475, 737, 750, 767, 768, 870, 871, 995, 997, 1000
  internally headed, 469
  reduced, 351, 468, 469, 480, 658
  restrictive, 658
Relativized Minimality, 56, 72, 97, 104, 120, 150, 248, 252, 430, 452, 600, 656, 657, 660, 670, 671, 672, 674, 687, 688, 847; *see also* minimality
RELATOR, 336, 339, 340, 420, 471; *see also* copula
remnant movement, 469, 470, 917
representational: *see* constraint; derivational vs. representational
restructuring, 413, 437, 585, 617, 685, 686
resultative construction, 279, 291, 301, 302, 315
resumption, resumptive pronoun, 16, 66, 333, 443, 570, 667, 668, 693, 694, 695, 820, 821
rewrite rules: *see* rules
rheme, 317
Right Node Raising, 372, 677
Right Roof Constraint, 660, **663**
Role and Reference Grammar, 168
roll-up movement, 419, 476, 919
root, 55, 83, 84, 141, 144, 151, 158, 182, 227, 230, 231, 232, 235, 239, 241, 242, 243, 244, 245, 254, 282, 301, 315, 316, 321, 358, 393, 416, 427, 430, 433, 434, 455, 500, 521, 533, 548, 558, 559, 563, 611, 613, 676, 685, 705, 717, 747, 787, 909, 949, 950, 970, 1004
  acategorial, 268, 314, 461, 560
rules, 487
  construction-specific, 49, 360, 488, 499

context-free, 227, 358, 359, 360
context-sensitive, 358
global, 49
language-particular/specific, 49, 51, 488, 495, 499
lexical, 53, 221
lexical redundancy, 268
ordering, 211, 213
phrase structure, 266, 358, 359, 360, 401
rewrite, **29**, 901, 902

scope, 20, 22, 23, 39, 75, 84, 167, 259, 442, 443, 446, 452, 468, 476, 568, 579, 619, 685, 741, 749, 750, 761, 782, 795, 804, 807, 813, 817, 818, 827, 964, 985; *see also* quantifier, quantification
scope freezing: *see* freezing
scrambling, 15, 73, 145, 196, 197, 410, 411, 452, 592, 623, 708, 851, 880, 883, 885, 886, 888, 943, 995
selection, selectional restrictions/requirements/ dependencies, 198, 279, 289, 314, 315, 316, 374, 375, 579, 581, 587, 921, 988, 990
  c(ategorial)-selection, 82, 354, 359, 375, 408
  c(ategory)-selection, 267
  s(emantic)-selection, 82, 267, 439, 446
sentence comprehension: *see* sentence processing
sentence processing, 690, 930, 971, 972, 976, 977, 981, 982, 985, 986, 987, 992, 995, 998, 999, 1002, 1004
Sentential Subject Constraint, 660, 663
sequence of tenses (SoT), 19, 751, 755, 756, 767, 769, 771, 784, 785, 786; *see also* tense
serial verb construction, 693
sideways/sideward movement, 570, 595, 605, 615
Single Complement Hypothesis, 416
Single Event Grouping Condition, 665, 668
slash (category), *209*, 714
sloppy vs. strict readings, **976**, 517, 522, 524, 527, 551, 552, 554, 741
sluicing, 49, 77, 706, 712, 713, 718, 719, 720, 721, 722, 723, 724, 726, 728, 729, 730, 731, 743, 744, 745; *see also* ellipsis, clausal
small clause, 183, 246, 247, 260, 279, 300, 301, 311, 328, 334, 335, 336, 338, 340, 341, 342, 344, 395, 416, 470, 679, 688
snowballing movement: *see* roll-up movement
sociolinguistics, sociolinguistic factors of variation, 918, 920, 922, 923
spading, 718, 719, 726, 727, 728, 729; *see also* ellipsis, clausal
specificity, 306, 347, 350, 351, 621, 622, 624
Specified Subject Condition, 71, 81, 529, 690
specifiers, 23, 42, 43, 45, 46, 59, 109, 130, 180, 181, 182, 183, 184, 298, 301, 302, 310, 313, 320, 334, 335, 339, 346, 351, 362, 366, 371, 373, 375, 380, 382, 384, 386, 387, 397, 398, 401, 402, 406, 408, 414, 416, 418, 420, 426, 429, 432, 435, 446, 458, 459, 466, 467, 469, 470, 471, 472, 473, 474, 475, 476, 481, 482, 499, 531, 554, 584, 598, 611, 612, 613, 614, 621, 623, 627, 673, 674, 676, 678, 680, 683, 684, 694, 801, 803, 804, 902
  multiple, 110, 120, 435
  outer, 133, 253, 254
Spec(ifier)-Head relation/agreement, 7, 56, 103, 104, 386, 406, 467, 481, 499, 500, 501, 612, 910, 918

spell-out, 100, 112, 909, 937, 941
  cyclic, 676, 687
  multiple, 8, 100, 101, 105, 909
  single, 100
split antecedents, 539, 558, 742
sprouting, 718, 721, 725; *see also* ellipsis, clausal
stage-level: *see* individual-level vs. stage level
Standard Theory, 35, 39
statistical learning, 932, 951, 952, 958, 959
Stranded/Stray Affix Filter: *see* filter
strength
  of constraint ranking, 138
  of features, 25 *see* features, strong; features, weak
stress, 23, **862**, 863, 882, 883, 884, 885, 886, 887, 888, 889
  nuclear, **878**, 879, 883, 889, 890
  phrasal, 865, 867, 879
  sentential, 865, 867, 882, 883
string-vacuous movement: *see* vacuous movement, Vacuous Movement Hypothesis (VMH)
stripping, 718, 719, 743, 744; *see also* ellipsis, clausal
Structuralism, structuralist linguistics, 10, 11, 26
structure preservation, structure preserving hypothesis: *see* preservation
stylistic inversion: *see* inversion
subcategorization, 7, 13, 211, 215, 266, 314, 328, 359, 361, 374, 375, 408
  frame, 267, 316, 359
Subjacency, 63, 64, 66, 116, 392, 419, 589, 656, 662, 663, 664, 665, 667, 691, 692, 833, 834, 937
subject-aux(iliary) inversion: *see* inversion
Subject Condition, 664, 672
subject control: *see* control
subject pronoun metathesis: *see* metathesis
subjunctive: *see* mood
Subset Principle, 534, 936, 937, 947, 950, 965, 966, 968, 969
substitution, 229, 230, 232, 241, 242, 243, 244, 251, 259
  selective, 233
successive-cyclic movement, 15, 16, 17, 102, 120, 237, 259, 503, 656, 662, 680, 681, 682, 686, 696, 708; *see also* escape hatch
successive-cyclic *wh*-movement, 496
superiority, Superiority Condition, 56, 114, 115, 503, 656, 691, 692
super-raising, 248, 250, 503, 670, 671, 690, 696; *see also* NP-raising
swiping, 718; *see also* ellipsis, clausal
syntax/semantics interface: *see* interface

T-marker, **32, 33**, 34, 36, 37, 39, 243
T-model, 18, 38
telic(ity), 290, 291, 292, 294, 295, 298, 409
tense, 19, 84, 141, 180, 186, 211, 306, 335, 336, 339, 340, 350, 355, 376, 409, 414, 423, 425, 426, 427, 428, 429, 431, 432, 433, 435, 436, 437, 439, 447, 480, 500, 507, 533, 534, 587, 608, 609, 610, 611, 612, 614, 618, 630, 634, 635, 637, 676, 746, 748, 799, 802, 859, 907, 917
Tensed-S Condition, 81, 529, 661, 662; *see also* Propositional Island Condition (PIC)

that-trace effect, filter, violation, 68, 453, 490, 669, 696, 903, 942
thematic hierarchy, 163, 167, 168, 269, 317
thematic roles: *see* theta-roles
Theta Criterion, 16, 18, 71, 82, 95, 99, 240, 241, 248, 249, 250, 252, 259, 260, 272, 274, 332, 377, 408, 468, 488, 494, 551, 585, 590, 674
theta-roles, 7, 304, 305, 306, 308, 312, 324, 331, 332, 333, 340, 350, 362, 376, 377, 380, 408, 446, 468, 494, 499, 507, 528, 543, 551, 578, 584, 585, 591, 592, 602, 635, 665, 907, 986
  as features, 106
Theta Theory, 370, 488
topic, 16, 22, 89, 171, 172, 176, 187, 198, 199, 281, 309, 316, 317, 325, 333, 335, 336, 337, 344, 345, 346, 396, 441, 442, 443, 444, 445, 446, 450, 451, 452, 453, 456, 457, 590, 594, 617, 648, 683, 684, 696, 705, 706, 829, 839, 842, 860, 995, 996; *see also* comment; discourse; focus; given(ness); pragmatic (function); presupposed, presupposition
  contrastive, 873, 885
tough-movement construction, 11, 333, 536, 580, 596, 602
trace, trace theory, 103, 105, 107, 199, 220, 378, 453, 491, 510, 550, 584, 599, 669, 711, 712, 725, 799, 841, 842, 853, 857
  traces as copies: *see* copy (theory of movement)
transformation, 10, 13, 27, 30, 32, 53, 81, 268, 273, 901, 902, 976
  generalized, 10, 14, 30, 33, 54, 99, 228
  singulary, 31, 228
Tree Adjoining Grammar (TAG), 14, 28, 31, 53, 224, 226, 680, 978, 996, 1000
trigger, 9, 20, 24, 53, 83, 85, 918, 919, 920, 921, 934, 935, 952

unaccusative, unaccusativity, 148, 150, 151, 153, 284, 286, 289, 294, 305, 317, 318, 319, 350, 377, 565, 566, 578, 648, 682, 695, 850
unbounded dependencies: *see* long-distance
underspecification, 216, 316, 547, 557, 558, 945, 947, 952, 953, 954, 955, 957, 969
unergative, 289, 305, 317, 318, 319, 340, 350, 377, 566, 682, 850
uniformity of chains: *see* chain
Uniformity of Theta Assignment Hypothesis (UTAH), **36**, 82, 273, 282, 316, 417
Universal Alignment Hypothesis (UAH), 273, 411, 417
Universal Base Hypothesis (UBH): *see* Linear Correspondence Axiom(LCA)
unselective binding: *see* binding

V2, Verb Second, 73, 140, 142, 143, 183, 200, 346, 376, 431, 443, 448, 456, 717, 801, 854, 909, 949
vacuous movement, Vacuous Movement Hypothesis (VMH), 885
vacuous projection, 109, 366, 415
vacuous quantification, 829, 857
valence, valency, 169, 203, 214, 215, 217, *218*, 221, 541
variation, 24, 163, 491, 556, 899, 909, 942
  intra-speaker, 9, 895, 899, 919, 920, 922, 923
vehicle change, 574, 714, 724

verb movement/raising, 54, 133, 140, 141, 144, 376, 388, 418, 427, 428, 432, 440, 441, 503, 512, 531, 642, 695, 715, 800, 824, 911
Verbal Identity Requirement, 705; *see also* ellipsis, VP/Verb Phrase (VPE)
Visser's Generalization, 603
vocative, 393
voice, 169, 211, 284, 313, 314, 317, 437, 438, 717, 741, 747; *see also* passive
VP ellipsis, 10; *see also* ellipsis
VP-internal subject hypothesis, 16, 183, 336, 346, 361, 362, 380, 381, 386

wh-copying, 681, 682, 852, 857
wh-in-situ, 21, 97, 108, 112, 113, 691, 832, 833, 834, 835, 840, 841, 843, 844, 845, 853, 940

Wh-Island Condition, 248, 503, 661, 662, 665, 671, 674, 691, 694
wh-scope marking, 682, 852, 854
word order: *see* linear order, linear precedence, linearity, linearization

X-bar structure, 207, 211, 666
X-bar Theory, 7, 13, 18, 41, 42, 43, 45, 46, 98, 109, 180, 213, 358, 360, 361, 362, 363, 374, 384, 385, 386, 396, 401, 408, 414, 416, 425, 488, 496, 499, 500, 501, 612, 649, 902, 904
   generalized (to functional categories), 46

Y-model: *see* T-model
yes/no-questions, 495, 720, 729, 800, 809, 950

Printed by Printforce, United Kingdom